Judgment and decision making:
An interdisciplinary reader

Judgment and decision making:
An interdisciplinary reader

Edited by

Hal R. Arkes
Ohio University

Kenneth R. Hammond
University of Colorado

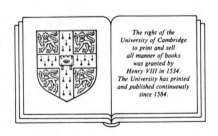

The right of the
University of Cambridge
to print and sell
all manner of books
was granted by
Henry VIII in 1534.
The University has printed
and published continuously
since 1584.

Cambridge University Press

Cambridge
London   New York   New Rochelle
Melbourne   Sydney

Published by the Press Syndicate of the University of Cambridge
The Pitt Building, Trumpington Street, Cambridge CB2 1RP
32 East 57th Street, New York, NY 10022, USA
10 Stamford Road, Oakleigh, Melbourne 3166, Australia

First published 1986

Printed in the United States of America

Library of Congress Cataloging-in-Publication Data
Judgment and decision making.
Bibliography: p.
Includes index.
1. Decision making. 2. Judgment. 3. Decision
making (Ethics) I. Arkes, Hal R., 1945–
II. Hammond, Kenneth R.
BF441.J79 1986   302.3   86–6084
ISBN 0 521 32617 6 hard covers
ISBN 0 521 33914 6 paperback

British Library Cataloging-in-Publication applied for

Contents

Contributors

Leonard Adelman *PAR Technology Corporation, McLean, Virginia*

Barry F. Anderson *Department of Psychology, Portland State University*

Norman H. Anderson *Department of Psychology, University of California at San Diego*

Hal R. Arkes *Department of Psychology, Ohio University*

Max H. Bazerman *Kellogg Graduate School of Management, Northwestern University*

Berndt Brehmer *Department of Psychology, University of Uppsala, Sweden*

Curtis A. Brown *Bureau of Reclamation, Denver, Colorado*

John S. Carroll *Sloan School, Massachusetts Institute of Technology*

D. M. Chaput de Saintonge *London Hospital Medical College, London, England*

Ray W. Cooksey *Centre for Behavioural Studies in Education, University of New England, Armidale, N.S.W., Australia*

H. L. F. Currey *London Hospital Medical College, London, England*

Graham R. Davidson *School of General Studies, Darwin Community College, Winnellie, N.T., Australia*

Krishna S. Dhir *Department of Management, University of Denver*

Ward Edwards *Social Science Research Institute, University of Southern California*

Hillel J. Einhorn *Center for Decision Research, Graduate School of Business, University of Chicago*

Baruch Fischhoff *Decision Research, a branch of Perceptronics, Inc., Eugene, Oregon*

Peter Freebody *Centre for Behavioural Studies in Education, University of New England, Armidale, N.S.W., Australia*

Gary J. Gaeth *Department of Marketing, University of Iowa*

Lewis R. Goldberg *Institute for Measurement of Personality, Eugene, Oregon*

John H. Greist *Department of Psychiatry, University of Wisconsin*

David H. Gustafson   *Centre for Health Systems Research and Analysis, University of Wisconsin*

Kenneth R. Hammond   *Department of Psychology, University of Colorado*

Reid Hastie   *Department of Psychology, Northwestern University*

Paul J. Hoffman   *COGITAN, Los Altos, California*

Robin M. Hogarth   *Center for Decision Research, Graduate School of Business, University of Chicago*

C. R. B. Joyce   *Medical Division, CIBA-GEIGY, Ltd., Basel, Switzerland*

Helmut Jungermann   *Institut für Psychologie, Technische Universität Berlin, Germany*

Daniel Kahneman   *Department of Psychology, University of British Columbia*

Robert F. Kidd   *Springer-Verlag, New York, New York*

J. R. Kirwan   *London Hospital Medical College, London, England*

Benjamin Kleinmuntz   *Department of Psychology, University of Illinois at Chicago*

Sarah Lichtenstein   *Decision Research, a branch of Perceptronics, Inc., Eugene, Oregon*

Darwyn E. Linder   *Department of Psychology, Arizona State University*

Lola L. Lopes   *Department of Psychology, University of Wisconsin at Madison*

Howard J. Markman   *Department of Psychology, University of Denver*

Barbara Marvin   *Center for Research on Judgment and Policy, University of Colorado**

Gary McClelland   *Department of Psychology, University of Colorado*

Barbara J. McNeil   *Department of Radiology, Harvard Medical School; Women's Hospital, Boston, Massachusetts*

Paul E. Meehl   *Department of Psychiatry, University of Minnesota*

Michael Mims   *Department of Psychology, University of Iowa**

John C. Mowen   *College of Business Administration, Oklahoma State University*

Margaret A. Neale   *Department of Management, University of Arizona*

J. Robert Newman   *Department of Psychology, California State University at Long Beach*

Stephen G. Pauker   *Department of Medicine, New England Medical Center Hospital, Boston, Massachusetts*

Lawrence D. Phillips   *Decision Analysis Unit, London School of Economics, London, England*

Robert Quinn   *IBM, San Jose, California*

Howard Raiffa   *Graduate School of Business, Harvard University*

John Rohrbaugh   *Graduate School of Public Affairs, State University of New York at Albany*

Leonard G. Rorer   *Department of Psychology, Miami University, Oxford, Ohio*

Jon C. Ross   *Children's Hospital, San Francisco, California*

* Asterisk indicates affiliation when article was originally published.

Michael J. Saks   *Psychology Department, Boston College*

Eric B. Schoomaker   *Department of Medicine, Walter Reid Army Medical Center, Washington, DC*

Richard H. Shachtman   *Psychology Department, Boston College*

Harriet Shaklee   *Department of Psychology, University of Oregon*

James Shanteau   *Department of Psychology, Kansas State University*

Herbert A. Simon   *Department of Psychology, Carnegie-Mellon University*

James C. Sisson   *Division of Nuclear Medicine, Department of Internal Medicine, University of Michigan Medical Center*

Paul Slovic   *Decision Research, a branch of Perceptronics, Inc., Eugene, Oregon*

Harold C. Sox, Jr.   *Department of Medicine, Stanford University*

Derick O. Steinmann   *American Banker/The Bond Buyer, New York, New York*

Thomas R. Stewart   *National Center for Atmospheric Research, Boulder, Colorado*

Jeffrey Sutherland   *Mid-Continent Computer Services, Denver, Colorado*

Richard H. Thaler   *Graduate School of Management, Cornell University*

Bruce Tianen   *Medicus Systems Corporation, Chicago, Illinois**

Amos Tversky   *Department of Psychology, Stanford University*

Detlof von Winterfeldt   *Social Science Research Institute, University of Southern California*

Friedrich Wilkening   *Institut für Psychologie, Johann Wolfgang Goethe-Universität, Frankfurt am Main, Germany*

George N. Wright   *City of London Polytechnic, London, England*

David L. Zalkind   *School of Government and Business Administration, Health Services Administration, George Washington University*

Editors' preface

Teachers of judgment and decision making can be found in psychology departments, business schools, economics departments, political science departments, medical schools, engineering schools, departments of social work, and, yes, other places. Therefore, it will be no surprise to learn that there are few books on this topic that are prepared for the general reader – one who wishes to be introduced to the topic without becoming fully immersed in the substantive details of any one area of application. But because the topic of judgment and decision making is of great interest to almost everyone, its applications touching almost every human endeavor, a general introduction to this topic is bound to be useful. Therefore, the Committee on Teaching of the Society for Judgment and Decision Making suggested that we prepare this volume with the assistance of the editorial committee named at the end of this Preface. Although we have profited greatly from the guidance of the editorial committee, the final selection and organization of the materials included have been ours. Our aim has been to provide a general, interdisciplinary introduction that will enable the reader to develop an appreciation of the nature of the new field of judgment and decision making.

We have also provided a very brief indication of the nature of two general approaches the reader will encounter in various chapters. Those teachers whose interests lead them to emphasize one or the other of these approaches will, of course, want to provide students with further reading. Those students who are reading this book "on their own" will find Suggested Readings that will enable them to explore each topic as far as they wish.

We have included 43 chapters organized in terms of 9 areas of application. Because our aim is one of introduction, we have not included any material (with the exception of one part) that requires anything more than an elementary understanding of algebra and statistics. Each part contains a brief introduction to the material included in it.

Thus, the reader should find in these pages a general introduction to one of our most important and interesting intellectual activities, as well as a series of illustrations of the empirical analysis of judgment and decision making in various fields of interest.

Ellipses in the text of an article indicate that material appearing in the original article has been omitted.

We wish to thank members of the Society for Judgment and Decision Making who served as editoral advisors for the selection of articles for this book: Norman Anderson, Berndt Brehmer, Robyn Dawes, Ward Edwards, Arthur Elstein, Baruch Fischhoff, Charles Gettys, Robin Hogarth, Daniel Kahneman, Robert Libby, Lola Lopes, Gary McClelland, Jeryl Mumpower, John Payne, James Shanteau, Paul Slovic, and Colleen Surber. We also wish to express our gratitude to Mary Luhring and Doreen Victor whose work on this book went far beyond the call of duty.

Hal R. Arkes

Kenneth R. Hammond

General introduction

All students like to believe that their particular subject is the center of the universe. Doubtless, students of judgment and decision making are no different, but they may have a good argument for their view. After all, they can claim that the great moments of history all turned on someone's judgment as to what should be done and someone's decision to do it. Moreover, they will claim that although their subject is as old as civilization it has been studied in a scientific, empirical way only within the very last quarter century. Indeed, most of the pioneers in this field are still alive and contributing to it. The fact that we are now able to study judgment and decision making in a scientific manner is, these students can claim, an exciting new discovery in and of itself.

Of course, the editors of this book and the authors of the chapters in it firmly believe in this view; judgment and decision making *are* of critical importance, and the fact that it is possible to study them in a scientific, empirical manner *is* a new and exciting event in the recent history of science.

Despite its central importance and long history, however, the field is still so new that it will be useful to turn to the dictionary to discover how these terms have been defined for common use. *Webster's Third New International Dictionary* says that *judgment* is "the mental or intellectual process of forming an opinion or evaluation by discerning and comparing," and the *capacity for judging* is "the power or ability to decide on the basis of evidence." Although the dictionary quotes E. L. Godkin as saying that "judgment is the highest of the human faculties," it also notes that Oliver Wendell Holmes said, "some of the sharpest men in argument are notoriously unsound in judgment." Apparently, we are to understand that the capacity to make sound judgments requires not only intelligence but wisdom and that the former does not guarantee the latter. *Webster's* definition of *decision*, "the act of settling or terminating ... by

1

giving judgment," suggests that there is little difference between *judgment* and *decision making* in ordinary discourse, so we shall not make a distinction here, although more advanced treatments of the topic do (see, e.g., Hammond, McClelland, & Mumpower, 1980, pp. 55–58).

Not only the sources but the nature of sound judgment have fascinated scholars since the beginning of self-reflection; the Greek intellectuals apparently mused about those topics every day. And the discussion continues today among philosophers, psychologists, political scientists, lawyers, management scientists, and others inside and outside of academia, because sound judgment is, of course, of great practical as well as academic concern. No question will be of greater importance to the board of directors of the industrial firm that evaluates candidates for the position of chief executive officer than the soundness of each candidate's judgment. And while members of all the above academic departments debate theories of rational choice (each group in happy ignorance of the activities of the others), members of the board of regents will be exercising their judgment as they select the new president of the university. Indeed, the capacity for sound judgment of every person who desires a high (or even not so high) place in almost every segment of society will be judged by those responsible for selecting them. That is because within both government and industry there is a strong correlation between the prominence and power of one's position, the amount of time that one spends on problems requiring judgment, and the salary one receives. At the other end of the scale, inability to make the simple judgments required in the ordinary circumstances of day-to-day living leads to the diagnosis of mental illness.

In short, judgment and decision making are pervasive, important intellectual activities engaged in by all of us in academic, professional, and social pursuits throughout every day. The ability to form good judgments and make wise and effective decisions generally is considered the mark of a successful person in the smaller as well as the larger matters of living. Apparently, the same has been true of every human society.

What do we know about this salient feature of our lives? This book will not try to answer that question completely, but it will provide a general introduction to our knowledge of judgment and decision making and provide guideposts for those who may wish to pursue their inquiry further. Although the study of judgment and decision making is a field in its own right, it finds application in virtually every known human endeavor. (A recent survey conducted by one of us showed that articles related to judgment and decision making appeared in more than 500 different professional journals.) Therefore, we have chosen to group studies of judgment and decision making within those major fields in which studies of judgment and decision making are currently being conducted. These include judgment and social policy, economics, law, clinical judgment, and other fields indicated in the Table of Contents.

It is easy to find examples of the importance of the "intellectual process of forming an opinion or evaluation by discerning or comparing" or "decid[ing] on the basis of evidence." The decision to drop the atomic bomb on Hiroshima without warning is perhaps the most dramatic example of an act of judgment in the 20th century. Other examples include changes in health policy (e.g., the decision to institute a National Health Service in Britain), economic policy (e.g., the deregulation of airlines in the United States), legal policy (e.g., the use of plea bargaining), and environmental policy (e.g., the protection of wildlife and pristine areas, the control of toxic waste), and the reduction of risk (e.g., the nationwide 55-mph speed limit in the United States); all provide examples of the attempt to exercise sound judgment. And in what follows we provide examples of efforts to study such judgments, both in the controlled conditions of the laboratory and in the world outside.

The reader will notice that all of these examples of studies of judgment and decision making are recent, from the 1970s forward. We could have provided examples from the 1950s (e.g., Edwards, 1954; Hammond, 1955) and at least one example from as far back as 1918 (Thorndike, 1918), but the systematic empirical study of judgment and decision making began to emerge as a discipline in its own right only in the 1960s. This occurred together with a strong surge of interest in the larger, more general field of cognitive psychology, which includes the study of memory, thinking, problem solving, mental imagery, and language. The explosion of research in cognitive psychology marked a sharp shift in interest from the concentration on motivation in psychological research to a concentration on "mental activity." There are two main reasons for this. First, something dropped out; by 1960 strict stimulus–response behaviorism lost credibility among many laboratory scientists, and Freudian psychology based largely on unconscious motivation lost credibility with almost everyone. Second, something dropped in, namely, the electronic computer, which immediately provided a credible metaphor for mental activity. Thus, within a decade of the introduction of the computer, psychologists were talking about and studying "human information processing." As one psychologist (George Miller) put it, "the mind came in on the back of the machine." The arrival of the computer made it possible to carry out research on human information processing (including judgment and decision making) in new and powerful ways. For example, those interested in problem solving were able to build computer models that simulated human information-processing activity, and this led rapidly to the creation of the new field of artificial intelligence. Those interested in constructing mathematical models of the judgment and decision-making process could rapidly test a variety of such models for their ability to represent and/or evaluate the rationality of human judgment and decision making. By the 1980s, work that would have been utterly impossible prior to the computer became commonplace.

Because two types of mathematical representations of judgment and decision-making behavior are frequently used, we present the basic ideas that underlie them in this General Introduction. The mathematical operations of both approaches are easy to grasp; a knowledge of simple algebra is all that is required. We first describe the approach known as *decision analysis* – which involves an a priori decomposition of the decision process – and, second, we describe the approach known as *judgment analysis* – which involves an a posteriori decomposition of the judgment process. Although the distinction between decision and judgment is somewhat arbitrary and need not concern us here, the distinction between a priori and a posteriori decomposition is important and should be kept in mind, for it will be illustrated often in the chapters that follow.

Decision analysis: A priori decomposition

A priori decomposition refers to separating the decision process into its components *before* the decision is made. Such components include (*a*) the *probabilities* or likelihood of occurrence of each alternative considered and (*b*) the *utility* attached to each alternative. The decision process is greatly aided when these concepts are used in the context of a *decision tree*.

Construction of a decision tree prior to making the decision is an easy way of guiding and simplifying the decision process because it *diagrams* the decomposition of the decision process into probabilities and utilities and thus provides a clear picture of the process and its components.

The decision maker needs only four types of information to construct a decision tree:

1. What are my possible courses of action?
2. What are the events that might follow from those actions?
3. What is the likelihood of each event?
4. What is the value of each event to me?

Here is a decision-making situation similar to one that actually confronted an elderly man known to us. The man had a very serious medical problem. His physician said that a difficult operation was necessary to remedy the situation. The physician added, however, that, given the man's very advanced age and the nature of the operation, there was a 40% *probability* that the patient would not recover from the operation. If the operation were not performed, the serious medical problem would linger, causing the patient discomfort and impairing his mobility. There was no chance that the problem would "go away," and there was a 20% probability that without the operation the man would die within the next 6 months. What should the man do? Should he have the operation?

Figure 1.1 depicts the decision tree for this situation. The box labeled "A" represents a "decision node." The two possible courses of action

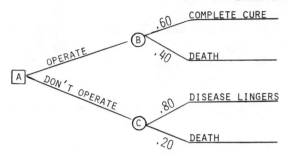

Figure I.1. Decision tree illustrating probabilities associated with alternative actions and outcomes.

emanate from this node. They are "operate" and "don't operate," and thus they comprise the first of the four types of information needed to construct a decision tree. The circles labeled "B" and "C" are chance nodes. (They are called chance nodes because no decision can be made to cause one of the outcomes to occur rather than the other. Their occurrence is therefore left to chance.) The events emanating from these circles are the possible events that might occur following the courses of action. This is the second type of information needed. Preceding each possible event is its probability of occurrence, based on the physician's best estimate. This is the third essential type of information. Finally, we need to know what value the patient places on each of these outcomes.

Because the value of any commodity is judged differently by everyone, the term *utility* rather than *value* is used. This term captures the subjective nature of the evaluation; a particular amount of money may have different utility for me than for you. Even health may have different utilities for different people. In order to calculate the utility of each outcome, we shall call the worst outcome 0.0 on a utility scale and the best outcome 1.0.

The patient assigned "death" the former value and "complete cure" the latter value. Using this range (0.0–1.0), the patient felt that living in discomfort and having decreased mobility was worth .6 to him. It was a state closer to "complete cure" than to "death," but not by much.

We now have all the information needed to make a decision tree. First, it is necessary to examine each outcome. The utility of each outcome needs to be weighted according to its likelihood. An outcome of 1.0 ("wonderful") that has a high probability of occurring should definitely be preferred to another outcome of utility 0.0 that has very little likelihood of occurring. In order to accomplish this mathematically, the utility of each outcome is multiplied by its probability of occurrence. This product is the *expected utility* of each outcome. Figure I.2 contains these calculations, which are located at the right edge of each branch of the decision tree.

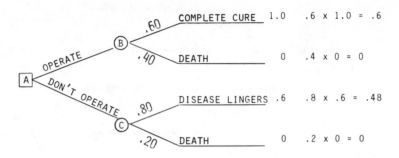

Figure I.2. Calculation of subjective expected utilities for alternative actions and outcomes: An a priori decomposition of a person's judgment process.

All that remains now is the process called "folding back," which consists of pruning all but the most preferred course of action at each decision node. There are two possible courses of action: operate and don't operate. For each of these two options we add together all of the expected utilities associated with that option. For example, the option "don't operate" has associated with it two expected utilities of .48 and 0. Their sum, .48, is the expected utility of the "don't operate" course of action. Because the "operate" course of action is higher (.6), the preferred course of action is to operate.

One immense virtue of a decision tree is that it is a wonderfully general decision aid. As long as the four types of information are available, any decision can be analyzed by use of the tree. Should I move to Minneapolis to accept this new job? Should I switch insurance policies from X to Y? Should we get a loan to get a new car now, or should we limp along with the one we have?

One difficulty often encountered in constructing a decision tree is that likelihoods and utilities are often not easy to assess. When an expert opinion is available, as in the case of our medical example, reasonable likelihoods can often be provided. Because the helpfulness of a decision tree is based largely on the accuracy of the likelihoods and utilities used, every effort should be made to obtain good estimates.

Occasionally the decision maker is uneasy about the "verdict" of the decision tree. In our medical example, the "operate" option was only .12 superior to the "don't operate" option. "What if I later decide that living with discomfort and decreased mobility isn't so bad? Maybe it's worth a .7 and not a measly .6," thinks the elderly man as the morning of the operation approaches. A quick calculation will reveal that "operate" is *still* the preferred choice, even if .7 is deemed the utility of an uncomfortable and immobile existence. Modifying the probabilities and utilities in this way is called a "sensitivity analysis," because such manipulating of the probabilities and utilities tests how sensitive the final choice is to the numbers initially assigned. Reasonable modifications of the probabilities and utilities often leave the decision unchanged. The decision maker can then rest comfortably with the decision that has been reached.

Concern about the assignment of accurate probabilities, the calculation of expected utilities, and the performance of various arithmetic tasks should not obscure what may be the greatest virtue of a decision tree: It forces the decision maker to make explicit all the bases for the decision. In the tree are contained all the courses of action, all the probabilities, all the utilities, and all the outcomes of which the decision maker is aware. Merely having to generate this information may force the decision maker to confront the situation in a much more organized and thoughtful way than would otherwise be the case.

Many of the chapters in this volume will employ this method. Some will be critical of its use. The first two chapters in Part I will provide the reader with a more detailed description of the approach to studying decision making. At this point we turn to judgment analysis.

Judgment analysis: A posteriori decomposition

If a priori decomposition implies decomposing the decision process *prior* to its occurrence, then a posteriori decomposition obviously implies that decomposition will take place *after* a series of judgments have been made. As we shall see, a person's *judgment policy* can be "captured" after judgments are made regarding hypothetical cases; the policy may then be applied to real cases.

The principal concepts of a judgment analysis are best illustrated by reference to the model of the judgment situation presented in Figure I.3, which indicates that judgment is a cognitive process similar to inductive inference. That is, judgment is a cognitive or intellectual process in which a person draws a conclusion, or an inference (Y_s), about something (Y_e), which *cannot* be seen, on the basis of data (X_i), which *can* be seen. In other words, judgments are made from *tangible* data, which serve as *cues* to *intangible* events and circumstances. The wide-ranging arc connecting Y_s and Y_e (labeled r_a in Figure I.3) indicates the degree to which the judgment Y_s was correct, that is, the extent to which the judgment coincides with the actual circumstance to be judged. A rough example can be found in the judgments of the weather forecaster who looks at certain tangible cues (X_i) such as wind speed, temperature, and barometric pressure and makes a judgment (Y_s) about what tomorrow's weather (Y_e) will be. The arc, r_a, indicates the degree of accuracy over a series of judgments.

Throughout any ordinary day one frequently encounters similar circumstances. Tangible data (e.g., events in the news, activities of the stock market, actions of friends and neighbors) evoke judgments as to the unperceived events that gave rise to the events perceived. *Causes* (Y_e) are

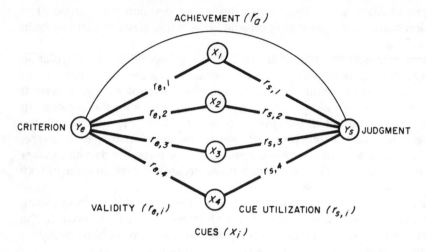

Figure I.3. Schematic illustration of the relation of achievement (r_a) and ecological validities; of cues ($r_{e,i}$) and cue utilization ($r_{s,i}$): an a posteriori decomposition of a person's judgment process.

frequently being inferred (Y_s) from those cue events (X_i), or *effects*, that are being observed. And the ability to make correct inferences (indicated by r_a) is, of course, an ability in which persons are believed to differ widely. High judgmental accuracy is considered to be an essential attribute of persons with high responsibility; low accuracy indicates persons very likely to be in difficulty with their social or physical surroundings.

The model in Figure I.3 also indicates the concept of *differential weight*. Cues may have differential weight in that they are of differential value in making inferences about events. That is, if a cue has a very strong relation (a high degree of covariation) with an event to be inferred, it will be more useful than one that has a weak relation. Therefore, cues with high degrees of covariation with the event to be inferred have a large degree of *ecological validity*; their weight is greater than those with low degrees of covariation.

The counterpart to the ecological validity (r_e) of a cue is its utilization (r_s) by the subject (see Figure I.3). Cues also may be used or depended upon to a larger or smaller degree, therefore, with regard to their *subjective utilization*. Thus an observer may compare the differential weights of a set of cues ($r_{e,i}$) in the task with the weights implicitly assigned to them by the person making the inference. Mismatches between ecological validities and subjective utilization of cues are one source of inaccurate judgments. In other words, one source of poor judgment lies in the failure to attach the correct relative weights or importance to cues.

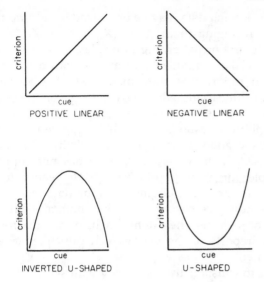

Figure I.4. Four commonly observed function forms between cues and a person's judgment.

Not only do cues have different task weights, but they may be related to the variable to be inferred (Y_e) by means of different functional relations, or *function forms*. These may include positive linear function forms, negative linear function forms, or a variety of curvilinear function forms (see Figure 1.4). Of course, cues may be related to judgment (Y_s) by means of various function forms also, and the comparison, or match, between task function form and subjective function form will also form the basis for accurate or inaccurate judgments.

Tasks that involve curvilinear functions are apt to be more difficult to learn than those with positive linear function forms, and people's judgments related to cues in curvilinear forms are apt to be more difficult for other people to understand. Moreover, people seldom make explicit to others exactly which function form they are employing in a given situation, simply because most people are not aware of this concept. It may appear in colloquial form, however. For example, one way to indicate that another person is using a positive linear function form when he or she should be using a curvilinear one is to say that the person's error lies in believing that "if a little is good, more is better" – a rule that, if followed in the taking of medicine, is apt to lead to disaster. The reader will find it easy to think of other examples of an inappropriate use of linear function forms. One should also consider the difficulties of *changing* a function form to fit the function form of a task, or to fit one preferred by a friend, a teacher, or a therapist.

The principles by which the cue data are organized into a judgment are of considerable importance. Such data may be organized by adding them, $Y_s = X_1 + X_2 + X_3$; by averaging them, $Y_s = (X_1 + X_2 + X_3)/3$; or by making use of some configural or patterning principles, $Y_s = X_1 + X_2X_3$.

When asked about how they organize information into a judgment, most persons are apt to report that they make use of a pattern or configuration of the data. Physicians who make a diagnosis, experts in investment, and others whose professional judgment is of great importance generally reply to questions about their judgment processes by referring more or less vaguely to their intuitive ability to recognize "patterns." Empirical research, however, in general has not supported these contentions; simpler organizing principles have been found to account for, or at least to predict, judgments from data better than patterns. Although it hardly seems doubtful that human beings *can* organize data by means of patterns, the extent to which they do in fact is unknown; in any event, reports of the use of such principles certainly cannot be taken for granted.

Finally, it is important to consider the *consistency* with which the same judgment is made in response to the same data. Although everyone is apt to assume that they always make the same judgments when confronted with the same facts, it is virtually certain that they will not do so except under the very simplest circumstances. That is, perfect consistency in judgments is apt to occur only when there is no uncertainty whatever in the task situation. Such simple task situations, of course, require little in the way of judgment, inasmuch as a given cue always evokes the same judgment.

The simplest and best way to discover the cues, differential weights, function forms, and consistency of a person's judgment process is to use a computer to present a number of cases to the person making the judgment. After the judgments have been made, a computer program can readily decompose the judgment process into weights, function forms, and consistency. Because this information is extracted *after* a series of judgments have been made, the decomposition is obviously a posteriori. But it is important to observe that, because the judgments can be made with regard to *hypothetical* cases, the person's *judgment policy* (consisting of specific weights and function forms) can then be applied to a real case or a series of real cases. In short, even though the method extracts the various components of the judgment policy after the judgments have been made, the policy may be applied to new cases or to any one judgment problem, just as in the situation where a priori decomposition takes place.

Examples of a posteriori judgment analysis may be seen in Chapters 3 and 21. A slightly different version of a posteriori decomposition can be found in Chapter 4. We trust that these brief remarks have proved to be informative to the reader and that they will provide a useful background for pursuing the principal contents of the book.

Part I
Introduction

We first present several sections of a monograph by Ward Edwards and J. Robert Newman that describes the application of Multiattribute Utility Technology (MAUT). Chapter 2, an article by Amos Tversky and Daniel Kahneman, challenges many assumptions of the rationality of our choices under uncertainty. Chapter 3, by Kenneth R. Hammond, Thomas R. Stewart, Berndt Brehmer, and Derick O. Steinmann, illustrates a different approach to judgment under uncertainty, and Chapter 4, an article by Norman H. Anderson, illustrates the research that uncovers the "cognitive algebra" by which information is integrated into a judgment. Most of the remaining chapters are based on the fundamental ideas presented in these introductory articles.

1. Multiattribute evaluation

Ward Edwards and J. Robert Newman

Evaluation of social programs

Evaluation is rapidly becoming Big Business. Questions like "Is this plan wise?" "Should I choose option A or option B?" "At what funding level should this program be supported?" "How well is this program doing?" have been asked of social programs since long before we were born. But the idea that one could answer such questions systematically and in a manner other than simply looking at the object of evaluation and making an intuitive judgment is a development of the 1960s and 1970s. As inflated costs and less-inflated program budgets come into steadily escalating conflict, the task of weeding out the programs worthy of support from those that are not, and of providing guidance for programs in existence, will continue to grow in importance – as will the resources and attention devoted to developing satisfying methods of performing that task.

What is evaluation?

The literature of evaluation is already huge, and grows daily. The purpose of this paper is not academic, and we do not intend more than the most cursory of references even to the literature on the method of evaluation that is our topic. For a recent and very scholarly presentation of evaluation methods and results from a broad spectrum of viewpoints, including our own, see Klein and Teilmann (1980). Edwards's chapter in that book will be of particular interest to scholars who find the ideas presented in this paper stimulating and potentially useful to them, since it discusses the same ideas in a far more technical way, reviews a significant amount of literature, and cites the literature of this and of other methods.

The purpose of this paper is to present one approach to evaluation: Multiattribute Utility Technology (MAUT). We have attempted to make a version of MAUT simple and straightforward enough so that the reader can, with diligence and frequent reexaminations of it, conduct relatively straightforward MAUT evaluations him- or herself. In so doing, we will frequently resort to techniques that professional decision analysts will recognize as approximations and/or assumptions. The literature justifying those approximations is extensive and complex; to review it here would blow to smithereens our goal of being nontechnical.

What is MAUT, and how does it relate to other approaches to evaluation? Edwards, Guttentag, and Snapper (1975) discussed that question in 1975, and we have little to add. MAUT depends on a few key ideas:

1. When possible, evaluations should be comparative.
2. Programs normally serve multiple constituencies.
3. Programs normally have multiple goals, not all equally important.
4. Judgments are inevitably a part of any evaluation.
5. Judgments of magnitude are best when made numerically.
6. Evaluations typically are, or at least should be, relevant to decisions.

Some of the six points above are less innocent than they seem. If programs serve multiple constituencies, evaluations of them should normally be addressed to the interests of those constituencies; different constituencies can be expected to have different interests. If programs have multiple goals, evaluations should attempt to assess how well they serve them; this implies multiple measures and comparisons. The task of dealing with multiple measures of effectiveness (which may well be simple subjective judgments in numerical form) makes less appealing the notion of social programs as experiments or quasi-experiments. While the tradition that programs should be thought of as experiments, or at least as quasi-experiments, has wide currency and wide appeal in evaluation research, its implementation becomes more difficult as the number of measures needed for a satisfactory evaluation increases. When experimental or other hard data are available, they can easily be incorporated in a MAUT evaluation.

Finally, the willingness to accept subjectivity into evaluation, combined with the insistence that judgments be numerical, serves several useful purposes. First, it partly closes the gap between the intuitive and judgmental evaluations and the more quantitative kind; indeed, it makes coexistence of judgment and objective measurement within the same evaluation easy and natural. Second, it opens the door to easy combination of complex concatenations of values. For instance, evaluation researchers often distinguish between process evaluations and outcome evaluations. Process and outcome are different, but if a program has goals of both kinds, its evaluation can and should assess its performance on both. Third, use of subjective inputs can, if need be, greatly shorten the time required for an evaluation to be carried out. A MAUT evaluation can be carried out from original definition of the evaluation problem to preparation of the evaluation report in as little as a week of concentrated effort. The inputs to such an abbreviated evaluative activity will obviously be almost entirely subjective. But the MAUT technique at least produces an audit trail such that the skeptic can substitute other judgments for those that seem doubtful, and can then examine what the consequences for the evaluation are. We know of no MAUT social program evaluation that took less than two months, but in some other areas of application we have participated in execution of complete MAUT evaluations in as little as two days – and then watched them be used as the justification for major decisions. Moreover, we heartily approved; time constraints on the decision made haste necessary, and we were very pleased to have the chance to provide some orderly basis for decision in so short a time.

Classes of purposes for evaluations

Evaluations can be done for various reasons; different reasons can and do lead to different forms of evaluative activities. The most common reason for evaluation is that it is required; perhaps by mandate from Congress or from a sponsor or perhaps by rules internal to the program organization.

The organizational requirement for an evaluation is normally based on the supposition that decisions need to be made. Sometimes the question is whether the program should be continued, modified, or scrapped. Sometimes it is simply what relatively minor changes, if any, should be made in program design, management, or functioning to improve its effectiveness. Sometimes no specific decisions are behind such mandated evaluations; the spirit of such evaluations is somewhat similar to the spirit that leads to annual external audit of corporate books.

Major evaluations are often required as a basis for potential major programmatic changes – up to and including the most major of all changes: the birth or death of a program. Sometimes such decisions are pure life-or-death choices; at least equally often, some social problem requires attention, and the decision problem is which of several alternative approaches to dealing with it looks most promising. Funding-level decisions are also programmatic choices; the same program at two sub-stantially different funding levels is really two different programs.

From this welter of considerations, we think we can distinguish four different classes of reasons for evaluations: curiosity, monitoring, fine tuning, and programmatic choice. Curiosity in itself is seldom a basis for wisely performed evaluations, since most programs are too specific in character for the kinds of generalizations to which wisely applied curiosity can lead, and generalized curiosity is a poor guide to choice of evaluative methods or measures.

Monitoring is both an appropriate and a necessary function for any program, and we believe MAUT offers useful tools for monitoring. Monitoring shades over into fine tuning; the same tools are relevant to both. Programmatic choice is the most important use to which evaluative information can be put, and the tools of MAUT are most directly relevant to it.

These reasons for evaluation share two common characteristics that make MAUT applicable to them all. The first is that, implicitly or explicitly, all require comparison of something with something else. This is most obvious in the case of programmatic choice. But even monitoring has the characteristic, since one normally wonders whether or not some minor change would change significantly one of the monitored values. An important implication of the comparative nature of virtually every evaluation is that some of the comparisons are inevitably between the program as it is and the program as it might be – that is, between real and imaginary programs or programmatic methods. The necessity of comparing real with imaginary objects is one of the problems that most approaches to evaluation find very difficult to solve. The normal approach of traditional methods is to make the comparison object real, typically by embodying it in an experimental (or control) group, locus, or program. We admire such comparisons when they can be made (e.g., in drug trials), but consider them impractical for most social program evaluations. MAUT deals with this problem by accepting data and judgments on equivalent footings; judgment is the most generally useful tool we know of for assessing the consequences of nonexistent programs. (Such judgments, of course, are best when based on relevant data, e.g., from other programs in other places.)

The second characteristic that the various reasons for evaluation share is that programs virtually always have multiple objectives; consequently, evaluations should assess as many of these as seem important.

We use the word "program" in a broader sense than has been common; we are concerned with many social programs other than social service delivery programs. We consider arms procurement, treaties among nations, labor contracts, choices made by businesses about such questions as where to locate new plants, and other similar public decisions with major impacts on people to be "programs," and to deserve evaluation. One version or another of the methods we discuss has been used for purposes as diverse as deciding whether to expand a Community Anti-Crime Program area, evaluating the Office of the Rentalsman in Vancouver as a dispute resolution mechanism, evaluating alternative school desegregation plans for Los Angeles, choosing among alternative sites for dams and nuclear power plants, evaluating competing bids for various kinds of military hardware, formulating U.S. negotiating positions in international negotiations, and assessing the combat readiness of Marine Corps brigades. For more information and a number of references to such applications, see Edwards (1980).

Since we claim that MAUT can be applied to evaluative problems of each of the kinds we can identify, are we asserting that it is a universally applicable mode of evaluation – perhaps a substitute for alternative modes? No. MAUT is, we believe, a very widely applicable method of organizing and presenting evaluative information. As such, it is compatible with any other evaluative activity designed to yield numbers as outputs. Since the ideas of MAUT do not limit the sources of the evaluative information, they can be combined with whatever data sources the evaluator finds satisfying and relevant to his or her problem ....

Steps in a MAUT evaluation

It may be helpful at this point to summarize concisely the steps involved in any MAUT evaluation. This will (1) summarize the remainder of this paper; (2) provide a brief procedural guide; and (3) identify, but not define, the technical terms ....

First, a note about technical terms. There are a lot of them, and many will seem nonstandard to those familiar with the MAUT literature. In every case that we can identify, use of a nonstandard term corresponds to a shading of difference between what this paper discusses and what previous publications (including many of which Edwards was an author) have discussed. Many more versions of MAUT exist than researchers active in developing it. While all depend on the same basic ideas, details of implementation change, and such changes produce corresponding changes in jargon. Many nontechnical readers will wish to skip this section and go on to the next.

Step 1. Identify the objects of evaluation and the function or functions that the evaluation is intended to perform. Normally there will be several objects of evaluation, at least some of them imaginary, since evaluations are comparative. The functions of the evaluation will often control the choice of objects of evaluation. We have argued that evaluations should help decision makers to make decisions. If the nature of those decisions is known, the objects of evaluation will often be controlled by that knowledge. Step 1 is outside the scope of this paper. Some of the issues inherent in it have already been discussed in this chapter. The next section, devoted to setting up an example that will be carried through the document, illustrates Step 1 for that example.

Step 2. Identify the *stakeholders*....

Step 3. Elicit from stakeholder representatives the relevant *value dimensions* or *attributes*, and (often) organize them into a hierarchical structure called a *value tree*....

Step 4. Assess for each stakeholder group the *relative importance* of each of the values identified at Step 3. Such judgments can, of course, be expected to vary from one stakeholder group to another, methods of dealing with such value conflicts are important....

Step 5. Ascertain how well each object of evaluation serves each value at the lowest level of the value tree. Such numbers, called *single-attribute utilities* or *location measures*, ideally report measurements, expert judgments, or both. If so, they should be independent of stakeholders and so of value disagreements among stakeholders; however, this ideal is not always met. Location measures need to be on a common scale, in order for Step 4 to make sense....

Step 6. Aggregate location measures with measures of importance....

Step 7. Perform *sensitivity analyses*. The question underlying any sensitivity analysis is whether a change in the analysis, e.g., using different numbers as inputs, will lead to different conclusions. While conclusions may have emerged from Step 6, they deserve credence as a basis for action only after their sensitivity is explored in Step 7....

Steps 6 and 7 will normally produce the results of a MAUT evaluation. ...

The relation between evaluation and decision

The tools of MAUT are most useful for guiding decisions; they grow out of a broader methodological field called decision analysis. The relation of evaluation to decision has been a topic of debate among evaluation researchers – especially the academic evaluation researchers who wonder whether or not their evaluations are used, and if so, appropriately used. Some evaluators take the position that their responsibility is to provide the relevant facts; it is up to someone else to make the decisions. "We are not elected officials." This position is sometimes inevitable, of course; the evaluator is not the decision maker as a rule, and cannot compel the decision maker to attend to the result of the evaluation, or to base decisions on it. But it is unattractive to many evaluators; certainly to us.

We know of three devices that make evaluations more likely to be used in decisions. The first and most important is to involve the decision makers heavily in the evaluative process; this is natural if, as is normally the case, they are among the most important stakeholders. The second is to make the evaluation as directly relevant to the decision as possible, preferably by making sure that the options available to the decision maker are the objects of evaluation. The third is to make the product of the evaluation useful – which primarily means making it readable and short. Exhaustive scholarly documents tend to turn busy decision makers off. Of course, nothing in these obvious devices guarantees success in making the evaluation relevant to the decision. However, nonuse of these devices comes close to guaranteeing failure.

By "decisions" we do not necessarily mean anything apocalyptic; the process of fine tuning a program requires decisions too. This paper unabashedly assumes that either the evaluator or the person or organization commissioning the evaluation has the options or alternative courses of action in mind, and proposes to select among them in part on the basis of the evaluation – or else that the information is being assembled and aggregated because of someone's expectation that that will be the case later on.

An example of a MAUT analysis

The Office of Community Anti-Crime Programs (OCAP) of the Law Enforcement Assistance Administration (LEAA) funded a number of community-based anticrime projects throughout the country. Decision Science Consortium, Inc. was hired to perform a large MAUT analysis of this whole program; the key people in that evaluation were Dr. Kurt Snapper and Dr. David Seaver....

The following discussion of a specific decision within that evaluation program is condensed from Snapper and Seaver (1978). One of the community projects within OCAP's program was that of the Midwood-Kings Highway Development Corporation (MKDC) in Brooklyn. The objectives (called *attributes* in this paper) of that particular project, and the *weights* given to them by its director, are given in Table 1.1. Note that all attributes are approximately equally important – a quite unusual finding. These attributes and weights were elicited in the first year of the MKDC project. The project was quite successful in improving on the preproject scores on these objectives in its area.[1]

In 1979, a decision problem arose. The City of New York adopted a "coterminality" policy; police and other service delivery areas were to become aligned or "coterminous" with community districts. Since MKDC served a part of the area served by the Midwood Civic Action Council

---

[1] Attribute 6, Option 1, in Table 1.2 shows a value of 105 on a 0–100 scale. This simply means that the project director judged 1981 performance on this dimension to be better than the best he thought could be expected when he defined endpoints of the dimension. Though such violations of the 0–100 range can occur, they should be rare.

Table 1.1. *MKDC CAC value attributes*

Number	Title of attribute	Importance weight
1	Reduce crime	.141
2	Reduce fear of crime	.140
3	Increase police responsiveness	.119
4	Serve community ombudsman role	.126
5	Increase resident involvement	.149
6	Institutionalize organization	.111
7	Provide technical assistance	.104
8	Integrate other social services	.110 1.000

(MCAC), the problem was whether to expand MKDC's area of service to include all of MCAC's area – a 50% expansion. No additional LEAA funds were expected for MKDC, so the concern was that expansion of the service area would lead to dilution of service quality and effectiveness. On the other hand, political considerations of various sorts argued for the expansion.

Working with Dr. Seaver and Dr. Snapper, the MKDC project director did a MAUT analysis of the two extreme options: to expand or not. The results are presented in Table 1.2. It is important to note that the measures on which Table 1.2 are based are judgments of the MKDC project director, and refer to the MKDC area alone. The baseline or *zero point* on each attribute is pre-MKDC project measures. The *100 point* on each dimension is the project director's judgment of the best that could be expected to be accomplished by the project. The weights used to combine the various utilities on each attribute into aggregate utilities come from Table 1.1. The aggregate utility serves as one basis for the evaluation – the higher these values, the better the option. Note that both are sets of judgments by the project director. A less abbreviated MAUT would have included other stakeholders.

The project director was relatively surprised by the results presented in Table 1.2; he had expected that expansion of the service area would lead to much more degradation of service than Table 1.2 shows. He therefore chose to go ahead and expand the area, since he felt that in the presence of such a relatively minor effect on service, the political considerations were compelling.

Political events in New York City have delayed implementation of coterminality, and there is some doubt about whether it will ever be

Table 1.2. *A MAUT analysis of the MKDC expansion decision*

Value attributes	1979	1980	1981
Option 1: *Expand to include all the MCAC area*			
1. Reduce crime	68	78	85
2. Reduce fear of crime	43	64	90
3. Increase police responsiveness	63	83	98
4. Serve ombudsman role	25	42	83
5. Increase resident involvement	28	69	95
6. Institutionalize organization	46	70	105
7. Give technical assistance	25	40	80
8. Integrate social services	75	88	97
Aggregate utility	46	67	92
Option 2: *Do not expand at all*			
1. Reduce crime	68	81	89
2. Reduce fear of crime	43	71	97
3. Increase police responsiveness	63	84	100
4. Serve ombudsman role	25	50	100
5. Increase resident involvement	28	85	100
6. Institutionalize organization	46	66	100
7. Give technical assistance	25	50	100
8. Integrate social services	75	90	100
Aggregate utility	46	73	98

implemented. However, MKDC is now considering petitioning LEAA to expand its target area to all of MCAC's area.

One reason for that decision is yet another version of the analysis. Recall that Table 1.2 is based only on predicted measures within the original MKDC area. If the area were to be expanded, it would be appropriate to take those measures over the whole MCAC area instead. Table 1.3 shows the result of a MAUT analysis based on predicted measures covering the whole MCAC area. Note that expansion of the area leads to severe initial degradation (for the year 1979) of the project effectiveness measures, since the new area includes a substantial region within which the old MKDC project, which had been very successful, had not been operating. However, the forecast leads to the conclusion that, although the figures are not as high as either of those in MKDC are alone, they show major improvement with time. This invites the idea that "the

Table 1.3. *Project effectiveness in the full MCAC area, assuming expansion*

Value attributes	1979	1980	1981
1. Reduce crime	−5	63	76
2. Reduce fear of crime	10	53	81
3. Increase police responsiveness	0	63	84
4. Serve ombudsman role	10	35	60
5. Increase resident involvement	15	43	90
6. Institutionalize organization	NA	66	70
7. Give technical assistance	0	25	50
8. Integrate social services	0	75	90
Aggregate utility	5	53	76

greatest good of the greatest number" is well served by expanding, even in the presence of constant funding.

The director also judged that a funding difference of only $60,000 would make the difference between leaving the original MKDC project ineffectual and giving it the necessary resources to serve all of the MCAC area as well as it was then serving MKDC. This is obviously an interesting assessment to report to LEAA in connection with any application to expand the MKDC area.

This is an example of a MAUT analysis carried out in a day. In spite of its brevity and omissions (e.g., of other stakeholders and of assessments of the political consequences of expanding or not expanding the area), it led a decision maker in a criminal justice project to change his mind, and provided him with the necessary information and analysis to defend that change of mind to sponsors, peers, and those he serves.

Summary

This section begins by defining the purpose of the paper: to present a version of Multiattribute Utility Technology (MAUT). The version chosen for presentation emphasizes multiple stakeholders, multiple program objectives, wholehearted acceptance of subjectivity, and linkage of evaluation to decision. The section distinguished four reasons for evaluation: curiosity, monitoring, fine tuning, and several forms of programmatic choice. MAUT is useful to them all because it implies comparison of something with something else with respect to multiple objectives. MAUT is not a mode of evaluation in itself; instead, it is a way of organizing and aggregating evaluative efforts. The section briefly lists the seven steps of a MAUT, discusses the relationship between evaluation and decision, and makes suggestions about how evaluative efforts can be made more likely to influence decisions. It concludes with an instance of a MAUT evaluation that led to a decision.

An example

We now present a fairly simple example of how to use multiattribute utility technology for evaluation. The example is intended to be simple enough to be understandable, yet complex enough to illustrate all of the technical ideas necessary for the analysis. . . .

Unfortunately, we cannot structure our discussion around the real example that we presented earlier. It does not have all of the features of MAUT that we need to examine. So we have invented an example that brings out all the properties of the method, and that will, we hope, be sufficiently realistic to fit with the intuitions of those who work in a social program environment.

The problem: How to evaluate new locations for a drug counseling center

The Drug-Free Center is a private nonprofit contract center that gives counseling to clients sent to it by the courts of its city as a condition of their probation. It is a walk-in facility with no beds or other special space requirements; it does not use methadone. It has just lost its lease, and must relocate.

The director of the center has screened the available spaces to which it might move. All spaces that are inappropriate because of zoning, excessive neighborhood resistance to the presence of the center, or inability to satisfy such legal requirements as access for the handicapped have been eliminated, as have spaces of the wrong size, price, or location. The city is in a period of economic recession, and so even after this prescreening a substantial number of options are available. Six sites are chosen as a result of informal screening for serious evaluation. The director must, of course, satisfy the sponsor, the probation department, and the courts that the new location is appropriate, and must take the needs and wishes of both employees and clients into account. But as a first cut, the director wishes simply to evaluate the sites on the basis of values and judgments of importance that make sense internally to the center.

The evaluation process

The first task is to identify stakeholders. They were listed in the previous paragraph. A stakeholder is simply an individual or group with a reason to care about the decision and with enough impact on the decision maker so that the reason should be taken seriously. Stakeholders are sources of *value attributes*. An attribute is something that the stakeholders, or some subset of them, care about enough so that failure to consider it in the decision would lead to a poor decision. . . .

In this case, to get the evaluation started, the director consulted, as

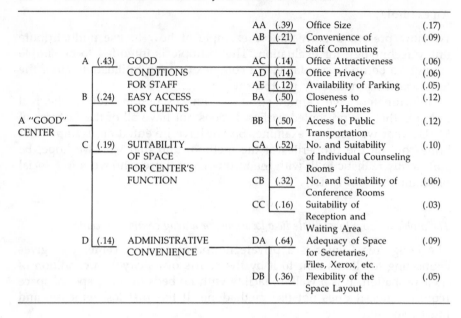

Figure 1.1. A value tree for the Drug-Free Center.

stakeholders, the members of the center staff. Their initial discussion of values elicited a list of about 50 verbal descriptors of values. A great many of these were obviously the same idea under a variety of different verbal labels. The director, acting as leader of the discussion, was able to see these duplications and to persuade those who originally proposed these as values to agree on a rephrasing that captured and coalesced these overlapping or duplicating ideas. She did so both because she wanted to keep the list short and because she knew that if the same idea appeared more than once in the final list, she would be "double counting"; that is, including the same value twice. Formally, there is nothing wrong with double counting so long as the *weights* reflect it. But in practice, it is important to avoid, in part because the weights will often not reflect it, and in part because the analysis is typically complex, and addition of extra and unnecessary attributes simply makes the complexity worse.

A second step in editing the list was to eliminate values that, in the view of the stakeholders, could not be important enough to influence the decision. An example of this type of value, considered and then eliminated because it was unimportant, was "proximity to good lunching places." The director was eager to keep the list of values fairly short, and her staff cooperated. In a less collegial situation, elimination of attributes can be much more difficult. Devices that help accomplish it are almost always worthwhile, so long as they do not leave some significant stakeholder feeling that his or her pet values have been summarily ignored.

The director was also able to obtain staff assent to organizing its values into four broad categories, each with subcategories. Such a structure is called a *value tree*. The one that the director worked with is shown in Figure 1.1. We explain the numbers shortly.

Several questions need review at this stage.

Have all important attributes been listed? Others had been proposed and could obviously have been added. The list does not mention number or location of toilets, proximity to restaurants, presence or absence of other tenants of the same building who might prefer not to have the clients of this kind of organization as frequent users of the corridors, racial/ethnic composition of the neighborhood, area crime rate, and various others. All of these and many more had been included in earlier lists, and eliminated after discussion. Bases for elimination include not only duplication and unimportance, but also that the sites under consideration did not vary from one another on that attribute, or varied very little. That is why racial/ethnic composition and crime rate were eliminated. Even an important attribute is not worth considering unless it contributes to discrimination among sites.

For program evaluation purposes, this principle needs to be considered in conjunction with the purpose of the evaluation. If the function of the evaluation is primarily to guide development of the program, then important attributes should be included even if they serve no discriminative function; in such cases, there may be no discriminative function to serve.

The director was satisfied with the list. It was relatively short, and she felt that it captured the major issues – given the fact that even more major requirements for a new site had been met by prescreening out all options that did not fulfill them.

An obvious omission from the attribute list is cost. For simplicity, we will treat cost as the annual lease cost, ignoring the possibility of other relevant differences among leases.

One possibility would be to treat cost as another attribute, and this is often done, especially for informal or quick evaluations. In such a procedure, one would specify a range of possible costs, assign a weight to that attribute, which essentially amounts to a judgment about how it trades off against other attributes, and then include it in the analysis like any other attribute. We have chosen not to do so in this example, for two reasons. First, some evaluations may not involve cost in any significant way (monitoring, for example), and we wish to illustrate procedures for cost-independent applications of MAUT. Second, we consider the kind of judgment required to trade off cost against *utility points* to be the least secure and most uncomfortable to make of all those that go into MAUT. For that reason, we like to use procedures, illustrated later, that permit extremely crude versions of that judgment to determine final evaluation.

While on the topic, we should discuss two other aspects of trading off dollars against *aggregated utilities*.

The first is budget constraints. If a budget constrains, in this example, the amount of rent the center can pay, then it is truly a constraint, and sites that fail to meet it must be rejected summarily. More common, however, is the case in which money can be used for one purpose or another. A full analysis would require considering also the loss, in this instance, that would result from spending more on rent and so having less to spend on other things. Such considerations are crucial, but we do not illustrate them here. In order to do so, we would have to provide a scenario about what budget cuts the director would need to make in other categories to pay additional rent. At the time she must choose among sites, she may not know what these are. Fairly often, the expansion of the analysis required to evaluate all possible ways in which a program might be changed by budget reallocations is very large indeed – far too large to make an easy example. So we prefer to think of this as a case in which the director's budget is large enough so that, for the range of costs involved, belt-tightening can take care of the difference between smallest and largest. A fuller analysis would consider the programmatic impact of fund reallocation, and could explore the utility consequences of alternative reallocations. The circumscription of the analysis in the interest of making it manageable is very common; relevant issues are and should be left out of every analysis. (An equivalent statement: If it can be avoided, no MAUT analysis should include every attribute judged relevant by any stakeholder.) ... The goal is to enlist stakeholder cooperation in keeping the list of attributes reasonably short.

The other issue having to do with cost but not with the example of this chapter is the portfolio problem. This is the generic name for situations in which a decision maker must choose, not a single option, but a number of options from a larger set. Typically, the limit on the number that can be chosen is specified by a budget constraint. The methods presented in this manual require considerable adaptation to be used formally for portfolio problems, because the decision maker normally wants the portfolio as a whole to have properties such as balance, diversity, or coverage (e.g., of topics, regions, disciplines, problems) that are not attributes of the individual options themselves. Formally, each possible portfolio is an option, and a value tree relevant to the portfolio, not to the individual options, is needed. But such formal complexity is rarely used. A much more common procedure in portfolio problems is to evaluate the individual elements using methods like those of this paper, choose from the best so identified, and then examine the resulting set of choices to make sure that it meets the budget constraint and looks acceptable as a portfolio.

You will have encountered such terms as benefit-cost analysis. Such analyses are similar in spirit to what we are doing here, but quite different in detail. By introducing into the analysis early assumptions about how nonfinancial values trade off with money, both benefits and costs can be expressed in dollar terms. We see little merit in doing so for social programs, since early translation of nonmonetary effects into money terms tends to lead to underassessment of the importance of nonfinancial consequences. The methods we present in this section ... are formally equivalent to doing it all in money, but do not require an equation between utility and money until the very end of the analysis, if then.

Back to our example. In the initial elicitation of values from the staff, the orderly structure of Figure 1.1, the value tree, did not appear. Indeed, it took much thought and trial and error to organize the attributes into a tree structure. Formally, only the attributes at the bottom of the tree, which are called *twigs*, are essential for evaluation. Figure 1.1 is a two-level value tree; that is, all second-level values are twigs. More often, different branches of a value tree will vary in how many levels they have. ... Examples with as many as fourteen levels exist.

Tree structures are useful in MAUT in three ways. First, they present the attributes in an orderly structure; this helps thought about the problem. Second, the tree structure can make elicitation of importance weights for twigs (which we discuss below) much easier than it would otherwise be, by reducing the number of judgments required. ... Finally, value trees permit what we call *subaggregation*. Often a single number is much too compressed a summary of how attractive an option is. Tree structures permit more informative and less compressed summaries. ...

Figure 1.1 contains a notational scheme we have found useful in value trees. Main branches of the tree are labeled with capital letters, A, B, and so on. Subattributes under each main branch are labeled with double letters, AA, AB, ..., BA, BB..., and so on. This is a two-level tree, so only double letters are needed.

Assignment of importance weights

The numbers in Figure 1.1 are *importance weights* for the attributes. Note that the weights in Figure 1.1 sum to 1 at each level of the tree. That is, the weights of A, B, C, and D sum to 1. Similarly, the weights of AA through AE sum to 1, as do those of BA and BB and so on. This is a convenient convention, both for elicitation of weights and for their use. The final weights for each attribute at each twig of the tree are easily obtained by "multiplying through the tree." For example, the weight .17 for twig AA (office size) is obtained by multiplying the normalized weight of A (.43) by the normalized weight for AA (.39) to yield .43 × .39 = .17. ...

The weights presented in Figure 1.1 emerged from a staff meeting in which, after an initial discussion of the idea of weighting, each individual staff member produced a set of weights, using the *ratio method*. ... Then all the sets of weights were put on the blackboard, the inevitable individual differences were discussed, and afterward each individual once again used the ratio method to produce a set of weights. These still differed, though by less than did the first set. The final set was produced by averaging the results of the second weighting; the average weights were acceptable to the staff as representing its value system.

The director had some reservations about what the staff had produced, but kept them to herself. She worried about whether the weights associated with staff comfort issues were perhaps too high and those associated with appropriateness to the function of the organization were perhaps too low. (Note that she had no serious reservations about the relative weights within each major branch of the value tree; her concerns were about the relative weights of the four major branches of the tree. This illustrates the usefulness of organizing lists of twigs into a tree structure for weighting.) The director chose to avoid argument with her staff by reserving her concerns about those weights for the sensitivity analysis phase of the evaluation.

Although a common staff set of weights was obtained by averaging (each staff member equally weighted), the individual weights were not thereafter thrown away. Instead, they were kept available for use in the later sensitivity analysis. In general, averaging may be a useful technique if a consensus position is needed, especially for screening options, but it is dangerous, exactly because it obliterates individual differences in weighting. When stakeholders disagree, it is usually a good idea to use the judgments of each separately in evaluation; only if these judgments lead to conflicting conclusions must the sometimes difficult task of reconciling the disagreements be faced. If it is faced, arithmetic is a last resort, if usable at all; discussion and achievement of consensus is much preferred. Often such discussions can be helped by a sensitivity analysis; it will often turn out that the decision is simply insensitive to the weights.

The assessment of location measures or utilities

With a value tree to guide the choice of measures to take and judgments to make, the next task was to make detailed assessments of each of the six sites that had survived initial screening. Such assessments directly lead to the utilities in multiattribute utility measurement. The word "utility" has a 400-year-old history and conveys a very explicit meaning to contemporary decision analysts. The techniques for obtaining such numbers that we present in this manual deviate in some ways from those implicit in that word. So we prefer to call these numbers *location measures*, since they simply report the location or utility of each object of evaluation on each attribute of evaluation.

Inspect Figure 1.1 again. Two kinds of values are listed on it. Office size is an objective dimension, measurable in square feet. Office attractiveness is a subjective dimension; it must be obtained by judgment. Proximity to public transportation might be taken in this example as measured by the distance from the front door of the building to the nearest bus stop, which would make it completely objective. But suppose the site were in New York. Then distance to the nearest bus stop and distance to the nearest subway stop would both be relevant and probably the latter would be more important than the former. It would make sense in that case to add another level to the value tree, in which the value "proximity to public transportation" would be further broken down into those two twigs.

As it happens, in Figure 1.1 all attributes are monotonically increasing; that is, more is better than less. That will not always be true. For some attributes, less is better than more; if "crime rate in the area" had survived the process of elimination that led to Figure 1.1, it would have been an example. On some attributes, intermediate values are preferable to either extreme; such attributes have a peak inside the range of the attribute. If "racial composition of the neighborhood" had survived as an attribute, the staff might well have felt that the site would score highest on that attribute if its racial/ethnic mix matched that of its clients. If only two racial/ethnic categories were relevant, that would be expressed by a twig, such as "percentage of whites in the neighborhood" that would have a peak at the percentage of whites among the center's clients and would tail off from there in both directions. If more than two racial/ethnic categories were relevant, the value would have been further broken down, with percentage of each relevant racial/ethnic category in the neighborhood as a twig underneath it, and for each of those twigs, the location measure would have a peak at some intermediate value. . . .

Figure 1.1 presented the director with a fairly easy assessment task. She chose to make the needed judgments herself. If the problem were more complex and required more expertise, she might well have asked other experts to make some or all of the necessary judgments.

Armed with a tape measure and a notebook, she visited each of the sites, made the relevant measures and counts, and made each of the required judgments. Thus she obtained the raw materials for the location measures.

However, she had to do some transforming on these raw materials. It is necessary for all location measures to be on a common scale, in order for the assessment of weights to make any sense. Although the choice of common scale is obviously arbitrary, we like one in which 0 means horrible and 100 means as well as one could hope to do.

Consider the case of the office size expressed in square feet. It would make no sense to assign the value 0 to 0 sq. ft.; no office could measure 0 sq. ft. After examining her present accommodations and thinking about those of other similar groups, the director decided that an office 60 sq. ft. in size should have a value of 0, and one of 160 sq. ft. should have a value of 100. She also decided that values intermediate between those two limits should be linear in utility. This idea needs explaining. It would be possible to feel that you gain much more in going from 60 to 80 sq. ft. than in going from 140 to 160 sq. ft., and consequently that the scale relating square footage to desirability should be nonlinear. Indeed, traditional utility theory makes that assumption in almost every case.

Curved functions relating physical measurements to utility are probably more precise representations of how people feel than straight ones. But fortunately, such curvature almost never makes any difference to the decision. If it does, the fact that the difference exists means that the options are close enough so that it scarcely matters which is chosen. For that reason, when an appropriate physical scale exists, we advocate choosing maximum and minimum values on it, and then fitting a straight line between those boundaries to translate those measurements into the 0 to 100 scale. . . . Formal arguments in support of our use of linearity are far too technical for this paper; see Edwards (1980) for citations leading to them.

The director did the same kind of thing to all the other attributes for which she had objective measures. The attribute "proximity to clients' homes" presented her with a problem. In principle, she could have chosen to measure the linear distance from the address of each current client to each site, average these measures, choose a maximum and minimum value for the average, and then scale each site using the same procedure described for office size. But that would have been much more trouble than it was worth. So instead she looked at a map, drew a circle on it to represent the boundaries of the area that she believed her organization served, and then noted how close each site was to the center of the area. It would have been possible to use radial distance from that center as an objective measure, but she chose not to do so, since clients' homes were not homogeneously distributed within the circle. Instead, she treated this as a directly judgmental attribute, simply using the map as an aid to judgment.

Of course, for all judgmental dimensions, the scale is from 0 to 100. For both judgmental and objective attributes, it is important that the scale be realistic. That is, it should be easy to imagine that some of the sites being considered might realistically score 0 to 100 on each attribute.

In this example, since the six sites were known, that could have been assured by assigning a value of 0 to the worst site on a given attribute and a value of 100 to the best on that attribute, locating the others in between. This was not done, and we recommend that it not be done in general. Suppose one of the sites had been rented to someone else, or that a new one turned up. Then if the evaluation scheme were so tightly tied to the specific options available, it would have to be revised. We prefer a procedure in which one attempts to assess realistic boundaries on each relevant attribute with less specific reference to the actual options available. Such a procedure allows the evaluation scheme to remain the same as the option set changes. And the procedure is obviously necessary if the option set is not known, or not fully known, at the time the evaluation scheme is worked out.

It can, of course, happen that a real option turns up that is more extreme than a boundary assigned to some attribute. If that happens, the evaluation scheme can still be used. Two possible approaches exist. Consider, for example, the attribute "access to public transportation" operationalized as distance to the nearest bus stop. One might assign 100 to half a block and 0 to four blocks. Now, suppose two new sites turn up. For one, the bus stop is right in front of the building entrance; for the other, it is five blocks away. The director might well judge that it scarcely matters whether the stop is in front of the building entrance or half a block away, and so assign 100 to all distances of half a block or closer. However, she might also feel that five blocks is meaningfully worse than four. She could handle the five-block case in either of two ways. She might simply disqualify the site on the basis of that fact. Or, if she felt that the site deserved to be evaluated in spite of this disadvantage, she could assign a negative score (it would turn out to be −29 . . .) to that site on that attribute. While such scores outside the 0 to 100 range are not common, and the ranges should be chosen with enough realism to avoid them if possible, nothing in the logic or formal structure of the method prevents their use. It is more important that the range be realistic, so that the options are well spread out over its length, than it is to avoid an occasional instance in which options fall outside it.

Table 1.4 represents the location measures of the six sites that survived initial screening, transformed onto the 0 to 100 scale. As the director looked at this table, she realized an important point. No matter what the weights, site 6 would never be best in utility. The reason why is that site 2 is at least as attractive as site 6 on all location measures, and definitely better on some. In technical language, site 2 *dominates* site 6. But Table 1.4 omits one important issue: cost. Checking cost, she found that site 6 was in fact less expensive than site 2, so she kept it in. If it had been as expensive as site 2 or more so, she would have been justified in summarily rejecting it, since it could never beat site 2. No other option dominates or is dominated by another. (Although she might have dropped site 6 if it had not been cheaper than site 2, she would have been unwise to notify the rental office of site 6 that it was out of contention. If for some reason site 2 were to become unavailable, perhaps because it was rented to someone else, then site 6 would once more be a contender.)

Aggregation of location measures and weights

The director now had weights provided by her staff and location measures provided either directly by judgment or by calculations based on measurements. Now her task was to aggregate these into measures of

Table 1.4. *Location measures for six sites*

Site number	Twig label											
	AA	AB	AC	AD	AE	BA	BB	CA	CB	CC	DA	DB
1	90	50	30	90	10	40	80	10	60	50	10	0
2	50	30	80	30	60	30	70	80	50	40	70	40
3	10	100	70	40	30	0	95	5	10	50	90	50
4	100	80	10	50	50	50	50	50	10	10	50	95
5	20	5	95	10	100	90	5	90	90	95	50	10
6	40	30	80	30	50	30	70	50	50	30	60	40

Table 1.5. *Calculation of the aggregate utility of site 1*

Twig label	Weight	Location measure	Weight x location measure
AA	.168	90	15.12
AB	.090	50	4.50
AC	.060	30	1.80
AD	.060	90	5.40
AE	.052	10	0.52
BA	.120	40	4.80
BB	.120	80	9.60
CA	.099	10	.99
CB	.061	60	3.66
CC	.030	50	1.50
DA	.090	10	0.90
DB	.050	0	0.00
Sums	1.000		48.79

Table 1.6. *Aggregate utilities and rents*

Site	Utility	Cost (rent per year)
1	48.80	$48,000
2	53.26	53,300
3	43.48	54,600
4	57.31	60,600
5	48.92	67,800
6	46.90	53,200

the aggregate utility of each site. The aggregation procedure is the same regardless of the depth of the value tree. Simply take the final weight for each twig, multiply it by location measure for that twig, and sum the products. This is illustrated in Table 1.5 for site 1. In this case, the sum is 48.79, which is the aggregate utility of site 1. It would be possible but tedious to do this for each site. All calculations like that in Table 1.5 were done with hand calculator programs; the discrepancy between the 48.79 for site 1 of Table 1.5 and the 48.80 of Table 1.6 is caused by a rounding process in the program. Table 6 shows the aggregate utilities and the costs for each of the six sites. The costs are given as annual rents.

Now a version of the idea of dominance can be exploited again. In Table 6, the utility values can be considered as measures of desirability and the rents are costs. Obviously, you would not wish to pay more unless you got an increase in desirability. Consequently, options that are inferior to others in both cost and desirability need not be considered further.

On utility, the rank ordering of the sites from best to worst is 425163. On cost, it is 162345. Obviously sites 1 and 4 will be contenders, since 4 is best in utility (with these weights) and 1 is best in cost. Site 5 is dominated, in this aggregated sense, by site 4, and so is out of the race. Sites 3 and 6 are dominated by site 1, and are also out. So sites 1, 2, and 4 remain as *contenders*; 2 is intermediate between 1 and 4 in both utility and cost. This result is general. If a set of options is described by aggregated utilities and costs, and dominated options are removed, then all of the remaining options, if listed in order of increasing utility, will turn out also to be listed in order of increasing cost. This makes the decision problem simpler; it reduces to whether each increment in utility gained from moving from an option lower to one higher in such a list is worth the increase in cost. Note that this property does *not* depend on any numerical properties of the method that will eventually be used to aggregate utility with cost.

A special case arises if two or more options tie in utility, cost, or both. If the tie is in utility, then the one that costs least among the tied options dominates the others; the others should be eliminated. If they tie in cost, the one with the greatest utility dominates the others; the others should be eliminated. If they tie in both utility and cost, then only one of them need be examined for dominance. If one is dominated; all are; if one is undominated, all are. So either all should be eliminated or all should survive to the next stage of the analysis. Note that a tie in aggregate utility can occur in two different ways: by accident of weighting, or because all location measures are equal. If all location measures are equal, the lower cost will always be preferable to the higher one regardless of weights, so the higher cost can be eliminated not only from the main analysis, but from all sensitivity analyses. If they tie in aggregate utility by accident of weighting, changes in weight will ordinarily untie them, and so the tied options must be included in the sensitivity analysis.

If the option that represents the tie emerges from the next stage of the analysis looking best, the only way to discriminate it from its twins is by sensitivity analysis, by considering other attributes, or both.

Nothing guarantees that the dominance analysis we just performed will eliminate options. If the ordering in utility had been 123456 and the ordering in cost had been 654321 (just the opposite) no option would have dominated any other, and none could have been eliminated. Such perfect relationships between cost and utility are rare, except perhaps in the marketplace, in which dominated options may be eliminated by market pressure.

The decision about whether to accept an increase in cost in order to obtain an increase in utility is often made intuitively, and that may be an excellent way to make it. But arithmetic can help. In this example, con-

Table 1.7. *Incremental utilities and costs for the siting example*

Site no.	Utility differences (increment)	Cost differences (increment)	Cost incr./ utility/incr.
1	0	0	
2	4.46	$5300	$1188
4	4.05	$7300	$1802

sider Table 1.7. It lists the three contending sites, 1, 2, and 4, in order of increasing utility and cost. In the second column, each entry is the utility of that site minus the utility of the site just above it. Thus, for example, the 4.05 utility difference associated with site 4 is obtained by subtracting the aggregate utility of 2 from that of 4 in Table 1.6: 57.31 − 53.26 = 4.05. Similarly, the cost difference of $7,300 for site 4 is obtained from Table 6 in the same way: $60,600 − 53,300 = $7,300. The other numbers in the second and third columns are calculated similarly. The fourth column is simply the number in the third column divided by the number in the second.

The numbers in the fourth column increase from top to bottom. This means that all three sites are true contenders. This is not necessarily the case....

The last column of Table 1.7 also serves another purpose. Since it is the increase in cost divided by the increase in utility, it is a dollar value for one utility point. Specifically, it is the dollar value for one utility point that would be just enough to cause you to prefer the higher cost site to the lower cost one. If the dollar value of a utility point is less than $1188, you should choose site 1; if it is between $1188 and $1802, you should choose site 2; and if it is above $1802, you should choose site 4.

But how can you know the dollar value of a utility point, for yourself or for other stakeholders? The judgment obviously need not be made with much precision – but it is, if formulated in that language, an impossible judgment to make. But it need not be formulated in that language. Consider instead the following procedure. Refer back to Figure 1.1. First pick a twig that you have firm and definite opinions about. Suppose it is DA, availability and suitability of space for secretaries, files, Xerox, and the like. Now, ask of yourself and of the other stakeholders, "How much money would it be worth to improve that twig by so many points?" The typical number of points to use in such questions is 100, so the question becomes: "How much would it be worth to improve the availability and suitability of space for secretaries, files, Xerox, and the like from the minimum acceptable state, to which I have assigned a location measure of 0, to a state to which I would assign a location measure of 100?"

Such a question, asked of various stakeholders, will elicit various

Table 1.8. *Aggregate utilities after subtracting penalties for excess cost*

Site no.	Value of a 100 point swing in DA (weight = .09)		
	$9,000	$13,500	$18,000
1	48.80	48.80	48.80
2	47.96	49.73	50.61
4	44.71	48.91	51.01

answers; a compromise or agreed-on number should be found. Suppose, in this example, that it turned out to be $13,500. Now, refer to Table 1.5 and note that the twig weight for DA is .090. Consequently, a 100-point change in DA will change aggregate utility by $100 \times .090 = 9$ points – for this particular set of weights. Note, incidentally, that while the 9-point number depends on the weights, the judgment of the dollar value of a 100-point change in DA does not. Consequently, if you choose to change weights ... you will need to recalculate the value of a utility point, but will not need to obtain a new dollar value judgment of this kind from anyone.

If a 9-point change in utility is worth $13,500, then a 1-point change in utility is worth $13,500/9 = $1500. So, using the weights on which this chapter is based, site 2 is clearly preferable to sites 1 and 4 since $1500 is between $1188 and $1802.

Let us verify that statement. One way to do so is to penalize the more expensive sites by a number of utility points appropriate for their increase in cost. Thus, if utility is worth $1500 per point, and site 2 costs $5300 more than site 1, then site 2 should be penalized $5300/1500 = 3.53$ utility points in order to make it comparable to site 1. Similarly, if utility is worth $1500 per point, then site 4 should be penalized by the increment in its costs over site 1, $5300 + $7300 = $12,600, divided by the dollar value of a point; $12,600/1500 = 8.40$ utility points. This makes all three sites comparable; by correcting each of the more expensive ones by the utility equivalent of the additional expense. So now the choice could be based on utility alone.

Table 1.8 makes the same calculation for all three sites and for three different judgments of how much a 9-point swing in aggregate utility is worth: $9000, $13,500, and $18,000; these correspond, with the weights used in this chapter, to utility values per point of $1000, $1500, and $2000, respectively. Table 1.8 is included here not because it is a calculation that the director would ever need to make, but because it demonstrates that the choices made on the basis of Table 1.7, which is a calculation she might well need to make, are appropriate.

As illustrated in Table 1.8, a utility value of $1000 per point makes site 1 best, a utility value of $1500 per point makes site 2 best, and a utility value of $2000 per point makes site 4 best. Note, however, that the differences in corrected utilities are relatively small. This is normal, and is one reason why we make no strong case for using such calculations to go from Table 1.6 to Table 1.8. Elimination of noncontenders is usually both more important and easier to do than selection among those that survive the elimination process, since the survivors are likely to be close enough to one another in attractiveness so that no choice will be disastrous.

Sensitivity analysis

The director of the center had some doubt about the weights her staff had given her. She therefore considered various other weights. She found a set of weights that make site 5 best in utility, and another for which site 2 is best.

. . . The director was relatively well satisfied with the location measures she was using, and felt no need to change them – and she also felt that there were so many that she was unsure which ones to change.

At this point the director felt she had enough information and analysis to make her recommendation of site 2. . . .

Summary

This section presents an example in detail. A social service center needs to move; six sites are available. Using staff weights applied to a value tree with twelve twigs, the director of the center is able to eliminate three of the six sites and to reach a conclusion among the other three.

Various technical problems arise and are discussed in presentation of the example. One is cost. The analysis treats cost as an evaluative attribute but keeps it separate from all other attributes until the end. Dominance techniques are used to eliminate options based on aggregated utilities and cost. An illustration is given of how judgments or trade-offs between cost and all other attributes can be used as a basis for a single multiattributed evaluation of what option is best. A second problem is how the nature of the context affects detailed definitions of values. A third is how to deal with options that fall outside anticipated ranges on one or more values. A fourth is how to go about operationalizing some values in order to obtain location measures. The last is what to do about ties in value, cost, or both.

2.   Judgment under uncertainty: Heuristics and biases

Amos Tversky and Daniel Kahneman

Many decisions are based on beliefs concerning the likelihood of uncertain events such as the outcome of an election, the guilt of a defendant, or the future value of the dollar. These beliefs are usually expressed in statements such as "I think that . . .," "chances are . . .," "it is unlikely that . . .," and so forth. Occasionally, beliefs concerning uncertain events are expressed in numerical form as odds or subjective probabilities. What determines such beliefs? How do people assess the probability of an uncertain event or the value of an uncertain quantity? This article shows that people rely on a limited number of heuristic principles which reduce the complex tasks of assessing probabilities and predicting values to simpler judgmental operations. In general, these heuristics are quite useful, but sometimes they lead to severe and systematic errors.

The subjective assessment of probability resembles the subjective assessment of physical quantities such as distance or size. These judgments are all based on data of limited validity, which are processed according to heuristic rules. For example, the apparent distance of an object is determined in part by its clarity. The more sharply the object is seen, the closer it appears to be. This rule has some validity, because in any given scene the more distant objects are seen less sharply than nearer objects. However, the reliance on this rule leads to systematic errors in the estimation of distance. Specifically, distances are often overestimated when visibility is poor because the contours of objects are blurred. On the other hand, distances are often underestimated when visibility is good because the objects are seen sharply. Thus, the reliance on clarity as an

This chapter originally appeared in *Science*, 1974, *185*, 1124–1131. Copyright © 1974 by the American Association for the Advancement of Science. Reprinted by permission.

indication of distance leads to common biases. Such biases are also found in the intuitive judgment of probability. This article describes three heuristics that are employed to assess probabilities and to predict values. Biases to which these heuristics lead are enumerated, and the applied and theoretical implications of these observations are discussed.

Representativeness

Many of the probabilistic questions with which people are concerned belong to one of the following types: What is the probability that object A belongs to class B? What is the probability that event A originates from process B? What is the probability that process B will generate event A? In answering such questions, people typically rely on the representativeness heuristic, in which probabilities are evaluated by the degree to which A is representative of B, that is, by the degree to which A resembles B. For example, when A is highly representative of B, the probability that A originates from B is judged to be high. On the other hand, if A is not similar to B, the probability that A originates from B is judged to be low.

For an illustration of judgment by representativeness, consider an individual who has been described by a former neighbor as follows: "Steve is very shy and withdrawn, invariably helpful, but with little interest in people, or in the world of reality. A meek and tidy soul, he has a need for order and structure, and a passion for detail." How do people assess the probability that Steve is engaged in a particular occupation from a list of possibilities (for example, farmer, salesman, airline pilot, librarian, or physician)? How do people order these occupations from most to least likely? In the representativeness heuristic, the probability that Steve is a librarian, for example, is assessed by the degree to which he is representative of, or similar to, the stereotype of a librarian. Indeed, research with problems of this type has shown that people order the occupations by probability and by similarity in exactly the same way (Kahneman & Tversky, 1973). This approach to the judgment of probability leads to serious errors, because similarity, or representativeness, is not influenced by several factors that should affect judgments of probability.

Insensitivity to prior probability of outcomes

One of the factors that have no effect on representativeness but should have a major effect on probability is the prior probability, or base-rate frequency, of the outcomes. In the case of Steve, for example, the fact that there are many more farmers than librarians in the population should enter into any reasonable estimate of the probability that Steve is a librarian rather than a farmer. Considerations of base-rate frequency, however, do not affect the similarity of Steve to the stereotypes of librarians and farmers. If people evaluate probability by representativeness, therefore, prior probabilities will be neglected. This hypothesis was tested in an experiment where prior probabilities were manipulated (Kahneman & Tversky, 1973). Subjects were shown brief personality descriptions of several individuals, allegedly sampled at random from a group of 100 professionals – engineers and lawyers. The subjects were asked to assess, for each description, the probability that it belonged to an engineer rather than to a lawyer. In one experimental condition, subjects were told that the group from which the descriptions had been drawn consisted of 70 engineers and 30 lawyers. In another condition, subjects were told that the group consisted of 30 engineers and 70 lawyers. The odds that any particular description belongs to an engineer rather than to a lawyer should be higher in the first condition, where there is a majority of engineers, than in the second condition, where there is a majority of lawyers. Specifically, it can be shown by applying Bayes' rule that the ratio of these odds should be $(.7/.3)^2$, or 5.44, for each description. In a sharp violation of Bayes' rule, the subjects in the two conditions produced essentially the same probability judgments. Apparently, subjects evaluated the likelihood that a particular description belonged to an engineer rather than to a lawyer by the degree to which this description was representative of the two stereotypes, with little or no regard for the prior probabilities of the categories.

The subjects used prior probabilities correctly when they had no other information. In the absence of a personality sketch, they judged the probability that an unknown individual is an engineer to be .7 and .3, respectively, in the two base-rate conditions. However, prior probabilities were effectively ignored when a description was introduced, even when this description was totally uninformative. The responses to the following description illustrate this phenomenon:

Dick is a 30 year old man. He is married with no children. A man of high ability and high motivation, he promises to be quite successful in his field. He is well liked by his colleagues.

This description was intended to convey no information relevant to the question of whether Dick is an engineer or a lawyer. Consequently, the probability that Dick is an engineer should equal the proportion of engineers in the group, as if no description had been given. The subjects, however, judged the probability of Dick being an engineer to be .5 regardless of whether the stated proportion of engineers in the group was .7 or .3. Evidently, people respond differently when given no evidence and when given worthless evidence. When no specific evidence is given, prior probabilities are properly utilized; when worthless evidence is given, prior probabilities are ignored (Kahneman & Tversky, 1973).

Insensitivity to sample size

To evaluate the probability of obtaining a particular result in a sample drawn from a specified population, people typically apply the representativeness heuristic. That is, they assess the likelihood of a sample result, for example, that the average height in a random sample of ten men will be 6 feet (180 centimeters), by the similarity of this result to the corresponding parameter (that is, to the average height in the population of men). The similarity of a sample statistic to a population parameter does not depend on the size of the sample. Consequently, if probabilities are assessed by representativeness, then the judged probability of a sample statistic will be essentially independent of sample size. Indeed, when subjects assessed the distributions of average height for samples of various sizes, they produced identical distributions. For example, the probability of obtaining an average height greater than 6 feet was assigned the same value for samples of 1000, 100, and 10 men (Kahneman & Tversky, 1972). Moreover, subjects failed to appreciate the role of sample size even when it was emphasized in the formulation of the problem. Consider the following question:

A certain town is served by two hospitals. In the larger hospital about 45 babies are born each day, and in the smaller hospital about 15 babies are born each day. As you know, about 50 percent of all babies are boys. However, the exact percentage varies from day to day. Sometimes it may be higher than 50 percent, sometimes lower.

For a period of 1 year, each hospital recorded the days on which more than 60 percent of the babies born were boys. Which hospital do you think recorded more such days?

▶ The larger hospital (21)
▶ The smaller hospital (21)
▶ About the same (that is, within 5 percent of each other) (53)

The values in parentheses are the number of undergraduate students who chose each answer.

Most subjects judged the probability of obtaining more than 60 percent boys to be the same in the small and in the large hospital, presumably because these events are described by the same statistic and are therefore equally representative of the general population. In contrast, sampling theory entails that the expected number of days on which more than 60 percent of the babies are boys is much greater in the small hospital than in the large one, because a large sample is less likely to stray from 50 percent. This fundamental notion of statistics is evidently not part of people's repertoire of intuitions.

A similar insensitivity to sample size has been reported in judgments of posterior probability, that is, of the probability that a sample has been drawn from one population rather than from another. Consider the following example:

Imagine an urn filled with balls, of which ⅔ are of one color and ⅓ of another. One individual has drawn 5 balls from the urn, and found that 4 were red and 1 was white. Another individual has drawn 20 balls and found that 12 were red and 8 were white. Which of the two individuals should feel more confident that the urn contains ⅔ red balls and ⅓ white balls, rather than the opposite? What odds should each individual give?

In this problem, the correct posterior odds are 8 to 1 for the 4:1 sample and 16 to 1 for the 12:8 sample, assuming equal prior probabilities. However, most people feel that the first sample provides much stronger evidence for the hypothesis that the urn is predominantly red, because the proportion of red balls is larger in the first than in the second sample. Here again, intuitive judgments are dominated by the sample proportion and are essentially unaffected by the size of the sample, which plays a crucial role in the determination of the actual posterior odds (Kahneman & Tversky, 1972). In addition, intuitive estimates of posterior odds are far less extreme than the correct values. The underestimation of the impact of evidence has been observed repeatedly in problems of this type (Edwards, 1968; Slovic & Lichtenstein, 1971). It has been labeled "conservatism."

Misconceptions of chance

People expect that a sequence of events generated by a random process will represent the essential characteristics of that process even when the sequence is short. In considering tosses of a coin for heads or tails, for example, people regard the sequence H-T-H-T-T-H to be more likely than the sequence H-H-H-T-T-T, which does not appear random, and also more likely than the sequence H-H-H-H-T-H, which does not represent the fairness of the coin (Kahneman & Tversky, 1972). Thus, people expect that the essential characteristics of the process will be represented, not only globally in the entire sequence, but also locally in each of its parts. A locally representative sequence, however, deviates systematically from chance expectation: it contains too many alternations and too few runs. Another consequence of the belief in local representativeness is the well-known gambler's fallacy. After observing a long run of red on the roulette wheel, for example, most people erroneously believe that black is now due, presumably because the occurrence of black will result in a more representative sequence than the occurrence of an additional red. Chance is commonly viewed as a self-correcting process in which a deviation in one direction induces a deviation in the opposite direction to restore the equilibrium. In fact, deviations are not "corrected" as a chance process unfolds, they are merely diluted.

Misconceptions of chance are not limited to naive subjects. A study of the statistical intuitions of experienced research psychologists (Tversky & Kahneman, 1971a) revealed a lingering belief in what may be called the "law of small numbers," according to which even small samples are highly representative of the populations from which they are drawn. The responses of these investigators reflected the expectation that a valid hypothesis about a population will be represented by a statistically significant result in a sample – with little regard for its size. As a consequence, the researchers put too much faith in the results of small samples and grossly overestimated the replicability of such results. In the actual conduct of research, this bias leads to the selection of samples of inadequate size and to overinterpretation of findings.

Insensitivity to predictability

People are sometimes called upon to make such numerical predictions as the future value of a stock, the demand for a commodity, or the outcome of a football game. Such predictions are often made by representativeness. For example, suppose one is given a description of a company and is asked to predict its future profit. If the description of the company is very favorable, a very high profit will appear most representative of that description; if the description is mediocre, a mediocre performance will appear most representative. The degree to which the description is favorable is unaffected by the reliability of that description or by the degree to which it permits accurate prediction. Hence, if people predict solely in terms of the favorableness of the description, their predictions will be insensitive to the reliability of the evidence and to the expected accuracy of the prediction.

This mode of judgment violates the normative statistical theory in which the extremeness and the range of predictions are controlled by considerations of predictability. When predictability is nil, the same prediction should be made in all cases. For example, if the descriptions of companies provide no information relevant to profit, then the same value (such as average profit) should be predicted for all companies. If predictability is perfect, of course, the values predicted will match the actual values and the range of predictions will equal the range of outcomes. In general, the higher the predictability, the wider the range of predicted values.

Several studies of numerical prediction have demonstrated that intuitive predictions violate this rule, and that subjects show little or no regard for considerations of predictability (Kahneman & Tversky, 1973). In one of these studies, subjects were presented with several paragraphs, each describing the performance of a student teacher during a particular practice lesson. Some subjects were asked to *evaluate* the quality of the lesson described in the paragraph in percentile scores, relative to a specified population. Other subjects were asked to *predict*, also in percentile scores, the standing of each student teacher 5 years after the practice lesson. The judgments made under the two conditions were identical. That is, the prediction of a remote criterion (success of a teacher after 5 years) was identical to the evaluation of the information on which the prediction was based (the quality of the practice lesson). The students who made these predictions were undoubtedly aware of the limited predictability of teaching competence on the basis of a single trial lesson 5 years earlier; nevertheless, their predictions were as extreme as their evaluations.

The illusion of validity

As we have seen, people often predict by selecting the outcome (for example, an occupation) that is most representative of the input (for example, the description of a person). The confidence they have in their prediction depends primarily on the degree of representativeness (that is, on the quality of the match between the selected outcome and the input) with little or no regard for the factors that limit predictive accuracy. Thus, people express great confidence in the prediction that a person is a librarian when given a description of his personality which matches the stereotype of librarians, even if the description is scanty, unreliable, or outdated. The unwarranted confidence which is produced by a good fit between the predicted outcome and the input information may be called the illusion of validity. This illusion persists even when the judge is aware of the factors that limit the accuracy of his predictions. It is a common observation that psychologists who conduct selection interviews often experience considerable confidence in their predictions, even when they know of the vast literature that shows selection interviews to be highly fallible. The continued reliance on the clinical interview for selection, despite repeated demonstrations of its inadequacy, amply attests to the strength of this effect.

The internal consistency of a pattern of inputs is a major determinant of one's confidence in predictions based on these inputs. For example, people express more confidence in predicting the final grade-point average of a student whose first-year record consists entirely of B's than in predicting the grade-point average of a student whose first-year record includes many A's and C's. Highly consistent patterns are most often observed when the input variables are highly redundant or correlated. Hence, people tend to have great confidence in predictions based on redundant input variable. However, an elementary result in the statistics of correlation asserts that, given input variables of stated validity, a prediction based on several such inputs can achieve higher accuracy when they are independent of each other than when they are redundant or correlated. Thus redundancy among inputs decreases accuracy even as it increases confidence, and people are often confident in predictions that are quite likely to be off the mark (Kahneman & Tversky, 1973).

Misconceptions of regression

Suppose a large group of children has been examined on two equivalent versions of an aptitude test. If one selects ten children from among those who did best on one of the two versions, he will usually find their performance on the second version to be somewhat disappointing. Conversely, if one selects ten children from among those who did worst on one version, they will be found, on the average, to do somewhat better on the other version. More generally, consider two variables X and Y which have the same distribution. If one selects individuals whose average X score deviates from the mean of X by k units, then the average of their Y scores will usually deviate from the mean of Y by less than k units. These observations illustrate a general phenomenon known as regression toward the mean, which was first documented by Galton more than 100 years ago.

In the normal course of life, one encounters many instances of regression toward the mean, in the comparison of the height of fathers and sons, of the intelligence of husbands and wives, or of the performance of individuals on consecutive examinations. Nevertheless, people do not develop correct intuitions about this phenomenon. First, they do not expect regression in many contexts where it is bound to occur. Second, when they recognize the occurrence of regression, they often invent spurious causal explanations for it (Kahneman & Tversky, 1973). We suggest that the phenomenon of regression remains elusive because it is incompatible with the belief that the predicted outcome should be maximally representative of the input, and, hence, that the value of the outcome variable should be as extreme as the value of the input variable.

The failure to recognize the import of regression can have pernicious consequences, as illustrated by the following observation (Kahneman & Tversky, 1973). In a discussion of flight training, experienced instructors noted that praise for an exceptionally smooth landing is typically followed by a poorer landing on the next try, while harsh criticism after a rough landing is usually followed by an improvement on the next try. The instructors concluded that verbal rewards are detrimental to learning, while verbal punishments are beneficial, contrary to accepted psychological doctrine. This conclusion is unwarranted because of the presence of regression toward the mean. As in other cases of repeated examination, an improvement will usually follow a poor performance and a deterioration will usually follow an outstanding performance, even if the instructor does not respond to the trainee's achievement on the first attempt. Because the instructors had praised their trainees after good landings and admonished them after poor ones, they reached the erroneous and potentially harmful conclusion that punishment is more effective than reward.

Thus, the failure to understand the effect of regression leads one to overestimate the effectiveness of punishment and to underestimate the effectiveness of reward. In social interaction, as well as in training, rewards are typically administered when performance is good, and punishments are typically administered when performance is poor. By regression alone, therefore, behavior is most likely to improve after punishment and most likely to deteriorate after reward. Consequently, the human condition is such that, by chance alone, one is most often rewarded for punishing others and most often punished for rewarding them. People are generally not aware of this contingency. In fact, the elusive role of regression in determining the apparent consequences of reward and punishment seems to have escaped the notice of students of this area.

Availability

There are situations in which people assess the frequency of a class or the probability of an event by the ease with which instances or occurrences can be brought to mind. For example, one may assess the risk of heart attack among middle-aged people by recalling such occurrences among one's acquaintances. Similarly, one may evaluate the probability that a given business venture will fail by imagining various difficulties it could encounter. This judgmental heuristic is called availability. Availability is a useful clue for assessing frequency or probability, because instances of large classes are usually recalled better and faster than instances of less frequent classes. However, availability is affected by factors other than frequency and probability. Consequently, the reliance on availability leads to predictable biases, some of which are illustrated below.

Biases due to the retrievability of instances

When the size of a class is judged by the availability of its instances, a class whose instances are easily retrieved will appear more numerous than a class of equal frequency whose instances are less retrievable. In an elementary demonstration of this effect, subjects heard a list of well-known personalities of both sexes and were subsequently asked to judge whether the list contained more names of men than of women. Different lists were presented to different groups of subjects. In some of the lists the men were relatively more famous than the women, and in others the women were relatively more famous than the men. In each of the lists, the subjects erroneously judged that the class (sex) that had the more famous personalities was the more numerous (Tversky & Kahneman, 1973).

In addition to familiarity, there are other factors, such as salience, which affect the retrievability of instances. For example, the impact of seeing a house burning on the subjective probability of such accidents is probably greater than the impact of reading about a fire in the local paper. Furthermore, recent occurrences are likely to be relatively more available than earlier occurrences. It is a common experience that the subjective probability of traffic accidents rises temporarily when one sees a car overturned by the side of the road.

Biases due to the effectiveness of a search set

Suppose one samples a word (of three letters or more) at random from an English text. Is it more likely that the word starts with r or that r is the third letter? People approach this problem by recalling words that begin with r (road) and words that have r in the third position (car) and assess the relative frequency by the ease with which words of the two types come to mind. Because it is much easier to search for words by their first letter than by their third letter, most people judge words that begin with a given consonant to be more numerous than words in which the same consonant appears in the third position. They do so even for consonants, such as r or k, that are more frequent in the third position than in the first (Tversky & Kahneman, 1973).

Different tasks elicit different search sets. For example, suppose you are asked to rate the frequency with which abstract words (thought, love) and concrete words (door, water) appear in written English. A natural way to answer this question is to search for contexts in which the word could appear. It seems easier to think of contexts in which an abstract concept is mentioned (love in love stories) than to think of contexts in which a concrete word (such as door) is mentioned. If the frequency of words is judged by the availability of the contexts in which they appear, abstract words will be judged as relatively more numerous than concrete words. This bias has been observed in a recent study (Galbraith & Underwood, 1973) which showed that the judged frequency of occurrence of abstract words was much higher than that of concrete words, equated in objective frequency. Abstract words were also jduged to appear in a much greater variety of contexts than concrete words.

Biases of imaginability

Sometimes one has to assess the frequency of a class whose instances are not stored in memory but can be generated according to a given rule. In such situations, one typically generates several instances and evaluates frequency or probability by the ease with which the relevant instances can be constructed. However, the ease of constructing instances does not always reflect their actual frequency, and this mode of evaluation is prone to biases. To illustrate, consider a group of 10 people who form committees of k members, $2 \leq k \leq 8$. How many different committees of k members can be formed? The correct answer to this problem is given by the binomial coefficient $\binom{10}{k}$ which reaches a maximum of 252 for $k = 5$. Clearly, the number of committees of k members equals the number of committees of $(10 - k)$ members, because any committee of k members defines a unique group of $(10 - k)$ nonmembers.

One way to answer this question without computation is to mentally construct committees of k members and to evaluate their number by the ease with which they come to mind. Committees of few members, say 2, are more available than committees of many members, say 8. The simplest scheme for the construction of committees is a partition of the group into disjoint sets. One readily sees that it is easy to construct five disjoint committees of 2 members, while it is impossible to generate even two disjoint committees of 8 members. Consequently, if frequency is assessed by imaginability, or by availability for construction, the small committees will appear more numerous than larger committees, in contrast to the correct bell-shaped function. Indeed, when naive subjects were asked to estimate the number of distinct committees of various sizes, their estimates were a decreasing monotonic function of committee size (Tversky & Kahneman, 1973). For example, the median estimate of the number of committees of 2 members was 70, while the estimate for committees of 8 members was 20 (the correct answer is 45 in both cases).

Imaginability plays an important role in the evaluation of probabilities in real-life situations. The risk involved in an adventurous expedition, for example, is evaluated by imagining contingencies with which the expedition is not equipped to cope. If many such difficulties are vividly portrayed, the expedition can be made to appear exceedingly dangerous, although the ease with which disasters are imagined need not reflect their actual likelihood. Conversely, the risk involved in an undertaking may be grossly underestimated if some possible dangers are either difficult to conceive of, or simply do not come to mind.

Illusory correlation

Chapman and Chapman (1967, 1969) have described an interesting bias in the judgment of the frequency with which two events co-occur. They presented naive judges with information concerning several hypothetical mental patients. The data for each patient consisted of a clinical diagnosis and a drawing of a person made by the patient. Later the judges estimated the frequency with which each diagnosis (such as paranoia or suspiciousness) had been accompanied by various features of the drawing (such as peculiar eyes). The subjects markedly overestimated the frequency of co-occurrence of natural associates, such as suspiciousness and peculiar eyes. This effect was labeled illusory correlation. In their erroneous judgments of the data to which they had been exposed, naive subjects "rediscovered" much of the common, but unfounded, clinical lore concerning the interpretation of the draw-a-person test. The illusory correlation effect was extremely resistant to contradictory data. It persisted even when the correlation between symptom and diagnosis was actually negative, and it prevented the judges from detecting relationships that were in fact present.

Availability provides a natural account for the illusory-correlation effect. The judgment of how frequently two events co-occur could be based on the strength of the associative bond between them. When the association is strong, one is likely to conclude that the events have been frequently paired. Consequently, strong associates will be judged to have occurred together frequently. According to this view, the illusory correlation between suspiciousness and peculiar drawing of the eyes, for example, is due to the fact that suspiciousness is more readily associated with the eyes than with any other part of the body.

Lifelong experience has taught us that, in general, instances of large classes are recalled better and faster than instances of less frequent classes; that likely occurrences are easier to imagine than unlikely ones; and that the associative connections between events are strengthened when the events frequently co-occur. As a result, man has at his disposal a procedure (the availability heuristic) for estimating the numerosity of a class, the likelihood of an event, or the frequency of co-occurrences, by the ease with which the relevant mental operations of retrieval, construction, or association can be performed. However, as the preceding examples have demonstrated, this valuable estimation procedure results in systematic errors.

Adjustment and anchoring

In many situations, people make estimates by starting from an initial value that is adjusted to yield the final answer. The initial value, or starting point, may be suggested by the formulation of the problem, or it may be the result of a partial computation. In either case, adjustments are typically insufficient (Slovic & Lichtenstein, 1971). That is, different starting points yield different estimates, which are biased toward the initial values. We call this phenomenon anchoring.

Insufficient adjustment

In a demonstration of the anchoring effect, subjects were asked to estimate various quantities, stated in percentages (for example, the percentage of African countries in the United Nations). For each quantity, a number between 0 and 100 was determined by spinning a wheel of fortune in the subjects' presence. The subjects were instructed to indicate first whether that number was higher or lower than the value of the quantity, and then to estimate the value of the quantity by moving upward or downward from the given number. Different groups were given different numbers for each quantity, and these arbitrary numbers had a marked effect on estimates. For example, the median estimates of the percentage of African countries in the United Nations were 25 and 45 for groups that received 10 and 65, respectively, as starting points. Payoffs for accuracy did not reduce the anchoring effect.

Anchoring occurs not only when the starting point is given to the subject, but also when the subject bases his estimate on the result of some incomplete computation. A study of intuitive numerical estimation illustrates this effect. Two groups of high school students estimated, within 5 seconds, a numerical expression that was written on the blackboard. One group estimated the product

$$8 \times 7 \times 6 \times 5 \times 4 \times 3 \times 2 \times 1$$

while another group estimated the product

$$1 \times 2 \times 3 \times 4 \times 5 \times 6 \times 7 \times 8$$

To rapidly answer such questions, people may perform a few steps of computation and estimate the product by extrapolation or adjustment. Because adjustments are typically insufficient, this procedure should lead to underestimation. Furthermore, because the result of the first few steps of multiplication (performed from left to right) is higher in the descending sequence than in the ascending sequence, the former expression should be judged larger than the latter. Both predictions were confirmed. The median estimate for the ascending sequence was 512, while the median estimate for the descending sequence was 2250. The correct answer is 40,320.

Biases in the evaluation of conjunctive and disjunctive events

In a recent study by Bar-Hillel (1973) subjects were given the opportunity to bet on one of two events. Three types of events were used: (i) simple events, such as drawing a red marble from a bag containing 50 percent red marbles and 50 percent white marbles; (ii) conjunctive events, such as drawing a red marble seven times in succession, with replacement, from a bag containing 90 percent red marbles and 10 percent white marbles; and (iii) disjunctive events, such as drawing a red marble at least once in seven successive tries, with replacement, from a bag containing 10 percent red marbles and 90 percent white marbles. In this problem, a significant majority of subjects preferred to bet on the conjunctive event (the probability of which is .48) rather than on the simple event (the probability of which is .50). Subjects also preferred to bet on the simple event rather than on the disjunctive event, which has a probability of .52.

Thus, most subjects bet on the less likely event in both comparisons. This pattern of choices illustrates a general finding. Studies of choice among gambles and of judgments of probability indicate that people tend to overestimate the probability of conjunctive events (Cohen, Chesnick, & Haran, 1972) and to underestimate the probability of disjunctive events. These biases are readily explained as effects of anchoring. The stated probability of the elementary event (success at any one stage) provides a natural starting point for the estimation of the probabilities of both conjunctive and disjunctive events. Since adjustment from the starting point is typically insufficient, the final estimates remain too close to the probabilities of the elementary events in both cases. Note that the overall probability of a conjunctive event is lower than the probability of each elementary event, whereas the overall probability of a disjunctive event is higher than the probability of each elementary event. As a consequence of anchoring, the overall probability will be overestimated in conjunctive problems and underestimated in disjunctive problems.

Biases in the evaluation of compound events are particularly significant in the context of planning. The successful completion of an undertaking, such as the development of a new product, typically has a conjunctive character: for the undertaking to succeed, each of a series of events must occur. Even when each of these events is very likely, the overall probability of success can be quite low if the number of events is large. The general tendency to overestimate the probability of conjunctive events leads to unwarranted optimism in the evaluation of the likelihood that a plan will succeed or that a project will be completed on time. Conversely, disjunctive structures are typically encountered in the evaluation of risks. A complex system, such as a nuclear reactor or a human body, will malfunction if any of its essential components fails. Even when the likelihood of failure in each component is slight, the probability of an overall failure can be high if many components are involved. Because of anchoring, people will tend to underestimate the probabilities of failure in complex systems. Thus, the direction of the anchoring bias can sometimes be inferred from the structure of the event. The chain-like structure of conjunctions leads to overestimation, the funnel-like structure of disjunctions leads to underestimation.

Anchoring in the assessment of subjective probability distributions

In decision analysis, experts are often required to express their beliefs about a quantity, such as the value of the Dow-Jones average on a particular day, in the form of a probability distribution. Such a distribution is usually constructed by asking the person to select values of the quantity that correspond to specified percentiles of his subjective probability distribution. For example, the judge may be asked to select a number, X_{90}, such that his subjective probability that this number will be higher than the value of the Dow-Jones average is .90. That is, he should select the value X_{90} so that he is just willing to accept 9 to 1 odds that the Dow-Jones average will not exceed it. A subjective probability distribution for the value of the Dow-Jones average can be constructed from several such judgments corresponding to different percentiles.

By collecting subjective probability distributions for many different quantities, it is possible to test the judge for proper calibration. A judge is properly (or externally) calibrated in a set of problems if exactly II percent of the true values of the assessed quantities falls below his stated values of Xn. For example, the true values should fall below X_{01} for 1 percent of the quantities and above X_{99} for 1 percent of the quantities. Thus, the true values should fall in the confidence interval between X_{01} and X_{99} on 98 percent of the problems.

Several investigators (Alpert & Raiffa, 1969; von Holstein, 1971; Winkler, 1967) have obtained probability distributions for many quantities from a large number of judges. These distributions indicated large and systematic departures from proper calibration. In most studies, the actual values of the assessed quantities are either smaller than X_{01} or greater than X_{99} for about 30 percent of the problems. That is, the subjects state overly narrow confidence intervals which reflect more certainty than is justified by their knowledge about the assessed quantities. This bias is common to naive and to sophisticated subjects, and it is not eliminated by introducing proper scoring rules, which provide incentives for external calibration. This effect is attributable, in part at least, to anchoring.

To select X_{90} for the value of the Dow-Jones average, for example, it is natural to begin by thinking about one's best estimate of the Dow-Jones and to adjust this value upward. If this adjustment – like most others – is insufficient, then X_{90} will not be sufficiently extreme. A similar anchoring effect will occur in the selection of X_{10}, which is presumably obtained by adjusting one's best estimate downward. Consequently, the confidence interval between X_{10} and X_{90} will be too narrow, and the assessed probability distribution will be too tight. In support of this interpretation it can be shown that subjective probabilities are systematically altered by a procedure in which one's best estimate does not serve as an anchor.

Subjective probability distributions for a given quantity (the Dow-Jones average) can be obtained in two different ways: (i) by asking the subject to select values of the Dow-Jones that correspond to specified percentiles of his probability distribution and (ii) by asking the subject to assess the probabilities that the true value of the Dow-Jones will exceed some specified values. The two procedures are formally equivalent and should yield identical distributions. However, they suggest different modes of adjustment from differecent anchors. In procedure (i), the natural starting point is one's best estimate of the quantity. In procedure (ii), on the other hand, the subject may be anchored on the value stated in the question. Alternatively, he may be anchored on even odds, or 50-50 chances, which is a natural starting point in the estimation of likelihood. In either case, procedure (ii) should yield less extreme odds than procedure (i).

To contrast the two procedures, a set of 24 quantities (such as the air distance from New Delhi to Peking) was presented to a group of subjects who assessed either X_{10} or X_{90} for each problem. Another group of subjects received the median judgment of the first group for each of the 24 quantities. They were asked to assess the odds that each of the given values exceeded the true value of the relevant quantity. In the absence of any bias, the second group should retrieve the odds specified to the first group, that is, 9:1. However, if even odds or the stated value serve as anchors, the odds of the second group should be less extreme, that is, closer to 1:1. Indeed, the median odds stated by this group, across all problems, were 3:1. When the judgments of the two groups were tested for external calibration, it was found that subjects in the first group were too extreme, in accord with earlier studies. The events that they defined as having a probability of .10 actually obtained in 24 percent of the cases. In contrast, subjects in the second group were too conservative. Events to which they assigned an average probability of .34 actually obtained in 26 percent of the cases. These results illustrate the manner in which the degree of calibration depends on the procedure of elicitation.

Discussion

This article has been concerned with cognitive biases that stem from the reliance on judgmental heuristics. These biases are not attributable to motivational effects such as wishful thinking or the distortion of judgments by payoffs and penalties. Indeed, several of the severe errors of judgment reported earlier occurred despite the fact that subjects were encouraged to be accurate and were rewarded for the correct answers (Kahneman & Tversky, 1972; Tversky & Kahneman, 1973).

The reliance on heuristics and the prevalence of biases are not restricted to laymen. Experienced researchers are also prone to the same biases – when they think intuitively. For example, the tendency to predict the outcome that best represents the data, with insufficient regard for prior probability, has been observed in the intuitive judgments of individuals who have had extensive training in statistics (Kahneman & Tversky, 1973; Tversky & Kahneman, 1971a). Although the statistically sophisticated avoid elementary errors, such as the gambler's fallacy, their intuitive judgments are liable to similar fallacies in more intricate and less transparent problems.

It is not surprising that useful heuristics such as representativeness and availability are retained, even though they occasionally lead to errors in prediction or estimation. What is perhaps surprising is the failure of people to infer from lifelong experience such fundamental statistical rules as regression toward the mean, or the effect of sample size on sampling variability. Although everyone is exposed, in the normal course of life, to numerous examples from which these rules could have been induced, very few people discover the principles of sampling and regression on their own. Statistical principles are not learned from everyday experience because the relevant instances are not coded appropriately. For example, people do not discover that successive lines in a text differ more in average word length than do successive pages, because they simply do not attend to the average word length of individual lines or pages. Thus, people do not learn the relation between sample size and sampling variability, although the data for such learning are abundant.

The lack of an appropriate code also explains why people usually do not detect the biases in their judgments of probability. A person could conceivably learn whether his judgments are externally calibrated by keeping a tally of the proportion of events that actually occur among those to which he assigns the same probability. However, it is not natural to group events by their judged probability. In the absence of such grouping it is impossible for an individual to discover, for example, that only 50 percent of the predictions to which he has assigned a probability of .9 or higher actually came true.

The empirical analysis of cognitive biases has implications for the theoretical and applied role of judged probabilities. Modern decision theory (De Finetti, 1968; Savage, 1954) regards subjective probability as the quantified opinion of an idealized person. Specifically, the subjective probability of a given event is defined by the set of bets about this event that such a person is willing to accept. An internally consistent, or coherent, subjective probability measure can be derived for an individual if his choices among bets satisfy certain principles, that is, the axioms of the theory. The derived probability is subjective in the sense that different individuals are allowed to have different probabilities for the same event. The major contribution of this approach is that it provides a rigorous subjective interpretation of probability that is applicable to unique events and is embedded in a general theory of rational decision.

It should perhaps be noted that, while subjective probabilities can sometimes be inferred from preferences among bets, they are normally not formed in this fashion. A person bets on team A rather than on team B because he believes that team A is more likely to win; he does not infer this belief from his betting preferences. Thus, in reality, subjective probabilities determine preferences among bets and are not derived from them, as in the axiomatic theory of rational decision (Savage, 1954).

The inherently subjective nature of probability has led many students to the belief that coherence, or internal consistency, is the only valid criterion by which judged probabilities should be evaluated. From the standpoint of the formal theory of subjective probability, any set of internally consistent probability judgments is as good as any other. This criterion is not entirely satisfactory, because an internally consistent set of subjective probabilities can be incompatible with other beliefs held by the individual. Consider a person whose subjective probabilities for all possible outcomes of a coin-tossing game reflect the gambler's fallacy. That is, his estimate of the probability of tails on a particular toss increases with the number of consecutive heads that preceded that toss. The judgments of such a person could be internally consistent and therefore acceptable as adequate subjective probabilities according to the criterion of the formal theory. These probabilities, however, are incompatible with the generally held belief that a coin has no memory and is therefore incapable of generating sequential dependencies. For judged probabilities to be considered adequate, or rational, internal consistency is not enough. The judgments must be compatible with the entire web of beliefs held by the individual. Unfortunately, there can be no simple formal procedure for assessing the compatibility of a set of probability judgments with the judge's total system of beliefs. The rational judge will nevertheless strive for compatibility, even though internal consistency is more easily achieved and assessed. In particular, he will attempt to make his probability judgments compatible with his knowledge about the subject matter, the laws of probability, and his own judgmental heuristics and biases.

Summary

This article described three heuristics that are employed in making judgments under uncertainty: (i) representativeness, which is usually employed when people are asked to judge the probability that an object or event A belongs to class or process B; (ii) availability of instances or scenarios, which is often employed when people are asked to assess the frequency of a class or the plausibility of a particular development; and (iii) adjustment from an anchor, which is usually employed in numerical prediction when a relevant value is available. These heuristics are highly economical and usually effective, but they lead to systematic and predictable errors. A better understanding of these heuristics and of the biases to which they lead could improve judgments and decisions in situations of uncertainty.

3.   Social Judgment Theory

Kenneth R. Hammond,
Thomas R. Stewart, Berndt Brehmer,
and Derick O. Steinmann

Why is judgment required?

Knowledge of the environment is difficult to acquire because of causal ambiguity – because of the probabilistic, entangled relations among environmental variables. Tolman and Brunswik called attention to the critical role of causal ambiguity in their article "The Organism and the Causal Texture of the Environment" (1935), in which they emphasized the fact that the organism in its normal intercourse with its environment must cope with *numerous, interdependent, multiformal relations* among variables which are *partly relevant* and *partly irrelevant* to its purpose, which carry only a *limited amount of dependability*, and which are *organized in a variety of ways*. The problem for the organism, therefore, is to know its environment under these complex circumstances. In the effort to do so, the organism brings a variety of processes (generally labeled *cognitive*), such as perception, learning, and thinking, to bear on the problem of reducing causal ambiguity. As a part of this effort, human beings often attempt to manipulate variables (by experiments, for example) and sometimes succeed – in such a manner as to eliminate ambiguity. But when the variables in question *cannot* be manipulated, human beings must use their cognitive resources unaided by manipulation or experiment. They must do the best they can by passive rather than active means to arrive at a conclusion regarding a state of affairs clouded by causal ambiguity. They must, in short, exercise their judgment. Human judgment is a cognitive activity of last resort. . . .

This chapter is an abbreviated version of one that originally appeared in Kaplan, M. F. & Schwartz, S. (eds.), *Human judgment and decision processes* (pp. 271–312). New York: Academic Press, 1975. Copyright © 1975 by Academic Press, Inc. Reprinted by permission.

Basic concepts

Relationships: The fundamental units of cognition

The fundamental concept ordinarily employed to describe an environmental "input" to the organism is the stimulus. That concept is rejected here. Although both Tolman and Brunswik used this term, they did not make a complete conceptual commitment to it; both argued that the objects and events apprehended by an organism do more – and less – than "impinge" upon it. Not only does the organism cognitively act on the "input," but the perceived object carries implications for *other objects.* That is why Tolman's position was labeled an S-S theory (that is, a "sign-significate" theory) and contrasted to an S-R (stimulus-response) theory by competing theoreticians of his time. And that is why Brunswik used the word "cue" to refer to various dimensions of the perceived world. Both these terms, "sign-significate" (or as Tolman also put it, "sign-Gestalt") and "cue," have in common the notion that the raw materials of perception point outward from the organism toward various aspects of the person's ecological surroundings. And whereas "sign-significate" and "cue" point *outward* from the organism to the environment, the concept of stimulus points *inward*. It is for this reason that S-R theories in general do not include concepts relating to the environment and that S-R judgment theories, in particular, do not include concepts referring to the properties of judgment tasks (see, for example, Anderson, 1971).

Because "cues" and "sign-significates" point outward, they involve a relation between two variables – proximal and distal, the given and the inferred. Choice of that relation as the fundamental unit of cognition has profound consequences, of course, and it was this choice that eventually led Tolman to introduce the concept of the "cognitive map" in 1948; he argued that cognition involves a subjective representation of the interrelations of goal paths in the organism's environment. Brunswik went further; he demanded a more detailed analysis of the *environment* and a less detailed analysis of the *organism*. Thus, for example, he remarked:

Both organism and environment will have to be seen as systems, each with properties of its own.... Each has surface and depth, or overt and covert regions.... It follows that, much as psychology must be concerned with the texture of the organism or of its nervous properties and investigate them in depth, it must also be concerned with the texture of the environment [1957, p. 5].

Brunswik's admonition to psychologists to "be concerned with the texture of the environment" gives clear direction to the student of human judgment; his first step must be to learn about and to understand the texture (and by that we mean the causal ambiguity) of the relationships among variables in the tasks which require human judgment. (The

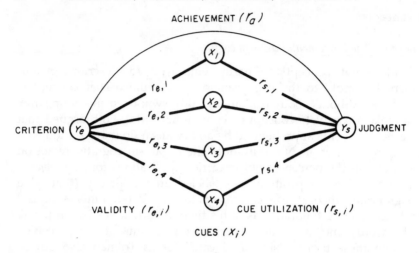

Figure 3.1. Brunswik's lens model.

methodological corollary is that such ambiguity among relations must be represented in the judgment tasks used to study human judgment.)

Principle of parallel concepts

As can be seen in the above quotation, Brunswik indicated that organismic and environmental systems should be described in symmetrical terms. That symmetry is represented in what Brunswik called the "lens model" of behavior indicated in Figure 3.1. (Space does not permit more than a cursory reference to the conceptual implications of the lens model; the best of several original sources is Brunswik's "The Conceptual Framework of Psychology," 1952; a secondary source which presents part of what is contained in several original articles is Hammond's *The Psychology of Egon Brunswik*, 1966.)

As Brunswik describes the lens model, it becomes clear that he employs a principle of parallel concepts, for each concept on one side is paralleled by a similar concept on the other. Thus, cues on the task, or ecological, side vary in *ecological validity*, and on the organismic side there is variation in *cue utilization* by the subject. And just as the relations between cues and distal variables on the ecological side may assume various (linear, curvilinear) *forms*, according to the principle of parallel concepts, the relations between cues and judgments may also assume various function forms on the organismic side. The investigator has similar interests with regard to both sets of variables: to what extent ecological validities are matched by cue utilization and to what extent ecological function forms are matched by subjective function forms. Social judgment theorists are also concerned with the extent to which the principles of organization that control the task system are reflected in the principles of organization that control the cognitive system of the subject.

It is the principle of parallel concepts, therefore, that produces the symmetrical relation between the descriptive terms applied to the organismic system and to the environmental system, and it is this principle that is responsible for the fact that Social Judgment Theory (SJT) includes a set of concepts which apply to task systems as well as person systems.

Distinction between surface and depth

This distinction is essential to SJT. It derives from the proximal-distal separation in perception theory and thus refers to the separation between what is given and what is inferred. *Surface* data are (given) cues to (inferred) *depth* conditions in the judgment task. By virtue of the principle of parallel concepts, this distinction also applies to organismic judgment systems (see Figure 3.1). Separation of surface and depth is critical to any theory of judgment (or inference), for it raises the question of the properties of the region that intervenes between them. Because of the importance of this region, we have named it the *zone of ambiguity*.

The zone of ambiguity. The region between depth and surface variables in a given judgment task involves the relations between cause (depth) and effect (surface). Because a single effect may be produced by several causes, as well as because multiple effects may be produced by a single cause, there is ambiguity from cause to effect and effect to cause. Because causes may be related, and because effects are interrelated, the network of task relations can be said to be entangled. Moreover, causal ambiguity is produced because (1) surface data are less than perfectly related to depth variables, (2) functional relations between surface and depth variables may assume a variety of forms (linear, curvilinear), and (3) the relations between surface and depth may be organized (or combined) according to a variety of principles (for example, additivity or pattern). These circumstances give more specific meaning to the term "causal texture," or causal ambiguity.

In short, causal ambiguity within the zone of ambiguity is the source of the human judgment problem, as well as a source of the misunderstandings and disputes that occur when judgments differ. As we shall see below, social judgment theorists direct themselves to reducing causal ambiguity in judgment tasks and in judgment policies by *externalizing* the properties of the zone of ambiguity in both systems.

Objectives of Social Judgment Theory

So far, we have set forth our assumptions about the environmental circumstances that create the need for human judgment. In addition, we have indicated the major concepts which SJT employs in the effort to understand the judgment process that must cope with these circumstances. The reader will have observed that these assumptions and concepts differ in fundamental ways from those offered by other theorists; he should also know that our research objectives differ rather markedly from those of other judgment theorists.

1. SJT is intended to be life relevant; that objective is a direct legacy from Brunswik.
2. SJT is not a law-seeking theory. It is not aimed at finding the laws of human judgment; rather, it is intended to be descriptive.
3. Social judgment theorists are interested in creating cognitive aids for human judgment – particularly for those persons who must exercise their judgment in the effort to formulate social policy and who will ordinarily find themselves embroiled in bitter dispute as they do so. Social judgment theorists intend not only to understand human judgment but to create and develop ways of improving it.

These objectives have led us to study disputes arising from differing judgments, and this research has in turn led us to invent a cognitive aid for persons involved in such disputes. More specifically, the theory described above, together with the results of empirical research, indicated that in order to be effective, a cognitive aid for persons exercising their judgment should be capable of *displaying pictorially* the weights, function forms, and uncertainty in persons' judgment policies as well as in judgment tasks. Without such displays, persons involved in dispute, or interpersonal learning, can do little besides exchange incomplete, inaccurate information about their judgment policies; verbal explanations of their introspections regarding their judgment processes are their only recourse. Social judgment theorists, on the other hand, can now offer persons the use of interactive computer graphics terminals which will display for them pictorial representations of their judgment policies, as well as the properties of task systems. These procedures have been developed from the quantitative method employed by social judgment theorists, a topic to which we now turn.

Quantitative method

Analysis of the cognitive system of an individual

The analysis of an individual's cognitive system proceeds in four steps:

1. *Identification of the judgment problem.* The substantive and formal properties of the judgment problem are identified.
2. *Exercise of judgment.* The individual makes judgments about a

representative set of cases of the judgment problem.

3. *Analysis of judgment.* The individual's judgments are analyzed to determine the components of his cognitive system.

4. *Display of results.* The results of the analysis are displayed graphically to the individual (ordinarily by interactive computer graphics techniques).

Description of the regression analysis approach

Identification of the judgment problem. This step consists of three parts: (1) defining the judgment to be made, (2) identifying the information (cues) on which the judgment is based, and (3) discovering the formal properties (for example, intercorrelations, distributions, and ranges) of the set of cue variables in the task. The procedures used in this critical step vary according to the type of judgment problem and the purpose of the analysis. A full-scale study involving extensive data gathering and multivariate analysis could be conducted, or a simple guided interview designed to elicit cue variables from the individual might suffice. Since methods used in this step are highly situation (and investigator) specific, we shall not attempt to describe them further here. This step is critical for the analysis, however, since the validity of all that follows depends on the proper identification of the judgment problem at this step. It is particularly important that all major cues are identified, since it is unlikely that the omission of a cue at this stage will be detected in later analysis. (But see Stenson, 1974, who shows that certain parameters of the judgment process can be ascertained even though the cues are not identified.)

Exercise of judgment. A judgment task is generated that consists of a number of cases representing the judgment problem. Each case consists of a profile representing a different combination or mix of values on the several cues. The individual indicates his judgments by rating several profiles on a numerical scale.

The judgment task may be conducted by pencil-and-paper procedures or by an interactive computer terminal, but the cue information must be presented unambiguously. All possible perceptual confusion must be eliminated from the display so that the task will be wholly judgmental in nature (unless, of course, the investigator is interested in studying the effects of perceptual ambiguity).

The formal properties of the judgment task (for example, distributions and interrelations) should correspond to the properties of the environment that gave rise to the problem. The correspondence of the judgment tasks to the environment (representativeness) is essential if the results of the analysis of the judgment task are to be generalizable.

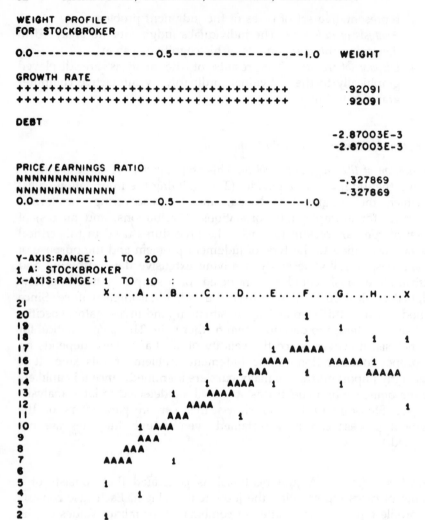

Figure 3.2. An example of a computer graphics display of weights and function forms.

Analysis of judgment. The judgment data are analyzed in terms of multiple regression statistics. The values of the cues are the independent variables in the analysis, and the individual's judgments constitute the dependent variable. The linear model that is fitted by this technique is

$$y_{ij} = \sum_{k=1}^{m} b_{ik}x_{jk} + c_i + e_{ij}'$$ (1)

where y_{ij} is the judgment of individual i for profile j, m is the number of

```
A: SMITH
B: JONES

WEIGHT   PROFILE

0.0----------------0.5---------------1.0      WEIGHT

WAGES
AAAAAAAAAAAAAAAAAAAAAAAAAAAAAAAAA             740226
BBBBBBBB                                      .195698

PRICES
AAA                                          -7.80695E-2
BBBBBBBBBBBBBBBBBBBBBBBBBBBBBBBBBBBBBBBB      -.887725

UNEMPLOYMENT
                                             5.93882E-3
BBBBBBB                                       -.167995
0.0-----------------0.5----------------1.0
```

Figure 3.3. A computer graphics display comparing two systems.

cues, b_{ik} is the raw score regression weight for individual i on cue k, x_{jk} is the value of cue k on profile j, c_i is the constant term for individual i, and e_{ij} is the residual error from the model of individual i for profile j. . . .

Display of results. The weights and function forms obtained from the analysis of judgment are presented to the individual immediately following his judgments by means of computer graphics displays. An example of a pictorial display of weights and function forms generated by a computer program is presented in Figure 3.2. In many applications it is necessary to compare two or more systems (an individual's cognitive system and a task system, or the cognitive systems of two or more individuals). A computer-generated pictorial display comparing two systems is shown in Figure 3.3.

Extensions of the method: Interactive computer graphics

The steps described above have been used with success in numerous studies of cognitive process and will continue to be important in future work. The availability of interactive computer graphics devices, however, provides flexibility and power for the analysis of cognitive systems far beyond what has been previously available. Some of the most promising new procedures are (1) subject-controlled revision of weights and function forms, (2) use of hierarchical judgment models, and (3) multi-method, multistage analyses. All of these are now being investigated; each will be briefly described below.

Subject-controlled revision of weights and function forms (at the computer console). If the individual wishes to change the weights and function forms in his judgment policy, he can do so by use of a light pen or by entering new weights and function forms directly from the keyboard. The computer can generate judgments consistent with the model newly specified by the individual and display to him these new judgments made in response to a set of profiles. The individual can then review the judgments which were derived from the weights and function forms he specified and can revise his judgment policy (for example, his weights and/or function forms) again if he is not satisfied with the new judgments. Thus, the computer provides the individual with complete control over his cognitive system during the exercise of his judgment. The development of this procedure as an aid for the person exercising his judgment illustrates clearly the sharp difference in research aims between social judgment theorists and other judgment researchers who focus their efforts on the search for the correct model of judgment processes....

Discussion of unique contributions in four cases

Social Judgment Theory distinguishes among four types of judgment situations. These are the single-system case, the double-system case, the triple-system case, and the N-system case. Space does not permit discussion of the research carried out within each case; therefore, only the unique contribution that SJT has made to each case will be mentioned.

The single-system case

This is the case ordinarily studied by judgment theorists (see, for example, Anderson, 1971; Edwards, 1968; Kelley, 1973). In this case the judgment processes of the person making the judgment are the only phenomena of interest. No task information other than the value of the cues (or "stimuli") and possibly their interrelations is considered by the researcher.

Unique contribution: Separating knowledge from cognitive control. The separation of knowledge and cognitive control (see the above section on quantitative method) has led to a new view of the competence of human judgment and to a shift in theory. Initially the concept of cognitive control was made equivalent to consistency (Hammond & Summers, 1972). That is, the random error in the subject's judgment system provided a measure of his *control* over, and thus his *consistency* in applying, his judgment policy. It is now clear that these terms should be separated, conceptually and mathematically (see above), due to the results of several recent studies.

These studies began with an effort to train two undergraduates to *exercise control* over their judgment processes in what were presumed to be a variety of highly complex tasks – tasks which involved differential weights and various function forms. For example, a simple judgment policy is one which requires only that the subject assign equal weights to, say, three cues, use the information from all three cues in terms of a positive linear function, and employ an additive organizational principle. A more difficult task would require the subject to assign differential weights to the cues and to employ different function forms (for example, a positive linear function form for cue 1, a negative linear function form for cue 2, and a U-shaped function form for cue 3).

The results from an initial study were surprising. The two students were able to exercise effectively various judgment policies over a wide range of tasks which had been presumed to be beyond their capacity. Gillis, Stewart, and Gritz (1975) found the same results with normal controls, and also found that methadone addicts and chronic schizophrenics (under medication) performed nearly as well. Steinmann's study (1974) of college students confirmed the results Gillis and his colleagues obtained with normal subjects. Further work by Weichselbaum (1975) confirmed their results with normals as well as with methadone addicts. In short, studies carried out by different investigators in different laboratories over a variety of subject populations have provided a clear result: Under the proper conditions, human beings can exercise control over their judgment processes with respect to far more complex relations than had been suspected.

To grasp the significance of these findings, one must remember that although the layman expects human judgment to have almost unlimited capacity, judgment researchers have stressed the limitations of human judgment again and again (for a recent example, see Tversky & Kahneman, 1974). The finding that human subjects *can* execute a judgment policy that requires them to organize information drawn from dimensions that vary widely in function form and in weights is, therefore, an important one. Whether human subjects in fact *execute* judgment policies of the complexity indicated above outside the laboratory is another question.

The double-system case

In this case (see Figure 3.1), one person makes judgments about one task system; in addition, task outcomes are *known* (in contrast to the single-system case, in which task outcomes are *unknown*), and, as a result, task structure is known. Moreover, the second task system might be a second *person* about which judgments are to be made. The immediate question raised by the double-system case is the accuracy of judgments, as well as the circumstances which enhance or impair it. In addition, the rate at which one learns to improve his judgment is an important matter. It is in this area that SJT has made a unique contribution.

Unique contribution: Providing cognitive feedback by means of interactive computer graphics. The traditional S-R approach to these problems is based on the provision of the correct answer after each trial. How else can people learn other than by observing task outcomes? Unfortunately, social judgment theorists who studied what during the 1960s was called "multiple-cue probability learning" accepted all too readily the traditional notion that learning is dependent upon receiving outcome feedback. A wholly fortuitous discovery by Newton (1965), however, that subjects might well be able to improve their performance without outcome feedback led Todd and Hammond (1965) to investigate an alternative type of feedback. They showed that if subjects were given feedback of a cognitive nature (that is, information about the properties of task systems and their judgment systems), they could rapidly improve their performance without outcome feedback (that is, without being told the correct answer after each trial). Moreover, they found that providing outcome feedback in addition to cognitive feedback did not improve accuracy. Indeed, Hammond, Summers, and Deane (1973) later showed that adding outcome feedback could result in the *impairment* of performance. These preliminary results, obtained from experimental situations involving only the crudest of equipment and materials, led to the search for an appropriate means for displaying (1) the properties of task systems, (2) the properties of cognitive systems of persons, and (3) the degree of match between them. Procedures involving interactive computer graphics techniques (mentioned above) were developed for this purpose and are now in use (see Hammond, 1971; Stewart & Carter, 1973; Hammond & Brehmer, 1973).

These procedures allow the subject not only to see the properties of his own judgment policy (the weights attached to cues, function forms employed, and the control with which he is executing his policy), but also to *compare* his policy with that of another person (or with the properties of the task to be dealt with if these are known; see Figure 3.3). Thus, interactive computer graphics techniques permit the human subject not only to see a representation of the "cognitive map" that Tolman (1948) spoke of, but to compare it with the causal texture of environmental (or task) systems Brunswik (1956) argued should be investigated in depth. Moreover, cognitive maps of several persons (or task systems) can be compared. Such cognitive material is, of course, appropriate to a cognitive theory intended to be free of stimulus-response concepts. Furthermore, as Lindell (1974) has shown, cognitive feedback enhances learning in those difficult judgment tasks in which task variables are intercorrelated and differential weights are involved.

This contribution by SJT – the development of a *cognitive aid* – has important practical applications, for it is now clear that it is no longer necessary to try to learn how to improve one's judgment by means of outcome feedback (indeed, if the task is complex and involves uncertainty, it will *never* be learned by means of outcome feedback), nor is it necessary to try to learn what the properties of another person's judgment policy are by interrogation on one person's part and intro-spection on the other's. Persons exercising their judgment can discover, immediately and in pictorial form (by means of computer graphics), the properties of their own judgmental system, as well as the properties of another person's judgmental system, and *change* those properties, if they desire, with complete control. That capability carries considerable significance for judgment situations in which more than one policy maker is involved and in which interpersonal conflict and interpersonal learning become significant phenomena, a point to be developed below. Learning with cognitive aids (in the form of other persons) is a more representative learning situation than the outcome feedback paradigm used in traditional learning studies. Our cognitive aids are only a superior version of what actually takes place when people learn, which they do on the basis of feedforward from other people and feedback from other people, rather than in terms of outcomes following specific judgments.

The triple-system case

There are two reasons for studying the case involving *two* persons and a task. First, as mentioned earlier, good methodology requires variations over different conditions; second, interpersonal conflict arising from different judgments and interpersonal learning were two highly important topics untouched by judgment theorists and, indeed, hardly investigated by anyone. Investigation of these problem areas is therefore a unique contribution made by social judgment theorists.

Unique contribution: Uncovering cognitive sources of interpersonal conflict. Social Judgment Theory differs sharply from all other approaches to the study of conflict because it focuses only on *cognitive* differences between persons who arrive at conflicting judgments, whereas all other approaches focus only on *differential gain* as the source of conflict; the latter approach has always dominated the field of conflict research. Strangely enough, neither psychologists nor others entertained the possibility that the properties of judgment processes may themselves produce conflict. The basis for the cognitive point of view was set forth by K. R. Hammond (1965) and elaborated by Hammond and Brehmer (1973).

The studies carried out by Brehmer and others (to be reported below) support the theory that cognitive differences in themselves are capable of producing conflict; they clearly show that it is unnecessary to appeal to motivational explanations in all cases of conflict. Indeed, it is clear that conflict can readily be increased, diminished, or elimianted by changes in task properties alone.

The research paradigm. The problem in extending SJT to engage this topic was, first, to create circumstances under which it would be possible to observe the interaction between persons whose judgments differ and, second, to discover whether the concepts of SJT in general, and the parameters of the lens model equation in particular, would provide new and useful information regarding the interaction.

Experiments within the SJT research paradigm for the triple-system case simulate a situation in which two persons make inductive inferences from uncertain information (cues). They use the cues differently, however, to arrive at their judgments – that is, they have different judgment policies. Differences in judgment policy can be created in the laboratory by *training* the persons to use the information differently, but it is also possible to *select* persons whose differences stem from differences in preexperimental experience. The training procedure has the advantage of allowing the investigator to create precisely whatever differences in judgment policy are required for the experiment; the selection procedure, on the other hand, allows the investigator to study socially induced rather than laboratory-induced differences. The findings so far, however, indicate that the same results are obtained regardless of whether training or selection is used (Hammond & Brehmer, 1973; Helenius, 1973; Rappoport, 1969).

The research focuses upon the changes in judgments that occur as the two persons interact with each other and with the task. Agreement and conflict are defined objectively in terms of the actual differences between the judgments made by the subjects for each problem rather than in terms of subjective factors (for example, in terms of whether the persons feel that they are in conflict or not). The experiments are conducted in two stages: a *training stage*, in which the subjects are trained to have different policies, and a *conflict stage*, in which the subjects are brought together in pairs to work on a set of problems. The problems in the conflict stage usually differ somewhat from the problems in the training stage, but the persons are not informed of this or of the fact that they have been differently trained. On each trial in the conflict stage, the subjects (1) study a set of cues, (2) make individual judgments from these cues which (3) they announce to each other, and if their judgments differ, (4) they discuss the case, until (5) they can reach a joint judgment, agreeable to both of them, after which (6) the correct answer for the problem is given. The relation between the individual judgments mentioned in (2) defines the amount of conflict and is thus the primary dependent variable.

Interpersonal conflict arising from differences in judgment. A first important question is whether it is possible to produce disagreement by means of the research paradigm described above, and if it is possible, whether persons resolve their judgmental differences as they interact with each other and with the task. The results of roughly 30 studies (including studies carried out in 12 different countries) show, first, that it is indeed possible to produce disagreement and, second, that the disagreement is not resolved (Hammond & Brehmer, 1973).

Analysis of conflict in terms of the lens model equation. The above-mentioned results lead to the question of why conflict is not resolved. The question can be answered through an examination of a measure of conflict based on the lens model equation. This measure expresses the effects of *two* sources of conflict: *systematic* as well as *nonsystematic* differences in judgment policy. Equation (2) disentangles the effects of these two sources. Recall that

$$r_a = GR_1R_2,\tag{2}$$

where r_a is the correlation between the judgments made by Subject 1 and those made by Subject 2 and the other terms are interpreted as in the quantitative discussion above.

In this equation, r_a is a measure of the amount of agreement between the judgments of Subject 1 and Subject 2, G indicates the extent to which the two judgment policies are similar with respect to their systematic aspects, and R_1 and R_2 indicate the consistency of each of the judgment policies and thus provide a measure of the nonsystematic differences in judgments.[1] As can be seen from the equation, perfect agreement (r_a = 1.00) can be reached only if the subjects are identical in the systematic aspects of their judgmnet policies (G = 1.00) *and* if their policies are executed with perfect consistency (R_1 = R_2 = 1.00). Thus, the two possible sources of disagreement, *differences* in judgment policy ($G < 1.00$) and *inconsistency* (R_1 and for $R_2 < 1.00$) in execution of policies, can be measured. This distinction shows that the mere observation that persons differ in their judgments does not allow the inference that there are fundamental differences between judgment policies. The two persons may lack perfect consistency, and thus their differences may be caused by inconsistent execution. The question, then, is whether subjects fail to reduce their conflict because they are unable to reduce the systematic differences between their policies or because they are unable to execute their judgments with perfect consistency.

Results. The results of a series of analyses of sources of conflict show that the relative importance of the two sources of policy conflict *changes* as

---

[1] In the following discussion, R is used as a measure of consistency for two reasons: (1) The term "consistency" was used exclusively in the original literature cited here. (2) In the studies discussed, the mean of a set of repeated judgments would coincide with the predictions based on the model, and therefore R is a valid measure of consistency. The training procedure resulted in subjects' using an additive policy, and the conflict procedure did not elicit a different type of model; only weights and function forms changed during conflict, with the organizing principle remaining unchanged. Consistency and control are thus identical.

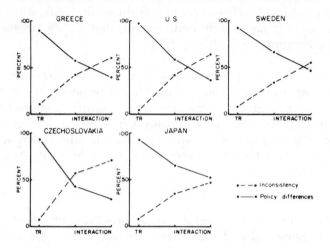

Figure 3.4. The relative contributions (percent) of policy differences (sums of differences in beta weights divided by 2) and inconsistency $[1 - (R^2_{s_1} + R^2_{s_2})/2]$ to disagreement as a function of blocks of trials for the five-nation study.

the subjects interact with each other and the task. At the beginning of the interaction, most of the conflict is caused by the systematic differences in policy, but these differences are rapidly reduced. At the same time, however, the consistency of the subjects' policies decreases so that at the end of a 20-trial conflict period, lack of consistency rather than systematic differences in policy is the main obstacle to agreement.

Replications. Some typical results are shown in Figure 3.4. These results have been replicated over subject conditions, such as nationality (Brehmer, Azuma, Hammond, Kostron, and Varonos, 1970) and sex (Hammond & Brehmer, 1973), and task variables, both with respect to *content* (Hammond & Brehmer, 1973) and with respect to *formal characteristics,* such as task predictability (Brehmer, 1973c, 1974e), the distribution of the validities of cues (Brehmer, 1974e), and the forms of the functions relating cues to criterion (Brehmer & Hammond, 1973; Brehmer & Kostron, 1973). The results obtained when the subjects have been selected because of their preexperimental differences are similar to those obtained when the subjects have been trained to have different policies (Rappoport & Summers, 1973).

Changes in cue dependencies: Negative consequences of good intentions. Subjects decrease their dependency on the cues used initially at a faster rate than they increase their dependency on the cues used by the other person (see, for example, Brehmer, 1972). This necessarily leads to a drop in consistency since R_1, which defines consistency, is related to the sum of the individual cue-judgment correlations which define the subjects' dependency on the individual cues. And a decrease in R means a decrease in r_a and thus a decrease in agreement, despite good intentions.

A study by Brehmer (1972) in which both subjects were trained to have *identical* judgment policies illustrates clearly the role of change and inconsistency. As the subjects tried to increase their judgmental accuracy in the conflict stage, they began to change; inconsistency developed (their R's decreased), and the subjects began to disagree (r_a decreased), yet their judgment policies remained virtually identical throughout the experiment (as shown by high G values). Thus, inconsistency will not only prevent subjects from reaching agreement but may also *introduce* disagreement where no prior disagreement existed. As this study indicates, however, disagreement may be *false*, since the judgment policies remained virtually identical.

Behavioral validation of the meaning of inconsistency. The first part of the hypothesis, that inconsistency leads to a lack of understanding, has gained support from two studies (Brehmer, 1974f, 1975) which show that subjects ask each other more questions when their policies are more inconsistent, thus indicating that inconsistency does indeed lead to lack of understanding and that inconsistency is not a mathematical fiction. (Whether inconsistency leads to distrust has still to be investigated.) A different type of behavioral validation has been carried out by Gillis (1975). He found that the phenothiazines commonly used as therapeutic agents in psychiatric hospitals have a deleterious effect on consistency. In short, inconsistency has been systematically related to behavioral observations.

Conflict reduction or task adaptation? The results of a series of studies using these conditions support the latter alternative: Only the subject with the incorrect policy shows any appreciable change in policy (Brehmer & Kostron, 1973: Brehmer, 1975; see also Brehmer & Garpebring, 1974).

These results show the important contribution of task characteristics to conflict arising from different judgments and support the value of analyzing conflict in terms of *three* systems rather than restricting the analysis to person characteristics, as is typical of an organism-centered psychology.

Effects of the characteristics of the task on conflict. We turn now to an examination of the effects of formal characteristics of the task on conflict.

Task consistency. If judgment policies in a conflict situation are affected by the characteristics of the task in the same way that they are in policy formation, these results lead to the prediction that subjects will develop less consistent policies in conflict tasks of high uncertainty, and, therefore, there will be less agreement under these conditions than when the task is highly predictable. This hypothesis has been confirmed repeatedly (Brehmer, 1973c, 1974b, 1974f, 1975).

Ecological validities of cues. When the tasks contain only linear relations, the distribution of the validities of the cues affects the consistency (R) but not the similarity (G) of policies. In this case, the policies tend to be more consistent when the subjects have to use only one cue than when they have to use multiple cues (Brehmer, 1975). However, both policy similarity and consistency are affected when the tasks contain both linear *and* nonlinear cues (Brehmer & Kostron, 1973). In the latter case, both policy similarity and consistency tend to be higher when the subjects have to use only one cue. These results are presumably due to the difficulties inherent in the use of nonlinear function forms (see Brehmer, 1971a, 1971b, 1973b, 1973c).

Task function forms. Nonlinear function forms lead to lower consistency, presumably because nonlinear functions are harder to execute (see Brehmer, 1971b). The degree of policy similarity (G) is not affected by the function forms, however (Brehmer & Hammond, 1973; Brehmer & Kostron, 1973).

Cue intercorrelations. Task characteristics also introduce certain constraints on the relation among agreement, judgmental accuracy, and policy similarity. For example, if the cues are positively intercorrelated, the subjects will reach a high level of agreement despite differences in policy. In addition, the intercorrelation between the cues will allow a subject who uses a cue that is in itself of no validity to reach a high level of judgmental accuracy, since the correlation between the cues will ensure that judgments become correlated with one another. When the cues are orthogonal, on the other hand, differences in policy will be directly reflected in disagreement, and dependency on nonvalid cues will lead to a lack of judgmental accuracy. In short, positive cue intercorrelations will lead to *agreement in fact*, despite *disagreement in principle*; they will also lead to judgmental accuracy, despite a faulty policy. This means that when the cues are intercorrelated, there will be less need for the subjects to change their policies, and this, in turn, leads to the hypothesis that the subjects will reach a lower degree of policy similarity when the cues are intercorrelated than when they are orthogonal. This hypothesis was supported in two experiments (Brehmer, 1974b).

These results, then, show that both the level of agreement and the relative contributions from the two sources of agreement vary in a predictable way with the nature of the task.

Summary. First, our results show that conflict arising from different judgments is not resolved even under the benign conditions prevailing in these experiments. Conflict can indeed be caused by purely cognitive factors; the commonsense notion that disagreement always involves motivational differences is incorrect.

Second, our results show that conflict does not persist because the subjects are determined to maintain the systematic differences between their policies; on the contrary, in these studies systematic differences between policies are usually rapidly reduced. But conflict persists, and it persists because of a lack of consistency. The lack of consistency, in turn, stems from the manner in which the subjects change their policies.

Third, the results illustrate the importance of task variables in conflict. The task is important, first, because it is the general focus of cognitive activity in the situation, second, because of its effects on the structure of the judgment policies of the participants and thus on agreement, and, third, because of the constraints it places on agreement, judgmental accuracy, and policy differences.

Interpersonal learning (IPL). Space permits only a brief summary of the rationale and results of the studies of interpersonal learning carried out by social judgment theorists. Research in this area is divided into two categories: IPL *from* the other and IPL *about* the other. Each is discussed in turn.

Interpersonal learning from the other. The research paradigm used in the triple-system case to study interpersonal conflict lends itself very readily to the study of IPL from the other because the investigator can specify the properties of the cognitive systems of both learners as well as the task to be learned.

Task variables and interpersonal learning. A series of studies has investigated the effects of task variables, such as task predictability (Brehmer, 1973b, 1974a, 1974b), function form (Brehmer, 1973a, 1973b; Earle, 1973; Hammond, 1972), the distribution of validities of the cues (Brehmer, 1973a, 1973b, 1974a, 1974b), and cue intercorrelations (Brehmer, 1974a). The results of these studies show that the effects of these variables are similar to those obtained in the individual learning studies, except that the learning of nonlinear relations in the task is more rapid in interpersonal learning than in individual learning. Thus, the results show (1) that subjects tend to have less optimal judgment policies when the task predictability is low than when it is high and (2) that although nonlinear functions are learned more rapidly in interpersonal learning than in individual learning, performance is nevertheless less optimal for tasks with nonlinear relations than for tasks with linear relations.

The effects of the characteristics of the cognitive systems of the learner and the other. A stable result in interpersonal learning studies (as well as those concerning conflict) is this: If one subject is trained to use a nonlinear relation and the other subject is trained to use a linear one, and if the interpersonal training task requires the subjects to use *both* the nonlinear cue and the linear cue to the same extent, the nonlinearly trained subject gives up his dependency on his trained cue faster than the linearly trained subject. The nonlinearly trained subject also learns to use the cue of the other faster than the linearly trained subject (Brehmer, 1969b, 1971a, 1973a, 1973b; Hammond, 1972; Brehmer & Hammond, 1973). Gillis (1975), Gritz (1975), and Zachariadis and Varonos (1975) have replicated these results in studies of the differential effects of psychoactive drugs on interpersonal learning.

Interpersonal learning about the other. The research paradigm used in the triple-system case also facilitates the study of this type of IPL; we describe one study (Mumpower & Hammond, 1974) which illustrates its use. This study was conducted by training two persons to have widely different judgment policies, as in the conflict studies described above. In the first case, pairs made judgments about a two-cue judgment task in which the two cues were highly intercorrelated. Each member of a pair was then asked to predict the judgments the other would make in 10 additional trials.

In the case in which subjects bring widely differing judgment policies to the joint task and the cues are highly intercorrelated in the joint task, subjects assume their judgment policies are highly similar because their judgments are similar. Unrestricted discussion does not lead them to detect the fact that their judgment policies are very different; they do not realize that their agreement is *false*, that they are agreeing in fact while disagreeing in principle. In short, they do not learn accurately about each other because the characteristics of the task impede such learning. As soon as the task variables are disentangled (that is, are uncorrelated) by the experimenter, the subjects rapidly learn that they have different judgment policies; assumed similarity decreases, actual similarity remains the same, but predictive accuracy increases. Counterbalancing of conditions shows that the effect is produced entirely by task characteristics – that is, by causal texture.

In sum, SJT has been applied effectively and productively to the study of interpersonal conflict produced by cognitive differences. It has also been successfully applied to two types of interpersonal learning, topics which have not previously been studied in a systematic way. Uncovering the cognitive sources of conflict and the cognitive barriers to interpersonal learning carries large implications for policy formation.

The N-system case

This case includes the situation in which a number of persons are studied, regardless of whether the properties of the task system are known. If a number of persons exercise their judgment, policy factions can be detected by means of cluster analysis. As indicated in the quantitative section, this procedure will not only provide information about which persons are arriving at similar judgments but also indicate the characteristics of the disparate policies. Thus, the cognitive bases of conflict within the group are indicated.

Unique contribution: Application of Social Judgment Theory to social policy formation. The unique contribution of SJT has been to bring the theory, quantitative procedures, results of research, and technological innovations (externalization of judgment policies by means of interactive computer graphics) to bear on social policy formation outside the laboratory.

Several applications of SJT to social policy show that SJT is indeed life-relevant, that the methodology and the cognitive aids produced by it are appropriate to a wide variety of judgmental problems and demonstrate that although judgment theory is not law seeking *per se*, the empirical regularities observed in the laboratory are also observed outside the laboratory. Such empirical regularities include the following general conclusions: (1) People do not describe accurately and completely their judgmental policies, (2) people are often inconsistent in applying their judgmental policies, (3) only a small number of cues are used, (4) it is difficult to learn another person's policy simply by observing his judgments or by listening to his explanations of them, (5) the cognitive aids described above can reduce conflict and increase learning, and (6) linear, additive organizational principles are often adequate to describe judgment processes.

Examples of the applications include: citizen participation in planning (Stewart & Gelberd, 1972); determining policies about community goals (Steinmann & Stewart, 1973); and modeling physicians' judgments (Stewart, Joyce, & Lindell, 1975). Stewart, West, Hammond, and Kreith (1975) describe the usefulness of SJT for technology assessment; Flack and Summers (1971) illustrate its application to water resource planning; Brady and Rappoport (1973) detail its relevance to policy about nuclear safeguards; and Smith (1973) provides a hierarchical model of the complex judgments of an investment analyst. Also, Balke, Hammond, and Meyer (1973) show its application to labor-management negotiations; Steinmann, Smith, Jurdem, and Hammond (1975) deal with public-land-acquisition policy; and Adelman, Stewart, and Hammond (1975) apply SJT to corporate policy formation.

Summary

The theory, methodlogy, and research findings described above are unconventional; they are not yet described in textbooks. But there appears to be a growing recognition on the part of conventional psychology that it must change its research approach. The recent presidential address (Jenkins, 1974) to the Division of Experimental Psychology of the American Psychological Association provides an example; Jenkins warned his colleagues that "a whole theory of an experiment can be elaborated without contributing in an important way to the science because the situation is *artificial and nonrepresentative* [italics ours]" (p. 794). In addition to this surprising statement of agreement with Brunswik (1943) and social judgment theorists who have been making precisely that point for at least a decade (K. R. Hammond, 1955, 1965, 1966), Jenkins advocated that research should be life-relevant; he urged his colleagues to "[relate their] laboratory problems to the ecologically valid [Brunswik's term!] problems of everyday life" (p. 794).

This striking departure from conventional methodology included no acknowledgment that Brunswik had called for a "fundamental, all-inclusive shift in our methodological ideology" as early as 1943 (p. 261; see also Hammond, 1966, p. 23; Hammond & Stewart, 1974) and that until 1955 he continued to carry out empirical research and to write articles and books in which he seriously and responsibly considered the many implications of the change Jenkins advocated (something Jenkins failed to do). Perhaps social judgment theorists should be heartened and their convictions strengthened by what appears to be an independent discovery of their methodological position. But it remains to be seen whether conventional psychologists will relinquish "artificial and non-representative" research designs or whether the need for representative design will have to be independently rediscovered periodically.

One might ask what social judgment theorists (who do not have to be convinced of the necessity for an "all-inclusive shift in methodological ideology" and who try to cope with the hard problems associated with that shift) intend to do in the second decade of their research. The foremost objective is to extend the limits of human judgment. We are particularly concerned with extending the limits of human judgment in the complex circumstances in which social policy is formulated. The reason for that is straightforward: Social, political, economic, and physical disasters of large scale appear to be imminent, and all of these problems require the exercise of human judgment. Estimates of the time remaining for human judgment to form effective social policies to cope with these problems range from a decade to a quarter- or perhaps a half-century. Social judgment theorists firmly believe that *all* students of human judgment should engage in research that will help provide better social policies and thereby increase our chances for a decent life on earth.

4. Algebraic rules in psychological measurement

Norman H. Anderson

Many kinds of measurement problems arise in psychology, but one that has caused unique difficulty is the problem of linear, or "equal unit," measurement. In the physical sciences, linear scales – such as the centimeter scale for length and the gram scale for weight – are taken for granted. In psychology, however, linear scales have been elusive. The subjective sensation of loudness is a classic example: no general agreement yet exists about the measurement of even so simple a sensory quality as loudness.

Intuitively, it seems that loudness ought to be measurable. If the physical intensity of a sound is varied, we experience corresponding variations in the sensation of "loudness." Since we can rank the loudnesses of different sounds, loudness is one-dimensional and so should be measurable on a linear scale. To measure loudness, then, we seek a method that assigns numbers to sounds as a linear function of their loudness. The problem is to find such a method.

Of course, the physical intensity scale is not a linear scale of loudness. Nature has wisely evolved the auditory system with a law of diminishing returns that makes it sensitive to extremely faint sounds, yet avoids overloading it even with sounds 10 million times more intense. Thus, each successive unit increase in physical intensity produces successively smaller increases in loudness. Because of this law of diminishing returns, the sensation of loudness is not a linear function of physical intensity. The logarithm of the intensity – the standard decibel scale – is an improvement but still is not a linear scale of loudness.

The unique difficulty, of course, is that loudness is a subjective

This chapter originally appeared in the *American Scientist*, 1979, 67(5), 555–563. Copyright © 1979 by Sigma Xi, The Scientific Research Society of North America, Inc. Reprinted by permission.

sensation. How then can we hope to find a linear scale of loudness, which is an intangible feeling inside another's head? How can we decide whether or not some given assignment of numbers is a linear scale of another person's private sensation?

Qualities that can be sensed, such as loudness and heaviness (as opposed to their corresponding physical qualities – sound intensity and weight, respectively), have received the most attention because it seems intuitively clear that linear scales of these sensations must exist. But cognitive qualities such as personal likableness, subjective probability, and deservingness are more important in daily life. A general theory of psychological measurement is needed that can provide linear scales of both sensory and cognitive qualities.

Various methods for psychological measurement have been proposed over the last century. One of these is the additive-unit method of physics, which reduces measurement to simple addition. The length of a line, for example, equals the number of unit lengths laid end to end to cover the line. The physicist Norman Campbell (1928) attempted to rationalize all physical measurement in terms of such additive operations. If analogous additive operations could be found in psychology, they would provide the sought-for linear scales. Unfortunately, the search for additive operations for loudness and other subjective quantities has not been very successful. Many scientists have therefore concluded that psychology could not attain true measurement.

Curiously enough, another physicist, Gustave Fechner (1860), had developed a unit method for sensation measurement almost at the beginning of scientific psychology. Fechner set the "just noticeable difference," or *jnd*, as the unit of sensation. Measurement of loudness would begin with a reference sound S_0 that would be assigned some arbitrary value, say, 0. Next, the sound S_1 that was just noticeably larger than S_0 would be determined experimentally; it would be assigned the value 1. Next, the sound S_2 that was just noticeably larger than S_1 would be determined; it would be assigned the value 2. And so on. The loudness value of any sound would then be calculated by the number of *jnd*'s between it and the reference sound. Thus the *jnd* would be the unit of measurement on the psychological scale.

Fechner's psychophysical investigations led to a striking outcome, commonly known as Fechner's "law." As the reference intensity increases, a greater physical increment is needed to become just noticeably larger. This phenomenon is easily illustrated with length – 1.5 cm is noticeably larger than 1.0 cm, but 100.5 cm is not noticeably larger than 100.0 cm. Empirically, the diminishing returns follows a roughly linear function, for the *jnd* increment in physical intensity is approximately proportional to the reference intensity. This empirical fact, coupled with Fechner's assumption that *jnd*'s could be treated as equal units, led to Fechner's "psychophysical law":

psychological sensation = log physical intensity

For the best part of a century, Fechner's method held the center of attention. It seems sensible because it implies, for example, that the logarithmic decibel scale of sound intensity provides a linear scale of loudness sensation, which is roughly correct. A more potent reason for Fechner's impact was that he seemed to provide a mathematical law in the psychological realm. This law, moreover, asserted a direct relation between the physical and psychological worlds, truly a "psycho/physical" law.

But the key element was missing. Fechner's assumption that *jnd*'s could be treated as equal units all along the loudness scale remained just an assumption, which he provided no way to validate. Although his approach was attractive, it remained untestable.

Another method for measuring loudness seems obvious: just ask the subject to assign a number to each sound in proportion to its loudness. Despite their simplicity, however, such numerical methods have generally been shunned. Empirically, they are known to be subject to various extraneous biases. Rationally, the number responses are really mere words, and to treat these words as true numbers on a linear scale seems very dubious. Thus the numerical methods face the same difficulty as Fechner's unit method. Some validational basis is needed – some method that allows proof or disproof of the key assumption that the response numbers assigned to the sounds are indeed a linear function of their subjective sensation value.

A "cognitive" algebra

In this article I shall describe a method for psychological measurement based on "cognitive" algebra. Many cognitive processes are expected to follow simple algebraic rules. If these rules hold empirically, they can provide true linear scales of subjective sensation.

The idea of a cognitive algebra is not novel, for many psychologists have speculated about simple algebraic rules. Sensory psychologists refer to the *summation* of loudness, brightness, skin warmth, etc. Workers in decision theory postulate that the value of a gamble should equal the *product* of its subjective likelihood and the value of the prize. Social psychologists think that group compromise should be an *average*, and that a fair share should be *proportional* to each person's contribution. The response in a conflict situation should be the *difference* between the approach and avoidance tendencies. Nor are animals neglected, for their behavior is often assumed to be a *product* of their motivation and the value of the reward.

But the study of algebraic rules in psychology has been limited by a fundamental difficulty – inability to measure subjective values. For example, consider the law of expected value for a gamble that gives a certain chance of winning a certain prize, with no penalty for losing. In mathematical decision theory, the expected value EV of the gamble is the product of the probability P of winning and the value V of the prize: $EV = P \times V$. Can we expect human judgment to obey this multiplying rule? Definitely not – if the three terms of the equation are measured in objective, or physical, scales. Thus an optimist and a pessimist will feel differently about the likelihood of winning a given gamble, and each one's attitude will affect his subjective expected value of the gamble.

Still, it is attractive to speculate that human judgment follows the same algebraic form, but with subjective, or personal, values. This subjective version of the law of expected value may be written $SEV = SP \times SV$, where S denotes subjective. To treat this as a genuine psychological equation entails measurement of subjective values for all three terms. Moreover, this subjective measurement must allow for different values for different persons. Without a method for measuring subjective values, this and other algebraic rules remain quasi-mathematical verbalisms.

In the traditional approach, psychological measurement is seen as logically prior to substantive inquiry. In the above SEV equation, for example, the traditional approach first seeks a method to measure the three quantities. If such a method could be found, substitution of these measured values into the equation would provide a ready test of its validity. This approach is reasonable and straightforward, seemingly much like the procedures used in other sciences, but it depends on having valid psychological scales of the stimulus and response quantities. Owing to a lack of methods for obtaining linear scales of subjective values, the traditional approach does not work very well.

The method on which I shall focus in this paper inverts the traditional approach and takes the structure of the algebraic rule as basic. Measurement is not prior to, but derivative from, the algebraic rule. This method is called "functional measurement," because the algebraic rule, or function, constitutes the base and the frame for the scales of measurement. Functional measurement makes it possible to transform verbalisms such as the SEV formula into true mathematical equations.

Additive rules will be discussed in the next two sections – first, the basic logic, and second, three empirical applications. Then the multiplying rule will be treated similarly.

Additive rules

The logic of functional measurement for additive models is simple: The algebraic additivity structure of the model corresponds to a graphical pattern of parallelism in the data. Hence the model can be tested directly by plotting the raw data and looking at the graph. If the graph exhibits parallelism, it supports the additive model and also provides linear scales of the subjective values of the stimulus variables. Readers may find it helpful to glance at the experimental examples of the next section before going over the logic of the parallelism analysis discussed here.

Parallelism depends on the experimental use of what is called factorial design. A factorial design can be considered to be a matrix in which the rows and columns represent two stimulus variables (factors) that are independently manipulated by the experimenter. The stimulus in row i will be denoted by S_{Ai}; the stimulus in column j will be denoted by S_{Bj}. Each cell of the design thus corresponds to a stimulus pair (S_{Ai}, S_{Bj}). Each of these stimulus pairs is presented to the subject, and his overt response is denoted by R_{ij}.

The hypothesis is that the stimulus values are added to produce the response. Of course, this additive hypothesis refers to the subjective values, not to the objective physical values. To represent this distinction, uppercase letters will denote physical values, and lowercase letters the corresponding subjective values. Thus, the additive hypothesis may be written

$$r_{ij} = s_{Ai} + s_{Bj} \tag{1}$$

The essentially psychological nature of this additive hypothesis may be emphasized by considering the subject as a "black box" whose internal workings are to be deduced. In the black box schematic, physical stimuli are applied to the subject, who emits the observed response R_{ij}. The question is what goes on in between, that is, inside the person's head. Schematically, the physical stimuli S_{Ai} and S_{Bj} are transformed into their psychological counterparts s_{Ai} and s_{Bj}. These subjective values are then integrated to form an implicit response r_{ij}. The implicit response is externalized to be measured by the experimenter:

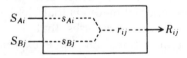

The hypothesis is that the integrator in the black box schematic is an adder, as specified by Eq. 1. Because all terms in the equation are in the subject's head, however, and not observable to the experimenter, it is not obvious that the additive hypothesis is testable.

Fortunately, there is a way to test the additive hypothesis, a way that requires nothing more than the matrix (R_{ij}) of observed responses. If the underlying process is additive, then this additive pattern will mirror itself in the observed data. The simplest and most useful case is covered by the parallelism theorem:

Suppose that the additive model of eq. 1 is true, and that the observable response R is a linear function of the implicit response r. Then the factorial plot of the observed response data will be a set of parallel curves; moreover, the row means of the factorial data table will be a linear scale of the subjective values of the corresponding row stimuli, and similarly for the column stimuli.

To prove the first conclusion of the parallelism theorem, it suffices to show that the entry in the first row minus the entry in the second row is constant – the same in every column of the design. By the assumption of response linearity, $R_{ij} = c_0 + c_1 r_{ij}$, where c_0 and c_1 are constants. By the additivity assumption of eq. 1, $R_{ij} = c_0 + c_1(s_{Ai} + s_{Bj})$. Hence, $R_{1j} - R_{2j} = c_1(s_{A1} - s_{A2})$. The last expression is independent of j and hence constant across columns. This algebraic constancy implies that the factorial plot will be a set of parallel curves, which proves the first conclusion. The proof of the second conclusion merely requires showing that the row means are a linear function of the s_{Ai}.

Both assumptions of the theorem are necessary. If r were nonadditive or if R were nonlinear, then parallelism would not in general obtain. There is, of course, a logical possibility that nonlinearity in R just counters nonadditivity in r to yield parallelism. Subject to this qualification, however, observed parallelism provides joint support to both assumptions of the theorem.

Observed parallelism thus accomplishes three simultaneous goals: (1) it supports the additive model, (2) it supports the linearity of the response measure, and (3) it provides linear scales of the stimulus variables. No prior stimulus scaling is needed; no statistical transformations are required. Hardly more is necessary than to do the experiment and graph the data.

Mathematically, the parallelism theorem is elementary; the difficulty lies in applying it. Parallelism analysis has no substantive relevance unless the two assumptions of the theorem are empirically true. It is important, therefore, to develop experimental methods that yield a linear response scale, and it is essential to find processes that are in fact additive. That this is possible is demonstrated by three experimental applications.

Empirical additivity

It is a well-known psychological fact that a pound of lead feels heavier than a pound of feathers. The effect is substantial and makes a surefire classroom demonstration. The size of an object influences its perceived heaviness; a larger object feels lighter even though it has the same physical weight as a smaller object. One interpretation of this phenomenon is that we expect the heaviness of an object to be in direct proportion to its size, and the contrast between the expected and experienced heaviness sensations produces the illusory effect. Analogous contrast effects are common in other areas of perception.

This effect is an illusion only in objective, physical terms; psychologically, it is quite real. The psychological sensation of heaviness is the integrated resultant of two stimulus cues, weight and size. The hypothesis to be tested is that this integration follows an additive model: heaviness = weight + size. The parallelism theorem treats this symbolic hypothesis as a true mathematical equation, with due allowance for the subjective values.

To test this hypothesis, the factorial experiment of Figure 4.1 was carried out. Instead of lead and feathers, the stimuli were gray cylinders of various heights and weights. Each curve in the figure corresponds to one level of weight; the five curves represent the five rows of the factorial design. Similarly, the five points on each curve correspond to the five levels of cylinder height; these points represent the columns of the factorial design. This 5 × 5 factorial design thus yields a total of 25 stimulus cylinders. Subjects lifted each cylinder and judged its heaviness on a rating scale of 1–20.

Each data point in the factorial graph represents the mean judgment of the heaviness of one stimulus cylinder. In the same way that a pound of lead feels heavier than a pound of feathers, the upward slope of each curve shows that shorter cylinders were judged heavier than taller cylinders of the same weight. For present purposes, of course, the important feature of this graph is the parallelism, which supports the hypothesis that the heaviness sensation results from an additive integration of weight and size.

Because the additive model appears to hold, it becomes possible to obtain the subjective heaviness values of the weights. In fact, the second conclusion of the parallelism theorem implies that the vertical elevations of the curves in Figure 4.1, which are equivalent to the row means, constitute a linear scale of heaviness for the corresponding physical weights. These curves are closer together for the heavier weights, which means that successive 100-gram increments produce successively smaller increments in heaviness. The psychophysical law that Fechner sought is defined by the graph of these psychological heaviness values as a function of physical weight. The key advantage of the functional measurement method over Fechner's method of adding *jnd*'s is that the parallelism property provides the necessary criterion to demonstrate the validity of the heaviness scale. This experiment, therefore, provides a solution, both in principle and in practice, to the problem that Fechner left unsolved.

The second empirical example comes from person perception, an activity that pervades our daily lives. We form impressions of a person's likableness, intelligence, motivation, etc., by adding up what we know about him. That our impressions are often wrong, that the person we hire doesn't pan out, for example, only emphasizes the need for systematic study of how we make judgments about others.

It is easier to study person perception if the stimulus information is

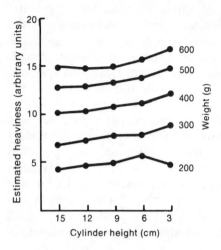

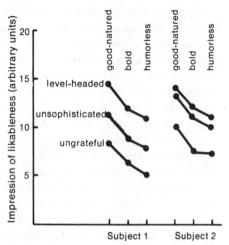

Figure 4.1 When subjects were asked to judge the heaviness of cylinders of various heights and weights on an arbitrary scale of 1–20, taller cylinders were judged less heavy than shorter cylinders of the same weight. Twenty-five cylinders were used; each data point represents the mean judgment of the weight of each cylinder. The parallel pattern exhibited on this graph supports an additive model for size-weight illusion. (The discrepant point at the lower right resulted from an error in the experimental procedures.)

Figure 4.2 Two subjects were asked to predict the likableness, on a scale of 1–20, of persons described by a combination of two traits, for a total of nine descriptions. The parallelism of the curves indicates that the predictions of the subjects are additive – that is, they are the sum of the values of the two adjectives that described the person. (After Anderson, 1962.)

under experimental control. For example, letters of reference about hypothetical but realistic people can be tailored to experimental need. In one experiment of this type, subjects were given pairs of adjectives that described persons unknown to them. They were instructed to form an impression of each person and to judge how likable the person would be on a scale of 1–20. There were nine such descriptions altogether, and they are specified by the matrix of adjectives given in Figure 4.2.

Data for two representative subjects are shown in the figure. Each data point represents the judged likableness of a person described by two personality traits. The essential feature of these data is that the three curves for each subject are practically parallel. This pattern tells us that both subjects obeyed an additive rule: their judgments can be represented as the sum of the values of the two adjectives that described the person. Although person perception certainly involves complex processes, this result points to an underlying simplicity.

Figure 4.2 also speaks to two problems of psychological measurement. First, it states that the rating response is a linear scale of subjective likableness; otherwise the second assumption of the parallelism theorem would not hold and parallelism would not be obtained. These ratings are not mere number words, therefore, but provide true quantification of the response on a linear ("equal-unit") scale. Second, the figure provides linear scales of the stimulus values. By virtue of the second conclusion of the parallelism theorem, the values of the three row adjectives are given by the elevations of the three curves. For subject 1, therefore, *unsophisticated* lies about midway in value between *ungrateful* and *level-headed*; for subject 2, however, *unsophisticated* has nearly the same value as *level-headed*.

Figure 4.2 makes yet another statement – one that has disturbed many investigators. Implicit in the additive model of Eq. 1 is the assumption that each stimulus adjective has a fixed value and meaning, regardless of what other adjective it is combined with. *Unsophisticated*, for example, is assumed to have the same value in all three descriptions represented in the middle curve of Figure 4.2. If *unsophisticated* changed its meaning and value from one description to another, systematic deviations from parallelism would occur.

The idea that meaning remains constant is strongly counterintuitive. Subjects and experimenters alike give confident, detailed reports of intricate interactions among the adjectives when they are combined in a description of a person. However, these introspective reports are a semantic illusion, as shown by the parallelism in Figure 4.2 and by considerable auxiliary evidence (Anderson 1974b). This experiment thus illustrates how functional measurement can probe beneath fallible introspections to delineate the actual processes that underlie our perceptions of other persons.

It is worth summarizing how much can be inferred from the pattern of parallelism in Figure 4.2. This pattern points to an additive rule that underlies person perception, and to the associated implication that the adjectives have the same meanings in different descriptions. Also associated with the additive rule are linear scales of the subjective values of the response, and of subjective values of the stimulus adjectives. These psychological scales are derivative from the additive rule, according to the logic of functional measurement.

The third empirical example comes from moral judgment, which is also a pervasive human activity. Concepts such as fair play, obligation, deservingness, and blame are integral aspects of social structure. Although such judgments have only recently begun to attract systematic experimental analysis, there is some evidence that a moral algebra is at work, as illustrated in a developmental study carried out by Leon (1980). Subjects of various ages were told stories about the intent of a boy who threw a stone, and how much damage the stone caused. Intent and damage varied in different stories. The subjects were then asked to judge how much the boy in each story should be punished.

The data for both children and adults, shown in Figure 4.3, exhibit the parallelism pattern. By virtue of the parallelism theorem, these data imply that information about intent and damage is integrated by an additive rule: deserved punishment = intent + damage. Other experiments also point to a moral algebra (Anderson, 1978b; Farkas and Anderson, 1979). Despite the subjective character of moral judgment, functional measurement can provide quantitative analysis within the value system of each individual.

Multiplying rules

Life is a succession of chances. Some people enjoy fool's luck, while others see their good risks turn bad. But, although chance limits our control of our lives, even chance can be handled wisely. The happiness we may expect along life's path depends on how well we play the cards that nature deals us, and on how wisely we place our bets.

In an experimental study of how people handle chance events, Shanteau (1974) asked subjects to judge the worth of lottery tickets that had printed on them the sentence "You have _____ chance to win _____," in which the two blanks contained information about the chance of winning and the object to be won. Figure 4.4 shows the design of this experiment. The chances to win were defined by probability phrases such as *unlikely* and *fairly likely*. Each curve represents some object to be won, such as a *watch* or *sandals*. Each data point represents the subjects' judged value of the corresponding lottery ticket.

The theoretical hypothesis in this experiment was that the judgments would obey the law of subjective expected value, $SEV = SV \times SP$. That is, the subject's judgment of each lottery ticket, which represents his subjective expected value SEV, should be the product of the subjective value SV of the object to be won and the subjective probability SP of winning. How can we decide whether or not the observed judgments plotted in Figure 4.4 obey this multiplying rule?

At first glance, the answer seems straightforward: if the multiplying model is correct, then the data should form a linear fan pattern of diverging straight lines. To visualize this fan pattern, suppose that the values of SP are laid out on the horizontal axis. Then the curve of data for each object to be won should form a straight-line function of SP, with slope equal to the corresponding subjective value SV. If only we knew the values of SP, we could test the model and, if it is successful, we could use it to measure SV.

But we do not know the values of SP. The values of SV would do equally well, but they also are unknown. Without a method for subjective measurement, the linear fan test is one vital step beyond our reach. However, there is a way to reach the goal. If the model is correct, then it can give us the subjective values we need. This follows from the linear

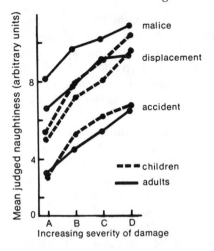

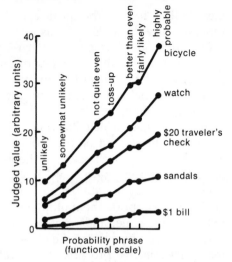

Figure 4.3 Children and adult subjects were asked to judge the naughtiness, on a scale of 1–12, of a fictitious child who threw a stone. In each story the child's intention differed (malice, displaced aggression, and accidental), and the amounts of damage differed. The data both for children, who were in the second, third, fifth, and seventh grades, and for adults exhibit parallelism and suggest that an additive rule applies in moral judgments: naughtiness = intent + damage. The greater slope and smaller vertical spread of curves for children imply that children attach more importance to damage and less importance to intention than do adults. (Data from Leon, 1980.)

Figure 4.4 Subjects were asked to judge the worth of lottery tickets that had marked on them the probability of winning a certain object. Each data point represents the subject's judged value, on an arbitrary scale of 1–40, of the lottery ticket. The linear fan pattern of diverging straight lines suggests that a multiplying rule operates. (After Shanteau, 1974.)

fan theorem for multiplying models, which is quite similar to the parallelism theorem for adding models and will be stated without proof:

Suppose that the multiplying model is true, and that the observable response R is a linear function of the implicit response r. Then the appropriate factorial plot of the observed response data will be a fan of straight lines diverging from a common origin; moreover, the row means of the factorial data table will be a linear scale of the subjective values of the corresponding row stimuli, and similarly for the column stimuli.

A vital feature of this theorem is that the second conclusion shows how to obtain the subjective values needed to attempt the linear fan plot. If *SEV* = *SV* × *SP*, then the column means of the data table provide a provisional linear scale for *SP*. Accordingly, the column stimuli would be spaced along the horizontal axis at the locations specified by the column means, thus forcing the mean curve to lie on a straight line. Then each separate curve will also plot as a straight line, if the theorem applies.

Of course, the linear fan pattern depends on both assumptions of the theorem being correct: if either one is incorrect, then the data will not generally plot as a linear fan. In practice, therefore, the column means are only provisional values of SV, but the actual plot provides the needed test of the multiplying model.

In Figure 4.4, which illustrates this method, the probability phrases have been spaced out on the horizontal axis at their functional SP values, as prescribed by the linear fan theorem. The resulting curves do form a linear fan, supporting the law of subjective expected value. As far as one experiment may go, therefore, this one simultaneously achieves three goals: (1) it supports the multiplying model; (2) it supports the linearity of the response scale; and (3) it provides linear scales of the two stimulus variables, thereby solving the classical problem of simultaneous measurement of subjective probability and value.

The relevance of this experiment to real-life situations deserves reflection. Life is a sequence of lottery tickets. Any course of action entails a spectrum of uncertain consequences, and each consequence corresponds to a lottery ticket with its own probability and value. In psychological decision theory, a choice between two houses, say, or two research projects, is viewed as a choice between two decks of lottery tickets. Shanteau's work shows how actual life choices can be subjected to exact analysis, within the value system of the individual.

Subjective probability

Mathematical theory yields simple addition and multiplication rules for probabilities of compound events, and many writers have speculated that human judgment obeys subjective versions of these same models. Methods of cognitive algebra were used to test one of these subjective probability models in two different experimental areas, poker playing and psycholinguistics.

Lopes (1976) studied betting behavior in a simplified, computerized version of five-card stud. On each trial, the subject saw the four up-cards and the bet of each of two computerized opponents, player A, who maintained a conservative playing style, and player B, who maintained an average playing style. The subject made an even-money side bet, between 1¢ and 30¢, that he could beat both opponents. The computer would then turn over the hole card of each opponent, determine the winner, and pay off or collect from the subject.

The theoretical hypothesis was the subjective analog of the multiplication rule for independent probabilities: subjective probability of beating both A and B = subjective probability of beating A × subjective probability of beating B. To test this model, the subjective probabilities of

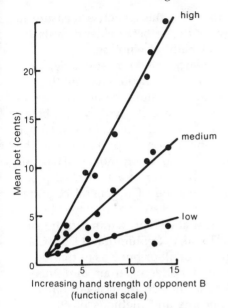

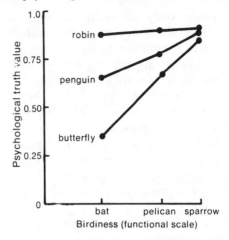

Figure 4.6 Subjects were asked to judge the truth value (on a scale of 0–1) of compound statements that either or both of two winged creatures is a bird. The answer requires that the truth values of the two components in each pair be integrated to form the truth value of the compound. The linear fan pattern suggests that the truth values of the components are integrated by a multiplication rule. (After Oden, 1977.)

Figure 4.5 In a computerized version of five-card stud, subjects were asked to make an even-money side bet that they could beat both of two opponents, A and B. On each trial the subject saw the four up-cards and the bet of each computerized opponent. The subjective probabilities of beating A and B were experimentally controlled by varying the strength of the opponents' visible hands and bets. The curve parameter represents the hand strength of opponent A. The linear fan pattern obtained by plotting the mean value of the subjects' side bets indicates that a multiplication rule applies in the area of subjective probability. (After Lopes, 1976.)

beating A and B were experimentally controlled by varying the strength of their visible hands and bets. In Figure 4.5, each curve represents one level of hand strength for A, while the values on the horizontal axis represent the hand strengths for B. The vertical axis gives the mean value of the subject's side bet.

The central feature of Figure 4.5 is the linear fan pattern. The subjects were experienced poker players, and every one showed the same pattern over the course of a long-term experiment. This linear fan pattern provides good support for the multiplication rule.

One odd, even irrational, feature of this experiment deserves notice. The multiplication rule applies to subjective probability, and in fact Lopes's other data show that the judged probability of winning does indeed obey the linear fan pattern. However, the response measure in Figure 4.5 is not subjective probability, but cash bet. Evidently subjects bet in proportion to their subjective probability of winning.

This betting strategy seems intuitively reasonable to most people, but a little reflection shows that it is irrational. If you feel you have less than an even chance of winning, you should bet the minimum, because the even-money bet represents a losing proposition. If you feel you have a better than even chance of winning, you should bet the maximum (of 30¢). Rationally, the curves in Figure 4.5 should be step functions. The subjects' actual strategy is suboptimal and costs them money. That this multiplying rule appears in the long-term behavior of experienced poker players gives further evidence for the operation of a general cognitive algebra.

A central problem in semantic theory is that of representing truth value as a continuous quantity (Zadeh, Fu, Tanaka, & Shimura, 1975). Class membership is usually a matter of degree, not all-or-none as in traditional propositional logic. Thus, a sparrow is a better or truer bird than a pelican, while a bat is not without some affinity to the class of birds.

Oden (1977) has shown how the concepts and methods of cognitive algebra apply to continuous truth value. In one of his experiments, subjects responded to compound questions of the form: How true is it that a sparrow is a bird, or a penguin is a bird, or both? The answer to this question requires that the truth values of the two components be integrated to form the truth value of the compound. One suggested integration rule is analogous to a multiplication rule from probability theory and can be stated thus: The falsity of the compound equals the product of the falsity values of the components.

To test this multiplication rule, Oden selected animals of different degrees of birdiness in a factorial design. The data in Figure 4.6 exhibit the linear fan pattern, thereby supporting the multiplication rule. Thus, "fuzzy logic" appears to obey the same cognitive algebra that has been found in other areas of psychological judgment theory. Oden's other results also illustrate the potential of cognitive algebra for obtaining numerical representations in logic and linguistics.

Case of nonlinear response

The success of the parallelism analysis depends on having a linear response scale, so that the observed numbers are a linear function of the unobservable sensation. Telling the subject to assign numbers to sensations is no guarantee of a linear scale, and, in any case, such numerical response methods are applicable only to certain experimental tasks. In this section I will indicate how the parallelism theorem can be extended to apply to response measures that are not linear.

A useful perspective on the issue of response linearity can be obtained by comparing the rating method, used in the above experiments, with a popular alternative – the method of magnitude estimation (Stevens 1974) – in which subjects are instructed to assign numbers to stimuli in proportion to their subjective magnitudes. If one object is assigned a heaviness number of 10, an object that feels half as heavy should be called 5, one that feels twice as heavy should be called 20, and so forth. This method differs from the rating method in that it imposes no upper bound on the response.

The rating method and the method of magnitude estimation seem rather similar. Both ask subjects to assign numbers to represent subjective magnitudes, and subjects find both methods natural and easy to use. Both methods ought to yield equivalent results, but, in fact, they typically yield quite different results.

The sharpness of this difference can be illustrated by the psychophysical laws for heaviness and grayness. The functional scale of heaviness shows a law of diminishing returns, as noted in the discussion of Figure 4.1. In contrast, Stevens claimed that a law of accelerating returns operates for heaviness. Functional measurement scales for grayness also show diminishing returns, whereas Stevens's method of magnitude estimation produces a law of accelerating returns. That is a radical difference for the operating characteristic of a sensory system.

When two plausible methods yield such discrepant results, both come under suspicion. Their disagreement underscores the essential problem: some criterion is needed to assess the validity of these numerical response methods. Cognitive algebra and functional measurement provide a validational criterion in the form of the parallelism and linear fan theorems. Functional measurement itself is neutral in the disagreement between the magnitude estimation and rating methods. The parallelism property and the linear fan property are impartial judges. Magnitude estimation and ratings have an equal opportunity to satisfy these validational criteria, but only one can succeed because they are nonlinearly related. Both could fail. By these criteria, magnitude estimation has failed, and the rating method has succeeded (Anderson, 1974a).

The success of the rating method has depended on the development of certain methodological precautions (Anderson 1974a, 1974b, 1982), which are necessary because ratings are subject to various well known biases that can cause deviations from the parallelism pattern. With suitable precautions, however, the rating method has been used successfully even with children four years of age and younger (Anderson, 1980; Butzin, 1978; Cuneo, 1978; Leon, 1980).

Of course, animals cannot give rating responses, nor can very young children. Moreover, behavioral measures such as amount of crying or duration of gaze, speed of running or food consumed, and voltage measures or pulse counts in physiological investigations are not likely to be linear scales in their raw form. These nonlinear response scales present a basic problem to the application of the parallelism theorem.

A frequent approach to nonlinear response measures has been to use only rank-order properties of the data as a basis for psychological measurement theory. The most systematic of these approaches is the conjoint measurement formulation of Luce and Tukey (1964), which has some similarities to functional measurement. Very few empirical applications of conjoint measurement have been made, however, in part because it was introduced more recently than functional measurement, and in part because it lacks an error theory for testing additive models.

It is desirable, therefore, to extend the parallelism theorem to handle nonlinear response measures and still provide a test of the additive model. This extension can be illustrated with an experiment on the century-old problem of grayness "bisection," in which the subject is presented with two gray chips (the stimuli) and instructed to select a third chip (the response) that lies midway in grayness between the two stimulus chips. In the previous notation, S_{Ai} and S_{Bj} denote the physical reflectance values of the stimulus chips; s_{Ai} and s_{Bj} denote their subjective grayness values. Similarly, R_{ij} and r_{ij} denote the physical and psychological values of the response chip, respectively.

The obvious hypothesis, implied by the instructions, is that the subject will choose the response chip so as to equate sense distances:

$$s_{Ai} - r_{ij} = r_{ij} - s_{Bj}$$

$$\text{or } r_{ij} = \tfrac{1}{2}(s_{Ai} + s_{Bj})$$

The hypothesis thus leads to a simple averaging model, and so the parallelism analysis should be applicable.

But the bisection model presents a critical problem. The response term r_{ij} denotes the subjective sensation value and so is not observable. The investigator must make do with the observable physical reflectances R_{ij}. Unfortunately, R is not a linear function of r, and so the physical reflectance measure will not exhibit parallelism. However, subjective grayness r is a monotone function of physical reflectance R. Hence some monotone transformation of the R_{ij} will yield the r_{ij}. This monotone transformation is determinate because it is the one (Aczel, 1966, p. 148) that transforms the observed responses in such a way that the factorial plot becomes parallel.

In practice, therefore, testing the bisection model reduces to two steps. First, compute the monotone transformation that transforms the physical measure so that the factorial plot is as parallel as possible, using procedures developed by Kruskal (1965) and de Leeuw, Young, and Takane (1976). If the bisection model is correct, then the remaining deviations from parallelism should be unsystematic – merely response variability. If the bisection model is not correct, then systematic deviations from parallelism must be expected. The second step, therefore, is to test whether the deviations from parallelism are systematic, using the general error theory for nonmetric, monotone analysis outlined in Anderson (1977).

In one grayness-bisection experiment, the physical reflectance values were markedly nonparallel. After the reflectance scale was transformed, the curves became virtually parallel, and the deviations from parallelism were not statistically significant. This outcome supports the bisection model and also solves the problem of measuring subjective grayness on a linear scale. Using similar procedures, Carterette and Anderson (1979) have successfully applied the bisection model to the measurement of loudness.

The implications of this method go far beyond the bisection task. Any additive model can be analyzed in the same way with no more than a rank-order, monotone response scale. This method, therefore, opens up the possibility of true quantification for behavioral and physiological response measures, and hence also for the psychological scales of the stimulus variables.

Problems and prospects

The parallelism analysis seems straightforward, but two perplexing problems have held back its development and use. The analysis requires that the response measure be linear and that the stimulus integration obey an additive rule. If either condition is not met, then the data will not in general exhibit parallelism. Nonparallelism is ambiguous, therefore, because it can result from a nonlinear response measure, from a non-additive integration model, or from some combination of both causes. Whereas observed parallelism has a straightforward interpretation, observed nonparallelism is often uninterpretable. This matter deserves consideration, because in practice nonparallelism is the rule, and parallelism is obtained only under special conditions.

If the stimulus integration does not obey an additive model, then parallelism will not generally be obtained. This has been a severe problem because, contrary to general expectation, true additive models have seldom been found. This issue was passed over in the previous discussion, but person perception (Fig. 4.2) and moral judgment (Fig. 4.3) actually obey an averaging model, not an additive model. Indeed, averaging processes appear to be predominant, but the averaging model yields parallel curves only when the various levels of each separate stimulus variable all have equal weight or importance (see, e.g., Anderson, 1974a, 1974b). Since they frequently do not have equal weight, the empirical results are frequently not parallel even when the response scale is linear. Against a prevailing expectation for additive models, however, observed nonparallelism was too easily attributable to nonlinear bias in the response.

If the response is not linear, then also parallelism will not generally be obtained. The seriousness of this problem has been illustrated by the sharp difference between results obtained from the rating method and the method of magnitude estimation. At least one of these numerical response methods must be nonlinear and therefore invalid, and a natural reaction is that neither can be trusted. The rating method, in particular, is subject to various biases and has been generally suspect. Successful application of the rating method, as illustrated in Figures 4.1–4.6, has depended on the development of experimental procedures to eliminate the biases. The development of these procedures, of course, has depended on empirical establishment of the parallelism property.

Thus the prevailing outlook at the beginning of the functional measurement research program was characterized by well-founded distrust of numerical response measures and by a general predilection for additive models that went cross-grain to the data. And of course there was substantial doubt that any algebraic model would hold. Because of these doubts and difficulties, it was not easy to work back from fallible data obtained with uncertain procedures to uncover the averaging model and the other algebraic models for stimulus integration.

Fortunately, the mind does seem to obey a fairly general cognitive algebra. The experiments I have discussed in this article come from an extensive research program on algebraic rules of stimulus integration (see Anderson, 1974a, 1974b; 1978b; 1979, 1980; 1982). Substantial evidence has been found for averaging, adding, subtracting, and multiplying models, as well as for certain ratio models. These algebraic models have been found at work in many substantive areas, including psychophysics, decision-making, psycholinguistics, social attitudes, person perception, and moral judgment. Not all judgmental processes obey simple models, nor should they be expected to. Nevertheless, the extent of the empirical evidence implies the operation of a general algebra of perception and cognition.

Cognitive algebra has intrinsic interest as a mode of thought. Beyond that, the algebraic models provide invaluable tools for psychological measurement and for cognitive analysis. They can dissect the integrated response to a complex stimulus field to delineate the underlying causal factors within the value system of the individual mind. This approach has thrown new light on old problems and has led to many interesting new problems. This brief overview cannot do justice to the empirical work or to the many problems that yet remain. I hope, however, that this discussion gives some indication of the promise and excitement of this line of investigation.

Part II
Judgment and social policy

Social policies arise out of human judgment; there is no other way. Some policies may be formed primarily on an analytical basis (e.g., prices to be charged for municipal services), and some may be formed primarily on intuitive grounds (e.g., whether to build an arts center or a gymnasium for the community). Whatever the mixture of intuition and analysis, all social policies are the result of some person's or persons' judgments that a certain course of action should or should not be undertaken. One can acquire information but not "judgment" in a book, a computer program, or a "how-to" course.

Therefore, from the point of view of a judgment/decision theorist the study of the judgment processes in the formation of social policy offers important and fascinating problems. Important, because policy judgments by those who represent the interests of the people – members of the city council, the county commission, the state and federal legislatures, the executive branch – are central to our democratic procedures. Fascinating, because if these social policies are to reflect the wisdom of the people, they must somehow integrate facts and values. Therefore, despite the difficulty – some would say impossibility – of studying social policy judgments empirically, some researchers in judgment and decision making have taken a keen interest in carrying out empirical studies of policy makers' judgments. In order to introduce students to these efforts, we present, first, a segment of the Nobel laureate Herbert A. Simon's recent lectures on rationality and human affairs, followed by an analysis by Paul Slovic, Baruch Fischhoff, and Sarah Lichtenstein of a major policy problem in modern societies, the problem of informing the public about risk. We then present a case study by Kenneth R. Hammond and Leonard Adelman of the use of a theory of judgment and decision making to settle a public policy dispute, and, finally, a case study by Curtis A. Brown of the conflict among the judgments of citizens, experts, and policy makers regarding social policy.

5. Alternative visions of rationality

Herbert A. Simon

Values

We see that reason is wholly instrumental. It cannot tell us where to go;
at best it can tell us how to get there. It is a gun for hire that can be
employed in the service of whatever goals we have, good or bad. It
makes a great difference in our view of the human condition whether we
attribute our difficulties to evil or to ignorance and irrationality – to the
baseness of goals or to our not knowing how to reach them.

Method in madness

A useful, if outrageous, exercise for sharpening one's thinking about the
limited usefulness of reasoning, taken in isolation, is to attempt to read
Hitler's *Mein Kampf* analytically – as though preparing for a debate. The
exercise is likely to be painful, but is revealing about how facts, values,
and emotions interact in our thinking about human affairs. I pick this
particular example because the reader's critical faculties are unlikely, in
this case, to be dulled by agreement with the views expressed.

Most of us would take exception to many of Hitler's "facts," especially
his analysis of the causes of Europe's economic difficulties, and most of
all his allegations that Jews and Marxists (whom he also mistakenly found
indistinguishable) were at the root of them. However, if we were to
suspend disbelief for a moment and accept his "facts" as true, much of
the Nazi program would be quite consistent with goals of security for the
German nation or even of welfare for the German people. Up to this
point, the unacceptability of that program to us is not a matter of evil

This chapter originally appeared in Simon, H. A., *Reason in human affairs* (pp. 7–35).
Stanford, CA: Stanford University Press, 1983. Copyright © 1983 by the Board of Trustees of
the Leland Stanford Junior University. Reprinted by permission.

goals – no one would object to concern for the welfare of the German people – or of faulty reasoning from those goals, but rests on the unacceptability of the factual postulates that connect the goals to the program. From this viewpoint, we might decide that the remedy for Nazism was to combat its program by reason resting on better factual premises.

But somehow that calm response does not seem to match the outrage that *Mein Kampf* produces in us. There must be something more to our rejection of its argument, and obviously there is. Its stated goals are, to put it mildly, incomplete. Statements of human goals usually distinguish between a "we" for whom the goals are shaped and a "they" whose welfare is not "our" primary concern. Hitler's "we" was the German people – the definition of "we" being again based on some dubious "facts" about a genetic difference between Aryan and non-Aryan peoples. Leaving aside this fantasy of Nordic purity, most of us would still define "we" differently from Hitler. Our "we" might be Americans instead of Germans, or, if we had reached a twenty-first-century state of enlightenment, our "we" might even be the human species. In either case, we would be involved in a genuine value conflict with *Mein Kampf*, a conflict not resolvable in any obvious way by improvements in either facts or reasoning. Our postulation of a "we" – of the boundary of our concern for others – is a basic assumption about what is good and what is evil.

Probably the greatest sense of outrage that *Mein Kampf* generates stems from the sharpness of the boundary Hitler draws between "we" and "they." Not only does he give priority to "we," but he argues that any treatment of "they," however violent, is justifiable if it advances the goals of "we." Even if Hitler's general goals and "facts" were accepted, most of us would still object to the measures he proposes to inflict on "they" in order to nurture the welfare of "we." If, in our system of values, we do not regard "they" as being without rights, reason will disclose to us a conflict of values – a conflict between our value of helping "we" and our general goal of not inflicting harm on "they." And so it is not its reasoning for which we must fault *Mein Kampf*, but its alleged facts and its outrageous values.

There is another lesson to be learned from *Mein Kampf*. We cannot read many lines of it before detecting that Hitler's reasoning is not cold reasoning but hot reasoning. We have long since learned that when a position is declaimed with passion and invective, there is special need to examine carefully both its premises and its inferences. We have learned this, but we do not always practice it. Regrettably, it is precisely when the passion and invective resonate with our own inner feelings that we forget the warning and become uncritical readers or listeners.

Hitler was an effective rhetorician for Germans precisely because his passion and invectives resonated with beliefs and values already present in many German hearts. The heat of his rhetoric rendered his readers incapable of applying the rules of reason and evidence to his arguments. Nor was it only Germans who resonated to the facts and values he proclaimed. The latent anti-Semitism and overt anti-Communism of many Western statesmen made a number of his arguments plausible to them.

And so we learned, by bitter experience and against our first quick judgments, that we could not dismiss Hitler as a madman, for there was method in his madness. His prose met standards of reason neither higher nor lower than we are accustomed to encountering in writing designed to persuade. Reason was not, could not have been, our principal shield against Nazism. Our principal shield was contrary factual beliefs and values.

De Gustibus Est Disputandum

Recognizing all these complications in the use of reason, hot or cold, and recognizing also that *ought*'s cannot be derived from *is*'s alone, we must still admit that it is possible to reason about conduct. For most of the *ought*'s we profess are not ultimate standards of conduct but only sub-goals, adopted as means to other goals. For example, taken in isolation a goal like "live within your income" may sound unassailable. Yet a student might be well advised to go into debt in order to complete his or her education. A debt incurred as an investment in future productivity is different from a gambling debt.

Values can indeed be disputed (1) if satisfying them has consequences, present or future, for other values, (2) if they are acquired values, or (3) if they are instrumental to more final values. But although there has been widespread consensus about the rules of reasoning that apply to factual matters, it has proved far more difficult over the centuries to reach agreement about the rules that should govern reasoning about inter-related values. Several varieties of modal logic proposed for reasoning about imperative and deontic statements have gained little acceptance and even less application outside of philosophy. (I state the case against modal logics in Section 3 of Simon, 1977, and in Simon, 1972.)

In the past half century, however, an impressive body of formal theory has been erected by mathematical statisticians and economists to help us reason about these matters – without introducing a new kind of logic. The basic idea of this theory is to load all values into a single function, the utility function, in this way finessing the question of how different values are to be compared. The comparison has in effect already been made when it is assumed that a utility has been assigned to each particular state of affairs.

This formal theory is called subjective expected utility (SEU) theory. Its construction is one of the impressive intellectual achievements of the first half of the twentieth century. It is an elegant machine for applying reason to problems of choice. Our next task is to examine it, and to make some judgments about its validity and limitations.

Subjective expected utility

Since a number of comprehensive and rigorous accounts of SEU theory are available in the literature (for example, Savage, 1954), I will give here only a brief heuristic survey of its main components.

The theory

First, the theory assumes that a decision maker has a well-defined *utility function*, and hence that he can assign a cardinal number as a measure of his liking of any particular scenario of events over the future. Second, it assumes that the decision maker is confronted with a well-defined *set of alternatives* to choose from. These alternatives need not be one-time choices, but may involve sequences of choices or strategies in which each subchoice will be made only at a specified time using the information available at that time. Third, it assumes that the decision maker can assign a consistent *joint probability distribution* to all future sets of events. Finally, it assumes that the decision maker will (or should) choose the alternative, or the strategy, that will *maximize the expected value*, in terms of his utility function, of the set of events consequent on the strategy. With each strategy, then, is associated a probability distribution of future scenarios that can be used to weight the utilities of those scenarios.

These are the four principal components of the SEU model: a cardinal utility function, an exhaustive set of alternative strategies, a probability distribution of scenarios for the future associated with each strategy, and a policy of maximizing expected utility.

Problems with the theory

Conceptually, the SEU model is a beautiful object deserving a prominent place in Plato's heaven of ideas. But vast difficulties make it impossible to employ it in any literal way in making actual human decisions. I have said so much about these difficulties at other times and places (particularly in the pages of *Administrative Behavior*) that I will make only the briefest mention of them here.

The SEU model assumes that the decision maker contemplates, in one comprehensive view, everything that lies before him. He understands the range of alternative choices open to him, not only at the moment but over the whole panorama of the future. He understands the consequences of each of the available choice strategies, at least up to the point of being able to assign a joint probability distribution to future states of the world.

He has reconciled or balanced all his conflicting partial values and synthesized them into a single utility function that orders, by his preference for them, all these future states of the world.

The SEU model finesses completely the origins of the values that enter into the utility function; they are simply there, already organized to express consistent preferences among all alternative futures that may be presented for choice. The SEU model finesses just as completely the processes for ascertaining the facts of the present and future states of the world. At best, the model tells us how to reason about fact and value premises; it says nothing about where they come from.

When these assumptions are stated explicitly, it becomes obvious that SEU theory has never been applied, and never can be applied – with or without the largest computers – in the real world. Yet one encounters many purported applications in mathematical economics, statistics, and management science. Examined more closely, these applications retain the formal structure of SEU theory, but substitute for the incredible decision problem postulated in that theory either a highly abstracted problem in a world simplified to a few equations and variables, with the utility function and the joint probability distributions of events assumed to be already provided, or a microproblem referring to some tiny, carefully defined and bounded situation carved out of a larger real-world reality.

SEU as an approximation

Since I have had occasion to use SEU theory in some of my own research in management science, let me throw the stone through my own window. Holt, Modigliani, Muth, and I constructed a procedure for making decisions about production levels, inventories, and work force in a factory under conditions of uncertainty (Holt, Modigliani, Muth, & Simon, 1960). The procedure fits the SEU model. The utility function is (the negative of) a cost function, comprising costs of production, costs of changing the level of production, putative costs of lost orders, and inventory holding costs. The utility function is assumed to be quadratic in the independent variables, an assumption made because it is absolutely essential if the mathematics and computation are to be manageable. Expected values for sales in each future period are assumed to be known. (The same assumption of the quadratic utility function fortunately makes knowledge of the complete probability distributions irrelevant.) The factory is assumed to have a single homogeneous product, or a set of products that can legitimately be represented by a single-dimensional aggregate.

It is clear that if this decision procedure is used to make decisions for a factory, that is very different from employing SEU theory to make decisions in the real world. All but one of the hard questions have been answered in advance by the assumption of a known, quadratic criterion function and known expected values of future sales. Moreover, this single set of production decisions has been carved out of the entire array of decisions that management has to make, and it has been assumed to be describable in a fashion that is completely independent of information about those other decisions or about any other aspect of the real world.

I have no urge to apologize for our decision procedure as a useful management science tool. It can be, and has been, applied to this practical decision task in a number of factory situations and seems to have operated satisfactorily. What I wish to emphasize is that it is applied to a highly simplified representation of a tiny fragment of the real-world situation, and that the goodness of the decisions it will produce depends much more on the adequacy of the approximating assumptions and the data supporting them than it does on the computation of a maximizing value according to the prescribed SEU decision rule. Hence, it would be perfectly conceivable for someone to contrive a quite different decision procedure, outside the framework of SEU theory, that would produce better decisions in these situations (measured by real-world consequences) than would be produced by our decision rule.

Exactly the same comments can be made about economic models formed within the SEU mold. Their veridicality and usefulness cannot be judged from the fact that they satisfy, formally, the SEU assumptions. In evaluating them, it is critical to know how close the postulated utilities and future events match those of the real world.

Once we accept the fact that, in any actual application, the SEU rule supplies only a crude approximation to an abstraction, an outcome that may or may not provide satisfactory solutions to the real-world problems, then we are free to ask what other decision procedures, unrelated to SEU, might also provide satisfactory outcomes. In particular, we are free to ask what procedures human beings actually use in their decision making and what relation those actual procedures bear to the SEU theory.

I hope I have persuaded you that, in typical real-world situations, decision makers, no matter how badly they want to do so, simply cannot apply the SEU model. If doubt still remains on this point, it can be dissipated by examining the results of laboratory experiments in which human subjects have been asked to make decisions involving risk and uncertainty in game-like situations orders of magnitude simpler than the game of real life. The evidence, much of which has been assembled in several articles by Amos Tversky and his colleagues, leaves no doubt whatever that the human behavior in these choice situations – for whatever reasons – departs widely from the prescriptions of SEU theory (see Tversky & Kahneman, 1974, and references cited there). Of course, I have already suggested what the principal reason is for this departure. It is that human beings have neither the facts nor the consistent structure of values nor the reasoning power at their disposal that would be required, even in these relatively simple situations, to apply SEU principles.

As our next task, we consider what they do instead.

The behavioral alternative

I will ask you to introspect a bit about how you actually make decisions, and I will make some assertions that you can check against your introspections. First, your decisions are not comprehensive choices over large areas of your life, but are generally concerned with rather specific matters, assumed, whether correctly or not, to be relatively independent of other, perhaps equally important, dimensions of life. At the moment you are buying a car, you are probably not also simultaneously choosing next week's dinner menu, or even deciding how to invest income you plan to save.

Second, when you make any particular decision, even an important one, you probably do not work out detailed scenarios of the future, complete with probability distributions, conditional on the alternative you choose. You have a general picture of your life-style and prospects, and perhaps of one or two major contemplated changes in the near future, and even of a couple of contingencies. When you are considering buying a car, you have a general notion of your use of automobiles, your income and the other demands on it, and whether you are thinking of getting a new job in another city. You are unlikely to envision large numbers of other possibilities that might affect what kind of car it makes sense to buy.

Third, the very fact that you are thinking about buying a car, and not a house, will probably focus your attention on some aspects of your life and some of your values to the relative neglect of others. The mere contemplation of buying a car may stimulate fond memories or dreams of travel, and divert your attention from the pleasures of listening to stereo or giving dinner parties for friends at home. Hence, it is unlikely that a single comprehensive utility function will watch over the whole range of decisions you make. On the contrary, particular decision domains will evoke particular values, and great inconsistencies in choice may result from fluctuating attention. We all know that if we want to diet, we should resist exposing ourselves to tempting food. That would be neither necessary nor useful if our choices were actually guided by a single comprehensive and consistent utility function.

Fourth, a large part of whatever effort you devote to making your car-buying decision will be absorbed in gathering facts and evoking possibly relevant values. You may read *Consumer Reports* and consult friends; you may visit car dealers in order to learn more about the various alternatives, and to learn more about your own tastes as well. Once facts of this sort have been assembled, and preferences evoked, the actual choice may take very little time.

Bounded rationality

Choices made in the general way I have just been describing are sometimes characterized as instances of *bounded rationality*. Good reasons can be given for supposing that evolutionary processes might produce creatures capable of bounded rationality. Moreover, a great deal of psychological research supports the hunch to which our introspections have led us, namely that this is the way in which human decisions – even the most deliberate – are made. Let us call this model of human choice the behavioral model, to contrast it with the Olympian model of SEU theory.

Within the behavioral model of bounded rationality, one doesn't have to make choices that are infinitely deep in time, that encompass the whole range of human values, and in which each problem is interconnected with all the other problems in the world. In actual fact, the environment in which we live, in which all creatures live, is an environment that is nearly factorable into separate problems. Sometimes you're hungry, sometimes you're sleepy, sometimes you're cold. Fortunately, you're not often all three at the same time. Or if you are, all but one of these needs can be postponed until the most pressing is taken care of. You have lots of other needs, too, but these also do not all impinge on you at once.

We live in what might be called a nearly empty world – one in which there are millions of variables that in principle could affect each other but that most of the time don't. In gravitational theory everything is pulling at everything else, but some things pull harder than others, either because they're bigger or because they're closer. Perhaps there is actually a very dense network of interconnections in the world, but in most of the situations we face we can detect only a modest number of variables or considerations that dominate.

If this factorability is not wholly descriptive of the world we live in today – and I will express some reservations about that – it certainly describes the world in which human rationality evolved: the world of the cavemen's ancestors, and of the cavemen themselves. In that world, very little was happening most of the time, but periodically action had to be taken to deal with hunger, or to flee danger, or to secure protection against the coming winter. Rationality could focus on dealing with one or a few problems at a time, with the expectation that when other problems arose there would be time to deal with those too. A simple formal model of such rationality is provided in Simon, 1956.

Mechanisms for bounded rationality

What characteristics does an organism need to enable it to exercise a sensible kind of bounded reality? It needs some way of focusing attention

– of avoiding distraction (or at least too much distraction) and focusing on the things that need attention at a given time. A very strong case can be made, and has been made by physiological psychologists, that focusing attention is one of the principal functions of the processes we call emotions. One thing an emotion can do for and to you is to distract you from your current focus of thought, and to call your attention to something else that presumably needs attention right now. Most of the time in our society we don't have to be out looking for food, but every so often we need to be reminded that food is necessary. So we possess some mechanisms that arouse periodically the feeling of hunger, to direct our attention to the need for food. A similar account can be given of other emotions.

Some of an organism's requirements call for continuous activity. People need to have air – access to it can be interrupted only for a short time – and their blood must circulate continually to all parts of their bodies. Of course, human physiology takes care of these and other short-term insistent needs in parallel with the long-term needs. We do not have to have our attention directed to a lack of oxygen in our bloodstream in order to take a breath, or for our heart to beat. But by and large, with respect to those needs that are intermittent, that aren't constantly with us, we operate very much as serial, one-at-a-time, animals. One such need is about as many as our minds can handle at one time. Our ability to get away with that limitation, and to survive in spite of our seriality, depends on the mechanisms, particularly emotional mechanisms, that assure new problems of high urgency a high priority on the agenda.

Second, we need a mechanism capable of generating alternatives. A large part of our problem solving consists in the search for good alternatives, or for improvements in alternatives that we already know. In the past 25 years, research in cognitive psychology and artificial intelligence has taught us a lot about how alternatives are generated. I have given a description of some of the mechanisms in Chapters 3 and 4 of *The Sciences of the Artificial* (Simon, 1981).

Third, we need a capability for acquiring facts about the environment in which we find ourselves, and a modest capability for drawing inferences from these facts. Of course, this capability is used to help generate alternatives as well as to assess their probable consequences, enabling the organism to maintain a very simple model of the part of the world that is relevant to its current decisions, and to do commonsense reasoning about the model.

What can we say for and about this behavioral version, this bounded rationality version, of human thinking and problem solving? The first thing we can say is that there is now a tremendous weight of evidence that this theory describes the way people, in fact, make decisions and solve problems. The theory has an increasingly firm empirical base as a description of human behavior. Second, it is a theory that accounts for the fact that creatures stay alive and even thrive, who – however smart they are or think they are – have modest computational abilities in comparison with the complexity of the entire world that surrounds them. It explains how such creatures have survived for at least the millions of years that our species has survived. In a world that is nearly empty, in which not everything is closely connected with everything else, in which problems can be decomposed into their components – in such a world, the kind of rationality I've been describing gets us by.

Consequences of bounded rationality

Rationality of the sort described by the behavioral model doesn't optimize, of course. Nor does it even guarantee that our decisions will be consistent. As a matter of fact, it is very easy to show that choices made by an organism having these characteristics will often depend on the order in which alternatives are presented. If A is presented before B, A may seem desirable or at least satisfactory; but if B is presented before A, B will seem desirable and will be chosen before A is even considered.

The behavioral model gives up many of the beautiful formal properties of the Olympian model, but in return for giving them up it provides a way of looking at rationality that explains how creatures with our mental capacities – or even, with our mental capacities supplemented with all the computers in Silicon Valley – get along in a world that is much too complicated to be understood from the Olympian viewpoint of SEU theory.

Intuitive rationality

A third model of human rationality has been much less discussed by social scientists than the two that I've considered so far, but is perhaps even more prominent in the popular imagination. I've referred to it as the intuitive model. The intuitive model postulates that a great deal of human thinking, and a great deal of the success of human beings in arriving at correct decisions, is due to the fact that they have good intuition or good judgment. The notions of intuition and judgment are particularly prominent in public discussion today because of the research of Roger Sperry and others, much supplemented by speculation, on the speciali-zation of the left and right hemispheres of the human brain.

The two sides of the brain

In the minds and hands of some writers, the notion of hemisphere specialization has been turned into a kind of romance. According to this romanticized account, there's the dull, pedestrian left side of the brain, which is very analytic. It either, depending on your beliefs, does the

Olympian kind of reasoning that I described first, or – if it's just a poor man's left hemisphere – does the behavioral kind of thinking I described as the second model. In either case, it's a down-to-earth, pedestrian sort of hemisphere, capable perhaps of deep analysis but not of flights of fancy. Then there's the right hemisphere, in which is stored human imagination, creativity – all those good things that account for the abilities of human beings, if they would entrust themselves to this hemisphere, to solve problems in a creative way.

Before I try to characterize intuition and creativity (they are not always the same thing) in a positive way, I must comment on the romantic view I have just caricatured. When we look for the empirical evidence for it, we find that there is none. There is lots of evidence, of course, for specialization of the hemispheres, but none of that evidence really argues that any complex human mental function is performed by either of the hemispheres alone under normal circumstances. By and large, the evidence shows that any kind of complex thinking that involves taking in information, processing that information, and doing something with it employs both of our hemispheres in varying proportions and in various ways.

Of course, brain localization is not the important issue at stake. Regardless of whether the same things or different things go on in the two hemispheres, the important question is whether there are two radically different forms of human thought – analytic thought and intuitive thought – and whether what we call creativity relies largely on the latter.

Intuition and recognition

What is intuition all about? It is an observable fact that people sometimes reach solutions to problems suddenly. They then have an "aha!" experience of varying degrees of intensity. There is no doubt of the genuineness of the phenomenon. Moreover, the problem solutions people reach when they have these experiences, when they make intuitive judgments, frequently are correct.

Good data are available on this point for chess masters. Show a chess position, from a mid-game situation in a reasonable game, to a master or grand master. After looking at it for only five or ten seconds, he will usually be able to propose a strong move – very often the move that is objectively best in the position. If he's playing the game against a strong opponent, he won't make that move immediately; he may sit for three minutes or half an hour in order to decide whether or not his first intuition is really correct. But perhaps 80 or 90 percent of the time, his first impulse will in fact show him the correct move.

The explanation for the chess master's sound intuitions is well known to psychologists, and is not really surprising. For a survey of the evidence, see Simon, 1979b, chapters 6.2–6.5. It is no deeper than the explanation of your ability, in a matter of seconds, to recognize one of your friends whom you meet on the path tomorrow as you are going to class. Unless you are very deep in thought as you walk, the recognition will be immediate and reliable. Now in any field in which we have gained considerable experience, we have acquired a large number of "friends" – a large number of stimuli that we can recognize immediately. We can sort the stimulus in whatever sorting net performs this function in the brain (the physiology of it is not understood), and discriminate it from all the other stimuli we might encounter. We can do this not only with faces, but with words in our native language.

Almost every college-educated person can discriminate among, and recall the meanings of, fifty to a hundred thousand different words. Somehow, over the years, we have all spent many hundreds of hours looking at words, and we have made friends with fifty or a hundred thousand of them. Every professional entomologist has a comparable ability to discriminate among the insects he sees, and every botanist among the plants. In any field of expertise, possession of an elaborate discrimination net that permits recognition of any one of tens of thousands of different objects or situations is one of the basic tools of the expert and the principal source of his intuitions.

Counts have been made of the numbers of "friends" that chess masters have: the numbers of different configurations of pieces on a chessboard that are old familiar acquaintances to them. The estimates come out, as an order of magnitude, around fifty thousand, roughly comparable to vocabulary estimates for native speakers. Intuition is the ability to recognize a friend and to retrieve from memory all the things you've learned about the friend in the years that you've known him. And of course if you know a lot about the friend, you'll be able to make good judgments about him. Should you lend him money or not? Will you get it back if you do? If you know the friend well, you can say "yes" or "no" intuitively.

Acquiring intuitions and judgment

Why should we believe that the recognition mechanism explains most of the "aha!" experiences that have been reported in the literature of creativity? An important reason is that valid "aha!" experiences happen only to people who possess the appropriate knowledge. Poincaré rightly said that inspiration comes only to the prepared mind. Today we even have some data that indicate how long it takes to prepare a mind for world-class creative performance.

At first blush, it is not clear why it should take just as long in one field as in another to reach a world-class level of performance. However, human quality of performance is evaluated by comparing it with the performance of other human beings. Hence the length of human life is a controlling parameter in the competition; we can spend a substantial fraction of our lives, but no more, in increasing our proficiency. For this reason, the time required to prepare for world-class performance (by the people whose talents allow them to aspire to that level) should be roughly the same for different fields of activity.

Empirical data gathered by my colleague John R. Hayes for chess masters and composers, and somewhat less systematically for painters and mathematicians, indicate that ten years is the magic number. Almost no person in these disciplines has produced world-class performances without having first put in at least ten years of intensive learning and practice.

What about child prodigies? Mozart was composing world-class music perhaps by the time he was seventeen – certainly no earlier. (The standard Hayes used for music is five or more appearances of recordings of a piece of music in the Schwann catalog. Except for some Mozart juvenilia, which no one would bother to listen to if they hadn't been written by Mozart, there is no world-class Mozart before the age of seventeen.) Of course Mozart was already composing at the age of four, so that by age seventeen he had already been educating himself for thirteen years. Mozart is typical of the child prodigies whose biographies Hayes has examined. A *sine qua non* for outstanding work is diligent attention to the field over a decade or more.

Summary: The intuitive and behavioral models

There is no contradiction between the intuitive model of thinking and the behavioral model, nor do the two models represent alternative modes of thought residing in different cerebral hemispheres and competing for control over the mind. All serious thinking calls on both modes, both search-like processes and the sudden recognition of familiar patterns. Without recognition based on previous experience, search through complex spaces would proceed in snail-like fashion. Intuition exploits the knowledge we have gained through our past searches. Hence we would expect what in fact occurs, that the expert will often be able to proceed intuitively in attacking a problem that requires painful search for the novice. And we would expect also that in most problem situations combining aspects of novelty with familiar components, intuition and search will cooperate in reaching solutions.

Intuition and emotion

Thus far in our discussion of intuitive processes we have left aside one of the important characteristics these processes are said to possess: their frequent association with emotion. The searching, plodding stages of problem solving tend to be relatively free from intense emotion; they may be described as cold cognition. But sudden discovery, the "aha!" experience, tends to evoke emotion; it is hot cognition. Sometimes ideas come to people when they are excited about something.

Emotion and attention

Hence, in order to have anything like a complete theory of human rationality, we have to understand what role emotion plays in it. Most likely it serves several quite distinct functions. First of all, some kinds of emotion (e.g., pleasure) are consumption goods. They enter into the utility function of the Olympian theory, and must be counted among the goals we strive for in the behavioral model of rationality.

But for our purposes, emotion has particular importance because of its function of selecting particular things in our environments as the focus of our attention. Why was Rachel Carson's *Silent Spring* so influential? The problems she described were already known to ecologists and the other biologists at the time she described them. But she described them in a way that aroused emotion, that riveted our attention on the problem she raised. That emotion, once aroused, wouldn't let us go off and worry about other problems until something had been done above this one. At the very least, emotion kept the problem in the back of our minds as a nagging issue that wouldn't go away.

In the Olympian model, all problems are permanently and simultaneously on the agenda (until they are solved). In the behavioral model, by contrast, the choice of problems for the agenda is a matter of central importance, and emotion may play a large role in that choice.

Emotion does not always direct our attention to goals we regard as desirable. If I may go back to my example of *Mein Kampf*, we observed that the reasoning in that book is not cold reasoning but hot reasoning. It is reasoning that seeks deliberately to arouse strong emotions, often the emotion of hate, a powerful human emotion. And of course, the influence of *Mein Kampf*, like that of *Silent Spring* or Picasso's *Guernica*, was due in large part to the fact that it did have evocative power, the ability to arouse and fix the attention of its German readers on the particular goals it had in mind.

A behavioral theory of rationality, with its concern for the focus of attention as a major determinant of choice, does not dissociate emotion from human thought, nor does it in any respect underestimate the powerful effects of emotion in setting the agenda for human problem solving.

Emotion in education

I would like to take a brief excursion at this point in order to consider the role of emotion in education. If literary and artistic works have a considerable power to evoke emotions, as they certainly do, does this power suggest any special role for them in the educational process?

We all know that the humanities feel a bit besieged today. A large proportion of the students in our universities appear to want to enroll in law, business, or medicine, and the humanities suffer neglect, benign or otherwise. One argument that is often advanced by those who would counter this trend is that it may be better, more effective, for students to learn about the human condition by exposure to the artist's and humanist's view of the world than by exposure to the scientist's. Of course my own professional identifications put me on the other side of the argument, but I think we should look at the issue quite carefully. What are the optimum conditions for efficient human learning about central and important matters? Which is better, cold cognition or hot? And whichever is better, will we find that this is the kind we associate with the sciences or the humanities?

I should say here that I have heard physicists argue for a strong infusion of hot cognition in teaching their subject. The problems that excite them, and motivate them to understand rather abstruse matters, are the cosmological and philosophical problems associated with the fundamental particles, and with astrophysics and the architecture of the universe. So perhaps I should not have associated science strictly with cold cognition.

But let me go to a domain where the point can be made more unequivocally and convincingly. Perhaps some of you are familiar with Arthur Koestler's *Darkness at Noon*. It is a novel that describes what happens to a particular person at the time of the Russian purge trials of the 1930s. Now suppose you wish to understand the history of the Western world between the two world wars, and the events that led up to our contemporary world. You will then certainly need to understand the purge trials. Are you more likely to gain such an understanding by reading *Darkness at Noon*, or by reading a history book that deals with the trials, or by searching out the published transcripts of the trial testimony in the library? I would vote for Koestler's book as the best route, precisely because of the intense emotions it evokes in most readers.

I could go down a long list of such alternatives: *War and Peace* versus a treatise on military sociology, Proust and Chekov versus a textbook on personality. If I were in a position where I had to defend the role of the humanities in education, to provide an argument for something like the traditional liberal arts curriculum of the early twentieth century, I would argue for them on the grounds that most human beings are able to attend to issues longer, to think harder about them, to receive deeper impressions that last longer, if information is presented in a context of emotion – a sort of hot dressing – than if it is presented wholly without affect.

But educating with the help of hot cognition also implies a

responsibility. If we are to learn our social science from novelists, then the novelists have to get it right. The scientific content must be valid. Freudian theory permeates a great deal of literature today – at the very time when Freudian theories are being revised radically by new psychological knowledge. There are few orthodox Freudians left in psychology today. Hence there is a danger, if we take this route of asking the humanities to provide an emotional context for learning, that a kind of warmed-over Freud will be served to our students in a powerfully influential form. We have to re-evaluate the great humanist classics to see to what extent they suffer from obsolescence through the progress of our scientific knowledge.

Homer is still alive because the *Iliad* and the *Odyssey* treat mainly of matters in which modern social science has not progressed much beyond lay understanding. Aristotle is barely alive – and certainly his scientific works are not, and his logic hardly. And we could have a great argument with philosophers as to whether his epistemology or his metaphysics has anything to say to students today. And Lucretius, of course, talking about atoms, has gone entirely.

The moral I draw is that, whereas works capable of evoking emotion may have special value for us just by virtue of that capability, if we wish to use them to educate, we must evaluate not only their power to rouse emotion but also their scientific validity when they speak of matters of fact.

If the humanities are to base their claims to a central place in the liberal curriculum on their special insights into the human condition, they must be able to show that their picture of that condition is biologically, sociologically, and psychologically defensible. It is not enough, for this particular purpose, that humanistic works move students. They must move them in ways that will enable them to live with due regard for reason and fact in the real world. I do not mean to imply that the humanities do not now meet this standard; a detailed assessment of the liberal curriculum in any existing university would certainly not give a simple yes-or-no answer to that question. But I do suggest that any examination of the appropriate roles of different fields of knowledge in providing the materials of a liberal education needs to give close attention both to the emotional temperature of material and to its empirical soundness.

Conclusion

In this chapter, I have sought to present three visions of rationality: three ways of talking about rational choice. The first of these, the Olympian model, postulates a heroic man making comprehensive choices in an integrated universe. The Olympian view serves, perhaps, as a model of the mind of God, but certainly not as a model of the mind of man. I have been rather critical of that theory for present purposes.

The second, the behavioral model, postulates that human rationality is very limited, very much bounded by the situation and by human computational powers. I have argued that there is a great deal of empirical evidence supporting this kind of theory as a valid description of how human beings make decisions. It is a theory of how organisms, including man, possessing limited computational abilities, make adaptive choices and sometimes survive in a complex, but mostly empty, world.

The third, the intuitive model, places great stress on the processes of intuition. The intuitive theory, I have argued, is in fact a component of the behavioral theory. It emphasizes the recognition processes that underlie the skills humans can acquire by storing experience and by recognizing situations in which their experience is relevant and appropriate. The intuitive theory recognizes that human thought is often affected by emotion, and addresses the question of what function emotion plays in focusing human attention on particular problems at particular times. . . .

6. Informing the public about the risks from ionizing radiation

Paul Slovic, Baruch Fischhoff, and Sarah Lichtenstein

Introduction

One dramatic change in people's outlook on life in recent years is a growing awareness of the risks encountered in daily experience. Radiation hazards, medicinal side-effects, occupational diseases, food contaminants, aviation accidents, fires, etc. increasingly fill our newspapers and our thoughts. One consequence of this awareness is pressure on the promoters and regulators of hazardous enterprises to inform people about the risks they face.

In May 1978, the White House directed the Secretary of Health, Education and Welfare to coordinate research on the health effects of radiation exposure, including the development of a public information program. The Interagency Task Force established to carry out this directive completed seven reports, including one on public information. The latter report focused on the need to provide information about radiation risks to the following audiences: medical and dental patients, workers exposed in their occupations, military personnel and civilians exposed to fallout from nuclear weapons testing, and the general public.

The task force recommended that messages developed for these audiences stress the following points:

- Low-level background radiation is a part of the earth's natural environment. Any man-made radiation exposure adds to that already received from natural sources.
- The degree of risk associated with exposure to low-level ionizing radiation is thought to be very low.

This chapter originally appeared in *Health Physics*, 1981, 41(4), 589–598. Reprinted by permission of the Health Physics Society.

- Scientists disagree about the precise magnitude of this risk.
- Unnecessary radiation exposure should be avoided.
- Any risk from radiation must be balanced against the benefits provided by the activity producing the radiation.

In addition, the public information report called for the development and presentation of information that describes the benefits and risks of radiation (and facilitates their comparison), outlines the scientific basis for risk estimates, and explains why such estimates are difficult to make for any given individual. Finally, the report called for a national survey of public attitudes and knowledge about radiation as an aid to designing public information materials.

Confronting human limitations

We strongly endorse the recommendation that programs be developed to inform patients, workers, and the general public. However, neither the report by the Interagency Task Force nor any other similar documents that we have seen adequately acknowledges the difficulties inherent in communicating highly technical information about risk.

Doing an adequate job means finding cogent ways of presenting complex, technical material that is clouded with uncertainty and may be distorted by the listeners' preconceptions (and perhaps misconceptions) about the hazard and its consequences. This section offers a brief overview of some of the problems facing any information program.

It is hard to think clearly about risk

Decisions about risk from radiation (or any other source) require sophisticated reasoning on the part of both experts and the public. Needed are an appreciation of the probabilistic nature of the world and the ability to think intelligently about rare (but consequential) events. As Alvin Weinberg observed in the context of managing nuclear power, "... we certainly accept on faith that our human intellect is capable of dealing with this new source of energy" (Weinberg, 1976, p. 21). Unfortunately, although the human intellect is deservedly held in high esteem in many contexts, numerous studies have shown that intelligent people have difficulty judging probabilities, making predictions, or otherwise attempting to cope with uncertainty. Frequently, these difficulties can be traced to the use of judgmental heuristics, mental strategies whereby people try to reduce difficult tasks to simpler judgments. These heuristics are valid in some circumstances, but in others, they lead to biases that are large and persistent (Slovic, Kunreuther, & White, 1974. Slovic, Fischhoff, & Lichtenstein, 1977; Tversky & Kahneman, 1974).

People's perceptions of risks are often inaccurate

Of the heuristics that people use in probabilistic thinking, one, the "avail-ability heuristic," has special relevance to risk perception. Users of the "availability heuristic" judge an event to be likely or frequent if it is easy to imagine or recall relevant instances of that event. Instances of frequent events are typically easier to recall than instances of less frequent events, and likely occurrences are easier to imagine than unlikely ones. Thus availability is often an appropriate cue for judging frequency and prob-ability. However, since availability is also affected by numerous factors unrelated to likelihood, reliance on it may lead to overestimation of probabilities for recent, vivid, emotionally salient or otherwise memorable or imaginable events. In the extreme, any factor that makes a hazard unusually memorable or imaginable, such as a recent disaster or a sen-sational film (e.g. *Jaws* or *The China Syndrome*), could seriously distort that hazard's perceived risk.

The biasing effects of availability may be seen in a study of the perceived frequency of various causes of death (Lichtenstein, Slovic, Fischhoff, Layman, & Combs, 1978). That study demonstrated that the frequencies of dramatic or sensational causes of death, such as accidents, homicide, cancer, botulism, and tornadoes, were greatly overestimated. Frequencies of undramatic causes, such as asthma, emphysema and diabetes, which take one life at a time and are common in nonfatal form, were greatly underestimated. News media coverage of fatal events has been shown to be biased in much the same direction, thus contributing to the difficulties of keeping proper mental accounts of everyday risks (Combs & Slovic, 1979).

Another important type of misperception is the tendency to consider ourselves personally immune to many hazards that we admit pose a serious threat to others. In a report titled, "Are We All Among the Better Drivers?", Svenson showed that most people rate themselves as among the most skillful and safe drivers in the population (Svenson, 1981). This effect does not seem to be limited just to driving. Rethans (1979) found that most people rated their personal risk from each of 29 consumer products (e.g. knives, hammers) as lower than the risk to other individuals. Ninety-seven percent of Rethans' respondents judged them-selves average or above average in their ability to avoid both bicycle and power mower accidents. Weinstein (1980) found that people were unreal-istically optimistic when evaluating the chances that a wide variety of good and bad life events (e.g., living past 80, having a heart attack) would happen to them.

Although the determinants of such personal optimism are not well understood, we believe that several contributing factors can be identified. First, the hazardous activities for which personal risks are underestimated tend to be seen (exaggeratedly) as under the individual's control. Second, they tend to be familiar hazards whose risks are low enough that the individual's personal experience is overwhelmingly benign. Automobile driving is a prime example of such a hazard. Despite driving too fast, tailgating, etc., poor drivers make trip after trip without mishap. This personal experience demonstrates to these drivers their exceptional skill and safety. Moreover, their indirect experience via the media shows them that when accidents do happen, they happen to others. Given such misleading experiences, people may feel quite justified in refusing to take protective action such as wearing seat belts (Slovic, Fischhoff, & Lichtenstein, 1978).

Risk information may frighten and frustrate the public

The fact that perceptions of risk are often inaccurate points to the need for educational programs. However, to the extent that misperceptions are due to reliance on imaginability as a cue for probability, such programs may run into trouble. Merely mentioning possible adverse consequences of radiation could enhance their perceived likelihood and make them appear more frightening. Anecdotal observation of attempts to inform people about recombinant DNA hazards supports this hypothesis (Rosenberg, 1978), but controlled research is needed to test it more adequately. To the extent that imaginability can blur the distinction between what is (remotely) possible and what is probable, information materials will have to be designed with great care.

Other psychological research shows that people have great difficulty making decisions about gambles, when they are forced to resolve conflicts generated by the possibility of experiencing both gains and losses, and uncertain ones at that (Lichtenstein & Slovic, 1973). As a result, people often attempt to reduce the anxiety generated in the face of uncertainty by denying the uncertainty, thus making the risk seem so small it can safely be ignored or so large that it clearly should be avoided. They rebel against being given statements of probability, rather than fact; they want to know *exactly* what will happen. Thus, just before hearing a blue-ribbon panel of scientists report being 95% certain that cyclamates do not cause cancer, former Food and Drug Administration Commissioner Alexander Schmidt said, "I'm looking for a clean bill of health, not a wishy-washy, iffy answer on cyclamates." Likewise, former Senator Muskie once called for "one-armed" scientists who do not respond "on the one hand, the evidence is so, but on the other hand . . ." when asked about the health effects of pollutants.

Given a choice, people would rather not have to confront the gambles inherent in living with radiation. They would prefer being told that radiation is managed by competent professionals and is thus so safe they need not worry about it. However, if such assurances cannot be given, they will want to be informed of the risks, even though doing so might make them anxious and conflicted (e.g., Fischhoff, 1983a; Weinstein, 1979).

Strong beliefs are hard to modify

The difficulties of facing life as a gamble contribute to the polarization of opinion about technologies such as nuclear power or genetic recombinations; some view these technologies are extraordinarily safe, while others view them as catastrophies in the making. It would be comforting to believe that such polarized positions would respond to informational and educational programs. Unfortunately, psychological research demonstrates that people's beliefs change slowly and are extraordinarily persistent in the face of contrary evidence. Once formed, initial impressions tend to structure the way that substantive evidence is interpreted. New evidence appears reliable and informative if it is consistent with one's initial belief; contrary evidence is dismissed as unreliable, erroneous or unrepresentative. Thus, depending on whether one is predisposed to favor nuclear power or oppose it, efforts to reduce nuclear hazards may be interpreted to mean either that the technologists are responsive to the public's concerns or that the risks are indeed great. Similarly, whereas opponents of nuclear power viewed the accident at Three Mile Island as proof that nuclear reactors are unsafe, proponents claimed that it demonstrated the effectiveness of the multiple safety and containment systems.

Presentation format is vitally important

The precise manner in which risks are expressed can have a major impact on perceptions. For example, an action increasing one's annual chances of death from 1 in 10,000 to 1.3 in 10,000 would probably be seen as much more risky if it were described, instead, as producing a 30% increase in annual mortality. Numerous effects of presentation format have been documented in the literature on risk assessment (Fishhoff, Slovic, & Lichtenstein, 1978; Tversky & Kahneman, 1981). Here, we shall present but two examples. The first is based on a pair of problems that Tversky and Kahneman (1981) gave to two groups of college students. Each problem had two options and respondents were asked to indicate which option they would choose.

Problem 1. Imagine that the U.S. is preparing for the outbreak of an unusual Asian disease, which is expected to kill 600 people. Two alternative programs to combat the disease have been proposed. Assume that the exact scientific estimate of consequences of the programs are as follows:

If Program A is adopted, 200 people will be saved.

If Program B is adopted, there is 1/3 probability that 600 people will be saved; and 2/3 probability that no people will be saved.

Which of the two programs would you favor?

Problem 2. (Same cover story as Problem 1.)

If Program C is adopted, 400 people will die.

If Program D is adopted, there is 1/3 probability that nobody will die, and 2/3 probability that 600 people will die.

Which of the two programs would you favor?

Seventy-five percent of these respondents chose Program A over Program B and 67% chose Program D over Program C, even though A and C are identical options, as are B and D. Thus, the preference patterns were reversed by the simple change from lives saved to lives lost. Groups of physicians have been found to exhibit similar reversals.

A second demonstration of the importance of presentation format comes from a study of attitudes towards the use of automobile seat belts (Slovic et al., 1978). Drawing upon previous research showing that the probability of loss was more important than the magnitude of loss in triggering protective action. Slovic *et al.* argued that motorists' reluctance to wear seat belts might be due to the extremely small probability of incurring a fatal accident on a single automobile trip. Since a fatal accident occurs only about once in every 3.5 million person trips and a disabling injury occurs only about once in every 100,000 person trips, refusing to buckle one's seat belt may seem quite reasonable. It looks less reasonable, however, if one adopts a multiple-trip perspective and considers the substantial probability of an accident on some trip. Over 50 years of driving (about 40,000 trips), the probability of being killed rises to 0.01 and the probability of experiencing at least one disabling injury is 0.33. Slovic *et al.* found that people who were asked to consider this lifetime perspective responded more favorably toward the use of seat belts (and air bags) than did people asked to consider a trip-by-trip perspective.

The fact that subtle differences in how risks are presented can have marked effects suggests that people who inform others have considerable ability to manipulate perceptions. Indeed, since these effects are not widely known, people may inadvertently be manipulating their own perceptions by casual decisions they make about how to organize their knowledge.

Placing radiation risks in perspective

We have attempted to demonstrate some of the difficulties people have in comprehending and estimating risks. Some observers, cognizant of these difficulties, have concluded that the problems are insurmountable. We disagree. Although the broad outlines of the psychological research just described seem to support a pessimistic view, the details of that research give some cause for optimism. Upon closer examination, it appears that people understand some things quite well, although their path to knowledge may be quite different from that of the technical experts. In situations where misunderstanding is rampant, people's errors can often be traced to inadequate information and biased experiences, which education may be able to counter.

There appears to be widespread agreement within the technical community that appropriate presentations of factual material, within a comparative framework, can go a long way towards educating the public and providing a sound basis for standard setting as well. In particular, comparisons of the radiation from different sources (including nature) or of the risks from radiation and other hazards have been advanced as exemplary methods for instilling proper perspectives. In this section, we shall briefly examine and critique three popular methods of comparison.

Sources of exposure

One type of comparative table partitions the average annual amount of radiation exposure according to source (natural vs technological; environmental, medical, occupational, etc.). Such tables indicate that the largest sources and the largest artificial exposures come from diagnostic X-rays. Of course, such presentations are only as useful as they are accurate. Recent research has revealed a major source of radiation not listed in most tables, namely that due to radon gas emanating from construction materials and accumulating in closed buildings. Myers and Newcombe (1979), for example, report that radon gas may be the major source of public radiation exposure, perhaps accounting for between 5 and 20% of all lung cancer deaths.

Natural standards

Another approach to placing risks in perspective assumes that the optimal (or acceptable) level of exposure to a hazard is the level characteristic of the conditions in which the species evolved. Radiation standards have been based on this principle. For example, Adler (quoted by Weinberg) proposed:

... rather than trying to determine the actual damage caused by very low radiation insult, and then setting an allowable dose, one instead compares the man-made standard with the background. Since man has evolved in the midst of a pervasive radiation background, the presumption is that an increment of radiation "small" compared to that background is tolerable and ought to be set as the standard. [Adler] suggests that small, in the case of γ radiation, be taken as the standard deviation of the natural background – about 20 mrad/yr (Weinberg, 1979, p. 16).

One attractive feature of such natural standards is that they can be set in the absence of precise knowledge of dose-response curves; another is that they avoid the problems of converting risks into a common unit (like workdays lost). Nonetheless, comparisons with the natural background, whether for purposes of education or standard setting, must face several criticisms. One is the fact that our natural exposure to many hazards has not diminished. Thus, whatever new exposure is allowed comes in addition to what we already receive from nature and thereby constitutes excess "unnatural" exposure. A second problem arises when the technology produces multiple sources of exposure. In principle, each such exposure could constitute a small, hence acceptable, increment over background exposures. Natural standards do not provide any clear criterion for deciding that the cumulative impact of a set of tolerable exposures is intolerable.

When defining as acceptable any activity whose risks are only slightly above natural levels, problems of definition become important. Aggregation of disaggregation of several sources of exposure can mean the difference between having several technologies, each within the limits of acceptance, or one technology outside the limits. Without clear guidelines, a consequential event could be redefined as a set of inconsequential events.

Cross-hazard comparisons

The third approach to risk education is to present quantified risk estimates for a variety of hazards. Presumably, the sophistication gleaned from examining such data will be useful not only for broadening one's perspective but for decision making as well. Wilson (1979) observed that we should "try to measure our risks quantitatively....Then we could compare risks and decide which to accept or reject" (p. 43). Likewise, Sowby (1965) argued that to decide whether we are regulating radiation hazards properly, we need to pay more attention to "some of the other risks of life."

Typically, such exhortations are followed by elaborate tables and even "catalogs of risks" in which diverse indices of death or disability are displayed for a broad spectrum of life's hazards. Thus Sowby (1965) provided extensive data on risks per hour of exposure, showing, for example, that an hour riding a motorcycle is as risky as an hour of being 75 years old. Wilson (1979) developed a table of activities (e.g., flying 1000 miles by jet, having one chest X-ray), each of which is estimated to increase one's annual chance of death by 1 in one million (which in the case of accidental death would decrease one's life expectancy by about 15 minutes). In similar fashion, Cohen and Lee (1979) ordered many hazards in terms of their reduction in life expectancy on the assumption that "to some approximation, the ordering should be society's order of priorities. However, we see several very major problems that have received very little attention ... whereas some of the items near the bottom of the list, especially those involving radiation, receive a great deal of attention" (Cohen & Lee, 1979, p. 720). A related exercise by Reissland and Harries (1979) compared loss of life expectancy in the nuclear industry with that in other occupations.

Although such risk comparisons may provide some aid to intuition, they may not educate as effectively as their proponents believe. For example, although some people may feel enlightened upon learning that a single takeoff or landing in a commercial airliner takes an average of 15 minutes off one's life expectancy, others may find themselves completely bewildered by such information. When landing or taking off, one will either die prematurely (almost certainly by more than 15 minutes) or one will not. From the standpoint of the individual, averages do not adequately capture the essence of such risks.

Furthermore, research on risk perception (e.g., Slovic, Fischhoff, & Lichtenstein, 1980) shows that perceptions and attitudes are determined not only by accident probabilities, annual mortality rates and losses of life expectancy, but also by numerous other characteristics of hazards such as uncertainty, controllability, catastrophic potential, equity and threat to future generations. Within the perceptual space defined by such characteristics, each hazard is unique. A statement such as "the annual risk from living near a nuclear power plant is equivalent to the risk of riding an extra 3 miles in an automobile" fails to consider how these two technologies differ on many qualities that people believe to be important. As a result, such statements are likely to produce anger rather than enlightenment.

In sum, comparisons across hazards and comparisons with natural levels of risk may be useful tools for educating the public. Yet the facts do not speak for themselves, except for those who already know what they want to hear. Comparative analyses must be performed with great care to be worthwhile. Even then, the insights they provide may be limited.

What can research tell us?

To be effective, any information program must be buttressed by extensive empirical research designed to indicate what people know, what they want to know, and how best to convey that information. For example, some have speculated that people shy away from information of a threatening nature. However, psychologist Neil Weinstein (1979) found the opposite reaction when people were given the opportunity to choose between a reassuring and a threatening message about environmentally induced cancer. Specifically, he found that:

- People were more interested in learning what the hazard might be than in receiving information minimizing its danger.

- Failure to seek information reflected a lack of interest in the topic rather than an attempt to avoid the topic because it was too threatening.
- Lack of information, even if acknowledged, did not necessarily lead people to seek out information.
- When conflicting messages were available regarding the existence of a hazard, people tended to select the message that agreed with their own point of view.

A study by Baruch Fischhoff (1983a) provides a detailed example of the way in which research can be carried out and the kinds of insights such research might provide. Fischhoff was concerned about how best to inform temporary workers in the nuclear industry about the radiation risks they faced when performing tasks in contaminated areas.

Design of the study

With the help of physicist Christoph Hohenemser, Fischhoff designed a pamphlet to inform temporary workers with the reading skills of high school graduates. This pamphlet included a definition of "maximum permissible quarterly dose" which included comparisons with other exposures, a best guess at the risks of death and genetic damage incurred by such exposure, and an acknowledgement that experts disagree on these effects, with the present "best guess" expressing less risk than that believed to be the case by a minority of experts.

Each of four versions of the statement was presented to a different group of 50–60 individuals. Respondents were recruited by advertising in a university newspaper and at a state employment office. Although a somewhat special population, these individuals are not entirely unrepresentative of the (unskilled) laborers who might be confronted with the nuclear work option. About 20% reported having worked in high-risk environments in the past.

After reading the statement, participants in the study made judgments in four categories: (a) appropriate pay for the job, (b) the nature and extent of the risks, (c) current and desired exposure standards, and (d) the quality of the statement and strategies for its administration.

Three factors were varied in creating the four versions:

1. Whether readers were told why temporary workers were being used. A long form included this information, a short form excluded it.
2. How the administration of the statement was described. Most readers were told nothing about its administration; one group was asked to imagine receiving it when arriving at the nuclear facility.

3. How pay questions were positioned. Most groups were asked to judge appropriate pay levels immediately after reading the statement; one group was asked about pay after answering questions on the other three topics. It was felt that answering the other questions might help elaborate the decision situation and affect respondents' attitudes towards pay.

Results

The pamphlet was moderately well regarded by readers. They viewed it as readable, straightforward, and fairly honest. Moreover, respondents were adamant about the need for presenting such information. More than 80% answered "definitely yes" to the question: "If you had taken such a job without being shown this pamphlet, would you feel that you had been deprived of necessary information?" A majority responded "definitely no" to the question: "Is this too much information?" Most wanted even more information than was in the pamphlet. As Weinstein's study also demonstrated, people want to be told.

Respondents also had definite ideas about when such information should be presented. Almost 90% said that it should be shown when workers originally report to the personnel office (off site); 88% viewed it as "very inappropriate" to present it only when workers asked for it explicitly. When asked how the presentation of risk information could have been improved, almost all respondents had definite opinions. They wanted more information and more elaborate presentations. The most common requests were for information about the specific plant and its safety record, additional research results, and a chance to discuss the topic with other workers and specialists.

In a variety of ways, the participants were asked to evaluate the nature and magnitude of the job's radiation risk. They generally felt that the risks were neither very well nor very poorly understood by themselves or by scientists. They judged the risks to be equivalent to those incurred in a similar period of time spent in a coal mine, but worse than those encountered in activities such as domestic work or driving. They generally believed that it was quite likely that the standards reported in the booklet would be exceeded by accident, that there was no amount of radiation so small as to present no danger, and that a worker would not be able to tell at the end of the job whether any damage had been suffered.

When asked about standards, these people felt that current standards were not stringent enough and that it was unreasonable to design plants calling for such exposure of temporary workers. Three-fifths believed that companies set standards; only one-fifth believed that they should. Perhaps even more surprising was that, whereas 87% believed that government officials currently set standards, only 55% believed that they should. What groups are judged to be underrepresented in standard setting? The public is one; 7% of respondents believed that the public was involved, 46% believed that it should be. Scientists and the courts were judged to be underrepresented to lesser extents.

When asked about fair pay for the job, the median response was $100 for one day. When asked about the lowest pay that they personally would require to take the job, half of all respondents reported being unwilling to take the job at any price. About half of those who categorically refused the job at the described risk levels were willing to accept it at $50 per day if the risks were reduced by a factor of 25–100. Wage demands (but not judgments of risk) were reduced by a variant of the pamphlet that asked respondents to imagine that they had received it upon reporting to work in the morning and by a variant that did not tell them that they were being exposed to save permanent workers.

Extensions

This particular pamphlet was but one attempt to present the facts fairly. Alternative versions could easily be prepared and it would be interesting to study their impact. For example, one might indicate who sets the standards and the likelihood that they will be exceeded by accident, what it is like to have cancer, or what the cure rates are. One could also detail the opinions of that minority of experts who believe that cancer risks from radiation exposures are higher than those indicated in the pamphlet or describe the views of those experts who believe that there is a threshold below which effects are absent. One could describe acceptance rates among other workers, the plant's financial situation (does it make a profit on the labor of these temporary workers?), other life events that cause cancer, or the risks from alternative jobs. Any of these variations could affect judgments of risk, equality, or bargaining power. Respondents' requests for additional information or alternative modes of presentation suggest that some such variations would be welcome. Nonetheless, the present pamphlet might not be too dissimilar in length and balance from what might eventually appear in real situations.

Although this particular study was concerned with informing just one particular category of worker, we believe that similar research should be done in conjunction with all programs to inform workers, patients, or members of the general public.

How and by whom should information be provided?

Radiation information programs have enormous potential to influence the behavior of workers, patients, and citizens. The stakes are high – jobs, electricity costs, willingness of patients to submit to treatments, public safety and health, etc. Potential conflicts of interest abound. Responsibility

for information programs should not be left solely to the natural trium-
virate of science, industry and government, lest these programs run the
risk of being viewed as propaganda campaigns. Since every decision
about the design of an information statement can influence perception
and behavior, extreme care must be taken to select knowledgeable and
trustworthy designers and program coordinators. We cannot propose a
general selection procedure here, as a competent and credible program
staff would have to be put together in consultation with representatives
of the people who were to be informed. If people do not trust their
informants, there is little point in pursuing the program.

7. Science, values, and human judgment

Kenneth R. Hammond and
Leonard Adelman

Scientists and policy-makers are uncertain how scientific facts are to be integrated with social values. For their part, scientists are uncertain whether their contributions should be restricted to presenting the facts, thereby leaving the policy judgment entirely to the political decision-makers, or whether they should also advise politicians which course the scientist believes to be best. And politicians, for their part, are uncertain how much scientific information they are supposed to absorb, and how much dependence they should place on scientists for guidance in reaching a judgment about policy.[1] As a result, "the scientific community continues its seemingly endless debate about the role of science and scientists in the body politic" (Curlin, 1975).

One principal reason for the "endless debate" is that scientific progress has increasingly come to be judged in the context of human values. These judgments find their ultimate expression in the forming of public policy because it is during that process that the products of science and technology are integrated, or aligned, with human values; it is during that process that scientific and technological answers to questions of what can be done are judged in the context of what ought to be done.

The key element, therefore, in the process of integrating social values and scientific facts is human judgment – a cognitive activity not directly observable and generally assumed to be recoverable only by (fallible) introspection and "self-report." These characteristics, among others, have led to the general belief that human judgment is beyond scientific

This chapter originally appeared in *Science*, 1976, *194*, 389–396. Copyright © 1976 by the American Association for the Advancement of Science. Reprinted by permission.

[1] See, for example, Public Law 92–484, which established the Office of Technology Assessment.

analysis and therefore little has been learned about the cognitive activity that produces crucial decisions. The integration of social values and scientific information in the effort to form public policy remains largely a mystery.

The fact that an essential element in the policy formation process remains a mystery has serious consequences, one of which is a search for safeguards. Means must be found to avoid both poor judgments and self-serving judgments. Two general methods have been recommended by scientists for these purposes: (i) the adversary method, in which scientists with differing judgments are pitted against one another in front of a judge or jury, or both, and (ii) the search for and use of scientists who have somehow gained a reputation for wisdom in the exercise of their judgment. Neither of these methods provide enlightenment with regard to the judgment process that produces the ultimate decision. Consequently, we reject both methods because they are "ascientific"; they leave the body politic at the mercy of a cognitive activity which remains as much a mystery as ever.

We contend that policy judgments can be brought under scientific study and, as a result, a process that is now poorly understood can be examined, understood, assisted, and thereby improved. To support this contention we describe a scientific framework for integrating (i) scientific information (the province of scientists) and (ii) social value judgments (the province of the electorate and their representatives) in a manner that is scientifically, socially, and ethically defensible, and offer an example of its use. First, however, we briefly consider two contrasting viewpoints concerning the role of science and scientists in the body politic.

Contrasting viewpoints of the role of the scientist

There are two main viewpoints: one is that scientists should merely present unbiased information, while the other is that scientists should provide advice with regard to the implications of scientific information. The first view can be illustrated by the comments of Phillip Handler, president of the National Academy of Sciences (NAS), in an interview with Otten, of the *Wall Street Journal*. Otten (1975, p. 12) writes: "Once the scientific community has presented the facts, however, it must leave final decisions to the policy-makers and the public, Mr. Handler asserts. 'Science can contribute much to enhancing agricultural production, but American policy with respect to food aid is not intrinsically a scientific question.' Similarly, science can study whether energy independence is technically feasible or whether Soviet underground nuclear tests can be detected, but [Handler] insists, [scientists] must then let regular policy-makers decide whether to try for energy independence or just what arms control proposals to put to the Russians." Otten concluded that "Both science and government seem well served by this reasonable man."

Handler's viewpoint as represented in the above quotation is exactly in accord with the two Executive Orders (1918, 1956) concerning the role of the National Research Council. These documents indicate that scientists are to render information to those who are entitled to receive it, but they do not imply that scientists should offer their judgment as to what public policy should follow from their studies.

In practice it may be impossible not to offer such judgments. With the ever-increasing reliance of society on science and technology it is difficult to imagine how modern scientific information could be conveyed to non-scientists without providing such judgments. In a recent editorial in *Science*, Boulding (1975) argued that if policy judgments were not offered by scientists, they would be demanded by politicians.

Every decision involves the selection among an agenda of alternative images of the future, a selection that is guided by some system of values. The values are traditionally supposed to be the cherished preserve of the political decision-maker, but the agenda, which involves fact or at least a projection into the future of what are presumably factual systems, should be very much in the domain of science.... [But] if the decision-maker simply does not know what the results of alternative actions will be, it is difficult to evaluate unknown results. *The decision-maker wants to know what are the choices from which he must choose* [italics ours].

Toulmin (1972, pp. 102–103) goes further than Boulding. Whereas Boulding notes that politicians may demand policy judgments from scientists, Toulmin argues that it may be part of the scientists' responsibility to offer policy judgments before such judgments are requested by political decision-makers. Thus, "In the early days, the picture was always of the politician as the man who *first* formulated for himself questions about the political options, about the choices he had to make: on this view, he *subsequently* turned to people called 'technical advisors' and asked them how to do this or that, how much each option would cost, and so on. A lot of people still see the relationship between the scientist or technologist and the politicians on this model...." But, Toulmin observes, "... even during [World War II] scientists were being transformed into people who could very often see a fresh range of policy options *before* the politicians could." Significantly, Toulmin notes that "To some extent, the institutional relationships between politics and science have not yet caught up with this change."

Thus, Toulmin points out that the decision-maker not only wants to know "the choices from which he must choose," as Boulding put it, but he also wants to know which choice the scientist thinks he should choose. Senator Muskie's call for a "one-armed scientist" (one who would not qualify his advice with "on the other hand") exemplifies the politician's demand for an unequivocal answer to the question of what ought to be done as well as to that of what can be done.

This situation has not escaped the attention of students of the role of scientists in the formation of public policy. The presence of, the demand for, and the exercise of value judgments has led to a sharp focus on the values, and thus on the motives, of the scientists who participate in the preparation of NAS reports that affect public policy.

The focus on scientists and their motives

In his book *The Brain Bank of America* (1975, p. 54) Boffey attributes self-serving motives to scientists who provide information and advice to the government within the framework of NAS committees, and thus questions their objectivity and honesty. For example:

The Academy claims that the most distinctive feature of its committees is that they are independent of any pressures of special interests.... But the Academy's record in recent years suggests that its protestations of Supreme Court impartiality should not be taken at face value. In actual practice, many of the Academy's reports have been influenced by powerful interests that have a stake in the questions under investigation.

Boffey admits, however, that "We found no cases of direct, personal conflict of interests at the Academy – no cases, for example, where a committee member profited financially as a direct result of the advice he rendered" (1975, p. 54). The charge that "many of the Academy's reports have been influenced by powerful interests" is directed toward the broader social and political motives which he claims influence scientists' judgments.

The NAS has already accepted the principle that the motives of scientists must be examined. Boffey (1975, p. 87) notes with approval that the NAS demands a "bias statement" from the scientists who provide information to the government, a report that is intended to reveal one's true interests, as may be inferred from a list of "all jobs, consultantships, and directorships held for the past 10 years, all current financial interests whose market value exceeds $10,000, or 10 percent of the individual's holdings; all sources of research support for the past five years, and any other information, such as public stands on an issue which 'might appear to other reasonable individuals as compromising of your independence of judgment.' " Thus the NAS has already fallen victim to the ethic of the lawyer (and the journalist). Trust no one, is the rule, unless they can offer this negative proof: I am not now, nor have I ever been, under the control of any incentive to lie, cheat, or otherwise compromise my judgment. Whereas this approach may begin with a request for a "self-report" on sources of bias, it seldom ends there, as scientists know all too well. Investigation is undertaken by others, and by other means, precisely because the focus has been successfully turned away from methods to persons and their motives.

The results of the focus on persons and their motives can be seen in

Polsby's review (1975) of Boffey's book. Polsby indicates what the results might have been had he taken a similar approach in his review by raising suspicions about Boffey's impartiality and thus his motives. That is, by using "Boffey's own primary method of demonstration: a glance at some-body's background gives a 'motive' for selected characteristics of his performance." Polsby finds that "Boffey's employer for the writing of this book was Ralph Nader (identified as 'consumer champion Ralph Nader' on p. 186), who of late has gotten rather heavily into the business of sponsoring exposés of establishment-type establishments.... Under these circumstances of employment, could Boffey have done other than to produce an attack, no matter how flimsily founded, on the Academy?" (1975, p. 666).

Polsby's review shows the customary result of such mutual destruction. Boffey's approach, he concludes, "is only good for so much mileage.... Arbitrarily imposing the symmetrical assumption ... that Boffey and the Academy are both fatally incapacitated by conflict of interest has the effect of condemning both the Academy and the book out of hand" (1975, p. 666). In short, because neither the critic nor those criticized can be trusted, the reader, the consumer, and the public remain buried in doubt as to where the truth lies. Thus, Polsby acknowledges that, "After reading *The Brain Bank of America* I do not know what to think about the Academy as an organization for evaluating the state of scientific knowledge" (1975, p. 666). In all likelihood, Polsby is not the only reader of Boffey's book who no longer knows what to think about the Academy.

It is precisely because scientists have learned that it is not only fruitless, but harmful, to focus on persons and their motives that they have learned to ignore them in their work as scientists. When scientists look for the truth and the truth appears to be in doubt, neither scientific work nor the scientific ethic requires the investigation of the characteristics of the person working on the problem: instead, they require the analysis of the method by which the results are produced. Unfortunately, in the confusion of the "endless debate" there has been a tendency to forget the scientific procedure and its associated ethics. The focus on persons and their motives has led not only to the filing of bias statements but to the advocacy of the adversary method for the settlement of disputes about the truth – a method which is ascientific not only in its procedure, but in its greater commitment to victory rather than to truth.

Scientists as adversaries

The concept of a "science court" reached Congress several years ago when Kantrowitz (in hearings before the House Committee on Rules and Administration in 1971) urged that members of Congress "appoint a science advocate for (each) side of the story...." He further suggested that a procedure be worked out which would be "modeled on the judicial procedure for proceeding in the presence of scientific controversy." The final judgment would be exercised by a group of scientific judges who would cross-examine each other and challenge each other's position. Kantrowitz's argument is currently being given serious consideration by members of the scientific community. *Physics Today* (published by the American Institute of Physics) recently indicated that a science court was worth trying, as did H. Guyford Stever, director of the National Science Foundation (see the article by Wilford, 1976).

Members of the scientific community are not unanimous, however, in their appraisal of the value of the adversary system, as the following interchange between Platt, Dror, and Waddington in a Ciba symposium indicates (Wolstenholme & O'Connor, 1975, p. 210):

PLATT: In the U.S. . . . we are beginning to have something called "adversary science," where scientists speak on public issues, doing their best, like lawyers, for a particular side, and then in a later case perhaps doing their best for the opposite side. The hope is that in this kind of open confrontation, as in a court of law, one comes closer to the truth than by having just accidents of committee structure or unanswered polemics decide the matter.

WADDINGTON: I would strongly oppose that way of advancing science.

PLATT: But somebody should make the total case for a nuclear plant, and somebody should make the total case against the plant for environmental reasons, so that we can see all of both sides before we decide.

DROR: Why shouldn't the two sides make two balanced presentations for and against? Why total . . . ?

PLATT: Do you know a better system?

DROR: Yes, reliance on professional judges in courts; and careful policy analysis on television for the public.

PLATT: Who judges the judges?

DROR: Who judges the juries?

WADDINGTON: That is a piece of politics, not a piece of learning. Learning is not advanced by legal procedures.

The above interchange not only indicates a divergence in viewpoint with regard to a science court and illustrates the morass (Who judges the judges? Who judges the juries?) into which scientists can be drawn because of the focus on persons, but it also points to the unproductiveness of the effort. Even if the concept of a science court were to be accepted by scientists, and even if scientists could be persuaded to make the "total case for (say) a nuclear plant" (Wolstenholme & O'Connor, 1975, p. 201), the adversary procedure would indicate only who had been judged to be the winner in the arena of competing scientific facts and scientific judgments. Integration of scientific judgments with social values would remain buried in the minds of the judges and the juries (and their judges): the "endless debate" would not be terminated.

It remains to be seen whether a science court, with its judges and juries and its ascientific adversary proceedings in which one scientist is pitted against another will be accepted by scientists. In any event, scientists not advocating the adversary method recommend a different ascientific method, the person-oriented approach.

Scientists' advocacy of the person-oriented approach

When scientists have addressed themselves to the function of human judgment in policy formation they have treated the unexamined intuitive abilities of persons as though they were somehow superior to the scientific method. For example, in its report on technology assessment to the House Committee on Science and Astronautics, the Committee on Public Engineering Policy (COPEP) of the National Academy of Engineering observed (Committee on Public Engineering Policy, 1969, p. 17) that "applying only cause-effect [i.e., scientific] methods to technology-initiated studies produces a mass of data but few broad conclusions." Apparently assuming that it had no other recourse, the committee called for "... contributions of talented individuals or groups who can intuitively perform analysis and evaluations...," an approach which "demands an integrated combination of information and value judgments that cannot always be formulated explicitly."

Not only does the COPEP report illustrate the advocacy of a person-oriented approach to the combination of "information and value judgments" that appeals to the mysterious as a substitute for the scientific method, it provides a clear case of the failure to recognize that it is precisely such person-oriented "combinations of information and value judgments that cannot always be formulated explicitly" that are defenseless against charges of self-serving bias.

Skolnikoff and Brooks (1975) were critical of the NAS study of science and public policy-making because it suggested that persons who provide science advice should have personal qualities of "intelligence, wisdom, judgment, humanity and perspective" on the ground that "These qualities are so obviously desirable for anybody in a high position that they are hardly helpful criteria." Yet they are as willing as COPEP or the NAS committee to let the process of combining facts and values remain subject to the unexamined vagaries of human judgment. For example (1975, p. 38):

Judgment on both technical and nontechnical issues and on their interaction is thus required [on policy issues]; a logically reasoned single answer is not possible. Judgment is necessarily affected by biases, policy preferences, ignorance differing estimates of the non-technical factors, and other vagaries. There is nothing wrong with this; it is unavoidable.

But there is something wrong with this, and this situation is avoidable. What is wrong is that both solutions indicated above focus on persons rather than on method, and both confuse scientific and valuative judgments. That is bad practice; it is bad for scientists, bad for leaders in government, and bad for the public that both are trying to serve. It is bad because it condones and encourages confusion of thought and function, substitutes an appeal to the unknown in place of the knowable, and makes scientists easy targets for charges of self-serving bias. The argument advanced by Skolnikoff and Brooks merely puts a brave face on a bad situation, for they imply that because scientific and valuative judgments cannot be separated there is nothing wrong with confusing them. That argument suggests that if such judgments could be separated, it would be wrong to confuse them. We argue that, from the point of view of science, it is not impossible in principle or in practice to achieve such a separation.[2]

A scientific approach toward the role of judgment would be quite different from the person-oriented approach that is embedded in the adversary system. A scientific approach would emphasize that judgment is a human cognitive activity and is therefore subject to scientific analysis, as are all natural phenomena. The premises of a scientific approach to the relation of science to public policy are: (i) human judgment is a critical part of the policy-making process; (ii) it is a part of the process that remains poorly understood; and (iii) it might well be improved through scientific study. Rather than searching for persons who possess mysterious talents, or indicating that the present situation is unavoidable, the scientific approach to this problem would be similar to the scientific approach to all problems: carry out theoretical and empirical analyses of the process in a manner that is subject to criticism and that provides cumulative knowledge.

The remainder of this article (i) provides an example that illustrates the social costs of employing the adversary system and the person-oriented approach and (ii) outlines a scientific framework for integrating scientific information and social values in the formation of public policy.[3]

An example of contrasting approaches

In 1974, the Denver Police Department (DPD), as well as other police departments throughout the country, decided to change its handgun ammunition. The principal reason offered by the police was that the

---

[2] There are clear indications that scientists are beginning to acknowledge the need for explicit methods for decision-making in areas where science and the public interest intersect. Two recent NAS committee reports (1975a, 1975b), as well as others mentioned in the latter describe the application of normative decision theory to such problems. Although these efforts represent a clear step forward through their insistence on the use of an explicit framework for decisions, they do not indicate how such decisions might be assisted or improved through the study of human judgment.

[3] For a general review of current research on judgment and decision-making see Slovic, Fischhoff, and Lichtenstein (1977). See also Kaplan and Schwartz (1975); Edwards, Guttentag, and Snapper (1975); Howard (1966); Raiffa (1968).

conventional round-nosed bullet provided insufficient "stopping effectiveness" (that is, the ability to incapacitate and thus to prevent the person shot from firing back at a police officer or others). The DPD chief recommended (as did other police chiefs) the conventional bullet be replaced by a hollow-point bullet. Such bullets, it was contended, flattened on impact, thus decreasing penetration, increasing stopping effectiveness, and decreasing ricochet potential.

The suggested change was challenged by the American Civil Liberties Union, minority groups, and others. Opponents of the change claimed that the new bullets were nothing more than outlawed "dum-dum" bullets, that they created far more injury than the round-nosed bullet, and should, therefore, be barred from use. As is customary, judgments on this matter were formed privately and then defended publicly with enthusiasm and tenacity, and the usual public hearings were held. Both sides turned to ballistics experts for scientific information and support.

Adversary, person-oriented approach

From the beginning both sides focused on the question of which bullet was best for the community. As a result of focusing on bullets and their technical ballistics characteristics, legislators and city councilmen never described the social policy that should control the use of force and injury in enforcing the law; they never specified the relative importance of the societal characteristics of bullets (injury, stopping effectiveness, or ricochet). Instead, the ballistics experts assumed that function. When the legislators requested their judgment as to which bullet was "best," the ballistics experts implicitly indicated the social policy that should be employed. That is, in recommending the use of a specific bullet, they not only implicitly recommended specific degrees of injury, stopping effectiveness, and ricochet, but also recommended a social policy regarding the relative importance of these factors. In short, the legislators' function was usurped by the ballistics experts, who thus became incompetent and unauthorized legislators – incompetent because of their lack of information about the social and political context in which a choice would be made; unauthorized because they assumed a function for which they had not been elected.

In parallel fashion, the ballistics experts turned their scientific-technical function over to those who should have formed social policy – the legislators. When the experts presented scientific information to policy-makers about various bullets, they found themselves disputing ballistics data with legislators who preferred a different type of bullet. Thus, the legislators, none of whom were ballistics experts, in their turn served as incompetent ballistics experts in the hearings.

When legislators and scientists accept the adversary system with its concomitant person-oriented approach as the primary means for integrating science and social values, they may expect to find a reversal of roles, and when scientists accept the person-oriented approach they may expect to be confronted by challenges to their objectivity.[4] The outcome is well represented by the comment of one legislator who said to an opponent (Public Broadcasting Service, 1975): "You have your expert and we have ours...."

A scientific approach

We now consider, by way of an example, a scientific method for integrating scientific information and social values that is scientifically, socially, and ethically defensible. This method was employed in solving the dispute about handgun ammunition for the police as described above. A broad outline of the method is presented (Hammond, Stewart, Adelman, & Wascoe, 1975).

The general framework of the method as it was applied to the above problem is shown in Figure 7.1. Basic to any policy involving scientific information are objectively measurable variables (Figure 7.1, left). Scientific judgments regarding the potential effects of technological alternatives are also required (Figure 7.1, middle). Finally, social value judgments by policy-makers or community representatives are necessary (Figure 7.1, right). The overall acceptability of an alternative is determined by how closely its potential effects satisfy the social values of the community.

Application of this framework to the bullet dispute involved three phases: (i) externalization of social value judgments; (ii) externalization of scientific judgments; and (iii) integration of social values and scientific judgments. Each phase is discussed in turn.

Phase 1: Externalizing social value judgments

The participants in phase 1 included the mayor and city council, other elected officials, representatives of the DPD (including the chief), and official representatives of community organizations, including minority groups and members of the general public. Each person was asked to

---

[4] Can the adversary system produce this confusion of roles at the national level, and does it have similar negative effects? Apparently it can, and does. For example, in Polsby's review of Boffey's book, Polsby (1975, p. 666) states: "Boffey notes, in criticizing a National Academy of Engineering committee on pollution abatement, that it was no more qualified than any other group of citizens to judge what should be 'wise' public policy." (In this instance, Boffey argues that scientists overstepped their bounds and should have confined their role to presenting the facts.) "Sound doctrine," observes Polsby, "and yet Boffey criticizes another of the Academy's committees for taking on an assignment pertinent to a naval communications project that did not include evaluating its 'desirability,' and for not venturing to raise 'questions as to the basic worth' of the space shuttle program." (In this instance, Boffey argues that scientists failed to help form social policy and thus failed in their responsibility to the public.) Thus, concludes Polsby, "the Academy is damned if it does pronounce on the overall wisdom of public policies, and damned if it doesn't."

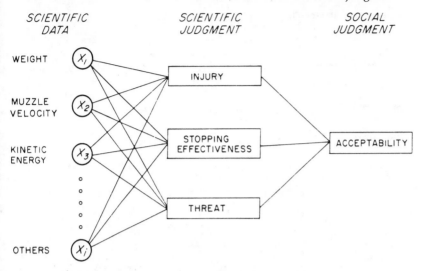

SCIENTIFIC
DATA

SCIENTIFIC
JUDGMENT

SOCIAL
JUDGMENT

Figure 7.1. A pictorial representation of a framework that combines scientific facts with social values.

make judgments concerning the relative desirability of hypothetical bullets, described in terms of their (i) stopping effectiveness, (ii) severity of injury, and (iii) threat to bystanders. These value judgments were made at the console of an interactive computer terminal. After their judgments were made, the participants were immediately shown the relative importance they gave to each of these three functional characteristics of bullets. That is, a statistical analysis was carried out on the data and the results were then displayed at the terminal for the participant to observe.[5] In addition, each participant was shown the form of the relation (linear, curvilinear) between his or her judgment and each of the three characteristics mentioned above. In this way, each participant saw the relative importance he or she attached to stopping effectiveness, injury, and threat to bystanders, as well as the optimal point for each (a typical display is shown in Figure 7.2).

After viewing the display, the participants were asked if the results reflected their considered judgment. The data, corrected when necessary, were then stored, and a cluster analysis was carried out in order to discover whether different groups held different judgment policies. Widely differing policies with regard to the relative importance of each

[5] To determine the relative importance a person places on each characteristic, linear multiple regression analysis was performed to obtain the beta weights on each of the three judgment dimensions, or factors. The absolute value of the beta weight for a factor was then divided by the sum of the absolute values of the beta weights over all factors to determine the relative weight, or importance place, on each factor. The relative weights were displayed on the computer console. For technical details on the procedure see Hammond, Stewart, Brehmer, and Steinmann (1975).

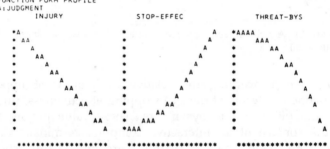

RELATIVE WEIGHT PROFILE

A : JUDGMENT
0.0------------------0.5------------------1.0   WEIGHT   FN FORM

INJURY
AAAAAAAAΛAAAAAAAAA   .41   NEGLIN

STOP-EFFEC
AAAAAAAAAAAAAAA   .34   NONLIN

THREAT-BYS
AAAAAAAAAΛ   .24   NONLIN

0.0------------------0.5------------------1.0

POLICY   CONSISTENCY
JUDGMENT   .95

FUNCTION FORM PROFILE
A:JUDGMENT
        INJURY   STOP-EFFEC   THREAT-BYS

Figure 7.2. A reproduction of a participant's interactive computer display of relative weights and functional relations. *FN*, function; *NEGLIN*, negative linear; *NONLIN*, nonlinear.

characteristic were found, although the functional relations between bullet characteristics and judgments were all found to be approximately linear in form.

The above procedure provides objective, visible data not otherwise available. The same procedure was used to externalize the required scientific judgments.

Phase 2: Externalizing scientific judgments

A panel was assembled that included one firearms expert, one ballistics expert, and three medical experts in wound ballistics. The judgments of these experts provided scientific information regarding the stopping effectiveness, severity of injury, and threat to bystanders of 80 bullets. The data for these bullets were obtained from the National Bureau of Standards. Each dimension (stopping effectiveness, injury, and threat to

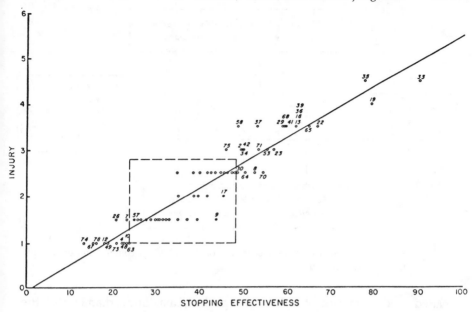

Figure 7.3. The average ratings of stopping effectiveness and injury are plotted above. Each point on the graph represents a bullet. The diagonal line, determined by linear regression analysis, indicates the average value of injury for bullets with a specific level of stopping effectiveness. Bullets above the line produce more injury than the average bullet with the same stopping effectiveness; bullets below the line produce less injury.

bystanders) was judged separately for each of the 80 bullets; agreement among the experts was found to be quite high.[6] Only the results for stopping effectiveness and injury are summarized here, as these were the central factors in the controversy.

Three factors were found to be important in judgments of stopping effectiveness: (i) The maximum diameter of the temporary wound cavity; (ii) the amount of kinetic energy lost by the bullet in the target; and (iii) the muzzle velocity of the bullet. The close, but not perfect, relation between stopping effectiveness and injury (shown in Figure 7.3) is reflected in the fact that independent judgments of potential injury were positively

[6] The judgment dimensions were defined as follows. (i) *Stopping effectiveness:* the probability that a 20- to 40-year-old man of average height (5'10") and weight (175 lbs) shot in the torso would be incapacitated and rendered incapable of returning fire. Judgments ranged from 0 to 100, indicating, on the average, how many men out of 100 would be stopped by a given bullet. (ii) *Severity of injury:* the probability that a man as described above, shot in the torso, would die within 2 weeks of being shot. (iii) *Threat to bystanders:* penetration was defined as a probability that a bullet would pose a hazard to others after passing through a person shot in the torso at a distance of 21 feet. Ricochet was defined as the probability that a bullet would pose a hazard after missing the intended target at a distance of 21 feet.

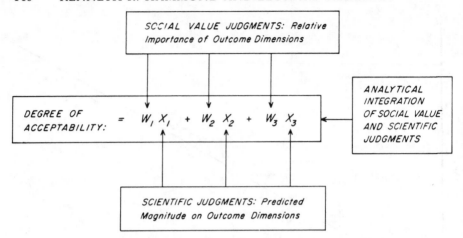

Figure 7.4. A schematic representation of the analytical combination of scientific facts and social values.

related to the amount of kinetic energy lost, maximum diameter of the temporary cavity, and degree of penetration.

The data in Figure 7.3 are important because they suggest that, contrary to previous, unexamined assumption, there is not a perfect relation between stopping effectiveness and injury; increasing one does not necessarily increase the other. These data illustrate the value of scientific information by indicating the possibility of finding a bullet that increases stopping effectiveness without increasing injury.[7]

Phase 3: Integrating social values and scientific information

Social value judgments and scientific judgments were combined by means of the equation in Figure 7.4, where the separation and combination of the judgments of policy-makers and scientists-technologists may be seen. We used the following algebraic form of this equation

$$Y_s = W_1X_1 + W_2X_2 + W_3X_3$$

where Y_s is the overall acceptability of a bullet; W_j, $j = 1.3$, indicates the weight, or relative importance policy-makers placed on stopping

[7] The separation of stopping effectiveness from injury that is indicated in the graph for bullet 9 was not due to inconsistencies and inaccuracies in the experts' ratings. The three medical experts agreed that the shape of the temporary cavity is an indicator of differences in severity of injury for bullets with the same stopping effectiveness. More severe wounds are produced by bullets that have a long, wide temporary cavity; less severe wounds localize the maximum diameter of their temporary cavity and do not penetrate deeply. According to all three experts, a temporary cavity that reaches a maximum diameter of 10 to 15 cm at 5 to 7 cm from the surface, and does not penetrate more than 15 cm, would provide the best compromise between stopping effectiveness and survivability.

effectiveness, injury, and threat to bystanders; and X_j, $j = 1$. 3 are the experts' judgments regarding stopping effectiveness, injury, and threat to bystanders.

Because phase 1 resulted in a variety of different weights on stopping effectiveness, injury, and threat to bystanders, the city council took all three factors into consideration by placing equal weight on each. As a result, when considering stopping effectiveness and severity of injury only, the appropriate bullet is one which lies farthest from the line of average relation in Figure 7.3, this distance from the line being measured perpendicularly from the point to the line. Bullet 9 in Figure 7.3 satisfies this criterion. It has greater stopping effectiveness and is less apt to cause injury (and less apt to threaten bystanders) than the standard bullet then in use by the DPD (bullet 57). In addition, bullet 9 (a hollow-point bullet) is less apt to cause injury than is bullet 17, the hollow-point bullet recommended by the DPD. Bullet 9 was accepted by the city council and all other parties concerned, and is now being used by the DPD.[8]

Finally, three points should be mentioned with regard to the application of judgment analysis to the above problem.

(1) Intense political and social conflict existed prior to our participation in the project. During the controversy a Denver police officer was killed by a hollow-point bullet; as a result, hundreds of policemen staged a march that ended in demands on both the police chief and the governor that the police be permitted to use hollow-point bullets. Members of the city council and others seemed convinced that the usual adversary methods had failed, and that they faced a dangerous impasse. The fact that the above procedures were used in these circumstances indicates that elected officials and special interest groups can accept a scientific approach to critical social problems, even when they have become immersed in sharp political dispute. Moreover, interviews with members of the city council and others not only indicated a high degree of satis-faction with the procedure but appreciation of its impersonal approach as well.

(2) The procedures were applied to complex technical judgments. As far as we could determine, at the time of the research no standard quantifiable definition of severity of injury (with regard to handgun ammunition) had ever been developed. Moreover, in developing such a definition, and in making their judgments, the ballistics experts con-sidered 11 distinct characteristics of handgun ammunition.

(3) The procedure is general in nature. Despite the apparent simplicity of the framework presented in Figure 7.4, judgment analysis can be

---

[8] The time, manpower, and cost of the handgun study were as follows. (i) The project was completed in 6 weeks and (ii) research personnel included four people of whom one worked full time. Total cost, including salaries of the project staff, did not exceed $6000; an additional $3500 was required to pay the travel and consulting costs of the ballistics experts.

applied to a variety of complex problems involving value judgments and scientific judgments by differentiating the elements in Figure 7.4 in a hierarchical fashion.[9]

Scientific defensibility

The above method is scientifically defensible, not because it is flawless (it isn't), but because it is readily subject to scientific criticism. It is vulnerable to such criticism (i) because its aim is to meet appropriate standards regarding replication, quantification, and logic for the problem under study (an aim all scientific efforts share) and (ii) because the procedure for achieving that aim is public (as all scientific effort must be). The locus and degree of imperfection in method and procedure are thus available for public inspection and subsequent improvement. In short, the process provides the opportunity for cumulative knowledge, as scientific efforts should.

Social responsibility

The above method is socially responsible because it provides a public framework for (i) separating technical, scientific judgment from social value judgments and (ii) integrating them analytically, not judgmentally. The separation phase permits elected representatives to function exclusively as policy-makers, and scientists to function exclusively as scientists. Neither role is confused or exchanged because policy-makers are not forced to become amateur scientists, nor are scientists required to make judgments on public policy. The integrative phase provides an overt, rather than covert, process for combining facts and values. Because the social values in the community are identified before the decision is implemented, the decision process is not seen to be a mere defense of a predetermined choice; rather it can be evaluated in terms of its rational basis before the final choice is made.

Ethical standards

Ethical and scientific standards converge in the process of combining facts and values because both scientific ethics and public ethics require controls against bias. Scientific control against bias is illustrated by the use of the double-blind control in experiments; in the above procedure public control against bias is carried out by a similar blindness. That is, the method described above has the advantage of situating all parties (policy-makers, scientists, and the public) behind what Rawls (1971, p. 136) calls

---

[9] For examples of the application of a hierarchical framework, see Hammond, Rohrbaugh, Mumpower, and Adelman (1977).

"a veil of ignorance." It fits Rawls' requirement that the participants should not "know how the various alternatives [would] affect their own particular case and they are obliged to evaluate principles solely on the basis of general considerations." In the approach described above, the technical experts were not aware of the relative importance the policy-makers placed on the three societal characteristics of bullets, nor were the policy-makers aware of the technical judgments made by the scientists-technologists in regard to specific bullets. In short, by implementing Rawls' veil of ignorance, both scientific and ethical standards were met.

Conclusion

Current efforts to integrate scientific information and social values in the forming of public policy are confused and defeated by the widespread use of ascientific methods – the adversary system and the person-oriented approach. The adversary system suffers from an ascientific commitment to victory rather than truth; the person-oriented approach suffers from an ascientific focus on persons and their motives rather than on the adequacy of methods. The reason for the widespread use of both lies in the failure to recognize that human judgment can be brought under scientific, rather than ad hominem, analysis. The argument advanced here is that a scientifically, socially, and ethically defensible means for integrating science and human values can be achieved.

8. The Central Arizona Water Control Study: A case for multiobjective planning and public involvement

Curtis A. Brown

This paper describes and evaluates the application of a multiobjective planning framework, incorporating substantial public involvement, to a major water resources development decision involving considerable conflict. The study helped to resolve more than a decade of controversy and bitter attacks and facilitated the development of broad support for a new plan. This study demonstrates the importance of a multiobjective approach to planning at a time when multiobjective planning is being de-emphasized in the Federal guidelines for water resources planning in favor of a greater emphasis on maximization of economic benefits. The study described is the Central Arizona Water Control Study (CAWCS), funded to examine water storage and flood control alternatives in the Phoenix, Arizona, metropolitan area.

Study setting

Historically, Phoenix has been subjected to flooding on the Salt River which flows through the center of the metropolitan area. In addition to structures for flood control, the State of Arizona has long sought additional reservoir storage for irrigation in the Phoenix area. These reservoirs, termed regulatory storage reservoirs, would hold water pumped from the Granite Reef Aqueduct during periods of low demand and release this water during the summer months. In 1976, the Bureau of Reclamation (Bureau) published an Environmental Impact Statement (EIS) proposing the construction of a flood control and regulatory storage structure, called Orme Dam, at the confluence of the Salt and Verde Rivers a few miles upstream from Phoenix (Bureau of Reclamation, 1976).

This chapter is a revision of an article that originally appeared in the *Water Resources Bulletin*, 1984, *20*(3), 331–337. Copyright © 1984 by the American Water Resources Association. Reprinted by permission.

For the 1976 EIS a number of alternative sites had been evaluated using the criteria of (1) storage capacity, (2) flood control, (3) recreation, (4) fish and wildlife benefits, and (5) power generation. The Orme site was recommended as the best of two possible alternatives that provided full flood control and storage benefits with a single structure.

Publication of the EIS and recommendation of the construction of Orme Dam brought strong public reaction. While Orme Dam would provide flood control and storage for irrigation, it would also require relocation of virtually the entire Yavapai Indian Tribe residing along the Verde River in the Fort McDowell Indian Reservation and inundation of streamside wildlife habitat that supports bald eagle nesting activities. The controversy and opposition to the proposed project were significant enough to halt the planning process. In April 1977, Orme Dam was 1 of 19 water projects halted by President Carter's "hit list."

Support for Orme Dam might have waned at this point if not for three major floods in 1978 and 1979 that caused approximately $200,000,000 in damages in the Phoenix area and the loss of seven lives. After the 1978 floods, pro-Orme groups blamed the Indians and environmentalists for the flood damages they felt could have been prevented by Orme Dam, and the opponents of the dam blamed the State and operators of the existing dams for "outmoded water policies" that prevented safe storage of the floodflows (Arizona Republic, 1978a, 1978d, 1978e; Arizona Daily Star, 1978; Scottsdale Daily Progress, 1978; State Press-ASU, 1978).

Public demands for a solution grew and political representatives pushed for reinstatement of Orme as part of the Central Arizona Project (Arizona Republic, 1978b, 1978c; Central Phoenix Sun, 1978). In response to these requests, a special planning study was initiated by the Bureau to study alternative solutions to the problem, including Orme Dam. The study, called the Central Arizona Water Control Study, began in July 1978.

The Central Arizona Water Control Study

The goal of the study was to find a plan that could address the various issues, including flood control, water storage, environmental concerns, and social concerns, and be acceptable to the many parties involved. The social context for the study presented many difficulties. The various interest groups were strongly polarized. At the start of the study, most local and state politicians strongly supported the Orme alternative, which had previously been halted because of the public controversy it generated. In addition, the recent floods put considerable pressure on the study team to develop a solution quickly.

To succeed, the study had to develop public support and trust, examine all reasonable alternatives, and yet not unduly delay selection of a plan. The general structure of the study was similar in many respects to the "iterative open planning process" (IOPP) proposed by Ortolano (1974). The IOPP is composed of four planning stages – problem identification, plan formulation, impact assessment, and evaluation – with continuous interaction between planners and the affected publics at each stage. The CAWCS design emphasized:

Multiobjective plan formulation and evaluation. The previous study, which had recommended Orme Dam, had employed multiple criteria to evaluate a number of plans that had been formulated primarily to address two objectives: flood control and regulatory storage. CAWCS was designed to use a broader set of objectives, including environmental and social objectives, to *formulate* plans, not just to evaluate plans. Emphasis was also placed on examining combinations of sites, not just single-structure alternatives.

An open planning process. While the previous study had obtained study review from a wide array of agencies and groups, public participation in the actual planning process was limited. The CAWCS study placed considerable emphasis on involving the public in all phases of the study process – from the generation to the evaluation of alternative plans. In addition, an independent consulting firm was hired to perform many of the sensitive environmental and social impact assessment studies and coordinate the public involvement program.

Public involvement

Public involvement is a systematic process that informs the public about decisions that may affect their lives and provides opportunities for the public to participate in the decision making process. Public involvement was a major aspect of the study, employing a wide range of activities. Many of the public meetings and workshops are discussed in the following description of the study. In addition to these activities, the public involvement program employed:

A Governor's Advisory Committee. Governor Babbitt appointed a 28-member committee, representing all major interest groups, to provide study guidance. Interests represented included municipalities, the business community, water development concerns, the League of Women Voters, environmental groups, Indian representatives, and public utilities. The committee, which met 19 times from June 1979 to October 1981, received numerous briefings on the study, provided comments, and served as a vehicle for obtaining public and political support for study findings.

The Technical Agency Group (TAG). This group was established as an advisory committee for technical aspects of the study, representing approximately 50 groups and agencies. The group met 24 times between

January 1979 and September 1981. The TAG facilitated discussion and resolution of technical problems as the study progressed. Comments made during the evaluation of the TAG process indicated that participants felt the TAG was unwieldy due to its size but necessary to resolve technical issues before facing the public. They felt that the TAG helped build credibility for technical aspects of the study and that it permitted review of the technical analyses without having to wait for the EIS (Bureau of Reclamation, 1982).

A mailing list. The mailing list of interest groups and individuals was continually updated and contained 4,386 entries by the end of the study.

Newsletters. Twenty-three newsletters were sent to the mailing list between January 1979 and November 1981. This was one of the most important and effective means for keeping the public appraised of study progress and upcoming activities, and public response to the newsletters was very favorable.

Factbooks. Four detailed factbooks were prepared for the public at key points in the study in order to provide information upon which to make a judgment or provide comments. While the newsletters provided general information and summaries of study findings, the factbooks carried the main burden of providing the public with technical detail and explanation. The final factbook was 150 pages and was accompanied by a 40-page summary. Providing these data throughout the study not only enhanced the quality of public input but also reduced the chances for the sort of unpleasant surprises and subsequent attacks which can occur when the public does not receive this information until publication of a draft EIS.

Briefings. Between July 1979 and November 1981, 26 briefings were held for elected officials and the media, including local city mayors, the Yavapai Tribal Council, the Governor, the State legislature, and the congressional delegation.

Public presentations. Over 150 presentations were given to civic groups, Government agencies, professional organizations, and other interested publics during the course of the study (Bureau of Reclamation, 1982).

Defining roles of study participants

The study process was designed to perform two parallel functions: fact identification and value identification. The goal of value identification was to identify the social objectives that the plans would address and to use that information in both the formulation and evaluation of plans. The primary source of value information was the public, through public involvement activities.

The goal of fact identification was to assess the technical feasibility of proposed plans and to determine their impact on the objectives. Technical facts were identified through studies performed by the Bureau of Reclamation, the Army Corps of Engineers, the U.S. Fish and Wildlife Service, and private consultants.

While planners should strive not to confuse judgments of fact with statements of value, the distinction between facts and values is blurred at the boundary. For example, while the public can specify that a riverine ecosystem is highly valued, technical specialists must make judgments about the best way to measure impacts to the ecosystem. Those judgments, such as which components of the ecosystem to measure, are not entirely value free. To maintain study credibility, such "boundary" judgments and assumptions must be well documented and subject to early public review (see, for example, Stewart, Dennis & Ely, 1984).

Also, planners must keep in mind that people have relatively few basic values (Rokeach, 1973) and cannot immediately apply these values to specific, often complex, alternatives. In order to reach a value judgment about a proposed action, individuals must be helped to understand how that action affects their own needs and goals. This requires both information about the action and time to consider its relationship to more basic values. If the public is rushed into making value statements about specific alternatives without sufficient time or information, unstable, unreliable responses may result which may misdirect the planning process (see Fischhoff, Slovic, & Lichtenstein, 1980). Therefore, time and information are two key components of any public involvement process.

Strategy for evaluation of alternatives

Most planning studies are a compromise between exhaustive analysis and practicality. While fully "rational" planning requires generation and evaluation of all potential alternatives, most studies must adopt economizing strategies to reduce the burden of data collection and evaluation. The CAWCS adopted the strategy of screening out poor alternatives as early as possible, subjecting only the most promising alternatives to full multiattribute analysis. The general design for CAWCS was:

1. Define study goals and generate potential plan elements (individual actions or structures) that might each partially meet the goals.
2. Screen out plan elements having unacceptable characteristics with respect to a set of critical factors (e.g. unsuitable damsite geology).
3. Combine remaining elements into 10 to 20 systems, or groups of elements that work together to address all goals.
4. Perform preliminary evaluation of systems on all objectives. Screen out poor performers.

5. Perform detailed multiattribute evaluation on remaining set of alternative systems.

This type of approach focuses the major effort on the most promising alternatives. As with all economizing strategies, it does carry some risk of desirable alternatives being screened out because they perform poorly on one "critical" factor. To guard against this possibility it is important that options are screened out only for "fatal flaws" – negative impacts that cannot be offset by any reasonable degree of benefits on other factors.

Description of the study

Stage I – June 1978

The goals of Stage I were to identify study objectives and potential actions that could achieve these objectives. Preliminary objectives identified by previous studies, the public, and interested agencies were:

1. Water supply
2. Flood control
3. Energy conservation and production
4. Water quality
5. Vegetation and wildlife
6. Recreation
7. Social considerations
8. Cultural resources
9. Preservation of water rights
10. Safety of dams

Three public meetings were held during Stage I to inform the public about the study process and to solicit their suggestions for study objectives and potential alternatives. A number of alternatives were suggested by the public and analyzed by the technical staff, including specific damsites, nonstructural alternatives for flood control, use of floodflows to recharge groundwater supplies, and changes in the operation of existing dams to provide additional flood storage. In all, over 30 structural (e.g., dams, levees) and nonstructural (e.g., floodplain management) elements were identified during Stage I. Fourteen of these elements were screened out as unfeasible on the basis of technical problems (e.g., geologic problems at the proposed damsite prevented a safe structure), or prohibitive cost, or ineffectiveness in meeting the objectives (Bureau of Reclamation, 1980).

Stage II – March 1980

Plan elements passing the screening were carried into Stage II where they were evaluated in more detail to determine their technical feasibility, cost, and environmental and social effects. Nine public workshops were held during this stage to report the results of the Stage I screening of individual plan elements and to obtain the public's suggestions for additional alternatives or additional factors that should be used to evaluate alternatives. Workshop participants generally agreed that all major alternatives had been identified, and helped to define the most critical aspects for the study objectives (for example, that transportation disruption was the most significant impact of flooding).

To this stage the study had examined only separate plan elements; that is, individual actions or structures that were sometimes redundant in purpose with other elements being evaluated. The next screening of alternatives was aimed at selecting the best element from each group of elements performing the same function, such as the best of the elements providing flood control on the Verde River, the best of the regulatory storage elements for the Agua Fria River, the best nonstructural flood control plan, and so on. Each set of elements was evaluated on the relevant subset of study objectives and the best performing element selected. Ten "best" elements remained, including eight structural and two nonstructural elements. Since no single element could achieve all of the study objectives, elements were next combined into 15 systems, each system composed of a set of elements that worked well together. For example, one system called for constructing a new dam on the Verde River and enlarging two existing dams on the Salt River. These structures, together with downstream flood plain management, would provide flood control, regulatory storage for the aqueduct, hydropower, and limited additional recreation facilities. At the close of Stage II, four public forums were held to present the alternative systems and obtain comments and questions from the public (Bureau of Reclamation, 1981a).

Stage III – January 1981

At the start of Stage III, more detailed evaluations of each system were performed. Some systems were eliminated because a constituent element had been found on further analysis to be prohibitively expensive. The remaining systems were rated on the basis of their performance on the study objectives, and clearly inferior systems were eliminated, i.e., plans were eliminated if they performed more poorly than other plans on most, if not all, objectives. This left eight "candidate" plans that all performed well on many objectives and represented the range of possible kinds of actions. As is standard practice, this group included a "no action" alternative.

Advanced technical studies for these eight plans were done in hydrology, sizing and operations of structures, design and cost estimation, economics, financial (cost repayment) analysis, recreation, environmental impacts, and social impacts. A detailed Factbook was

Table 8.1 *Plan evaluation factors for the public values assessment*

Water quality	Non-Indian relocations
Stream habitat	Flood control
Lake habitat	Stream recreation
Threatened and endangered species	Lake recreation
Prehistoric cultural resources	Net economic benefits
Historic sites	Total cost
Indian relocations	Regulatory storage

prepared for public distribution comparing the impacts of each plan on the study objectives. Over 75 specific characteristics of the plans were assessed, ranging from the level of flood protection provided at the Phoenix Municipal Airport and the number of bridges that would remain in service during a flood, to the number of families relocated from the reservoir sites and the number of bald eagle nesting sites inundated (Bureau of Reclamation, 1981a).

Of the remaining alternatives, no plan was clearly outperformed by a better plan, because each plan performed very well on some objectives. In order to choose among plans that have different benefits and costs on multiple objectives, it is necessary to specify the relative importance of the various objectives. Without this information, plan selection cannot proceed.

To obtain information on the relative importance of the study objectives, public participation in a "public values assessment" (PVA) was solicited in August 1981. Representatives from 60 public groups and organizations participated in the process (Bureau of Reclamation, 1981b). The set of plan characteristics was first reduced to a set of 14 major factors that were both important to the public and differentiated between plans (Table 8.1). Representatives then assigned "importance weights" to the factors to reflect their own values (i.e., which factor did they consider most important, second in importance, etc.). The group representatives were divided into seven clusters sharing similar views, and a values profile was developed and approved by each cluster. These seven profiles were then used to evaluate the performance of the eight plans as measured on the 14 factors. This produced ratings of the eight plans for each of the seven clusters as shown in Figure 8.1. This type of public values analysis has been used successfully to aid decisionmakers in other public policy conflicts (Dennis, Stewart, Middleton, Downton, Ely, & Keeling, 1983; Rorhbaugh & Wehr, 1978; Hammond & Adelman, 1976; Gardiner & Edwards, 1975). The PVA process is described in more detail in Rozelle (1982).

The results of the analysis were striking (Figure 8.1). First, none of the plans involving Orme Dam (plans 3, 4, and 5) was rated high by any of the value policies, not even by the cluster of groups representing water

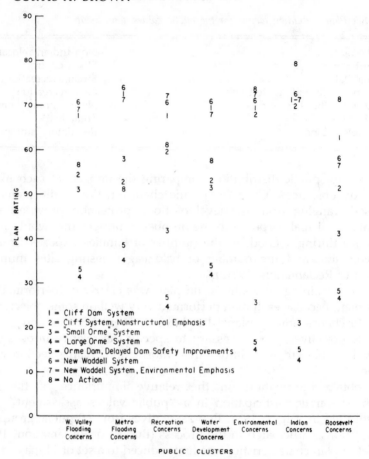

Figure 8.1 Plan ratings for each public cluster.

development concerns or by the two clusters most concerned with flood control. This indicated that, in spite of longstanding public promotion of Orme Dam by these groups, other alternatives were available that fit more closely with their value positions. The poor performance of the Orme Dam alternatives was due to two things: (1) Orme performed poorly on factors that many groups considered very important (environmental and social impacts and cost) and (2) other plans were available that performed nearly as well as Orme Dam on the other critical factors (flood control, regulatory storage).

It appeared that, at the very least, Orme Dam could be eliminated as a viable alternative based on this analysis. This was a remarkable finding considering the continuing strong support expressed for Orme Dam by some public groups and the great majority of local and State politicians, including the congressional delegation (Arizona Republic, 1981a; The Times, 1981).

Further analysis suggested that Plan 6 might be a viable compromise plan; four of the seven value policies ranked it first, and it was highly ranked for the remaining three. This plan avoided the major environmental and social impacts associated with the confluence (Orme) damsite, the impacts that had created opposition to the original Orme proposal. Regulatory storage would be provided by an enlarged reservoir (New Waddell) on the Agua Fria River, west of Phoenix, and flood control would be provided by one new, one enlarged, and one rebuilt dam on the Salt and Verde Rivers. The results of the public values assessment were presented to the PVA participants in a followup meeting in September 1981 and in a newsletter to all study participants.

On October 2, 1981, the Governor's Advisory Committee voted 19 to 1 to recommend Plan 6 to the Governor (Phoenix Gazette, 1981). On November 12, 1981, the Secretary of the Interior confirmed Plan 6 as the Bureau's recommended plan, stating, "The logic for the selection of Plan 6 as the proposed action is the strong local support, the functional ability to meet statutory obligations required by the authorizing legislation and the fact that impacts on the Fort McDowell Indian Tribe are avoided" (Department of the Interior, 1981).

In a short span, many public groups and politicians, longtime supporters of Orme Dam, chose to support Plan 6 (known as the Waddell Plan) (Scottsdale Daily Progress, 1981; Arizona Republic, 1981b). Said Senator Barry Goldwater, "I don't know why someone didn't dream up the Waddell Dam a long time ago" (New York Times, 1981). And Congressman Morris Udall reflected, "The Orme Dam was a critically important issue to Arizona.... But we finally ended up, to my utter amazement, with the whole Arizona establishment agreeing we really didn't want the dam" (Gendlin, 1982).

Afternote

Following the selection of a preferred alternative by the Secretary, an EIS was prepared and formal EIS hearings held in June 1983. Some conservation groups continue to oppose Cliff Dam, one of the flood control components of Plan 6. However, there appears to be continuing, broad support for Plan 6 as a whole. Perhaps the most enduring result of the study is the virtually unanimous agreement that an Orme Dam alternative is not needed, that a better alternative exists. It is this shift in opinion that probably contributed most to the reduction in conflict.

Discussion

What made CAWCS work? It cannot be argued that just any type of study would have succeeded – a previous study had produced only conflict. The combination of the previous study, followed by CAWCS, approximated a naturalistic experiment testing the efficacy of planning methods used in CAWCS but not the earlier study, primarily the increased emphasis on public involvement and multiobjective planning. It is unusual in the policy sciences to have such a test of basic planning principles. One seldom gets to make a major decision twice, using different methods, and observe the outcome.

A summary of factors that appear to have promoted success include:

Motivation to seek a solution. Because of the longstanding concern for flood control and the recent flooding events, almost every party to the decision was motivated to find a solution. A major difficulty for CAWCS was to keep this motivation from precipitating a rush to select an alternative prematurely.

Public involvement. The public involvement program was largely successful in achieving the goals of public information and participation, as delineated by Kauffman and Shorett (1977), and Schierow and Chesters (1983). For example, of those responding to a post-CAWCS evaluation, 84 percent felt their views had been considered in the study decisions (Bureau of Reclamation, 1982). Broad-based public involvement gave the public a feeling of commitment to the study process and its results. By using public values in plan formulation and selection, the study increased the likelihood of citizen support for the study recommendations, even when such recommendations were not exactly to an individual group's liking.

Multiobjective planning. CAWCS emphasized the importance of multiobjective planning characterized by multiobjective plan *formulation*, not just evaluation. The earlier study had formulated plans primarily on the basis of two objectives and later evaluated them on five criteria. CAWCS both formulated and evaluated plans on a much larger set of objectives that had been selected to reflect public concerns. It is notable that the final decision hinged on social impacts, a factor that had not been included as an objective in the previous study.

The interaction between the setting of objectives and the generation of alternatives is illustrated by the case of the New Waddell damsite. The previous study, which recommended Orme Dam, formulated plans on the basis of flood control and regulatory storage. At that time the Waddell site was rejected on the basis of a preliminary engineering judgment that the site geology was not suitable (Bureau of Reclamation, 1976, p. 322). However, since one of the objectives of CAWCS was to minimize adverse social impacts, the Waddell site was reexamined because it avoided those negative impacts. On reexamination, a suitable placement of the New Waddell Dam was found nearby.

The multiobjective framework thus led to the development of a superior alternative for two reasons. First, by broadening the set of objectives it forced the analysis of a broader set of alternatives to meet those objectives. The alternatives also became more complex, since no single structure could meet all of the study goals. Second, the identification of additional objectives forced reconsideration of previously unacceptable tradeoffs. Alternatives previously rejected, based on a few factors, now performed well, based on the full set of objectives. A multiobjective approach does not guarantee that a good plan can be found, but it improves the odds of finding such a plan, if it exists.

While accepting the Waddell Plan represented a compromise on the part of some groups, the Plan addresses virtually all major concerns. This underscores the fact that formulation of good alternatives is fundamental to production of compromise or consensus. Public involvement is necessary to develop support for even the best alternative, but it cannot "sell" a poor plan.

Sufficient resources committed. CAWCS was a large study, among the largest conducted by the Bureau. While only a dozen Bureau people comprised the core planning staff, hundreds of Bureau, Army Corps of Engineers, and contract staff were involved in aspects of the study. The amount of resources committed to social and environmental impact assessment and to public involvement was larger than for most studies because of the significance of these issues. Such a study requires staff, time, and money, and, when time is short, more money. For example, in CAWCS the tight schedule for getting information to the public often required rush printing of documents, which doubled printing costs.

Involvement of key decisionmakers. The survival of any recommendation depends upon the support of key decisionmakers. Considerable effort was made in CAWCS to maintain the involvement and support of important officials and decisionmakers. As noted, the GAC was important for maintaining involvement of not only the Governor but a wide range of influentials in the State. Regular briefings of local and State politicians and the Congressional delegation kept these individuals apprised of study developments so that they were not surprised by the release of study results that might contradict their public positions.

Patience and flexibility of decisionmakers. In the face of strong pressure to adopt the Orme Dam solution to the frequent floods, key decisionmakers within the Bureau and without, allowed the study to proceed in an open, deliberate fashion. While CAWCS may have been a case of "speaking truth to power" (Wildavsky, 1979), it was also an example of decisionmakers showing the flexibility to change long held personal and public positions in response to changing information and public attitudes.

The cost of CAWCS

Study costs for the June 1978 to March 1983 period were approximately $14,000,000 and public involvement costs were approximately $1,000,000. The cost for constructing Plan 6 is estimated at approximately $1 billion. This makes the study costs and public involvement costs roughly 1.4 percent and 0.01 percent of the construction cost, respectively. Was this money well spent?

In answering such questions, one can only try to estimate the economic efficiency of study expenditures in achieving study goals. How much is it worth to achieve resolution of a problem? Will a proposed study achieve resolution? While it is impossible to precisely estimate the benefit/cost ratio for a planning study, these types of questions should be asked when designing or evaluating any program. For CAWCS, the benefits of resolution, or of avoiding each additional year of delay, might be considered roughly equivalent to the annual Plan 6 net benefits, presently estimated at $20,000,000 (Bureau of Reclamation, 1981a). It is harder to estimate the likelihood of further delays and possible litigation if less money and effort had been spent. The only point of comparison is the earlier study which resulted in a delay of at least five years.

Implications for Federal water resources planning

On February 3, 1983, the President signed the new Principles and Guidelines for Federal Water and Land Resources Planning (P&G) (U.S. Water Resources Council, 1983). Among the many changes made from previous Federal guidelines, the P&G restructured the set of objectives for water resources planning. The previous guidelines (U.S. Water Resources Council, 1973) specified two co-equal objectives: national economic development and environmental quality. Plans were formulated to meet these objectives and were then evaluated on those two criteria plus regional economic development and contribution to social well-being. The P&G now emphasize a single planning objective, instructing that "the Federal objective of water and related land resources project planning is to contribute to national economic development consistent with protecting the Nation's environment" (Section IIa), and "The alternative plan with the greatest net economic benefit consistent with protecting the Nation's environment (the NED Plan), is to be selected unless the Secretary of a department or the head of an independent agency grants an exception to this Rule" (Section X 1.10.1).

While it is possible to interpret this language as restricting plan formulation to National Economic Development, the P&G in fact encourages considerable latitude in the formulation of plans to meet multiple, local objectives (see P&G, 1.6.4, 5b-5c). It should also be noted that achieving multiple objectives is not necessarily inconsistent with attaining National

Economic Development. The New Waddell Plan, for example, has among the highest net economic benefits of any plan considered. If water resources planners narrowly construe the P&G and formulate plans only to maximize the NED objective, they may very well miss those alternatives that meet the NED objective and also address other issues that affect a plan's social, environmental, and political viability.

Part III
Economics

Economists generally think of people as individuals who must spend their money in order to obtain desired goods. Obviously, good judgment and careful decisions are essential to this endeavor. Indeed, economists have usually assumed that humans are not only rational decision makers but fully informed consumers who want to maximize their happiness and well-being through careful allocation of their limited resources. Research in judgment and decision making has brought this optimistic view of our economic decision-making ability under attack, however, for being too simple and not in conformity with the facts.

In the 1950s Herbert Simon coined the term *bounded rationality* to denote our inability to think completely rationally about all facets of an economic situation. In the 1960s and 1970s Slovic and Lichtenstein found that people might prefer to play gamble *A* rather than gamble *B*; yet these same people would assign a higher monetary value to gamble *B*! Research findings such as these suggested that strict dollars-and-cents considerations alone could not explain economic behavior. If these were the only considerations people used, Las Vegas would be a dusty town in the desert, and insurance companies would be nonexistent. Because gamblers and insurance policy holders in the aggregate lose millions of dollars every year, psychological factors must exert some influence over economic ones.

As early as the 18th century Daniel Bernoulli noted the discrepancy between the theory of the rational actor and behavior in the marketplace and suggested one way to explain what might appear to be economic irrationality. He hypothesized that people might not try to maximize the *value* they received for their money and effort. Instead, people would try to maximize *utility*. For example, $10 might be twice as useful to me as $5, but $10,000 is not twice as useful as $5,000. The marginal utility of money lessens as one gets wealthier. Due to factors such as these, utility (subjective) and value (objective) might not always correspond.

Bernoulli was not the last theoretician who attempted to introduce psychological factors into the analysis of economic decision making. The most recent and most influential attempt is "Prospect Theory," devised by Daniel Kahneman and Amos Tversky. The first article, by Richard H. Thaler, shows how one economist was influenced by research in judgment and decision making. The chapter by Slovic illustrates how such research can uncover information about the judgment processes of investment bankers. Finally, the chapter by Kahneman and Tversky will bring the reader up to date with regard to the psychology of choosing and deciding.

9. Illusions and mirages in public policy

Richard H. Thaler

Like most people, I have always found optical illusions fascinating. Figure 9.1 is a scale drawing of the world's largest man-made optical illusion – the Gateway Arch in St. Louis. Although it appears to be at least 50 percent taller than it is wide, the height and width are actually equal. This optical illusion is an example of what I will call "judgmental illusions": Somehow the mind is fooled into making an error of judgment. We all erroneously judge the arch's height to be greater than its width.

Another type of optical illusion is the mirage. We have all experienced the illusion of "seeing" water on a perfectly dry highway on a hot day. Such mirages on the desert are commonplace. Mirages, like judgmental illusions, fool the mind. We are fooled into believing that an object exists when it does not.

The subject of this essay is not optical illusions, but rather the related concept of cognitive illusion. Like optical illusions, cognitive illusions can be of two types. Judgmental cognitive illusions induce people to misestimate magnitudes, and in a specific direction. Other cognitive illusions are like mirages: A situation is structured such that we are fooled into thinking we have many choices when in fact only one really exists. Both kinds of cognitive illusions have powerful influences on how people make choices – in their private lives and in the realm of public policy.

Four illusions

The following example of a judgmental cognitive illusion will be familiar to anyone who has taken a course in probability theory:

This chapter originally appeared in *The Public Interest*, 1983, *73*, 60–74. Copyright © 1983 by National Affairs, Inc. Reprinted by permission.

Figure 9.1. The Gateway Arch in St. Louis (scale drawing).

A class has 25 students in it. What is the chance that at least two students will have a common birthday?

Most people guess that the chance of a match is pretty small, perhaps one in ten or one in 20. In fact, the chance of at least one pair of students having the same birthday is better than 50–50.

The interesting thing about this problem is that it affects almost everyone the same way. We all judge the chance of a match to be smaller than it really is. This is the defining characteristic of a judgmental cognitive illusion: The problem induces predictable errors in a particular direction.

Can such cognitive illusions that create errors in judgment also create errors in contemporary public policy debates? Yes – and to illustrate this I have selected several examples that relate to our perceptions of risk and uncertainty. The first tests one's ability to estimate magnitudes:

What is the relative frequency of homicides and suicides in the United States?

Most people think homicides are much more common, when in fact suicides are more common – in one recent year there was 27,300 suicides and 20,400 homicides. (This is true in spite of the fact that the official statistics understate the true level of suicides. Many suicides are classified as accidental deaths.) Why do we guess that homicides are more common? Well, often when we have to estimate the frequency of an event or class of events we do so by judging the ease with which we can recall instances of it. Psychologists Daniel Kahneman and Amos Tversky call this the *availability heuristic* (Kahneman, Slovic, & Tversky, 1982). The availability heuristic is usually a good way to estimate frequency because ease of recall is usually highly correlated with actual frequency. Sometimes, however, availability and frequency diverge. Since homicides receive more publicity than suicides, they are more available, and thus are erroneously judged to be more common.

The next example, first devised by Daniel Ellsberg, consists of an imaginary lottery:

You are shown three urns, each containing 100 balls. Urn A has 50 red and 50 black balls, urn B has 80 red and 20 black balls, and urn C has 20 red and 80 black balls. You are given *a choice between two lotteries. You can take lottery A, in which a ball will be picked at random from urn A. If the ball picked is red you win $100, otherwise you win nothing. Alternatively, you can take lottery BC. In this case the lottery has two stages. The first step is to flip a coin. If it comes up heads you must choose a ball from urn B. If it comes up tails you must choose from urn C. The second step is to pick a ball from the urn determined by the coin flip. Again, if the ball is red you win $100, otherwise you win nothing. Which lottery do you prefer?*

Simple multiplication will confirm that the chance of winning either lottery is 50 percent, yet most people say that they prefer lottery A. Why? Two characteristics of the BC lottery make it unattractive. First, lottery A is simpler. Complexity itself is aversive. Second, the chance of winning the BC lottery is more ambiguous: Depending on the outcome of the coin flip it might be 80 percent or 20 percent. This ambiguity is also aversive. The moral is that most people – if forced to gamble – would prefer a simple, well-defined risk to a complex, ambiguous risk (Ellsberg, 1961).

The next set of three situations relates to the value people place on their lives. How much would someone pay to avoid a risk to his life? How much would he charge to take an additional risk?

Risk Situation 1: *While attending the movies last week you inadvertently exposed yourself to a rare, fatal disease. If you contract the disease, you will die a quick and painless death in one week. The chance that you will contract the disease is exactly .001 – that is, one chance in 1000. Once you get the disease there is no cure, but you can take an innoculation now which will prevent you from getting the disease. Unfortunately there is only a limited supply of innoculation, and it will be sold to the highest bidders. What is the most you would be willing to pay for this innoculation? (If you wish, you may borrow the money to pay at a low rate of interest.)*

Risk Situation 2: *This is basically the same as situation 1 with the following modifications. The chance you will get this disease is now .004 – that is, four in 1000. The innoculation is only 25 percent effective – that is, it would reduce the risk to .003. What is the most you would pay for the innoculation in this case? (Again, you may borrow the money to pay.)*

Risk Situation 3: *Some professors at a medical school are doing research on the disease described above. They are recruiting volunteers who would be required to expose themselves to a .001 (one chance in 1000) risk of getting the disease. No innoculations would be available, so this would entail a .001 chance of death. The 20 volunteers from this audience who demand the least money will be taken. What is the least amount of money you would require to participate in this experiment?*

I have asked these questions to numerous groups. The typical median responses are that people would pay $800 in Situation 1; pay $250 in Situation 2; and charge $100,000 in Situation 3. Obviously, people treat these as three quite different questions. Yet economists would argue that the answers should all be about the same. (They would allow for a small difference between Situation 3 and the other two, but nothing like the magnitude observed.) Essentially each situation presents the subject with a choice between more money or a greater chance of living. If Situations 1 and 2 are compared, we can see that people will pay over three times as much to reduce a risk from .001 to zero than to reduce a risk from .004 to .003. While the increase in the chance of living is the same in each case, the change is more attractive in Situation 1 because the risk is eliminated altogether. Generally, people will pay more to eliminate a risk than to achieve an equivalent reduction of a risk. Daniel Kahneman and Amos Tversky call this the *certainty effect* (Tversky & Kahneman, 1981).

If we compare the responses to Situation 3 with those given to Situations 1 and 2, we see that the median response to Situation 3 is several times larger. Yet this implies that a typical individual would refuse to pay $5000 to eliminate a risk, *and* would refuse to take $5000 to accept the same risk. How can $5000 be both better and worse than bearing some risk?

This comparison illustrates another behavioral regularity which I have called the *endowment effect* (Thaler, 1980). The endowment effect stipulates that an individual will demand much more money to give something up than he would be willing to pay to acquire it. The endowment effect can be observed in cases that do not involve any risk. Suppose you won a ticket to a sold-out concert that you would love to attend, and the ticket is priced at $15. Before the concert you are offered $50 for the ticket. Do you sell? Alternatively, suppose you won $50 in a lottery. Then, a few weeks later, you are offered a chance to buy a ticket to the same concert for $45. Do you buy? Many people say they would not sell for $50 in the first case and would not buy for $45 in the second case. Such responses are logically inconsistent.

Policy deceptions

These illusions can affect policy decisions in many ways. Take the endowment effect: Essentially it says that once people have something it is very hard to take it away. Residents of communities with declining school populations know how this has created problems for their school boards. People who would be unwilling to pay for a tax increase to add a school in their neighborhood nevertheless become incensed if an existing school in their neighborhood is closed in order to avoid a tax increase.

Similarly, most people know that when social security benefits were indexed, the formula used was inadvertently generous. The result has been that benefits have grown much faster than wages in recent years – clearly an unintended outcome. Nevertheless, any politician who dared to suggest a reduction in the rate at which benefits increase was considered an enemy of senior citizens. Just because it was a mistake to give people something does not mean it can be easily taken away. Even the most recent solution to this problem – a one-time postponement of cost of living increases for six months – is a curious sort of deception. We did not take anything away – we just postponed it!

An issue that is particularly interesting in the present context is nuclear power, the debate over which involves all of the illusions discussed so far. The specific question I wish to discuss is: Why is nuclear power so unpopular? I do not intend to evaluate the advantages and disadvantages of nuclear and conventional power plants, since I have no particular insights to offer. The question is why nuclear power generates so much vocal, emotional opposition. This *is* a puzzle, since the experts seem at least evenly divided. Yet how many demonstrations do we see opposing coal-fired plants? Surely it is not because conventional power sources are without risk to humans or to the environment. Coal mining accidents could be (but are not) attributed indirectly to coal-fired power plants. And acid rain is partly attributed to conventional power plants, but nuclear power is rarely suggested as a solution to the problems of acid rain. So why is nuclear power so unpopular? The four cognitive illusions each play a role:

Availability

As with homicide, the risks from nuclear power are widely publicized, while as with suicides, the risks from conventional sources are not as well known. The Three Mile Island incident and the popular movie *The China Syndrome* have helped keep the nuclear risks very "available," even though, so far as we know, there has not been a single death related to nuclear power.

Complexity and ambiguity

As with the Ellsberg urn, the risks from nuclear power are complex and ambiguous. People are not confident that they have been estimated correctly. Future risks, such as those related to waste disposal, are especially ambiguous. The Ellsberg effect shows that such risks are particularly aversive. (It is rather ironic that Ellsberg is now so active in the anti-nuclear power movement. Has he fallen into his own trap?)

The certainty effect and the endowment effect

The responses to the three risk situations demonstrated that people are least willing to pay to decrease an existing risk (Situation 2) and demand great compensation for the introduction of a new risk (Situation 3). The way the nuclear power issue is generally discussed, replacing a conventional power plant with a nuclear power plant would reduce an existing risk and add a new risk – the least attractive combination possible.

I am not saying that opposition to nuclear power is silly or irrational. Rather, I have just tried to show how four cognitive illusions all happen to be working to make nuclear power seem highly unattractive, which may help explain why opposition to nuclear power is so widespread.

There is a good book on optical illusions by Stanley Coren and Joan Girgus called *Seeing is Deceiving*. That title might be applied to thinking: Seeming is deceiving. But like optical illusions, cognitive illusions can be overcome. We can measure the height and width of the Gateway Arch; similarly, we can look in the almanac to find out how many homicides and suicides there are. Nevertheless, there is no practical way of preventing cognitive illusions from influencing policy decisions. Cognitive illusions influence representatives, senators, presidents – even so-called experts are not immune. A physicist may fall for a cognitive illusion just as easily as an economist might fall for an optical illusion. But since informed judgment and explicit analysis can in principle mitigate the effects of illusions, we must encourage the use of scientific research, cost-benefit and cost-effectiveness analyses, and expert commissions in the making of policy decisions.

Mirages

The second class of policy problems involves mirages. Rather than illusory objects, these mirages are illusory choices, choices we perceive that do not really exist.

Economists tell us that we should keep our options open, and that we should prefer having more choices to having fewer. This is good advice, like "buy low and sell high," but like all good advice it has exceptions. One exception would arise when the costs of deciding are exceptionally high, in which case any decision may be better than more costly pondering.

A second, more interesting, exception is illustrated by the following true story. A group of economists was sitting around having cocktails, awaiting the arrival of dinner. A large can of cashews was placed on the cocktail table, and within 90 seconds one half of the cashews were gone. A simple linear extrapolation would have predicted the total demise of the cashews and our appetites in another 90 seconds. Leaping into action, I grabbed the can and (while stealing a few more nuts on the way) hid it in the kitchen. Everyone seemed relieved, yet puzzled. How could removing the can, and thus removing a choice, have made us better off? Let us analyze this case with the help of the simple decision tree shown in Figure 9.2.

At time 1 we have a decision: to have the bowl or to remove it. If we remove the bowl, we have no further choices to make, and no more nuts to eat. We obtain Option C. If we leave the bowl, we must then decide how many more nuts to eat. Suppose we would most like to eat a few nuts (Option A) but that we would prefer to stop (Option C) rather than to end up eating the whole bowl (Option B). Given these preferences the rational thing would be to leave the bowl and pick Option A. But it is

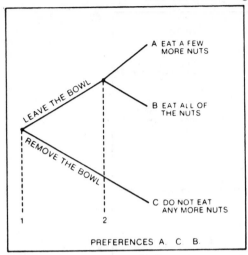

A EAT A FEW
   MORE NUTS

LEAVE THE BOWL

B EAT ALL OF
   THE NUTS

REMOVE THE BOWL

C DO NOT EAT
   ANY MORE NUTS

1   2

PREFERENCES A. C. B.

Figure 9.2. Cashew nut decision tree.

rational only so long as Option A is really feasible. At the dinner party, Option A was a mirage. As much as we might have liked at time 1 to eat only a few more nuts, at time 2 we would have devoured the whole can. If Option A is a mirage, then Option C becomes the rational choice. I will call taking Option C an act of *precommitment:* commiting oneself to a particular choice in advance.

The first recorded act of precommitment was that taken by Ulysses in his encounter with the Sirens, a popular singing group in Ulysses's time whose songs were highly addictive. Anyone on the seas who heard their songs would feel compelled to draw ever nearer to land, inevitably crashing on the rocks near shore. Ulysses's strategy was to have himself tied to the mast so he could not alter the course of his ship.

Ulysses's method of dealing with the Sirens and my act of removing the cashews were both acts of *rational precommitment.* They both satisfy the two conditions that are necessary for precommitment to be rational: (1) a change of preferences is anticipated; and (2) the change will be for the worse. Ulysses knew that he would alter the course of his ship if he had the option, and that the change of course would be for the worse.

A common precommitment institution is the Christmas club. Christmas clubs have three distinguishing features: They pay little or no interest; they require weekly deposits at some inconvenience; and they do not allow the customer to withdraw any money before Thanksgiving. This institution clearly seems inefficient. But is it irrational? The decision tree in Figure 9.3 shows once again that C is a rational choice only if A is a mirage. But for the individuals or families on a tight budget who would otherwise not save enough, a Christmas club could be rational. The fundamental point is that a rule (which is what a precommitment strategy

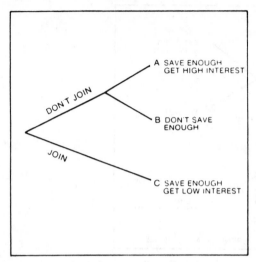

Figure 9.3. Christmas club decision tree.

is) must *necessarily* be crude and inflexible, and may also be inefficient. Nevertheless, these drawbacks, in and of themselves, should not lead us to the conclusion that a particular rule is undesirable. To evaluate a rule we must compare it with the alternatives. Normally a rule specifying that the captain of the ship may not alter the ship's course would be judged unacceptable. But for Ulysses, that rule was better than any other feasible alternative.

Public uses of precommitment

Rational precommitment is highly important in the domain of public policy. Take terrorism or airplane hijacking, for example: As all airline passengers know, we spend millions of dollars and countless hours of time screening airline passengers for bombs, guns, keys, lighters, and calculators. Film is ruined, people miss planes, and we all pay more for plane tickets. What do we gain from this? Since any security system can be beaten, planes are still occasionally hijacked. As an alternative to all the equipment I propose we adopt the following rule: "Never make concessions to hijackers." Hijackers would be given a choice: Give up or be shot. One might say, "Won't that be a dangerous rule? Won't many innocent people be hurt or killed?" The answer is no. First, if no one ever gets anything from hijacking a plane, then the incidence will fall almost to zero. Second, there is no defense against a crazed terrorist. If someone wants to kill himself and a lot of other people he can do it, and we cannot stop him. Anyone can hijack a bus or blow up an office building at will.

A different criticism of this rule is that there might be situations in which society would want to make concessions. Suppose someone hijacks a caravan of school buses – would we not want to make concessions in this case? But such examples simply illustrate the value of the rule: If an exception is made for a school bus once, no school bus would ever be safe again. To enforce this rule we could decide now that anyone not personally at risk who grants a concession to a hijacker would be guilty of a felony. (A jail sentence would be mandatory, of course.)

Another example of rational precommitment is mandatory retirement. Mandatory retirement rules normally have two separate provisions. First, an organization will announce that it is under no obligation, moral or legal, to keep a worker past the age of 60 (or 65, or 70). One reason organizations adopt such a policy is that for most workers, though not all, productivity reaches its peak some time before retirement. Wages, on the other hand, usually rise throughout a worker's employment. These two factors together suggest that just before retirement most workers are earning more than they produce. Clearly a firm would not want to allow that state of affairs to go on indefinitely (Lazear, 1979).

The second provision, while not universal, frequently accompanies the first. It provides that no worker may remain employed after the normal retirement age; this might be called "mandatory mandatory retirement" (or MMR for short). Since the adoption of MMR eliminates some future options for an organization, it qualifies as precommitment. But is it rational? It is easy to criticize an MMR rule since it might force a university to lose a Nobel laureate who is still active. Nevertheless, I believe such rules make good sense because it is so difficult to tell anyone he is no longer productive. Thus the option to keep some people can, and will, become a practice of keeping almost anyone who wants to stay on. So for every Nobel laureate who is kept for an extra couple of years, the organization must retain several others who are no longer productive.

I am not advocating any particular age for mandatory retirement; clearly that should differ across jobs. What I do oppose is the recent federal law that declared mandatory retirement illegal for ages under 70. I believe this is an unnecessary and ill-advised intrusion into private organizations' affairs. In many cases these rules were arrived at through an explicit process of collective bargaining. The abolition of mandatory retirement is sometimes posed, improperly, as a civil rights issue. But old age is a state we all hope to attain. Young people benefit when mandatory retirement creates new openings, but those same young people will face those rules later. Mandatory retirement makes sense for some organizations, and they should be given the freedom to enforce their own rules.

The federal budget as dinner check

I would also encourage the federal government to impose some precommitment rules on itself, in particular fiscal caps such as

Proposition 13 in California. Several proposed constitutional amendments would impose such rules on the federal government either by restricting future growth of spending to no more than the growth rate of real GNP, and/or by requiring a balanced federal budget. Such ideas are not new. In 1798 Thomas Jefferson wrote, "I wish it were possible to obtain a single amendment to our Constitution. I would be willing to depend on that alone for the reduction of the administration of our government to the genuine principles of its Constitution; I mean an additional article, taking from the government the power of borrowing."

Since these proposed amendments would greatly restrict the government's flexibility (though exceptions are made for declarations of war), it must be demonstrated that such precommitment would be rational. Though the growth in government's share of GNP in the last 55 years should be evidence enough, let me describe some of the mirages that led to this explosion.

Suppose we consider the behavior of a hypothetical group of 500 people going to an expensive restaurant for drinks and dinner. Compare their expected behavior under two different rules: Each person pays his own bill; or, the total bill is divided evenly. Under which rule will people spend more? The latter of course. If I order a shrimp cocktail for $5.00 and it is split 500 ways, I pay only one cent. I am more likely to order a shrimp cocktail at one cent than at $5.00. This "check-splitting effect" is what leads to so-called pork barrel legislation (Buchanan & Tullock, 1962). The amount a district will pay toward a particular local project can be very small indeed, so it is in the interest of every Representative to get as many projects into his district – just as it is my interest to order dessert if everyone else is chipping in.

Suppose the larger dinner party comes up with a clever idea: The check will still be divided evenly, but to save time, the ordering will be done by committee. There will be separate committees for drinks, appetizers, entrees, salads, and desserts. Each person can serve on the committee of his choice. How will people allocate themselves to committees? You guessed it – the lushes will be on the drinks committee, the vegetarians on salad committee, the sweet-tooths on the dessert committee, etc. (After all, we do want the people with expertise on the relevant committees.) Of course such an arrangement will exacerbate the tendency toward over-ordering. The lushes will have a bottle of wine with each course, the sweet-tooths two rounds of dessert, and if by chance a lush finds himself on the dessert committee we can be sure that rum cake will be served. Unfortunately, this metaphor closely resembles the structure of the U.S. Congress, where the committee process reinforces the tendency toward excessive spending (Niskanen, 1971).

Suppose further that each of our diners can put his bill on a credit card – a special credit card that does not have to be paid if the diner loses his job or retires. This rounds out the story nicely. To a representative more concerned with getting re-elected than with posterity, "buy now, pay later (maybe)" is a very appealing process.

How can we control the budget? I advocate random committee assignments, but that is probably politically infeasible. Failing that, we need both a limit on the rate at which government spending can grow, and an enforced balanced budget.

Such rules have been criticized on numerous grounds: They are rightly described as crude and inflexible, and the definition of a balanced budget is far from obvious. Nonetheless, the spirit of such amendments is worth supporting, and the criticisms are not persuasive. The issue is not whether such rules are perfect, but rather whether they are an improvement over the current situation. As Richard Wagner and Robert Tollison recently wrote:

Annual budget balance is a good idea because it places useful and meaningful constraints on political choice. This is not to say that it is a *perfect* rule for the conduct of government, for there are no perfect rules for the conduct of something as massive as our government. The problem is to search for feasible, workable rules that encourage political decision makers to act as if they had good common sense. A rule of annual budget balance and careful up-front monitoring of the viability of long-term government projects seems to be the wisest course of action (Wagner, Tollison, Rabuska, & Noonan, 1982).

No thyself

By definition, precommitment must be done in *advance*, before we actually face temptation. We always resolve to go on a diet – next week. "Lord give me strength – but not now." So we should not be surprised to find that we, or our organizations, want to break rules that were established earlier, even if the rules are desirable. Indexation of the federal income tax is a good illustration of this principle.

Because we have a progressive income tax with marginal rates that increase with income, inflation automatically produces real tax increases. In 1981, Congress passed a law that instituted indexing of the personal income tax beginning in 1985. The way the law works, the personal exemption (now $1000), the zero-tax bracket (now $3400), and all other bracket levels would automatically rise with inflation. This would be particularly helpful to lower income families, since the brackets are much closer together at lower levels. Not surprisingly, some in Congress now want the law repealed. As Martin Feldstein, chairman of the President's Council of Economic Advisors, argues in a recent *Wall Street Journal*:

If tax revenue must be raised, the repeal of indexing isn't a satisfactory substitute for an explicit tax increase. Because the repeal of indexing is a *hidden* way of increasing taxes, it removes the pressure to choose between spending cuts and more taxes. And unlike voting an explicit tax increase, repealing indexing doesn't provide a fixed amount of additional tax revenues but starts a money machine that will squeeze more and more money from taxpayers in years ahead. The repeal of indexing is politically *tempting* to many in Congress because it increases revenue without explicitly increasing taxes. But it is the very opposite of responsible budgeting [emphasis added].

Feldstein's choice of language is quite apt. First, he describes the tax increases in the absence of indexation as *hidden*. This is right on target. To keep government spending under control we should want tax increases to be visible, not hidden. Second, he says the repeal of indexation would be *tempting* to Congress. Congress recognized its addiction to hidden tax increases and resolved to break the addiction – starting in four years. It is important that this resolution be kept. Indexation is particularly important in the absence of spending restrictions or a balanced budget amendment, since it will help keep government from growing.

My proposal can perhaps best be summarized in the dictum Thomas Schelling set down in these pages several years ago: "No Thyself." This is good advice for individuals, organizations, and governments. If we make rules to enforce the "no," we must remember that all rules are imperfect, and that they must not be lightly abandoned. Not even Ulysses could count on self-restraint.

10. Psychological study of human judgment: implications for investment decision making

Paul Slovic

You are – face it – a bunch of emotions, prejudices, and twitches, and this is all very well as long as you know it. Successful speculators do not necessarily have a complete portrait of themselves, warts and all, in their own minds, but they do have the ability to stop abruptly when their own intuition and what is happening Out There are suddenly out of kilter.

If you don't know who you are, this is an expensive place to find out.

—Adam Smith, *The Money Game*

Introduction

Just as the stock market has been described as "The Money Game," security analysis, whether by expert or novice, might aptly be labeled "The Information Game." In no other realm are such vast quantities of information from such diverse sources brought to bear on so many important decisions. Careful accumulation and skilled interpretation of this information is said to be the *sine qua non* of accurate evaluation of securities.

The basic tenet of those in charge of helping the investor to make market decisions seems to be "the more information, the better." Bernhard, writing in 1959, noted that,

Large brokerage houses undertook big advertising campaigns to acquaint investors with the 'research services.' Of what did the research consist? Primarily, it was represented as a careful compilation of all the facts deemed relevant to an understanding of the subject company and its stock. That done, the customer was left to his own devices to evaluate the facts (1959, p. 34).

Modern technology has contributed its share to the information explosion by making vastly greater quantities of elegant data readily

This chapter originally appeared in the *Journal of Finance*, 1972, 27(4), 779–799. Copyright © 1972 by the American Finance Association. Reprinted by permission.

available to the analyst, broker, and investor. However, little attention has been given to the problems of interpreting this information skillfully. Graham et al., in their classic treatise on security analysis, recognized the proper use of information as a key element of investment decision making. They observed, "After the anlayst has learned what information he can get and where to get it, he faces the harder question: What use to make of it (Graham, Dodd, Cottle, & Tatham, 1962, p. 85)?"

Many aspects of investment analysis are said to be psychological in nature; certainly, the appraisal of man's capabilities for integrating information into a judgment or decision is one such aspect. Because of a lack of relevant psychological knowledge, security analysts have all too often been forced to become amateur psychologists themselves. For example, G. A. Drew asserted in 1941 that,

> In fact, simplicity or singleness of approach is a greatly underrated factor of market success. As soon as the attempt is made to watch a multiplicity of factors, even though each has *some* element to justify it, one is only too likely to become lost in a maze of contradictory implications....The various factors involved may be so conflicting that the conclusion finally drawn is no better than a snap judgment would have been (1941, p. 86).

Is Drew's speculation correct? What are man's limitations as a processor of information? The purpose of this paper is to acquaint the reader with psychology's recent endeavors to answer this general question. Along the way we shall touch on a number of related topics, including studies of the accuracy and reliability of judgment; techniques for modeling the judgment process and making intuition explicit; biases in judgments of probability, variability, and correlation; experimental studies of risk-taking behavior; and discussion of the relative merits of scientific versus intuitive approaches to making judgments and decisions. Wherever possible, implications of this work for investment decision making will be noted. If, as we proceed, we expose some warts, prejudices, and twitches, it is done in the belief that a full understanding of human limitations will ultimately benefit the decision maker more than will naive faith in the infallibility of his intellect.

Scientific vs. subjective prediction in finance

To set the stage for a discussion of the relevant psychological literature, I would like to review briefly current opinion within the domain of investment analysis pertaining to the analyst's use of information.

The analyst is called upon to make predictions, forecasts, diagnoses, evaluations, etc., on the basis of fallible information, and with regard to such qualities as expected returns, growth rates, variability, and correlation. There is a branch of applied mathematics, namely statistics, whose purpose is to help men make these kinds of judgments. Most of the time, however, we bypass formal statistical procedures when making judgments, and when we do this we are acting as "intuitive statisticians."

The relative merit of scientific or statistical vs. subjective or intuitive methods of prediction is a controversial issue. The intuitive approach is the traditional and predominant method. Here decisions are seen as based more or less on a state of mind, on feelings or attitudes, on knowing, without the conscious use of well-defined reasoning. For example, consider the following quotations:

> This is no science. It is an art. Now we have computers and all sorts of statistics, but the market is still the same and understanding the market is still no easier. It is personal intuition, sensing patterns of behaviour. (Smith, 1968, p. 20)
>
> What is it the good [money] managers have? It's a kind of locked-in concentration, an intuition, a feel, nothing that can be schooled. (Smith, 1968, pp. 25–26)

In the opposite corner are advocates of a scientific approach to investment analysis. Bauman (1967) defines the scientific approach as one which consistently applies investment theory or a set of decision rules to a variety of investment situations, taking advantage of theoretically-derived or empirically-determined quantitative relationships between market factors and security performance. Although subjectivists criticize the scientific approaches as being too static and insensitive to subtle factors, scientific methods are rapidly gaining in popularity due to the availability of sophisticated mathematical and statistical techniques and the development of high-speed computers by which to implement them. Lorie (1966) observed that a tremendous amount of research is in progress on such diverse subjects as insider trading, the effect of stock splits, portfolio selection, prediction of stock prices and earnings, etc. He concluded that much of this research work has already had the effect of discrediting beliefs – and even some relatively sophisticated ones – about the behavior of security prices.

Judgmental accuracy in investment analysis

Gray (1966) has recently warned security analysts that unless they develop procedures for measuring the validity of their efforts they are likely to have such assessments imposed upon them by those outside the profession. Despite the need for such appraisal, there have been relatively few attempts to assess the results of decisions made by analysts or investors under the harsh light of scientific scrutiny. And, in these investigations, the performance of man's inferences has appeared rather mediocre.

Cowles (1933) made one of the first and most extensive attempts to determine the validity of "expert" forecasting. He found that sixteen financial services, making some 7500 recommendations on individual stocks between 1928 and 1932, compiled an average record that was worse than that of the average common stock by 1.4% annually. Cowles' close analysis of the forecasts of William D. Hamilton, editor of the *Wall Street Journal,* over the 26 years between 1904 and 1929, showed that they achieved a result poorer than a representative sample of stocks. Similarly, poor results were achieved by 24 financial publications between the years 1928 and 1932. A follow-up study in 1944 produced further negative findings along with the observation that more than 80% of all forecasts were bullish despite the fact that bear markets predominated during the period studied (Cowles, 1944).

Treynor and Mazuy (1966) evaluated the performance of 47 mutual funds and the sensitivity of their portfolio managers to market fluctuations. They reasoned that, if fund managers were able to anticipate major turns in the stock market, they would adjust the proportion of high and low-risk securities in their portfolios accordingly. Treynor and Mazuy found no evidence of such adjustments and they concluded that perhaps no investor, professional or amateur, can outguess the market. Several other investigations also indicate that the market has performed as well or better than a considerable number of professionally managed funds (Bauman, 1965; Fama, 1965; Jensen, 1968; O'Brien, 1970; Wharton School of Finance and Commerce, 1962).

Perhaps the most extensive studies of the validity of individual investors' judgments are the several "Value Line Contests" in which individuals pit their own portfolios against those selected by Value Line and against the market averages. The 1969 contest attracted 65,000 entrants (Murphy, 1970). There appeared to be a greater number of superior portfolios among these than could be expected by chance. However, the majority of submitted portfolios were not analyzed in enough detail to permit a careful evaluation of contestants' abilities. Unfortunately, the results of two earlier Value Line Contests were also inconclusive regarding investors' ability to outperform the market averages (Bernard, 1967; Hausman, 1969).

A study by Cragg and Malkiel (1968) examined earnings projections for 185 corporations made by five different forecasting firms. The correlations between predicted and actual earnings turned out to be quite low, leading Cragg and Malkiel to conclude that the careful, painstaking efforts of the analysts performed little better than simple projections of past growth rates.

On the basis of this brief review, several conclusions seem warranted. First, there have still been relatively few studies concerned with the forecasting ability of sophisticated investors and analysts. Second, even these studies have not directly addressed the subjective vs. scientific issue. For example, the extent to which the analysts and fund managers evaluated by Cragg and Malkiel, Cowles, or Treynor and Mazuy used statistical as opposed to intuitive methods is not known. With the exception of Cowles' work, interest in these issues is of relatively recent origin. In contrast, these and related questions have been studied extensively for several decades within psychology and medicine. The following discussions of relevant psychological research may place the results from securities analysis into broader perspective while suggesting worthwhile avenues for further investigation.

Psychological studies of human judgment

Psychologists have a dual reason for studying the types of judgmental processes involved in stock market decisions. First, such processes are obviously within the proper domain of psychological inquiry. Second, clinical psychologists are forced to use similar processes in their role as diagnosticians of mental disorders and predictors of human behavior. Much of the psychological research relevant to investment decision making comes from the study of the judgmental processes of clinical psychologists, i.e., "clinical judgment." For a comprehensive review of research on clinical judgment see Goldberg (1968).

Accuracy and reliability of clinical judgment

Over the past 20 years, numerous studies have tested the accuracy of clinical judgments. The results, like those of investment judgments, have been quite discouraging. Goldberg references nine studies that not only demonstrated a marked lack of validity but also yielded the surprising finding that the judge's length of professional training and his experience often showed little relationship to his accuracy. Equally disillusioning are the 15 experiments cited by Goldberg which showed that the amount of information available to the judge was not necessarily related to the accuracy of his inferences. Typical of these is a study by Oskamp (1965) who had 32 judges, including eight experienced clinical psychologists, read background information about a patient's case. The information was divided into four sections. After reading each section of the case, the judge answered 25 questions about the personality of the subject. The correct answers were known to the investigator. The clinician also rated his confidence in his answers. Oskamp found that, as the amount of information about the case increased, accuracy remained at about the same level while the clinicians' confidence increased dramatically and became disproportionately great. These findings may explain, in part, the prevailing tendency to provide the investment decision maker with as much information as possible. It makes him feel more confident, but will it improve his decision? This type of study would seem worth replicating within the context of security analysis.

   The lack of validity of clinical judgments has led to a number of studies of their reliability. Goldberg distinguished among three types of reliability: (a) *consistency*, or stability across time for the same judge using the same data; (b) *consensus,* or agreement across judges using the same data; and (c) *convergence,* or agreement when one judge makes several judgments of the same case but uses different data each time. Studies reviewed by Goldberg indicate that consistency tends to be moderately high but consensus and convergence leave much to be desired. The reliability of investment forecasts would seem to merit systematic study. For one such attempt see Cragg and Malkiel (1968).

Even in medicine, studies of clinical judgment have often revealed a surprising degree of unreliability and inaccuracy. Bakwin (1945) reported an experiment which showed that there was no correlation whatsoever between the estimate of one physician and that of another regarding the advisability of tonsillectomy. These and similar results prompted Bakwin to conclude that, although the superstitions and magic rites that prevailed in the 17th Century had largely been forgotten, some theories and practices persisted in the scientific era of medicine even though their falsity was patent. Garland (1960) has provided similar and more recent examples of unreliability and inaccuracy in medicine. For example, numerous studies of radiologists showed that they failed to recognize the presence of lung disease that was defintely visible on the X-ray film about 30 per cent of the time when reading X-rays. They also found that a radiologist changed his mind about 20 per cent of the time when reading the same film on two occasions.

This work in psychology and medicine, along with the previously described research in finance, implies that we must never take for granted the reliability and accuracy of a judge, no matter how expert. Whenever possible, empirical studies should be conducted to determine whether judgmental performance is satisfactory.

Clinical vs. statistical prediction

When one considers the typical findings of unreliability, lack of validity, and insensitivity to information, it is not surprising to find clinical judgments increasingly under attack by those who wish to substitute statistical prediction systems for the human judge. Thus psychology has its own version of the scientific vs. subjective controversy. This issue was popularized by Meehl's classic book titled *Clinical vs. Statistical Prediction* which was published in 1954. Goldberg (1968) summarized the vast amount of research stimulated by Meehl's book by pointing out that over a very diverse array of clinical tasks, some of which were selected to show the clinician at his best and the statistician at his worst, rather simple actuarial formulae typically performed at least as well as the clinical expert. All this, of course, pertained to repetitive situations where historical data existed for the statistician to use. It would be interesting to pit clinical vs. statistical prediction methods in investment situations, although it is unlikely that the statistician's superiority would be any less there than in the many studies in clinical psychology. Recent studies by Sawyer (1966), Pankoff and Roberts (1968), and Einhorn (1972) indicate that a combination of clinical and statistical methods, with the clinician gathering the data and the statistician processing it, may be the optimal procedure to follow in many judgment situations.

Descriptive analysis of the judgment process

Foresightful investment analysts have long recognized the need to understand more clearly the detailed processes underlying investment decisions – especially decisions made by acknowledged experts. For example, Bernhard (1959) observed that, if the mental processes of consistently successful investors are intuitional, that intuitional reasoning must be made understandable. In a similar vein, Bauman (1967) has argued that by compelling the investment analyst to translate his vague attitudes, opinions, and reasons into explicit quantities, the analyst's thoughts are brought out into the open where they can be observed, evaluated, and tested.

Researchers in the areas of economics, finance, and psychology have recently taken up the challenge of simulating and describing the judgment process. At present, there are a number of new methods that should be of interest to persons concerned with the dynamics of investment decisions.

Complex simulation. It is interesting that some of the most important analyses of complex judgment processes were undertaken within the context of financial decision making. Perhaps the outstanding example is the work of Clarkson (1962) who undertook to simulate the portfolio selection processes of a bank's trust investment officer. Clarkson followed the officer around for several months and studied his verbalized reflections as he was asked to think aloud while reviewing past and present decisions. Using these verbal descriptions as a guide, the investment process was translated into a sequentially branching computer program. When the validity of the model was tested by comparing its selections with future portfolios selected by the trust officer, the correspondence between actual and simulated portfolios was found to be remarkably good. A similar research plan designed to simulate the decision processes of bank officers when granting business loans was outlined by Cohen, Gilmore, and Singer (1966).

Linear models. Clarkson's work shows that, given patient and intelligent effort, many of the expert's cognitions can be distilled into a form capable of being simulated by a computer. However, there is still another approach – one that attempts to provide less of a sequential analysis and more of a quantified, descriptive summary of the way that a decision maker weights and combines information from diverse sources. This approach aims to develop a mathematical model of the decision maker and requires less time and effort on the part of investigator, subject, and computer. It forms a nice compromise between Clarkson's complex, sequentially branching model and the relatively naive approaches of the pre-computer era – such as simply asking the decision maker how he makes his judgments. The rationale behind these mathematical models and techniques for building them are reviewed by Slovic and Lichtenstein (1971).

The basic approach requires the decision maker to make quantitative evaluations of a fairly large number of cases, each of which is defined by a number of quantified cue dimensions or characteristics. A financial analyst, for example, could be asked to predict the long-term price appreciation for each of 50 securities, the securities being defined in terms of cue factors such as their P/E ratios, corporate earnings growth trend, dividend yield, etc. Just as investigators interested in modeling the characteristics of the market have suggested using multiple correlational procedures to capture the way in which the market weights and responds to these factors, one could also fit a regression equation to the analyst's judgments to capture his personal weighting policy. The resultant equation would be:

$$\hat{J}_{pa} = b_1X_1 + b_2X_2 + \ldots b_kX_k \tag{1}$$

where J_{pa} = predicted judgment of price appreciation; X_1, $X_2 \ldots X_k$ are the quantitative values of the defining cue factors (i.e., P/E ratios, earnings, etc.); and b_1, $b_2 \ldots b_k$ are the weights given to the various factors in order to maximize the multiple correlation between the predicted judgments and the actual judgments. These weights are assumed to reflect the relative importance of the factors for the analyst. Equation (1) is known as the *linear model*.

Psychologists have found linear models to be remarkably successful in predicting judgments of such diverse phenomena as psychiatric diagnoses, malignancy of ulcers, job performance, and the riskiness and attractiveness of gambles; and political scientists have found linear models useful for describing judicial decision processes in workmen's compensation and civil liberties court cases (Slovic & Lichtenstein, 1971). Researchers interested in simulating financial and managerial decisions have independently discovered the value of linear models. For example, Bowman (1963) and Kunreuther (1969) successfully fit linear models to decisions concerned with production scheduling, and Hester (1966) used regression analysis to develop a "loan offer function" representative of the lending policy of a particular bank. Hester's function makes explicit the weighting of such factors as the applicant's profits, his deposit balance, his current ratio of assets to liabilities, etc. Such a function could be compared with the bank's formally-stated policy guidelines. Functions of different loan officers could also be compared.

Large individual differences among weighting policies have been found in almost every study that reports individual equations. A striking example of this in a task demanding a high level of expertise comes from a study of nine radiologists by Hoffman, Slovic, and Rorer (1968). The stimuli were ulcers, described by the presence or absence of seven roentgenological signs. Each ulcer was rated according to its likelihood of being malignant. There was considerable disagreement among the judgments of the radiologists, as indicated by a median interjudge correlation, across stimuli, of only .38. Examination of each radiologist's linear equation clearly pinpointed the idiosyncratic weightings of the various signs that led to the observed disagreements in diagnosis.

Nonlinear models. Although the linear model does an impressive job of predicting judgments, when one asks individuals how they are processing information their comments suggest that they use cues in a variety of nonlinear ways. Researchers have attempted to capture these nonlinear processes by means of more complex equations. One type of nonlinearity occurs when an individual cue relates to the judgments in a *curvilinear* manner. For example, this quote from Loeb suggests a curvilinear relation between the volume of trading on a stock and its future prospects:

If you are driving a car you can get to your destination more quickly at 50 mph than at 10 mph. But you may wreck the car at 100 mph. In a similar way, increasing volume on an advance up to a point is bullish and decreasing volume on a rally is bearish, but in both cases only up to a point. (1965, p. 287)

Curvilinear functions such as this quote suggests can be modeled by including exponential terms (i.e., X^2_i, X^3_i, etc.) as predictors in the judge's policy equation.

When an analyst associates good investment decisions with complex and interrelated decision rules, chances are that he envisages types of patterned or *configural* relationships rather than the linear combination rule discussed above. Configurality means that the analyst's interpretation of an item of information varies depending upon the nature of other available information. This example of configural reasoning involving price changes, volume, and market cycle is given by Loeb:

Outstanding strength or weakness can have precisely opposite meanings at different times in the market cycle. For example, consistent strength and volume in a particular issue, occurring after a long general decline, will usually turn out to be an extremely bullish indication....On the other hand, after an extensive advance which finally spreads to issues neglected all through the bull market, belated individual strength and activity not only are likely to be shortlived but may actually suggest the end of the general recovery. (1965, p. 65)

Since analysts believe that factors relevant to investment decisions should often be interpreted configurally, it is important that techniques used to describe judgment be sensitive to such processes. The linear model can be made sensitive to configural effects by incorporating cross-product terms into the policy equation of the judge. Thus, if the meaning of factor X_1 varies as a function of the level of factor X_2, the term $b_{12}X_1X_2$ can be added to the equation. A number of studies have employed a statistical technique, analysis of variance, to identify configural processes in judgment. For example, Slovic, Fleissner, and Bauman (1972) used this technique to isolate configural processes used by stockbrokers when evaluating the attractiveness of common stocks. A number of interesting instances of configural uses of information were found in these studies and large differences in the policy equations for individual brokers were also evident.

Subjective weights and self-insight

Thus far we have been discussing weighting policies that have been assessed by fitting an algebraic model to the judge's responses. We think of these as "computed" or "objective" policies. Judges in a number of studies were asked to estimate the relative weights they had been using in the task. The correspondence between these "subjective weights" and the computed weights indicated the judge's insight into his own policy. One type of error in self-insight has emerged in all of these studies (Slovic & Lichtenstein, 1971). Judges strongly overestimate the importance they place on minor cues (i.e., their subjective weights greatly exceed the computed weights for these cues) and they underestimate their reliance on a few major variables.

In a recent study of 13 stockbrokers, Slovic, Fleissner, and Bauman (1972) found an intriguing result that needs to be tested further. The longer a broker had been in the business, the less accurate was his insight into his weighting policy.

Bootstrapping. Can a system be designed to aid the decision maker that is based on his own judgments of complex stimuli? One possibility is suggested by the finding that algebraic models, such as the linear model, can do a remarkably good job of simulating such judgments. An important hypothesis about cooperative interaction between man and machine is that the model of the man may be able to make better predictions than the man himself. Dawes (1971) has termed this phenomenon "bootstrapping."

The rationale behind the bootstrapping hypothesis is quite simple. Although the human judge possesses his full share of human learning and hypothesis-generating skills, he lacks the reliability of a machine. As Goldberg (1970) has noted:

He is subject to all these human frailities which lower the reliability of his judgments below unity. And, if the judge's reliability is less than unity, there must be error in his judgments – error which can serve no other purpose than to attenuate his accuracy. If we could ... [eliminate] the random error in his judgments, we should thereby increase the validity of the resulting predictions. (p. 423)

The algebraic model captures the judge's weighting policy and applies it consistently. If there is some validity to this policy to begin with, filtering out the error via the model should increase accuracy. Of course, bootstrapping preserves and reinforces any misconceptions or biases that the judge may have. Implicit in the use of bootstrapping is the assumption that these biases will be less detrimental to performance than the inconsistencies of unaided human judgment.

Bootstrapping has been explored independently by a number of different investigators. Bowman (1963) outlined a bootstrapping approach within the context of managerial decision making that has stimulated considerable empirical research. Other applications of bootstrapping have been described by Dawes (1971), Goldberg (1970), and Wiggins and Kohen (1971).

Studies of probabilistic inference

Conservatism. There is a rapidly developing school of thought called "Decision Theory" which asserts that we ought to cast our opinions about the world in probabilistic terms (Edwards, Lindman, & Phillips, 1965; Raiffa, 1968). For example, rather than predicting that a stock will sell at a specific price six months from now, we should estimate a probability distribution across a set of possible prices. These probabilities can then be used, in combination with information about the payoffs associated with various decisions and states of the world, to implement any of a number of decision rules, including the maximization of expected value or expected utility.

When we translate our opinions into probabilities, a mathematical formula, Bayes' theorem, dictates the optimal way that our estimates should change upon receipt of new information. Led by the efforts of Edwards (Edwards et al., 1965; Edwards, Phillips, Hays, & Goodman, 1968), many psychologists have compared man's subjective probability revisions with those of Bayes' theorem in a variety of experimental and real-life situations. This research shows that men are conservative processors of fallible information. Upon receipt of new data, subjects revise their probability estimates in the direction prescribed by Bayes' theorem, but the revision is typically too small; subjects respond as though the data are less diagnostic than they truly are. In some studies subjects have required from two to nine data observations to revise their estimates as much as Bayes' theorem would prescribe after just one observation. A number of experiments have attempted to explain this finding. The results are controversial, but in Edwards' view (1968) the major cause of conservatism is human misaggregation of the data. That is, men perceive a datum accurately and are well aware of its individual diagnostic meaning, but are unable to combine its meaning properly with their prior opinions and with the diagnostic meaning of other data when revising their estimates.

Intuitions about sampling variability. There is a different type of probabilistic inference in which decision makers turn out to be very nonconservative. This work is described by Tversky and Kahneman (1971a) who analyzed the decisions psychologists make when planning their scientific experiments. Despite formal training in statistics, psychologists usually rely upon their educated intuitions when they decide how large a sample of data to collect or whether they should repeat an experiment to make sure their results are reliable. Tversky and Kahneman distributed a questionnaire to psychologists in the audience at the meetings of several professional societies. Typical of the questions was the following:

Suppose you have run an experiment on 20 subjects, and have obtained a significant result which confirms your theory ($z = 2.23$, $p < .05$, two-tailed). You now have cause to run an additional group of 10 subjects. What do you think the probability is that the results will be significant, by a one-tailed test, separately for this group? (1971a, p. 105)

From the answers to this and a variety of other questions, Tversky and Kahneman concluded that people have strong intuitions about random sampling; that these intuitions are wrong in fundamental ways; that they are shared by naive persons and sophisticated scientists alike; and that they are applied with unfortunate consequences in the course of scientific inquiry. They found that the typical scientist gambles his research hypotheses on small samples without realizing that the odds against his obtaining accurate results are unreasonably high; has undue confidence in early trends from the first few data points and in the stability of observed patterns; has unreasonably high expectations about the replicability of significant results; and rarely attributes a deviation of results from expectations to sampling variability because he finds a causal explanation for any discrepancy.

Tversky and Kahneman summarized these results by asserting that people's intuitions seemed to satisfy a "law of small numbers" which means that the "law of large numbers" applies to small samples as well as to large ones. The "law of large numbers" says that very large samples will be highly representative of the population from which they are drawn. Thus, small samples were also expected to be highly representative of the population. Since acquaintance with logic or probability theory did not make the scientist any less susceptible to these cognitive biases, Tversky and Kahneman concluded that the only effective precaution is the use of formal statistical procedures, rather than intuition, to design experiments and evaluate data.

In a related study of college undergraduates, Kahneman and Tversky (1972) found that many of these individuals did not understand the fundamental principle of sampling, i.e., the notion that the error in a sample becomes smaller as the sample size gets larger. Kahneman and Tversky concluded: "For anyone who would wish to view man as a reasonable intuitive statistician, such results are discouraging."

Biases in judgments of probability, variability, and covariation

What can be done to help the decision maker interpret and combine information appropriately? Bootstrapping is one answer to this question. Most of the other answers involve some version of the decomposition principle:

The spirit of decision analysis is divide and conquer: Decompose a complex problem into simpler problems, get your thinking straight in these simpler problems, paste these analyses together with a logical glue, and come out with a program for action for the complex problem. Experts are not asked complicated, fuzzy questions, but crystal clear, unambiguous, elemental, hypothetical questions. (Raiffa, 1968, p. 271)

There seems to be general agreement that we cannot do away with the human element in judgment, so the decomposition approach attempts to obtain relatively simple judgments that can be integrated by some optimal combination model. In this way, it relieves the judge from having to integrate his basic opinions and expectations. For example, certain information-processing systems require men to estimate the probability that each of various items of data would be observed, given a certain state of the world. These estimates are then processed mechanically via Bayes' theorem to produce an estimate of the probability of that state, given that this data was observed (Edwards et al., 1965; Edwards et al., 1968). In the realm of finance, portfolio selection models require that analysts estimate expected returns, variances, covariances, etc., which are then combined via an optimal model (Ahlers, 1966; Markowitz, 1959). Similarly, models of common stock valuation require an analyst to make estimates of future balance-sheet and income data, which can be combined by an empirically-derived or theoretically-based model (Ahlers, 1966; Wendt, 1965). The use of decision trees to analyze complex investment problems is another example of decomposition (Magee, 1964; Raiffa, 1968).

Decomposition is certainly a reasonable approach, although it is still too early to know how successful it will be. Critics claim that the decision maker may be able to make good judgments and choices without being able to introspect accurately about the values and expectations that underlie his actions. A decision maker who has developed an expertise in a particular area may find it extremely difficult and unnatural to respond to elemental questions about which he has never thought and with which he has had no direct experience. In addition, there are a number of biases that distort even the simplest kinds of judgments of probability, variance, or correlation, as the remainder of this section will illustrate.

Biased judgments of probability. Some of the inadequacies of probabilistic judgment have already been discused. In addition to conservatism and the belief in the law of small numbers, there is yet another source of distortion, "availability bias," that affects simple probability estimates. According to Tversky and Kahneman (1971b), the essence of this bias is that judgments of an event's probability are determined by the number of instances of that event that are remembered and the ease with which they come to mind. The *availability* of instances is affected by such factors as recency, salience, and imaginability, all of which may or may not be related to the correct probability. For example, the letter k is three times as likely to appear as the third letter of an English word as the first letter, yet most persons judge it as more likely to be a first letter. Tversky and Kahneman hypothesize that, when subjects make this judgment, they try to think of words either beginning with k or having k as the third letter. It is easier to think of words that begin with k, and if we use that fact as a cue on which to base our intuitive probability estimates, these words will be perceived as more probable than words with k in the third position. In general, the harder it is to recall or imagine instances of an event, the lower the judged probability of that event.

The effects of availability bias are not likely to be limited to the psychological laboratory. An analyst who attempts to evaluate the likelihood of a recession may do so by recalling economic conditions similar to those of the present or by recalling recessions. The latter are easier to retrieve because they are more sharply defined, whereas states of the economy are more difficult to characterize and, therefore, harder to remember. The resulting probability estimate is likely to be greatly dependent upon which of these two mental sets the analyst adopts. Even the form of the question may be important. Consider the following questions:

(a) How likely is it that there will be a recession soon?
(b) How likely is it that, with the present tightening of credit, there will be a recession soon?

The first question may focus attention on past instances of recession, whereas the latter may cause the analyst to think about previous credit conditions.

There are numerous other instances of systematic biases in our judgments of probabilities. Cohen and Chesnick (1970) and Slovic (1969b) found that subjects systematically misperceived the probabilities of compound events. For example, in the study by Cohen and Chesnick, some people preferred the opportunity of drawing a winning lottery ticket out of a population of 10 tickets (with one attempt) to the chance to draw the winner out of 100 tickets, even when they had up to twenty draws of the latter kind (with replacement after each draw). Other studies have found that the desirability of an event biases its subjective probability (Slovic, 1966b), although the effects are complex and differ from person to person. Some people are overly optimistic, tending to attribute greater probability to highly-desired events than to undesired events, other factors being equal. Other persons consistently overestimate the likelihood of unpleasant events.

Biased judgments of variance. Several factors seem to influence a person's judgment of the variance of a sequence of values about the mean of that sequence (Beach & Scopp, 1968; Lathrop, 1967). The first of these factors is the mean itself. Perceived variance increases as the mean decreases. A standard deviation of two feet for a group of saplings would be perceived as larger than the same standard deviation for a group of fully-grown trees. Greater irregularity in a sequence also leads to an illusion of greater variance. Sequences in which the values progress in an orderly fashion (e.g., ascending or descending or ascending up to a point, then descending, etc.), with little difference between successive values, are perceived to have less variance than sequences whose adjacent values are less regular (Lathrop, 1967). The stimuli in experiments on perceived variance have been sets of line lengths and numbers. It would be interesting to determine whether these same sorts of biases would occur when the variance of a sequence of stock prices or earnings reports was being judged.

Biased judgments of correlation and causality. There have been a number of studies relating to judgments of correlation and causality. The results of these studies suggest that even if the random walk theory of security price changes were absolutely true, we probably would not believe it and would find, upon observing random price changes, what appear to be meaningful patterns upon which to base our forecasts.

Several lines of psychological research appear relevant here. The first stems from a classic experiment by Skinner (1948). Skinner found that hungry birds, given food at brief random intervals, developed very idiosyncratic, repetitive actions. The precise form of this behavior varied from bird to bird, and Skinner referred to these actions as superstitions. What happened to these birds can be described in terms of the concept of positive reinforcement. The delivery of food increased the likelihood of whatever form of behavior happened to precede it. Food was then presented again. Because the reinforced behavior was occurring at an increased rate, it was more likely to be reinforced again. The second reinforcement caused a further increase in the rate of this particular behavior which improved its chances of being reinforced again, and so on. After a short while the birds were found to be turning rapidly counter clockwise about the cage, hopping from side to side, making odd head movements, etc. Because such behaviors are reinforced less than 100 per cent of the time during learning, they persist even when reinforcement stops altogether. Animals trained in this way have been known to make as many as 10,000 attempts to obtain a reward that was no longer forthcoming.

The environment of the stock market seems to provide exactly the right conditions for the development and maintenance of superstitious behavior. That is, there has been a favorable expected return and thus a predominance of positive reinforcement (at least in the past) which is administered intermittently. And there is always the hope that if enough people harbor the same superstitions, and the game is to anticipate the actions of the crowd, then knowing the superstitions and acting on them may be quite rewarding. At any rate, one chartist may have been correct when he said, "If I hadn't made money some of the time, I would have acquired market wisdom quicker" (Lefevre, 1968, p. 30).

The superstitions developed in Skinner's pigeons were highly individualistic. Yet the behavior and the lore of Wall Street is often commonly agreed upon. How can this consensus be reconciled with the notion of stock-price changes as a random walk? Several recent experiments by Chapman and Chapman (1967) may provide a possible answer to this question along with further insight into the pitfalls awaiting human intuition.

The Chapmans, studying a phenomenon they have labeled illusory correlation, have shown how our prior expectations of relationships can lead to faulty observation and inference, even under seemingly excellent conditions for learning. They presented naive subjects with human figure drawings, each of which was paired with a statement about the personality of the patients who allegedly drew the figures. These statements were randomly paired with the figure drawings so that the figure cues were unrelated to the personality of the drawer. They found that most subjects learned to see what they expected to see. In fact, naive subjects discovered the same relationships between drawings and personality that expert psychologists report observing in their clinical practice, although these relationships were absent in the experimental materials. The illusory correlates corresponded to commonly-held expectations, such as figures with big eyes being drawn by suspicious people, muscular figures being drawn by individuals who worried about their manliness, etc.

The Chapmans noted that in clinical practice the observer is reinforced in his observation of illusory correlates by the reports of his fellow clinicians, who themselves are subject to the same illusions. Such agreement among experts is, unfortunately, often mistaken as evidence for the truth of the observation. They concluded that the clinician's cognitive task may exceed the capacity of the human intellect and they suggested that subjective intuition may need to be replaced, at least partially, by statistical methods of prediction.

The research on illusory correlation suggests parallel experiments using stock prices. One hypothesis is that, if we provide a stream of random price changes to intelligent but naive subjects, say undergraduate students in a finance course, they might discover in these random sequences some of the same rules that we see accepted by chartists or other analysts. Although the influence of illusory correlation in financial analysis remains to be demonstrated, there is no reason to believe that it will be less here than in clinical psychology.

Finally, a number of studies have investigated subjects' perceptions of correlation and causality in simple situations involving just two binary variables. Consider a 2×2 table in which variable A is the antecedent or input variable and B is the consequent or output variable; and the small letters are the joint frequencies.

	B_1	B_2
A_1	a	b
A_2	c	d

A correlation or contingency exists between A and B to the extent that the probability of B_1 given A_1 differs from the probability of B_1 given A_2: that is, to the extent that $a/(a + b)$ differs from $c/(c + d)$.

Research indicates that subjects' judgments of contingency are not based on a comparison of $a/(a + b)$ versus $c/(c + d)$. For example, Smedslund (1963) had students of nursing judge the relation between a symptom and the diagnosis of a disease. He found that the judgments were based mainly on the frequency of joint occurrence of symptom and disease (cell a in the table), without taking the other three event combinations into account. As a result, the judgments were unrelated to actual contingency. Similar results were obtained by Ward and Jenkins (1965) who concluded:

In general ... statistically naive subjects lack an abstract concept of contingency that is isomorphic with the statistical concept. Those who receive information on a trial by trial basis, as it usually occurs in the real world, generally fail to assess adequately the degree of relationship present. (p. 240)

Experimental study of risk-taking behavior

There is a great deal of experimental research on risk-taking behavior that may have implications for investment decision making. In this research, subjects are asked to indicate their preferences and opinions among various gambles. Gambles are studied because they represent, in abstract form, important aspects of real-life decisions – namely, probabilities, incentives, and risks. By using gambles, the basic dimensions of risk-taking situations can be manipulated and hypotheses can be tested in a rigorous way. Whether the results generalize to real-life gambles must, of course, be checked by further research.

The influence of variance on risk taking

Theorists such as Allais (1953), Fisher (1906), and Markowitz (1959) have argued that the variance of returns on an investment should be considered as an investment criterion in addition to the mean or expected return. High variance is typically equated with high risk.

Does variance influence the perceived attractiveness of a gamble? Subjects in several psychological experiments have exhibited what seemed to be strong preferences for playing high or low variance gambles (for example, see Coombs & Pruitt, 1960). However, recent evidence suggests that the subjects in these experiments were choosing according to decision rules such as "minimize possible loss" or "maximize possible gain," rather than basing their preferences on variance per se. Variance appears to have correlated with the preferences only because it also correlated with these other strategies (Slovic & Lichtenstein, 1968).

Another study has found that perceived risk was not a function of the variance of a gamble (Slovic, 1967). Instead, riskiness was more likely to be determined by the probability of loss and the amount of loss. This result is in accord with comments made by Lorie (1966) who complained that it was absurd to call a stock risky because it went up much faster than the market in some years and only as fast in other years, while a security that never varies in price is not risky at all, if variance is used to define risk. The importance of understanding how risk is perceived is stressed by Lepper (1967), who pointed out the crucial role of investors' perceptions of risk in determining the impact of various taxes. Taxes, of course, can alter markedly the variance of the potential returns for an investment.

Response mode and information use

A study by Lichtenstein and Slovic (1971) found that subtle changes in the manner in which the decision maker reported his evaluation of a gamble had a strong influence on the way that he processed information about probabilities and payoffs. For example, consider the following pair of bets:

Bet A: .90 to win $ 4 and .10 to lose $2.
Bet B: .30 to win $16 and .70 to lose $2.

Bet A has a much better probability of winning but Bet B offers a higher winning payoff. Lichtenstein and Slovic's subjects were shown many such pairs of bets. They were asked to indicate, in two ways, how much they would like to play each bet in a pair. First they made a simple choice, A or B. Later they were asked to assume they owned a ticket to play each bet, and they were to state the lowest price for which they would sell this ticket.

Presumably these selling prices and choices are both governed by the same underlying quality, the subjective attractiveness of each gamble. Therefore, the subject should state a higher selling price for the gamble that he prefers in the choice situation. However, Lichtenstein and Slovic found that subjects often chose Bet A, yet stated a higher selling price for Bet B. Why should this happen? Lichtenstein and Slovic have traced it to the fact that subjects used different cognitive strategies for setting price than for making choices. Subjects choose Bet A because of its good odds, but they set a higher price for B because of its large winning payoff.

A "compatibility" effect seemed to be operating here. Since a selling price is expressed in terms of monetary units, subjects apparently found it easier to use the monetary aspects of the gamble to produce this type of response. Such a bias did not exist with the choices. When faced with their inconsistent decisions, many subjects had a very hard time changing either of their conflicting responses. They felt that the different strategies they used for each decision were appropriate. However, strict adherence to an inconsistent pattern of prices and choices can be termed irrational, since the inconsistent subject can be led into purchasing and trading gambles in such a way that he continually loses money.

The message in this research is that integrating information is quite a difficult cognitive task, and there may often be a very subtle interaction between the form of the information we have to use and the form of the judgmental response we have to make. This may well generalize beyond experimental gambling situations. For example, a financial analyst who is forecasting a stock's market price six months hence might be led to overweight previous price information, simply because of the compatibility factor. And if he were asked to forecast percentage price increase rather than price itself, he might then give more weight to other variables in the company report that were expressed in terms of percentages. Experiments testing this hypothesis would seem to be worth conducting, so that steps could be taken to minimize compatibility biases if they are found.

Is willingness to take risks a stable personality trait?

An understanding of risk-taking propensity as a personality characteristic could prove valuable in the selection and training of portfolio managers, investment counselors, or brokers. It would also help these individuals to better understand and service their clients. Although knowledge of the dynamics of risk taking is still limited, there is one important aspect that has been fairly well researched – that dealing with the stability of a person's characteristic risk-taking preferences as he moves from situation to situation. Typically, a subject is tested in a variety of risk-taking tasks involving problem solving, athletic, social, vocational, and pure gambling situations. The results of close to a dozen such studies indicate little correlation, from one setting to another, in a person's preferred level of risk taking (Slovic, 1972b). Only those tasks highly similar in structure and involving the same sorts of payoffs (e.g., all financial, all social, etc.) have shown any generality and, as similarity decreases, these cross-task consistencies rapidly decline. Thus an individual who takes risks by guessing often on a mathematics exam (when guessing is penalized) is likely to be a high risk taker in other exams as well, but that does not imply that he would prefer a high-risk occupation. In sum, the majority of evidence argues against the existence of risk-taking propensity as a generalized characteristic of individuals. A person's previous learning experiences in specific risk-taking settings seem much more important than his general personality characteristics.

As an example of one implication of this work, consider the problem of selecting a portfolio manager. Suppose that one desires a manager who has the propensity to invest at high levels of risk. The best predictor of this characteristic would be the individual's demonstrated performance in a position highly similar to the one under consideration. Evidence of his risk-taking propensity gleaned from other forms of behaviors is unlikely to predict how he would behave in an investment situation.

Comparison of group and individual risk taking

Many decisions are made not by individuals, but by groups. Over the past decade, comparison of group versus individual risk-taking tendencies has been the subject of an extensive body of research. The typical finding is that decisions made by groups are riskier than the average of the individual members' decisions prior to group discussion. Individual risk-taking levels also increase following group discussion. This phenomenon has been labeled the "risky shift."

One of the leading explanations of the risky shift is the "diffusion of responsibility" hypothesis. It asserts that each group member feels less personal blame if his choice fails, thus he is not afraid to recommend or accept riskier courses of action.

Another explanation of the risky shift is the "cultural value" hypothesis which assumes that moderate riskiness is a stronger, more widely held cultural value than caution. This value leads individuals to perceive themselves as being at least as willing as their peers to take risks. In this regard, the group discussion provides information that allows group members to compare their own positions with those of their peers. Members whose initial positions were less risky than those of the group average come to learn that they are not as risky as they thought and as they want to be. To remedy this, they increase their level of risk taking.

Both of these explanations, and others as well, have received experimental verification. For more detailed discussion of group influence on risk taking see reviews by R. D. Clark (1971) and Kogan and Wallach (1967).

Concluding remarks

Several facts are important about the research described in this paper. First, most of the work is of very recent origin. Second, with only a few exceptions, this research has been done without explicit consideration of problems in business and finance. As a result, there is a great need to replicate the various types of studies in specific financial settings. Studies of high-level decision makers and analysts, in their natural working environment, are particularly needed. Besides contributing to the understanding of financial decisions, such research would also benefit psychology, much as Clarkson's simulation of the trust investment officer provided important insight into the nature of complex thought processes. Obviously, this kind of research would benefit greatly from interdisciplinary collaboration among psychologists, economists, financial analysts, computer scientists, and others.

If research in financial settings verifies the early indications of man's information-processing limitations, the next phase of research must certainly emphasize the development of techniques to help decision makers overcome their cognitive biases. Will informing an analyst about his biases make him less susceptible to them or will it lead him to overcompensate, perhaps with even greater error? Would computer simulation be effective in conveying an appreciation of sampling variability and probabilities? The past decade of research has uncovered some fascinating questions. The next decade should provide some extremely interesting and important answers.

11. Choices, values, and frames

Daniel Kahneman and Amos Tversky

Making decisions is like speaking prose – people do it all the time, knowingly or unknowingly. It is hardly surprising, then, that the topic of decision making is shared by many disciplines, from mathematics and statistics, through economics and political science, to sociology and psychology. The study of decisions addresses both normative and descriptive questions. The normative analysis is concerned with the nature of rationality and the logic of decision making. The descriptive analysis, in contrast, is concerned with people's beliefs and preferences as they are, not as they should be. The tension between normative and descriptive considerations characterizes much of the study of judgment and choice.

Analyses of decision making commonly distinguish risky and riskless choices. The paradigmatic example of decision under risk is the acceptability of a gamble that yields monetary outcomes with specified probabilities. A typical riskless decision concerns the acceptability of a transaction in which a good or a service is exchanged for money or labor. In the first part of this article we present an analysis of the cognitive and psychophysical factors that determine the value of risky prospects. In the second part we extend this analysis of transactions and trades.

Risky choice

Risky choices, such as whether or not to take an umbrella and whether or not to go to war, are made without advance knowledge of their consequences. Because the consequences of such actions depend on uncertain events such as the weather or the opponent's resolve, the choice of an act

This chapter originally appeared in the *American Psychologist*, 1984, 39(4), 341–350.

may be construed as the acceptance of a gamble that can yield various outcomes with different probabilities. It is therefore natural that the study of decision making under risk has focused on choices between simple gambles with monetary outcomes and specified probabilities, in the hope that these simple problems will reveal basic attitudes toward risk and value.

We shall sketch an approach to risky choice that derives many of its hypotheses from a psychophysical analysis of responses to money and to probability. The psychophysical approach to decision making can be traced to a remarkable essay that Daniel Bernoulli published in 1738 (Bernoulli 1738/1954) in which he attempted to explain why people are generally averse to risk and why risk aversion decreases with increasing wealth. To illustrate risk aversion and Bernoulli's analysis, consider the choice between a prospect that offers an 85% chance to win $1000 (with a 15% chance to win nothing) and the alternative of receiving $800 for sure. A large majority of people prefer the sure thing over the gamble, although the gamble has higher (mathematical) expectation. The expectation of a monetary gamble is a weighted average, where each possible outcome is weighted by its probability of occurrence. The expectation of the gamble in this example is .85 × $1000 + .15 × $0 = $850, which exceeds the expectation of $800 associated with the sure thing. The preference for the sure gain is an instance of risk aversion. In general, a preference for a sure outcome over a gamble that has higher or equal expectation is called risk averse, and the rejection of a sure thing in favor of a gamble of lower or equal expectation is called risk seeking.

Bernoulli suggested that people do not evaluate prospects by the expectation of their monetary outcomes, but rather by the expectation of the subjective value of these outcomes. The subjective value of a gamble is again a weighted average, but now it is the subjective value of each outcome that is weighted by its probability. To explain risk aversion within this framework, Bernoulli proposed that subjective value, or utility, is a concave function of money. In such a function, the difference between the utilities of $200 and $100, for example, is greater than the utility difference between $1200 and $1100. It follows from concavity that the subjective value attached to a gain of $800 is more than 80% of the value of a gain of $1000. Consequently, the concavity of the utility function entails a risk averse preference for a sure gain of $800 over an 80% chance to win $1000, although the two prospects have the same monetary expectation.

It is customary in decision analysis to describe the outcomes of decisions in terms of total wealth. For example, an offer to bet $20 on the toss of a fair coin is represented as a choice between an individual's current wealth W and an even chance to move to W + $20 or to W − $20. This representation appears psychologically unrealistic: People do not normally think of relatively small outcomes in terms of states of wealth

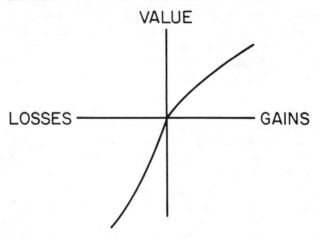

Figure 11.1. A hypothetical value function.

but rather in terms of gains, losses, and neutral outcomes (such as the maintenance of the status quo). If the effective carriers of subjective value are changes of wealth rather than ultimate states of wealth, as we propose, the psychophysical analysis of outcomes should be applied to gains and losses rather than to total assets. This assumption plays a central role in a treatment of risky choice that we called prospect theory (Kahneman & Tversky, 1979b). Introspection as well as psychophysical measurements suggest that subjective value is a concave function of the size of a gain. The same generalization applies to losses as well. The difference in subjective value between a loss of $200 and a loss of $100 appears greater than the difference in subjective value between a loss of $1200 and a loss of $1100. When the value functions for gains and for losses are pieced together, we obtain an S-shaped function of the type displayed in Figure 11.1.

The value function shown in Figure 11.1 is (a) defined on gains and losses rather than on total wealth, (b) concave in the domain of gains and convex in the domain of losses, and (c) considerably steeper for losses than for gains. The last property, which we label *loss aversion*, expresses the intuition that a loss of $X is more aversive than a gain of $X is attractive. Loss aversion explains people's reluctance to bet on a fair coin for equal stakes: The attractiveness of the possible gain is not nearly sufficient to compensate for the aversiveness of the possible loss. For example, most respondents in a sample of undergraduates refused to stake $10 on the toss of a coin if they stood to win less than $30.

The assumption of risk aversion has played a central role in economic theory. However, just as the concavity of the value of gains entails risk aversion, the convexity of the value of losses entails risk seeking. Indeed, risk seeking in losses is a robust effect, particularly when the probabilities of loss are substantial. Consider, for example, a situation in which an individual is forced to choose between an 85% chance to lose $1000 (with a 15% chance to lose nothing) and a sure loss of $800. A large majority of people express a preference for the gamble over the sure loss. This is a risk seeking choice because the expectation of the gamble (−$850) is inferior to the expectation of the sure loss (−$800). Risk seeking in the domain of losses has been confirmed by several investigators (Fishburn & Kochenberger, 1979; Hershey & Schoemaker, 1980; Payne, Laughhunn, & Crum, 1980; Slovic, Fischhoff, & Lichtenstein, 1982). It has also been observed with nonmonetary outcomes, such as hours of pain (Eraker & Sox, 1981) and loss of human lives (Fischhoff, 1983b; Tversky, 1977; Tversky & Kahneman, 1981). Is it wrong to be risk averse in the domain of gains and risk seeking in the domain of losses? These preferences conform to compelling intuitions about the subjective value of gains and losses, and the presumption is that people should be entitled to their own values. However, we shall see that an S-shaped value function has implications that are normatively unacceptable.

To address the normative issue we turn from psychology to decision theory. Modern decision theory can be said to begin with the pioneering work of von Neumann and Morgenstern (1947), who laid down several qualitative principles, or axioms, that should govern the preferences of a rational decision maker. Their axioms included transitivity (if A is preferred to B and B is preferred to C, then A is preferred to C), and substitution (if A is preferred to B, then an even chance to get A or C is preferred to an even chance to get B or C), along with other conditions of a more technical nature. The normative and the descriptive status of the axioms of rational choice have been the subject of extensive discussions. In particular, there is convincing evidence that people do not always obey the substitution axiom, and considerable disagreement exists about the normative merit of this axiom (e.g. Allais & Hagen, 1979). However, all analyses of rational choice incorporate two principles: *dominance* and *invariance*. Dominance demands that if prospect A is at least as good as prospect B in every respect and better than B in at least one respect, then A should be preferred to B. Invariance requires that the preference order between prospects should not depend on the manner in which they are described. In particular, two versions of a choice problem that are recognized to be equivalent when shown together should elicit the same preference even when shown separately. We now show that the requirement of invariance, however elementary and innocuous it may seem, cannot generally be satisfied.

Framing of outcomes

Risky prospects are characterized by their possible outcomes and by the probabilities of these outcomes. The same option, however, can be framed or described in different ways (Tversky & Kahneman, 1981). For example, the possible outcomes of a gamble can be framed either as gains and losses relative to the status quo or as asset positions that incorporate initial wealth. Invariance requires that such changes in the description of outcomes should not alter the preference order. The following pair of problems illustrates a violation of this requirement. The total number of respondents in each problem is denoted by N, and the percentage who chose each option is indicated in parentheses.

Problem 1 ($N = 152$): Imagine that the U.S. is preparing for the outbreak of an unusual Asian disease, which is expected to kill 600 people. Two alternative programs to combat the disease have been proposed. Assume that the exact scientific estimates of the consequences of the programs are as follows:

If Program A is adopted, 200 people will be saved. (72%)

If Program B is adopted, there is a one-third probability that 600 people will be saved and a two-thirds probability that no people will be saved. (28%)

Which of the two programs would you favor?

The formulation of Problem 1 implicitly adopts as a reference point a state of affairs in which the disease is allowed to take its toll of 600 lives. The outcomes of the programs include the reference state and two possible gains, measured by the number of lives saved. As expected, preferences are risk averse: A clear majority of respondents prefer saving 200 lives for sure over a gamble that offers a one-third chance of saving 600 lives. Now consider another problem in which the same cover story is followed by a different description of the prospects associated with the two programs:

Problem 2 ($N = 155$): If Program C is adopted, 400 people will die. (22%)

If Program D is adopted, there is a one-third probability that nobody will die and a two-thirds probability that 600 people will die. (78%)

It is easy to verify that options C and D in Problem 2 are undistinguishable in real terms from options A and B in Problem 1, respectively. The second version, however, assumes a reference state in which no one dies of the disease. The best outcome is the maintenance of this state and the alternatives are losses measured by the number of people that will die of the disease. People who evaluate options in these terms are expected to show a risk seeking preference for the gamble (option D) over the sure loss of 400 lives. Indeed, there is more risk seeking in the second version of the problem than there is risk aversion in the first.

The failure of invariance is both pervasive and robust. It is as common among sophisticated respondents as among naive ones, and it is not eliminated even when the same respondents answer both questions within a few minutes. Respondents confronted with their conflicting answers are typically puzzled. Even after rereading the problems, they still wish to be risk averse in the "lives saved" version; they wish to be risk seeking in the "lives lost" version; and they also wish to obey invariance and give consistent answers in the two versions. In their stubborn appeal, framing effects resemble perceptual illusions more than computational errors.

The following pair of problems elicits preferences that violate the dominance requirement of rational choice.

Problem 3 ($N = 86$): Choose between:

E. 25% chance to win $240 and
   75% chance to lose $760   (0%)

F. 25% chance to win $250 and
   75% chance to lose $750   (100%)

It is easy to see that F dominates E. Indeed, all respondents chose accordingly.

Problem 4 ($N = 150$): Imagine that you face the following pair of concurrent decisions. First examine both decisions, then indicate the options you prefer.

Decision (i) Choose between:
A. a sure gain of $240   (84%)
B. 25% chance to gain $1000 and
   75% chance to gain nothing   (16%)

Decision (ii) Choose between:
C. a sure loss of $750   (13%)
D. 75% chance to lose $1000 and
   25% chance to lose nothing   (87%)

As expected from the previous analysis, a large majority of subjects made a risk averse choice for the sure gain over the positive gamble in the first decision, and an even larger majority of subjects made a risk seeking choice for the gamble over the sure loss in the second decision. In fact, 73% of the respondents chose A and D and only 3% chose B and C. The same pattern of results was observed in a modified version of the problem, with reduced stakes, in which undergraduates selected gambles that they would actually play.

Because the subjects considered the two decisions in Problem 4 simultaneously, they expressed in effect a preference for A and D over B and C. The preferred conjunction, however, is actually dominated by the rejected one. Adding the sure gain of $240 (option A) to option D yields 25% chance to win $240 and 75% to lose $760. This is precisely option E in Problem 3. Similarly, adding the sure loss of $750 (option C) to option B yields a 25% chance to win $250 and 75% chance to lose $750. This is precisely option F in Problem 3. Thus, the susceptibility to framing and the S-shaped value function produce a violation of dominance in a set of concurrent decisions.

The moral of these results is disturbing: Invariance is normatively essential, intuitively compelling, and psychologically unfeasible. Indeed, we conceive only two ways of guaranteeing invariance. The first is to adopt a procedure that will transform equivalent versions of any problem into the same canonical representation. This is the rationale for the standard admonition to students of business, that they should consider each decision problem in terms of total assets rather than in terms of gains or losses (Schlaifer, 1959). Such a representation would avoid the violations of invariance illustrated in the previous problems, but the advice is easier to give than to follow. Except in the context of possible ruin, it is more natural to consider financial outcomes as gains and losses rather than as states of wealth. Furthermore, a canonical representation of risky prospects requires a compounding of all outcomes of concurrent decisions (e.g., Problem 4) that exceeds the capabilities of intuitive computation even in simple problems. Achieving a canonical representation is even more difficult in other contexts such as safety, health, or quality of life. Should we advise people to evaluate the consequence of a public health policy (e.g., Problems 1 and 2) in terms of overall mortality, mortality due to diseases, or the number of deaths associated with the particular disease under study?

Another approach that could guarantee invariance is the evaluation of options in terms of their actuarial rather than their psychological consequences. The actuarial criterion has some appeal in the context of human lives, but it is clearly inadequate for financial choices, as has been generally recognized at least since Bernoulli, and it is entirely inapplicable to outcomes that lack an objective metric. We conclude that frame invariance cannot be expected to hold and that a sense of confidence in a particular choice does not ensure that the same choice would be made in another frame. It is therefore good practice to test the robustness of preferences by deliberate attempts to frame a decision problem in more than one way (Fischhoff, Slovic, & Lichtenstein, 1980).

The psychophysics of chances

Our discussion so far has assumed a Bernoullian expectation rule according to which the value, or utility, of an uncertain prospect is obtained by adding the utilities of the possible outcomes, each weighted by its probability. To examine this assumption, let us again consult psychophysical intuitions. Setting the value of the status quo at zero, imagine a cash gift, say of $300, and assign it a value of one. Now imagine that you are only given a ticket to a lottery that has a single prize of $300. How does the value of the ticket vary as a function of the probability of winning the prize? Barring utility for gambling, the value of such a prospect must vary between zero (when the chance of winning is nil) and one (when winning $300 is a certainty).

Intuition suggests that the value of the ticket is not a linear function of the probability of winning, as entailed by the expectation rule. In particular, an increase from 0% to 5% appears to have a larger effect than an increase from 30% to 35%, which also appears smaller than an increase from 95% to 100%. These considerations suggest a category-boundary effect: A change from impossibility to possibility or from possibility to certainty has a bigger impact than a comparable change in the middle of the scale. This hypothesis is incorporated into the curve displayed in Figure 11.2, which plots the weight attached to an event as a function of its stated numerical probability. The most salient feature of Figure 11.2 is that decision weights are regressive with respect to stated probabilities. Except near the endpoints, an increase of .05 in the probability of winning increases the value of the prospect by less than 5% of the value of the prize. We next investigate the implications of these psychophysical hypotheses for preferences among risky options.

In Figure 11.2 decision weights are lower than the corresponding probabilities over most of the range. Underweighting of moderate and high probabilities relative to sure things contributes to risk aversion in gains by reducing the attractiveness of positive gambles. The same effect also contributes to risk seeking in losses by attenuating the aversiveness of negative gambles. Low probabilities, however, are overweighted, and very low probabilities are either overweighted quite grossly or neglected altogether, making the decision weights highly unstable in that region. The overweighting of low probabilities reverses the pattern described above: It enhances the value of long shots and amplifies the aversiveness of a small chance of a severe loss. Consequently, people are often risk seeking in dealing with improbable gains and risk averse in dealing with unlikely losses. Thus, the characteristics of decision weights contribute to the attractiveness of both lottery tickets and insurance policies.

The nonlinearity of decision weights inevitably leads to violations of invariance, as illustrated in the following pair of problems:

Poblem 5 ($N = 85$): Consider the following two-stage game. In the first stage, there is a 75% chance to end the game without winning anything and a 25% chance to move into the second stage. If you reach the second stage you have a choice between:

A. a sure win of $30	(74%)
B. 80% chance to win $45	(26%)

Your choice must be made before the game starts, i.e., before the outcome of the first stage is known. Please indicate the option you prefer.

Problem 6 ($N = 81$): Which of the following options do you prefer?

C. 25% chance to win $30	(42%)
D. 20% chance to win $45	(58%)

Because there is one chance in four to move into the second stage in Problem 5, prospect A offers a .25 probability of winning $30, and prospect B offers .25 × .80 = .20 probability of winning $45. Problems 5 and 6 are therefore identical in terms of probabilities and outcomes.

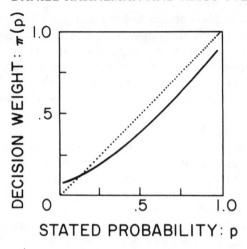

Figure 11.2. A hypothetical weighting function.

However, the preferences are not the same in the two versions: A clear majority favors the higher chance to win the smaller amount in Problem 5, whereas the majority goes the other way in Problem 6. This violation of invariance has been confirmed with both real and hypothetical monetary payoffs (the present results are with real money), with human lives as outcomes, and with a nonsequential representation of the chance process.

We attribute the failure of invariance to the interaction of two factors: the framing of probabilities and the nonlinearity of decision weights. More specifically, we propose that in Problem 5 people ignore the first phase, which yields the same outcome regardless of the decision that is made, and focus their attention on what happens if they do reach the second stage of the game. In that case, of course, they face a sure gain if they choose option A and an 80% chance of winning if they prefer to gamble. Indeed, people's choices in the sequential version are practically identical to the choices they make between a sure gain of $30 and an 85% chance to win $45. Because a sure thing is overweighted in comparison with events of moderate or high probability (see Figure 11.2) the option that may lead to a gain of $30 is more attractive in the sequential version. We call this phenomenon the *pseudo-certainty* effect because an event that is actually uncertain is weighted as if it were certain.

A closely related phenomenon can be demonstrated at the low end of the probability range. Suppose you are undecided whether or not to purchase earthquake insurance because the premium is quite high. As you hesitate, your friendly insurance agent comes forth with an alternative offer: "For half the regular premium you can be fully covered if the quake occurs on an odd day of the month. This is a good deal because for half the price you are covered for more than half the days." Why do most people find such probabilistic insurance distinctly unattractive? Figure 11.2 suggests an answer. Starting anywhere in the region of low probabilities, the impact on the decision weight of a reduction of probability from p to $p/2$ is considerably smaller than the effect of a reduction from $p/2$ to 0. Reducing the risk by half, then, is not worth half the premium.

The aversion to probabilistic insurance is significant for three reasons. First, it undermines the classical explanation of insurance in terms of a concave utility function. According to expected utility theory, probabilistic insurance should be definitely preferred to normal insurance when the latter is just acceptable (see Kahneman & Tversky, 1979b). Second, probabilistic insurance represents many forms of protective action, such as having a medical checkup, buying new tires, or installing a burglar alarm system. Such actions typically reduce the probability of some hazard without eliminating it altogether. Third, the acceptability of insurance can be manipulated by the framing of the contingencies. An insurance policy that covers fire but not flood, for example, could be evaluated either as full protection against a specific risk (e.g., fire), or as a reduction in the overall probability of property loss. Figure 11.2 suggests that people greatly undervalue a reduction in the probability of a hazard in comparison to the complete elimination of that hazard. Hence, insurance should appear more attractive when it is framed as the elimination of risk than when it is described as a reduction of risk. Indeed, Slovic, Fischhoff, and Lichtenstein (1982) showed that a hypothetical vaccine that reduces the probability of contracting a disease from 20% to 10% is less attractive if it is described as effective in half of the cases than if it is presented as fully effective against one of two exclusive and equally probable virus strains that produce identical symptoms.

Formulation effects

So far we have discussed framing as a tool to demonstrate failures of invariance. We now turn attention to the processes that control the framing of outcomes and events. The public health problem illustrates a formulation effect in which a change of wording from "lives saved" to "lives lost" induced a marked shift of preference from risk aversion to risk seeking. Evidently, the subjects adopted the descriptions of the outcomes as given in the question and evaluated the outcomes accordingly as gains or losses. Another formulation effect was reported by McNeil, Pauker, Sox, and Tversky (1982). They found that preferences of physicians and patients between hypothetical therapies for lung cancer varied markedly when their probable outcomes were described in terms of mortality or survival. Surgery, unlike radiation therapy, entails a risk of death during treatment. As a consequence, the surgery option was relatively less attractive when the statistics of treatment outcomes were described in terms of mortality rather than in terms of survival.

A physician, and perhaps a presidential advisor as well, could influence the decision made by the patient or by the President, without distorting or suppressing information, merely by the framing of outcomes and contingencies. Formulation effects can occur fortuitously, without anyone being aware of the impact of the frame on the ultimate decision. They can also be exploited deliberately to manipulate the relative attractiveness of options. For example, Thaler (1980) noted that lobbyists for the credit card industry insisted that any price difference between cash and credit purchases be labeled a cash discount rather than a credit card surcharge. The two labels frame the price difference as a gain or as a loss by implicitly designating either the lower or the higher price as normal. Because losses loom larger than gains, consumers are less likely to accept a surcharge than to forego a discount. As is to be expected, attempts to influence framing are common in the marketplace and in the political arena.

The evaluation of outcomes is susceptible to formulation effects because of the nonlinearity of the value function and the tendency of people to evaluate options in relation to the reference point that is suggested or implied by the statement of the problem. It is worthy of note that in other contexts people automatically transform equivalent messages into the same representation. Studies of language comprehension indicate that people quickly recode much of what they hear into an abstract representation that no longer distinguishes whether the idea was expressed in an active or in a passive form and no longer discriminates what was actually said from what was implied, presupposed, or implicated (Clark & Clark, 1977). Unfortunately, the mental machinery that performs these operations silently and effortlessly is not adequate to perform the task of recoding the two versions of the public health problem or the mortality-survival statistics into a common abstract form.

Transactions and trades

Our analysis of framing and of value can be extended to choices between multiattribute options, such as the acceptability of a transaction or a trade. We propose that, in order to evaluate a multiattribute option, a person sets up a mental account that specifies the advantages and the disadvantages associated with the option, relative to a multiattribute reference state. The overall value of an option is given by the balance of its advantages and its disadvantages in relation to the reference state. Thus, an option is acceptable if the value of its advantages exceeds the value of its disadvantages. This analysis assumes psychological – but not physical – separability of advantages and disadvantages. The model does not constrain the manner in which separate attributes are combined to form overall measures of advantage and of disadvantage, but it imposes on these measures assumptions of concavity and of loss aversion.

Our analysis of mental accounting owes a large debt to the stimulating work of Richard Thaler (1980, 1985), who showed the relevance of this process to consumer behavior. The following problem, based on examples of Savage (1954) and Thaler (1980), introduces some of the rules that govern the construction of mental accounts and illustrates the extension of the concavity of value to the acceptability of transactions.

Problem 7: Imagine that you are about to purchase a jacket for $125 and a calculator for $15. The calculator salesman informs you that the calculator you wish to buy is on sale for $10 at the other branch of the store, located 20 minutes drive away. Would you make a trip to the other store?

This problem is concerned with the acceptability of an option that combines a disadvantage of inconvenience with a financial advantage that can be framed as a *minimal, topical,* or *comprehensive* account. The minimal account includes only the differences between the two options and disregards the features that they share. In the minimal account, the advantage associated with driving to the other store is framed as a gain of $5. A topical account relates the consequences of possible choices to a reference level that is determined by the context within which the decision arises. In the preceding problem, the relevant topic is the purchase of the calculator, and the benefit of the trip is therefore framed as a reduction of the price, from $15 to $10. Because the potential saving is associated only with the calculator, the price of the jacket is not included in the topical account. The price of the jacket, as well as other expenses, could well be included in a more comprehensive account in which the saving would be evaluated in relation to, say, monthly expenses.

The formulation of the preceding problem appears neutral with respect to the adoption of a minimal, topical, or comprehensive account. We suggest, however, that people will spontaneously frame decisions in terms of topical accounts that, in the context of decision making, play a role analogous to that of "good forms" in perception and of basic-level categories in cognition. Topical organization, in conjunction with the concavity of value, entails that the willingness to travel to the other store for a saving of $5 on a calculator should be inversely related to the price of the calculator and should be independent of the price of the jacket. To test this prediction, we constructed another version of the problem in which the prices of the two items were interchanged. The price of the calculator was given as $125 in the first store and $120 in the other branch, and the price of the jacket was set at $15. As predicted, the proportions of respondents who said they would make the trip differed sharply in the two problems. The results showed that 68% of the respondents ($N = 88$) were willing to drive to the other branch to save $5 on a $15 calculator, but only 29% of 93 respondents were willing to make the same trip to save $5 on a $125 calculator. This finding supports the notion of topical organization of accounts, since the two versions are identical both in terms of a minimal and a comprehensive account.

The significance of topical accounts for consumer behavior is confirmed by the observation that the standard deviation of the prices that different stores in a city quote for the same product is roughly proportional to the average price of that product (Pratt, Wise, & Zeckhauser, 1979). Since the dispersion of prices is surely controlled by shoppers' efforts to find the best buy, these results suggest that consumers hardly exert more effort to save $15 on a $150 purchase than to save $5 on a $50 purchase.

The topical organization of mental accounts leads people to evaluate gains and losses in relative rather than in absolute terms, resulting in large variations in the rate at which money is exchanged for other things, such as the number of phone calls made to find a good buy or the willingness to drive a long distance to get one. Most consumers will find it easier to buy a car stereo system or a Persian rug, respectively, in the context of buying a car or a house than separately. These observations, of course, run counter to the standard rational theory of consumer behavior, which assumes invariance and does not recognize the effects of mental accounting.

The following problems illustrate another example of mental accounting in which the posting of a cost to an account is controlled by topical organization:

Problem 8 ($N = 200$): Imagine that you have decided to see a play and paid the admission price of $10 per ticket. As you enter the theater, you discover that you have lost the ticket. The seat was not marked, and the ticket cannot be recovered.
Would you pay $10 for another ticket?
  Yes (46%)   No (54%)

Problem 9 ($N = 183$): Imagine that you have decided to see a play where admission is $10 per ticket. As you enter the theater, you discover that you have lost a $10 bill.
Would you still pay $10 for a ticket for the play?
  Yes (88%)   No (12%)

The difference between the responses to the two problems is intriguing. Why are so many people unwilling to spend $10 after having lost a ticket, if they would readily spend that sum after losing an equivalent amount of cash? We attribute the difference to the topical organization of mental accounts. Going to the theater is normally viewed as a transaction in which the cost of the ticket is exchanged for the experience of seeing the play. Buying a second ticket increases the cost of seeing the play to a level that many respondents apparently find unacceptable. In contrast, the loss of the cash is not posted to the account of the play, and it affects the purchase of a ticket only by making the individual feel slightly less affluent.

An interesting effect was observed when the two versions of the problem were presented to the same subjects. The willingness to replace a lost ticket increased significantly when that problem followed the lost-cash version. In contrast, the willingness to buy a ticket after losing cash was not affected by prior presentation of the other problem. The juxta-position of the two problems apparently enabled the subjects to realize that it makes sense to think of the lost ticket as lost cash, but not vice versa.

The normative status of the effects of mental accounting is question-able. Unlike earlier examples, such as the public health problem, in which the two versions differed only in form, it can be argued that the alter-native versions of the calculator and ticket problems differ also in substance. In particular, it may be more pleasurable to save $5 on a $15 purchase than on a larger purchase, and it may be more annoying to pay twice for the same ticket than to lose $10 in cash. Regret, frustration, and self-satisfaction can also be affected by framing (Kahneman & Tversky, 1982c). If such secondary consequences are considered legitimate, then the observed preferences do not violate the criterion of invariance and cannot readily be ruled out as inconsistent or erroneous. On the other hand, secondary consequences may change upon reflection. The satisfac-tion of saving $5 on a $15 item can be marred if the consumer discovers that she would not have exerted the same effort to save $10 on a $200 purchase. We do not wish to recommend that any two decision problems that have the same primary consequences should be resolved in the same way. We propose, however, that systematic examination of alternative framings offers a useful reflective device that can help decision makers assess the values that should be attached to the primary and secondary consequences of their choices.

Losses and costs

Many decision problems take the form of a choice between retaining the status quo and accepting an alternative to it, which is advantageous in some respects and disadvantageous in others. The analysis of value that was applied earlier to unidimensional risky prospects can be extended to this case by assuming that the status quo defines the reference level for all attributes. The advantages of alternative options will then be evaluated as gains and their disadvantages as losses. Because losses loom larger than gains, the decision maker will be biased in favor of retaining the status quo.

Thaler (1980) coined the term "endowment effect" to describe the reluctance of people to part from assets that belong to their endowment. When it is more painful to give up an asset than it is pleasurable to obtain it, buying prices will be significantly lower than selling prices. That is, the highest price that an individual will pay to acquire an asset will be smaller than the minimal compensation that would induce the same individual to give up that asset, once acquired. Thaler discussed some examples of the endowment effect in the behavior of consumers and entrepreneurs. Several studies have reported substantial discrepancies between buying and selling prices in both hypothetical and real transactions (Gregory, 1983; Hammack & Brown, 1974; Knetsch & Sinden, 1984). These results have been presented as challenges to standard economic theory, in which buying and selling prices coincide except for transaction costs and effects of wealth. We also observed reluctance to trade in a study of choices between hypothetical jobs that differed in weekly salary (S) and in the temperature (T) of the workplace. Our respondents were asked to imagine that they held a particular position (S_1, T_1) and were offered the option of moving to a different position (S_2, T_2), which was better in one respect and worse in another. We found that most subjects who were assigned to (S_1, T_1) did not wish to move to (S_2, T_2), and that most subjects who were assigned to the latter position did not wish to move to the former. Evidently, the same difference in pay or in working conditions looms larger as a disadvantage than as an advantage.

In general, loss aversion favors stability over change. Imagine two hedonically identical twins who find two alternative environments equally attractive. Imagine further that by force of circumstance the twins are separated and placed in the two environments. As soon as they adopt their new states as reference points and evaluate the advantages and disadvantages of each other's environments accordingly, the twins will no longer be indifferent between the two states, and both will prefer to stay where they happen to be. Thus, the instability of preferences produces a preference for stability. In addition to favoring stability over change, the combination of adaptation and loss aversion provides limited protection against regret and envy by reducing the attractiveness of foregone alternatives and of others endowments.

Loss aversion and the consequent endowment effect are unlikely to play a significant role in routine economic exchanges. The owner of a store, for example, does not experience money paid to suppliers as losses and money received from customers as gains. Instead, the merchant adds costs and revenues over some period of time and only evaluates the balance. Matching debits and credits are effectively cancelled prior to evaluation. Payments made by consumers are also not evaluated as losses but as alternative purchases. In accord with standard economic analysis, money is naturally viewed as a proxy for the goods and services that it could buy. This mode of evaluation is made explicit when an individual has in mind a particular alternative, such as "I can either buy a new camera or a new tent." In this analysis, a person will buy a camera if its subjective value exceeds the value of retaining the money it would cost.

There are cases in which a disadvantage can be framed either as a cost or as a loss. In particular, the purchase of insurance can also be framed as a choice between a sure loss and the risk of a greater loss. In such cases the cost-loss discrepancy can lead to failures of invariance. Consider, for example, the choice between a sure loss of $50 and a 25% chance to lose $200. Slovic, Fischhoff, and Lichtenstein (1982) reported that 80% of their subjects expressed a risk-seeking preference for the gamble over the sure loss. However, only 35% of subjects refused to pay $50 for insurance against a 25% risk of losing $200. Similar results were also reported by Schoemaker and Kunreuther (1979) and by Hershey and Schoemaker (1980). We suggest that the same amount of money that was framed as an uncompensated loss in the first problem was framed as the cost of protection in the second. The modal preference was reversed in the two problems because losses are more aversive than costs.

We have observed a similar effect in the positive domain, as illustrated by the following pair of problems:

Problem 10: Would you accept a gamble that offers a 10% chance to win $95 and a 90% chance to lose $5?

Problem 11: Would you pay $5 to participate in a lottery that offers a 10% chance to win $100 and a 90% chance to win nothing?

A total of 132 undergraduates answered the two questions, which were separated by a short filler problem. The order of the questions was reversed for half the respondents. Although it is easily confirmed that the two problems offer objectively identical options, 55 of the respondents expressed different preferences in the two versions. Among them, 42 rejected the gamble in Problem 10 but accepted the equivalent lottery in Problem 11. The effectiveness of this seemingly inconsequential manipulation illustrates both the cost-loss discrepancy and the power of framing. Thinking of the $5 as a payment makes the venture more acceptable than thinking of the same amount as a loss.

The preceding analysis implies that an individual's subjective state can be improved by framing negative outcomes as costs rather than as losses. The possibility of such psychological manipulations may explain a paradoxical form of behavior that could be labeled the *dead-loss effect*. Thaler (1980) discussed the example of a man who develops tennis elbow soon after paying the membership fee in a tennis club and continues to play in agony to avoid wasting his investment. Assuming that the individual would not play if he had not paid the membership fee, the question arises: How can playing in agony improve the individual's lot? Playing in pain, we suggest, maintains the evaluation of the membership fee as a cost. If the individual were to stop playing, he would be forced to recognize the fee as a dead loss, which may be more aversive than playing in pain.

Concluding remarks

The concepts of utility and value are commonly used in two distinct senses: (a) *experience value*, the degree of pleasure or pain, satisfaction or anguish in the actual experience of an outcome; and (b) *decision value*, the contribution of an anticipated outcome to the overall attractiveness or aversiveness of an option in a choice. The distinction is rarely explicit in decision theory because it is tacitly assumed that decision values and experience values coincide. This assumption is part of the conception of an idealized decision maker who is able to predict future experiences with perfect accuracy and evaluate options accordingly. For ordinary decision makers, however, the correspondence of decision values between experience values is far from perfect (March, 1978). Some factors that affect experience are not easily anticipated, and some factors that affect decisions do not have a comparable impact on the experience of outcomes.

In contrast to the large amount of research on decision making, there has been relatively little systematic exploration of the psychophysics that relate hedonic experience to objective states. The most basic problem of hedonic psychophysics is the determination of the level of adaptation or aspiration that separates positive from negative outcomes. The hedonic reference point is largely determined by the objective status quo, but it is also affected by expectations and social comparisons. An objective improvement can be experienced as a loss, for example, when an employee receives a smaller raise than everyone else in the office. The experience of pleasure or pain associated with a change of state is also critically dependent on the dynamics of hedonic adaptation. Brickman and Campbell's (1971) concept of the hedonic treadmill suggests the radical hypothesis that rapid adaptation will cause the effects of any objective improvement to be short-lived. The complexity and subtlety of hedonic experience make it difficult for the decision maker to anticipate the actual experience that outcomes will produce. Many a person who ordered a meal when ravenously hungry has admitted to a big mistake when the fifth course arrived on the table. The common mismatch of decision values and experience values introduces an additional element of uncertainty in many decision problems.

The prevalence of framing effects and violations of invariance further complicates the relation between decision values and experience values. The framing of outcomes often induces decision values that have no counterpart in actual experience. For example, the framing of outcomes of therapies for lung cancer in terms of mortality or survival is unlikely to affect experience, although it can have a pronounced influence on choice. In other cases, however, the framing of decisions affects not only decision but experience as well. For example, the framing of an expenditure as an uncompensated loss or as the price of insurance can probably influence the experience of that outcome. In such cases, the evaluation of outcomes in the context of decisions not only anticipates experience but also molds it.

Part IV

Law

"Justice for all" has been a primary goal of our society and many others. Yet rendering justice is an immensely difficult task. Not everyone has the wisdom of a King Solomon, and legal issues today are dealt with by mortals whose judgments are regularly called into question.

Attempts to assist legal decision making and judgment have only recently begun. In the 1960s some psychologists and statisticians sought to improve the jury's decision making by quantifying the evidence. In one of the most famous cases (*People* v. *Collins*, 1968), a robbery victim could not positively identify the culprit but did testify that the robber was certainly a woman with a blond ponytail who entered a yellow convertible driven by a black male with a moustache and beard. The prosecution produced an expert who testified that the probability that these characteristics would co-occur in any given couple was one in 12 million. Therefore the prosecution insisted that the accused woman who corresponded to this description was guilty beyond a reasonable doubt. Modern research, however, has focused mainly on the manner in which judges and juries use information. For example, Ebbesen and Konečni (1975) carefully described the factors that a judge considered in setting the amount of bail. This research is not *prescriptive*; that is, it does not presume to tell a judge how to behave. Instead, it is *descriptive*; the researchers analyze the judge's behavior in order to describe it and thus perhaps determine the cause(s) of it.

Recent research, some of which has received a great deal of publicity, has indicated that when left to their own devices, witnesses and jurors may depart from strictly legal, or normative, standards. In the 1970s several researchers demonstrated that eyewitness testimony was much less accurate than was commonly supposed. Many social psychologists demonstrated that "extralegal" factors such as the attractiveness of the defendant exerted a strong influence on the verdict and the severity of the sentence. Findings such as these suggest that research on judgment and decision making in the courts would be highly useful.

Our first selection in this part, by Michael J. Saks and Robert F. Kidd, is an excellent summary of the use of "cognitive heuristics" (simple rules of thumb for inferring guilt or innocence) by jurors. The second article, by

John S. Carroll, examines parole decisions. The final selection, by Michael Saks and Reid Hastie, illustrates a test of the juror's ability to ignore evidence that the judge has ruled inadmissible in court.

12. Human information processing and adjudication: Trial by heuristics

Michael J. Saks and
Robert F. Kidd

While a trial is many things, it most surely is a social invention for deciding between disputed alternatives under conditions of uncertainty. The values this invention seeks to maximize may be manifold and contradictory, but one of the most important among them is accuracy or correctness. Through legal decision making we seek to avoid the classic errors of convicting an innocent defendant or acquitting a guilty one, or finding liability when there is none or failing to find liability when it is present. Whatever justice may be, surely it is not error.

Various commentators have proposed, and various advocates have sought to introduce at trial, mathematical or statistical tools to guide the trier of fact and to reduce the number of inevitable errors (e.g., Baldus & Cole, 1979; Broun & Kelly, 1970; Cullison, 1969; Fairley & Mosteller, 1974; Finkelstein & Fairley, 1970; Kaplan, 1968; Meyer, 1973; Wigmore, 1940; EEOC Guidelines, V.29, Code of Federal Regulations, 1979: §§1607.1 and 1607.5[c]; Cohen, 1977, 1979, 1980; Schum, 1979). A limited amount of sharply reasoned and intriguing debate has taken place over these issues both in law reviews and in appellate courts (e.g., *People v. Collins*, 1968; *Smith* v. *Rapid Transit, Inc.*, 1945). Perhaps the most thorough critique of these proposals has been that of Lawrence Tribe in his article, "Trial by Mathematics: Precision and Ritual in the Legal Process" (1971). In that paper, Tribe seeks to persuade us that "the costs of attempting to integrate mathematics into the factfinding process of a legal trial outweigh their benefits" (1971, p. 1393).

Tribe does not object to the introduction of quantitative evidence, though he is decidedly wary of it and its aroma of certitude. What he advocates is that such data be used, if they must, in their most descriptive

This chapter originally appeared in the *Law and Society Review*, 1980, 15(1), 123–160. Copyright © 1980 by the Law and Society Association. Reprinted with permission.

and raw form, that the judge or jury not be told how these data might be analyzed and what inferences might be drawn from the results of such analysis. The kinds of analysis and mathematical models used by all sorts of scientists, engineers, administrators, planners, and others in order to put questions to their data is what Tribe would ban from legal fact finding. His objections to such mathematizing of evidence are based on his opinion that it leads to imprecise estimates that are inevitably probabilistic, that soft variables are dwarfed in favor of more easily quantifiable variables, that it is difficult to apply background probability estimates to deciding specific instances, and that the trial process would be dehumanized. Tribe argues, in essence, that keeping a trial as intuitive, as elemental, as the Anglo-Saxon trial can be will preserve the symbolism and humanness, thereby best serving the courts and society.

In a fundamental criticism of using the somewhat more precise language and meaning of mathematics, Tribe eloquently defends the value of legal symbolism and the resulting mask of certainty.

The system does *not* in fact authorize the imposition of criminal punishment when the trier recognizes a quantifiable doubt as to the defendant's guilt. Instead, the system dramatically – if imprecisely – insists upon as close an approximation to certainty as seems humanly attainable in the circumstances. The jury is charged that any "reasonable doubt," of whatever magnitude, must be resolved in favor of the accused. Such insistence on the greatest certainty that seems reasonably attainable can serve at the trial's end, like the presumption of innocence at the trial's start, to affirm the dignity of the accused and to display respect for his rights as a person – in this instance, by declining to put those rights in deliberate jeopardy and by refusing to sacrifice him to the interests of others.

In contrast, for the jury to announce that it is prepared to convict the defendant in the face of an acknowledged and numerically measurable doubt as to his guilt is to tell the accused that those who judge him find it preferable to accept the resulting risk of his unjust conviction than to reduce that risk by demanding any further or more convincing proof of his guilt.

...That some mistaken verdicts are inevitably returned even by jurors who regard themselves as "certain" is of course true but is irrelevant; such unavoidable errors are in no sense *intended*, and the fact that they must occur if trials are to be conducted at all need not undermine the effort, through the symbols of trial procedure, to express society's fundamental commitment to the protection of the defendant's rights as a person, as an end in himself. On the other hand, formulating an "acceptable" risk of error to which the trier is willing deliberately to subject the defendant would interfere seriously with this expressive role of the demand for certitude – however unattainable real certitude may be, and however clearly all may ultimately recognize its unattainability. (1971, p. 1374)

A trial may indeed be more than a search for the truth in a given matter; but surely it is not less. We will seek to demonstrate, contrary to Tribe, that while certain errors and harm may be inherent even in the proper use of probabilistic tools, even more harm may be inherent in not using them.

The present paper has two aims and consequently is divided into two major sections. The first aim is to cast altogether new light on this debate by challenging Tribe's assumptions from an empirical point of view. We will do this by presenting the conclusions of a family of theories of human decision making known as "behavioral decision theory" and some of the empirical research findings on which they stand. These are fascinating in themselves and highly relevant to the question of whether intuitive decision making by humans and explicit calculation of probabilities will lead a trier of fact closer to the correct conclusion.

Influential as Tribe's paper has been, like much legal scholarship, it is a Swiss cheese of assumptions about human behavior[1] – in this case human decision-making processes – which are asserted as true simply because they fall within the wide reach of the merely plausible, not because any evidence is adduced on their behalf. The present article makes available to this important and increasingly unavoidable debate some important findings about human decision processes and their implications for the trial process and for the role of mathematical tools in the fact-finding portion of that process. While the other debaters have focused on mathematics and make facile assumptions about what humans do with such information, we focus on the human decision-making machinery. By enumerating its characteristic problems, we invite legal policy makers and other observers to decide not between flawed mathematics and unspecified, black-box human cognitive processes, but between two imperfect systems for reaching decisions.

The second goal of this article is to explore still other implications of these findings for the trial process, going even to its fundamental structure. These implications include the effect of the trial's format on the fact finder's subjective certainty of guilt, the costs of relying upon human intuition, the unstoppable growth of scientific and technical evidence in trials, the limited influence on fact finders of statistical relative to anecdotal information, the question of whether particularistic information really exists for the legal fact finder, the associated problem of applying background base-rate probabilities to reaching decisions in specific instances, the problem of evaluating witness credibility, and the use of heuristic biases by lawyers to be more persuasive trial advocates.

---

[1] Consider the following examples: people have great difficulty translating their subjective feeling of certainty into statements of probability (at 1358). Presented with a "mathematically powerful intellectual machine," people will tend to disregard soft nonquantifiable variables in favor of quantified variables (Tribe, 1971, pp. 1360–1362). When jurors vote to convict, many/most would describe their state of mind as "completely sure" or "as sure as possible" (Tribe, 1971, p. 1374). In the face of quantitative data, few jurors will perform or even recall their "humanizing function, to employ their intuition and their sense of community values to shape their ultimate conclusions" (Tribe, 1976, p. 1376). These premises, sometimes important to Tribe's thesis, stand without any supporting evidence. If these seem picky, consider this major thesis: that symbolic functions of the trial are often more important than accurate fact finding. This too stands without evidence.

Decision making under uncertainty

Most legal decision making, like that in many other areas of complex activity, is done under conditions of uncertainty.[2] Events must be classified, predicted, or post-dicted in circumstances where the correct choice is more probable than zero but less probable than unity. If one wished to choose a given product with the lowest unit price, the fastest transit route between two cities, or which manner of calculating one's taxes results in the least liability, one could, through proper information gathering and analysis, identify the correct solution with certainty (or something bordering on certainty). Other problems, by virtue of their complexity, the limitations of available information, or the inadequacy of our conceptualizations for dealing with them, have best solutions that cannot be known with certainty to be correct. Judges and jurors are called upon, for example, to assess the likelihood that a witness's report is congruent with the actual event; the probability, given certain evidence, that a defendant committed an alleged offense; the risk of harm that reasonably should have been foreseen as associated with certain design features of a product; the probability that a pollutant caused certain damage; or the likelihood that a person in jeopardy of civil commitment is dangerous to self or others.[3] Thus, the nature of the questions and the information available to judicial decision makers defines their task as an uncertain and probabilistic one.[4]

Abundant evidence from psychological research, however, suggests that in many contexts decision makers' intuitive, common-sense judgments depart markedly and lawfully (in the scientific sense) from the actual probabilities. People use a number of simplifying operations, called "heuristics," to reduce the complexity of information which must be

[2] One of the simplest ways to think about uncertainty is to consider predicting a simple event. If the event (say, the sun shining tomorrow) *always* occurs, we would be certain it will happen ($p = 1.00$); if it *never* occurs, we would be certain it will not happen ($p = 0.00$); if it occured 60 percent of the time, our confidence in predicting its next occasion would reflect something other than certainty, and our prediction would most likely reflect the relative frequency of occurrence ($p = 0.60$). See Raiffa, 1968; Savage, 1950.

[3] Many of the rules of evidence and procedure are designed precisely to deal with the uncertainty of knowledge that guides adjudications, most evident in the standard of proof required to reach a finding. When the available information comes to be recognized as systematically defective, the standard of proof has been lowered to meet it (*Addington v. Texas* [1979]).

[4] That probabilistic thinking is inherent in the law and familiar to lawyers is evident from even a casual reading of the notes and commentaries to the Federal Rules of Evidence or the lawyer's role as defined by the Code of Professional Responsibility:

In serving a client as adviser, a lawyer in appropriate circumstances should give his professional opinion as to what the ultimate decisions of the courts would *likely* be as to the applicable law.

The advocate may urge any permissible construction of the law favorable to his client, without regard to his professional opinion as to the *likelihood* that the construction will ultimately prevail [emphasis added] (ABA Code of Professional Responsibility EC7-3 and 7-4).

integrated to yield a decision. These simplifying strategies often lead to errors in judgment. Consider the following examples:

1. After observing three consecutive red wins, a group of people playing roulette start to switch their bets to black. After red wins on the fourth and fifth spins, more and more players switch to black, and they are increasingly surprised when the roulette wheel produces a red win the sixth, and then the seventh time. In actuality, on each spin the odds of a red win remain constant at 1:1. The shifting of bets to black was irrational, as was the strong subjective sense that after each successive red win, black became more likely.

2. The following description is of a man selected at random from a group composed of 70 lawyers and 30 engineers. "John is a 30-year-old man. He is married and has two children. He is active in local politics. The hobby that he most enjoys is rare book collecting. He is competitive, argumentative, and articulate." A large group of respondents was asked to estimate the probability that John is a lawyer rather than an engineer. Their median probability estimate was .95. Another group of respondents was asked the same question, except that they were first told that the group from which John was selected consisted of 30 lawyers and 70 engineers. The second group's median estimate of the likelihood that John is a lawyer was also .95. Information about the composition of the group from which John was selected logically should have affected the estimated probability, but it had no effect at all on the decision makers' judgment. (This problem is taken from Kahneman and Tversky, 1973.) Only at the extremes of the distributions, where the group approaches 100 lawyers and 0 engineers (or the converse) do the decision makers become sensitive to the information about group composition.

3. A cab was involved in a hit-and-run accident at night. Two cab companies, the green and the blue, operate in the city. A witness reports that the offending cab was blue, and legal action is brought against the blue cab company. The court learns that 85 percent of the city's cabs are green and 15 percent are blue. Further, the court learns that on a test of ability to identify cabs under appropriate visibility conditions, the witness is correct on 80 percent of the identifications and incorrect on 20 percent. Several hundred persons have been given this problem and asked to estimate the probability that the responsible cab was in fact a blue cab. Their typical probability response was .80. In actuality, the evidence given leads to a probability of .41 that the responsible cab was blue.[5] (This problem is taken from Tversky and Kahneman, 1980.)

The first example illustrates the simplest and best known of errors in human probability judgment, the "Gambler's Fallacy." In a sequence of

[5] The indispensability of such base rates to making sense out of evidence is not recognized in the law, but it is elsewhere. In medicine, for example, laboratory tests constitute a major source of evidence for decision making. Each test has a known or knowable "sensitivity" and "specificity." Specificity means the probability that a person who is said by the test not to have a disease actually does not have it. Sensitivity means the probability that a person who is said by the test to have a disease actually does have it. These parameters tell us the probable accuracy of the test results in an individual case, and the accuracy "is related fundamentally to the incidence [i.e., base rate] of the disease" (Krupp, Sweet, Jawetz, Biglieri, Roe, & Camargo, 1979; Krieg, Gambino, & Galen, 1975).

independent events, outcomes of prior events do not affect the probability of later events. Each event is independent of the other. On the seventh spin, the roulette wheel neither remembers nor cares what it did on the preceding six spins. People know that in the long run, half the wins will be red and half black. They err in believing that a small local sequence of events will be representative of the infinite sequence. "Chance is commonly viewed as a self-correcting process in which a deviation in one direction induces a deviation in the opposite direction to restore the equilibrium. In fact, deviations are not 'corrected' as a chance process unfolds, they are merely diluted" (Tversky & Kahneman, 1974). Although intuition in this context is out of harmony with reality, we all feel it compellingly, and continue to hear that baseball players who have not had a hit in some time are "due" for one, and that lightning will not strike twice in the same place.[6] These common-sense judgments are, nevertheless, dead wrong.

The second example illustrates how human decision making tends to be insensitive to base rates when case-specific information is available.[7] Given only the group base rates – 30 lawyers: 70 engineers – people rely heavily on this information to make their judgments. They correctly say the probability is .30 that the person selected is a lawyer. When descriptive case-specific information is added, they tend to ignore the numerical base rate and rely instead on the degree to which the description of John is representative of their stereotype of lawyers. Subjects base their estimate of the probability that John is a lawyer on the degree of correspondence between his description and their stereotype of lawyers as argumentative, competitive, and politically aware. Given the base-rate data in this example, it is 5.44 times as likely that John is a lawyer when the group is composed of 70 lawyers and 30 engineers than when the opposite membership distribution holds.[8]

The third example also demonstrates insensitivity to base-rate information, this time in a context where both the base-rate and the case-specific information are given numerically. The actual low probability that

---

[6] This reflects belief in a "law of small numbers," even though nature's design is limited to the "law of larger numbers" (i.e., as sample sizes become increasingly large, they will more closely approach the parameters of the population; the "law" of small numbers would hold that this works also for small samples) (Tversky & Kahneman, 1971a).

[7] Note that this is precisely the opposite of what is assumed by many commentators (cf. Tribe, 1971).

[8] The solution may be calculated by Bayes' rule, in odds form. The rationale is not complicated. The person is either a lawyer or an engineer. The odds that he is a lawyer are 70:30, that he is an engineer, 30:70. The ratio of the former odds to the latter is

$$\frac{\frac{70}{30}}{\frac{30}{70}} = \left(\frac{70}{30}\right) = 5.44.$$

For a discussion of Bayes' Theorem, see Finkelstein and Fairley, 1970.

the cab is blue is due to the fact that the base rate for blue cabs is very low, and the witness is of dubious acuity. Indeed, the base rate is more extreme than the witness is credible. But, fact finders apparently are unable simultaneously to relate the color of the hit-and-run cab to two different concerns, namely, the sampling of cabs from the city's cab population and imperfect color identification by the witness. They ignore the base-rate information and treat the accuracy of the witness as equal to the probability of a correct identification.[9]

These illustrations demonstrate the gap between the judgments people make intuitively and the probabilities yielded by explicit calculation (or by empirical observation of actual outcomes[10]). People do not always err, but in particular decision making situations they tend predictably to be incorrect. Because these errors of intuition are systematic and lawful, they are called biases. Because these biases result from the simplifying strategies used by decision makers, whose cognitive capacities cannot otherwise efficiently process the information, they are known as heuristic biases.[11]

[9] Again, by Bayes' rule,

$$\frac{P(B/W)}{P(G/W)}$$

that is, the ratio of the probability that the cab was blue, given the witness's statement; to the probability that the cab was green, given the witness's statement

$$= \frac{P(W/B)\ P(B)}{P(W/G)\ P(G)} = \frac{(.8)\ (.15)}{(.2)\ (.85)} = \frac{.12}{.17}$$

$$P(B/W) = \frac{.12}{.12 + .17} = .41$$

Graphically,

		In reality, cab is G	B	
Probability W is	Right	.68	.12	.80
	Wrong	.17	.03	.20
		.85	.15	

Thus, given that W says "the cab was blue," there is a probability of .12 that the cab was blue and the witness is right, and a probability of .17 that the cab was green and the witness wrong. Thus, given that the witness says "blue," the probability is .12/(.12 + .17) = .41 that the cab was in fact blue.

[10] If the actual experiments were carried out, and some have been, the empirical observations would confirm, and have confirmed, the explicit calculation rather than the implicit judgment. That such "statistical" decision making is more accurate than "clinical" judgment, is a well settled question (Meehl, 1954; Sawyer, 1966).

[11] A heuristic is a strategy, usually a simplifying strategy, which provides aid and guidance in solving a problem. A heuristic is the opposite of an algorithm. In deciding what move to make in a chess game, one could systematically consider and evaluate every possible move. This would be an algorithmic strategy. Or one could evaluate only the positions of pieces in the center of the board and the most important pieces. That would be a heuristic strategy.

These heuristic biases are not limited to decision making in legal contexts, nor are they limited to the simple illustrations cited above. The same errors have been observed for bankers and stock market experts predicting closing stock prices (von Holstein, 1972; Slovic, 1969a), for Las Vegas casino patrons making bets (Lichtenstein & Slovic, 1971, 1973), for psychiatrists and clinical psychologists predicting behavior (see reviews in Meehl, 1954; Mischel, 1968), for statistically sophisticated researchers estimating statistical values (Brewer & Owen, 1973; Cohen, 1962; Tversky & Kahneman, 1971a), for military intelligence analysts (Brown, Kahr, & Peterson, 1974b), for engineers estimating repair time for inoperative electric generators (Kidd, 1970), for flood plain residents estimating the probability of floods (Slovic, Kunreuther, & White, 1974), for physicians making diagnoses and prognoses (Einhorn, 1972; Gilbert, McPeek, & Mosteller, 1977), and in business decision making (Bowman, 1963). One can summarize these diverse findings by concluding that "people systematically violate the principles of rational decision making when judging probabilities, making predictions, or otherwise attempting to cope with probabilistic tasks" (Slovic, Fischhoff, & Lichtenstein, 1976a).

In many areas, decision aids are being developed to compensate for the fact that ". . . man's cognitive capacities are not adequate for the tasks which confront him" (Hammond, 1974). These aids range from the advice to engage in explicit calculation of probabilities (Tversky & Kahneman, 1971a; Kahneman & Tversky, 1979b), to decision analysis (Howard, Matheson, & Miller, 1977; Raiffa, 1968; Schlaifer, 1969), to human/machine systems (Davis, Weisbrod, Freedy, & Weltman, 1975; Edwards, 1962; Hammond, 1971; Hammond, Stewart, Brehmer, & Steinmann, 1975). We hope it is not unduly optimistic to suppose that the law could be another area in which less than reliable, less than accurate decision making can be identified and corrective strategies developed.

We now turn to a closer examination of decision heuristics – what they are, why they exist, their impact on human judgmnet, and their implications for decision making in legal contexts.

Heuristics

The leading research in decision heuristics is that of Amos Tversky and Daniel Kahneman.[12] These two research psychologists have identified a limited number of principles which seem to guide the simplification of complex information-processing tasks. For many purposes these simplifying heuristics result in reasonable judgments; however, they often lead to distorted and systematically erroneous decisions. The three funda-

---

[12] We have borrowed heavily from these researchers, and must credit them with the basic discoveries. We have applied these findings to legal concerns, and any errors in doing so are ours. For some of their original research reports, see Kahneman and Tversky, 1972, 1973; Tversky, 1975; Tversky and Kahneman, 1971a, 1973, 1974, 1980.

mental heuristics involved in making probabilistic judgments are: representativeness, availability, and anchoring and adjustment.

Representativeness

Often probability statements concern the likelihood that an event, behavior, or object originated from or caused another event, behavior, or object. For example, what is the probability that person P committed a murder, given that his fingerprints are found on the murder weapon? What is the probability that a firm intended to discriminate in hiring, given that none of its 14 employees is a member of an ethnic minority? In answering some of these types of questions, people sometimes rely on the representativeness heuristic.

With this "cognitive shorthand," people assess the likelihood that event A causes or is associated with event B by the degree to which A is representative of B, or in other words, the degree to which A resembles B. People connect events A and B by assessing the degree of similarity between them. This assessment invariably leads to the inference that A and B are connected probabilistically simply because they bear some resemblance to each other in terms of their descriptive features. For a great many purposes, this is a useful strategy – namely, those occasions when probability is highly correlated with similarity. One might choose livestock by assessing the degree to which the offspring are similar to other animals that grew to be prized adults. One might admit applicants to law school by assessing the degree to which they are similar to others who were successful in the past.

But judging the probability of an event based on its similarity to or representativeness of other events may lead to defects in judgment, because similarity is not influenced by facts that should affect probability judgments. One major factor that should affect probability judgments is the *prior probability* or the prior frequency of the occurrence of an event. In the example of the cab accident, the subjects' likelihood estimates were not affected by the fact that only 15 percent of the cabs in the hypothetical city were blue. This prior probability makes it much more likely that the hit-and-run accident was committed by a green cab.

A common example of this kind of information in court arises from evidence presented by experts in scientific or technological fields. Many of the facts typically presented, which can be highly diagnostic for the fact finder, are of this probabilistic sort: the risk of death due to anesthesia is 1 in 5000; a palmprint of a particular type occurs with a frequency of 1 in 1000; one-third of suicide victims leave a note. Particularly well studied are the errors made by psychiatrists and clinical psychologists (and then judges) in predicting dangerousness (Ennis & Litwack, 1974; Steadman & Cocozza, 1974; Ziskin, 1975). The consistent overprediction of dangerousness is in part due to experts' insensitivity to the low frequency of such behavior and reliance on the representativeness heuristic wherein the person threatened with commitment is compared to the stereotype of a dangerous person (Kahneman & Tversky, 1972). The greater the degree of similarity, the greater the clinician's confidence in predicting dangerousness. But, however much person P may resemble the clinician's stereotype of the dangerous person, the extremely low base rate of violent behavior (either in the population or for this individual) means that the probability that person P will be violent is very low. Clinician's errors are thus expected to be high and in the direction of massive overprediction of dangerousness (Dershowitz, 1968; Livermore, Malmquist, & Meehl, 1968; also see references in Ennis & Litwack, 1974; Ziskin, 1975).

In addition to uses (or should we say non-uses?) of base-rate information for deciding conventional cases in the courts, we find growing numbers of scientific and technological cases. These include litigation in the areas of antitrust, economic programs, nuclear regulation, products liability, environment and pollution, rate making, new drugs, consumer law, energy policy and others.[13] Many of these cases are appeals from regulatory agency decisions, in which the very meaning of the data is at issue. (See, e.g., *Essex Chemical Co.* v. *Ruckelshaus*, 1973; *Ethyl Corporation of America* v. *EPA*, 1976; *Greater Boston Television Corp.* v. *FCC*, 1970; *International Harvester Co.* v. *Ruckelshaus*, 1973; *Portland Cement Association* v. *Ruckelshaus*, 1973; also see Stewart, 1975; Bazelon, 1977.) In all of the kinds of cases mentioned, base-rate information – the form in which many legislative facts often exist (e.g., *Ballew* v. *Georgia*, 1978; *Gregg* v. *Georgia*, 1976; and cases cited above; also see Leventhal, 1974) – is typically presented as evidence along with case-specific information. As we have seen, the base-rate information, despite its considerable value to rational decision making, is likely to be given less weight when the fact finder has to integrate it with case-specific information.

Some solutions have already been proposed for the law. Perhaps the minimum solution is already present: allowing the information to be testified to by experts (Federal Rules of Evidence 702, 703, 704, 705). Clever experts could turn the representativeness heuristic to advantage in their testimony or appendices to briefs by supplementing their base-rate information with anecdotal examples or illustrations, which are more case-specific and hence ought to be more persuasive to the heuristic decision maker. Another suggestion has been to have an additional expert – for example, a statistician – give the fact finder guidance in what the base-rate evidence means or how it can be combined optimally with whatever the fact finder thinks about the case-specific information

---

[13] See the recent bibliography, Cohen, Ronen, & Stepan, 1978, especially the sections on Science and the Adjudicatory Function of Law, Computers, Medicine, Public Health and Safety, Natural Resources and Environmental Controls, and Science and International Law.

(Finkelstein and Fairley, 1970). Some commentators have taken so seriously the general problem of handling scientific and technical data in the courts that they have suggested more extensive solutions, such as special masters (Beuscher, 1941; Federal Rules of Civil Procedure 53; *LaBuy* v. *Howes Leather Co.*, 1957; *Avco Corp.* v. *A.T.T.*, 1975; *Vermont* v. *N.Y.*, 1974; *U.S.* v. *I.B.M.*, 1976; *Omnium Lyonnais D'Etancheite* v. *Dow Chemical Co.*, 1977; *Hobson* v. *Hansen*, 1971), court advisers (e.g., *Reserve Mining* v. *U.S.*, 1975; Federal Rules of Evidence 706), and special courts.

Another important variant of the representativeness heuristic is human *insensitivity to sample size*. In the world of reality, larger samples are more likely than smaller samples to approximate the characteristics of the population from which they were drawn. "This fundamental notion of statistics is evidently not part of people's repertoire of intuitions" (Tversky & Kahneman, 1974; p. 312). A clear instance of this error in judicial policy making is provided by the U.S. Supreme Court in *Williams* v. *Florida* (1970). In deciding whether reductions in jury size from twelve to six would reduce the jury's ability to provide a representative cross-section of the community, the court concluded:

[W]hile in theory the number of viewpoints represented on a randomly selected jury ought to increase as the size of the jury increases, in practice the difference between the twelve-man and the six-man jury in terms of the cross-section of the community represented *seems* likely to be negligible [emphasis added]. (*Williams* v. *Florida*, 1970: 101)

The Court's intuitive sampling theory was found to be in error when compared to explicit calculation. For example, sampling randomly from a community composed of a stratified population (90 percent one group and 10 percent another), 72 percent of 12-person juries would include at least one member of the minority while only 47 percent of six-person juries would include at least one minority person (Saks, 1977; Zeisel, 1971; *Ballew* v. *Georgia*, 1978). In this example, the "negligible" difference is 25 percent. Because intuitive decision makers expect samples of any size to be representative of the population from which they originate, they will often be wrong.

The *illusion of validity* is a third example[14] of the representativeness heuristic. As shown above, people tend to make intuitive predictions by selecting the outcome that is more similar to their stereotype. People express great confidence in such predictions, ignoring factors which limit predictive accuracy. Given a brief personality description, people rely on their stereotypes, or implicit personality theory,[15] and go from the description – however scanty, unreliable, or outdated – to the prediction.[16] Even when decision makers are knowledgeable about the factors limiting

---

[14] Other kinds of representativeness heuristics the human mind is heir to include misconceptions of chance, insensitivity to predictability, and misconceptions of regression. See Tversky and Kahneman, 1974.

the accuracy of predictions, their intuitions press them compellingly toward error.

> It is a common observation that psychologists who conduct selection interviews often experience considerable confidence in their predictions, even when they know of the vast literature that shows selection interviews to be highly fallible. The continued reliance on the clinical interview for selection, despite repeated demonstrations of its inadequacy, amply attests to the strength of this effect. (Tversky and Kahneman, 1974, p. 1126)

One of the major determinants of the strength of the illusion (i.e., the degree of unwarranted confidence) is the pattern of internal consistency among the inputs. If the information on which the conclusion is based is seen as highly consistent (it all "points in the same direction" or "hangs together"), the decision maker's confidence in the stereotype's accuracy is greatly increased. Unfortunately, this pattern of consistency will often be the result of redundant information, rather than additional information. When actual data are collected to develop predictive models, as by social scientists and others, the elementary statistics of correlation show that input variables that are highly correlated, or redundant, do not improve the accuracy of the prediction. Predictions achieve greater accuracy when they are based upon informational inputs which are independent of each other. "Thus, redundancy among inputs decreases accuracy even as it increases confidence, and people are often confident in predictions that are quite likely to be off the mark" (Tversky & Kahneman, 1974, p. 1126).

The skillful attorney may trade on this defect of intuition by trying to paint a consistent personality picture of a party to a case, whether it be through character testimony, through other evidence, or in argument. Given our susceptibility to such illusions of validity, the rules of evidence are fortunate in their exclusion of evidence of "character" traits.[17] And, while FRE 403 excludes the "needless presentation of cumulative evidence" because it wastes time, the rule will also tend to avoid the problems inherent in increasing fact finders' confidence without increasing their accuracy. We should note, however, that FRE 403 asserts that such evidence is relevant, but should be excluded anyway. To the extent that evidence is redundant, it is *not* relevant, that is, it does not have "any tendency to make the existence of any fact . . . more probable

---

[15] "Implicit personality theory" is the set of beliefs each person holds concerning the behavior and personality of others – that is, which characteristics occur together, predict other characteristics, predict behavior, etc. One's implicit personality theory will be partly culturally determined, partly idiosyncratic, but in any case is an untested, unconfirmed collection of ideas that people rely on to explain or predict others. See Bruner and Tagiuri, 1954.

[16] That is, they do not take into account the inaccuracy of their implicit personality theories.

[17] Federal Rules of Evidence, Rule 404. While the rule excludes "character" evidence for reasons of relevancy, it has the corollary advantage of avoiding the activation of character-behavior stereotypes, which are strong, and the likely impact of illusory validity on the fact finder.

or less probable than it would be without the evidence" – except subjectively (Federal Rules of Evidence 401; also see Lempert, 1977). And that, of course, is the very issue on which the illusion of validity principle casts light. Redundant information makes certain facts *seem* intuitively more probable, but in actuality it does not increase their likelihood.

Availability

A second heuristic discussed by Tversky and Kahneman is availability. According to this heuristic, people are likely to judge the probability or frequency of an event based on the ease with which they can recall instances or occurrences of the event. Availability, as noted by these researchers, may be a helpful cue when assessing probability, because events that are more frequent may be recalled more readily than events that occur less frequently. However, factors other than simple objective frequency may affect intuitive probability estimates.

In an elementary demonstration of this effect, subjects heard a list of well-known personalities of both sexes and were subsequently asked to judge whether the list contained more names of men than of women. [In actuality, the numbers of men and women were equal.] Different lists were presented to different groups of subjects. In some of the lists the men were relatively more famous than the women, and in others the women were relatively more famous than the men. In each of the lists, the subjects erroneously judged that the class (sex) that had the more famous personalities was the more numerous. (Tversky & Kahneman, 1974, p. 1127)

Because they were more readily available to memory, people thought they were more numerous, and consequently made erroneous judgments. Factors such as familiarity, salience, and recency of the occurrence of the event affect the retrievability of information and enhance the potency of the availability heuristic.

The availability heuristic raises important concerns for the presentation of certain kinds of evidence to a fact finder. The subjective estimates of the likelihood that a particular event did occur or that particular consequences would follow from certain actions will be influenced not only by the actual frequencies of those events, but by their availability in memory. Expert witnesses reporting scientific and/or statistical data are likely to have less impact on a fact finder than does a person who reports a case study, relates a compelling personal experience, or offers anecdotal evidence. That which is more concrete, vivid, emotion-arousing, and otherwise more salient will be more accessible when a fact finder ponders the decision to be made (Nisbett & Temoshok, 1976).

Using this lesson ourselves, we offer the following two anecdotal illustrations. We have two colleagues who are experts on the psychology of eyewitness identification and occasionally testify in criminal trials. She testifies as the scholar, describing factors affecting sensation and perception, storage, retention, and retrieval, memory decay curves, and the findings of experimental research on perception and memory. He presents a slide show in which he explains a few things about the psychology of perception and memory, shows more pictures and fewer graphs, tells some stories about faulty police procedures and eyewitness inaccuracy, and most important of all, by way of the slide show gives jurors an opportunity to experience their own perceptual errors.[18] In terms of persuading juries to be more skeptical of eyewitness testimony, he is a more successful expert than she. The salience of their own experience is more persuasive to jurors than data reporting on the behavior of many others.

Assumptions about the way people think lead lawyers to plan particular trial strategies. Erroneous assumptions may lead to ineffective or counterproductive strategies. In one recent case (*Mashpee Wampanoag Indians* v. *Assessors*, 1980), a critical issue was whether plaintiff Native Americans did indeed constitute a tribe. The plaintiffs had their expert, an anthropologist armed with anecdotal observational evidence, and the defense had theirs, a sociologist with computer analyzed survey data. Fearing the overpowering effect of the sociologist's quantitative data, the plaintiffs moved to have the data excluded. On persuading the judge that the data were flawed by methodological and analytic errors, the plaintiffs succeeded in having the defense expert limited to testifying only to her anecdotal personal observations. We believe the plaintiff's strategy was a mistake on two counts. First, based on what we know about the availability heuristic, we would predict that the quantitative data of the sociologist would have been *less* persuasive than the anthropologist's anecdotal report, because the latter would generally be more concrete and salient, and therefore more accessible. Second, and somewhat beside the present point, if the data were flawed, then exposing it to adversary cross-examination would lead the jurors to give it even less weight than their own cognitive processing would normally have given it. The plaintiffs threw away an opportunity to expose the flaws in the defense data and won a motion requiring the defense expert to give only the more salient evidence. The defense won.

Beyond issues concerning the presentation of evidence, judges making sentencing and commitment decisions use heuristics. Instead of relying on all of the events in their experience, the availability principle tells us they will more readily recall and therefore believe to be more probable, the more salient experiences. Experiences are more likely to be salient because they are bizarre or exteme. Thus, they are the poorest instances on which to construct decision-making policies.

For example, physicians making rational treatment decisions should

---

[18] Part of one's confidence may stem from a lack of reality testing, or sloppy testing.

consistently play the odds established by empirical research or long experience. Instead they have been found to deviate in their treatment recommendations as a function of recent, salient, more cognitively available experiences. In particular conditions Treatment A may be the choice over Treatment B. But, if the last few times the physician prescribed A it failed to work, on the next few decisions that physician will (irrationally) shy away from prescribing it (Bowman, 1963; Dawes & Corrigan, 1974; Dawes, 1979; Goldberg, 1970; Wiggins & Kolen, 1971). This will, of course, hold for any decision maker relying on intuitively derived probabilities – physicians, football coaches, stockbrokers, lawyers, and judges. It is nearly always instructive for decision makers to compare their subjective impressions to data objectively summarizing the actual events they are deciding about. Reality usually holds some surprises.[19]

Another [20] interesting kind of error based on the availability principle is the notion of *illusory correlation* (Chapman & Chapman, 1967, 1969), a bias in the judgment of the frequency of co-occurrence of two events. An illusory correlation is a report by an observer of a correlation between two classes of events which in reality (a) are not correlated, (b) are correlated to a lesser extent than reported, or (c) are correlated in the opposite direction of that which is reported (Chapman & Chapman, 1967, 1969; Tversky & Kahneman, 1974).

In many areas of judgment, people are asked to estimate co-occurrences, such as that between personality characteristics and patterns of behavior. For instance, judges instruct jurors to rely on their life experiences to assist them in judging the credibility of witnesses, assigning weight to testimony, and so on. In the case of an illusory correlation, a person's estimate of co-occurrence departs systematically from the evidence they actually experience. In one study of this phenomenon researchers provided subjects with clinical diagnoses and drawings of a person made by hypothetical psychiatric patients. The subjects were asked to estimate the correlations between certain diagnoses and features of the patients' drawings. Many of the correlations they reported perceiving – such as size and emphasis on the eyes being associated with diagnoses of paranoia and suspiciousness – reproduced much of the common but unsubstantiated clinical lore concerning the interpretation of such drawings. People "perceived" these stereotypical correlations even though there was no evidence for them. Indeed, the illusory correlations were so resistant to contradictory evidence that they persisted even when the actual correlation between diagnosis and

---

[19] By "reality" we do not mean to become entangled in philosophical undergrowth. We mean simply what is observable, what may be empirically confirmed – as opposed to what we may speculate on or hope or wish to be true.

[20] The various kinds of availability heuristics include biases due to the retrievability of instances, biases due to the effectiveness of a search set, biases of imaginability, and illusory correlation (Tversky & Kahneman, 1974).

symptom was negative. Moreover, the illusory correlations prevented subjects from detecting relationships that actually were present.

An availability interpretation of this phenomenon would be that the judgment of covariation between the two events (the diagnosis and the drawing) is determined simply by the stereotypic association between these two events. The stronger the assumed association between the two, the more likely it is judged that they will co-occur. The nature and strength of the association flow from cultural norms, stereotypes, or observers' direct experience with a limited number of similar events. Like similar effects we have discussed, the more cognitively available associates are not necessarily the ones that actually occur at a high frequency or, indeed, with any frequency at all.

Lifelong experience has taught us that, in general, instances of large classes are recalled better and faster than instances of less frequent classes; that likely occurrences are easier to imagine than unlikely ones; and that the associative connections between events are strengthened when the events frequently co-occur. As a result, [people have] at [their] disposal a procedure (the availability heuristic) for estimating the numerosity of a class, the likelihood of an event, or the frequency of co-occurrences, by the ease with which the relevant mental operations of retrieval, construction, or association can be performed. However, as the preceding examples have demonstrated, this valuable estimation procedure results in systematic errors. (Tversky and Kahneman, 1974, p. 1128)

Adjustment and anchoring

To round out our discussion of heuristics we will mention two final rules. These decision heuristics are known as adjustment and anchoring. When making certain types of judgments, people often start with an initial estimate and then make adjustments or revisions of these initial estimates. However, it is often the case that the adjustments depend heavily on initial values.[21] It is not surprising that different initial values often lead to different final estimates. This phenomenon is known as anchoring.

To illustrate the anchoring principle two groups of high school students were given one of two problems to solve. One group was asked to estimate, without the aid of paper and pencil, the product of the following sequence:

$$8 \times 7 \times 6 \times 5 \times 4 \times 3 \times 2 \times 1 = ?$$

The other group was asked to estimate the product of these same numbers presented in ascending order.

Usually the students simply multiplied together the first two or three numbers and then extrapolated from this product to the final guess. If

[21] Cf. Tribe, 1971; pp. 1358–1359, on "the elusive starting point."

this is indeed how they performed the calculations to arrive at a final product, then the anchoring principle should have caused the first, descending group to judge the final product as larger than the second, ascending group. In fact, this was the case. The median estimate for the ascending sequence was 512, while the median estimate for the descending sequence was 2250. The correct answer is the same in both cases, 40,320. This illustrates *insufficient adjustment* from the initial anchor (Slovic & Lichtenstein, 1971).

Trivial in its obviousness is the suggestion that fact finders asked to estimate amounts should be expected to insufficiently adjust from the initial anchoring quantity they receive. Systematic errors are likely to occur, and clever advocates could turn this heuristic to forensic advantage.

A more intriguing aspect of the adjustment and anchoring heuristic has to do with *biases in the evaluation of conjunctive and disjunctive events*. A study by Bar-Hillel (1973) clearly illustrates the matter. Subjects could bet on several kinds of events:

(a) simple events (e.g. drawing a red marble from a bag containing 50 percent red marbles and 50 percent white marbles).
(b) conjunctive events (e.g., drawing a red marble seven times in succession, with replacement, from a bag containing 90 percent red marbles and the rest white).
(c) disjunctive events (e.g., drawing a red marble at least once in seven successive tries, with replacement, from a bag containing 10 percent red marbles and the rest white).

In the above examples, a significant majority of subjects preferred to bet on the conjunctive event over the simple event, and the simple event over the disjunctive event. Actually, the conjunctive event has a .48 probability of occurrence, the simple event a .50 probability, and the disjunctive event a .52 probability. In making both choices, people erroneously placed more confidence in the less likely event. This example illustrates a more general phenomenon, namely, over- and underadjustment to the initial anchor. People tend to overestimate the probability of the occurrence of conjunctive events and to underestimate the probability of disjunctive events.

In estimating probabilities involving compound events, decision makers are likely to make systematic errors of the anchoring kind. In judging the likelihood that an enterprise involving a series of interconnected events will succeed, people will tend to overestimate the probability of success. Even if each of the individual events has a high probability of occurrence, the overall probability for the enterprise can be extremely small if the number of elements is large. Intuitive judgments fail to adjust adequately for such conjunctive events. Decision makers estimating subjective likelihoods for the success of business ventures, surgical procedures, technological efforts, or the likelihood that a project will be completed on schedule or at the agreed upon price will be more optimistic about the chances of success than is in fact warranted by reality.

Disjunctive events, by contrast, are commonly encountered in the assessment of risks. Complex systems, such as nuclear reactors or human bodies, will malfunction if any essential component fails.[22] Even if each component has only a very small probability of malfunction, the probability of a system breakdown will be great if the system has many components. Again, intuitive decision makers underadjust departures from the anchor, and underestimate the likelihood of a system failure.

Overconfidence in judgment

At the beginning of this section, we stated that heuristics often result in erroneous decisions. On other occasions decision heuristics may facilitate proper and efficient decision making. The accuracy of the judgments produced by heuristic processes depends to a great extent on the nature of the question at hand. Accuracy may also depend on how divergent different approaches to the same problem are. This major question – knowing when and under what circumstances these heuristic judgments vitiate decision making or facilitate it – are not completely known and cannot be answered here.

One fact, however, can be unambiguously derived from the extensive literature on the psychology of decision making. People tend to be overconfident in their judgments. Not only do individuals tend to overestimate how much they already know,[23] but they also tend to underestimate how much they have just learned from facts presented in a particular context. Once they do know an outcome, people fail to appreciate how uncertain they were before learning of it.

A number of studies by Baruch Fischhoff and his associates (Fischhoff, 1975; Fischhoff & Beyth, 1975) demonstrate this knew-it-all-along effect. In one experiment, Fischhoff took a number of general knowledge questions from almanacs and encyclopedias. Various groups of people were asked to answer a set of these questions, were given the right answers, and asked to recall what their original answers had been. The findings showed that the subjects overestimated how much they knew initially, and tended to forget their initial errors.[24] Surprisingly, this tendency to overestimate what they knew persisted in the face of

---

[22] That is why both nature and people build back-up systems or redundancy into their complex creations, to improve the probability of continued function of the system in the face of component breakdowns. As the calculations – and experience – show us, system breakdown is unlikely to be postponed forever. A computable and real margin of failure must exist.

[23] For an example showing that physicians overestimate what they know and can predict, see Gilbert, McPeek and Mosteller, 1977.

attempts to undo the knew-it-all-along effect. Further experiments showed that these overestimation effects were produced even when subjects were exhorted to be as correct as possible in their estimates of how much they did or did not know, or when they were actually told about the bias. Informing people about the tendency toward such judgmental distortions did not serve to eliminate them.

In related studies, Fischhoff found a "hindsight" effect. Evidence was perceived as leading more surely to a conclusion once that conclusion was known. For example, suppose people are given information about the parties and events surrounding an actual military conflict and are asked to predict the outcome and to state the certainty of their prediction. Other people are told the outcome and asked how certain they would have been that that was the outcome had they been given only the input information. People who have been told the outcome are about twice as certain that that would have been the outcome compared to those not told. This occurs even when the "outcome" they are told about is *not in fact the true one*. The input information is perceived as far more predictive of the outcome once the outcome is known than when the outcome is still in doubt.

Essentially, people find it difficult to disregard information that they already possess. Telling people that an event has occurred causes them to report that the event was more likely to have happened. Furthermore, hearing such information does not also cause them to report that the information affected their perceptions or decisions. People do not appreciate the extent to which hearing new information has an effect on their judgments.

Why do people tend to be overconfident in their judgments? One possibility is that individuals reinterpret previous information in light of new information, so that the two sets of information are integrated into a coherent whole. The "old" view of these events is assimilated into the "new" correct view in such a natural and immediate fashion that the assimilator is unaware that his or her perspective has been altered. The outcome psychologically is that the person reports that he or she really knew the answer or held the same opinion previously, and that a discrepancy never existed between initial reactions and the apparent conclusions.

These findings have strong implications for the legal process. Fischhoff's principle may be operating when jurors are presented with evidence that is subsequently ruled inadmissible. Though they may not

---

[24] The study was more complicated than our summary of it, including a "memory" group which was asked to answer a set of the questions, told the correct answers, and then asked to recall their own initial responses; a "reliability" group which was asked to answer the questions and then to recall their answers without an intervening step; and a "hypothetical" group which was shown the same group of questions with the answer indicated and asked what their answers would have been had they not been told the answers.

incorporate the evidence in later decisions, the judgments that preceded the information may be irretrievably altered (Sue, Smith, & Caldwell, 1973; Loftus & Loftus, 1976). Another extension of the phenomenon may go to the heart of some judicial proceedings. Typically, when solving a problem or answering a question, we first get the relevant information and then try to generate a solution or choose from among several alternative solutions. In a criminal trial, people are first given the "answer" – that is, the defendant. Then, the evidence is provided, and the fact finder is asked whether the evidence does in fact prove the conclusion. This arrangement seems especially prone to hindsight. Each of the bits of evidence will appear more likely to lead to the defendant than they would have if the defendant were not already known. Analogizing from the hindsight experiments to the "fact finders" at trial, the evidence will seem to point more surely to the answer than it did when the investigators were developing the evidence. It may be that the high standard of proof required for a finding of guilt makes up for the peculiarity (and consequent distorting effects) of the way the question is posed: answer first. It is noteworthy that only criminal proceedings are framed this way and only criminal proceedings require the highest standard of proof. An interesting alternative procedure might be to experiment with trials in which the evidence is presented first and fact finders are asked which of several defendants, if any, is the guilty party. Under such conditions, fact finders, lacking the judgmental bias produced by hindsight, would probably be less sure of their judgments than is true with the existing criminal trial structure.

Further implications for the trial process

Differential accuracy

As society becomes increasingly sophisticated in its use of science and mathematics, statistical and other types of quantitative data will increasingly find their way into court. The entry way may vary – through forensic sciences in criminal proceedings, through civil actions in which substantive technical evidence is relevant (such as we already see in antitrust [Areeda, 1974], products liability [Schreiber, 1967], or employment discrimination [Baldus & Cole, 1979]) or through the increasing number of "science and technology cases" prompted by regulatory agency actions, and in other ways. Through whichever door these data enter the courtroom, once there, humans will have to deal somehow with the relevant information in making their decisions. The fact that humans are heuristic information processors and consequently will make systematic errors in raw intuitive judgment confronts the courts with challenges to their role as a fact finding agency.

Any solution to this challenge may, however, be an unsatisfying one. As Tribe has argued, the trial is not only a search for truth, but also a social ritual which supports certain values and helps litigants and the society as a whole to accept the judgments of courts (Tribe, 1971, p. 1376). Tribe goes so far as to argue that the more formal mathematical processing departs from intuition, the more it should be eschewed by the courts (1971, p. 1376). As we have seen, under specifiable circumstances, intuition is a poor guide and may lead to incorrect conclusions. To accept the dilemma posed by Tribe and adopt his preference for intuition is to choose a comforting ritual over accurate decisions, much like a patient who would rather have a human physician make a wrong diagnosis than allow a computer to make a correct one. The discovery of heuristic decision processes sharpens this dilemma by clarifying the costs of truth seeking: the decision maker whose only tool is intuition will often err.

One may be unconvinced of this if we attend only to judicial proceedings, where the criterion of accuracy is permanently elusive. (If some ultimate truth were available against which to test the fact finder's accuracy, there would be little need for the trial.) In many other decision-making contexts, such as where medical diagnoses are testable against later and better evidence, or where psychiatric predictions are testable against future behavior, or where predictions about weather or economic behavior or the performance of physical materials are testable against easily observable criteria, it is possible to evaluate the intuitive decision maker's accuracy in comparison to other decision-making devices, notably formal decision models. It has been well established for some time now that when the same information is available to intuitive humans or a good mathematical model, the human's decisions are consistently less accurate.[25] These studies have been conducted in a variety of decision-making contexts and we think it safe to generalize these processes to human judgment in legal settings.

We might ask how human decision making differs, if at all, in its processes or products, when contrasted to decision making by mathematical models. That differences exist seems universally accepted.[26] Even when mathematical tools are modeled after human decision processes, the copy works better than the original. One can "capture the decision

---

[25] This is not to say that computers are always better. But for defined decision-making tasks, they certainly make better "judgments." In the 1940s, when statistical decision models were introduced to aid clinical psychologists, the rationale was to provide a "floor" of statistical accuracy below which the clinical diagnostician could not fall. But, the floor turned out to be a "ceiling." The intuitive diagnosis could not reach above it. See Dawes and Corrigan, 1974; Goldberg, 1970; Meehl, 1954.

[26] Critics of explicit computation urge us to reject mathematical tools because they can point to flaws. They fail to ask the question "compared to what?" Compared to perfection, these tools do leave something to be desired. Compared to intuitive decision-making, they look better.

policies" of individuals, converting their choice behavior into a mathematical statement which links the input evidence to the decision.[27] This "paramorphic linear representation" of the human decision maker can be directly compared with the individual's judgments. Consistently, the paramorphic linear representation of the human decision maker is more accurate than the decision maker, a phenomenon known as "bootstrapping" (Dawes & Corrigan, 1974, p. 101). Even then, models using random weights do better than both the human or the human's model (Dawes & Corrigan, 1974, p. 102). One learns a few things about human information processing from such comparisons. The mathematical model of a person's own decision policies is more accurate than the person because it consistently applies the same logic, while the human decision maker fluctuates, being over-influenced by fortuitous, attention-catching pieces of information that vary from time to time, and processing a too-limited set of variables.[28] Unaided individuals tend to have great difficulty incorporating quantified variables, give excessive weight to bits and pieces that happen for whatever reason to be salient, base their decisions on less information (often the less useful information) than do mathematical models, and apply their decision policies inconsistently (Dawes & Corrigan, 1974). This presents an interesting set of concerns about human decision making that contrasts with Tribe's concerns about mathematical decision making. The problems associated with drawing inferences from probability evidence, problems Tribe would like to see the courts avoid, are not avoided by dumping the data, quantitative as well as nonquantitative, into the mental laps of human decision makers, armed only with their intuition.

Moreover, the choice is not really between computers and people. It is between explicitly presented computing and subjective computing, or between more and less accurate computing. This is not to degrade humans. It is merely to recognize, on the one hand, our information processing limitations and, on the other, our capacity to invent tools that can do the job better.[29] After all, many people trust their pocket calculators and the light meters in their cameras, whose workings they do not begin to comprehend; yet their faith is well placed, because these devices make decisions and judgments faster and more accurately than

---

[27] One of the first to suggest doing this was Henry Wallace, before becoming vice president under Roosevelt (Wallace, 1923).

[28] See Bowman, 1963. For example, suppose a physician applying a correct decision rule has observed a poor outcome in the last several patients. The physician may, consequently, modify the decision rule in the next several patients. That idiosyncratic fluctuation will reduce accuracy. The "bootstrapped" model will inexorably play the best odds and minimize error.

[29] That people can invent tools that do a better job than the humans who invented them should come as no surprise to people who have used such devices as radios, light meters, or hammers. Indeed, the adversary process is just such a tool. It seems intuitively wrong to many people, but it is capable of accomplishing certain purposes that intuitive individuals cannot. See Thibaut and Walker, 1975.

people do.[30] The comparison is not between humans and mathematics, but between humans deciding alone and humans deciding with the help of a tool. (See review of person/machine systems in Slovic, Fischoff & Lichtenstein, 1977, p. 25; also see Saks, 1976.)

Our suggestion is modest, and most lawyers should find it comfortingly traditional. Namely, experts ought to be permitted to offer their data, their algorithms, and their Bayesian theorems. The errors that may be introduced will be subjected to adversarial cross-examination. Various formal mathematical models do have room for errors – variables omitted, poor measurements, and others that Tribe has cogently presented. But so do intuitive techniques. Properly employed and developed, the former can have fewer. It is up to opposing counsel to unmask the errors. Moreover, as a matter of developing and introducing new tools from what might be called decision-making technology, the identification of flaws does not imply that the tools ought not be used. The proper question is whether the tool, however imperfect, still aids the decision maker more than no tool at all.

Under-incorporating statistical information

Another contribution of behavioral decision research to this debate is the challenge it poses to what seems to be a unanimous assumption held both by advocates and opponents of the introduction of mathematical and statistical data and tools to the judicial fact-finding process. This widespread assumption is that the tools and the numbers they produce are unduly persuasive (Tribe, 1971, pp. 1334, 1376). Upon hearing the technical pronouncement, it is said, fact finders doubt their intuition and more or less blindly accept the conclusions given them.

Research demonstrates, however, that people do not process probabilistic information well, that in the face of particularistic information, they cannot integrate the statistical and anecdotal evidence and consequently tend to ignore the *statistical* information. Intuitive, heuristic, human decision makers must dispense with certain information, and that tends strongly to be the quantitative information. While commentators' arguments have been that the data are inordinately persuasive, the evidence says that the reverse is true. The implications are several. First, statistical data need not be regarded as so overwhelming as some have supposed, and therefore they ought not to be considered prejudicial. The more realistic problem is presenting statistical evidence so that people will incorporate it into their decisions at all.

---

[30] Trust in the pocket calculator is based on experience with it. People who acquire experience with mathematical decision making in management, operations, planning, science, economics, and so on, develop a similar trust in these other computational aids.

Aggregate probabilities

A third and related implication has to do with the role of aggregate probabilities (base rates) in making decisions in a specific case. The problem usually posed is: how can information about a general state of affairs, background information, legislative facts, base rates, serve as evidence about a specific event? Several examples may help to clarify the question (drawn from Tribe, 1971):

1. A person is found guilty of heroin possession. The next question is whether the drug was domestic or illegally imported. It can be shown that 98 percent of all illegally possessed heroin is illegally imported. May this fact be used in deciding the question in this case?

2. A physician sued for malpractice is accused of having dispensed a drug without warning of what he knew to be its tendency to cause blindness in pregnant women. Should he be allowed to introduce evidence that 95 percent of all physicians are unaware of that side effect (as evidence that he did not know)?

3. A plaintiff is negligently run down by a blue bus. The question is whether the blue bus belonged to the defendant who, it can be shown, owns 85 percent of the blue buses in town. What effect may such evidence be permitted to have?

We know from the research described earlier that when a decision involves only simple base-rate data, people make (approximately) the correct probability estimate. The legal question is whether such evidence may be offered as proof. The argument for admitting it rests largely on the contribution such evidence will make to reaching a correct finding based on available information. The argument against it rests on the premise that base rates are uninformative about specific cases.[31] "[I]t has been held not enough that mathematically the chances somewhat favor a proposition to be proved; for example, the fact that colored automobiles made in the current year outnumber black ones would not warrant a finding that an undescribed automobile of the current year is colored and not black, nor would the fact that only a minority of men die of cancer warrant a finding that a particular man did not die of cancer" (*Sargent* v. *Massachusetts Accident Co.*, 1940). [Such cases] are entirely sensible if understood ... as insisting on the presentation of *some* non-statistical and 'individualized' proof of identity before compelling a party to pay damages, and even before compelling him to some forward with defensive evidence, absent an adequate explanation of the failure to present such individualized proof" (Tribe, 1971, p. 1344 n.37).

The assumption in these decisions is that somehow particularistic

---

[31] Poor use of statistics and probability theory is beside the point. As Tribe points out, the possible costs of correct use are the issue.

evidence is of greater probative value, that is, is more diagnostic. The studies we have described can be seen as making some enlightening points about such a seeming distinction. If neither case-specific nor base-rate data are available, the fact finder has no real way to evaluate a witness's statement. In the absence of internal or external contradiction, they probably accept it as credible. When only case-specific information is present, the fact finder regards the probability that proposition X is true as equal to the credibility of the witness. This is a condition which exists *only* when the base rate is 50:50.[32] If no base-rate data are available, and this is common, the fact finders are doing the best they can; in essence, placing an even bet.

Now consider what is gained when base-rate information is added. The value of the base-rate information is that it provides a context in which the case-specific information has meaning. Once one knows that 85 percent of the buses are blue, and that the witness is 80 percent accurate in the appropriate color identification task, then one can, with the proper tools, evaluate the probative force of the statement "I saw the bus, and it was blue."[33] Contrary to the speculations of many commentators, the research on heuristics suggests that errors are massively in the direction of being seduced by case-specific information and failing to employ base-rate information to temper belief in a witness's credibility.[34]

The myth of particularistic proof

Perhaps the most serious error is an epistemological one: the assumption that case-specific information is really *qualitatively* different from base-rate information. The courts, commentators, and we through most of this article have categorized them separately. And, indeed, it seems obvious that background base-rate information is about other cases while particularistic information is about *this* case. Whatever meaning the distinction may have, it is not one that pertains to the probability of an accurate decision on the facts. Much of the testimony that is commonly thought of as particularistic only seems so. It is far more probabilistic than we normally allow jurors (or judges) to realize. This includes eyewitness identification (e.g., Buckhout, 1974; Gardner, 1933; Munsterberg, 1976; Levine & Tapp, 1973), fingerprints (Galton, 1965), and anything else we could name. This follows not from the nature (and fallibility) of these particular techniques, but from the nature of the logic of classifying and identifying. All identification techniques place the identified object in a

---

[32] *Cf.*, medical laboratory testing example, supra note 5. By ignoring the base rate or by refusing to admit it into evidence, the decision maker substitutes a false base rate (50:50) for the correct one and necessarily reaches a distorted conclusion.

[33] If 95 percent of the buses are blue, and the witness is 80 percent accurate, when a witness reports seeing a blue bus, this yields a .98 probability that the bus was, indeed, blue.

[34] Our experts on eyewitness accuracy, supra, have been trying to do just this tempering. Unfortunately, as we have seen, their base rates tend to be ignored.

class with others (Tribe, 1971, p. 1330 n.2). There is little, if any, pin-pointed, one-person-only evidence in this world. In fairness to Tribe, he notes that non-distinction, then promptly ignores its implications by saying, "I am, of course, aware that *all* factual evidence is ultimately statistical, and all legal proof ultimately probabilistic, in the epistemo-logical sense that no conclusion can ever be drawn from empirical data without some step of inductive inference – even if only an inference that things are usually what they are perceived to be.... My concern, how-ever, is only with types of evidence and modes of proof that bring this 'probabilistic' element of inference to explicit attention in a quantified way. As I hope to show, much turns on whether such explicit quantifica-tion is attempted" (Tribe, 1971, p. 1330 n.2). The problems of probability do not come into existence only when we become aware of them. Making them explicit does not create the problems, it only forces us to recognize them and enables us to begin dealing with them. Burying them in implicitness is no solution; revealing their existence is not the problem.

Suppose we must decide if a person on trial for possession of heroin is guilty also of possessing illegally imported heroin. And suppose we can learn either that 90 percent of all heroin in the U.S. is illegally imported or that a witness whom we judge to be 80 percent credible (e.g., knows and tells the truth 80 percent of the time) asserts that he (or she) observed the delivery and it was an illegal importation.

The usual argument, recall, is that the particularistic evidence tells us something on which we can base a decision, while the base-rate data are all but irrelevant to the case at hand. But, from the viewpoint of a disinterested fact finder, all information is indirect, distant, abstract, and imperfectly credible. The fact finders, in terms of their truth-seeking role, simply have a set of input information on which to base a judgment, and depending on the characteristics of the evidence and the way it is processed, that finding will have a greater or lesser probability of being correct. The simple fact in this example is that the fact finder can be 80 percent sure of being right or 90 percent sure. Consequently, in this instance it is the base-rate information that is more diagnostic, more probative, and more likely to lead to a correct conclusion.

Making this argument with the relatively concrete images of a case hampers our consideration of the concept. Let us try to make the point with one of those concretely abstract statistical anecdotes. Suppose you are at a state fair and approach a kind of shell game. You are presented with two overturned cups, each hiding a marble. One of the marbles is red. Your task is to bet on which cup is covering the red marble. You learn that under one cup is a marble drawn randomly from a bag contain-ing 90 percent red marbles. A bystander, whom you know to tell the truth 80 percent of the time tells you, "I saw the marble placed under the other cup, and it was red." Placing your bet, the base-rate vs. case-specific character of the evidence is irrelevant. The odds of betting correctly, of maximizing the likelihood of winning, are dictated only by the content of the information. The question for the decision maker is which is more informative, an imperfectly credible witness, or an imperfectly pinpointed set of base-rate information. One choice offers a .90 probability of being correct, the other only .80. The diagnostic value of the information is not affected by whether it appears to report background facts or "case-specific" facts. Even so-called particularistic evidence is probabilistic. Invariably, all information is really probability information. Only if we neglect to uncover, or otherwise conceal from a fact finder the base rates of witness (or other evidence) reliability, will the case-specific information seem more informative. Only if we conceal from the bettor the fact that the witness who says "I saw the marble and it was red" is only .80 truthful or .50 accurate in color perception, will the assertion seem to have special probative force. The distinction between what one can learn from case-specific as opposed to base-rate information is more imaginary than real. In terms of accurate fact finding, it is a difference that makes no difference.

Similarly mistaken are distinctions between certain kinds of identifications. Descriptions which lead to a probability of correct classification of a person (e.g., "a completely bald man with a wooden left leg, wearing a black patch over his right eye and bearing a six-inch scar under his left, who flees from the scene of the crime in a chartreuse Thunderbird with two dented fenders") are treated as different from the "particularistic" type where a witness says, "Yes, that's the person." Some have argued that evidence that the above description fits only one person in 64 million ought not to be used in the trial of a person fitting that description, because it merely specifies the class to which he belongs and its size; it does not identify him. The latter identification would be more welcome, because it singles out a unique individual. The identifying witness may be confident that the identification is correct, but the fact finder ought to appreciate the inherently probabilistic nature of perception, storage, recall, and identification. Apparently, fact finders (like legal commentators) fail to appreciate this point. They act as though the eyewitness identification is highly accurate, when in reality it may be far more likely than once in 64 million to be in error. Indeed, the probability of correct eyewitness identification has been found to be far lower than commonly assumed (Buckhout, 1974; Loftus, 1980).

The most meaningful difference between these two kinds of identification is that in one we allow the identifying witness to make the decision instead of letting the fact finder do so. But to think we have here evidence that is somehow uniquely diagnostic is only to conceal from ourselves the probabilistic nature and limited accuracy of the identification process.[35] In

[35] This parallels the concern that a statistician using Bayes' Theorem to reach a probability of guilt determination is making the decision for the fact finder. If we have eyewitnesses, let us also have appropriate experts to offset the eyewitness's inordinate impact.

both kinds of identifications we are dealing with classes containing more than one person, and there is no guarantee that the "particularistic" approach yields smaller classes.

By disposing of the false distinction between probabilistic and particularistic evidence, we also obviate the interesting worry that probability evidence cannot support a finding of liability or guilt in the way that particularistic evidence can, by virtue of the latter's ability to pinpoint. To the extent that the goal of adjudication includes accuracy, the background data are not without probative force. Like it or not, base-rate information can be helpful to a decision maker. We may for other reasons lament this state of affairs, but it remains a fact of life in making decisions under uncertainty.

Evaluating witness credibility

Probability evidence can address quite usefully the credibility of a witness. Such data are probably most available and most useful in this sphere – informing about the witness more so than about the defendant. As we saw earlier, heuristic decision makers tend to equate the probability that a conclusion is correct with the credibility of a witness. Consider two examples of how such background data can inform a fact finder about the reliability and validity of a witness's testimony.

1. A forensic scientist testifies that a paint sample matches the defendant's automobile, a blood stain on the upholstery matches that of the victim, and the fatal bullet was fired from the defendant's gun. Such scientific evidence is often highly credible testimony. Most critics of probability evidence would be pleased that it is particularistic; it pinpoints the defendant (or at least the defendant's property); it does not merely define a class to which the defendant belongs. First of all, as we have argued, particularistic evidence is nothing of the sort. This expert's evidence, like all evidence, rests on a foundation of reality that is necessarily probabilistic. The same or another expert could testify as to the probability of an accurate identification – that is, the size of the class to which the defendant's car's paint, the victim's blood, and the defendant's gun belong, relative to the respective universes of paint, blood, and firearms. Or the expert could testify to the joint probability of all three occurring. Furthermore, this or another expert could testify to the probability that the paint, blood, and ballistics really do match, given that the test for a match was positive. And although the expert may be confident of the conclusions testified to, this or another expert could inform the court about relevant background findings such as those of the Forensic Sciences Association in a national study (Peterson, Fabricant, & Field, 1978) showing that as many as 51 percent of police laboratories misidentified paint samples, 71 percent misidentified blood samples, and 28 percent misidentified firearms. None of these is what we might call a

pinpoint of accuracy. In such light, the testimony takes on a different appearance.

2. In appropriate circumstances it would be informative to a fact finder to be advised of the diagnostic error rates of physicians or of the laboratory tests on which they often base their diagnoses. Virtually every medical test has an error rate. Virtually every test has a known specificity (the percentage of negative results among people who do not have the disease – that is, the true negatives), and this value is not uncommonly 80 percent or lower. Similarly, virtually every test has a known sensitivity (the percentage of positive results among people who do have the disease – that is, the true positives), and this value is not uncommonly 70 percent or lower.[36] Add to this any evidence of additional error due to laboratory inaccuracy (that is, errors over and above those inherent in the test, available from quality control studies), and the fact finder may have a quantitative sense of how many grains of salt to include when weighing such expert testimony.

All testimony, including eyewitness accounts as well as such expert testimony, may be tempered by the introduction of relevant background base-rate probabilities. It is noteworthy that these error rates and base-rate probabilities, these ubiquitous limiting features of all evidence, not only recognized but also *measured* by every scientific discipline, are often simply ignored by legal commentators on the use of such evidence in court.

Conclusion

Tribe advocates, in short, the maintenance of a fantasyland of apparent certainty in a world of patent uncertainty. Regarded from only a mildly different angle, such a deliberate turning away from reality may serve neither the law nor the defendant. First of all, the symbolism is so at variance with the objective reality as well as with the conceptualizations of legal scholars (certainly including Tribe himself) and the subjective experience of judges and jurors, that this may be one more of the legal fictions that tend to undermine the law's own credibility. An institution that would so deliberately ignore real, measurable doubt and assert not that it has made the best decision it was able to but that it is "certain" it is correct, is unlikely to keep the masquerade going forever or to fool everyone. That is the harm that may be done the court.[37]

The harm that may be done a defendant is that behind this mask of certainty can hide not only minute quantities of uncertainty, but *massive* quantities. Relevant evidence might be weak indeed, but so long as it is

[36] What has been said here is true of *all* test instruments, including judges and juries. *Cf.* Krieg *et al.*, 1975.
[37] One major survey of the low esteem in which the public holds the courts is Yankelovich, Skelly, and White, 1978.

kept fuzzy, a finding against a defendant could be rendered and claimed to be certain. Is this an affirmation of the accused's dignity?

Candid announcement of unavoidable margins of error may be a greater service to individual defendants and to the legal system. With such awareness we may be motivated to modify one of our most important social inventions to make it work better (err less); we may recognize that truth is not merely anything that a court asserts it to be; and both legal policy makers and case-by-case fact finders will not be able to hide from the implications and consequences of their own decisions nor from the context in which they must decide.

Cases cited

Addington v. *Texas*, 47 LW 4473, 1979.
Avco Corporation v. *A.T.T.*, 68 F.R.D. 532, 1975.
Ballew v. *Georgia*, 435 U.S. 223, 1978.
Essex Chemical Co. v. *Ruckelshaus*, 486 F2d 427, 1973.
Ethyl Corporation of America v. *E.P.A.*, 541 F2d 1, 1976.
Greater Boston Television Corp. v. *F.C.C.*, 444 F2d 841, 1970.
Gregg v. *Georgia*, 428 U.S. 153, 1976.
Hobson v. *Hansen*, 327 F. Supp. 844 D.C., 1971.
International Harvester Co. v. *Ruckelshaus*, 478 F2d 615, 1973.
La Buy v. *Howes Leather Co.*, 352 U.S. 249, 1957.
Mashpee Wampanoag Indians v. *Assessors*, Mass., 398 N.E. 2d 724, 1980.
Omnium Lyonnaise D'Etancheite v. *Dow Chemical Co.*, 73 F.R.D. 114, 1977.
People v. *Collins*, 66 Ca. Rptr. 497, 438 P2d 33, 1968.
Portland Cement Association v. *Ruckelshaus*, 486, F2d 375, 1973.
Reserve Mining Co. v. *U.S.*, 514 F2d 492, 1975.
Sargent v. *Massachusetts Accident Co.*, 307 Mass. 246, 250, 29 N.E.2d 825, 827, 1940.
Smith v. *Rapid Transit, Inc.*, 317 Mass. 469, 58 N.E.2d 754, 1945.
U.S. v. *I.B.M.*, 72 F.R.D. 532, 1976.
Vermont v. *New York*, 417 U.S. 270, 1974.
Williams v. *Florida*, 399 U.S. 78, 1970.

13. Causal theories of crime and their effect upon expert parole decisions

John S. Carroll

Introduction

For over a century, the criminal justice system has been centrally concerned with why crime occurs, under the theory that crime can best be stopped and offenders rehabilitated when the causes of crime are known. The parole process, for example, is based on the principle that imprisonment and prison programs are ameliorating criminogenic factors in the offender. The parole board in most states is therefore charged to assess the progress of these rehabilitative effects on whatever is considered to be the causes of crime in the individual offender, assess the appropriate moment for release, and tailor further supervision and programs in the community to ensure continued progress (cf. Miller, 1972).

Although parole boards try to accomplish these goals, the available evidence suggests that the means are not yet at hand. The effects of various correctional or rehabilitative programs on offenders are largely unknown or null (Gottfredson, 1975; Martinson, 1974). Nor are parole boards very good at predicting recidivism (Hakeem, 1961). Pressed by high volume and low funds, parole boards simply do the best they can in an important and difficult situation. Board members use common sense, years of experience with offenders, and what they have heard from experts to construct inferences about the nature of the offender, the etiology of his criminal behavior, the prospects for treatment, and predictions of future behavior.

In contrast, the law seeks the objective causes that are assumed to actually have produced a criminal act. For example, the law distinguishes accidents from intended acts, and further divides those acts whose conse-

This chapter originally appeared in *Law and Human Behavior*, 1978, 2(4), 377–388. Copyright © 1979 by Plenum Publishing Corporation.

quences were intended (motive or malice) from those whose consequences were simply foreseen as possible results (Holmes, 1881). Yet,
legal scholars readily admit that "probable intent" is judged by social
norms – what we assume the "reasonable man" would have done or not
done in such circumstances (Marshall, 1968). These discriminations rest
on subjective judgments including attributions made by people at various
points in the criminal justice system (e.g., prosecutor, judge, jury) and
hence are amenable to study using attribution theory. Attribution theory
also has dealt with the distinctions among levels of responsibility
(causality–foreseeability–intentionality, Heider, 1958; Shaw & Sulzer,
1964) and has proposed that the normative, socially desirable, or con-
sensual act is less informative of intent and dispositions than the non-
normative act (Jones & Davis, 1965; Kelley, 1973). Thus, the attributional
approach can serve to separate legal philosophy from normative or
general knowledge, and to specify the antecedent information leading
people to infer particular causes of crime. Ultimately, we may be able to
improve the quality of justice by understanding how subjective human
judgments form the basis for the way the legal and criminal justice
systems deal with crime and criminals.

It is the purpose of this article to review the nature and prevalence of
causal attributions about crime in laypeople and experts. These attributions will be organized into a framework from which predictions are
derived regarding the effect of particular kinds of attributions upon
reactions to the crime and criminal. Using research on parole decisions as
an example, the discussion will include the kinds of attributions made
about parole applicants, their effects upon parole decisions, and the
sources of these attributions in case material and individual attitudes.

Causal theories about crime

The public

Public opinion polls have inquired about public perceptions of crime
causation for several decades. Major causes of crime that have been
mentioned in these polls include: (a) parental upbringing and the breakdown of family life, (b) bad environment, (c) leniency in the laws and
criminal justice system, (d) drugs, (e) mental illness, (f) permissiveness in
society, and (g) poverty/unemployment (Erskine, 1974).

Sociopolitical ideologies exemplify the way segments of our society
integrate their ideas about the causes of criminal behavior and suggestions for combatting crime (Miller, 1973). The conservative political right
holds the view that the bulk of serious crime is committed by people who
lack self-control and moral conscience. The control of crime demands that
fear be the impetus for self-control instilled by the severe punishment of
criminals. When criminals are not punished, such as when society's

liberal values encourage the defiance of legal authority and leniency in the criminal justice system, then crime increases. In contrast, the liberal political left holds social conditions of inequality and discrimination at fault for crime. Criminals are victims of the system, and they are further victimized because law enforcement is selective in punishing the crimes committed by the poor but ignoring the crimes of the rich. Liberals advocate system reform and rehabilitation of persons who have been victimized by social and economic misfortune.

The experts

Although some experts endorse variants of the above ideological positions, others espouse a range of differing opinions. Scientific theories typically focus either on the biological or psychological abnormalities of the individual offender or on factors in the environment or social milieu of the person that promote crime (Schrag, 1971). For example, contrast a psychiatric view that criminal behavior is a symptom of an underlying mental condition, with a sociological view that criminal behavior is a product of differential association with criminal role models.

Advocates of various correctional philosophies within the criminal justice system also exhibit diversity. Deterrence focuses on the educative value of punishment: the offender will choose not to commit a crime if there is enough risk of unpleasant consequences. In essence, this implies that crime is due to the choices made by offenders and the punitiveness of the environment. Incapacitation establishes the idea that society can be protected by separating out bad risks who would be expected to cause future crimes. Rehabilitative programs operate on the idea that something has gone awry in the person's social history to cause criminal behavior and that the provision of new training and new settings will encourage new noncriminal behavior. Retribution argues that the criminal has wronged society, and must in turn be hurt in order to maintain the morality of the social order, regardless of whether this is helpful or harmful to the criminal.

Parole decision makers

Whatever is the correct approach, it is clear that there are numerous and widespread opinions and theories about the causes of crime and the purposes and value of corrections. A detailed example of the prevalence of such causal theories comes from research with expert decision makes. For example, Carroll and Payne (1977a) observed five experts examining actual parole cases. These experts were instructed to "think out loud" during this process and their remarks were tape-recorded, transcribed, and coded. Attributions were found to represent the single largest category of statements going beyond the factual information being read.

Twenty-two percent of coded statements were attributions. Thus, causal theories do appear prevalent in expert judgment.

As an illustration, one expert described the events around a crime of breaking into a food market and stealing 37 cartons of cigarettes in the following way:

OK, you know, what he did was so, was done so impulsively, man. He was out. He had been drinking with this cat and uh, they were drunk, and they needed cigarettes. And he went into this place and he got the cigarettes.

This offender had a prior record, but no problems for ten years prior to this crime. The expert felt that "the difficulties that the guy had in the past – the records would show that it was due to alcoholism you know." He stated that "the guy has the ability to be stable out there," referring to his ten years of staying straight and an expectation of a possible future. And why the reemergence of an alcoholism problem? "He indicated to the counselor that when he found himself out of work that he started hitting the bottle, which is, you know, that's his, you know, reason for doin' it. For going to the alcohol, as to why, why there would be some alcohol abuse."

This expert decision maker was concerned not only with the crime, but also with the causes of the crime. He gradually built a picture of the offender as a person who had controlled an earlier alcohol problem, but was set off by frustrations over losing his job. This causal attribution provided a consistent way of interpreting the crime, the criminal record, participation in Alcoholics Anonymous in the institution, and even directed the preparation of treatment plans: "I think the area that we're gonna be concerned with, or the parole agent should be concerned with this man is that of his alcohol problems."

A subsequent study provides more extensive information about the nature of causal attributions in parole decisions (Carroll, 1978). The five members of the Pennsylvania Board filled out a questionnaire immediately following 272 actual parole hearings over a two-month period. Two items on the questionnaire served to measure attributions regarding the crime: "Opinion on underlying cause for offense committed" and "Opinion on reason for criminal record/history."

Five hundred and fifty-seven attribution statements were produced from these cases and grouped into categories. The most frequent causes given for offenses and the percentage of such causes they represented were as follows:

a.	drug abuse problem	15%
b.	alcohol abuse problem	12%
c.	long-term greed for money	9%
d.	sudden desire to get money	7%
e.	victim precipitation	7%

f. drunk at time of crime   7%
g. influence of associates   6%
h. lack of control   4%
i. mental problems   4%
j. domestic problems   4%

The most frequent causes given for the criminal history were the following:

a. drug abuse problem   23%
b. alcohol abuse problem   19%
c. influence of associates   11%
d. long-term greed for money   7%
e. immaturity   6%
f. lack of control   5%
g. easy influencibility   4%
h. aimlessness   4%

Along with directing attention at the importance and prevalence of causal attributions about crime, attribution theory also suggests that the diverse attributions can be organized into categories or types of attributions, and that each type has predictable effects upon evaluations of past behavior and expectations for future behavior.

Attribution theory framework

Carroll and Payne (1976) suggested that Weiner's (1974) model of attributions in achievement settings could be adapted as a framework for attributions about crime and criminals. Weiner's model proposes that there are three dimensions or aspects upon which attributions vary: (a) whether the cause of the event is located within or internal to the actor or externally in the environment around the actor; (b) whether the cause is stable and enduring over time or relatively unstable and temporary; and (c) whether the cause is under the control of or intended by the actor or by other people, or is relatively unintentional.

The causes of crime which were previously discussed can be arranged on the above attributional dimensions. Internal causes would include all those that are inside or properties of the offender such as mental illness, drunkenness, drug addiction, laziness, greed, youth, or a decision to commit the crime. External causes would include all those that are outside the offender such as the victim, the offender's parents, the economy, the breakdown of society, the leniency of the criminal justice system, and the offender's associates. Some of the internal causes are stable and enduring over time, such as a pathological personality, whereas other internal causes are more transitory, such as drunkenness. Similarly, some external causes are stable (e.g., a poverty environment) whereas others are unstable (e.g., the victim starts a fight). The final attributional dimension, intentionality, can cut across all combinations of internal–external and stable – unstable causes. For example, a decision to seek money is intentional, as is being coerced by other people to participate in a crime. Having an aggressive personality or a poverty environment, on the other hand, are unintentional.

Attributional research utilizing the Weiner model has revealed that the attributional dimensions have consistent predictable effects upon evaluations and expectations. Studies have shown that good events receive more praise, and bad events more blame, when attributed internally to the actor, and especially when attributed internally and intentionally (e.g., Shaw & Reitan, 1969; Sosis, 1974; Weiner & Kukla, 1970). Expectations for future behavior are based on past behavior to the extent that the perceived cause is stable over time (e.g., Valle & Frieze, 1976; Weiner, Nierenberg, & Goldstein, 1976).

Following the above reasoning and evidence, Carroll and Payne (1976) proposed that the internality and intentionality of attributed causes for crime should affect evaluations of an offender, whereas the stability of the attributed causes should affect predictions of future crime. They further proposed that evaluations and predictions relate directly to research showing that parole boards *evaluate* the seriousness of criminal behavior and use time in prison as a punishment for the offense and also *predict* whether or not an offender is a good risk and withhold release from those whom they expect to commit new crimes (Hoffman, 1973; Stanley, 1976). Thus, attributions should affect the desire to punish and/or to incapacitate the offender. The precise response in a parole decision would depend upon the attribution and the relative salience of punishment and incapacitation goals to the decision maker.

The influence of causal attributions upon expert parole decisions

These predictions about expert parole decision makers were first tested by having college students and parole experts evaluate crime reports each consisting of one of eight crime descriptions (e.g., robbery, rape, burglary, drugs) and one of eight pieces of background information designed to suggest a causal attribution about the crime (Carroll & Payne, 1977a, 1977b). Backgrounds were in a 2 × 2 × 2 design of internal vs. external, stable vs. unstable, and intentional vs. unintentional causal attributions. An example of one crime report from the study was the following:

Mr. Green is a 25-year-old male convicted of second-degree murder. He was in a bar having a drink and talking to the victim when they began to argue, push and punch each other. He pulled out a gun and shot the victim several times; the victim was pronounced dead on arrival at the hospital. Mr. Green surrendered himself to police called by the bartender. He has no previous record of convictions. Interviews indicated that he could not find a good job because his skill had been replaced by mechanization. The circumstances around the crime had been acting on him for some time.

The results showed that students' judgments did conform to the predictions. Attributions to causes internal to the offender led to generally more negative evaluation – less liking, higher ratings of crime severity, responsibility, and purpose of prison is punishment, and longer prison term. Internal-intentional causes were judged the highest on responsibility. Attributions to stable, long-term causes led to higher expectations for recidivism, higher ratings of criminality, purpose of prison is incapacitation, and of responsibility, and the longer prison term. Prison term was assigned on the basis of both punishment and risk factors, and was an additive sum of internal-external judgments and -unstable judgments. For example, crimes with internal-stable causes were given an average prison term of 9.1 years, crimes with internal-unstable causes were given 6.6 years, external-stable causes received 5.2 years, and external-unstable causes were given an average of 3.7 years.

In contrast, when using this same procedure with parole experts, the pattern of results was different. There was a clear tendency for the experts to respond differently on nearly all judgments to internal-stable causes as compared to any other types of causes. These causes led to higher judgments of both crime seriousness and recidivism risk than any others. For example, recommended prison term was 5.9 years for internal-stable causes, but the other combinations of internality and stability averaged between 3 and 4 years in prison. Thus, while attributional information was important to both students and experts, only the students clearly showed the predicted separability of the attributional dimensions in the resultant punishment and risk judgments. Further, the impact of the attributional information on nearly all judgments was much greater for students than for experts (Carroll & Payne, 1977b).

Examination of subjects' comments about the task suggested that the experts felt uncomfortable making decisions based upon so little information, and this may have lessened their reliance upon the more subjective causal information. Despite the fact that past studies of parole boards have indicated that they *use* only a few pieces of information in their decision making (Wilkins, Gottfredson, Robison, & Sadowsky, 1973), the experts *wanted* to have subjectively more complete case material. Thus, this study was flawed by the use of controlled but artificial materials. However, two subsequent studies of expert decisions used more valid operations.

In one study, already described in this article, expert decision makers were tape-recorded while "talking aloud" about a small number of actual cases (Carroll & Payne, 1977a). Analyses of the attribution statements found in the verbal protocols revealed that those cases that received favorable parole decisions consistently received the lowest proportion of internal attributions. This suggests that attributing the crime to the offender rather than to the environment leads to a less favorable disposition of the offender.

Further evidence comes from the postdecision questionnaire study of 272 parole hearings (Carroll, 1978) that was also described earlier. Parole release recommendations were examined in a multiple regression analysis using as independent variables: (a) four objective characteristics from each case – minimum sentence, crime type, number of prior convictions, and Board Member; (b) six attribution variables – attributions made about the offense and the criminal history each coded for internality, stability, and intentionality; (c) 26 subjective variables consisting of ratings of the importance of 22 decision considerations, ratings of the severity of the offense and of the record, and ratings of the risk of a new offense and of a new dangerous offense: and (d) 144 bilinear interaction terms computed as the product of the objective and attributional variables in standardized form. Interaction terms were not computed for the subjective variables.

This analysis revealed that the primary determinants of the parole recommendations were subjective decision considerations reflecting concerns with risk of future crime, rehabilitative potential, and special deterrence. The stability of the cause of the offense was a significant determinant of judgments of the risk of future crime, and thereby significantly influenced parole recommendations. Specifically, crimes attributed to more stable causes received higher ratings of risk and poorer recommendations.[1]

These results also revealed that crime seriousness, crime type, length of sentence, and record did not relate to parole release recommendations. However, the minimum sentence was significantly and strongly correlated with crime seriousness, crime type, and record but not correlated with risk of future crime. In short, it appears that the punitive considerations in a case are dealt with by the length of sentence given by the judge. At the time of the release decision, the Board does not evaluate crime and record in order to punish but rather uses predictions of the risks to the community and the benefits to the client as considerations in parole decisions. For these reasons, stability was related to parole recommendations but internality and intentionality were not, because the punishment aspect is not present in Pennsylvania.

---

[1] The importance of risk judgments in Pennsylvania parole decisions was verified in an experiment by Carroll (1980). Statements regarding risk were systematically introduced into actual case materials in a place where they often are found. Favorableness of risk statements was significantly related to favorableness of parole release recommendations.

The sources of attributions

An understanding of the role of causal attributions in expert parole decisions must include not only the effects of attributions on decisions, but also a description of how the experts make these attributions. It is reasonable to assume that attributions arise from the interaction of case information with the attitudes and knowledge of the individual attributor.

Case information. Research on the antecedents of attributions in criminal justice settings has been summarized by Pepitone (1975) and Perlman (1980). Illustrative of the antecedents that would be found in parole case information are the nature of the crime and prior record. For example, using college students who evaluated descriptions of crimes, Rosen and Jerdee (1974) found that crimes with more serious consequences led to more attribution to the offender. Lussier, Perlman, and Breen (1977) found a prior record produced more attribution to the offender.

Dan Coates and I are now in the process of analyzing data on roughly 1000 parole cases, the first group of which were analyzed and reported in Carroll (1978). Our preliminary analyses of the antecedents of attributions have focused upon case information that significantly correlates with the three attributional dimensions of internality, stability, and intentionality. We have found that the attribution to more internal (rather than external) causes for a crime is associated with cases where the offender had a history of drug abuse, a more serious criminal record, and was an actor rather than an accomplice in the crime. The crimes of men were also attributed to more internal causes than were the crimes of women. The attribution to more stable (rather than unstable) causes occurred when the offender was involved in serious drug abuse, particularly a recent history of heroin use, and had a greater number of previous parole violations. The attribution to more intentional (rather than unintentional) causes for crime was associated with offenders having better job skills but less stable employment histories.

These analyses did not reveal the simple relationships between crime seriousness or criminal record and attributions that other studies have shown. Most indices of crime or record were unrelated to attribution; the most serious crime, murder, was also considered most external and least stable, a complete reversal. We should note that few criminologists consider offense type useful for categorizing offenders (Megargee, 1975). If we examine the nature of what was said in the attributional statements, we might surmise that aspects of the offense description other than the offense type and elements of the offender's social history are important sources of attributions. The attributions are typically drugs, alcohol, get money, poor associates, personality problems, interpersonal hostilities, or environmental stress. It could be that rather specific information is used to infer these specific attributions (e.g., drug use history, presence of accomplices, psychological reports). Thus, causal attributions may have a similar structure to schemas (Abelson, 1976); certain case information triggers a "drug habit" schema which contains suppositions about past social history and criminal behavior, suggestions for treatment, and predictions about future behavior.

Individual differences. Our data, some of which were analyzed and reported in Carroll (1978), also reveals substantial individual differences among decision makers in their attributions, their average recommendations, and the case information related to their judgments. Differences among individuals are not at all unusual in criminal justice research, and researchers often focus upon individual correctional philosophies as the precursor of differences. For example, Hogarth (1971) found that judges' sentences were related to the perceived purposes of incarceration in the specific case, particularly incapacitation and punishment. Analyses based on how the individual judge perceived and understood the "facts" of the case were several times more predictive than analyses based on facts in the case files coded "objectively" by the researcher. He concluded that "one can explain more about sentencing by knowing a few things about the judge than by knowing a great deal about the facts of the case" (1971, p. 350).

An assumption of the attributional approach is that individual correctional philosophies reflect individual assumptions about the causes (and therefore the necessary cures) of crime (Carroll & Payne, 1976, 1977a). For example, people whose personal ideological or scientific beliefs about the nature of crime lead them to make generally internal attributions about crime (something about the offender) are likely to proffer retributive sentences (especially for intentional attributions), incapacitative sentences (if stable attributions are made), or therapeutic programs focusing on personal problems. People who make external attributions would avoid retribution, and focus on system reform and rehabilitation (providing opportunities lacking in the previous environment), with lesser emphasis on incapacitation (stable environment) as necessary but somewhat unjust to the offender.

Studies have related individual differences in attributional beliefs directly to reactions to criminals. Sosis (1974) classified subjects by their scores on Rotter's (1966) Locus of Control Scale as Internals, who view people as potent causal agents, or Externals, who view the environment as causally potent. She found that Internals judged offenders more harshly than did Externals, presumably a reflection of the Internal's attribution of crime to the offender. Carroll and Payne (1976, 1977a) gave subjects a simulated parole task in which they had to ask for information about the parole applicant from a list of categories (e.g., age, offense). Results showed that Internals looked at information earlier that dealt with the crime (crime description, cooperation with police, time served, time left on sentence) and with the person (age, prior arrests, previous parole revocations, education level, susceptibility to influence). Externals looked earlier at information about the environment (release job plans, recent employment) and the prison (disciplinary problems, changes in attitude noted, prior convictions). Thus, the attributional bias of the individual subject seemed to induce a *confirmatory set*, in which information to confirm the hypothesized cause of criminal behavior was looked at earlier than information about other possible causes. This biased information seeking undoubtedly makes confirmation more likely (cf. Snyder, Tanke, & Berscheid, 1977), and supports an attributional basis for individual differences in responses to crime. Insofar as the attributional bias makes hypothesized causes more salient, these salient causes would be more likely to be implicated as the attributions for a crime (cf. Taylor & Fiske, 1979).

Summary and implications

This article has presented a framework for analyzing judgments about crime and criminals and has argued that causal attributions are prevalent and important in the way laypeople and experts understand crime. The role of attribution in parole decisions was extensively described in order to illustrate this approach. Specifically, research has demonstrated that expert parole decision makers make causal attributions in the process of deliberating about the release of offenders, with the most typical attributions regarding the causes of crime being substance abuse (drugs and alcohol), profit, victim precipitation, influence of associates, personality deficiencies (lack of control, mental problems, immaturity, easily influenced, aimless) and domestic problems.

The attributional framework categorizes attributions about crime in regard to whether the perceived cause is internal to the offender or in the external environment, enduring or temporary, and intentional or not on the part of the offender or others. In general, blameworthiness and punitive responses were expected to be mediated by the internality of the attribution, with crimes attributed to internal-intentional causes receiving the most punishment. Crime prevention through incapacitation of dangerous offenders was expected to be mediated by the stability of the attributed cause. The studies on expert parole decisions in Pennsylvania indicated that punishment was not an important consideration, but risk was. For this reason, internality of attributed causes did not influence parole decisions, but offenders whose crimes were perceived as due to more stable causes were judged worse risks on parole (more likely to commit subsequent crimes) and received less favorable parole recommendations.

Some preliminary analyses of the antecedents of attributions in parole decisions have revealed that we do not yet fully understand how case information and individual differences in beliefs combine to produce attributions. Future research must address this topic as well as the effects of attributions upon decisions.

The attributional analysis of responses to crime has several potential implications for the criminal justice system. First, the criminal justice system in general (and, as we have seen, parole decision makers) is faced with poorly defined and conflicting goals which are based upon assumptions of what causes and cures criminal behavior. The attributional approach is useful in providing the idea that the imputed causes are due not only to the facts of a case, but also to the ideas and attitudes of the evaluators. Attribution theory further contributes by describing how correctional goals, philosophies, individual attitudes, and case information fit together. Thus, the attribution framework may help us to recognize and sharpen policy issues, speeding up the process of creating a policy that deals with discretionary human judgments and seeks a greater level of justice for all.

Second, the attribution approach can provide a means of evaluating the attributional biases of individual decision makers or of entire segments of the criminal justice system. The approach suggests how to characterize people and policies in terms of their underlying causal assumptions. Thus, differences among decision makers could be detected, as could differences between decision makers and legislated policy. This enhanced ability to examine current practices could be tied to attempts at changing policy, improving decisions, or training decision makers.

Most important of all is the implication that the criminal justice system can be studied in a systematic and meaningful way that relates social psychological theory to complex real-world judgments. The criminal justice system is the aggregated acts of individuals whose judgments and decisions reflect causal theories about crime and criminals. Although the experts have been shown to differ markedly from laypeople in the knowledge they possess, the principles of attribution theory apply to them as well as to the "naive" individual.

14. Social psychology in court: The judge

Michael J. Saks and Reid Hastie

Overview of the judge's role

In the public eye, the judge is the central actor in the courtroom. Of all the participants in the legal process, he or she is the most prominent symbolically, the most prestigious, and the most powerful during the trial itself. To begin this chapter we will review the judge's major activities in the criminal trial process.

Every person arrested must appear before a judge within a few hours of the arrest. During this initial presentment to the court the defendant is informed of legal rights, the criminal charges are explained, and the judge makes a preliminary decision about whether there is enough evidence to continue to hold the defendant in jail. At this preliminary hearing or shortly afterward the judge is required to set bail for the defendant, the bail being an amount of money that the defendant must pay to guarantee reappearance at subsequent court proceedings. Often the defendant is released without a monetary bail on his or her "own recognizance" or promise to return for further proceedings.

During the bail hearing or shortly before it, the judge presides over the arraignment, during which the accused is formally charged and enters a plea of guilty or not guilty. If the accused pleads guilty, the judge may interrogate him or her to ensure that the consequences of the plea are fully understood, and that it is entered without coercion by the police or others. Following a guilty plea, the judge usually decides on a sentence (often a fine, a short jail sentence, or probation) immediately.

If the defendant enters a not guilty plea, a trial date is set – usually several months after the date of the arraignment. During the interval

This chapter originally appeared in Saks, M. J., & Hastie, R., *Social psychology in court* (pp. 23–46). New York: Van Nostrand Reinhold, 1978. Copyright © 1978 by Litton Educational Publishing, Inc. Reprinted by permission.

between arraignment and trial most defendants, if they have not already done so, change their pleas to guilty. When this happens, the judge again assumes control of the proceedings, and the sentencing process begins. Most guilty pleas are entered after negotiations ("plea bargaining") take place between the prosecution and defense lawyers. The result of these negotiations is an agreement that the defendant will plead guilty to a lesser charge or that the prosecuting attorney will recommend reduced sentences to the judge during the pre-sentence hearing. Judges usually respect the terms of these bargains by following the prosecution's recommendations in sentencing. In some jurisdictions the judge actually participates in the bargaining process, acting as a mediator between the two attorneys.

If the case reaches trial, the judge (usually not the same judge who conducted the pretrial proceedings) presides over the case. If it is a jury trial he or she directs the impanelment of jurors, "umpires" the attorneys' presentations, and gives the jury final instructions on the law and evidence before they begin deliberation. In a few rare cases the judge exercises the court's power to intervene in the jury's decision either by directing them to return a particular verdict or even by reversing their judgment (this is called a judgment *non obstante verdicto*).

If the verdict is acquittal, the defendant leaves the criminal process. If the verdict is conviction, sentencing takes place. Usually the judge sentences the defendant a few days after the trial, allowing for a review of the facts of the case and a pre-sentence report prepared by the court's probation department.

On the surface we have presented an image of a powerful, autonomous trial judge. Of course, this picture is a simplification and even somewhat misleading. The judge's behavior is constrained by a great number of forces operating in the criminal justice system. First, there are conventions, rules, and laws that limit freedom. These factors specify the ordering and protocol for most of the events in the court's operation. For example, the law determines which hearings must be held, sets limits on bail levels for bailable offenses, controls the selection and instruction of juries, determines courtroom procedure, and limits or even prescribes sentences for various crimes. Second, relationships with other court officials, especially prosecutors and police, place limits on the judge's freedom. This is clear when we consider the paramount importance of the plea-bargaining process. Finally, the sheer weight of the caseload in most courts will diminish the judge's role still further. To avoid even greater congestion in the criminal justice system, the judge is forced to hold brief hearings and constantly to press attorneys and juries for swift, decisive action within the law's formal procedural requirements.

Although these numerous unobtrusive constraints limit the judge's autonomy, he or she is still the most powerful actor in the legal system. A judge's personal predispositions determine which cases reach the courtroom, and influence prosecution and defense attorneys before the trial.

The judge's discretion to set bail and determine sentences is still very broad. And the court[1] usually has recourse to exercise his or her prerogatives by reversing decisions made by others.

Judicial backgrounds

There is bewildering variety in the methods used to recruit trial judges. The variety chiefly reflects the workings of historical accidents and the great range of tasks that judges perform. Most state and municipal jurisdictions select judges through public elections; many depend on political officeholders such as governors, mayors, and legislators to appoint judges; and an increasing number of jurisdictions have panels composed of lawyers, citizens, and politicians to select judges on the basis of their professional records. Federal judgeships are filled by presidential appointment with a senate review. Each of these paths to the bench is tortuous and obscure, and each selection method serves some interests while neglecting others. The point for the present discussion is that this complexity is certain to produce a great diversity in the personal characteristics of judges.

There are numerous surveys of the characteristics of men and women serving on the bench (see Abraham, 1975, for a sampling), which provide a sense of the diversity in the profession. However, relatively little research has been devoted to the relationship between judicial background or personal differences and judicial performance.

Given the central role of the judge and the emphasis on rationality and impartiality in the legal system, social scientists have been interested in the manner in which individual differences influence the quality and direction of their decisions. Most of this research has focused on "sociological" rather than psychological variables. For example, Nagel (1962) conducted a large-scale study of the influence of background on state and federal supreme court judicial decisions. Nagel constructed an index of each judge's tendency to decide cases in favor of the defense or prosecution. He found that political party affiliation (Republican), bar association membership, high income, Protestant religious affiliation, low scores on a test of liberal political attitudes, and experience as a prosecuting attorney were all associated with a bias to favor the prosecution side of a case under appellate court review.

There have also been several efforts to characterize "personal styles" of judges and to relate style to family and educational background. An example of this approach is in the work of Smith and Blumberg (1967), who used a participant observation method to examine the differences among nine judges on the bench in a major criminal court. They developed a typology of six major judicial role patterns, which is perhaps best summarized by listing their labels: Intellectual-Scholar, Routineer-Hack,

---

[1] "The court" is sometimes synonymous with "the judge."

Political Adventurer-Careerist, Judicial Pensioner, the Hatchet-Man, the Tyrant-Showboat-Benevolent Despot. Smith and Blumberg discovered that the majority of the work-load of the entire bench was handled by two justices, an Intellectual-Scholar and a Routineer-Hack. The authors noted that it was typical of large urban court systems to find one or two "workhorse" judges handling cases at a far higher rate than the other justices. However, they found it quite remarkable that the two "work-horses" in their study exhibited such great stylistic differences – the well-educated Intellectual-Scholar conducting an almost frenzied court, working weekends and evenings, and arousing antagonism from the rest of the bench; the more prosaic Routineer-Hack running a more traditional, but nonetheless efficient court.

To date there is no research on the effects of traditional personality variables on judicial decision making. To some extent this is due to judges' reluctance to open their profession to psychologists' scrutiny. Almost all of the research on individual differences has been ac-complished by examining public records or by observing judges at work in the courtroom. However, it is also true that the current primitive state of the personality field provides a rather weak base for studying naturally occurring individual differences. Most personality constructs are as yet poorly developed, and reliable and valid assessment instruments are almost completely lacking (Mischel, 1968). The focus on social, attitudinal, and behavioral style differences is a conservative but sound beginning.

Arraignment and bail

Judges are first involved in most criminal cases when they are called on to oversee arraignment and bail-setting hearings. In some cases a judge approves a warrant for the arrest of a suspect; but most arrests are made without a warrant, and in any case a warrant is issued routinely if the police do request one. The initial presentment of a defendant usually occurs within a day of arrest. During this proceeding the judge's duties are quite straightforward, although there is a wide range in the conscien-tiousness with which they are performed in the lower courts (President's Commission, 1967). Ordinarily the judge informs the defendant of the charges that led to the arrest, apprises him or her of legal rights, and arranges to have a defense attorney assigned to the case. Many minor cases are disposed of at this point; if the defendant pleads guilty, the judge imposes sentence at once. In most felony cases a brief hearing is held at this time to determine whether the prosecution has enough evidence to show probable cause to hold the defendant for trial.[2] In these

---

[2] In some jurisdictions a grand jury hearing replaces the probable cause hearing with a specially selected jury (usually of twenty-five persons) deciding if the prosecution case is strong enough to "indict" the defendant.

cases, following the probable cause hearing, the prosecutor's office prepares an "information" describing the charges against the defendant, and a formal arraignment is held. Many, probably most, defendants plead guilty at this point, and the sentencing process is started. For those defendants who plead innocent as charged, a trial date is set, usually months from the arraignment data, and the issue of bail is raised.

Bail, as we have said, is a monetary payment to ensure that the defendant will appear in court when required to do so. The legal object of the bail system is to ensure reappearance, but a number of factors that are not relevant to the risk of the defendant's fleeing probably enter into the judge's bail decision.

There are a multitude of problems with the bail system, most of them deriving from the fact that while its object is to guarantee the defendant's appearance in court, the means to secure the appearance is monetary. First of all, psychologists and other behavioral scientists have not developed prediction techniques powerful enough reliably to distinguish the high-risk defendants from the low-risk ones. Second, the effects of the monetary bail system are critically dependent on the defendant's economic condition. In fact, the bail payment is probably an effective sanction for only a small proportion of the defendants: many defendants cannot afford any bail costs no matter how low, and many are wealthy enough so that the bail payment is no guarantee of later appearance in court. Third, it seems unjust to jail a person, who is presumed to be innocent until proven guilty, merely because he or she is unable to meet the costs of bail.

Research on defendants' behavior between arraignment and trial suggests that the likelihood a person will commit further crimes in the interval or flee is typically overestimated. Efforts to reform bail laws (the 1966 federal bail reform law) and bail-setting practices such as the famous Manhattan Bail Project (Ares, Rankin, & Sturz, 1963) have promoted the use of "on own recognizance" releases, where the defendant is not required to post bail money but is released on his or her promise to return. This method seems more consistent with the premise that a defendant is "innocent until proven guilty," and in practice an over-whelming number of recognizance-release defendants appear for trial.

In addition to the research by social scientists designed to predict the behavior of defendants awaiting trial, there are several studies of judges' bail-setting policies. The research by Ebbe Ebbesen and Vladimir Konečni on bail-setting decisions is an excellent example of the application of social science methods to a natural domain. We will spend some time on their research because it illustrates several theoretical, methodological, and substantive points.

Ebbesen and Konečni (1975) designed two studies to examine judges' decision making in the bail-hearing situation. Typically the bail hearing in a minor case lasts a few minutes following arraignment. A lower court judge reviews a terse summary of the charges against the defendant, his or her economic status, ties to the local community, and prior criminal record. Both attorneys present recommendations for bail and occasionally briefly emphasize details of the case in support of their recommendations. Then in a matter of seconds the judge renders a decision based on the information in the probation officer's case file and the two recommendations.

The relative simplicity of the situation appealed to the two psychologists, and in their first experiment they enlisted the cooperation of eighteen lower court judges. They asked each judge to review several model cases designed to mimic real case files and including written attorney's recommendations, and then to set bail as though they were actually in court. The simulation method allowed the experimenters to prepare case reports in which several variables were systematically manipulated. Several levels of district attorney bail recommendations and defense recommendations were presented, along with information implying weak or strong local community ties and a previous criminal conviction record or no record. Thirty-six files were created, so that every level of every variable occurred with every level of each other variable. Other factors were presented at fixed levels in every case; for example, only robbery charges were included, the defendants always entered not guilty pleas, and they were always between the ages of twenty-one and twenty-five. Finally, other details of the case, such as the exact nature of the stolen goods, were varied to increase the realism of the cases.

The advantages of the experimental plan are fairly obvious. Any systematic variations in the judge's final bail levels can be unequivocally attributed to variations in the independent variables. The relative effects of these experimenter-controlled variables can be assessed and clearly separated from the influences of the constant background variables (for example, type of crime).

Ebbesen and Konečni were not content with merely demonstrating that some variables influence bail levels while others do not. They hoped to "capture the judge's decision policy" by developing a simple mathematical equation that would predict actual final bail levels from information about each case. In this situation they made the following theoretical assumptions about their judges:

1. The facts of each case can be viewed as forces acting on the judges' final bail decisions.

2. The strength of each fact's influence force on the final bail level can be characterized as acting in a specific *direction* with a particular *weight*. For example, if we consider only the two attorneys' recommendations, we can imagine that they will differ in *direction*, with the value of the district attorney's recommendation being "high" (he would urge the judge to set a high bail) and the defense recommendation being "low"

(urging the judge to set a low bail or release the defendant on his own recognizance). The second, *weighting*, factor refers to the weight the judge gives to each recommendation. A prosecution-oriented judge might tend to weigh the district attorney's recommendations more heavily than those of the defense. Consequently we would expect his final decision to fall in the direction of the higher recommendation. The notion of weight in this sense is very close to the everyday usage of the term: the district attorney's recommendation has a greater weight in the judge's final decision.

3. Although it is fairly easy to think of the attorney's recommendations as variables in an equation to predict final bail level – after all, the recommendations and the final bail are all stated in comparable dollar-value terms – it is not so easy to accept the authors' contention that factors such as prior record and local ties can also be represented quantitatively. Even psychologists who are eager to quantify or "scale" these apparently nonnumerical entities believe that the road to a successful mathematical formulation is steep and thorny. Suffice it to say for our present purposes that modern psychological measurement theory and scaling techniques provide a practical, although cumbersome, solution to the problem of quantifying variables such as local ties and prior record (see Dawes, 1972, and Anderson, 1974b, for an introduction to these methods).

4. Next the authors proposed that the typical judge's bail decision could be described or modeled as a *weighted sum* of the values and weights of each of the types of information in the case. Since many background variables were fixed at constant levels in the experiment, the psychologists needed only to consider a simplified form of the model to account for the judges' decisions. The experimenters proposed a model of the following form:

$$[WEIGHT_1 \times DISTRICT\ ATTORNEY'S\ RECOMMENDATION]$$
$$+\ [WEIGHT_2 \times DEFENSE\ ATTORNEY'S\ RECOMMENDATION]$$
$$+\ [WEIGHT_3 \times STRENGTH\ OF\ LOCAL\ TIES]$$
$$+\ [WEIGHT_4 \times PRIOR\ CONVICTION\ RECORD]$$

$$=\ FINAL\ BAIL\ LEVEL$$

Notice that although we have been quite precise about the conceptual meanings of the weights and scale values and the form of the model we have not committed ourselves to exact number values for these variables. The experimenter gives the model several advantages when he applies it to the data from an experiment. First, he tests only the general form of the model, assigning values to the four weights ($WEIGHT_1$ ... $WEIGHT_4$) and the scale values (DISTRICT ATTORNEY'S RECOMMENDATION ... PRIOR RECORD) to maximize the fit of the model to the data (and to satisfy a few constraints imposed by the measurement and scaling methods). Second, he is willing to assume that if the form of the model is successful in the simplified case, he can generalize it by merely adding new terms as new variables enter the judgment task (for instance, WEIGHT$_5$ × AMOUNT STOLEN).

(The model of the judge proposed by Ebbesen and Konečni is actually a special case of a very general mathematical model, called the linear multiple regression model by statisticians. This model is usually used to summarize the relationship between a single to-be-predicted dependent variable [the judge's bail decision in the Ebbesen and Konečni case] and a number of predictor independent variables [the information about attorney's recommendations, crime severity, strength of community ties, and so forth, in this case]. Details of the statistical model are available in many elementary texts on multivariate analysis.)

5. Finally, Ebbesen and Konečni assumed that the final bail judgment is not only a *weighted sum* but that it is a *weighted average* of the scale values of the case information. This final assumption is the most restrictive and the most controversial. The so-called averaging model has proved to be a valid representation in a number of decision-making situations similar to the bail-setting task (for instance, as a model of first-impression judgments in social acquaintance situations), but it has also failed as a psychological model (for instance, in predicting evaluations of economic and gambling problems).

The averaging constraint takes the form of an assumption that the sum of the weights in the model is equal to unity:

$$\text{WEIGHT}_1 + \text{WEIGHT}_2 + \text{WEIGHT}_3 + \text{WEIGHT}_4 = 1$$

The conception of a judge comprehending or "evaluating" and then weighting each fact relevant to a decision seems intuitively reasonable. Even the averaging rule, which implies that the weight given to each piece of information is dependent on the nature of the other facts in the case, is quite plausible. Resistance to the model usually arises because of its simplicity. Most experts, legal judges or otherwise, feel that their decisions are byzantine inferential masterpieces and that the prosaic averaging model is an insult to the richness of their intellectual creativity. There are several responses to this objection. First, experts almost always overestimate the complexity and sensitivity of their personal judgment strategies. Slovic and Lichtenstein (1971) reviewed several studies of expert decision making. They concluded that experts such as medical diagnosticians, stockbrokers, admission officers, and clinical psychologists have relatively poor insight into their decision policies. Generally these experts believed that they utilized many more sources of information and more complex judgment rules than they actually used. Interestingly, these experts appeared to become even less insightful as they gained professional experience: young judges were more accurate in assessing their personal decision policies than older ones. Second, the averaging model is not expected to reflect every detail of the judge's behavior. The model is a first approximation, which aims to capture the general features of the decision strategy while missing or ignoring the fine structure. After all, psychological research on expert judges is very new, less than ten years old, and the initial models must by necessity be overly simple.

Returning to Ebbesen and Konečni's experimental method, eighteen judges read the experimental materials for thirty-six arraignment-bail files and assigned a dollar-value bail to each case. The resulting judgments are displayed in Figure 14.1. The pattern of results shows that the district attorney's recommendation is important (all of the lines slope up to the right) and that both the local-ties variable and the prior-record variable have significant impacts on the final bail decision. The defense attorney's recommendation had no influence on the judge – a fact which corresponds to the condition of an averaging model where this information receives no weight at all (WEIGHT$_2$ = 0).

Table 14.1 presents values for weights and scale values that might be derived to account for the present results (actually Ebbesen and Konečni proposed a slightly more elaborate model and analysis). We can use the weights and values in this table in conjunction with the averaging model to "predict" (actually *post*dict) the judges' decisions. For instance, the predicted bail for a defendant with strong local ties and a prior-conviction record, for whom the district attorney recommends a bail of $2250, and the defense recommends $1100 would be represented as follows:

[.50 × $2000] + [.00 × $1100] + [.30 × $0] + [.20 × $6000] = $2200

This result is quite close to the actual figure obtained in the experiment ($1800).

Ebbesen and Konečni next attempted to apply their model to bail decisions occurring in actual arraignment hearings. They sent several observers to the courtrooms of the same judges who had participated in the pencil-and-paper laboratory study. These observers recorded information on the variables that had been manipulated in the laboratory along with the final bail set in hundreds of real bail hearings. The experimenters added a new variable, severity of the crime with which the defendant was charged, to the analysis.

Again they applied the averaging model. As before they found that the district attorney's recommendation had the greatest influence on the final bail value. They discovered that in the actual courtroom setting that strong or weak community ties and presence or absence of a prior criminal record did not have any simple effect on bail decisions. They also found that the defense attorney's recommendations had little or no in-

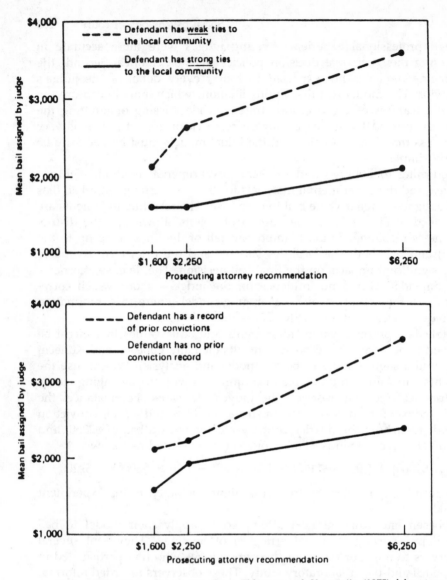

Figure 14.1. Summary of data from Ebbesen and Konečni's (1975) laboratory bail-setting experiment. The vertical axis represents the amount of the judge's bail decision, the dependent variable in the study. The horizontal axis represents the prosecuting attorney's recommendation, one of the independent variables. The fact that all four lines slope upward to the right indicates that these recommendations had an impact on the judgment; when the attorney recommended higher bail levels, the judge assigned higher bail requirements. The upper panel splits the data according to the "community ties" independent variable. The separation on the two lines indicates that this variable also had an effect on assigned bail levels: if the defendant had weak ties to the community, bail was set at a higher level than if his ties were strong. Finally, the lower panel shows that the existence of a record of prior criminal convictions affected bail levels: if the defendant had a record, bail was set higher than if his record was clean. Effects of the defense attorney's recommendation are not represented here because this independent variable had no reliable impact on the judge's bail decision.

Table 14.1. *Example weights and scale values for the simple averaging model for the data from Ebbesen and Konečni, Experiment 1*

	Weights	Subjective scale values		
District attorney's recommendation	.50	recommendation: $1600 scale value: $1600	recommendation: $2250 scale value: $2000	recommendation: $6250 scale value: $4000
Defense attorney's recommendation	.00	recommendation: $0 scale value: $0	recommendation: $550 scale value: $550	recommendation: $1100 scale value: $1100
Strength of local ties	.30	Strong local ties scale value: $0	weak local ties scale value: $3000	
Prior conviction record	.20	No prior convictions scale value: $0	Record of prior convictions scale value: $6000	

fluence on the judges' decisions. They concluded that although the weights on the factors of the case had shifted from the laboratory setting to the courtroom, the averaging model was still valid.

Ebbesen and Konečni also found that the severity of the crime which the defendant was alleged to have committed was important, but the influence of this variable was indirect. Severity of the crime affected both attorneys' recommendations, and it is through these recommendations that the final decision was influenced. Note that one implication of these conclusions is that the judge does attend to the factors which predict the risk that the defendant will not reappear in court: local ties, attorneys' recommendations, and crime severity. Also it seems that the judge does ignore the existence of a prior record per se. Further, since the averaging model based on only these five factors does a good job of predicting the judge's decisions, it follows that the influence of irrelevant factors (such as press coverage, desire to punish the defendant immediately, favoritism for the district attorney) is relatively small.

One problem with the field study in contrast to the controlled laboratory experiment is that it is impossible completely to eliminate alternative accounts for the results based on the effects of "hidden" or "unmeasured" variables. For example, Anderson (1976b) speculates that the Ebbesen and Konečni results reflect the effects of the defendants' race on bail decisions. Since Ebbesen and Konečni did not record defendants' race, and since race is plausibly related to some of the variables that were studied (e.g., prior record, crime severity), they cannot confidently eliminate interpretations of their results based on hypothetical race effects. (Of course this essential ambiguity is always present in nonexperimental field research. The conscientious researcher must be continually vigilant for plausible "hidden variable" explanations to turn them into testable hypotheses as best he can. Probably the best research strategy available is exemplified by Ebbesen and Konečni's approach: yoke the powerful, but unrepresentative, laboratory experiment to the inferentially weaker, but realistic, field study.)

Actually the hidden-variable problem is several subproblems. First, it could be that the researcher has completely missed the variable that is controlling the judge's decisions. The example outlined above illustrates this possibility. Anderson speculated that judges could be sensitive to the defendant's race, but Ebbesen and Konečni completely ignored the race variable in their analysis. If race were a crucial variable (and we don't know that it was), Ebbesen and Konečni's analysis would be flawed. Second, it could be that the researchers have defined a variable in one way (e.g., strength of community ties), but the judge is sensitive to a conceptually related but distinct variable (e.g., socioeconomic class). Here the problem is not that the researcher has failed to detect a relationship, but that he has "mislabeled" the relationship. Other researchers and theorists who do not carefully scrutinize the original data may then generate conclusions about residence patterns, geographical mobility, and so forth, while a correct analysis would have emphasized income, occupation, and the like. The solution to this problem is to consider a variety of empirically observable indices of a construct, such as "strength of community ties." The use of "multiple converging empirical operations" (i.e., many related measures of a construct) protects us from missing the correct conceptualization of measured variables.

Third, the researcher may have defined a dimension that is not treated as a single continuum by the judge. For example, although Ebbesen and Konečni defined severity of crime as a single dimension in their analysis, it is quite plausible that the judge distinguishes two (or more) categories of crime (violent v. nonviolent, or murder v. other crimes) and treats the two in very different ways as they appear in the arraignment docket. In fact, there was some evidence that the community-ties variable had one sort of effect for less severe crimes and exactly the opposite pattern of effects for more severe crimes in the Ebbesen and Konečni study.

To summarize, bail decisions in the laboratory setting reflected the prosecutor's recommendation, strength of local ties, and prior record. However, in actual bail hearings, the judge's final bail was directly related only to the prosecutor's recommendation. First, there are two ways to account for the correlation between the final bail and the prosecutor's recommendation: the judge depends heavily on the recommendation, or the judge and the prosecutor have highly similar decision policies (both depending on crime severity as the major cue to set bail). In this case both the direct-dependence and use-of-similar-cues hypotheses are almost certainly valid. Second, how can we account for the differences in policy, for the same judges, in the laboratory and the courtroom settings? One rather unflattering possibility suggested by Ebbesen and Konečni is that the judges are on their best behavior in the laboratory, and they adopt an unnatural bail-setting policy carefully weighting prior record and community-ties information as they feel a proper judge should. However, when they are back on the bench, unaware of the psychologists' scrutiny, they return to their irresponsible habits and listen only to the prosecutor. This interpretation is probably incorrect. A more likely account follows from an analysis of the flow of information in the disjointed, complex arraignment hearing. The judge does his best to attend to all the sources of information relevant to his decisions. Unfortunately, the irregular, muddled presentation of information and conflicting attention demands in the courtroom foil the judge's efforts to be open-minded, and leave him dependent on one or two inputs. One implication of this interpretation is that the defense attorney, completely ignored in Ebbesen and Konečni's study, could exert more influence on the judge if he or she would clearly highlight the facts of a case that favor lower bail. That is, we should not blame the overloaded judge but the defense attorney who fails to bring community ties and prior record to the court's attention when these variables are in favor of the accused.

We have invested so much time in reviewing the Ebbesen and Konečni paper because we feel that it foreshadows coming developments in psychological research on the trial judge. The method is especially appealing because it allows comparisons between highly controlled laboratory settings and the actual courtroom. The authors' arguments for the validity of the averaging model are very persuasive because of the convergence of results obtained in the two settings. The theoretical section of their paper is also exemplary in that the model of the judge is plausible, precise, and empirically flexible. It is interesting to see that the general form of the model, the averaging rule, is valid in both settings, but that details such as the weights vary with changes in the setting. One rather encouraging conclusion is that laboratory simulations are a useful method to explicate the judge's performance in the natural setting.

Plea bargaining

Most criminal cases (approximately 80%) end during the period following arrest before the trial begins, with a plea of guilty by the defendant. Without this high rate of "plea copping" there would be no way for the present court systems to handle the volume of criminal cases that would reach the trial stage. There are numerous sociological and participant observation studies of the plea bargaining process (Rosett & Cressey, 1976; Newman, 1956). Most jurisdictions enjoin judges from participating in the negotiations for pleas, and the two attorneys deal with one another directly. Recently there has been a shift in the procedure, and judges in some states (for example, parts of California and Minnesota) mediate discussions between the attorneys. To date there is no research by psychologists on this problem. It would seem that the Ebbesen and Konečni method for studying bail setting could be easily adapted for studying some aspects of the negotiated guilty plea. Another approach is suggested by the simulation method employed by Thibaut and Walker (1975) in their experiments on conditions in pretrial settlement conferences in civil cases.

The judge's instructions to the jury

Once the trial begins, the judge takes a more prominent directive role. The judge usually conducts the voir dire proceedings during which the trial jury is selected if the defendant has not waived rights to a jury trial. The judge reviews and decides on motions by the lawyers usually concerned with the admission of exhibits of evidence, deposition statements by witnesses who cannot be present at the trial, expert testimony, and so forth. Finally, once the actual trial begins, the court assumes the role of "umpire," ruling on objections raised by the attorneys and occasionally directing attorneys and witnesses to improve the quality of the trial.

There has been no research on the variables that control the judge's behavior during the trial itself. However, there are a number of experiments on the impact of the judge's instructions to the jury on the jury's behavior. Most of this research has focused on the effect of a judge's instruction to disregard a portion of the testimony on the jury's later use of the testimony.

Doob and Kirshenbaum (1973) conducted one of the neater experiments on this issue. In their simulation experiment, college-student subjects read a summary of a burglary case. For half of the subjects the case included information about the defendant's past record indicating that he had been convicted, five times, of breaking and entering charges. Subjects receiving this information were consistently more likely to judge the defendant guilty in the case. Of more interest to us is the fact that it made no difference whether or not the judge instructed the subject that the past-record evidence was only relevant to evaluating the witness's credibility and not relevant to deciding on his guilt or innocence. Clearly subjects ignored the judge's instructions; otherwise the instruction would have caused the subjects receiving it to judge the defendant as less likely to be guilty as charged than they did.

Sue, Smith, and Caldwell (1973), also using college-student subjects in a simulation of juror decision making, found that evidence ruled inadmissible had a significant effect on subjects' verdicts and assignments of punishment. The effects of inadmissible evidence were especially strong when the remaining, admissible, evidence was weak.

The disturbing implication of the Doob and Kirshenbaum and Sue, Smith, and Caldwell results, that jurors will typically ignore or misunderstand instructions from the bench, is echoed by a number of other empirical studies. Even more disquieting is contemplation of the fate of the judge's final instructions and charge to the jury at the end of the trial. Almost no research has been conducted on the extent to which jurors comprehend and apply the long difficult summary instructions. One section of the renowned "American Jury" study by Harry Kalven and Hans Zeisel of the University of Chicago bears on this issue indirectly (Kalven & Zeisel, 1966, 1967).

In this classic survey study, the two researchers mailed questionnaires to state and federal trial judges asking for information about recent case outcomes. The design of the survey emphasized comparisons between the juries' actual verdicts and the judges' (private) judgments. The general conclusion of the study was that in an overwhelming majority of cases judges' and juries' decisions were in agreement. The researchers went on to demonstrate that numerous characteristics of the trial – e.g., case difficulty, strength of evidence, length – affected both the jury and the judge similarly. For example, trial length was directly related to deliberation time, and judges' ratings of case difficulty predicted the likelihood that juries would request additional instructions from the judge during their deliberation. Judges' ratings of closeness of the case were related to the probability of disagreement between judge and jury on the verdict. Jury acquittal rates were related to judges' evaluations of the strength of the prosecution case, and so on. Taken together all of these correlations suggest that the jury and the judge are sensitive to the same characteristics of the case. Since the judge's instructions are the major communication between judge and jury, it seems plausible that jurors follow the case correctly and do a conscientious job of comprehending and applying rules of law outlined in the judge's final instructions. Unfortunately the logic behind this conclusion is not irresistible, and even in the Kalven and Zeisel survey there was a nonnegligible rate of judge-jury disagreements.

A few experiments have looked more directly at jurors' reactions to the judge's instructions, and the conclusions from this research are rather pessimistic. Several simulation experiments (DeSloovere, 1933; Forston, 1970; Henney, 1947; Hunter, 1935) assessed jurors' comprehension of the final instructions. All of these investigators concluded that the typical juror's grasp of the principles of law was weak at best and that legal definitions and rules were more often misapplied than used correctly.

There is currently considerable interest in developing more comprehensible "pattern instructions" and procedures that will deliver instructions to a jury in a maximally useful manner. Two promising suggestions are to present instructions before as well as after the trial evidence (Prettyman, 1960) and to allow jurors to take a written summary of the instructions into the deliberation room. In addition to these procedural improvements, researchers are studying ways in which psycholinguistic theory can be applied to render difficult instructions more understandable (Sales, Elwork, & Alfini, 1977).

Following the judge's final instructions, the case is in the jury's hands. Upon the jury's request, the judge may be called on to decide whether to send evidence exhibits, sections of the trial transcript, or additional instructions to the deliberation room. Should the jury return without reaching a verdict or "hang," the judge would exhort them to attempt once again to reach agreement.

When the jury returns with a verdict, the judge thanks them and dismisses them to return to the jury waiting room. If the verdict is an acquittal, the legal process is finished and the defendant is released. The prosecution side of the case has no rights to appeal the verdict. If the verdict is for conviction, the judge begins a review of the guilty defendant's record to determine the disposition of the case.

Sentencing

Thus far in the legal process the judge's behavior has been strongly constrained by laws, court rules, and the roles of other participants in the legal system; however, the matter of sentencing is almost completely in the judge's hands. In this country the judge reviews the facts of the case, a pre-sentence report prepared by a probation officer, and then simply determines the sentence. It is something of an embarassment to observe the great range of sentences that different judges assign to apparently indistinguishable crimes. Penologists, of course, have to live with these disparities, and they are particularly acerbic about sentencing practices. James V. Bennett, former Director of the Federal Bureau of Prisons, has observed:

In one of our institutions a middle-aged credit union treasurer is serving 117 days for embezzling $24,000 in order to cover his gambling debts. On the other hand, another middle-aged embezzler with a fine past record and a fine family is serving 20 years, with 5 years probation to follow. At the same institution is a war veteran, a 39-year-old attorney who has never been in trouble before, serving 11 years for illegally importing parrots into this country. Another who is destined for the same institution is a middle-aged tax accountant who on tax fraud charges received 31 years and 31 days in consecutive sentences. In stark contrast, at the same institution last year an unstable young man served out his 98-day sentence for armed bank robbery. [cited in Kaplan, 1973]

Federal and state laws provide limits that set upper and lower bounds on the penalties which can be imposed by the judge. But these boundaries usually allow wide lattitude for the judge's discretion to operate. For example, in Massachusetts a conviction for armed robbery can carry a sentence from five years to life in prison, and a conviction for manslaughter a sentence from two and one-half to twenty years in prison; and of course the judge may always grant a suspended sentence, allowing the defendant to return to society immediately. Furthermore, there is almost no appeals court review of sentences. Neither the prosecution nor the defense has a right to appeal the trial judge's sentence in most cases.

This lack of limitations and lack of review is accompanied by lack of control, leaving even the most conscientious judge at sea in an ocean of inconsistent standards and shifting guidelines. For example, at least four conflicting theories of sentencing policy are popular today:

(a) Case disposition should satisfy the victim's, friends of the victim's, and the public's need for *vengeance* on the criminal.
(b) Case disposition should demonstrate publicly the penalty a wrongdoer pays for his crime, to *deter* other potential offenders.
(c) Case disposition should aim to *protect* society from additional crimes by convicted criminals.
(d) Case disposition should aim to *rehabilitate* the criminal to prevent him or her from choosing to commit further crimes after leaving the correctional system.

Judges are left to their own devices to adopt or create sentencing policies. The result is that sentences in apparently identical crime circumstances vary widely. An early survey study by Gaudet (1938) found large disparities in the sentences assigned to similar offenders in lower courts in New Jersey. Gaudet found that judges tended to be consistent in assigning harsh or lenient sentences, but he was unable to isolate any relationships between sentencing policies and personal experience, local economic conditions, or imminence of reappointment.

The Gaudet result has been replicated in many other survey studies; however, we cannot conclude that this evidence for variation in sentences across similar *but different* cases proves that there is injustice in sentencing. It is possible that judges are attempting to sentence defendants justly and that the different circumstances of each case require considerable flexibility in sentencing. Unfortunately, a number of studies demonstrate that there is also great variation in the sentences imposed on the *same* defendants by different judges.

An experimental study in the Second Circuit of the federal court system (federal trial courts in New York, Connecticut, and Vermont) provides a clear demonstration that a defendant's sentence depends on the individual trial judge (Partridge and Eldridge, 1974). The study asked fifty federal judges to impose sentences on twenty different defendants charged with a range of offenses. Some example results are presented in Table 14.2. First, it is clear that there is enormous disagreement between judges. The authors of the report concluded that, "for the most part, the pattern displayed is not one of substantial consensus with a few sentences falling outside the area of agreement. Rather, it would appear that absence of consensus is the norm." Second, the most troubling sentencing inequities occur when one person receives a prison sentence and another, charged with the same offense, does not. Judges in the Second Circuit study disagreed on the issue of incarceration in sixteen out of the twenty cases studied. Third, sentencing disparities were not related to the length of a judge's service. There was no evidence that more experienced judges were closer to one another than less experienced judges.

There has been almost no research by psychologists on the problem of identifying and modeling individual differences in trial judges' sentencing behavior. Ebbesen and Konečni (1976) have started to apply their techniques to the problem, but the trial judge is still the least well-understood actor in the courtroom.

Although the larger problem of modeling the trial judge's decision policy is still untouched, sociologists have pursued the problem of identifying the influences of "extralegal" factors (for instance, the defendant's race, sex, and socioeconomic status) on sentencing ever since the publication of a pioneering monograph by Sellin in 1928. Sellin argued that although factors such as the defendant's race and economic status are legally irrelevant to the determination of sentence, the judge cannot escape their subtle influence.

Research on the problem has all followed a single methodological strategy. One or more extralegal factors are isolated, and cases in which

Table 14.2. *Second Circuit Sentencing Study. The numbers in the table indicate the federal judges' sentence assignments for seven cases. The range in sentences, the difference between the most and least severe figures for each case, is quite large, implying that disagreement between judges is high even when they review the same cases*

Experimental case	Most severe sentence	Median sentence	Least severe sentence
Extortionate credit transactions; income tax violations	20 yr prison $65,000	10 yr prison $50,000	3 yr prison
Bank robbery	18 yr prison $5,000	10 yr prison	5 yr prison
Sale of heroin	10 yr prison 5 yr probation	5 yr prison 3 yr probation	1 yr prison 5 yr probation
Theft and possession of stolen goods	7.5 yr prison	3 yr prison	4 yr probation
Operating an illegal gambling business	1 yr prison $3,000	3 yr probation $10,000	1 yr probation $1,000
Mail theft	6 mos prison 18 mos probation	3 yr probation	1 yr probation
Perjury	1 yr prison $1,000	2 yr probation $500	$1,000

the defendant was convicted are classified on the basis of the factors. Then the researcher employs statistical techniques to determine if the sentence imposed in each case is reliably correlated with the extralegal factor. For example, Sellin hypothesized that when sentences are imposed, the most severe sentences will be assigned to blacks and other members of racial minorities. The difficulty with this approach is that although a superficial survey of cases may appear to confirm the hypothesis, a thorough, convincing analysis must not only demonstrate that there is a relation between the extralegal factor and sentence severity, but further that the true source of the relationship is not another legally relevant factor (for instance, prior conviction record). In Sellin's example, he needed to show that race and sentence are correlated, and in addition he needed to demonstrate that a correlation between race and prior record (black defendants were likelier than whites to have prior criminal convictions) did not exist, or did not account for the relation between race and sentence. As it turns out, Sellin did not accomplish either objective. He neither established the existence of a strong race-sentence correlation, nor did he attempt to rule out other legally relevant variables as competing explanations. The statistical logic required to establish a variable as causal and to rule out explanations based on "co-varying" factors is extremely complex. In a recent review paper Hagan (1974) concludes that none of the thirty-odd studies to date has established the significance of extralegal attributes in criminal sentencing. Of course, this does not mean that extralegal considerations are negligible, but only that a clear case for their importance has yet to be advanced.

The appellate court judge

In addition to the research we have just reviewed on the psychology of the trial judge, there is a literature on appellate court judges. The most prominent and most studied judges in the country are the nine justices of the Supreme Court of the United States, which is exclusively concerned with cases on appeal. Unlike the trial judges we have discussed above, most appellate judges meet to make their decisions collegially. Any successful analysis of these judges' behavior must consider the dynamics of these small groups as well as the judges as individuals. Social scientists and legal scholars have focused on four topics in collegial justice: first, the development of quantitative models to predict individual supreme court justices' decisions; second, comparisons between judges' behavior making decisions alone and (the same) judges' decisions as members of judicial tribunals; third, theoretical analyses of the relative accuracy of individual and group decisions; fourth, historical analyses of the patterns of clique formation and inter-judge influence in the Supreme Court.

Ulmer (1971) has written an excellent monograph introducing research on "courts as small groups." We will not discuss appellate court decision making in this text because the procedures and functions of an appellate court are so different from those of the trial courtroom, which is the focus of our presentation.

Summary

This chapter on the psychology of the trial judge began with a review of the tasks performed by the judge in the courtroom. There followed a short section on the nature of individual differences between judges, emphasizing the diversity of personal characteristics to be found on the bench. Next the bail-setting process was explored in an extensive analysis of two studies by Ebbesen and Konecni. Experimental and correlational methods were compared, and a mathematical averaging model of the trial judge's decision-making policy was examined. A short review of research on the judge's communications with the trial jury, instructions during the trial, was presented. The general conclusion that the trial judge's instructions could be improved in comprehensibility and effectiveness was advanced. Finally, the chapter concluded with a summary of research on sentencing policies.

Part V
Interpersonal conflict

Why do people find it so difficult to reconcile their differences? Why so much wrangling and dispute among us? Our failure to answer these questions and to discover how to reduce conflict may eventually lead us to nuclear war. It has certainly led to war since time immemorial. And, of course, scientific advances have now brought us to the point where all of humanity and all it holds dear are at the mercy of the judgments of the persons in dispute. Somehow we must increase our competence in understanding and coping with conflicts between persons – before it is too late.

Even small disputes have enormous psychological, social, and economic costs. Strikes, boycotts, litigation, the health effects of stress, the sheer unhappiness of people involved in domestic conflict are all consequences of our ignorance regarding conflict resolution. Society at large has no less a stake in scientists' understanding of conflict resolution than it does in research on cancer and heart disease.

Prior to 1964 studies of conflict were predominantly concerned with motivational differences, that is, disputes about who gains and who loses. But judgment and decision researchers are now learning that interpersonal conflict is frequently caused by cognitive differences, that is, differences in judgments about values (what *ought to be*), facts (what *is*), action (what *to do*), history (what *has been*), and predictions (what *will be*). Studies of how such cognitive differences lead to and prolong dispute are relatively recent and have not yet become a part of the mainstream of research in the study of conflict resolution. The first article to describe how cognitive differences could be studied in terms of judgment and decision making appeared in 1965 (Hammond, 1965). It was followed by replication of the same study carried out in Eastern and Western Europe, Australia, and Japan in which essentially the same results were obtained; namely, differences in judgments created by different experiences were not reduced by ordinary verbal discourse. That meant that the conventional wisdom is wrong: If cognitive differences *alone* lead to dispute that is not resolved, the removal of motivational differences will not necessarily lead to the removal of dispute. The fact that these results were achieved in a number of countries and were produced by a number of independent investigators indicates that they are not peculiar to one society.

One important discovery from research on cognitive differences is that people in general do not effectively describe their judgment policies to one another; that is, they do not know how to describe the manner in which they organize information into a judgment. As a result, they are poor at discovering where their cognitive differences lie and, therefore, poor at reducing them. They are as inept at describing their dispute – "We just can't agree" – as the the driver who, knowing nothing about automobile mechanics, sees an engine problem in terms of "It just won't work." As a result, not only are people slow to learn what another person's judgment policy is, but serious misunderstanding and conflict persist. A recent review of the research on cognitive rather than motivational differences can be found in Hammond and Grassia (1985).

We present four chapters in this part. The first, by Krishna S. Dhir and Howard J. Markman, describes how the results of judgment and decision research can be used to help settle marital disputes. The second, by Berndt Brehmer, focuses on understanding and resolving conflict in small groups. The third, by Max Bazerman and Margaret A. Neale, is directed toward the process of bargaining and illustrates the application of findings of Tversky and Kahneman (see Chapter 2). A selection from Howard Raiffa's *Art and Science of Negotiation* shows that a person skilled in the techniques of decision theory can often reduce such disputes amicably and effectively.

15. Application of social judgment theory to understanding and treating marital conflict
Krishna S. Dhir and
Howard J. Markman

Theories of marital distress have long emphasized the role of conflict in the etiology, maintenance, and treatment of marital and family problems (Barry, 1970; Coser, 1956; Deutsch, 1969; Gottman, 1979; Raush, Barry, Hertel, & Swain, 1974; Scanzoni, 1979; Sprey, 1969; Straus & Tallman, 1971; and Strodtbeck, 1951). These conceptions of conflict have in common the assertion that couples are interdependent and experience problems due to their interdependency that need to be resolved. Well-functioning couples rely on their interactional abilities or agreed-upon norms to arrive at solutions that maximize the rewards and minimize the cost for the couple (Thibaut & Kelley, 1959; Kelley & Thibaut, 1978). Conflict occurs when solutions are reached that are not satisfying for the partners. That is, conflict results from failure of problem-solving strategies to solve problems due to the couples' interdependency. Recently, in fact, Braiker and Kelley have assigned to conflict the central role in understanding the development and dissolution of close relationships. Conflict is seen as the "window through which we can observe close relationships function" (1979, p. 2).

Despite the fact that theorists have long recognized the importance of understanding the role of conflict in relationships, until recently there has been little systematic research examining the couples' interaction in conflict situations. The advent of behavioral marital therapy, (Gottman, Notarius, Gonso, & Markman, 1976; Jacobson & Margolin, 1979; Stuart, 1969) with its focus on modifying couples' interaction process, stimulated several research groups to begin systematically examining couples' interaction in conflict situations.

Couples in these studies were asked to resolve, through discussion,

This chapter originally appeared in the *Journal of Marriage and the Family*, 1984, 46(3), 597–610. Copyright © 1984 by the National Council on Family Relations. Reprinted by permission.

conflict tasks including the Inventory of Marital Conflicts (Olson & Ryder, 1970), and their top personal problems in their relationships (e.g., Gottman, Notarius, Markman, Bank, Yoppi, & Rubin, 1976). While talking, couples' interactions were videotaped and coded with one of several behavioral observation systems (see Markman, Notarius, Stephen, & Smith, 1981 for a review). These studies found that there were systematic differences in how distressed (unhappy) and nondistressed (happy) couples resolved conflict tasks. The basic differences were that distressed, as compared with nondistressed, couples use more negative and less positive communication behaviors (Billings, 1979; Birchler, Weiss, & Vincent, 1975; Gottman, Markman, & Notarius, 1977; Raush et al., 1974). One longitudinal study also has indicated that negative communication was predictive of later relationship unhappiness (Markman, 1979, 1981).

The results of these studies have been interpreted to suggest that effective conflict resolution is related to couples' use of communication and problem-solving skills (e.g., Jacobson, 1977; Jacobson & Margolin, 1979). In addition to increasing our understanding of the process of problem solving in conflict situations, these studies also produced well-validated assessment instruments to facilitate the study of couples' interaction in laboratory and home situations (Weiss, 1980). To summarize, behavioral observation studies of couples' interaction have shed light on the role of conflict in close relationships.

Recently, a number of studies have indicated that cognitive/perceptual factors are at least as important as the actual behaviors exchanged in understanding and resolving marital conflict (Floyd & Markman, 1983; Christensen, 1981; Baucom, 1982; Braiker & Kelley, 1979; Jacobson, McDonald, & Folletee, 1981; Weiss, 1980). These studies have focused on two areas. First, the impact of couples' communication on each partner (i.e., how couples perceive their partners' communication). Second, the attributions that couples make concerning the cause of the other's behaviors (Braiker & Kelley, 1979; Jacobson et al., 1981; Orvis, Kelley, & Butler, 1976; Kelley, 1979). These studies have focused on the *outcome* of perceptual processes and have increased our knowledge about how couples feel about and explain conflict. However, little attention has been paid in couples research to the *determinants* of how couples perceive events in their relationships.

It is perhaps an important first step for understanding and helping couples in conflict to understand the role of discrepancies at a cognitive level, before focusing on communication and problem-solving skills at the behavior level. In other words, if couples do not understand the source of their misunderstandings, then communication training is probably not the best choice of intervention. Under these conditions a focus on communication behavior may actually aggravate the conflict rather than resolve it. This certainly has been the experience of many marital and family therapists who have used communication approaches in therapy (Farrell & Markman, 1986).

Thus, understanding the pathways towards perceptual outcomes and patterns of marital interaction should increase our understanding of how conflict develops and how it can be treated and prevented. There is a vast literature, both theoretical and empirical, on how *individuals* perceive the world (e.g., Bruner, 1957; Kelly, 1955) that can be fruitfully applied to couples. These contributions suggest that *cognitive sets* determine, to a large degree, one's perceptions and behaviors. Applied to couples, we can assert that the cognitive sets that individuals bring to the relationship may be important determinants of conflict in close relationships. However, there have been major problems defining and measuring cognitive sets (Markman, 1984).

An important theoretical advance was provided by Sager (1976) who asserted that marital problems were due to the fact that spouses had different marriage "contracts." These "contracts" were essentially a way of describing the couples' expectations about their relationships, particularly in terms of what they were willing to give to the relationships and what they wanted out of them. The major assumption, inherent in Sager's work, is that spouses are not aware of a good percentage of their own and their spouses' expectations. According to Sager, marital conflict results as a function of couples arguing about issues without really knowing the true origins of the current topics of conflict. This is similar to the concept of "hidden agendas" as discussed by Gottman, Notarius, Gonso and Markman (1976). Application of Sager's work to a cognitive theory of marital conflict suggests that (a) couples have different cognitive sets, (b) couples are not always aware of their cognitive sets and, thus, (c) are not able to communicate their understanding of their cognitive/perceptual sets to their partners. Therefore, a major basis for miscommunication and conflict lies in the cognitive/perceptual arena.

Sager provides some valuable clinical tools for assessing and helping couples understand their differing perceptual sets concerning their relationships. Unfortunately, due to problems in measuring these constructs, there has been no research on how cognitive sets influence conflict resolution. Thus, research methods are needed to assess the cognitive sets (i.e., expectations) that each couple member brings to the relationship.

The present paper argues that social judgment theory (e.g., Hammond, 1965) provides both a theoretical framework and a research paradigm to measure cognitive sets. To our knowledge, only one previous study (Royce & Weiss, 1975) has heretofore provided a link between social judgment theory and marital conflict. Royce and Weiss (1975) were interested in identifying the behavioral cues that untrained judges used in evaluating the marital satisfaction of distressed and nondistressed couples. Judges made global ratings of marital satisfaction after watching tapes of couples interacting and then stated the cues they used to make their judgments. A different set of the trained observers used a behavioral observation system to obtain measures of the rates of occurrence of these cues. The results indicated that judgments of untrained observers were based on cues that actually occurred in the couples' interactions. Thus, the untrained judges' "cognitive sets" about marital distress received validation. Unfortunately, the Royce and Weiss study sparked little interest from marital and family researchers in using social judgment paradigms. The reasons for this outcome may have involved several factors: (a) the prevailing theory of marital distress at that time (social learning theory) did not emphasize the role of cognitive factors; (b) consistent with the social learning orientation, the focus of the Royce and Weiss (1975) study was on observers, not couples; and (c) the authors did not link their methods with the large body of research available in the social judgment literature.

Below, we present a brief overview of the history of social judgment theory for those readers who may be unfamiliar with this approach, since with only one notable exception (Royce & Weiss, 1975) it has not found its way into the marital and family field. Next, a formal application of social judgment theory to the study of the marital conflict is presented. Finally, we present a case study in order to exemplify both research and clinical applications of social judgment theory. It is hoped that this will stimulate studies with larger samples and systematic application of a social judgment approach to the understanding, treatment, and prevention of marital and family distress.

History of social judgment theory

Social judgment theory emerges from several other theories of conflict. Traditionally, theories of conflict have focused on motives of the parties involved; however, this approach to the study of conflict has not contributed adequately to our ability to analyze, manage, and ameliorate situations of human conflict. These theories seek self-serving behavior on the part of the parties involved in conflict and, consequently, are inherently divisive. Thus, application of these theories to clinical situations may aggravate conflict rather than resolve it. In addition, preoccupation with motives and gain as the prime causes of conflict diverts attention from other possible causes.

Hammond presented a new research paradigm for the study of cognitive conflict and its resolution. Of his paradigm, Hammond wrote:

The research paradigm produces the following situation: two persons who (1) attempt to solve problems which concern both of them, (2) have mutual utilities (their gain or loss derives from their approximations to the solution of the problem), (3) receive different training in the solution of a problem involving certain inference, are then brought together and find themselves dealing with a familiar problem which their experience apparently prepared them for but, (4) find that their answers differ, and that neither answer is good as it has been although each answer is logically defensible, (5) and who provide a joint decision as to the correct solution, and therefore (6) must adapt to one another as well as to the task if they are to solve their problems. (1965, p. 50)

The situation described by Hammond appears in many problem areas, and the paradigm has been applied to numerous research efforts. Examples of applications include: water resource planning (Flack & Summers, 1971); citizen participation in planning (Stewart & Gelberd, 1972); labor-management negotiations (Balke, Hammond, & Meyer, 1973); policy evaluation for nuclear safeguards (Brady & Rappoport, 1973); investment analysis (Smith, 1973); determining policies about community goals (Steinmann & Stewart, 1973); corporate policy formulation (Adelman, Stewart, & Hammond, 1975); public land acquisition (Steinmann, Smith, Jurdem, & Hammond, 1975); modeling physicians' judgments (Stewart, Joyce, & Lindell, 1975); improving technology assessment (Stewart, West, Hammond, & Kreith, 1975); and implementation of models (Dhir, 1976). However, with the one exception mentioned above, the paradigm has not heretofore been directly applied to marital interaction.

Marriage produces a situation to which Hammond's paradigm can be applied. As mentioned earlier, couples' attempts to solve interdependency problems in their day-to-day living may be limited by differing cognitive sets. In terms of Hammond's paradigm, they have different utilities and orientations and must adapt to one another in order to arrive at joint decisions. These concepts are clearly compatible with Kelley and Thibaut's (1978) analysis of dyadic interdependency. Below we discuss human judgment analysis (Hammond, 1965; Hammond, Stewart, Brehmer, & Steinmann, 1975) and modern computer graphics technology (Hammond, Stewart, Brehmer, & Steinmann, 1975; Stewart & Carter, 1973) as they apply to understanding and treating marital conflict. Let us begin with an examination of the nature of human judgment and its limitations.

The process of human judgment

Human judgment is a process through which an individual uses social information to make decisions. The social information is obtained from an individual's environment and is interpreted through the individual's "cognitive image" of the environment. The cognitive image or set provides a representation of the environment based on past experiences and essentially predisposes the person to respond to social information in predictable ways. These patterns are represented by an individual's "policies" or beliefs about the environment (Brunswik, cited in Hammond, 1965). Human judgments are based then upon one's biased interpretation of available information. This leads to judgments considered as probability statements about one's environment and how one reacts to it. This condition leads to the human judgment process being inherently limited. In order to understand the limitations of this process, let us examine its characteristics.

Characteristics of human judgment

The human judgment process has three fundamental characteristics. It is (a) covert, (b) inaccurately reported, and (c) inconsistent (Hammond, 1971; Hammond & Brehmer, 1973). *Covertness* means that reports of one's judgment process are subjective. It is seldom possible for an individual to describe his or her judgment process accurately. Ordinarily, introspection or observation of the judgments and guessing at the reasons for them are the only means of actually "uncovering" and "explaining" judgments. *Inaccurate reporting* means that such explanations are incomplete and misleading. This is not due to evil intent but rather because of the fallibility of subjective reporting. *Inconsistency* of the judgment process means that identical circumstances do not always lead to identical judgments. When judgments made by one individual are noticed as being inconsistent by another, the observer may conclude that the individual making judgments is either incompetent or has hidden motives. Motivational explanations have assumed that the individual's inconsistency arises from his or her self-serving behavior; however, the psychological theory of human judgment described by Brunswik (K. R. Hammond, 1966) finds such assumption unnecessary. Judgment is inconsistent because human judgment is not a fully analytical and controlled process; therefore, inconsistency is an inherent characteristic.

These three characteristics may not completely describe the concepts of the psychological theory of human judgment; but they make clear that the limitations of the human judgment process offer enormous potential for mistrust and conflict and suggest that cognitive aids, designed to overcome these limitations, would prove invaluable in management of conflict situations in which human judgment plays a major role. Let us now examine how the psychological theory of human judgment can be applied to understanding and treating marital conflict.

Application of social judgment theory to marital conflict

Social judgment theory, as the psychological theory of human judgment has come to be called, is described pictorially by a "lens model" shown in Figure 15.1. This figure represents a typical situation of interpersonal conflict in which there is an environmental system and two person's cognitive systems. Each system is composed of one distal variable (Y_m for the environmental system, and Y_w and Y_h for the two cognitive systems) and a group of proximal variables, called cues, common to all three systems. Y_w and Y_h, therefore, provide an operational definition of

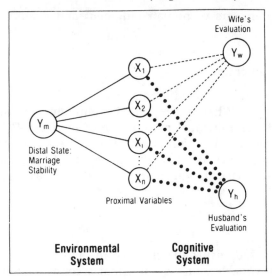

Figure 15.1. A lens model representation of interpersonal conflict.

partners' cognitive sets about a domain of marital and family relationships. Marital conflict occurs when partners utilize the same cue information in such manner that they arrive at different judgments; e.g., Y_w is different from Y_h. For the purposes of the present paper, Y_m represents a measure of the stability of a marriage system, proximal variables X_is represent attributes of that marriage system, and Y_w and Y_h represent the judgments made by the wife and the husband respectively in regard to the stability of the marriage system.

The criterion of judging stability was chosen because it represents an important part of the decision process that couples go through when evaluating the viability of their relationship. However, stability is only one of many important dimensions that couples use to evaluate their relationships. The reader should consider the dimension of stability as exemplary of a set of judgments that couples continuously make about their relationships. Similarly, the attribution or cues that we have chosen are based on typical dimensions that emerge in sociological studies of marital conflict (e.g., Burgess & Wallin, 1953). Once again, this list is not intended to be exclusive. Rather, we want to provide an example that can be helpful to researchers in their own work, investigating the role of cognitive variables in marital conflict.

Social judgment theory contends that disagreements may flow from mere exercise of human judgment (Hammond & Boyle, 1971; Hammond & Brehmer, 1973). Consequently, any attempt at amelioration of a human conflict situation must try to analyze the human judgment process and its limitations. Cognitive aids developed for this purpose must explain and make explicit the parameters of human judgment and components of disagreement.

Parameters of the judgment process

The judgment process of an individual may be explored by posing the following questions: (a) What *factors* influence judgment? (b) What relative *emphasis* does the individual put on each of the factors? (c) How does the individual *integrate* the information regarding each cue to arrive at an overall judgment? (d) What is the *consistency* with which the individual is able to make judgments? Let us now explore these questions.

Factors

What *factors* influence judgment? In reference to Figure 15.1, we must identify the proximal variables, or the cues, that account for the individual's judgment.

Emphasis

What relative *emphasis* does the individual put on each of the factors considered by him? When using cue information about an environmental system to arrive at a judgment about it, the individual attaches various weights to the proximal variables. One source of disagreement arises from the fact that different weights are likely to be attached by different individuals to the proximal variables (Slovic & Lichtenstein, 1973).

Integration

How does the individual integrate the information regarding each cue to arrive at an overall judgment? This involves identification of the mathematical relationship that describes the dependence of the overall judgment (variables Y_w and Y_h in Figure 15.1) on the cues (variables X_1 through X_n in Figure 15.1). The relationship between each cue and the overall judgment may be linear or nonlinear, and the contribution of each cue to the overall judgment may be positive or negative. The nature of dependence of the overall judgment on each cue is referred to as that cue's *function form*. When evaluating the stability of marriage, for example, the judgments of a marriage partner may be related to the various cues in different ways. Some aspects of the marriage may be related to overall judgments of stability in a positive linear form: the more of a certain attribute in the marriage, the greater its stability; or in a negative linear form: the more of a certain attribute in the marriage, the lesser its stability. Other aspects may be related in a nonlinear form: a small amount of a certain cue may cause the marriage system to be judged as having low stability, a moderate amount may cause it to be judged as highly stable, and an excessive amount may again cause it to be judged as having low stability. Differences may occur in function forms for the same cue from one individual to another: the wife might relate her judgments of the marriage system's stability to a given cue in a positive linear manner (the more the better), while the husband might relate his judgments of stability to the same cue in a U-shaped manner (the more the worse – up to a point – beyond which the more the better).

Consistency

What is the *consistency* with which the individual is able to make judgments? An individual may make different judgments about the same situation on different occasions. A major cause of inaccuracy in unaided exercise of the judgment process is that an individual is seldom aware of the specific weights and function forms he or she employs with respect to the various cues. Because of general unawareness of the degree of inconsistency in one's judgment process, it ought to be measured whenever possible. Furthermore, an aid to judgment must offer the individual an opportunity to improve his or her consistency.

Modern computer devices can provide immediate analysis of the judgment process with pictorial, nontechnical feedback describing the parameters of the judgment process (Hammond & Summers, 1972; Hammond & Brehmer, 1973) in terms of weights, function forms, and inconsistency. They make it possible for the user to change his or her weight with respect to any cue while keeping others unchanged and to eliminate his or her inconsistency entirely. The computer program used in the present study is called POLICY (Stewart & Carter, 1973), which is available through General Electric's Marks III Network System, by the name of POL3. It may be used interactively, with or without computer graphics.

A case study

The objectives of this study were to (a) investigate the accuracy of the wife's and the husband's knowledge of their own and their partner's judgment processes, (b) measure the nature and the amount of real or actual (as opposed to apparent) conflict between the spouses, and (c) determine whether the application of judgment theory and computer graphics techniques would result in increased agreement between spouses. The case study provides an example of how social judgment theory can be used for both research and clinical purposes.

Subjects

A couple, married for eight years, was invited to participate in a single subject study. The husband was 34 years old and the wife 32 years.

Procedures

Choice of cue variables. Both the wife and the husband were asked the following question: "Suppose that you were to evaluate the stability (distal variable) of a marriage. What attributes (proximal variables) of the marriage would you consider in making your judgment regarding its stability?" Stability of a marriage was defined as the likelihood of its not ending up in a divorce or breakdown. The couple then discussed the attributes of a marriage that each considered important in making judgments of marital stability. After discussion both agreed that the following list exhausted all the attributes they would consider in making their judgments:

  i. Degree of *communication,*
  ii. Degree of *sexual compatibility,*
  iii. Degree of *mutual respect,*
  iv. Adequacy of *finances,*
  v. Degree of *common interests,*
  vi. Similarity of *family and social background.*

Design of cue profiles. The computer graphics system was used to randomly generate 20 different profiles, each representing a hypothetical marriage. A sample profile is shown in Figure 15.2.

In these profiles each cue variable may be assigned a minimum value of 1, corresponding to a very low level of the cue variable, and a maximum value of 10, corresponding to a very high level of the cue variable. Consequently, an assignment of a value of 1 to "mutual respect" in a profile would imply that the cue profile represents a marriage in which mutual respect between the partners is at a very low level. Similarly, an assignment of a value of 10 to "communication" would imply that the degree of communication in that marriage is excellent.

Subjects' tasks. The wife and the husband were isolated from each other at this point. Both were asked to indicate their a priori subjective estimates of the weights they expected to place on each cue variable when making judgments about the stability of hypothetical marriages to be described later by the 20 cue profiles, as well as their estimates of the weights of their own marriage partners. These estimates were indicated by distributing 100 points among the six cue variables identified so that the points awarded to each cue variable indicated its importance relative to the others. Subsequently, the estimates were divided by 100 to add up to 1. These are reported in section A of Table 15.1.

Both participants also were asked to indicate their a priori estimates of function forms for each cue, for their own judgments and their partner's. Then each participant was separately given the same set of 20 profiles of hypothetical marriages. They were asked to specify their evaluations on a scale from 1 to 10, where 1 corresponded to very low marital stability and

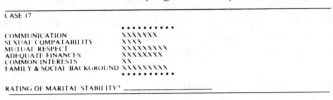

Figure 15.2. A cue profile display for participants' judgment.

Table 15.1. *Weights assigned to cue variables*

	Cue Variables					
Source	Communi-cation	Sexual compati-bility	Mutual respect	Ade-quate finances	Common interests	Family & social back-ground
A. *A priori subjective estimates of cue weights*						
Wife's estimates for own judgments	0.30	0.25	0.30	0.05	0.10	0.00
Husband's estimates for own judgments	0.20	0.50	0.15	0.03	0.02	0.10
Wife's estimates for husband's judgments	0.10	0.40	0.10	0.10	0.30	0.00
Husband's estimates for wife's judgments	0.20	0.20	0.30	0.20	0.05	0.05
B. *Relative weights used in making judgments*						
Wife's relative weights	0.33	0.29	0.16	0.03	0.14	0.05
Husband's relative weights	0.23	0.38	0.22	0.02	0.07	0.08
C. *Revised subjective estimates of cue weights*						
Wife's estimates for own judgments	0.30	0.28	0.28	0.02	0.12	0.00
Husband's estimates for own judgments	0.20	0.45	0.20	0.05	0.04	0.06
D. *Relative weights used in making second set of judgments*						
Wife's relative weights	0.24	0.12	0.32	0.06	0.01	0.24
Husband's relative weights	0.18	0.33	0.16	0.03	0.13	0.17

10 represented very high marital stability. After all cue profiles had been separately evaluated, the judges reviewed the twenty profiles and made whatever changes they considered appropriate in their evaluations.

Intervention. After both participants had expressed satisfaction with their respective evaluations, these were analyzed through the computer system, POLICY.[1] The participants were given feedback on their performance through four measures. First, they were shown the relative weights associated with each cue variable as a result of their own evaluations of the 20 profiles and also the relative weights associated with each cue variable as a result of their partner's evaluations. This display is shown in section B of Table 15.1. They were asked to compare the weighting system each actually used in making evaluations against the weighting system used by the other and also against the a priori subjective estimates of weights they had expected to use.

The second measure of the participants' performance was the function forms showing the relationship between each cue variable and their respective overall judgments of stability. These are shown in Figure 15.3. The participants were asked to compare their function forms with those of their partner. These comparisons, both of weighting system and of function forms, allowed the participants to identify the components of their judgment process that accounted for differences between a priori estimates and actual measures.

The third measure of their performance was their respective cognitive consistency in making their judgments. Each participant was informed that the wife's consistency in her evaluation was 0.94 and that the husband's consistency in his evaluation was 0.92. Lastly, the participants were informed that the measure of their mutual agreement in regard to the stability of the 20 profiles evaluated by each was 0.54 (i.e., 29.2% of the variance in judgments made by one partner could be explained by the judgments made by the other). This measure included the effects of cognitive inconsistencies of the participants. The participants also were told that, with this effect eliminated, their mutual agreement was found to be 0.65 (i.e., 42.3% of the variance in judgments made by one partner could be explained by the judgments made by the other).[2] The former measure, 0.54, is referred to as the *apparent* mutual agreement; and the

---

[1] The analysis consisted of multiple regression analyses, treating the participants' evaluations of marital stability as the dependent variable and the six cue variables as the independent variables. The regression model used consisted of first- and second-order terms for each cue variable. The relative weights for the cues were obtained from the regression coefficients. The cognitive consistency in making judgments was measured by multiple correlation coefficient. Measurement of mutual agreement also was obtained from the correlation matrix. For detailed description of the mathematical basis for these measures, see Hammond et al. (1975, pp. 277, 284).

[2] The effect of cognitive inconsistency is eliminated by computation of participants' evaluation from the regression model obtained through multiple regression analyses.

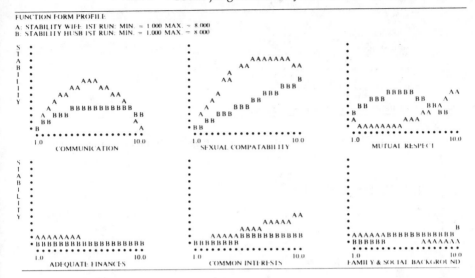

FUNCTION FORM PROFILE
A: STABILITY WIFE 1ST RUN: MIN. = 1.000 MAX. = 8.000
B: STABILITY HUSB 1ST RUN: MIN. = 1.000 MAX. = 8.000

Figure 15.3. The computer graphic display comparing wife's and husband's function forms.

latter, 0.65, is referred to as the *actual* mutual agreement.[3] The participants discussed these results with each other.

The participants then were asked to revise their a priori estimates of the weights and function forms to indicate those weights and function forms that they now felt ought to be placed on each cue variable when evaluating the stability of marriages. The weights thus obtained are reported in section C of Table 15.1. The revised function forms were all positive linear.

The spouses now were given a different identical set of 20 profiles of hypothetical marriages. This time, however, with each profile they also were given two ratings for marital stability, computed by POLICY, based on their *revised* estimates of weights and function forms, respectively. A sample display is shown in Figure 15.4. They were asked to evaluate these profiles in terms of marital stability, as before. Again they received feedback in terms of the same four measures used before. The relative weights obtained this time are shown in section D of Table 15.1, and the function forms obtained are shown in Figure 15.5.

The wife's cognitive consistency in her evaluations for this second run was 0.99. The corresponding figure for her husband was 0.95. Their apparent mutual agreement through the second run was 0.75 (or 56.3%)

[3] Mutual conflict between the wife and the husband may be measured as follows:

$$\text{Mutual conflict} = \sqrt{[1 - (\text{Mutual agreement})^2]}.$$

Corresponding to apparent and actual mutual agreements, one would obtain apparent and actual mutual conflict, respectively.

CASE 7

```
                                      • • • • • • • • • •
COMMUNICATION                    XXXX
SEXUAL COMPATABILITY             XXXXXXX
MUTUAL RESPECT                   XXXX
ADEQUATE FINANCES                XXXXXXXXX
COMMON INTERESTS                 XXXXXXXX
FAMILY & SOCIAL BACKGROUND XX
                                      • • • • • • • • • •

COMPUTED RATING — WIFE: 4.9
COMPUTED RATING — HUSB. 6.3

RATING OF MARITAL STABILITY? _____
```

Figure 15.4. A cue profile display for participants' second set of judgments.

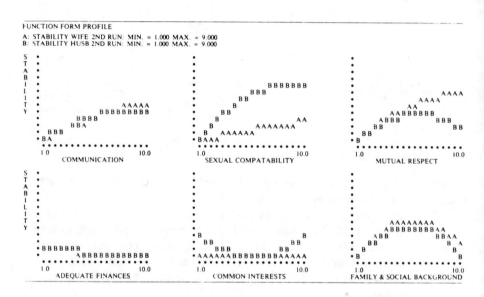

Figure 15.5. The computer graphic display comparing wife's and husband's function forms obtained through second set of judgments.

compared with 0.54 in the first run. The actual mutual agreement this time was 0.81 (i.e., 65.6%), compared with 0.65 in the previous run.

Discussion

One of the objectives of this case study was to investigate the accuracy of the wives' and the husbands' knowledge of their own and their partners' judgments. By correlating (a) the judgments specified by the participants a priori and (b) the judgments predicted with complete consistency by the "policy," statistically derived from their sets of judgments in the first and second runs, respectively, it is possible to determine the extent of dissimilarity between subjective and objective judgmental policies. The measure of agreement between the wife's subjective judgments, predicted from a priori estimates of cue weights for her own judgments, and those predicted with complete consistency by the policy, derived from her judgments made during the first run, was 0.80. The corresponding figure for the second run was also 0.80. Similarly, in the husband's case the agreement between the subjective judgments, based on a priori estimates of cue weights for his own judgments, and his objective judgments, derived with complete consistency from his judgments made during the first run, was 0.91. The corresponding measure for the second run was 0.86.

Similar analyses were performed to examine each participant's understanding of the partner's judgments. The agreement between the wife's subjective judgments and those predicted with complete consistency by the policies, derived from the husband's judgments made during the first and second run, were 0.78 and 0.57, respectively. Similarly, the agreements between the a priori estimates of the husband for his wife's judgments, and those predicted with complete consistency by the policies, derived from the wife's judgments made during the first and the second runs, were 0.72 and 0.75, respectively.

Figure 15.3 indicates that the cue variables contributing to conflict between the wife and the husband during the first set of judgments were primarily communication, sexual compatability, and mutual respect. Figure 15.5 indicates, however, that conflict due to communication was eventually eliminated and that the contribution of mutual respect at lower levels was also eliminated. The main source of conflict between the spouses during the second set of judgments was sexual incompatibility.

The results indicated that the wife and the husband participating in this study were found to have an imperfect understanding of their own judgment process, as well as of their partner's judgment process in regards to the evaluation of marital stability. However, the tools described in this paper made it possible to describe the judgment processes involved. Furthermore, these tools facilitated identification, measurement, and reporting of some of the sources of conflict between the wife and the husband: namely, (a) cognitive inconsistency in their respective judgments, (b) differences in the set of cue weights assigned by them to the various cue variables in making their judgments, and (c) differences in the set of function forms associated with the cue variables in their respective judgments. Recognition of cognitive inconsistency as an inherent characteristic of the human judgment process allowed for differentiating between apparent conflict and actual (or real) conflict. The most suggestive result obtained in the case study was that the implementation of the procedure described in this paper led to increase in their apparent agreement from 29.2% to 56.3% in their actual agreement from 42.3% to 65.6%.

Conclusions

There are certain limitations implicit in the procedure of marital conflict analysis described in the case study. First, it is clear that weights assigned to the cue variables constituting a set of profiles depend upon the set of cue variables chosen. It is conceivable that different sets would lead to different weights being assigned to the cues. It is likely that different sets of cue variables would be appropriate for different pairs of spouses. Therefore, in representing hypothetical marriage profiles, the selection of cue variables is a crucial step. Furthermore, when generating the hypothetical marriage profiles to be evaluated by the participants, care should be taken to ensure that the values assigned to the various cue variables are not intercorrelated. In this study the highest correlation coefficient was 0.334, with a corresponding t statistic of 1.50.

Second, the procedure described in the case study has certain inherent limitations. The major problem is that it does not represent an example of a typical interaction situation which previous researchers have used in studying marital conflict (e.g., Gottman et al., 1977; Markman, 1979; Raush et al., 1974). However, the reader should keep in mind that goals of the present procedure involved identifying the couples' cognitive set of judgment patterns which may underlie conflicts, not how they interact to solve conflicts. In future research it would be interesting to measure both the discrepancies in judgment and the ensuing interaction.

Third, as with any case study, the results must be interpreted with caution in terms of the utility of the procedure for either research or interaction. Future research clearly needs to use a larger sample size to provide more meaningful estimates of the variables under study (e.g., stability of judgments, results of intervention). Such studies are currently being planned.

Finally, there is the question of how research participants or marital therapy candidates will react to the computerized technology involved in the POLICY procedure. Our experience using similar methods with over 150 couples has indicated that couples are not intimidated by this type of technology. In fact, they found the experience to be enjoyable and worthwhile (e.g., Markman, Jamieson, & Floyd, 1983). With the increased popularity of computers and video games, the public is probably becoming accustomed to the role of computerized technology in their lives.

To summarize, we have presented a conceptual framework, research paradigm, and intervention procedure generated from an application of social judgment theory to the understanding and treatment of marital conflict. The social judgment paradigm should be useful to marital and family researchers and theorists, given the current emphasis on the roles of cognitive discrepancies in causing marital conflict and the interplay between cognitive and behavioral factors in marital distress.

16. The role of judgment in small-group conflict and decision making

Berndt Brehmer

Those who want to understand and explain a decision made by an individual or a group face what seems to be an unsolvable problem: that the important determinants of the decision cannot be observed. We recognize two such determinants: the decision-maker's motive or goal, and his understanding of the decision problem. Neither of these can be observed. What can be observed is the relation between some description of the decision problem and the actual decision or the consequences of the decision. Thus, we face an impossible problem: we have *two* unknowns, but only *one* equation. The problem can be solved only if we eliminate one of the unknowns. The only way of doing this is by making some assumption about the decision-maker's goal or about his understanding of the decision problem.

The customary assumption, made by scientists and non-scientists alike, is that of rationality. That is, one assumes that the decision-maker has perfect understanding of the decision problem. Consequently, he is able to select that course of action which leads to his goal. His decision, therefore, mirrors his motives perfectly, and the actual consequences of the decision are the consequences that the decision-maker intended. This solves the problem of explanation, because we are now able to ignore one of the unknowns, and we can concentrate on the other unknown, that is the decision-maker's motives. Explanation now becomes a matter of inferring these motives. Once the motives have been inferred, the decision-maker's behaviour is fully explained.

We recognize this paradigm as the general paradigm of lay psychology, as well as the paradigm of most sciences. In political science, for example, the paradigm is called the 'rational actor paradigm' and guides important

This chapter originally appeared in Stephenson, G. M., & Davis, J. H. (Eds.). *Progress in applied social psychology* (Vol. 2), pp. 163–183). New York: Wiley, 1984. Copyright © 1984 by John Wiley & Sons, Ltd. Reprinted by permission.

research on international and national politics (e.g. Allison, 1971). In psychology, the paradigm is a well-known explanatory device in clinical psychology. Psychoanalysis despite its reputation of being a science of the irrational is also founded on the rational actor paradigm. Thus, psychoanalysts assume that although a person's behaviour may look irrational, it is nevertheless an expression of rational cognitive processes; the problem is that these rational processes are employed to pursue irrational motives. However, using the assumption of rationality, the psychoanalyst is nevertheless able to infer what these motives are, despite the fact that the person being so explained may strenuously object to explanation.

As pointed out by Allison (1971), the rational actor paradigm provides us with efficient means to handle problems in the area of international politics. It always leads us to expect the worst, and as a consequence, we are not likely to be taken by surprise. It may be conjectured that the paradigm serves similar objectives in the everyday lives of people. It does so, however, only at the cost of fostering distrust, and it makes lack of trust a primary motive when dealing with our fellowmen. It does, of course, not take too much effort to find self-serving motives that explain the behaviour of others, so the rationality assumption is not easily refuted.

Even though the rational actor paradigm is so common that it may seem almost self-evident, it cannot, however, account for any but the simplest decisions. First, it seems unlikely that people have the perfect understanding of what will lead to what in a decision problem assumed in the rational actor paradigm. For example, decisions are often based on projections of what the future may be and many unforeseen things may intervene between the decision and that future state. This introduces an element of uncertainty in the relation between the decision and the consequences. For example, the increase in the price of oil since 1973 obviously came as a surprise to many decision-makers and made it impossible to achieve many of the things expected when the decisions were made. Therefore, the decision-maker's motives cannot be inferred from the consequences of his decisions.

Second, decisions often require the decision-maker to rely on new and perhaps unique configurations of information. Consequently, the decision-maker cannot rely on any particular past experience, and if he turns to science, he will often find that theories there are not powerful enough to deal with the complexity of the problems facing him; recall, for example, the problems now facing Keynesian (and other) economists trying to deal with stagflation.

Third, decision problems often require the decision-maker to integrate a considerable amount of information. Given that he has but a limited capacity for processing information, he may not always be able to find the decision that would lead to exactly those consequences which he sought to achieve. Consequently, his decisions would not reflect his motives with any great fidelity.

Thus there are good reasons for doubting that a decision-maker's motives can be inferred from his decisions. Therefore the usefulness of the rational actor paradigm for explaining the behaviour of real people in real decision problems is in doubt also and we would do well to look for an alternative.

To develop such an alternative we take as our point of departure the consequences of the purely epistemological problems mentioned above, which are to force the decision-maker to rely on something other than facts and a full understanding of the decision problem for his decisions. Instead of facts, he will have to rely on what Hammond (1974) has so aptly called 'the cognitive process of last resort': human judgment. Consequently, the basic premise of the rational actor paradigm, that the decision-maker has perfect understanding of the decision problem, cannot be upheld for any but the simplest and most trivial of decision problems. Therefore this paradigm is not likely to serve us well in solving the problems in the real world either. This conclusion is certainly not contradicted by any great number of success stories from social scientists helping to solve important decision problems.

The purpose of the present chapter, therefore, is to argue for an alternative to the rational actor paradigm for analysing decision-making. Provisionally, we will call this alternative paradigm the judgment paradigm to underline its most important feature: that it sees decisions as based on judgment rather than on fact, and that it considers the analysis of these judgments to be the key to understanding decisions. This entails giving up the basic tenet of the rational actor paradigm: that decisions are based on a complete understanding of the decision problem (which amounts to the same thing as assuming that judgments are based on fact).

Analysis of decisions using the judgment paradigm requires that the decision-maker's motives are presumed to be known. Such an assumption is no more problematic than the basic assumption in the rational actor paradigm. It is only by the fruitfulness of the analyses that follow from it, that the value of an assumption can be assessed.

The move away from the rational paradigm is currently gaining popularity in psychology, mainly as a result of the work of Tversky and Kahneman (e.g., 1974) on probabilistic reasoning, which has shown that judgments based on probabilistic information often do not follow the rules of probability theory. Another important source has been Simon's (e.g., 1953) work on "bounded rationality," that is the hypothesis that people often do not strive to do what is best because this requires too much effort. Instead, they just try to get what is good enough, that is, in the words of Simon (1953) people are "satisficers" rather than "optimizers." Dawes (1976) summed up these developments when he called for a "shallow psychology" of cognitive processes instead of a depth psychology of motives to explain behaviour.

The present chapter, however, does not have these traditions as its point of departure. Instead, it is grounded in an earlier tradition, that of Social Judgment Theory, SJT (Hammond, Stewart, Brehmer, & Steinmann, 1975). SJT stems from Brunswik's probabilistic functionalism (e.g. Brunswik, 1952), which has been adapted to the task of analysing human judgment and decision-making by Hammond and his collaborators.

SJT and the analysis of judgment

SJT defines human judgment as the process of using information from probabilistic cues to arrive at an inference which can serve as a basis for a decision. An example is the cognitive activity of a physician making a diagnosis on the basis of a set of symptoms to guide his selection of a treatment, or a stockbroker inferring what the future value of some stocks may be to provide a basis for deciding whether or not to buy.

In problems requiring judgment, there is no fail-safe algorithm for computing the answer (not much of a restriction when it comes to real decision problems). Judgment, therefore, becomes a matter of relying on two sources of information: whatever rules may be available from textbooks and the like, and one's experience with cases of a similar kind. This amalgam of analytical knowledge of rules and specific case-by-case experience defines the process of judgment in SJT. The details of this process are not known, but there seems to be general agreement about at least one aspect of the process: that it is covert, that is to say, although a person may be able to make judgments, he may nevertheless not be able to report on how he actually arrived at these judgments (see e.g. Slovic & Lichtenstein, 1971 for a review of the evidence).

The covert nature of the process is the source of three kinds of problems:

1. It is impossible to ascertain whether or not a person has taken a certain factor into account or not. Consequently, it is impossible to assess whether or not a person's judgment is biased.
2. It is difficult to teach judgment. Even though an expert diagnostician may be able to make successful diagnoses, he often cannot teach his students to make these diagnoses, leaving the students to learn from their own experience, which in no way guarantees that the students will become experts (see Brehmer, 1980b).
3. Conflicts are hard to resolve. Suppose that two persons, A and B, have arrived at different decisions and start questioning each other. A then finds that B's explanations of his decisions cannot account for these decisions. What could A then possibly conclude? Following the rational actor paradigm, he must assume

that if B does not give a satisfactory explanation, this is because there is something B does not want him to know. And what B does not want him to know is probably something that is going to hurt him. Consequently, A can only conclude that B is up to no good, and that he cannot be trusted. Thus, something that started as a simple disagreement develops into a full-scale conflict which becomes impossible to solve because it is perceived incorrectly.

These three problems could presumably be solved if the judgment process could somehow be made overt.

At first, this may seem like an unsolvable problem. However, the problem is no worse than that facing most other sciences: many of the phenomena of interest to, for example, physics, are covert and cannot be observed directly. There is a solution to the problem. It takes as its point of departure that if one knows a person's judgments and the information upon which they are based, it is possible to develop a mathematical model which relates the judgments to the information. If one is successful in this enterprise, the model, when given the same information as a person, will produce the same judgments as the person. The model may then be said to simulate the person's judgment process. But because it is a simulation, it has a great advantage; it is overt, rather than covert. Consequently, it is possible to inspect the model and find out how it works. By doing so, one can learn about the covert system being modelled.

The problem, then, is to select a mathematical model. For reasons that we shall not go into here (but see Brehmer, 1976c, 1979), Social Judgment Theorists have chosen linear statistical models for the purpose of modelling human judgment.

A linear model describes a judgment, J, as a weighted sum of the cues, x_i, upon which it is founded.

$$J = b_0 + b_1x_1 + b_2x_2 + \ldots + b_nx_n \tag{1}$$

when $b_1 \ldots b_n$ are weights determined by fitting the model to the judgments and b_0 is the intercept.

Such a model gives information about four aspects of the judgment process:

1. What cues are used. This is shown by what cues receive significant weights in the analysis.
2. The relative weights given to different cues.
3. The functional relation between each cue and the judgments. This relation may be linear, that is, the higher the value of the cue, the higher the judgment, or it may be non-linear, for example, quadratic, so that there is an optimum value, leading to a high judgment with values above and below this optimum leading to lower values.

4. The organizing principle, that is, the rule used for combining the information from the different cues. This rule may be additive and compensatory, or configural, such that the weight given to one cue depends on the value of another cue. Given the form of Equation (1), it may not seem possible to assess configural rules. However, Equation (1) can easily be expanded to include higher order terms, for example cross-product terms. If these terms receive a significant weight in the analysis, deviations from additivity are indicated.

These four aspects of the process as described by a linear model are easy to understand, and it is clear that an analysis by this kind of model answers exactly the kind of questions anyone would want to ask:

1. What factors did the judge use?
2. What was the relative importance of these factors?
3. How were the factors used?
4. How did the person put the different factors together?

There may be some doubt about exactly which of the measures available should be used (see Brehmer & Qvarnström, 1976, for a study of what people understand by the concept of weight), but it is clear that the linear model will provide answers to the kinds of questions anyone would want to ask about the judgment process. However, these kinds of analysis also give information about an aspect which people may not think of asking about: the *consistency* of the process.

Basically, the term consistency refers to the degree to which a person makes his judgments in the same manner from case to case. If the person is inconsistent, this means that she/he will not make the same judgment when the same case is presented over again. Thus the rules used for making judgments will differ from case to case. The degree of consistency is usually measured by inserting replicates among the cases presented for judgment. The degree of consistency is then given in the manner of a test-retest reliability coefficient by the correlation between the judgments for the replicates. Alternatively, if there is evidence that a linear model adequately describes the process, the degree of non-consistency is simply given by the proportion of variance that cannot be accounted for by the model (see Brehmer, 1978). The actual estimation of the parameters of the judgment process by means of multiple regression offers a number of problems not mentioned here, and anyone who wants to use these techniques should start by consulting a good textbook on the subject.

Overview of results from studies of judgment

Linear models have been used to analyse judgment processes in a variety of experts, including stockbrokers (Slovic, 1969a), clinical psychologists

(Goldberg, 1970; Hammond, 1955; Hoffman, 1960), radiologists (Hoffman, Slovic, & Rorer, 1968), and physicists (Hammond & Marvin, 1981); see Goldberg (1968), or Slovic and Lichtenstein (1971), for reviews.

The results are easily described because the results of all of the analyses so far are quite similar. They can be summarized under four headings.

The judgment process is simple

First, it is simple in the sense that judges seem to rely on very little information. Thus, a judge may ask for a lot of information, say ten or more cues, but s/he is usually found to use no more than three or four cues. Second, the process is simple in that it usually follows a simple linear model. If deviations from an additivity are found, they are usually small and have little systematic importance (e.g. Hoffman et al., 1968; Wiggins & Hoffman, 1968). However, the fact that a linear model fits the judgments must not be interpreted to mean that the judge simply adds up the information from the various cues. An additive model is only a paramorphic representation of the process (Hoffman, 1960). Thus it may be consistent with different kinds of psychological process. One likely candidate is a general compensatory process where different cues are traded-off against one another (see Einhorn, Kleinmuntz & Kleinmuntz, 1979, for a discussion of this problem). This trade-off may, of course, not be perceived by the judge as a particularly simple process, despite the fact that the mathematical description of the result is simple.

The process is inconsistent

A typical finding in these analyses is that the judges are inconsistent. Thus, judgment processes are not perfectly regular, and there is a measure of unpredictability, or randomness, in these processes. The nature of this inconsistency is not known. Inconsistency is, however, not a constant, but varies with the characteristics of the judgment task. At least two characteristics are known to affect consistency: task complexity and task uncertainty. As for task complexity, the results show that consistency is lower when the task has many cues, rather than few cues, and lower when the task requires the subjects to use non-linear rules, rather than linear rules (Brehmer, Hagafors, & Johansson, 1980). This has been interpreted to mean that judgment, at least in part, may be seen as a matter of skill. This means that even though a person intends to use a certain rule, his judgments may not necessarily follow that rule, just as wanting to make a certain stroke in tennis does not automatically produce that particular stroke. However, in the case of tennis, it is immediately apparent that the results are not what one intended. In the case of judgment, this is not always true because there may be no immediate feedback informing the judge about his success. Furthermore, it is not possible, for a judgment task of even very moderate complexity, to ascertain what rules were actually followed. Therefore it is usually not possible for a person to detect that his judgment does not follow the rule s/he intended it to follow. This is illustrated in the study by Brehmer *et al.*, (1980).

In this study, subjects were asked to use specified configural rules for making judgments. Despite the fact that they tried to use these rules and believed that they had used them, their judgments nevertheless tended to follow a simple additive model without any configural components. That is, the subjects' judgments did not follow the rule that the subjects intended to use, but they were not aware of this.

Task predictability is a measure of the extent to which the criterion can be predicted from the cues, for example, the degree of certainty with which a disease can be diagnosed from the symptoms. A common measure is the multiple correlation between the cues and the criterion.

According to statistical decision theory, which is the appropriate normative theory for these kinds of tasks, task predictability should not affect the utilization of the cues; regardless of the predictability of the task, the cues should be used maximally, that is to say, such that the multiple correlation between the cues and the criterion is unity. Human judges do not follow this recommendation, however. First, they are inconsistent: that is, the multiple correlation between cues and judgments is not unity. Moreover the consistency varies with the predictability of the task, such that as predictability decreases, so does consistency (Brehmer, 1976b). This result has been obtained in a wide variety of circumstances, both in laboratory studies of learning (e.g., Brehmer, 1978) and conflict (Brehmer, 1973c) and in studies of clinical judgment (Brehmer, 1976b). The explanation for these results is not clear. Two hypotheses about possible explanations have been investigated.

The first of these hypotheses is that people simply do not know that they have to use statistical rules, rather than deterministic rules, when faced with probabilistic cues, or that they do not recognize a probabilistic task when they see one. This hypothesis has been tested in a series of studies (Brehmer & Kuylenstierna, 1978, 1980; Johansson & Brehmer, 1979; Kuylenstierna & Brehmer, 1981) in which subjects have been given various kinds of information about the nature of the task, thus relieving them of the requirement to ascertain that the task is, in fact, probabilistic, and of deciding whether they should use a statistical rule or not. This has not affected their behaviour. When information about the nature of the rule to be used has been given, this has led to some improvement in performance. However, even with this information, subjects remain inconsistent, and the relation between inconsistency and task predictability does not change. This suggests that lack of knowledge about the appropriate rule is at best part of the explanation for the effects of task predictability on the subjects' behaviour in judgment. This leads to the second hypothesis, which is that subjects lack the cognitive capacity required to perform optimally in these kinds of tasks. Specifically, to find the optimal statistical rules, it is necessary not only to have the correct kind of rule, it is also necessary to use rather large amounts of data; to focus on single hits and misses can only lead the person astray.

To test this hypothesis, the effects of various means of decreasing the cognitive strain imposed by these tasks have been investigated. Hagafors and Brehmer (1980a, 1980b) studied the effects of how information was presented, and Kuylenstierna and Brehmer (1981) the effects of memory aids. Again, some effects were found, but the subjects still behaved in a fundamentally non-optimal way. Thus lack of optimality cannot be explained in terms of cognitive strain.

A possible explanation for these results, and one that would tie them to other results on how people handle uncertain information, is what Tversky and Kahneman (1971a) have called "Belief in the law of small numbers"; that is the belief that the characteristics of the task can be inferred from small samples. This may be interpreted to mean that people have adapted their rules of inference to their limited capacity for processing information; if one has limited processing capacity it does one no good to use rules which require large amounts of information such as the full-fledged statistical rules.

Because the judges rely on small samples, their rules change and they become inconsistent, and more so the greater the inconsistency of the task. This hypothesis thus explains the results on inconsistency, as well as those from a variety of other statistical tasks of the kind used by Tversky and Kahneman.

There is considerable disagreement

This is true also when the subjects are experts who are making the kinds of judgments they usually make, and have been making for years and years. That there will be disagreement follows from the fact that people are inconsistent. If two persons are inconsistent, their judgments cannot be perfectly correlated, even if they use the same rules for making their judgments. However, lack of consistency is not the only explanation for the disagreement among experts. There are also systematic differences, and experts such as physicians are found not only to rely on different symptoms, but also to give different weights to the same symptoms and, occasionally, to use different rules for combining the information from different symptoms (e.g., Hoffman *et al.*, 1968).

This means, in fact, that people who work at the same task, for example diagnosing a set of diseases, may learn very different things from what they have to learn from experience in probabilistic tasks. This is not surprising. In such a task (as in any inference task) the hypotheses that the persons bring to the task are as important as the information, but the hypotheses cannot, of course, be derived from the information. Therefore there is no guarantee that people will learn the correct rules from a given task, or even that they will learn the same rules (see Brehmer, 1980b, for a discussion of this issue). For the physicians studied by Hoffman *et al.*, it was indeed shown that no physician used the most useful of the available symptoms:

Subjects lack insight into their own rules

In many cases, investigators have collected not only judgments from their subjects but also subjective descriptions of how they have been making these judgments. From these descriptions, it has then been possible to construct models of the judgment process, and these models have then been compared to the models fitted to the actual judgments. The extent to which these models agree gives a measure of the degree of insight people have into their own judgment processes. An alternative is to compare subjective reports about specific aspects of the process, for example about the relative weights they give to different cues, by comparing what the model fitted to the judges' judgments yields. The results of both these kinds of studies (e.g. Hoffman, 1960; Summers, Taliaferro, & Fletcher, 1970; Stewart & Carter, 1973; Slovic, 1969a) show that subjects do not have very good insight into their judgment processes, a finding in line with many other studies using retrospective reports about cognitive processes (Nisbett & Wilson, 1977).

Taking all of the available results in this field into account, an interesting pattern emerges: objective models fitted to the actual judgments tend to be simpler than subjective models. That is, people seem to believe that their judgment processes are more complex than they actually are. There are at least two possible explanations for this.

First, as pointed out by Einhorn *et al.* (1979), many different kinds of processing information will result in a linear model. A linear model is a compensatory model, implying that the person makes trade-offs. The process of making trade-offs may very well be experienced as being quite complex.

Second, as shown by Brehmer *et al.* (1980), lack of cognitive skill may prevent a person from actually following the rule s/he intends to use. Specifically, the results show that even when subjects are trying to follow a configural model, and believe that they are following such a model, their judgments nevertheless fail to exhibit configural properties. That is, the subjects are simply unable to follow the model they intend to follow. It is possible that verbal descriptions of judgment processes give information about what model a person intends to follow but not necessarily about the actual process.

In summary, the results from studies on judgment indicate that judgment processes are simple and inconsistent and that people have limited insight into these processes.

Hammond and Brehmer (1973) have termed such processes *quasi-rational processes*, and hypothesized that their characteristics stem from their being midway between analytical and intuitive thinking. Basically, a quasi-rational process is seen as a process that is partially rule-bound (analytical thinking) and partly relying on specific experience (intuitive thinking). Thus a person may have rules for making judgments, but the judgments derived by these rules are checked against specific experience from cases similar to that at hand. If the rule-derived judgment does not agree with whatever specific case that the person happens to remember, the judgment is modified. As a consequence, the process is not completely determined by the rules, that is, it is inconsistent.

Although this is an attractive explanation for inconsistency, it is admittedly *ad hoc*. However, whatever the explanation, the fact of inconsistency remains, and it has unfortunate consequences for human social interaction, as we shall see as we now turn to the problem of conflict.

Cognitive conflict in small decision-making groups

One reason for letting a group, rather than an individual, make decisions is that many kinds of expertise may be needed, or because experts differ in their opinions. Another reason is, of course, that there are conflicting interests that may be involved and need to be reconciled, but such a case will not be considered here.

Within SJT, differences in expertise are interpreted in terms of differences in how the cues in a judgment task are used. Thus one expert may know how to use some cues, while another may know how to use some others. These experts may then need to co-operate to produce an optimal decision for a decision problem which requires the use of both sets of cues. This will entail the reconciling, or integration, of judgmental differences which stem from differences in how the cues are used. Such a reconciling will, of course, often imply a change in judgmental strategies.

However, judgmental differences may also occur in the absence of any real differences in expertise. As described above, experts may also differ within their area of expertise, especially when the expertise is derived from their own experience, either because they have learned different rules from this experience, or because they are inconsistent. Of course, people do not have to be experts to make different judgments; this can also happen when ordinary people make decisions about everyday problems, such as when a husband and wife try to agree on where their vacation should be spent.

As should be clear from what has been said above, both of the cases described, that involving persons with different expertise, and that involving persons with the same kind of expertise, may lead to conflict caused by judgmental differences.

Conflicts of this kind have not received very much attention from social and behavioural scientists, presumably because the prevalence of the rational actor paradigm leads them to focus on conflicts caused by motivational factors, and to interpret cases of conflict in terms of motivational differences. An additional reason for the relative neglect of these kinds of conflicts may be that there has not been any well-developed experimental paradigm comparable to those developed for the study of conflict of interest, such as the prisoner's dilemma game.

Hammond (1965) has, however, developed a paradigm for the study of judgmental conflicts and this paradigm has now generated a considerable number of empirical results both in the laboratory and in applied settings. In the next section we will describe this paradigm and give a brief overview of the results obtained.

The SJT paradigm for the study of interpersonal conflict

The SJT interpersonal conflict (IPC) paradigm was first suggested by Hammond (1965) as a simulation of the essential characteristics of judgment conflicts. Experiments in this paradigm are conducted in two stages. The first stage serves to create, or assess, the relations between the cognitive systems of the persons involved. In most laboratory studies, this first step is a training stage in which two or more persons are trained to have the judgmental policies required for the experiment. The training usually follows a multiple-cue probability learning (MPL) paradigm.

Experiments in an MPL paradigm require subjects to learn to infer the state of a criterion variable from that of a set of cue variables which are imperfectly correlated with the criterion, thus introducing uncertainty into the task.

The MPL paradigm incorporates many of the important features of the situations requiring judgment, as these situations are conceptualized within SJT. Most important are (i) that the subjects have to learn to use uncertain information, and (ii) that a number of cues have to be used.

The policies acquired in MPL share the important features of the cognitive systems involved in judgment as these features have been revealed in, for example, studies of clinical judgment. Thus, the policies acquired in the MPL are inconsistent (e.g., Brehmer, 1976b), and the subjects have limited insight into their policies; they cannot fully describe how they arrive at their judgments (Brehmer, Kuylenstierna, & Liljergren, 1974). Thus the MPL paradigm produces cognitive systems which have the important features of quasi-rational cognition.

However, training is not the only method of obtaining subjects with different cognitive systems. It is also possible to select subjects whose policies towards some issues differ as a consequence of their pre-experimental experience. It does not seem to make any difference in the results of these experiments if subjects are trained to have different policies or if they are selected because of different policies (Hammond & Brehmer, 1973).

Conflict stage

In the conflict stage pairs of subjects are brought together to work on a new task for which their policies are only partly relevant. This may be arranged in different ways. One possibility, used in many experiments, is to train subjects to use different cues and then put them together in a situation requiring the use of all the cues. This may be seen either as a situation where two persons with different expertise are brought together to co-operate and benefit from each other's specialist knowledge, or as a situation where two persons with different ideologies have to resolve differences in how they view the world. The general context will determine which of these possibilities is relevant, but so far, experiments have generally been set up to study the latter possibility, which is how people who see the world differently are able to resolve their differences.

In the conflict stage, subjects are given a series of problems of the same kind. For example, they may receive a series of 20 different countries, each described in terms of the same economic indices, and asked to predict the future economic growth for each of these countries. In those cases about which the subjects disagree, they are asked to discuss their differences until they can reach a joint answer agreeable to both of them.

The trial then usually ends with a feedback, when the subjects are informed of the correct answer for the trial, but this feedback may be omitted (see e.g., Brehmer, 1971).

In the conflict stage, as in the training stage, probabilistic tasks, that is tasks in which the correlation between the cues and the feedback values is less than unity, are used in accordance with the general analysis of the nature of judgment tasks in SJT.

Experiments in this paradigm yield a variety of measures (Hammond, 1965), but in actual practice only the relation between the initial judgments is analysed as this provides a measure of the amount of conflict. In addition, analyses of the subjects' policies – how they use the cues, and their consistency – are performed.

In the early experiments, various distance measures were used, such as the absolute differences between the initial judgments, $S_1 - S_2$, often weighted by the expected difference, $T_1 - T_2$, where T_1 and T_2 are the judgments predicted from regression equations fitted to the subjects' responses in the final part of the first stage, for example the last 15 trials in training or selection (see e.g., Miller Brehmer, & Hammond, 1970). These kinds of measures were later called "surface measures." They were found to have unfortunate characteristics and were later abandoned (see Brehmer, 1969a, 1974b), in favour of a correlational analysis, using the so-called "lens model equation," LME (Hursch, Hammond, & Hursch, 1964; Tucker, 1964). This equation was first developed to analyse the relation between the cognitive system of a person and a cognitive task, but was adapted to the analysis of cognitive conflict by Brehmer (1969b).

For analyses of conflict, the LME takes the following form

$$r_A = GR_{S1} R_{S2} \tag{2}$$

where r_A is the correlation between the judgments made by subject S_1 and those made by subject S_2, G is the correlation between the linearly predictable variance in the cognitive systems of the two subjects, that is, $G = r_{\hat{J}S1/\hat{J}S1}$ is the judgment predicted for subject S_1 from a regression equation fitted to the relation between the judgments of S_1 and the cues, and $\hat{J}_{S2}$ the judgment predicted for S_2 from a regression equation fitted to the judgments of S_2 and the cues, R_{S1} the multiple correlation between the judgments of S_1 and the cues, and R_{S2} the corresponding multiple correlation for the judgments of S_2.

In Equation (2), r_A is a measure of the level of agreement between S_1 and S_2 and G shows the extent to which the systematic aspects of the policies of S_1 and S_2 are similar, that is, the extent to which they use the cues in the same way. R_{S1} and R_{S2}, finally, show the consistency of the policies of S_1 and S_2.

Equation (2) shows that two things are required for perfect agreement, that is, for r_A to reach unity: that the subjects use the cues in the same way, that is, so that $G = 1.00$, and that they are perfectly consistent, that is, so that $R_{S1} = R_{S2} = 1.00$. Therefore it is not sufficient that the subjects have the same policies, they must also apply these policies with perfect consistency. Disagreement does not therefore imply that there are fundamental policy differences; because of inconsistency, we may have cases of agreement in principle but disagreement in fact. Indeed, inconsistency may also produce the opposite problem, agreement in a concrete instance, despite fundamental policy differences. This means that it is not possible to draw any firm conclusions about the nature of a conflict from observations of the relations between the decisions of two persons: a structural analysis of the kind provided by the LME is needed. Yet most analyses of conflict outside SJT usually rely only on the actual decisions and no structural analysis is performed. This is, of course, especially true in analyses performed in the rational actor paradigm. In this paradigm, inconsistency is, of course, totally unthinkable, so a structural analysis may not seem all that necessary.

Overview of results obtained with the SJT paradigm

There have been a number of quite detailed reviews of the results from various perspectives (Brehmer, 1976c; Brehmer & Hammond, 1977; Hammond, Stewart, Brehmer, & Steinmann, 1975; Hammond, Rohrbaugh,

Mumpower, & Adelman, 1977), so we will only give a brief overview of two of the most important results: those pertaining to the structure of conflict and those concerning the importance of the task, before we turn to a review of some of the applied work.

The structure of conflict

The early results obtained with the SJT paradigm were surprising in that they yielded no evidence of conflict reduction over a 20-trial conflict sequence (e.g. Hammond et al., 1968; Miller, Brehmer, & Hammond, 1970). Thus it seemed that people were unable to change their policies.

However, these studies were limited in that they used only surface measures of conflict. The first studies using LME analyses gave an entirely different picture (Brehmer, 1968), and showed that although there was little reduction in surface conflict, there was a radical change in the structure of the conflict. Specifically, the results showed that the systematic differences between the subjects' policies decreased rapidly. At the same time, however, the consistency of the policies also decreased. Thus in the beginning of the conflict stage, most of the conflict was caused by systematic differences in policy, that is by a low G value, but at the end, most of the conflict was caused by lack of consistency, that is, by low values of R_{S1} and R_{S2}.

Further analysis showed that the decrease in consistency was due to the manner in which the subjects changed their policies as a consequence of their interaction with each other and with the task. Thus, contrary to expectation, the subjects did not stick to their initial policies, but gave up these policies and acquired new ones. However, they gave up their old policies faster than they learned new ones, and as a consequence, their consistency decreased.

These results have subsequently been replicated over a wide variety of circumstances, including subject characteristics such as their sex (Hammond & Brehmer, 1973) and nationality (Brehmer, Azuma, Hammond, Kostron, & Varonos, 1970), and task characteristics, both with respect to substantive characteristics, such as task content (Hammond & Brehmer, 1973) and formal characteristics such as task predictability (Brehmer, 1973c), the distribution of the validities of the cues (Brehmer, 1974e; Brehmer & Kostron, 1973), the forms of cue-criterion relations (Brehmer & Hammond, 1973) and the intercorrelation between the cues (Brehmer, 1974a).

The adverse effects of inconsistency are also obtained when the subjects start with similar policies, but are required to change because their policies are not optimal for the task at hand. Under these circumstances, inconsistency causes persons who start out with near perfect agreement to disagree more and more as they change their policies, even though they do not develop any systematic differences in policy (Brehmer, 1972). These results suggest a new kind of explanation for why groups break up when their environment changes.

Inconsistency is not an artifact, caused by the particular way in which the data from the experiments are analysed; it also has behavioural consequences. Thus Brehmer (1974f) showed that when inconsistency is high the subjects ask their partners more questions about what they are doing and what their policy is. This indicates that inconsistency leads to lack of interpersonal understanding. In a reanalysis of some data collected by Brown and Hammond (1968), Hammond and Brehmer (1973) found that inconsistency hindered the subjects in four-person groups in identifying who had the same policy and who had a different policy with respect to the evaluation of presidential candidates. This is a remarkable result given that the four-person groups were composed of two students from the radical Students for a Democratic Society and two students from the conservative Young Americans for Freedom.

Hammond and Brehmer (1973) have discussed these results in detail, and hypothesized that inconsistency will prevent the persons from realizing the true nature of their conflict, and because they are likely to employ the rational actor paradigm, they are likely to explain their differences in motivational terms, rather than in cognitive terms. As a consequence, they will not only fail to resolve their conflict, but attempts to resolve the conflict may actually lead to exacerbation when the subjects start searching for the motives that will explain their differences. This attribution process has, however, not yet been investigated empirically.

The importance of the task

In standard analyses of conflict following the rational actor paradigm, conflicts are seen as involving only the two persons in conflict. According to the present analysis, this is not sufficient. Instead, the analysis must involve three systems: the two parties to the conflict and the task for which the conflicting policies have been developed. This is because the characteristics of this task will have important effects on the policies of the people in conflict. In the earlier part of this paper, we mentioned two important task characteristics that affect the consistency of policies: complexity and uncertainty. Since the policies in the conflict stage are changed to cope with the task in that stage, we would expect that the characteristics of the task would affect the consistency of the policies developed and that the level of conflict would vary with the characteristics of the task. This prediction is supported in studies by Brehmer (1973) and Brehmer and Hammond (1973). The former study shows that conflict varies with task predictability, and that disagreement is greater when predictability is lower because the subjects' policies are then less consistent. The study by Brehmer and Hammond (1973) suggests that complex non-linear tasks tend to lead to higher conflict because of lower consistency.

These results are important because they show that the level of conflict cannot be understood only in terms of the persons in conflict and their characteristics. The nature of the task facing the persons has to be considered as well. In short, the analysis of conflict must involve three, rather than just two, systems. Clearly, it may be just as reasonable to look for an explanation of conflict in the task as to look for it in the people in conflict.

Summary

The results obtained with the SJT paradigm in the laboratory show that interpersonal conflict can be caused by purely cognitive factors, that is, by differences in policies, and that the level of conflict can be understood in terms of the cognitive systems involved. An important determinant of the level of conflict is the nature of the task which affects the conflict by its effects on the policies of the persons involved.

These results were, however, all obtained in laboratory simulations of conflict. We now turn to some applications of these results in real settings.

Studies in applied settings

There have been a number of studies in applied settings. These studies have been reviewed in Brehmer and Hammond (1977) and Hammond *et al.* (1977). Later studies add little to what is in these reviews, except to add to the variety of settings in which SJT methods have been applied.

Except for the first study by Balke, Hammond, and Meyer (1973), which was a re-enactment of a labour-management conflict, the applied work has been concerned with real conflict which had existed for some time before the Social Judgment Theorists became involved. The conflicts studied include, among other things, disagreement over the choice of handgun ammunition for a metropolitan police force (Hammond & Adelman, 1976), conflict over policy in a governmental organization (Adelman, Stewart, & Hammond, 1975), and disagreement among experts over judgments of cancer risk (Hammond & Marvin, 1981).

In all of these studies, it proved possible to identify the cognitive differences that caused the conflicts by means of the kinds of techniques for judgment analysis described in this paper. These results thus give evidence that these techniques are useful, but, more important, they demonstrate the utility of analysing conflict in terms of cognitive differences, and not only in terms of differences in interest. In short, they underline the importance of developing an alternative to the rational actor paradigm for understanding decision-making and conflict.

As would be expected from the laboratory results, the judgment policies in these studies were found to be inconsistent, and the parties to the conflicts had little insight into the real causes of their disagreement and what differences actually existed between their policies (see Balke *et al.*, 1973, for a particularly clear demonstration of this).

These results suggest that it is important to develop new methods for communication to help resolve conflict. A first step in this direction was taken by Hammond and Brehmer (1973). They developed a computer graphics system which presents cases for judgment, accepts judgments via a keyboard, performs a judgment analysis according to the principles described in this paper and displays the results graphically so that the parties to the conflict can see what their differences actually are with respect to what cues are used, which weights are given to these cues, the functional relations between each cue and the judgments, and their consistency, thus relieving the persons of having to rely on their limited insight and on the imprecise medium of words for communicating about their policies. The current version of this system (Stewart & Carter, 1973) is available through the General Electric international time-sharing system.

The system has been used in many of the applied studies referred to above, but there has been no evaluating of its usefulness compared to other techniques for communication, nor has there been any study comparing conflict reduction with the system and without the system. Despite the fact that there are good theoretical reasons for expecting positive effects from the system on conflict reduction through improved communication there are, as yet, no empirical results to demonstrate that the system actually serves the function it is supposed to serve. To perform such an evaluation is a task of utmost importance for future studies in SJT.

Conclusions

The main argument in this paper is that the complexity of the problems facing decision-makers prevents them from having the complete understanding presumed in the rational actor paradigm. As a consequence, decisions have to be based on judgment, rather than on fact, that is to say, cognitive processes intervene and have to be taken into account. Clearly, the characteristics of the judgmental processes involved contribute to conflict, and judgmental differences seem sufficient to create disagreement, even in the absence of motivational differences, as is demonstrated in both laboratory and applied studies. These results substantiate the claim that an alternative to the rational actor paradigm is needed to supplement the analysis performed in this paradigm. While it is clear that considerably more theoretical and empirical work is needed before we achieve any reasonably complete understanding of human judgment and its role in decision-making and conflict, I hope that this chapter has at least convinced the reader that work conducted towards this end will prove worthwhile.

17. Heuristics in negotiation: Limitations to effective dispute resolution

Max H. Bazerman and Margaret A. Neale

Negotiation is a decision-making process in which multiple parties jointly make decisions to resolve conflicting interests. The research literature typically classifies the study of negotiations in organizations as part of labor/management relations. However, negotiations extend over a much broader range of organizational processes, occurring in the acquisition of supplies, salary negotiation, personnel transfers within organizations, performance appraisal, budget determination, the acquisition of financing, selling output, and so on. In addition to limiting its application to labor/management relations, the literature has concentrated on two major categories of research: the industrial relations approach and the social psychological approach (Kochan, 1980). The industrial relations approach encompasses three major components of negotiating: (1) legal issues, (2) the historical/institutional aspects, and (3) the neoclassical economic. The social psychological perspective focuses on the individual differences of the negotiators (e.g., interpersonal orientation) and structural interventions (e.g., forms of third-party interventions). Further, both these lines of investigation have emphasized the *outcomes* of negotiation (resolution or impasse, value of the contract, and so forth) to the virtual exclusion of the *process* involved in negotiation. The purpose of this chapter is to suggest an alternative direction for negotiation research – that of defining the negotiator as a decision maker, focusing on the effects of the negotiator's decision-making process on the negotiator's success and the likelihood of reaching a negotiated settlement. Specifically, five decisional biases will be suggested that systematically and predictably alter negotiator performance and dispute resolution behavior.

To more clearly understand how these inferential biases work, it is useful to make the argument that negotiator behavior often deviates from rationality. To allow us to discuss the existence of systematic deviations from rationality by negotiators, consider Walton and McKersie's (1965) "bargaining zone" concept. Their framework can be illustrated through the use of the following simplified diagram:

M_t = management's target
U_r = union's resistance point
M_r = management's resistance point
U_t = union's target

Walton and McKersie suggested that each negotiator has a resistance point, below which he or she would choose to sustain a strike (or whatever alternative exists when an impasse is reached) rather than settle. Further, they suggested that the resistance points typically represent greater compromise than is suggested by the two parties' target points and initial offers/demands. If a gap exists between resistance points – that is, the employer's (in a labor/management context) resistance point is less than the union's resistance point – a "*negative* contract zone" exists. Where the resistance points overlap (e.g., the above diagram), a "*positive* contract zone" exists. If the negotiators are rational, a settlement would never occur when a negative contract zone exists, while a settlement would always occur when a positive contract zone exists. In contrast, common observation is that the two parties often fail to agree despite overlapping resistance points. Walton and McKersie asserted that "intangibles," or psychological factors and conflict dynamics, result in the disappearance of the bargaining zone during negotiations. *If it is rational for a settlement to occur whenever a positive contract zone exists, what specific processes account for negotiators failing to reach an agreement despite overlapping resistance points?* The alternative direction to understanding the negotiation process that we propose here offers some answers to this question. . . .

Following March and Simon's (1958) concept of bounded rationality, the literature on behavioral decision theory has identified a number of ways in which systematic biases bound a decision maker's rationality. This chapter proposes five specific biases that affect negotiators and demonstrates how these biases may explain the paradox defined above. For each bias, logic and empirical evidence will be presented to demonstrate the effect and examine the impact of that bias in the negotiation domain.

The framing of negotiation

Bazerman's (1982) adaptation of Kahneman and Tversky's (1979b) prospect theory presents the following question:

A large car manufacturer has recently been hit with a number of economic difficulties and it appears as if three plants need to be closed and 6000 employees laid off. The vice-president of production has been exploring alternative ways to avoid this crisis. She has developed two plans:

Plan A: This plan will save 1 of the 3 plants and 2000 jobs.

Plan B: This plan has a ⅓ probability of saving all 3 plants and all 6000 jobs, but has a ⅔ probability of saving no plants and no jobs.

Which plan would you select?

Organizational behavior research has identified a number of content issues that are relevant to consider in evaluating the plans. However, a more fundamental question underlies this subjective situation and the resulting decision. Reconsider the above problem, replacing the choice options provided above with the following alternative choices:

Plan C: This plan will result in the loss of 2 of the 3 plants and 4000 jobs.

Plan D: This plan has a ⅔ probability of resulting in the loss of all 3 plants and all 6000 jobs, but has a ⅓ probability of losing no plants and no jobs.

Which plan would you select?

Close examination of the two sets of alternative plans finds them to be *objectively* the same. For example, saving 1 of 3 plants and 2000 of 6000 jobs (Plan A) is the same objective outcome as losing 2 of 3 plants and 4000 of 6000 jobs (Plan C). Empirically, however, *most* (80+ percent) individuals choose Plan A (objectively the same as Plan C) in the first set, while *most* (80+ percent) individuals choose Plan D (objectively the same as Plan B) in the second set. While the two sets of choices are objectively identical, changing the description of the outcome states from job and plants saved (gains) to jobs and plants lost (losses) was sufficient to shift prototypic choice from risk averse (taking the sure thing) to risk seeking.

These findings are consistent with a growing body of literature (Tversky & Kahneman, 1981; Thaler, 1980; Kahneman & Tversky, 1979b) that indicates that individuals treat the prospect of gain (e.g., saving jobs and plants) differently from the prospects of losses (e.g., losing jobs and plants). Kahneman and Tversky's (1979b) prospect theory states that potential gains and losses are evaluated relative to their effect on current wealth. Choice is explained by an S-shaped value function – a value function that is convex (indicating a risk-averse orientation) for gains and concave (indicating a risk-seeking orientation) for losses.

Figure 17.1 shows that the value individuals typically place on *saving* one plant and 2000 jobs is more than one-third of the value placed on *saving* three plants and 6000 jobs. In contrast, the "value" of a loss

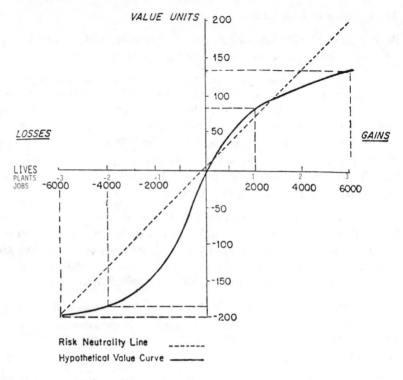

Figure 17.1. Hypothetical value function accounting for framing.

suffered by *losing* three plants and 6000 jobs is not three times as great as the "value" of losing one plant and 2000 jobs.

Now consider a prototypic labor/management situation: The union claims it needs a raise to $12 per hour and that any lesser raise would represent a *loss* to members given the current inflationary environment. Management, in contrast, claims that it cannot pay more than $10 per hour and that any greater payment would impose an unacceptable *loss* to the company. Given this simplified, one-issue case, imagine what would happen if each side had the option of settling for $11 per hour or going to arbitration? Since each party is viewing the negotiation in terms of what it has to lose, following Kahneman and Tversky's basic propositions, each will respond in a risk-seeking manner and arbitration is likely to be chosen. Presenting the same objective specified above but changing the *subjective* gain/loss situation results in a very different predicted outcome. If the union views anything about $10/hour as a gain and management views anything under $12/hour as a gain, a positive frame will exist, risk aversion will tend to dominate, and a negotiated settlement will generally occur (Neale & Bazerman, 1983b). Empirically, Neale and Bazerman found that a positive frame led to significantly greater concessionary behavior and more successful performance than a negative frame did.

The implications of the above framework are of critical importance. Both sides in negotiations often talk in terms of why they *need* a certain wage, thus setting the referent point (the benchmark by which gains or losses are determined) along the same lines as their public target goals. If this is indeed the case, the negotiators would adopt negative frames, exhibit risk-seeking attitudes, and be less likely to reach a settlement. Because of the tendency to view the potential outcome from this perspective, a critical aspect of the potential success of the negotiation hinges upon how various participants in the interaction are able to influence the position of the referent point and thus the frame of the negotiation. A critical role of interested third parties may therefore be their skill at influencing the parties to alter their negative frame (and concomitant risk-seeking orientation) toward a neutral or positive frame that is more conducive to a negotiated settlement. Thus as Rubin (1980) suggests, the primary role of the third party may not be simply to add uncertainty associated with third-party intervention strategies but to increase the options of the participants by altering the situational frame of the parties in conflict. Second, in collective bargaining it is generally recognized that the actual participants negotiate not only with identified opponents but also with their constituencies to influence the position of the referent points (and thus the frame) through intraorganizational bargaining (Walton & McKersie, 1965). Negotiator skill in interaction with the constituency to manipulate their aspirations levels – as the equivalent third-party skill at influencing negotiator frame – is likely to result in a higher settlement rate because the referent point is altered thus allowing a greater range of settlement options to be viewed as gains (i.e., from a positive frame). Finally, while this framework was developed in the labor/management negotiating domain, the importance of the frame of a dispute is relevant to *any* negotiation context in which two parties have the option of accepting a settlement or in some way risking the escalation of the dispute (e.g., divorce, transfer pricing, salary negotiation).

Overconfidence in judgment

A substantial amount of research on clinical judgment, decision making, and probability estimation has demonstrated many systematic deviations from rationality. Yet evidence also shows that individuals have unwarranted confidence in their fallible judgments (Einhorn & Hogarth, 1978; Einhorn, 1980b). Laboratory subjects are known to be overconfident in their assessment of the probability (confidence judgment) that their response to uncertain decisions will be accurate. Because it is hard to observe overconfidence based on a single confidence judgment, research has examined the quality of a set of confidence judgments, each representing the subjective probability that a response to a two-choice question (e.g., yes/no) is correct (Lichtenstein, Fischhoff, & Phillips, 1977). An appropriately confident individual within this methodology should, for example, be accurate on 80 percent of the judgments to which they give confidence judgments of 80 percent. Typical laboratory studies, in contrast, find overconfidence to be the commonly observed finding (Fischhoff, 1982). For example, with a large group of two-choice questions for which subjects were 75 percent confident that their judgment was correct, typically only 60 percent of the questions would have been answered correctly. For confidence judgments of 100 percent, it is common for subjects to be correct only 85 percent of the time (Fischhoff, 1982). Finally, when people put confidence intervals around numerical judgments (e.g., "I am 95 percent certain that there are between 500 and 700 pennies in that jar"), it is common for the actual number (of pennies) to fall outside the 95 percent boundaries for 50 percent of all subjects.

In the negotiation context, Farber (1981) discusses this problem in terms of the existence of divergent expectations by negotiators. That is, each negotiator has an optimistic view of the point at which a neutral third party will choose to adjudicate the dispute. For example, assume the union is demanding $8.75 per hour, while management is offering $8.25 per hour. In addition, assume that the "appropriate" wage is $8.50 per hour. Farber (1981) suggests that the union will typically expect the neutral third party to adjudicate at a wage somewhat over $8.50/hour, while management will expect a wage somewhat under $8.50/hour. Given these divergent expectations, neither side is willing to compromise on $8.50/hour (or on any other mutually agreed upon wage). Both sides will thus incur the costs of impasse and aggregately do no better than they would through the use of a third party.

In general, existing research demonstrates that negotiators tend to be overconfident that their positions will prevail if they do not "give in" during negotiations. Specifically, Neale and Bazerman (1983a, 1983b) show that negotiators consistently overestimate by 15 percent the probability that, under final-offer-by-package arbitration, their final offer will be accepted by the arbitrator. That is, while only 50 percent of all final offers submitted to the arbitrator can be accepted, the average subject estimated that there was a much higher probability that his or her own offer would be accepted. In terms of Walton and McKersie's bargaining zone, overconfidence may inhibit a variety of settlements, despite the existence of a reasonable bargaining zone. Neale and Bazerman (1983b) found "appropriately" confident negotiators to exhibit more concessionary behavior and to be more successful than overly confident negotiators. Once again, while these arguments have been developed relative to an industrial relations perspective, they can be generalized to suggest that any joint venture may fail to occur as each side is overconfident that the other side will eventually give in to one's own "superior" position/argument.

The lack of perspective taking

The biases of framing and overconfidence just presented suggest that individuals are generally affected by systematic deviations from rationality. Yet experience and empirical evidence suggest that there are some individuals who are more accurate in their interpersonal judgments (Bernstein & Davis, 1982; Davis, 1981) or less influenced by the frame of the situation. These individual differences may be related to the ability of a negotiator (individual) to take the perspective of his or her opponent. It is important to note that taking the perspective of an opponent is not done for purely philanthropic reasons; rather, in achieving any set of objectives, there is valuable information to be gleaned from taking the perspective of the other negotiating party. Davis (1981) recently developed a construct and measure of the ability to take others' perspective and see things from their point of view. He found that individuals with high perspective-taking ability (PTA) are more accurate than are those with low PTA in judging others. Further, the accuracy with which those with high PTA judge others increased with experience, while those with low PTA did not exhibit similar improvement in accuracy (Bernstein & Davis, 1982). Interestingly, this systematic limitation to effective interpersonal judgment is not related to standard measures of intelligence.

In a bargaining context, it is expected that individuals with high PTA would be better able to adopt the perspective of their bargaining opponents. They would also be more aware of the perspective of the opponent's constituency (e.g., labor or management) than would individuals with low PTA. This added information from perspective taking should increase one's ability to predict accurately the opponent's goals and expectations. This is extremely important in developing bargaining strategy (Siegel & Fouraker, 1960; Rubin & Brown, 1975) and facilitating compromise. Neale and Bazerman (1983a) found that perspective-taking ability positively affects the concessionary tendencies of negotiators and the likelihood that a settlement will be reached. In addition, perspective-taking ability was found to affect positively the outcome obtained by a negotiator. Further, Bazerman and Neale (1982) have suggested that training mechanisms should be developed to increase the perspective-taking ability of negotiators. This is consistent with the literature on negotiator role reversal – that having each bargainer verbalize the viewpoint of the other increases the likelihood of a negotiated resolution (see Pruitt, 1981). Perhaps increasing the tendency of negotiators to take their opponents' perspective is the central focus of mediators. Research (Kochan & Jick, 1978; Neale & Bazerman, 1983a) suggests that increased information that is derived in this way often results in behavior that is more conducive to a negotiated settlement.

Escalation

There are many organizational contexts in which an employee can become trapped into a costly course of action. The escalation of commitment to a failing course of action has recently become a topic of interest among decision researchers (Bazerman, Beekun, & Schoorman, 1982; Brockner, Shaw, & Rubin, 1979; Conlon & Wolf, 1980, Staw, 1976, 1981; Teger, 1979). Individuals and groups who are personally responsible for negative consequences consistently commit the greatest amount of resources to a previously chosen course of action. America's involvement in Vietnam is often cited as a classic example of escalation (Teger, 1979). Policymakers of that time gradually increased the nation's commitment in such a manner that no major political force could retrospectively argue that the actions taken were rational.

Staw (1976) provided initial experimental evidence of the escalation effect. In this study, one group of subjects (high responsibility) was asked to allocate research and development funds to one or two operating divisions of an organization. Subjects were then told that after three years, the investment had either proved successful or unsuccessful and that they were faced with a second allocation decision concerning the division to which they had previously given funds. A second group (low responsibility) was told that another financial officer of the firm made a decision that had been either successful or unsuccessful (the same content information was provided to both groups of subjects) and that they were to make a second allocation of funds concerning that division. When the outcome of the previous decision was negative (an unsuccessful investment), high-responsibility subjects allocated significantly more funds to the original division in the second allocation than did low-responsibility subjects. For successful initial decisions, the amount of money allocated in the second decision was not related to responsibility.

Following the logic of the escalation literature, negotiators can be expected to escalate nonrationally their commitment to a previous course of action. Unfortunately, the most common form of distributive negotiation leads both sides to make extreme demands initially. If negotiators become committed to their initial public statements, we can expect them nonrationally to adopt a nonconcessionary stance. Further, if both sides incur losses as a result of a lack of agreement (e.g., a strike), their commitment to their respective positions will increase and the willingness to change to a different course of action (i.e., compromise) may decrease. For example, it could be argued that in the Malvinas/Falklands conflict, once Argentina had suffered the initial loss of life, it had the information necessary rationally to pursue a negotiated settlement. The escalation literature, in contrast, accurately predicts that the loss of life (a significant commitment to a course of action) would lead Argentina to a further escalation of its commitment not to compromise on the return of the Malvinas to Britain.

One important result from the escalation literature is that public announcement of one's commitment increases one's tendency to escalate nonrationally (Staw, 1981). Once this general public (or constituency) is aware of the commitment, the decision maker is far less likely to retreat from his or her previously announced position. This suggests that escalation can be reduced if negotiators and third parties avoid the formation of firmly set public positions, for this provides the ignition for the nonrational escalation of conflict. Implementation of this recommendation is, however, contradictory to everything known about how negotiators (e.g., labor leaders, representatives of management) behave when they represent constituencies. A firmly set public position is typically perceived as necessary to build constituency support and allegiance. Thus it may be that what is best for the constituency is not the same as what the constituency will reward.

The mythical fixed pie

Walton and McKersie (1965) suggested four models of negotiation. Two of them present drastically different perspectives of the bargaining process. The distributive bargaining model views the bargaining process as a procedure for the division of a fixed pie of resources. That is, what one side gains, the other side loses. In contrast, the integrative bargaining model focuses on the means of making tradeoffs or solving problems to the mutual benefit of both sides. Walton and McKersie suggest that most negotiators view the bargaining process as a distributive task.

We argue that Walton and McKersie's observation of the perceptions of labor/management negotiators represents a fundamental bias in human judgment. It is common to take a win/lose perspective. Some people would argue that acting as if all conflicts are of a fixed pie nature is likely to be perceived as hard-headed, tough-minded, and realistic. It may be that the competitive nature of our education, athletic activities, and the like fosters fixed pie conflict behavior. Regardless of the basis for this mythical fixed pie perception of bargaining, we agree with Pruitt that most conflicts are not purely distributive problems. Why?

Most conflicts have more than one issue at stake, with the parties placing different values on the differing issues. Once this condition exists, the conflict is objectively no longer a fixed pie. Consider a Friday evening on which you and your spouse are going to dinner and a movie. Unfortunately, you prefer different restaurants and different movies. It is easy to adopt a distributive attitude toward each event to be negotiated. In contrast, if you do not assume a fixed pie, you may find out that you care more about the restaurant selection and your spouse cares more about the movie choice. Similarly, purchasing goods is often treated as a distributive problem. Often, however, a retailer is suddenly willing to reduce the purchase price if payment is made in cash (no receipt, and so on). While you care only about price, he or she also cares about the form of payment. In a tight, inflationary housing market, many deals are possible when it becomes clear that the seller cares more about the sales price while the buyer is largely concerned about the existence of secondary sources of financing. Again, tradeoffs to both sides may be possible.

Reaching a negotiated settlement in the above situations is likely to depend on determining the favorable tradeoffs that are viable. Such solutions, however, are possible only when the negotiators eliminate fixed pie perceptions. The literature on creativity (Wickelgren, 1974) points out that we are often limited in finding creative problem solutions by the false assumptions that we make. We apply this position to negotiation by arguing that the fixed pie perception is a fundamentally false assumption that hinders the resolution of conflict, despite the potential existence of mutually agreeable resolutions. A fundamental role of mediators should be to break such false assumptions and to look for mutually favorable tradeoffs.

Conclusion

While negotiation is often defined as a decision-making process, the research literature has failed to consider the critical role of the social-cognitive decision processes of negotiators and its impact on their behavior. This chapter has attempted to highlight conceptually the negative impact of limitations in human judgment on the performance of negotiators and the likelihood that these negotiators will reach a mutually agreed-upon solution to their conflict. Specifically, five unique systematic biases that affect the judgments of negotiators have been identified. Future research is needed to provide empirical support for the existence of these biases in actual and varied negotiation contexts. Further, it is likely that these biases are merely a sampling of the population of systematic deficiencies in human judgment. Thus continued research is necessary to identify these biases and to provide possible solutions to the problems they present.

The description of systematic biases that affect negotiators is a critical step in the development of the conflict literature. However, research on this topic needs to advance to provide prescriptive recommendations for improving resolution behaviors. While systematic research is needed to explore alternatives for improving the personal and societal effectiveness of the process of negotiation, some guidelines for such improvement can be provided. In the literature on behavioral decision theory, Nisbett and Ross (1980) have begun to focus on remedies for these decision-making limitations. With respect to the negotiation context, there are at least two approaches to overcoming the biases of negotiators in probability assessment: (1) improve the selection criteria used for negotiators and (2) train negotiators to eliminate decision-making biases. In developing selection criteria, it is important to select for the defined task – negotiating. Thus it becomes particularly important to have, at hand, remedies for the biases to which negotiators are particularly vulnerable. Choosing negotiators on characteristics other than job title or elected position may provide considerable relief for the observed deviations from rationality identified here. Second, a number of systematic decision biases exist due to the effects of statistics and their interpretation on the human inference process. If individuals can be trained to deal with the common task of negotiating in a "rational" manner, the probability of reaching a negotiated settlement will be enhanced. This chapter identifies a number of specific items that should affect the training of negotiators. The remaining question concerns how to train negotiators to eliminate the biases identified. The first step would be awareness – most negotiators are not aware of these biases. Most scholars in the area of creating change would quickly point out, however, that it is far easier to identify behavioral dispositions than to change them. To respond to this criticism, we advocate using an unfreezing-change-refreezing approach to improving the judgment of negotiators. That is, before negotiators change their judgmental strategies, their current strategies need to be unfrozen. How? One change strategy adopted by the authors in the classroom is to develop negotiation exercises that lead to failure because of the manner in which the participants deviate from rationality. Once a negotiator attends to the fact that his or her biases led to failure, the likelihood increases that change will occur and persist. Finally, an aware mediator can facilitate the negotiation process by using the information in this chapter to point out to the parties the judgmental deficiencies in each side's arguments.

In conclusion, this chapter has identified a new direction for increasing the likelihood that negotiators will achieve a resolution by improving the quality of their decision-making processes. This area of inquiry complements the existing literature that has identified structural interventions and relevant personality characteristics of negotiators (Rubin & Brown, 1975; Pruitt, 1981) as predictors of their success.

18. The Camp David negotiations

Howard Raiffa

The historic Camp David negotiations will be used here to illustrate the role of a third-party intervenor with mediating clout, and as a basis for discussing a recently developed technique for structuring the negotiation process – a technique that employs what is known as a "single negotiating text."[1]

In early 1977 President Jimmy Carter and Secretary of State Cyrus Vance, abandoning Henry Kissinger's step-by-step approach to mediating the Egyptian-Israeli conflict, tried to convene another Geneva Conference to be jointly chaired by the United States and the Soviet Union. Several key parties, however, were reluctant to attend: Syria because of the Palestinian issue; Israel because it did not want to deal with the Palestinian Liberation Organization (PLO); Egypt because it had reservations about an increased Soviet role. In an effort to impart momentum to the stalled peace process, Egypt's President Anwar-el Sadat on November 19, 1977, made his celebrated trip to Jerusalem, and conferred with Israel's Prime Minister Menachem Begin on Christmas of that year at Ismailia, Egypt.

Sadat, insisting that he was acting as spokesman for all Arab interests, asked for the return of all occupied territories (Egypt's Sinai Peninsula, Jordan's West Bank, Syria's Golan Heights) as well as for the return of East Jerusalem, in exchange for peace and normalization of relations with Israel. His inability, though, to evoke from Begin a "grand gesture"

---

[1] The historical account in this chapter is based extensively on "Middle East Negotiations – Camp David Summit," a case study prepared by Mark G. McDonough. Kennedy School of Government, Harvard University: C 14–79–261.

comparable to his own caused mounting opposition from his fellow Arabs. Sadat was not deterred by the vociferous opposition of the "steadfast front" of Arab states allied against him, but he was undoubtedly angered by the terrorist operations of the PLO, some of which he believed were directed against him.

Begin appeared to be pleased with the prospect of direct negotiations with Egypt, as long as they focused on bilateral issues and addressed the Palestinian issue only in broad terms. A separate peace with Egypt would give Israel military advantages relative to its other Arab neighbors and would avoid the security risks involved in the return of the Golan Heights to Syria and the West Bank to Jordan. Nevertheless, there were indications that in return for peace, Sadat would attempt to get Israel's agreement to a set of principles that would give the Palestinians wide-ranging autonomy rights on the West Bank and Gaza Strip. The nature of these rights evoked the possibility that a Palestinian state might evolve out of the accords. This sort of provision would help Sadat defend himself against charges that he had sold out his brethren by making peace with Israel.

The United States was surprised by Sadat's trip to Jerusalem, but soon saw the merits of this initiative and offered its mediating services. Carter's effort to bring about a settlement, on which he had staked so much of his domestic and international prestige, depended in large measure on Sadat's ability to carry it off. The United States, in playing its mediating role, was bound to be extremely sensitive to his problems and his needs. But its decision to support Sadat's bilateral initiative and renege on its commitment to a comprehensive approach ran a high risk of antagonizing the other Arab states – including Saudi Arabia, upon whom the United States was depending for political support not only for its Middle East peace efforts but also for its own national energy requirements. Furthermore, the United States was taking a calculated risk in excluding the Russians from the negotiating process. It was becoming obvious that the Soviet Union was working with the rejectionist Arab states in an effort to sabotage U.S. initiatives. Nevertheless, the United States was still hoping that the principles of any agreement it helped to mediate would eventually draw in the Arab states that were now boycotting the negotiations.

In order to simplify the negotiation process, Sadat and Begin agreed at Ismailia to convene two ministerial-level committees. A Military Committee would deal primarily with Egyptian-Israeli bilateral issues (especially Israeli withdrawal from the Sinai) leading to a peace treaty between the two states. A Political Committee would address the multilateral Arab-Israeli issues, including the form of Palestinian autonomy on the West Bank and Gaza Strip, and would design a Declaration of Principles that could serve as a "framework" for peace negotiations.

On January 10, 1978, the Military Committee convened in Cairo, but bogged down rapidly when the Israelis demanded at the outset that they be allowed to retain civilian settlements and military air bases in Sinai, while giving sovereignty to Egypt. Starting on January 16 the Political Committee, with Vance in attendance, had an abortive two-day meeting. Sadat recalled his delegation because of (in his view) Israel's hard line.

Acrimony developed between Sadat and Begin. In February Sadat was invited to Washington and received U.S. backing for his contention that Israel should agree to give up all the territory it had gained in the 1967 war. The Israelis, though, remained adamant about the West Bank and Gaza Strip, which Begin regarded as an integral part of Israeli territory.

The following month Begin came to Washington, where he and Carter differed strenuously about the territorial issues. Part of the problem was the interpretation of United Nations Security Council Resolution 242. This resolution, which had been approved unanimously by the Security Council on November 22, 1967, called for: (1) the withdrawal of Israeli forces from occupied Arab areas; (2) an end to the state of belligerence between the Arab nations and Israel; (3) acknowledgment of and respect for the sovereignty, territorial integrity, and political independence of every nation in the area; (4) the establishment of secure and recognized national boundaries; (5) a guarantee of freedom of navigation through international waterways in the area; and (6) a just settlement of the refugee problem. Since the United States had repeatedly said that it interpreted Resolution 242 as requiring Israeli withdrawal on all fronts from Arab territories occupied in 1967, Sadat apparently hoped that as a "full partner" in the negotiations, the United States could pressure Israel into giving up the territories. On the other hand, Israel, wary of this interpretation, insisted that the U.S. role remain that of mediation and therefore opposed the presentation of "American peace plans."

On July 18, 1978, Vance met with Moshe Dayan, foreign minister of Israel, and Mohammed Ibrahim Kamel, foreign minister of Egypt. Vance was encouraged by their flexibility and reported this to Carter. After meeting with his senior policy advisers, Carter decided that without his presidential intervention the Egyptian-Israeli peace process would collapse, and that given Vance's report about glimmers of flexibility, a three-nation summit would be a reasonable gamble.

On August 4 Vance flew to the Middle East in an effort to break the impasse that had developed during the previous few months. His trip, however, had a more specific purpose than the American public was led to believe. In an attempt to revive the momentum toward peace that had been created by Sadat's visit to Jerusalem, Vance carried with him personal invitations from Carter to Begin and Sadat to join him at Camp David, Maryland. On August 8, the White House issued the following statement: "The President is pleased to announce that President Sadat and Prime Minister Begin have accepted an invitation to come to Camp David on September 5 for a meeting with the President to seek a framework for peace in the Middle East.... Each of the three leaders will be accompanied by a small number of their principal advisors and no specific time has been set for the duration of the meeting."

To prepare for the upcoming U.S. mediating effort, Carter set up a task force that included Zbigniew Brzezinski and William Quandt of the National Security Council, and, from the State Department, Harold H. Saunders and Alfred L. Atherton, Jr. (both assistant secretaries for Near Eastern and South Asian Affairs), as well as Vance. The task force was to derive methods or tools of mediation to be used by the president, to "invent" solutions, and to identify compromise language acceptable to both Egypt and Israel.

What were the United States' interests in the upcoming summit discussions? In 1975 a report entitled *Toward Peace in the Middle East*, prepared by a Brookings Institution group that had included Brzezinski and Quandt, had presaged the Carter administration's comprehensive approach to the settlement of the conflict in that region. The report had reached five main conclusions. First, the United States had a strong moral, political, and economic interest in the resolution of the Middle East conflict. Second, unless the core issues of the Arab-Israeli dispute (such as the Palestinian issue) were addressed soon, the risk of another war would increase. Third, future negotiations should make use of informal multilateral meetings or a reconvened Geneva Conference. Fourth, the United States, "because it [enjoyed] a measure of confidence on both sides and [had] the means to assist them economically and militarily," should remain actively involved in the settlement. Fifth, the United States "should work with the U.S.S.R. to the degree that Soviet willingness to play a constructive role [would] permit." The report had also suggested guidelines for accords on seven specific issues:

(a) *Security.* All parties to the settlement commit themselves to respect the sovereignty and territorial integrity of the others and refrain from the threat of the use of force against them.

(b) *Stages.* They withdraw to agreed boundaries and that the establishment of peaceful relations be carried out in stages over a period of years, each stage being undertaken only when the agreed provisions of the previous stage have been faithfully implemented.

(c) *Peaceful relations.* The Arab parties undertake not only to end hostile actions against Israel, but also to develop normal regional and international political/economic relations.

(d) *Boundaries.* Israel undertakes to withdraw by agreed stages to the June 5, 1967, lines with only such modifications as are mutually accepted. Boundaries will probably need to be safeguarded by demilitarized zones supervised by UN forces.

(e) *Palestine.* There should be provision for Palestinian self-determination, subject to Palestinian acceptance of the sovereignty and integrity of Israel within agreed boundaries. This might take the form either of an independent Palestine state or of a Palestine entity voluntarily federated with Jordan.

(f) *Jersualem.* The report suggests no specific solution for the particularly difficult problem of Jerusalem but recommends that, whatever the solution may be, it meet with the following criteria: there should be unimpeded access to all of the holy places and each should be under the custodianship of its own faith; there should be no barriers dividing the city which would prevent free circulation throughout it; and each national group within the city should, if it so desires, have substantial political autonomy within the area where it predominates.

(g) *Guarantees.* It would be desirable that the UN Security Council actively endorse the peace agreements.

At the time of the Camp David meeting in early September 1978, the idea of a reconvened Geneva Conference with a Soviet role was a thing of the past.

Preparations for negotiations: The U.S. role

The members of the team advising Carter were not new to the Egyptian-Israeli situation. They had already thought deeply about their preferred solutions. They knew what issues had to be debated at Camp David and they knew how the Military Committee and the Political Committee had already structured the issues dividing the two sides. In addition, the members of the U.S. team were familiar with the Israeli proposal of December 31, 1977, called the "twenty-six-point self-rule plan," as well as the Egyptian proposal of July 5, 1978, called the "six-point plan." They knew a lot about both sides; they could have assessed – but evidently did not assess – a multiattribute value function for each side and even one for the United States, as well as reservation values on packages and on individual issues. Keep in mind that the set of negotiators from each side did not have a monolithic position – to say nothing about the contending factions back home – and that there were many concerned parties on the fringes: the Arab states, the PLO, the Soviet Union, and a number of oil-starved developed and developing nations. Crisp formalization was hardly the crucial issue.

Carter and his team decided that progress could not be made in a fishbowl atmosphere: privacy during the negotiations was vital. Carter also tried desperately (futilely, as it turned out) to create a cordial ambience for negotiations and to get the contending parties to approach the problem as a joint problem-solving exercise. In addition, it was critical for the world, and especially the political forces within Israel and Egypt, to know that three very important world figures were isolating themselves from all other duties in order to devise a compromise accord – an accord that could only be acceptable to Egypt and Israel if it did not come easily. Any quick, realistic agreement was destined to meet trouble at home.

The U.S. mediators did not want both sides to come to the negotiating table with fixed packages. A dance of packages had already been tried, and the gaps were formidable. The mediators tried initially to get the principals to construct a package on an issue-by-issue basis, but they expected that this strategy would not work. It didn't. By day two Begin and Sadat would not talk to each other. What could be done?

The conflict was mediated through the use of a single negotiation text (SNT), a device suggested by Roger Fisher of Harvard Law School, who knew some of the key U.S. players (Atherton, Quandt, and Brzezinski). The use of some sort of SNT is often employed in international negotiations, especially with multiparty negotiations. The U.S. team devised and proposed an entire package for the consideration of the two protagonists. They made it clear that the United States was not trying to push this first proposal, but that it was meant to serve as an initial, single negotiating text – a text to be criticized by both sides and then modified and remodified in an iterative manner. These modifications would be made by the U.S. team, based on the criticisms of the two sides. The SNT was to be used as a means of concentrating the attention of both sides on the same composite text.

Neither side formalized its value tradeoffs; but if they had, then the United States might have generated a set of feasible joint evaluations and an efficient frontier, as shown in Figure 18.1. Assume that the ranges on each of the issues have been specified in advance; that each side has scored the worst possible agreement for its side at zero and the best agreement as 100; and that both sides have monolithic preferences. It is not necessarily true that the agreement that is worst for Israel is best for Egypt, or vice versa.

The United States starts the ball rolling by offering its first single negotiating text (point SNT-1 in the figure). Both Begin and Sadat protest that the proposal is ridiculous, whereupon the mediators reassure them that SNT-1 is not intended as a serious final settlement, but as a document to be criticized and improved upon: Why, they ask, is it so unacceptable? The mediators know very well why each side is so vehement in its rejection of SNT-1. This is part of the ritual. After some of the most egregious flaws have been pointed out by each side, the U.S. team comes up with SNT-2. Begin and Sadat, although they may agree that this text is marginally better than SNT-1, still claim that it's so far from being acceptable that they feel they're wasting their time. Sadat packs his bags and gets ready to go home, but Carter persuades him to stay for a few more rounds.

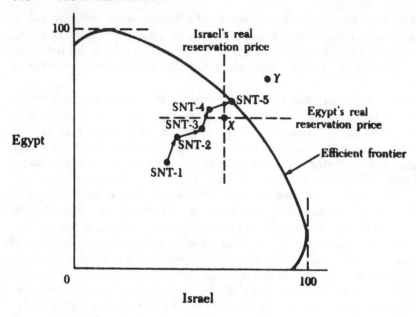

Figure 18.1. A hypothetical march of joint evaluations of successive SNTs.

After SNT-2 United States offers a new SNT, but the Israelis feel that this "improved" text is marginally a step backward – and a step backward from a hopelessly unfair starting point. So the United States comes up with a revised SNT-3; then with SNT-4 and SNT-5. Now let's imagine that the improvement from SNT-3 to SNT-4 was a critical jump for the Egyptians because the transition pierced their real reservation value – that is, Egypt truly preferred no agreement to SNT-3, but preferred SNT-4 to the no-agreement state. There still may be joint gains to be had, and if Egypt announces that SNT-4 is acceptable whereas Israel does not, then the ensuing gains are going to be tilted toward the Israeli side. That would not be a disaster for Egypt if that's the only way Israel can get over its reservation hurdle, but Sadat might think that the Israelis are already satisfied and are just trying to squeeze out more at Egypt's expense. So he still maintains that SNT-4 is unacceptable, but his protests are less vehement than before.

With the proposal of SNT-5, Israel's reservation value, too, is pierced. Will Begin announce this? Probably not, for the same reasons Sadat did not. But now it is no longer possible to squeeze out additional joint gains. If SNT-5 is modified to the advantage of one side, it is only at the expense of the other side. In Figure 18.1, SNT-5 is on the efficient frontier and no achievable joint evaluations are northeast of it. Point X represents a composite reservation value: Egypt would rather have no agreement than any deal that yields an evaluation south of X; Israel would rather have no agreement than any deal that yields an evaluation west of X; both sides would prefer to have any point northeast of X rather than the no-agreement state. But each, acting strategically, does not announce that SNT-5 is better than no agreement. Of course, if the composite reservation value were at Y rather than X, then they would be acting sincerely in their rejections of SNT-5. We're dealing with idealizations here. The reservation values are vague, and a politically acceptable agreement is usually one that has been difficult to negotiate.

Assume that both sides claim that they cannot settle for SNT-5, and that it proves impossible for the mediating team to squeeze out further joint gains. What now? The mediators are very discouraged, since the United States, too, has a stake in the negotiations. It may now be propitious for President Carter to give up something. Perhaps Israel could accept SNT-5 if the United States funded the construction of new airfields in Israel to replace those of the Sinai. No? Well how about some oil guarantees also? And might Egypt accept SNT-5 if the United States provided some financial aid for Egypt's ailing economy? So the president applies pressure and offers sweeteners, and a deal is struck.[2]

Did Egypt and Israel expect the United States to sweeten the pie? Did they gamble by declining SNT-5 in anticipation of a U.S. contribution? Did the United States anticipate that it might have to offer inducements to each side in order to generate an agreement? In preparing for the meetings, did all three sides think hard about what the United States could offer and about their tradeoffs and reservation values with potential U.S. contributions? Did Egypt and Israel agree to come to Camp David because this would put pressure on the United States to get an agreement? Did the U.S. team know that they were thinking this way? Did they know that the mediators knew that they knew? Did Egypt and Israel engage in tacit collusion to squeeze the United States?

Most of these questions probably have affirmative answers, at least to some degree. Is this morally wrong? Some might be tempted to say that it is, because they are not pleased with the outcome of the Camp David accords. But trying to leave that aside, would it be morally reprehensible, in principle, for statesmen to behave so strategically? My general answer is that it is not morally reprehensible – that leaders who do not act strategically may not be behaving in the best interests of their constituencies. But – and this is an important "but" – strategic misrepresentations can lead, as we have seen, to inefficiencies in outcomes and to ensuing mistrust. So the challenge is: How can we devise negotiating

---

[2] In reality, the negotiations at Camp David were a bit different from those described here. The number of iterations of the single negotiation text was not five, but more like twenty-five. Magnanimous U.S. offers to each side were not made exclusively at the end of the play; they were sprinkled along the way to keep the protagonists from quitting the negotiating game.

processes that will encourage more honest revelations and less strategic behavior?

Generating a single negotiating text

Let's look at how a negotiator or mediator might successfully combine a number of issues into a single composite text for discussion.

Suppose that Negotiator B persuades his adversary, Negotiator A, to *tentatively* consider an opening package that B himself has suggested as a point of departure for potential improvement. The joint evaluation of B's proposal is represented by point SNT-1' in Figure 18.2. Actually, B lures A into this position by arguing that it is easier for them to talk about a single negotiating proposal (text) than about two proposals simultaneously. Although SNT-1' is certainly not acceptable to A, Negotiator B suggests that no harm will be done if they jointly try to see if it could lead to some acceptable conclusion. The first improvement to SNT-1' favors A. Then A and B become so involved in generating successive improvements that A forgets where they started from (B's opening proposal); or perhaps A runs out of time. Figure 18.2 depicts what might happen: the negotiations starting from SNT-1' end up with a joint evaluation at X. If the roles were reversed and if A started with proposal SNT-1", they might have ended up at Y.

The conclusion should be clear: where one ends up depends in large part on where one starts. The question that remains is how to go about getting started – how to generate an SNT.

At Camp David the U.S. team generated an SNT. They probably tried not to start too close to the efficient frontier, aiming for a starting point that would appear to be "neutral" (as interpreted by the U.S. team). If the mediators had privately informed one side of the U.S. negotiating strategy, that side might have tried to influence the United States to start with an alternate SNT more favorable to themselves. A lot depends on the starting point.

Here are some ways in which an SNT can be generated. Suppose that A and B negotiate through a dance of packages. In Figure 18.3 successive offers by A are denoted as A_1, A_2, A_3, and by B as B_1, B_2, B_3. The offers seem to be converging on some package X, but the negotiators each want more. As a tactic, they might agree to accept X as their SNT and look for successive joint gains from that vantage point. Or A and B might agree to negotiate cordially and loosely on all issues and not to log-roll while looking for joint gains; this results in a joint *tentative* package, X, that is treated as the starting SNT. As a variation on this theme, the negotiators themselves might identify a bargaining range for each factor. They then agree to choose a focal point (for example, the mid-value on each continuous factor). They might have to haggle a bit in the process; but

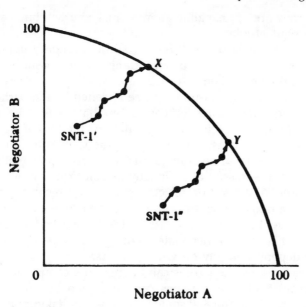

Figure 18.2. Dependence of final outcome on the choice of the SNT.

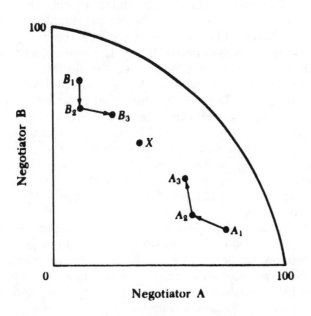

Figure 18.3. A dance of packages leading to an agreed-upon SNT.

they know that they are not haggling about a final contract, but a starting point for the pursuit of joint gains.

Suppose there are a host of small issues, all of secondary importance and all of comparable magnitude of importance. If one issue seems to loom large, it might be broken into separate issues or staggered over time. Or the importance of an issue might be lessened by the parties first narrowing the range of possible outcomes on that issue. The parties might then agree to resolve each issue separately by the toss of a coin. Or they might agree to take turns, each resolving the issue of its choice, of those remaining, in its favor (within mutually agreed-upon bounds, of course). A coin might be tossed to designate the starter. For example, the coin falls heads and A starts. She selects issue 17 and resolves it in her favor – but within a range preset by both before the process starts. B goes next, choosing issue 12, and resolves it in his favor. And so on. The parties, of course, first have to negotiate bounds on each issue or else the outcome might depend critically on who goes first.

There is no reason why the parties can't agree on a composite scheme for determining an SNT. Some issues can be settled by using central values; some by a random process; some by the parties' taking turns. The parties can be ingenious about the schemes they devise. The important thing is that this process appear to be fair to both sides and not be divisive. The parties should keep in mind that they are agreeing merely on the SNT which, in turn, will only loosely influence the final outcome.

Recall from our discussion of final-offer arbitration how the process works with a single continuous issue (distributive bargaining): if A and B can't settle, the arbitrator calls for final offers from both negotiators simultaneously and then chooses one of these. The same procedure can be used when there are several issues. One way to do this, which has been adopted by some states, requires each side to submit a final-offer *total package*; the arbitrator selects one of these two packages. A second way, adopted by other states, allows the arbitrator to break up packages – to accept A's final offer on some issues and B's final offer on other issues. Some arbitrators try to look at each issue separately and to resolve each in isolation without log-rolling, in their minds, between issues. It's easy to see how these procedures could be jointly inefficient, becase the essence of squeezing out joint gains lies in log-rolling between issues. Perhaps the best method would be to encourage both sides to use the arbitrated solution as an SNT for an ensuing round of negotiations, perhaps with a mediator; if they can't agree on how to squeeze out further joint gains, the arbitrated solution holds. If an SNT were to be generated by a final-offer arbitrator process, then it would probably be better if the SNT were created by using final-offer resolution on each issue separately, rather than on the package of issues collectively.

Part VI

Clinical judgment in medicine and psychology

One of the cornerstones of judgment and decision-making research was laid in the 1940s and 1950s with the early studies of clinical judgment described in Paul Meehl's classic volume *Clinical versus Statistical Prediction: A Theoretical Analysis and a Review of the Evidence* (1954; see Chapter 33). Clinical judgment is the name given to the cognitive activity of skilled professionals (e.g., clinical psychologists, medical doctors, nurses, social workers), who review a large amount of clinical data (signs, symptoms, laboratory reports, etc.) regarding a patient's or client's situation, organize the information in their minds according to their training and experience, and offer a diagnosis or prognosis. Clinical judgment thus provided researchers with an excellent research site for studying complex cognitive activity in a rigorous, scientific manner. For one thing, they could directly investigate the judgments of mature, professional persons, thereby avoiding the artificiality of social experimentation in the laboratory. Additionally, because clinicians routinely make judgments about many patients or clients, powerful methods of statistical analysis (e.g., multiple regression), which must be implemented over a large number of observations, could be used to study each clinician individually. Each clinician's judgment process could be "externalized" and thus understood. This method has enormous advantages over comparing the "mean response" of subjects in experimental and control groups.

Interest in judgment and decision making was sparked by the startling results of the initial studies of clinical judgment. Researchers developed mathematical formulas that were intended to be "models" of the judgment process and then tested the ability of clinical psychologists to predict behavior against the performance of mathematical formulas, given the same data. Although it seemed a foregone conclusion at the time that sophisticated clinical psychologists would provide more accurate predictions than the mechanical operation of mathematical formulas, the reverse was found to be true. The question was addressed again and again, but the early studies withstood repeated attempts by researchers to discover artifacts and methodological flaws.

Part VI begins with an article by Lewis R. Goldberg that was highly influential in establishing the validity of judgment and decision-making research. We have included this article not only because it provides a useful summary of the judgment and decision-making field as it stood in 1968 but also because by that time Goldberg could refer to research that demonstrated *why* an equation could make more accurate predictions than clinical judgment. Empirical observations were enhanced by understanding.

The study of clinical judgment soon spread from psychology to medicine, to the medical and behavioral judgments of doctors and nurses, and now there is a professional society and journal dedicated to the study of "medical decision making." We have included four articles that show the impact of the conclusions reviewed by Goldberg on medical decision making. The study by James C. Sisson, Eric B. Schoomaker, and Jon C. Ross directly addresses the common fallacy that "more information is always better." The article by J. R. Kirwan, D. M. Chaput de Saintonge, C. R. B. Joyce, and H. L. F. Currey documents the validity and utility of the "paper patient," which is commonly used in judgment and decision research, and shows how much can be learned about clinical judgments in medicine from judgments about hypothetical patients whose signs and symptoms are presented as data profiles. David L. Zalkind and Richard H. Shachtman's article shows the application of decision analysis to an important episode in the history of medical decision making – the "swine flu" vaccination decision. Finally, we include the article by Barbara J. McNeil and her colleagues that not only demonstrates that the manner in which information is presented to patients influences the choice of alternate therapies but, perhaps equally important, demonstrates that research in medical decision making is now acceptable for publication in the prestigious *New England Journal of Medicine*.

The conclusions reviewed by Goldberg in 1968 have been strengthened by work in the 1970s and 1980s that has uncovered other limitations in human judgment (see, e.g., Chapter 2). It is now conceded that several types of behavior are better predicted by equations than by professionally trained practitioners. For example, the American Psychiatric Association now goes so far as to plead that its members *not* be asked by the courts to predict whether defendants are likely to commit acts of violence at a future time. A discussion of the wide-ranging moral and legal implications of the fallibility of clinical judgments can be found in Alan Stone's *Law, Psychiatry, and Morality* (1984; see Suggested Readings).

19. Simple models or simple processes? Some research on clinical judgments

Lewis R. Goldberg

Imagine the following situation: You are sitting unobserved in a physician's office watching a week of his professional activities. During the course of the week, some 100 patients come to his office, each telling him of his symptoms, which you record; after each patient leaves the office, and any requested laboratory findings have arrived, the physician records his diagnosis for that patient. At the end of the week you have collected a set of 100 symptom configurations, one for each patient, and a set of 100 corresponding diagnoses.

Alternatively, you are sitting unobserved in the office of a personnel officer of a large manufacturing concern. He has 100 folders on his desk, each containing information about a different applicant for 50 sales positions with his company. He spends his week carefully looking through the application materials for each applicant – examining the applicant's test scores, the ratings made by each of the company's three initial interviewers, and the reference forms from each of the applicant's past employers. When he has completed examining the materials for each applicant in turn, he records his selection decision. At the end of the week each of the 100 folders of application data has a corresponding personnel recommendation associated with it.

Again alternatively, you are watching a clinical psychologist function over the course of a month at a busy outpatient psychiatric clinic. Most of his day he spends administering tests and interviewing patients. But, for a few hours at the end of every day he gathers together all of the information he has collected on one patient, examines it all carefully, and proceeds to write a report of his findings. In this report he includes some descriptive statements about the patient and his problems, the patient's

This chapter originally appeared in the *American Psychologist*, 1968, 23(7), 483–496. Copyright © 1968 by the American Psychological Association, Inc. Reprinted by permission.

diagnosis, and some predictions of the likelihood of certain important consequences for the clinic (e.g., the probability of the patient committing suicide, his probable response to treatment, etc.). The data collected from the patient (test scores, interview notes, etc.) are stored in one folder; the resulting reports are sent elsewhere in the clinic. At the end of the month, you can gather together 100 patient folders, plus the 100 corresponding psychological reports.

Each of these three professional activities has as its central core a reliance upon what the practitioner might call "clinical wisdom," but which in psychology is more modestly called "clinical judgment." Each is an important human cognitive activity, typically carried out by a professional person, aimed at the prediction of significant outcomes in the life of another individual. When the same type of prediction is made repeatedly by the same judge, using the same type of information as a basis for his judgments, then the process becomes amenable to scientific study. And, not surprisingly, over the past 20 years the clinical judgment process has begun to be studied intensively by investigators all over the world.

The focus on accuracy

Historically, the earliest research efforts centered on the accuracy of such clinical judgments. And, since World War II had sparked the emergence of clinical psychology as an applied speciality area (in which, at least at first, clinicians spent a good deal of their professional time making diagnostic judgments), it was natural that the first major focus of accuracy research was upon the diagnostic acumen of clinical psychologists themselves. Over the past 20 years, a flurry of such studies has appeared, the most dramatic and influential being the early ones reported by Kelly and Fiske (1951) and Holtzman and Sells (1954).

Studies of the accuracy of these sorts of judgments have yielded rather discouraging conclusions. For example, one surprising finding – that the amount of professional training and experience of the judge does not relate to his judgmental accuracy – has appeared in a number of studies (e.g., Goldberg, 1959; Hiler & Nesvig, 1965; Johnston & McNeal, 1967; Levy & Ulman, 1967; Luft, 1950; Oskamp, 1962, 1967; Schaeffer, 1964; Silverman, 1959; Stricker, 1967). Equally disheartening, there is now a host of studies demonstrating that the amount of information available to the judge is not related to the accuracy of his resulting inferences (e.g., Borke & Fiske, 1957; Giedt, 1955; Golden, 1964; Grant, Ives, & Ranzoni, 1952; Grigg, 1958; Hunt & Walker, 1966; Jones, 1959; Kostlan, 1954; Luft, 1951; Marks, 1961; Schwartz, 1967; Sines, 1959; Soskin, 1959; Winch & More, 1956). Let us look at Oskamp's (1965) study as one example of some of these findings.

Oskamp had 32 judges, including 8 experienced clinical psychologists, read background information about a published case, divided into four sections. After reading each section of the case in turn, and thus before seeing any other information, each judge answered a set of 25 questions about the personality of the target (questions for which the correct answers were known to the investigator). For each question, the judge also indicated his confidence in the accuracy of his prediction by indicating the percentage of questions answered with that much confidence that he would expect to answer correctly. Oskamp found that as the amount of information about the target increased, accuracy remained at about the same level, while confidence increased dramatically. In general, the average judge was slightly overconfident when he had only one-fourth of the total amount of data available to him (he estimated that he would be correct on 33% of the questions, while he was actually correct on 26%); by the time he had seen all of the information, however, he was extremely overconfident (53% estimated correct versus 28% actually correct). Oskamp (1965) concluded:

the judges' confidence ratings show that *they become convinced of their own increasing understanding of the case*. As they received more information their confidence soared. Furthermore, their certainty about their decisions became entirely out of proportion to the actual correctness of those decisions. (p. 264)

For another demonstration of this same phenomenon, see Ryback (1967).

Such findings relative to the validity of clinical judgments obviously raise questions as to their reliability. Within the judgment domain, we can distinguish at least three different types of inferential reliability (Goldberg & Werts, 1966): (a) *stability*, or reliability across time (for the same judge using the same data); (b) *consensus*, or reliability across judges (for the same data and the same occasion); and (c) *convergence*, or reliability across data sources (administered on the same occasion and interpreted by the same judge). While the relatively few investigations of judgmental stability have concluded that judges may show substantial consistency in their judgments over time, the vast majority of reliability studies have focused upon judgmental consensus and have come to widely disparate conclusions. Findings have ranged from extremely high consensus on some judgmental tasks (e.g., Bryan, Hunt, & Walker, 1966; Goldberg, 1966; Hunt & Jones, 1958a, 1958b; Hunt, Jones, & Hunt, 1957; Hunt, Walker, & Jones, 1960; Weitman, 1962; Winslow & Rapersand, 1964) to virtually no consensus on other tasks (e.g., Brodie, 1964; Grosz & Grossman, 1964; Gunderson, 1965a, 1965b; Howard, 1963; Marks, 1961; Ringuette & Kennedy, 1966; Watley, 1967; Watson, 1967).

The classic study of the convergence among clinical inferences was carried out by Little and Schneidman (1959), who concluded that the reliability of clinicians' judgments leaves "much to be desired" (a most dramatic understatement if one examines their important findings). In a more recent study, Goldberg and Werts (1966) concluded that "an experienced clinician's judgments from one data source do *not* correlate with another clinician's judgments from another data source, even though both clinicians are diagnosing the very same patient on – ostensibly – the very same trait" (p. 205). Most of the other studies of judgmental convergence (e.g., Howard, 1962, 1963; Phelan, 1964, 1965; Vandenberg, Rosenzweig, Moore, & Dukay, 1964; Wallach & Schooff, 1965) have tended to confirm this somewhat dismal general picture.

If one considers the rather typical findings that clinical judgments tend to be (*a*) rather unreliable (in at least two of the three senses of that term), (*b*) only minimally related to the confidence and to the amount of experience of the judge, (*c*) relatively unaffected by the amount of information available to the judge, and (*d*) rather low in validity on an absolute basis, it should come as no great surprise that such judgments are increasingly under attack by those who wish to substitute actuarial prediction systems for the human judge in many applied settings. Since I assume that virtually all psychologists are acquainted with what has come to be known as the "clinical versus statistical prediction controversy" (e.g., Gough, 1962; Meehl, 1954, 1956, 1957, 1959, 1960; Sawyer, 1966), I can summarize this ever-growing body of literature by pointing out that over a rather large array of clinical judgment tasks (including by now some which were specifically selected to show the clinician at his best and the actuary at his worst), rather simple actuarial formulae typically can be constructed to perform at a level of validity no lower than that of the clinical expert.

The focus on the judgment process

As a consequence of these sorts of findings, the research focus among judgmental investigators has begun to turn from validity studies to investigations of the process of clinical inference, the aim of which is to "represent" (or "simulate" or "model") the hidden cognitive processes of the clinician as he makes his judgmental decisions (Hoffman, 1960). Hopefully, by understanding this process more completely than we do today, clinical training programs can be made more effective and judgmental accuracy can thereby be increased.

An investigator of the clinical judgment process might express his aims through the following questions: By what psychological model can one best depict the cognitive activities of a judge? More specifically, what model allows one to use the same data available to the judge and combine these data so as to simulate most accurately the judgments he actually makes? To return to the three illustrative examples described at the beginning of this paper, these questions could be reformulated, respectively:

1. By what model can the 100 symptom configurations from each of the 100 patients be combined so as to generate most accurately the physician's resulting diagnoses?
2. By what model can the information extracted from the 100 applicant folders be combined so as to produce the most accurate prediction of the personnel officer's selection decisions?
3. By what model can the information from the psychological folders of the 100 psychiatric patients be combined so as to most accurately reproduce the material found in the 100 psychological reports?

All of these questions have some common elements, namely, (a) a search for some formal (i.e., specifiable) model, which (b) uses as its "input" the information (data, cues, symptoms, etc.) initially presented to the judge, and (c) combines the data in some optimal manner, so as to (d) produce as accurate as possible a copy of the responses of the judge – (e) regardless of the actual validity of those judgments themselves. Note that such a model is always an intraindividual one; that is, it is intended as a representation of the cognitive activities of a single judge. Moreover, the test of the model is not how well it works as a representation of the state of the world (e.g., how well it predicts who will or will not be a successful employee), but rather how well it predicts the inferential products of the judge himself.

In mathematical terms, one begins with a cue matrix of size $M \times N$, where M = the number of variables presented to the judge and N = the number of targets for which the judge is asked to predict. One wishes to discover some combinatorial model which will reproduce as accurately as possible the vector of N responses produced by the judge to the same cue matrix. For this process to be amenable to mathematical analyses, the original cue matrix and the terminal judgmental response vector should be in a quantified format (or in a format easily transformable into a set of numbers). While it is fashionable to lament about the difficulty of transforming "behavioral" data into quantitative form, this difficulty may be more apparent than real. For if the cues (and resulting judgments) can be represented in even so simple a form as a binary digit (e.g., the patient has characteristic X versus the patient does not have this characteristic), then quantification is straightforward (e.g., $X = 0$; non-$X = 1$). Since a good deal of the data available to many clinicians is already in quantitative form (e.g., test scores, laboratory findings) or can be easily transformed quantitatively with no apparent loss of information (e.g., trait ratings), it is typical for most judgmental investigators to simply present the data to the judge and ask for the judgmental responses in a previously quantified format.

What sort of judgmental model should one try? Since introspective accounts describe the clinical judgment process as curvilinear, configural, and sequential (e.g., McArthur, 1954; Meehl, 1954, 1960; Parker, 1958), one possible strategy is to begin with fairly complex representations, perhaps with an eye to seeing how they may eventually be simplified. For example, Kleinmuntz (1963a, 1963b, 1963c) had a clinician "think aloud" into a tape recorder as he made judgments about the adjustment of college students on the basis of their MMPI profiles. Kleinmuntz then used these introspections to construct a computer program simulating the clinician's thought processes. The resulting program was a complex sequential (e.g., hierarchical or "tree") representation of the clinician's verbal reports.

The research of investigators at two major centers for research on clinical inference – Oregon Research Institute and the Behavior Research Laboratory of the University of Colorado – has proceeded from a diametrically opposite strategy (see Hammond, Hursch, & Todd, 1964; Hoffman, 1960), namely, to start with an extremely simple model and then to proceed to introduce complications only so far as is necessary to reproduce the inferential responses of a particular judge. Rather than beginning with a model which is already complex (e.g., curvilinear, configural, sequential) as Kleinmuntz did, we have opted to start with what is perhaps the simplest of all models: a linear, additive, regression model (of the sort now used rather universally for a host of applied prediction problems). That is, we begin with the hopefully naive assumption that the responses of a person in a judgment task can be reproduced by a mathematical model of the form:

$$Z = b_1X_1 + b_2X_2 + \ldots + b_kX_k$$

where Z is the vector of judgmental responses, $X_1 \ldots X_k$ are the values of the matrix of K cues by N targets presented to the judge, and $b_1 \ldots b_k$ are constants representing the "weight" of each cue in the judgmental model. In practice, the X values (the $N \times K$ matrix of cues) are known to the investigators (they are the stimulus or input variables presented to the judge) and the Z values are produced by the judge during the course of the experiment. The b values (regression weights) are found from one subset of the judge's responses by a standard linear regression analysis, and the "accuracy" of this linear model can then be ascertained by cross-validating these regression weights on the other subset of the judge's responses. The resulting correlation coefficient (R_a) represents the extent of agreement between the linear model and the inferential products of the judge.

Since we routinely ask each judge to make his judgments on two occasions (typically these "retest" protocols are sandwiched among the original protocols so that the judge is unaware of the fact that he is ever judging the exact same protocol twice), it is possible to compute a reliability coefficient (r_{tt}) to represent the stability of the judge's responses (or, alternatively, the extent to which one can predict his judgments from his own previous judgments of the same stimuli). This reliability coefficient can be viewed as the upper limit to the predictability of any model which we might construct. To the extent that the value of R_a approaches the value of r_{tt}, the model can be seen as representing the cognitive processes of the judge. When R_a and r_{tt} are identical for a particular judge, we have a perfect "paramorphic representation" of his judgment processes. Hoffman (1960) introduced this term to indicate that we do not pretend to be mapping any mind in an "isomorphic" fashion, but are merely seeking to discover some model which accurately generates the judgmental responses themselves.

Since clinicians generally describe their cognitive processes as complex ones involving the curvilinear, configural, and sequential utilization of cues, one might expect that the linear additive model would provide a rather poor representation of their judgments. Consequently, we might anticipate the need to introduce into the model mathematical expressions to represent these more complex processes. For example, if the judge is using a particular cue (X) in a curvilinear fashion (e.g., a personnel officer may feel that applicants who score in the middle range of a standardized intelligence test will be more successful salesmen than those who score at either extreme), then we may be able to approximate this judgmental process by adding to the model terms like X^2, or X^3, X^4, etc. That is, we can represent curvilinear cue utilization generally by introducing into the more basic equation terms of the form bX^a, where X represents the cue value, a is a power constant reflecting the particular curvilinear use of that cue by the judge, and b is once again the weight of the entire term in the overall judgmental model.

While clinicians frequently attest that they use cues in a curvilinear fashion, even more commonly do they call attention to their use of cues in a configural (or interactive) manner. What they mean is that their judgments are not simply dependent on the value of a particular cue, but rather that the relationship between cue X_1 and their response is dependent upon (i.e., interacts with) the value of a second cue, X_2. For example, a physician might feel that body temperature is positively related to the likelihood of some disease if a patient has symptom Y, while temperature has no relevance for this diagnosis if the patient does not have symptom Y. Therefore, once again we must find mathematical expressions which approximate such configural cue usage. One way to express the interactive use of two cues, X_1 and X_2, is by the product term, $X_1 \cdot X_2$. Higher order interactions could be introduced into the basic equation by using even more complex cross-products (e.g., $X_1 \cdot X_2 \cdot X_3$, a term analogous to the three-way interaction line in the classical analysis of variance).

What should be clear from these examples is that we can systematically begin to introduce more complex terms into the basic multiple regression model and see whether the new models are more adequate representations of the judge's mental processes than was the original linear one. In general, we can introduce curvilinearity in cue utilization, for example,

$$\sum_{i=1}^{k} b_i X_i^{ai}$$

configurality, for example,

$$\sum_{i=1}^{k-1} \sum_{j=2}^{k} b_{ij} X_i \cdot X_j \qquad (i < j)$$

and, of course, much more complex sets of terms, for example,

$$\sum_{i=1}^{k-1} \sum_{j=2}^{k} b_{ij} X_i^{ai} \cdot X_j^{aj} \qquad (i < j)$$

While the introduction of additional terms into the model can never serve to decrease its accuracy in the sample of judgments used to derive the b weights, these extra terms may simply serve to explain chance characteristics of the particular judgments from the derivation sample and thus can severely attenuate the accuracy of the resulting model upon its cross-validation in another sample of judgments. However, when the judge is actually using the cues in a curvilinear or in a configural manner, then the introduction of the mathematical approximations of these processes should serve to improve the model.

While the preceding discussion has focused primarily on the use of multiple regression techniques, it could just as easily have been formulated in terms of the fixed-model analysis of variance (ANOVA), both systems simply being alternative formulations of a general linear model. Since the structural elements underlying both the multiple regression and the ANOVA model are formally equivalent, it is often possible to use the latter in judgment studies – thereby capitalizing on the well-known descriptive and inferential properties of ANOVA (Hoffman, Slovic, & Rorer, 1968). However, the ANOVA model imposes two important restrictions on the cue values to be used in judgment research: (a) the cues must be treated as categorical rather than continuous variables; and (b) the cues must be orthogonal (uncorrelated). While these restrictions make the ANOVA model less suitable for some real life judgment situations (for example, differential diagnosis from the profile of highly correlated MMPI scale scores), there are many real situations – plus a host of contrived situations – where the restrictions are not too severe. In some of these cases, it is possible to use a completely crossed experimental design (all possible combinations of each of the cue levels), provided that neither the number of cues nor the number of levels per cue is too large.

When judgments are analyzed in terms of the ANOVA model, a significant main effect for cue X_1 implies that the judge's responses varied systematically with X_1 as the levels of the other cues were held constant.

Provided sufficient levels of the factor were included in the design, the main effect may be divided into effects due to linear, quadratic, and cubic (i.e., curvilinear) trends. Similarly, a significant interaction between cues X_1 and X_2 implies that the judge was responding to particular patterns of those cues (i.e., the configural effect of variation of cue X_1 upon judgment differed as a function of the corresponding level taken by cue X_2). Moreover, it is possible to calculate an index of the importance of individual or configural use of a cue, relative to the importance of other cues. The index ω^2, described by Hays (1963), provides a rough estimate of the proportion of the total variation in a person's judgments which can be predicted from a knowledge of the particular levels of a given cue or of a configural pattern of cues. An alternative technique for expressing the extent of configural cue usage in the judgment process has been proposed by Hammond et al. (1964).

The search for configural judges

With this technical digression now out of the way, let us return to some empirical studies of the clinical judgment process. You will recall that while our research strategy forces us to begin with a simple linear additive model, this model should soon give way to more complex ones, as configural and curvilinear terms are added to fit the judgmental processes of each particular judge. However, in study after study our initial hopes went unrealized; the accuracy of the linear model was almost always at approximately the same level as the reliability of the judgments themselves, and – no doubt because of this – the introduction of more complex terms into the basic equation rarely served to significantly increase the cross-validity of the new model. Hammond and Summers (1965) have reviewed a series of studies in which the same general finding has emerged: for a number of different judgment tasks and across a considerable range of judges, the simple linear model appeared to characterize quite adequately the judgmental processes involved – in spite of the reports of the judges that they were using cues in a highly configural manner.

Three possible hypotheses spring to mind to account for these findings: (a) human judges behave in fact remarkably like linear data processors, but somehow they believe that they are more complex than they really are; (b) human judges behave in fact in a rather configural fashion, but the power of the linear regression model is so great that it serves to obscure[1] the real configural processes in judgment; (c) human judges

---

[1] In the same way, a straight line can provide an excellent approximation of many curved lines, exemplified by the fact that we often use a straight line to navigate between two cities even though the real route is along a curved arc. For an excellent discussion of this point, see Ghiselli (1964, pp. 3–7). For a more complete treatment of this topic in judgment research, see Hoffman (1968).

behave in fact in a decidedly linear fashion on most judgmental tasks (their reports notwithstanding), but for some kinds of tasks they use more complex judgmental processes.

During the past few years, my colleagues at Oregon Research Institute and I have been systematically experimenting to see which of these three hypotheses is the most plausible. Our general goals have been (a) to discover and use some alternative judgmental models which allow more rigorous checks on the process of cue utilization (e.g., Hoffman, 1967), and (b) to discover and study some new judgmental tasks – tasks where configural cue utilization is most likely to be necessary for making accurate inferences and therefore where configural judgmental processes are most likely to be found. The remainder of this paper will focus primarily on our efforts to achieve this latter goal.

The search for inherently configural tasks has led to three major fields: physical medicine, psychiatry, and clinical psychology. Subject matter experts in each of these fields were consulted in search of diagnostic decisions of a clearly configural nature, and three judgmental tasks – one from each field – were finally selected for intensive study. Experienced medical gastroenterologists chose the first purportedly highly configural task: the differential diagnosis of a benign versus malignant gastric ulcer from the signs which are visible on a stomach X ray. The staff of a large psychiatric hospital provided a second important clinical judgment task: the decision to permit temporary liberty for a chronic patient committed to a psychiatric hospital. And finally, Paul Meehl (1959) chose the third purportedly highly configural judgment task: the differential diagnosis of psychosis versus neurosis from a patient's MMPI profile.

Let us begin with the problem from medicine, the diagnosis of benign versus malignant gastric ulcers (Hoffman et al., 1968). Physicians have assured us that there are seven major signs which can be seen in X rays of gastric ulcer patients and that this diagnostic problem can be assessed only by the configural (interactive) use of these seven cues. The seven cues are either present or absent in a given X ray, and one of the cues can only occur when another one is present; consequently, two of the seven cues can be combined into one variable having three levels, while each of the other five cues has two levels (absent versus present). There are thus 3×2^5, or 96, possible combinations of all seven cues. Nine judges, six experienced radiologists and three radiology residents, were asked to make differential diagnoses for 192 presumably real, but actually hypothetical, patients (two administrations of each of the 96 possible cue combinations). The judges made their diagnoses on a seven-point scale, from "definitely benign," through "uncertain," to "definitely malignant." The inferences of each judge were analyzed by the ANOVA model to ascertain the proportion of the variance in his diagnoses associated with each of the 6 possible main effects (i.e., linear use of the cues), each of the 15 possible two-way interactions, each of the 20 possible three-way interactions, each of the 15 possible four-way interactions, each of the 6 possible five-way interactions, and the 1 six-way interaction.

The major finding was that the largest of the 57 possible interactions, for the most configural judge, accounted for but 3% of the variance of his responses. In the investigators' own words (Hoffman et al., 1968):

the largest main effect usually accounted for 10 to 40 times as much of the total variance in the judgments as the largest interaction. On the average, roughly 90% of a judge's reliable variation of response could be predicted by a simple formula combining only individual symptoms in an additive fashion and completely ignoring interactions. (pp. 343–344)

it should be noted that the performance of the judges in this study was rather adequately accounted for in terms of linear effects, in spite of the fact that a deliberate attempt had been made to select a task in which persons would combine cues configurally. (p. 347)

While these findings may be disheartening to judgment researchers, another finding could be more generally terrifying. When one examines the degree of agreement between physicians for this diagnostic problem, these interjudge correlations were distressingly low. Of the 36 coefficients of consensus, 3 were negative – the median correlation being only .38. The intrajudge test-retest correlations were reasonably high (ranging .60–.92, Mdn = .80), and the task itself was certainly not seen as an impossibly difficult one. Yet, these findings suggest that diagnostic agreement in clinical medicine may not be much greater than that found in clinical psychology – some food for thought during your next visit to the family doctor.[2]

Let us turn now to some ANOVA analyses of another judgmental task, the decision whether or not to grant temporary liberty to a psychiatric patient (Rorer, Hoffman, Dickman, & Slovic, 1967). The six presumably most relevant variables for making this decision were used in this study. With two levels of each variable (e.g., "Does the patient have a problem with drinking?" "Yes" versus "No"), there were thus 2^6, or 64, possible cue combinations. Twenty-four members of the professional staff of a psychiatric hospital – 6 physicians, 12 nurses, 3 clinical psychologists, and 3 psychiatric social workers – served as judges. Each of them decided whether 128 presumably real, but actually hypothetical, patients (two administrations of each of the 64 possible cue configurations) should be granted the privilege of leaving the hospital for 8 hours on a weekend. Again, as in the previous study, the judgments from each judge were analyzed individually to ascertain the proportion of his response variance, which was associated with each of the six main effects and each of the possible two-way, three-way, four-way, five-way, and six-way interactions.

---

[2] For some intriguing corroborative evidence concerning this seemingly subversive statement see Garland (1959, 1960).

The results were, unfortunately, remarkably similar to those from the previous study. On the average, less than 2% of the variance of these judgments was associated with the largest interaction term, these percentages ranging across the 24 judges from virtually zero to less than 6%. And again, one of the most striking findings was the great diversity – the startling lack of interjudge agreement – among clinicians for this judgment task.

Let us now turn to the third purportedly configural judgment task, the differential diagnosis of neurotic from psychotic patients by means of their MMPI profiles. Paul Meehl (1959) initially focused research on this task on the grounds that: "the differences between psychotic and neurotic profiles are considered in MMPI lore to be highly configural in character, so that an atomistic treatment by combining single scales linearly should theoretically be a very poor substitute for a configural approach" (p. 104). Meehl collected 861 MMPI profiles from seven hospitals and clinics throughout the United States; each of these profiles was produced from the MMPI responses of a psychiatric patient who had been diagnosed by the psychiatric staff as being rather clearly either psychotic or neurotic – the total sample containing approximately equal numbers of both diagnostic groups. Twenty-nine clinicians (13 PhD clinical psychologists, plus 16 advanced graduate students in clinical psychology) attempted to diagnose each of the 861 patients from their MMPI profiles; the 29 judges rated each profile on an 11-step forced-normal distribution from least to most psychotic. After making some preliminary comparisons of the validity of the clinicians' judgments with the validities achieved by various actuarial techniques (Meehl, 1959), Meehl generously turned over these valuable data to Oregon Research Institute for further analyses.

An extensive investigation of the validity of the clinicians' judgments, as compared to that of numerous MMPI signs and indexes, has already been published (L. R. Goldberg, 1965). As in many previous judgment studies, accuracy on this task was not associated with the amount of professional experience of the judge; the average PhD psychologist achieved a validity coefficient identical to that of the average graduate student. Moreover, an unweighted composite of five MMPI scale scores $(L + Pa + Sc - Hy - Pt)$ achieved a validity coefficient $(r = .44)$ greater than that of the average judge $(r = .28)$, greater than that of the pooled ratings of all 29 clinicians $(r = .35)$, and even greater than that of the single most accurate judge $(r = .39)$. Moreover, I recently discovered a moderator for the above index, namely another unweighted linear composite $(D + Pd + Sc - F - Hs - Pa)$; when some 1248 patients were divided into three subsamples on the basis of their scores on the moderator variable (i.e., high versus medium versus low moderator scores), the validity coefficients for the three groups were .27, .42, and .58, respectively.

When one turns from analyses of validity to those focused on the judgment process, conclusions become more difficult. For unlike the two previously described judgmental tasks, this one has some serious limitations. Two of these problems are inherent to the task, while a third stems from Meehl's (1959) experimental procedures: (*a*) the 11 MMPI scale scores presented to the judges are not orthogonal (the 55 intercorrelations range up to almost .80 – for example, *Hs* versus *Hy* – 8 of them being higher than .50); (*b*) each scale score is a relatively continuous variable covering a considerable range of scale values; and (*c*) the 29 clinicians in Meehl's original study judged each of the 861 profiles only once (i.e., no repeated profiles were presented). For reasons *a* and *b* the ANOVA model is inappropriate for these data, and for reason *c* it is impossible to ascertain to what extent various judgment models approach the reliability of the judges' responses, since these reliability values are not known. Nonetheless, it has been possible to make some estimates about the nature of these clinical judgments (Wiggins & Hoffman, 1968).

Wiggins and Hoffman (1968) compared – as representations of the cognitive processes of each of the 29 clinicians – the following three models: (*a*) the standard linear regression model; (*b*) a quadratic model, which added to the first model all squared terms (e.g., X_1^2) and cross-product terms (e.g., $X_1 \cdot X_2$); and (*c*) a "sign" model, which included a set of 70 MMPI diagnostic signs from the psychometric literature. While Wiggins and Hoffman (1968) interpreted their findings as indicating that, for some judges, one of the non-linear models provided a slightly better representation of their judgments than the linear model, nonetheless, the most overwhelming finding from this study was how much of the variance in clinicians' judgments could be represented by the linear model. For example, if one compares the judgment correlations produced by the linear model with those from each of the two configural models (see Wiggins & Hoffman, 1968, Table 3), one finds that (*a*) the linear model was equal to, or superior to, the quadratic model for 23 of the 29 judges (and at best, for the most configural judge, the quadratic model produced a correlation with his judgments which was only .03 greater than that of the linear model); and (*b*) the linear model was equal to, or superior to, the sign model for 17 judges (the superiority of the sign model being but .04 for the single most configural judge). In the authors' own words,

A note of caution should be added to the discussion of differences between linear and configural judges. Though the differences appear reliable, their magnitude is not large; the judgments of even the most seemingly configural clinicians can often be estimated with good precision by a linear model. (pp. 76–77)

Once again, the linear model provided an excellent representation of the judgments of most of these clinicians, even for a task which they believed to be a highly configural one.

The point of this discussion is *not* to assert that clinicians, including the many clinicians studied in the experiments already described, cannot and do not use cue relationships more complex than simple linear ones. In the first two of these studies, for example, there were one or more statistically significant interactions in the judgment models of at least some of the clinicians, and in the third study there were clinicians whose judgments were at least slightly better represented by a model other than the linear one. Moreover, Paul Slovic (1968) has recently demonstrated that the judgments of each of two professional stockbrokers, asked to predict future stock prices from 11 dichotomized indexes, showed significant interactions which are explainable in terms of the theoretical orientations of the brokers themselves. And, in a number of other judgmental studies (e.g., Slovic, 1966a), evidence of configural cue utilization has been uncovered. Clearly, clinical judgments *can* involve the configural utilization of cues. What are, then, the implications from these judgmental investigations?

First of all, it is important to realize that the very power of the linear regression model to predict observations generated by a large class of nonlinear processes can serve to obscure our understanding of all but the more gross types of configural judgments. Yntema and Torgerson (1961) and Rorer (1967) have both demonstrated rather dramatically how observations generated by nonlinear processes can become interpreted as linear ones when analyzed by standard regression and ANOVA methodology; Hoffman et al. (1968) and Hoffman (1968) provide an excellent discussion of this problem as it applies to the judgment process. If we return once again to the three competing hypotheses which provided the framework for launching these judgmental investigations, I would now assert that our original hypothesis (b) – that judges can process information in a configural fashion, but that the general linear model is powerful enough to reproduce most of these judgments with very small error – is, at this point, certainly the most compelling one.

Consequently, if one's sole purpose is to reproduce the responses of most clinical judges, then a simple linear model will normally permit the reproduction of 90%–100% of their reliable judgmental variance, probably in most – if not all – clinical judgment tasks. While Meehl (1959) has suggested that one potential superiority of the clinician over the actuary lies in the human's ability to process cues in a configural fashion, it is important to realize that this is neither an inherent advantage of the human judge (i.e., the actuary can include nonlinear terms in his equations), nor is this attribute – in any case – likely to be the clinician's "ace in the hole." If the clinician does have a long suit – and the numerous clinical versus statistical studies have not yet demonstrated that he has – it is extremely unlikely that it will stem from his alleged ability to process information in a complex configural manner.

Learning clinical inference

If "clinical wisdom" results in linearly reproducible judgments of rather low validity, it becomes sensible to ask whether these judgments could not be improved through training. Leonard G. Rorer and I reasoned that the major cause of the low validity coefficients reported for the judgments of practicing clinicians is the fact that in most, if not all, clinical settings there is no realistic opportunity for the clinician to improve his predictive accuracy. For learning to occur, some systematic feedback regarding the accuracy of the judgmental response must be linked to the particular cue configuration which led the clinician to make that judgment. But, in clinical practice feedback is virtually nonexistent, and in the relatively rare cases when feedback does occur the long interval of time which elapses between the prediction and the feedback serves to ensure that the initial cue configuration leading to the prediction has disappeared from the clinician's memory. As an example, say a clinician infers the prognosis "high suicide potential" from the MMPI profile of Patient A and writes in his report a statement like "Patient A has a high risk of committing suicide and therefore should be carefully watched." In most cases Patient A eventually returns to the community or moves to another hospital, and the clinician does not know whether the patient ever attempted suicide (accurate inference) or not (inaccurate inference). And if in 3 years the clinician happens to read in the newspaper that Patient A committed suicide, he is unlikely to be able to recall the particular MMPI profile configuration which initially led to his (successful) prediction, with the result that the "cue configuration → suicide inference" link is in no way strengthened.[3]

What is necessary for clinical inference to be learned, Rorer and I reasoned, is that the clinician obtain immediate feedback concerning the accuracy of his judgments – ideally feedback which occurs after the judgmental response has been formulated but before the removal of the cue configuration which led the clinician to that response. Moreover, if the cues are related to the criterion in some curvilinear and/or configural manner, then the clinician should be able to learn these more complex relationships, modify his own judgmental processes to incorporate such configural elements, and thereby begin to make judgments for which the best representation is a more complex model than the linear one.

To test this hypothesis, Rorer and I designed a study in which judges were given immediate feedback on the same task previously described, namely, the differential diagnosis of psychosis versus neurosis from

---

[3] B. F. Skinner (1968) has made much the same point in rebutting the belief in the accumulated wisdom of the classroom teacher: "It is actually very difficult for teachers to profit from their experience. They almost never learn about their long-term successes or failures, and their short-term effects are not easily traced to the practices from which they presumably arose" (pp. 112–113).

MMPI profiles. Three groups of judges – termed expert, middle, and naive – were studied. The expert group was composed of three clinical psychologists who had had extensive MMPI experience. The naive group was composed of 10 non-psychologists who were unfamiliar with the MMPI and who were told only that their task was to learn to differentiate "N" from "P" profiles. The middle group was composed of 10 psychology graduate students who had at least a passing familiarity with the MMPI and some idea of the difference between a neurotic and a psychotic patient.

The judges received alternate weeks of training and testing. Five sets of 60 training profiles, each of which contained the criterion diagnosis on the back of the profile sheet, were assembled from 300 profiles drawn at random from one hospital sample. Thirty of these profiles in each set were repeated so that there was a total of 90 profiles in each training set. Ten testing sets were constructed, each set including profiles from a different clinical sample (one of which was the same as that used in the training set). Whenever possible, the testing set was composed of 100 profiles, 50 of which were then repeated, so that there was typically a total of 150 profiles in each testing set. Judges were instructed to diagnose the profiles from one set per day for 5 days per week. The judges were asked to classify each profile in turn and also to indicate their confidence in each of their judgments.

While all of the analyses of these data have not been completed, some preliminary results are available (Goldberg & Rorer, 1965; Rorer & Slovic, 1966). Let us first look at the levels of accuracy achieved after 9 weeks of daily training and 8 alternate weeks of daily testing. By this point, the judges had already received 90 training profiles per day (450 per week) for a total of over 4000 training profiles (each followed by immediate feedback), plus another 6000 testing profiles – over 10,000 profiles in all. But, while all three groups of judges manifested some learning on the training profiles, only the naive group showed *any* generalization of this training is improving their accuracy on the testing profiles. The average naive judge was correct about 52% of the time at the beginning, and after 17 weeks he had increased his accuracy to about 58%. The middle and expert judges were virtually indistinguishable, both groups achieving an average accuracy percentage around 65% at the beginning of training and the same figure after 17 weeks. Thus, even after 4000 training profiles, the average accuracy percentage for the naive judges was still substantially below that manifested by the expert and middle judges. For the expert and middle judges, training on this task turned out to almost completely sample specific; there was virtually no cross-sample generalization of learning as a result of intensive training on over 4000 MMPI profiles!

Faced with these startling findings, a number of experimental variations in the training procedures were introduced in an effort to increase judgmental accuracy. Two naive and two middle subjects were assigned to each of the following five sub-groups:

Standard condition

These subjects continued what they had been doing all along. They were therefore a control group for the other four experimental variations.

Group training

Two subjects worked together and agreed on a response. There was one naive pair and one middle pair. They were tested both individually and as a pair.

Generalization training

Subjects in the generalization training group were given training on previously unused profiles from those installations on which the judges had achieved their poorest results.

Formula training

These subjects were given the formula $(L + Pa + Sc - Hy - Pt)$ and told that it would increase the accuracy of their judgments. They were encouraged to use the formula as a guide to indicate the scales to which they might profitably attend.

Value training

The judges in this group, including all three experts, were given the numerical value of the formula for each profile and the optimum cutting score. They were told that this formula would achieve approximately 70% accuracy and that it would be more accurate for extreme values than for values close to the cutting score. They were free simply to report the formula diagnosis for every profile (a procedure which in every case would have allowed them to increase their judgmental accuracy), though they were encouraged to try to find ways in which they might improve on the formula decision.

After 8 more weeks (4 of training and 4 of testing), we found that those groups given value training (including all of the experts) had, on the average, increased their accuracy to a bit below 70% correct. But, none of the other experimental groups showed any substantial learning. Giving judges the optimal formula (formula training) resulted in a rapid increase in diagnostic accuracy (especially for the naive group), but this effect gradually wore away over time. By the end of the study of formula training groups were again achieving approximately the same level of accuracy as the standard training control groups. On the other hand, giving judges the actual values of the optimal formula for each profile (value training) did result in a stable increase in diagnostic accuracy, though the accuracy of these judges' diagnoses was not as high as would have been achieved by simply using the formula itself.

The thousands of judgments collected during those months of intensive training should yield many more nuggets than these few which I have scraped off the top. But, I doubt whether the conclusions we can already draw will have to be drastically changed. It now appears that our initial formulation of the problem of learning clinical inference was far too simple – that a good deal more than outcome feedback is necessary for judges to learn a task as difficult as the present one. The research of Chapman and Chapman (1967) serves to reinforce this belief by providing an even more stunning example of the pitfalls of relying solely upon feedback to improve the accuracy of clinical inferences.

In what is perhaps the most ingenious series of studies of clinical judgment ever carried out, Chapman and Chapman (1967) have demonstrated how prior expectations of the relationships between cues and criteria can lead to faulty observation and inference, even under seemingly excellent conditions for learning. The Chapmans exposed subjects to human figure drawings, each of which was paired with two criterion statements concerning the characteristics of the patients who allegedly drew the figures. Though these training materials were constructed so that there was no relationship between the cues and the criterion statements, most subjects erroneously "learned" the cue-criterion links which they had expected to see. In fact, the "illusory correlation" phenomena demonstrated by the Chapmans was such a powerful one that many subjects trained on materials where the cue-criterion relationships were constructed to be the opposite of those expected still persisted in "learning" the erroneous relationships! For further documentation of this pervasive source of bias in the learning of clinical (and other) types of inference see Chapman (1967).

The intriguing research of the Chapmans illustrates the ease with which one can "learn" relationships which do *not* exist. Our own MMPI learning research, plus that of others (e.g., Crow, 1957; Sechrest, Gallimore, & Hersch, 1967; Soskin, 1954), demonstrates the problems which can be encountered in learning those relationships which *do* exist. What now seems clear is that at least three conditions – all of which are are missing from the typical clinical setting – must hold if more complex clinical inferences are to be learned. First of all, some form of feedback (e.g., Skinner, 1968; Todd & Hammond, 1965) is a necessary, though not necessarily a sufficient, condition for learning to occur. Second, at least for problems of the complexity of many encountered in clinical practice, it may be necessary to be able to disturb the natural sequence of cue presentations – to rearrange the order of cases – so that one's hypotheses can be immediately verified or discounted. It does little good to formulate a rule for profile Type A, only to have to wait for another 100 profiles before an additional manifestation of Type A appears; what one must do is group together all Type A profiles in order to be able to verify one's initial inference. In the clinical setting this means studying those patients who manifest some particular cue configuration of interest, rather than taking patients as they come in the door. Finally, as the Chapmans' (1967) clever research so vividly demonstrates, it may often be necessary to *tally* the accuracy of one's hypotheses, thereby letting some variant of a paper-and-pencil boxscore substitute for the more ephemeral storage capacities of the unaided human brain.

But, what do we call this process which is characterized by a disruption of the naturally occuring order of observations, plus immediate feedback on cue-criterion links, followed by some concrete form of tallying the accuracy of one's hypotheses? We call it RESEARCH.

20. Clinical decision analysis: The hazard of using additional data

James C. Sisson, Eric B. Schoomaker, and Jon C. Ross

A little knowledge is a dangerous thing. Yet, the apparently obvious remedy for the deficiency – the acquisition of new information – may create a more hazardous state. In the practice of medicine, the numerous and rapidly proliferating diagnostic measurements provide attractive resources for the uncertain physician. Two major restraints on the use of procedures to gain information are the physical risk incurred and the cost. The latter has been a subject of numerous cost-benefit appraisals (Krieg, Gambino, & Galen, 1975; Griner & Liptzin, 1971; Neuhauser & Lewicki, 1975). However, transcending the problems posed by risk and cost of acquiring data is the possibility that the use of new information, generated by processes accepted by the medical community, may lead to a course of action that does more harm than good to patients. Delineation of this frequently overlooked danger in clinical practice and proposing a method to avoid it are the purposes of this communication.

The concept that additional knowledge may be deleterious to health is poorly understood by most physicians. It is derived from the nature of medical decision-making. To a large extent, clinical judgment is reached by intuition. In past decades, the number of variables observed in a patient were fewer, and the experienced physicians summated the importance of illness manifestations with remarkable accuracy. The capacity of clinicians to investigate disease processes (and thereby create data) has expanded enormously in recent years. Concomitantly, the potential to help and harm has been enhanced. When the factors from which clinical judgment is evolved become numerous and interacting, a physician using intuitive thinking may be unable to comprehend their

This chapter originally appeared in the *Journal of the American Medical Association*, 1976, 236(11), 1259–1263. Copyright © 1976 by the American Medical Association. *Reprinted by permission.*

aggregate meaning. Consequently, more data applied to a clinical problem may make the decision on management an inferior one.

Decision analysis

The dilemma of whether or not to obtain additional knowledge can be resolved by decision analysis, a well-established method for dealing with complex problems, including those of medical practice (Schwartz, Gorry, Kassirer, & Essig, 1973; Gorry, Kassirer, Essig, & Schwartz, 1973; McNeil, Varody, Burrows, & Adelstein, 1975; McNeil & Adelstein, 1975). The following two examples show how decision analysis can aid in attaining optimal clinical judgment.

Pancreatic cancer

Patients with cancer of the pancreas almost invariably die of the neoplasm. One reason for the inability to effect cure by surgical excision is the inability to establish the diagnosis early in the course of the disease. Metastases develop at a time when clinical findings are nonspecific and laboratory assays are insensitive.

The group most likely to have cancer of the pancreas consists of patients more than 40 years of age who have experienced midabdominal pain for one to three weeks. Assume that, in a retrospective study, 12 of 1000 in this group harbored pancreatic neoplasm.

Also assume that a new and virtually risk-free test has been developed to uncover carcinoma of the pancreas at an earlier stage than any currently available technique. In evaluations, this procedure detected an abnormality in 80% of patients with early pancreatic cancer; for individuals with similar symptoms but who ultimately were found to have no neoplasm, the test was abnormal in 5%. In a series of cases, the diagnosis was established so promptly that 50% of the cases were deemed cured after total pancreatectomy. Unfortunately, the results of the test can be confirmed only by careful histologic examination of the entire pancreas, and complete removal of the organ, whether for benign or malignant disease, carries a 10% mortality. To many physicians, this diagnostic procedure would appear to offer a reasonable approach, not unlike many others employed today to solve difficult clinical problems.

Accepting that actions will be directed by the information obtained from the new test, a decision analysis tree for the problem is constructed (Fig. 20.1). The assigned numbers are derived from a patient base of 1000, using the probabilities already noted at each branch. The square indicates a decision node, a branching point under control of the physician. The possible outcomes and the number of patients who would be expected to experience each outcome are summarized in Table 20.1

Use of the new data provided by the hypothetical test increases the

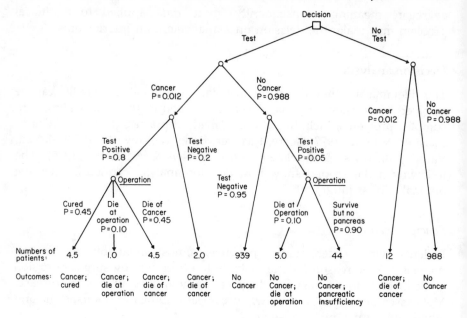

Figure 20.1. Beginning with a 1000-patient base at decision node (square), probabilities at each branch give number of patients arriving at each probability node (circles). Numbers of patients are recorded at bottom for each outcome and add up to 1000 for each decision: test or no test.

Table 20.1. *Testing for cancer of the pancreas: Possible outcomes*

| | Value of outcome | | |
	Better	Worse	Dead
Test ordered			
Patients with cancer of the pancreas			
Cured	4.5	...	...
Die at operation	...	...	1.0
Die of cancer	...	...	6.5
Patients without cancer of the pancreas			
Die at operation	...	...	5
Iatrogenic pancreatic insufficiency	...	44	...
Test not ordered			
Patients with cancer of the pancreas			
Die	...	...	12

Note: Patient base of 1000. Patients whose health or disease was not altered are not listed.

death rate (12.5 vs 12), and among the group who die are included five with benign disease. Moreover, the application of the new information also leads 44 patients without neoplasm to lifelong pancreatic insufficiency. Thus, additional knowledge, acquired through scientific and safe methods and no more imperfect than that available for many clinical judgments can, under some circumstances, cause more harm than good.

A major contributor to the undesirable outcomes when the test data are used is the 5% rate of false-positive results. In a subpopulation of those who have the disease for which testing is done, responses that are in the diagnostic range (outside the normal limits) are called true-positive; responses in the same subpopulation that are not in the diagnostic range are false-negative. The sum of the two values gives the entire subpopulation with the disease. Conversely, in the subpopulation who do not have the disease for which testing is being done, results that are in the diagnostic range are false-positive; responses outside the diagnostic range are true-negative. These two values sum to give the entire subpopulation without the disease.

One is tempted to adjust the point of separation (cutoff point) of normals from "abnormals" so that a smaller percent of those without cancer fall outside the normal limit. However, movement of the cutoff point changes the fractions of false-positives and false-negatives in opposite directions; a reduction in the former (noncancerous patients diagnosed as having cancer) is accompanied by an increase in the latter (cancerous patients escaping detection). Depending on the relationships of the cancer and noncancer populations, adjustment in the cutoff point may be unacceptable (Figure 20.2).

A second confirming test (also with negligible risk) might be welcome, but decision analysis would again be necessary to determine the optimum course of management. For example, a second test used after the first might result in 10% false-positives and 10% false-negatives in the population at risk for pancreatic cancer. A decision analysis tree will now show that of those patients with cancer, 4.5 will recover and eight will die of the cancer or at operation; and of those without cancer, only 0.5 will be killed by the pancreatectomy, but 4.5 will be handicapped with permanent pancreatic insufficiency. Are these outcomes, in aggregate, better than the 12 deaths from cancer expected without the employment of the two new diagnostic procedures? Such a question is not easily answered; many ethical considerations must be weighed to provide the best response, and this response could vary from time to time and patient to patient. But the question would not have been asked, or at least not so clearly formulated, had not a systematic prospective analysis been exercised.

Some physicians may contend that laboratory results that cannot be easily reconciled with the current appraisal of a patient's problem can properly be ignored; in fact, this appears to be common practice

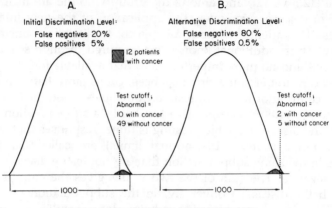

HYPOTHETICAL RELATIONSHIP OF CANCER AND
NON-CANCER POPULATIONS WITH RESPECT TO
TEST FOR CANCER OF THE PANCREAS

Figure 20.2. Hypothetical relationship of cancer and noncancer populations with respect to test for cancer of pancreas. Test cutoff point in A gives approximately 5% false-positives and 20% false-negatives. When cutoff point is moved (B) to reduce the false-positives to 1% or less, false-negatives rise to 90% or more; a condition that may not be acceptable. Results obtained from changing cutoff points depend on sizes and relationships of disease and nondisease populations; calculations of effects from change may be made for each given situation.

(Schneiderman, DeSalvo, Baylor, & Wolf, 1972). However, the intuitive abrogation of data may lead to as many errors in clinical judgment as the little-considered use of new information.

Liver scan and bronchogenic cancer

A patient who was found to have a solitary pulmonary nodule on chest roentgenogram also produced sputum that contained cells characteristic of squamous cell bronchogenic carcinoma. The tests usually employed to search for metastatic disease before surgical therapy have given negative results. A liver scan is contemplated as an additional assessment of neoplasm status. If there is no evidence of metastatic deposits, a thoracotomy and resection of the nodule will be accomplished. If metastases are found, only symptomatic care will be given.

A reasonable assumption would be that as yet undetected liver metastases are present in 20% or less of patients for whom comparable data have been obtained; we will begin with this percent and consider a different figure later. When screening for metastatic neoplasms, interpretations of liver scans have been associated with false-negative rates of 40% (Lunia, Parthasarathy, Bakshi, & Bender, 1975). (Because false-positive and false-negative results were not defined in the conventional manner [Lunia, Parthasarathy, Bakshi, & Bender, 1975] they were recalculated.) When scans were employed to search for general liver abnormalities, false-negative rates as low as 7.5% have been recorded. Since, in this clinical situation, if metastatic deposits are present they are likely to be small, a 25% false-negative rate is a reasonable figure with which to begin calculations. False-positive diagnoses have been rendered for liver scans at rates of 9.5% (Lunia, Parthasarathy, Bakshi, & Bender, 1975) and 8% to 15% (Nishiyama, Lewis, Ashare, & Saenger, 1975); therefore, 10% seems to be an acceptable approximation for the decision analysis.

Again, assuming that the interpretation of the laboratory test will appropriately influence the choice of management, the impact of using this new information on the outcome can be computed. (The efficacy of surgical therapy for bronchogenic carcinoma, another problem for decision analysis, will not be investigated here.)

Analysis of this problem demands that the multiple possible outcomes be assigned relative values which, although they are arbitrary, must relate to one another as better or worse. The assigned outcome values reflect the impact of physicians' efforts on a particular patient's disease and well-being. Magnitudes may vary according to the attitudes of physician and patient.

The analysis tree for this problem contains relatively few branches (Fig. 20.3). For each of the possible choices (to scan or not to scan), a *decision value* can be obtained by a "folding back" process (Raiffa, 1968, p. 21). In this process, each outcome value is multiplied by the probability of its occurrence (and noted on the preceding respective branch) to give branch products that are then summed at each preceding probability node. The computations are repeated for the next preceding branches and nodes until the original decision branches are reached; the numbers determined for these branches are the decision values. For example, in Fig 20.3 the outcomes 1 and 2 give, respectively, $+2000 \times .75$ and $-2000 \times .25$ which, when summed, give a value of $+1000$ for the immediately preceding chance node. Complete "folding back" gives a relative value of $+3400$ for the decision to scan, and $+3600$ for the decision not to scan. It is better patient care to reject a request for liver scans for patients who fall into the described clinical situation.

The difference in the two decision values is small and, realizing the bias involved in assigning outcome values, may not be persuasive. Nevertheless, there is no advantage accrued to scanning the liver and this costs time and money.

Modification of the assigned values and probabilities is not only possible but a virtue of the process. If future studies show that the probability of liver metastases in the given clinical situation were actually .1 instead of .2, the relative decision values would then more clearly favor not scanning ($+4300$) over scanning ($+3700$), while a probability of metastases greater than .2 would have the opposite effect. If the interpretations

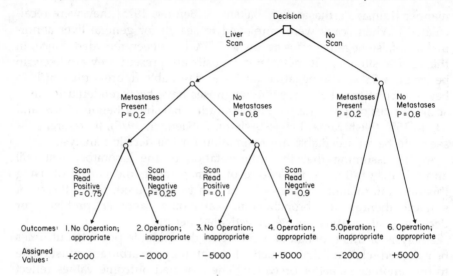

Figure 20.3. "Folding back" process is opposite of that used in Fig. 20.1: outcome value is multiplied by immediately preceding probability and values obtained summated at each probability node. Ultimately, a value is obtained for each decision: liver scan and no scan.

of liver scans could be adjusted so that the false-positive ratio was reduced to .05 while increasing the false-negative rate to .30, then the relative decision outcomes would be to scan, +3760; not to scan, +3600. From these figures, it is apparent that major differences in the errors of interpretation would be necessary to appreciably alter the relative decision values.

Comment

The dilemma of whether or not to obtain and use more data in clinical management problems is often resolved in favor of the former, a choice which, to the uncritical eye, incurs only the obvious, but often modest physical risks and monetary costs. As shown in both problems here, the use of additional information poses another hazard to optimal medical practice.

Since the practice of medicine remains an inexact science, complications of management and even permanently undesirable results are to be anticipated. Nevertheless, the inevitability of such events should not be used to excuse shoddy thinking and inept strategy. Only by planning within the framework of what is possible and what is likely can we maximize benefit and minimize injury. Alvan Feinstein (1970) articulated the challenge a few years ago:

Physicians have developed a splendid clinical science for explanatory decisions, and a magnificent technologic armamentarium of therapy, but our managerial decisions generally continue to be made as doctrinaire dogmas, immersed in dissension and doubt.

The tactics of decision analysis should help us overcome this impediment to logical patient management.

Data from the literature and some reasonable assumptions enable the analysis of the problem of possible liver metastases from bronchogenic cancer (Fig. 20.3). Although there are only two branches at each decision and chance node in the problem, more are possible. Additional branches would permit the inclusion of intermediate groups in terms of test results and of therapeutic outcomes (since many tests give a continuum of responses and several values, each abnormal to a different degree, may be associated with different probabilities for the event or disease under study).

Pauker and Kassirer (1975) have developed a relatively simple formula that may be used to determine which of two courses of action is preferable. However, the formula applies only to binary decisions. Although more complex calculations of a similar nature may aid in choosing from several options, we believe that the construction of a modest tree, with as many branches as are appropriate at any decision or chance node, and the "folding back" process will more readily serve physicians in many of the medical practice problems that require decision analysis.

The inevitable gaps in knowledge will make some branches of the analysis trees tenuous, but our ignorance will be explicit. Critical assumptions about diagnosis and treatment will be recognizable. Both the essential but missing information and the requisite accuracy of this information can then be sought. When doubt persists, calculations using the extremes of a range of probabilities will establish limits for decision values which, within the identified uncertainty, may still indicate the preferable course. The best guess of an expert will usually suffice as an estimate of probability for a set of events in specialized areas of disease. (Gorry et al., 1973). Indeed, a new role for the consultant may be to provide primary care physicians with reasonably accurate figures on incidence and prevalence of diseases, specificity and sensitivity of diagnostic procedures, and the probabilities of success with specific therapeutic programs. Primary care physicians, in turn, will find it necessary to determine more clearly the appropriate outcome values when planning the management of illness for individual patients; as patients are better informed, they can cooperate more intelligently in this process.

The problem of the patient with possible cancer of the pancreas was hypothetical, but, basically, posed choices not unlike the many to be decided by physicians each day: to collect or not to collect more information. This particular problem was selected because each possible outcome is valued in numbers of patients with distinctive end points, and the significance of a decision is therefore easily understood.

Generally, the results of clinical decisions are less well-defined, as seen in the example of the patient with possible metastases from bronchogenic cancer. Although qualitative distinctions among outcomes are integral features of everyday clinical judgments, the assignment of quantitative values to these same end points is a task not easily comprehended. Quantitative assessments of the outcomes involve ethical, sociologic, and economic factors as well as scientific measurements (Lusted, 1975). Designating a unit in terms of "healthy person-years of life" is a step in the right direction, but mensuration must become considerably more refined to be useful in most medical decisions. The construction of an acceptable taxonomy in this area of personal and social values may provide an impetus for further progress.

It is appropriate to designate any values that are consistent throughout the analysis, reflect how physicians have altered illness or health, and take into account the patients' own appraisals of outcomes. One practice is to assign a zero value to any outcome when the patient does not have the disease in question, and when neither diagnostic measures nor therapy are aimed at this disease. Positive values would be given to outcomes where the patient has a disease and the natural course is altered to provide the patient with lesser morbidity or mortality. Negative values would be assigned to outcomes that are worse than the natural history of the disease, or are the same as the natural history, but which, in our present state of knowledge, should be favorably modified. For a mathematical basis for assigning outcome values, see Barnoon and Wolfe (1972).

Criticism of decision analysis as a tool of the everyday practice of medicine has been aimed at the lack of experimental evidence that shows improved clinical results, and at the paucity of prevalence rates that apply to specific situations. We believe that the problem of assessing metastatic cancer before thoracotomy is an example of how decision analysis can help the physician reach an optimal clinical judgment. However, this obviously was not a scientific investigation that clearly determined the superiority of decision analysis. In fact, research that evaluates alternate strategies for handling patient problems is virtually impossible to carry out in a clinical practice where patients with different diseases and variations of the same disease are seen, but where the outcomes, which may only be appreciated over years, are the sole measurement for comparison.

Because of the basic differences in approach to patients and their diseases, the results derived from the use of decision analysis by specialists who are able to see many patients with similar illnesses cannot be compared to those obtained by practitioners whose professional encounters are more varied. The relative merits of decision analysis and conventional methods in choosing courses of management can be more easily compared in terms of costs or risks to patients, but such assessments are not the purposes of this communication. Much as has been the case for problem-oriented records, decision analysis will have to be accepted on the basis of appeal to the physician's logic.

Complete analysis of complicated medical problems may require the aid of a computer (Schwartz et al., 1973, Gorry et al., 1973). At the other extreme, excellent clinical judgments for many patients are derived from one of two diagnostic variables and the associated weights of two outcomes without a formalized strategy. But between these ends of the spectrum, and arising from a pool of ever-increasing numbers of diagnostic procedures and therapies, optimal choices demand more than instinctive behavior from physicians. To help solve these problems of intermediate complexity, we believe that modest decision analysis trees can be constructed in the outpatient office or at the bedside.

21. Clinical judgment in rheumatoid arthritis: II. Judging "current disease activity" in clinical practice

J. R. Kirwan, D. M. Chaput de Saintonge, C. R. B. Joyce, and H. L. F. Currey

Clinicians differ in the importance they claim to attach to measures of disease activity in rheumatoid arthritis (Kirwan, Chaput de Saintonge, Joyce, & Currey, 1983a), but it is not known whether their stated opinions reflect actual practice when making clinical decisions about patients. Using "paper patients" – a convenient technique developed for presenting standard patient data to several doctors on different occasions (Kirwan et al., 1983a) – and judgment analysis – a form of multivariate analysis of the information on which decisions are based (Hammond, Stewart, Brehmer, & Steinmann, 1975) – the present study investigates how clinicians use information to help them make judgments of "current disease activity" in rheumatoid arthritis. It aims to answer the following questions: (a) How can rheumatologists' decision policies be adequately described or modelled? (b) How do such models of actual behavior compare with their own view of their policy?

Materials and methods

Two rheumatologists saw between them 19 patients with RA at routine outpatient consultations over a 2-week period and noted the information that they considered contributed to their assessment of the patient's disease activity. This information was used to construct paper patients as previously described (Kirwan et al., 1983a). Some weeks later "current disease activity" was assessed in these patients by making judgments on a visual analogue scale (VAS) 100 mm long marked "no disease activity" at the left end and "maximum possible disease activity" on the right. A

This chapter originally appeared in *Annals of the Rheumatic Diseases*, 1983, 42, 648–651. Copyright © 1983 by British Medical Association House. Reprinted by permission.

similar judgment had also been made at the time the clinician first saw the real patient.

Judgment policy models were extracted from the decisions by the method of all possible subsets regression analysis on a computer (Frane, 1981). Briefly, all possible combinations (subsets) of the data in the "paper patients" are correlated with the judgments made by the doctor. The combination which produces the regression line best fitted to the judgments is taken as the model. The relative contribution of each clinical variable (or cue) to the model indicates the importance (or weight) of the cue in question. Here the weight is assessed by calculating the loss of explained variance when each cue in turn is omitted from the regression equation and is thus the "relative contribution to R^2" for that cue. Those cues for which the relative contribution to R^2 is low could be omitted from the model with little loss of its ability to represent actual practice; on the other hand cues with a high relative contribution are obviously essential elements.

In addition to judging paper patients the clinicians then recorded the importance they attached to the same cues as measures of disease activity by dividing 100 marks between them, higher scores indicating a greater relative weight.

Results

Although the physicians were given an opportunity to record a large number of clinical variables, in practice they noted only 5 for each of the patients seen: early morning stiffness, patient's global assessment, patient's pain score, functional capacity, and articular index. Details of the data collected are shown in Table 21.1 together with VAS judgment scores for both real and "paper" patients and including duplicated judgments for some of the "paper patients." There is a good agreement between scores for real and the equivalent "paper" patients when judged by the same clinician, and between the duplicated judgments, as has been observed previously (Kirwan et al., 1983a). The models were based on all the judgments made by each clinician (28 judgments by Doctor A and 21 by Doctor B), and the extracted policy model equations, together with the proportion of the variance each explains, are:

> *Doctor A*
> J = 3.9 × articular index + 9.7 × functional capacity + 5.6 ×
> pain score − 8.7.
> $R^2 = 0.949$.

> *Doctor B*
> J = 24.1 × patient's global assessment + 8.5 × functional capacity
> + 7.8 × pain score − 36.7.
> $R^2 = 0.939$.

Table 21.1. "Paper patient" information collected by clinicians and their real patient and "paper patient" VAS judgments

Patient information						Judgments (mm from left of VAS)			
						Doctor A		Doctor B	
Patient code	Early morning stiffness (mm)	Patient's global assessment (0–4)*	Patient's pain score (0–4)*	Functional capacity (1–4)*	Articular index (0–16)*	Real patient	Paper patient†	Real patient	Paper patient†
C1	80	1	1	1	3	27	23 22		7
C2	30	1	1	1	4	8	21		5
C3	60	2	2	2	8	52	63 52		37
C4	180	1	1	2	4			11	14 23
C5	30	1	2	2	0			3	26
C6	60	2	2	2	12			28	47 43
C8	30	2	2	3	6	53	48		52
C9	120	3	3	2	12	68	78 74		75
C15	300	3	4	3	12	79	98		100
C17	60	2	2	2	3	33	32 43		
C43	0	1	1	1	1			3	3
C44	30	2	2	2	6			54	49 48
C48	30	3	2	3	10			73	77
C84	0	1	0	1	3	5	14		
C85	180	4	3	2	16	85	96 90		
C87	0	2	2	1	3	15	22 19		
C88	0	1	1	1	1	23	12		

* Lowest number indicates most favourable response.
† Where 2 entries are shown they represent judgments of duplicate cases (see "Materials and methods" section).

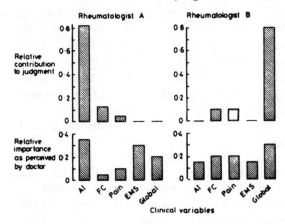

Figure 21.1. Actual and perceived contributions of clinical variables to judgments. Actual contributions are the relative contributions to R^2 derived from the computed judgment models. Perceived contributions are the proportion of 100 marks allocated to each variable by each clinician (see "Materials and methods" section).

The value of the indices in the equations as shown depends on the units of measurement for each cue. The relative importance of the cues to the judgment policies of the doctors (see "Materials and methods" section) is shown in Fig. 21.1 as the relative contribution to R^2. The doctors' own scores for the importance of the cues are also shown.

Discussion

Judgments based on paper patients have been shown to agree closely with face-to-face judgments made on the real patients from whom the data were obtained (Kirwan et al., 1983a), and it is therefore reasonable to assume that the paper policies calculated here model actual practice policies. The policy models contain only 3 cues but explain 95% and 94% of the variance in clinical judgments of the 2 physicians. These remarkably high proportions indicate that most of the information required to arrive at the judgments has been included in the models. The surprisingly small number of cues or clinical variables is consistent with other work in the social sciences (Hammond, Stewart, Brehmer, & Steinmann, 1975) and medicine (Fisch, Hammond, Joyce, O'Reilly, 1981) showing that, in general, very few cues are needed to describe judgment policies adequately. Even so, the policies of the 2 clinicians are quite different. That of Doctor A can be described largely by the contribution of the articular index, whereas for Doctor B the patients' global assessment is most important. Similar results have recently been obtained in diagnosis of the severity of depression by general physicians (Fisch et al., 1981) and psychiatrists by Fisch et al. (1982) using hypothetical patient data, and were foreshadowed by a brief early report in rheumatology (Joyce, Berry, Chaput de Saintonge, Domenet, Fowler, & Mason, 1977).

The models derived from the doctors' actual decisions and the relative importance of the cues as seen by the doctors themselves (Fig. 21.1) also differ. For Doctor A, early morning stiffness and global assessment by the patient appeared strongly in his own perceptions but did not appear at all in the judgment model, and for Doctor B the same was true of pain and early morning stiffness.

Given only the similarity of the doctors' own beliefs about their clinical behaviour we should find it difficult to discover why they differ in their assessments of some patients. The models based on their actual judgments of cases on the other hand allow a better insight into their areas of disagreement. The intention here has not been to specify a "correct" policy but, after identifying the reasons for disagreement, to make possible rational discussion of their importance and implications.

In this study the 2 clinicians made judgments on many common patients. It is not necessary, however, for judges to review the same cases when comparing computed policy models, only for the subsets of cases to be broadly similar. Within this limitation judgment policies can be compared even if there are no cases in common. In this way the clinical decisions of different investigators – for example, in a multicentre drug trial – can be analysed, and by identifying systematic differences in assessment policies between centres disparate results from similar investigations may be explained and used more effectively.

22. A decision analysis approach to the swine influenza vaccination decision for an individual

David L. Zalkind and Richard H. Shachtman

The federally-sponsored swine influenza vaccination campaign that was unexpectedly and abruptly aborted highlights the current ethical and legal problems attendant to informed consent by medical patients. There is a need for mechanisms that provide patients with the information and tools to be active decision makers in the medical care process.

Decision analysis provides a systematic framework for rational decision making that can be utilized by knowledgeable health care personnel to inform a patient about potential consequences of medical actions, and that can be used with the patient's own values to help make a decision that is best for him. In other words, individuals can use the tool of decision analysis, perhaps under the guidance of specially trained health technicians, to educate themselves to make more rational decisions in the face of hard data, soft data, nonexistent data and personal preferences. Equally important, public health analysts can use decision analysis to help determine whether advice about what actions individuals should take is rational from the viewpoint of each individual being advised to take the action. Such an understanding may be of use in devising both one-on-one and mass media educational efforts for preventive health measures.

There are at least four different viewpoints for the decision, or four different decisions. The first is the federal government decision of whether to have such a program and, if so, who should fund it. Schoenbaum, McNeil, and Kavet (1976) have discussed the first part of this decision from an economic viewpoint. The second is that of a local health administrator who must decide how to pay for the program. We do not consider these problems here. A health professional who must

This chapter originally appeared in *Medical Care*, 1980, *18*(1), pp. 59–72. Copyright © 1980 by J. B. Lippincott Co. Reprinted by permission.

advise individuals whether or not to receive the vaccine has a third viewpoint. The individuals who would receive the vaccine have the fourth viewpoint. For the latter two viewpoints, certain parameters characterizing the individual's values for consequences and probabilities for outcomes may affect the decision. Factors to take into consideration include the probability of an epidemic, reaction to receiving the vaccine, etc. Thus, this article proposes a rational procedure for an individual to follow in deciding whether to obtain a swine influenza vaccination. Many Americans made this decision during the fall of 1976 and similar decisions will be made year after year as new or altered viral strains threaten to cause national epidemics,[1] for which acceptance of the vaccine is not mandated by law.

The methodology developed here can be used in several contexts. First, with the aid of an easy-to-use computer package or programmable calculator, a patient in conjunction with medical personnel can use informed consent to its fullest extent. Second, the systematic approach to problem solving inherent in decision analysis makes it an excellent tool for training of health care personnel. We will not review the use of decision analysis in medical care here. The interested reader can find an extensive bibliography in Albert (1978). An example of a typical application in the literature is that of Plisken and Beck (1976) describing how a physician and a patient incorporate some of their subjective feelings and value judgments in a decision analysis model used to determine the treatment of end-stage renal failure.

An individual is faced with a choice – receive the vaccine, or decline to receive the vaccine. In large part, the consequence of such a choice depends on whether the individual in question is exposed to swine influenza virus, or is never exposed to swine influenza virus. In the terminology of classical statistics, one might say that receiving the vaccine and not being exposed to the virus is a Type I error and that not receiving the vaccine and being exposed to the virus is a Type II error. Although classical statistics develops trade-offs between probabilities of committing Type I and Type II errors, the methodology of decision analysis, described in this paper, goes further, because it allows the individual decision maker to incorporate his own values (and probabilities) for the potential consequences of his actions and the true state of nature that is unknown at the time the decision is made. For example, at the time the immunization decision is made, the individual does not know whether he will be exposed to the virus. Furthermore, this technique provides the opportunity for the decision maker to explore the sensitivity of his decision to alternative probability estimates and value assessments.

---

[1] As this is being written, the upcoming example appears to be the "Russian Influenza" (A/USSR).

The A/New Jersey[2] virus is antigenically[3] similar to both the swine influenza virus and the virus assumed to cause the pandemic[4] of 1918, for which the death toll was 20 million. Public health officials mounted the swine influenza program because, like the A/Japan ("Asian") influenza of 1957, the A/New Jersey virus represented a radically different strain from recently prevalent strains, and excess mortality during the A/Japan pandemic was the highest of all influenza epidemics in the past 20 years. Also, there was a theory that the next epidemic would come from a swine influenza type virus.

We structure the decision tree and indicate parameters for individuals in any age/sex cohort within the age range 20 to 45. Some of the probabilities used are for the authors' cohort of healthy males in their early thirties. Similar calculations may be made for other age/sex cohorts. We construct the tree in the first section and derive probabilities and scale values in the second and third sections, respectively. We then enumerate conditions under which the individual can make the vaccination decision without specifying a personal value of death. In the fourth section, we report the results of a method we have developed for determining the value of death (or life) to the individual in this context and show how this method may be used to complete the decision. We represent the decision regions graphically.

Because the possibility of contracting the Guillain-Barré syndrome was not widely known by the public at the time individual decisions were made to receive the vaccine, we did not include this possibility in the main part of the analysis. However, public health officials now recognize that an outbreak of Guillain-Barré syndrome cases might occur with any mass viral immunization program. In the fifth section, we modify the decision tree to take the Guillain-Barré syndrome into account. Thus, in the future, a person can include this possible consequence when making a decision.

The basic decision tree

When the government decided to provide swine influenza vaccine injections to the public free of charge, individuals were faced with the decision of whether to receive it. Although the authors are not experts on swine influenza, we show in this paper how the methodology known as decision analysis can be used as an aid in making the decision. In the age

---

[2] Hattwick, O'Brien, Hoke, and Dowdle (1976) contains a description of standardized nomenclature for describing influenza viruses.

[3] An antigen is any substance capable of inducing antibody formation and of reacting specifically in some detectable manner with the antibodies so induced.

[4] A pandemic is a major epidemic due to a single virus type which sweeps around the world in a short period of time and causes marked increases in mortality.

group we consider, it was the belief of experts at the Center for Disease Control (CDC), that the vaccine would be efficacious for at least 1 year and perhaps as long as 2 or 3 years. This period is also a function of the change in the strain of virus to which the individuals are susceptible. Thus it is realistic to fix a 1-year time period for the decision.[5] The basic data for the decision will be those available in October 1976, when individuals were deciding whether to receive the vaccine.

The problem has four basic components:

1. The decision by an individual of whether to receive the vaccine.
2. Values[6] and probabilities associated with having a reaction to the injection.
3. Value and probabilities associated with contracting swine influenza.
4. Values and probabilities associated with dying as a direct result of having swine influenza.

The decision problem is represented in the decision tree of Figure 22.1. The square, called the decision node, represents the *human* decision of whether or not to receive the vaccine. The circles, called the chance nodes, represent chance events (nature's decisions). There are nine different consequences represented in the tree, labeled "A" through "I." For example, "A" represents the human choice to receive the vaccine, followed by a reaction to the vaccine, followed by contracting swine influenza, followed by dying as a direct result of swine influenza. Consequence "B" is the same as "A" except that the decision maker does not die as a result of getting swine influenza (a rather important difference). Note that consequence "B" does not preclude the possibility of the decision maker dying from something else during the upcoming year. Similarly, we can see that consequence "C" involves taking the vaccine and not getting swine influenza; thus we do not have to consider dying as a result of getting swine influenza. We interpret the other consequences in a similar manner.

In order to analyze the decision tree we must assign probabilities to the branches emanating from each chance node (the circles representing nature's decisions) and assign a personal value to each consequence. These are explained in the section on values. The methodology of decision analysis prescribes that we make the choice of Shot (receiving the vaccine) versus No Shot (not receiving the vaccine) that yields the highest *expected value*.[7]

We use information available from CDC to determine some of the appropriate probabilities and values. When "objective" probabilities and

---

[5] The potential additional benefit of added protection from getting additional vaccination in subsequent years is not considered in our analysis because of the 1-year time horizon.

[6] Relative values will be determined on a fixed scale in the section on values.

[7] For our purposes, expected value is the same as weighted average. The weights are calculated from the probabilities we assign to potential consequences. The quantities to be "averaged" are the scale values we will assign to the consequences.

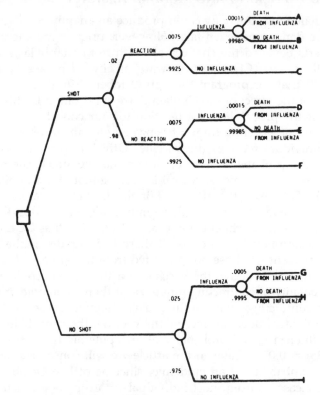

Figure 22.1. Decision tree for individual decision to receive swine influenza shot with probabilities, assuming the epidemic probability is 0.1.

values are unavailable, decision analysis relies on the use of subjective or personal judgments of the decision maker. Of course, the decision maker may wish to rely heavily on "expert" opinion. The probabilities and values we use were valid as of October 1976 for healthy males in their early thirties.[8] We assume that only the monovalent shot (providing protection against one strain of influenza) is available to us.

Probabilities

Although as many as 50 percent of vaccine recipients might get sore arms, the swine influenza vaccination field trials indicated that only slightly more than 2 percent of those getting the vaccine would suffer some other kind of side effect. These additional reactions might include fever, headache or malaise ranging from mild to severe, usually lasting no longer than one day. Moreover, any type of foreign protein injected,

[8] It is straightforward to substitute values for individuals in other groups. Any conclusions drawn are only for individuals not allergic to eggs, with no current respiratory problems or other current medical contraindications. We do not consider the problem for ages younger than 25 or older than 45, although the approach would be the same.

ingested or inhaled into the body could produce an anaphylactic[9] reaction which could be dangerous, even fatal. However, prior to the vaccination program, experts believed the chances of death from anaphylaxis would be quite small; in fact, CDC was unaware of any such case occurring during the field trials or program through October 1976. (See, however, our discussion of the effect of the Guillain-Barré syndrome.) In this paper we use 0.02 for the probability of a reaction for our cohort.

The probability of suffering from influenza is, of course, dependent on whether an individual receives the vaccine. Other factors affecting this probability are the probability of an epidemic and the attack rate for our cohort if there is an epidemic. A typical expert estimate for an epidemic, as of August 1976, was 0.1 (R. J. O'Brien, L. Schoenberger, D. J. Bregman, & R. Goodman, personal communications, 1976 and 1978). Using the information in Schoenbaum et al. (1976), as well as CDC expert opinion, the assumption is made that if there is an epidemic the attack rate will be 25 percent for those not protected from the disease. That is, if an individual does not receive the vaccine and there is an epidemic, he has a 0.25 probability of contracting influenza. If there is no epidemic, the probability of contracting swine influenza is assumed to be negligible. Thus, if the individual does not receive the vaccine, the probability of his contracting influenza is the probability of an epidemic times the attack rate: $(0.1)(0.25) = 0.025$. (Later in the article we will consider a range of values for the probability of an epidemic, since as of late October 1976, the lack of new cases caused most individuals to estimate a much lower probability of an epidemic occurring. We analyze the decision using a range of epidemic probability from 0.01 to 0.1.)

We assume, based on expert advice, the vaccine has 70 per cent efficacy for the cohort under consideration. That is, if an individual chooses to get the shot, the probability of his contracting influenza is reduced by a factor of 0.7. Thus, assuming that an epidemic occurs with probability 0.1, if he takes the shot his probability of contracting swine influenza is $(0.3)(0.025) = 0.0075$. Our assumptions also rely on expert judgment that there is no significant chance of death from the shot itself, and that a reaction to the shot will not affect its efficacy; see however, the section on the Guillain-Barré Syndrome.

We next assess the probability of dying from swine influenza. If the individual does not get the shot and eventually contracts influenza, expert opinion is that the probability of dying is about 0.0005 for our cohort (which is between 0.004 for the 1918–19 pandemic and 0.00014 for the 1968 "Hong Kong" influenza). Experts believe the shot will reduce the severity of a case if contracted and will reduce the probability of dying from influenza by about 70 percent. Hence, the probability that an

---

[9] Anaphylaxis is an exaggerated reaction of an organism to a foreign protein or other substance to which it has previously become sensitized.

individual dies from influenza, given that he received the vaccine but contracts it anyway, is 0.00015. (It is straightforward to test the sensitivity of our decision to this assumption.) The probabilities discussed above appear on the tree in Figure 22.1 for an epidemic probability of 0.1.

Values

The consequences of the decision tree of Figure 22.1 naturally cluster in three groups according to relative "value" to the individual. These clusters are: no influenza (consequences C, F and I), influenza but not death from it (consequences B, E and H) and death from influenza (consequences A, D and G). A reasonable preference ordering for the consequences that do not involve death is, from best to worst, I, F, C, E, H, B. For purposes of computation and interpretation these consequences will be assigned values from 0.0 to 1.0. In the first group assign a value of 1.0 to I, since it is the *best* consequence. Assign (somewhat arbitrarily) slightly lower personal values for F and C, namely 0.98 and 0.90 respectively.[10] (Because the decision will be found to be sensitive to the value assigned to F, and F may plausibly have a value as high as I, i.e. 1.0, we will subsequently solve the decision tree using values for F from 0.98 to 1.0.)

In the second group of consequences, we believe B should be assigned the value 0.0 since it is the *worst* consequence. For the other consequences in this group we decided that values of 0.2 and 0.1 for E and H, respectively, would be appropriate for the authors as decision makers. This judgment is based on the supposition, supported by expert opinion, that even though the shot would not prevent us from contracting influenza, it would enable us to have a milder case than we would have had otherwise. We tested the sensitivity of our decision to ranges around the above values of E and H and found that the decision is relatively insensitive to changes of these values.

In the third group, the consequences involve dying during the upcoming year as a result of contracting swine influenza. As we have discussed (Zalkind & Shachtman, no date), we assume it is not consequential to differentiate values among them and so assign a value of $-X$ to each of the consequences A, D and G. The value $-X$ is a large negative number reflecting the individual's value of death and is a point on a scale which includes the values for consequence I (assigned a value of 1.0) and consequence B (assigned a value of 0.0). The decision tree now looks like Figure 22.2. The (conditional) probabilities in the right hand column are

[10] It has been suggested that we are ignoring a moral obligation to contribute to "herd immunity" by getting the shot and shouldn't rate consequence I as high. Also, we are not taking potential medical care costs or lost personal income into account in our analysis here. For our current purposes, we are just considering our attitudes about our own health and mortality. These other factors can be taken into account.

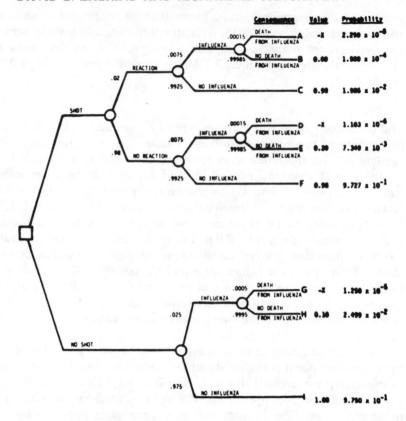

Figure 22.2. Swine influenza decision tree with probabilities and values, assuming the epidemic probability is 0.1.

calculated by multiplying the probabilities along the path leading to each consequence. For example, the probability of consequence A, *given that an individual gets the shot*, is written as P(A/shot) and is calculated as:

$$
\begin{aligned}
P(A/Shot) &= P(Reaction/Shot) \\
&\times P(Influenza/Shot, Reaction) \\
&\times P(Death/Shot, Reaction, Influenza) \\
&= (0.02)\,(0.0075)\,(0.00015) = 0.0000000225 \\
&= 2.25 \times 10^{-8}.
\end{aligned}
$$

At this point decision analysis calls for evaluating the tree by the method known as "averaging out and folding back" (Raiffa, 1968; Shachtman & Blau, 1974; Zalkind & Shachtman, 1976a, 1976b). E(S) and E(NS) denote the expected values associated with getting the shot and with not getting the shot, respectively. Assuming an epidemic probability of 0.1, these values are:

$$E(S) = (-X) (2.25 \times 10^{-8}) + (.0) (1.5 \times 10^{-4}) + (0.9) (1.985$$
$$\times 10^{-2}) + (-X) (1.103 \times 10^{-6}) + (0.2) (7.349 \times 10^{-3})$$
$$+ (0.98) (0.97265)$$
$$= (1.125 \times 10^{-6}) (-X) + 0.97253$$

and

$$E(NS) = (-X) (1.25 \times 10^{-5}) + (0.1) (2.496 \times 10^{-2}) + (1.0) (0.975)$$
$$= (1.25 \times 10^{-5})(-X) + 0.9775.$$

A rational decision maker would choose to receive the vaccine if and only if $E(S)$ is greater than (or, perhaps, equal to) $E(NS)$. This is equivalent to $(1.25 \times 10^{-6})(-X) + 0.97253 \geq (1.25 \times 10^{-5})(-X) + 0.9775$, which reduces to approximately $X \geq 437$. Thus the decision depends on the numerical value a person assigns to X.

Before further specification of X, we point out two possible conclusions not requiring specification of X:

1. If the value 1.0 was assigned to consequence F, the expected value of getting the shot is $E(S) = 1.125 \times 10^{-6} (-X) + 0.99198$ and the expected value of not getting the shot is $E(NS) = 1.25 \times 10^{-5}(-X) + 0.9775$. For all negative values of $-X$, $E(S) > E(NS)$ and the individual should decide to get the shot, since the expected value for this action is always greater than that for not getting the shot.[11] There are other values of F for which this conclusion also holds. Figure 22.3 shows regions of values for F and for the personal probability of having a reaction (possibly different from 0.02[12]) where the choice of the shot does not depend on X. These regions are bounded by lines that depend on the subjective probability estimate for an epidemic actually occurring during the coming year. Using the notation e = probability of an epidemic, r = probability of a reaction and f = value assigned to consequence F, the decision is automatic for any pair of values (r, f) falling in a shaded region *above* the curve corresponding to a given epidemic probability, e. If the individual's values do not fall into one of these automatic decision regions, he should continue the analysis.

2. One can observe that the sum of the coefficients of $-X$ in the expressions for $E(S)$ and $E(NS)$, respectively, are the probabilities of dying from swine influenza, depending on whether or not the shot is taken. Thus, one can see that receiving the vaccine reduces the (subjective) probability of dying from the swine influenza from about 12.5 out of a million to slightly more than one out of a million. (Naturally, these figures would be altered if we had used different probabilities in the

---

[11] $E(S) \geq E(NS)$ if and only if $1.375 \times 10^{-5}(X) \geq (0.9775 - 0.99198)$. But the right hand side of the last inequality is negative and admissible values of X are non-negative. Hence the inequality is true for any admissible value assigned to X.

[12] Some individuals assess their personal probability of a reaction, r, to be much higher than the field trials indicated.

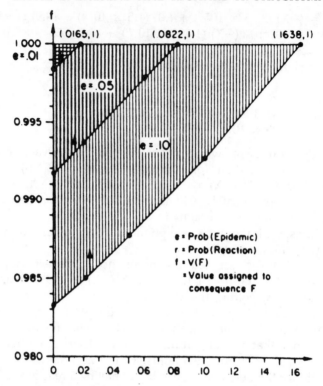

Figure 22.3. Decision regions for automatic choice of receiving the vaccine (not requiring specification of value of death).

decision tree.) Some decision makers may wish to stop at this point. They may feel that consideration of the relative probabilities of death is sufficient for making the decision (with other potential consequences taken into account in some "intuitive" manner). However, we believe that a more thorough analysis including a personal estimation of the value of X should be carried out.

Personal value of death (or life)

We have presented (Zalkind & Shachtman, no date) the derivation of a personal value of life relative to other values in the swine influenza vaccination decision tree (See Figure 22.2) using the tree structure presented here.

A brief description of the approach used follows. Using a simplifying assumption, the derived value of X depends on only two parameters–s, the probability of death for the cohort under investigation during the upcoming year in the absence of a swine influenza epidemic, and p, a fractional reduction of s, more fully described below. Given these two parameters, the value of X is derived as

$$X = (1/s - 1)/p = (1 - s)/ps.$$

Note that X does not depend on any consequence values or other probabilities used in the original tree (i.e. reaction, epidemic, attack rate, efficacy of vaccine or dying from swine influenza). Values of s are available from the National Center for Health Statistics (1976) for most cohorts which would be analyzed, since s is an overall probability of dying during the upcoming year, assuming no special risk such as contraction of swine influenza.

Briefly, the death rate reduction factor p is derived in the following way: Let $t = ps$, so that $s - t = s(1 - p)$ is the (reduced) probability of dying resulting from using a special therapeutic agent (TA) which enhances one's chances of living during the coming year. However, TA also has a negative effect: taking it will definitely make one temporarily ill with the same reaction as one might get from the swine influenza shot, including any immediate reaction such as a temporary malaise plus an illness with symptoms that mimic swine influenza symptoms. The interpretation of t is that it is a decrement in the probability of death that is sufficient to induce one to take a TA. This situation is represented by the decision tree in Figure 22.4.

Each individual decision maker must find a probability decrement t sufficiently large so that he is indifferent between taking TA and not taking TA. If $t = 0$, one clearly would not take TA. If t is very close to s, the authors believe most people in their cohort would choose to take TA. Hence, somewhere between 0 and s there exists a t for which the decision maker is indifferent between the two possible actions. In Zalkind & Shachtman (no date) we derive a value for X as a function of s and t, namely $X = (1 - s)/t$. Since it may be easier for an individual to think about a *reduction* in the probability of death as a proportional factor rather than a difference we write $t = ps$ and ask the decision maker to make a personal estimate for p rather than directly for t. Then the expression for X becomes $X = (1/s - 1)/p$.

For the authors' cohort at the time the decision was made, $s = .002$ and $X = (1/s - 1)/p = 499/p$. In Section 3 we found that the shot should be taken for $X > 437$ when the probability of an epidemic is 0.1. Since for $p \leqslant 1$ we have $X \geqslant 499$, it is clear that the "correct" decision is to get the vaccination.

We can also resolve the decision problem assuming that the probability of an epidemic is only 0.01. The numerical values for the probabilities of the various consequences are given in Table 22.1. For the values in Table 22.1, we can calculate that

$$E(S) = 1.1255 \times 10^{-7} (-X) + .97780828, \text{ and}$$
$$E(NS) = 1.25 \times 10^{-6} (-X) + .997749875.$$

From these figures we see that the shot should be taken if $X \geqslant 17,532$, which is equivalent to $499/p \geqslant 17,532$ or $p \leqslant 0.02846$. Therefore, in this

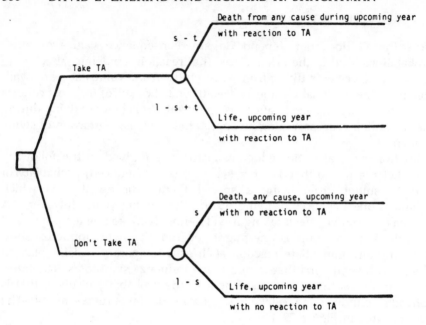

Figure 22.4. Decision tree used to derive the reduction probability t.

Table 22.1. *Values and probabilities for decision tree consequences for an epidemic probability of 0.01*

	Receive vaccination			Decline vaccination		
Consequence	Value	Probability		Consequence	Value	Probability
A	$-X$	2.25×10^{-9}		G	$-X$	1.25×10^{-6}
B	0.0	1.5×10^{-5}		H	0.1	2.4988×10^{-3}
C	0.9	1.9985×10^{-2}		I	1.0	9.975×10^{-1}
D	$-X$	1.103×10^{-7}				
E	0.2	7.349×10^{-4}				
F	0.98	9.7926×10^{-1}				

case, an individual following the expected value model should receive the vaccination if the proportional reduction in the probability of death which is sufficient to induce him to take action TA is only about 3 percent.

The values of the proportional reduction p sufficient to imply that action TA should be taken are shown in Figure 22.5 for varying (subjective or objective) probabilities e for the occurrence of an epidemic. The swine influenza vaccine should be taken for any point (e, p) in the shaded region. For example, if one believes that the probability of an epidemic is less than 0.02 and if one requires a reduction proportion for death during

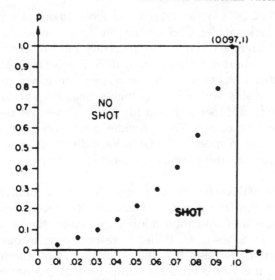

Figure 22.5. Decision region for choice of receiving the swine influenza shot given epidemic probabilities and reduction proportions.

the upcoming year of at least 0.25 to induce him to take action TA, then he should choose not to take the swine influenza vaccination.

It can be seen in Figure 22.5 that for the consequence values on the right hand side of Figure 22.2 the vaccine should be taken by the individual for any personal probability estimate for an epidemic greater than 9.7 per cent, regardless of the reduction proportion value.

The Guillain-Barré Syndrome

The Guillain-Barré Syndrome (GBS) is a neurologic disease which may be induced by the introduction of foreign matter into the body, for example, by a swine influenza vaccination. Possible outcomes for a victim of GBS include death, permanent disabling paralysis, temporary disabling paralysis or other less severe permanent or temporary effects. Intensive respiratory care may be required for the paralysis outcomes.

Before October 1976, most individuals facing the vaccination decision would not have been aware of the additional risks due to GBS. We indicate a modification of the decision tree of Figure 22.1 which reflects GBS outcomes.

Attached to the ends of each of the consequences labeled B, C, E and F in Figure 22.1 are the additional branches shown in Figure 22.6. We will analyze the personal cost for these branch modifications using information about probabilities and types of health outcomes provided by CDC (R. J. O'Brien, L. Schoenberger, D. J. Bregman, & R. Goodman, personal communications, 1976 and 1978).

By mid-January 1977, CDC gave an estimate of about 10 out of a million for the augmented attack rate of GBS during the first few weeks after receiving the swine influenza vaccine. The mortality rate for those contracting the GBS in our cohort is approximately 0.05. Precise estimates for the probabilities of other outcomes are not available; hence, we proceed with the analysis below using both relatively high probabilities and highly negative personal values (approaching that for death) as well as nominal estimates for the severe outcomes. This provides a risk averse analysis, i.e. fairly conservative with respect to the GBS, for individuals specifically wanting to take into account the potential iatrogenic[13] effect of receiving the vaccine.[14]

We can estimate the values for the consequences of the branches of Figure 22.6 by first finding the expected value for the set of branches using the above probabilities and then adding this value to the values already computed for branches B, C, E and F, respectively, in our basic tree in Figure 22.2. The hypothesis that these values can be summed is fairly innocuous, since it is based on the assumption that the occurrence of influenza, GBS and other reaction outcomes are independent events and that the probability associated with non-GBS outcomes when the shot is taken is of the order of 10^{-6}, which is much larger than the probability of dying from GBS induced by the shot. Although the GBS could occur for branches A and D representing death from influenza following vaccination, the probability of such an event is of the order of 10^{-11}. Hence, corresponding values are insignificant relative to all other outcome values. Moreover, we will show the ultimate decision about taking the vaccine to be rather insensitive to the values assigned to consequences of these branches. For this reason, we have not further disaggregated paralysis outcomes.

We give "reasonable" upper and lower bounds for values of the branches of Figure 22.6 as well as probabilities of each consequence *conditional* on the fact that we have already reached the end of the corresponding branches in Figure 22.2. The value ranges for consequences involving paralysis were determined by considering typical decision analysis "lottery" questions involving the outcomes. Using Figure 22.7 we assessed a value for temporary paralysis by considering sequential choices between contracting swine influenza for certain and a hypothetical lottery between the status quo and temporary paralysis where the probabilities q and $1 - q$, respectively, of the latter two outcomes were varied until a range was established. From Figure 22.7, we see that

$$0 = q(1.0) + (1 - g) (k), \text{ or}$$
$$k = -q/(1 - q).$$

---

[13] An iatrogenic effect is an abnormal state or condition produced by a physician, other health care provider or intervention in a patient by inadvertent or erroneous treatment.
[14] It is taken as given that a person has not contracted GBS unless there is physiological muscle involvement, e.g. at least some temporary paralysis.

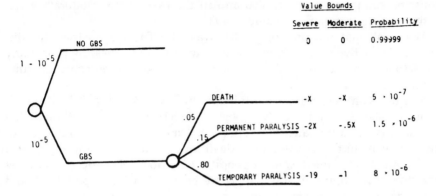

Value Bounds		
Severe	Moderate	Probability

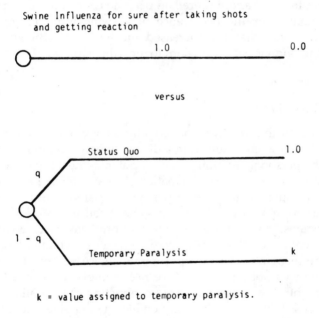

Figure 22.6. Additional branches for Guillain-Barré Syndrome with associated probabilities and ranges of values.

k = value assigned to temporary paralysis.

Figure 22.7. Lottery to determine value range for temporary paralysis.

The authors feel that their probability q is between 0.5 and 0.95 implying that k is between −1.0 and −19.0. This procedure is a standard one for assessing subjective values for decision analysis. Thus, the expected value to be added to branches B, C, E and F of Figure 22.2 is between 3.5×10^{-6} (−X) − 1.52×10^{-4} and 1.25×10^{-6} (−X) − 8.0×10^{-6}, where (−X) is the personal value of death. Returning to the calculation in Section 4, we see that in the case of the severe value estimates, the value to which X must be compared becomes 650 and in the case of the moderate value estimates, the comparable value is 492.

We recall that the previous value was 437. The reason that this difference is relatively small is that relative to other outcomes the probability of actually contracting GBS and suffering a severe outcome is quite small.[15]

The decision here remains automatic since $X = 499/p \geqslant 492$ for $p \leqslant 1$; that is, take the shot. For $X = 499/p \geqslant 650$, $p \leqslant 0.767$; although the decision is not automatic, we believe that if a proportional reduction of three-fourths in the probability of death during the upcoming year could be obtained by taking TA, most people would do so. Therefore, following the line of reasoning in this paper, we believe that most people should take the swine influenza vaccination.

Hence, rather surprisingly, for the authors' cohort, probabilities and values, analysis of the tree augmented with GBS branches indicates no change in the decision. That is, if the original decision were clearly in favor of getting the shot and if there had been no concomitant drop in the subjective estimates for the occurrence of a swine influenza epidemic about the same time that the increased incidence of GBS was being recognized, the individual's decision to get the shot might not have changed.

Summary and conclusions

We have illustrated that the systematic methodology of decision analysis can be applied to problems viewed in a distinctly non-economic manner – in this case, the personal decision based on potential health consequences of whether to get an influenza vaccination. It was shown that once the problem was formulated, the "best" personal decision might be evident without having to make value judgments about conceptually difficult-to-measure outcomes, such as death. Furthermore, we used a (derived) personal non-economic value of the decision maker's own life in making a decision where recognition of the appropriate choice without knowledge of such a value was not automatic. One rather unexpected result is that the inclusion of the possibility of contracting the Guillain-Barré Syndrome, a possibility that effectively ended the massive federal swine influenza vaccination program, was unlikely to alter the *personal* decision about getting the vaccine.

Public health authorities have been concerned with "high-risk groups" when considering influenza immunization policy and programs. In general, high-risk groups have been characterized by age, respiratory ailments and certain chronic diseases (Gregg, Bregman, O'Brien, &

---

[15] In fact, in the past the probability of getting GBS from a "typical" influenza vaccine (other than for swine influenza) was thought to be negligible and had never been a serious consideration in the decision of whether or not to take such vaccines.

Millar, 1978; Housworth & Langmuir, 1974; Housworth & Spoon, 1971; R. J. O'Brien, L. Schoenberger, D. J. Bregman, & R. Goodman, personal communications, 1976 and 1978; Sabin, 1977). In the case of swine influenza, no specific identification of high risk was made (R. J. O'Brien, L. Schoenberger, D. J. Bregman, & R. Goodman, personal communications, 1976 and 1978). However, for individuals who ordinarily would receive influenza vaccine, a bivalent vaccine (including A/New Jersey) was recommended. Accordingly, to employ our methodology to such cohorts, one would alter the probabilities of morbidity and mortality in the decision tree and perform sensitivity analyses. Clearly, such individuals may also reflect their attitudes about consequences by adjusting the corresponding values in the tree.

Currently, HEW officials are revaluating federal policy on influenza immunization. There is an ensuing controversy on the key cost-effectiveness issue, which involves the estimation of excess morbidity and mortality from influenza viruses with and without consideration of high risk (Gregg et al., 1978; Housworth & Langmuir, 1974; Housworth & Spoon, 1971; R. J. O'Brien, L. Schoenberger, D. J. Bregman, & R. Goodman, personal communications, 1976 and 1978; Sabin, 1977). Regardless of the outcome of federal discussions, including, possibly, revised estimates of risks and benefits, our analysis remains appropriate for individuals faced with the decision of using available vaccines.

A relatively inexpensive package could be developed which would allow a para-professional, working with a patient in any risk group, to use personal values in evaluating the decision. The authors hope that this paper will contribute toward making informed consent by patients about medical care more prevalent as they become intelligent participants in decisions about their own health care.

23. On the elicitation of preferences for alternative therapies

Barbara J. McNeil, Stephen G. Pauker,
Harold C. Sox, Jr., and Amos Tversky

There is a growing appreciation in the general public and the medical profession of the need to incorporate patients' preferences into medical decision making. To achieve this goal, the physican must provide the patient with data about the possible outcomes of the available therapies, and the patient must be able to comprehend and use these data. In this paper we investigate how people use statistical information regarding the possible outcomes of alternative therapies. We have focused on a particular medical problem (operable lung cancer) and asked the participants to choose between surgery and radiation therapy on the basis of simple descriptions of their possible consequences. Four variables were investigated: the input data presented to the subjects (life expectancy or cumulative probability), the characterization or framing of the outcomes (in terms of mortality or in terms of survival), the identification of the treatments (surgery or radiation therapy vs. unidentified treatments labeled "A" and "B"), and the population of respondents (physicians, patients, and graduate students).

Methods

The clinical problem

Lung cancer was selected for study because it offers a clear-cut choice between two alternative therapies – irradiation and surgery – that yield different patterns of survival probabilities. A previous study of this problem, using a formal decision-analytic approach (Raiffa, 1968; Keeney & Raiffa, 1976), found that an appreciable number of patients preferred radiation therapy to surgery despite the lower long-term survival

This chapter originally appeared in the *New England Journal of Medicine*, 1982, *306*, 1259–1262. Copyright © 1982 by the Massachusetts Medical Society. Reprinted by permission.

associated with radiation therapy (McNeil, Weichselbaum, & Pauker, 1978), presumably because it does not involve the risk of perioperative death.

As in the previous study on lung cancer, we used data reported by Mountain and his colleagues on the results of surgery (Mountain 1974, 1976; Mountain, Carr, & Anderson, 1974) and data reported by Hilton (1960) on the results of radiation therapy for operable lung cancer. These reports and others indicate that for 60-year-old patients treated with surgery the average operative mortality rate is 10 per cent, and the average five-year survival rate is about 34 per cent. The survival rates at one, two, three, and four years are 68, 51, 40, and 35 per cent, respectively. For radiation therapy there is essentially no treatment mortality, and the five-year survival rate is 22 per cent; survival rates at one, two, three, and four years are 77, 44, 28, and 23 per cent, respectively. Other data from the National Cancer Institute on the excess risk of death from lung cancer and on age-specific annual mortality rates were used to adjust the survival data to other age groups (Axtell, Cutler, & Myers, 1972). The comparison of the two treatments shows that surgery offers better long-term prospects at the cost of a greater immediate risk.

Input data

Two types of data were used. The first type, called cumulative-probability data, included the probability of survival (or death) immediately after the treatment, one year after the treatment, and five years after the treatment. The one-year point was chosen because it represents the short-term range in which survival after radiation therapy is higher than survival after surgery; the five-year point was chosen because it is commonly used in medicine to evaluate and compare alternative treatments. The second type, called life-expectancy data, included the probability of survival (or death) immediately after the treatment and the life expectancy associated with each treatment – that is, the average number of years lived after the treatment.

The survival curve describing the results after surgery has a long tail (i.e., it is more skewed to the right) than the survival curve for radiation therapy. Thus, the proportion of patients who will survive more than 10 years, for example, is greater for surgery than for radiation therapy. Consequently, the use of life expectancy, which is affected by the long tail, is expected to make surgery appear more attractive than it would with the use of one-year and five-year survival rates, which are not affected by the long tail.

Identification of treatment

For about half the respondents, the input data were identified as resulting from surgery or radiation therapy; for the remaining respondents, the treatments were not identified and the alternatives were labeled "A" and "B." The input data describing the results of A were identical to the results of surgery, and the data describing the results of B were identical to those of radiation therapy. This variation was introduced to assess the extent to which choices are determined by prior conceptions (or misconceptions) about surgery and radiation therapy.

Framing of outcome

The cumulative probabilities presented to about half the subjects referred to survival after a particular time – e.g., to a 68 percent chance of living for more than one year. The cumulative probabilities presented to the rest of the subjects referred to mortality – e.g., to a 32 percent chance of dying by the end of one year. Recent work by cognitive psychologists on the framing of decision problems indicates that the characterization of outcomes in terms of the probability of survival rather than the probability of death can have a substantial effect on people's preferences (Kahneman & Tversky, 1979b; Tversky & Kahneman, 1981). More specifically, this work suggested that the impact of perioperative mortality on the comparison between the two treatments would be greater when it was framed as a difference between mortality rates of 0 percent and 10 percent, than when it was framed as a difference between survival rates of 100 percent and 90 percent. Because the risk of perioperative death is the major disadvantage of surgery relative to radiation therapy, we hypothesized that surgery would be selected more frequently when the problem was described in terms of the probability of living than when it was described in terms of the probability of dying.

Subject population

Three groups of respondents were investigated: patients, physicians, and students. None of the subjects was known to have lung cancer. The patients were 238 men with chronic medical problems who were being treated as outpatients by internists at the Palo Alto Veterans Administration Medical Center. Their ages ranged from 40 to 80 years, with an average age of 58 years, which is similar to the age distribution of patients with lung cancer. The physicians were 424 radiologists whose ages ranged from 28 to 67 years, with an average age of 43 years; these subjects were taking postgraduate courses at the Harvard Medical School and the Brigham and Women's Hospital. Since physicians normally have an essential role in the choice of therapy, their own preferences are of considerable interest. The third group consisted of 491 graduate students from Stanford Business School, who had completed several courses in statistics and decision theory. Their average age was 29 years. They were

Table 23.1. *Numbers of subjects given data in various ways.*

Population	Outcome presented as probability of dying		Outcome presented as probability of living	
	Treatment identified	Treatment unidentified	Treatment identified	Treatment unidentified
Patients	60	60	59	59
Physicians	80	135	87	122
Students	196	64	101	130

included in the study so that we could examine the effects of age and analytic training.

We expected the students, who were younger than both the patients and the physicians, to choose surgery more often than the other two groups. We also expected the physicians and the students, who had more formal training than the patients, to be less affected by the variation in framing.

Procedure

Each subject was assigned to one of four conditions defined by the combinations of label (identified or unidentified) and frame (living or dying). The number of subjects in each group is shown in Table 23.1. All subjects received both cumulative-probability data and life-expectancy data, in that order. All subjects received the input data appropriate for their age group. Subjects who received the input data in an identified format and with outcome presented as the probability of dying were given the following instructions.

Surgery for lung cancer involves an operation on the lungs. Most patients are in the hospital for two or three weeks and have some pain around their incisions; they spend a month or so recuperating at home. After that, they generally feel fine.

Radiation therapy for lung cancer involves the use of radiation to kill the tumor and requires coming to the hospital about four times a week for six weeks. Each treatment takes a few minutes and during the treatment, patients lie on a table as if they were having an x-ray. During the course of the treatment, some patients develop nausea and vomiting, but by the end of the six weeks they also generally feel fine.

Thus, after the initial six or so weeks, patients treated with either surgery or radiation therapy feel about the same.

Next, the subjects were presented with the following cumulative probability data, which were also displayed in a table.

Of 100 people having surgery, *10* will die during treatment, *32* will have died by one year and *66* will have died by five years. Of 100 people having radiation therapy, none will die during treatment, *23* will die by one year and *78* will die by five years.

Which treatment would you prefer?

After the subjects made a choice, they were told that the above data summarized the experience of many hospitals and that they would now be asked to consider new information pertaining to a specific hospital and to make a new choice on the basis of these data.

At this single hospital, 10 percent of the patients who have surgery die during the perioperative period. The patients who survive treatment have a life expectancy (e.g., average number of remaining years) of *6.8* years. The life expectancy of all patients who undergo surgery (including those who die in the postoperative period) is *6.1* years. With radiation therapy, nobody dies during treatment, and the life expectancy of the patients who undergo radiation therapy is *4.7* years.

Which treatment would you prefer?

The subjects who received the data in an unidentified format were presented with different background information:

Both Treatment A and Treatment B are medications which are administered to the patient hospitalized for cancer. Both are given intravenously and neither one has significant side effects. Treatments A and B are considered equal except in their survival rates.

The input data concerning cumulative probability and life expectancy were the same as those for the identified treatments except that sugery and radiation therapy were replaced by "A" and "B," respectively. For the subjects who received the input data expressed in terms of the probability of survival, the probability of dying was replaced throughout by the probability of living. The patients were interviewed individually. The physicians and the students responded to a written questionnaire.

Results

The percentages of respondents who chose radiation therapy rather than surgery are shown in Table 23.2 for each of the experimental conditions. The results for the cumulative-probability condition and for the life-expectancy condition were submitted to two separate 3-by-2-by-2 analyses of variance after an arcsin transformation (Snedecor & Cochran, 1967). The effects of all four independent variables were significant ($P < 0.001$). Moreover, Table 23.2 reveals a highly regular pattern: with one minor exception there are no "cross-over" interactions among the major dependent variables – input data, identification of treatment, and the outcome frame. For example, all entries under "cumulative probability" exceed the corresponding entries under "life expectancy." We shall summarize the main effects in turn.

Table 23.2. *Percentages of subjects choosing radiation therapy over surgery.*

Type of data	Outcome and treatment variables				Overall
	Dying		Living		
	identified treatment	unidentified treatment	identified treatment	unidentified treatment	
(No. of subjects)	(336)	(259)	(247)	(311)	(1153)
*Cumulative probability**					
Patients	40	68	22	31	40
Physicians	50	62	16	51	47
Students	43	53	17	27	35
Overall	44	61	18	37	40
Life expectancy[†]					
Patients	35	50	19	27	28
Physicians	28	39	9	41	31
Students	21	41	9	24	22
Overall	25	42	11	31	27

* Immediately after treatment and at one and five years thereafter.
† Probability of surviving or dying from immediate treatment plus life expectancy thereafter. The dichotomy between probability of dying and probability of living in this group applies only to the data concerning the immediate treatment period.

Input data

As expected, subjects who had received life-expectancy data chose radiation therapy less frequently overall (27 percent) than did subjects who had received cumulative-probability data (40 percent). An examination of individual choices revealed that 59 percent of the subjects chose surgery under both types of data and 26 percent chose radiation therapy under both types. Hence, 85 percent of the respondents made the same choice under both conditions. Fourteen percent of the respondents chose radiation therapy in the cumulative-probability condition and surgery in the life-expectancy condition; only 1 percent made the opposite choices.

Identification of treatment

Overall, radiation therapy was chosen 42 percent of the time when it was not identified and only 26 percent of the time when it was identified. Evidently, identification of the two treatments favors surgery over radiation therapy.

Framing of outcome

As predicted, surgery was relatively less attractive in the mortality frame (probability of dying) than in the survival frame (probability of living). On the average, radiation therapy was preferred to surgery 42 percent of the time in the mortality frame and 25 percent of the time in the survival frame.

Subject population

Radiation therapy was least popular among the students (28 percent of all responses), somewhat more popular among the patients (34 percent), and most popular among the physicians (39 percent). The general pattern of preferences, however, was very similar in all three groups despite large differences in age, income, and lifestyle.

Discussion

We presented a large number of outpatients, physicians, and graduate students with information describing the possible outcomes of two alternative therapies for lung cancer. The respondents appeared to comprehend and use these data. An interview with the patients after the experiment indicated that they understood the data and were able to recall important items of information. However, the choices of both naive subjects (patients) and sophisticated subjects (physicians) were influenced by several variations in the nature of the data and the form in which they were presented.

The finding that data on life expectancy favored surgery whereas data on cumulative probability favored radiation therapy is not surprising in view of the fact that the survival distribution for surgery is much more skewed than the survival distribution for radiation therapy. However, this result illustrates the difficulty of selecting appropriate summary data; seemingly reasonable statistics (e.g., the mean or the median of a distribution) are likely to bias the decision maker in favor of one therapy or another.

The finding that radiation therapy was less attractive when the treatments were identified indicates that people relied more on preexisting beliefs regarding the treatments than on the statistical data presented to them. We do not know, however, whether these beliefs were based on valid evidence or reflected a widely shared bias against radiation therapy. In the former case, the input data should be expanded to include additional information that was presumably used by the subjects in the identified format only. In the latter case, subjects should be informed before the elicitation process in an attempt to reduce their biases.

Perhaps our most notable finding is the effect on people's choices of presenting the data in terms of survival or death. Surgery appeared to be much more attractive when the outcomes were framed in terms of the probability of survival rather than in terms of the probability of death. We attribute this result to the fact that the risk of perioperative death looms larger when it is presented in terms of mortality than when it is presented in terms of survival. Unlike the preceding effects, which can be justified or at least rationalized, this effect of using different terminology to describe outcome represents a cognitive illusion. The effect observed in this study is large (25 percent vs. 42 percent) and consistent: It holds for both cumulative-probability and life-expectancy data, for both identified and unidentified treatments, and for all three populations of subjects. Much to our surprise, the effect was not generally smaller for the physicians (who had considerable experience in evaluating medical data) or for the graduate students (who had received statistical training) than for the patients (who had neither).

One might be tempted to conclude from this study that there is no point in devising methods for the explicit elicitation of patients' preferences, since they are so susceptible to the way the data are presented, and to implicit suggestions and other biases. However, it should be noted that the preferences expressed by the physicians, which are likely to play an important part in the advice they give to patients, were subject to the same biases. In addition, there is little reason to believe that more informal procedures in which the treatments are described in general terms without quantitative statistical data are less susceptible to the effects of different methods of presentation.

Variations in types of data presentation can be used to assess the sensitivity of preferences with respect to the available alternatives. If a patient prefers surgery over radiation therapy, for example, whether the data are presented as cumulative probabilities or as life expectancy and whether the probabilities are presented in terms of mortality or in terms of survival, the preference may be assumed to be reasonably certain. If, on the other hand, a change of presentation leads to a reversal of preference, then additional data, discussions or analyses are probably needed. We suggest that an awareness of the effects of presentation among physicians and patients could help reduce bias and improve the quality of medical decision making.

Part VII

Social prediction and judgment

The majority of judgments we make are everyday decisions about our social environment and the people in it. Our judgments about other people and their ideas (as well as ourselves) are among the main elements of social life.

Some of the earliest research in the areas of judgment and decision making focused on social judgments. For example, a large number of investigators demonstrated the importance of first impressions; subsequent data about a person usually seemed to be interpreted in a way consistent with the initial opinion one had formed about that person. Partisan views, of course, have strong effects on social judgments. Albert Hastorf and Hadley Cantril showed, for example, that the Dartmouth fans had a drastically different evaluation of what had happened during the Dartmouth–Princeton football game than the Princeton fans did. A more serious and eventually famous study was done by Gordon Allport. Subjects were shown a picture of a subway scene in which a white male was holding a razor while speaking with a black male who held nothing in his hand. Many subjects later recalled that the scene contained a black male holding a razor. All of these early classic studies showed that preconceived notions exert powerful effects on the interpretation and recall of data.

Much of this research concerned what has been termed *hot cognition*, judgments made by biased or otherwise aroused subjects. In recent years there has been an increase in the investigation of errors made under normal conditions. These are errors that occur as a consequence of normal cognitive functioning, unencumbered by prejudice or emotion. As an example, suppose I am asked whether more people die from asthma or from tornadoes. As Paul Slovic and his colleagues have shown, most people think that tornadoes are more lethal than asthma, although the reverse is true. That is because every deadly tornado receives considerable publicity. But when did you last see a headline that shouted: "Asthma Kills Two in Kansas"? Bigotry, bias, or hot cognition is not the only reason for poor judgment about what is going on around us.

The first two readings we have chosen for this part demonstrate errors in social prediction and judgment. These selections reveal substantial human conceit: We think our judgment is more accurate than it really is, and we think we exert more control over a situation than we really do. Finally, we present an article that examines cross-cultural differences in judgment.

24. Knowing with certainty: The appropriateness of extreme confidence

Baruch Fischhoff, Paul Slovic, and Sarah Lichtenstein

Two aspects of knowledge are what one believes to be true and how confident one is in that belief. Both are represented in a statement like, "I am 70% certain that Quito is the capital of Equador." While it is often not difficult to assess the veridicality of a belief (e.g., by looking in a definitive atlas), evaluating the validity of a degree of confidence is more difficult. For example, the 70% certainty in the above statement would seem more appropriate if Quito is the capital than if Quito isn't the capital, but that is a rather crude assessment. In a sense, only statements of certainty (0% or 100%) can be evaluated individually, according to whether the beliefs to which they are attached are true or false.

One way to validate degrees of confidence is to look at the calibration of a set of such confidence statements. An individual is well calibrated if, over the long run, for all propositions assigned a given probability, the proportion that is true is equal to the probability assigned. For example, half of those statements assigned a probability of .50 of being true should be true, as should 60% of those assigned .60, and all of those about which the individual is 100% certain. A burgeoning literature on calibration has been surveyed by Lichtenstein, Fischhoff, and Phillips (1977). The primary conclusion of this review is that people tend to be overconfident, that is, they exaggerate the extent to which what they know is correct. A fairly typical set of calibration curves, drawn from several studies, appears in Figure 24.1. We see that when people should be right 70% of the time, their "hit rate" is only 60%; when they are 90% certain, they are only 75% right; and so on.

People's poor calibration may be, in part, just a question of scaling.

This chapter originally appeared in the *Journal of Experimental Psychology: Human Perception and Performance*, 1977, 3(4), 552–564. Copyright © 1977 by the American Psychological Association, Inc. Reprinted by permission.

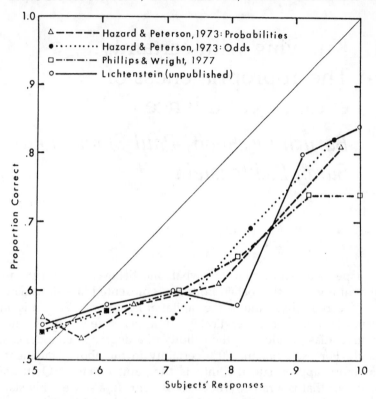

Figure 24.1. Some representative calibration curves. (Taken from Lichtenstein, Fischhoff, & Phillips, 1977. Copyright 1977 by D. Reidel Publishing Co. Reprinted by permission.)

Probabilities (or odds) are a set of numbers that people use with some internal consistency (e.g., the curves in Figure 24.1 are more or less monotonically increasing) but not in accordance with the absolute criteron of calibration. Miscalibration can have serious consequences (see Lichtenstein et al., 1977), yet people's inability to assess appropriately a probability of .80 may be no more surprising than the difficulty they might have in estimating brightness in candles or temperature in degrees Fahrenheit. Degrees of certainty are often used in everyday speech (as are references to temperature), but they are seldom expressed numerically nor is the opportunity to validate them often available (Tversky & Kahneman, 1974).

The extremes of the probability scale are, however, not such foreign concepts. Being 100% certain that a statement is true is readily understood by most people, and its appropriateness is readily evaluated. The following studies examine the calibration of people's expressions of extreme certainty. The studies ask, How often are people wrong when they are certain that they are right? In Experiment 1, the answer is sought in probability judgments elicited by questions posed in four different ways.

Experiment 1

Method

Stimuli. The questions covered a wide variety of topics, including history, music, geography, nature, and literature. The four formats used were the following:

1. Open-ended format. Subjects were presented with a question stem, which they were asked to complete; for example, "Absinthe is a _____" After writing down an answer, they estimated the probability that their answer was correct, using a number from .00 to 1.00.

2. One-alternative format. Subjects were asked to assess the probability (from .00 to 1.00) that simple statements were correct; for example, "What is the probability that absinthe is a precious stone?" The statement of fact being judged was sometimes true and sometimes false.

3. Two-alternative format (half range of responses). For each question, subjects were asked to choose the correct answer from two that were offered. After making each choice, they judged the probability that the choice was correct; for example, "Absinthe is (a) a precious stone or (b) a liqueur." Since they chose the more likely answer, their probabilities were limited to the range from .50 to 1.00.

4. Two-alternative format (full range of responses). Instead of having subjects pick the answer most likely to be correct as in Format 3, the experimenters randomly selected one of the two alternatives (e.g., [b] a liqueur) and had subjects judge the probability that the selected alternative was correct. Here the full range [.00, 1.00] was used. As in Format 3, one answer was correct.

Subjects and procedure. The subjects were 361 paid volunteers who responded to an ad in the University of Oregon student newspaper. They were assigned to the four groups according to preference for experiment time and date. Each group received the questions in only one of the four formats. Besides the differences in question format, the specific questions used differed somewhat from group to group. Instructions were brief and straightforward, asking subjects to choose or produce an answer and assign a probability of being correct in accordance with the format used.

Results

Lichtenstein and Fischhoff (1977) and Fischhoff and Lichtenstein (1977) have reported on the calibration of the entire range of probability

Table 24.1. *Analysis of certainty responses in Experiment 1*

Question format	No. items	No. subjects	Total no. responses	Certainty responses (p)	% certainty responses	% correct certainty responses
1. Open ended	43	30	1,290	1.00	19.7	83.1
2. One alternative	75	86	6,450	1.00	14.2	71.7
				.00	13.8	29.5
3. Two alternative (half range)	75	120	9,000	1.00	21.8	81.8
4. Two alternative (full range)	50	131	6,500	1.00	17.3	80.7
				.00	19.1	20.5

responses of subjects in Experiment 1. Here we examine only their extreme responses. Table 24.1 shows (a) the frequency with which subjects indicated 1.00 or .00 as the probability an alternative was correct and (b) the percentage of answers associated with these extreme probabilities that were, in fact, correct. Answers assigned a probability of 1.00 of being correct were right between 20% and 30% of the time. Answers assigned a probability of .00 were right between 20% and 30% of the time. In Formats 2 and 4, where responses of 1.00 and .00 were possible, both responses occurred with about equal frequency. Furthermore, alternatives judged certain to be correct were wrong about as often as alternatives judged certain to be wrong were correct. The percentage of false certainties ranged from about 17% (Format 1) to about 30% (Format 2), but comparisons across formats should be made with caution because the items differed. Clearly, our subjects were wrong all too often when they were certain of the correctness of their choice of answer.

Experiment 2

Experiment 1 might be faulted because of the insensitivity of the response mode. With probabilities, subjects using the stereotypic responses of .50, .55, .60, and so on, have few possible responses for indicating different degrees of high certainty. At the extreme, most subjects restricted themselves to the responses .90, .95, and 1.00, corresponding to odds of 9:1, 19:1, and ∞:1. Perhaps with a more graduated response mode, subjects would be better able to express different levels of certainty. In Experiment 2, subjects were presented with general-knowledge questions concerned with a single topic – the incidence of different causes of death in the United States – and asked to express their confidence in their answers in odds. The odds scale is open ended at the extremes, easily allowing the expression of many different levels of great certainty (e.g., 20:1, 50:1, 100:1, 500:1, etc.).

Method

Stimuli. All items involved the relative frequencies of the 41 lethal events shown in Table 24.2. They were chosen because they were easily understood and had fairly stable death rates over the last 5 years for which statistics were available. The event frequencies appearing in Table 24.2 were estimated from vital statistics reports prepared by the National Center for Health Statistics and the "Statistical Bulletin" of the Metropolitan Life Insurance Company. These frequencies provided the correct answers for the questions posed to our subjects.

From among these 41 causes of death, 106 pairs were constructed according to the following criteria: (a) Each cause appeared in approximately six pairs and (b) the ratios of the statistical rates of the more-frequent event to the less-frequent event varied systematically from 1:25:1 (e.g., accidental falls vs. emphysema) to about 100,000:1 (e.g., stroke vs. botulism).

Procedure. Subjects' instructions read as follows:

Each item consists of two possible causes of death. The question you are to answer is: Which cause of death is more frequent, in general, in the United States?

For each pair of possible causes of death, (a) and (b), we want you to mark on your answer sheet which cause you think is more frequent.

Next, we want to decide how confident you are that you have, in fact, chosen the more frequent cause of death. Indicate your confidence by the odds that your answer is correct. Odds of 2:1 mean that you are twice as likely to be right as wrong. Odds of 1000:1 mean that you are a thousand times more likely to be right than wrong. Odds of 1:1 mean that you are equally likely to be right or wrong. That is, your answer is completely a guess.

At the top of the answer sheet we have drawn a scale that looks like this:

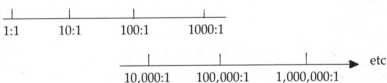

This scale is used to give you an idea of the kinds of numbers you might want to use. You don't have to use exactly these numbers. You could write 75:1 if you think that it is 75 times more likely that you are right than you are wrong, or 1.2:1 if you think that it is only 20% more likely that you are right than wrong.

Do not use odds less than 1:1. That would mean that it is less likely that you are right than that you are wrong, in which case you should indicate the other cause of death as more frequent.

Table 24.2. *Lethal events whose relative frequencies were judged by subjects in Experiments 2 and 3*

Lethal event	Actual deaths per 100 million[a]
Smallpox	0
Poisoning by vitamins	0.5
Botulism	1
Measles	2.4
Fireworks	3
Smallpox vaccination	4
Whooping cough	7.2
Polio	8.3
Venomous bite or sting	23.5
Tornado	44
Lightning	52
Nonvenomous animal	63
Flood	100
Excess cold	163
Syphilis	200
Pregnancy, childbirth, and abortion	220
Infectious hepatitis	330
Appendicitis	440
Electrocution	500
Motor vehicle – train collision	740
Asthma	920
Firearm accident	1,100
Poisoning by solid or liquid	1,250
Tuberculosis	1,800
Fire and flames	3,600
Drowning	3,600
Leukemia	7,100
Accidental falls	8,500
Homicide	9,200
Emphysema	10,600
Suicide	12,000
Breast cancer	15,200
Diabetes	19,000
Motor vehicle (car, truck, or bus) accident	27,000
Lung cancer	37,000
Cancer of the digestive system	46,400
All accidents	55,000
Stroke	102,000
All cancers	160,000
Heart disease	360,000
All diseases	849,000

[a] Per-year death rates are based on 100 million United States residents.

In case some of the causes of death are ambiguous or not well defined by the brief phrase that describes them, we have included a glossary for several of these items. Read this glossary before starting.

Subjects. The subjects were 66 paid volunteers who answered an ad in the University of Oregon student newspaper.

Results[1]

Table 24.3 shows the percentages of correct answers, grouped across subjects, for each of the most frequently used (major) odds categories. At odds of 1:1, 1.5:1, 2:1, and 3:1, subjects were reasonably well calibrated. However, as odds increased from 3:1 to 100:1, there was little or no increase in accuracy. Only 73% of the answers assigned odds of 100:1 were correct. Accuracy jumped to 81% at 1000:1 and to 87% at 10,000:1. For the answers assigned odds of 1,000,000:1 or greater, accuracy was 90%. For the latter responses, the appropriate degree of confidence would have been odds of 9:1. The 12% of responses that are not listed in Table 24.3 because they fell between the major odds categories showed similar calibration.

As in Experiment 1, subjects in Experiment 2 exhibited great over-confidence. They were frequently wrong at even the highest odds levels. Moreover, they gave many extreme odds responses. Of 6996 odds judgments, 3560 (51%) were greater than 50:1. Almost one fourth of the responses were greater than 1000:1.

Experiment 3

Although the tasks and instructions for Experiments 1 and 2 seemed reasonably straightforward, we were concerned that subjects' extreme overconfidence might be due to lack of motivation or misunderstanding of the response scale. Experiment 3 replicated Experiment 2, giving more care and attention to instructing and motivating the subjects.

Method

Experiment 3 used the 106 causes-of-death questions and odds response format of Experiment 2. The experimenter started the session with a 20-minute lecture to the subjects. In this lecture, the concepts of probability and odds were carefully explained. The subtleties of expressing one's feelings of uncertainty as numerical odds judgments were dis-

---

[1] A more detailed description of subjects' performances on this task and several related ones can be found in Lichtenstein, Slovic, Fischhoff, Combs, and Layman (1976).

Table 24.3. *Percentage of correct answers for major odds categories*

Odds	Appropriate % correct[a]	Lethal events						General-knowledge questions		
		Experiment 2			Experiment 3			Experiment 4		
		N	% N	% correct	N	% N	% correct	N	% N	% correct
1:1	50	644	9	58	339	8	54	861	19	53
1.5:1	60	68	1	57	108	2.5	59	210	5	56
2:1	67	575	8	64	434	10	65	455	1	63
3:1	75	189	2	71	252	6	65	157	3.5	76
5:1	83	250	4	70	322	8	71	194	4	76
10:1	91	1,167	17	66	390	9	76	376	8	74
20:1	95	126	2	72	163	4	81	66	1.5	85
50:1	98	258	4	68	227	5	74	69	1.5	83
100:1	99	1,180	17	73	319	8	87	376	8	80
1,000:1	99.9	862	13	81	219	5	84	334	7	88
10,000:1	100	459	7	87	138	3	92	263	6	89
100,000:1	100	163	2	85	23	.5	96	134	3	92
1,000,000:1	100	157	2	90	47	1	96	360	8	94
Total		6,098	88		2,981	70		3,855	75	
Overall % correct				71.0			72.5			73.1

Note: % N refers to the percentage of odds judgments that fell in each of the major categories. There were 66 subjects in Experiment 2, 40 in Experiment 3, and 42 in Experiment 4.
[a] For well-calibrated subjects.

cussed, with special emphasis on how to use small odds (between 1:1 and 2:1) when one is quite uncertain about the correct answer. A chart was provided showing the relationship between various odds estimates and the corresponding probabilities. Finally, subjects were taught the concept of calibration and were urged to make odds judgments in a way that would lead them to be well calibrated. (The complete text of the instructions is available from the authors.)

The subjects for Experiment 3 were 40 persons who responded to an ad in the University of Oregon student newspaper. As in previous experiments, they were paid for participating. Group size was held to about 20 to increase the likelihood that subjects would ask questions about any facet of the task that was unclear.

Results

The proportion of correct answers for each of the most frequent odds categories is shown in the center portion of Table 24.3. The detailed instructions had several effects. First, subjects were much more prone to use atypical odds such as 1.4:1, 2.5:1, and so on. Only 70% of their judgments fell within the major odds categories of Table 24.3, as compared to 88% for Experiment 2. Second, their odds estimates tended to be smaller. About 43% of their estimates were 5:1 or less, compared to 27% for this category in Experiment 1. Third, subjects in this experiment were more often correct at odds above 10:1 and thus were better calibrated.

Nevertheless, subjects again exhibited unwarranted certainty. They assigned odds greater than or equal to 50:1 to approximately one third of the items. Only 83% of the answers associated with these odds were correct. When subjects estimated odds of 50:1, they were correct 74% of the time and thus should have been giving odds of about 3:1. At 1000:1, they should have been saying about 5:1.

Although only 70% of the responses fell in the major odds categories of Table 24.3, inclusion of the remaining 32% would not have changed the picture. Odds estimates falling between major categories were calibrated similarly to estimates within those categories. Elaborate instruction tempered subjects' extreme overconfidence, but only to a limited extent.

Experiment 4

Is there something peculiar to the causes-of-death items that induces such overconfidence? Experiment 4 replicated Experiment 3 using general-knowledge questions (of the type used in Experiment 1) matched in difficulty with the 106 causes-of-death items. In addition, subjects' faith in their odds judgments was tested by their willingness to participate in a gambling game based on those judgments.

Method

The questionnaire consisted of 106 two-alternative items covering a wide variety of topics; for example, "Which magazine had the largest circulation in 1970? (a) *Playboy* or (b) *Time*"; "Aden was occupied in 1839 by the (a) British or (b) French"; "Bile pigments accumulate as a result of a condition known as (a) gangrene or (b) jaundice." These items were taken from a large item pool with known characteristics. Availability of this pool allowed us to select items matched in difficulty, question by question, with the 106 items about lethal events studied in Experiments 2 and 3.

The subjects were 42 paid volunteers, recruited by an ad in the University of Oregon student newspaper. The instructions paralleled those of Experiment 3. Subjects first received the detailed lecture describing the concepts of probability, odds, and calibration. They then responded to the 106 general-knowledge items, marking the answer they thought to be correct and expressing their certainty about that answer with an odds judgment.

After responding to the 106 items, they were asked whether they would be willing to accept gambles contingent on the correctness of their answers and the appropriateness of their odds estimates. If subjects really believe in their extreme (extremely overconfident) odds responses, it should be possible to construct gambles that they are eager to accept but which, in fact, are quite disadvantageous to them. The game was described by the following instructions:

The experiment is over. You have just earned $2.50, which you will be able to collect soon. But before you take the money and leave, I'd like you to consider whether you would be willing to play a certain game in order to possibly increase your earnings. The rules of the game are as follows.

1. Look at your answer sheet. Find the questions where you estimated the odds of your being correct as 50:1 or greater than 50:1. How many such questions were there? _____ (write number)

2. I'll give you the correct answers to these "50:1 or greater" questions. We'll count how many times your answers to these questions were wrong. Since a wrong answer in the face of such high certainty would be surprising, we'll call these wrong answers "your surprises."

3. I have a bag of poker chips in front of me. There are 100 white chips and 2 red chips in the bag. If I reach in and randomly select a chip, the odds that I will select a white chip are 100:2 or 50:1, just like the odds that your "50:1" answers are correct.

4. For every "50:1 or greater" answer you gave, I'll draw a chip out of the bag. (If you wish, you can draw the chips for me.) I'll put the chip back in the bag before I draw again, so the odds won't change. The probability of my drawing a red chip is 1/51. Since drawing a red chip is unlikely, every red chip I draw can be considered "my surprise."

5. Every time you are surprised by a wrong answer to a "50:1 or

greater" question, you pay me $1. Every time I am surprised by drawing a red chip, I'll pay you $1.

6. If you are well calibrated, this game is advantageous to you. This is because I expect to lose $1 about once out of every 51 times I draw a chip, on the average. But since your odds are sometimes higher than 50:1, you expect to lose less often than that.

7. Would you play this game? Circle one. Yes No

Subjects who declined were then asked if they would play if the experimenter raised the amount he would pay them to $1.50 whenever he drew a red chip, while they still had to pay only $1 in the event of a wrong answer. Those who still refused were offered $2 and then a final offer of $2.50 for every red chip. Since the experimenters expected the game to be unfair to subjects (by capitalizing on a "known" judgmental bias), it was not actually played for money.

Results

The proportion of correct answers associated with each of the most common odds responses is shown in the right-hand column of Table 24.3. Compared with the previous studies, subjects in Experiment 4 gave a higher proportion of 1:1 odds (19% of the total responses). A few difficult items led almost all of the subjects to give answers close to 1:1, indicating that they were trying to use small odds when they felt it was appropriate to do so. However, this bit of restraint was coupled with as high a percentage of large odds estimates as was given by the untutored subjects in Experiment 2. About one quarter of all answers were assigned odds equal to or greater than 1000:1.

Once again, answers to which extremely high odds had been assigned were frequently wrong. At odds of 10:1, subjects were correct on about three out of every four questions, appropriate to odds of 3:1. At 100:1, they should have been saying 4:1. At 1000:1 and at 100,000:1, estimates of about 7:1 and 9:1 would have been more in keeping with subjects' actual abilities. Over the large number of questions for which people gave odds of 1,000,000:1 or higher, they were wrong an average of about 1 time out of every 16.

The gambling game. Of the 42 subjects, 27 agreed to play a gambling game described above for $1. Six more agreed when the stakes were raised to $1.50 every time the experimenter drew a red chip. Of the holdouts, 3 subjects agreed to play at $2 for every red chip and 2 more agreed when the final offer of $2.50 was made. Only 3 subjects refused to participate at any level of payment per red chip.

After subjects had made their decisions about playing the game, they were asked whether they would change their minds if the game were to be played, on the spot, for real money. No subject indicated a desire to change his or her decision. Two subjects approached the experimenter after the experiment requesting that they be given a chance to play the game for cash. Their request was refused.

Of course, this game is strongly biased in favor of the experimenter. Since subjects were wrong about once for every eight answers assigned odds of 50:1 or greater, the game would have been approximately fair had the experimenter removed 86 of the white chips from the bag, leaving its contents at 14 white and 2 red chips.

The expected outcome of playing the game with each subject was simulated. Every wrong answer on a "50:1 or greater" question was assumed to cost the subject $1. The experimenter was assumed to have drawn 1/51 of a red chip for every answer given at odds greater than or equal to 50:1; his expected loss was then calculated in accordance with the bet the subject had accepted. For example, if a subject accepted the experimenter's first offer ($1 per red chip) and gave 17 "50:1 or greater" answers, the experimenter's simulated loss was 17/51 dollars (33¢).

The subjects who agreed to play averaged 38.3 questions with odds greater than or equal to 50:1. Thirty-six persons had expected monetary losses, and three had expected wins. Individual expected outcomes ranged between a loss of $25.63 and a gain of $1.84. The mean expected outcome was a loss of $3.64 per person and the median outcome was a loss of $2.35. Ten persons would have lost more than $5. The 39 subjects would have lost a total of $142.13 across 1,495 answers at odds greater than or equal to 50:1, an average loss of 9.5¢ for every such answer. The two persons who earnestly requested special permission to play the game had expected losses totaling $33.38 between them.

Experiment 5: Playing for keeps

Subjects in Experiment 4 viewed their overconfident odds judgments as faithful enough reflections of their state of knowledge that they were willing to accept hypothetical bets more disadvantageous than many that can be found in a Las Vegas casino. Before concluding that there is money to be made in "trivia hustling," we decided to replicate Experiment 4 with real gambling at the end.

Method

Nineteen subjects participated in Experiment 5. It differed from Experiment 4 only in that the gambling game was presented as a real game. After responding to the 106 items, subjects heard the gambling game instructions and decided whether or not they would play. They were told that they could lose all the money they had earned in the experiment and possibly even more than that. After they made their decisions about playing the game, subjects were told that any earnings from the game would be added to their pay for the experiment, but that if they lost money, none of the money initially promised them for participating would be confiscated. The game was then played on those terms.

Six of the 19 subjects agreed to play the game as first specified (with a $1 payment for each "experimenter's surprise"). Three more agreed to play when the experimenter offered to increase the payment to $1.50 per red chip. Increasing the payment to $2 brought in one additional player, and three more agreed to play at $2.50. Six subjects consistently refused to participate; some because they felt they were not well calibrated, others because they did not like to gamble.

Results

When the game was actually played, the 13 participating subjects missed 46 of the 387 answers (11.9%) to which they had assigned odds greater than or equal to 50:1. All 13 subjects would have lost money, ranging from $1 to $11 (in part because, by chance, no red chips were drawn). When the experimenter's part of the game was simulated as in Experiment 4, four subjects would have lost more than $6, and the average participating subject would have lost $2.64. Thus, the hypothetical nature of the gamble in Experiment 4 apparently had minimal influence on subjects' willineess to bet.

General subject and item analyses

Is undue confidence found only in a few subjects or only for a few special items? If cases of extreme overconfidence are concentrated in only a few subjects, then the generality of our conclusions would be limited. Pathological overconfidence on the part of a small sector of the public would be worth exploring further but would not tell us much about cognitive functioning in general. The results of the gambling games reported above show that this was not the case. Most subjects were willing to play and most would have lost money because they were too often wrong when using extreme odds. The left columns of Table 24.4 show the distribution of cases of extreme overconfidence (defined as giving odds of 50:1 or greater and being wrong) over subjects for Experiments 3 and 4. The great majority of subjects had one or more cases of extreme overconfidence. The median number was 4 in Experiment 4 and between 3 and 4 in Experiment 3, well over what would be expected with well-calibrated subjects. In each experiment, one subject appeared to be an outlier (those subjects having 32 and 27 cases). Reanalyzing the data after removing those two subjects had no effect on our conclusions.

The right columns of Table 24.4 show the distribution of cases of extreme overconfidence over items. If most cases were concentrated in only a few items, the situation would be rather different than if a broad

Table 24.4. Frequency of extreme overconfidence (odds greater than or equal to 50:1 that were assigned to wrong answers)

No. cases of extreme overconfidence	Number of subjects Experiment 3	Number of subjects Experiment 4	No. extremely overconfident subjects	Number of items Experiment 3	Number of items Experiment 4
0	5[a]	3	0	33[b]	41
1	3	7	1	25	20
2	6	5	2	19	16
3	6	5	3	13	10
4	4	9	4	3	8
5	1	1	5	2	2
6	4	1	6	4	1
7	2	2	7	1	3
8	1	0	8	1	0
9	0	3	9	0	0
10	2	2	10	2	3
11	0	1	11	1	0
12	1	0	12	0	0
13	1	0	13	1	1
14	0	0	14	1	0
15	0	2	15	1	1
16	2	0			
17	1	0			
More than 17[c]	1(32)	1(27)			

[a] There were five subjects in Experiment 3 who never showed extreme overconfidence.
[b] There were 33 items in Experiment 3 for which no subject showed extreme overconfidence.
[c] Actual number of cases is in parentheses.

section of items fooled some of the people some of the time. It would not necessarily be less interesting, for it would remain to be explained why people went astray on those few items. As the results in Table 24.4 indicate, both situations seem to have been true. There are some items on which many people gave high odds to the wrong answer, but most items did show a few such cases.

The items on which six or more subjects showed extreme over-confidence were all items that might be described as "deceptive," ones which less than 50% of the subjects answered correctly. Some correlation between deceptiveness and extreme overconfidence is inevitable; many subjects must get an answer wrong before many can get it wrong *and* be certain that they are right. There were 18 items in Experiment 3 and 17 items in Experiment 4 answered correctly by less than 50% of our subjects.

Table 24.5 shows the incidence of cases of extreme overconfidence with deceptive and nondeceptive items. Although extreme overconfidence is disproportionately prevalent with the deceptive items, it is still abundant with the nondeceptive ones. If the deceptive items are removed from the sample, then the remaining distribution of cases of extreme over-confidence over items closely resembles a Poisson distribution, which is what one would expect if such cases were distributed at random over items. One third of the easiest items, those answered correctly by 90% or more of our subjects, had at least one case of a subject answering wrongly and giving odds of being correct of 1000:1 or greater. Deleting the one extreme subject from each of Experiments 3 and 4 had little effect on this result. Clearly, a few subjects or items are not responsible for the extreme overconfidence effect.

Table 24.5. *Percentage wrong with deceptive and nondeceptive items*

Experiment and item	Percentage wrong association with odds of		
	≥50:1	≥100:1	≥1000:1
Experiment 3			
All items (106)	16.6	14.1	12.9
Deceptive items (18)	73.9	75.5	72.3
Nondeceptive items (88)	8.9	6.7	6.9
Experiment 4		13.1	10.8
All items (106)	13.8	76.7	70.6
Deceptive items (17)	73.2	6.8	5.2
Nondeceptive items (89)	7.6		
Expected with perfect calibration	≤1.96	≤.99	≤.10

General discussion

These five experiments have shown people to be wrong too often when they are certain that they are right. This result was obtained with both probability and odds responses, with minimal and extensive instructions and with two rather different types of questions. Subjects were sufficiently comfortable with their expressions of certainty that they were willing to risk money on them in both hypothetical and real gambles. Finally, cases of extreme overconfidence were widely distributed over subjects and items.

Although these studies have shown the effect to be a robust one, they have certainly not closed the topic. Further research with different subjects, different items, and different instructions would be most useful. Some moderately informed guesses at the results of such additional studies are possible. Lichtenstein and Fischhoff (1977) have found that the calibration of probability responses associated with general-knowledge questions is relatively invariant with regard to several factors not considered here, including subjects' intelligence, subjects' expertise in the subject-matter area of the questions and subjects' reliance on the stereotypic responses of .50 and 1.00. They did, however, find that calibration varies with item difficulty.

A crucial question for generality is how well the level of item difficulty found in these experiments represents the level found in the world. Although no simple answer to this question is possible, it is worth noting that the items in Experiments 2 and 3 were not constructed with the intention of eliciting extreme overconfidence. Rather, they were constructed to vary in difficulty from very hard to very easy, as defined by the ratio of the statistical frequencies of death from each of the two causes. Items in Experiments 4 and 5 were matched to these items in difficulty.

To explain these results, we must understand both how people answer questions and how they assess the validity of their answering process. Collins (Collins, Warnock, Aiello, & Miller, 1975; Collins, 1976) has shown that people use many different strategies in answering questions. We suspect, therefore, that extreme overconfidence can come from a variety of sources. Every answering procedure may have its own ways of leading people astray and its own ways of hiding that misguidance when people try to assess answer validity. Some possible pathways to over-confidence are described below.

Many of the items we presented to our subjects are on topics for which they do not have a ready answer stored in memory. They must infer the answer from other information known to them. But people may be insufficiently critical of their inference processes. They may fail to ask "What were my assumptions in deriving that inference?" or "How good am I at making such inferences?" For example, when people draw a few instances of a category from memory to get an idea of the properties of the category, they may not realize that readily available examples need not be representative of the category (Tversky & Kahneman, 1973). Wason and Johnson-Laird (1972) have shown that people have considerable confidence in their own erroneous syllogistic reasoning. Collins et al. (1975) have described a variety of inferential strategies that people use in producing answers without realizing their limitations. Summarizing her studies on the inference process in perception, Johnson-Abercrombie (1960) concluded, "The[se erroneous] inferences were not arrived at as a series of logical steps but swiftly and almost unconsciously. The validity of the inferences was usually not inquired into; indeed, the process was usually accompanied by a feeling of certainty of being right" (p. 89). Pitz (1974), who also observed overconfidence in probability estimates, elaborated a similar hypothesis. He proposed that people tend to treat the results of inferential processes as though there was no uncertainty associated with the early stages of the inference. Such a strategy is similar to the "best-guess" heuristic that has been found to describe the behavior of subjects in cascaded inference tasks (e.g., Gettys, Kelly, & Peterson, 1973).

For other questions, people believe that they are answering directly from memory without making any inferences. People commonly view their memories as exact (although perhaps faded) copies of their original experiences. However, considerable evidence has demonstrated that memory is more than just a copying process (e.g., Neisser, 1967). According to this view, people reach conclusions about what they have seen or what they remember by reconstructing their knowledge from fragments of information, much as a paleontologist infers the appearance of a dinosaur from fragments of bone. During reconstruction, a variety of cognitive, social, and motivational factors can introduce error and distortion into the output of the process. Examples of this are the foibles of eyewitness testimony documented by Buckhout (1974), Loftus (1974), Münsterberg (1908), and others.

If people are unaware of the reconstructive nature of memory and perception and cannot distinguish between assertions and inferences (Harris & Monaco, 1978), they will not critically evaluate their inferred knowledge. In general, any process that changes the contents of memory unbeknownst to people will keep them from asking relevant validity questions and may lead to overconfidence. In his classic studies of reconstructive processes in memory, Bartlett (1932) found that subjects not only created new material but were often highly certain about that which they had invented.[2]

---

[2] An example of the subtle role of assumptions in the reconstruction of knowledge comes from the experience of one of the authors who became embroiled in a friendly debate with a colleague about the dates of a forthcoming conference. Both parties agreed that the conference was to last about 4 to 5 days. But the dispute centered about whether these dates were March 30 to April 3 or April 30 to May 3. The author was certain of the former dates because he specifically recalled the date March 30 in the organizer's letter. His

Table 24.6. *Deceptive items in Experiment 3*

Causes of death compared[a]	Percent correct	No. cases of extreme overconfidence[b]
Pregnancy, abortion, childbirth versus appendicitis	15	15
All accidents versus stroke	17.5	14
Homicide versus suicide	25	12
Measles versus fireworks	25	5
Suicide versus diabetes	27.5	8
Breast cancer versus diabetes	30	1

[a] Subjects judged the first cause of death listed to be less frequent than the second.

[b] Data are the number of subjects (out of 40) who gave odds greater than or equal to 50:1 to the wrong alternative.

We present these ideas more as a framework for future research and conceptualization than as an explanation for our results. Nonetheless, if these speculations have some validity, it should be possible to find apparent examples in our data. Tables 24.6 and 24.7 present the most deceptive items from Experiments 3 and 4, respectively. Although cases of extreme overconfidence were distributed over most items, these "deceptive" items produced a disproportionate share. In the absence of detailed protocols from subjects, these cases where many people went astray may provide better clues to our intuitions than situations where just one or two subjects had trouble with an item.

Looking at the deceptive items in Experiment 3 (see Table 24.6), we find that in many cases the cause of death incorrectly judged to be more frequent (the first one listed in each pair) is a dramatic, well-publicized event, whereas the underestimated cause is a more "quiet" killer. Considering the first three examples, (a) pregnancy, abortion, and childbirth, (b) accidents, and (c) homicide seem disproportionately more newsworthy and better reported than their comparison cause of death.[3] In these cases, people may be relying on the greater availability in memory of examples of the "flashier" causes of death without realizing that availability is an imperfect inferential rule (Tversky & Kahneman, 1973).[4]

colleague was certain of the latter period because he specifically recalled the date May 3 in the letter. Bets were placed, and the letter was consulted to resolve the dispute. To the surprise of both parties, the letter stated the dates as March 30 to May 3, an obvious mistake. Thus, both parties were correct regarding the fragment of information they recalled, but one fragment led to the wrong conclusion.

[3] This speculation has been empirically affirmed by Lichtenstein, Slovic, Fischhoff, Combs, and Layman (1976).

[4] Subjects in Experiment 3 were asked to select one answer about which they were certain and to write a short statement indicating why they were so confident. One subject explained odds of 2000:1 that death from pregnancy was more frequent than deaths by appendicitis by writing "I've never heard of a person dying of appendicitis, but I have many times heard of persons dying during childbirth and abortion."

Table 24.7. *Deceptive items in Experiment 4*

General-knowledge question[a]	Answers[b]	Percent correct	No. cases of extreme over-confidence[c]
1. Three fourths of the world's cacao comes from	Africa* or South America	4.8	15
2. Which causes more deaths in the U.S.?	Appendicitis* or pregnancy, abortion, and childbirth	19.0	13
3. When was the first air raid?	1849* or 1937	26.2	10
4. Adonis was the god of	Love or vegetation*	31.0	10
5. Kahlil Gibran was most inspired by which religion?	Buddhist or Christian*	33.3	7
6. *Dido and Aeneas* is an opera written by	Berlioz or Purcell*	33.3	2
7. Potatoes are native to	Ireland or Peru*	35.7	10

[a] Some questions have been abbreviated slightly.
[b] Correct answer carries an asterisk.
[c] Data are the number of subjects (out of 42) who gave odds greater than or equal to 50:1 to the wrong alternative.

Other items suggest other answering processes. Subjects' confident – but erroneous – beliefs (not shown in Table 24.6) that there were fewer deaths from smallpox vaccine than from the disease itself may have been based on the generally valid assumption that vaccines are safer than the diseases they are meant to prevent. With smallpox, however, the vaccine has been so successful that no one has died of the disease in the U.S. since 1949, while from 6 to 10 people have died annually from complications arising from vaccination.

For the general-knowledge questions of Experiment 4 in Table 24.7, we will give a few interpretations of the varied ways that unrecognized or inadequately questioned assumptions can obscure the tenuousness of erroneous beliefs; the reader can surely provide others. Regarding Item 1, cacao is native to South America. Subjects who knew this fact (or guessed it from the Spanish-sounding name) may have been misled by assuming that the continent of origin is also the continent of greatest production. Similar reasoning may have been involved with Item 7. The potato's prominence in Irish history does not mean that it originated there. Regarding Item 3, it may not have occurred to subjects that an air raid could be conducted by balloons, which were used by Austria to bomb Venice in 1849. The fact that Adonis was a handsome youth who had an affair with Venus, the Goddess of Love, may have suggested that he, too, was a deity of love (Item 4). And so on.

Finally, let us add a warning that extreme overconfidence cuts both ways. Our sources for the answers to general-knowledge questions were a variety of encyclopedias and dictionaries. We viewed the answers they provided with great confidence. Much to our chagrin, we discovered on several occasions that these authorative sources disagreed, a possibility we had never considered. Fortunately, our own overconfidence was discovered before conducting these experiments; the offending items were deleted and the remaining ones double- and triple-checked until we were *certain* of their accuracy.

25. Cultural variation in probabilistic thinking: Alternative ways of dealing with uncertainty

George N. Wright and
Lawrence D. Phillips

Bruner, Goodnow, and Austin (1956) devoted a chapter of "A study of thinking" to categorizing with probabilistic cues. They concluded, speculatively:

Cultural differences and individual differences in venturesomeness with respect to the use of cues doubtless exist. The speed with which one person will pigeonhole another on the basis of slender external cues – this is one of the most characteristic aspects of man's general cognitive style: willingness to sustain indecision, whether it be equated to "tolerance for ambiguity" or not – gives the appearance of being a relatively consistent trait.

Independently in the 1950's subjective probability estimates replaced objective or relative frequency based probability as input to decision theory (see Edwards, 1954). Under this approach, the probability of an outcome, given an act by a decision maker, and the attractiveness or utility of that outcome *determine*, in a normative sense, optimal act choice (see Lindley, 1971; Raiffa, 1968, for outlines of decision theory, and Brown, Kahr, and Peterson, 1974a, for the related technology, decision analysis). A probability entered into a decision analysis is usually a subjective "degree of confidence" (Bernoulli, 1713). Even though people may differ in their probability assessments, each is equally "correct" provided that the probabilities so assessed conform to the axioms of probability theory (De Finetti, 1937; Savage, 1954).

However, probability assessments can be examined for their accuracy, given hindsight, that is, in the light of subsequent events. Winkler and Murphy (1968) thus identified two measures of a probability assessor's adequacy; normative goodness, which reflects the degree to which the

This chapter is an abbreviated version of an article that originally appeared in the *International Journal of Psychology*, 1980, *15*, 239–257. Copyright © 1980 by the North Holland Publishing Company. Reprinted by permission.

assessments conform to the axioms of probability and substantive goodness, which reflects the amount of knowledge of the topic area contained in the assessments. Lichtenstein, Fischhoff, and Phillips (1977) delineated a further aspect of a probability assessor's adequacy, "calibration." A probability assessor is "well calibrated" if, over the long run, for all propositions assigned the same probability, the proportion that are true is equal to the probability assigned.

This study examines cultural and intra-cultural differences in calibration and, more generally, in probabilistic thinking. By probabilistic thinking we mean the tendency to adopt a probabilistic set, discrimination of uncertainty and the ability to express the uncertainty meaningfully as a numerical probability. Before presenting new data we will review previous research.

Phillips and Wright (1977) and Wright, Phillips, Whalley, Choo, Ng, Tan, and Wisudha (1978) have reported cultural differences in probabilistic thinking using British, Hong Kong, Malaysian and Indonesian samples. The largest cultural difference was found between Asian and British student groups. The British adopted a more finely differentiated view of uncertainty, both verbally and numerically, than the Asians in response to uncertain situations. These differences are predictable neither on the basis of the relative abundance of probability expressions in the Indonesian language nor by the Malay samples' ability to discriminate English probability words on a meaningful probability discrimination dimension. For numerical probabilities assigned to almanac questions, the British were less extreme and better calibrated than the Asian students. However, the British students were still more extreme than that required for perfect calibration getting an average of 84 per cent correct for the hundred per cent assessments given. Slovic, Fischhoff, and Lichtenstein (1976b) found this effect with American students and labelled it the "certainty illusion."

In an attempt to account for the strong cultural differences in probabilistic thinking, Phillips and Wright (1977), Wright et al. (1978) have suggested a causal relationship with the "fate-orientation" of a culture. Wilson (1970) supports the assertion that Asian culture is, in general, fate-orientated relative to British culture. Unfortunately, no psychological studies have attempted to verify this assertion. Use of Rotter's (1966) Internal–External control scale is inappropriate in such an enterprise due to its dichotomy of "active" and "passive" approaches to life, respectively. As Kluckhohn and Strodtbeck (1961) point out, harmony with nature rather than subjugation to nature seems to have been the dominant orientation in many periods of Chinese history.

The question of possible antecedents of probabilistic thinking will be discussed later after a presentation of recent cross-cultural data using a wide variety of Asian and British samples. These samples were obtained in order to test the generality of previous findings of cultural differences in probabilistic thinking.

The experiment

Method

Instruments (1) View of Uncertainty Questionnaire (VUQ). The View of Uncertainty Questionnaire (VUQ), detailed in Phillips and Wright (1977) asks 45 questions such as "Will you catch a head cold in the next three months?" or "Is Bagdad the capital of Iraq?" Half the questions are about events that have not yet happened while the others concern factual matters that most people are not sure about (e.g., "Is the Suez Canal over 100 miles long?"). The instructions asked respondents to "Write in the space provided a reasonable and appropriate response to the following questions."

Responses on the VUQ were classified into five categories: (1) number of yes/no responses; (2) number of don't know responses; (3) number of probability responses; (4) number of different probability responses used by that subject, and (5) catch-all responses (e.g., "I hope not"). The percentage correct or hit-rate for any Yes or No responses given to the factual questions were also calculated. This coding of the VUQ gives an indication of verbal probabilistic set and discrimination.

The View of Uncertainty Questionnaire and the Probability Assessment Questionnaire (described below) were administered in English for the English, Hong Kong and Malay samples and translated into Indonesian samples using the back-translation method (after Brislin, 1970). We considered translating the Malaysian version of the questionnaires into Malay, but decided against it as we knew that most courses at the University of Malaysia are taught in English. Wright *et al.* (1978) lend support to this decision by showing that Malaysian student samples have the ability to arrange English probability words on a meaningful probability discrimination dimension.

(2) Probability Assessment Questionnaire (PAQ). The Probability Assessment Questionnaire (PAQ), as detailed in Phillips and Wright (1977), presented 75 questions with two choice alternative answers, such as:

Which is longer?
(a) Panama Canal
(b) Suez Canal

*S*s are asked to choose the right answer and also to indicate how sure they are by writing a percentage between 50 and 100.

Several measures were taken from the PAQ: number of 100 per cent assessments, number of correct 100 per cent assessments, percentage correct (hit-rate) for any 100 per cent assessments given, and number of 50 per cent assessments. Also calculated was the entropy measure, H, for the distribution of the 75 probability assessments given on the PAQ. Specifically,

$$H = - \sum_{i=1}^{i-M} \frac{n_i}{N} \log_2 \frac{n_i}{N},$$

where n_i is the number of assessments of a given probability, M is the number of *different* probability assessments made by the S, and $N = \Sigma n_i = 75$. The H measure is relatively large when many different assessments are given, and when they are made equally often. The H measure would be relatively small for an individual who gave only assessments of 50 per cent and 100 per cent, particularly if most of the assessments were just one of those probabilities. . . .

Samples.[1] The data reported here are a comparison of: Malay Malaysians ($n = 96$), Chinese Malaysians ($n = 104$) and Indian Malaysians ($n = 90$) attending the University of Malaysia; Moslem Indonesians ($n = 52$) and Christian Indonesians ($n = 41$) attending the University of Indonesia; British civil servants ($n = 55$); Hong Kong managers ($n = 33$) and Indonesian managers and company directors ($n = 39$) in business in the Jakarta area.

The Malaysian student samples were also analysed for arts/science differences and they were compared with a new sex analysis of a previous sample of the general British population ($n = 143$).

Procedure

Each S was first asked to read, or was read, a brief statement of the general purpose of the experiment. The statement discussed decision making in general and made no reference to probabilistic thinking. The S was then given the View of Uncertainty Questionnaire. When that was completed it was removed and replaced with the Probability Assessment Questionnaire, which includes instructions for its use. Finally, each S was given a personal inventory which asked for such information as age, sex, race, course followed, and so forth.

For the British, Hong Kong and Malaysian samples all instructions and questionnaires were given in English. The Indonesian sample received instructions and questionnaires written in the Indonesian language.

[1] We are indebted to Mr. T. Casey at the Hong Kong University, Dr. S. Sadli and Dr. E. Markhum at the University of Indonesia and Dr. Awang Had Salleh and the heads of department and housemasters at the University of Malaysia for their invaluable assistance with the experiment.

Table 25.1. *Comparisons on probabilistic set and discrimination: Malaysian sub-cultural analysis*

Measure	Sample			
	Malay Malaysians (MM) ($n = 95$)	Chinese Malaysians (CM) ($n = 104$)	Indian Malaysians (IM) ($n = 90$)	British students (B) ($n = 43$)
No. of probability word responses				
M	6.98	6.29	7.43	9.23
S	5.79	4.45	4.33	6.12
$p < 0.01$		B		CM
$p < 0.05$	B	IM	CM, B	MM, IM
No. of different probability word responses				
M	3.12	3.4	3.82	6.84
S	2.31	2.36	2.36	4.70
$p < 0.01$	B	B	B	MM, CM, IM
$p < 0.01$	IM		MM	
H				
M	1.73	1.83	1.91	2.84
S	0.794	0.73	0.77	0.593
$p < 0.01$	B	B	B	MM, CM, IM
$p < 0.05$				

Note: Letters next to standard probability levels refer to differences between the groups at the head of the table.

Results

Malaysian sub-cultural student samples. Malaysia has a plural society in which Malays form 49.8 per cent of the total population, Chinese 37.2 per cent and Indians 11.2 per cent.[2] Previously, Wright *et al.* (1978) compared Malay Malaysians with other Asian and British samples. Table 25.1 gives the means and standard deviations for measures taken from the VUQ and PAQ using new student samples from the Malaysian Chinese and Indian sub-cultures, along with mean differences that reach significance at the 0.01 and 0.05 level.[3]

Across the measures of probabilistic set and discrimination the Malaysian sub-cultural groups do show differences but these are not

[2] Department of Statistics, Kuala Lumpur, 1967. Population Census of the Federation of Malaya, Report No. 14.

[3] By the 0.01 significance level we mean that, using the student-*t* distribution, the 99% credible interval for the difference between the means does not include zero. Similarly for the 0.05 significance level. For details of the Bayesian analyses, see Phillips (1973, pp. 283–286).

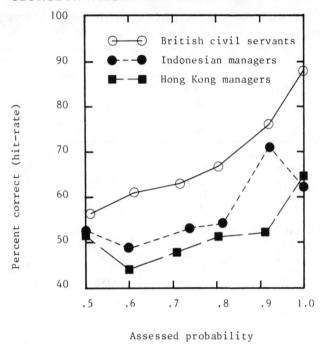

Figure 25.1. Calibration curves – Malaysian sub-cultural analysis.

systematic. This finding contrasts sharply with the strong differences shown by Wright *et al.* (1978) comparing the Malay sample with a British student sample. Similarly the Malaysian sub-cultural samples show similar group determined calibration curves in Figure 25.1. This similarity was confirmed in individual subject analysis.

The general similarity of the Malaysian sub-cultures on our measures of probabilistic thinking supports our earlier deduction that Rotter's I-E Control scale will be a non-correlate of probabilistic thinking, for Indian students have been found to be highly "internal" relative to most other cultures (Carment, 1974; Parsons & Schneider, 1974).

Indonesian religious groups. This analysis was performed on the Indonesian student sample employed previously in Wright *et al.* (1978). The sample was divided into those of Moslem faith (*n* = 52) and those of Christian faith (*n* = 41) by considering the students' response to the question: "What was the religion taught in your family when you were a child?" asked in a personal inventory presented after the VUQ and PAQ. The remainder of the Indonesian students who were classified as Buddhists (*n* = 7) or of no religion (*n* = 1) were not included in the data analysis.

Parkinson (1967) argues that:

Table 25.2. *Comparisons on probabilistic set and discrimination: religion analysis*

Measure	Sample	
	Indonesian Moslem (IM) Students ($n = 52$)	Indonesian Christian (IC) Students ($n = 41$)
No. of probability word responses		
M	8.23	7.54
S	4.51	6.02
$p > 0.05$	–	–
No. of different probability word responses		
M	3.90	2.98
S	2.33	2.22
$p > 0.05$	IC	IM
H		
M	1.73	1.75
S	0.678	0.615
$p > 0.05$	–	–

Note: Letters next to standard probability levels refer to differences between the groups at the head of the table.

The Islamic ... is very prone after receiving a set back, to give up striving and say that he has no luck, that it is the will of God.... Such an attitude constitutes a significant drag on economic development.... All this forms part of their impotence in the force of more powerful influences which shape their destiny.

On the basis of such a view of Islamic belief, the Moslem students could perhaps be categorised as "external" or "passive" in the context of Rotter's I-E control scale. The Christian Indonesians could perhaps be viewed as more similar to the British in their beliefs. Accordingly we would expect the Moslem sample to show less evidence of probabilistic thinking than the Christian sample *if* religious belief affects the ability to think probabilistically. Table 25.2 reveals that this expectation is ill-founded; the Moslem students, relative to the Christian students, tended to give more different probability word responses to the VUQ, showed similar differentiation of numerical probability, and showed similar calibration as revealed by group determined calibration curves and individual subject analysis.

British, Hong Kong, and Indonesian managers. Many decisions are made under uncertainty. Indeed the rationale of decision analysis is to deal with uncertainty in decision making in an optimal way. Managers deal with uncertainty as their occupation, therefore, if cultural differences in probabilistic thinking exist between managers from the cultures studied previously, there is strong evidence for more general cultural influences.

Table 25.3. *Comparisons on probabilistic set and discrimination: managerial analysis*

Measure	Sample		
	British civil servants (B) ($n = 55$)	Hong Kong managers (HK) ($n = 31$)	Indonesian managers (I) ($n = 39$)
No. of probability word responses			
M	10.95	7.45	7.67
S	7.49	5.03	5.24
$p < 0.01$	HK,1	B	B
No. of different probability word responses			
M	6.31	3.23	3.72
S	4.75	2.16	2.79
$p < 0.01$	HK, 1	B	B
H			
M	2.61	1.77	1.66
S	0.420	0.615	0.607
$p < 0.01$	HK, 1	B	B

Note: Letters next to standard probability levels refer to differences between the groups at the head of the table.

Table 25.3 compares Hong Kong middle managers, British civil servants of administrative grade and Indonesian businessmen working in the Jakarta area. The direction of differences on the probabilistic thinking measures confirm the differences found by Wright *et al.* (1978) using student samples.

The relevant calibration curves are shown in Figure 25.2. The British civil servants are much better calibrated than the Asian managers, who differ little, both in the group determined calibration curves and individual calibration parameters.

Arts/science orientation within Malaysia. Since Phillips and Wright (1977) and Wright *et al.* (1978) have suggested that differences in probabilistic thinking may be influenced by arts/science orientation, the Malaysian student samples described above were subdivided *within* the sub-cultural groups into those following a general arts course as opposed to a science or social science course. As Table 25.4 illustrates, arts/science differences do exist but these differences are not systematic or readily interpretable.

Sex differences. Subdivision of the Malaysian student samples and Wright and Phillips' (1979) sample of the general British population by sex revealed no systematic sex differences indicating that the differential sex composition of the samples reported earlier and above has no obvious

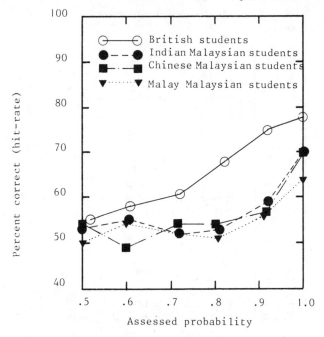

Figure 25.2. Calibration curves – managerial analysis.

influence upon the reported findings (see Table 25.5 for a summary of the sex differences).

A further analysis of the general British population (n = 143) examined age differences and probabilistic thinking. The mean age of this sample was 36 years old with a standard deviation of 14.3. Two non-zero correlations emerged:

Number of 100 percent assessments on the PAQ correlated 0.28 (p = 0.04)[4] with age, suggesting that as one gets older one becomes more sure of onself, although this certainty is not reflected in reality shown by the near-zero correlation of age with per cent correct for any 100 per cent assessments given; age also gave a correlation of −0.35 (p < 0.001) with H on the PAQ suggesting, similarly, that as one gets older one makes less-fine distinctions in uncertainty.

Age analysis was not applicable to the Asian samples due to the small age variations present in the student samples.

The "certainty illusion." Another aspect of probabilistic thinking showing strong differences between Britain and Asia, and noted by Wright *et al.*

[4] Numbers in parentheses are the posterior probabilities associated with the null hypothesis of zero correlation when the alternative hypothesis is "non-zero correlation," assuming 50–50 priors for the hypotheses and uniform distribution of prior opinion on the diffuse hypothesis.

Table 25.4. *Comparisons on probabilistic set and discrimination: arts/science analysis*

Measure	Sample					
	Chinese arts (CA) (n = 48)	Chinese science (CS) (n = 56)	Indian arts (IA) (n = 48)	Indian science (IS) (n = 42)	Malay arts (MA) (n = 46)	Malay science (MS) (n = 50)
No. of probability word responses						
M	7.27	5.45	7.21	7.69	4.76	9.02
S	4.22	4.52	3.76	4.94	5.33	6.26
$p < 0.01$		MS			MS	CS, MA
$p < 0.05$	CS, MA	CA, IS, IA	CS, MA	CS, MA	CA, IS, IA	
No. of different probability word responses						
M	3.98	2.91	3.75	3.90	2.43	3.72
S	2.20	2.41	2.10	2.32	1.81	2.54
$p < 0.01$	CS, MA	CA	MA	MA	MS, CA, IS, IA	MA
$p < 0.05$		IS		CS		
H						
M	1.51	0.210	1.85	1.98	1.50	1.94
S	0.706	0.640	0.864	0.650	0.719	0.792
$p < 0.01$	CS, MS, IS	CA, MS, MA, IS, IA	CS	CS, CA, MA	MS, IS, CS	MA, CA, CS
$p < 0.05$	IA		CA, MA		IA	

Note: Letters next to standard probability levels refer to difference between the groups at the head of the table.

Table 25.5. *Comparisons on probabilistic set and discrimination: sex analysis*

Measure	Sample					
	Chinese Malaysian females (CMF) (n = 40)	Chinese Malaysian males (CMM) (n = 56)	Indian Malaysian females (IMF) (n = 20)	Indian Malaysian males (IMM) (n = 63)	British females (BF) (n = 101)	British males (BM) (n = 42)
No. of probability word responses						
M	7.47	5.52	7.45	7.51	7.82	7.79
S	4.60	4.34	4.12	4.50	5.3	7.28
$p < 0.01$	–	–	–	–	–	–
$p < 0.05$	CMM	CMF	–	–	–	–
No. of different probability word responses						
M	4.03	2.93	4.2	3.83	5.5	5.0
S	2.51	2.21	1.99	2.32	4.07	4.78
$p < 0.01$	–	–	–	–	–	–
$p < 0.05$	CMM	CMF	–	–	–	–
H						
M	1.99	1.90	2.27	1.92	2.4	2.5
S	0.638	0.654	0.793	0.672	0.59	0.578
$p < 0.01$	–	–	–	–	–	–
$p < 0.05$	–	–	IMM	IMF	–	–

Note: Letters next to standard probability levels refer to differences between the groups at the head of the table. The Malay Malaysian students and the British students could not be included in this data analysis due to their high constituent proportion of males.

(1978), was the strong tendency for Asian students to say "100 percent sure," on the PAQ although this certainty was not reflected in per cent correct for the 100 per cent assessments given. Table 25.6 gives means and standard deviations for these two variables.

The result replicates Wright *et al.*'s original findings; there is a strong tendency for the Asian samples to use 100 per cent assessments overconfidently. The British samples, by contrast, use 100 per cent assessments relatively infrequently but more accurately.

Discussion and conclusion

Our finding that Malaysian Indian students performed more similarly to Malay and Chinese Malaysian students than to the British students, suggests that the concept of internal-external control may not be related to probabilistic thinking. This conclusion is reinforced by the strong similarities between Moslem and Christian Indonesians, the former being presumed to be more passively external than the latter, in our measures

Table 25.6. *The certainty illusion*

Measure	Sample							
	British students (B) (n = 43)	Malay Malaysian students (MM) (n = 95)	Chinese Malaysian students (CM) (n = 104)	Indian Malaysian students (IM) (n = 90)	British civil servants (BC) (n = 55)	Hong Kong managers (HK) (n = 31)	Indonesian businessmen (I) (n = 39)	British general population (BG) (n = 143)
No. of 100% assessments given								
M	12.88	42.06	40.2	39.05	20.9	37.9	37.05	18.05
S	10.12	17.4	16.7	15.95	10.2	13.4	12.24	12.09
$p < 0.01$	MM, CM, IM, BC, HK, I, BG	B, BC, BG	B, BC, BG	B, BC, BG	B, CM, IM, MM, HK, I	B, BC, BG	B, BC, BG	B, MM, CM, IM, HK, I
$p < 0.05$	–	I	–	–	–	–	MM	–
Percentage correct for any 100% assessments given								
M	84.2	65.0	72.0	71.7	88.8	65.9	61.8	80.3
S	13.4	13.0	10.0	12.0	14.2	10.6	11.7	15.4
$p < 0.01$	MM, CM, IM, HK, I	B, BC, BG, CM, IM	B, BC, BG, I, MM, HK	B, BC, BG, HK, MM, I	MM, CM, IM, HK, I	B, BC, BG, CM, IM	B, BC, BG, CM, IM	MM, CM, IM, HK, I
$p < 0.05$	–	–	–	–	–	–	–	–

of probabilistic thinking. Extrapolating further, religious orientation may not be an important factor influencing probabilistic thought; Indonesian Christians and Western Christians (our original British student sample) showed pronounced differences in probabilistic thinking.

Arts/science and sex differences in probabilistic thinking were apparent across cultures although these differences are not systematic. Any attempt at interpretation is, on the basis of present knowledge, problematic.

Intracultural differences in probabilistic thinking between students and managers from Britain and Asia are small compared with the strong inter-cultural differences. Whether these differences are accountable in terms of the relatively general "fatalism" of Asian culture remains speculation. Adaption of Kluckhohn and Strodtbeck's (1961) value-orientation concept into a questionnaire form might be one way to test this possibility.

Investigation of possible child-rearing antecedents of probabilistic thinking may also be fruitful. For instance, Kriger and Kroes (1972) note that there is some evidence that Chinese mothers are more restrictive in their child rearing attitudes than American mothers. Similarly, Swift (1965) and Dyamour (1959) note the tendency of Malay parents to encourage indulgence on the part of their young children, hence discouraging them from becoming self-reliant. Conversely, Carstairs (1957) found that maternal indulgence and self-dependency, especially with regard to sons, were characteristic of Indian family life. Whether this pattern of child rearing is found in Indian Malaysian parents is as yet unknown. As cultural differences in probabilistic thinking are extended and replicated, analysis of child rearing and socialization patterns in the search for antecedents of probabilistic thought will become more appropriate.

Our major conclusion at this stage of the research is that strong differences exist between people raised within Asian and British culture on our measures of probabilistic thinking: these differences outweigh any influence of sub-culture, religion, occupation, arts/science orientation or sex, at least within the contexts studied. Generally, Asians adopt a less finely differentiated view of uncertainty, both numerically and verbally than do the British. In cases where a numerical probabilistic set is adopted by Asians the probabilities assessed are much more extreme and much less realistic[5] than those assessed by the British. This finding has clear implications for communication of uncertainty across cultures and to the

[5] Realism of probability assessments does not bear a simple relationship to the amount of knowledge the groups studied here possess, as Lichtenstein et al. (1977) would suggest, as there is no sharp distinction between the British and Asian groups in overall proportion of items answered correctly (0.64, 0.62, 0.79, 0.57, 0.58, 0.59, 0.62, 0.62, 0.53, 0.58 for the British students, British general population, British civil servants, Hong Kong students, Hong Kong managers, Malay Malaysian students, Indian Malaysian students, Chinese Malaysian students, Indonesian students and Indonesian managers, respectively).

potential inapplicability of decision analysis as a means of decision making to Asian culture.

Redding and Martyn-Johns (1978) have noted that, "... the commonest of the phrases used by the Western practising manager dealing with his Asian equivalents – 'they think differently' ..." and "if probability is seen differently, then this will materially effect the process of management thinking and in turn it will effect management action." Non-probabilistic thinking may result in a lack of long-term future planning. Events in the future may be seen as "uncertain" rather than "probable" or "improbable." For instance, Penny (1967) notes about Indonesian agricultural planning, "Too great a willingness on the part of the government to forego future gains for the sake of smaller immediate ones can mean the rejection of extremely profitable development opportunities." The successful non-probabilistic thinker, realizing his inability to think probabilistically, may remain flexible in response to an uncertain future. The unsuccessful non-probabilistic thinker may make confident predictions of the future and often be wrong. Conversely, the probabilistic thinker may predict the future in terms of probabilities assigned to events but still be unprepared for actual events due to lack of perfect calibration.

As Redding (1978) notes:

Why is it that the Chinese form of business is predominately the small scale, owner-dominated enterprise, *with a reputation for flexibility* and a capacity for survival? ... Instead of surveys of product markets, it relies instead for its strategic thinking on personal recommendations, keeping an ear to the ground, having a highly developed sense of the complete context in which it operates, and following hunches. It takes risks but not based on probability theory.... It goes without saying the Chinese have a flair for business. It also seems evident that their managerial methods are not the same as are found in a Western company. The contrast seems to be between the Western sense of order and rationality and the Oriental sense of all-embracing contextual thinking in which the *options are always open, the view can change* and sense or feel takes over from calculation. It is arts versus science.

Table 25.7 presents data from the present study which confirms this assertion.

Asian managers are more likely to respond "don't know," both verbally and numerically, to uncertain situations compared to British civil servants who, as Table 25.3 revealed, adopt a probabilistic view.

The data presented in Table 25.6, however, indicated that the picture is more complicated, for the Asian managers are also more susceptible to the certainty illusion. Using a British sample Wright and Phillips (1979) have found that "yes/no" *versus* "don't know" is one psychological set for viewing uncertainty, whilst "yes/no" *versus* a probability assessment is another world view. Clearly the "yes/no – don't know" view of uncertainty is prevalent in Asian culture and as such may account for the description of Asian decision making quoted above.

Table 25.7. *Managerial response to uncertainty*

Measure	Sample		
	British civil servants (B) ($n = 55$)	Hong Kong managers (HK) ($n = 31$)	Indonesian managers (I) ($n = 39$)
No. of don't know responses			
M	2.53	8.48	4.82
S	3.09	6.36	4.8
$p < 0.01$	HK, I	B, I	B, HK
$p < 0.05$	–	–	–
No. of 50% assessments			
M	11.53	17.03	20.97
S	7.45	10.23	10.25
$p < 0.01$	HK, I	B	B
$p < 0.05$	–	–	–

26. A computer-based system for identifying suicide attemptors

David H. Gustafson, Bruce Tianen, and John H. Greist

Introduction

During the fall of 1972 a collaborative effort was undertaken at the University of Wisconsin–Madison by the Departments of Industrial Engineering and Psychiatry to design and evaluate a computer-based system for collecting legible and standardized patient and therapist information which could be used for measuring suicide risk and referring patients to appropriate therapy. The system designed, along with the results of the tests made to evaluate it, are discussed in full in "*A Probabilistic* System for Identifying Suicide Attemptors" (Gustafson, Griest, Strauss, Erdman, & Laughren, 1977). In brief, the suicide detection system's principal components are a computer-based interactive interview and a computer decision making model. After the patient has taken the computer interview, the probabilities referring to two diagnostic states [1] patient will attempt suicide and [2] patient will not attempt suicide are printed. These, along with a summary of the interview, are then made available to the therapist to assist him in his decision concerning the proper evaluation of the suicide potential and the type of therapy to be prescribed.

It was found that this risk prediction system does predict attempts well (Griest, Gustafson, Strauss, Rowse, Laughren, & Chiles, 1973) but that it does not successfully measure the lethality of the attempt; that is, whether the suicide attempt will lead to death. Since an effective measure for predicting the lethality of a potential suicide attempt is also necessary for accurate patient diagnosis and treatment, further work was indicated. The following is a report of the development and implementation of a complementary system which addresses the problem of predicting lethality if a suicide attempt is made.

This chapter originally appeared in *Computers and Biomedical Research*, 1981, *14*, 144–157.

The system is set up to employ either a Bayesian or a multiple regression model. Both models are built upon subjective judgments rather than empirical data. Subjective judgments are relied upon because reliable empirical data are not available in the form needed for development of predictive models. The rationale for using subjective rather than empirical estimates is discussed in detail in other papers (Gustafson, Edwards, Phillips, & Slack, 1969; Slovic & Lichtenstein, 1971; Hursh, Hammond, & Hursch, 1964; Grinell, Keeley, & Doherty, 1971). Suffice it to say that there are problems in gaining access to empirical data from medical records, and that when the data are available, they are often incomplete, illegible, and sometimes inaccurate. More will be said about the subjective estimation process later. The next paragraphs will discuss the Bayesian and regression models.

The multiple regression model is a linear additive model of the form

$$y = a + b_i x_i + \ldots + b_n x_n, \tag{1}$$

where x_i are the independent attributes used to predict y (in our case, survival or death from a suicidal attempt), a is a constant, and b_i are the coefficients that distinguish the importance of the attributes in predicting suicide attempts. The coefficients are estimated by asking judges to estimate the chances of death for a set of hypothetical patients. Each hypothetical patient is described by one level from each attribute. The set of hypothetical patients is created by taking a random sample of all possible combinations of attribute levels. Once survival estimates and attribute levels are available, a statistical least-squares technique is used to derive the attribute coefficients.

The second model selected for this research was the Bayesian model. While the regression model is additive, the Bayesian model is multiplicative. The Bayesian model has been more extensively applied in medical diagnosis, starting with Ledley and Lusted's suggestion (Ledley & Lusted, 1959b) and Warner's application of the tool (Toronto, Veasey, & Warner, 1963). A review of the literature (Albert, 1978) – which will not be repeated here – discussed these and other successful uses of the Bayesian approach to medical diagnosis. Another reason for selecting the Bayesian model is that it is a formally optimal method of revising prior opinion in the light of new evidence. Finally, the Bayesian model is also used in our suicide diagnostic system. Therefore a Bayesian risk/rescue scale would be easy to adapt to that system.

System development

The regression model

To develop the regression model two sets of information were required: (1) a sample of patient profiles and (2) an estimate of the chance of death for the group of patients whose profiles were used. The first set of information, the patient profiles, was obtained by creating 56 profiles of hypothetical patients, using the process described in the introduction to the regression model. Each profile consisted of 15 independent variables. These independent variables had been identified, through a survey of the relevant literature and through discussion with experienced clinicians, as the major factors contributing to a suicidal death. A sample patient profile with information regarding all fifteen predictor cues is shown in Fig. 26.1.

The second set of information needed for the development of the regression model was an estimate of the chance of death for the patients whose profiles were used. This information was obtained by giving a group of four third-year psychiatric residents and a group of four mental health center clinicians the sample profiles and asking the members of each group to estimate the probability that each patient died as a result of the suicide attempt. The dependent variable (chance of death) and the independent variables (e.g., age) were used in a step-wise multiple regression procedure to create a linear regression model based on the predictions of each group. The models, one for each group, were validated by comparing their predictive results with the estimates of the two clinician groups and with the actual outcomes of the patients whose profiles were used.

The Bayesian model

To develop a Bayesian model, there are three requirements: (1) conditionally independent symptoms, (2) prior probability estimates, and (3) likelihood estimates.

Conditional independence of symptoms conceptually means that assuming a particular outcome, the occurrence or nonoccurrence of one symptom is not dependent on the occurrence or nonoccurrence of another symptom. Four psychiatrists were given a stack of cards each containing the name of one symptom, e.g., age. The psychiatrists individually sorted the cards into piles, such that two cards in the same pile meant that knowing one symptom makes it substantially easier to estimate the occurrence or nonoccurrence of another symptom. After an individual sorting of cards, the psychiatrists discussed their sorting and then revised them as seemed appropriate. When two symptoms were placed together by 75% of the psychiatrists, the symptoms were considered conditionally dependent and one of the two was eliminated. This process has been shown by Glackman (1970) to be an effective means of dealing with the conditional independence issue.

The methods of estimating the prior probabilities and likelihoods for the Bayesian model are shown in Figs. 26.2 and 26.3. In both cases, four psychiatric residents from the University of Wisconsin Department of Psychiatry and four staff members from the Dane County Mental Health Center provided the subjective estimates. The prior probabilities, likeli-

PATIENT NO. __2__

SEX—Male
AGE—30 to 39
EXTENT OF SUICIDE PLANS—I have a plan but have not obtained the means.
ATTITUDE TOWARDS LIVING—I do not want to continue living.
FINAL ACTS IN ANTICIPATION OF DEATH (E.G., WILLS, GIFTS, INSURANCE)—
None.

ACTION TO GAIN HELP DURING/AFTER ATTEMPT—Did not contact or notify potential
helper.

PREMEDITATION OF SUICIDE—Suicide contemplated for more than three hours.
LOCATION OF THE ATTEMPT—Familiar (home, place of work, etc.)
PROBABILITY OF DISCOVERY DURING THE ATTEMPT—Accidental discovery, low.
AGENT OR METHOD USED—Drugs

CONCEPT OF METHODS LETHALITY—Patient was certain of death as a result of his act.
CONCERN ABOUT DIFFICULTIES WITH HEALTH—Low concern.
DEGREE OF ISOLATION—No one nearby or in visual or vocal contact.
TIMING—Timed so that rescue is unlikely.
PRECAUTIONS AGAINST DISCOVER/INTERVENTION—Active precautions (as locked
door).

THE PERCENT CHANCE THAT THIS PATIENT
DIED AS A RESULT OF THE ATTEMPT _____

Figure 26.1. A sample of the patient profiles used in developing the regression model. (Independent variables or "predictor cues" are on the left. The information to the right describes the patient.)

ASSUME THAT __ALL__ YOU KNOW ABOUT 100 PATIENTS IS THAT THEY ATTEMPTED
SUICIDE.

OF THE 100 PATIENTS HOW MANY WERE IN EACH OF THE FOLLOWING CATEGO-
RIES AS THE RESULT OF THEIR ATTEMPT:

	RESIDENTS	MENTAL HEALTH CENTER STAFF
1. DEAD DUE TO SUICIDE	14	17
2. SURVIVED THEIR ATTEMPT	86	83
	100	100

Figure 26.2. Task description for subjective estimation of prior probabilities. The numbers entered in the blanks are the average prior probability estimates obtained from the residents and the mental health center staff.

ASSUME THAT IN COLUMN 2 ALL YOU KNOW IS THAT A TOTAL OF 100 PEOPLE ATTEMPTED SUICIDE AND DIED AS A RESULT; THEN ESTIMATE THE NUMBER WHICH WOULD FALL IN EACH OF THE CATEGORIES. ASSUME IN COLUMN 3 THAT 100 PEOPLE ATTEMPTED SUICIDE AND SURVIVED THE ATTEMPT; THEN ESTIMATE THE NUMBER WHICH WOULD FALL IN EACH OF THE COLUMN 3 CATEGORIES.

Symptom level description (Column 1)	Residents		Mental health center staff		Actual patients	
	(Column 2) Dead	(Column 3) Not dead	(Column 2) Dead	(Column 3) Not dead	Dead	Not dead
Sex of patient						
1. Male*	29	69	25	66	6(0.33)	8(0.56)
2. Female*	71	31	75	34	12(0.67)	6(0.44)
TOTAL	100	100	100	100	18	14
Age						
1. 10 to 19	17	7	13	9	3(0.16)	0(0)
2. 20 to 29	23	14	27	16	9(0.50)	2(0.14)
3. 30 to 39	19	12	20	14	2(0.12)	5(0.36)
4. 40 to 49	14	17	13	18	3(0.13)	4(0.28)
5. 50 to 59	12	20	12	21	1(0.06)	2(0.14)
6. 60 to 69	9	18	9	15	0(0)	1(0.07)
7. 70 and over	6	12	7	7	0(0)	0(0)
TOTAL	100	100	100	100	18	14
Was the location where the attempt occurred						
1. Familiar (home, place of work, etc.)*	48	64	44	69	14(0.78)	12(0.86)
2. Non-familiar, non-remote	21	26	16	20	2(0.11)	0
3. Remote (isolated or hidden spot)	31	10	40	10	2(0.11)	2(0.14)
TOTAL	100	100	100	100	18	14

Symptom level description	Residents		Mental health center staff		Actual patients	
(Column 1)	(Column 2) Dead	(Column 3) Not dead	(Column 2) Dead	(Column 3) Not dead	Dead	Not dead
Probability of discovery How probable was it that you would be discovered or rescued during the attempt						
1. High, almost certain	11	56	8	69	0	9(0.50)
2. Uncertain discovery	28	32	25	22	5(0.36)	6(0.33)
3. Accidental discovery, low	61	12	67	9	9(0.64)	3(0.17)
TOTAL	100	100	100	100	14	18
Extent of suicide plans						
1. I have no plans	6	36	6	36	4(0.28)	3(0.18)
2. I have a plan but have not obtained the means	20	28	18	30	4(0.28)	5(0.27)
3. I have a plan and have already obtained the means*	74	36	76	34	6(0.44)	10(0.55)
TOTAL	100	100	100	100	14	18
Difficulties with health						
1. None	24	49	16	41	3(0.21)	7(0.39)
2.	13	17	13	23	4(0.28)	0
3. Moderate	19	16	15	17	3(0.21)	3(0.17)
4.	21	10	21	11	1(0.07)	4(0.22)
5. Extreme	23	10	35	8	3(0.21)	4(0.22)
TOTAL	100	100	100	100	14	18

Figure 3 Continued

Symptom level description (Column 1)	Residents		Mental health center staff		Actual patients	
	(Column 2) Dead	(Column 3) Not dead	(Column 2) Dead	(Column 3) Not dead	Dead	Not dead
Degree of isolation						
1. Someone present	4	19	11	47	1(0.07)	1(0.06)
2. Someone near	19	46	21	32	3(0.21)	10(0.55)
3. No one near	77	35	68	21	10(0.62)	7(0.39)
TOTAL	100	100	100	100	14	18
Timing						
1. Timed so rescue probable	8	60	7	68	0(0)	13(0.72)
2. Timed so rescue unlikely	32	27	19	21	5(0.36)	3(0.17)
3. Timed so rescue very unlikely	60	13	74	10	9(0.64)	2(0.11)
TOTAL	100	100	100	100	14	18
Precautions against discovery						
1. None	14	47	9	62	2(0.14)	8(0.44)
2. Passive	31	39	21	26	7(0.50)	9(0.50)
3. Active precautions	55	14	70	12	5(0.36)	1(0.06)
TOTAL	100	100	100	100	14	18
Attitude toward living						
1. Wants to live	5	22	5	36	2(0.14)	3(0.16)
2. Doesn't want to live	69	29	68	31	5(0.36)	3(0.16)
3. Ambivalent*	26	49	27	33	7(0.50)	12(0.64)
TOTAL	100	100	100	100	14	18
Final acts in anticipation of death						
1. None*	27	52	13	63	8(0.58)	15(0.83)
2. Made some arrangements	31	34	26	26	3(0.21)	3(0.17)
3. Completed arrangements	42	14	11	11	3(0.21)	0
TOTAL	100	100	100	100	14	18

Figure 2 Continued

Symptom level description (Column 1)	Residents		Mental health center staff		Actual patients	
	(Column 2) Dead	(Column 3) Not dead	(Column 2) Dead	(Column 3) Not dead	Dead	Not dead
Action to gain help during and after attempt						
1. Notified potential helper	14	41	8	67	1(0.07)	5(0.28)
2. Gave clues to potential helper	24	34	20	20	1(0.07)	4(0.22)
3. No contact with potential helper*	62	25	72	13	12(0.86)	9(0.50)
TOTAL	100	100	100	100	14	18
Degree of premeditation						
1. None—impulsive	10	25	14	42	2(0.14)	4(0.22)
2. Contemplated for less than three hours	13	30	24	26	2(0.14)	8(0.44)
3. Contemplated for more than four hours*	77	45	62	32	10(0.72)	6(0.33)
TOTAL	100	100	100	100	14	18
Agent/method used						
1. Drugs*	26	48	27	52	5(0.36)	11(0.61)
2. Cutting/Stabbing	9	37	8	29	0	2(0.11)
3. Drowning/Strangling or gas	18	8	16	11	2(0.14)	1(0.06)
4. Jumping	14	4	13	4	1(0.07)	0(0)
5. Shooting	33	3	36	4	6(0.42)	3(0.17)
TOTAL	100	100	100	100	14	18
Concept of method lethality						
1. Thought death unlikely	11	56	10	65	0(0)	2(0.11)
2. Uncertain	21	37	21	26	3(0.21)	13(0.72)
3. Felt death was certain	68	7	69	9	11(0.79)	3(0.17)
TOTAL	100	100	100	100	14	18

* The numbers entered in the columns reflect the average likelihood estimates obtained from psychiatric residents, mental health center staff, and (for comparison purposes only) from 32 actual patients.

Figure 3 Continued

hoods, and probability of death estimates could all have been estimated empirically by collecting a data base of actual cases. Unfortunately, the data needed for this model were not available in current medical records. Moreover, even if the data were available there is reason to believe that, given present data collection systems, there would be problems with accuracy and legibility. This means that to obtain an empirical data base sufficient to provide the needed estimates, there would have to be prospective data collection. This is entirely possible assuming that patients are followed to determine if they made a suicide attempt to determine the outcome of that attempt. And in fact, one of the advantages of the computer-based interviewing process under discussion is that data are collected from subjects, whose cases will be followed to determine the outcome. Over time, the data from these case records will accumulate to the point where there will be sufficient empirical data to replace the subjective estimates. Until then, the empirical data accumulated can be used to refine the subjective estimates. Such a refinement could take place by making an assumption of equivalent sample size for the subjective estimate. For instance, one might, by examining the variance in subjective estimates, decide that the subjective estimates were equivalent to an empirical data base of 100 cases. Then, as real empirical data are collected, those empirical cases could simply be added to the subjective sample.

Figures 26.2, 26.3 also include numbers which are the average estimates of prior probabilities and likelihoods. Figure 26.2 contains two columns of numbers. The first column shows the estimates of the four Department of Psychiatry residents in the Department of Psychiatry at the University of Wisconsin. The second column shows the estimates made by the four Mental Health Center staff.

Figure 26.3 presents six columns of estimates. The first two columns show the residents' likelihood estimates given death (column 2) and not death (column 3). The next two columns represent the likelihood estimates by the Mental Health Center staff. The final two columns show the frequency and likelihood estimates based on 14 actual suicides and 18 surviving suicide attemptors. These figures may be useful in comparing the accuracy of subjective versus empirical estimates. The statistic of comparison is chosen as the likelihood ratio

$$\frac{P(S_i/\text{Death})}{P(S_i/\text{Not Death})}.$$

The likelihood ratio is chosen because it provides an indication of the extent to which a datum revises prior opinion. A likelihood ratio of 1.0 has no effect. A ratio of 10/1 has a substantial effect. Twelve data items were chosen for comparison. These were the 12 items where $P(S_{ij}/D_i)$ had at least five observations for each D_i, these were the items that in our opinion had begun to stabilize the likelihood ratio even with the small

Data item	Residents	Mental Health Center Staff	Actual patients
		Likelihood ratio estimates from	
Male	2.8	2.3	1.7
Female	1/2.4	1/2.1	1/1.5
Familiar location	1/1.3	1/1.6	1.1
Discovery uncertain	1/1.1	1.1	1.1
Plan and means obtained	2.1	2.2	1/1.25
Isolated location	2.1	3.2	1.6
Passive protection against discovery	1/1.3	1/1.2	1.0
Ambivalent attitude towards living	1/1.9	1/1.2	1/1.3
No final acts	1/1.9	1/4.8	1/1.4
No attempt to contact potential helper	2.5	5.5	1.7
More than four hours of planning	1.7	1.9	2.2
Method was drugs	1/1.8	1/1.9	1/1.7

Figure 26.4. A comparison of subjective and empirical likelihood ratio estimates for the 12 data items where at least five observations were found in each cell used to calculate the empirical likelihood ratio.

sample size. Each datum chosen is identified by an asterisk. Figure 26.4 presents a comparison of the subjective and empirical estimates. The selection of these data items tends to bias the estimates toward 50/50 since there were only 18 live and 14 dead patients studied. Results indicate the subjective estimates were very similar to each other. Both subjective estimates were generally in the same direction and in similar magnitude to the empirical estimates. In our opinion this comparison must be considered preliminary because a much larger sample size is needed before much credibility can be placed in the empirical estimates.

Two Bayesian models were developed. One used uniform priors. This model assumes life and death are equally likely from a suicidal attempt if nothing else is known about the attempt. The other Bayesian model used the prior probability estimates collected using the description in Fig. 26.2. There are good arguments to take either approach. Our past experience (Gustafson, Kestly, Greist, & Jensen, 1971) suggests that the uniform priors tend to be somewhat more accurate.

The study had six sets of survival estimates available on each of 32 test cases whose outcomes were known (18 lived; 14 died).

1. The estimates of psychiatric residents given the patient profiles previously described.
2. The estimates of staff from the Dane County Mental Health Center.

3. The estimates of the regression model developed by psychiatric residents.
4. The estimates of the regression model developed by staff of Dane County Mental Health Center.
5. The estimates of the Bayesian model developed by psychiatric residents.
6. The estimates of the Bayesian model developed by staff of Dane County Mental Health Center.

Evaluation

The system was evaluated by comparing the actual outcome of suicide attempts with the predicted outcome of the attempts made by three prediction agents: two clinician groups, the Bayesian models, and the regression models. A comparison with Weisman–Worden risk–rescue ratings (see Glackman, 1970) (from factors used) would be interesting. The Bayesian and regression models were compared with the two clinician groups (psychiatric residents and mental health clinicians) by diagnosing 14 actual cases of patients who had completed suicide. The performance of the Bayesian models was also compared with the performance of the regression models by diagnosing 32 actual cases of patients, 14 of whom completed suicide and 18 of whom attempted suicide but survived the attempt. (It should be noted that all predictions were made on profile sets or data sets which are distinct from those used in the development of the regression models.)

Three measures of effectiveness were employed: (1) the percentage of cases in which the outcomes were correctly assigned the highest probability, (2) the average probability assigned to the correct outcome, and (3) the average probability assigned to the correct outcome when the incorrect outcome was predicted. All three measures are expressed in terms of percentages. The first two are self-explanatory. In the case of the third, a relatively high level of probability indicates less confidence in the incorrect prediction so that, as with the two other measures, the higher the percentage, the better.

Table 26.1 summarizes the results of the analysis. Six models are shown: clinician estimates, regression estimates, and Bayesian estimates, each employing judgments from either psychiatric residents or mental health center staff. Table 26.1 also has six columns. The first two columns portray the percentage of cases in which the model assigned a greater than 50% chance to the actual outcome. The first column addresses the 14 suicide attemptors who "died." The second column addresses the 18 attemptors who "lived." Columns 3 and 4 portray the average probability assigned to the correct diagnosis. The rationale for this measure is that the less equivocal a prediction the more likely the clinician would be to respond. Columns 5 and 6 portray the average probability assigned to the

Table 26.1. *Comparison of the performance of clinicians, regression, and Bayesian models in terms of accuracy, certainty when correct, and certainty when wrong*

	Accuracy (number and percentage)		Probability assigned to correct outcome		Probability + number of correct outcome when prediction was wrong	
Clinicians						
Residents	37/56[a](66%)	NA[b]	0.62	NA	0.25(19)	NA
Mental health center	50/56[a](89%)	NA	0.76	NA	0.35(6)	NA
Regression						
Residents	11/14(79%)	14/18(78%)	0.63	0.67	0.38(3)	0.36(4)
Mental health center	14/14(100%)	11/18(61%)	0.74	0.55	NA	0.38(7)
Bayesian						
Residents	13/14(98%)	14/18(78%)	0.90	0.78	0.23(1)	0.19(4)
Mental health center	14/14(100%)	14/18(78%)	0.94	0.78	NA	0.23(4)
Actual outcome	Died	Lived	Died	Lived	Died	Lived

[a] Four clinicians of each type predicted outcomes for each of the 14 attemptors.
[b] NA means these data are not available.

correct diagnosis when the model predicted wrong. The rationale here is that one would like the model to be equivocal when it is wrong. Note there are no entries in the clinician model for attemptors who lived. These data were not collected.

In terms of accuracy, both models seem to predict quite well. The regression and Bayesian models using mental health center estimates identified all 14 attemptors who died. The Bayesian model built on resident estimates missed 1 of 14 and the regression model built on resident estimates missed 3 of 14. This compares favorably to direct clinician estimates where mental health center staff missed an average of 1.5 and residents missed an average of almost 5 of 14. We conclude that both the regression and Bayesian models performed at least as well as the clinicians.

Comparisons with clinician estimates are not available for the attemptors who lived. However, the results indicate the model performance drops off somewhat. The two Bayesian models and the resident regression model identified 14 of 18 attemptors who lived. The mental health regression model correctly identified only 11 of 18. This model identified all deaths correctly so there may be a systematic bias in that direction.

In terms of probability assigned to the correct outcome it appears that the Bayesian model assigns higher probabilities (in the 90s). Regression and clinicians seem to profess equal certainty on attemptors who died

(0.63 for residents and 0.74 for mental health center staff). The Bayesian model seems to assign higher certainty to attemptors who lived (high 70s versus 50s and 60s). This is another positive feature of the Bayesian model's performance.

Up to this point the Bayesian model performance is impressive. The trend is reversed somewhat in examining the incorrect predictions. One would be happier to find a model's predictions to be equivocal when it is wrong. For instance, if an attemptor died and the model predicted survival one would prefer to see the probability of death be substantial, e.g., 0.48, rather than very small, e.g., 0.02. The regression model did this. On the average it assigned probabilities in the high 30s to the correct outcome when it predicted outcome wrong. The Bayesian and clinician made predictions in the 20s and 30s for attemptors who actually died. There are no entries for the mental health center regression and Bayesian models because there were no errors. But for attemptors who actually lived the story is different. The Bayesian model predicted death for four of the attemptors who survived and gave all of them 0.19 and 0.23 chances of surviving.

One other way of looking at the data is to compare the estimates of the residents and mental health center staff. When there was a difference, that difference generally favored the mental health center staff. The only exception is in the regression model for attemptors who lived. In that case the resident model seems superior for accuracy and for probability assigned to correct diagnosis.

Discussion

This study suggests that both Bayesian and regression models are promising methods for predicting outcome of a suicide attempt. In all cases the models performed at least as well as clinicians. Where differences occur these differences seem to favor the models. Where model differences occur the differences seem to favor the Bayesian model, except on the criterion "probability assigned to correct diagnosis when the incorrect outcome was favored."

The effectiveness of this model cannot be compared directly with the Weisman and Worden model because the model developed here does not require a history of previous attempt(s) to be useful, whereas the Weisman and Worden model can only be used when the patient has a history of previous attempts. The Weisman and Worden model (Glackman, 1970) indicates that their model predictions differed from chance at the 0.35 level. The Bayesian model and regression model predictions differed from chance at the 0.0001 and the 0.0019 levels, respectively.

While these figures are encouraging for the Bayesian and regression models, one must remember that the Weisman–Worden risk–rescue scale was not promoted as a patient management tool.

Like any technology, this model needs to be field-tested carefully before full scale implementation. Such a field test is about to take place. The Bayesian model is being added to the interactive suicide attempt prediction system so the clinician will receive these products from the system: a history of the patient's problem, a prediction of suicide attempt and now a prediction of outcome if the attempt is made. It will take years to fully evaluate the effectiveness of such a system. However, the results are encouraging.

Part VIII
Experts

Nowhere is the role of judgment more important than in the work of the expert, for the essential value of experts lies in their judgment. When a problem is routine, when a simple extrapolation from past or present can be made, when a "how-to" book tells us what to do, no expert is needed. But it is precisely when the problem cannot be solved by these methods that somebody – the expert – whose professional training and/or experience makes him or her particularly knowledgeable about the problem is needed. Invariably, experts exercise judgment; that is, they seek out, select, organize information, and offer, on the basis of their expertise, a judgment – a diagnosis, a plan – that could be produced in no other way. If the expert's judgment is right, we are grateful – and pay the bill. But occasionally, some would say frequently, the experts are wrong, and we then denigrate expert judgment and wish we had never consulted the expert. Moreover, experts are known to disagree. And if we consult more than one, we may be left with two opposing experts who will defend themselves by resorting to "That's my best professional judgment," and we are forced to choose between them. The justices of the Supreme Court, for example, are experts in the law, yet they almost always disagree; unanimous verdicts are rare indeed. Unless we believe truth is discovered by 5–4 votes, there is bound to be doubt about the wisdom of experts.

Those who take a negative view of expert judgment are apt to agree with the aphorism that "an expert is one who knows more and more about less and less." And when expert witnesses disagree in courts of law or in front of legislative committees, the value of their expertise is often ridiculed.

Nevertheless, experts are needed because experts *do* know more than nonexperts about their subject matter. And if we want to make a claim for rational decision making, then we want the most knowledgeable person available to help with the problem. Consequently, we must consult an expert or be accused of making decisions based on ignorance, whim, or bad faith. When a mistake is made without expert advice, it is hard to defend the decision-making process as the best possible effort.

Thus ambivalence about the value of experts' judgment is widespread and has become increasingly so since the 1970s. On the one hand, we often need it, often seek it out, and usually pay a lot for it. On the other hand, once we get the expert's judgment we often regard it with suspicion, jeer at disagreement among our experts, and wind up doing what we (nonexpert as we may be) judge to be best, often relying on nothing more than what is inelegantly called a "gut feeling" – and, more often than not, claiming its superiority. In a society growing ever more complex and developing ever-increasing dependency on technology, experts are becoming indispensable. Nevertheless, the question remains: How good are the experts, anyway? How good is expert judgment? More specifically, how much better are the experts than novices?

It will not, therefore, be surprising to the reader that researchers in the field of judgment and decision making should attempt to study the judgments of experts. Not only would they make an effort to find out how *accurate* the experts' judgments are and to discover why they disagree so often, but the study of expert judgment offers an excellent opportunity to learn about judgment itself. For example, what is the difference in cognitive activity between experts and novices? Do they look at different information? Organize it differently? There is now a large and flourishing field of research that addresses these questions, and that is why we have a section on this topic.

Of course, it is not so easy to study expert judgment. For one thing, experts are busy and their time is expensive and they are not inclined to have the value of their judgments scrutinized, often by methods they do not understand or appreciate. Nor can experts be studied in brief periods of time; their work is complex, and therefore understanding their judgment processes takes time – their time. Nevertheless, research on expert judgment can be done and has been done. It began with the studies of expert clinical psychologists and has included a wide variety of studies of expert medical judgment (see Part VI). Because clinical judgment has been awarded a section of its own, we include in this part studies of experts other than those judging the conditions of patients: (*a*) a study of agricultural experts who judge soil samples, (*b*) a study of epidemiologists, and (*c*) a study of medical pathologists.

27. Reducing the influence of irrelevant information on experienced decision makers

Gary J. Gaeth and James Shanteau

A fundamental and critical component of expert judgment is the ability to appropriately use available information which varies in its relevance. Ideally, experts would select and use only information which is the most relevant. There is, however, a great deal of evidence which indicates that the presence of irrelevant information can influence judgment adversely in a variety of situations. If this influence extends to experienced decision makers, then one reasonable approach to improving judgmental skill would be to train judges to reduce the use of irrelevant information. Accordingly, the four purposes of this paper are (a) to determine whether experienced agricultural judges are influenced by irrelevant information, (b) to compare the effectiveness of two training procedures designed to reduce this influence, (c) to evaluate what impact irrelevance and training have on the accuracy of the judgments, and (d) to investigate the long-term effect of the training through a follow-up study.

Previous studies of irrelevance

Basic research

In a recent search of the literature of Gaeth and Shanteau (1981), over 250 published reports were found from a variety of psychological areas which investigated the influence of irrelevance. We will briefly consider a few of these studies for illustrative purposes.

In a prototype study, Williams (1974) had subjects make "same-different" judgments of visual stimuli which varied on multiple dimensions. He found that reaction times were longer when the stimuli differed on

This chapter originally appeared in *Organizational Behavior and Human Performance*, 1984, 33, 263–282. Copyright © 1984 by Academic Press, Inc. Reprinted by permission.

irrelevant dimensions than when they were the same. Similar perceptual demonstrations of the influence of irrelevant information have been obtained in scaling tasks (Besner & Coltheart, 1976; Bundesen & Larsen, 1975), reaction time analyses (Gordon, 1979; Larsen & Bundesen, 1978), and signal recognition studies (Montague, 1965).

In addition, several studies using concept formation or problem solving paradigms have concluded that the ability to ignore irrelevance is a cognitive skill (Kausler & Kleim, 1978; Rabbitt, 1965). This ability appears to depend on individual-difference factors such as age. For older adults, evidence points to an age-related decrement in the ability to separate relevant from irrelevant (Ford, Hink, Hopkins, Roth, Pfefferbaum, & Kopell, 1979; Hoyer, Rebok, & Sved, 1979). Additional research seems to indicate that very young or mentally retarded children may have greater difficulty distinguishing between relevant and irrelevant dimensions than older or normal children (Bush & Cohen, 1970; Eimas, 1966; Evans & Beedle, 1970; Low, Coste, & Kirkup, 1980; Shantz, 1967).

Applied research

Only a few studies have been found which dealt with the role of irrelevance in applied (i.e., nonlaboratory) settings. In one industrial study, irrelevant biodemographic information was shown to influence the evaluation of prospective teachers by school administrators (Rice, 1975). In another study on personnel selection, information on the sex, age, and physical attractiveness of hypothetical job applicants was shown to be inappropriately used by experienced business students (Nagy, 1981; also see Beach, Mitchell, Deaton, & Prothero, 1978; Griffitt & Jackson, 1970).

In the judicial setting, irrelevant information may also play a critical role. As an example, indications are that inadmissible (irrelevant) evidence has an inappropriate influence on the decisions of juries (Mitchell & Byrne, 1972; Sue, Smith, & Caldwell, 1973).

In all, irrelevant information has been found to influence psychological judgments in a variety of basic and applied research areas. The influence on experienced decision makers is especially noteworthy and will be the focus of this research.

Soil judgment

Soil judgment was chosen as the content area for this research for three reasons. First, the task is important, yet heavily based on psychological skills. Hand soil analysis is performed routinely as part of road and dam construction, agricultural land testing, etc. Any contribution that psychology can make to soil judgment may, in itself, have important consequences.

Second, previous experience has shown that trained agricultural students are skilled and cooperative subjects (Shanteau & Phelps, 1977).

Specifically, previous work with student soil judges has confirmed both their expertise and willingness to participate (Gaeth & Shanteau, 1979; Gaeth & Shanteau, 1980). Moreover, the students were highly motivated to participate in this training research because they were attempting to qualify for the school soil judging team (a prestigious accomplishment in an agriculturally oriented program).

Finally, in contrast to many other applied areas in which irrelevance has been studied (i.e., law, personnel selection), soil judgment lends itself nicely to quantitative research. A limited description of the soil judgment task is necessary to understand this latter point.

The soil judgment task

By definition, soil texture is derived directly from the proportion of three basic constituents in the soil. These are: sand (particles between 2 and .05 mm), silt (particles between .05 and .002 mm), and clay (particles less than .002 mm). Based on the naturally occurring percentages of each of these constituents, any soil can be placed into one of 12 soil texture categories. The texture categories are specified by the USDA (United States Department of Agriculture) soil texture triangle presented in Figure 27.1. For illustration, a soil containing 40% sand, 40% silt, and 20% clay has been plotted on the soil triangle. As can be seen, it is part of the texture category "loam."

A soil analysis to determine the percent of sand, silt, and clay can be performed physically in a soils laboratory; however, the process is relatively expensive (up to $100 per sample) and time consuming (up to several months). Because of these constraints, the vast majority of field soil judgments are performed using the "feel method" (Clarke, 1936), a tactile method for determining soil composition. The laboratory analyses thus serve only as a criterion or standard. The goal for professional soil judges therefore is to produce assessments using the feel method which are equivalent to the laboratory results.

Student soil judges are indirectly trained to this standard by learning to emulate the judgments of an instructor; these instructors are usually established professional soil scientists. Therefore, the instructor both teaches the students the soil judgment process and provides the standard to which the students are typically compared.

Irrelevant factors in soil judgment

As a direct consequence of the definition of soil texture, any material in the soil other than sand, silt, and clay is irrelevant. Based on a survey of USDA soil scientists and other evidence (Gaeth & Shanteau, 1980), it was found that coarse fragments (particles in the soil which are larger than 2.0 mm) and excessive moisture (the presence of water in excess of what is used when evaluating soil) were among a number of irrelevant factors

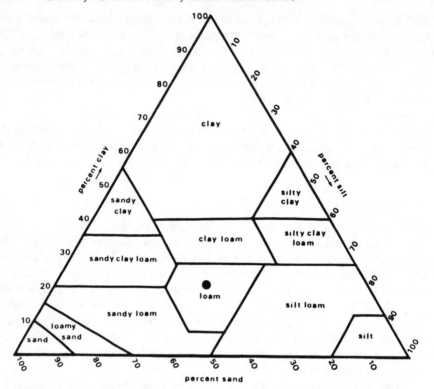

Figure 27.1. USDA Soil Classification Triangle. Soil plotted with 40% sand, 40% silt, and 20% clay is a "loam."

which may adversely influence soil judgment. These two materials, excessive moisture and coarse fragments, were then chosen for this investigation because they occur naturally and can be controlled in specially prepared soils.

Training procedures

It is beyond the scope of this paper to review the previous studies on the various procedures for training decision makers (see Einhorn & Hogarth, 1981; Slovic, Fischhoff, & Lichtenstein, 1977; Slovic & Lichtenstein, 1971). Rather, we will present four general "rules" which guided the design of the two training techniques used in the research.

First, the training periods had to be fairly short, i.e., less than half an hour. We were constrained because of having skilled participants whose time was at a premium; this of course is not an uncommon limitation when working with experienced decision makers.

Second, the training programs had to be as parallel as possible to the general type of training normally given to soil judges. This was done

(a) to keep our training "natural," (b) to increase the credibility of our research, and (c) to allow for its possible adoption in soil education programs.

Third, the training procedures rested on the fundamental idea that the most effective way to teach the judges to "ignore" irrelevance is to concentrate on it. This somewhat counterintuitive approach was grounded in notions from selective attention (Kahneman, 1973); you must pay at least some attention to information before you can decide not to pay attention.

Finally, the training procedures should not depend on conventional outcome feedback, i.e., the "correct" answer. Because most applied judgment problems do not have objective standards (indeed, if objective measures are readily available, expert judgment is generally unnecessary), we wanted to use a training approach with maximum generality.

Based on these four principles, two training procedures were developed: lecture training and interactive training.

Lecture training. This training was designed to be roughly equivalent to the usual approach taken in the classroom. Basically the judges were warned verbally that excessive moisture and coarse fragments are irrelevant and therefore should not be allowed to influence their judgments. Thus, in accord with many other studies (e.g., Fischhoff & Slovic, 1980; Fischhoff, Slovic, & Lichtenstein, 1977; Harris, 1977), our first approach to training was to warn the soil judge about the detrimental influence of irrelevance.

Interactive training. This training was designed to be similar to the experience gained from a laboratory class. Although past research has consistently shown that verbal warnings (lecture training) are not very successful (Fischhoff, 1975; Harris, 1977), there are some examples of successful training approaches from which we could build; these include the "discovery" method (Slovic & Fischhoff, 1977; Bruno & Harris, 1980) and the use of extended practice (Lichtenstein & Fischhoff, 1980). Also, an analysis of the soil judgment task demonstrates that it requires both cognitive and perceptual skill. Therefore, the interactive training, involving "hands-on" practice with soils, was intended to help the judges discover that the irrelevant factors had in fact influenced their own soil judgments.

Method

Participants and stimuli

Participants. Twelve soil judges (two females; ten males) were recruited from an advanced soil morphology class taught at Kansas State

Table 27.1. *Percentage of sand, silt, clay, coarse fragments, and excessive moisture for each evaluation and training soil*

Soil no.	Usage	% Sand	% Silt	% Clay	% C.F. natural	% C.F. used	% E.M. used
2	Base	5(5)	66(70)	29(25)	30	23	20
4	Base	17(20)	60(60)	23(20)	25	26	30
6	Base[a]	52(20)	29(55)	19(25)	38	33	25
1	Filler	62	10	28	–	–	–
7	Filler	22	49	29	–	–	–
8	Filler	8	63	29	–	–	–
9	Filler	7	65	28	–	–	–
3	Training	23	61	16	44	–	–
5	Training	26	48	26	82	–	–

Note: C.F. = coarse fragments, E.M. = excessive moisture. Values in parentheses reflect the estimates made by the professional soil science instructor. The percentages are based on a mechanical analysis conducted by the Front Range Laboratory, Fort Collins, Colo.
[a] Soil 6 was also used as a training soil.

University.[1] Coupled with this class, all judges had previous experience with soil judgment through various combinations of personal work experience, laboratory work, other classes, and prior membership on soil judging teams (college, high school, or 4H club). They were paid $12 for their participation and were each run individually through the research.

Soil stimuli. Nine Kansas soil samples were used in this experiment (see Table 27.1). These nine soils included five which contained naturally occurring coarse fragments and four filler soils which did not contain coarse fragments. This collection of nine soils was separated into two sets: (a) evaluation soils and (b) interactive training soils.

For the evaluation soils, a factorial set of 12 soils was created by making 4 variations of each of 3 "base" soils; these soils all originally contained coarse fragments (2, 4, 6 in Table 27.1). The set was generated by preparing each soil according to a two levels of coarse fragments (present – not present) × two levels of moisture (present – not present) design. For the *not-present* level of coarse fragments, the sieved "base" soil was used, i.e., all coarse fragments were removed; when *present*, the level of coarse fragments was roughly equal to the amount found in the soil naturally. For the moisture factor, the *not-present* level was chosen as the dried base soil containing virtually no moisture; the *present* level was deliberately set

[1] All but one of the class members agreed to participate. One judge who participated was dropped from the analysis because of his inadequate familiarity with the USDA soil texture classification system. This judge had recently come from Europe and was taking the course as an introduction to the USDA soil judgment system.

as an amount of moisture greater than what is normally used when assessing the soil texture by hand.

Added to these 12 soils were 4 fillers yielding an evaluation set of 16. The fillers (1, 7, 8, 9) were included to disguise the factorial design. Also, the responses to several of these soils were used in the interactive training procedure as feedback.

One hundred grams of each soil was prepared and stored in 8-ounce airtight plastic containers; the containers were marked with a code number used as identification. Due to concern over the evaporation of water from the samples, the soils with moisture were prepared each day they were used.

Procedure

Each judge attended five sessions as follows: Session 1, *preevaluation;* Session 2, *lecture training;* Session 3, *midevaluation;* Session 4, *interactive training;* and Session 5, *postevaluation.* Three different procedures were used in these sessions: one for the evaluation sessions (pre-, mid-, post-), and one for each of the two training sessions.

Evaluation procedure. In each evaluation session, the judge was asked to use the "feel method" to estimate the percentage of sand, silt,[2] and clay, and to report the textural classification of each of the 16 evaluation soils. The experimenter repeated the judge's responses aloud in order to guarantee accurate recording. In addition, the time required for the soil judgments was recorded with a stopwatch; however, this dependent measure will not be considered here.[3] Finally, the judge was asked to indicate the likelihood that the texture judgment was correct; these likelihood ratings do not pertain to the issue of training efficacy and so will not be considered further here. Once the judge was satisfied with the responses, he/she was not allowed to change them. This same procedure was repeated in the mid- and postevaluation session for each of the 16 soils.

Training procedures. The lecture training was given first followed within a period of 7 days by the midevaluation and interactive training. For half of

---

[2] The judges generally determine the amount of silt in a soil by first calculating the percent of sand and clay, and then subtracting from 100% to get the silt percentage. Thus, the silt values are both psychologically and statistically dependent on the sand and clay values. Because of this dependency, none of the analyses for the silt estimates will be reported.

[3] Timings were taken of all soil assessments. It was hoped that these could be used as a measure of cognitive effort spent on each soil judgment. Unfortunately, because the judges were each run individually, some had a tendency to discuss what they were doing with the experimenter. It was decided that it was more important to maintain a cooperative environment and allow them to verbalize in a natural fashion than to demand silence.

the judges, the content of both training procedures dealt with the influence of coarse fragments; for the other half, the content dealt with excessive moisture. Although the training content was different, the training procedures were parallel in structure. The results indicated that the training generalized from one irrelevant factor to the other. Therefore, the two groups were combined in the analyses.

Lecture training. A 30-min lecture training session consisted of verbal instructions recited to the judge by the experimenter. A set of concealed cue cards was used to produce uniformity.

In the first section of the lecture training procedure, evidence was presented that the irrelevant factor involved could cause erroneous judgments. Second, a formal definition of what constitutes the irrelevant factor was given. In the last section, seven suggestions were presented, each designed to help the soil judge deal with problems caused by the irrelevant factor. These were both physical ("remove as much water as possible") and cognitive ("make a judgment as to how much clay has been lost"). After completion of the three sections, the judge was asked to summarize the essentials of the training instructions in his/her own words. Any deletions or misunderstandings were corrected to ensure that the desired information had been communicated.

Interactive training. A 30-min interactive training session was divided into four sections. In the first section, the judge was shown an outline of the seven suggestions from the prior lecture training and asked to paraphrase them. Training suggestions which were forgotten or mistakenly recalled were corrected.

The next part of the interactive training required the judge to assess a soil containing added irrelevant materials (either excessive moisture or coarse fragments). This soil had been shown earlier as a filler with the irrelevant material removed. Then the judge's current response was compared to the earlier response in an unfavorable light.[4] The point was made that any difference in the responses could only be due to the presence of the irrelevant factor; the differences were frequently quite large.

The third section of the interactive training involved the presentation of a set of three soils, two of which had never been analyzed by the judge (3 and 5); a third soil (6) was included to determine whether familiarity with

---

[4] There were two possible comparison responses available from the preevaluation session which could be used. In the initial stages of the interactive training, the preevaluation response which was the most distant from the training response was selected to impress upon the judge that the irrelevant information had a major influence. At the end of the interactive training, the preevaluation response which was closest to the training response was used in order to provide encouragement.

specific evaluation soils influenced training effectiveness. The basic training strategy was based on the concept of successive approximations. To implement this strategy, each soil was initially assessed without any of the irrelevant factors present. Then, in successive stages, increasing amounts of irrelevant material were added and the soil was assessed again. The judge was reminded that the percentage judgments should not change as the irrelevant material increased. At each stage in order to focus attention on the irrelevance, the judge was also asked to estimate the amount of the irrelevant factor present in the soil sample.

In the last section, the judge reassessed a soil which had been seen in the first session as a filler. Then, however, the soil did not contain any irrelevant factors. In the training session, it contained a relatively large amount of irrelevant material. The training response was then compared to the one made earlier in as favorable a light as possible (see note 4). This was done to provide encouragement and to help the judge leave the training with a feeling of accomplishment. The interactive training procedure was followed by the postevaluation session and debriefing.

Derivation of dependent measure

To evaluate both the influence of the irrelevant factors and the impact of the training procedures, analyses based on response differences were used. The use of a derived dependent measure is necessary because individual differences in the judges' raw responses can bias the analyses at the group level. Derived scores were computed on an individual soil/judge basis: the response to the "irrelevance-absent" for each base soil was used as a standard, and the absolute difference between it and each of the three "irrelevance-present" instances to the soil was then obtained. Thus, the derived scores reflected the discrepancies between the base, or irrelevance-absent response, and irrelevance-present responses (calculated for each soil and judge).

Results

The results relate directly to the first three issues raised in the introduction. First, do the irrelevant factors influence the judges' soil estimates? Second, do either of the training procedures reduce the influence of the irrelevant factors? Third, what influence does irrelevance and the subsequent training have on the accuracy of the judgments? (The fourth issue, related to long-term impact, will be taken up at the end of the section.) After presenting the results pertaining to these three main questions, some additional findings will be considered. All reported efforts were significant at $p < .05$.

Influence of irrelevant factors

The initial influence of the irrelevant factors was reflected in the size of the preevaluation derived scores. The mean values for the three irrelevance conditions (coarse fragments, no moisture; no coarse fragments, excessive moisture; and coarse fragments, excessive moisture) were 12.1, 12.2, and 13.5 for sand, and 7.1, 10.2, and 7.1 for clay, respectively. For each of these conditions, a one-tail *t* test against zero difference was significant. When present, therefore, the irrelevant materials caused both the sand and clay estimates to be different than those given for the otherwise identical base soil.

Impact of training

The training efficacy was examined by looking at changes in the derived scores across the evaluation sessions for both sand and clay. The resulting means are shown in Figure 27.2.

For both sand and clay, the means of the scores decreased ($F(2,20) = 4.41$ and $F(2,20) = 3.92$, respectively). A Newman–Keuls comparison of the means showed that for both scores, the decrease was significant only in the third evaluation session, i.e., following interactive training.

Accuracy

The soil laboratory analysis (see Table 27.1) was used to compute an accuracy score based on the absolute difference between the judges' estimates for each soil and the corresponding laboratory analysis. It should be pointed out that examination of accuracy is quite important since it is possible for the training to reduce the influence of irrelevance, but not to improve accuracy.

Figure 27.3 shows the assessment errors for each of the three base soils for sand. The sand means for soils 2 and 4 became more accurate, while the estimates for soil 6 became less accurate. A significant session × soils interaction was obtained, $F(4,40) = 5.20$ for sand; there was no significant change in the accuracy for clay.

Additional accuracy results

Although the laboratory analyses remain the accepted standard for soil judgments, student judges are seldom able to compare their responses against this standard. Instead, the criterion to which they are routinely trained is their soil instructor's judgments. The estimates from the students' instructor appear in parenthesis in Table 27.1 for each soil. In the case of soils 2 and 4, his estimates are quite close to the laboratory

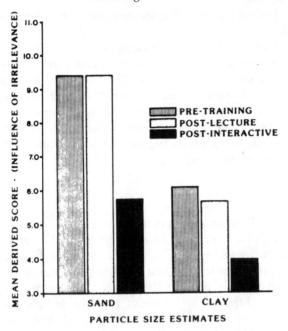

Figure 27.2. Impact of training on influence of irrelevance as reflected in magnitude of derived scores.

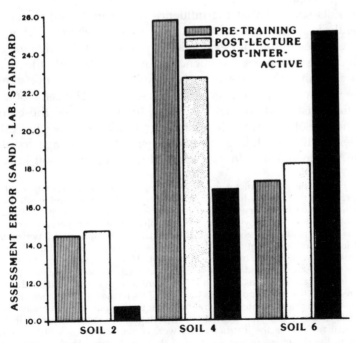

Figure 27.3. Change in assessment errors across evaluation sessions when laboratory analysis is used as standard.

analyses. However, his values for soil 6 are noticeably different from the laboratory standard.[5]

A set of accuracy analyses parallel to those presented earlier, but using the instructor as the standard, was conducted. The mean assessment errors for this analysis are given in Figure 27.4 for sand. In this case, the "instructor-based" accuracy increased significantly across sessions ($F(2,20) = 4.85$) and was greatest following interactive training. Moreover, the convergence toward increased agreement occurred for all soils, including soil 6. As with the analysis based on the laboratory criterion, there was no significant change for clay.

Follow-up

In order to evaluate the long-term effects of training, an effort was made to recontact the judges at a later time. Five of the original 12 soil judges agreed to participate in the follow-up. They were contacted from 12 to 21 months after the completion of the original training study and were asked to judge the same set of soils used in the initial evaluations; however, they believed it was a different set. Two of the five judges were not available in person and so were sent the soils through the mail. This seemed to pose no problem because they were still familiar with the procedure and simply filled out their responses in a booklet rather than responding verbally.

The results showed that the influence of the irrelevant materials was consistently less than it was prior to the training. Figure 27.5 gives the difference scores in the four evaluation sessions for these five judges. A t test comparing the pretest influence of irrelevance with the follow-up showed a significant decrease for sand and a large, but nonsignificant, decrease for the clay percentages (5.08 versus 3.35). The issue of accuracy was again considered in the follow-up. In the case of these five soil judges the size of the errors decreased significantly for the sand estimates (18.42 versus 12.72) while there was no significant change for the clay errors (6.50 versus 7.45). In summary, at least for these soil judges, the

---

[5] At a later time, the soil instructor was given an opportunity to reevaluate soil 6. At this time he reported that he may have initially misinterpreted the fine sand as silt. Consideration of the detailed laboratory results (which he was not aware of) showed that a large portion of sand was indeed very fine, i.e., the physical size difference in these particle classes is very small. This gives some idea of the highly developed perceptual skills needed for the soil judgment task. Almost all the soil judges were "fooled" by the fine sand present in soil 6 and interpreted it as silt. However, when the soils instructor estimates were used as a standard, the accuracy increased across the evaluation session for all soils, including soil 6. Thus, the soil judges were converging to what, to them, may be considered to be the more appropriate standard. This relationship between the instructor and the students bears an interesting resemblance to previous work in animal science by Phelps (1977). She found that the judgment strategies of student livestock judges were quite similar to those of the instructor they were currently training with. In some cases, this was to the detriment of the accuracy of their judgments. Thus, the students were making their judgments in a fashion consistent with their current instructor, regardless of the absolute accuracy standard.

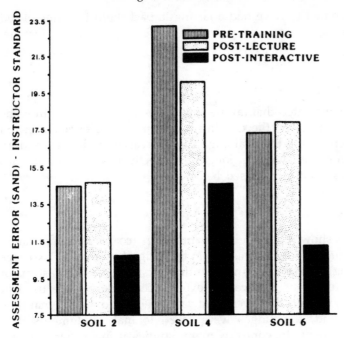

Figure 27.4. Change in assessment errors across evaluation sessions when soil instructor's responses are used as standard.

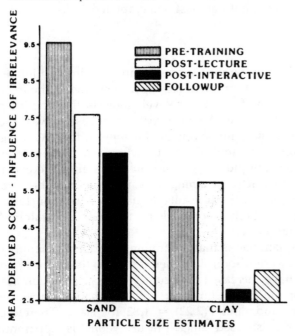

Figure 27.5. Impact of training on influence of irrelevance as reflected in magnitude of derived scores for subjects in follow-up session.

training seemed to have had a lasting impact, both in terms of reducing the influence of irrelevance and in increasing accuracy for the sand estimates.

Discussion

The results indicated that (a) the soil judges were adversely influenced by irrelevant factors, (b) the training procedures were effective in reducing this influence, (c) the training also increased accuracy, and (d) the training shows evidence of long-term effectiveness. Several implications of these results are discussed below.

Impact of irrelevance

Our results show that both irrelevant factors (coarse fragments and excessive moisture) produced changes in the judges' estimates. Two aspects of this finding are especially noteworthy. First, unlike the vast majority of previous studies of irrelevance, experienced judges were used here as subjects; moreover, they were motivated and cared about what they were doing. Second, the judges were asked to make judgments that were natural for them. In contrast, many studies using experts require that they work on unfamiliar tasks. This lends credence to the notion that the adverse influence of irrelevance, although typically demonstrated in laboratory studies, extends to at least some applied tasks.

Efficacy of training

As shown here, the training was successful in reducing the influence of irrelevant information both in the initial experiment and in the follow-up. Moreover, the evidence at the group level suggests that the interactive training played a critical role. A similar pattern of results was also seen for individual soil judges; for seven of the nine judges who were influenced by training, the improvement occurred following interactive training. In addition, the judges' verbal statements after the experiment revealed that the interactive training was more memorable than the lecture training. However, these results do not allow the conclusion that interactive training is entirely responsible for the impact of training; there are at least three alternatives.

One potential explanation is that the training impact was simply due to practice. If practice were responsible, then it follows that the responses to filler soils should have increased in accuracy across evaluation sessions. The judgments for the fillers, however, did not change across sessions ($F(2,22) = .43$ for sand, and $F(2,22) = 1.82$ for clay). Therefore, this explanation can be dismissed since practice alone is apparently not sufficient to account for the training efficacy.

A second possible explanation is that interactive training may have an effect because of the repetition of the lecture training suggestions; the basic ideas in lecture training were summarized as a part of interactive training. This explanation cannot be immediately dismissed; indeed, there is research which shows that repeated lecture training can be successful (Bruno & Harris, 1980; Lichtenstein & Fischhoff, 1980).

A final possibility is that training works because of a combination of the lecture and interactive approaches. The lecture may have supplied neces- sary cognitive knowledge, while the interactive training provided the perceptual skill needed to use this knowledge. This possibility also deserves some consideration. Thus additional research is needed to establish the locus of the training effect.

Nonetheless, there was both a substantial reduction in the influence of irrelevance and an increase in accuracy following the interactive training in this study. Given the ineffectiveness of prior training procedures, this result is quite encouraging and, in itself, represents a major accomplish- ment. It would be interesting to determine whether the success of the present approach to training expert judges generalizes to other decision tasks.

Effects on accuracy

The answer to the question, does the training improve accuracy, leads to a qualified "yes" for the sand estimates; training did not effect the clay estimates. The reason for the qualification stems from the choice of an accuracy standard. For the laboratory-derived standard, the accuracy increased for soil 2 and 4, and decreased for soil 6. However, for the instructor-derived standard, accuracy increased for all three soils. The situation which occurred with soil 6 is interesting in its own right and reveals the critical importance of selecting an appropriate accuracy stan- dard in applied research studies.

Long-term effects

The finding of a long-lasting impact of training is especially encouraging. Since previous efforts at training decision makers have frequently failed, the finding of continued impact up to a year and a half later is certainly noteworthy.

Of course, it might be argued that the judges may have simply recalled their prior training session when they were recontacted; in practice, however, this training may have otherwise been forgotten. Although such partial forgetting is certainly possible, what is nonetheless signifi- cant is that judges could still recall their training experience. Indeed, several follow-up judges reported having clear memories of the interactive phase a year or more after training. Therefore, the training apparently had a considerable impact on the judge's memory.

Implications of training

Focus on irrelevance. Taking an extreme position, there are two diametrically opposed approaches to training to reduce the influence of irrelevance. The common-sense approach dictates that concentration on the relevant dimensions will, by default, result in a decreased influence in irrelevant dimensions. Without question this position has logical merit. For example, the physician concerned with a diagnosis is unlikely to be influenced by the weather. Clearly, exclusive concentration on relevant dimensions successfully diminishes the use of irrelevant dimensions which are not related to the judgment at hand.

When the relevant and irrelevant dimensions are perceptually similar, however, the problem is different. For example, in a concept formation task, the subject may know that one dimension, e.g., texture, is irrelevant to the concept of, e.g., shape. Nevertheless, reaction time analyses show that subjects cannot simply ignore the irrelevant dimension through concentration on the relevant dimension (Williams, 1974). In the present case, distinguishing coarse fragments from sand is often quite difficult. Simply telling subjects to concentrate on the relevant information does not suffice as training.

The alternative approach which we adopted suggests that the training is more effective when the judges pay active attention to misleading irrelevant information. They are then told how to compensate for the effects of irrelevance. In addition, the suggestions which presumably helped them do this also increased accuracy.

Generality. The training procedures used in this study were designed to be useful in other applied judgment problems; most critically, the procedures do not depend on outcome (accuracy) feedback. A brief distillation of the interactive session may provide some additional insights into the training strategy.

The interactive training used a set of test stimuli which varied on only the irrelevant dimensions. In this case, a factorial design was used which contained stimuli with the irrelevant information both present and not present. However, a formal design is not necessary; if two stimuli differ by only irrelevant information, and the judge responds differently to them, then an influence of irrelevance has been established. This comparison can then be shown directly to the judge. In the case of the soil judges, we found this demonstration to have a considerable impact. Indeed, some of the follow-up judges commented that even after more than a year, this part of the personalized feedback was quite memorable.

The next phase of the interactive training involved practicing the lecture suggestions with real stimuli. A test set was used which contained stimuli varying only on the degree to which the irrelevant information is present. The judges then practiced responding to this stimulus set with the goal of learning to make exactly the same response even when the irrelevant material varied.

Finally, the judge looked at a new set of stimuli to determine if the influence of irrelevance had been reduced. Assessing the effectiveness of the training and recycling through it again may be necessary if the desired goals have not been met or if a refresher is needed.

Several other aspects of the training may also influence its potential for generality. First, outcome feedback was not used as part of the training procedures. When available, however, this may provide a useful addition. The judges could then be shown that the irrelevant information not only changed their judgments, but made them less accurate.

Second, our training relied heavily on the prior training and the previous experience of the judges. Because of that, we did not assume that any single suggestion would work for all the judges; rather we depended on the judges' skill to help them discover which one of the suggestions worked best. Hence, it may be very important to construct a set of suggestions from which the trainees can choose. Most likely, this contributed to the long-term success of this training.

Extensions. Without question the success of the training procedures used in this study depended heavily on specific tailoring to the soil judgment task. In fact, because soil judgment is largely "perceptual" in nature, the training (especially the interactive procedure) reflected a perceptual emphasis.

This may create some concern over the generalizability of the training to other less perceptually based judgment problems. However, we have recently been successful in adapting these training procedures to the problem of bias in personnel selection; sex, age, race may be considered as irrelevant, but influencing, factors. Similar training was useful in reducing the influence of these factors (Gaeth & Shanteau, 1982). Interestingly, it appears that in this more cognitively oriented task the lecture training may be nearly as effective as the interactive training.

Therefore, the training approach outlined in this study is apparently not restricted to perceptually based tasks. Instead, the approach seems to be generalizable to other types of judgment situations which involve various types of irrelevant information.

28. Improving scientists' judgments of risk

Kenneth R. Hammond,
Barry F. Anderson, Jeffrey Sutherland,
and Barbara Marvin

Introduction

Despite the high concern about the risks from scientific and technological developments, little progress has been made toward providing the public with usable information about such risks. As a result, doubt, confusion, and uncertainty hamper formation of public policies concerning the further development of nuclear power, the disposal of toxic waste, the use of food additives and insecticides, the causes and consequences of acid rain, and other scientific and technological issues. Moreover, policy makers who rely on scientists for information about such issues are often frustrated by conflicting counsel. For example, commenting on the report from the Ford Foundation Energy Project, Brooks complained that, "The whole thing presents a divergence of values and political prejudices which is truly depressing. If experts are so at loggerheads, how can the public and the politicians fail to be confused? The expert views seem to leave almost unlimited scope for all possible national energy policies" (Brooks, 1975).

Disagreement about values, or what *ought* to be, is inevitable and deserves more analytical treatment than it currently receives.[1] In the present article, however, we consider only scientific dispute about *facts*, when such dispute directly bears on the public interest. We do so for three reasons: (a) determination of the scientific facts is the scientists' primary responsibility, (b) disagreement among scientists regarding the

[1] There is a growing literature on the role of values in science; for reviews see *Science, Technology and Human Values*, a quarterly journal published by MIT Press; for an example of the integration of science and social values in policy making, see Hammond and Adelman (1976).

This chapter originally appeared in *Risk Analysis*, 1984, 4(1), 69–78. Copyright © 1984 by the Society for Risk Analysis. Reprinted by permission.

facts frustrates the development of public policy regarding risk, confuses members of the public, and reduces their confidence in science, and (c) such disagreement, we believe, can be reduced through cooperation between cognitive psychologists and the scientists in dispute. The first two points are hardly debatable, but the third invites testing. Therefore, we analyzed a situation in which scientists' disagreement about facts had for several years effectively blocked the efforts of a quasi-official citizens' committee to inform its constituents about threats to their health and safety from toxic emissions from a nearby, federally-owned industrial plant. The scientists' dispute had also prevented formation of public policy regarding the plant by state and federal agencies directly involved. In what follows, we: (1) identify the *primary source* of persistent disagreement among scientists; (2) indicate a *remedy* that requires the interaction between cognitive psychologists and disputing scientists; (3) test that remedy in the context of a *worked-out example*.

The primary source of disagreement among scientists

When citizens and their representatives demand to know "How much risk does a given installation or action impose on the population likely to be affected?" scientists and engineers can seldom immediately perform the experiments, or carry out the statistical studies, that will provide rigorously derived answers. Rather, they must almost invariably extrapolate and generalize from the pure science of the laboratory to circumstances not yet studied. To do so, they must resort to "judgment." Without the cognitive safeguards provided by the fully analytical methods of logic and experimentation, scientists who exercise judgment are reduced to employing the same *quasi-rational* cognitive processes that laypersons must use, with much the same consequences, uncertainty, misunderstanding, and persistent dispute that leads to personal animosity – epiphenomena which frustrate, delay, and often misdirect the development of public policy (Brooks, 1975; Hammond, 1978b; Hammond, Mumpower, Dennis, Fitch, & Crumpacker, 1983).

The pervasive role of intuitive judgment in ascertaining risk

Scientists prefer to base their judgments on a common, delimited, and well-defined set of data, as many National Research Council Committee reports have demonstrated. But scientists are frequently required to judge the relative risk of various alternatives without reference to a specific, delimited set of data (e.g., "Dr., what is your judgment of the risk posed by ...?"). In such situations reliance on intuitive judgment often results in conflicting and self-contradictory results, induces nonproductive dispute, leads people to converge on mutually destructive strategies, and blocks the formation of a rational public policy (Hammond & Brehmer,

1973; Brehmer & Hammond, 1977). Lowrance's widely-cited remark that "A thing is safe if its risks are judged to be acceptable" indicates the key role of intuitive judgment in risk assessment (Lowrance, 1976; Okrent, 1980; Kletz, 1981; Lowrance, 1981).

Remedy

Providing information for citizens and public policy makers ordinarily forces scientists to give up the analytical mode of cognition, and requires them to use the modes of cognition in which their analytical skills are no longer applicable. When experimentation is not feasible, scientific judgment must be used to: (a) *select* the data to be considered in forming a judgment of risk, (b) decide how the criteria should be *weighed,* (c) determine the *functional relations* between criteria and risk, and (d) most important, decide how such material should be aggregated, or *organized* into a judgment of risk. The latter parameter is of particular importance in scientific judgments because principles that implicitly organize data into a judgment are, in fact, covert, untested scientific theories.

Techniques developed from empirical research in judgment can be, and have been, successfully used to achieve greater awareness of the four parameters of judgment processes. Externalizing these parameters and their values makes it possible to discover and compare the source of differences in scientists' judgments, and thus to aid in their revision when appropriate.

The following example illustrates this process.

An example

The Rocky Flats Plant (RFP) is a federally-owned industrial plant near Denver, Colorado that has been under suspicion since 1953 of discharging plutonium into the atmosphere and thus creating a risk to the health and safety of thousands of nearby citizens. The uncertainty regarding the risk from the operation of the RFP led the governor of Colorado and the congressman representing the district in which the RFP is located to form in June, 1978, the Rocky Flats Monitoring Committee (RFMC). Its stated purposes included the following:

to provide state and local government officials with continuous *advice* (regarding) ... the welfare of local citizens; to conduct an extensive *information* program to educate the public about the Rocky Flats Plant; to study and *evaluate* reports, accidents and various health standards applicable to the Rocky Flats Plant and to *educate* the public about the same. (Governor's Executive Order, 8 June 1978; emphasis added.)

Fulfillment of these objectives clearly rests on the assumption that scientists can and will provide the RFMC with information regarding the possible risk from the RFP; advice, information, evaluation, and education are wholly dependent upon scientific sources.

The RFMC encountered a serious obstacle in its effort to carry out its mission. Scientists, local and national, provided different and thus confusing judgments regarding the risk to health and safety from the RFP. Several years of increasingly acrimonious dispute among scientists made it impossible for the RFMC to inform itself or its constituents about the risk from the RFP. Consequently, in February, 1981, the RFMC approached the Center for Research on Judgment and Policy (CRJP) at the University of Colorado and requested assistance in resolving the dispute.

Steps to solution. The effort to reduce the dispute among scientists was carried out in three Phases.

Phase I. The specific aim of Phase I was to determine whether differences among scientists did in fact exist, and, if so, whether such differences were due simply to differences in disciplinary background (e.g., epidemiology vs. radiology).

Eleven scientists were chosen for study on the basis of their knowledge about and interest in risks to health from plutonium emissions from the RFP. The scientists agreed that the proper method for studying the effect of their respective disciplines on their judgments was to provide relevant information about a number of persons with differential exposure to plutonium radiation, ask each scientist to judge the risk of cancer for each person described, and to compare the judgments by discipline. This work was undertaken; a report to the RFMC concluded that the eleven scientists did in fact:

make different judgments of cancer risk from identical information, that the differences among scientists were stable, and were not due to differences in professional background and training, but due to differences in the way in which the judgments were made. Specifically, in a study of scientists' judgments of 40 (hypothetical) individuals exposed to cancer risk, large differences were found in the relative weights (importance) they assigned to the six factors (e.g., smoking, diet, etc.) deemed causative of cancer. Additionally, differences in implicit theories of risk, i.e., differences in principles for organizing information from several causative factors, may also be a source of differences in judgments of cancer risk.

It is therefore concluded that the principal sources of disagreement are locatable, if not already located by the present study, and that it is feasible to reduce disagreement and thus to remove this impasse from the work of the RFMC. Because these tentative conclusions are based on a brief pilot study, limitations are indicated and recommendations regarding future work are included (Hammond & Marvin, 1981).

Thus the utility of applying the above framework to the analysis of scientists' judgments of risk was demonstrated. (1) It was discovered that agreement on the factors to be considered could be achieved and that these factors could then be made explicit. (2) Once the factors were defined, a straightforward application of judgment analysis using a form of multiple regression statistics, aided by an interactive computer program designed specifically for judgment analysis could be employed (Hammond, Stewart, Brehmer, & Steinman, 1975; Hammond, Rohrbaugh, Mumpower, & Adelman, 1977). This analysis made it possible to ascertain quickly (a) the relative weights each scientist attached to each factor, (b) functional relations between factors and judgments, (c) self-consistency of judgments, and (d) inter-judge agreement. It was therefore possible to provide a report for the RFMC and the eleven participating scientists within a work-period of one month. (3) It became obvious that a nonretraceable process of organizing information into a judgment of risk for the hypothetical persons exposed to radiation was being employed instead of an explicit principle derived from research findings. The scientists' judgments in this situation could therefore be described as *quasi-rational* (Anderson, Deane, Hammond, McClelland, & Shanteau, 1981). That is, their public disagreements were produced not by clear, fully-documented differences in methods or aggregating the common information but by cognitively implicit methods of aggregating information.

Phase II. The purpose of Phase II was to determine whether disagreement could be removed by assisting the scientists to construct an agreed-upon, defensible, organizing principle for aggregating data into a prediction of risk. That is, an attempt would be made to develop an explicit theory of risk of cancer from plutonium emissions from the RFP.

The CRJP research group asked five of the most widely disagreeing scientists among the eleven studied in Phase I to participate in Phase II. The aim was to find a wholly analytical method of defining predictor variables, their functional relations with cancer, interactions among the variables, and, most important, a defensible and explicit method of aggregating information over the predictor variables. Such a method would not include subjective weighting of variables. Instead, each variable to be included would have to be defended by a specific reference to directly related studies. Furthermore, each scientist's suggestion for each step of the process would be checked by the other four scientists; differences would be settled by reference to the relevant literature.

Phase II thus began with an analytical approach to the structuring of the problem itself. (1) Different kinds of cancers were distinguished, and it was agreed that different cancers should not be grouped together, but should be considered separately. (2) The scientists agreed that the most important cancer to be considered in relation to the RFP should be lung cancer. (3) Predictor variables were then considered; the goal was to arrive at a set of predictors that would maximize validity and minimize redundancy. The set of predictor variables used in Phase I was re-examined and revised from this perspective.

Factors considered. *Plutonium* was included as an important predictor variable, because it is clearly relevant to both the presence of the RFP and lung cancer. *Medical x-radiation* was included because the scientists agreed that it is the most important of the lung cancer producing agents involving radiation, other than plutonium. *Smoking* was included because of its causal relevance to lung cancer. It was also agreed that, except for smoking, the most important lung cancer producing agent that does not involve radiation is asbestos. Asbestos was not included because it was learned that there is no appreciable exposure to asbestos in the Rocky Flats area. *Age of exposure* to radiation was also included in the set of predictor variables because of the long latency period between exposure and the appearance of the disease.

The final step in the problem-structuring portion of Phase II was to separate epidemiological problems from problems in health physics. The question of how best to measure the level of respirable plutonium was therefore reserved for the final phase of the project.

Phase II thus differed from Phase I in the more analytic approach taken to structuring the prediction problem, and in selection of the set of predictor variables. In Phase I, hypothetical individuals were presented for judgment, each individual having been characterized by a measurement on each variable deemed to be associated with cancer. In Phase II, however, variables, not individuals, were presented one at a time for evaluation, and the functional relationship between probability of lung cancer and each of the predictor variables was specified directly by the scientists. The predictor variables were then presented in pairs, and principles for combining them were put forward, criticized, and revised on the basis of the research literature.

Results

The approach taken in Phase II produced a much more satisfactory level of agreement than had been achieved in Phase I. The five scientists agreed on: (a) the factors to be considered; (b) the general forms of the functional relations between plutonium and lung cancer (close to linear), smoking and lung cancer (convex downward but close to linear over the range of concern), and x-radiation and lung cancer (convex downward but close to linear over the range of concern); (c) the latency period for the development of lung cancer (should be taken to be 25 years). Agreement on these conditions made it possible to construct an analytical principle for aggregating the data into the prediction.

The principle was derived from the following information:

1. The annual probability of lung cancer in nonsmokers is taken to be 7/100,000 (Doll & Hill, 1964; E. C. Hammond, 1966; Doll & Peto, 1978).

2. The effects of smoking are predicted by the equation in Doll and Peto. (1978)
3. The effects of exposure to plutonium and smoking are obtained by modifying these probabilities by ratios taken from a study by Archer, Gillam, Wagoner, and James. (1978)
4. The effects of x-radiation are determined by relating the dosage in question to the equivalent plutonium dosage in terms of REMs. (U.S. Department of Energy, 1980)
5. The effects of age of exposure to plutonium are based on mortality figures taken from the U.S. Department of Health and Human Services Life Tables, page 25.

Agreement on this analytical principle established an explicit, defensible method for organizing the relevant facts into a judgment of risk. For example, if the amount of respirable plutonium in the atmosphere downwind from RFP is known, then persons living in that area who know (a) the number of cigarettes they smoke each day, (b) the amount of radiation they have received and are receiving from medical or occupational sources, and (c) their age at initial exposure, could readily find in a table the effect of measured plutonium in the atmosphere on their personal-annual risk of lung cancer.

In addition, policy makers who must judge the acceptability of the increase in the amount of risk placed on their constitutents as a result of atmospheric plutonium can now base their decision on an agreed-upon scientific analytic principle (Anderson, Hammond, Berg, Hamman, Johnson, Marine, & Sutherland, 1981). The advantage of such an analytical principle is that, unlike pooled intuitive judgments, its rationale and empirical base is clear. Therefore, it is readily subject to modification if it should be found to be in error, and as new scientific findings made modification appropriate.

Phase III: Development of tables of estimated risk

The purpose of this phase of the study was to use the above principle, together with the results of previous empirical research, to develop risk tables which could be easily understood by the general public. These tables would be entered by level of plutonium exposure, current age, and smoking habits, to yield the relative risk of lung cancer during the next year for a specific individual compared to a person of the same age who is a nonsmoker and has never been exposed to Rocky Flats plutonium.

Use of the analytic principle developed in Phase II requires converting an ambient air level of plutonium to dose in REMs to the lung. The ambient air level of Pu239 + 240, in microcuries per cubic meter of air, is measured, reported, and published by the Rocky Flats Plant (RFP), the Department of Energy (DOE), and the Colorado Department of Health

(CDH). A panel of four experts in health physics was recruited to develop a valid dose estimation procedure (Sutherland, 1983).

Tables of risk were then developed using the following procedure:

1. Specify individual age, average number of cigarettes smoked per day, average ambient air level of Pu239 + 240 in microcuries per cubic meter of air, and age at initial exposure to this ambient air level.[2]

2. Calculate the expected incidence of lung cancer for persons of the same age and smoking status using the equation of Doll and Peto (1978). This equation is valid for persons who began smoking at ages 16–25.

3. Determine the cumulative dose in REMs to the lung from Pu239 + 240 inhalation. Assume six REMs of plutonium inhalation exposure is equivalent to one working level month of radon exposure as estimated in the BEIR III report (Advisory Committee on Biological Effects of Ionizing Radiation, 1979). (Doses from x-radiation should be added.)

4. Adjust expected incidence of lung cancer for persons of same age and smoking status for working-level months of equivalent exposure using Fig. 1 of Archer, Gillam, Wagoner, and James (1978). The method of adjustment is specified in detail by Sutherland. (1983)

5. Calculate relative risk of lung cancer by dividing the incidence rate calculated in procedure #4 by the expected incidence of lung cancer in nonsmokers with no Rocky Flats plutonium exposure.

The equation for determining the probability of lung cancer during the next year for a person of specified age a and who smoked c cigarettes per day starting at age 16–25 is:

$$I = (0.273 - 10^{-7})(C + 6)^2(A - 22.5)^{4.5} \times \exp(0.00018(\text{DOSE}))$$

The first three terms of the equation represent risk from smoking alone (Doll & Peto, 1978). The last ($\exp(0.00018 (\text{DOSE}))$) represents the increased risk from plutonium exposure and the interaction effect between cigarette smoking and plutonium inhalation. The method of dose calculation for a person exposed to a continuous ambient air level of Rocky Flats plutonium is specified in detail by Sutherland (1983).

Eight ambient air levels of Rocky Flats Pu239 + 240 were chosen for analysis (see Table 28.1). The first level presented (level(0)) is for no Rocky Flats plutonium exposure. Relative risks in Tables 28.2–28.4 for

[2] In the tables, exposure to Rocky Flats plutonium since birth was assumed. For periods of exposure less than the entire life span, risk may be extrapolated from values in the tables, by multiplying the fraction of life span at risk by the difference between risk for level of exposure of interest and risk for zero plutonium exposure, and adding this value to risk at zero plutonium exposure.

Table 28.1. *Ambient air levels of Pu239 + 240*

Description	Level	Microcuries/CU M
No exposure	(0)	0.0
Typical background fallout	(1)	0.1×10^{-9}
Low RFP sample east gate	(2)	0.5×10^{-9}
Typical RFP sample east gate	(3)	0.1×10^{-8}
Typical EML sample east gate	(4)	0.2×10^{-8}
Typical CDH sample east gate	(5)	0.5×10^{-8}
DOE/CDH guideline	(6)	0.6×10^{-7}
Less than 1/50th of the 1957 release at the stack	(7)	0.1×10^{-5}

this level reflect age and smoking risk only. Level (1), 0.1E − 9 microcuries of Pu239 − 240 per cubic meter of air, is a typical background level recorded at CDH in metropolitan Denver (Colorado Department of Health, 1976). No increase in risk is noted at background fallout levels. (Compare levels (0) and (1) in Tables 28.2–28.4.)

Risk and living near the RFP during 1974–1978

Level (2), 0.5E − 9 microcuries per cubic meter, was the *lowest* average reading reported from RFP east gate samples during the years 1974–1978 (Barker, 1981). Levels (3), (4), and (5) are typical levels reported from RFP, EML (DOE Environment Measurements Laboratory) and CDH samplers respectively during the same period (see Figure 28.1).

No increase in radiation is noticeable at these levels of plutonium exposure in any age group at any smoking level. Under normal operating conditions during 1974–1978, the Plant presented no noticeable radiation hazard to persons living in its vicinity. (Compare levels (2), (3), and (4) in Tables 28.2–28.4)

Risk of plutonium exposure at DOE/CDH guidelines

Level (6), 0.6E − 7 microcuries per cubic meter, is the DOE/CDH guideline for release of soluble plutonium aerosols in controlled areas. At this level of exposure, a 1% increase in relative risk is noted for nonsmokers. A similar percentage increase is noted for smokers. Since no noticeable increase in risk should be observable at DOE/CDH guideline exposures, this guideline needs more careful evaluation by federal and state regulatory authorities.

During 1957, a fire and explosion at the plant produced unmonitored plutonium releases during the fire and for six days thereafter due to power outage. Monitoring resumed seven days after the fire, and a release was recorded equal to 50 times level (7) (Johnson, 1981). Actual release may have been an order of magnitude or more greater.

Table 28.2. *Lung cancer relative risk for nonsmoking white males*

Age	Plutonium ambient air levels							
	(0)	(1)	(2)	(3)	(4)	(5)	(6)	(7)
40	1.00	1.00	1.00	1.00	1.00	1.00	1.00	1.06
45	1.00	1.00	1.00	1.00	1.00	1.00	1.00	1.06
50	1.00	1.00	1.00	1.00	1.00	1.00	1.00	1.07
55	1.00	1.00	1.00	1.00	1.00	1.00	1.00	1.08
60	1.00	1.00	1.00	1.00	1.00	1.00	1.01	1.09
65	1.00	1.00	1.00	1.00	1.00	1.00	1.01	1.10
70	1.00	1.00	1.00	1.00	1.00	1.00	1.01	1.10
75	1.00	1.00	1.00	1.00	1.00	1.00	1.01	1.11

Table 28.3. *Lung cancer relative risk for white male smokers, 20 cigarettes per day*

Age	Plutonium ambient air levels							
	(0)	(1)	(2)	(3)	(4)	(5)	(6)	(7)
40	2.82	2.82	2.82	2.82	2.82	2.82	2.83	2.98
45	5.34	5.34	5.34	5.34	5.35	5.35	5.36	5.69
50	8.50	8.50	8.50	8.50	8.50	8.50	8.53	9.11
55	12.11	12.11	12.11	12.11	12.11	12.12	12.17	13.08
60	16.04	16.04	16.04	16.04	16.05	16.05	16.12	17.46
65	20.18	20.18	20.18	20.18	20.18	20.19	20.29	22.12
70	24.44	24.44	24.44	24.44	24.45	24.45	24.59	26.99
75	28.76	28.76	28.76	28.76	28.76	28.77	28.94	31.99

Table 28.4. *Lung cancer relative risk for white male smokers, 40 cigarettes per day*

Age	Plutonium ambient air levels							
	(0)	(1)	(2)	(3)	(4)	(5)	(6)	(7)
40	8.82	8.82	8.82	8.82	8.82	8.83	8.85	9.33
45	16.73	16.73	16.73	16.73	16.73	16.73	16.79	17.81
50	26.60	26.60	26.60	26.60	26.60	26.61	26.71	28.53
55	37.91	37.91	37.91	37.91	37.92	37.92	38.09	40.95
60	50.22	50.22	50.22	50.22	50.23	50.24	50.47	50.64
65	63.17	63.17	63.17	63.18	63.18	63.20	63.52	69.24
70	76.50	76.50	76.51	76.51	76.52	76.54	76.96	84.47
75	90.02	90.02	90.02	90.03	90.04	90.07	90.60	100.12

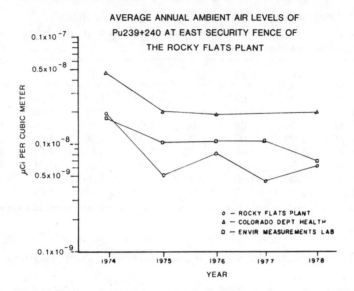

Figure 28.1. Average annual Pu239 + 240 ambient air levels at the east security fence of the Rocky Flats Plant for 1974–1978. Levels were measured by three different agencies (RFP, CDH, DOE) using three different procedures. Redrawn after Barker (1981).

Therefore, some individuals downwind from the plant may have received the cumulative dose in 1957 equivalent to more than 50 years exposure at level (7) due to the 1957 fire. As Tables 28.2–28.4 indicate, the increase in risk for lifetime exposure varies from 4% for 40-year-old males to 11% for 75-year-old males. It is essential, therefore, that the Rocky Flats Emergency Response Plan allow for evacuation of persons living near the plant in the event of an accident. Careful consideration should be given to zoning regulations by public officials for development near the plant, since it is much easier to evacuate a business office than families and small children from residential dwellings and schools.

Relationship between plutonium risk and smoking habits

While radiation risk percentage increases are similar for smokers and nonsmokers, *smoking alone* increases the risk of lung cancer far more than possible increases in risk from past Rocky Flats Plant operations. Figure 28.2 illustrates this phenomenon for a 75-year-old male. Relative risk is shown for various levels of plutonium exposure and cigarette consumption. Only levels (5), (6), and (7) are labeled on the figure because the first four levels produce no noticeable increase in risk.

For nonsmokers, the relative risk of lung cancer varies from 1.0 at level (5) to 1.11 at level (7). For persons smoking 20 cigarettes per day, relative

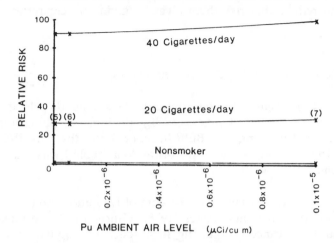

Figure 28.2. Relative risk of lung cancer for a 75-year-old male smoking 0, 20, or 40 cigarettes per day from age 16–25 and lifetime exposure to ambient air plutonium at levels (5) (normal operation), (6) (DOE guidelines), and (7) (accident levels).

risk increased from 28.77 at level (5) to 31.99 at level (7). For persons smoking 40 cigarettes per day, the relative risk increased from 90.07 at level (5) to 100.12 at level (7). In all cases, for a 75-year-old male, the increase was 11% over this range of plutonium exposures.

From a public health perspective, an 11% increase in lung cancer risk to nonsmokers will produce less than one additional lung cancer case per 100,000 of the population per year. For smokers, that increase will be 3 to 10 per 100,000 additional lung cancer cases per year. From an individual smoker's perspective, then, the first precautionary action to take if working or living near Rocky Flats is to stop smoking.

The achievement of this study is that, using Tables 28.2–28.4, individuals can now determine their annual relative risk from living or working near the Plant for ambient air plutonium levels measured and published by the CDH. The tables will also be important to public officials responsible for overseeing development of the Rocky Flats environs and for protecting the health of workers and the public. These officials can now see that there is a small possible increase in risk at the DOE/CDH guideline level and a larger increase in risk from accidents. In addition, they must grapple with the dilemma posed by risk to smokers. Unlike nonsmokers, smokers incur significant risk of lung cancer from an accident at the RFP. But that risk is a direct result of their voluntary acceptance of an even greater absolute risk of lung cancer from cigarette smoking. The question is whether the public should bear the huge costs of reducing the involuntary risk of lung cancer for smokers, when smokers could reduce that risk themselves by giving up cigarettes.

Errors of estimate

The error of estimate in Table 28.1 is a function of:

(1) Error induced by the dose estimation procedure. This depends primarily on the relative biological effectiveness (RBE) of inhaled plutonium in producing cancer of the lung. The BEIR III report states that this RBE is in the range 8–15 based on review of historical data. Table I was calculated with an assumed RBE of 10.

(2) Error due to population sampling in the data of Doll and Peto (1978) and Archer, Gillam, Wagoner, and James (1978). Cancer incidence rates are based on counts of cancers occurring in a specified population which follow a Poisson distribution. Confidence limits on the curves from these studies vary from 0.871–1.154 times the dose-response rates in smokers estimated by Doll and Peto to 0.459–2.73 times the dose-response rates for nonsmoking uranium miners estimated by Archer, Gillam, Wagoner, and James where the sample size is smallest (Bailar & Ederer, 1964).

(3) Error of unknown magnitude introduced by using data from health effects of human radon exposure to estimate effects of plutonium exposure. Both radon daughters and plutonium particles are alpha emitters. However, the distribution of particles in the lung is slightly different for different isotopes. No data are available in the literature to allow estimation of resulting differences in the rate of lung cancer induction in humans. The latter source of error is of unknown magnitude because it was introduced by the judgment of a panel of epidemiologists that the data on human radon exposure is the best available data for use in estimation of plutonium inhalation effects. This is precisely where the mode of inquiry moves from intuitive judgments to explicit, retraceable principles.

Conclusion

Scientists' judgments of risk should be improved through the use of judgment analysis because: (a) it describes scientists' cognitive activity rather than their motives, (b) externalizes parameters of the scientists' judgment process that otherwise remain obscure, and (c) assists in the development of explicit, rather than implicit, theories that are open to criticism and modifications based on the scientific literature. All of these advantages are part of the scientific tradition of employing cognitive safeguards against systematic and unsystematic errors.

Addendum

Following the completion of the above study, a report by Cobb, Eversole, Archer, Taggart, and Efurd included the following abstract:

A study was conducted to determine whether the tissues of people who lived near to or downwind from the Rocky flats nuclear weapons facility in Colorado contained more plutonium than the tissues from people who lived farther away. Information was collected on the age, sex, smoking history, residence history, presence of disease, and plutonium level in selected tissues from individuals autopsied in various Eastern Colorado hospitals. The 236, 238, 239, and 240 isotopes of plutonium were determined.

Plutonium levels in lung and liver tissues were affected by age and smoking history more than by distance from the Rocky Flats Plant. Though the measured 240/239 isotope ratio indicated a small contribution from Rocky Flats, the total amount of plutonium in the samples was no different than in similar samples collected from other areas of the U.S. (1982).

We interpret these findings as providing clear support for our methods and conclusions.

29. Expert judgment: Some necessary conditions and an example

Hillel J. Einhorn

In an age of increasing specialization, it is quite likely that greater numbers of people will have to rely on expert judgment. It is therefore an important matter to discuss some of the conditions that produce "expertise." Is an expert simply one who is very skillful with training and knowledge in some specialized field or are there perhaps more objective criteria that can be used? The purpose of this study is to discuss and illustrate some necessary, if not sufficient, conditions for defining expertise within a given situation. The type of situation to be considered is one in which several judges have to deal with multidimensional information. This information has to be measured and combined into a decision or global judgment. This is a very general task, specific examples of which might include: (a) radiologists viewing an X ray and coming to a diagnosis; (b) businessmen making a sales forecast for a new product; (c) art critics viewing a painting and judging its quality, etc.

The expert must *identify* information or cues from the multidimensional stimulus he encounters. These cues are diagnostic (i.e., contain information) about the final decision or judgment. The expert's ability to identify cues can be seen as a problem of extracting weak signals from a background of noise (e.g., Green & Swets, 1966). While each cue is related to the final categorization, it also serves the function of leading the expert to other cues that will also be of importance in the determination of the final categorization. For example, consider the cue of "product safety." While this cue can be related to how much sales we can expect, it is also indicative of other cues in the product (its price may be higher due to safety features). When one considers that the expert may deal with

This chapter is an abbreviated version of an article that originally appeared in the *Journal of Applied Psychology*, 1974, *59*(5), 562–571. Copyright © 1974 by the American Psychological Association, Inc. Reprinted by permission.

many cases in the course of time, it is not unreasonable to assume that he builds up expectations regarding both what variables typically covary together and the strength of this covariation.

Consider that the expert must measure two cues that he considers to be highly related, for example, the degree of workmanship and the quality of material in a particular product. If he believes that these cues covary together, it is quite likely that his measurement of one cue will affect his measurement of the other. This is similar to what has been termed a *logical error* (Guilford, 1954); that is, traits that logically go together are rated in similar ways. The relationship different experts expect between cues may vary due to their different experience and training. Furthermore, this is not an error but reflects each expert's way of *organizing information into clusters or dimensions*.[1] From a psychological point of view, this clustering of information serves to reduce the dimensionality of the information one has to process; that is, instead of having to process many cues, one only has to deal with a smaller number of general factors.

While cues are being identified and clustered together, the expert is *measuring the amount* of the cue. The businessman may say that a product is "tasty," but how "tasty"? In many types of situations the expert will have to serve as a measuring instrument for cues that cannot be measured in more objective ways (cf. Sawyer, 1966).

There are three issues that are important in discussing the measurement of cues: (a) intrajudge reliability, (b) construct validity (Cronbach & Meehl, 1955), and (c) judgmental bias. With regard to intrajudge reliability, it should be obvious that unless the expert can reproduce his measurements of the cues, there is little more that can be said in defense of his expertise. Therefore, high intrajudge reliability is a necessity for expertise. With regard to construct validity, it should be the case that the cues being measured should have status as explanatory concepts. Operationally, we would expect that the cues show both convergent and discriminant validity when they are considered as traits (judges are considered methods) in a multitrait-multimethod matrix (Campbell & Fiske, 1959). Finally, with regard to judgmental bias, we should expect that expert judges will not show such well-known biases as *leniency, halo,* etc. (Guilford, 1954; Ghiselli & Brown, 1955). All three of the above criteria should be considered in evaluating expertise.

After cues are identified, measured, and clustered, the important cognitive work of *weighting and combining* to form a global evaluation follows. This part of the judgment task has received the greatest amount of attention (Slovic & Lichtenstein, 1971). The results of a large number of studies have shown that judges are quite poor at weighting and

---

[1] It has been noted that in situations where an objective measure of the relationship between cues is given, subjects find it very difficult to learn them if they are different from their preconceived ideas of what "go together" (Chapman & Chapman, 1969).

combining information accurately, that is, in accord with the objective validity of the information. However, objective validity implies that the criteria used as the bases for comparing the global evaluation were themselves relevant to the ultimate criteria in question (Thorndike, 1949). In many cases, availability of criteria, not relevance, was used to define the objective measure. It is therefore possible that global judgments have more validity than it has been possible to demonstrate thus far.

Since questions of criterion relevance cannot be fully answered, and since some situations contain no criteria, is there some other way of evaluating global judgments? Let us take the same line of inquiry that was used in the measurement of traits; that is: Is the global evaluation an operational concept in the sense of possessing convergent validity? While it would seem important that experts agree on their evaluations (as a condition for expertise), the issue is considerably more complicated. The concept of agreement can itself be thought of in two ways: (a) agreement "in fact" and (b) agreement "in principle." The former refers to actual agreement of evaluation, whereas the latter refers to agreement with respect to weighting and combining policy, that is, *how* the global evaluation is to be formed once the inputs are specified. Although one may have agreement in principle, there may be disagreement with respect to the coding of input (note that coding of input is also dependent on the perceived covariation of the cues). Therefore, agreement in fact will be a function of weighting and combining similarity *and* similarity in coding cues. On the other hand, it should not be assumed that agreement in principle is easy to achieve. This is due to the fact that learning probabilistic relationships in the natural environment may be quite difficult. This implies that there is great room for individual differences in the evaluation of the diagnosticity of cues and subsequently, large differences in the weights assigned to those cues. Furthermore, even when training is rigorous and the conditions for learning optimal, similar weighting policies may reflect training in a particular school of thought. It seems that policies would be very similar within but not between competing schools (a practical application of this is Naylor & Wherry's, 1965, technique for grouping judges on the basis of similarity of their weighting policies).

Although the difficulty of achieving either type of agreement is great, it should be the case that there is at least a common core of knowledge which is germane to a particular area of inquiry. Furthermore, expertise consists, to some extent, of knowing that common core. Therefore, as a practical guide it is proposed that there be at least some agreement, both in fact and in principle, for the global evaluation.[2]

With the discussion of the factors involved in expert judgment, there is

---

[2] In cases where experts are from competing schools, we might expect high negative correlations.

a need to illustrate, in a concrete manner, how the various criteria discussed in this study can be used in evaluation of real experts. The purpose of the present study is to make explicit the processes assumed to be present in the preceding discussion. The details of the study to be described appear in Coppleson, Factor, Strum, Graff, and Rappaport (1970) and Einhorn (1972).

Method

Subjects

The judges we considered were three medical pathologists. This specialty requires considerable training and is of special importance since the pathologists' report is often the ultimate criterion that is used for the diagnosis of various diseases.

Procedure

The three pathologists independently viewed 193 biopsy slides taken from patients having Hodgkin's disease, a cancer of the lymph system. The biopsies were taken when the patient first entered the hospital. The only information given to the pathologists was the biopsy slide. All the slides used in this study were taken from patients who had died and from whom complete data were available with respect to the ratings to be described.

For each slide, the pathologist had to give his judgment of the amount of nine histological characteristics that were chosen, a priori, to be important. The histological signs were as follows: benign histiocytes, malignant histiocytes, eosinophils, necrosis, plasma cells, neutrophils, lymphocytes, Sternberg-Reed distribution, and Sternberg-Reed cells. For each of these signs, with the exception of Sternberg-Reed distribution (which was measured on a 2-point scale), a 6-point scale was used, which was developed by the pathologists.

In addition to the judgments of the amounts of the histological characteristics, a global judgment concerning the classification of the disease in terms of severity was also made. This judgment was measured on a 9-point scale (higher values representing greater severity). The global judgment was made after the judgments of the histological signs. Finally, 26 of the slides were repeated twice each so that estimates of test-retest reliability (the ability to reproduce the judgments) could be obtained.

Although the judges picked out the signs they expected to measure, one would expect that experts with experience in this task would have little difficulty in recognition of attributes, whereas the judgment of amount would be of most concern. However, definitions of each sign were not given so that any differences the judges had in this regard

484 HILLEL J. EINHORN

would be revealed in the later analyses. Of special importance is the fact that the multidimensional stimulus was viewed intact, so that interactions, context effects, etc. could play whatever role they normally did in the task.

Results

The first question addressed was whether the ratings or cue measurements were reliable; that is: Could the expert, when viewing exactly the same slide on two occasions, give the same response? Mean intrajudge reliability for the signs ranged from .19 to .93 (over the three judges), while the mean global judgment reliability was .63 (over the three judges). The mean reliability for the three judges (over signs) ranged from .64 to .74. Judge 2 had a slightly higher reliability for the signs, but his reliability on the global judgment (.46) was considerably lower than that of the other judges (.69, .71). The average reliability over both judges, signs and global judgments was .69.

Convergent and discriminant validity were examined for evidence of construct validity. Convergent validity refers to the fact that different methods (judges) should converge in measuring the same trait (sign); the correlation between judges for the same sign should be greater than zero. Discriminant validity, on the other hand, is defined by three conditions: (a) The correlation between the same traits (signs) for different judges should be higher than the correlation between different traits as measured by different judges. (b) The correlation between the same signs as measured by different judges should be higher than the correlations between different signs as measured by the same judge. (c) The pattern of correlations should be the same in the submatrices of the multitrait–multimethod matrix. This refers to the ordering in both sign and magnitude of the correlations in the heterotrait–heteromethod matrices.[3]

The multitrait–multimethod (multisign–multijudge) matrix is shown in Table 29.1.

Looking first at convergent validity, 29 of the 30 correlations between judges' measures of signs were significant at $p < .01$. Furthermore, the average of these correlations was .56 – evidence of convergent validity. It should be noted that convergent validity, in situations where a single judge is defined as a method, is the same as *inter*judge reliability, or agreement. The amount of agreement was considerably different for the

---

[3] These conditions can be expressed formally. Let, x_{ijs} = rating on ith slide by jth judge for sth sign. Let $i \neq i'$, $j \neq j'$, $s \neq s'$. Convergent validity then refers to $\rho_{x_{js}, x_{j's}} > 0$ (correlating over i). The two conditions for discriminant validity are:

$$(a) \ \rho_{x_{js}, x_{j's}} > |\rho_{x_{js}, x_{j's'}}|; \ (b) \ \rho_{x_{js}, x_{j's}} > |\rho_{x_{js}, x_{js'}}|.$$

Absolute value operators are used, since it is the magnitude rather than the sign of the correlation that is important.

various signs (.33 to .80). Notice should be given to the fact that the greatest amount of disagreement was with respect to the global judgment (.27). This finding is in accord with earlier remarks about the global judgment being a composite variable. As far as the mean agreement for the three pair of judges, over all signs, Judges 1 and 2 agreed with each other most (.64), with Judges 1 and 3 next (.52), and Judges 2 and 3 agreeing least (.50).

In analyzing discriminant validity of 540 comparisons, there were only 20 violations (or 4%) of the requirement that the correlation between the same signs for different judges be higher than the correlation between different signs as measured by different judges. Additionally, there were only 32 violations of the 540 comparisons (or 6%) of the requirement of discriminant validity that correlations between the same signs as measured by different judges be higher than the correlations between different signs as measured by the same judge. Given that this requirement is quite stringent and the percentage of violations small, it seems fair to conclude that this condition was also met. Examination of the submatrices further showed that the pattern of correlations was the same in the submatrices, indicating that the third condition for discriminant validity had been met. Therefore, it seems fair to conclude that this data showed both convergent and discriminant validity.

Guilford (1954) presented an analysis of variance approach for dealing with judgmental biases found in the use of rating scales. While the situation that this approach was originally developed for involved raters rating employees on various traits, the general idea is applicable to any situation where judges rate objects on a number of dimensions (Stanley, 1961, also discusses this basic design). Although Guilford's procedure is applicable to the present data, there is a slight difference. In Guilford's example (pp. 280–288), each rater rates each ratee on each attribute only once. In the present study, using the 26 repeat slides, we have a Judges × Slides × Signs design with two replications. The last two factors are repeated and therefore an appropriate way to analyze this data is given by Winer (1962, pp. 319–337). This analysis of variance is presented in Table 29.2.

Note first that the main effect for judges is not significant. Since this effect represents the judges' overall tendency to rate the amount of the signs, this indicates a lack of a *leniency* error. (Leniency in this case refers to a tendency to overvalue or undervalue the slides in general). The lack of an effect in the present context is more in accord with what one would expect from expert judges. The two other main effects simply indicate that different slides and different signs have varying means. What is of major concern are the interactions involving the judges' factor. These involve the differential effect of judges on slides (A × B), on signs (A × C) and on Slides × Signs (A × B × C). These interactions should be nonsignificant; that is, differential effects due to judges are not consistent

Table 29.1. *Multitrait (signs) – multimethod (judges) matrix*

	Judge 1										Judge			
	Lukes	BH	MH	Eos.	Nec.	PC	Neut.	Lymph.	S-R D.	S-R C.	Lukes	BH	MH	Eos.
Judge 1														
Lukes	(690)													
BH	−044	(430)												
MH	302	−061	(820)											
Eos.	217	−116	138	(860)										
Nec.	058	100	370	134	(840)									
PC	126	−035	061	104	105	(470)								
Neut.	212	114	193	294	302	189	(490)							
Lymph.	−310	−212	−447	−420	−288	−159	−422	(850)						
S-R D.	280	−094	539	172	160	007	184	−339	(220)					
S-R C.	306	−131	449	027	191	029	129	−139	461	(590)				
Judge 2														
Lukes	400	016	135	−091	116	038	−086	−021	160	275	(460)			
BH	−041	446	049	−108	190	−012	027	−231	−017	−083	051	(710)		
MH	241	−096	634	071	144	060	082	−318	484	402	179	−036	(860)	
Eos.	109	−037	114	824	099	069	266	−387	119	−048	−113	−021	015	(900)
Nec.	121	128	382	142	858	069	301	−320	230	195	108	102	180	129
PC	013	−098	−047	132	069	600	161	−157	−115	−100	−051	031	−086	131
Neut.	239	−007	235	294	368	217	655	−471	270	153	033	095	139	339
Lymph.	−217	−133	−356	−348	−316	−088	−424	686	−264	−120	−062	−237	−282	−407
S-R D.	160	−078	285	−037	056	072	056	−118	489	266	169	−031	451	−033
S-R C.	156	−093	315	−018	080	044	031	−115	332	596	169	−113	511	−074
Judge 3														
Lukes	209	069	233	090	170	093	101	−225	141	229	199	−022	232	054
BH	−037	305	−093	−072	−129	020	−103	−104	072	−042	−040	327	−047	−020
MH	222	053	500	084	354	111	214	−351	365	412	184	042	503	−005
Eos.	190	−058	075	776	094	050	322	−409	169	049	−035	−017	027	783
Nec.	118	031	282	188	572	154	479	−442	194	140	029	076	097	158
PC	139	−008	−004	086	094	420	189	−180	−061	011	−015	122	−019	057

	Neut.	Lymph.	S-R D.	S-R C.	Lukes	BH	MH	Eos.	Nec.	PC	Neut.	Lymph	S-R D.	S-R C.
Neut.	265	004	195	277	362	159	674	−516	206	100	016	076	080	261
Lymph.	−188	−239	−324	−245	−318	−115	−393	614	−215	−131	−052	−182	−195	−220
S-R D.	255	−080	252	319	162	086	272	−260	365	295	075	−043	179	251
S-R C.	275	−087	298	120	221	049	215	−173	386	558	267	−151	275	022

2

Judge 3

	Nec.	PC	Neut.	Lymph.	S-R D.	S-R C.	Lukes	BH	MH	Eos.	Nec.	PC	Neut.	Lymph	S-R D.	S-R C.
Nec.	(840)															
PC	053	(530)														
Neut.	374	191	(640)													
Lymph.	−305	−127	−536	(760)												
S-R D.	100	−109	076	−088	(170)											
S-R C.	043	−065	045	−072	386	(830)										
Lukes	168	049	054	−197	049	193	(710)									
BH	−137	032	−126	−031	130	056	−159	(400)								
MH	367	−009	224	−279	291	323	335	−119	(720)							
Eos.	094	082	315	−406	017	009	119	−006	072	(950)						
Nec.	561	106	510	−393	115	142	086	−060	309	191	(550)					
PC	032	527	191	−170	−071	048	175	100	028	136	165	(570)				
Neut.	341	102	652	−446	136	105	113	−016	186	343	672	162	(550)			
Lymph	−331	−046	−386	629	−126	−102	−229	−089	−436	−331	−443	−158	−455	(730)		
S-R D.	141	045	327	−231	124	201	056	011	250	306	351	002	345	−164	(160)	
S-R C.	245	−129	207	−169	278	423	343	080	−427	133	258	−043	276	−302	407	(590)

Note: Correlations are based on $n = 193$. Validity diagonals are circled. Correlations in parentheses are intrajudge reliabilities ($n = 26$). Lukes = judgment of severity; BH = benign histiocytes; MH = malignant histiocytes; Eos. = eosinophils; Nec. = necrosis; PC = plasma cells; Neut. = neutrophils; Lymph. = lymphocytes; S-R D. = Sternberg-Reed distribution; S-R C. = Sternberg-Reed cells.

Table 29.2. *Analysis of variance for judges × slides × signs*

Source	SS	df	MS	F
Judges (A)	2.38	2	1.19	< 1
Subjects × within	3.88	3	1.29	
Slides (B)	160.70	25	6.43	14.61**
A × B	21.10	50	.44	1.47
B × subjects within	22.75	75	.30	
Signs (C)	975.63	8	187.80	257.26**
A × C	26.37	16	1.65	2.26*
C × subjects within	17.62	24	.73	
B × C	976.08	200	4.88	13.94**
A × B × C	159.15	400	.40	1.14*
B × C × subjects within	208.93	600	.35	

Note: All factors are assumed fixed.
 * $p < .05$.
** $p < .001$.

with the fact that the shared core of expertise is influencing their measurement. Consider the Judges × Slides (A × B) interaction. This interaction involves the particular judge's tendency to overvalue or undervalue particular slides. This can be conceptualized as a *halo* effect; that is, a general tendency dominates the ratings of the particular attributes. In this situation, a halo effect would mean that the pathologists first get a general impression of severity and then work at rating the signs in accord with this general impression. However, this interaction is not significant indicating the absence of any halo. Both the Judges × Signs (A × C) and the Judges × Signs × Slides (A × B × C) are significant, although the magnitude of these interactions is quite small. The former interaction indicates that the judges differentially rate the signs; that is, some judges *see* more or less of some signs than others. The three-way interaction indicates that judges differentially rate signs depending on what slide the sign appears in. This is a type of context effect that is specific to the judges. However, it should be stressed that the significant interactions are all quite small. For these particular experts then, there seems to be only slight bias in their judgmental ratings.

One final analysis is necessary to complete the results on bias. Because of the qualitative difference between the global judgment and the individual cues, a separate one-way analysis of variance (repeated measures on each slide for the three judges) was performed on the global judgments. The results showed a significant effect with Judges 1 and 2 being most different ($\bar{Y}_1 = 2.98$, $\bar{Y}_2 = 4.61$). Therefore, Judge 2 saw more severity generally than did Judge 1, although both judges did *not* see different amounts of the signs. As has been pointed out before, this is consistent with the remarks made concerning the difficulty of achieving agreement on global variables....

In order to examine the weighting process, the combining function was assumed to be additive (Dawes & Corrigan, 1974). The weights given to the cues were determined by regressing the global judgment on the nine cues, for each judge.... The results of this analysis are shown in Table 29.3.

It can be seen that the ability to model the judge varies among these three judges. The multiple correlation for Judge 2 is low, as compared to the other two judges. What is most important is the fact that the weights for the cues vary greatly across the three judges. Consider Experts 1 and 2. As we have previously seen, these two experts have very similar factor structures, yet, they weight the cues quite differently in coming to their global judgment. As a matter of fact, the cue that is weighted most heavily by Judge 1, Sternberg-Reed cells, is not weighted significantly by Judge 2. Consider the weighting policies of Judges 1 and 3. They do agree that Sternberg-Reed cells should be weighted most highly yet. Judge 3 weights three other cues as being important (benign histiocytes, malignant histiocytes, and plasma cells), while Judge 1 does not. Clearly then, in addition to there being low agreement in fact, there is also low agreement in principle. From our previous results we can say that disagreement in fact is mostly accounted for by disagreement in principle, since the judges seem to code the data in very similar ways.

Discussion

The implications of the results on information weighting for defining expertise are problematic. If one requires that experts have similar weighting policies, the problem of adequately defining *similarity* is immediately raised. For example, Judges 1 and 3 do agree on the importance of Sternberg-Reed cells, yet they do not agree on the weighting of the other cues. On the other hand, Judge 2 is clearly different from either Judges 1 or 3. It should be mentioned that Judge 2 was a resident of Judge 1 and was learning this task to some extent. His low correlation suggests another possible criterion for expertise – experts should have at least one significant cue weight. The reason for this is that at least some information in the cues should be used in forming the global judgment.

Although requiring experts to have similar weighting policies would be a very stringent requirement, it would seem that the combining of information lies at the core of expertise. Learning the important relationships between cues and criteria should be one of the most important kinds of learning that is involved in mastering a particular area. Therefore, it is tentatively suggested that experts should exhibit similar weighting policies.

It was stated at the outset that the conditions discussed in the present

Table 29.3. *Beta weights for cues in predicting global judgment*

Judges	Cues									
	BH	MH	Eos.	Nec.	PC	Neut.	Lymph	S-R D.	S-R C.	Multiple R
1	.00	.12	.11	−.13*	.08	.08	−.16*	.05	.22***	.46***
2	.04	.07	−.13*	.08	−.03	.00	−.05	.09	.09	.27*
3	−.14**	.22***	.07	−.11	.19***	.02	−.07	−.11	.29***	.49***

Note: Results are based on regressions with $n = 193$. BH = benign histiocytes; MH = malignant histiocytes; Eos. = eosinophils; Nec. = necrosis; PC = plasma cells; Neut. = neutrophils; Lymph. = lymphocytes; S-R D. = Sternberg-Reed distribution; S-R C. = Sternberg-Reed cells.
* $p < .10$.
** $p < .05$.
*** $p < .01$.

study were necessary but not sufficient. This clearly implies that other factors are indicative of expertise. Consider our example of businessmen making a forecast of sales for a new product. Whereas they may agree on what some of the relevant attributes of the product are, the real expert may discern/form cues that no one has ever seen before. Similarly, the expert may be the one who can discern and use contingent relationships between cues, that is, complex interactions among cues. These aspects of cue formation and utilization may be an important aspect of expertise.

A second consideration not discussed in this study is how alternatives are first formed in the decision/judgment process. For example, although there may be several ways to market a new product, the expert may be able to elucidate alternatives that have not been thought of before. Again, this is a creative process that we know little about.

A third consideration, somewhat related to the first two, is how the task is *structured*. By this is meant how the problem is defined and the manner in which a solution will be attempted. For example, the process of information search will greatly structure the task. Kleinmuntz (1968) suggests that the expert searches his environment for those cues that yield the greatest amount of information, and this leads to a shortening of the "decision tree" used to reach a judgment. These types of problems have not been discussed in this study since the experiment served to structure the task. However, in nonexperimental settings, this structuring will undoubtedly be of great importance.

A major criticism of the conditions for expertise stated in the present context may be that too much stress has been put on agreement. This agreement has been with respect to clustering, measuring, and weighting cues. As is well known, the history of science is replete with oddballs who did not agree with anyone, yet, were proved to be correct by subsequent events. This criticism has value, yet it conceals the fact that eventually some relevant criterion other than agreement became available (possibly due to new instrumentation or unusual events). However, from a practical point of view, we cannot afford to wait long periods of time to see who may be correct. Actions and decisions have to be taken within a limited time perspective. Therefore, although agreement is by no means the only criterion, it is one that seems relevant to the discussion of expertise.

Where a relevant, or partially relevant criterion can be known within a reasonable time period, expertise can be determined by one's track record. If it is found that two experts do equally well in terms of matching a criterion (and this is significantly higher than some base rate value), yet they do not meet the requirements discussed in the present study (especially that of similar weighting), What are we to say? We can only say that in a highly probabilistic world, there may be many routes to the same goal (cf. Hammond, 1955) and that there may be more than one way to perform the cognitive tasks involved in judgment.

Part IX
Development and learning

Almost everything we know about how people make judgments and arrive at decisions has come from studies of adults. This is changing as more researchers discover the fascinating changes that occur as children progress from immature to mature thought. In order to investigate the path from immature to mature thought, however, it is necessary to examine performance on a task that is appropriate for all age groups.

Harriet Shaklee and Michael Mims, the authors of our first selection, have chosen a most ubiquitous task for this purpose: covariation estimation. Covariation estimation is simply a judgment as to what extent two factors are related to each other. Does my health vary regularly with the amount of vitamin C I ingest? Does Mom pay more attention to me when I make more noise? Does my spouse become distant every time I bring up the topic of my future career goals? Social interaction, scientific investigation, and most of our everyday interactions with the environment are predicated on accurate assessment of covariation. Shaklee and Mims show that adults are more accurate than children because they perform covariation estimation in a more sophisticated way. In addition, the careful methodology used by the authors enables them to discover what factors may cause adults to revert to childlike cognitive strategies.

Rather than choosing a single specific task, such as covariation estimation, which can be performed at nearly any age, other researchers have examined those fundamental concepts whose acquisition must begin at a very young age. For example, the well-known Swiss psychologist, Jean Piaget, studied children's understanding of space, time, and causality. Our second chapter in this part, by Friedrich Wilkening, uses information integration theory (described in Part I) to discover exactly how children combine the concepts of distance and time to gauge velocity.

The final chapter in this part deals not with the judgments *of* children but with judgments *about* children. Ray W. Cooksey, Peter Freebody, and Graham R. Davidson asked teachers to consider test scores of several children in order to predict each child's early reading achievement level. By examining the pattern of each teacher's judgments, the authors were able to deduce which cues each teacher felt were important in arriving at his or her prediction. The authors could then determine whether the teachers were basing their predictions on those cues that truly were

493

related to early reading performance. Thus, this type of analysis not only can provide a precise description of each teacher's judgments but can potentially provide guidance by informing the teachers which predictors of performance have the most validity.

30. Development of rule use in judgments of covariation between events

Harriet Shaklee and Michael Mims

Many psychologists (Heider, 1958; Inhelder & Piaget, 1958; Kelley, 1967) suggest that everyday causal judgment is based on the identification of covariation between events. That is, people search for likely causes of events by identifying event covariates from the past experience of individual "data" instances. The complexity of evaluating event relationships from individual instances raises questions about children's competence at the judgment. A well-defined understanding of development in covariation judgment may be important to a successful model of children's causal judgment.

However, the problem is complicated by disparity among investigations of mature covariation judgment (Shaklee, 1979). In each case, investigators presented subjects with individual data instances illustrating one of two states (e.g., presence/absence) for two potentially related events (e.g., germs and disease). Inhelder and Piaget (1958) and Seggie and Endersby (1972) find adolescent and adult subjects to be accurate at identifying relationships between such events. Other investigators (Jenkins & Ward, 1965; Niemark, 1975; Smedslund, 1963) find such accuracy to be rare among comparably aged subjects.

While the evidence indicates that covariation judgments are often erroneous, those judgments may be rule governed nonetheless. Specifically, subjects may evaluate relationships between events according to a variety of rules, each of which should produce a characteristic performance pattern. Four rules are proposed as possible judgment strategies.

Least sophisticated of our proposed rules is judgment according to the frequency with which the target events co-occur (A_1B_1, cell a in a

This chapter originally appeared in *Child Development*, 1981, 52, 317–325, Copyright © 1981 by the Society for Research in Child Development, Inc. Reprinted by permission.

traditionally labeled contingency table), failing to consider joint event nonoccurrences (A_2B_2, contingency table, cell d) in defining the relationship. A subject using this strategy would identify a positive relationship between events if cell a frequency was the largest of the contingency table cells, a negative relationship if it was the smallest (cell a strategy). Inhelder and Piaget (1958) cite this as the form of reasoning used by young adolescents; Smedslund (1963) considers the rule to be typical among adults as well. This strategy does consider some relevant information and may result in better-than-chance performance. However, the rule is a limited one and would be especially misleading when there is a large difference between frequencies in contingency table cells a and d.

A second possible rule, also suggested by Inhelder and Piaget (1958) as a precursor to mature reasoning, would compare the number of times target events A_1 and B_1 co-occur with the times A_1 occurs with B_2 (comparison of frequencies in contingency table cells a and b, strategy a vs. b). Again this strategy considers some of the relevant information and may result in accurate judgment of many event contingencies. However, failure to consider frequencies in cells c and d (event combinations A_2B_1, A_2B_2) would be a particularly costly error when the direction of that frequency difference is the same as the difference between cells a and b.

A much improved approach would be the strategy defined by Inhelder and Piaget (1958) as formal operational. Specifically, covariation would be defined by comparing frequencies of events confirming (cells a and d) and disconfirming (cells b and c) the relationship. Thus, the rule would compare the sums of the diagonal cells in the contingency table (sum of diagonals strategy). Jenkins and Ward (1965), however, suggest that this strategy has its limits as well. Specifically, the rule is an effective index only when the two states of at least one of the variables occur equally often. Otherwise, a correlation may be indicated when, in fact, independence is the case.

Instead, Jenkins and Ward (1965) suggest that covariation is more appropriately evaluated by comparing the probability of event A_1, given event B_1 [$p(A_1/B_1)$], with the probability of A_1, given that B_2 has occurred [$p(A_1/B_2)$]. By definition, independence is indicated by equivalence between these conditional probabilities; nonindependence is indicated by any difference (conditional probability strategy). This is the most sophisticated of our proposed strategies and should result in accurate judgment of any contingency problem.

Thus, four alternative strategies are proposed to account for subjects' judgments, each with a distinctive judgment pattern. Problems can be identified which would be accurately judged by all four strategies. Alternatively, error rates may be high on problems solved only by the more sophisticated strategies. According to this analysis, solution accuracy may be problem specific. Thus, past performance variability may be a function of the particular covariation problems used by the experimenter.

At the same time, this conceptualization suggests a powerful tool for identifying strategies actually used in covariation judgment. Since different rules produce different judgments, covariation problems might be identified which would differentiate among those rules. In fact, careful structuring of a problem set should allow us to identify the specific strategy a subject is using.

A set of such problems is illustrated in Figure 30.1. Problems are structured hierarchically such that cell *a* problems are correctly solved by all strategies; strategy *a* versus *b* problems are correctly solved by *a* versus *b*, sum of diagonals, and conditional probability strategies. Sum of diagonal problems will be accurately judged by sum of diagonal and conditional probability strategies. Conditional probability problems would be correctly solved by the conditional probability strategy alone. Solution accuracy is indexed by the direction of the judged relationship (i.e., A_1 more likely given B_1, B_2, or no difference). A subject's solution pattern on the set of 12 problems indicates the strategy used. Table 30.1 summarizes the solution pattern congruent with each strategy type. Subjects who fail to solve problems of any strategy type may be using some other strategy or no consistent strategy at all (strategy 0).

In two experiments, Shaklee and Tucker (1980) employed this strategy index to identify judgment rules of high-school and college subjects. Subjects judged relationships in 9–12 problems, each of which consisted of 24 instances in which event states were defined for two events. Problems were set in contexts of everyday events (e.g., cake rises or falls at high or low oven temperature). Subjects' performances indicated general conformity to the strategy set. Congruence with the cell *a* strategy pattern was frequent among the high-school subjects (17%) but rare in the college sample (1%). Response patterns matched that of the *a* versus *b* strategy for 18% of the college sample (use of this strategy was not tested among the high-school subjects). Judgment patterns were congruent with the conditional probability strategy for 17% of the high-school subjects and 33% of the college sample. In each experiment, the modal response pattern conformed to that of the sum of diagonals rule (35% of the college subjects, 41% of the high-school subjects). Thus, generally, subjects demonstrated at least some sophistication about appropriate covariation judgment. However, the optimal judgment rule was used by a minority of subjects in the two samples.

These initial investigations demonstrate the general success of this rule diagnostic approach. Subject judgment patterns indicated strong intraindividual consistency in rule use. Furthermore, the variety of rules evident in these results suggests that characterization of group judgment by any single rule would be inappropriate. Our use of a diagnostic problem set to identify rule use is similar to Siegler's approach (Siegler, 1976; Siegler & Vago, 1978) to analyzing other formal reasoning skills. The approach is a particularly informative method for study of developmental questions,

	Cell a Problems		a versus b Problems		Sum of Diagonal Problems		Conditional Probability Problems	
	B_1	B_2	B_1	B_2	B_1	B_2	B_1	B_2
A_1	11	4	4	1	4	4	2	12
A_2	1	8	3	16	1	15	0	10
	B_1	B_2	B_1	B_2	B_1	B_2	B_1	B_2
A_1	6	6	4	4	9	5	1	5
A_2	6	6	8	8	7	3	3	15
	B_1	B_2	B_1	B_2	B_1	B_2	B_1	B_2
A_1	1	8	4	11	4	4	12	2
A_2	11	4	8	1	15	1	10	0

Figure 30.1. Cell frequencies used for each problem type.

Table 30.1. *Strategy use and resultant patterns of problem accuracy*

	Problem strategy type			
Subject strategy type	Cell *a*	*a* vs. *b*	Sum of diagonals	Conditional probability
Conditional probability	+	+	+	+
Sum of diagonals	+	+	+	0
a vs. *b*	+	+	0	0
Cell *a*	+	0	0	0
Strategy 0	0	0	0	0

Note: + = accurate; 0 = inaccurate.

since it allows one to identify specific judgment rules which might be precursors of more mature judgment competence. That is, the steps in our strategy hierarchy may represent a developing sequence of increasingly sophisticated rule use in judgments of event contingencies. There are a couple of reasons to suspect that such judgments might follow a reliable developmental progression.

First, two of our proposed strategies, cell *a* and *a* versus *b*, are identified by Inhelder and Piaget (1958) as characteristic of younger adolescents. The sum of diagonals strategy was believed to develop in later adolescence. Our rule diagnostic approach should allow us to track such shifts in strategy use.

Second, our own previous investigation hints at such a developmental trend. Although modest changes in experimental procedure prevent direct comparison between our high-school and college samples, the college-aged subjects were somewhat more likely to be categorized as using the most sophisticated rule, the conditional probability strategy (33% of college subjects vs. 19% of high-school subjects). Conversely, use of the least general rule, cell *a*, was almost nonexistent among the college subjects (1%), while several of the high-school subjects (17%) were so categorized. This investigation was planned to use our rule index to clarify developmental trends in covariation judgment.

Method

Subjects

Subjects included 24 fourth graders (age range 9–2 to 10–2, mean 9–8), 24 seventh graders (age range 12–4 to 13–2, mean 12–9), and 26 tenth graders (age range 15–0 to 16–7, mean 15–9) from public and parochial schools. Twenty-nine college students (age range 18–1 to 21–7, mean 19–4) participated as one option in fulfillment of a requirement for a course in introductory psychology. Subjects included 12 males and 12 females at the fourth grade, 8 males and 16 females at the seventh grade, 6 males and 20 females at the tenth grade, and 13 males and 16 females in the college sample.

Problems

Twelve different problem contents were developed, each of which consisted of a set of observations picturing one of two states for two potentially related everyday events. Three problems pictured bakery products which either rose or fell in association with the presence or absence of yeast, baking powder, or "special ingredient." In three other problems, plants were pictured as healthy or sick as a possible function of presence or absence of plant food, bug spray, or "special plant medicine." In three problems, people (or animals) were pictured as sick or healthy as a possible function of presence or absence of a shot, liquid medicine, or a pill. The remaining three problems pictured a possible association between space creatures' moods (happy/sad) and the presence or absence of one of three weather conditions (snow, fog, or rain).

For each problem, data instances were pictured in a 2 × 2 table. Actual frequencies used are listed in Figure 30.1. Tabled frequencies indicate one noncontingent and two contingent relationships for each strategy problem type.[1] Direction of relationship (A_1 more likely given B_1, B_2, or no difference) was counterbalanced across subjects for each problem content.

Each problem was introduced with a paragraph describing a context in which several observations were made on two potentially related variables. Subjects were asked to look at the pictured information and identify the relative likelihood of one of the events when the second event was either present or absent. An example problem:

Spacemen from Earth landed on another planet and found creatures called the blockheads. They wanted to see what blockheads were like, so they watched them closely. Every Saturday they would look outside to check the weather and see how the blockheads were doing. Sometimes it was snowing and sometimes it was not. Sometimes the blockheads were happy and sometimes they were not. In the picture you will see how many times each of these things happened together. The picture indicates that when it was snowing blockheads were (circle one):

    a) more likely to be happy than
    b) just as likely to be happy as
    c) less likely to be happy than

when it was not snowing.

A similar paragraph and response form was developed for each problem content. In each case, subjects indicated whether A_1 given B_1 was more likely, just as likely, or less likely than A_1 given B_2.

Problems were grouped in blocks including a problem of each of the four strategy types. Order of problems within blocks was random. The three problem blocks were then sequenced in one of two orders. In this way the 12 problems were formed into a problem booklet.

Procedure

Subjects were tested in small groups (2–10) within each age level. Instructions introduced the concept of covariation in the context of "things which tend to go together." Real world examples were given of positive relationships (i.e., tall people are more likely to be heavy than short people), negative relationships (i.e., it is less likely to rain when the sun is shining than when it is cloudy), and unrelated events (i.e., a green truck is just as likely to run out of gas as a red truck). Subjects were told that they were to do some problems about hypothetical events that may

---

[1] We had some difficulty defining a noncontingent relationship for the sum-of-diagonals problems. The problem we included (middle problem, col. 3, fig. 30.1) deviates slightly from independence ($p[A_1/B_1] - p[A_1/B_2] = -.06$) by the conditional probability rule. As a result, we scored responses as correct if subjects concluded that A_1/B_1 was either less likely or just as likely as A_1/B_2. The problem does discriminate appropriately among the other judgment rules. Cell a and a vs. b judges should say that A_1/B_1 is more likely than A_1/B_2; sum-of-diagonal judges should say the two outcomes are equally likely.

or may not tend to occur together. A sample problem was used to explain stimulus materials and problem format. Subjects progressed through the problems at their own pace and were encouraged to use the storybooks for scratch paper if needed.

Results

For each subject, response accuracy was summed across problems within problem strategy type, resulting in a score ranging from 0 to 3 for each of the four problem types. Since the design includes within-subject comparisons, a profile analysis was done on the data (McCall & Applebaum, 1973; Morrison, 1976). Factors included four levels of age, two orders, and four problem strategy types.

The analysis indicates that age did significantly influence judgment accuracy ($F[3,95] = 19.08$, $p < .001$). Table 30.2 lists the mean judgment accuracy for each grade on each of the problem types. Accuracy was also reliably affected by problem strategy type ($F[3,93] = 94.93$, $p < .001$, see table 30.2). Univariate follow-up tests indicate that differences were significant in comparisons between each adjacent pair in the strategy hierarchy (all $F[1,95] > 4.0$, $p \leq .05$). Problem sequence did not significantly influence judgment accuracy. No interactions between factors were significant.

Most informative about strategy use is the categorization of judgment records for individual subjects. Subjects were said to have passed criterion for any given problem strategy type if they accurately judged at least two of the three problems of that type. Table 30.1 lists the judgment patterns congruent with each of the proposed strategies. Subjects comparing conditional probabilities should pass criterion on all problem types. Subjects using the sum-of-diagonals strategy should fail on conditional probability problems alone. Subjects comparing cell a and b frequencies should judge cell a and a versus b problems correctly, but fail sum-of-diagonal and conditional probability problems. The cell a strategy should result in correct judgment on cell a problems alone. The probability of meeting each of these criteria by chance alone is .08 for cell a, .03 for a versus b, .02 for sum-of-diagonal, and .007 for the conditional probability strategy. People who passed no criteria were labeled strategy 0. Records matching none of these patterns were labeled unclassifiable.

Using this categorization procedure, 18% of the judgment patterns matched that of the conditional probability strategy, 39% matched the sum-of-diagonal strategy, 24% were congruent with the a versus b strategy, 3% matched the cell a pattern, 5% passed no criteria (strategy 0), and 11% were unclassifiable. Table 30.3 lists the frequency of each judgment pattern at each age level.

Comparisons among ages were made by assigning each subject a performance score according to the number of problem strategy levels

Table 30.2. *Mean accuracy: Grade by problem strategy type*

Grade	Problem strategy type				
	Cell *a*	*a* vs. *b*	Sum of diagonals	Conditional probability	All types
College	2.90	2.83	2.21	1.17	2.27
Tenth	2.81	2.76	2.08	.92	2.14
Seventh	2.83	2.42	1.67	.79	1.91
Fourth	1.83	1.79	1.21	.54	1.35
All grades	2.59	2.45	1.79	.85	1.92

Table 30.3. *Frequency of judgment patterns at each grade level*

Grade level	Strategy					
	Strategy 0	Cell *a*	*a* vs. *b*	Sum of diagonals	Conditional probability	Unclassi-fiable
College	0 (0)	0(0)	6(21)	11(38)	11(38)	1 (3)
Tenth	0 (0)	0(0)	6(23)	13(50)	7(27)	0 (0)
Seventh	0 (0)	1(4)	6(25)	12(50)	1 (4)	4(17)
Fourth	5(21)	2(8)	7(29)	4(17)	0 (0)	6(25)
All ages	5 (5)	3(3)	25(24)	40(39)	19(18)	11(11)

Note: Numbers in parentheses are percentages.

passed in the strategy hierarchy (strategy 0 = 0; conditional probability patterns = 4). Unclassifiable subjects were not included in the comparison. Mean strategy level was 1.56 for fourth-grade subjects, 2.65 for seventh graders, 3.04 for tenth graders, and 3.17 for college subjects. An analysis of variance indicated a significant effect of age on strategy use ($F[3,88] = 16.12$, $p < .001$). Differences were significant between fourth- and seventh-grade subjects ($F[1,88] = 16.60$, $p < .01$), but were not significant between seventh- and tenth-grade performance ($F[1,88] = 2.57$, $p > .05$). College subjects were not significantly different from tenth graders ($F[1,88] = .34$, N.S.), but were significantly different from seventh graders in strategy use ($F[1,88] = 4.77$, $p < .05$).

Since the strategy index was structured hierarchically, the set of judgment patterns should conform to a Guttman scale (Guttman, 1967). The pass-fail records of all subjects on the four problem types were compared to a Guttman standard of scalability. Analysis of these data yielded a coefficient of reproducibility of .97, demonstrating close conformity to the Guttman pattern.

Discussion

Results offer strong support for the set of proposed strategies. Analysis indicates that strategy problem types were differentially difficult in the pattern that would be predicted by the hierarchical structure. The conformity of the set of judgment patterns to a Guttman scale further suggests a hierarchical strategy set.

The strongest support for our specific proposed strategies comes from the categorization of individual judgment records. The dominant pattern in the data was congruent with the sum-of-diagonals strategy (39%). Smaller minorities of the sample used the more limited a versus b (24%) rule and the optimal conditional probability strategy (18%). The low frequency of cell a and strategy 0 patterns indicates that most subjects have at least some sophistication about appropriate covariation judgment.

Unclassifiable judgment records were examined for suggestions of alternative judgment strategies. Records were compared among subjects to identify any shared judgment patterns. None of the judgment patterns replicated among subjects, indicating that any underlying strategies were idiosyncratic.

Analyses further suggested that judgment patterns did show a reliable developmental progression toward the use of increasingly accurate rules. The a versus b strategy was used by sizable groups of subjects at all ages (21%–29% of subjects for each of the grades). Sum-of-diagonals solution patterns characterized a few fourth graders (17%) but were more common among the older subjects (38%–50% for seventh through college grades). Conditional probability patterns were rare until the tenth grade (27% at tenth grade, 38% at college).

The fourth-grade subjects were the least likely of the age groups to conform to the proposed strategies. A sizable group of subjects' judgments (29%) did suggest use of the a versus b strategy, and a few subjects showed sum-of-diagonals judgment patterns (17%). However, the large number of unclassifiable (25%) and strategy 0 (21%) records raises questions about the remaining subjects' understanding of event covariation. Whether these younger judges would be better characterized by some simpler strategy remains to be seen. However, the failure of these patterns to show shared features among subjects suggests that a common, underlying strategy is unlikely.

Evidence in this investigation suggests a developmental trend with some of the elements predicted by Inhelder and Piaget (1958). The a versus b strategy does seem to be one of the earliest developing strategies. Comparison of the sums of diagonal cells becomes common by seventh grade, somewhat earlier than Inhelder and Piaget might have predicted. Judgment of mature subjects, however, is not congruent with the Piagetian position. The sum-of-diagonals approach does seem to be used by many of our oldest subjects, but the more limited a versus b strategy is common as well. The conditional probability strategy, evidenced by a sizable group of tenth grade and college subjects, was not anticipated by Inhelder and Piaget.

The absence of cell *a* judgment patterns among our subjects is an intriguing outcome. The strategy had been proposed by Inhelder and Piaget (1958) as a precursor of mature judgment. In fact, Smedslund (1963) suggested that the strategy was characteristic of adults as well. In contrast, our evidence indicates that the strategy is rare even among our youngest subjects. However, it is important to note that strategy use may vary with judgment conditions. Subjects in this experiment experienced favorable conditions for evaluating event relationships. Data instances were organized for them in a 2 × 2 matrix and were available at the time covariation judgments were made. Conditions increasing memory and/or organizational demands might produce evidence of less accurate judgment rules. In fact, previous work (Shaklee & Tucker, 1980) yielded evidence of some cell *a* judgment patterns among tenth graders (17%) in a paradigm where subjects organized the data for themselves. Thus, it would be premature to drop the cell *a* strategy from our rule hierarchy without further investigation.

As in all rule modeling, congruence between predicted and actual judgment patterns requires cautious interpretation. That is, subject's judgments may be the product of an alternative rule that mimics a proposed rule on our diagnostic problem set. In fact, one such approach to covariation judgment would be to compare the frequencies in contingency table cells *a* and *c* (strategy *a* versus *c*).[2] Conceptually, the strategy is similar to our *a* versus *b* strategy, but with our particular problem set the *a* versus *c* strategy would produce a pattern of judgment accuracy close to that of our sum-of-diagonals rule. The reader can compare judgments by the two rules for the problems in Figure 30.1. Five of the problems in our set should produce different judgments by sum-of-diagonals and *a* versus *c* rules. These include the noncontingent problem for *a* versus *b* (sum of diagonals: $[4 + 8] - [4 \times 8] = 0$; *a* versus *c*: $4 - 8 = -4$) and sum-of-diagonal (sum of diagonals: $[9 + 3] - [7 + 5] = 0$; *a* versus *c*: $9 - 7 = 2$) problems. The two rules also produce different errors on all of the conditional probability problems. Thus, judgment on these five problems can be used to test the relative viability of the two rules. Records of the subjects in our sum-of-diagonals classification were examined for evidence of the two rules. Judgments on each of the five problems were classified as congruent with sum-of-diagonal, *a* versus *c*, or neither of the two rules. The rule with the greatest number of supportive judgments was taken as the best index of likely rule use for each subject. Of the 32 subjects originally categorized as sum-of-diagonal rule users, 44% were categorized as *a* versus *c* judges by this analysis; 44% showed

[2] Thanks to Hayne Reese for suggesting this alternative rule.

a dominance of sum-of-diagonals judgments. The remaining subjects' records either showed equal support for the two rules (9%), or showed a dominant pattern congruent with neither of the rules (3%). Thus, a subsequent analysis of differentiating problems has produced substantial support for both of the proposed rules. Problems identifying a versus c rule use should be incorporated into our problem set in future research.

Other rules might be proposed which may be mathematically so similar to our proposed rules as to be difficult to differentiate by this procedure. This is particularly likely for our optimal rule, comparison of conditional probabilities. Statisticians have identified a variety of ways to assess event contingencies (e.g., X^2, ϕ) which should produce the same judgments as our conditional probability rule. Subjects with fully accurate judgments may be using one of these alternative approaches (or some component, e.g., $ad-bc$) in judging the relationships in our problems. Subjects' explanation of their judgments may be useful in discriminating among use of mathematically similar rules. However, the utility of such protocol analysis hinges on subjects' awareness of their own rule use and their ability to express those rules verbally.

Although a few alternative judgment strategies remain to be investigated, our rule diagnostic approach has drastically narrowed the set of possibilities. Furthermore, the developmental trend evidenced in our results suggests that it may be useful to think of covariation judgment in terms of approximations to optimal judgment rules. Precursors of mature judgment rules may result in accurate judgment of many forms of event contingencies. With development, shifts in rule use result in improved judgment accuracy. However, that developmental trend may terminate short of optimal rule use for the majority of people.

While our evidence describes a developmental sequence, analyses of the source of that trend must be speculative at best. One immediate possibility is that our age shifts in rule use represent no more than a measurement sequence (Brainerd, 1978). A measurement sequence may occur when later developing rules incorproate and build on strategies acquired earlier in the sequence. Since such rules are structurally hierarchical, the sequence of rule acquisition is logically predetermined. One could make such an argument about our own strategy set. For example, the addition and subtraction of four quantities involved in our sum-of-diagonals rule incorporates and adds to the operations involved in our a versus b rule (i.e., subtraction of one quantity from another). Similarly, our conditional probability rule requires knowledge of ratios and fractions in addition to the understanding of subtraction involved in the earlier rules. Thus, given our proposed rules, it could be argued that our obtained sequence of acquisition may be the necessary outcome of the structural interdependence of underlying competencies.

However, the argument breaks down when one considers the ages of the children involved in this developmental trend. That is, children at the ages included in this study should have encountered all of these arithmetic operations in previous course work. Certainly, by the seventh grade, children should be showing competent use of addition and subtraction and should be able to make comparisons between ratios. Children who have the competence for optimal judgment continue to use faulty judgment rules. Our evidence indicates that substantial use of the conditional probability rule does not occur until the tenth grade, and then by only a minority of the subjects. This evidence is congruent with other research indicating that problems in application of ratio concepts are common among adults as well as children (Capon & Kuhn, 1979; Karplus & Peterson, 1970; Kurtz & Karplus, 1979). By this analysis, the developmental trend evidenced in this study should have little to do with acquisition of underlying skills. Instead, age shifts are more likely due to children's developing awareness of the relevance of those skills to the evaluation of event covariations.

The faulty judgment rules evidenced in this experiment should have implications for development in causal reasoning. Previous evidence indicates that children as young as 6 years of age show a preference for event covariates as likely causes of events (DiVitto & McArthur, 1978; Shultz & Mendelson, 1975; Siegler, 1975). Our evidence, however, indicates that children's search for event covariates will be a systematically error-prone process. That is, use of less-than-optimal judgment rules will lead children to see relationships between events which are, in fact, independent, or fail to note relationships between true event covariates. Furthermore, the nature of those errors should shift with age. Thus, developmental trends in covariation judgment may set an upper limit to competence in identifying cause-effect relationships.

The relative impact of this problem depends on the types of contingencies actually encountered. Some relationships may be accurately evaluated by even the simplest of our rules. The sum-of-diagonals rule, in particular, will result in accurate judgment of a variety of relationships. However, that rule is most likely to be misleading when the frequencies of the alternative states of each of the two variables are unequal. Consider an individual with a prior expectation about the nature of a relationship (e.g., cloud seeding tends to produce rain). Past research demonstrates a propensity to search for evidence confirming that expectation (e.g., Snyder & Swann, 1979; Wason & Johnson-Laird, 1972). Such a tendency would lead the individual to extensively sample evidence about the outcome of the target event state (cloud seeding), gathering little information about the effect of the alternative state (no cloud seeding). Differential sampling of this sort would produce precisely the circumstance under which the sum-of-diagonals rule is most limited. In this way, problems in covariation judgment may interact with the effects of other reasoning biases, producing serious errors in identifying cause-effect relationships.

31. Integrating velocity, time, and distance information: A developmental study

Friedrich Wilkening

Velocity, time, and distance can be conceptualized as a set of interrelated dimensions. In classical mechanics, velocity is defined as a relation between time and distance. The definitional interdependency is even stronger in relativity theory in which neither dimension can be defined independently of the others. Are these physical relations reflected in our cognitive structure and, if so, how does our integration of the dimensions develop? The present article is an attempt to investigate these questions.

Previous research on the development of velocity, time, and distance concepts has nearly exclusively been carried out within the theoretical framework of Piaget (1946/1969, 1946/1970, 1970). According to this theory, velocity, time, and distance concepts are not a priori ideas for young children but undergo a lengthy developmental construction. At the beginning, the child's representations of time and velocity are thoroughly confounded with representations of space. Young children assume, for example, that an object going a longer distance always goes for the longer time, regardless of speed, or that it goes at the faster speed, regardless of the time traveled. After having passed several stages of progressive decentration from distance cues, the child enters the stage of mastery. In this stage, velocity, time, and distance are conceived as separate entities and, further, can be coordinated in the classical metric sense. According to Piaget, this coordination "requires ... formal or hypothetico-deductive operations" (1946/1970, p. 206), and it "appears very late in child development, about 9 or 10 years of age" (1970, p. 62).

Piaget's notions have been supported with few modifications in later studies (e.g., Berndt & Wood, 1974; Crépault, 1979; Levin, 1977; Montangero, 1977; Rothenberg, 1969; Siegler & Richards, 1979; Weinreb &

This chapter originally appeared in *Cognitive Psychology*, 1981, *13*, 231–247. Copyright © 1981 by Academic Press, Inc. Reprinted by permission.

Brainerd, 1975). A common feature to all of these subsequent studies is the adoption of Piaget's choice method (see below for an example). This method was believed to be capable of assessing the child's concept of velocity, time, or speed.

The problem with the Piagetian paradigm can be demonstrated by analysis of one of the more systematic studies, an experiment by Siegler and Richards (1979). Using Siegler's (1976) rule assessment methodology, Siegler and Richards wanted to study children's knowledge of time, speed, and distance concepts. To this end, two toy trains traveled on parallel tracks for different times, at different speeds, and over different distances. The child was asked "to watch the trains closely and then tell ... which train goes (for a longer time) (a longer distance) (a faster speed) ... or if they go the same (amount of time) (distance) (speed)" (p. 292). Mastery of the time concept was assumed when the child correctly identified the train which traveled for the longer time, mastery of the distance concept when the child correctly identified the train which traveled the longer distance, and mastery of the speed concept when the child correctly identified the train with the greater speed. Based on these criteria, the following conclusions were drawn: 5-year-olds do not master any concept. On the other hand, 20-year-olds master all three concepts. Within the age range from 5 to 20 years, both speed and distance concepts are mastered before the concept of time.

There are various problems inherent in this task. The most serious one, which will be elaborated below, is that the task does not reveal what children understand about the relationships among the variables. Therefore, it remains unclear whether or not the child understands the concepts in question. This is true because logical concepts like those of interest here are generally characterized not only in terms of their relevant features but also in terms of the rule that integrates those features (e.g., Bourne, Dominowski, & Loftus, 1979, p. 164). Applied to the concept of velocity, for example, it follows that a child "having" the concept should know that distance and time information are relevant features and that this information has to be integrated according to some (algebraic) rule.

In the Piagetian studies, just the opposite appears to have been investigated. In each of the three tasks for the assessment of time, speed, and distance concepts, the easiest way for the child to give correct answers is to completely ignore the two defining dimensions. For example, no time and speed information is at all necessary to judge which of the two trains traveled the greater distance. In this task, time and speed information serve the function of distracting the child's attention from the distance cues rather than providing the basis necessary for a distance judgment. The analogous argument applies to the tasks for the assessment of time and speed concepts. It appears, therefore, that the previous studies did not investigate children's understanding of the interrelationships that exist between time, speed, and distance but, in contrast, investigated children's ability to ignore the variables that define each concept.

In principle, therefore, it would not have been necessary in these studies to use dimensions out of the time, speed, and distance set as distracting variables. Any other variable not logically related to time, speed, or distance could have been used as well. Evidence for this argument comes from a study by Levin (1979) who has shown that the intensity of a light has the same distracting effect on young children's time judgments as has logically related speed information.

In addition to the conceptual problem discussed so far, there are two problems of a more technical character inherent in the choice tasks. First, children's performance on these tasks very often requires auxiliary abilities such as language development (see Gelman, 1978, for a review). When velocities, distances, and/or travel times have to be compared in choice tasks, relational terms such as *faster* and *longer* can hardly be avoided. Research on developmental linguistics has shown that many of these terms are ambiguous for young children and have a different meaning for them than for adults. This applies particularly to the comparative adjectives *same* and *different* (e.g., Donaldson & Wales, 1970) and to the temporal-reference terms *before* and *after* (e.g., Amidon & Carey, 1972; E. V. Clark, 1971; French & Brown, 1977) which are almost always necessarily included in the instructions. A direct demonstration of the confounding effect of the language variable on the assessment of time and velocity concepts has been given by Mori (1976) in a comparison of Japanese and Thai children.

Second, apart from the language problems mentioned above, choice tasks are hardly capable of detecting a whole class of rules that children might use to integrate velocity, time, and distance information. A reasonable working assumption is that the psychological rules mirror the physical laws that exist between the variables. These are algebraic rules, such as multiplication and division. As has been recently shown by Wilkening and Anderson (1980), rule assessments based on responses obtained in the Piagetian choice tasks tend to severely misrepresent children's knowledge when they actually use algebraic rules.

In the present study, the problems with previous tasks are avoided. In each of three tasks, information about two dimensions is presented in two separate events, and the child has to infer the value of the third dimension. This contrasts with previous tasks which intermix velocity, time, and distance information into one event and ask successive questions about one of the variables presented.

Techniques of functional measurement (Anderson, 1974a, 1981) are of particular use for the present purpose. Functional measurement methodology has been explicitly developed to handle rules by which people integrate information from different dimensions. Moreover, this approach has been successfully applied in recent studies in the developmental area. For example, Anderson and Cuneo (1978), Cuneo (1982), and Wilkening (1979) have shown that children as young as 5 years integrate stimulus dimensions such as height and width or height and diameter in judgments of area and volume, and length and density in judgments of numerosity (see Anderson, 1980, for an overview and for further results). Given this high level of integrational capacity, it seems possible that young children can also integrate velocity, time, and distance information. The present study tests this hypothesis.

Method

General design

Three tasks were designed, each involving velocity, time, and distance dimensions. One of these three dimensions served, in turn, as a dependent variable which was to be judged: distance in Task 1, time in Task 2, and velocity in Task 3. The two remaining dimensions were the independent variables, the integration of which was studied. Three levels on each dimension were used; their combinations were presented in a 3 × 3 within-subjects design.

To make the experimental situation realistic to the child, the levels of velocity were represented by a turtle, a guinea pig, and a cat. These animals were portrayed as fleeing from a barking dog, and the children had to judge either how far an animal would have run, how long the dog would have barked, or which animal would have run that distance over that time.

Task 1: Velocity and time integration

Apparatus. A frightful-looking dog was sitting close to the exit of his den which was shown on the left side of a screen 3 m long and 1 m high, mounted on the wall at the subject's eye level. A straight footbridge, crossing a small lake, led away from the den to the right. This footbridge served as the judgment scale. A metal strip was fixed on it, containing a centimeter scale not visible to the subject.

Three cardboard pieces, each measuring about 10 × 6 cm in outline, showed pictures of a turtle, guinea pig, or cat. At the back of each cardboard piece, a small magnet was mounted, which allowed the animal pictures to be attached anywhere on the judgment scale.

A tape had been recorded with the barking of a shepherd's dog for periods of 2, 5, and 8 sec. These time periods were recorded in a random order, with 10 replications for each period and an interval of 10 sec between each barking. The loudspeaker of the tape recorder was mounted behind the screen close to the dog, so that the barking could easily be associated with the dog.

Procedure. At the beginning of the experiment, the child was shown the screen with the turtle, guinea pig, and cat. These animals were sitting in a random order near the dog. The child was told that all three animals were extremely frightened by the barking of the dog, that each animal would start fleeing over the footbridge when the dog began to bark, but would stop when he became silent. The child was acquainted with the fastening function of the magnet and asked to rearrange the animals according to their order of natural speed. All children produced the order: turtle, guinea pig, and cat.

After this introduction, three practice trials were run. For each practice trial, only one of the three animals was placed on the screen. The child was told to imagine that the animal started running as fast as possible when the dog began to bark and stopped immediately when he became silent. The experimenter then started the tape recorder, and the dog barked for 2, 5, or 8 sec. After that, the child was asked to put the animal at that position on the footbridge he or she thought that animal would have reached. This distance judgment was read in centimeters by the experimenter. The three velocity and time levels each occurred once in the practice trials.

Following the practice, the nine velocity–time combinations were presented in three replications for each child. The order of presentation was random except that the same velocity or time level did not appear in succession.

In each trial, the eye movements of the children were observed during the time the dog barked. Since the visual angle taken by the screen was large, it could be determined relatively easily without using an apparatus whether the children (a) did not look at the screen at all, (b) "centered" on a specific point on the screen, (c) scanned the screen in an unsystematic manner, or (d) followed an imaginary, linear movement on the footbridge with their eyes.

Task 2: Velocity and distance integration

Apparatus. The apparatus was the same as that for Task 1, except for the following modifications. The tape was recorded with continuous barking, and the tape recorder was connected to a key on the table in front of the child. On pressing this key, the dog began to bark and, at the same time, a stopwatch started which was visible to the experimenter only. On releasing the key, the dog stopped barking, and the barking time could be read in milliseconds on the stopwatch.

Procedure. The introductory procedure paralleled that of Task 1. The judgment task was changed as follows. For each trial, the turtle, guinea pig, or cat was placed at a distance of 70, 140, or 210 cm away from the dog on the footbridge, and the child was asked how long the dog would have barked to cause the animal to run that distance. The children made their judgments by pressing the key to let the dog bark for a certain time. Details of the procedure were the same as those in Task 1.

Task 3: Distance and time integration

Apparatus. The apparatus was again the same as that in Task 1, except for the following changes. A white cardboard piece with a magnet on its back served for the presentation of distance levels on the footbridge. Velocity judgments were obtained by the following response scale. Pictures of seven animals were painted on cardboard pieces: a snail, turtle, guinea pig, mouse, cat, deer, and horse. Each animal lay on a board 180 cm long and 40 cm wide in one of seven 25 × 25-cm fields. The board lay on a table in front of the child, and the animals were arranged in the above order from left to right. Pressing a key on the board in front of each animal caused that animal to stand up.

These particular seven animals were selected on the basis of pilot-study results. In this study, eight 5-year-olds were asked to arrange various combinations of animals out of a total of 15 according to their natural speeds. The seven animals used here seemed to be most spontaneously associated with a certain speed, and all children produced the above order after a few trials.

Procedure. The introductory story paralleled that of Tasks 1 and 2, with the following modification. The child was told that all seven animals would play in the den exit as long as the dog was silent, but that all of them would start fleeing when the dog began to bark. For each trial, first the dog barked for 2, 5, or 8 sec, and then the experimenter put the white cardboard piece on one of the 70-, 140- or 210-cm distance levels. The child was asked which out of the seven animals would have run that distance over that time; this judgment was given by pressing the key which caused that animal to stand up. Details of the procedure were the same as those in Tasks 1 and 2.

In all three tasks, the procedure for the adults was similar to that used with the children. The main difference was that the adults were informed of the reasons for the childlike character of the experiment.

Subjects

A total of 135 subjects participated in the experiment, 45 in each of three age groups. Within each age group, 15 subjects were assigned to one of the three tasks. Age group 1 consisted of children in the age range from 5 years, 0 months to 6 years, 6 months (mean age: 5.7). The children in Age group 2 were in the age range from 9 years, 0 months to 10 years, 11 months (mean age: 10.2). Most children in Age group 1 were 5 years old, and most children in Age group 2 were 10 years old. For purposes of brevity, therefore, these two age groups are referred to here as 5-year-olds and 10-year-olds, respectively. Age group 3 consisted of adults in the age range from 17 to 34 years (mean age: 25). Each age group contained approximately equal numbers of males and females. The 5-year-olds and 10-year-olds were attending kindergarten or fourth grade of a primary school in the Frankfurt area. The adults were mostly students at the University of Frankfurt, West Germany.

Results

Figure 31.1 shows the results of all three tasks. Mean distance, time, or velocity judgments, each calculated over 15 subjects, are plotted as a function of time or distance, with one curve for each level of velocity or time.

Task 1: Velocity and time integration

Task 1 tested the multiplying model:

$$\text{Judged distance} = \text{time} \times \text{velocity}. \tag{1}$$

This model implies that the data should form a diverging fan of straight lines. With distance plotted as function of time, the curve for the lowest velocity level (turtle) should have the smallest slope, and the curve for the highest velocity level (cat) should have the steepest slope. In other words: The difference in distance between the animals should linearly increase with increasing levels of time.

The upper panel of Figure 31.1 shows that the data of all three age groups in Task 1 follow this fan pattern very closely. Each age group took account of both dimensions and integrated them multiplicatively.

The interaction of time and velocity was highly significant, $F(4,56) = 8.11$. 17.82, and 33.91, $p < .01$, for the 5-year-olds, 10-year-olds, and adults, respectively. An exact test of the multiplicative model would require a breakdown of this interaction into its bilinear and residual components (Anderson, 1974a). In the present case, this decomposition seemed unnecessary, since it is evident from each of the three fan patterns that the bilinear, i.e., multiplicative, component is the principal source of the interaction. Besides the interaction terms, all main effects of time, $F(2,28) = 36.40$, 43.24, and 55.47, as well as of velocity, $F(2,28) = 15.09$, 28.56, and 47.94, were significant, $p < .01$, in the above order for the three age groups.

To test the possibility that the multiplicative model found for the age groups may be an artifact of averaging over subjects, the individual graphs were visually inspected. The far majority of them followed a clear bilinear pattern, although these graphs were not as smooth as the group

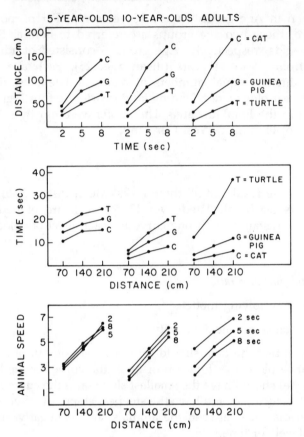

Figure 31.1. Mean judgments of distance as a function of time and velocity in Task 1 (upper panel), time as a function of distance and velocity in Task 2 (middle panel), and velocity as a function of distance and time in Task 3 (lower panel) for the three age groups.

data. To test the integration rules at the individual level statistically, an analysis of variance was computed for each subject. These analyses provided not much information; most F values failed to reach the critical value. For the design used in this experiment, the response variability was apparently too high to yield clear inference statistics at the single-subject level.

Task 2: Velocity and distance integration

Task 2 tested the dividing model:

Judged time = distance ÷ velocity.   (2)

This model also implies that the data should form a diverging fan of straight lines. Since it has the dividing form, it differs from the multiplying model of Task 1 in that the order of the curves for the velocity levels should be reversed. According to this model, the differences in time that animals of different speeds need to cover the same distance should linearly increase with increasing distance.

The middle panel of Figure 31.1 shows that the data of the 10-year-olds and adults follow this diverging fan pattern. These two age groups took account of both dimensions and integrated them according to the physically correct dividing rule. The interaction distance and velocity was significant, $F(4,56) = 13.22$ and 9.66, $p < .01$, as were the main effects of distance, $F(2,28) = 47.84$ and 27.32, and of velocity, $F(2,28) = 69.94$ and 9.17, $p < .01$, for the 10-year-olds and adults, respectively.

The data of the 5-year-olds, on the other hand, seem not to follow the dividing rule. The curves do not diverge, but are approximately parallel. Parallelism is an indication of an adding-type rule. In the present case, with the same velocity order as required by the dividing rule, this would mean a subtracting rule:

$$\text{Judged time} = \text{distance} - \text{velocity.} \tag{3}$$

In the analysis of variance, main effects should be significant but not the interaction. This pattern of results was found in this age group, $F(2,28) = 4.65$ and 11.75, $p < .01$, for distance and velocity, respectively, and $F(4,56) = 1.47$, $p < .05$, for the interaction.

As in Task 1, the visual inspection of the individual graphs showed that the age group results in Figure 31.1 are valid representations of the individual subjects' data in the respective age group.

Task 3: Time and distance integration

Task 3 tested the dividing model:

$$\text{Judged velocity} = \text{distance} \div \text{time.} \tag{4}$$

The data obeying this model should form a diverging fan of straight lines, with the judgments for the shortest time level forming the top line and those for the longest time level forming the bottom line. The model implies, for instance, that when time intervals are held constant, the differences in velocity will linearly increase with increasing levels of distance.

For these velocity judgments, no age group follows the fan pattern (see lower panel of Figure 31.1). For the 5-year-olds, the upward slope shows a clear effect for the distance dimension; the curves for the three time levels are, however, not clearly separated. This pattern agrees with a distance-only rule:

$$\text{Judged velocity} = \text{distance.} \tag{5}$$

In this task, the 5-year-olds apparently did not take the time dimension into account.

The effect of distance was highly significant, $F(2,28) = 77.41$, $p < .01$, but neither the effect of time, $F(2,28) = 1.77$, nor the distance − time interaction, $F(4,56) = 1.62$, approached significance, $p > .05$.

In contrast, the three time-level curves for the 10-year-olds and adults appear to be separated. The curves do not, however, diverge as required by the dividing model, but seem to be parallel. Parallelism pattern implies a subtracting rule:

$$\text{Judged velocity} = \text{distance} - \text{time}. \tag{6}$$

Parallelism was supported by the analysis of variance. Both the effect of distance, $F(2,28) = 161.29$ and 161.13 and the effect of time, $F(2,28) = 8.32$ and 79.92, were significant, $p < .01$, but not the interaction, $F(4,56) = 1.40$ and 2.27, $p > .05$, for the 10-year-olds and adults, respectively.[1]

Discussion

Knowledge of dimensional relations and integration rules

Integration of velocity, time, and distance information was found in all age groups and in all tasks. Completely new results were found in the youngest age group. Children as young as 5 years were able to infer the values of one dimension from information about the other two. Moreover, these children showed remarkable knowledge of how the dimensions are interrelated. Five-year-olds showed knowledge – at least tacitly – that distance is directly related to time and velocity, and that time is directly related to distance but inversely related to velocity. Although the understanding of the relationships between the dimensions may not be complete, young children do know that velocity, time, and distance are distinct entities and that they interact in some way.

Previous studies have claimed that young children's understanding of velocity, time, and distance concepts is undifferentiated (e.g., Piaget, 1946/1969, 1946/1970; Siegler & Richards, 1979). However, the tasks used in these studies did not tap children's understanding of velocity, time,

---

[1] Task 3 differed from Tasks 1 and 2 in that the response scale was not objectively linear, and this may give rise to doubts about the results obtained in the present task. A particular nonlinear scale deserves special mention. This is the logarithmic scale. Suppose that the covert integration of distance and time follows a dividing rule and that the overt response is a logarithmic function of the covert response. Since the logarithm of a ratio equals the difference between the single logarithms, the overt response, then, would form a parallel pattern. For the present task, this would mean that the subtractive model assigned to the 10-year-olds and adults would reflect a dividing rather than a subtracting integration process. Note, however, that the above reasoning would require a downward bowing of the curves in Fig. 31.1 and decreasing intervals between the curves for increasing time levels. For the 10-year-olds, this is clearly not the case, thus supporting the interpretation of a linear scale and a subtracting integration process. For the adults, a slight downward bowing of the curves as well as a decreasing curve separation from 2 to 8 sec is visible, thus leaving the possibility of a logarithmic response function and a covert dividing process open.

and distance interrelations. The previous studies, all being in the Piagetian tradition, asked a quite different question. The tasks were addressed to whether the child can judge one dimension independently of the others, when velocity, time, and distance information is intermixed. This, however, appears to be an issue of selective attention and perceptual learning rather than an issue of conceptual knowledge at which the studies were supposedly aimed. Given the present results, one might argue that it is not children's understanding of velocity, time, and distance that is undifferentiated but only their perception of these dimensions.

The present findings were enabled by a method which contrasts with the traditional Piagetian choice-task approach. Instead of intermixing all three dimensions into one event, the three dimensions were separated. Furthermore, instead of asking questions about information on a dimension that was physically present, the values on that dimension had to be inferred from information about the other two. Methods of information integration theory and functional measurement (Anderson, 1974a, 1981) proved to be of particular use in investigating the rules used to combine the dimensions in these inferences.

The use of functional measurement methodology made it possible to show that the integration of velocity, time, and distance information followed algebraic rules. The form of the rules depended on age and task. For the distance = time × velocity task, all age groups obeyed the physically correct multiplication rule. The other two tasks, in contrast, showed different rules and sharp developmental trends.

For the time = distance ÷ velocity task, the rule shifted developmentally from subtraction to division. The 5-year-olds, again, took account of both relevant stimulus dimensions but, instead of using the normative dividing rule for distance and velocity integration, they followed the simpler subtracting rule. The normative dividing rule appeared in the 10-year-olds and adults.

For the velocity = distance ÷ time task, the rules shifted from a distance-only model to subtraction. This condition was the only one in which the 5-year-olds showed no integration of the dimensions. Furthermore, it was the only condition in which even the judgments of the adults did not follow the correct integration model. They fell back to a subtracting rule, analogous to that found for the 5-year-olds in the time = distance ÷ velocity task.

Processes underlying the integration rules

As to the "cognitive algebra" of integrating the information, perhaps the most striking result is that the 5-year-olds judged distance by the correct multiplication rule: Distance = time × velocity. A multiplying integration rule at this age has not yet been reported in the literature for any dimensions. What processes enabled these 5-year-olds to produce such seemingly sophisticated judgments? Observations of the eye movements provide an answer. The children followed the imaginary movement of the animal on the footbridge with their eyes for the time the dog barked. When he stopped barking, they pointed to that position on the scale the imaginary movement had reached. Since the eye movements were slowest for the turtle and fastest for the cat, this strategy produced data following the diverging fan pattern.

The same judgment strategy was employed by the 10-year-olds and adults. Furthermore, these older subjects showed a similar strategy for distance and velocity integration in judging time (Task 2). Time had to be judged by letting the dog bark on a tape recorder. These subjects started the tape recorder and, at the same time, started following the imaginary movement of the fleeing animal with their eyes. When the imaginary movement had reached the distance level presented on the scale, they stopped the dog's barking. These time judgments necessarily follow a diverging fan pattern when different speeds are associated with the animals.

It might be questioned, however, whether the judgments based on the eye-movement strategy reflect a genuine integration of the dimensions. In the usual meaning of the term, this would require initial estimates of the values on each dimension followed by an integration of these estimates according to the operative rule. But, in the distance = time × velocity task, subjects employing the eye-movement strategy did not estimate elapsed time and multiply it with the velocity estimate. Rather, the child first determined the speed of each animal; this could be done in terms of some unit of distance/time or in terms of a constant innervation of the eye muscles. Then, when the barking started, the child moved her eyes at the determined speed until the barking stopped. This yielded a multiplicative function for velocity and time on the distance scale. The reason is that the child could tacitly translate the speed of each animal into speed of eye movements and maintain this speed for each unit of time.

The level of understanding revealed by the eye-movement strategy may be classified as an implicit one. For the assessment of an explicit understanding, a higher level of awareness of applying the multiplication principle or the ability to explain it independently from the particular strategy would be required (Greeno, 1980). Of course, this argument applies also to the adults, who apparently used the same mechanism. Their integration ability, however, will probably not be disputed (e.g., Ebbesen, Parker, & Konečni, 1977; Svenson, 1970).

The data of the 5-year-olds in the time = distance ÷ velocity task show that these children can integrate the dimensions also without using the eye-movement strategy. In this task, time was to be judged on the basis of distance and velocity information, and the data exhibited a pattern of parallelism. This parallelism means that the 5-year-olds did not use the eye-movement strategy; that would have produced a diverging fan pattern. This conclusion is consistent with observations made during the experiment. Some 5-year-olds apparently tried an eye-movement strategy, but they were apparently too distracted by the key-pressing device and the distance stimulus on the scale to be able to maintain this strategy throughout the experiment. Instead, they combined distance and velocity according to a subtracting rule, time = distance − velocity.

This subtracting rule may be seen as another instance of the general-purpose adding rule suggested by Anderson and Cuneo (1978). The main feature of an adding rule is that the dimensions contribute independently to the overall judgment; the same is true, of course, for a subtracting rule. The general-purpose adding rule seems to operate in young children across a variety of situations (Anderson, 1980; Wilkening, 1980). The nature of the processes underlying this rule is still unclear. However, it seems obvious that quantitative estimates of the values on each dimension are involved. Otherwise, algebraic rules would hardly appear.

Thus, the finding of a subtracting rule in this age group not only shows that children as young as 5 years can integrate the dimensions, but also that they can conceptualize velocity, time, and distance in a metric manner. This follows because the algebraic rules require some metric of the dimensions involved. So far, metric representations of velocity, time, and distance at this age have not been reported in the literature. All previous studies in this area seem to have adopted Piaget's view that metric concepts are not possible before the stage of formal operations and that younger children, if at all, can only conceptualize the dimensions in terms of ordinal, i.e., nonmetric, relations.

Integration failure and memory demands

The 5-year-olds did not integrate the dimensions when velocity had to be judged on the basis of time and distance information. Here, a distance-only rule was found for the young children. Theoretically, an eye-movement strategy was possible in this task also but it would be very complex. It would require imagining the movement of all seven animals simultaneously, all starting at the same time and fleeing over the foot-bridge with different speeds. After the dog had stopped barking, the imaginary positions of the seven animals on the footbridge would be stored until the distance level was presented. Then, the animal nearest to that point would be selected for the velocity judgment. The information processing demands imposed by this strategy are extremely high, and even the 10-year-olds and adults did not employ it. The 10-year-olds and adults fell back on a subtracting rule, analogous to that found for the 5-year-olds for distance − velocity integration.

Why did the 5-year-olds not integrate the time information, but only rely on distance information when judging velocity? A simple answer is that the time information was not visually present at the moment of judgment, but had to be retrieved from memory. Research in other areas of cognitive development has shown that such memory demands play a crucial role in determining children's ability to combine pieces of information (e.g., Trabasso, 1977). The distance-only rule found for the young children may, therefore, most simply be interpreted as a manifestation of a memory problem.[2]

It seems not unlikely that analogous memory problems are the main reason for children's failure in the Piagetian choice tasks. As an example, the study by Siegler and Richards already mentioned in the Introduction may again be considered. When asked which of the two trains went faster, for the longer time, or over the longer distance, 5-year-olds based their choices on stopping points for all three judgments: Whichever train ended farther ahead was judged as having traveled at the faster speed, for the longer time, or over the greater distance. The stopping points of the trains were the only information that was visually present at the moment of judgment; the information about all other variables would have to be retrieved from memory. Given the well-known finding that young children have difficulties in remembering the premises necessary for logical inferences (Bryant & Trabasso, 1971), the 5-year-olds' reliance on stopping points is not surprising. However, the conclusion that this is all that young children know about the relations between velocity, time, and distance appears to be unwarranted – even without taking into account the results of the present experiment.

The 11-year-olds in the Siegler and Richards study predominantly gave correct answers when they had to compare the speeds of the two trains but not when they had to compare their traveling times. The authors conclude that the concept of speed is mastered well before the concept of time. However, it may have been much more difficult for these children to remember the starting times of the trains than their different speeds. Speed information was more recent; probably it was perceptually more salient also. This example shows that caution is especially necessary when conclusions on the development of knowledge structures are drawn from children's answers in tasks that differ in information processing demands.

---

[2] A reviewer suggested an interesting alternative interpretation: Rather than due to high memory demands, the distance-only rule might reflect a peculiarity of the response scale. On the velocity scale, the response alternatives, i.e., animals, were arranged as a linear array in space. Because of this correspondence between velocity and distance, the young children might have "centered" on distance. This possibility was tested in a subsequent experiment with ten 5-year-olds. The velocity scale was changed by arranging the animals circularly instead of linearly. Essentially the same results as in the original experiment were obtained, the only major difference being that the effect of distance information was relatively low for some children. In any case, this task variation did not help the children to "decenter" from distance and to consider the time information.

Acquisition order of velocity, time, and distance concepts

The question of the order in which the concepts of velocity, time, and distance are acquired in the course of development has intrigued many researchers. Unfortunately, an unequivocal answer is harder to find than has previously been assumed. To answer the question clearly, requires the assessment of velocity, time, and distance concepts in tasks that do not systematically differ in information processing demands. This has never been the case. As in the example above, memory demands, in particular, have always been a confounding variable.

In the present study, too, the tasks differed as to their memory demands. In view of this fact, unwarranted conclusions will be avoided. However, some discussion about a probable acquisition order should be made. Assuming for the moment that all the confounding variables could be eliminated, there are reasons to argue that concepts involving direct relations are easier to understand than those involving inverse relations. From this argument, which will be elaborated below, it follows that the distance concept, involving a multiplying integration rule, should generally develop before the velocity and time concepts, each of them involving a dividing integration rule.

Why are processes which require multiplication easier than those that require division? For purposes of illustration, the distance = time × velocity rule will be considered first. Assume that you know that an object going at velocity v_1 covers distance d_1 in time t_1. When you wish to know what distance d_2 it will cover in time $t_2 = 3 \times t_1$, you may find the easiest solution by applying the principle of repeated addition. That is, you can use d_1 as a unit and put three units one after another to find $d_2 = 3 \times d_1 = d_1 + d_1 + d_1$ – like measuring with a yardstick.

Imagine now that distance were inversely related to time or velocity, so that a dividing rule, distance = velocity ÷ time (or distance = time ÷ velocity) would hold. In this case, you would have to divide distance d_1 by 3 if you wished to know what distance d_2 the object covered in time t_2 (or at velocity v_2). The important difference to the strategy for a multiplying rule outlined above is that a perceptual solution of dividing a distance unit involves a trial-and-error process, the end product of which can only be an approximation to the true result.

Instead of a dividing process, a strategy of repeated subtraction could be employed, analogous to the principle of repeated addition for a multiplying rule. But even then, an important difference remains: The distance unit d_1, which is known, cannot be used as a basis for the subtraction, for this would lead to negative distance values. Rather, a new unit, an arbitrary segment of d_1, has to be found. Furthermore, when the responses produced by repeated subtraction are to result in responses following a dividing rule, additional knowledge is required: You have to know that different, i.e., increasing, units have to be subtracted for increasing values of time or velocity. Lack of this knowledge of inter-action between the dimensions may result in a subtracting rule as found in Tasks 2 and 3 of the present study.

The foregoing analysis, although very preliminary, has shown that dividing processes are more difficult than both multiplying and sub-tracting processes. It may be of interest to note that the pattern of results obtained in the present study is in line with the theoretical arguments developed here.

32. Social Judgment Theory: Teacher expectations concerning children's early reading potential

Ray W. Cooksey, Peter Freebody, and Graham R. Davidson

Issues surrounding the nature and effects of teachers' expectations have led to some of the more engaging and divisive debates in educational research. Many of these debates have arisen from research conducted by Rosenthal and Jacobson (1968). They claimed to have demonstrated that the expectations that teachers develop or have presented to them about students' "potentials" for academic achievement tend to act as "self-fulfilling prophecies." One popular explanation has been that, in line with varying expectations, differing patterns of interaction develop with differing students (for reviews of relevant findings, see Brophy & Good, 1974; Dusek & Joseph, 1983). These different patterns, it has been argued, in turn partly account for actual subsequent differences in performance, which are highly correlated with the original expectations, hence reinforcing them.

Since the original studies by Rosenthal and Jacobson, many cogent attacks on their work have been presented. These have been variously concerned with the methodology, theoretical assumptions, analyses, ethical implications, and replicability of the experiments (Brophy & Good, 1974; Dusek & Joseph, 1983; Elashoff & Snow, 1971). Many researchers, on the basis of these attacks, have dismissed or minimized the significance of the original studies. However, the number and diversity of compatible findings reported sinced those original studies have ensured that the notion of self-fulfilling teacher expectations has retained its momentum in the educational research community. Brophy and Good reached a representative conclusion:

Regardless of where one stands concerning Rosenthal and Jacobson's original data, work by a large number of investigators using a variety of methods over the past several years has established unequivocally that teachers' expectations can and do function as self-fulfilling prophecies, although not always or automatically. (1974, p. 32)

In addition, the notion of self-fulfilling teacher expectations has influenced, though sometimes covertly, the detailed documentary and interpretive efforts of some classroom ethnographers (e.g., McDermott, 1976; Rist, 1970). It has also motivated some extensive examinations of the verbal and nonverbal cues emitted by teachers in their interactions with students (e.g., Brophy & Good, 1970, 1974). In all, it forms an often important part of the intuitive accounts many educators give for the still alarming underrepresentation of individuals from ethnic minorities and from the lower socioeconomic strata among the ranks of high achievers at all stages of the schooling process (Rist, 1970; Rubovits & Maehr, 1971).

Unfortunately, much of the broad-scale research conducted under the heading of teacher expectations has carried with it the connotation that the teacher is inadequate to the complexity of the teaching task and that the development of and reliance on expectations are covertly motivated and inappropriate responses to this inadequacy. As Borko, Cone, Russo, and Shavelson (1979) have pointed out, however, a teacher's expectations concerning the interests, abilities, and dispositions of students are not only appropriate but also important elements in the process of arriving at instructional, diagnostic, and management decisions. It is antithetical to even the crudest notion of how a teacher might deal constructively with a room full of students to suggest that he or she must somehow operate without expectations. It is when those expectations become impervious to new communications from students that the operations of expectations become problematic.

The formation of expectations can, therefore, be seen as an essential and useful cognitive activity for the teacher. The nature of the development and operation of expectations is, perhaps, best understood as a judgmental process. Based on certain available student cues (e.g., socioeconomic status, ethnicity, past achievement levels, behavior patterns, physical appearance), the teacher arrives at judgments regarding how particular students are likely to perform or behave in the class. Such judgments are typically informal in nature and, often, cannot even be articulated by the teacher, although the effects of the expectation may frequently be observable. Thus we can conceive of teacher expectations as a sort of informal cognitive policy which, when exercised, permits the teacher to reduce the complexity and uncertainty present in the classroom context (Cooksey & Freebody, 1983, 1984; Shulman & Elstein, 1975). It provides the teacher with a measure of "psychological" control over the situation by, in essence, "categorizing" students according to anticipated performance levels. The utility of enhanced psychological control rests in the notion that once a student's achievement potential has been initially identified the teacher can more readily decide how best to interact with that student. The above depiction can be seen to apply irrespective of whether these informal judgments or expectations have been appropriately formed. In addition, such informal judgmental policies vary widely among teachers in terms of their flexibility and openness to modification based on subsequent feedback.

Given this judgment-based interpretation of the expectation formation process, three key questions emerge: First, which cues among the myriad available are most salient for teachers in the development of their expectations, and how are the cues combined in their use? Second, how accurate are such informal judgment policies in an empirical sense? Third, how can we go about obtaining information regarding such informal policies?

A range of techniques have been employed to address the first question, which raises the issue of cue *utility*. Many of these studies have been summarized by Shavelson and Stern (1981). They reported, among other things, ten studies that examined the cues teachers use in forming estimates related to students' future academic achievement. The specific criteria ranged from descriptions of the "ideal" student to promotion/retention expectations and generalized estimates of school achievement. Three studies comprised semistructured interviews (Barr, 1975; Long & Henderson, 1972; Willis, 1972); five others used a questionnaire/checklist methodology (Goodwin & Sanders, 1969; Morrison & McIntyre, 1969; Schafer, 1973; Silberman, 1969; Yamamoto, 1969). Of the remaining studies, one was an analysis of report cards (Caplan, 1973) and one an observational study (Good & Brophy, 1972).

The findings from these studies were quite equivocal. Goodwin and Sanders (1969), for instance, reported that teachers found socioeconomic status (SES) the most important variable in the prediction of academic success, whereas Long and Henderson (1972) found that SES did not relate at all to teachers' predictions.

Most researchers, however, reached agreement on the somewhat more predictable salient cues for teachers. Many studies have reported that "general ability" is a highly salient cue for teachers in the formation of their expectations. Although it would be surprising if this were found not to be the case, it is somewhat puzzling that so few researchers have attempted to analyze the subcomponents of the construct of "general ability." The few that have done so found that teachers focus on a student's attentiveness (Long & Henderson, 1972; Willis, 1972), independence or originality of thought (Caplan, 1973; Morrison & McIntyre, 1969; Schafer, 1973), receptiveness to the ideas of others (Caplan, 1973; Schafer, 1973), and capacity for working in class without constant teacher supervision (Morrison & McIntyre, 1969; Willis, 1972). Only two studies have reported significant teacher use of standardized tests of achievement or academic readiness in the formation of expectations (Barr, 1975; Long & Henderson, 1972).

There were also, secondarily to our purposes here, a number of social/behavioral cues that teachers seemed to find relevant to their estimates of achievement. Among these were considerateness, determination, sense of humor (Caplan, 1973), activity level (Long & Henderson, 1972), carelessness, cooperativeness, courtesy (Morrison & McIntyre, 1969), maturity and self-confidence (Willis, 1972), punctuality, and obedience (Yamamoto, 1969).

The studies summarized above leave unanswered a number of questions relating to teachers' use of ability factors in the development of expectations of academic success. The first problem is the generalized nature of the construct of "ability." Even those ability-related attributes found to be important (attentiveness, independence of thought, receptiveness to the ideas of others, and capacity for unsupervised work) have a strongly social flavor. They are, to some degree at least, learned aspects of acceptable classroom behavior, without any necessary relationship to cognitive competence. It would seem useful to adopt a more analytic approach to teacher expectations within a given area of achievement.

A second shortcoming concerns the lack of provision for relative weightings of cues used in estimates. The data reported by Willis (1972), for instance, permit comparisons of rankings of various students on several attributes with their projected achievement levels. Comparing simple zero-order correlations, however, does not yield a clear picture of the relative weightings of the cues, nor does it allow possible cases of interactive trade-offs and cue intersubstitutability to emerge.

Third, in these studies no attempt has been made to compare the cues used by teachers in expectation formation with sources of information that empirically predict academic achievement, either generally or in a particular domain. Cues may vary in their actual predictive utility depending on the particular context. Variables such as the area of academic achievement, the type of curriculum package, the instructional style of the teacher, and the climate of the classroom may well affect learning outcomes and, hence, have predictive value. Generalized accounts of salient attributes, therefore, without reference to the actual appropriateness of their selection or weighting, may be of comparatively limited value.

A fourth concern surrounding the studies summarized is that teachers' explicit reports of cues salient in the prediction of achievement (elicited in interviews, questionnaires, and checklists) may, like many cases of self-reports of decision criteria, convey only part of the story. Apart from distortions in line with perceived social desirability, some aspects of the processes of expectation formation (a) simply may not be accessible to the respondents for self-report, (b) may not yield valid formulations of the experience of impression formation, and (c) may not be consistently applied from one occasion to another, particularly when very general or vague labels are used.

Understanding teacher's informal expectation policies through Social Judgment Theory

Thus far we have considered the issues of cue salience and utility in the formation of teacher expectations. However, the second and third questions posed earlier remain as critical issues to be addressed. How accurate are such informal judgment policies with respect to actual student achievement, and how can we best go about gaining insights into such informal policies? The task before us then is to *display objectively* the informal, largely covert, expectation policy of a teacher and to study the policy's *accuracy* with respect to predictions of academic potential.

Social Judgment Theory (SJT; see Hammond, Stewart, Brehmer, & Steinmann, 1975) provides the theoretical and methodological machinery with which to carry out this task. In addition, we will show that SJT offers a framework within which the above four problems arising from previous studies of teacher expectations may be minimized.

Social Judgment Theory. We present here a brief discussion of the SJT approach to teacher expectations. For more complete theoretical and technical treatments of SJT, the reader is referred to Cooksey and Freebody (1983, 1984), Hammond, Stewart, Brehmer, and Steinmann (1975), and Hammond and Wascoe (1980).

The general theoretical stance taken by SJT is founded in principles advanced by the psychologist Egon Brunswik (1955) and centers around the notion of causal ambiguity in the environment – generally termed the judgment *ecology*. The information with which people making judgments must deal is only partly relevant to their purposes, is limited in its dependability, and is organized and patterned in very diverse ways. In most cases, this ambiguity cannot be removed by systematic control, experimentation, or analysis on the researcher's part without damaging the representativeness of the task being studied. Therefore, a judgment or the formation of an expectation must, in these cases, take place in the face of the ambiguity of available information. A second critical notion in this approach is the distinction between what is *given* in the environment and what is *inferred*. Often the person's task is to conclude, decide, or develop an expectation related to an inferred trait, state, or unobserved event. This is particularly the case in the study of interpersonal perception, attributive judgments, and, relevant to our purposes, the estimation of future events.

The essential paradigm of SJT is embodied in the so-called lens model. Figure 32.1 clarifies the nature of the SJT lens model by depicting the

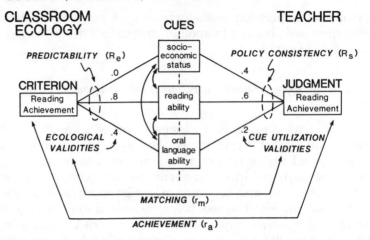

Figure 32.1. The SJT lens model and its associated parameters.

analysis of a simulated classroom situation concerning teacher expectations of students' year-long reading achievement. A teacher considers a number of student profiles and makes an estimate of some criterion, say, end-of-year reading achievement, for each student. The teacher's estimates are represented on the right side of the model. For each student, there is some objective criterion value (e.g., standardized test score) for his or her reading success at the end of the year. This is represented on the left side of the lens. The teacher's task is to make the "best" judgment possible of the value of this criterion for each student, based on available pieces of information, or *cues*, that are perceived to be related to or predictive of end-of-year reading success. The cues are represented in the center of the lens diagram. These cues are then somehow integrated by the teacher to form a judgment. It is these cues and their properties that are the critical features in the development of expectations.

Different cues have different degrees of relationship or correlation with the actual, or *ecological*, criterion being judged. Thus we say the cues have differing *ecological validities*. Some cues are more highly correlated with the criterion than others, whereas certain other cues may be totally unrelated, thus carrying zero weight. This merely reflects the fact that the teacher is operating in an uncertain environment – that is, that no single cue or even set of cues will perfectly predict the criterion.

From the teacher's perspective, the cues are there to be used in whatever way seems appropriate to form an acceptable judgment. The cues will usually differ in importance (weight) and relevance to the teacher's judgments. We say here that the cues differ in *cue utilization validity*. The utilization validities for the cues, although they may or may not be the same as their corresponding ecological validities, reflect the teacher's judgment policy or method of integrating the cue information.

Several correlational indexes arise from the lens model that reflect the quality and accuracy of a teacher's judgments. The ecological validities are the correlations of each cue with the ecological criterion of interest. The cue utilization validities are the correlations of each cue with the teacher's judgment of the criterion value. For ease of interpretation, these validity indexes can be expressed either as standardized regression weights or as squared semipartial correlations (the "usefulness" index discussed by Darlington, 1968). In addition, the cues themselves are generally correlated with each other to some degree (thus, the double-ended arrows interconnecting the cues in Figure 32.1).

On the ecology side, regressing all cues on the criterion yields a specific degree of predictability (i.e., a multiple correlation) for reading achievement. This *predictability* index (R_e) sets the upper limit on how well the teacher can expect to do in judging the criterion within the given ecology. More predictability is generally not possible unless more cues or better cues are available. On the judgment side of the lens, the teacher formulates a policy utilizing the three available cues. The *policy consistency* index (R_s – the multiple correlation obtained by regressing the cues on the judgments) tells us how consistently, across students, the teacher has implemented his or her policy in forming judgments. The *achievement* index (r_a) tells us how accurate the teacher's judgments are by correlating the actual criterion values with the teacher's judgments of those criterion values. The *matching* index (r_m) tells us how well the teacher's policy matches the optimal policy in the ecology and is found by correlating the *predicted* values from the ecology and judgment regression equations.

There is a straightforward mathematical relationship that ties together all of these correlational indexes and formally expresses the links between the ecology and the teacher's expectation policy. This lens model equation (see Hammond, Stewart, Brehmer, & Steinmann, 1975) is

$$r_a = r_m \cdot R_e \cdot R_s + C \cdot \sqrt{1 - R_e^2} \cdot \sqrt{1 - R_s^2} \tag{1}$$

The equation shows achievement correlation to be composed of two components: The first component, defined by the product of the predictability, consistency, and matching indexes, is termed the linear component, as it summarizes that portion of achievement that is *linear* in nature. In most lens model applications, it is this linear term that has accounted for the major portion of achievement in judgment tasks. From a practical standpoint, it becomes clear that there are at least two ways a teacher could improve his or her policy within an ecology having a given amount of predictability. First, the teacher could increase the degree of match between his or her policy and the optimal policy in the ecology (thus increasing r_m and enlarging the linear component of achievement). Second, and perhaps in association with increasing r_m, a teacher could try to apply his or her policy with more consistency (thus, increasing R_s).

The second component is termed the configural component and represents that portion of achievement that can be attributed to configural or nonlinear cue usage. The C coefficient in Equation 1 represents configural matching (whereas r_m represents linear matching) and is found by correlating the residuals from the ecology and judgment regression systems. With configural matching, we are considering the extent to which the teacher's judgment policy utilizes nonlinear cue relationships in the same way that they operate within the ecology itself. The two terms following the radical signs in Equation 1 represent unexplained linear and nonlinear variance in the ecology and policy regression systems, respectively.

The parameters of the lens model along with the ecology and policy cue weights provide a comprehensive description of an individual teacher's judgment process in a particular ecological context. The lens model can characterize individual as well as group estimation processes, allowing natural individual variations in information use to come to the fore. However, in many contexts including the classroom, teachers may be involved in making multidimensional judgments from the same information base; that is, there may be multiple criteria being judged.

Cooksey and Freebody (1985) have presented the details of a generalized multivariate lens model that can be applied in such multiple criteria contexts. The multivariate analysis jointly considers judgmental accuracy on all criteria to give a *general* depiction of a teacher's overall performance. The analysis results in a multivariate equation exactly paralleling Equation 1, but all the lens model parameters are based on canonical correlations rather than on multiple regressions. Generally speaking, in multidimensional judgment contexts, the logic of analysis is to move from general to specific in considering judgmental performance. The multivariate lens model yields a general depiction, the force of which is specified by considering analyses of each criterion separately (i.e., univariate analyses). Depending upon the purpose of the research, either or both multivariate and univariate levels may be needed to depict adequately judgmental performance. For example, concise depiction may be obtained if one evaluates the general accuracy and adequacy of a teacher's multidimensional judgments by (*a*) interpreting the parameters from the *multivariate* lens model equation, then (*b*) utilizing the regression weights (or a similar "importance" index) that emerge from the *univariate* criterial analyses to represent the specific policies being employed by the teacher. (The univariate lens model parameters are automatically available from the multivariate lens analyses [see Cooksey & Freebody, 1985] for use as supplemental information.)

The lens model of teacher expectations. If we return to the four problems with current research on teacher expectations outlined earlier, it can be seen that the lens model permits (*a*) the use of cues of varying levels of specificity, (*b*) explicit comparison among weightings given to cues, and (*c*) the relating of cue utilization to ecological validity.

The lens model approach can be useful on a number of additional counts. First, the researcher can present teachers with many profiles of actual, clearly defined student characteristics, rather than using contrived accounts or checklists containing ill-defined labels. The researcher can in this way present, for judgment, a broad, ecologically representative sample of profiles having realistic combinations of cue values.

Further, a lens model of the formation of teacher expectations is compatible with recent characterizations of the nature and functions of knowledge. Essentially, any decision can be seen to rely on the decision maker's knowledge of the generalized concept at hand. Cognitive scientists have found useful the notion that knowledge can be thought of as being embedded in flexibly organized data structures, which contain both general and specific information on the relevant topic. A variety of terms have been used in discussions of knowledge structures, including vocabulary derived from computer models, such as knowledge "frames" (e.g., Minsky, 1975), "scripts" (Schank & Abelson, 1977), and "schemas" (see Bobrow & Norman, 1975; Rumelhart & Ortony, 1977). Theorists have characterized "schemas," for example, as hypothetical knowledge banks that (*a*) have as subcomponents variables that can be filled by ranges of values, (*b*) can be embedded within other schemas, (*c*) can relate generic concepts to one another at varying levels of abstractions, and (*d*) represent knowledge rather than logic or definitions and hence postulate normative and probabilistic relationships between variables (Rumelhart & Ortony, 1977). There is a strong sense, then, in which educing expectations in a lens model study can be seen as making concrete an individual's generalized schema for the construct at hand – in our case, early reading achievement. Weightings for various salient components influence the estimates of criterion values, based on generalized patterns of relationships among those components and between them and the criterion.

It must also be stressed that a judgment needs to be viewed as the result of knowledge and decisional *systems* and that such systems are coherent and integrated at the level of the individual. SJT, as a working theoretical framework for conceptualizing human judgment and decision making, is explicitly *idiographic* in its emphasis. Apart from the SJT work by Hammond, Brehmer, and others (e.g., Hammond, Stewart, Brehmer, & Steinmann, 1975; Hammond & Wascoe, 1980), the study of judgment and decision making has tended to remain in the methodological traditions for nomothetic design and analysis. In any system, the workings of each part need to be viewed in the context of the entire operation. If this principle is applied to decision systems, then the aggregation of data across individuals can be seen to yield only a partial account of the factors relating to judgment. It is our contention that an individual's decision system needs to be viewed in isolation and as a coherent whole *before* aggregation across judges occurs. Once we have a clear picture of individual policies in a particular context, we can then proceed to examine the commonalities and differences among various policies through the use of cluster analysis or some other typology-generating technique.

Criticisms of the lens model in educational research

To date, there has been very little work in applying SJT and the lens model to educational policy and decision making, despite some insightful discussions of the lens model's potential by Shulman and Elstein (1975) and Snow (1968). Shavelson and Stern (1981) reviewed the few studies that have employed the lens model or its simpler relative, policy capturing. In their review of methodologies for studying teacher judgment processes, Shavelson and Stern cited three criticisms of lens model/ policy capturing, which we would like to address here. The three criticisms presented were (a) that studies in this tradition have, until recently, typically been conducted in artificial, laboratory contexts with hypothetical judgment tasks, thus raising the question of generalizability; (b) that researchers typically aggregate data across subjects in their analyses, on the false assumption that all subjects are operating with the same policy; and (c) that individuals may not "actually take a weighted sum of variables" in the formation of judgments but, rather, the lens model must be seen as highly speculative and hypothetical, constituting an "as if" model (Shavelson & Stern, 1981, p. 458).

The first criticism is only partly applicable – mainly to the earlier laboratory studies done during the developmental stages of SJT's evolution. The current focus in applying SJT is to examine natural judgment ecologies using ecologically representative cues and cue configurations (see the review by Hammond, Rohrbaugh, Mumpower, & Adelman, 1977, for examples). The second criticism is patently incorrect with respect to research in the SJT paradigm: Aggregation can occur but only *after* individual judgmental policies have been completely specified. As mentioned above, SJT is an explicitly idiographic theory, the strong assumption being that individuals are so diverse that any one individual's judgment policy must be recognized and understood as a unique cognitive process that is not necessarily like that of any other person. Only after understanding the uniqueness of judgment policies will we be in a position to talk about the commonalities among policies, that is, aggregation.

The final criticism issued by Shavelson and Stern concerning the lens model is, as we interpret it, that, experientially, individuals may not "actually" (that is, consciously) combine weighted variables in the formation of their judgments and that, therefore, all that such an approach can hope to yield is an "as if" model. There are in fact two issues here. The first issue concerns whether or not judges "actually" weight and combine various pieces of information in the formation of judgments. Put simply, the point is debatable. In many circumstances – for instance, a teacher's surveying a set of test scores to decide on grades or promotion or even in-class groupings – it is entirely likely that some weighting/integrating system will be used. Other circumstances may lead to qualitatively different decision systems being invoked. This, in the end, is an empirical question. It is at least arguable that a lens model study is no more artificial than some of those that present judges with anecdotes about students and ask the judges to express various opinions. In many such studies there are at least three sources of artificiality: (a) the judges are often asked to respond "as if" they were teachers, (b) the set of anecdotes themselves are often constructed to conform to a complex orthogonal design, and (c) the results are often aggregated across judges and discussed in purely nomothetic terms (Shavelson, Caldwell, & Izu, 1977, is an example of a study with all three of these characteristics). Our point here is not to challenge the conclusions of such studies but rather to caution against simplistic and inconsistently applied notions of generalizability.

Treating the "as if" aspect of Shavelson and Stern's final criticism, the point is well taken but must apply to some extent to almost all studies of judgment or any other especially complex cognitive phenomena. As soon as the researcher presents someone with a report, a profile, or an account of the object of the judgment (a person or a phenomenon) rather than with an instance of the actual object itself, the "reality" of the process is in question. Similarly, when responses are aggregated across people (e.g., teachers), the experiential reality of each individual's judgmental process is lost. In short, any model is best seen as a heuristic representation even though certain models may be more promising in their relationships to overt behavior. In particular, for our purposes, the parameters of the lens model system have been shown to have direct and predictable implications for behavior in, for example, judgmental ecologies that induce policy conflict and quarreling and in certain clinical contexts (see Brehmer, 1980c, for an overview; see Kirwan, Chaput de Saintonge, Joyce, & Currey, 1983b, for an example in a clinical context).

Purpose of the present study

The example reported in this section has three purposes. First, we aim to demonstrate the applicability and utility of SJT as a way of understanding teacher expectations and what may underly them. Second, we want to comment on the apparent nature of specific expectation policies held by novice teachers (with little or no prior teaching experience) as a way of examining how they might be thinking when they first enter a classroom. Third, we want to examine the accuracy of such policies in the context of the classroom ecology.

To accomplish these goals, we provided novice teachers with a large number of actual student profiles, thus enhancing the representativeness of our decision context and thereby the generalizability of findings. Such profiles contained the sort of information (e.g., indexes of early cognitive performance, SES, and nature of instructional program) that would be available to teachers when taking over a new class, for example, or beginning their teaching service. We also began our analyses at the idiographic level, treating the data from each individual as a unique system of estimation before exploring the possibility of clustering teachers in the search for common types of policies. Finally, to enhance ecological representativeness, we examined teacher expectation policies for *two* important criteria relating to early reading achievement in the context of the multivariate lens model.

Method

Subjects

Participating in the present study were 20 volunteer teachers-in-training from a teacher's college in a small rural city. The student teachers were in various stages of their training: Nine were first-year teacher trainees, eight were second-year, and three were third-year. Only one of the 20 student teachers had any teaching experience in the elementary grades, but all intended to teach at that level. Thus the sample permitted examination of the judgment policies of *novice* teachers, that is, those policies that may initially be operating when the teacher-in-training first enters the classroom ecology.

Student profiles

The ecology of interest in the present study was that of a kindergarten classroom and, specifically, the potential reading achievement of kindergarten children. The particular cues of interest were selected on the basis of previous research (Freebody & Rust, 1985), which suggested their relevance to the prediction of children's early reading achievement. The five cues selected were:

1. *SES*, an index (based on Congalton, 1969) of the socioeconomic status of the child's family, quantified in a numerical rating ranging from 1 (low SES) to 7 (high SES).
2. *RPROG*, the type of reading instructional program or curriculum

in which the child was to be taught reading. There were two types of program. One was a highly structured and sequential program with controlled vocabulary and an emphasis on phonics learning (the SKILLS program). The other was less structured and focused more on encounters with meaningful sentences, highlighting books as interesting objects (the MEANING program).

3. *CAP*, percentile score on the Concept about Print test (see Clay, 1977), which reflected a child's general knowledge of books and print conventions such as which way a book should be held, where the words are on the page, and how illustrations relate to the text.

4. *LETTER*, percentile score on a test of Letter Knowledge (Clay, 1979), which reflected the child's knowledge of the alphabet: letter names and sounds.

5. *ORAL*, numerical score on a test of oral Language Comprehension Ability, reflecting the child's ability to understand orally presented stories.

All the above measures were obtained at the beginning of the kindergarten school year.

There were two criterion measures of interest in this ecology: a child's end-of-year vocabulary development or word knowledge (WK, incorporating both word articulation and picture vocabulary knowledge) and end-of-year reading comprehension achievement (RC, incorporating measures of both literal and inferential comprehension). (The interested reader is referred to Freebody & Rust, 1985, for further discussion of these criterion measures.) Both criterion measures were considered important because the focus of the reading programs was to promote development in both these areas. A child's performance on each criterion was represented as a percentage score when used in the lens model analyses.

In order to obtain a realistic depiction of novice teacher expectation policies, a representative sample of actual children was required whose end-of-year reading achievement levels were known (thus providing the criterion values for the ecology side of the lens model). Thus profiles of 118 kindergarten children were obtained from the data base assembled by Freebody and Rust (1985). The sample size is large relative to the number of cues to provide more stable estimates of cue weights in the lens model analysis. The naturally occurring intercorrelations among the five cues for this sample of the ecology are reported in Table 32.1. Note that the three cognitive cues (CAP, LETTER, ORAL) are fairly highly correlated, indicating some cue redundancy and potential intersubstitutability.

Each child's profile thus contained his or her values for the five cues. The profiles were typed in a standard format on separate sheets and

Table 32.1. *Intercorrelations among the five cues in the reading classroom ecology*

Cue	SES	RPROG	CAP	LETTER	ORAL
SES	1.000				
RPROG	.065	1.000			
CAP	.337	−.001	1.000		
LETTER	.228	.160	.700	1.000	
ORAL	.176	.235	.406	.457	1.000

Note: Correlations are based on $n = 118$ profiles of kindergarten children.

assembled into a notebook. Each profile provided two blank lines on which the student teacher could enter his or her judgments of scores for the two criteria (see Figure 32.2 for a sample student profile).

Procedures

Each teacher was given a notebook and instructed to consider the beginning-of-year information presented in each profile and then to estimate what he or she felt that child would obtain on an end-of-year test of word knowledge and a test of reading comprehension. Each estimate was to be in the form of a percentage score with possible values ranging from 0% to 100%. The participants were told that the profiles were of actual children. They were provided with clear explanations of what each cue represented. They were to proceed with making their estimates at their own pace and, when finished, were asked to rank-order the cues in terms of their importance, first, to estimation of word reading comprehension achievement.

To control for potential order effects, the sample of 118 profiles was randomly split into two blocks of 59 profiles each (blocks A and B). Ten of the student teachers rated the profiles in block order AB, and the remaining ten rated them in block order BA. Subsequent analysis revealed no detectable blocks effects; therefore, all analyses reported here will concentrate on the entire set of 118 profiles.

Analysis of expectation policies

The analysis of the expectation policies proceeded in three stages, the first two being idiographic analyses, the third being more nomothetic in nature. First, to capture the *overall* expectation policy system of each student teacher, the entire system of judgments (incorporating both the WK and the RC criteria) was analyzed using generalized multivariate lens model procedures (see Cooksey & Freebody, 1985, for procedures and

Information about student   1

Socio-economic Status (1=lowest; 7=highest) 3

Type of Reading Scheme student will be taught under . . . MEANING

Knowledge about books and print conventions 87.5%

Letter-name and letter-sound knowledge 100.0%

Oral language comprehension ability . . . . HIGH

>>Your judgment of this student's end-of-year performance on:

    (1) a test of Word Knowledge: ____%

    (2) a test of Reading Comprehension: ____%

Figure 32.2. Sample student profile for the reading judgment tasks.

information on computer programs used for this type of analysis). Second, the univariate judgment systems for each criterion were analyzed to evaluate specifically the expectation policies concerning the individual criterion measures. Note that for all lens model analyses the five cues entered the canonical or regression equations (as referred to in the discussion of the SJT model in the introduction to this chapter) simultaneously, thus yielding what Cooksey and Freebody (1985) have termed a *standard* lens model analysis. Finally, the policy cue weights, reported as squared semipartial correlations, for each student teacher on each criterion were cluster-analyzed to see if common policy types could be detected.

Results and discussion

Multivariate lens model analysis of expectation policies

The results of the generalized multivariate lens model analysis of each student teacher's judgment system and its interaction with the ecology system is shown in Table 32.2. Note that a unique set of multivariate lens model parameters (refer back to Equation 1) is reported for each student teacher. As reflected by the multivariate estimate of R_E, the ecology system was not perfectly predictable from the five cues (median R_E = .720). (The estimates for R_E in Table 32.1 differed slightly for each student teacher due to the canonical nature of multivariate estimation procedure.) Thus, even if a student teacher had been perfectly consistent (R_S = 1.0) and had perfectly matched his or her own policy system to the ecological

Table 32.2. *Summary of multivariate lens model parameters for 20 student teachers, jointly considering word knowledge and reading comprehension predictions*

Student teacher	Multivariate lens model parameter[a]						
	R_A	R_E	R_S	R_M	C	Linear	Config
16A	.656	.719	.984	.946	−.105	.669	−.013
3A	.594	.711	.852	.878	.169	.532	.062
6A	.631	.705	.842	.986	.121	.585	.046
11A	.631	.721	.958	.921	−.026	.636	−.005
26A	.640	.726	.965	.925	−.044	.648	−.008
14A	.564	.719	.858	.938	−.043	.579	−.015
13A	.643	.727	.884	.939	.125	.603	.040
7A	.647	.725	.975	.917	−.099	.649	−.001
19A	.648	.727	.947	.914	.084	.630	.018
20A	.633	.720	.955	.951	−.103	.654	−.021
9B	.657	.721	.958	.945	.023	.653	.005
1B	.671	.714	.991	.942	.048	.666	.005
17B	.605	.715	.971	.916	−.185	.636	−.031
10B	.638	.718	.898	.946	.092	.610	.028
23B	.646	.713	.939	.943	.061	.632	.015
2B	.670	.720	.951	.943	.112	.646	.024
4B	.654	.723	.975	.934	−.028	.658	−.004
8B	.702	.721	.979	.955	.196	.674	.028
5B	.697	.716	.969	.975	.117	.676	.020
15B	.639	.723	.973	.926	−.079	.651	−.013

Note: Abbreviations used are: R_A = multivariate achievement; R_E = multivariate predictability; R_S = multivariate policy consistency; R_M = multivariate policy–ecology matching; C = configural matching; Linear = total linear component of R_A; Config = total configural component of R_A.
[a]All values are interpreted as correlations.

policy system (R_M = 1.0), the best achievement level obtainable, assuming negligible nonlinear matching (i.e., C = 0), was specified by R_E. In this regard, we note that all 20 student teachers achieved at a reasonably high level (median R_A = .645; interquartile range [IQR] = .023) relative to R_E. There was some individual variability, though not extreme, in consistency (median R_S = .958; IQR = .056) and, to a lesser extent, matching (median R_M = .941, IQR = .023).

Configural matching values were clearly the most variable parameters (median C = .036; IQR = .148), perhaps reflecting uncertainty as to interactive or nonlinear relationships that might be useful in predicting the ecological criteria. The primary contributor to multivariate achievement in each student teacher's policy was the linear component (R_M × R_E × R_S: median *linear* value = .647; IQR = .036). Policy consistency was generally quite high as was policy–ecology matching (both generally exceeding correlation values of .9).

The overall impression from the multivariate lens model analysis is that all of the 20 student teachers coped reasonably well with the judgment task. Statistically, this impression is strengthened by looking at the discrepancy between R_E (setting the limit for linear achievement in this task) and R_A for each student teacher in Table 32.2. For example, student teacher 8B had the smallest discrepancy, $.721 - .702 = .019$, whereas student teacher 14A showed the greatest discrepancy, $.719 - .564 = .155$: Clearly all the student teachers were reasonably close to the limits set by R_E. However, some degree of individual differences in expectation policy formation was evident, particularly in the degrees of configural matching and policy consistency.

Univariate lens model analysis of expectation policies

Thus far, we have established the overall expectation policy parameters in the reading ecology. Although we generally conclude adequate performance in the task as a whole by all participants in the study, further univariate analyses of the criteria would be highly instructive, particularly as regards specific expectation policies.

Table 32.3 summarizes the lens model parameters for each criterion (word knowledge and reading comprehension) generated by each student teacher. By examining these univariate components of the multivariate lens model analysis over and above what the multivariate analysis has shown us, we obtain specific impressions of the expectation policies in the vocabulary development and reading comprehension domains. Inspection of Table 32.3 gives the general impression that, although many of the student teachers had essentially equivalent achievement in predicting either criterion (median difference between respective (WK–RC) r_a parameters = .00; IQR = .06), teachers 13A, 19A, and 20A showed a lesser level of achievement in predicting reading comprehension (r_a = .51, .48, and .48, yielding r_a differences of .10, .10, and .16, respectively). This could primarily be attributed to the lesser degree of policy–ecology matching on the reading comprehension criterion attained by these three student teachers (r_m = .79, .84, and .79, respectively) relative to the rest. Generally, the linear component was the main contributor to achievement on both criteria although several student teachers did have some configural contribution in their reading comprehension policies (see student teachers 3A, 13A, and 5B). In general, the student teachers tended to be slightly less consistent in applying their RC policies but, at the same time, tended to be better at matching that policy to the ecological RC criterion. This suggests that the student teachers were a bit more knowledgeable about predicting kindergarten children's potential reading comprehension

Table 32.3. *Summary of univariate lens model parameters for 20 student teachers: Separate policy models for word knowledge and reading comprehension measures*

Student teacher	Univariate lens model parameters											
	Word knowledge						Reading comprehension					
	r_a	R_s	r_m	C	Lin	Con	r_a	R_s	r_m	C	Lin	Con
16A	.58	.99	.83	−.09	.59	−.01	.60	.97	.96	−.04	.61	−.01
3A	.51	.85	.80	.08	.49	.03	.51	.80	.86	.13	.45	.06
6A	.54	.84	.89	.02	.54	.01	.56	.83	.99	.04	.54	.02
11A	.57	.94	.85	−.01	.58	−.01	.57	.95	.95	−.08	.59	−.02
26A	.61	.97	.90	−.05	.62	−.01	.53	.91	.95	−.15	.57	−.04
14A	.52	.86	.90	−.08	.55	−.03	.52	.83	.94	.02	.51	.01
13A	.61	.85	.97	.05	.59	.02	.51	.88	.79	.15	.46	.05
7A	.61	.98	.89	−.05	.62	−.01	.56	.94	.91	.00	.56	.00
19A	.64	.95	.92	.07	.62	.02	.48	.92	.84	−.08	.50	−.02
20A	.58	.95	.90	−.16	.61	−.03	.48	.92	.79	−.01	.48	.00
9B	.60	.96	.87	.00	.60	.00	.60	.94	.97	−.01	.60	.00
1B	.52	.98	.75	−.04	.53	−.01	.59	.99	.89	.06	.58	.01
17B	.54	.96	.84	−.19	.58	−.04	.57	.94	.94	−.03	.58	−.01
10B	.58	.89	.87	.09	.55	.03	.55	.88	.96	−.01	.55	.00
23B	.57	.94	.86	−.02	.58	−.01	.56	.90	.92	.05	.54	.02
2B	.55	.92	.80	.08	.53	.02	.57	.93	.90	.07	.55	.02
4B	.59	.99	.84	−.04	.59	.00	.60	.98	.95	−.05	.61	−.01
8B	.65	.96	.89	.19	.61	.04	.63	.93	.98	.11	.60	.03
5B	.62	.97	.89	.03	.62	.00	.63	.92	.92	.19	.58	.06
15B	.57	.98	.83	−.06	.58	−.01	.53	.91	.89	−.01	.53	.00
Median	.58	.96	.87	−.02	.58	−.00	.56	.92	.93	−.00	.56	.00
IQR	.06	.07	.06	.10	.06	.03	.07	.05	.06	.10	.07	.03

Note: For all student teachers, the ecological predictability (R_e) for word knowledge = .715; the ecological predictability for reading comprehension = .657. Abbreviations used are: r_a = achievement; R_s = policy consistency; r_m = ecology–policy matching; c = configural matching; Lin = total linear component of r_a; Con = total configural component of r_a; and IQR = interquartile range.

achievement from the five cues. There were sizable individual differences in configural matching for both ecological criteria.

Table 32.4 presents the individual policy cue weights for each judgment criterion. Also shown are the optimal policy weights determined from the ecology itself. The individual differences among student teachers clearly reveal themselves here. Not only do WK and RC policy weights differ widely across the sample, they differ in comparison to the ecological cue weights as well. The reason that such weighting discrepancies emerged despite the rather high levels of policy–ecology matching noted earlier rests with the intercorrelations among the cues themselves. Referring

Table 32.4. *Univariate policy weights for each cue, separately considering word knowledge and reading comprehension predictions*

Student teacher	Word knowledge					Reading comprehension				
	SES	RPROG	CAP	LETTER	ORAL	SES	RPROG	CAP	LETTER	ORAL
16A	—[a]	—	—	46.6	—	10.8	—	32.3	—	—
3A	6.6	—	—	18.5	—	—	—	6.2	10.8	6.6
6A	—	—	9.3	3.9	3.9	—	—	—	7.0	—
11A	—	—	—	29.8	—	—	—	—	26.0	—
26A	—	—	—	32.6	—	3.9	—	—	17.1	7.0
14A	—	—	—	22.4	—	—	—	—	15.4	15.4
13A	—	11.4	—	15.4	2.6	—	14.4	—	5.1	5.6
7A	—	—	—	38.1	—	—	—	—	28.3	9.4
19A	—	4.5	—	28.8	5.0	—	6.5	—	19.6	38.7
20A	—	—	—	20.6	5.2	—	—	—	5.1	5.2
9B	—	—	—	25.7	—	—	—	2.7	13.8	—
1B	—	—	41.2	—	—	—	—	—	41.6	11.5
17B	—	—	12.1	41.5	—	—	—	—	15.4	—
10B	—	—	—	9.0	—	—	—	—	17.9	23.8
23B	—	—	22.8	26.1	3.3	—	—	—	4.7	—
2B	—	—	—	—	—	—	—	—	36.1	—
4B	—	—	—	39.8	—	—	—	—	27.4	—
8B	—	—	—	28.7	—	—	—	18.6	3.8	—
5B	—	—	4.2	19.4	—	—	—	5.7	—	20.4
15B	—	—	—	36.5	—	—	—	—	12.3	20.4
Ecology	—	10.0	2.7	4.2	—	—	—	6.1	2.6	—

Note: All policy weights reported as squared semipartial correlations (i.e., Darlington's, 1968, usefulness index) multiplied by 100 to yield *percentage* of reduction in R^2 if cue was removed from the policy equation. The larger the index, the greater the importance of the cue.
[a] refers to an essentially zero weight, i.e., a weight less than 2.5%.

back to Table 32.1, we note that the three cognitive cues (CAP, LETTER, ORAL) were fairly highly correlated. Thus, to some extent, these cues were intersubstitutable such that shifting one's focus from one cue to another would not necessarily detract from overall policy performance. Thus reasonable functional achievement within the ecology could be attained even if the optimal cue weights for the cognitive cues were not closely approximated – trade-offs among these cues (particularly the CAP and LETTER cues) could be tolerated without unduly altering the rank-ordering of predictions that ultimately result from an individual's expectation policy. For example, lens model parameters for predicting reading comprehension remained at a generally high level in spite of the fact that only two student teachers (16A and 8B) gave the greatest policy weight to the CAP test when the CAP score really was the most predictive cue for RC in the ecology. If, however, undue weight was given to SES or RPROG (which have much lower intercorrelations with the other cues), this was likely to detract from potential achievement and policy–ecology matching. For example, student teacher 3A placed greater emphasis on the SES cue (6.57 for WK; 10.76 for RC) than did anyone else in the sample and showed somewhat lower values for r_a and r_m (consistency, R_s, was lower for this person as well). Student teacher 13A placed heavy emphasis on the RPROG cue in predicting reading comprehension (cue weight was 14.38) when, in the ecology, it had trivial predictive validity, resulting in the lowest observed level of policy–ecology matching ($r_m = .79$).

It is interesting to note that the rank order of policy weights objectively derived through multiple regression analysis did not often agree with what student teachers subjectively reported as their order of importance. For the WK policies, the correlations among the ranks of objective and subjective cue weights ranged from $-.20$ to 1.00 with a median correlation of .55. Similarly, for RC policies, the correlations ranged from $-.70$ to 1.00 with a median correlation of .60. These results tend to support the findings of previous studies (that, to some extent, judges tend not to be either aware of or able to correctly report their own policy weights (see, e.g., Summers, Taliaferro, & Fletcher, 1970). However, there were some student teachers (20A, 4B, 5B) who correctly reported their own policy emphases on at least one criterion. Hence, generalizing the inability to report one's policy weights to all student teachers would clearly not be appropriate.

The search for common policy types

It was evident, in inspecting the policy weights in Table 32.4, that certain types of expectation policies tended to be utilized by the student teachers. To capture empirically the common policy types employed by this sample of student teachers, the 20 sets of univariate policy weights for the

WK and RC criteria were separately cluster-analyzed. The clustering procedure employed was a modified version of the ISODATA minimum squared error clustering algorithm (Ball & Khanna, 1977; Cooksey, 1982). The modified version evaluated sequential numbers of clusters from 1 to 10, and, at each stage, produced estimates of variance in policy weights accounted for by the clusters (the estimate used was the correlation ratio – η^2 – from analysis of variance). By plotting $1 - \eta^2$ against the number of clusters, a scree-type test (see Gorsuch, 1983) was performed to detect the most appropriate number of clusters to interpret. Once the appropriate number of clusters was decided, the cluster memberships were independently confirmed using the iterative relocation procedure of the CLUSTAN cluster analytic system (Wishart, 1978). Figure 32.3 depicts, using profiles of average cue weights, the types of policies identified by the clustering procedure. Five distinct policy types were isolated for expectations of word knowledge development, and six types of policy were identified for expectations of reading comprehension achievement. On the average, the identified clusters accounted for over 80% of the variance in policy weighting for both the WK and RC criteria ($\eta^2_{WK} = .8196$; $\eta^2_{RC} = .8664$). To simplify presentation and highlight the policy variations, the average policy weights were categorized into None, Slight, Moderate, or Strong weight categories (the actual values for the weights appear in parentheses on each profile). The policy for each criterion in the ecology is also shown for comparative purposes.

Several points are of interest in this typological policy analysis. In general, the types of policies utilized are very diverse and differ widely from the ecology profiles. For each criterion, there are two unique expectation policies held by single individuals, 3A and 13A (for WK: policies D_{WK} and E_{WK} for RC: policies E_{RC} and F_{RC}). The policies held by student teacher 3A placed emphasis on SES as a cue for predicting performance, whereas policies E_{WK} and F_{RC} emphasized the RPROG cue (which was quite appropriate in the case of WK judgments).

The major WK policy was A_{WK}, where 11 of the 20 student teachers placed emphasis only on the LETTER cue. Policy C_{WK} emphasized the CAP score as the major cue with minor emphasis on the LETTER score. There were two major RC policies, B_{RC} and C_{RC}. Policy C_{RC} had major emphasis on LETTER and minor emphasis on ORAL, whereas policy B_{RC} focused totally on the LETTER cue. Policy D_{RC} was alluded to earlier, where only two student teachers utilized the CAP test as a valid predictor of RC. Thus we note that some types of expectation policy were rather simplistic (focusing on a single cue) whereas others showed some complexity in distributing utility weights. Some student teachers show sensitivity to the possibility of different policies applying to the different criteria by actually employing different policies (e.g., note differing WK and RC policy types for student teachers 20A, 23B, 16A, 8B, 1B, and 2B).

An interesting further investigation might be to examine the role of

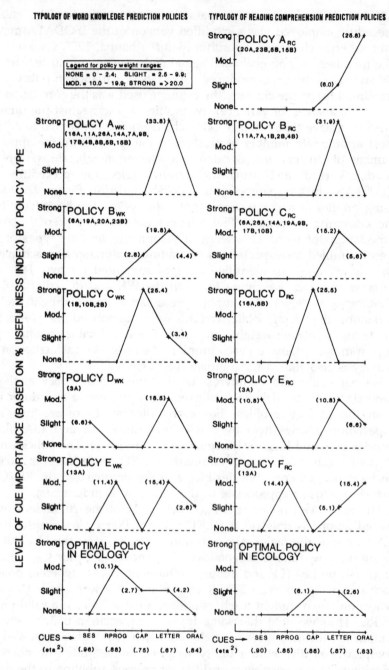

Figure 32.3. Profiles of policy types identified through cluster analysis for the WK and RC prediction criteria (each cue's eta-squared value is provided below that cue's label on the abscissa).

cognitive complexity in the formation of expectation policies. Even in the small sample of the present study, the idiographic diversity of policy formation becomes clear. Such diversity would have been completely clouded by a nomothetic analysis of the entire sample.

General discussion

We have attempted to demonstrate the utility of Social Judgment Theory as both a theory and a method for understanding and externalizing covert expectation policies used by educators. Relative to the reading ecology itself, the student teachers in the sample performed quite well in both policy consistency and policy–ecology matching. Achievement levels were reasonably close to their theoretical maximums for most student teachers on both prediction criteria. Analysis of policy weights for the WK and RC prediction criteria revealed great diversity in types of policies applied and in sensitivity to different policies applying to different criteria. Many student teachers had difficulty in correctly reporting the importance of the various cues in their judgments of criterion values.

Lest we overstate the implications of this policy diversity, recall that the three cognitive ability cues (CAP, LETTER, and ORAL) were substantially intercorrelated (LETTER and CAP particularly so at $r = .70$; see Table 32.1). Thus, as we stated earlier, these three cues are, at least partially, intersubstitutable. With this in mind, it is clear that much of the diversity in WK and RC policies arises out of particular student teacher preferences for one or two measures of reading readiness over the others. Thus one could argue that policies A to D for both the word knowledge and reading comprehension criteria really reflect the same general type of policy – high emphasis on a preferred reading readiness measure. The intersubstitutability of these three measures helps to ensure that, overall, utilizing a preferred reading readiness measure does not substantially influence or bias a student teacher's performance characteristics.

Although the summarization of results from an idiographically oriented approach such as that embodied in SJT is somewhat complex, it is a vital step in the analysis of expectation policies. There was no a priori reason to expect different teachers to be using the same informal policies in the classroom. The advantage of the SJT approach is that individual policies were understood first, before the search for common policies commenced.

As our study has demonstrated, SJT can make explicit the covert informal expectation policies of teachers in a given classroom ecology and can provide information as to their accuracy and consistency in application. And, as Hammond et al. (1977) have shown, because people often are not aware of or cannot verbalize their own policy systems, an important second step in the application of SJT should be the provision of cognitive feedback to the policy maker. Clearly this should be a further step in our applications of SJT to expectation policy analysis. The form of such cognitive feedback has been discussed elsewhere (e.g., Cooksey & Freebody, 1984). The potential benefit of such feedback is to provide information to the teacher regarding appropriateness or inappropriateness of certain expectation policies in the classroom.

Although the present study focused on a rather restricted sample, we have shown that the methodology of SJT, long in use in many other policy-making contexts, provides some new tools with which we can move into educational contexts (ranging from classroom and counseling ecologies to larger administrative ecologies) and begin to analyze critically and attempt to improve the decisions and policies made in such areas.

Part X

Research techniques

Making a judgment or decision may seem to be more of an art than a science. The number of factors to be weighed may seem immense. Their combination and distillation may seem to be a mysterious endeavor even to the brain doing the combining and distilling. Can a process such as this really be made amenable to scientific investigation?

The answer – in the abstract – might well be, why not? But, in fact, all of us hold our judgment in high esteem. As the French essayist La Rochefoucauld put it, "Everyone complains of his memory . . . and no one complains of his judgment." As a result, the idea that human judgment should be brought under scientific study has not always been greeted with enthusiasm. The idea met with resistance when it began to appear that even the professional judgments of highly skilled persons could be described mathematically and – worse still – by rather simple equations. Very early, Paul Meehl (1954) pointed out the misconceptions "held by the more tender-minded clinicians which prevent clear thinking" about this topic. Because his remarks are as relevant now as then, our first selection includes brief excerpts from his attempt to clear away these misconceptions. The article by Benjamin Kleinmuntz provides an up-to-date review of research in clinical judgment in psychology and medicine.

The final four chapters in this part describe research techniques used in the analysis of judgment. Although they were not originally written with the intent of describing a research technique, the usefulness of the techniques will become apparent as they are used to analyze medical and legal situations. The article by Paul Hoffman, Paul Slovic, and Leonard Rorer, for example, represents a classic use of analysis of variance to describe judgment policies. This technique enables the researcher to discover which cues are used and which are ignored by the decision maker. The next article, by Hal Arkes, contains a description of the use of Bayes's theorem. This theorem describes the way in which probabilities should be updated as new information is received. The chapter by John C. Mowen and Darwyn E. Linder reviews signal detection theory, whose application is illustrated in a legal setting. These authors also provide a brief review of the application of information integration theory. Finally, John Rohrbaugh, Gary McClelland, and Robert Quinn show how utilitarian and egalitarian values can be studied.

33. General remarks on quantification of clinical material

Paul E. Meehl

In discussing the problem of actuarial prediction one often comes across certain misconceptions held by the more tender-minded clinicians which prevent clear thinking. For instance, there is still the misconception that mathematical descriptions of persons in terms of scores *require* that persons achieving identical scores should be identical or indistinguishable with respect to the traits so quantified. We sometimes hear this view expressed by such statements as "A human being is more than just a set of numbers." It is pointed out that two persons who achieve a score of 1.5 sigmas above the mean on an introversion test do not manifest their introversion in precisely the same way, and that they did not arrive at it via the same sequence of experiences. The first thing to see about such a statement is that it is true. But this indubitable uniqueness of the single case is no more fatal to psychology than it is to physics. To see it as fatal to psychological quantification is to forget that the class character of concepts and dimensions is found in all descriptive enterprises. As Cattell says, "It seems that one must subscribe to the extreme sense of Allport's argument and admit that *all* traits are in some way unique" (Cattell, 1946, p. 61). No two individuals are exactly alike, and no verbal or mathematical characterization can do complete justice to their individuality. No two explosions are identical nor can any system of equations give a description of any of them which is exhaustive. As Thurstone has pointed out, those who object to assigning the same score to two introverts because their introversion is distinguishable should in all consistency object to saying that two men have the same income since one of them works and the other steals (Thurstone, 1947, p. 54). A cannon ball falling

This chapter is an abbreviated version of one that originally appeared in Meehl, P. E. *Clinical versus statistical prediction: A theoretical analysis and a review of the evidence* (pp. 129–135). Minneapolis: University of Minnesota Press, 1954. Copyright © 1954 by the University of Minnesota. Reprinted by permission.

through the air is "more than" the equation $S = \frac{1}{2} g \, t^2$, but this has not prevented the development of a rather satisfactory science of mechanics. The exhaustive description of an individual event is not aimed for in the scientific analysis of the world *nor can it be hoped for in any descriptive enterprise* (Hempel, 1949; Nagel, 1952). All macroscopic events are absolutely unique. It is a further mistake to exaggerate the degree to which this lack of concreteness reflects a special failing of the scientist, since there is *no* kind of human knowledge which exhaustively characterizes direct experience by a set of propositions. No set of percentile ranks, no graphical representation of personality components, *and no paragraph of characterological description* can contain all the richness of our immediate experience. The abstractive or summarizing character of descriptions is shared by differential equations, maps, gossip, and novels alike. So-called scientific description, however, abstracts those things which are most relevant in terms of causal-analytic and predictive aims; and, secondly, employs a language (mathematical when possible, but not always!) which minimizes ambiguity.

Further objections associated with the one just mentioned imply that quantitative descriptions cannot yield a unique person. Stouffer (1941) has pointed out that with only ten traits, each of which may take on only four values, there are somewhat over a trillion possible unique individuals. It is well known that the science of fingerprinting makes use of a small number of dimensions and is nevertheless capable of identifying the unique case. In the quantitative case of continuous variables this is even more obvious. . . .

A major research need is further empirical comparison of the two methods of prediction, with the elimination of the disturbing factors mentioned previously. On the formal side, we shall have to wait for the logicians to achieve a clarification of the nature of the concept of probability, especially the probability of hypotheses, and the general formulation of inductive logic. Systematic studies should be undertaken of the success frequency of certain *subjects* of the clinician's predictions. For instance, at what type of prediction is he best? What importance should be assigned to his own subjective degree of confidence? When the clinician and the actuary are in disagreement, to whom should we listen? This latter is important because one commonly hears it said by psychiatrists that they are predicting for the individual case, so that the greater success frequency of the actuary, even if clearly established, is treated as of no importance in practice. This thinking is, of course, thoroughly muddled. In any given instance, we must decide on whom to place our bets; and there is no rational answer to this question *except* in terms of relative frequencies. If, when the clinician disagrees with the statistics, he tends to be wrong, then, if we put our bets *in individual instances* upon him, we will tend to be wrong also.

34. The scientific study of clinical judgment in psychology and medicine

Benjamin Kleinmuntz

In the lead article written to launch *Clinical Psychology Review,* Jerry Wiggins (1981) provided a superb retrospective and prospective view of the clinical and statistical prediction issue. One of his objectives was to rekindle interest among clinical psychologists in the extensive research on clinical judgment. He has certainly rekindled my interest in this area. But perhaps in a way different than he intended. His paper inspired me to reflect on the history and current state of the art of clinical judgment from the perspective of someone who has researched this area in medicine as well as in clinical psychology. The main purpose of this paper, therefore, is to complement the Wiggins piece with the hope of introducing clinical psychologists to similar research in other disciplines. Secondarily, this paper aims at providing clinical psychologists with a view of a variety of possible ways of proceeding in the study of clinical judgment.

Five main developments have contributed to the relatively recent interest in the scientific study of clinical judgment. Interestingly, three of these have their origins in psychology; and all began in the early and mid-1950s: (1) The clinical versus statistical prediction controversy of clinical psychology which was launched with a theoretical analysis and a review of the evidence of the relative accuracy of statistical and intuitive clinical predictions; (2) an interest of cognitive psychologists, particularly of the then emerging information processing psychologists, in the computer's ability to think intelligently; (3) The behavioral decision theorists' interest in the importance of the human's decision strategies as well as the complexity of the decision task; (4) the focus of physicians, in collaboration with statisticians and computer scientists, on formal approaches to medical reasoning; and (5) the emergence of the computer as an information machine. Let us begin with the first of these, which also served as Wiggins' (1981) jumping off point.

Clinical versus statistical prediction

In 1954, Paul E. Meehl wrote his now classic monograph, "Clinical Versus Statistical Prediction: A Theoretical Analysis and a Review of the Evidence." In it, he argued that many clinical predictions can best be made by statistical rather than intuitive means. He reviewed a number of empirical studies in which predictions made intuitively (i.e., in the head) were compared with those made more formally (i.e., by using statistics or other formal procedures) and showed that in 24 of these instances the latter outperformed human clinical judgment. He later increased this boxscore tally to 35 studies (Meehl, 1973).

Meehl's analysis spawned many studies (Goldberg, 1959, 1968; Grebstein, 1963; Kleinmuntz, 1963b; Oskamp, 1962) which further added to the evidence that formal or mechanical methods surpass in accuracy those which rely on judgment. Most of the studies dealt with predictions made from psychological test data using a variety of applied decision tasks, including predicting college success, aviator school dropout rates, psychodiagnosis, and prison parolee recidivism.

But Meehl's extreme actuarial stance did not go unchallenged. The most persistent argument on the clinical side of the controversy has been that of Robert R. Holt (1958, 1978), who has steadfastly maintained over the years that persons cannot be understood or measured meaningfully without the subjective judgments as the clinician perceives, empathizes, intuits, as well as integrates and synthesizes information, and constructs a theory of the person under consideration. Holt's main argument with Meehl's and others' boxscore tallies is that clinicians predicted outcomes (i.e., college grades, diagnoses, job success, parole violation) that put the clinician at a considerable disadvantage vis-a-vis statistics. He would prefer to have clinicians predict behavioral outcomes that are more clearly determined by personality traits, motives, defenses, or other inner states that clinical psychologists are trained to assess (tasks, in the opinion of Holt, that a computer probably could not perform adequately) (Goldberg, 1968; Kleinmuntz, 1967; Lindzey, 1965; Meehl, 1965).

Commenting directly on the limitations of computers, Holt (1978) had this to say: "What I have been opposing all these years is not formal methods ... but attempts to denigrate and eliminate judgment.... Attempts to computerize diagnosis in internal medicine have been going on for some years, but they still fail to yield definite results in many cases, so that the physician still has to fall back on his judgment. If that judgment is constantly derogated ... will he be able to accept the responsibility of using it when it is most needed?" (pp. 14–15).

Thus, we see that Meehl's analysis of the empirical evidence supporting formal methods is disconcerting to Holt because it uses studies that place clinical intuition at an unfair disadvantage and because it challenges the dignity and worth of human intelligence. Unfortunately, the counterintuitive fact of the matter is that much of what clinicians do, particularly physicians who typically process hard data from laboratory and other tests and exams, entails combining these data according to learned decision rules and facts they have in memory. And this is precisely where intuitive strategies are most flawed, regardless of our opinions about the dignity of human judgment.

In this regard, Elstein, Shulman, & Sprafka (1978), who have studied physicians' diagnostic problem solving extensively, list several reasons why clinical judgment is flawed. *First,* diagnostic problems are usually solved by formulating a finite set of alternative solutions and testing them. Humans tend to be misled by these alternatives because they focus on irrelevant features of the problem, or because they are guided by faulty biases, and expectations. *Second,* clinical reasoning is inaccurate because human clinicians tend not to think probabilistically or, if they do, their weightings of certain data are inappropriate, again possibly because of their biases in favor of certain hypotheses. *Third,* clinicians tend to collect too much data on the belief that such redundancies improve their decisions, whereas in point of fact (Koran, 1975; Neuhauser & Lewicki, 1975) these data overload the clinician's cognitive capacity to interpret those data. Finally, according to Elstein, studies on the human's ability to revise subjective probabilities (Edwards, 1968; Kahneman & Tversky, 1973; Slovic, Fischhoff, & Lichtenstein, 1977) have shown that people are exceedingly poor and nonoptimal decision makers.

All of this is not to say that Elstein favors the use of formal procedures or computers as clinical decision makers. But a good argument can be made on these grounds for using the best available decision makers and, if it so happens that programmed decision rules in a computer are the best means available, then these should be used. This coincides with what Meehl wrote in 1954 when he anticipated the use of computers for clinical decision making, "in no case do ... (the clinician's) ... eyes and brains do anything fundamentally different from what is done by the Hollerith machine ..." (p. 38). And if there are clinical decision tasks, as Holt suggests there are in internal medicine, in which humans excell, the important lesson to keep in mind is that, in principle at least, the computer is a better decision maker than humans when the latter attempt to do what they are ill-equipped to do. This principle does not assert, however, that all human clinical decision making necessarily entails strategies for which the computer is better equipped than humans.

As our historical survey progresses, the question of the computer's capabilities and limitations will come up in various ways, although it is not the purpose of this paper to compare the relative superiority of one over the other. It so happens, however, that in the next set of studies which, incidentally, were directly inspired by Meehl's monograph, the computer was shown to be the better clinician.

Computer predictions: An example

The main goal of a series of studies conducted at Carnegie-Mellon University in the 1960s was to formalize a set of decision rules designed to interpret the profiles of a personality test (see Kleinmuntz, 1967, 1975). The way this was accomplished was to model an expert clinical psychologist's "thinking aloud" while he was interpreting the results of the Minnesota Multiphasic Personality Inventory (MMPI). These studies, in addition to being inspired by the clinical versus statistical controversy, were conducted in an environment that was influenced by the information processing viewpoint of Newell and Simon (1972), about which I shall comment later.

The MMPI yields a multivariate profile and was designed to help identify persons with known psychiatric disorders. Clinicians diagnosing patients typically scan the 16 or so profile dimensions of the MMPI and, after a subjective tour de force, pronounce their diagnostic verdict. But profile interpretation is a complex task not unlike that which confronts the physician interpreting an EEG, EKG, or histopathology slide. The task in the case of the MMPI would be simpler if the diagnosis depended merely on the elevation of a single scale, but this is not the case. Our studies have shown that a correct interpretation depends on an accurate reading of the pattern of the MMPI profile, a task that only one out of about ten clinicians does well.

In order to capture the decision rules used by one clinician, we devised a scheme that enabled and even forced the test interpreter to think aloud. Thereby he yielded a running commentary of his thinking while solving 126 MMPI profile problems. The Q-sort technique developed by William Stephenson (1953) at the University of Chicago lent itself well to the task. Conventional use of Stephenson's method calls for the preparation of a set of phrases covering, for example, descriptive personality traits. These phrases are then prepared on a deck of cards and the rater is instructed to sort the cards by placing a specified number of cards in each of several piles. The number of cards and the piles into which they are to be sorted vary from one study to the next; but an invariant of the method is that the cards must be placed along the continuum of a forced normal distribution. In our study, instead of using cards with printed phrases or statements, MMPI profiles were used as the cards to be sorted. The experienced MMPI user was instructed to Q-sort the profiles of emotionally maladjusted ($n = 45$) and adjusted college students ($n = 81$) along a 14-step continuum. He or she was told to place the two least maladjusted profiles on the farthest lefthand pile, and to place to the right of these three slightly less maladjusted profiles, and so on until the two most adjusted profiles were placed on the farthest pile to the right. The test interpreter was encouraged to think aloud, placing the profiles while rank-ordering them. In other words, the sorter was instructed to give reasons for placing particular profiles along the continuum of piles.

So that we could learn as much as possible about MMPI profile decision making, we found it imperative not to allow the sorter to make any decisions without giving a rationale. Typically, a statement would be made such as the following: "Now I'm going to divide these into two piles . . . on the left (least adjusted) I'm throwing MMPI's with at least four scales elevated above the score of 70. . . ." These "thinking aloud" sessions were tape-recorded, and the protocols of one expert (there were ten experts in all) were studied in detail.

The information that was obtained from the test interpreter after about 30 hours of Q-sorting was edited, compiled, a flow chart prepared, and then programmed into computer language so that the machine could make decisions about profiles similar to those made by the Q-sorter. In other words, the computer was given the sorter's information and strategies for processing the information. The success rate of the programmed decision rules was quite similar to that of the MMPI expert. They both had about an 80% hit (true positive) rate in classifying correctly the profiles of persons who were maladjusted; and they had about a 70% hit (true negative) rate in the correct classification of the adjusted persons. Thus far, then, the Q-sorter's protocol was used as the raw data upon which to build a theory of one expert's processing of MMPI information. In that sense, the computer program statements become the elements of a theory of how one person processes such information, a topic about which we will have more to say when we discuss information processing psychology below. However, in this series of studies, the main focus was on building a better mousetrap, not on formulating a theory of MMPI decision making. With this in mind, therefore, the 16 rules (Figure 34.1) were subsequently improved by increasing them to 35 decision rules that included well-known strategies for capturing several complex configural features of MMPI profiles. The new decision rules then easily outperformed the clinical psychologist originally used to generate the 16 rules and, in a separate study (Kleinmuntz, 1969) were shown to be superior to most psychologists analyzing a new set of MMPI's.

According to the latest *Mental Measurements Yearbook* (Buros, 1978), there are currently about a dozen automated personality test interpretation programs now commercially available. Most of these, according to Wiggins (1981, p. 8), follow a logic similar to the one described above. Unfortunately, however, as one critic has already noted (Butcher, 1978), many of these interpretative programs rely more heavily on their vendors' and users' testmonials than on sound psychometric evidence of accuracy and validity. In order to improve this state of affairs, I heartily join Wiggins (1981) in suggesting that clinical psychology now

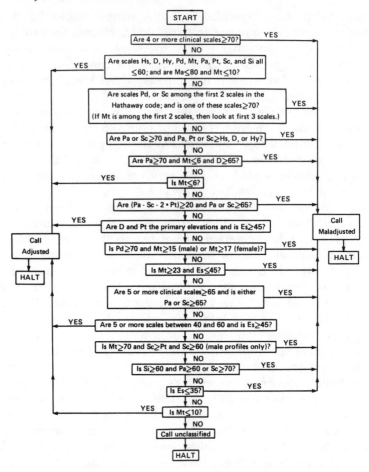

Figure 34.1. Flowchart of MMPI decision rules prior to computer programming.

direct its attention to "the development of better assessment devices ... (as well as) ... the development of procedures that will increase the accuracy of clinical judgment and prediction" (p. 11).

Information processing psychology

The second influence on the study of clinical reasoning comes from the information processing psychology group which, again, also in the mid 1950s had its beginning in the work of Allen Newell and Herbert A. Simon (Newell, 1958, 1961; Simon & Newell, 1964) of Carnegie-Mellon University. Newell and Simon and their students and others working on artificial intelligence projects have been exerting a continuing effort since that time to construct psychological theories using computer program statements as the basic components of a theory of human problem solving. They argue that one can undertake to construct theories about thinking and reasoning using an information processing language, just as one can construct theories of chemical reactions using systems of differential equations, or models of genetics using probabilistic assumptions.

Newell and Simon used the term "simulation" in reference to these theories because they provide soft-ware facsimiles of the phenomena they explain. Information processing theories are sufficiently detailed to perform the actual cognitive tasks of the human with whom they are concerned. For example, an information processing theory of human chess playing is sufficiently complete and detailed to predict the actual moves the human player will consider in a particular situation as well as the problem solving behaviors leading up to that choice. All of this is accomplished, of course, in terms of the basic components of the particular information processing system that was devised to simulate the chess player. In the following study, I attempt a simulation of the diagnostic problem solving of a clinical neurologist.

An illustrative simulation study in medicine

Methodoligically, the information processing approach generally uses direct observations of behavior combined with introspective reports not unlike those used in the MMPI study described earlier. The observations and introspections may be collected in real time or they may be photographed or videotaped for future analysis. The data in the following example occurred in real time and were collected, as we indicated earlier, in order to simulate the strategies of clinical neurologists. A more detailed description appears elsewhere (Kleinmuntz, 1968, 1972, 1975). The choice of clinical neurology as a medical specialty to be studied was made because of the highly structured nature of the clinical data within neurology, and the emphasis among neurologists on coming up with the correct diagnosis. In order to encourage neurologists to think aloud during diagnostic decision making, a scheme was devised that served a similar purpose as the Q-sort procedure in the MMPI study described earlier. A variant of the game of "Twenty Questions" was used by having one player, invariably an experienced neurologist, think of a disease while the other player, the diagnostician, tries to discover what disease the first has in mind. The neurologist pretending to be the patient was able, over a set of different experiments, to assume any of a number of different roles. For example, this person could pretend that he or she is a patient suffering with symptoms a, b, and c; or he or she could assume the role of the omniscient neurologist who is thinking of a disorder which is characterized by symptoms a, b, and c. The diagnostician's task in either case is to ask about the presence or absence of other symptoms, signs, or biographical data, and to call for specific laboratory tests and

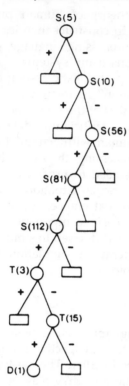

Figure 34.2. A summary tree structure describing the clinical judgment of a neurologist diagnosing several disorders.

inquire about their results. Again, as in the case of the MMPI study, the subject's questions and the experimenter's answers were tape-recorded.

The end product of the diagnostic neurology game resembles a tree structure (see Figure 34.2). The way the game was described above, one would obtain a binary tree in which each point or node in the tree has exactly one connection to a point closer to the root of the tree. The starting point, or the root of the tree, is the subject's first question; all subsequent questions are tests that are performed at the various nodes of the tree. Unless a node is an endpoint – that is, unless a diagnosis has been made on the basis of the questions asked (i.e., tests performed up to that point) – it is connected to two lower nodes, and through them to any number of still lower nodes. A test is associated with each nonterminal node, and depending on the result of the test, a particular branch to left or right is taken. A path is a collection of lines from the root of the tree to an endpoint or terminal node; and the path is the representation of the search strategy that the clinician used in arriving at the diagnostic solution.

For illustrative purposes, consider the game represented in Figure 34.2

in which the experimenter asserted that he has a disease in mind, let us call it D(1), and the subject, inquiring about the presence or absence of a number of symptoms, asks whether a certain symptom is present in that disease. The subject's first question is whether S(5) is present in the particular disease the experimenter has in mind. He or she receives a negative reply. Then the subject asks whether S(10) is a symptom of the disease. Again he or she receives a negative reply. The next question, presumably based on information obtained from prior questions, concerns the presence of S(56). An affirmative reply to that question leads to the query about the presence of S(81) and S(12). Confirmation of the presence of these symptoms then leads the subject to call for laboratory tests T(3) and T(15). The experimenter in this example replied that the results of the first test were negative, but that T(15) yielded positive results. The subject then ventures a diagnosis, D(1), which in our example happens to be a correct diagnosis, and the game is terminated. Since the game was tape-recorded, the tree structure is ready for computer programming.

From an inspection of this tree we can readily see the number and types of questions that the subject had to ask to arrive at a diagnosis. In the game represented in Figure 34.2, the binary tree that begins with the root S(5) has exactly eight nodes, all except the last of which are test nodes. The path from S(5) to D(1) has seven branches, of which three are negative and all the rest are positive. In this way, the computer allows us to construct a model of the clinical decision maker which, if the model is a good one, functions in precisely the same manner as the human diagnostician. Once we have a collection of one subject's tree structures, it is possible to write programs that enable the machine to utilize diagnostic search strategies in much the same manner as did the human decision maker. In principle, if we have a large enough collection of trees from one subject, or from a group of diagnosticians, and if this collection includes most of what is known about clinical neurology, then we can challenge the machine in the same way that patients challenge neurologists when they confront them with a set of symptoms and complaints.

The importance of the computer in this work is that it provides a convenient storage bin that permits ready access to medical knowledge as well as to the decision rules to be used in processing that knowledge. More importantly, however, for the information processing viewpoint is that the rigors of computer programming forces the experimenter to devise schemes that compel the clinician to carefully articulate his or her thought processes. In addition, the computer permits a refinement that would be impossible without the machine. It allows the scientist to construct a model of the clinical decision maker that, if the model is a good one, functions in precisely the same manner as the human decision-maker.

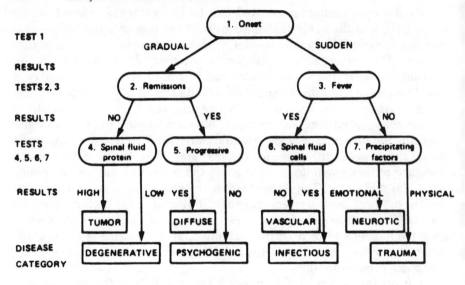

Figure 34.3. Tree of trees resulting from a summary of several actual neurology games.

In fact, that is exactly what was done in the clinical neurology study just described. The thinking aloud information was collected from one neurologist who diagnosed many disorders during the experimental sessions of Twenty Questions. Figure 34.3 is a "tree of trees" that depicts, in a summary way, the overall diagnostic strategies of that clinician. This tree indicates that when presented with most sets of symptoms, the neurologist typically began her inquiry by asking about whether the symptoms were of gradual or sudden onset (this program is in fact based on a woman neurologist's protocols). If the answer was "gradual," she then pursued a specific line of inquiry (e.g., left branch) that ultimately led her to diseases that were either tumor, degenerative, diffuse, or psychogenic. If the answer to the first set of questions was "sudden," the possible diseases were of vascular, infectious, neurotic, or traumatic origin. The important feature to note about such tree of trees is that, given enough neurological knowledge from games such as Twenty Questions or similar techniques of eliciting information from many neurologists, it is possible to build a Neurology machine that thinks like a sophisticated neurologist.

The implications of this study for clinical psychology should be obvious. Clearly, the parallel to the MMPI study was no coincidence since both studies were conducted by the same investigator. Hence, one way to find out in great detail what a clinician does in solving *any* diagnostic problem (i.e., not just the MMPI) is to ask him or her. As blatantly introspective as this may sound, the end-product, or the protocols, can be validated against real-world criteria. It is therefore perfectly possible that a clinician, either intentionally or not, may not give an accurate "thinking aloud" account of his or her clinical problem solving. That is not too critical. The important test of the protocols' accuracy is whether it solves the n + 1 problems that confront it.

Behavioral decision theory

At about the same time that Meehl was writing his treatise on clinical versus statistical prediction, and that Newell and Simon were developing their information processing psychology, the Berkeley psychologist, Egon Brunswik, wrote his 1952 book called, *The Conceptual Framework of Psychology*. Among other important contributions, Brunswik, in this book and in later papers (1955, 1956), was the first to propose that in studying judgment it is equally important to model the task environment as it is the cognitions of subjects. Moreover, Brunswik emphasized the fallible and probabilistic nature of both the environment and the judgments made therein.

Brunswik's students and followers focused on a number of judgment-task interactions, which he called "probabilistic functionalism," and they launched a series of studies that focused on how judges use stimulus cues in uncertain environments. Brunswik had developed the idea of the "lens model" which, under the leadership of Kenneth Hammond of the University of Colorado, proved to be a valuable tool for studying clinical judgment (Hammond, 1955, 1966).

The lens model, as later modified by several investigators, who detailed its relationship to multiple regression statistics (Dudycha & Naylor, 1966; Hursch, Hammond, & Hursch, 1964; Tucker, 1964), is shown in Figure 34.4. The model uses the analogy of the convexity of a lens to describe the relation between a judge's perception of an environment (Y_s) and the object or criterion of perception (Y_e). The variables $X_1, X_2 \ldots X_n$ are cues or information sources that define each stimulus object. For example, if the stimuli being evaluated are patients whose disorders are to be predicted, the X can represent symptoms, laboratory tests, and so on. Each cue dimension has a relevance to the true state of the world (Y_e), which is the patient's actual disorder. But since the cues are related probabilistically to both the judgment and the true state which is being evaluated, the judge's predictions are less than perfect. The arc r_a, also called validity, reflects the degree to which a clinician's judgment (Y_s) coincides with the actual event to be judged. Hence the lens model equation,

$$r_a = GR_eR_s + C \sqrt{1 - R_e^2} \sqrt{1 - R_s^2}$$

represents the validity (overall accuracy) of the judge's or clinician's decisions, as measured by the correlates between judgments, Y_s, and the criterion, Y_e. The statistical properties of the environment are represented

STATISTICAL VS CLINICAL DETECTION

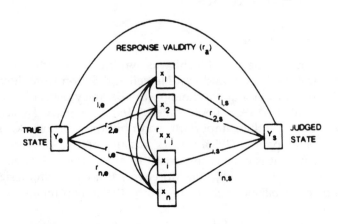

Figure 34.4. The lens model.

by R_e (i.e., the criterion's predictability from the cues), and the statistical properties of the clinician's judgments are represented by R_s (i.e., the judge's ability to apply his or her knowledge).

A wide variety of papers have dealt with the lens model, or aspects of that model, which may be relevant for clinical judgment. One of the earliest such papers was Hammond's (1955) proposal for the use of probabilistic functionalism in the study of clinical judgment. Hoffman (1960) later showed that a linear model derivation of the lens model can be used to study a judge's predictions. Most recently, Julian Szucko and I (Szucko & Kleinmuntz, 1981) used the lens model, in conjunction with the Theory of Signal Detection, to study the clinical accuracy of polygraph protocol interpretation in lie detection. These statistical techniques were sensitive enough to indicate that for polygraph interpretation, clinicians would be performing more nearly optimally if they used formal processing procedures rather than intuitive judgments.

In the opinion of several researchers in behavioral decision theory (Edwards, 1971; Slovic & Lichtenstein, 1971), it is unfortunate that

Brunswik was not a mathematician because otherwise he might have used Bayesian statistical decision theory to study clinical judgment. This approach in the study of medical reasoning was used by Leonard Savage (1972), who stated that the Bayesian viewpoint forms a good framework in which to discuss and to develop a language for diagnosis that is more sensitive to the complexities of diagnostic decision making than the very crude language of "maybe" and "surely." Savage's example of its use in medicine will suffice here. Along with the subjective probability of events, according to Savage, there is the utility of consequences. When a physician is confronted with a case, the physician may reason as follows: The patient is almost surely in one of the three mutually exclusive states A, B, or C with probabilities $P(A)$, $P(B)$, and $P(C)$, perhaps .01, .09, and .9, respectively; if I do not perform an emergency operation now, he will die in case of A, recover very badly in case of B, and be fine tomorrow in case of C; if I do operate, he will recover but rather uncomfortably and be out of pocket half a year's salary.

According to the theory of utility, any tenable decision of this physician can be represented by attaching numbers U_4, U_3, U_2, and U_1 to the four possible consequences: death, nonpostoperative recovery with its costs, speedy recovery, and postoperative recovery with its costs – all without regard for the probabilities of A, B, and C – in such a way that the operation is preferred if and only if

$$U_4 > U_1 P(A) + U_2 P(B) + U_3 P(C).$$

Unfortunately, it will be more difficult to apply utility theory to clinical judgments in psychology. In the first place, the consequences of our decisions are not always easily apparent to us. Second, the probabilities of A, B, C – if these are considered as treatment options – are almost never as clear in psychiatric as in medical cases. And finally, most clinical psychologists do not have the mathematical wherewithall to reason quantitatively. If the last of these problems is resolved – preferably in graduate admissions decisions – the other difficulties will be resolved also.

Formal approaches to medical reasoning

In 1957, Lusted, a physician at the National Institutes of Health, and Ledley, a dentist at the National Bureau of Standards, became interested in the possibility of automating medical problem solving. Their Science article "Reasoning Foundations of Medical Diagnosis" (1959a), outlined an ambitious attempt to formalize what Sir William Osler a half century earlier called "a science of uncertainty and art of probability." Using a combination of symbolic logic and conditional probability theory, Ledley and Lusted formulated the concept of symptom-disease complexes (SDC) in which a symptom complex is a list of the symptoms that a patient does and does not posess; a disease complex is a similar list of diseases. An

SDC is a list of both symptoms and diseases that a patient does and does not have.

An illustration of Ledley and Lusted's analysis is given below, and it is well to keep in mind that their approach was inspired by the realization that some sort of device is needed to aid physicians in their diagnosis because of the complexity of the clinical judgment task. They proposed that medical diagnosis might be viewed in terms of symbolic logic and conditional probability. To this, they added value theory, chosen principally from von Neumann and Morgenstern's game theory as indicated earlier, in order to aid the physician in the choice of an optimum treatment plan. In what follows, I shall describe only that part of Ledley and Lusted's SDC concept which deals with symbolic logic and truth-table analysis of diagnosis. It is highly suggestive for psychiatric diagnosis because of its simplicity and all-or-none categorization strategy.

An example of the truth table approach to diagnosing an SDC is presented in Figure 34.5, where two symptoms, S(1) and S(2), and two diseases D(1) and D(2) are presented. Each column represents an SDC, where a unit in the row signifies that the patient has the corresponding symptom or disease, and zero indicates that the patient does not have the symptom or disease. Thus the column in the rectangle of Figure 34.5 represents the SDC of the patient having S(1), not having S(2), having D(1), and having D(2). The columns of this figure represent all conceivable SDCs (by applying the truth-tables of symbolic logic) that can be formed from two symptoms and two diseases.

One more example may clarify the SDC concept. Using the reduced logical basis of SDC's (i.e., reduced by available medical knowledge) presented in Figure 34.5, suppose a patient presents the following symptom complex: he does not have S(1), but does have S(2), written symbolically, this is:

$$\overline{S(1)}. S(2)$$

where the bar over S represents NOT S, and the dot represents AND. To make the diagnosis, consider Figure 34.6, which contains the reduced basis of all possible SDC, for those columns that include the symptom complex $\overline{S(1)}$. S(2). There is one such column (rectangle), and this informs the diagnostician that the patient with this symptom complex has D(1). D(2), or D(1) and not D(2).

The intent of developing this formal analysis of medical reasoning which, incidentally could be equally applicable in clinical psychology for diagnosing the behavior disorders delineated in DSM II or DSM III, was to use the computer's memory and retrieval capabilities to store and supply logical analyses that would detect, from an examination of the SDC possibilities, the correct diagnosis for given cases. However, these researchers early on realized the computational complexity of this task even for modern day computers. As Ledley (1972) later wrote, with 20

S(1)	1111	1 111	0000	0000
S(2)	1111	0 000	1111	0000
D(1)	1100	1 100	1100	1100
D(2)	1010	1 010	1010	1010

Figure 34.5. Logical truth table basis for two symptoms, S(1) and S(2), and two diseases, D(1) and D(2).

S(1)	111	101	0	0
S(2)	111	000	1	0
D(1)	110	110	1	0
D(2)	101	101	0	0

Figure 34.6. Reduced logical basis after applying medical knowledge to the truth table of Fig. 34.5. The rectangle is the case of a patient having S(1), S(2).

symptoms there are 2^{20}, or 1,048,576 possible symptom complexes; therefore it is best to develop a hierarchical structure of possible (i.e., according to medical knowledge) symptom-disease complexes. The advantage of this hierarchy is to reduce the truth-table matrix to only those symptom complexes that actually exist rather than include all conceivable symptom (or disease) complexes. And since Ledley and Lusted (1959a, 1965) also suggested that decision theory as well as value theory be applied to the analyses of these truth tables, the computational burden of this task almost surely is beyond the capability of anything but computers, which is the subject of the next several pages.

Enter the computer

The fifth and final development that occurred in the 1950s was the emergence of the computer as an information processing machine. Until the 1950s the name given these machines had obscured the fact that they were capable of performing tasks that go beyond mere computation. It was the physicist, L. N. Ridenour (1952), who at that time was the first to observe that they are called computers simply because computation is the only significant job that had been given them. He suggested that to describe its potentialities, the computer needs a new name – perhaps it can be called an information machine. And, as such, as we have already shown, the influence of the computer has been considerable.

But its impact has been less on research in clinical judgment than it has on some other areas. The computer has had resounding successes in some of these. Let us briefly mention these successes and then attempt to account for the computer's difficulties in clinical information processing.

One such area is the computer's ability to play masters level chess. Although grandmaster level computer programs are not yet available, the information processing group at Carnegie-Mellon and others (deGroot, 1965, 1966) are making substantial headway toward that goal. There are some important differences between chess and clinical information processing of course, but in many respects, the game of chess is similar to information management in clinical psychology or medicine. As Herbert A. Simon of Carnegie-Mellon recently noted (1979a), a good chess player needs to know some 1300 patterns of chess pieces and their positions in order to play well; masters and grandmasters must know some 50,000 patterns and configurations. These patterns and their complexity seem on a par with those that exist in clinical psychology or medicine. But this analogy should not be pushed too far. There are no "game" rules in these clinical disciplines, and there are no opponents as in chess whose board moves change in predictable ways. It is probably also the case that computer programs in clinical psychology and medicine are comparable to class A chess players, which is acceptable in chess playing but unacceptable in the clinical disciplines where one should insist on master and grandmaster performance. In other words, in clinical psychology and medicine we are dealing with problems in which there is considerably more at stake than in chess (or Go, cryptarithmetic, symbolic logic, and so on), and computer programs must be more than just clinically competent or acceptable – they must be first rate. But, I am of the opinion that, given more resources, initiative, and time, computer programs in clinical psychology and medicine soon will be playing at the masters and grandmasters levels. Progress in this area, which is the topic of another paper (Kleinmuntz, in press) is impressive.

Summary and conclusions

Our survey has delineated the five main developments that contributed to the contemporary scientific interest in clinical judgment and has presented some representative research in this area. These developments include the clinical versus statistical prediction controversy, information processing psychology of the Carnegie-Mellon University group, behavioral decision theory which focuses on both the judgment strategy as well as the task environment, the attempt by physicians to formalize medical reasoning, and introduction of the computer as an information machine. All of these efforts occurred at about the same time and, although seemingly independent of one another, were influenced by a mutual cross-fertilization of ideas that occurred at various symposia and conferences.

The current state of clinical information processing still awaits further computer software and hardware advances, but seems to be progressing in several directions. Admittedly, the computer has not had the impact on clinical information management that was optimistically anticipated 20 years ago, but a glimpse at advances in other problem solving spheres that resemble diagnostic judgment suggests that equally impressive developments in the clinical sciences may be expected soon.

35. An analysis-of-variance model for the assessment of configural cue utilization in clinical judgment

Paul J. Hoffman, Paul Slovic, and Leonard G. Rorer

Studies of clinical judgment can be divided into two groups. Those in the first group focus upon outcome, that is, the accuracy or the reliability with which judgments can be made. The results of these studies indicate that, for many kinds of inferences which individuals are called upon to make, both accuracy and reliability leave much to be desired (Bendig, 1955; Goldberg, 1959, 1965, 1966; Grebstein, 1963; Holtzman & Sells, 1954; Howard, 1962; Hunt, Jones, & Hunt, 1957; Sawyer, 1966). Studies in the second group focus upon the judgment process itself, particularly the manner in which cues are weighted and combined by the judge. The results of these studies indicate that judgments can be predicted with a high degree of accuracy from a simple linear combination of the cues (Hammond, Hursch, & Todd, 1964; Hoffman, 1960; Naylor & Wherry, 1965).

Hammond and Summers (1965) cite more than a dozen studies of clinical or quasi-clinical judgment in which the accuracy of prediction derived from linear regression analyses was sufficiently great as to suggest that judges are primarily linear in their mode of combining cues. Yet, no one really believes this to be the case. The argument for the efficacy of clinical judgment rests heavily on the clinician's reputed ability to take advantage of nonlinear relationships (Meehl, 1954), and our daily experience leads us to believe that that ability is not slight. Furthermore, the studies cited by Hammond and Summers do not eliminate the possible existence of meaningful nonlinear cue use. They simply indicate that it has not yet been exhibited in the experimental situation. In view of the practical and theoretical importance of the issue, it is surprising that

This chapter is an abbreviated version of an article that originally appeared in the *Psychological Bulletin*, 1968, *69*(5), 338–349. Copyright © 1968 by the American Psychological Association, Inc. Reprinted by permission.

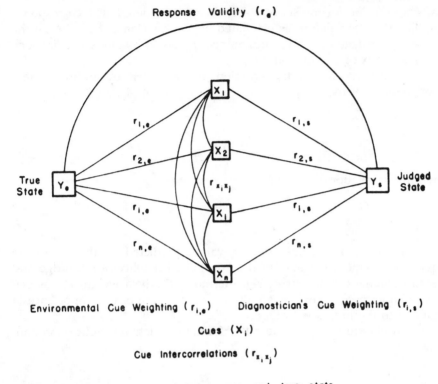

Figure 35.1. The lens model.

there have not been more studies focusing specifically on the degree to which the judge operates in a configural manner, taking advantage of patterned relationships existing between cues and a criterion, as opposed to using some weighted combination of the individual cues. Those studies which have considered this problem can all be described within the framework of the lens model.

The lens model has been suggested by Brunswik (1952) and by Hammond and his associates (Hammond, 1955; Hursch, Hammond, & Hursch, 1964) as a useful framework for conceptualizing the judgment process for an individual judge. The elements of the model are defined as in Figure 35.1. The r_a is the overall response accuracy, the correlation between the criterion diagnosis and the judged diagnosis. It is the value usually reported in studies of diagnostic or judgmental accuracy. Each cue has a specific degree of relevance to the true state of the world. This environmental validity is estimated by the correlation $r_{i,e}$ between the cue and the criterion for the set of objects being considered. The corresponding "judgmental validity" is estimated by the correlation $r_{i,s}$ between the cue and the diagnostician's judgments. These correlations provide one possible index of cue utilization.

If the judgments and the criterion are predicted by additive linear combinations of the cues, as indicated in Equations 1 and 2,

$$\hat{Y}_e = \sum_{i=1}^{n} \beta_{i,e} X_i \tag{1}$$

$$\hat{Y}_s = \sum_{i=1}^{n} \beta_{i,s} X_i \tag{2}$$

then the correlations R_s and R_e

$$R_s = r_{Y_s \hat{Y}_s} \tag{3}$$

$$R_e = r_{Y_e \hat{Y}_e} \tag{4}$$

between the actual values and the values predicted by the regression equation provide a measure of the linear predictability of the judge and the environment, respectively. Furthermore, the beta weight $\beta_{i,s}$ associated with each cue provides an alternative measure of the importance of that cue to the individual judge.

Still another index is provided by Hoffman's relative weight (Hoffman, 1960)

$$RW_{i,s} = \frac{\beta_{i,s} r_{i,s}}{R_s^2} \tag{5}$$

$$RW_{i,e} = \frac{\beta_{i,e} r_{i,e}}{R_e^2} \tag{6}$$

which is designed to indicate the relative importance of each of the cues, even when the cues are intercorrelated. Since the sum of the relative weights is one, Hoffman's index can be used to describe the relative contribution of each of the predictors as a proportion of the predictable linear variance.

The above measures all apply to the linearly predictable variance. However, within the framework of the lens model, Hursch et al. (1964) have developed an index of nonlinear cue usage which they call C. If that variance which cannot be linearly predicted is labeled Z_e for the true state and Z_s for the judged state, then the following relationships hold

$$Y_e = \hat{Y}_e + Z_e \tag{7}$$

$$Y_s = \hat{Y}_s + Z_s \tag{8}$$

Now define G as the correlation between the linearly predictable variances

$$G = r_{\hat{Y}_e \hat{Y}_s}$$

Define C as the correlation between the residual variances

$$C = r_{Z_e Z_s}$$

Tucker (1964) has shown that the overall validity r_a may be represented as

$$r_a = GR_e R_s + C \sqrt{1 - R_e^2} \sqrt{1 - R_s^2} \tag{9}$$

An alternative form of this equation

$$r_a = \frac{1}{2}(R_e^2 + R_s^2 - \Sigma d) + C \sqrt{1 - R_e^2} \sqrt{1 - R_s^2} \tag{10}$$

where

$$\Sigma d = \sum_i^n (\beta_{i,e} - \beta_{i,s})(r_{i,e} - r_{i,s})$$

was earlier presented by Hursch et al. (1964). In either case, the right-hand side of the equation is composed of two parts, the first having to do with linear accuracy, and the second having to do with configural accuracy. If C is zero, the judge may be using a random, a linear, or an invalid configural strategy. However, positive values of C indicate valid, nonlinear cue utilization, although they do not indicate the form of the nonlinear cue utilization.

One possible way in which particular sources of nonlinearity might be identified has been described by Hoffman (1960), who suggested the utilization of configural terms within the regression model itself. The contribution of products of the original predictors, or more complex terms involving other combinations of the predictors, may be assessed by determining the extent to which predictive accuracy is improved when such terms are added to the basic regression model. Examples of increases in predictive accuracy as a result of the inclusion of such terms are scarce, but some do exist (e.g., Goldberg, 1965; Wiggins & Hoffman, 1968).

This paper describes an analysis-of-variance (ANOVA) approach to the discovery and description of nonlinear cue usage. The structural models underlying the fixed effects and random effects designs are quite similar to the multiple regression model. These ANOVA models seem intuitively descriptive of many judgment situations, yet they have not previously been used to represent the judgment process. If judgment stimuli (cues) are regarded as categorical treatment factors rather than as continuous random variables, and if the judgments made to the cues are considered as dependent variables, then the elegant inferential and descriptive capabilities of the ANOVA technique can be applied to the study of judgment. The application is simple and direct: one prepares multidimensional judgmental stimuli by constructing all possible combinations (patterns) of the cue levels in a completely crossed factorial design. Such a set of patterns is of necessity orthogonal in the cue dimensions.

When judgments are analyzed in terms of an ANOVA model, a significant main effect for Cue 1 implies that the judge's responses varied systematically with Cue 1. Similarly, a significant interaction between Cues 1 and 2 implies that the judge was responding to particular patterns of these cues, that is, that the effect of variation of Cue 1 upon the judgments differed as a function of the level of Cue 2. Provided sufficient levels of a factor are included in the design, an effect may be divided into subeffects due to linear, quadratic, cubic, etc., trends. In general, the model represents judgments as a weighted additive combination of the factors, both main effects and interactions.

Significance tests can provide an indication of the judge's utilizations of a particular cue individually or in combination with one or more other cues. If one is interested in generalizing his results only to the particular set of cues and the particular levels of those cues from which the stimuli were constructed, then a fixed effects ANOVA model applies and F ratios may be constructed accordingly.

The ANOVA model is being proposed not because it provides a convenient way to calculate tests of significance, but rather because of its potential for describing both the linear and the nonlinear aspects of the judgment process. Within the framework of the model, it is possible to calculate an index (ω^2) of the importance of individual or patterned use of a cue, relative to the importance of other cues (Hays, 1963). The index ω^2 provides an estimate of the proportion of the total variation in a person's judgments that can be predicted from a knowledge of the particular levels of a given cue or a pattern of cues. Its interpretation is analogous to the interpretation of the squared product-moment correlation as a proportion of variance explained and to Hoffman's index of relative weight when the latter is calculated for orthogonal cues. The ω^2 makes possible the interpretation of the effects of ANOVA variables in terms of degree, rather than in terms of level of significance.

In the following experiment an ANOVA structural model was applied to a problem of differential diagnosis in medicine. The experiment illustrates the adequacy of the model for describing the judgments made by a gastroenterologist as he decides whether a gastric ulcer is benign or malignant.

The differential diagnosis of ulcer malignancy

Consultation with a gastroenterologist led to the selection of seven signs, some of which are presumed by experts to combine in a configural manner for this diagnostic task. These signs were:

1. Ulcer is extraluminal. (Yes or No)
2. Associated filling defect is present. (Yes or No)
3. Ulcer contour is regular. (Yes or No)

Case No. 037	Yes	No
1. Extraluminal	x	
2. Filling Defect		\
3. Regular Contour	x	
4. Rugal Pattern		x
5. Duodenal Symptoms	x	
6. On Greater Curvature		x
7. Small Crater	x	

Benign						Malignant
1	2	3	4	5	6	7

Figure 35.2. One of the 96 stimulus cases. (The diagnostician circled one of the numbers provided, on the basis of the above information. The information was ostensibly taken from roentgenological reports.)

4. Rugal pattern is preserved around ulcer. (Yes or No)
5. Evidence of associated duodenal ulcer is present. (Yes or No)
6. Ulcer is located on the greater curvature. (Yes or No)
7. Ulcer crater is small. (Yes or No)

Hypothetical ulcer patients were constructed by forming all possible combinations of the seven signs. Since each sign could take one of two levels (present or absent), this produced 2^7 or 128 cases. A typical case is shown in Figure 35.2

Because the plausibility of the cue patterns was a matter of some importance, all of the 128 possible patterns were reviewed by a competent gastroenterologist, who was asked to indicate whether any of them were sufficiently implausible as to cast doubt upon the meaningfulness of the study. This gastroenterologist eliminated exactly 32 of the patterns, all because they paired "Ulcer is extraluminal (No)" with "Associated filling defect (No)." Apparently an intraluminal ulcer is by definition one with an associated filling defect. However, all of the remaining 96 profiles, or cases, were considered plausible. Sign 1 and Sign 2 were, therefore, combined into a single variable treated at three levels:

Level 1. Ulcer is extraluminal (No) and associated filling defect (Yes).
Level 2. Ulcer is extraluminal (Yes) and associated filling defect (No).
Level 3. Ulcer is extraluminal (Yes) and associated filling defect (Yes).

This resulted in a 3×2^5 complete factorial arrangement of case patterns.

Table 35.1. *Means, standard deviations, reliabilities, and interjudge correlations for each subject*

Radiologist	Radiologist									Mean judgment	SD
	1	2	3	4	5	6	7	8	9		
1	(.82)									3.3	1.8
2	.61	(.61)								3.9	1.0
3	.83	.58	(.91)							3.3	2.0
4	.74	.55	.76	(.80)						4.2	1.2
5	.00	.05	−.01	−.09	(.70)					3.0	1.3
6	.27	.40	.22	.17	−.02)	(.60)				3.9	1.9
7	.40	.13	.32	.18	.37	−.07)	(.88)			3.9	2.0
8	.52	.38	.49	.53	.24	.02	.20	(.73)		3.5	1.7
9	.73	.66	.78	.69	−.11	.47	−.01	.46	(.92)	3.7	1.8
Average	.56	.44	.55	.49	.06	.19	.20	.36	.51		

Note: Interjudge correlations are based on 192 cases. Numbers in parentheses are the intrajudge correlations between the two administrations of the 96 cases (reliabilities).

Each of the resulting 96 cases was presented twice during the experiment so that each subject had 192 cases to judge. The profiles for the second replication were randomly interspersed within the first. This method offers two advantages. First, the interspersion of duplicate profiles within a single administration of the task minimizes order effects. Second, it reduces temporal effects, since identical profiles are in closer proximity than would be the case if the two replications were completely separated. It was not the purpose of the experiment to assess the stability of judgments over time, but rather to assess the reliability of the behavior at a given period in time.

The judgments were made on a 7-point scale ranging from 1 (definitely benign) to 7 (definitely malignant). The subjects were six practicing radiologists and three radiologists-in-training at the University of Oregon Medical School.

Table 35.1 presents for each radiologist the mean, standard deviation, and reliability of his judgments, and the correlations between his judgments and those of the eight other judges. The most striking feature of these data is the low degree of agreement among the various judges. The highest correlation was .83, the lowest was −.11, and the median was only .38. The correlation between the two replications for each diagnostician is shown as the diagonal entry in the table. These reliabilities range from .60 to .92, indicating considerable variation in judgmental consistency. Nevertheless, the coefficients are high enough to contraindicate the hypothesis that the lack of agreement between judges is due solely to inconsistency or unreliability. Twenty-one of the 36 interjudge coefficients are .40 or less, and 15 of them are .25 or less. Even if corrected for attenuation due to unreliability, these coefficients would be considerably less than 1.0. Thus, the differences among judges appear to be real, and it remains to be seen if they can be accounted for in terms of differences in underlying judgmental processes.

In order to provide a model of those processes, a separate ANOVA was performed on each judge's responses. Sums of squares and mean squares were computed for each of the six main effects (individual symptoms), 15 two-way interactions, 20 three-way interactions, 15 four-way interactions, six five-way interactions, and one six-way interaction. Table 35.2 presents a frequency count of the number of statistically significant main effects and interactions for each radiologist. All but one radiologist can be described by significant main effects for three or more symptoms and by three or more combinations of symptoms.

Table 35.3 shows the individual symptoms and cominations of symptoms which were most frequently found to be statistically significant. Each of the individual symptoms was considered relevant by three or more radiologists. A subset of only 17 configurations, out of 57 possible patterns of cues, accounted for 43 of the 57 instances in which the radiologists exhibited interactive use of cues. Thus, a subset of cues and cue patterns appears to be of consistent importance among radiologists.

The values of the ω^2 index for the statistically significant main effects and for the largest of the 57 interactions are presented in Table 35.4. Inspection of this table reveals that the largest main effect usually accounted for 10 to 40 times as much of the total variance in the judgments as the largest interaction. On the average, roughly 90% of a judge's reliable variation of response could be predicted by a simple formula combining only individual symptoms in an additive fashion and completely ignoring interactions.

The above analyses indicate that there was substantial, but by no means unanimous, agreement among the radiologists, either with regard to final diagnosis (Table 35.1) or with regard to the importance of individual symptoms (Table 35.4). In order to determine the significance of these differences, one large ANOVA, using the data from all nine radiologists, was run. Radiologists were considered to be a random sample from a larger population of expert judges, and replications to be nested within radiologists. Since the symptoms were considered to be fixed effects (nonsampled), the appropriate error terms for the F tests in this analysis were governed by a mixed model (Winer, 1962).

The results for the main effects and significant interactions are listed in Table 35.5. The first source of variance listed in the table, that due to radiologists, was statistically significant. This indicates that the radiologists differed in their mean judgments across the 192 stimuli. The significant main effects for Symptoms 1 and 3 indicate that, when data were averaged over radiologists, the mean judgments varied systematically with the levels of these cues. A significant interaction between radiologists and an individual symptom indicates that the radiologist differed among themselves in the extent to which they relied on this

Table 35.2. *Number of statistically significant main effects and interactions for each radiologist*

| Source of variation | Total number of possible effects for each radiologist | Radiologist | | | | | | | | | Sum |
		1	2	3	4	5	6	7	8	9	
Main effects	6	3[a]	5	3	3	6	5	4	6	2	37
2-way interactions	15	0	3	5	1	5	3	5	1	1	24
3-way interactions	20	1	1	2	2	4	2	4	0	1	17
4-way interactions	15	2	0	1	3	4	0	3	1	0	14
5-way interactions	6	0	0	1	0	0	0	0	0	0	1
6-way interactions	1	0	0	0	0	0	0	0	1	0	1
Total interactions		3	4	9	6	13	5	12	3	2	57

[a] Cell entries are the number of effects that are significant at $p < .05$, as determined by F tests made on the analyses of each radiologist.

Table 35.3. *Symptoms and symptom combinations (interactions) used by two or more radiologists to a statistically significant degree*

Symptom combination	Number of radiologists using this symptom	Symptom combination	Number of radiologists using this symptom
1	9	123	4
2	6	126	2
3	9	134	2
4	5	245	2
5	3		
6	5		
		1234	2
		1236	2
12	2	1245	2
13	3	1246	2
14	4	1346	2
23	3		
24	2		
34	5		
36	2		
46	2		

Note: The criterion of statistical significance was $p < .05$ as determined by F tests made on the analyses of each radiologist.

Table 35.4. *The relative use of six symptoms and their 57 interactions (values of the ω^2 index)*

Symptom	Radiologist									Average
	1	2	3	4	5	6	7	8	9	
1 Extraluminal & filling defect	.50	.48	.56	.46	.05	.40	.02	.22	.91	.40
2 Regular contour	.03	.01	.03		.03		.48	.03	.01	.07
3 Rugal pattern	.28	.03	.25	.22	.05	.02	.29	.04		.13
4 Duodenal symptoms		.01			.31	.01		.23		.06
5 On greater curvature					.04	.07		.01		.01
6 Small carter		.01		.07	.03	.02		.18		.04
Largest interaction	.01	.02	.02	.02	.03	.02	.02	.02	.003	.017

Table 35.5. *Analysis of variance performed on the combined data from all radiologists*

Source of variation	df	MS	F
Radiologists (R)	8	25.8	46.1**
Symptom 1	2	576.7	11.5**
Symptom 2	1	163.2	4.5
Symptom 3	1	411.2	10.2*
Symptom 4	1	62.6	2.8
Symptom 5	1	9.3	1.2
Symptom 6	1	3.1	0.2
R × 1	16	49.8	82.7**
R × 2	8	36.6	61.0**
R × 3	8	40.4	67.3**
R × 4	8	22.3	37.2**
R × 5	8	7.7	12.8**
R × 6	8	18.8	31.3**
1 × 4	2	3.6	4.2*
2 × 4	1	4.6	5.6*
R × 1 × 3	16	2.1	3.6**
R × 2 × 3	8	2.6	4.3**
R × 3 × 4	8	3.2	5.3**
1 × 2 × 5	2	1.4	2.3*
1 × 5 × 6	2	3.1	3.8*
3 × 4 × 5	1	2.4	4.0*
4 × 5 × 6	1	2.3	3.8*
R × 1 × 2 × 3	16	1.8	3.0**
R × 1 × 3 × 4	16	1.5	2.5**
R × 1 × 4 × 6	16	1.4	2.3**

* $p < .05$.
** $p < .01$.

symptom. This could be a difference in direction as well as in degree, that is, some may have thought a symptom to be a positive indicator of malignancy, while others may have considered it a contraindicator. The significance of individual differences in the use of each of the six individual symptoms is of more than passing interest.

In similar fashion, the two-way interactions between cues indicate whether or not a particular pair of cues was employed configurally by the group as a whole; the three-way interactions, with radiologists as one of the factors, tell whether there were individual differences in the configural use of a pair of cues, etc. All in all, there were some pairs of cues and some three-symptom patterns that were used configurally by the group as a whole, and other two- and three-element patterns whose use differed among radiologists, No configurations involving more than three cues reached significance in this analysis. . . .

Discussion

Studies of judgment have typically tried to formulate models descriptive of the process by which information of varying reliability and relevance is combined into a unitary judgment. In oder to do so, it is necessary to be able to identify the cues available to the clinician. This is possible in the experimental situation, where the judge is provided with a specifiable set of cues on the basis of which he is to make his judgments. This procedure rules out the possibility that there were unidentified cues which may have influenced the judge to some unknown extent. The clinician may choose not to use some of the cues which are available to him; but this, then, is a problem of cue utilization, rather than cue availability.

Once the cue set can be specified, it is then possible to tackle the problem of cue utilization. Since there is an infinite number of ways of combining even two cues, there is an infinite number of possible strategies available to the judge for any specified cue set. The problem is to identify, out of that infinite set, the one that he used. It would seem that the simplest way to do that would be to ask the clinician for an account of what he did. Unfortunately, subjective accounts of the decision-making process are typically incomplete, unreliable, and inaccurate. The alternative is to use the judgments as the data from which to infer the strategy (model) that must have been used. One is then faced with the problem that there is an infinite number of models that will fit to any desired degree of accuracy. The optimum strategy seems to be one that combines the two approaches: one can use the judge's subjective reports as a basis for selecting the form of the model to be tried. That is, one can start with a model which, on rational grounds, seems representative of the situation.

In the present situation it seemed reasonable to assume that a diagnostician assigns to a duodenal ulcer, not further described, some prior probability of malignancy. There are some signs which, if present, will have the effect of either increasing or decreasing that prior probability. Furthermore, certain combinations of signs may cause revisions greater than could be accounted for by summing their independent contributions. This is the kind of situation that would be appropriately represented by an ANOVA model. In the real world situation, where signs are likely to become available one at a time, the process may be more obviously sequential than in the present experimental situation, where the cues were all made available to the judge at the same time. Even here, it seems likely that the diagnosticians probably used the cues sequentially, making a number of successive revisions before arriving at their final diagnostic judgment. The model itself is equally applicable whether the process is sequential or not.

On the other hand, it is erroneous to assume a parallelism between the model and the underlying cue utilization process of the judge solely on the basis of reasonableness or descriptive adequacy. As Hoffman (1960) has stressed with regard to multiple regression procedures, there are bound to be several subsets of terms which will lead to essentially the same degree of predictive accuracy if included in the regression function. Even though the inclusion of a particular term in the linear regression function may enhance the accuracy of estimate of the judgments, thereby providing what must in some sense be termed a "better fitting model," it does not necessary follow that the judge was, in fact, using that particular term at all, much less in the way stipulated by the model. It is for this reason that Hoffman termed his models "paramorphic."

With the above considerations in mind, it should be noted that the performance of the judges in this study was rather adequately accounted for in terms of linear effects, in spite of the fact that a deliberate attempt had been made to select a task in which persons would combine cues configurally. Although there were a substantial number of statistically significant interaction terms, and although judges sometimes differed in their configural use of symptom patterns, these effects accounted for a rather small proportion of the total variability of a judge's responses. This result is consistent with the findings of a large number of studies (see Hammond & Summers, 1965, for a list) in which data were fit quite well by a linear model.

While the validities of individual cues are a sufficient condition for the finding of linear effects, strong configural or interactive effects will be found only when the implication of a particular cue is radically different when associated with one pattern of other cues, rather than with another. In particular, the presence of Sign X might imply malignancy when Signs A, B, and C are present, whereas the *absence* of Sign X might imply malignancy when Signs A, B, and C are absent. For interactive effects to account for a substantial portion of the total predictable variance, such reversals would have to be the rule, rather than the exception. This seems highly unlikely within the framework of the present task, or for that matter, within the framework of most tasks familiar to human experience. What is more likely is that certain patterns augment or attenuate the importance of particular signs without reversing the implication. As the data from the present study show, these types of configurality can be well approximated by main effects (see also Yntema & Torgerson, 1961).

Nevertheless, one cannot completely discount the importance of inter-action effects, even when their contributions are as small as in the present study. Though the total amount of variance attributable to interactions may be small, the inclusion of those interaction terms may enhance diagnostic accuracy in several cases out of 100. If one considers the possibility that it is his ulcer that is being evaluated, it becomes clear that these terms should not be excluded simply because their overall effect may be small. In general, whenever the payoffs contingent upon accurate diagnosis are high, they will repay the effort involved in obtaining knowl-edge of even small effects.

Hopefully, the present study has demonstrated some of the advantages of the ANOVA model for describing the microstructure of judgment processes. Unfortunately, the applicability of the procedure is limited to those situations for which an experiment can be designed so that all cue patterns are orthogonally arranged within a factorial design. Therefore, ANOVA models will not be useful for analyzing judgments about many types of natural stimuli, unless these appear in sufficient number to allow an orthogonal subset to be selected for analysis. Furthermore, a complete crossing of all possible combinations of cues becomes an unmanageable task when the number of cues increases above a relatively small number, or when it is desirable to include many levels of each cue. However, if one is willing to assume that some of the higher order interactions are zero, then it is possible to evaluate the importance of the main effects and lower order interactions with a considerably reduced number of stimuli. For example, by eliminating the within cells replications of an n-way factorial design, one can study main effects and interactions up to the order $n - 1$. Alternately, one could construct stimuli by a fractional replication design (Cochran & Cox, 1957). In this method, the experimeter confounds those higher order interactions presumed to have negligible effects with main effects and lower order interactions. This is accom-plished by judiciously omitting certain of the stimulus combinations from the set of all possible patterns. For many judgment situations, the assumption that higher order interaction effects are negligible is probably a very reasonable one.

Another disadvantage of the ANOVA technique arises from the possibility that, by orthogonalizing a set of cues which are correlated in nature (and whose correlated properties are known and expected by the judge), one might alter the judge's conceptualization of the environment, causing him to alter his judgment model at the same time. Recent studies by Slovic (1966a) and Dudycha and Naylor (1966) have demonstrated such an effect for specific judgment tasks, and this potential source of bias must be considered by anyone contemplating use of the ANOVA technique. However, the magnitude of this problem can be diminished simply by telling the judge that he will be dealing with a selected, rather than a random, sample of cases, and that he might, therefore, expect a high proportion of unusual cases.

The substantive results of the study warrant brief comment. Perhaps the most striking result of the present study was the lack of agreement among diagnosticians who are presumably experts at the task to which they were assigned. The individual ANOVA models showed clearly that this disagreement was not random, but was attributable to underlying differences in cue utilization. Almost as surprising was the lack of reliability with which the judgments were made. In defense of the judges it might be noted that such a diagnosis would not ordinarily be made on the basis of the data used here. Their judgments based on other data may be more reliable. On the other hand, the signs or symptoms encountered in real life are invariably fallible, and unreliability in the symptoms would itself produce a component of unreliability in the diagnoses. But the present study emphasized an error free set of symptoms. Thus, the obtained estimates of reliability may be larger than those encountered in real situations. Finally, the experimental task imposed a degree of uniformity that would not otherwise exist. In real life, clinicians differ in their prior expectations of the validities of individual signs or symptoms. This often results in individual selectivity of signs and in diagnoses which are not therefore comparable. Thus, the degree of agreement among the experts of this study is in part due to the uniformity imposed by the task itself. Real world disagreement should be even more pronounced.

In any event, it seems quite likely that application of the ANOVA technique to the analysis of expertise, in this and other areas, might provide even the expert diagnostician with new insight into his inferential processes. It might also be a valuable teaching device that would enable trainees to see exactly how their inferential strategy differs from that of their expert model (e.g., see Todd & Hammond, 1965). Such analayses could lead to marked improvement in the quality of many kinds of complex inferences.

36. Impediments to accurate clinical judgment and possible ways to minimize their impact

Hal R. Arkes

The investigation of clinical judgment began in earnest in the 1950s due in large part to the "statistical versus clinical" controversy engendered by Meehl's 1954 book. The controversy was fueled by several studies which suggested that the reliability of clinicians' judgments was low (e.g., Goldberg & Werts, 1966; Little & Schneidman, 1959; Phelan, 1964; Wallach & Schooff, 1965). The purpose of this article is not to enter into that controversy but instead to analyze clinical judgment from the perspective of a cognitive psychologist. I have two goals in attempting this analysis: first, to point out several factors that make diagnosis such a difficult task, and second, to suggest ways in which improved diagnostic accuracy might be achieved.

Impediments

Covariation misestimation

The first impediment to high diagnostic accuracy is the inability to assess covariation accurately. Figure 36.1 depicts a prototypical situation. A clinician notes that some people have Symptom S while others do not. The clinician then attempts to determine if the presence of the symptom is diagnostic of some future outcome (e.g., psychotic episode). Research by Arkes and Harkness (1980a), Nisbett and Ross (1980), and Smedslund (1963) suggests that people base their assessment of covariation largely on the number of instances in Cell A. For example, Arkes, Harkness, and Biber (1980) showed subjects 12 pieces of evidence from Cell A, 6 from B, 6 from C, and 3 from D. Subjects estimated the relation between the row factor and column factor to be 54 on a 0–100 scale of contingency (0 = no relation, 100 = complete relation). However, the actual relation is zero, since the outcome is twice as likely to occur whether or not the symptom

This chapter originally appeared in the Journal of *Consulting and Clinical Psychology*, 1981, 49(3), 323–330. Copyright © 1981 by the American Psychological Association, Inc. Reprinted by permission.

Outcome

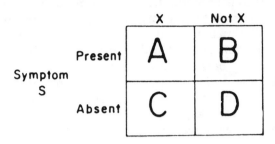

Figure 36.1. Prototypic diagnostic situation.

is present. It is the large magnitude of Cell A that apparently causes the badly biased estimate of contingency.

Consideration of information in the bottom row of Figure 36.1 is mandatory in order for a diagnostician to determine whether a symptom and disease are related. Yet, Arkes, Harkness, and Biber (1980) have shown that in the typical covariation estimation situation, such information is ignored. Augmenting the salience of instances in Cell B helped reduce the contingency to a more accurate level; increasing the salience of the information in Cell C had no effect, even though information in Cell C mathematically lowers the true contingency as much as the information in Cell B does. We believe that subjects perceived the information in Cell C to be completely irrelevant of contingency estimates (Meehl & Rosen, 1955).

Placing oneself in the role of a diagnostician may heighten the appreciation of how unimportant Cells C and D appear to be. Assume that you suspect that a certain MMPI (Minnesota Multiphasic Personality Inventory) profile is diagnostic of an impending psychotic break. To check this suspicion, you keep track of how many people with this profile do or do not have a subsequent psychotic episode. Would you also consider keeping track of those without that profile in order to test the hypothesis? Since the hypothesis deals only with people having a certain profile, disregarding those without it appears sensible. Yet those instances need to be recorded to test the hypothesis adequately. Therefore, increasing the utilization of such information will be one way to improve diagnostic accuracy. A way to accomplish this will be discussed later.

Preconceived notions

The second major impediment to accurate clinical judgment is the influence of preconceived notions or expectancies. The classic study in this area (Chapman & Chapman, 1967) is so famous that only a brief overview is needed. When drawings were randomly paired with personality traits presumably characteristic of the person who did the drawings, subjects fabricated illusory correlations between drawing features and personality traits. For example drawings containing large eyes were said by subjects to be frequently done by people who were said to be suspicious. Chapman and Chapman (1967) suggested that these false relations were due to a prior association between eyes and suspicion. This prior association warped the perception of incoming data so much that a positive correlation was seen even when the true relation between a drawing feature and a trait was negative.

Prior associations do not merely warp the perception of correlation; at a more basic level, they impede the accurate processing of an individual datum. Perhaps the most powerful example is by Shweder (1977), who reanalyzed data collected by Newcomb (1929). Newcomb had asked camp counselors to monitor and record the behavior of each camper every day. At the end of the 24-day camping session, the counselors were asked to recall the behaviors performed by each camper. The correlation between the initial recording of the behaviors and subsequent memory for the behaviors was −.27. In an attempt to explain this abysmal correlation in the 1929 data, Shweder asked undergraduates (almost a half century later) to fill out a simple questionnaire. Each question was of the form, "Assume that a boy is aggressive. How likely is it that he is also friendly?" Subjects were to answer on a 0–100 scale. By looking at answers to numerous questions such as this one, Shweder was able to tap the general "implicit personality theory" (Bruner & Tagiuri, 1954). Most people probably think that aggressive people are not likely to be friendly or charitable but are likely to be cold and self-centered. Shweder found that the various correlations between such traits were very highly related to the counselors' memories of the campers' behaviors. Shweder suggests that when a counselor tried to recall the behavior of camper Joey, the counselor might have recalled an incident such as Joey's inverting the oatmeal bowl over his friend's head. Recall of this behavior triggered the inference that Joey was also aggressive, cold, and self-centered but not friendly or charitable. The implicit personality theory thus guided the counselor's recall of Joey's behavior. This preconceived matrix of assumptions simply overwhelmed whatever the data might actually have been. This explains the enormous correlation of .84 between the implicit personality theory matrix of behavior and remembered camper behavior.

The influence of such preconceived ideas also influences the perception of current as opposed to remembered data. Lord, Ross, and Lepper (1979) found that proponents and opponents of capital punishment found arguments supporting their own viewpoints to be more convincing and probative than arguments against. Mahoney (1977) found the same type of bias among journal referees reviewing articles consistent with or opposed to their own theoretical persuasion. This research gains added importance when one realizes that clinicians' Q-sorts of clients stabilize after only two to four sessions (Meehl, 1960). It is quite likely that all subsequent data gleaned from the client will be biased by whatever opinions have been formed during this brief initial period. Data consistent with the tentative diagnosis will be given added credence; data inconsistent with the hypothesis will be disregarded. The fact that the initial hypothesis or diagnosis is merely tentative does not decrease its biasing influence (Ross, Lepper, Strack, & Steinmetz, 1977).

Lack of awareness

No matter what bias a diagnostician demonstrates, attempts to eliminate it would be fostered by awareness of one's own clinical judgment process. Research by Brehmer, Kuylenstierna, and Liljergren (1974), Oskamp (1967), and Summers, Taliaferro, and Fletcher (1970) suggests that we have negligible awareness of the factors that influence our judgment. For example, Summers et al. (1970) presented subjects with four economic indicators for each of several countries. Subjects were asked to use these cues to predict the future economic growth of each country. At the conclusion of the task, subjects were asked to report how much they used each of the four economic indicators in making their predictions. These self-reports of cue usage were not closely related to the actual extent of cue usage. In short, subjects were unaware of the impact each symptom had on their diagnosis (see also Nisbett & Wilson, 1977).

A study by Gauron and Dickinson (1966) makes the same point using a clinical judgment task. Clinicians asked for information previously collected from a client. As each category of information was received, the clinician announced a tentative diagnosis and the confidence level with which that diagnosis was held. Gauron and Dickinson deemed a piece of information to be important if that information either caused the clinician to switch to the final diagnosis or if it increased the confidence in the diagnosis that proved to be the final one. This measure of importance was not significantly related to the clinicians' own estimates of the importance of each piece of information. In other words, the clinicians had minimal awareness of which factors actually influenced their judgment.

Overconfidence

Another factor that impedes the improvement of clinical judgment is the serious overconfidence that diagnosticians have in their diagnoses. Oskamp (1965) has shown that providing a judge with more information increases his or her confidence in the decision without necessarily increasing the accuracy of the decision. Worse yet, Holsopple and Phelan (1954) have shown that the most confident diagnosticians tend to be the least accurate.

Numerous factors undoubtedly contribute to this overconfidence. Einhorn and Hogarth (1978) demonstrated that treatment effects are one such factor. To use one of their examples, suppose a granting agency wishes to check the validity of their own granting procedures. It checks the quantity and quality of the research it has funded. If the proportion of satisfactory research projects among those funded is high, the agency might conclude that the judgmental procedures used to decide among the grant applicants were excellent. However, funding of a grant request enables a researcher to buy equipment, hire assistants, and do other things that enable him or her to perform successful research. Even if the agency's judgment procedures were woefully inadequate, most of its funded applicants might have successful research programs due to the benefits derived from receiving the grant. This high proportion of successes might be interpreted by the agency as a validation of their procedures, thereby instilling overconfidence in those procedures. Note that a similar problem can occur whenever there is a placebo effect. As long as a group or individual improves in performance for any reason, the therapist or experimenter administering the treatment may attribute the improvement to the treatment. This Hawthorne effect scenario, probably relatively common in psychological situations, would lead to over-confidence in the treatment.

Snyder (1981) has demonstrated that people selectively seek evidence that confirms the hypothesis currently under consideration. Such biased information gathering will lend support to the hypothesis. For example, when testing the hypothesis that a person is an introvert, questions such as "What factors make it hard for you to really open up to people?" are asked. When testing the hypothesis that a person is an extravert, questions like "In what situations are you most talkative?" are more probable. Those questions generate answers that will in turn lead to overconfidence in the current hypothesis. Similarly, Koriat, Lichtenstein, and Fischhoff (1980) presented evidence that people disregard evidence that contradicts their current judgment. Given selective seeking of confirmatory evidence and selective censoring of disconfirmatory evidence, a hypothesis simply cannot fail to be well substantiated. Such a hypothesis is very unlikely to be modified or discarded.

Hindsight bias

There is always enough evidence in a rich source of data to nurture all but the most outlandish diagnosis. This impediment to optimal judgment is manifested in the hindsight bias, which was systematically investigated first by Fischhoff (1975). Fischhoff asked one group of subjects, the fore-sight group, to read psychotherapy case histories and then judge the likelihood of four possible circumstances that may have followed therapy. One hindsight group was shown the case history and then was told that a certain outcome, A, occurred. The group was then asked whether they would have been able to predict the occurrence of A had they been asked to do so. These hindsight subjects assigned probabilities to Event A that were 49% higher than the probability assigned to A by the foresight group. Thus, the occurrence of A was obvious only in hindsight. Other hindsight subjects were told that Event B actually occurred. These subjects claimed that B would have been relatively easy for them to predict. Of course, the foresight group, not having outcome knowledge, did not consider B to be a likely outcome. Arkes, Wortmann, Saville, and Harkness (1981) have found this same effect in the area of medical diagnosis. The foresight group was shown an actual case history and was asked to assign probabilities to four possible diagnoses. Each of four hindsight groups was told that a different one of the four diagnoses was true. The hindsight groups then assigned probabilities to each of the four diagnoses. Even in the area of medical diagnosis, presumably where the symptom–disease relation is more exact than in psychology, the hindsight bias emerged. Given enough data, many diagnoses can appear obvious.

Possible debiasing techniques

One technique that has proven to be absolutely worthless is telling people what a particular bias is and then telling them not to be influenced by it (Fischhoff, 1977: Kurtz & Garfield, 1978; Wood, 1978). If people truly do have limited awareness of the factors that influence their judgments, exhortations to increase or decrease the impact of these factors may be dommed to ineffectiveness.

Chapman and Chapman (1967) attempted to reduce the illusory correlations reported by their subjects by creating a negative correlation between the symptoms and diagnoses that prior subjects had perceived to be positively correlated. This debiasing technique was not very successful: The illusory correlation was reduced but not eliminated. Also, it is not possible to rearrange correlations in the real world to promote the debiasing of diagnosticians; therefore, this debiasing technique is not practical.

Consider alternatives

A debiasing technique that has shown some success has been demonstrated by Slovic and Fischhoff (1977). In an effort to reduce the hindsight bias, Slovic and Fischhoff asked hindsight subjects to explain why Outcome A might have been expected from the prior events and how alternative Outcome B might be explained had it occurred instead of A. Being forced to consider B reduced (but did not completely eliminate) the hindsight bias toward A. Using a similar technique, Koriat et al.

(1980) presented people with two-alternative questions and asked them to list reasons for and against each of the two possible options. Only then could the subjects choose one of the answers and state their confidence in the correctness of their choice. This procedure produced a marked improvement in confidence ratings compared to the ratings given by control subjects.

Research by Ross et al. (1977) helps us to understand the relative effectiveness of the Slovic and Fischhoff (1977) and Koriat et al. (1980) debiasing techniques. Ross et al. showed that given a body of prior events, any purported outcome that a subject is asked to explain is perceived by the subject as more likely to occur. This effect takes place even if the subject knows the outcome to be explained is merely hypothetical. Thus, when Slovic and Fischhoff (1977) asked a subject to concoct a scenario for both purported Outcome A and hypothetical Outcome B, the authors were really using the Ross et al. bias on B to offset the hindsight bias on A. As a result, the hindsight bias was reduced. Similarly, when Koriat et al. (1980) asked their subjects to list reasons against the option that was eventually not chosen, overconfidence was largely eliminated.

Considering alternatives may be an effective means of reducing unwarranted overconfidence in a number of contexts divorced from the hindsight situation. Problem solvers from Benjamin Franklin to Wayne Wickelgren (1974) have suggested that decision making is improved if one ensures that all alternatives are given substantial consideration. Consistent with this, Elstein, Shulman, and Sprafka (1978) have found that the most accurate diagnosticians tend to arrive at their final diagnosis later than do less accurate diagnosticians. Premature closure results in the biased processing of subsequent data. Perhaps the most dramatic example of this may be found in a series of studies by Dailey (1952). Subjects were first asked to read an autobiography of a person and then were asked to predict how that person would have answered each item on a personality inventory. The criterion was how the writer of the autobiography actually did respond to each inventory item. Dailey had some subjects make some predictions after reading half of the autobiography and the rest of the predictions at the end. A second group made all of their predictions at the end. Dailey found that the latter group performed significantly better on the questions both groups answered at the end. Presumably, asking some subjects to predict in the middle forced the formulation of premature hypotheses. The final half of the data were then biased by these hypotheses based on inadequate data. This interpretation is supported by the results of a second experiment. Merely having subjects pause halfway through the autobiography to think about the data resulted in inferior performance on the final predictions. From data such as these, it would appear that one way to improve accuracy and reduce bias would be to entertain alternative hypotheses for a long period of time. As Slovic and Fischhoff (1977) have shown, active consideration of such hypotheses may be particularly beneficial in combating bias.

Think Bayesian

To improve judgment by increasing the impact of usually ignored information, some researchers (e.g., Galen & Gambino, 1975; Lusted, 1968; Schwartz, Gorry, Kassirer, & Essig, 1973) have presented what amounts to a tutorial in Bayesian statistics. This example, taken from Schwartz et al., demonstrates diagnosticians' need for some statistical guidance:

A total of 290 subjects were asked to assume that a test for cancer was available that has the following characteristics: (1) The test is positive in 95 of 100 patients with cancer. (2) The test is negative in 95 of 100 patients without cancer. They were also asked to assume that, on the average, 5 people in a population of 1,000 have previously undetected cancer.

The problem posed was as follows: if the test described is given to a randomly selected patient from this population and the test is positive, what is the probability that the patient actually has cancer? (1973, p. 467)

The great majority of the subjects (medical students and physicians) answered with values of 50% or greater. The correct answer is 9%. A Bayesian analysis will help us discover why this typical diagnostic problem is so difficult.

Bayes's theorem enables one to examine the impact of information on a hypothesis or diagnosis. The prior odds are expressed as a ratio of the likelihood of the hypothesis being true divided by the likelihood of the hypothesis being not true, or $p(H)/p(\bar{H})$. If a piece of information is now obtained (e.g., a test score), these prior odds must be modified in light of this information. The prior odds are multiplied by the likelihood ratio. This ratio is simply the probability of obtaining that piece of datum if the hypothesis were true divided by the probability of obtaining the datum if the hypothesis were false, or $p(DIH)/p(DI\bar{H})$. When the prior odds are multiplied by the likelihood ratio, we obtain the posterior odds. This final product is the probability that the hypothesis is true given this piece of information divided by the probability that the hypothesis is not true given this piece of information, or $p(HID)/p(\bar{H}ID)$. The whole formula is

$$\frac{p(HID)}{p(\bar{H}ID)} = \frac{p(DIH)}{p(DI\bar{H})} \times \frac{p(H)}{p(\bar{H})}$$

Let us examine the example presented by Schwartz et al. The prior odds of having cancer are

$$\frac{p(H_c)}{p(\bar{H}_c)} = \frac{5}{995},$$

since 5 out of every 1000 people have the disease. These are the odds before any test information is obtained. The likelihood ratio is

$$\frac{p(DIH_c)}{p(DI\overline{H}_c)} = \frac{95}{5},$$

since a positive test result is obtained 95% of the time when cancer is present and 5% of the time when cancer is absent. The posterior odds are

$$\frac{p(H_cID)}{p(\overline{H}_cID)} = \frac{95}{5} \times \frac{5}{995} = \frac{475}{4975}.$$

Since this fraction is an expression of odds, it means that out of every 5450 positive tests results, 475 will be from a patient with cancer, and 4,975 will be from a patient without cancer. The probability that a positive test is from a patient with cancer is

$$\frac{475}{475 + 4975} = 9\%.$$

The physicians who grossly overestimated the probability of cancer were probably impressed by the wonderfully high diagnosticity of the test for cancer: Fully 95% of those who tested positively had the disease. Diagnosticity is reflected in the likelihood ration of 95/5. The gross overestimation by the physicians ignores the prior odds, which are a reflection of the base rate, the proportion of the population having cancer. Abundant evidence in the judgment (Kahneman & Tversky, 1973) and social psychology (Nisbett & Borgida, 1975) literatures indicates that base rates are grievously underutilized in many instances. If there were some way to get diagnosticians to attend more to the prior odds, immense improvement in diagnostic accuracy would be achieved. One way to achieve this is by asking diagnosticians to pit the prior odds and likelihood ratio against each other. An example will illustrate this technique.

Following the reported diagnosis of a patient at a mental institution as a multiple personality, I asked a class of graduate students what the probability would be of a true multiple personality at that institution. The class settled on 1 out of 100,000. The prior odds are thus:

$$\frac{p(Hmp)}{p(\overline{H}mp)} = \frac{1}{99,999}.$$

I then asked the class to imagine the type of testing and interviewing that had gone on at the institution in the diagnostic process. I told them to imagine the type of responses a person with multiple personalities might have made. Finally, I instructed the class to divide the probability that a multiple personality would provide those data by the probability that a nonmultiple personality would provide those data. The class settled on 100 to 1. The likelihood ratio is thus:

$$\frac{p(\text{DIHmp})}{p(\text{DI}\overline{\text{H}}\text{mp})} = \frac{100}{1}.$$

Thus, the posterior odds are

$$\frac{p(\text{HmpID})}{p(\overline{\text{H}}\text{mpID})} = \frac{100}{1} \times \frac{1}{99,999} = \frac{100}{99,999}.$$

The probability that the diagnosis of multiple personality was correct was a paltry .1%. In order for the probability of being correct to have exceeded 50%, the likelihood ratio would have to have exceeded 99,999/1. There are two crucial rules to be gleaned from this. First, if the prior odds are x/y, the likelihood ratio must be larger than y/x in order for the hypothesis to be correct more than 50% of the time. Since no student was convinced that any group of psychological tests could have provided data that overwhelming, all students agreed that the diagnosis of multiple personality was probably not correct.

The second rule to be learned from this example is that the more unlikely the hypothesis, that is, the lower the prior odds are, the greater the likelihood ratio must be to justify that hypothesis. For example, if the prior odds are $\frac{1}{2}$, a likelihood ratio of 4/1 makes the hypothesis likely ($p = .67$). If the prior odds are 1/100, the same likelihood ratio still leaves the hypothesis in the longshot category ($p = .04$).

As long as the posterior odds are viewed as a contest between the prior odds and the likelihood ratio, the base rate cannot be ignored: This will lead to much more accurate assessment of covariation. Note also that this technique requires that attention be paid to $p(\text{DI}\overline{\text{H}})$, the denominator of the likelihood ratio. This is precisely the data that Arkes et al. (1980) found were disregarded by their subjects, leading to poor judgmental performance.

Decrease reliance on memory

A final strategy to increase judgmental accuracy is predicated on the fallibility of recall: Try to decrease reliance on memory. Arkes and Harkness (1980b) found that unpresented symptoms consistent with a diagnosis tended to be remembered as having been presented. Under some circumstances, previously presented symptoms inconsistent with the diagnosis were not remembered as having been presented. Both types of memory errors would lead to overconfidence in the diagnosis. Without access to a list of those symptoms that actually did not did not occur, one tends to remember the facts supportive of the hypothesis under consideration and to forget the facts inconsistent with the hypothesis.

Another cost of relying on memory rather than records is discussed by Ward and Jenkins (1965). Estimates of covariation were grossly incorrect when the individual pieces of datum were presented one at a time. When box-score summaries were presented based on the four categories of Figure 36.1, the estimates were much more accurate. The box scores impose no memory load, since all past instances are represented in the summary (Shaklee & Mims, 1980).

A third way in which excessive reliance on memory may lead to poorer clinical judgment was recently discovered by Lueger and Petzel (1979). Using the Chapman and Chapman (1967) task, Lueger and Petzel found that the illusory correlation became more pronounced when greater amounts of information had to be processed by the subjects. It is important to note that in all three of these examples, memory losses did not merely result in less information with which to make a judgment. Memory loss resulted in more biased judgment. Hopefully a more humble view of one's own memory will result in less of a need to be humble about the accuracy of one's judgment.

37. Discretionary aspects of jury decision making

John C. Mowen and Darwyn E. Linder

Discretion is defined as the power of free decision, individual judgment, and undirected choice (Merriam-Webster, 1961). As applied to the criminal justice system, it refers to areas of choice in which a criminal justice official is able to make a decision dictated by his or her own judgment and conscience (Black, 1968). While the decision is made within the confines of rules and principles of law, the discretionary judgment involves the application of the individual's own beliefs, attitudes, and personal perception of the situation and circumstances.

Even though writers such as Shaver, Gilbert, and Williams (1975) have discussed the use of discretion in the criminal justice system from the perspective of the police, prosecution, courts, and corrections, little attention has been given to an analysis of jury discretion. At first glance the role of discretion in jury decision-making may seem minimal. After all, the role of the jury in America is to determine the facts and apply the law to them. However, the fact-finding process itself involves the use of discretion in determining the credibility of a witness. In addition, the psychological integration of facts into weight of evidence against the defendant involves the interpretation of the importance of various pieces of evidence. Finally, the jury has the inherent power to ignore and nullify laws. In the general verdict of guilty or not guilty, the jury does not have to give reasons or explanations for the finding. Such a power to abrogate laws, though controversial, represents jury discretion at its maximum. The jury, then, has choice in several aspects of the decision-making process, from the nullification of laws to the interpretation of the relative importance of the evidence in the case.

This chapter originally appeared in Abt, L. E., and Stuart, I. R. (Eds.). *Social psychology and discretionary law* (pp. 219–239). New York: Van Nostrand Reinhold, 1979. Copyright © 1979 by Litton Educational Publishing, Inc. Reprinted by permission.

In this chapter we propose that two theories, when utilized together, account for the general jury decision-making process. Discretion in jury decision-making is represented in the theories by components that allow for the influence of attitudes, beliefs, and situational factors in the decision. We will first present the Theory of Signal Detection as a model within which the final jury decision may be analyzed. The model, however, fails to account for how the jury determines the total amount of evidence against the defendant. Information integration theory was developed to explain the process of combining disparate pieces of information to arrive at a judgment and is, we argue, well suited to fill this explanatory gap. Jury decision-making, as well as discretion, is discussed in terms of each model, and an empirical study is presented that provides support for the application of the Theory of Signal Detection to jury decision-making.

In this chapter it will be assumed that the jury functions much as a single individual. Therefore, the same factors that have been shown to influence an individual will be assumed to influence a group. Such an assumption has been made previously (e.g., Fried, Kaplan, & Klein, 1975) and is an important step in simplifying and bringing into investigatory focus a complex process. In addition, previous research has shown that mock jury decisions can be predicted with good accuracy from the preliminary decisions of the individual jurors (Bray, 1974; Davis, Kerr, Atkin, Holt, & Meek, 1975). Thus we believe that the ecological validity of the model will not be severely tarnished by our concentration upon the factors influencing individual decisions.

The Theory of Signal Detection

The Theory of Signal Detection (TSD) evolved from statistical decision theory and psychophysics; its lineage can be traced from Blackwell to Thurstone to Fechner (Swets, 1973). An important catalyst to its development was the need to understand the process of detecting electromagnetic signals; for example, how can one explain the decrement in performance of radar operators attempting over long periods of time to locate a signal (enemy aircraft) amid the noise (clouds, etc.) appearing on the radar scope?

A two-component model, TSD views the precision of the observer in distinguishing signal from noise (d') as independent of the observer's criterion or bias (B) in reporting the presence or absence of a signal. An observer's sensitivity is related to his general ability to discriminate the "blip" of the aircraft from various false readings on the scope. The observer's criterion represents the amount of certainty which he must have in order to indicate that the "blip" is a signal. The presence of the criterion biasing a decision is exemplified by the radar operator who will tend, when uncertain, to state that a "blip" is a signal in order to avoid

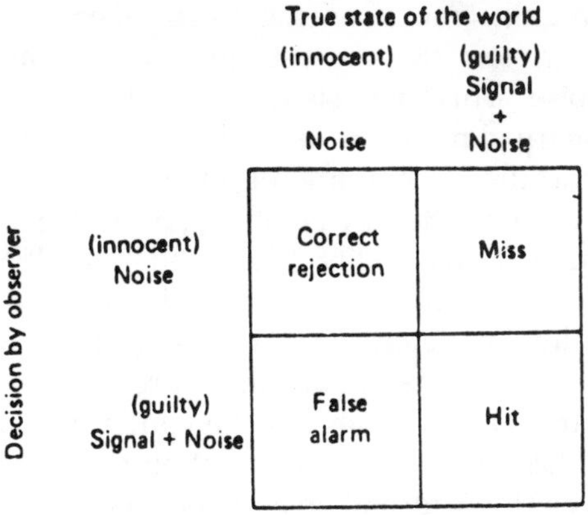

True state of the world

(innocent)   (guilty)
                    Signal
                    +
Noise   Noise

		Noise	Signal + Noise
(innocent) Noise		Correct rejection	Miss
(guilty) Signal + Noise		False alarm	Hit

Decision by observer

Figure 37.1. The 2 × 2 response matrix utilized in the Theory of Signal Detection to analyze the decisions of observers.

letting an enemy aircraft pass undetected. The theory assumes that observers make mistakes and that the judgmental factors of the perceived prior probability of a signal and of the relative rewards and costs of making certain types of mistakes influence the type of error made. The error of stating that a signal occurred when it was absent is called a "false alarm," while the error of stating that no signal occurred when it was present is called a "miss." Correct responses are labeled either a "hit" or a "correct rejection," giving the 2 × 2 response matrix presented in Figure 37.1. When certain assumptions are met, d' is independent of B. Thus manipulations of the a priori probability of a signal, or of the response payoff matrix, have been found to affect B while leaving d' constant.

Swets (1973) has described succinctly the history, computational procedures, and applications of TSD. He noted that TSD has been successfully applied to the study of vigilance, perceptual defense, recognition memory, attention, learning, personality, speech, and other topics. In each case an organism attempts to detect a stimulus under circumstances where the signal probability or the benefits and costs of the stimulus-response outcomes may influence the decision to report a stimulus as either a signal or a noise.

TSD and jury decision-making

We propose that the tasks facing a juror and a radar operator are conceptually similar. Each makes a binary decision under uncertainty. While the radarman must determine if a "blip" indicates an enemy aircraft or only a cloud, a juror must decide if the amount of evidence presented by the prosecution is sufficient to indicate the defendant's guilt. The juror utilizes the underlying continuum of "evidence against the defendant" to detect guilt, much as the radar operator uses the amount and quality of light on the radar scope to determine if the stimulus was signal or noise. This analysis assumes that a defendant's "guiltiness" lies on a unitary dimension labeled "evidence against the defendant." The idea that the dichotomy of guilt and innocence is artificial has previously been submitted by Feinberg (1972). He suggested, for pedagogical purposes, that the ability to defend oneself is a continuum and that factors such as an alibi, a good lawyer, and so on, generate a differential ability to defend. Feinberg's analysis, however, would lead one to conclude that a defendant must prove his innocence. To avoid this misconception, we have labeled the continuum "evidence against the defendant," indicating that the prosecution must prove guilt.

We have, then, a relatively tight formal analogy between TSD and jury decision-making. A juror (observer) is confronted by a trial (the stimulus) that can vary from a small amount of evidence against the defendant (only noise present) to a very great amount of evidence (an unmistakable enemy plane "blip"), and must decide whether the defendant is innocent or guilty.

Factors affecting a jury's criterion for guilt

If the isomorphism between TSD and jury decision-making exists, factors affecting a jury's criterion and sensitivity should be identifiable. In fact, the trial seems structured to ensure that the jury sets a high criterion for finding guilt. When the guilt threshold is set very high, an increased amount of evidence is required to convict, resulting in a lower probability of conviction. If the observer in Figure 37.1. makes many fewer "guilty" decisions, the number of false alarms will be reduced, but so will the number of hits, while both correct rejections (an innocent person found not guilty) and misses (a guilty person set free) will increase. One principal way of setting the criterion is through reasonable doubt instruction. As shown by Kerr, Atkin, Stasser, Meek, Holt, and Davis (1976), if the instruction sets a lax standard for guilt (i.e., criterion is set low), an increased number of guilty verdicts results. Conversely, setting severe standards for guilt results in a lower number of guilty verdicts. [In the Kerr et al. study, the lax criterion was that "a reasonable doubt must be a substantial one," and the stringent criterion was that "essentially any doubt about the defendant's guilt qualified as a reasonable one" (p. 285)]. In TSD terminology, setting a high criterion for guilt decreases the probability that an innocent person will be found guilty (a false alarm).

Note that the bias in the American jury system to avoid the false alarm differs from that of the radarman. Our judicial system abhors making a false alarm, while for the radar operator it only scrambles the jet interceptors with time and money lost. Conversely, a miss for the radarman results in potential catastrophe with an enemy plane undetected, and for the jury results in freeing a guilty individual. Such variations in criteria are based upon the differential reward-cost structure operating in the two situations. For the jury, the cost of convicting an innocent person is higher than the cost of letting a guilty person go free. Conversely, the cost of scrambling the jets is low for the radarman, while the cost of missing an enemy plane is high.

Manipulation of the 2×2 payoff matrix affects the jury's criterion in additional ways. The perceived severity of the sentence that the defendant will receive if found guilty may affect the criterion. For example, much more evidence may be required to convict if the death penalty rather than life imprisonment results from a guilty verdict. The death penalty is, of course, assumed to increase the cost of false alarms. The heinousness of the crime may work conversely, however. Hendrick and Shaffer (no date) found that a heinous crime increases the probability that a jury will find the defendant guilty. Such a crime may cause the costs of a miss to be perceived as highly noxious, thereby lowering the criterion for guilt. The relative impact of a conviction on the defendant may also affect the costs of either type of error. For example, the cost of convicting an individual with a job and family may be greater than for an individual without such socially approved responsibilities. Another case was the requirement to find the "smoking gun" in order to impeach Richard Nixon. The costs to the defendant and potentially to the United States of impeaching a President were so great that no evidence short of a "smoking gun" would suffice to find guilt.

Another factor that can affect the placement of the criterion is the prior probability of a signal's occurring, and several variables may operate similarly in the courtroom. Pretrial publicity may act to create an a priori expectation of the defendant's guilt (see Hoiberg & Stires, 1973). The use of character witnesses seems directed at convincing the jury that, despite the evidence, the likelihood that the defendant committed the crime is low. The physical attractiveness of the defendant may act similarly to create an expectation among jurors that a particularly attractive individual would not have resorted to crime (Sigall & Ostrove, 1975; Landy & Aronson, 1969; Reynolds & Sanders, 1973). Finally, the prior probability of a previously convicted offender committing a second crime will probably be perceived as greater than the probabililty of an individual committing his first offense, resulting in a greater likelihood for conviction because a lower criterion is set (see Doob, 1976).

Factors affecting a jury's sensitivity

Factors affecting a jury's ability to detect a guilty individual also exist in the courtroom. The trend to allow jurors to take notes and for juries to request information while deliberating is clearly related to increasing sensitivity. The method and quality of the presentation of the respective cases by the prosecution and defense attorneys can also affect sensitivity. The adversary system of American courtroom procedure is a method of ensuring a high-quality presentation of the prosecution and defense cases. Also of critical importance is the quality of the police investigation. A sloppy investigation will result in a lack of evidence or evidence of poor reliability, which can be harmful to both defense and prosecution cases. The ability of the judge to control the courtroom and to ensure the proper execution of the trial proceedings can also affect the sensitivity of the jury. Finally, studies investigating the impact of varying the order of the testimony (e.g., Walker, Thibaut, & Andreoli, 1972) may identify factors influencing the sensitivity of the simulated jury.

Note that all of the above factors are external to the jury. An appropriate analogy is a comparison of the sensitivity of the radar operator who must work with a vintage 1950 radar and an operator working with a 1970 radar. Because of superior equipment, the latter operator will be more sensitive in distinguishing signal from noise. Similarly, properly presented cases, good police investigation, and proper handling of the courtroom by the judge increase the resolution of the process of presenting the evidence of the case. However, factors internal to the jury may also affect sensitivity. The intelligence of the individual panel members, the mix of dominant and submissive individuals, and perhaps the mix of personality types can influence the jury's ability to distinguish signal from noise.

The importance of analyzing jury decision-making in terms of TSD can be demonstrated by the following example. Suppose court officials decided that their goal was to maximize the percentage of correct judgments made by juries. To do this, they could try to have each jury set a criterion that placed equal importance on avoiding either a false alarm or a miss. This procedure, however, would result in an increase in the number of innocent individuals found guilty. Paradoxically, then, if criminal justice officials decided that the percentage of correct responses should be increased by eliminating, to the extent possible, the discretionary aspects of jury decision-making, the probability of false alarms (convictions of innocent persons) occurring would increase. To satisfy their goal, officials must ensure that the criterion remains fixed while the sensitivity of the process is increased.

Figure 37.2 may help to clarify this example. The two matrices are composed of hypothetical innocent and guilty verdicts crossed by the hypothetical true state of the world. In matrix A note that the number of false alarms is very low and that the number of misses is quite high. When the calculations are made of sensitivity (d') and bias (B) (see Hochhaus, 1972), one finds that $d' = 1.70$ ($d' = 0$ if the matrix is random) and that the criterion is set at 3.31, revealing a bias to avoid finding an innocent person guilty ($B = 1$ if no such bias existed). In matrix B note that the number of false alarms and the number of misses are equal,

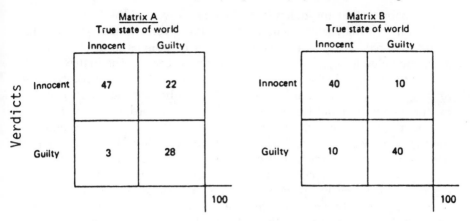

Figure 37.2. Frequencies of verdicts in the 2 × 2 response matrix. Matrix A reveals a criterion set to avoid a false alarm. Matrix B reveals a criterion set to maximize the proportion correct.

indicating that $B = 1$, and that no bias exists to avoid either type of error. The sensitivity is equal to 1.68, indicating the same ability to discriminate noise from signal + noise as in matrix A. Also, note that the percentage correct has increased from 75 percent in matrix A to 80 percent in matrix B. The point of the example is that, in moving the criterion, the sensitivity remained essentially unchanged, the proportion of correct responses increased from 75 percent to 80 percent, and the probability of finding an innocent person guilty increased from 6 percent to 20 percent. Thus, moving the criterion to a point at which the types of errors are balanced increases the probability of finding an innocent person guilty, while increasing the overall proportion of correct verdicts. Such an example reveals the importance of conceptualizing jury decision-making in the form of a two-component process. Increases in the total percentage correct can result from either increasing sensitivity or changing the criterion so that the two types of errors are equally weighted. Because the bias to avoid convicting innocent persons is essential to the American system of justice, gains in accuracy must be achieved by increasing the sensitivity of the process, which is not necessarily measured by increases in the percentage of correct verdicts.

Two alternative models resembling TSD

Prior to the discussion of the application of information integration theory to determining the weight of the evidence, two conceptual models bearing some similarity to TSD should be mentioned. Fried, Kaplan, and Klein (1975) introduced a decision theory model that resembles TSD. Their approach assumes that a juror determines a verdict by calculating the probability that the defendant is guilty as well as the "... values or utilities for voting for conviction or acquittal given the true states of the world" (p. 58). Within the model a matrix of utilities is developed that gives the value for each of the four decision outcomes. The matrix is quite similar to the one developed in Figure 37.1. The utilities are combined to form a criterion or standard of reasonable doubt that must be surpassed by the perception of the probability of guilt in order to convict. The probability of guilt is determined by assessing the evidence presented in the trial and closely approximates the concept in the TSD formulation of determining the weight of the evidence against the defendant. The formation of a decision criterion by assessing the matrix of utilities for outcomes also closely approximates the process of setting the decision threshold in TSD by analyzing the reward-cost outcome matrix. Thus the Fried et al. model resembles the TSD formulation in these two important respects. Their model, however, does not contain a parameter relevant to the sensitivity or accuracy of jurors in decision-making, nor does the model utilize the jurors' view of the prior probability of guilt in explaining jury decision-making. In summary, the decision theory model of Fried, et al. contains components strongly resembling those of TSD, but offers a less differentiated view of jury decision-making.

A second model similar to the TSD approach was developed by Thomas and Hogue (1976). As in TSD, the model assumes that jurors calculate an apparent weight of the evidence and that a decision criterion exists which the weight of the evidence must surpass in order to convict. As structured, the model, with but one exception, can account for all of the influences on jury decision-making with which TSD deals. The model is unable to develop an index of juror sensitivity. The approach, though, has strength in that with some simplifying assumptions, it can empirically identify movements in a juror's criterion. Thus while lacking the overall explanatory ability of TSD, the model developed by Thomas and Hogue can be empirically tested in a trial setting in a more stringent manner than can currently be done with TSD.

Determining the weight of the evidence

The Theory of Signal Detection gives promise of adequately explaining the factors influencing the final binary decision of the jury. However, one component of the decision task which the jury faces diverges substantially from that encountered by the radio operator. To determine the amount of evidence against the defendant, the jury must intergrate a complex set of stimuli presented over a period of days or even weeks. Conversely, the radar operator in a brief period of time, lasting only a few seconds, must determine the intensity of the signal. TSD, then, provides only a partial explanation of jury decision-making. Another theoretical model is required to explain how the jury determines the weight of the evidence against the defendant.

In order to determine the weight of evidence, the jury must integrate the information provided by the witnesses and by the quality and force of the lawyer's arguments. In other words, the amount of evidence is a total of all of the evidence presented during the trial for and against the defendant. Information integration theory (Anderson, 1971) explicitly addresses the question of how individuals or groups combine information in order to reach a decision. We propose that in order to determine the amount of evidence against the defendant, the jury utilizes an information integration process. Only after the jury determines the weight of the evidence is TSD utilized to reach the final decision.

Information integration theory

Norman Anderson and his colleagues have applied information integration theory to an astonishing variety of areas over the past 15 years, in experimental as well as social psychology. Theoretical formulations to which integration theory has been applied in social psychology include judgments of motivation and ability, moral judgments, attitudes and opinions, impression formation, and group decision-making. Integration theory has even been applied to jury decision-making (Kaplan & Kemmerick, 1974).

Based on a simple but highly flexible algebraic judgment model, integration theory distinguishes between the scale value and weight of a piece of information and then describes alternative methods of how the pieces are integrated into a judgment. The scale value(s) of an informational stimulus refers to its location on a judgmental dimension. For example, the scale value of a highly attractive individual would be 8 or 9 on a scale of attractiveness with 10 as the very attractive boundary. The weight (w) of an informational stimulus refers to its psychological importance in the final decision. In other words, in the overall judgment the weight indicates how much a particular scale value counts.

The basic theoretical model (Anderson, 1971) is:

$$R = C + \Sigma W_i S_i$$

In the equation, R is an overt response on a scale, C is a scaling factor to allow for an arbitrary zero point, W is the weight, and S is the scale value. The first term of this summational model, $W_0 S_0$, is the initial attitude or opinion of the individual prior to receiving the informational stimuli. In an attitude change experiment, S_0 can be conceived of as the target person's initial position, and W_0 represents his personality characteristics, persuasibility, strength of opinion, and so on. The quantity S_i gives the scale values of the communications, and W_i gives the importance of each communication in the final judgment. The weight of each communication is influenced by such factors as the communicator's status, reliability, and expertise.

Anderson (1971) specified several basic integration rules. One stated that "... the total effect of a communication to be the product of its weight and value" (p. 175). A second rule specified that when two communications are combined, they follow some form of an averaging rule.

Integration theory and determining the weight of evidence

If the task of determining the weight of evidence in a jury trial is viewed as analogous to an impression formation task, information integration theory is directly applicable. In impression formation tasks, the subject is provided information, often in the form of a series of adjective traits. It is hypothesized that each piece of information is given a scale value and a weight and then combined with other information to yield a value on a unitary trait dimension. The jury is faced with a similar task. Information is given in the form of witness testimony and of the attorneys' arguments. In processing the information, the jury assigns a scale value and a weight to the testimony of each witness and integrates the information, probably via an averaging process, to obtain a stimulus value on the unitary dimension of evidence against the defendant. The averaging model, in which each piece of evidence has different scale value and weight, is presented in the simple algebraic expression below:

$$E = \frac{W_0 S_0 + \Sigma W_e S_e}{W_0 + \Sigma W_e}$$

The quantity E is the judgment of the amount of evidence, S_0 is the preexisting scale value of the impression of the evidence, S_e are the scale values assigned to the pieces of evidence, and W_0 and W_e are the respective weights.

The scale value of the testimony of a witness represents the extent to which the information given is indicative of guilt. For example, in a murder case if a witness testifies that he saw the defendant pull the trigger of the pistol and saw the victim fall from the impact of the bullet, the scale value of this evidence will be very high. However, the importance of this information in the final judgment is determined by the weight assigned to it. The characteristics of the source of information are, in theory, independent of the content of the information, and such source characteristics function to weight the evidence provided. If the source person was a known liar, turned state's evidence to avoid prosecution, or was nearly blind, and so forth, his credibility would be low and his information would be given little weight. Another example of a factor influencing the weighting of evidence occurs when inadmissible evidence is presented in the courtroom. In asking the jury to disregard the testimony, the judge may be viewed as telling the jury to assign it a weight of zero so that it will not influence their final judgment.

The jurors may also have an initial opinion regarding the guilt of the defendant. Such an initial opinion will enter the final judgment and have a scale value and weight. For example, pretrial publicity will result in jurors' having formed some opinion of the defendant's guilt. Another factor which may influence a juror's initial opinion is the fact that the defendant was brought to trial. Jurors are aware that prosecutors will not bring a person to trial unless good evidence of guilt exists. The judicial instructions to presume the defendant innocent may be viewed as an attempt to influence the weighting of the scale value for this piece of evidence.

Discretion in jury decision-making

A model of jury decision-making has been proposed in which evidence or information is first integrated into a judgment of the amount of evidence against the defendant. The final binary decision is made by comparing this judgment to the amount of evidence necessary to convict, in a manner proposed by the theory of signal detection. From this general model the discretionary components of jury decision-making may be derived. Because the model of decision-making proposed consists of two components, sources of discretion are viewed as occurring in both the integration phase and in the binary decision phase.

Discretion in determining the weight of the evidence

The process of determining the amount of evidence against the defendant was hypothesized to consist of the jury's assigning a scale value and a weight to the information provided by each witness and lawyer. In such a judgmental process, we propose that determining the scale values of each piece of testimony is relatively impervious to the influence of an individual's own beliefs, attitudes, and idiosyncracies, and thus relatively free of influence of discretionary processes. We do propose, however, that the process of weighting of information is influenced by discretionary forces. The factors previously hypothesized to influence the weighting of information are those related to the introduction of attitudes and beliefs in the decision. In particular, attitudes regarding the believability of certain types of witnesses (e.g., minorities or ex-convicts) should function to influence the weighting of the evidence and, therefore, involve the application of discretionary judgment.

To test empirically the hypothesis that the weighting of information is viewed as influenced by personal values and beliefs while the determination of the scale value of the information is not, an experiment was performed. College students were asked to play the role of jurors and were given information on an individual charged with first degree murder. The evidence against the defendant was held constant in the two conditions of the study. In one condition a key piece of evidence was supplied by the deceased's twin brother, who possessed poor eyesight (80–20 when corrected). In the other condition the evidence was furnished by an impartial observer (a respected store owner). Subjects in independent groups rated the witnesses' testimony on two dependent variables – "How indicative of guilt was the testimony?" (a measure of scale value) and "How much weight would you give to this evidence in your decision?" (a measure of the weighting of the scale value). The results revealed that the evidence against the defendant was rated as about equal in the two conditions ($t < 1$), and that the evidence supplied by the impartial observer would be rated as having more weight, $t(25) = 1.75$, $p < .05$, one-tailed. These results support the hypothesis that factors related to discretion, such as the characteristics of the witness, should influence the weighting of the scale value, but not the scale value itself.

Discretion in the binary decision task

In assessing the role of discretion in the jury's decision task of determining guilt or innocence, it is necessary to determine how beliefs and attitudes interact with the decision process. As noted previously, two factors determine the decision – the jury's sensitivity and the criterion for the amount of evidence necessary to convict. Sensitivity refers to the ability of the individual to discriminate noise and signal + noise and is independent of the judgmental factors of the reward-cost matrix of the decision and of the prior probability of either signal or noise occurring. In the theory of signal detection the observer's discriminatory ability is considered to be a perceptual process, not influenced by judgmental factors. In the jury's task, sensitivity refers to the ability of the jury to assess accurately the weight of the evidence against the defendant. The sensitivity of a jury was noted previously to depend upon such external factors as the quality of the police investigation. Internal factors were also noted, such as the collective intelligence of the jury. Such factors are largely unrelated to the role of attitudes and beliefs in personal judgment. Thus the sensitivity of the jury is hypothesized to be unrelated to discretion in decision-making.

In contrast, in TSD setting the criterion is conceptualized as specifically influenced by judgmental factors. As applied to the jury, then, discretion in the binary decision task involves the influence of the reward-cost outcome matrix and the perception of the prior probability of the signal. When discretion is conceptualized in this manner, some of the court rules and procedures as well as tactics of attorneys appear focused upon reducing (or increasing) the influence of discretion in jury decision-making. This conceptualization is illustrated by the judicial instructions for the jury not to consider the potential sentence a factor influencing the reward-cost matrix. Similarly, prosecutors may attempt to influence the reward-cost matrix by emphasizing the heinousness of the crime through lurid photographs. Another example of a trial procedure designed to minimize discretion is the rule that the prosecution cannot itself introduce the defendant's prior record into evidence. Such a rule helps to reduce the likelihood that subjective prior probabilities will spuriously influence setting the criterion.

In summary, discretion in jury decision-making is hypothesized to occur when personal attitudes and beliefs enter into the decision process. Thus, within the model of jury decision-making developed in this chapter, discretion occurs in determining the importance of individual items of testimony utilized in assessing the total weight of the evidence and in setting the criterion for the amount of evidence required to convict.

In the introduction to this chapter, we briefly discussed the extreme use of discretion in which the jury acts "lawlessly" to nullify a law. Within the model developed in this chapter, such behavior results from the placement of a criterion so high as to make it extremely difficult for the prosecution to gather enough evidence to surpass the threshold for guilt. Kalven and Zeisel (1966) discussed four reasons for the nullification of laws by juries: (1) the penality was too severe; (2) enforcement of the law was not being applied evenhandedly; (3) the jurors themselves sometimes committed the same crime (e.g., gambling or hunting violations); (4) the jurors resented laws regulating their behavior on social or moral grounds (e.g., victimless crimes). In each case a high threshold for guilt seems to exist. In the first case an extremely severe sentence should lead to the perception of even greater costs for convicting an innocent person than would normally be the case. In the last three instances the criterion is raised because the costs of releasing a guilty individual are low. One, the inequity of charging some individuals and not others makes the cost of releasing a guilty person low. Two, the juror knows that he is not a threat to society for having committed the offense; so the individual being tried should not be a threat, with a resultant extremely low cost for a "miss." Finally, in a victimless crime, the harm is borne predominantly by the defendant himself, thereby lowering the cost of a miss to society.

An empirical test of the TSD model

Research by Kaplan and his colleagues has demonstrated the utility of applying information integration theory to jury decision-making. However, except for the theoretical article developed by Mowen and Linder (1976) and the related work of Fried et al. (1975) and Thomas and Hogue (1976), TSD has not previously been applied to jury decision-making. In this section we will reanalyze a study reported by Vidmar (1972), which investigated the dynamics behind the jury's verdict in the Algiers Motel trial. The reanalysis reveals that certain aspects of the study's results support hypotheses derived from TSD. A conceptual replication of the Vidmar study is then presented, which gives additional support for the TSD model.

Vidmar (1972) conducted a study inspired by the infamous Algiers

Table 37.1. *Frequency of verdicts as a function of experimental condition in Vidmar (1972)*

Possible verdicts	Condition #						
	1	2	3	4	5	6	7
1st	11			2	7		2
2nd		20		22		11	15
MS			22		16	13	5
NG	13	4	2	0	1	0	2

Note: Blank cells indicate that the verdict alternate was not allowed for subjects under the condition.

Motel incident (see Hersey, 1968), in which three young blacks were killed during the Detroit riots of 1967. A white policeman was brought to trial for the death of one of the men. In his final instructions to the jury, the judge gave the jurors the verdict alternatives of guilty of first degree murder or not guilty, omitting the middle ground verdicts of second degree murder and manslaughter. Such instructions are unusual, though legal, and represent another example of judicial discretion. The jury returned with a verdict of not guilty, despite considerable evidence against the defendant. A number of questions of a psychological nature arose from the trial. Did omission of the middle ground verdict alternatives lower the probability of the jury finding the defendant guilty of something? And does varying the number of decision alternatives influence the type of decision reached by the jury?

   The experimental approach utilized by Vidmar consisted of having simulated jurors (college students) read a trial summary weighted so that the average juror viewed the defendant as guilty of either manslaughter or second degree murder. The four decision alternatives – first degree murder (1st), second degree murder (2nd), manslaughter (MS), and not guilty (NG) – were then arranged into seven conditions defined by the seven combinations of guilty verdicts and not guilty (see Table 37.1). In analyzing the results of the study, Vidmar focused entirely on the three two-choice conditions (1st v. NG, 2nd v. NG, and MS v. NG). For these conditions the results revealed that the probability of a guilty verdict decreased as one moved from MS v. NG to 2nd v. NG to 1st v. NG. Vidmar identified a mechanism possibly responsible for such results in his introduction: "One might hypothesize that in the instance of a choice between a guilty verdict which carries too severe a penalty or a not guilty verdict, jurors will say 'the penalty is too severe even though the defendant is guilty, and hence I will find him to be not guilty'" (p. 212).

   As explained by Vidmar, the effects found in the comparison of the two-choice conditions closely match the effects that excessive penalties have on the criterion for the amount of evidence required for guilt. With high penalties the jurors will not want to risk finding an innocent man guilty of the crime. TSD, then, accounts for Vidmar's interpretation of these results. However, Vidmar failed to consider that in addition to variations in the penalty for the various two-choice cases, there are also variations in the amount of evidence required to prove guilt. Proof of MS requires evidence of a wrongful killing; proof of 2nd requires evidence of malice, and proof of 1st requires evidence of premeditation. Thus the decrease in the number of 1st verdicts could have resulted from the fact that proof of 1st requires additional evidence, not from a penalty perceived as excessive. Thus TSD does not provide the only explanation for the patterns of results Vidmar obtained, and, while the model is not contradicted by the data, it is not unambiguously supported.

Other aspects of the results of the study, however, offer much stronger support for the TSD analysis. TSD may be applied to the situation of multiple decision alternatives in the following manner. The evidence required to convict of MS, 2nd, and 1st may be viewed as forming a Guttman scale. To prove 1st, the prosecution must prove both 2nd and MS, and in order to convict of 1st the jury must determine that the killing was wrongful, with malice, and premeditated. Thus the verdict alternatives are aligned on a scale of evidence against the defendant, with each separate verdict alternative having a different criterion for the amount of evidence necessary to convict. As usual, these criteria may be affected by differential reward-cost outcome matrices or by variations in the probability of the signal.

In Table 37.1, the verdict of 1st was paired with either one, two, or three other verdicts (i.e., 1st-NG, 1st-MS-NG, 1st-2nd-NG, 1st-2nd-MS-NG). Analyzing the likely costs of finding either an innocent person guilty or a guilty person innocent of 1st across the three sets of conditions leads to a straightforward prediction based upon the following reasoning. With no other verdict alternatives available, the cost of finding an innocent person guilty of 1st is high, and particularly so for the verdict of 1st because of the severe punishment associated with it. However, with no other guilty alternatives available, the cost of not convicting a guilty person is also great, because a murderer can possibly be set free. With the cost of releasing a guilty person and of convicting an innocent person both high in the two-choice case of 1st-NG, the two types of costs will balance. The criterion will then be set to require a middle range of evidence to convict of 1st. For the three-choice alternatives of 1st-2nd-NG and 1st-MS-NG, the costs of failing to convict a person guilty of 1st are lower because he can still be convicted of a lesser charge. This results in the cost of convicting an innocent person of 1st becoming relatively greater than the costs of failing to convict a guilty person of 1st. The result is a higher threshold for guilt, consequently making it more

Table 37.2. *Analysis of the effects of the number of verdict alternatives available on the frequency of first degree murder verdicts*

	2-choice condition	3-choice conditions	4-choice conditions
Frequency of 1st	11 (45%)	9 (19%)	2 (8%)
Frequency of other verdicts	13 (55%)	39 (81%)	22 (92%)

Note: Conditions 4 and 5 shown on Table 37.1 were collapsed to form the 3-choice condition above.

difficult for the prosecution to obtain a conviction of 1st in the three-choice conditions than in the two-choice condition. With four choices an additional guilty alternative is available, which will further increase the relative cost of convicting an innocent person of 1st. This analysis leads to the prediction that a linear trend should exist such that the probability of finding a person guilty of 1st degree murder should be greatest in the two-choice condition and least in the four-choice condition with the three-choice conditions falling in between.

The prediction can be tested by utilizing the Vidmar data. His data were entered into a 2×3 matrix, given in Table 37.2. The columns represent the two-choice, three-choice, and four-choice conditions (with conditions 4 and 5 from Table 37.1 collapsed for the three-choice conditions). The top row shows the number of 1st verdicts, and the second row shows the frequency of all other verdicts. The statistical analysis consists of first testing for a linear trend and then for a quadratic component. The test for linear trend was significant, ($X^2 = 10.2$, $df = 1$, $p < .001$), and the quadratic component was not significant, ($X^2 = .24$, $df = 1$), supporting the hypothesis that reducing the number of decision alternatives increases the probability of a 1st verdict.

Attention can also be focused on the influence of the number of decision alternatives on obtaining an acquittal. In order to avoid the confounding element of type of guilty charge, we will deal only with conditions having MS as the least severe guilty alternative. Again an analysis of the reward/cost structure of the decision outcomes allows for a straightforward prediction. In the two-choice condition of MS/NG, the costs of finding an innocent person guilty and of a guilty person innocent balance themselves in a manner similar to those for 1st degree murder. In three-choice cases, however, with the alternative of 2nd or 1st also available, we propose that the perceived costs of finding an innocent person guilty will decrease. The reason is that with 1st or 2nd or both available (i.e., in the four-choice condition), a verdict of MS will be perceived as a less severe outcome in a manner analogous to a perceptual contrast phenomenon. Thus members of the jury will respond as though they felt that "Well, the defendant could have been convicted of 1st (2nd), so a conviction of MS is not so severe." If our hypothesis is correct, a linear trend should be found such that as the number of decision alternatives increases, the probability of a NG verdict will decrease even with the least severe guilt alternative held constant as MS.

Again the data from the Vidmar study were entered in a 2×3 matrix with the two rows consisting of (1) NG verdicts and (2) all other verdicts. However, a visual inspection revealed that no differences existed. It was apparent that so much evidence was brought against the defendant that nearly all the simulated jurors found the defendant guilty when MS was given as an alternative. With such a ceiling effect the hypothesis could not be tested. A test can be made, though, by utilizing 2nd degree murder as the least severe guilt alternative. Thus condition 2 (2nd v. NG) was compared to condition 4 (1st and 2nd v. NG). The comparison was made utilizing the Fisher Exact Probability Test because two of the cells contained expected frequencies of less than five (Siegel, 1956). The exact probability that the observed distribution, or one more extreme, could occur was $p = .055$, supporting the hypothesis that as the number of decision alternatives increased, the probability of a NG verdict decreased, even with the least severe guilty alternative held constant. However, full support for the model required that we obtain similar results with MS as the least severe guilty alternative. Thus, an experiment was conducted in which the strength of the evidence was lowered in order to avoid the ceiling effect found in the Vidmar study. In addition, two trials were utilized in order to obtain some data on the generalizability of the results.

The experiment

Serving as simulated jurors were 675 students in introductory psychology. Subjects listened to audio-taped summaries of and reached verdicts on two trials – a version of the Vidmar (1972) trial with some evidence removed and a trial summarized from Norris (1965). The contents of the trials were recorded on audio cassette tape by a single narrator, and subjects reached their verdicts individually, without a group decision process. The experimental sessions were run with groups of from 6 to 31 subjects, with an average of 20. Because of the high cost of using large numbers of subjects, only four conditions from the Vidmar experiment were utilized (1st-NG, 2nd-NG, MS-NG, and 1st-2nd-MS-NG). The subjects were randomly assigned to one of the four verdict conditions in each trial, and the order of the presentation of the trials was counterbalanced across sessions.

Subjects were introduced to the experimental situation by being instructed to imagine that they were in a courtroom with a judge, witnesses, and so on. They were also reminded that in the future they would probably serve as jurors. They then heard the cassette tape

Table 37.3. *Frequencies and percentages of verdicts in the experiment*

Verdict chosen	Verdicts available to jurors			
	1st-NG	2nd-NG	MS-NG	1st-2nd MS-NG
1st	40 (30%) / 103 (68%)			0 (0%) / 56 (32%)
2nd		83(56%) / 108 (70%)		48(34%) / 30 (17%)
MS			100 (68%) / 116 (70%)	73 (52%) / 50 (29%)
NG	93 (70%) / 54 (34%)	64 (44%) / 46 (30%)	48 (32%) / 50 (30%)	18 (13%) / 37 (21%)

Note: Frequencies above diagonals are for the Vidmar trial replication. Frequencies below diagonals are for the second trial, extracted from Norris (1965).

recordings of the trials (lasting 7 and 14 minutes, respectively) and recorded their verdicts on forms supplied by the experimenter. After all simulated jurors had reached a verdict, the second trial was played. The experimental situation appeared to elicit a high level of involvement, and subjects indicated great interest in the study, evidenced by the fact that only two failed to complete the experimental questionnaire. Subjects were given the definition of "reasonable doubt" and the definitions of the verdict alternatives and were instructed not to consider the possible sentence in reaching a verdict. At the conclusion of the experiment all subjects were asked if they were aware that the commission of a homicide while committing another felony is automatically considered to be first degree murder. Individuals who were aware of this fact and who indicated that it affected their verdict were discarded from the analysis of the Vidmar trial (88 total). In this trial the defendant allegedly committed a homicide while performing an armed robbery.

Results and discussion of the experiment

In each trial the two predictions developed from TSD were supported; the results are presented in Table 37.3. For the prediction that as the number of verdict alternatives increased, the probability of a guilty verdict would increase, the respective one-tailed tests of significance were: Trial 1 − X^2

= 31.4, *df* = 1, *p* < .001; Trial 2 – X^2 = 2.94, *df* = 1, *p* < .05. Thus with the least severe guilt alternative of manslaughter held constant, adding the verdicts of first and second degree murder increased the chances that the defendant would be found guilty, from 68 percent to 87 percent in Trial 1 and from 70 percent to 79 percent in Trial 2. The prediction that as the number of verdict alternatives increased, the probability of a verdict of first degree murder would decrease was also supported in each trial: Trial 1 – X^2 = 46.6, *df* = 1, *p* < .001; Trial 2 – X^2 = 31.4, *df* = 1, *p* < .001. The frequency of 1st verdicts decreased from 30 percent to zero (Trial 1) and from 67 percent to 32 percent (Trial 2) as the number of alternatives increased from two to four.

The support obtained for each of the predictions derived from TSD has theoretical and practical importance. Although other explanations of the results of the Vidmar study are possible (see Larntz, 1975),[1] the findings can be interpreted to provide evidence that the reward/cost decision matrix can be influenced by the types of other decisions available. TSD, a theoretical formulation of considerable explanatory power, has therefore been shown empirically to account for some aspects of jury decision-making.

On the practical side, the results imply that the discretion of the judge to select the number of verdict alternatives may have important consequences for the defendant. By adding decision alternatives, the probability of a guilty verdict increased by an average of 14 percent in the two cases, but 1st verdicts decreased by about 30 percent for both trials when 2nd and MS were added to 1st and NG as possible verdict alternatives.

The results of the experiment reveal the utility of applying TSD to jury decision-making. The theory's distinction between sensitivity and criterion setting has potential importance in developing court procedures that maximize the overall probability of convicting those who are guilty while concomitantly avoiding the serious error of convicting a larger proportion of innocent defendants. This point is an important one in understanding the application of TSD to jury decision-making. Merely moving the criterion to a point at which the two types of errors are given equal weight will not, in theory, influence the sensitivity of the jurors. However, it will increase the number of innocent individuals found guilty, as was shown by the example presented earlier in the chapter.

There is an additional advantage when the information integration approach is used in combination with TSD. To conceptualize discretion in jury decision-making as occurring in setting the criterion in the final judgment and in determining the weight of the items of evidence is a first step in the process of more clearly defining an elusive concept. In

---

[1] Larntz (1975) was able marginally to fit Vidmar's (1972) study with a mathematical conditional probability model. The model was applied to the data obtained in the two trials and was found not to fit with *p* < .01 in each case.

previous work, discretion has generally been treated as a broad concept, and no attempt has been made to define it precisely. Until the term is narrowed and related to specific behaviors or components of a theory or model, research on discretion in jury decision-making will be difficult. Our attempt to define discretion in terms of the judgmental aspects of setting decision thresholds and of determining weighting of evidence, though somewhat arbitrary, fulfills the function of narrowing the concept to the point at which the variables influencing it can be specified, and its impact on decision-making identified. Future research in this area should focus on additional factors that influence weighting evidential information and setting the criterion.

38. Measuring the relative importance of utilitarian and egalitarian values: A study of individual differences about fair distribution
John Rohrbaugh, Gary McClelland, and Robert Quinn

Previous attempts to study value systems usually have been based on a limited number of values ordered according to relative importance. Allport, Vernon, and Lindzey (1951) identified 6 classes of values and developed standardized scales for their measurement. Rokeach (1973) listed 18 terminal values and 18 instrumental values and devised an instrument that permits individuals to rank them in order of personal importance. Scott (1965) suggested 12 values relevant to a college population and validated scales for each. The present article identifies two general values, utility and equity; proposes alternative but convergent methods for their measurement; and indicates significant differences between individuals with regard to the relative importance of these values.

Frankena (1963) has suggested that "there are at least two basic and independent principles of morality, that of beneficence or utility which tells us to maximize the total amount of good in the world ... and that of justice" (p. 35). In a value system based on utilitarianism, a social state that provides the greatest amount of individual good, satisfaction, or happiness is preferred. Justice is emphasized in an egalitarian value system, which has as its primary objective the most homogeneous distribution of individual utility. Because utilitarian and egalitarian values are concerned with the amount and distribution of individual happiness or satisfaction, they may encompass a wide variety of other values, such as pleasure or freedom. For example, certain individuals may express the primary importance of utility by advocating a tax reform that reduces taxes by the greatest dollar amount (assuming the marginal utility of

This chapter is an abbreviated version of an article which appeared in the *Journal of Applied Psychology*, 1980, 65(1), 34–49. Copyright © 1980 by the American Psychological Association, Inc. Reprinted by permission.

income is constant), whereas others may express the primary importance of equity by endorsing legislation that attempts to more evenly allocate state and local funds to public schools based on enrollment estimates. Thus, utility and equity are superordinate values determining the parameters of the distribution of objects or events on which other values are placed.

Utility and equity are independent values, as Frankena has suggested. Only if all individuals had identical utility functions (i.e., if everyone were made equally happy or satisfied by the same objects or events) would the social states preferred by either utilitarian or egalitarian values be isomorphic. In such a unique situation, promoting the greatest good of the greatest number would yield a distribution acceptable to both utilitarian and egalitarian values, since total utility would be achieved only by providing total equity. In the more common situations in which individual utility functions differ, utilitarian and egalitarian values compete; maximum utility does not promote maximum equity, nor does maximum equity promote maximum utility. For example, a completely equitable distribution of land in Monaco would result in less than ⅟₅₀ of an acre per citizen, thereby reducing the overall utility of the separate parcels.

The competition between utilitarian and egalitarian values has not been addressed explicitly in the social-psychological value literature, although utility and equity have been considered as identifiable components of a value system. For example, Becker and McClintock (1967) discussed as the basis for behavioral decision theory "in a very broad manner ... the utility component of value ... as whatever it is that the individual attempts to 'maximize'" (p. 240). The value placed on the equitable allocation of rewards in society is a major focus of equity theory (Adams, 1965; Homans, 1961; Walster, Berscheid, & Walster, 1973).[1] A fundamental proposition of equity theory is that over time groups can maximize collective reward by equitably apportioning rewards and costs among members (Austin, Walster, & Utne, 1976). The question left specifically unanswered by equity theory is the extent to which the overall utility of the group membership should be forfeited to provide more equitable allocations.

Keeney and Raiffa (1976, pp. 532–536) have pointed to the problem of integrating utility and equity in decision theory, but they provide no specific models. Instead, they conclude that individual judgment is required: "The Decision Maker is faced with the tradeoff of amount of equity versus degree to which the narrow interpretation of Pareto

---

[1] The use of the term *equity* in this article is not in ignorance of the important distinction between equity and equality norms in group allocation decisions (Leventhal, 1976, pp. 108–117). The use of equity is preferred here, under the assumption that the input or performance of all recipients is the same.

optimality[2] is violated" (p. 534). Perhaps only in the area of welfare economics has the conflict between utilitarian and egalitarian values been clearly traced (Harsanyi, 1976; Rawls, 1971; Sen, 1973). Social welfare economists have constructed a variety of preference functions that rank order alternative combinations of individual utilities. Harsanyi (1975) has argued that the ideal social welfare function is the arithmetic mean of the individual utilities. Rawls (1958) has suggested that the welfare level of society should be measured solely by the utility level of the most unfortunate individual.

It is clear that Rawls (1971) places considerably more importance on equity in his social welfare function than does Harsanyi (1975). To specify how much more he values equity, we formulate an example. Let us assume that a labor negotiator and a management negotiator are reviewing alternative contracts that might settle a strike. Both negotiators rate the alternative contracts on a scale of 0–20, which is used to roughly indicate the utility each contract provides for them. The total utility of each contract might be defined as the sum of the individual utilities (see Keeney & Raiffa, 1976, for a discussion of the aggregation of individual utilities),

$$u_1(x) + u_2(x),$$

where u_i designates the utility of individual i. Similarly, the inequity of each contract might be defined as the absolute difference between the individual utilities (see Sen, 1973),[3]

$$|u_1(x) - u_2(x)|.$$

Thus, the total utility of any contract potentially can range from 0 to 40; the inequity of the contract potentially can range from 0 to 20. The full set of possible ordered pairs of inequity and utility is contained within the boundaries of the triangle shown in Figure 38.1.

For any pair of ratings produced by the labor and management negotiators, a corresponding ordered pair of inequity and utility can be located in Figure 38.1. For example, a contract rated 14 by the labor negotiator and rated 10 by the management negotiator (14–10) corresponds to the ordered pair of inequity and utility (4,24). The social

---

[2] A Pareto optimal alternative is one for which no individual can increase his or her utility without simultaneously decreasing the utility of another. To prefer an alternative that is not Pareto optimal implies that an individual is losing some utility, since his or her utility could be increased without negatively affecting the utility of another. Thus, a violation of Pareto optimality also implies that the sum of the individual utilities is not at its maximum.

[3] McClelland and Rohrbaugh (1978) tested four social welfare functions incorporating equity considerations: Sen's (1973) absolute deviation model, Sen's variance model, Keeney and Kirkwood's (1975) multilinear model, and Rawls's (1958) maximin principle. The findings suggested that arbitration judgments are best described by Sen's absolute deviation model.

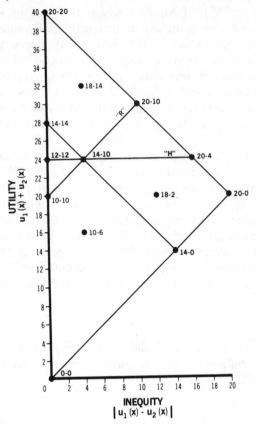

Figure 38.1. Ordered pairs of inequity and utility.

welfare functions of both Harsanyi (1975) and Rawls (1971), with regard
to this particular example, are illustrated in Figure 38.1. Harsanyi would
be indifferent to this contract (4,24) and any contract yielding ordered
pairs of inequity and utility on the "H" line of Figure 38.1; he would
prefer any contract yielding ordered pairs of inequity and utility above
the line because it would provide greater average utility. Rawls would be
indifferent to this contract (4,24) and any other contract on the "R" line of
Figure 38.1; he would prefer any contract above the line because it would
increase the utility of the more unfortunate negotiator. The darkened
areas in Figure 38.1 are relevant to the Pareto criterion. Any contract on
or above the lines marking off the top of the darkened areas would be
preferred, according to the Pareto criterion, to the contract located at the
ordered pair (4,24); any contract on or below the lines marking off the
bottom of the darkened areas would be suboptimal according to the
Pareto criterion.

It is clear from Figure 38.1 that the alternative contracts preferred by the social welfare functions of Harsanyi (1975) and Rawls (1971) are not in violation of Pareto optimality. It is also clear, however, that there are an infinite number of social welfare functions (i.e., indifference lines between utility and equity) that violate the Pareto criterion, as well as an infinite number of social welfare functions between those proposed by Rawls and Harsanyi. Each social welfare function is unique because of its implicit statement about the relative importance of utilitarian and egalitarian values, that is, the trade-off that should be made between utility and equity in making a wide variety of social welfare decisions.

Study 1

Problem

The application of utilitarian and egalitarian values is relevant to any social decision involving the possible distribution of objects or events. Decisions about food supplies, fuel allocations, federal contracts and grants, job promotions, and health care to some extent include an implicit consideration of the trade-off between utility and equity. Study 1 was intended to illustrate the applicability of utility and equity considerations to a major social problem area, the arbitration of labor–management disputes. Furthermore, Study 1 was designed to demonstrate that the relative importance of utilitarian and egalitarian values for an individual decision maker could be precisely measured. The relative importance of these values was hypothesized to vary significantly across participants in the study.

Method

Participants. Participants were 42 male and female students in the Graduate School of Public Affairs at the University of Colorado. They had not been previously exposed to the theoretical issues relevant to the study. Approximately 60% of the participants were between 20 and 29 years of age; the remaining participants were 30 years of age or older. A majority of the participants were part-time graduate students. Approximately 75% of the participants were employed; 60% of the participants worked in the public sector.

Procedure. Participants were shown ratings (given by one hypothetical labor negotiator and one hypothetical management negotiator) of the acceptability of 25 alternative contracts that might be ratified to end a strike. Participants were not shown the original contracts, but only the paired ratings, made on a scale of 0 (a completely unacceptable contract) to 20 (a completely acceptable contract). The ratings were not specifically identified as labor or management. Participants were asked to assume the role of an arbitrator and to evaluate each contract on the basis of its suitability as an arbitrated solution to the conflict. By considering each pair of ratings, the arbitrators gave each hypothetical contract a rating to indicate its quality as an arbitrated settlement. These ratings were also on a scale of 0 (a completely unacceptable settlement) to 20 (a completely acceptable settlement). Figure 38.2 depicts 25 pairs of hypothetical ratings by Negotiators I and II used as the basis for Study 1. Here the participant playing the role of arbitrator has rated the first contract as a slightly more acceptable settlement than the second contract.

The overall utility of each hypothetical contract is computed by adding the ratings of labor and management. Thus, the utility of any contract can range from 0 (a contract rated with a 0 by both negotiators) to 40 (a contract rated with a 20 by both negotiators). The inequity of each contract is computed as the absolute difference in the ratings of labor and management. Thus, the inequity of any contract can range from 20 (a contract rated with a 20 by one negotiator and with a 0 by the other) to 0 (a contract rated identically by both negotiators). For example, the first contract in Figure 38.2 has a utility of 20 and an inequity of 4; the second contract has a utility of 16 and an inequity of 8.

The pairs of ratings were varied across three conditions to which the participants were randomly assigned. In the first condition, the 25 alternative contracts were systematically selected from a set in which the ratings of management and labor were in serious conflict ($r = -.60$). In the second condition, the 25 alternative contracts were systematically selected from a set in which the ratings of management and labor were in little conflict ($r = .60$). In the third condition, the 25 alternative contracts were randomly selected from a set in which the ratings of management and labor were in moderate conflict ($r = .00$). The latter set of ratings is shown in Figure 38.2. Because the three experimental conditions produced no differences with respect to the results discussed in this article, the data have been collapsed into one set.

These measures of utility and equity for each of the hypothetical contracts were used statistically as predictors of each participant's arbitration ratings. This use of multiple regression as a basis for describing an individual's judgment process (social judgment analysis) has been widely reviewed (see Hammond, Stewart, Brehmer, & Steinmann, 1975; Slovic & Lichtenstein, 1971). The size of the resulting standardized regression coefficients (beta weights) for the measures of utility and equity provides an indication of their relative importance for each participant in the judgment of contract settlements. The size of the multiple correlation coefficient provides an indication of the extent to which these two measures of equity and utility were being used consistently by the participant as the basis for rating the acceptability of the contracts.

Contract Number	Rating I	Rating II	Arbitration Judgment
1	8	12	9
2	12	4	7
3	6	12	___
4	18	2	___
5	14	14	___
6	9	15	___
7	19	18	___
8	5	8	___
9	18	10	___
10	14	18	___
11	10	4	___
12	6	14	___
13	3	2	___
14	12	16	___
15	5	5	___
16	7	3	___
17	2	14	___
18	9	1	___
19	10	13	___
20	11	10	___
21	7	17	___
22	12	2	___
23	1	4	___
24	17	14	___
25	7	15	___

Figure 38.2. Hypothetical labor–management ratings of alternative contracts.

Results

Of the 42 participants in the study, 40 produced coefficients of multiple correlation of at least .80, which indicates that at least 64% of the variability in their ratings as arbitrators could be attributed to the consistent application of utilitarian and/or egalitarian values. Over half of these participants produced coefficients of multiple correlation that exceeded .90. No cut-off point in the size of the multiple correlation has been suggested as assuring that the representation of the judgment process is a statistically adequate model. In practice, multiple correlations between .70 and .80 are generally employed (see Hammond, Rohrbaugh, Mumpower, & Adelman, 1977). Anderson (1976a) and Shanteau (1977) have argued that the correlation coefficient is not a good index of fit for a judgment model because it systematically ignores interaction effects. Kerlinger and Pedhazur (1973) demonstrated how interaction effects can be included in regression equations to test for a judge's tendency to multiply rather than to add information. In the present study, only 3 of the participants produced significant interaction terms in the regression model of their judgments. In none of the 3 instances did the interaction term increase the proportion of explained variance by more than .04.

Large individual differences existed in the application of utilitarian and egalitarian values. The size of the standarized regression coefficients associated with utility ranged between .09 and .99; the size of the standardized regression coefficients associated with equity ranged between −.15 and .90. These results are shown graphically as a histogram in Figure 38.3. Although the ranges were similar for both utilitarian and egalitarian values, the mean sizes of the standardized regression coefficients were dissimilar, .75 for the utility factor and .30 for the equity factor. In general, then, utility was shown to be over twice as important as equity in participants' determination of acceptable contract settlements. A statistical test of the regression coefficients (Kerlinger & Pedhazur, 1973) showed that approximately 95% of the participants placed significant weight on utility ($p < .05$) and 57% of the participants placed significant weight on equity; over half of the participants placed significant weight on both values. Almost 75% of the participants placed significantly greater importance on utility than on equity ($p < .05$), whereas about 13% of the participants placed significantly greater importance on equity than on utility.

The implication of these striking individual differences is graphically displayed in Figure 38.4. The social welfare function of each participant, based on the explicit trade-off between utility and equity represented by the standardized regression coefficients, is displayed in relation to those of Harsanyi (1975), Rawls (1971), and the Pareto criterion. The array of social welfare functions produced by the participants covers a wide spectrum. Of the 40 social welfare functions, 20% were almost identical to that advocated by Harsanyi, another 20% were relatively close to that advocated by Rawls, and 25% ranged between them. The remaining social welfare functions (approximately 35%) were even more egalitarian than that advocated by Rawls; the Pareto criterion was routinely violated as a result of these arbitration judgment policies....

Conclusion

The present study is one of a series of studies investigating the trade-off between utility and equity in arbitration and social welfare judgments. McClelland and Rohrbaugh (1978) and Rohrbaugh, McClelland, and Quinn (1980) report the details of these studies. All the studies provide convergent results, which may be surprising to students of both decision theory and equity theory. Students of decision theory may be surprised to find that so much importance was placed on equity by participants. A clear majority placed significant weight on equity in Study 1 and in the subsequent studies. Equity was treated as such an important value to the participants, in fact, that Pareto optimality – the principle that says that a policy that makes everyone better off should be preferred – was routinely violated (see McClelland & Rohrbaugh, 1978, for details). Students of equity theory may be surprised to find that so much importance was

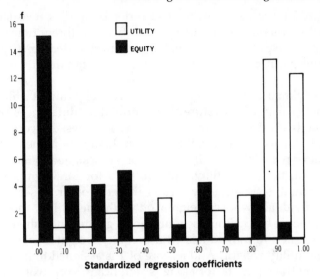

Figure 38.3. Histogram of standardized regression coefficients of equity and utility produced in Study 1. (f = frequency.)

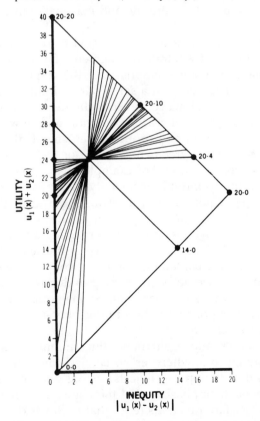

Figure 38.4. The social welfare functions produced in Study 1.

placed on utility by the participants. The series of studies revealed that the utility factor was typically treated as two to three times more important than the equity factor in making arbitration decisions. In fact, over 40% of the participants in Study 1 placed no significant weight on equity.

The large individual differences in the relative weighting of utility and equity are most striking. To capture these individual differences we can construct a rough U−E scale using the following rules: A score of 5 is assigned to individuals whose weight on the utility factor alone is statistically significant or reliable ($p < .05$). A score of 4 is assigned to individuals whose weights on both the utility and equity factors are significant but whose utility weight is significantly greater than the other. A score of 3 is assigned to individuals whose weights on both the utility and equity factors are significant but neither is significantly greater than the other. A score of 2 is assigned to individuals whose equity weight is significantly greater than the utility weight. And a score of 1 is assigned to individuals whose weight on the equity factor alone is significant. Approximately 3% of the participants were coded as 1, 10% as 2, 3% as 3, 43% as 4, and 40% as 5. The relationship between the U−E scale derived in this manner from the regression analysis and other attitude and personality measures can be easily examined.

Researchers interested in conflict resolution may wish to explore the implications of the wide range of arbitration judgments found in these studies. Luce and Raiffa (1957) have emphasized the importance of obtaining agreement among disputants on a set of fair arbitration axioms prior to actual arbitration efforts. However, even if the disputants could agree on such matters as the limits of feasible solution and how much utility each side would receive from any proposed settlement, they still might not be able to reach a final agreement because of their divergent views of what constitutes a just solution. For example, management may prefer a solution with high utility and minimal equity, whereas labor may prefer a solution with perfect equity even if it results in lower utility for each. Future research in this area might explore how these results are related to findings in the extensive literature on bargaining and conflict resolution. For instance, McClintock (1972) has proposed several motivational orientations within a bargaining context: own, joint, relative, and other gain maximization. It would be interesting to discover whether the U−E scale can predict the particular motivational orientation of bargainers in a variety of situations in addition to the labor–management scenario of the present research.

The application of utilitarian and egalitarian values is important, not only in bargaining situations but wherever social decisions are made regarding the possible distribution of objects, goods, resources, or penalties. The present research emphasizes that there are not merely two or three competing social welfare functions (e.g., that of Rawls or that of

Harsanyi) on which such decisions about distribution can be based but an unlimited number of possible intermediate trade-offs between utility and equity. Furthermore, other studies in this research series (see especially Study 3 in Rohrbaugh, McClelland, & Quinn, 1980) suggest that the advocacy or application of a particular social welfare function reflects a certain individual value system that at least in part may be associated with personality characteristics such as religiosity and conservatism.

The relative importance of utilitarian and egalitarian values to the individual decision maker is implicit within graduate school admissions and municipal budgets, insurance premiums and television programming, political caucuses and ticket sales for sporting events. Trade-offs between utility and equity are being made implicitly every day, sometimes with major social consequences. The present research provides a first step toward making such consequential value judgments more explicit and, thereby, more subject to further investigation.

Part XI
Overview

In the General Introduction to this book we warned the reader that the topic of judgment and decision making is of wide and compelling interest, that scholars in many disciplines are intrigued with this important aspect of human behavior, and that as a result many different talents and special interests from many fields are brought to bear on it; in short, we warned that the complexity of the topic meant that rich and varied approaches to a number of different areas would be encountered. There should be no doubt about the relevance of that warning at this point.

The diversity the reader has experienced calls for an effort to "bring it all together" – somehow. And so we have included an Overview that attempts to do that. But again we must issue a warning: Different scholars "bring it all together" differently. Helmut Jungermann differentiates "two camps" of researchers and describes the different interests and conclusions of each. Ward Edwards and Detlof von Winterfeldt take a firm stand in one of those camps and indicate why they believe that the conclusions from the research on "cognitive illusions" should be treated with great caution. Robin M. Hogarth expresses similar cautions but in a different way; he notes that most conclusions about heuristics and cognitive illusions are based on judgments and decisions made in "static" rather than "dynamic" tasks. Berndt Brehmer organizes yet a different set of materials in his review, where he argues against the value of experience. Finally, we include a note from Lola L. Lopes that strikes at the very heart of a concept – randomness – hardly ever examined by the researchers themselves.

It is clear, then, that this "overview" will not bring to the reader that strong feeling of coherence that an overview should. And there lies the challenge and the promise. Certainly, the effort to understand human judgment and decision making offers a challenge; certainly, there is promise of great progress in self-understanding, should we be able to meet the challenge. The field is in its infancy; much remains to be done. We hope that these readings will inspire the reader to accept the challenge and confirm the promise.

39. The two camps on rationality

Helmut Jungermann

The status of the rationality concept

If one postulates that people are generally *rational*, one meets today usually objection or, at best, scepticism; biases, errors and faults are described and illustrated to prove that the postulate has little empirical justification. If one declares a person *irrational*, however, one equally will meet usually protest from this person; he or she will explain that there were good reasons for the judgment or decisions questioned. The contradiction might be due to the words "generally" and "usually" in the above statements: People are not *always* rational and people will not *always* claim to be rational. However, the present debate about the quality of human judgment and decision indicates that the controversy is not only about generalizations and exceptions (e.g., Einhorn & Hogarth, 1981; Nisbett & Ross, 1980; Cohen, 1979; Kahneman & Tversky, 1982; Edwards, 1983; Fischhoff, 1983c; Berkeley & Humphreys, 1982; Phillips, 1983). The participants in this debate tend to avoid the term "rationality" because it is overloaded with many connotations, but just for that reason I find it useful as an umbrella under which most contributions fit fairly well; they all treat one or another definition or meaning of rationality.

Rationality is not a genuine term of scientific psychology but rather a concept of philosophy and economics. The most common, and in this context most relevant, definition says that an action is rational if it is in line with the values and beliefs of the individual concerned; or more precisely, if it is "logical" or "consistent" as stated in a set of axioms. This definition specifies rational behavior normatively. Empirical research can

This chapter originally appeared in Scholz, R. W. (Ed.). *Decision Making under Uncertainty* (pp. 63–86). Amsterdam: Elsevier, 1983. Copyright © 1983 by Elsevier Science Publishers B.V. (North Holland). Reprinted by permission.

study whether actual human behavior is rational in the sense that it obeys the norm.

To measure human behavior with a normative yardstick is not the rule but rather the exception in cognitive psychology. In the psychology of *perception*, for instance, the physical world is taken as a standard when perceptual illusions are investigated. Normally, however, the physical stimuli are used to provoke responses; one tries to understand and explain these responses and they are not evaluated as "deviant from" or "consistent with" something. The psychology of *language* worked for some time on the assumption that human language could be evaluated with the linguistic yardstick of an ideal speaker or hearer. But this assumption turned out to be not very helpful in understanding actual human language, and research began to focus on psychological models like semantic networks. Finally, the psychology of *thinking* used, and to some extent still uses, formal logic as a yardstick for the study of deductive reasoning. But not only is this merely a small area within the psychology of thinking, the approach itself has increasingly been disputed as mistaken. Similarly to the development in psycholinguistics, the focus has been directed increasingly on the content rather than on the formal characteristics of thinking. In all these areas of research, the use of a physical or logical yardstick plays only a minor role today or has been abandoned altogether.

In the psychology of *judgment and decision*, on the other hand, normative models have been the most important research tools since its beginnings in the late fifties. Research has been primarily concerned with studying, explaining and interpreting discrepancies between predictions derived from normative models and actual judgments and decisions. The most prominent models of judgment are probably Bayes' theorem and the multiattribute utility models, and the normative model of decision is the SEU model. Most research is still oriented towards these models and the debate about the quality of human judgment and decision is still centered around the idea of rationality embodied in these models.

In a somewhat exaggerated manner, I will distinguish two camps in this debate, one that points to the deficiency and one that argues for the efficiency of human judgment and decision. The *pessimists*, as I will call the members of the first camp, claim that judgment and decision making under uncertainty often show systematic and serious errors, due to in-built characteristics of the human cognitive system. Violations of rationality, particularly of the SEU model, are interpreted as true deficits of the decision maker. The *optimists* of the other camp claim that judgment and decision are highly efficient and functional even in complex situations. Observed violations of rationality axioms are interpreted as unjustified evaluations based on inappropriate theoretical assumptions or empirical approaches on the part of the researcher. In the following, I will describe the approach to rationality taken in both camps, each of which has various factions, and discuss some points that make the debate so complicated and, sometimes, obscure. The description cannot be as differentiated as the approaches are, of course, but I hope that it is essentially correct; the interested reader is referred to the original sources.

The pessimists: Biases are in people

Since Simon (1955) proposed the concept of "bounded rationality," the strongest attacks against human rationality came from Tversky and Kahneman (e.g., 1974), Slovic (1972), Janis and Mann (1977), and Nisbett and Ross (1980). The general tendency of this research was that human judgment and decision making ability and capacity is indeed limited, leading to violations of rationality principles. There are three variants in this camp in explaining these violations: As results of *judgmental biases*, of *representational faults*, and of *coping defects*.

Judgmental biases

The most extensive and influential work of interest in this context has been the research of Tversky and Kahneman on probabilistic thinking. While in the sixties, Peterson and Beach (1967) in their review came to the conclusion that people form and revise their beliefs according to the normative principles of statistics, Tversky and Kahneman (e.g., 1974) offered a different conception: Judgments of probabilities are often severely biased because people in many situations rely on heuristics which, although generally efficient, can sometimes lead to systematic errors. For example, people often judge the probability of an event according to the *representativeness* of the event for the underlying population or for the generating process. However, "this approach to the judgment of probability leads to serious errors, because similarity or representativeness is not influenced by several factors that should affect judgments of probability" (Tversky & Kahneman, 1974, p. 1124). Such factors are, for instance, base rates, sample size and the reliability of information. Another heuristic people use is the saliency or *availability* of information, i.e., how easily instances of the event whose probability is to be assessed can be retrieved from memory. Since ease of retrieval is also influenced by other factors than the actual frequency of the event (e.g., recent occurence) the use of this heuristic can likewise result in systematic judgmental errors. Other heuristics described in this research are "anchoring and adjustment" and "simulation" (for a collection of the most important papers on biases and heuristics see the recent book by Kahneman, Slovic, & Tversky, 1982).

Judgmental biases may produce inconsistent decisions. Such inconsistencies would then not reflect violations of assumptions of the model (e.g., SEU model) but rather incorrect input. However, the discussion has mostly been restricted to the quality of the judgment itself. The judgment is compared to a standard like relative frequency or the inference based on a statistical model for which the researcher has defined the relevant data (e.g., what the base rates are). In both cases, deficiency means deviation of the judgment from some "objective" quantity, and the "objectivity" is rooted in the real world, or rather the researcher's view of the real world. The implicit notion of rationality, then, is not consistency but realism; it is less *formal* rationality that is questioned than *substantive* rationality: People use cognitive inference and retrieval strategies which often lead to (in the researcher's view) substantively incorrect judgments about the world.

Implicitly, this meaning of rationality pervades the discussion on biases and heuristics in probabilistic thinking. It is interesting to find it made *explicit* with respect to judgments which are equally important for decision making but much less debated, namely, utility judgments (March 1978). Tversky and Kahneman (1981) question the rationality of utility judgments that turn out to have been unrealistic anticipations of satisfaction at the time when the consequences actually incur. But biases and heuristics in the judgment of utility are still unexplored, maybe due to the lack of a yardstick like relative frequency it offers for probability judgments. A different approach is needed here, maybe taking the work of Ainslie (1975) on preferences as a function of time delay of satisfaction and the economic approach to "rational expectations" as a starting point. Rationality in this sense, i.e., as realism, certainly comes close to the meaning of this term in common sense: We often call hopes and fears "irrational" which we consider as extremely unrealistic. The question, of course, is who is to define reality.

Representational faults

A more recent argument against rationality, raised by the same group of researchers, concerns the effect of different frames for the decision problem on people's decision making behavior (Tversky & Kahneman, 1981; cp. also Payne, 1982). A striking example is the experiment in which a majority of subjects behaved risk averse when they had to decide between two options that were formulated in terms of lives saved, but behaved risk seeking when the options were formulated in terms of lives lost – although the (expected) values of the options were in both cases identical. This violation of rationality, i.e., of the SEU model, is interpreted by the assumption that people code the possible outcomes as gains and losses rather than as final states, and the framing of the options induces in one case coding in terms of gains and in the other case coding in terms of losses, i.e., it induces subjects to focus on different parts of their utility functions. Since the utility functions are different below and above the reference point, apparently inconsistent preferences result.

Coding outcomes in terms of gains and losses is, according to Kahneman and Tversky (1979b), only one of several cognitive mechanisms which people use to edit, or represent, decision problems before the options will be evaluated, and these operations can also lead to violations of rationality. Other editing mechanisms are, for instance, the segregation of riskless components of prospects and the cancellation of components which are shared by two prospects.

The representational errors resulting from the application of such mechanisms are likened to perceptual illusions (Tversky & Kahneman, 1981). This implies the assumption that there exists one and only one correct representation of the problem, as there exists only one veridical representation of the physical world. Inconsistent preferences are understood as results of a deficient perception and interpretation of the decision problem.

It is interesting to note that with this argument, the context for discussing rationality is being enlarged. Previously, the domain of theoretical and empirical research was judgment and evaluation only, but *not* the cognitive activities which forego these steps, e.g., how the problem structure is generated. Only recently, interest has shifted to these early phases of the decision making process (e.g., Pitz, Sachs, & Heerboth, 1980; Jungermann, von Ulardt, & Hausmann, 1983), but this research has not been generally linked to the discussion about the deficiency/efficiency of judgment and decision.

Coping defects

The third attack on rationality comes from Janis and Mann (1977) who look at people's decision making behavior from a motivational perspective. They distinguish various coping patterns that people use in handling stress of decision situations, and only one of them corresponds to the rational behavior as explicated in decision theory. The other four patterns lead to defective decision making. For example, if the coping pattern is "defensive avoidance," the person escapes the decisional conflict by procrastinating, shifting responsibility to someone else, or constructing wishful rationalizations to bolster the least objectionable alternative, remaining selectively inattentive to corrective information. Although these patterns, as Mann and Janis (1982) concede, can occasionally be adaptive in saving time and effort, they often lead to defective decision making. "Deficiency" is here not directly defined in relation to some normative model, e.g., the SEU model, but more generally by the failure of people "to assimilate and combine information relating to outcome expectations and values" (p. 347) and particularly "to make use of the resources available to them for engaging in effective search for and appraisal of alternatives – within the limits of their cognitive capabilities and within limits imposed by powerful social constraints" (p. 346). In a large number of experimental studies, Janis and Mann (1977) have collected evidence for these coping defects, and they have tried to identify the conditions under which people exhibit different types of information processing behavior in decision situations.

Thus, Janis and Mann also emphasize the deficiences of human judgment and decision, but in their perspective, the sources are motivational, not cognitive in nature: "We see man not as a cold fish, but as a warm-blooded mammal, not as a rational calculator always ready to work out the best solution but as a reluctant decision maker – beset by conflicts, doubts, and worry, struggling with incongruous longings, antipathies, and loyalties ..." (1977, p. 15). This latter statement illustrates that, although the focus is explicitly on decision making under stress, the authors tend to generalize their theory to human decision making in general.

A similar approach, though from a cognitive standpoint, has been taken by Dörner who examined how people operate in highly complex and dynamic situations (e.g., Dörner, 1983; Dörner, Kreuzig, Reither, & Stäudel, 1983). In one of the studies, for instance, he used a computer model of a little town and had the subjects reign this town as mayor for ten simulated years in interaction with the computer. Having to cope with such ill-defined problems, subjects often apparently use a number of heuristic procedures which might be considered deficient. Dörner et al. do not compare the observed behavior with normative models of judgment and decision, however, but rather check whether the subjects' behavior meets certain demands of the situation. For example, requirements resulting from characteristics of the aspired goal are often managed by "redefining" or "forgetting" the final goal, by thematic vagabonding (e.g., swinging from one area of pursuit to another), or by encapsulation (e.g., sticking obstinately to a theme irrespective of the changing situation). Although the deficiencies displayed in these experiments are probably largely due to cognitive overload, some of the heuristics might well be used also in less complex situations.

In summary, the members of this camp view human judgment and decision making as deficient in several respects: Judgments are sometimes systematically biased, due to the use of heuristics; decisions are sometimes inconsistent, due to errors in the representation of the problem; and information search and combination is often defective, due to motivational factors. Mostly, this deficiency is not seen simply as a consequence of cognitive overload in highly complex or unfamiliar situations, but as rooted in mechanisms working within the human information processing system itself. People are prone to violate principles of rationality. A key assumption of at least the cognitive variants described is that there is a reliable and valid yardstick for the evaluation of judgment and decision, namely, the objectively reality, and consequently that there is some kind of objectively veridical mode of information processing which is mapped in the respective normative model.

The optimists: Biases are in research

In the last few years, a kind of counter-movement has developed. The members of this new camp partly question the validity of the other camp's findings, and partly emphasize the implicit rationality of human judgment and decision behavior. The biases, they argue, are not in human behavior but in the analysis of this behavior in the other camp (Berkeley & Humphreys, 1982). Interestingly enough, a leading representative of this camp has been a founder of the other camp with his research on conservatism in human information processing (Edwards, 1968); other researchers I include in this camp are Beach and Mitchell (1978), Einhorn and Hogarth (1981), Berkeley and Humphreys (1982), and Phillips (1983). Three theoretical arguments are raised in particular, which I will call the *meta-rationality* argument, the *continuity* argument and the *structure* argument.

The meta-rationality argument

The essence of this argument is that decision behavior which violates principles of rationality as, for instance, the principle of maximizing subjectively expected utility, can be described as perfectly rational if the cognitive *costs* of being rational are taken into account. To illustrate the point, when somebody wants to buy a book at the train station for a long ride, he will probably not check all available books in order to find the best of all but he will look at a few and then buy the first that he finds reasonably attractive. This person can be described as working on the satisficing principle, i.e., as not behaving fully rational from a SEU model perspective. But to many people, that is counter-intuitive. They would probably call a person non-rational if he *would* check all books in the store. With finite time and resources available, it is not rational to spend infinite effort on the exploration of all potential consequences of all options. Rather, the decision costs are weighted against the potential benefits resulting from the application of a decision strategy, and this may lead to violations of SEU model rationality which are, however, perfectly rational.

This point has been made by various authors (e.g., Miller & Starr, 1967; Einhorn & Hogarth, 1981; Janis & Mann, 1977; Hogarth, 1980; Montgomery & Svenson, 1976; cp. Payne, 1982). It is most explicitly and clearly represented in the contingency model of Beach and Mitchell (1978). In this model it is assumed that people make meta-decisions between the various decision strategies they have in their repertoire. Strategies differ with respect to the cognitive effort required and the probability with which they lead to an optimal solution (i.e., SEU maximizing, satisficing, elimination-by-aspects, coin flipping). Strategy selection is seen as contingent upon a (cost/benefit) compromise between the decision maker's desire to make the best decision and his or her negative feelings about investing time and effort in the decision making process. The strategy that is perceived as yielding the maximum net gain is the one selected. The specific choice depends on characteristics of the situation (e.g., familiarity of the problem, time pressure) and of the subject (e.g., knowledge, ability). Various hypotheses derived from this model have been experimentally investigated and have generally been confirmed (e.g., Christensen-Szalanski, 1978; McAllister, Mitchell, & Beach, 1979; Christensen-Szalanski, 1980).

The rationality cost, i.e., the cognitive effort associated with each strategy, is not formalized in Beach and Mitchell's (1978) model. For the comparison of multidimensional alternatives, Johnson (1979) has proposed a process model which allows the computation of the number of mental operations required. A similar method has been proposed by Shugan (1980). In both models it is assumed, however, that the researcher knows the number of attributes. For more simple strategies, a formal approach might be more difficult.

In the model of Beach and Mitchell (1978), maximizing of subjectively expected utility is only one of several available strategies each of which may be chosen rationally as the best strategy under the given conditions, even coin flipping. Violations of "classical" rationality are considered as errors that the subject anticipates and, more important, tolerates. People are global maximizers with local inconsistencies (Elster, 1979). Renunciation of cognitive effort might not only result, however, from the calculation that the costs outweigh the expected benefits but also from the knowledge that *"the very act of deliberating* can modify the character for the worse, and in ways judged even more important, through the stultifying effects on spontaneity"* (Elster, 1979, p. 40). Thus, to save spontaneity, which in itself has a value, a person might rationally select a strategy possibly leading to violations of SEU rationality.

The continuity argument

The core of this argument is the conceptualization of judgment and decision as moments in a continuous process. They sometimes may appear biased or deficient if treated or tested as discrete events, while they might in fact be very functional when considered as moments in a continuous and changing environment (Hogarth, 1981). An experiment by Ronen (1973), described in Hogarth (1981), can serve as an illustration: Subjects had to choose between two options with identical (positive) payoffs and probabilities of success. The outcomes were dependent on the results of two sequential events. In one option, there was a higher probability of success in the first step and a lower probability in the second step, while it was the other way around with the alternative option. Since the SEUs of the two options were equal, rationality would imply indifference. However, subjects preferred the option with the higher probability in the first step. Hogarth (1981) provides the following explanation: If people are used to a changing environment, they might give less weight to the probability of the second step since the situation might have changed when this phase has been reached; it might be attractive to stay in the game as long as possible, and therefore to choose the option with the higher probability of success in the first phase.

More generally, many experiments on probabilistic information processing have excluded the possibility of feedback and redundancy which, however, is characteristic of the environment and thus relevant for judgment and decision. Models have been tested under the assumption of stabile environment, while subjects might have operated under the assumption of a changing environment. A number of biases, demonstrated with the discrete approach, can be interpreted as indicators of cognitive mechanisms and strategies which are actually very functional in a continuous environment. Hogarth (1981) discusses several assumptions underlying prescriptive models which explicitly do not take this continuity into account, e.g., the *existence of a stabile time horizon:* An example given by Tversky and Kahneman (1973) for the use of availability resulting in a biased judgment is reinterpreted by Hogarth (p. 206) with the argument that in the specific experimental situation under time pressure, the application of this heuristic could be considered as very functional: People use the cues which are most available first, because in normal life one can expect to have a chance to correct such a judgment. It is therefore important to specify under which conditions the application of a heuristic is functional and under which it is not. Another assumption discussed is the *stability of preferences and goals* which may be wrong for various reasons (March, 1978): First, preferences develop over time. Choices imply, however, anticipations of future preferences, i.e., preferences at the time when the consequences incur (a point I discussed earlier in Section 2). Secondly, preferences are formed by experiences, and these experiences are often sought actively by people, sometimes in order to know more about their preferences. Thirdly, preferences are usually characterized by a high degree of ambiguity. Such ambiguity can be functional, because the person is open for further information and saves mental energy to clarify the ambiguity. Other assumptions discussed are the *stationarity of probabilistic processes,* the *independence of judgmental effects on consequences,* and the *abstraction from the competition character of action.* The continuity argument is raised by Hogarth (1981) not only against the contention of judgmental biases but also against the contention of representational errors.

The attack on the pessimists' camp can take two forms. Demonstrations of deficient judgment and decision can either be attributed to inadequate assumptions of the model, like fixed time horizons; the observed behavior was in fact efficient and functional, the model was wrong. Or, one can claim that the experimental situations used for testing the model had a very low ecological validity and that therefore biases and errors were possibly artifacts, encouraged by the researcher.

The structure argument

The third argument against the other camp has been raised in particular by Berkeley and Humphreys (1982) and Phillips (1983). The claim is that demonstrations of cognitive deficiency are questionable due to the neglect of the subjects' internal structural representation of the problem. The characterization of the observed behavior as biased rests on the assumption that the subjects share the experimenter's understanding of the problem structure. A common understanding of the problem structure can be assumed to be established by the use of process tracing methods or through the experimental instructions; or, it can be assumed to exist a priori because of the objective nature of the task, as illustrated by Tversky and Kahneman (1981) in their use of the analogy of perception.

As an example, Berkeley and Humphreys (1982) discuss the problem presented to subjects by Tversky and Kahneman (1981) in which two options are formulated either in terms of lives lost or in terms of lives saved. In the first case, subjects behaved risk averse, in the second case they behaved risk prone, interpreted by Tversky and Kahneman as inconsistent preferences since "it is easy to see that the two problems are effectively identical" (p. 453). Berkeley and Humphreys question this interpretation because the "uncertainty, concerning human agency in affecting subsequent states of the world, is left unresolved" (p. 222) in Tversky and Kahneman's formulation of the problem. Berkeley and Humphreys offer a different structural representation the subjects might have developed in order to resolve this uncertainty which would result in preferences perfectly consistent with SEU theory. A similar reasoning is found in Hogarth (1981) and Phillips (1983).

The second approach, in which the problem structure is imposed under the assumption of a common understanding, does not investigate experimental data in their own right as products of the subjects' reasoning, but compares them with data resulting from the application of a normative model to the problem in question, "the assumption being that the model represents the basis for rational choice (or inference) in the presented problem" (Berkeley & Humphreys, 1982, p. 230). Two implications of this assumption are questioned by the authors: First, the naturalization of small worlds, which means the exclusion of the subjects' individual "goal-closing" of his or her large world into the small world of the experimental moment and presenting the observed departures from veridicality as *cognitive* rather than motivational biases (p. 233). Second, the utilization of normative models as ideal types, i.e., as standards of comparison with the intuitive model of the subject; this requires, however, the investigation of whether there is a common understanding of the way in which the problem universe is to be goal-closed and thus does not permit imposition of a problem structure (p. 234).

This argument, then, focuses on the structural representation of the task and its significance for the interpretation of judgments and decisions. The representation depends strongly, however, on the context within which it is developed. Different contexts evoke different knowledge – elements and structures of knowledge – and thus will often lead to different behaviors. Each behavior might be consistent within the given context although inconsistent with some behavior towards the same task in a different context. The description of behavior as deficient or non-rational is not justified if it is not invariant over multiple contexts; to the contrary, invariant behavior would be deficient.

Two views are still possible here: One can go as far as Phillips (1983) and argue phenomenologically that there is no criterion for defining some "objective" problem representation as implied in Tversky and Kahneman's (1981) analogy between judgmental errors and perceptual illusions. Or one can assume such a criterion but conclude that "task representation may be of more importance in defining errors than the rules they (the people) use within that representation" (Einhorn & Hogarth, 1981, p. 60), e.g., if one considers the case of a paranoid person. In both views, however, the problem of structure is essential for a discussion of deficiency/efficiency.

In summary, the members of this camp challenge the view that human judgment and decision is cognitively deficient. They question this conclusion with different arguments: Because an important parameter has been neglected, namely, the cost of a decision strategy; because judgments and decisions are treated as discrete events and not as moments in a continuous process; and because no attention has been paid to the internal structural representation of the problem as the person- and context-dependent basis of judgment and decision. The emphasis in all three positions is less on demonstrating efficiency of human behavior than on studying more carefully under what conditions people show which kind of behavior, and not "too easily to adopt a crude view of human rationality" (Slovic, 1972a).

Résumé and outlook

It seems that the history of research on human judgment and decision making in the last thirty years represents a typical example of scientific progress. Against the once dominant model of rational man, the camp I have called pessimistic formed and questioned this conception by demonstrating deficiencies in judgment and decision. Now after this camp has ruled decision research for many years, it comes under attack by a new group that I have called optimistic which points to weaknesses in the former concepts and suggests even more differentiated perspectives of judgment and decision. Both camps have gained their impetus from the critique of the respective prevailing conception. Some of the criticisms, particularly of the optimists' camp against the pessimists' camp, have already been mentioned in the previous section. However, I will briefly sum up these points and add those more general arguments which have been exchanged between the two camps more recently.

The critique of the pessimists' position focuses on the following points: First, the experiments are of low ecological validity in the sense that they do not represent the majority of situations in which people have to give judgments and make decisions. Second, the experiments were designed such that biases and errors are not surprising since the situations and problems were taken out of any real life context. Third, important parameters like cognitive effort have not been accounted for in the models used as yardsticks. Fourth, whether subjects cognitively represented the problem in the way the researcher assumed is rarely investigated. A more general, fifth argument is that this research has focused too much on errors rather than on the cognitive processes per se; not only is it hard to define what errors are, they also constitute atypical behavior samples.

The rejoinder of the pessimists' camp is: First, meta-theories on the selection of strategies according to cognitive effort considerations are methodologically more or less immune to charges of "irrationality"; any behavior that violates the SEU model can be "rationalized" by recurring to some higher level of rationality. Second, demonstrations of differences between the experimental and real world situations do not prove that these differences matter. Third, speculations that subjects might have represented a problem cognitively differently than the researchers do not prove that they have done so. Fourth, the focus on errors is justified because (a) "they expose some of our intellectual limitations and suggest ways of improving the quality of our thinking," (b) they "often reveal the psychological processes and the heuristic procedures that govern judgment and inference," and (c) they "help the mapping of human intuitions by indicating which principles of statistics or logic are non-intuitive or counter-intuitive" (Kahneman & Tversky, 1982, p. 124). Clearly, these are defensive arguments but therefore not less reasonable than the offensive arguments of the authors. It is not to be expected that this camp will capitulate as easy under the attack as did the "rational man" when that concept was besieged by today's defenders.

As Heraclit said, war is the father of all and the king of all. The theoretical and empirical work in both camps as well as the dispute between them has generated many data, insights and ideas. The understanding of judgment and decision making has been dependent and differentiated and has opened new, more comprehensive research perspectives. I will characterize briefly some essential aspects of the present state of the debate and of the direction future research might take.

For almost all arguments, the theoretical point of reference is still the SEU model or some variant of it (e.g., prospect theory), despite some harsh critique (e.g., Fischhoff, Goitein, & Shapira, 1982). While one side provides evidence that people do not behave as the model predicts, the other side demonstrates that with different theoretical assumptions or experimental settings the same behavior might not violate the model at all. Pitz said (in 1977) that "models based upon some variant of expected value theory have the attraction of being familiar and easy to work with, and inertia is one of the strongest forces in nature" (p. 421); another reason is probably that the SEU model is hard to falsify since "with sufficient ingenuity, one can always find something that a particular decision maker has maximized in a particular situation" (Fischhoff et al., 1982, p. 317). Pitz also said that "until a well developed, systematic alternative to the normative model is available, it is likely that new approaches will have no more lasting success than did Gestalt psychology" (1977, p. 421). This still seems to be a fairly valid description of the present situation. However, that no real alternative has been offered might also be taken as an indicator of the strength of the model as a core of theories of judgment and decision. The wide use of expectancy-value models also in other areas of psychology, particularly in motivation research, is a further indicator (cp. Feather, 1982).

The issue is not anymore what the limitations of the human cognitive system are. All approaches assume that there are boundaries for rationality in situations of cognitive overload due to the capacity and processing limits of the system. The issue is how people form judgments and make decisions, and particularly whether they operate rationally *within* the constraints. While one side focused on errors, biases and fallacies, the other side considers this a theoretically questionable and also too negative approach. In this view, research on judgment and decision making has been driven too much by a concern for errors relative to a normative standard the validity of which one can doubt with good arguments (Einhorn & Hogarth, 1981).

The focus on errors has recently been defended by Kahneman and Tversky (1982) by pointing towards various advantages of this approach (see above). Kahneman and Tversky also argue that "the emphasis on the study of errors is characteristic of research on human judgment, but it is not unique to this domain: we use illusions to understand the principles of normal perception and we learn about memory by studying forgetting" (1982a, p. 123). I don't quite agree, for two reasons: First, because, although illusions are a subject of interest in the psychology of perception, the *emphasis* has certainly not been on errors. Second, memory research is not interested in errors *as such* but uses them as a dependent variable for testing models about storing or retrieval of information, i.e., about the "normal" memory processes and structures; researchers on memory do not demonstrate errors in their research, as do many researchers on judgment and decision. However, the recent discussion of the issue seems to have led to some rapprochement of positions. Kahneman and Tversky concede that "although errors of judgment are but a method by which some cognitive processes are studied, the method has become a significant part of the message" (1982a, p. 124), and they accentuate stronger than before, e.g., that the notion of judgmental heuristics should "provide a common account for both correct and incorrect judgments" (1982b, p. 325). If it is agreed, then, that "theoretically it is necessary to understand *all* reasoning data, regardless of their conformity to a normative rule system" (Evans, 1982, p. 319), the study of errors becomes a question of research strategy. Kahneman and Tversky, in their reply to Evans, argue that "errors may sometimes be more informative than correct judgments, which can be produced *either* by an initial valid intuition *or* by a subsequent correction" (1982b, p. 325).

Another important progress is to be seen in the now generally accepted conceptualization of judgment and decision as parts of a multi-stage cognitive process. Actually, activities that precede the "moment of decision" seem presently to be the prevailing object of theoretical and empirical work – in particular the acquisition and processing of information, or, in other terms, the generating and structuring of knowledge. Some work on predecisional cognitive processes is already available (cp. Einhorn & Hogarth, 1981), but new questions have come up. For instance, what are the implications of using the "conversational paradigm" (Berkeley & Humphreys, 1982; Kahneman & Tversky, 1982a)? How can we elicit or infer the cognitive representation of problems? We need theories of problem representation that explain the use and the results of particular judgmental and decision making strategies. There is also increasing interest in post-decisional processes, particularly the implementation of decisions (cp. Gasparski, 1980). Again, research has focused primarily on "errors," i.e., on the phenomenon that people often do not implement their mental decisions due to motivational and emotional factors (e.g., Sjöberg, 1980; Elster, 1979). Elster has analyzed the various strategies that people use to overcome this "weakness of will," interfering between decision and action (using Ulysses as a prominent example who bound himself to the mast in order not to give in to the temptation by the sirens. He put this problem in the context of the rationality debate: "Man often is not rational, and rather exhibits *weakness of will*. Even when not rational, man knows that he is irrational and can *bind himself* against the irrationality. This second-best or imperfect rationality takes care both of reason and passion. What is lost, perhaps, is the sense of adventure" (Elster, 1979, p. 111).

A final lesson to be learned from the debate might be that one should avoid the term rationality in psychology at all. Obviously, the concept is used with different meanings; it is certainly no longer defined exclusively by formal coherence and consistency. An alternative way of handling this difficulty is, however, to distinguish explicitly various meanings of the term. Besides formal rationality, concepts like substantive rationality and procedural rationality might be useful for a theory of judgment and decision (Simon, 1978). *Substantive* rationality captures an important aspect of the term as it is used in common language, namely, how realistic, correct, adequate some judgment or decision is with respect to the real world – the paranoid with his perfectly consistent beliefs and values provides an example. Rationality is not only a question of whether a choice is in line with a person's belief and preferences, but also a question of what sort of preferences and beliefs the person holds, a point elaborated also by Einhorn and Hogarth (1981). Differently stated, a decision might be consistent (and thus formally rational), but the judgments that provide the input for the decision might be very poor (and thus the choice might be substantively not rational). *Procedural* rationality can be linked to sustantive rationality easily if one asks what information is searched for and used by a person to form values and beliefs, whether the person tried hard enough to anticipate future consequences of current actions and future preferences for those consequences, etc. What Janis and Mann (1977) describe as "vigilant information processing" might be considered one aspect of this kind of rationality. Particularly in a social context, when decisions have to be justified, procedural rationality can be much more important than substantive matters about which agreement often cannot be reached.

My conclusion from the debate between the two camps with respect to the rationality problem is threefold: *First*, we should be liberal (which does not mean vague) in our use of the rationality concept. The different meanings that I have briefly described (and others, cp. March, 1978) are all useful tools in analyzing judgment and decision processes. *Second*, we may use the concept in its prescriptive sense legitimately in situations where prescription is asked for, like in decision aiding or in decision training. Criteria for defining rationality in a prescriptive sense can be taken from our knowledge about the real world, from our intellectual system and from the social consensus – however relative these criteria are in a historical or cultural sense. *Third*, we should use the concept in descriptive research more cautiously because it too easily entices to label all behavior that does not meet the criteria as deviant or deficient, as errors, biases, or whatever. I subscribe to Kahneman and Tversky's balanced advice that we "should avoid overly strict interpretations, which treat reasonable answers as errors, as well as to overly charitable interpretations, which attempt to a rationalize every response" (1982a, p. 124). *Finally*, the recognition of the conditionality of normative models on assumptions about the environment as well as the cognitive representation of that environment, most convincingly elaborated by Einhorn and Hogarth (1981) and Payne (1982), is in my opinion the synthesis emerging from the debate between the (pessimistic) thesis and the (optimistic) antithesis. Implicitly or explicitly, it is agreed to by members of both camps.

40. On cognitive illusions and their implications

Ward Edwards and Detlof von Winterfeldt

Psychologists, and a few others, have been producing a literature on systematic errors in human performance of inference and decision-making tasks. The topic is large and complex, and the literature is unmanageable. The focus on human error in general is a folkway of psychology, particularly of experimental psychology (see Edwards, 1983). The fact that human beings sometimes make systematic intellectual errors is clearly a topic for psychological research, whereas the fact that other human beings under other circumstances can produce right answers to the same questions is ordinarily the subject matter of some other discipline, usually the one that discovered how to find the right answers. The motivation for the greater part of the research we will discuss has been clearly described by Kahneman and Tversky.

There are three related reasons for the focus on systematic errors and inferential biases in the study of reasoning. First, they expose some of our intellectual limitations and suggest ways to improve the quality of our thinking. Second, errors and biases often reveal the psychological processes that govern judgment and inference. Third, mistakes and fallacies help the mapping of human intuitions by indicating which principles of statistics or logic are non-intuitive or counter-intuitive. (1982a, p. 494)

This research strategy has led to many insights into human information-processing abilities and limits.

This essay is derived from a more extensive treatment in *Decision Analysis and Behavioral Research* (von Winterfeldt & Edwards, in press). Both focus on some kinds of errors to the exclusion of others. Specifically, they explore four kinds of intellectual tasks: probability assessment and revision, decision making, intuitive physics, and logic and mental arithmetic. We call the kinds of errors with which this essay deals "cognitive illusions." The first half of that phrase emphasizes the intellectual nature of the tasks; the second is intended to suggest that these phenomena are quite similar to a variety of perceptual illusions extensively studied by psychologists.

Because we are not lawyers, our speculations about the relevance of the cognitive illusions to what lawyers and courts do are not likely to be worth much. We produce them, more for your entertainment than as serious thinking, at the end of the essay. More important by far is the topic of human cognitive competence. The publication of paper after paper about easily predictable human intellectual errors is bound to produce in some of their readers the impression that such errors are both widespread and inevitable. The main intent of this essay, aside from reviewing some of the literature, is to explore the extent to which that impression may be justified; that is, to try to find a meaningful perspective, in the light of this research, from which to assess what to expect from people faced with difficult intellectual tasks.

A thorough review of the literature requires a book, not an essay. Fortunately, such a book appeared in 1982: *Judgment under Uncertainty: Heuristics and Biases*, edited by Daniel Kahneman, Paul Slovic, and Amos Tversky. In a slightly earlier book, Hogarth (1980) defined at least 27 sources of bias or error in judgment and decision making. A number of older sources have also reviewed the aspects of this literature that are concerned with probability assessment and decision making. We are not familiar with any reviews of the research on intuitive physics. Extensive reviews of errors in mental arithmetic can be found in the literature of educational psychology but are directed almost entirely to errors made by children as they relate to instruction and learning. One or two are cited later.

The research paradigm for finding cognitive illusions

Webster's Third New International Dictionary defines *illusion* as, among other things, "the state or fact of being intellectually deceived or ... misled." The cognitive illusions fit the definition exactly.

The elements of every cognitive illusion are the same.

1. A formal rule that specifies how to determine a correct (usually, *the* correct) answer to an intellectual question. The question normally includes all information required as input to the formal rule.
2. A judgment, made without the aid of physical tools, that answers the question.

3. A systematic discrepancy between the correct answer and the judged answer. (Random errors do not count.)

Sometimes it takes two or three questions to demonstrate the presence of a cognitive illusion; the principle is the same.

This exposition of cognitive illusions will use relatively simple examples and demonstrations, usually taken verbatim from the early experiments that identified them. It will then speculate about possible intuitive remedies, using whatever relevant experimental and applied literature we know of. We consider it self-evident that by far the best remedy for such errors is to use the formal rules that lead to the right answers rather than unaided intuition to answer questions to which they apply.

Though our background is in psychology, our profession is decision analysis. This means that we set out to use a combination of formal analytic tools, psychological skills, and tricks of our trade to help people and organizations make valid inferences and wise decisions. Decision analysis is an applied discipline, and we are appliers as well as researchers. Our focus on helping people and organizations to act wisely in the presence both of irreducible uncertainties and of values that must be traded off against one another in making decisions dominates the expository part of this essay.

Cognitive illusions in probability and inference

The research on probability assessment and inference to be discussed here grows out of the Bayesian point of view about those topics (see, e.g., Edwards, Lindman, & Savage, 1963). Those familiar with that viewpoint should skip the highly condensed précis that follows.

A probability is a number between 0 and 1. Probabilities describe propositions about events; for expository convenience we shall discuss only finite sets of events, though the generalization to infinite sets is straightforward. Probabilists agree that probabilities are in some sense measures of uncertainty. Bayesians hold that the sense is quite straightforward: A probability is an appropriate description of your (or our, or someone's) uncertainty about the truth of a proposition asserting that the event will happen, or perhaps that it has happened. This means that probabilities describe *opinions* about the truth or falsity of propositions about events. Because an opinion must be some person's opinion, and because it describes the person as well as the proposition that the opinion is about and the event to which the proposition refers, such probabilities are usually called "personal." The term *subjective* is also often used; we avoid it, both because in a technical sense many personal probabilities are not very subjective, for there can be little disagreement about them, and because many scientists, not including us, find that word pejorative.

A major competitor to the Bayesian position is the frequentistic view.

Frequentists hold that probabilities are the limiting values that relative frequencies approach as the number of observations of a random variable increases without limit. Although Bayesians would often regard information about relative frequencies as crucial to forming their opinions, they disagree with frequentists both about how such relative frequencies should be used to estimate probabilities and about what to do when relative frequencies are unavailable or even unimaginable. Bayesian and frequentistic approaches lead to quite different conclusions about the rules for statistical inference, and statisticians of these persuasions have engaged in running arguments since the early 1960s.

An important consequence of our Bayesian position is that it is entirely meaningful to assess the probability of a unique event. How likely is it, for you, that the 20th president of the United States was a Republican? He either was or was not, and no relative frequency seems relevant. But unless you are better informed about 19th-century presidents than we are, you are not sure whether he was or was not. You do have relevant information. You probably know that the 20th president served after Lincoln and before Theodore Roosevelt and that the Republican party existed and was quite successful during that period. You may be unsure what number would best describe the degree of uncertainty you feel about that assertion, but on the basis of the information you now have you would surely regard .5 as an underestimate. As the example illustrates, one way of finding out your probability that a proposition is true is to ask you. Psychologists have studied procedures for asking such questions and the merit of the resulting answers extensively; we review a bit of the relevant literature later.

Opinions change in the light of evidence. Let $P(H)$ be your opinion about how likely hypothesis H is before you receive datum D, and let $P(H|D)$ be your opinion about H now that you know D. Then

$$P(H|D) = P(D|H) \, P(H)/P(D).$$

This equation is one of the many ways of writing Bayes's theorem. $P(D|H)$, the probability that the datum would be observed if the hypothesis were true, is its essence. The denominator, $P(D)$, is an unimportant normalizing constant that forces the values of $P(H|D)$ to sum to 1 over the set of hypotheses being considered. If, for example, you are considering H and not-H, then

$$P(D) = P(D|H) \, P(H) + P(D|\text{not-}H) \, P(\text{not-}H).$$

Bayes's theorem is trivial and uncontroversial; it is simply a consequence of the fact that the probabilities of an exhaustive set of mutually exclusive events must sum to 1. Its importance results from the fact that it is a normatively optimal rule for thinking; it tells you exactly how much you should revise your prior opinions (represented as $P(H)$) in the light of relevant new evidence (represented as $P(D|H)$ and $P(D|\text{not-}H)$) to form your posterior opinions (represented as $P(H|D)$). That is, it is one of the rules for getting the right answer specified by the cognitive illusions paradigm. Indeed, it is an especially significant one, because the task of revising opinions in the light of new evidence, sometimes called by such names as inference, diagnosis, or trial by jury, is of very considerable human importance.

Conservatism

In the late 1950s, mostly as a result of Savage's work (1954), psychologists became aware of Bayes's theorem and of its importance as a normative rule for inference. The cognitive illusions paradigm had been invented much earlier, but this seemed to be an especially attractive context in which to apply it.

Phillips, Hays, and Edwards (1966) did the first study. In an unnecessarily complex task they found that no subject revised opinions nearly so much as the optimal Bayesian rule required. This inability has come to be called conservatism in probabilistic inference. Phillips and Edwards (1966) thereupon developed the simplest task they could invent that still embodies the basic Bayesian idea, the bookbag-and-pokerchips task. A subject is presented with two bookbags. One contains, for example, 70% red chips and 30% blue chips; the other has the opposite composition. One bag is chosen at random, so that the prior probability of the predominantly red bag is .5. Then a sample is taken with replacement, generating, for example, six red chips and four blue chips. The subjects are asked to provide posterior probabilities or odds in favor of the bag favored by the data. Typical responses in the above example are .6–.7, quite different from the normatively correct .84. The finding, strong and robust in experiments like these, has been that human inference is routinely conservative.

Early explanations of this phenomenon included response bias (people do not like to respond with extreme numbers), misperception (people underestimate the diagnostic impact of the data), and misaggregation (people perceive the impact of a single datum correctly but fail to aggregate properly the joint impact of several data). (See Edwards, Phillips, Hays, & Goodman, 1968; Wheeler & Edwards, 1975.) These explanations, together with the orderly nature of the conservatism phenomenon, led to relatively straightforward designs of tasks and procedures to avoid conservatism. Two are of particular interest. A system called PIP (for Probabilistic Information Processing; see Edwards, 1962; Edwards et al., 1968) separated the two tasks of assessing the diagnostic impact of particular data and aggregating diagnostic impacts into posterior opinions, assigning the former to human judgment and the latter to Bayes's theorem. Another way to reduce conservatism is to use response modes that call for responses in the midst of, rather than far away from, the numerical representations of the information to be aggregated (Eils, Seaver, & Edwards, 1977).

In the 1970s, the conservatism literature encountered a host of criticisms that challenged both the previous explanations and the corrective mechanisms they suggested. (For examples, see Beach, Wise, & Barclay, 1970; Kahneman & Tversky, 1972; Marks & Clarkson, 1972; Slovic & Lichtenstein, 1971; Vlek & Wagenaar, 1979.) The crux of many of these criticisms was that the Bayesian inference task is too complex for unaided human performance and consequently that subjects asked to perform Bayesian tasks seek and find simplifying strategies. A number of such strategies were suggested and explored in experiments, but none seemed to explain a broad range of studies of Bayesian tasks successfully.

A more general criticism, not only of conservatism experiments but of other experiments on probability assessment, also arose in the 1970s. Its essence is that laboratory experiments use contrived inference problems of types that occur rarely outside the laboratory and are misleading in their structure (Navon, 1978; Winkler & Murphy, 1973). In particular, real-world inference problems usually involve unreliable source data and conditional dependencies among data and among intermediate hypotheses. (Two data are conditionally independent, given a hypothesis, if the probability of either, given the hypothesis, is unaffected by knowledge that the other occured. In symbols, if D_i and D_j are two data, then

$$P(D_i|H) = P(D_i|H, D_j)$$

for all values of i and j and for all hypotheses being considered. Conditional independence is so demanding a requirement on the relationships among data and hypotheses that it virtually never describes anyone's opinions except in the special contexts of laboratory experiments and other statistical inferences based on random sampling.)

We now believe that simple cures for conservatism are probably less useful than detailed structuring of actual inference problems to reflect facts of life such as the unreliability of many data and the existence of complex, conditionally dependent inference structures. Such structures call for disaggregated judgments of probabilities, but the appropriate combination rules for these probabilities are much more demanding than the simple single-stage formulation of Bayes's theorem.

Ignoring base rates

Bayes's theorem specifies that proper inference from fallible evidence should combine that evidence with prior probabilities, that is, the opinions the person making the inference held before the new evidence became available (see Edwards et al., 1963). Often, though not always, the relevant prior information takes the form of base rates. Before you get close enough to the approaching blonde to recognize eye color, you may consider it likely that she has blue eyes, simply because so many blondes do. In recent years, a number of experiments have called into question whether people actually use base rates in probability judgments.

The seminal study of neglect of base rate was done by Kahneman and Tversky. One group of subjects was given the following cover story:

A panel of psychologists have interviewed and administered personality tests to 30 engineers and 70 lawyers, all successful in their respective fields. On the basis of this information, thumbnail descriptions of the 30 engineers and 70 lawyers have been written. You will find on your form five descriptions, chosen at random from the 100 available descriptions. For each description, please indicate your probability that each person described is an engineer, on a scale from 0 to 100. (1973, p. 241)

Subjects in another large group were given the same story except that it referred to 30 lawyers and 70 engineers. Both groups were then presented with five descriptions. For example:

Jack is a 45-year-old man. He is married and has four children. He is generally conservative, careful, and ambitious. He shows no interest in political and social issues and spends most of his free time on his many hobbies, which include home carpentry, sailing, and mathematical puzzles.

On the basis of this description, the subjects were expected to judge the probability that Jack is a lawyer (or, for some subjects, an engineer). The data indicate that base rates did not make much difference, although when the same subjects were asked what their judgment would be in the absence of the personality description, they indicated that they would in fact use the base rates. Kahneman and Tversky concluded that in the presence of specific individuating evidence, prior probabilities, by which they meant base rates, are ignored.

This neglect of base rates has been replicated in a number of studies using various stimuli, including some in which the numerical diagnosticity could be inferred, thus providing the ingredients for a straightforward Bayesian calculation. (See, e.g., Bar-Hillel, 1980; Carroll & Siegler, 1977; Hammerton, 1973; Lyon & Slovic, 1976.) Although these studies generally supported the existence of a base-rate fallacy, they also showed that based rates are sometimes taken into account: when the link between base rate and target event is causal, when base rates appear relevant, when the base rates relate to individuating information, and when both diagnostic and base-rate information are essentially statistical.

This body of experimental evidence combines with a number of real-world observations to generate a picture of a robust phenomenon. The seminal paper about the real-world consequences of that neglect was written by Meehl and Rosen (1955). Dershowitz (1971) and McGargee (1976) have called attention to the consequences of failure to consider base rates in judicial contexts. Lykken (1975) noted the contribution of that failure to misinterpretations of lie detector tests. Oskamp (1965) complained of it in connection with interpreting case studies. Eddy (1982), in a very stimulating article, showed how not only medical doctors but also their teachers and textbooks fall into the base-rate trap.

Bar-Hillel (1980) put all this evidence and thought together in a most orderly and persuasive way. She summed it up as follows:

People integrate two items of information only if both seem to them equally relevant. Otherwise, high relevance information renders low relevance information irrelevant. One item of information is more relevant ... than another if it somehow pertains to it more specifically.

She suggests that this can happen in two ways:

(1) the dominating information may refer to a set smaller than the overall population to which the dominated items refer ... (2) the dominating information may be causally linked to the judged outcome, in the absence of such a link on behalf of the dominated information. This enhances relevance because it is an indirect way of making general information relate more specifically to individual cases.

Thus, Bar-Hillel sees the Tversky – Kahneman findings about causality as a special case of her more general principle of relevance.

In real-world applications of Bayesian inference models, one constructs a problem structure that appropriately reflects the statistical properties of the environment and that meets the analytic requirements of the Bayesian model. We believe that appropriate structures go a long way toward avoiding the base-rate bias. In almost every experimental situation that we reviewed, a little help in structuring the inference problem would have enormously improved the subjects' performance (or shown that subjects had, indeed, a different problem structure in mind). One part of problem structuring is to identify classes of hypotheses and events that are useful for decision making and that allow discrimination among data. Often such classes are constructed so that the prior distribution is relatively flat; that is, the hypotheses being considered are a priori fairly close to being equally likely. (If a prior distribution is very steep, one often tries to find subdivisions of the high-probability hypothesis.) Flat or gently sloping priors can be ignored. The structuring process also decomposes the problem in a way that highlights the separate relevance of priors, diagnostic information, reliability information, and their dependencies. This decomposition alone should enhance the inference maker's awareness of base rates, priors, diagnosticities, and their inter-linkages.

In addition, we are convinced from everyday experience that professionals working at their professions make extensive use of base rates. Doctors routinely make diagnoses of upper respiratory ailments on the basis of history and physical data combined with base-rate information. Lawyers concerned with criminal defense routinely assess statements by their clients on the basis of base rates. Accountants use base-rate information in deciding what to explore carefully in audits. And so on. In a sense, sophisticated awareness of and use of base rates is a key element of what we mean by expertise.

Once the problem is appropriately structured, the simplest way to avoid the base-rate fallacy is by modeling priors explicitly, assessing likelihoods or likelihood ratios, and using Bayes's theorem to aggregate. Subjects thus would never be asked to aggregate base rates and diagnostic information intuitively. But sometimes intuitive aggregation cannot be avoided, and if Bar-Hillel's explanation is correct, aggregation of two nonequally relevant items of information can lead to distortions when done in the head. In such a case, the literature suggests the following strategies.

First, if both diagnostic information and base-rate information are essentially statistical, their statistical nature and interlinkages should be stressed. Second, if both can be related causally to the target event, the causal chains should be pointed out for both. Third, one could provide individuating information about base rates (as is usually implicit in diagnostic information). Fourth, Nisbett and Borgida (1975) suggested and Nisbett, Borgida, Crandall, and Reed (1976) demonstrated that one can make the base-rate information more dramatic and less abstract by using a few concrete examples instead of a set of descriptive statistics. All of these strategies essentially attempt to put base-rate and diagnostic information on an equal footing. Of course, the same strategies apply if two pieces of information of the same kind (e.g., two pieces of base-rate information; two pieces of diagnostic information) have different degrees of relevance.

Ignoring sample size

A series of experiments by Tversky and Kahneman (1971a, 1973, 1974) showed that subjects tend to ignore the sample size when constructing subjective sampling distributions and that even experienced and statistically trained psychologists fail to appreciate the power (or lack of power) of a small sample test. The result is what they call a human "belief in the law of small numbers." Tversky and Kahneman argue that this effect is due to the representativeness heuristic according to which a sample that is similar in features to the population is considered to be more likely than one that is dissimilar. Similarity thus can override other considerations like sample size.

In a particularly striking demonstration, Kahneman and Tversky (1972) asked subjects to construct sampling distributions for the mean height of

10, 100, and 1000 males drawn randomly from a population with mean 170 cm (the variance was not specified explicitly). Subjects gave individual probability estimates for five equal 5 cm intervals between 160 cm and 185 cm, plus estimates of the probabilities that the respective means would fall below 160 cm or above 185 cm. Sampling theory would, of course, prescribe that the variance of the subjective sampling distributions decrease with N. However, in Kahneman and Tversky's experiment, the median sampling distributions were, in fact, constant across N. Thus subjects appeared to be insensitive to sample size. Kahneman and Tversky (1972) report similar results for binomial sampling distributions, as well as for simpler questions about the probability that the proportion of elements in a sample would exceed a specified amount. For example, when subjects were asked to judge the probability that a random sample of newborn babies would contain at least 60% males, 56% of them gave the same answer independently of whether the sample was generated in a large hospital (large daily N) or a small hospital (small daily N), and the rest split evenly between the two hospitals.

These findings apply to sophisticated as well as naive subjects. Mathematical psychologists, trained in statistics, were found to be too confident in the replicability of statistically significant results. For example, they though that a sample of 10 subjects is very likely to reproduce a result that was previously found to be significant with 20 subjects at the .05 level (Tversky & Kahneman, 1971a).

Where the "law of small numbers" occurs, several precautions can be taken against it. One, as usual, is an appropriate problem structure, decomposing samples, data, and hypotheses to avoid judgments prone to the bias. This is especially true for the confidence judgments about samples, which can be structured and modeled in various ways (see, e.g., the two structures that Tversky and Kahneman, 1981, propose to construct a normative model for the significance test replication – there are many more of this sort). The findings by Bar-Hillel indicate that it is important to discuss with the experts and decision makers the nature of the sampling process, in particular considering replacement versus non-replacement, proportions of samples to populations, and the effect of sample sizes on sample statistics. Especially important is a search for reasonable hypotheses about parent populations, given particular samples. One of the first things experts and inference makers may do, when faced with questions about the likelihood of a sample, is to generate hypotheses that make the data likely. If the sample makes the hypotheses about the population proposed by experiment or scenario seem absurd, it is entirely predictable that subjects will consider others. Every model of a data-generating process should be judged on its merits; none ever deserves unlimited credence. For a detailed discussion of such issues, see Edwards et al. (1963).

Nonregressive prediction

When experts or statistically unskilled human subjects have to predict a variable y from knowledge of another variable x, and the correlation between x and y is less than perfect, traditional statistical models require that estimate to be regressive. In the extreme, if there is a zero correlation between the variables, the conditional estimate of y given x should coincide with the unconditional mean of y. The higher the correlation, the closer the estimate should fall to the 45-degree line (assuming standardized variables) in the graph of y as a function of x. Normative regressiveness of prediction makes several assumptions about the nature of the prediction task, but these are general enough so that, in most situations, predictions of imperfectly correlated variables should be regressive.

Several studies have found that subjects instead tend to predict by matching the dependent to the independent variable and do not sufficiently account for the lack of perfect correlation. Kahneman and Tversky (1973) found this effect when asking subjects to predict a student's grade point average given information about aptitude test scores. In this task, as in others, subjects showed marked lack of regressiveness. As with the base-rate and the sample-size biases, Tversky and Kahneman attribute nonregressiveness to the representativeness heuristic in that "the degree of confidence one has in a prediction reflects the degree to which the selected outcome is more representative of the input than are other outcomes" (1973, p. 455).

Several other studies found nonregressive prediction in a variety of settings (see, e.g., Jennings, Amabile, & Ross, 1982; Nisbett & Ross, 1980). These studies also included findings that subjects typically overestimate the amount of covariation between two variables; in other words, they have "illusions of reliability and validity" (see, e.g., Chapman & Chapman, 1967, 1969). This illusion is stronger when covariation is estimated on theoretical grounds and prior expectations, smaller when based on data (Jennings et al., 1982).

Real-world evidence also suggests nonregressiveness. Teachers of statistics often find the notion of regressive estimates to be difficult to teach. Statistically experienced psychologists often cling to arguments about test validities in spite of contrary statistical evidence. Less sophisticated social scientists interpret regressive data as meaningful effects.

Kahneman and Tversky (1979a) propose a heuristic procedure to correct nonregressive predictions. It consists of five steps. The first is to identify the reference class (the relevant population). The second is to assess the distribution of y in that class. (Some of the language of the paper suggests, appropriately, that several different distributions should be assessed conditional on several different values of x or of the x vector.)

The third is to obtain an estimate of the correlation between x and y, preferably by statistical means. The fourth is to correct the intuitive estimate of y by means of a computation based on that correlation. Kahneman and Tversky (1979a) do not expect that suggestion to lead to immediate acceptance of the revised estimate; instead, they hope that it can be used as a basis for persuasion.

Overconfidence

You would like any probability assessment to have two characteristics that relate to the outside world. One is obvious: You would like it to be extreme. An assessment close to 1 or 0 is far more useful guidance about what to expect, and therefore what to do, than an assessment near .5. The same thought for continuous distributions is that you would like probability density functions to be as peaked as possible.

The other property you would like probability assessment to have is called calibration, and it is much subtler than extremeness. You cannot assess the calibration of any single assessment. But if you have a number of probability assessments all of .6, then you would feel better about them if about 60% of the propositions so assessed turned out true and the other 40% turned out false than if, say, 10% or 90% turned out true. The same thought for any continuous distribution over a parameter is that you would like the area of the density function between any two cutoff points to correspond to the relative frequency with which the true value of the parameter falls between them.

Calibration and extremeness pull in opposite directions. Consider a weather forecaster who must every day specify a probability of rain. One way to proceed would be to inspect records, note that last year it rained on 60% of all days in that city, and so make each day's assessment for this year 60%. Such assessments (called climatological in meteorology) are likely to be well calibrated, because the percentage of rainy days changes relatively little from year to year. But they would be almost useless, because they do not differentiate among days.

The alternative of saying either that it will rain or that it will not rain is better, but not much. It makes no distinction between days on which you think it a bit more likely than not that it will rain and days on which you can see the puddles accumulating in the street while you formulate your forecast.

In order to balance the inward pull of the desire for good calibration against the outward pull of the desire for extremeness, you must use the evidence at hand – exactly what the weather forecasters do.

Research evidence about calibration is abundant but singularly hard to understand. Lichtenstein, Fischhoff, and Phillips (1982) have done an exceptionally good job of reviewing the experimental studies, which reach back all the way to Adams (1957). Most of the numerous experiments they review show excessively high assessments of probabilities over .5.

An important conclusion from Lichtenstein et al.'s review is that people are much less likely to be overconfident about easy probability judgments than about difficult ones. Pitz (1974) found that very difficult judgments produce most overconfidence. Lichtenstein and Fischhoff (1977), asking subjects to discriminate between such stimuli as drawings made by Asian or European children, found essentially no calibration at all; virtually any response meant about .5. Using various other stimuli and manipulations that made the discriminations easier, they found much better performance. Indeed, Lichtenstein and Fischhoff (1980) found underconfidence for easy judgments, as have several others. A particularly encouraging finding by Koriat, Lichtenstein, and Fischhoff (1980) is that respondents are less overconfident even on difficult questions if asked to write down reasons why the answer they prefer might be wrong.

Response modes may help reduce overconfidence, at least in the continuous case. Numerous studies have shown that probability distributions over continuous variables elicited using the fractile method are far too tight (see, e.g., Alpert & Raiffa, 1969; for reviews, see Lichtenstein, Fischhoff, & Phillips, 1977, 1982). Seaver, von Winterfeldt, and Edwards (1978) used direct probability assessment methods to construct continuous probability distributions and found that overconfidence and excessive tightness vanished.

Expertise helps too, even in experiments. Sieber (1974) and Pitz (1974) both found good calibration for students taking tests on the subject matter of courses they were then taking – about which they might be assumed to be fairly expert. However, Lichtenstein and Fischhoff (1977) found that graduate students in psychology did no better on psychology-related items than on general knowledge items. Perhaps expertise needs to be more specific than that.

Yet another conclusion implicit in the literature that Lichtenstein et al. review is that subtle verbal and other methodological issues may well have a lot to do with how such experiments come out, even though they mean nothing about the intellectual content of the task. A happy fourth conclusion suggested by some of the studies they review is that training in and experience at probability estimation can improve matters.

The facts that easy assessment tasks produce better calibration than difficult ones and that both training in probability estimation and experience at it improve performance help to explain other findings. Zlotnick (1968) found relatively good calibration for intelligence analysts, hampered primarily by a tendency to overestimate the probabilities of occurrence of dire events. That finding about overestimating the probability of dire events is widely reported in the real-assessments literature. The standard and plausible interpretation of it is that it is a by-product of

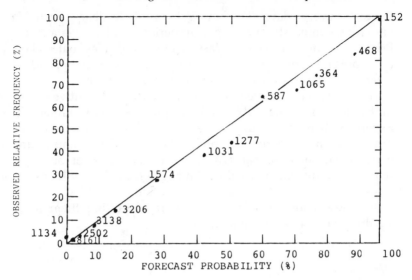

Figure 40.1. Calibration curve for weather forecasters. (*Source:* Murphy & Winkler, 1977a.)

utilities associated with the job. An intelligence analyst, or a doctor, would much rather warn of a dire event and later be proven wrong than to miss it in the first place.

Ludke, Stauss, and Gustafson (1977), in a study focused primarily on response modes, found relatively high quality of performance in calibration terms as well as others for all response modes studied; the respondents were trained medical personnel answering questions about familiar physiological topics like blood pressure. Lusted et al. (1980), reporting a very large field study of probability assessments by emergency room attending physicians, found generally good calibration except for the warning effect mentioned above. DeSmet, Fryback, and Thornbury (1979) also report good performance by medical respondents.

But the world's probability assessment championship clearly belongs to weather forecasters. Murphy and Winkler (1974, 1977a, 1977b) find average deviations of only .028 from perfect calibration for credible interval temperature forecasts. U.S. weather forecasters have been making probabilistic forecasts of rain since 1965. Figure 40.1 from Murphy and Winkler (1977a) shows the calibration data for 24,859 judgments made in Chicago during the four years ending June 1976. The number associated with each point is the number of observations it represents. A. H. Murphy (personal communication, SPUDM, 1983) reports data that are even better. He believes that forecasters learn to do better with experience, and other data support that belief. Among numerous reasons why weather forecasters are so good are: (*a*) they make forecasts every day; (b) they get event feedback each day about yesterday's forecast; (c) they get numerical feedback via a rule called the Brier score, an example of a class of numerical rules that make it optimal to report one's true opinion as one's probability estimate; and (d) to some extent their Brier scores bear on promotion and pay.

In sum: These data seem to us to argue that substantive expertise helps probability assessment by making the task easy rather than hard. Expertise about probability assessment helps too, probably because the proficient and experienced probability estimator simply understands better what such estimates mean. Feedback both of outcomes and of scoring rule information helps. And, given these conditions, probability assessors can be expected to do a good job.

But these conditions are rare. Short of putting them in place, can anything be done? Not much.

Hindsight

Two cognitive illusions have been cleverly studied by Fischhoff (1975, 1976; Fischhoff & Beyth, 1975); they are called the hindsight illusions. Fischhoff (1980) summarizes them as follows:

In hindsight, people consistently exaggerate what could have been anticipated in foresight. They not only tend to view what has happened as being inevitable, but also to view it as having appeared "relatively inevitable" before it happened. People believe that others should have been able to anticipate events much better than was actually the case. They even misremember their own predictions so as to exaggerate in hindsight what they knew in foresight.

These phenomena seem to be a probabilistic version of "I told you so." Fischhoff's studies leave no doubt about their reality.

Of all cognitive illusions, the hindsight illusions would seem to be easiest to correct: Simply make and write down the probability estimate before the event occurs or before the estimator learns the answer. But Fischhoff was motivated by the plight of the historian, condemned to look backward at events that have already occurred and to wonder what chance, if any, they had of occurring otherwise. (See Fischhoff, 1980, for a detailed discussion of these problems.) Writing history is an exercise in hindsight. Are the hindsight illusions an inevitable occupational disease for historians?

Perhaps. Still, the Bayesian position may have something to contribute. A formulation like "Twenty-four hours before the battle started, how probable was it that Napoleon would lose at Waterloo?" is at worst nonsense and at best incomplete, because it specifies neither whose the probability is nor the information on which it is based. The question "Twenty-four hours before the battle started, how probable did Napoleon consider it to be that he would lose at Waterloo?" is at least well framed;

historians might try to answer it. To do so, they would have to find out what Napoleon then knew about his own past record of successes and failures and about the state of his enemies' forces, and what scenarios he was considering about how the battle would go. This strips the problem down to at least potentially manageable size. The sunken wall, for example, is irrelevant; Napoleon did not know it was there. Thus formulated, the apparent inevitabilities of history look less inevitable.

Proper formulation of the probability question is not necessarily a cure. Fischhoff's studies imply that the historian's post hoc point of view fairly well assures the first bias. They are silent about what would happen if the historian were to try to see the world the way Napoleon saw it on the spot – admittedly an extraordinarily difficult exercise of imagination.

Debiasing

Von Winterfeldt and Edwards (in press) say,

Assessing uncertainties that may control significant decisions is serious business, and should be done in the right atmosphere. The analyst should work either one-on-one or in a small group. . . . Classroom settings are inappropriate. . . . [The respondent] should understand the techniques to be used, as much as time and other limits permit. . . . Good elicitation practice is never to rely on only one way of asking. Instead, ask the same or related questions in various ways, looking for inconsistencies. If you find some, be glad. They can be fed back to the respondent, who must then be asked to think some more, in order to get rid of them. Anything that promotes hard thought and insight helps. . . . We recognize some idealism in this set of prescriptions. Time, respondent patience, or cost may not permit. If they do, the enhanced accuracy may not be worth while. . . . Our advice has two purposes: to specify standards of skilled performance for an analyst, and to provide a check-list against which to assess the conditions of experimental studies that conclude that respondents do a poor job of uncertainty assessment. We are not very impressed with evidence that performance is poor unless the analyst went to great pains to try to help the respondent do well.

Virtually none of the experimental literature so far reviewed conforms to these criteria. Indeed, the criteria are inconsistent with the part of the cognitive illusions paradigm that calls for intuitive, unaided judgments. Because much of that literature has in various ways argued that people make systematic errors in assessing uncertainties, it is natural to dismiss such studies by saying "Oh, they didn't do it right." But a number of studies have in fact tried out, one by one, some of the ways of improving elicitation procedures explicit or implicit in this essay. Fischhoff (1982) has written an extraordinarily thoughtful and insightful review of such studies in the context of overconfidence and the hindsight biases.

Consider Table 40.1, taken from Fischhoff (1982). Fischhoff's proposed list of debiasing strategies bears a very close resemblance indeed to the rules for probability estimation we have proposed already and to some

Table 40.1. *Debiasing methods according to underlying assumption*

Assumption	Strategies
Faulty tasks	
Unfair tasks	Raise stakes
	Clarify instructions/stimuli
	Discourage second-guessing
	Use better response modes
	Ask fewer questions
Misunderstood tasks	Demonstrate alternative goal
	Demonstrate semantic disagreement
	Demonstrate impossibility of task
	Demonstrate overlooked distinction
Faulty judges	
Perfectible individuals	Warn of problem
	Describe problem
	Provide personalized feedback
	Train extensively
Incorrigible individuals	Replace them
	Recalibrate their responses
	Plan on error
Mismatch between judges and task	
Restructuring	Make knowledge explicit
	Search for discrepant information
	Decompose problem
	Consider alternative situations
	Offer alternative formulations
Education	Rely on substantive experts
	Educate from childhood

Source: Fischhoff, 1982.

that emerged from our discussion of calibration. One omission compared with our list is the idea of convergent operations: asking the same or related questions in such a way as to elicit inconsistencies and then using these inconsistencies as stimuli to reelicitation. The omission is major, because it is the most important thing a decision analyst does during probability elicitation. A second major omission is that Fischhoff rules out significant computational assistance. Still, Fischhoff's list is a very serious attempt to examine methodological deficiencies of probability elicitation experiments.

Fischhoff proceeds to review a rather large number of studies that attempt to correct one or another of the faults he lists by using one or more of the strategies he lists. His review is both detailed and discouraging. Such corrections, at the level of intensity at which they have been tried, on the whole do very little to correct the two biases he examines. The two most effective procedures seem to be to make the task easier (or, equivalently, to enhance the substantive abilities and information that the respondent brings to it) and to teach probability estimation skills. The review seems to us to slight somewhat the earlier literature on effects of response modes.

Fischhoff's summing-up is a gem of balanced thought. One point it makes is especially important to the perspective taken by this essay. We have assumed all along that probability assessments are important enough that one should work hard to get them right.

[T]he relative validity of casual and work-hard laboratory experiments depends upon the real world situations to which their results are to be extrapolated. Each has its place. Understanding the laboratory-world match requires good judgment in characterizing both contexts. For example, work-hard situations are not necessarily synonymous with important situations. People may not work hard on an important problem unless they realize both the centrality of a judgment to the problem's outcome and the potential fallibility of that judgment. (Fischhoff, 1982, p. 441)

Probability judgments are often not central to important decision problems of which they are a part. And, clearly, the overwhelming majority of our uncertainties bear either on trivial decisions or on no decisions at all. In a sheer numerical sense, instances in which it is important to get the measurement of uncertainty just right are quite rare, and the kinds of uncertainty judgments studied in typical experiments are much more common, though still rare.

Anchoring

When people are asked to generate an estimate, they frequently anchor on an obvious or convenient number (e.g., the mean, the mode) and then adjust upward or downward if there is a reason to believe that the correct number should be moved in either direction. In many situations that strategy works well, in particular when anchors are finely graded over the scale of estimates. Diamond evaluation is an example. The four standard dimensions for such evaluations are cut, color, clarity, and carats. Carats are, of course, easily measured on a balance. Diamond experts disagree about whether cut should be evaluated by a complex formula based on physical measurements or by intuitive judgments. But all agree that color and clarity must be assessed judgmentally. The training process uses many exemplars; the judgment reduces to assessing the similarity of the new diamond to remembered or currently available exemplars.

In other situations, anchoring and adjustment can lead to misjudgments. Slovic, Fischhoff, and Lichtenstein (1977) reviewed a number of studies showing the effect. Tversky and Kahneman (1974) argued that in probability judgments people frequently underadjust and thereby produce predictable biases in their numerical estimates.

Bar-Hillel (1973) and J. J. Cohen (1972) show that the probability of compound events is typically overestimated, and this seems to be an anchoring effect. People anchor on one event and fail to appreciate that multiplying two probabilities less than 1 by each other will produce a number less than either of them.

The previously discussed overconfidence bias has also been interpreted as an anchoring and adjustment bias (see, e.g., Slovic & Lichtenstein, 1971). By centering judgments around some median or modal value, subjects may attempt to find fractiles that are not sufficiently far removed from the anchor values.

In decision analytic practice, the key to reducing anchoring and adjustment biases is the use of multiple anchors and convergent validation techniques. When assessing continuous probability distributions, for example, one may begin by identifying the mean, the mode, and the plausible range of the random variable. In addition, the analyst could use two different assessment techniques: fractiles and direct probability estimation. The inevitable inconsistencies should lead to insights, discussions, and resolution. Sometimes an analyst may have a suspicion that respondents will anchor on some value like the most likely value or on a very low or very high value. In that case it is good practice to provide respondents with "counter-anchors" to "break" their intuitive anchors. In other cases it is useful to construct probabilities over different random variables, which can be formally related but invite anchors that produce divergent assessments.

Retrieval and scenario-based availability

Tversky and Kahneman (1973) presented a number of studies concerned with the effect of various kinds of availability of instances or answers on judgments. Because we are trying to categorize instances according to the nature of the normative principle that leads to the right answer, rather than according to the underlying psychological mechanism, we shall discuss only some of those studies here, along with others conducted since.

The form of availability we discuss here has been called a bias, but the name may be inappropriate. Subjects tend to estimate a higher probability for those events for which they can easily generate or recall instances. The most familiar real-world examples are those in which extensive publicity about some atrocious crime or unusual kind of disaster much enhances lay assessment of how probable the event is. Every light-plane pilot knows that the true statement "The most dangerous part of the flight is the drive to and from the airport" is shocking and objectionable to most nonpilots, because plane crashes are normally publicized whereas automobile crashes, except for unusual ones, are not.

Tversky and Kahneman (1973) asked subjects to state whether words that begin with R are more or less likely in the English language than those that have an R as the third letter. Most subjects said that words that begin with an R are more likely. The statistical fact is the reverse. Words that begin with R are easier to recall or generate than words that have an R in the third place. One interpretation of availability is that people overassess the probability of easily retrieved events and fail to recognize that is an error.

An even more complex collection of problems arises when judgments of probability must be based on scenarios about the future. This form of probability assessment has been formalized by the technical device known as "fault trees," which attempts to assess the probability of a low-probability event by drawing out a schematic of all the ways in which that event may occur and assessing the likelihood of each. (For a full technical presentation, see Green & Bourne, 1972; for the most famous application, see U.S. Nuclear Regulatory Commission, 1975.) The method is in extensive use. Anxieties about its validity among the engineers who developed it seem to focus primarily on whether its assumptions are satisfied. A much more dramatic set of possible problems is implied by a study by Fischhoff, Slovic, and Lichtenstein (1978), which showed that experienced automobile mechanics, asked to deal with various representations of the possible reasons why a car might not start, did not recognize the omission of major branches of the fault tree. Kahneman and Tversky (1982) have discussed other problems with simulations as bases for probability assessment.

Evidence for successful statistical intuitions in inductive reasoning

Rather recently, a countercurrent to the line of research summarized so far has begun to appear. By far the best summary of its thinking and content is contained in an important paper by Nisbett, Krantz, Jepson, and Kunda (1983).

The authors, starting from the premise that some intuitive judgments that should depend on statistical principles do and some do not, attempt to explore what problem and respondent characteristics favor the use of statistical principles. They note the important work of Piaget and Inhelder (1941/1975), which shows that children develop statistical intuitions as they grow older and that understanding of the behavior of physical objects that obviously behave randomly emerges as a function of age. They suggest that, here as elsewhere in development, the development of the individual to some extent resembles the development of human understanding in general. They identify three task variables that can influence the ease with which adults can think statistically: the degree to which the random nature of the data-generating device or process is visible and obvious, familiarity with the randomness of a sequence of events resulting from past experience with it or comparable sequences, and cultural prescriptions to reason statistically (e.g., the incessant baseball season bombardment with statistical information, implying random variability, about aspects of individual and team performance).

They conducted some very stimulating experiments. In one, subjects were far more willing to generalize from a very small number of consistent instances about what seems to be a nonrandom process (electrical conductivity of a metal) than about an obviously more variable one (obesity of a Pacific island dweller). Another showed that enumeration of a sample space and recognition that a subset of observations from it was in fact a sample made that sample less important and thus enhanced the importance of other conflicting information. Yet another showed that experienced athletes and actors were more likely to recognize that a poor performance could be random than inexperienced ones. They conclude from these and other arguments and data that

some of our subjects showed ... an appreciation of the statistical principles that in previous work other subjects failed to appreciate. It seems more reasonable to explain [this success] by saying that they are more skilled at statistical reasoning than the other subjects than by saying that they saw through the experimenters' tricks.... We see a powerful argument in the work we have reviewed for the role of cultural evolution. It does not require unusual optimism to speculate that we are on the threshold of a profound change in the way that people reason inductively.... Most people today appreciate entirely statistical accounts of sports events, accident rates, and the weather.... Will our own descendants differ as much from us as we do from Bernoulli's contemporaries? (Nisbett et al., 1983, pp. 360–362)

These conclusions are perhaps an even more dramatic message of hope than the one we are offering. Our emphasis on understanding and expertise is like that of Nisbett, Krantz, Jepson, and Kunda, as is our recognition of gradual emergence of inductive skills during maturation and education. We think of decision analysis as a technique that can help hone those skills when they are lacking and needed. If we take the argument about cultural evolution seriously, we might look for the disappearance of decision analysts. There is precedent. At one time, professional scribes wrote for those who could not. Later, professional arithmeticians served the needs of merchants deficient in arithmetical skill. Both professions have disappeared.

Other classes of cognitive illusions

Violations of SEU

There are many axiomatic treatments of decision making. The axioms purport to be, and usually are, rules of behavior that no one would wish to violate if the stakes are high. Most such sets of axioms lead to a simple theorem, known as the SEU model. SEU stands for Subjectively Expected

Utility, and the model simply asserts that, from various alternative actions available, one either should or does choose the one that has the largest SEU. In the preceding sentence "should" applies if the model is considered as normative or prescriptive; "does" applies if the model is considered as descriptive of actual behavior. The distinction, here and elsewhere in this essay, is far more slippery than it appears. People often do what they should do. Because under general though not universal circumstances the SEUs of the available options can be discovered (this is a major function of almost all decision analyses), one way in which people can behave wisely if the stakes are high enough to justify the effort is to discover the SEUs of the actions available to them (perhaps with the help of a decision analyst) and to maximize SEU deliberately. In special circumstances other rules for decision making are appropriate; examples include the famous minimax rule for some kinds of games and the less famous but more often applicable rule of avoiding gambler's ruin. Such rules can be interpreted as ways of maximizing SEUs in the situations to which they apply.

An expectation of anything is simply a weighted average. In this case the numbers being averaged are utilities. A utility is a subjective measure of the attractiveness of a possible outcome to the decision maker(s). Most actions can have various outcomes, depending on what chance or Nature or any other agency beyond the decision maker's control may do as a result of or after the action. These possible outcomes have personal probabilities. Take the utility of each possible outcome, multiply it by the probability that outcome will occur, sum these products over an exhaustive set of mutually exclusive outcomes, and you have an SEU.

Few thinkers about decision making have questioned the normative appropriateness of maximizing SEU, though some have questioned the feasibility of implementing the normative rule. But many theorists and experimenters have questioned whether people in fact do so and have sought and found contexts in which they do not. The literature is large, and we cannot do justice to it here. See von Winterfeldt and Edwards (in press) for a chapter-length discussion.

Labile values. An assumption implict in both normative and descriptive versions of the SEU model is that decision makers know what they would like to maximize. Fischhoff, Slovic, and Lichtenstein (1980) have challenged that assumption, arguing that phrasing and response mode variations have substantial effects on value judgments. A number of experiments support this view – but its implications for the SEU model are unclear because the status of the model is unclear. If it is taken to mean that people in fact routinely make decisions that maximize SEU, then it is clearly wrong, as a long history of experimentation and argument shows. The decision analytic position is that people can be helped to maximize SEU by suitable elicitation and computations. The fact that the numbers obtained depend to some extent on the method used to elicit them by no means implies that they cannot or should not be the basis for decisions. The practice of decision analysis is inherently iterative, and procedures that produce inconsistencies are valuable as incentives to more iteration and harder thought (see Fischer, 1979). Various studies in which decision analytic techniques have been used to elicit utilities and various methods have been used to validate the numbers thus elicited have been generally encouraging; see von Winterfeldt and Edwards (in press) for a review.

Preference reversals. A particularly interesting finding of a response mode effect in conflict with SEU maximization is the preference reversal effect. Lichtenstein and Slovic (1971, 1973) constructed gambles in which a subject could win either a medium amount of money with a high probability (*A*) or a large amount with a low probability (*B*). But student subjects playing for small amounts and gamblers in a casino produced inconsistent judgments: When asked to choose between *A* and *B* they chose *A*, but when asked to bid for these bets they bid more for *B*. Experiments by Grether and Plott (1979), Pommerehne, Schneider, and Zweifel (1982), and Reilly (1982) found variants of the same effect. Slovic and Lichtenstein (1983) have reviewed the literature that is building up. They interpret the findings as reflecting different information-processing strategies induced by the response modes. So far as we know, no one has explored the effect on such patterns of preference either of careful guidance or of exploitation. It should not be too difficult to arrange iterative repetitions of such situations so that a subject determined to maintain preference reversals becomes a money pump. For example, let the subject choose *A*. Then, exploiting the fact that the subject is willing to bid more for *B*, offer to permit *A* to be traded in for *B* and a small fee. Now once again offer to exchange *B* for *A*; because the subject prefers *A*, the trade should be attractive. Continue until the subject rebels or goes broke. If, as we believe, no subject would stand still for such a rooking, that fact calls into question not the robustness of the experimental finding but the firmness of the judgments on which it depends. On a priori grounds one would expect considerable lability in such preferences, because the options in such experiments must necessarily be quite close to one another in SEU, or the reversal effect will not occur. Those who take preference as a primitive in thinking about human decisions have more difficulty in dealing with such effects than those who, like us, believe that preferences, like bids, are constructed out of more elementary, more subjective assessments.

Cognitive illusions in physics

Probably the most famous errors in intuitive physics were originally reported by Piaget and Inhelder (1941) and are known as conservation errors. Suppose a beaker of a colored liquid is first shown to a young child and then poured into another glass container of a different shape. Will the child recognize that the amount of liquid has not been changed? Piaget and Inhelder found that the answer is no, not if the child is under 7.

Over many years, Piaget and his colleagues studied a wide variety of physical conservation tasks: conservation of quantity, of length, of number, and so on. None of these conservation rules taken so for granted in adult thinking is demonstrable in young children. We seem to learn such simple physical principles. (See Inhelder & Piaget, 1958; Piaget & Inhelder, 19841/1975.)

Adults also show lack of appreciation of physical rules that they might reasonably be expected to have learned in the course of a lifetime of observation, combined with some classroom teaching. McCloskey, Caramazza, and Green (1980) conducted some very ingenious experiments on intuitive assessments by college student subjects of motions and trajectories. Thus, consider a stimulus like Figure 40.2. It represents a view from above of a ball attached to the end of a string. The string is attached to something (with a swivel; it does not roll itself up around a pole), and the ball maintains a circular trajectory. Now, imagine that the string breaks. Draw a line representing the direction in which you think the ball will subsequently move.

The physical principle involved is that an object will continue in a straight line unless affected by an external force. Once the string is broken, the only external force affecting the ball is gravity, which does not show its effect in a view from above. Consequently, the correct answer is that the ball should continue on a straight line tangent to the circular path it had been following prior to the moment at which the string broke. The authors report that more than 30% of their student subjects failed to recognize this fact. Caramazza, McCloskey, and Green (1981) studied a more sophisticated prediction-of-motion problem and found that only about 25% of their college student subjects produce right answers. We ourselves have tried the task presented in Figure 40.2 informally on respondents in the Social Science Research Institute and found that even graduate students with considerable prior training in physics get it wrong. We also tried a manipulation not reported in the other studies: We tried explaining the reasoning that would lead to the correct answer. In every instance, an adequate explanation was successful in causing the respondent to produce the right response.

Although this class of cognitive illusions seems particularly fragile, in the sense both that some versions appear only if the respondents are children and that others are easy to correct by explanation, this may well be because the physical principles explored so far are matters of daily experience. More complex principles of physics are surely less intuitive. Those of relativistic physics, if intuitive to anyone, have become so only during the 20th century. The existence of billiard and pool sharks and of

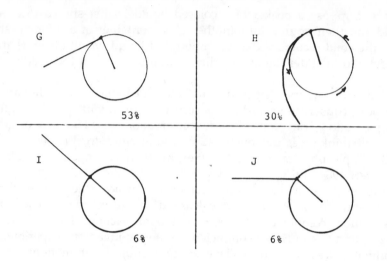

Figure 40.2. Illustration of a physical illusion. After the string breaks, the ball is moving in the direction indicated in (G). Only 53% of the subjects chose G as the correct answer. (*Source:* McCloskey et al., 1980 Copyright © 1980 by the AAAS.)

skilled ship handlers shows that originally nonintuitive principles of physics can become intuitive by extensive experience; the existence of professors of physics shows that they can become intuitive by precept. Intuitive physics seems to share with intuitive arithmetic the property of presenting a much wider range of intellectual difficulty than intuitive Bayesian inference, for example. The thrust of this comment is not that intellectual tasks like Bayesian inference cannot become intuitive. We offer ourselves and many others we know well as counterexamples. The point is simply that the extent to which a normative rule becomes "intuitively obvious" depends, among other things, on the inherent difficulty of the rule.

Cognitive illusions in logic and arithmetic

We group these topics, studied for different purposes and at different times, because they represent the application of particularly explicit formal rules, the violation of which seems especially shocking.

The conjunction fallacy. Perhaps the most shocking example is presented in very recent work by Tversky and Kahneman (1983) on what they call the conjunction fallacy. They presented 260 students at the University of British Columbia and Stanford University with the following problem:

Consider a regular six-sided die with four green faces and two red faces. The die will be rolled 20 times and the sequence of greens (G) and reds (R) will be

recorded. You are asked to select one sequence, from a set of three, and you will win $25 if the sequence you chose will appear on successive rolls of the die. Please check the sequence of greens and reds on which you prefer to bet.
1. RGRRR
2. GRGRRR
3. GRRRRR

The paper goes on to explain to its readers:

Note that Sequence 1 can be obtained from Sequence 2 by deleting the first G. By the conjunction rule, therefore, Sequence 1 must be more probable than Sequence 2. Note also that all three sequences are rather unrepresentative of the die, since they contain more R's than G's. However, Sequence 2 appears to be an improvement over Sequence 1, because it contains a higher proportion of the more likely color. [Tversky & Kahneman, 1983, p. 303]

About half of the 260 subjects actually played the bet chosen, for real payoffs. The percentages of subjects choosing the dominated Sequence 2 were 65% with real payoffs and 62% in the hypothetical format. Only 2% in both groups chose Sequence 3.

This dramatic finding of a violation of dominance produced by an inclusion relation is reproduced in various forms in the paper from which the previous example was quoted. It is only a minor consolation that when the logic of the situation was presented 76% of subjects (Stanford students for this study) found it persuasive. One wonders about the other 24%. The arguments were presented in written form, and students were asked which they found correct. We suspect that their lack of agreement represents lack of understanding rather than obstinate adherence to a logically untenable judgment. But the argument that such errors are attributable to sheer naiveté is wrong. Appropriate versions of the same logical structure were presented to trained physicians and to professionals involved in forecasting and planning. Varying but substantial percentages of them showed the same kind of error. We can only hope that an attempt to reproduce these results on professional logicians would fail.

A weaker form of the same kind of phenomenon had been studied by Bar-Hillel (1973), Beyth-Marom (1981), Cohen and Hansel (1957), Goldsmith (1978), and Wyer (1970).

Errors in arithmetic

The literature on errors in arithmetic is enormous; we cannot hope to summarize it here. Arithmetic is a major element of early education. Apparently, every single isolable skill that goes into it, from counting on up, is a product of early learning. Consequently, virtually any arithmetical error that one can think of can be found at some age or another, in some task or another. Many such errors are systematic, but their nature depends sensitively on experimental arrangements. A review of the literature on numerical skills and concepts in children appears in Flavell (1977, pp. 86–97).

Adults make errors in arithmetic too. Tversky and Kahneman (1973) asked college students to multiply, within 5 seconds, either the numbers from 1 through 8 or the numbers 8 through 1. The product is 40,320. All subjects grossly underestimate it, but those who work with the descending sequence are far less in error than those who work with the ascending sequence. The reqirement that the subjects respond within 5 seconds, of course, prevents them from actually doing the required multiplications, either on paper or in their heads. (The latter is perfectly possible. Try it, Solution time was about 90 seconds for one of us.)

In the same paper, Tversky and Kahneman ask respondents to perform much more difficult mathematical tasks. Subjects made systematic errors in assessing permutations, combinations, and binomial distributions. Tversky and Kahneman explain all of these errors as illustrating the effects of the availability heuristic. For example, subjects routinely judge that more different two-person committees than eight-person committees can be formed from a total of 10 people. The two numbers must obviously be identical, because a two-member in-group automatically defines an eight-member out-group. In this problem, the dramatic result was not the difference between small and large committees but rather the very large discrepancy between judged and correct number of committees for all sizes of membership greater than two. Tversky and Kahneman argue that "people estimate combinatorial values by extrapolating from an initial impression. What a person sees at a glance or in a few steps of computation gives him an inadequate idea of the explosive rate of growth of many combinatorial expressions. In such situations, extrapolating from an initial impression leads to pronounced underestimation" (1973, p. 214).

A closely related group of studies compares intuitive with calculated extrapolations of exponential growth. Wagenaar and Sagaria (1975) asked subjects to extrapolate from the early terms (usually 5) of an exponential-growth process and found that the resulting extrapolations were dramatically too small. Nor did either prior instruction or simply experience with exponential growth processes help much. Wagenaar and Timmers (1978b) point out that such inability to recognize the consequences of exponential growth is a matter of great social concern, because exponential-growth processes are so common in the environment.

Arithmetic and mathematics are clearly the best topics to use in introducing the idea of intellectual tools and their embodiment in physical tools. Virtually every new idea acquired in the course of learning arithmetic and mathematics depends on tools. In the early stages of learning to count, children use pebbles or other physical objects that they can manipulate (Inhelder & Piaget, 1958). Later, counting is easy, but a convenient representational system, the decimal system, is needed to facilitate the tasks of arithmetic. Few casual users of calculus can get along without tables of integrals. The tools required to perform arithmetic and other forms of mathematics are numerous, diverse, and effective. We do not believe that those facts make them any different in kind from the tools used to perform other intellectual tasks. They simply make them more familiar and easier to use and understand.

Reflections on the cognitive illusions

Making sense of cognitive illusions

We have found it extraordinarily difficult to make sense of the cognitive illusions, and this essay and others related to it have been through many previous unsuccessful versions. Several thoughts seem to have helped us.

1. The paradigm of cognitive illusions has been difficult to get into sharp focus, perhaps in part because the work with which we have been most familiar has concentrated on intellectual tasks that lie at or beyond the limits of ability of most adults. It has been very helpful to think about intuitive arithmetic and intuitive physics – both easier tasks, at least in the forms in which we have thought about them. Obviously, both arithmetical and physical tasks can easily be devised that are well beyond the reach of adult human intuition. The point is that intuitively easy tasks of these kinds can also be devised. We know of no intuitively easy version of Bayesian inference. It has been helpful to us to be able to consider a full range of task difficulty.

2. We started out believing that we knew what the word *intuition* means. We also started out believing that a *cognitive process* is a fixed method of doing intellectual business. Both ideas now seem absurd. We can find no agreed-on definition of intuition in the literature, and we found that we ourselves disagreed about what the word means. Cognitive researchers better acquainted than we with the literature of developmental psychology helped us to understand that cognitive processes are not givens. They develop and change over time as a function of maturation, experience, and training.

Research on cognitive processes as it is normally done using adult subjects gives the appearance of reporting static processes for two reasons: because we like to describe those processes by means of static models, and because the time periods of such studies are normally short relative to the periods over which development and learning take place. Consequently, such experiments study "snapshots," pictures of how the cognitive process being studied works at a given level of development and training.

These two lines of thought have helped us. Many cognitive psychologists interested in cognitive illusions in adults say that they study them in order to learn more about intuitive cognitive processes; we quoted Kahneman and Tversky to that effect earlier. It is very helpful to recognize that, as Hammond and his colleagues put it, "Intuition is what analysis is not" (Hammond, Hamm, Grassia, and Pearson, 1984, p. 2), and that cognitive processes are responsive to maturation, experience, and education, even if we do try to capture them by means of static models that imply the contrary.

3. Yet another crucial recognition has been that the notion of intellectual effort is central to understanding thought. Because "intellectual effort" is a thoroughly subjective concept, experimentalists have tended to use objectively measurable stand-ins for it; the most common of these are incentives.

4. The notion of intellectual tools is important. Decision analysis is a collection of intellectual tools. Only recently did we come to think about the relation of intellectual tools to physical tools that implement them. Intellectual tools, we feel, are used if the user knows that they exist, knows how to use them, and considers it worthwhile to make the intellectual effort. If they are useful they become embodied in physical tools. Often, after the embodiment has occurred, the former user of an intellectual tool delegates the task performed by it to the physical tool and may even forget how to use the intellectual tool.

The topic of intellectual tools relates to expertise. Experts become expert in the use of intellectual tools as well as acquiring factual knowledge. They may use physical tools to implement the intellectual ones; experts on Bayesian statistics, though they have no difficulty recognizing a Bayesian problem, may need a hand calculator or even a computer to get the right answer.

If an experiment requires its subjects to perform a task that even an expert would need physical tools to perform but forbids their use, that fact at least implies that getting the answer right is not important enough to require a major intellectual effort.

Task difficulty, mental effort, and intellectual tools

The crucial question, it seems to us, presented by any cognitive illusions study is: What is the difference between the experimenter and the subject, other than that the former gets the answers right and the latter gets them wrong? We see two ways of thinking about this question. One is to focus on the processes that produce wrong answers. The literature reviewed in this chapter has for the most part addressed this question and has proposed a number of processes of this kind.

Our focus is different: What are the processes that permit a respondent to a problem (e.g., the experimenter) to be correct?

As long as the tasks we considered were so difficult that most adults without physical tools produced wrong answers, the only answer we could come up with was that physical tools are important – hardly an astonishing discovery. But consideration of a sequence of tasks that ranged from trivially easy to impossible helped us to a better understanding of our question.

Our insights began to develop when we considered mental arithmetic. We would like to take you through a series of problems in mental arithmetic, in the hope that they will lead you to the same lines of thought to which they led us.

In so doing, we will be exploiting the fact that the examples can be presented on the page. This idea dates back at least to the Gestalt psychologists who used examples on the page to study visual illusions. The experimental cognitive psychologists of the present day collect data, but they also present the examples on which they base their arguments as part of the text of each article. We assume that they expect the examples on the page to support, or perhaps to be even more compelling than, the experimental evidence. We use our examples for the same reason. Please, therefore, do not just read each problem as we present it. Make a genuine mental effort to solve it, and do not read on until it is solved. If you must, you can use paper and pencil – but through problem 8 it should not be necessary, and to do so will destroy some of the vividness of the example.

In order to discuss our examples, we must first examine what the word *intuition* means. We propose four definitions, bearing a family resemblance to but not exactly the same as the three proposed by Kahneman and Tversky (1982a).

Intuition-I is the dictionary definition of intuition. Different dictionaries phrase it differently, but the key idea is that of immediate, effortless understanding. It is often contrasted with reason or deliberate inference. *Webster's New Collegiate Dictionary*, for example, gives two relevant definitions: "immediate apprehension or cognition"; "the power ... of attaining to direct knowledge or cognition without evident rational thought and inference."

Intuition-R is a judgment that is a rough cut, an approximation. Although this does not correspond to the dictionary meaning, it does most closely corresond to what experimenters on cognitive illusions study. Such experimenters often encourage mental effort but do not permit the use of physical tools. As later examples will suggest, such conditions often produce partial answers or approximations.

Intuition-M is our name for a situation in which the method of attack on the problem is obvious and intuitive even though the answer requires the use of physical tools. Long division is a good example for problems of reasonable difficulty.

Intuition-V is the kind of judgment you make when you say, looking at the sum of a long column of figures, that you do not plan to do the arithmetic but that the answer looks reasonable. This is an intuitive verification of an answer arrived at by other means. Perhaps the most extreme, fully subjective version of it is the tip-of-the-tongue phenomenon in which you know what someone's name is but cannot remember it. You usually can reject wrong answers proposed by yourself or anyone else without trouble and feel embarrassed at your stupidity when you finally have to ask for the right name.

Some arithmetic problems. The following text presents 13 arithmetic problems graded in difficulty. When each is presented, please stop reading and try to solve it in your head. Note both what you do and how well you do. Try to compare your intuitions with ours.

> 1. $2 + 2 =$
> 2. $8 \div 4 =$
> 3. $\sqrt{9} =$

All three of these problems seem completely Intuitive-I. They require no effort, the answers are transparent, and any adult with reasonable education will get them right. It is helpful to remember that the same comment does not apply to children. It might be as much as two or three years before a child who found problems 1 and 2 Intuitive-I could even understand what problem 3 means. For most of you the answer to all three of these problems comes not from knowing how to do arithmetic but from memory.

Next, consider these problems.

> 4. $37 + 28 =$
> 5. $78 \div 13 =$
> 6. $\sqrt{441} =$

None of these problems is Intuitive-I, at least for us. We can get all three right, but it takes mental effort. A cognitive process, which might as well be called mental arithmetic, is clearly required. Problem 6 is interesting both because it requires more mental effort than 4 or 5 and because the effort is of a different kind. We do not know how to extract square roots in our heads – or on paper, for that matter. To solve 6, it helps to combine search with mental multiplication. First, note that $20 \times 20 = 400$. Search the integers upward from there. The first trial after that gives the right answer, so search stops. Had the problem been 529, you might have used the same starting point but skipped a number or two in the search, recognizing that the difference between 400 and 529 is large enough so that trying 21 is unnecessary. With harder thought you might also have recognized that the last digit of the square root of 529 must be odd and can only be 3 or 7, and consequently trying 22 is unnecessary also. If you find that comment nontransparent, as many will, read no further until you see why it must be so. This will give you direct experience of what mental effort is. It took one of us some time, after recognizing the specific point, to discover the underlying principle and to see why no square can end in 2, 3, 7, or 8. We needed paper and pencil to understand that. Do you?

These problems are effortful. For some, problem 6 may be Intuitive-R; why bother with more than an approximation? For all, they are Intuitive-M and Intuitive-V. Many of those tempted by the fact that problem 6 is very Intuitive-R, might settle for the thought that the answer is more than 20, but not much more – unless some good reason for getting the answer right provided an incentive for harder thought.

The next three problems are:

7. $48{,}512 + 659{,}871 =$
8. $2{,}365 \div 43 =$
9. $\sqrt{20{,}449} =$

Problems 8 and 9 push us almost beyond our abililty to do mental arithmetic. We can do problem 7 in our heads but need more mental effort than we would normally be willing to use in order to remember the digits of the answer in the right order, because we arrive at them from right to left. But little mental effort is involved in 7 or 8 if pencil and paper is allowed.

Problems 7 and 8 are naturals for Intuition-R. Problem 7 is obviously roughly 700,000. Problem 8 is a little less obvious. A first approximation is $3000 \div 40 = 50$. For a more thoughtful approximation, note that $50 \times 43 = 2150$. So 50 is really too small. Really hard thought can produce an answer without any physical tool. Still more thought is needed to approximate the answer to problem 9. A first thought is that $150 \times 150 = 22{,}500$, so that answer must be near to but smaller than 150. Try 140 next; its square is 19,600. Now we have the answer trapped. Using the principle that you figured out in connection with problem 6, you can see that the answer must be either 143 or 147, and obviously 147 is too large. But this is really harder intellectual work than almost anyone routinely does without physical tools. As usual, these problems are Intuitive-M and Intuitive-V.

Problem 9 presents another issue about tools. A few of you may know how to figure square roots using only paper and pencil. We do not, though Edwards was taught how in high school and von Winterfeldt could figure it out. We doubt that many contemporary schoolchildren learn in this era of the hand calculator. For such problems paper and pencil have become technologically obsolete.

Previous problems focused attention on the meanings of intuition. This set focuses attention on the meaning of the notion of cognitive process. Is an intellectual process that *requires* external physical tools for its correct execution a cognitive process or not? We say yes. We think a cognitive process is a learned intellectual or judgmental skill executed using whatever tools seem necessary.

The implications of this definition are dramatic. Children learn to do arithmetic. These problems might do a fairly good job of sorting children by age and grade level. Only the simplest are Intuitive-I to us, though we consider it quite likely that problems 4, 5, and 6 might be Intuitive-I to someone who does arithmetic all day for a living. For young children, none is intuitive in any of the four senses. For those without access to (or knowledge about) calculators, 9 may not be Intuitive-M. For most educated adults, all are Intuitive-V and Intuitive-R.

Consider another set of problems.

10. $e + \pi =$
11. $\pi \div e =$
12. $\sqrt{\pi e} =$

Most of you could answer these three problems but would have to look up π and e first. Now the source of that information becomes an intellectual tool.

Is looking up something in a book an acceptable element of a cognitive process? Though we feel lonely and exposed doing so, we feel that we have no choice but to say yes.

Now we should test the limits of the definition of cognitive process that admits physical tools. To do problem 12, even with π and e readily available, is tedious if, say, 8 significant digits are desired. But a sophisticated hand calculator can do the task, including the looking up, in seven keystrokes. This clearly exploits Intuition-M where Intuition-I is absent and Intuition-R is very weak.

Is this still a cognitive process? A great deal of responsibility for the thinking has now been delegated. The symbols in problem 12 each specify a task. The only thinking required is exploitation of Intuition-M: ability to recognize what each task is and to identify the sequence of keystrokes that accomplishes it. These identification and sequencing tasks are clearly cognitive processes, but they are not mental arithmetic.

A further complication: the calculator is programmable. The seven button pushes can be reduced to one. This separates the task of recognizing the visual input of problem 12 from the task of knowing the appropriate sequence of keystrokes required. Delegation of intellectual effort by the mind doing the recognizing of the task is now not only to the calculator but also to the mind, which may reside in a different head, that entered the program into the calculator.

Computers can perform extraordinarily complex cognitive tasks at the (figurative) push of a button. The man–computer system is clearly thinking. But is the man? Which man – the button pusher, the programmer, the task analyst, the user of output? This definition of cognitive processes is misty at the upper end. Once any object external to one person's skin is allowed into it, no clear lines can be drawn. Those who write about or experiment on cognitive processes ordinarily forbid physical tools. The reason why has now emerged. Once you allow any physical tool at all, even a book, to be used, where do you stop?

It would be misleading to focus too much attention on physical tools. Consider problem 13.

13. LXIV ÷ IV =

In working on it, please remember that you are a Roman, familiar with the symbols ÷ and = but not with the decimal system. A bit of casual historical reading led us to believe that Roman mathematicians could do some but not all division problems and that Roman merchants found such problems hard. The secret seems to have been to find tricks to make the problem convenient. This example offers one: LXIV = XX + XX + XX + IV. XX ÷ IV = V, and of course IV ÷ IV = I. So the answer must be V + V + V + I = XVI.

To a Roman mathematician, this problem was Intuitive-V but probably not intuitive in any other way. (Multiplication by successive addition was well known.) To many of us, 64 ÷ 4 = 16 is Intuitive-I. The difference is a convenient notational system – an intellectual tool so deeply ingrained that we forget it is there. Good intellectual tools are crucial to good intellectual performance. Their embodiment in physical tools is a by-product of that importance.

For us, at least, the preceding discussion of mental arithmetic has clarified understanding of the cognitive illusions. A fairly seamless sequence of intellectual tasks, and of methods for their performance, exists. At one end, the task is simple, easy, and intuitive. At the other, it is massive, difficult, and may involve many people and complex physical machinery. No obvious boundary exists on the intellectual continuum defined by the idea of a tool. Simple arithmetic can easily be done in the head. If the problem is simple enough, it normally is. More complex arithmetic may or may not be done in the head, depending on training, ability, need, willingness to make an effort, and the availability of physical tools. Really complex arithmetic absolutely requires physical tools. Where is the boundary between cognitive processes and use of tools? Tradition answers: at the skin. But the idea of intellectual tools challenges the tradition. Intellectual tools have no clear residence. Do they reside inside the head? If so, they are presumably cognitive pro-cesses. But tools resident inside the head at one time may later move out, as the examples illustrate. The notion of an intellectual tool makes the boundary of the skin, of such great philosophical and psychological importance, less and less meaningful. This seems to be an intellectual trap.

Let us be radical for a moment and ask why the skin is such an important boundary. Senses exist in order to make it easy for information to pass from one side of it to the other. The issue is where that information and its processing reside.

The sharp delineation of the boundary at the skin was unsatisfactory because the process of education moves both information and information processing from one side of the skin to the other. As problems 9 and 12 illustrate, technological innovation moves both back outside. It would be easier to think about the problem if we ignored the boundary.

That, of course, is exactly what many serious thinkers do. Few lay people care much what information is processed inside the head and what outside. What seems critical is that the processing be done, and done well. The tool-using human species has no hesitation about inventing and using tools, including intellectual tools that make possible information processing that otherwise no head could possibly perform.

Yet the distinction between what the mind does and what the computer does matters enormously to us all. Most of us stridently insist that computers cannot think but never say what thinking is.

These few pages have started from trivial arithmetical problems and moved to philosophical dilemmas. They have made at least one important point. The argument is often made (e.g., by Edwards et al., 1968) that one should deal with human cognitive limitations by designing intellectual tools and consequently that the research on, for example, cognitive illusions strengthens the case for intellectual tools like decision analysis. From our point of view, the case for intellectual tools, like that for physical tools, is that tool building and tool using are as natural to human beings as is the desire to be right rather than wrong. Tools may transcend intellectual limitations; calculators can do things that are beyond the reach of mental arithmetic. Tools may transcend other tools; computers transcend calculators. Computers were not designed because mental arithmetic is difficult. Linear programming was not designed because intuitive allocation is difficult. Human beings build tools because the reach of their minds exceeds their present grasp – because they want to do better than they now can. Awareness of what is possible, not dissatisfaction with what exists, stimulates tool building, intellectual or physical. And in our experience resistance to the use of any tool, physical or intellectual, is produced almost entirely by reluctance to make the effort necessary to learn how. Skilled tool users are proud of the tools they use and of the results that use produces.

To return to the topic of this essay, perhaps it is appropriate to accept the psychological tradition that establishes the skin as an important boundary. But the function of education is to move information and processing skills from outside the boundary to inside. We still can find no intelligible meaning to the notion of a cognitive process other than as a learned intellectual skill.

Can the available literature offer any substantiation? Yes. The most important substantiation is simply that the literature exists. If the authors of the papers on cognitive illusions did not know how to find the right answers to the questions they ask, the literature would not exist. If the respondents responded correctly, it might exist but would be much smaller and less interesting.

It would be unfair to say that such researchers exploit the differences in expertise between themselves and their respondents, for many reasons. (1) Their key point is that errors are systematic, not that they occur. (2) Experts as well as naive respondents make these errors.

What are the differences between the researchers and their respondents? Two suggest themselves. One is that the researchers need to, and do, make the mental effort required to get the right answers. The other is that, in doing so, the researchers have access to, and use, whatever intellectual tools they need – including books, calculators, computers, and whatever else the intellectual task requires.

Implications of the argument. The preceding pages have erected a lot of philosophical scaffolding on the rather shaky foundations of intuitive arithmetic. What lessons, if any, emerge from this line of thought?

1. The seamless nature of the intuitive arithmetic task, by presenting a spectrum of task difficulty ranging from trivial to impossible, has made it possible to disentangle ideas that we normally mix up. For example, it disentangles expertise from mental effort, it distinguishes between checking operations that are heuristics and checking operations that are exact, and it enables us to understand intuition as coming in at least four different brands.

2. The obvious fact that we learn a wide variety of mental operations in order to perform intuitive arithmetic, and that we must be able to perform all of these operations well in order to get correct answers, invites attention to learning. The facts that mental arithmetic can be learned and that skills at doing it are gained both by formal precept and by experience invite the speculation that the same thing applies to other cognitive operations. Just as ability to perform mental arithmetic is labile, so other cognitive skills are probably labile. And just as the amount of time required to learn how to do mental arithmetic is measured in years, so the amount of time required to acquire other cognitive skills is probably measured in years.

3. Thought about mental arithmetic has helped to differentiate expertise from mental effort. Obviously, no amount of mental effort can create expertise where it does not exist. But an expert not making a mental effort is likely to come up with fewer good answers than one who is making a mental effort.

4. Mental effort almost always requires the use of tools. Tools must, then, characterize almost every serious task in our mental life. Most cognitive tasks require numerous tools, and usually numerous heads, for effective execution. . . .

Summary

A cognitive illusion arises when (*a*) some formal rule specifies a (usually *the*) correct answer to an intellectual question, (*b*) human subjects, usually naive and always working without tools, are asked to perform the task intuitively, and (c) systematic discrepancies appear between the intuitive and the correct answers. This research paradigm has a 100-year history but has been extensively used since 1968 to study human probability assessment, inference, and risky decision making. This paper reviews a number of familiar and less familiar cognitive illusions and attempts to examine what they do and do not imply about human intellectual competence in general.

When performing intuitively Bayesian probabilistic inferential tasks, human beings seem routinely to modify their opinions less than they should on the basis of the evidence and to make less use of base-rate information than they should. They also sometimes pay less attention than they should to the diagnostic implications of varying sample size.

Predictions typically should be regressive and very often are not. Probability assessments should be well calibrated and sometimes are when the probabilities are low. Many probabilities of over .5 are over-assessed; the evidence about the effect of expertise, both about the topic at hand and about probability assessment, is conflicting. In hindsight, people tend to consider what actually happened as more inevitable than it was.

In assessing uncertain continuous quantities, people tend to use an anchoring-and-insufficient-adjustment procedure, which causes the probabilities of rare events to be underestimated.

Much research designed to improve intuition by such techniques as encouraging people to "work hard" or by raising the stakes has had generally discouraging results. Researchers have, however, been able to find both stimuli and forms of expertise that seem conducive to good performance in probability assessment.

Research on risky decision making has clearly shown that people do not maximize Subjectively Expected Utility (SEU) in choosing among gambles. This may be because of labile values or for other reasons, including in particular the fact that gambles can be packaged in various ways, and different packages lead to different relations of the gamble to the reference events with which it is compared.

Children make many mistakes in understanding simple physical principles, such as conservation of volume or number. Adults have been shown to make more sophisticated mistakes in understanding less obvious and familiar (but no less ubiquitous) physical principles.

Cognitive illusions can also be demonstrated in intuitive performance of problems in logic and arithmetic.

Exploration of arithmetic problems turns out to be helpful in understanding the cognitive illusions because they vary continuously in difficulty from obvious to very hard. Exploration of a sequence of such problems suggests at least four different interpretations of the notion of intuition: immediate and correct apprehension, a good approximation, intuitive knowledge of method for solving the problem but not of the solution, and intuitive ability to verify answers. Such exploration also raises the question of the boundaries of cognition. Are tasks performed with the aid of physical tools cognitive? Are tasks performed with the aid of more than one mind cognitive? Many aids to cognition (e.g., the decimal system) are taught to schoolchildren and so come to reside in the head; many also are designed into physical tools designed to facilitate cognitive work. Aids that once resided in the head may cease to do so as physical tools make them more accessible. The whole issue of how good human intuitive performance is may be more or less irrelevant to the broader question of human intellectual competence, because if the problem is important and the tools are available people will use them and thus get right answers. Indeed, this is the main difference between experimenters and subjects in experiments on the cognitive illusions.

41. Beyond discrete biases: Functional and dysfunctional aspects of judgmental heuristics

Robin M. Hogarth

The crucial role of predictive judgment (or anticipations) for understanding behavior has been recognized by many psychologists. For example, Kelly's (1955) first postulate states, "A person's processes are psychologically channelized by ways in which he anticipates events" (p. 46). Attribution theory, social judgment theory, and attitude research also concern the importance of predictive judgments (e.g., Brehmer, 1976c; Ross, 1977; Triandis, 1971). Furthermore, expectations play a prominent role in social learning and personality theories (e.g., Mischel, 1973; Rotter, 1966) as well as in Bandura's (1977) self-efficacy theory.

Recently a growing literature in behavioral decision making has revealed that people often make predictive judgments that are biased relative to normative standards (Hogarth, 1975a, 1980; Slovic, Fischhoff, & Lichtenstein, 1977; Slovic & Lichtenstein, 1971; Tversky & Kahneman, 1974). For example, base rate information is ignored (Kahneman & Tversky, 1973; Nisbett, Borgida, Crandall, & Reed, 1976); revision of opinion is conservative (Edwards, 1968); people indicate excessive confidence in their judgment (Fischhoff & Slovic, 1980; Lichtenstein, Fischhoff, & Phillips, 1977; Oskamp, 1965); they are subject to hindsight biases (Fischhoff, 1975), and so on. Furthermore, these findings have influenced other areas of psychology (Fischhoff, 1976; Mischel, 1979; Nisbett & Borgida, 1975; Nisbett & Ross, 1980).

The literature paints a depressing picture of human judgmental ability. Nonetheless, as stated by Toda (1962):

Man and rat are both incredibly stupid in an experimental room. On the other hand, psychology has paid little attention to the things they do in their normal habitats; man drives a car, plays complicated games, and organizes society, and rat is troublesomely cunning in the kitchen. (p. 165)

This chapter originally appeared in the *Psychological Bulletin*, 1981, *90*(2), 197–217. Copyright © 1981 by the American Psychological Association, Inc. Reprinted by permission.

However, to dismiss recent evidence on the grounds that its external validity has not been adequately demonstrated would be naive. People do make mistakes. The more serious criticism is the failure to specify conditions under which people do or do not perform well. There are many interesting phenomena but few attempts at theoretical integration. Without such integration, it is difficult both to evaluate and improve judgmental ability.

This article emphasizes the continuous, adaptive nature of the judgmental processes used to cope with a complex, changing environment (cf. Neisser, 1976). With few exceptions, however, judgment researchers have focused on discrete incidents (particular actions, predictions, and choices) that punctuate these continuous processes; furthermore, task environments are typically conceptualized to be stable. The failure to study and evaluate judgment and choice as continuous processes has had two important, negative consequences. First, insufficient attention has been paid to the effects of feedback between organism and environment. Second, although judgmental performance has been evaluated according to the principles of optimal behavior implied by decision theory and the probability calculus, few researchers have questioned whether the assumptions of such models apply to continuous processes.

It would be misleading to suggest that psychologists have ignored the continuous nature of judgment and choice and, in particular, the role of the feedback. Within the paradigm of social judgment theory, Hammond, Brehmer, and their co-workers (Brehmer, 1976c; Hammond, 1965; Hammond & Brehmer, 1973; Hammond, Stewart, Brehmer, & Steinmann, 1975) have explored processes of learning and interpersonal conflict resolution where judgments made across time by one party provide information (feedback) to another, and vice versa, in what amounts to a continuously changing environment. In this article, I raise issues that have not been explicitly addressed within that paradigm.

A second approach, known as dynamic decision theory and stimulated by the seminal papers of Edwards (1962) and Toda (1962), has compared human decision making across a series of temporally related decisions with optimal solutions yielded by mathematical models (for an overview, see Rapoport, 1975). Performance in this multiple-incident paradigm has been shown to be effective (see also Corbin, 1980; Peterson & Beach, 1967). These results are paradoxical if one believes difficulty of performance to be inversely related to the mathematical complexity of defining optimal responses. However, it is to precisely the interaction between environment and organism that Rapoport attributes successful performance. That is, in the experimental paradigms used, the structure of tasks is such that deviations from optimal analytic solutions are not heavily penalized. Errors made at one stage can be attenuated by the end of the task. The implications of these results, however, have not been pursued with the attention they merit. One reason, suggested by Slovic, Fischhoff, and Lichtenstein (1977), is that the operational difficulty of defining optimal solutions for complex tasks has limited the number of psychologists studying sequences of behavior. I argue that the conceptual issues raised by considering ongoing decision processes are crucial for understanding judgment and choice and that sophisticated mathematics and statistics are unnecessary.

This article is organized as follows. The importance of environmental characteristics in determining judgmental performance is first explored by examining the role of feedback in continuous processes. Second, several assumptions used to evaluate judgment in discrete incidents are critically examined. In so doing, evidence is summarized to support the hypothesis that judgmental biases revealed in discrete incident research are often indicative of processes that are functional in continuous environments. Third, different sources of judgmental bias are briefly discussed before considering methodological issues relevant to studying judgment and choice as continuous processes. Finally some normative implications are derived.

Importance of feedback in continuous processes

Important psychological insights have been gained from the recognition that organisms adapt to their environments (Brunswik, 1952; Piaget, 1970; Simon & Newell, 1971). To understand behavior, one must characterize (a) the nature of the environment, (b) the nature of the organism, and (c) the means the organism has developed for coping with the environment.

The environment can be considered complex and distinguished by uncertain (i.e., probablistic) relations. However, it also contains considerable redundancy (i.e., intercorrelation between cues) (Brunswik, 1943, 1952). The human information-processing system that has evolved to cope with the environment is characterized by essentially sequential processing, limited memory, selective perception, and reliance on cognitive simplification mechanisms (i.e., heuristics). Central to these means is the role played by feedback.

It is important to emphasize that judgment is primarily exercised to facilitate action (Einhorn & Hogarth, 1978). Furthermore, most actions induce feedback that is often immediately available. Consider, for example, motor activities such as walking along a corridor. One does not make an a priori judgment as to the best path; rather, a series of incremental judgment-action–outcome feedback loops monitor progress during the activity of walking. Similarly, judgments made in social interaction also involve judgment-action–outcome feedback loops; for instance, a smile induces a smile, or the judgment to make a particular comment provokes a reaction that is interpreted before responding in turn (cf. Duncan & Fiske, 1977). Although feedback is crucial to behavior (see also Norman, 1981), its very ubiquity may have blinded investigators of its presence. As stated by Powers (1973):

All behavior involves strong feedback effects, whether one is considering spinal reflexes or self-actualization. Feedback is such an all-pervasive and fundamental aspect of behavior that it is as invisible as the air we breathe. Quite literally it is behavior – we know nothing of our own behavior but the feedback effects of our own outputs. (p. 351)

Receiving and acting on feedback in continuous fashion increases the number of cues and responses available to the organism and thus their intersubstitutability. The importance of such environmental redundancy to performance was stressed by Brunswik (1952) through the principles of vicarious functioning and mediation, which imply that different sets of probabilistic cues can be used to predict the same criterion (see Armelius & Armelius, 1976; Einhorn, Kleinmuntz, & Kleinmuntz, 1979; Hammond, 1955; Hammond, Stewart, Brehmer, & Steinman, 1975; Postman & Tolman, 1959).[1] Continuous processing is thus not only consistent with the characteristics of the human information-processing system, it is functional for the organism to treat tasks in this manner.

Many discrete judgment tasks studied in the literature take place in environments degraded by the lack of both feedback and redundancy (cf. Winkler & Murphy, 1973). As examples, consider studies of Bayesian probability revision (Edwards, 1968), the use or neglect of base rates (Lyon & Slovic, 1976), and studies where available cues induce reliance on a single judgmental heuristic (e.g., representativeness; Kahneman & Tversky, 1972). Feedback and redundancy, however, are critical to achievement. In particular, the role of feedback highlights several issues: (a) the level of predictive accuracy required in dealing with a complex environment, (b) the degree of commitment implied by choice, (c) the importance of learning and the acquisition of judgmental expertise, and (d) the nature of cue-criterion relations.

Judgmental accuracy

The different degrees of judgmental accuracy required in discrete and continuous processes can be formalized with the aid of the following analogy. Imagine that judgment can be likened to aiming at a target, and let choice represent the selection of a particular trajectory (i.e., shooting). For example, consider Figure 41.1 and imagine that you are at point A. The precise target is the point D, and the line BC shows the amount of allowable error. As concrete examples, imagine predicting future values of an economic variable (e.g., sales, gross national product) or level of success in a job or graduate school. In both cases, choice is represented

---

[1] The importance of this is captured precisely by von Neumann's (cited in Beer, 1966) *principle of redundancy*, which asserts that reliable communication systems can be established from large combinations of components, each of which is relatively unreliable (see, e.g., Beer, 1966, chap. 9), a link that was also specifically noted by Brunswik (1952, p. 92).

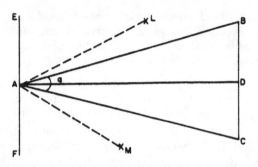

Figure 41.1. Diagram of a judgmental task. (The person positioned at point A wants to hit the target D and can err between B and C.)

by the selection of a particular level of the variable. Now consider the probability of hitting the target in Figure 41.1 at random (i.e., in the absence of predictive ability). Provided that you are "pointed" in the appropriate direction – indicated in Figure 41.1 by drawing EF parallel to BC – the probability of hitting the target BC at random in a discrete incident is equal to the ratio of the angle α (i.e., BAC) to 180°. However, α is a function of BC (size of target) to AD (distance from target). Specifically, $\alpha = 2 \tan^{-1}$ (BD/AD), where BD = .5 BC. Therefore, the probability of hitting the target without predictive ability is an increasing function of BC/AD (i.e., size of target/distance from target). For example, when the ratio of target to distance is .10, the probability of hitting the target at random in a discrete incident is .032. However, starting from the same point, a continuous process represents an easier task. By simply moving toward the target and checking periodically on direction, the judge can transform the initial probability of .032 to almost a certainty, without exercising much predictive ability. For instance, the probability of accurately predicting the economic variable or level of job success increases as one approaches the target date. Continuous processing, however, necessitates receiving feedback between the starting point (A) and the target (BC). When available, such feedback could be sampled occasionally at the will of the organism; alternatively, it could be received periodically in the form of outcomes of a temporal sequence of actions (as in dynamic decision theory).

How appropriate is the target analogy? The continuous model certainly applies to many simple and complex motor tasks (e.g., walking through a door, or skiing), as well as more cognitive tasks that induce feedback through actions. For example, monitoring the performance of a trainee in a new job provides intermediate feedback that can be used to modify predictions and/or actions. More importantly, the target analogy highlights two critical dimensions of judgmental achievement: (a) the degree of commitment implied by particular actions and (b) that the availability and interpretation of feedback are often more important than predictive ability per se.

Commitment

Feedback plays a crucial role in the organism's capacity to make adaptive responses by reducing the commitment implied by any particular action. In the judgment literature, however, this aspect of feedback has hardly been recognized. In discrete incident research, for example, two types of feedback have been identified; outcome feedback and process feedback (Hammond et al., 1975). Outcome feedback is simply knowledge of the outcome of a judgment, whereas process feedback is information concerning the relations between the cues in the environment and the criterion.

In continuous processing, on the other hand, outcome feedback can become corrective (so-called negative feedback in the cybernetic sense of the term) in that it permits adjustments to the general direction of judgment. In particular, corrective feedback allows the organism to appear as though complex sequences of behavior had been planned in detail when, it fact, only relatively simple actions need to be coordinated across time. An everyday example has been provided by Connolly (1980) in the context of clipping an overgrown hedge. One does not make complex, a priori calculations involving, for instance, the cantilever characteristics of branches or differential weight of various woods. Rather, one proceeds incrementally, snipping and observing, thereby reducing the level of commitment implied by particular actions as compared with a more discrete, analytic approach.

The hedge-clipping example highlights the differential nature of task complexity in discrete and continuous environments. In discrete incident research, definitions of task complexity have typically focused on variables such as amount of information, redundancy, and task familiarity (see, e.g., Hogarth, 1975b; Payne, 1976). However, in the presence of corrective feedback the importance of such variables may be significantly diminished insofar as feedback affects the commitments implied by particular actions. Indeed, from a continuous perspective, conditions concerning feedback largely determine task complexity. The frequency and speed of possibilities for corrective judgment are thus important variables by which judgmental tasks should be characterized (cf. Powers, 1978).

A recent study by Mackinnon and Wearing (1980) illustrates this point. Subjects were required to make a series of decisions to manage a simulated welfare administration project over time (with feedback) under varying conditions of task complexity (defined by the number of elements in the system, connections between elements, and levels of random variation). Performance varied little as a function of complexity; in particular, the more complex systems (as conventionally defined) did not always lead to poorer levels of performance than simpler systems. Indeed, Mackinnon and Wearing (1980) commented:

The complex situation may be different (i.e., require or allow a completely different approach) from the simple one.... Heuristic methods which may be applicable and successful in dynamic systems may not be applicable to the static decision-making tasks that have been widely studied. (p. 295)

Commitment is also relevant to possible differences between the concepts of judgment and choice and whether and when these involve different processes (Einhorn & Hogarth, 1981; Einhorn et al., 1979; Hammond, McClelland, & Mumpower, 1980). When viewed as discrete incidents, judgment and choice are often indistinguishable in that they cannot be reversed and thus commit the individual. How, for example, can one distinguish in the discrete case between a predictive judgment and the choice of a particular value of an unknown quantity (e.g., when predicting future sales or grade point average)? In continuous processing, however, judgment can be thought of as providing a temporal background of mental activity that is punctuated by particular choices. This is exemplified in the target model, where aiming is used as the analogy for judgment, and the actual shooting is analogous to choice. This does not, of course, deny that one can shoot without aiming, just as one can ignore judgment in choice (Einhorn & Hogarth, 1981).

The distinction between judgment and choice in continuous environments can be clarified by considering instances where judgment is exercised to delay the commitment implied by choice. For example, consider various strategies one can use when faced with a choice between two jobs at a particular time. The anticipation of commitment frequently induces conflict that can be confronted directly (e.g., through the use of a compensatory choice rule) or avoided by adopting a nonconfronting perspective on the problem (e.g., by choosing an alternative simply to escape the conflict implied by the choice situation itself; cf. Shepard, 1964). Alternatively, one can delay choice. This judgment, however, will involve neither commitment nor conflict unless the failure to choose also closes one's options. In the latter case, the judgment becomes a choice. Corbin (1980) has suggested that choice is often delayed until information reduces the level of uncertainty below a certain threshold. Hogarth, Michaud, and Mery (1980) have stated more generally that mechanisms that reduce the regret associated with taking the wrong decision will induce action. Both analyses, however, emphasize that the moment of action, and thus commitment, is influenced by the way information is acquired and processed across time.

It is difficult to give a precise definition of the differences between judgment and choice. However, by noting the moment of commitment, a continuous perspective provides a clearer framework for noting their interrelations. That is, judgment can lead to choice, and choice induces feedback, which is interpreted via judgment prior to further choice.

Learning and expertise

Learning involves the use of feedback to generate, modify, maintain, or abandon hypotheses, a process that occurs across time. In discrete tasks, however, the methodological constraints of technique (e.g., regression analysis) typically force investigators to assume that subjects are applying a single judgmental rule. Thus in the multiple-cue probability learning paradigm, for example, the learning of judgmental rules is investigated by comparing rules inferred from performance achieved in different blocks of trials as opposed to monitoring behavior over time on a trial-by-trial basis (see e.g., Castellan, 1977). An important aspect of both judgment and learning masked by this approach concerns the meaning of inconsistency observed in judgmental strategies (see e.g., Brehmer, 1978). Whereas inconsistency is dysfunctional in that it reduces achievement (Brunswik, 1952) in the form of predictive accuracy (Goldberg, 1970), emphasis on prediction hides the fact that in adapting to the environment, it is the identification of relevant variables that is of paramount importance. As stated by Dawes and Corrigan (1974), "the whole trick is to decide what variables to look at and then to know how to add" (p. 105). Indeed, Campbell (1960) has emphasized that random variation (observed inconsistencies in judgment) and selective retention (of cues that have been useful) is not only the basic model of natural selection but is inherent in the trial-and-error nature of much human perception, learning, and creative thought. From one individual's viewpoint, there is always an unexpected element in the environment (e.g., the reactions of others in a social context). Thus, willingness to deviate from a consistent policy may well both facilitate learning and be adaptive in responding to the unexpected (see also Fiske, 1961). A discrete perspective obscures the point that prior commitment can reduce opportunities for learning (cf. Einhorn, 1980).

Feedback is also central to the learning of expertise. In this respect, since continuous feedback characterizes the development and execution of sensorimotor skills (Slovic, 1972a), an analogy between the acquisition of conceptual and physical expertise seems appropriate. In fact, Piaget (1970) has argued that intellectual skills develop from the establishment of sensorimotor capabilities, and it is certainly parsimonious to postulate that both develop from the same principles. Two recent studies speak to these issues. Schmidt, Zelaznik, Hawkins, Frank, and Quinn (1979) have proposed a theory for rapid motor acts based on Woodworth's (1899) thesis of how the accuracy of voluntary movement is achieved. Central to this work is the idea that initial impulses are followed by corrective feedback. Hoffman, Earle, and Slovic (1981) have further demonstrated that learning within the multiple-cue probability paradigm can be considerably facilitated when subjects are provided with a form of continuous feedback (so-called tonal feedback achieved through a sound-producing device). An important implication of the Hoffman et al. study is that conceptual learning can be aided through mimicking the continuous conditions of motor skill acquisition.

Is it possible to generalize from these studies? First, it should be noted that forecasting accurately in discrete incidents is not impossible. Weather forecasters, for example, have been shown to be well calibrated (Slovic, Fischhoff, & Lichtenstein, 1977). However, their forecasting activity takes place in conditions characterized by accurate feedback received frequently and often shortly after making forecasts. Moreover, these favorable conditions emphasize that feedback is not necessarily corrective. It can be ambiguous, misleading, and difficult to discern. For example, are the outcomes of a decision to be attributed to chance or skill, or some combination of both (Langer, 1977)? Are predictive successes and failures to be attributed to the variables selected for judgment, the weights assigned the variables, or to the information-combining rule used? Furthermore, depending on task characteristics such as levels of base rates and selection ratios, or the inability to see outcomes of actions not selected, feedback may even reinforce inappropriate behavior (Einhorn & Hogarth, 1978). Judgment may also induce "self-fulfilling prophecies" of which the individual is unaware (Einhorn, 1980a; Weick, 1977). Whereas the task environments of weather forecasters are relatively simple to interpret in terms of these variables (e.g., there can be no self-fulfilling prophecies), this is not the case in many other situations (e.g., clinical prediction or job selection).

The preceding comments emphasize the importance of determining the limits of predictive ability imposed by the nature of feedback available in particular tasks. Such an analysis may often suggest reducing the length of the forecast horizon and lead to adopting an incremental, or more continuous approach. For example, in assessing ultimate career success of recent PhDs, it is probably more appropriate to predict short-term performance (say over 2 years) rather than making career-length forecasts. If the situation permits mastery of the first step, one can learn to predict two stages ahead, and so on. However, in many situations it is unlikely that sufficient cases will be observed to establish expertise unless one also induces valid causal models of the phenomena. In chess or billiards, for example, the ability to predict several moves ahead requires several years of practice (cf. Thaler, 1980). An appropriate analogy concerns the distinction between matching and optimizing in probability learning (Estes, 1972). The advantages of optimizing can only be achieved by recognizing one's lack of knowledge and abandoning a matching strategy.

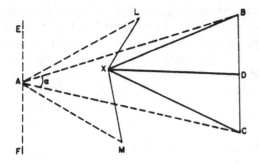

Figure 41.2. Diagram of a judgmental task when a person moves from point A to X. (The base rate increases, BXC > BAC, but the validities of L and M decrease, since LXM > LAM.)

Cue-criterion relations

Although some studies have investigated judgmental processes with unstable cue-criterion relations (see, e.g., Ruffner & Muchinsky, 1978), there has been little recognition of the ubiquity of such phenomena and how they are often a consequence of continuous processing. As a concrete example, imagine a sensitive interview where one would not want to pose the direct question of interest before acquiring a more complete appreciation of the situation. This can be illustrated by comparing Figures 41.1 and 41.2.

Recall from Figure 41.1 that the base rate of hitting the target is given by the angle $\alpha/180°$. However, consider the effects of recognizing that the positions of the cues L and M provide information; in particular, that an action to the right of L, and to the left to M, is appropriate. In this case, the probability of hitting the target at random conditional on this knowledge is α divided by the angle LAM. Thus, the joint validity of the cues L and M can be measured by the differential predictive information they provide over the base rate (i.e., $\alpha/\text{LAM} - \alpha/180°$).

Now consider Figure 41.2 in which the person has moved from position A to position X (i.e., after receiving feedback from initial directing questions). This has two effects: first, the base rate of hitting the target has increased, since angle BXC is greater than angle BAC; second, the predictive validities of L and M have decreased relative to Figure 41.1 (angle LXM is greater than angle LAM). Of course, it is unclear that as a person moves toward a target he or she would continue to rely on the same cues. In an interview, for instance, one formulates new questions as a result of prior feedback. However, the key point to note is that action (movement) not only affects the base rate of predictive judgment but also the validity of cues used in judgment. Thus, the use of cue-criterion relations is quite different in continuous and discrete environments.

Indeed, Neisser (1976) has made the point that "the act of locomotion, which *requires* more information if it is to be carried out successfully, also *produces* more information for the moving perceiver" (p. 114). Parenthetically, note that the ability to attribute different validities to the same cue as a function of spatiotemporal distance is an important aspect of constancy (Brunswik), or conservation (Piaget), in intellectual achievement.

Discrete assumptions and continuous environments

Research documenting the existence of judgmental heuristics in discrete incidents has acknowledged that these may be functional in specific contexts (see, e.g., Slovic et al., 1977, p. 4; Tversky & Kahneman, 1974). However, neither the characteristics of such tasks nor their ecological distribution has been specified (cf. Einhorn et al., 1979). In this section, these issues are considered by examining the implications of some assumptions used to evaluate judgment and choice in discrete incidents. I aruge that several biases revealed through such discrete evaluations are, in fact, indicative of mechanisms that are functional in more prevalent continuous environments. The following assumptions are considered: (a) the existence of a finite horizon at which the consequences of decisions can be evaluated, (b) the modeling of task uncertainty by stationary probabilistic processes, (c) the requirement of stable preferences or goals, (d) treating the effects of judgment as conditionally independent of outcomes, and (e) abstraction from competitive aspects of behavior.

Fixed decision horizons

One cannot determine the optimal solution to a decision problem, only the optimal solution to a *model* of that situation (cf. Einhorn & Hogarth, 1981). Savage (1954) referred to such models as "small worlds," in which it is necessary to make various simplifying assumptions. One important assumption is the fixed decision horizon at which outcomes are evaluated. The limitations of fixed horizons are examined here with respect to (a) mechanisms for coping with posthorizon consequences and (b) the interaction of judgmental heuristics and continuous feedback.

Coping with posthorizon consequences. The use of an optimal decision model necessitates creating temporal discontinuities in continuous processes. For example, consider whether one should invest in a real estate venture. The wisdom of the action depends on both the price at the moment of purchase and the estimated value of the real estate at a specific future date. However, from a continuous viewpoint, how can one evaluate such a venture? Moreover, since actions have consequences beyond small worlds (e.g., the investment could limit future possibilities or leave one vulnerable to emergencies), how should one act to gain advantage through immediate action yet achieve a position facilitating future actions?

Evidence reveals two mechanisms suited to continuous processing. First, judgments and choices are made relative to momentary reference points; that is, evaluations of choice options are better described by considering differences between potential gains and losses relative to a reference point rather than the normatively appropriate comparison of "terminal wealth states" (Kahneman & Tversky, 1979b). Whereas one might imagine these to be equivalent, this is not the case if the displeasure of a loss is evaluated differently from the pleasure of an objectively comparable gain. In fact, there is evidence that losses are weighted more heavily than gains (Kahneman & Tversky, 1979b; Tversky & Kahneman, 1981) and that whether something is seen as a loss or a gain depends on the reference point (e.g., is a tax cut a gain or less of a loss?) From a continuous perspective, a gain increases one's future options, whereas a loss is restrictive. For example, although it is more "economic" to settle one's tax liabilities by making a payment as opposed to receiving a refund, at the time of settlement many prefer the latter.

The second mechanism is the use of aspiration levels to evaluate future positions implied by actions (Simon, 1955, 1959). For example, consider whether a person should stick to a long-term career plan. The use of intermediate aspiration levels to handle this complex task not only reduces information processing to within feasible limits but prepares the person to anticipate what can reasonably be expected, thus modifying preferences to reality across time. Moreover, since aspiration levels are set relative to one's current reference point, they implicitly frame choices both in terms of gains and losses and the ability to face the future consequences implied by choice. For example, what does one gain or lose in changing jobs? The use of aspiration levels has been demonstrated recently in both laboratory and field studies of decision making (Hogarth et al., 1980; Kahneman & Tversky, 1979b; Laughhunn, Payne, & Crum, 1980; Payne, Laughhunn, & Crum, 1980). More generally, Toda (1976) has noted that sequences of behavior can be simplified through hierarchical planning. That is, there is no need to specify the implications of all possible paths several stages ahead; rather, one makes a rough first estimate (of small world consequences) and then simply handles the details of paths subsequently encountered.

Decomposing discrete tasks into sequential form also reveals tendencies to think in terms of incremental gains leading to positions more favorable to future actions. In a simple gambling task, Ronen (1973) presented subjects with the choice between two mutually exclusive actions characterized by identical (positive) payoffs and probabilities of success. The payoffs, however, depended on the outcomes of two sequential events where the "paths" to success differed in that one had a higher first-stage probability of success but a lower second-stage probability. These probabilities were known to the subjects. Since the expected utilities of the actions were equal, people should have been indifferent to choosing between them. However, they were not. Subjects favored the action with the larger first-stage probability. Why? A plausible hypothesis is that people are used to functioning in a manner where the immediate goal is to reach a better position from which the ultimate target can be attained. Moreover, if people are accustomed to environments changing across time, less confidence should be given to the second stage probability. Thus, staying in the game as long as possible is attractive and favors the action with the larger first-stage probability of success.[2]

A similar phenomenon has been reported by Kahneman and Tversky (1979b) in their investigations of the "isolation effect" in prospect theory. This refers to the tendency to cancel out common aspects of choice alternatives and to attend to differences and can be highlighted by decomposing choice options in sequential manner. For example, in two-stage problems with common outcomes at the first stage, choices are seen to depend on preferences at the second stage conditional on success at the first (see also Tversky & Kahneman, 1981). That is, since the options are seen to be identical at the first stage, the sequential formulation focuses attention on the second stage. In certain cases, this leads to violations of expected utility theory in that end states are not compared in the normative way (Kahneman & Tversky, 1979b; Tversky & Kahneman, 1981).

To illustrate the power of such sequential formulations, consider Figures 41.3 and 41.4, which represent the choice situations of Allais's paradox (Slovic & Tversky, 1974) presented as two-stage problems. In this formulation, respondents are asked to choose between actions at Stage 2 *before* knowing the outcome of Stage 1. For example, they are asked to imagine the decision they would entrust to an agent if they were unable to observe the outcome of Stage 1 themselves. If one considers end states, Figure 41.3 represents a choice between a certain 1 million dollars and an uncertain prospect. In Figure 41.4, the choice is between two uncertain prospects. However, as demonstrated by Slovic and Tversky (1974), when end states are explicitly highlighted (i.e., the problem is not presented in sequential form), the modal choices correspond to A (Figure 41.3) and D (Figure 41.4) and violate the expected utility principle. In the sequential formulation, on the other hand, almost no violations of expected utility

---

[2] An implication of these statements is that when the payoff is negative, people will choose the action with the lower first-stage probability of success. I have verified this prediction in classroom and seminar settings (with master of business administration [MBA] students and faculty) on at least six independent occasions and even when presenting two versions of the same problem involving positive and negative payoffs, respectively.

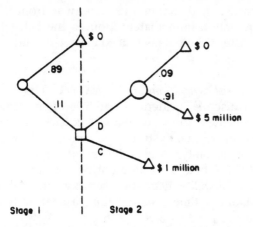

Figure 41.3. Situation 1 of Allais's paradox (Slovic & Tversky, 1974), presented in sequential form. (Respondents are asked to choose between actions B and A at Stage 2 before knowing the uncertain outcome of Stage 1. For example, respondents are asked to imagine the decision they would instruct an agent to take if they were unable to see the outcome of Stage 1. Circles indicate uncertain events and squares indicate action points.)

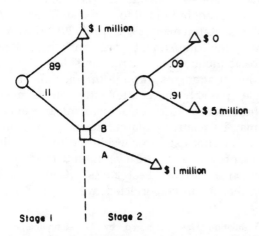

Figure 41.4. Situation 2 of Allais's paradox, to be interpreted in the same manner as Figure 3. (Responses consistent with expected utility theory are A [Situation 1] and C [Situation 2], or B [Situation 1] and D [Situation 2].)

theory are observed.[3] That is, by directing attention away from the first stage, the sequential formulation immediately induces the belief that A and C or B and D are consistent choices (as indeed expected utility theory also implies).

Interaction of judgmental heuristics and continuous feedback. The temporal location of the horizon in discrete incident research is often artificial in that the organism is prevented from receiving feedback. When this restriction is relaxed, however, the dysfunctional effects of two well-publicized heuristics – availability, and adjustment and anchoring (Tversky & Kahneman, 1974) – take on a different perspective.

As an example of the availability heuristic, Tversky and Kahneman (1973) have reported that under time pressure (i.e., a specific temporal horizon), people evaluate the product $8 \times 7 \times 6 \times 5 \times 4 \times 3 \times 2 \times 1$ more accurately than the reverse order (i.e., $1 \times 2 \times 3 \times 4 \times 5 \times 6 \times 7 \times 8$), although both presentations induce underestimation. The point of the availability heuristic is that one takes direction from the cues that are more available. Thus, the descending series leads to a larger value than the ascending series. However, under what conditions is the heuristic functional? If the availability heuristic gives direction to judgment that can be corrected subsequently, it can be most effective, and particularly when speed of judgment/action is important.

In discussing the adjustment and anchoring heuristic, Tversky and Kahneman (1974) have argued that it can account for biases observed in evaluating the joint probabilities of several events. The typical result is overestimation of the probabilities of conjunctive events and under-estimation of disjunctive events (Bar-Hillel, 1973; Cohen, Chesnick, & Haran, 1971, 1972). Subjects are assumed to fix (i.e., anchor) on the probability of one elementary event but to fail to adjust sufficiently for the other events (see Tversky & Kahneman, 1974, p. 1129). However, in continuous environments, the adjustment and anchoring heuristic essentially provides the basic mode of judgment. Consider, for instance, how one forms impressions of strangers through interaction. That is, in discrete incidents a single (possibly inaccurate) judgment is made. In continuous processing, however, a series of adjustment and anchoring responses, all of which may be relatively inaccurate, takes one progressively to the target. People are not used to considering the probabilities associated with sequences of several future events and often progress incrementally conditional on a current "best guess" (Gettys, Kelly, & Peterson, 1973), knowing that it can be corrected over time. Parentheti-

[3] The possibility of this formulation was suggested by D. Kahneman (personal communication, October 1979). In presenting this form of the problem to classes of approximately 55 MBA students on at least six occasions, the rate of choices inconsistent with expected utility theory is of the order of 3%. Indeed, the sequential formulation induces less inconsistency with expected utility theory than Savage's (1954) rephrasing of Allais's problems.

cally, adjustment and anchoring strategies have even been shown to yield accurate judgment in tasks involving two stages (Lopes & Ekberg, 1980).

A further well-documented bias is the conservatism effect in Bayesian revision tasks (Edwards, 1968; Slovic & Lichtenstein, 1971). However, in continuous environments there is good reason for opinion change to be slower than the optimal prescription. Specifically, imagine a body with momentum headed toward a target (the direction being the prior opinion). Information is received that implies a change in direction (the data in the form of the likelihood). If the change is small, it is easy to make the adjustment; and, in fact, the conservatism effect is negligible in such conditions. However, if the required change is large, immediate implementation can be dysfunctional (imagine trying to change the direction of an airplane or car suddenly by 60°). Work on systems dynamics indicates that such changes must be introduced gradually; otherwise overshooting and other related problems can occur (see, e.g., Coyle, 1977). Although there are other explanations for conservatism (e.g., Navon, 1978; Winkler & Murphy, 1973), the analogy does illustrate that changes may have to be implemented differently in continuous and discrete environments. The human tendency to resist sudden, dramatic changes could well be functional in continuous environments. In particular, if one has imperfect understanding of the task environment, dramatic as opposed to incremental changes can have large, unanticipated and dysfunctional consequences (cf. Lindblom, 1959).

Stationary probabilistic processes

In small worlds, the calculation of optimal responses assumes specific probabilistic models, the parameters of which do not change across time. In dealing with naturally occurring phenomena, however, people have to face many different types of processes. For example, observations can increase or decrease linearly across time, exhibit random fluctuations around a mean level, follow patterns and/or cycles, change their characteristics, or even be random. Moreover, although the detection of patterns for prediction is crucial, there is no certainty that observations do follow a particular pattern. Rather, pattern must be induced through experience. These issues are examined here with respect to (a) the regression fallacy, as a paradigmatic case, and (b) analog mechanisms for prediction in unstable environments.

Regression fallacy. It is easy to condemn failures to comprehend regression effects (Campbell, 1969; Kahneman & Tversky, 1973), yet care must be exercised to understand the effects of misspecified hypotheses. Whereas extreme observations can be generated by stable processes (although by definition rarely), they can also signal changes in the underlying process (Einhorn & Hogarth, 1981). When advising "trapped administrators" how to make successful interventions, for example, Campbell (1969) has suggested that they "pick the very worst year, and the very worst social unit. If there is inherent instability, there is nowhere to go but up, for the average case at least" (p. 414). However, the validity of this advice depends on the observed instability being generated by a stationary process, and in many instances it is not evident that this is the case. In fact, "the worst unit" could well subsequently exhibit both instability and a sharp downward trend, thus exacerbating the administrator's position. Without knowledge of the relative costs of different errors in the natural ecology (i.e., misinterpreting an extreme observation as signaling a change vs. failing to detect a change), it is unclear that predicting extreme responses is in fact an "error."

Analog mechanisms for prediction in unstable environments. From a continuous perspective, much judgmental activity can be likened to extrapolation of multiple time series. It is therefore appropriate to consider the burgeoning statistical literature on this subject (for reviews see Armstrong, 1978b; Makridakis, 1976, 1978). Results may be summarized as follows. When a series is well behaved in that its characteristics satisfy certain statistical properties, complex and sophisticated mathematical models can accurately predict future values. In addition, simple models may also predict quite well. However, when series are "ill behaved" in that they do not conform closely to known models or their characteristics change, the predictive ability of the more complex models deteriorates. Instead, simpler models provide more accurate forecasts (for an instructive example, see Makridakis & Hibon, 1979, as well as the survey by Armstrong, 1978a).

These results are significant in that the simple models require neither much computational ability nor memory capacity and, in this respect, are within human capabilities. (It is not claimed that people actually use these models, only that the models can produce fairly accurate short-term predictions in complex environments. See also Cyert & March, 1963, chap. 7.) The simple models are based on only a few values, such as predicting the next period by the most recent observation (adjusted, if necessary, for seasonal factors). Alternatively, exponential smoothing models are used which involve differentially weighting the most recent predictions and realizations. These models, however, like judgment in continuous situations, rely on the relative inertia of most processes which induce high correlations between successive observations. Indeed, it is interesting to note that people have difficulty in understanding that some series are effectively generated at random (J. Cohen, 1972; Wagenaar, 1972).[4] Since the immediate future is usually similar to the present, minor adjustments effected at frequent intervals can keep one on course. Paren-

---

[4] Lopes (1980) points out that these assessments are based on the assumption of the existence of well-defined criteria of randomness. Furthermore, she goes on to show that the assumption is unfounded.

thetically, many anticipations of this kind are exhibited in tracking, a task in which people can develop a high degree of skill (Poulton, 1974).

The relative success of simple models to handle complex predictive tasks speaks to the interpretation of studies that have indicated deficiencies in the extrapolation of exponential growth patterns (Timmers & Wagenaar, 1977; Wagenaar & Sagaria, 1975; Wagenaar & Timmers, 1978a, 1978b, 1979). People systematically underestimate growth processes, whether these are presented numerically, by graphs, or even in non-numerical diagrammatic form. Furthermore, sensitivity to such processes is neither enhanced by mathematical training nor by experience with them. On the other hand, bias is less severe for descending as opposed to ascending series, and people tend to be less inaccurate when they observe fewer data points.

Three comments help to place these results in perspective. First, subjects are asked to predict a value that is several stages distant (e.g., predict 1986 in 1981). Second, the "correct" answers are given by a precise exponential formula known only to the experimenter even though one could fit several curves to the past data. Third, in a replication it was found that accurate estimates could be obtained by giving subjects continuous feedback, thereby inducing adjustment and anchoring strategies (i.e., step-by-step prediction with feedback at each step; e.g., predict 1982, feedback; predict 1983, feedback; ...).[5]

Wagenaar and Timmers's (1978a, 1978b) finding that people are better at long-range extrapolation with fewer data points (that is, when sampling the process with greater intervals between observations) appears at first to contradict the notions of corrective feedback developed earlier in this article (cf. Figure 41.1). However, the apparent inconsistency can be reconciled by noting that if judgment is based only on recent observations, the slope of an exponential growth curve is more evident the greater the distance between observations. More generally, one can draw an analogy between this process and that of continual as opposed to intermittent adaptation to change. When you live with someone (e.g., spouse or child), you are not aware of the process of aging. However, for people you see intermittently (e.g., distant relatives), the changes are perceptible (see also Wagenaar & Timmers, 1978a). Furthermore, although attention is limited, the number of time series one is effectively tracking in the process of living is quite large. Thus, since only few processes can be tracked continuously, it is reasonable that larger and usually more important changes attract greater attention.

Stable preferences

In small worlds, preferences are necessarily assumed to be stable. For example, when deciding between two jobs, relative preferences for

---

[5] Details of this experiment appeared in an earlier version of this article.

different attributes of the jobs are deemed not to change between the moment of decision and its horizon. Difficulties in justifying this assumption have been elaborated by March (1978): (a) Preferences are not stable but may evolve over time. Thus, choices made in the present involve guesses about future preferences (and so violate, incidentally, the decision theoretic requirement of independence between preferences and beliefs). (b) Preferences are formed across time through experience and habit. Furthermore, people often experiment and determine preferences through actions. That is, actions determine preferences rather than vice versa (see also Koopmans, 1964; Simon, 1955). (c) Ambiguity in preference is the rule rather than the exception. Furthermore, ambiguity, as well as inconsistency, can be functional both from a personal viewpoint (permitting a wider range of experiences) and in social interaction where it is often not advantageous to reveal true preferences (e.g., in negotiations). Furthermore, the mental effort required to imagine and delineate future preferences is considerable (Koopmans, 1964). Thus, if people believe environments and preferences to be unpredictable, expending mental energy on such activity will be deemed unproductive.

How do people manage possible changes in preferences? One mechanism is not to have precise preferences but to let these adapt to changing circumstances (e.g., through the use of aspiration levels). Indeed, precision may often be unnecessary in that knowing the direction of a target can be more important than exact knowledge of its location. In addition, the target may often be hidden or changing, eventualities for which flexibility is suited. A corollary of such flexibility, however, is lability in the expression of preferences (Fischhoff, Slovic, & Lichtenstein, 1980). Furthermore, although people might need to express clear preferences at the moment of particular decisions, they allow these to change with subsequent frames of mind (cf. Shepard, 1964; Tversky & Kahneman, 1981).

A further mechanism is, on the contrary, proactive and involves taking action to inhibit possible future changes. Thaler and Shiffrin (1981) have given examples of such precommitment strategies that are often used to provide protection from future temptations (e.g., consider the "uneconomic" use of Christmas clubs and whole-life insurance, or the fixed sum appeal of package holidays) (see also Schelling, 1978; Thaler, 1980). Toda (1980) has noted the use of precommitment strategies in the form of metadecisions taken both to avoid possible future choice conflicts (e.g., whether to smoke) and to provide moral guidelines (e.g., never steal). Although both these mechanisms can also induce dysfunctional consequences (e.g., can an 18-year-old really imagine the cumulative effects of smoking for 50 years?), they do facilitate the control of preferences across time.

Finally, the evolution of preferences through physical maturation, experience, and learning raises important issues for theories of judgment and choice, which discrete conceptualizations have ignored (Einhorn & Hogarth, 1981). For example, how does type of experience with activities affect preferences? A recent theory proposed by Solomon (1980) links types of reinforcement schedules to the strength of acquired motivations and thus bears on these issues. Solomon has reported that low levels of reinforcement induced through regular participation in an activity spaced across time lead to less addiction (e.g., to drugs, sexual activity, or sports such as jogging or parachute jumping) than irregular participation within short periods, which is accompanied by heightened levels of reinforcement. The implications of this work for decision research are important and await further development.

Conditional independence between judgments and outcomes

Discrete incident research assumes that judgments are conditionally independent of outcomes. However, as the continuous processing model (Figure 41.1) indicates, possibilities for corrective action invalidate this assumption. Einhorn and Hogarth (1978) have explicitly examined the implications of treatment effects that moderate the relation between judgments and outcomes (and can also be considered similar to self-fulfilling or defeating prophecies). For example, if grants aid researchers in their work, how can the allocation process be evaluated without also giving grants to researchers deemed unworthy of support? Depending on task structure, the presence of such treatment effects can complicate the learning of predictive relations, contribute to illusions (e.g., over-confidence), and render problematic the evaluation of judgments and actions. In economics, for example, theorists now recognize that government announcements can affect, and even offset, the policies they are supposed to foster (Lucas, 1976). The extent, therefore, to which people are aware and/or use treatment effects in prediction (explicitly or implicitly) is an open and intriguing question.

Abstraction from competitive behavior

An important ecological dimension missing from most research on judgment and choice is that decisions are often made in competitive and other social situations. Thus, response tendencies that are dysfunctional within isolated, discrete incident models could be useful in interaction. Two instances have, in fact, been mentioned previously: First, inconsistency in behavior can be important in competitive situations where it pays to be unpredictable; second, ambiguity in the expression of preferences preserves greater freedom of action.

Concern with competitive behavior also helps to define standards to evaluate actions in complex environments. In competitive situations optimal responses are not necessary for survival. Instead, responses only have to be better than those of competitors or sufficiently differentiated (Einhorn, 1980a; Hammond, 1972).

Sources of judgmental bias

The adaptive nature of continuous processing suggests an evolutionary perspective in considering judgmental abilities. In a review of systematic judgmental errors, Campbell (1959) stated that many communication (i.e., decision) systems are artificially designed, with the result that people make errors they would not commit in their natural habitats. However, he added that "where the constant errors have this origin, they will be found to be part-and-parcel of psychological processes of general adaptive usefulness" (p. 340). Cognitive "biases" may therefore also indicate what people can do well.

Implicit in an evolutionary perspective is the notion that the human design has evolved as a compromise among conflicting demands of the environment. Thus, when an organism exhibits a response bias in its natural environment, one should also ask how many different errors could have been committed and which would have been the more frequent and/or costly (Campbell, 1959; Russo, 1978). Furthermore, the human body first evolved to enhance physical survival in an environment lacking the technology developed in recent centuries. Certain dysfunctional tendencies could well represent vestiges of responses that were functional in previous eras (cf. Skinner, 1966).

Judgmental biases probably have several origins. The extant empirical evidence does not permit a single explanation. First, bias may reflect sensitivity to payoffs in the environment. Killeen (1978), for example, has shown how the so-called superstitious behavior of pigeons can arise from appropriate discrimination of the relative losses implicit in different types of error. Second, and as argued here, several biases revealed in experimental situations can result from response tendencies that are functional in the natural ecology of the organism (see also Bar-Hillel, 1979). For example, consider the "illusion of control" (Langer, 1975) whereby people believe that, through skill, they exert greater control over events than is in fact the case. Although such beliefs can induce suboptimal behavior in discrete incidents, they can also lead to functional, proactive behavior across time, which, given the difficulty of attributing outcomes to skill or chance, is preferable to overestimating the latter. In fact, persistent underestimation of skill can lead to "learned helplessness" (Seligman, 1975).

Both the recognition of asymmetries in error and the adoption of a functional viewpoint are useful in considering judgmental phenomena, yet care must be exercised in invoking such arguments (Lewontin, 1979). It is facile to define costs and benefits after the fact so that behavior appears to be optimal, or at least reasonable. Furthermore, the persistence of dysfunctional behavior is not incompatible with evolutionary notions (Einhorn & Hogarth, 1981). Finally, whereas cognitive limitations do undoubtedly play a role in how decisions are formulated (cf. Simon, 1955), systematic "errors" have also been demonstrated in situations that do not exceed human information-processing ability (Grether & Plott, 1979; Tversky & Kahneman, 1981). The mechanisms by which such responses are produced remain unknown.

Methodology and normative issues

Methodology

How should one study judgment and choice in continuous environments? In this article I have emphasized the importance of task characteristics to performance; thus, conceptual analysis of these variables is a first priority.

The discrete-continuous distinction suggests at least four important task variables: (a) The cost of making an erroneous judgment/choice. This can be affected by the level of commitment implied by particular actions and/or competitive considerations. Errors may also have differential short- and long-term effects. (b) The availability of feedback (speed and frequency) and the extent to which it is or is not misleading. (c) The level of redundancy in the environment. (d) The stability of environmental cue-cue and cue-criterion relations. The importance of these variables lies in their effects on the demands made of a relatively limited organism dealing with a complex environment. Judgmental heuristics, for example, can be expected to work well when some or all of these task variables are at favorable levels. There is no need for organisms to respond at levels of accuracy exceeding task demands, nor would one expect them to learn how to do so.

The definition of rational behavior in continuous environments is problematic and raises the issue of determining appropriate performance criteria. The view taken here adopts an evolutionary perspective and emphasizes adaptation, since this highlights the ability to interpret feedback, learn, and act in consequence. Moreover, rather than defining optimal benchmarks, this view suggests studying the relative performance of different types of decision behavior (i.e., strategies or rules) in different types of environments characterized, for example, by varying levels of the task variables discussed previously. It should be particularly stressed that such decision rules may be simple (e.g., naive or even arbitrary/random strategies) and thus provide operational mechanisms for studying decision behavior in a wide range of tasks, either in simulations or as comparisons with human decisions. Indeed, the use of simple decision rules has already proved illuminating in several discrete paradigm tasks by providing baselines for assessing more complex strategies. Consider, for example, baselines for assessing the quality of group judgment (Einhorn, Hogarth, & Klempner, 1977), picking investment portfolios (Cowles, 1933), and selecting weighting schemes in linear models (Dawes & Corrigan, 1974; Einhorn & Hogarth, 1975).

Several recent studies have embodied these ideas in continuous tasks. Hogarth and Makridakis (1981), for example, monitored performance (and thus adaptation) across time of human teams playing in a dynamic, competitive business simulation game by comparing achievement against the baseline of artificial teams managed by sets of arbitrarily chosen, nonadapting decision rules. The artificial teams outperformed, on average, 30% of the human teams and thus shed some light on the value of the time the human teams spent on decision making. Furthermore, by varying the level of consistency in the rules of the artificial teams, the advantages and disadvantages of rule consistency in a dynamic environment could also be investigated. In a simulated, multistage medical decision-making task involving the interpretation of symptoms and the effects of previously administered treatments, Kleinmuntz and Kleinmuntz (1981) studied the performance of three decision rules varying in cognitive sophistication (an expected utility maximizer using Bayes's theorem, a heuristic search strategy that accepted satisfactory solutions, and a generate-and-test strategy that used random, trial-and-error search procedures). Overall, the Bayesian strategy proved most effective; however, in several cases differences were not significant, results which are important in the context of possible tradeoffs between the complexity of decision rules and ease in their use. In a further simulation study, Findler (1977) has cleverly explored the effects of different hypothese concerning strategies for learning in poker.

These studies are indicative of useful mechanisms for studying decision behavior in continuous environments; however, they also reinforce the need for prior conceptual analysis mentioned earlier. The number of different task environment-decision strategy combinations is so large that empirical simulations alone will not suffice to provide generalizable results. In particular, the effects of different types of combinations of environments and strategies will need to be linked theoretically to the abilities and limitations of the human information-processing system. Furthermore, since certain strategies can be robust across a range of environmental conditions (cf. Thorngate, 1980), the importance of determining the ecological distribution of types of tasks, discrete and continuous, in terms of both frequency and relative payoffs, is emphasized.

At the level of more traditional experiments, that researchers should use "representative" (Brunswik, 1956) as opposed to "systematic" designs has already been emphasized within the discrete framework (Ebbesen & Konečni, 1980; Hammond, 1978a; Hammond & Stewart, 1974). However, it should be noted that the within-subjects emphasis of representative design is inherently continuous in nature. When sampling situations within subjects, the researcher necessarily samples across time. Furthermore, by ignoring the nature of situational transitions, between-subjects designs can be misleading unless it is specifically desired to generalize to situations where judgments and choices are made in unique circumstances. Consider, for example, experiments that have explored naive appreciations of the statistical concept of variance (for a review see Hogarth, 1975a). The notion of variance is, it seems, more accurately represented by the coefficient of variation than by the variance itself. However, to the extent that the means and variances of naturally occurring phenomena are positively correlated (cf. Pearson, 1897), the coefficient of variation and the variance will also be highly correlated. In continuous situations, where people are accustomed to responding quickly and frequently, the use of such ecological correlations is clearly functional. Representative design is even more important in assessing human capabilities in continuous as opposed to discrete situations.

Normative issues

If behavior consistently violates normative standards (which are themselves defined in discrete manner), then an important implication of this article is to question such models. Indeed, March (1978) has stated:

For if there is sense in the choice behavior of individuals acting contrary to standard engineering procedures for rationality, then it seems reasonable to suspect that there may be something inadequate about our normative theory of choice or the procedures by which it is implemented. (p. 589)

Einhorn and Hogarth (1981) have pointed out that no authority can reveal whether optimal models or human representations capture the essence of a decision problem more adequately. One cannot overcome the fact that the validity of the axioms underlying the optimal models against which unaided judgment is tested rests on judgment itself. Nonetheless, research has revealed important flaws that should not go unheeded. What can be done?

First, the assumptions and limitations of the predominantly discrete, prescriptive decision models must be clearly stated (see also Ackoff, 1979).

Second, the limits of human predictive ability and the difficulties of learning valid predictive relations need to be established (for a start, see Einhorn & Hogarth 1978). Crucial to this is development of the ability to interpret feedback.

Third, ways of conceptualizing discrete tasks in continuous form should be investigated. For example, a suggestion by Bray (1975) in the context of economic planning has interesting implications. Taking the view that forecasts are necessarily inaccurate, Bray likened planning to that of guiding the economy on a certain trajectory over time (cf. Figures

41.1 and 41.2). This involves setting control parameters and steering the economy on the implied course. In a simulation study, Bray compared this strategy with the successive "stop-go" policies followed by the British government since World War II and found that if a discrete perspective had not been followed, Great Britain would be considerably better off today. Despite considerable technical difficulties implicit in this approach, the notion deserves further development.

Fourth, the kinds of incremental, adaptive judgmental strategies discussed in this article often avoid looking ahead and suggest that, relative to environmental demands, "cognitive myopia" is probably the most common form of judgmental bias. Thus, in training decision makers, the development of imagination and creativity may well be more important than teaching the statistical reasoning implicit in the discrete paradigm. As emphasized by Campbell (1960), deliberately investing in "thought trials" to induce "random variations" is a crucial aspect of both evolutionary and creative processes. Thought trials are precisely a means of simulating the conditions of corrective feedback.

Finally, it is appropriate to conclude by noting that one result dominates the extensive descriptive research on decision making carried out in recent decades: Judgment and choice depend crucially upon the context in which they occur and the cognitive representation of that context. However, both environment and mind interact in continuous fashion. The major contention of this article, therefore, is that theories of judgment and choice that lack a continuous perspective exclude one of the most important determinants of the behavior they purport to explain.

42. In one word: Not from experience

Berndt Brehmer

In 1959, Goldberg published a study in which he compared experienced clinical psychologists and secretaries with respect to their ability to make diagnoses of brain damage. The diagnoses were made from the Bender Gestalt Test, an instrument widely used for making diagnoses of this kind. The results were as clear as they were surprising: there were no differences between the two groups, clinical psychologists were no better than secretaries in making these diagnoses.

Although these results are particularly striking, Goldberg's study is but one of many studies showing that even considerable experience with a clinical task does not make people very good at making the decisions required by this kind of task (see, for example, Goldberg, 1968, for a review of this research).

One reaction to this kind of findings has been to consider them confirmation of one's worst suspicions about clinical psychologists and psychiatrists. A more interesting way of looking at them is, however, to remind oneself that even psychiatrists and clinical psychologists are people just like the rest of us, and to note that we have in this literature a solid body of evidence that people do not always learn from experience, at least not when the experience consists of a series of cases. This may be a startling conclusion and certainly one that goes against some of our most cherished beliefs: that experience improves our judgments and decisions.

It is possible to understand the conviction that we learn from experience in terms of its roots in British Empiricist philosophy, but the strength of the conviction suggests that it may serve not only our scientific understanding, but that it has ideological functions as well (see

This chapter originally appeared in *Acta Psychologica*, 1980, 45, 223–241. Copyright © 1980 by North-Holland Publishing Company. Reprinted by permission.

Greeno, James, Da Polito, & Polson, 1978, for a discussion of this point). It is, however, a conviction that at least psychologists have not been able to keep without considerable cost. Part of this cost is that we have come to have what can only be called a perverse conception of the nature of experience.

This conception is very clearly illustrated in the model of experience which is manifest in psychological experiments on learning, and it is nowhere more clearly expressed than in the so called paired-associates paradigm. In experiments in this paradigm, the subject is given a list of word pairs and asked to learn to give the second member of each pair as his response when presented with the first member as a stimulus. This is a task which subjects learn with little difficulty, thus seemingly vindicating the hypothesis that experience leads to valid knowledge. What these results show, however, is only that experience can lead to a modification of a person's mind. It does not show that the knowledge obtained in this manner will be valid, for as an object of knowledge, there is something very special about a list of paired associates. This is that we know exactly what there is to be learned from this list. In the words of Karl Popper (*e.g.*, 1963), the peculiar thing about such a list is that truth is manifest. The process of acquiring knowledge therefore becomes a simple matter of creating a mental picture of the task, and if this picture is a faithful one, it also constitutes knowledge about the world. Thus, in this case, experience does indeed lead to valid knowledge.

But note why this is the case. The guarantee of validity is *not* in experience itself. There is nothing in the subject's experience with the task that even suggests that a given stimulus work will be followed by the same response word on each and every trial. Clearly, the guarantee of validity does not come from experience. It comes from the *experimenter* who has assured the subjects, not only that there *is* something to learn, but also *what* there is to learn. This, rather than experience as such, guarantees the validity of the knowledge acquired in this paradigm. The paradigm may thus very well model the situation in teaching, where the teacher decides for the pupil what the truth should be in a given case, but it certainly does not model the situation in which a person is learning from experience.

Take the case of a clinical psychologist learning about diagnoses and treatment from his personal experience with patients. In this case, nobody will be able to tell him what there is to learn, or even whether there is anything for him to learn. He may learn what his colleagues think the correct diagnosis and treatment should be, but this is only learning about what another person thinks that he knows, but not about the patients. And just because the kind of treatment selected turns out to lead to recovery does not mean that the decision was correct, for this recovery may have many causes other than the treatment given and, of course, many other kinds of treatment might have been just as effective. Take, for example, the belief in the efficacy of penicillin as a cure for sore throats! Penicillin, as we know, is a good cure for diseases caused by bacteria, but sore throats are usually caused by viruses rather than bacteria and for these, penicillin is not effective. Nevertheless, the patient recovers, but not because of the penicillin but because of the body's general ability to fight disease.

In these kinds of situations, then, turth is no longer manifest. Indeed, this is only the beginning of our problems. It is not only the case that the truth is not readily apparent; we may also distort the situation by our actions, so that what we could have learned will not be learned. We will return to this problem later in the paper, and we will start with the simpler case when we do not act but learn from just observing the world.

Learning from observing the world

The problem of induction

The psychological problem of learning from experience is, of course, only the old philosophical problem of induction. As philosophers after Hume have agreed, inductive judgment cannot be justified in the way deductive judgment can be justified. The judgment may very well be true, and serve as a guide to action, but it cannot be *shown* to be true. The fact that it works says little about its truth, it just tells us that it works, and the explanation for why it works may be very different from what we think it is.

Whereas philosophers have given a lot of thought to the problem of induction, psychologists have generally not given much thought to the corresponding problem of learning from experience. They have been content to note that the behavior of people changes as a result of experience, but they have not considered whether the persons also have acquired more valid knowledge; this has been taken for granted. Nor have they considered the problem of where our faith in experience may come from, given that the things we learn cannot be justified. Instead, they have just accepted Hume's psychological theory of induction. This theory holds that as we experience many things of a similar kind, a "habit of mind" makes us believe that we will see even more things of this kind. Thus, when we have seen five white swans, we tend to believe that the next swan will also be white.

The objections to this theory are well known and have to do with the problem of similarity (Popper, 1963). It is all very well to say that our belief is strengthened when we see many similar things, but how do we know that the things that we encounter are really similar and instances of the same phenomenon? This may not be very much of a problem in a traditional psychological experiment on induction, such as a concept learning experiment where the things are colors and simple geometrical figures, stimuli that our evolutionary history has taught us to recognize. But what about the more complex stimuli encountered in the real world such as psychiatric patients, or political decision problems? Here, we have to contribute to the learning process by first deciding what things are similar and what things are not similar to form a basis for our induction. But for that, we need to have an idea of what the relevant characteristics are, *i.e.*, we need to know what characteristics will lead to a useful classification. In short, we need to define what we are to learn, before we are able to learn it.

The learning process, therefore, cannot simply be a case of forming a mental picture of the world. It must be an active process of hypothesis testing. This leads to two problems for research; *viz.*, the problem of where our hypotheses come from, and that of how we test our hypotheses. We now turn to a brief review of what psychological research has to say on these two problems.

Hypothesis testing theories

Hypotheses testing theories have a long history in experimental psychology. Interesting enough, the first theory of this kind was developed for discrimination learning in the white rat (Krechevsky, 1932) at a time when most psychologists would not allow a person to think or have hypotheses for fear of being of accused of mentalism. This theory then came to set the pattern for subsequent theories of this kind in psychology especially those within the area of concept learning. The most well known is, of course, that of Bruner, Goodnow, and Austin (1956).

The distinguishing characteristic of the situation for which these theories have been developed, is that the subjects' task is to discover which of the dimensions of a series of stimulus objects are useful for dividing them into two or more classes.

For these situations, it is not difficult to decide where the subjects' hypotheses come from. The hypotheses are simply sampled from the stimuli. The theories assume that the subjects are able to analyze the stimuli into their relevant components, and that they then try the usefulness of these components, either one by one, or in some combination. These theories are thus only new versions of the old abstraction theories for concept formation. In their actual application, the theories tend to bypass the problem of abstraction, however, in that they are applied to the learning of stimuli, the components of which are already well formed concepts, such as color and form. These experiments, therefore, are set up in such a way that the experimenter is certain that the subjects already have the hypotheses relevant to the task. This means, however, that these experiments do not tell us what we need to know, and the extension of these theories to situations where the components are not well learned concepts becomes very problematical. In short, we do not know whether these theories really apply to the learning of new concepts (see Bolton, 1972).

This is not the place to review all the results obtained with the experimental paradigm that have grown out of this conceptualization of concept learning, especially since there are already good reviews available (see, for example, Bourne, 1966, for a short introduction). One result, however, is of great interest in the present context. This is that subjects learning these kinds of tasks do so by trying to confirm hypotheses, rather than by trying to refute incorrect hypotheses. Furthermore, they rely mainly on those tests which provide them with positive information about the concept, *i.e.*, information telling them what the concept is, but neglect negative information, *i.e.*, information telling what the concept is not (see Bruner *et al.*, 1956, and the paper by Mynatt, Doherty, & Tweney, 1977).

Confirmation will, of course, not teach the subjects about the actual validity of their hypotheses; it will only tell which hypotheses work, although the reason why the hypotheses work may be very different from what the subject thinks. In fact, it is clear that this kind of strategy may actually prevent the subjects from discovering even rather simple relations in the task. An experiment by Wason (1960) gives a good illustration of this. In Wason's experiment, subjects had to find a simple rule by generating triplets of numbers. The rule was a simple monotonic series, so that any three numbers in an ascending order was correct, *e.g.*, 1, 2, 3, or 1,501, 10,000. However, an infinite number of complicated series will fulfill the condition of monotonicity, and subjects would use all sorts of rules, which fulfilled this condition, thus arriving at correct answers. Nevertheless, their rules would, however, not be the correct rule, and a majority of subjects actually failed to find the simple rule of monotonicity because they sought confirmation of a rule they believed to be correct, rather than refutation of a possibly incorrect hypothesis.

In concept learning experiments, the neglect of negative information leads to slow and inefficient learning, but the strategy makes sense when one considers the conditions under which people usually have to learn in the so-called real world. Negative information is clearly useful in a concept learning experiment where the subjects know the dimensions of the "world." For example, if there are red and green squares, knowing that a green square is not an instance of the concept immediately tells us what the concept is. But to be told that a cat is not an elephant when one does not even know how many different kinds of animals there are, will not teach us very much about elephants. Being told what an elephant is, on the other hand, is highly useful. But note that this is the case only because there is a guarantee of truth in the very fact of being told. This can be given because this statement informs a person, not about the world as such, but about the kinds of concepts people have.

When we have to learn from outcomes, it may, in fact, be almost impossible to discover that one really does not know anything. This is especially true when the concepts are very complex in the sense that each instance contains many dimensions. In this case, there are too many ways of explaining why a certain outcome occurred, and to explain away failures of predicting the correct outcome. Because of this, the need to change may not be apparent to us, and we may fail to learn that our rule is invalid, not only for particular cases but for the general case also. This is very clearly demostrated in a series of experiments by Fischhoff and Slovic (1980). Their experiments show that even very limited amounts of experience with complex stimuli, such as handwriting samples and common stocks, lead to a highly unwarranted confidence in one's ability to classify these stimuli when the subjects believe that they are in possession of a good rule for making the classifications. Indeed, these results suggest that the mere fact that they are able to find a rule is sufficient for the subjects to believe that they can make the appropriate discriminations even though they have no experience indicating that the rule is valid.

However, even though the hypothesis-testing theories mentioned above are a step towards a general theory of how people classify stimuli, and thus also a step towards a theory of how people learn from experience, they are clearly not sufficient. This is because they do not cover the important problem of how relations between variables are learned. We now turn to this problem.

Learning relations between variables

A typical judgment task, such as a diagnostic problem in clinical psychology, requires not only that one learns to classify patients but also, and perhaps to a greater extent, that one learns the relations between variables, *e.g.*, the relations between various symptom configurations and treatment outcomes. The process of learning the relations in tasks of this sort, *e.g.*, the relation between MMPI scores and degree of illness, is made difficult by the fact that the relations among the variables are probabilistic rather than deterministic.

These tasks differ from the classification tasks discussed above in that it is not even theoretically possible to construct hypotheses by sampling aspects from the stimulus configurations. A relation between two variables is not defined by any single instance, and even if multiple instances are available, they have to be ordered before the relation can be detected. Such an ordering does, of course, presuppose a hypothesis about the nature of the relation being looked for, so ordering does not provide any automatic solution.

Since the hypotheses about the nature of the relation between variables cannot come from the stimulus objects, they have to come from the subjects. That is, the subjects have to contribute the hypotheses. It is thus clear that what will be learned in this case will very much depend on what kinds of hypotheses the subjects will bring to the task.

In a series of studies, we have used various forms of probabilistic inference tasks to investigate this problem. The tasks have required the subjects to learn to use one or more cues to infer the state of a criterion variable which is imperfectly correlated with the cues. The only information given to the subject is the correct criterion value on every trial, so learning takes place on the basis of outcome feedback only.

The first few studies (Brehmer, 1874c; Brehmer, Kuylenstierna, & Liljergren, 1974) were directed at the problem of how subjects find the functional relations between two variables. The results agreed quite closely with the predictions from a hypothesis sampling model based on the assumption that subjects have a limited number of hypotheses which are ordered in a hierarchy according to strength, and that they sample and test hypotheses in the order determined by the relative strengths of these hypotheses. Later experiments have shown, however, that subjects are also able to construct some new hypotheses not in their hypothesis hierarchy, and that they are thus not limited to learning only the few rules about which they have hypotheses in their hierarchy (Brehmer 1976a, 1980a; Brehmer & Kuylenstierna, 1979). But even though such constructions are possible, linear hypotheses are by far the dominant ones. This has been interpreted to mean that linear relations are the most common relations in real world inference tasks and subjects have therefore learned to try this rule first (Brehmer, 1974c). However, this hypothesis would go against the main thesis of this paper. The results of Dawes and Corrigan (1974) suggest a different interpretation more in line with the present argument that people do not learn from experience.

Dawes and Corrigan showed that a linear model, and even one with unit weights, provides a good approximation to most judgment tasks. If equipped with such a model, the person is simply not likely to find any better model. It is only in the, probably rare, case when the relations between the cues and the criterion are not conditionally monotone, that the subjects may find that there is a better alternative to their linear model. Thus, if the cognitive system had only one model to use for judgment, a linear model is what it ought to use. Under these circumstances, it is hardly surprising that this is indeed the most common model used by subjects. At the same time, using such a model is clearly very useful since it allows the subjects to make reasonably good predictions even if they have not learned from experience with the task.

Further studies showed, however, that functional rules, such as linear and U-shaped functions were by no means the only rules considered by subjects in these tasks, even though they tended to prefer these kinds of rules. Figure 42.1 gives a summary of the results of our experiments.

As is shown in this figure, subjects prefer to assume that there is a rule, rather than that there is no rule, that this rule is deterministic, rather than

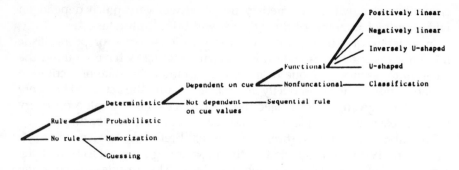

Figure 42.1. Summary of results from studies on probabilistic inference tasks. Note that there is no further breakdown of probabilistic rules. This is because no such rules are observed in the experiments. The heavy line in the figure indicates the most common path.

probabilistic, that the values to be predicted from the cue values do in fact depend on these cue values, rather than on other aspects such as trial number, that the rule is functional, rather than nonfunctional, and that the rule is a positive linear function, rather than any other function. If the hypothesis about linearity fails, the subjects try some of the other functional rules before backtracking their decision tree, trying a nonfunctional rule, or a rule that does not assume cue dependence, such as a sequential rule, meaning that the ordinal number of the cue values, rather than their actual values, are used to form their hypothesis. For example, the subjects may believe that low criterion values are regularly followed by high criterion values, or *vice versa*. When these rules also fail, the subjects tend to assume that there is no rule at all, rather than to seriously consider the possibility that the rule may be probabilistic in character. Therefore, they go to a memorization strategy, or they may just give up and guess.

The result that the subjects do not seem to consider the task to be probabilistic, or to use a strategy appropriate to a probabilistic task, agrees with that obtained under other kinds of circumstances by Tversky and Kahneman (1980). In this and other papers, they have shown that when subjects have to estimate probabilities, they generally do not follow the rules of probability calculus. Instead, they use various heuristics such as representativeness and availability. The results in Tversky and Kahneman (1980) strongly suggest that the subjects believe that the relations in the experiment are causal, rather than statistical in nature. Consequently, they use inference rules appropriate to deterministic tasks, rather than the rule appropriate to probabilistic tasks. In this context, it is interesting to note that Wason and Johnson-Laird (1972) earlier invoked the same kind of hypothesis to explain why subjects failed to follow adequate logical rules in another kind of task also requiring the use of a formal schema for making inferences. Specifically, Wason and Johnson-Laird found that subjects did not understand the logical relation of implication ("if, then") and that they tended to consider this relation equivalent to a double implication ("if, and only if"), as would be appropriate for a causal task. They also showed that task content had a very strong effect on the subjects' inference rules, a finding consistent with those of Tversky and Kahneman (1980), but which has only rather limited support in probabilistic inference tasks requiring the subjects to use cues for making inferences (Brehmer & Kuylenstierna, 1980). Taken together, however, these results provide considerable evidence that determinism, or causality, is a very basic schema used by people to make sense of the world.

While this may be a useful schema in many circumstances, it nevertheless leads to rather dramatic errors in many circumstances (see Tversky and Kahneman 1980), so it is clearly not universally applicable.

This leads to the important question of whether it is possible to improve the subjects' performance by informing them of the basic probabilistic character of the task. In a series of experiments we have studied the effects of giving this kind of information in inference tasks requiring the subjects to use probabilistic cues to make inferences about a criterion variable (Brehmer & Kuylenstierna, 1978, 1980; Johansson & Brehmer, 1979). Specifically, we have used various forms of instructions to explain to the subjects that the task is probabilistic, ranging from a simple statement that it is impossible to make perfect inferences on every trial because the task is probabilistic to explicit graphical explanation in terms of scatter diagrams. This has not led to any improvement in performance or to any change in strategy. We have then tried to explain to the subjects, not only that the task is probabilistic, but also what kind of strategy is applicable to these kinds of tasks, i.e., that they should look for the regression function and use it consistently. When this also failed, we thought that this may be because the subjects could not test their hypotheses about the rule for the task, so we therefore also informed the subjects about the magnitude of the errors to expect, given that they had found the optimal rule to help them evaluate their performance. Again the results were negative, as they were also when the tasks were given a content which clearly suggested that the relations between cues and criterion were probabilistic, and which was interpreted by the subjects to mean that the task was probabilistic, as assessed in a separate experiment. Regardless of instruction or task content, the subjects showed the typical behavior for these kinds of inference tasks: suboptimal performance due to inconsistent inference strategies with inconsistency being a monotone function of the uncertainty of the task.

These results, taken as a whole, strongly suggest that people simply do not have the cognitive schemata needed for efficient performance in probabilistic tasks. These experiments are, of course, laboratory experiments using college students as subjects. However, there is evidence that these results are not limited to the laboratory. Experienced clinicians behave in the same manner as the subjects in these experiments when making inferences in tasks with which they have years of experience (Brehmer, 1976b).

One possible explanation why people do not learn in these tasks is that they are unable to test their hypotheses when the information comes in a nonsystematic way. However, this is, at best, only part of the explanation. There are results (P. Slovic, personal communication) indicating that subjects do not learn probabilistic inference tasks more efficiently when the information is presented in a systematic way calculated to give them maximum information or when they are given an opportunity to select instances in whatever order they wish.

These results, then, support the earlier results on clinical inference in that they show that people do not learn optimal strategies from experience even if they are given massive amounts of practice. The reason why the subjects fail to improve in these tasks seems to be that they lack the necessary basic schemata to help them understand and use the information provided by their experience. Rather than using the appropriate statistical schemata, subjects use an inappropriate causal or deterministic schema. Even though this does not, of course, prevent them from learning anything at all, the deterministic schema may be a good approximation to what is to be learned, it will certainly prevent them from learning as much as they could. However, even when subjects are using the appropriate statistical schemata, their performance is not better than when they are not using these schemata (Brehmer & Kuylenstierna, 1979, 1980), perhaps because the subjects are not used to this way of dealing with inference tasks.

These findings raise the problem of why the subjects fail to detect the probabilistic nature of these tasks, which is so obvious to the experimenter.

Upon reflection this is, perhaps, not so strange. The characteristic of probabilism is, of course, not manifest, but it has to be inferred. This means, first, that the subject has to have an adequate notion of probabilism among this schemata for organizing his experience, and, second, that he has some criterion for when a task should be considered probabilistic. There is, of course, no absolute criterion of probabilism, so it can only be evaluated in comparison with some deterministic hypothesis. One way of doing this is to assume a functional, or other, rule and evaluate the fit of this rule. However, it is clear that this will put the subject in quite a bind, for to evaluate his rule, he has to make some assumption about the error in this system, and to evaluate the error, he has to make assumptions about the rule. It would seem, therefore, that the only way in which a subject could do this would be to try all his rules, and then shift to a statistical strategy, when he can find no more rules to try. Although the subjects certainly seem to follow the first part of this strategy, they fail to switch to the statistical rule when they have run out of deterministic rules. Instead the subjects seem to think that there is some deterministic rule for the task, but that they cannot find it. It is, of course, impossible to prove them wrong; the fact that they cannot find the rule does not prove that there is no rule. This illustrates that for a person with a firm belief in the deterministic character of the world, there is nothing in his experience that would force him to discover that the task is probabilistic and to give up the notion of determinism. To detect the probabilistic nature of the task, the subject clearly has to have the hypothesis that it is probabilistic.

If a subject cannot detect that a given task is probabilistic, it is not surprising that he does not have a general statistical approach. On the other hand, the notion of determinism is just as hidden from experience. It is therefore legitimate to ask why subjects do not have the opposite approach, *i.e.*, why they do not have probabilism as a basic schema and fail to detect when the task is deterministic. Such an approach ought to be at least as compatible with their experience as the deterministic approach.

Some observations by Piaget and Inhelder (1975) are relevant here. They point out that the notions of chance and probability cannot develop until a person has reached the stage of formal operations, and that it can develop only in contrast to the schema of order, or causality. They then document in a series of experiments that the notion of probability is indeed dependent on the nature of the person's general cognitive structures, and that it develops only after the schema of causality has been firmly established around the age of 11 to 12 years.

These results, then, suggest that the notion of order is developmentally prior to that of probabilism. If so, it is no longer surprising that the subjects in our experiments do not entertain probabilistic hypotheses, especially in consideration of all the results which show that not very many people enter the stage of formal operations.

To summarize, our discussion shows that subjects do not seem to be able to learn to perform optimally in probabilistic inference tasks, and that this is due to lack of adequate schemata for handling the probabilistic aspect of the world. This may seem surprising, but it can be understood if we remember that the probabilism of task is not manifest, and that it can be detected only by a person who already has the notion of probabilism in his cognitive equipment. In short, probabilism must be invented before it can be detected. This, in turn, requires considerable cognitive development on the part of the person. We may get some appreciation for how hard it is to make this invention if we remember that probability calculus was not invented until the seventeenth century. One explanation why it has to take so long, consistent with the interpretation by Piaget and Inhelder of the development of the child, is that it was only at this point in time that the notion of causality had reached such a level that it could provide a suitable contrast against which to evaluate disorder. Be that as it may, the fact that probability calculus is such a late invention, despite that it would have been useful long before it was invented, is evidence that an adequate understanding of probabilism is very hard to come by from our experience.

Learning when the outcomes are dependent upon judgment

So far, we have considered only the case when a person learns passively by observing the world. This, however, is not the only, or perhaps even the most common, case. Often, and this is certainly the case in clinical situations, a person has to act on his judgment, *i.e.*, by prescribing a cure, and the outcome from which he is to learn will depend not only on the quality of the person's judgment but also on the nature of his actions. The most fundamental characteristic of action is its selective nature; doing one thing precludes doing another. Thus, giving one kind of therapy precludes giving another. Furthermore, action may be selective also in that it is directed only at some of those who could have received it. For example, scarce resources may force us to treat only a limited number of all those who apply for treatment. As we shall see, the possibilities of learning from experience may be extremely limited in this case. Specifically, there will be a number of factors that prevent us from detecting that our judgment is fallible.

Consider the case where a psychologist has invented a new form of therapy. He now wishes to show its usefulness. However, he cannot give therapy to everyone who wants it, so he makes the reasonable decision to give therapy only to those who need it the most, *i.e.*, to those he judges to be most ill. He then goes on to give his therapy to those people and then makes a new judgment concerning the status of his patients. Almost inevitably, he will now find that they have improved, and he will be led to conclude that his treatment was useful, and that he made the correct judgment concerning his patients. The problem is that there is a very likely alternative explanation: that the improvement he observed is simply a regression effect. Since his judgment is likely to be unreliable (indeed, the results from studies on clinical inference would suggest that his judgment would most likely be grossly unreliable), it will change from the first to second time so that those patients given low judgments on the first occasion will, on the average, be given higher judgments on the second occasion, and *vice versa*. This is likely to be a common mechanism for it must often be the case that the resources are limited, forcing us to select cases for treatment, and if we select extreme cases, the regression effect will automatically insure that our method will appear useful. Under these circumstances, nobody should be surprised that old methods of therapy are never given up but always found useful by clinical experience, and abandoned only for new methods presumably found useful for the very same reason as the old ones. Nor should anyone be surprised that as a treatment becomes more widely available, and thus is given to less severely disturbed patients, its effect will seem smaller.

Kahneman and Tversky (1973) have pointed to some tragical consequences of the regression effect: that it makes us use punishment rather than reward for influencing behavior. This is because punishment is likely to be given to those judged to be bad, *i.e.*, to those who appear to be low with respect to the characteristic being judged. These people are, of course, exactly those who would be judged to have improved from the first to the second occasion simply because of the regression effect. Rewards, on the other hand, are likely to be given to those who are judged to be good, *i.e.*, to those judged to have a high value. For these people, the regression effect will work in the opposite direction, so that they will seem to have a lower score on the second occasion. Thus, it is clear that one's experience will tend to prove that punishment is an effective means for improving performance, and that reward is not only ineffective, but perhaps even harmful. Kahneman and Tversky document by examples that this is indeed what people learn from their experience, contrary to what a person who has studied the psychological literature on the effects of reward and punishment would expect. A person's experience, it seems, will not necessarily tell the truth.

Let us now consider the opposite case, that our judgment has little or no validity, but we have a powerful and efficient treatment. This case has recently been analyzed in detail by Einhorn and Hogarth (1978). In their interesting and important paper, they show how, under these circumstances, we may easily be led to overestimate the validity of our judgment.

In part, the problems with this case should be well known to social scientists: it is simply the case of self-fulfilling prophesies. Einhorn (1980a) uses the example of the effects of deciding to fund a grant application. Regardless of the validity of the judgment of value or deservedness of the research application, it is clear that those who get grants are going to produce more and probably also better research than those who do not get grants, thus confirming the judgment of the granting agency that those who got the grants were indeed those who should have had them. There is, of course, no ground for saying anything about the validity of the judgment of the basis of these outcomes. To do so, it is necessary to disentangle the effects of the treatment, *i.e.*, giving the grant, from the judgment. But this can be done only by *not* acting on one's judgment, and by using some other means of resource allocation, *e.g.* random distribution. But this is, of course, exactly what is not likely to happen, especially when the resources are scarce. In such a situation we are thus not likely to find the true validity of our judgment.

As we have already pointed out, the problem of learning from our experience when we also have to act upon our judgment is that the very fact that we do something will preclude getting the information we need to evaluate our judgment. Action is always selective, meaning that as we select certain cases for treatment, we by that very act also select other cases who do not get treatment. The only cases we can observe, therefore, are the true positives and the false positives.

In many situations, this may not be such a problem. Given that the selection ratio is extreme, it is clear that we may actually get only true positives, even if the validity of our judgment is extremely low. Scarce resources thus tend to give us an inflated sense of judgment ability. As the resources get less scarce, and the selection ratio less extreme, our judgment is going to appear less and less good. Perhaps this is the reason why we now have so much more concern about unnecessary surgery than we had 20 years ago when the resources for hospital care were less adequate than they are today.

While the need to act may logically preclude learning about the validity of one's judgment, the psychological effects may not be as great as one might expect. The problem of learning about the validity of one's judgment in the present case is basically that of learning about the relation between two dichotomous variables. The judgment dichotomizes the independent variable into two categories: those who do and those who do not get treatment, and the dependent variable is dichotomized into those who succeed and those who do not, *e.g.*, those who get well and those who do not.

This particular learning task has received considerable attention (Jenkins & Ward, 1965; Smedslund, 1963; Ward & Jenkins, 1965). The results show that the subjects, when learning these tasks, tend to focus only on the number of true positives, *i.e.*, they follow the same strategy of using only confirming evidence as we have observed earlier. This is, of course, not very satisfactory from a logical point of view. It makes sense, however, when we consider that under natural circumstances, *e.g.*, when people have to learn about the validity of their judgment, they will not have access to all four outcomes. Thus, it may not be so surprising that people have not learned the optimal way of coping with tasks of this sort.

So far, we have mentioned two aspects of the task that may give us a false sense of judgmental ability: the efficiency of our treatments and the selection ratio. However, it should also be clear that the base rate of the trait being judged is extreme, this will also affect our sense of judgmental ability. For example, if 90% of the patients who come to a clinical hospital are schizophrenic, it is not a great achievement to be able to correctly identify 80% of all patients as schizophrenic although an 80% hit rate may sound impressive when we do not consider the base rate, and may thus lead us to trust our judgment.

It should also be clear that there will be interactions among judgmental validity, selection ratio, base rate, and the efficiency of our treatment, and that the rate of positive hits will vary with all four of these factors.

Einhorn and Hogarth (1978) present a formal model of how these factors interact. The importance of this model for future research on judgment and decision-making can hardly be overestimated. It provides a needed first step towards a more adequate conception of what a person's experience really is like, and this is, of course, a prerequisite for a more adequate conception of what a person may learn from that experience. Hopefully, the work of Einhorn and Hogarth will inspire others to continue their work and provide us with a more complete picture of the nature of experience.

Conclusion

We started this paper by discussing some results that seemed to contradict one of our deepest convictions: that experience leads to better judgment and decisions. Our further analysis of the problem has shown, however, that our faith in experience is, if not totally without foundation, so at least far from well grounded. This is because it stems from an untenable conception of the nature of experience, a conception that assumes that truth is manifest and does not have to be inferred. A more adequate understanding of the nature of experience leads to a more pessimistic view of what its effects may be. This, in turn, leads to less surprise about the results of studies on judgment and decision making. It seems that these results are exactly what they should be, and if we do not learn from experience, this is largely because experience often gives us very little information to learn from.

43. Doing the impossible: A note on induction and the experience of randomness

Lola L. Lopes

In standardized tests of reasoning ability, one often finds questions like this:

What digit should go in the space at the end of the series below?
1 2 2 3 3 3 4 4 4 4 5 5 5 5 5 6 6 6 6 6 ?

Almost certainly, test makers and proficient test takers would agree that the answer is 6. Another question that might be asked is the following:

Below are three hypotheses concerning the source of the series above. Rank order the hypotheses from most to least likely.
a. The test maker made up the series.
b. The series is digits 676,512 through 676,531 of Rand's *One Million Random Digits*.
c. The series is digits 500,000 through 500,019 of Rand's *One Million Random Digits*.

Although the question is unusual, most people world rank the hypotheses exactly as given. The series seems almost certainly to have been constructed by human agency, but if by some extraordinary coincidence, it did happen to occur in Rand's (1955) table of radom digits, then it seems far more likely to have been at some relatively anonymous position than exactly in the middle of the table.

Consider, however, what would happen if the same two questions were asked about another series:

2 2 1 2 1 5 9 1 7 9 1 7 6 8 3 1 5 8 6 7 ?

In this case it is not at all clear how the series ought to be completed, nor is it clear how the source hypotheses ought to be ordered. Why do we

This chapter originally appeared in the *Journal of Experimental Psychology; Learning, Memory, and Cognition*, 1982, 8(6), 626–636. Copyright © 1982 by the American Psychological Association, Inc. Reprinted by permission.

have such different intuitions about these two series? The answer is obviously that the first series has a readily discernible pattern whereas the second does not. It is this pattern that underlies our *mistaken* intuition that the first series is less likely than the second to be generated by a random process. And it is also this pattern that underlies and enables our inductive inference that the first series should end with a 6.

Induction is how we discover for ourselves what the world is like. It occurs when we generalize past experience with particular even patterns to new and as yet unobserved instances (Harré, 1970). Scientists do it; lay people do it; even birds and beasts do it. But the process is mysterious and full of paradox (cf. Gardner, 1976), for as Hume (1748/1977) showed long ago, induction cannot be justified on logical grounds: No matter how strongly available evidence may seem to support our current beliefs about the world, the possibility always remains that new evidence will prove us wrong. Thus, to do induction is necessarily to run the risk of error, and this, it will be argued, makes it difficult to evaluate how well the process is being done. For if induction cannot be justified rationally, then what criteria can be used to judge whether it is being done rationally?

For human beings, induction has two relatively distinct stages: the act of conceiving a new idea or theory and the act of testing or justifying that theory. An extensive literature now exists on the logical analysis, formalization, and, some would hope, the eventual improvement of the second of these stages (e.g., on scientific method: Harré, 1970; Lakatos, 1970; Popper, 1959; on statistical inference: Hacking, 1965; Kyburg, 1970; Levi, 1967). But little corresponding effort has been directed at the first stage. Popper (1959), in fact, argued that the initial stage contains an irrational element that seems neither to call for logical analysis nor to be susceptible of it. As he said, "Such processes are the concern of empirical psychology but hardly of logic" (p. 31).

The present note comments on the psychological foundations of an essential, but often overlooked, part of the initial stage: the act of noticing a pattern against a background of noise. To illustrate the potential significance of such acts, I draw on a problem in induction sketched originally by Ball (1980) in an article that speculated on the means by which Earth people might discover the existence of extraterrestrial intelligence. According to Ball, it is unlikely that alien beings are trying to communicate with us. Instead, it is much more likely that Earth scientists will stumble on evidence of alien existence inadvertently by "eavesdropping" on their "waste energy," a possibility that can be easily appreciated if we reverse perspective and consider the fate of some of our own waste energy.

In the early days of television, the antennas used for broadcasting TV signals were very nearly omnidirectional. This allowed much of the transmitted signal to be lost to space where, as any science fiction fan knows, it is traveling still. It is possible, then, and perhaps even likely, that intelligent space beings, with their receivers turned to space, might someday intercept a fragment of one of those old broadcasts. But – and this is the critical question – would they know what they had? Would they even know that they had a signal of some sort? Not necessarily, for a fundamental problem facing extraplanetary eavesdroppers – human or otherwise – is how one is to know, having intercepted some stray energy, that it has been generated by intelligent beings rather than by a natural process. As Ball put it, "We need not decode the signal, but we must determine, somehow, that it is a signal" (1980, p. 662). And this is not as simple as it sounds.

In its very first stage, induction demands what, strictly speaking, cannot be done: Pattern must be distinguished from noise, order from disorder; randomness must somehow be discriminated from non-randomness. In this article I discuss the fundamental relation between people's ability to do induction and their beliefs about randomness or noise, and I illustrate the special difficulties that psychologists face when they try to evaluate the rationality of these beliefs. The presentation is divided into four sections. The first describes the traditional experimental approach to evaluating people's conceptions of randomness and summarizes the data that have been taken to support the conclusion that people have a very poor conception of randomness. The second contrasts the relatively narrow conception of randomness that seems to underlie these experimental studies with the broader and far less well agreed upon conception of randomness that one finds in philosophical and mathematical treatments of the topic. The third outlines some benefits for psychologists to be gained from thinking about induction as a problem in signal detection. And the fourth presents the argument that any adequate evaluation of ordinary people's conceptions of randomness must consider the role that these conceptions play in inductive inference, that is, in distinguishing between random and nonrandom events.

Experimental studies of subjective randomness

Two kinds of studies in the psychological literature bear on the beliefs people have about randomness. The first sort was prompted by a remark of Reichenbach (1934/1949) that people untrained in probability theory would be unable to produce random series of events but would instead, produce too many *alternations*, that is, too few long runs of a given event and too many short runs.[1]

In brief, Reichenbach was right. At least 15 experiments (reviewed by Wagenaar, 1972) have been performed in which subjects were explicitly instructed to produce random series. These were of sufficient length (i.e., 20–2520 events) to preclude complete memorization of the series. Some

---

[1] The string 0 1 1 0 0 0 1 1 *alternates* between 1 and 0 three times. This is exactly equivalent to saying that the string has four *runs*.

experiments used binary events, such as asking subjects to produce series that would mimic tosses of a coin. Others used larger event sets, including the 6 sides of a die, the 10 single digits, the 26 letters of the alphabet, and various subsets of digits and letters. Response modes were also diverse and included speaking, writing, and a variety of manual responses such as pointing and button pushing.

Despite the lack of standardization among these experiments, one result was apparent for virtually all: Series produced by human subjects failed in various mathematical tests of randomness. These included not only the comparison of expected and observed numbers of runs that Reichenbach proposed but also tests based on expected and obtained event frequencies, expected and obtained bigram and trigram frequencies, autocorrelation functions of the generated series, and various measures of redundancy, stereotypy, and information content. In addition, more recent research (Kubovy & Psotka, 1976) suggests that subjects even have difficulty in generating a *single* random response when asked to report the first digit that comes to mind. Instead, the digits they generate, with 7 being a very common choice, appear to be chosen not because they are actually spontaneous but rather because they seem to the subject to comply with the experimenter's request.

The second kind of psychological study is the set of demonstrations by Kahneman and Tversky (1972) showing people's reliance on a *representativeness heuristic* to answer questions about random events. This heuristic refers to a general tendency for people to judge the subjective probability of an event by the degree to which it (a) is similar in essential characteristics to its parent population and (b) reflects the salient features of the process that generated it.

Kahneman and Tversky used problems in probability theory to show how use of the representativeness heuristic can cause people's intuitions about probability to deviate qualitiatively from what is normatively correct. In one problem, for example, subjects were told that in a particular city there were 72 families with six children in which the birth order is GBGBBG. They were asked to estimate the number of families in that city in which the birth order was BGBBBB. The median estimate was 30 (rather than the normatively correct 72), a result indicating that people consider the latter sequence to be considerably less likely than the former. This reflects the fact that the proportion of boys to girls in the latter sequence deviates markedly from the characteristics of the parent population.

In another problem, five children were described as playing a game in which 20 marbles are distributed among them randomly. Two distributions were shown, one in which the five children get 4 marbles each and one in which Children A, B, and D get 4 marbles each while Child C gets 5 and Child E gets 3. Subjects were asked which of the two distributions would occur more often in repeated plays of the game. They chose, incorrectly, the distribution with unequal outcomes since it reveals the randomness in the game.

The foregoing experimental studies show clearly that naive subjects have systematic difficulties in producing random series and in answering questions about random events. But does this imply a more general problem with their conceptions of randomness? For some, the answer is unequivocally yes. Kahneman and Tversky (1972, p. 450) wrote, "In our daily life we encounter numerous random processes ... which obey the binomial law, for example, to a high degree of approximation. People, however, fail to extract from these experiences an adequate conception of the binomial process." Slovic, Kunreuther, and White (1974, p. 192) put the case even more strongly: "People have a very poor conception of randomness; they don't recognize it when they see it and they cannot produce it when they try."

To conclude, however, that naive people's conceptions of randomness are poor in general implies that randomness is clearly defined and well understood by those who are not naive. Nothing could be farther from the truth. In the next section I sketch a few of the ways in which the seemingly erroneous notions people have about randomness are related to the issues and paradoxes that arise when mathematicians and philosophers try to say exactly what randomness is.

Randomness visited and revisited

The most commonly cited definition of randomness is probably one originated by von Mises (1928/1957). For von Mises, a sequence of events was random if, in an infinitely long series, the relative frequencies of the various attributes possess limiting values and if these limiting values remain the same in all infinite subsequences selected by an arbitrary rule. Von Mises's definition has been criticized by some because of its reliance on the concepts of infinite series and limiting values, but for present purposes there is no need to get into these issues. Instead, it is sufficient to consider a logical problem with von Mises's definition (and all like) that was pointed out by Spencer-Brown (1957) in his book *Probability and Scientific Inference.*

Spencer-Brown noted that when we say a series is random, we mean two different things. In the first place, we mean that the series has primary randomness, which is to say that the atomic (or elementary) events in the series are unpredictable. However, we also mean that the series has secondary randomness, which is to say that all molecular units (such as groups of 10 atomic events considered as a unit) have primary randomness as well. In other words, every molecular unit of particular length, say the 10-event unit 0000000000, must be just as likely to occur as any other equivalent molecular unit.

Concerning this, Spencer-Brown reflected on a random series of

$10^{1,000,007}$ 0's and 1's in which about 10 separate subseries of a million consecutive zeroes each would be expected to occur. He wrote,

Now let us consider an observer with a machine for making random numbers, having arrived at the beginning of one of these subseries of a million consecutive noughts. Will he be calling the series random? If he is accustomed to checking long series of $10^{1,000,007}$ digits, he might. But if he is a normal observer, dying at about 70, he will be mildly surprised after five consecutive noughts; after ten he will begin to suspect the machinery; after twenty he will call for his laboratory assistants to see to it; and, if he happens to be compiling a table of random numbers for scientific uses, he will certainly regard the records from where the noughts began as unpublishable. (pp. 55–56)

Thus we, along with the observer, are faced with a dilemma. For if we assume the primary randomness of atomic events, then random series will contain predictably extraordinary events that cannot be called "random" in the common sense of the word. But if in pursuit of practical ends we prevent the occurrence of such extraordinary events, then we necessarily violate the assumption of secondary randomness. Which, then, is it to be? Do we want our machine to be random, or do we want our table to be random?

Random processes

In his series on computer algorithms, Knuth (1969) introduced the topic of random number generators by asking playfully, "Is 2 a random number?" The joke, of course, is that in most technical usages, randomness is a property of processes and not of products. But the rub is that the randomness of processes cannot be observed directly. Thus, the only way we can confirm that a particular process is random is to sample a sequence of output from the process and test whether it has the properties of random sequences, which brings us right back to talking about the randomness of products.

The epistemological impasse between process and product is nowhere more apparent than in the production of tables of random numbers. Typically, one begins with a physical process that, if current physical theory is correct, should yield a random sequence of digits. (Rand's table of random digits, for example, was initially produced by driving electronic counters with electronically generated noises.) Then the provisional sequence of digits is subjected to various tests of randomness, among which are the very sorts of test (described above) that have been used when testing the randomness of sequences produced by human subjects.

What is surprising is that sequences produced by presumably random processes do not seem to have much better luck in passing tests of randomness than sequences produced by people, although the deficiencies of the former may be more subtle than the deficiencies of the latter. In the case of the Rand table, for example, the original sequence of 1 million digits contained certain unacceptable distributional biases that forced Rand scientists to systematically construct a new (and, as it turned out, improved) table from the original one by adding pairs of adjacent numbers and keeping only the least significant digit (Tompkins, 1956). In the same vein, distributional troubles also plagued Fisher and Yates (1938) and Kendall and Babington Smith (1939) in the production of their now-classic tables of random numbers. And just as with the Rand table, these earlier tables were also "corrected" by their authors before publication, although by somewhat simpler expedients: Fisher and Yates merely altered their numbers by hand until they were random enough to pass the tests, whereas Kendall and Babington Smith threw out 10,000 of theirs (Spencer-Brown, 1957).

Another odd relation between process and product turns up with pseudorandom sequence generators, which are known in computing circles as "random number generators." What is noteworthy about random number generators is that there is nothing random about them: They are completely deterministic algorithms for generating digit sequences whose only claim to randomness is the *appearance* of randomness, relative to a specified set of tests and relative to a finite, although usually large, cycle length. And odder still are the algorithms that are used to compute the decimal expansions of certain irrational numbers (such as e, π, and $\sqrt{2}$) to aribitarily many places. Although these algorithms are also completely deterministic, the expansions they produce are "as ugly and disordered as any randomly generated list of numbers" (Gardner, 1979a, p. 22), and it has been conjectured that the numbers are actually random in the sense that each individual digit (or atomic event) as well as each subseries of fixed length (or molecular event) occurs equally often in the expansion (Gardner, 1979b). But if this is correct, then these particular algorithms produce as mere by-product at least as good a "grade" of randomness as humankind has achieved intentionally by the most sophisticated application of either computational or physical expertise. It hardly seems fair.

Random products

Random number tables serve a great many important scientific functions, and those of us who use them for simulation or for ordering experimental stimuli can probably sympathize with the Rand scientists and their predecessors in the judgment that some numbers, no matter how randomly generated, are simply not random enough for practical purposes. But there is more than practicality to the idea that products can be characterized in terms of randomness. In *The Logic of Scientific Discovery*, Popper (1959) argued that it is essential for probability theory to have an objective characterization of disorder or randomness as a *kind of order*. Accordingly, he suggested that ideally disordered sequences be developed that can serve as standards against which to test the randomness of empirical sequences.

But where did Popper think we should get such ideal sequences? Certainly not from machines that are random in von Mises's sense of the word. Popper was shocked at definitions of randomness that (like von Mises's) admit sequences that start off with, say 00   11   00   11 and so forth for 500 million places, and become irregular only in the long run. Instead, Popper insisted that random strings ought to start random – and stay random – from beginning to end. And to show what he meant, he gave an algorithm (Popper, 1959, Appendix iv) that can be used to construct a binary string that is equidistributed (i.e., has equal numbers of 1's and 0's) and *n*-free (i.e., free of sequential effects for all *x*-tuples, with $x \leq n + 1$) for all initial segments having length

$$m = 2^{2^{2}}$$

where the *number* of powering steps ≥ 0 and $n = (\log_2 m) - 1$.

For illustration, consider a sequence that begins with the 16 digits shown below:

0 1 1 0 1 0 1 1 1 1 0 0 0 0 1 0 ....

The first 2 digits (the smallest initial segment, $m = 2$) are equidistributed and (trivially) 0-free. The first 4 digits (the next smallest segment, $m = 2^2$) are also equidistributed and, in addition, 1-free. That is to say, if we treat the sequence as wrapping around on itself, then each of the four possible 2-tuples occurs exactly once. In the same way, the first 16 digits of the sequence ($m = 2^{2^2}$) are equidistributed and 3-free: Each possible 2-tuple occurs exactly four times; each 3-tuple, exactly twice; and each 4-tuple exactly once. The next shortest initial segment would be 65,536 digits long, and it would be both equidistributed and 15-free.

Popper's argument is complex and technically sophisticated. But his conviction that random strings should be random from their very start has a familiar, representativeness-like ring to it, and it is likely that naive people would have no difficulty sympathzing with his intuition that there is something fundamentally wrong about calling a string "random" that alternates between 00 and 11 for the first 500 million places. Another approach to randomness that should also appeal to naive people is the algorithmic approach of Chaitin (1975) and of Martin-Löf (1966). The algorithmic approach starts with the simple intuition that a random sequence is one that has no pattern and then gives this intuition formal substance by characterizing patterns in terms of the complexity of the computer programs that would be capable of generating them on an idealized computing machine. Patterned or nonrandom strings are those that can be generated by programs that are much shorter than the strings themselves. In other words, nonrandom strings are compressible. (The sequence that was used to begin this article, for example, can be generated by a simple program that says, For $n = 1$ to 6, print n n times.) Random strings, in contrast, are noncompressible. To generate them would require programs very nearly as long as complete enumerations of the strings.

Before closing this section, it is worth making explicit that these various definitions of randomness are not so much in competition with one another as they are intended to serve different purposes. Thus, no one would argue that the algorithmic definition of randomness would be suitable for testing whether a particular series, such as a table of random numbers, has the statistical properties of random series. Instead, the algorithmic definition was developed to complement classical definitions of randomness by "giving precise meaning to concepts that had been intuitively appealing but that [previously] could not be formally adopted" (Chaitin, 1975), p. 48). Likewise, Popper's notion of ideal strings was intended to bridge the gap between the constraints implicit in the intuitive concept of irregularity or patternlessness and the equally defensible mathematical constraints of equidistribution and n-freedom.

In certain respects, the problem of trying to define randomness is like the problem faced by the committee of blind men who were sent to find out what elephants are like: One, feeling the tail, said an elephant is like a rope; another, feeling a leg, said an elephant is like a tree; a third, feeling an ear, said an elephant is like a sail; and so forth. Small wonder that they, being sightless, disagreed so heartily among themselves. But a critical difference between the problems is that, unlike the situation with elephants, *no one at all* has ever seen what randomness is like. Nor will they, for in principle there can be no observer blessed with the ability to perceive randomness directly. Thus, there is no alternative but to characterize randomness in terms that reflect the narrow and sometimes competing concerns of human life. This much is clear: No definition yet advanced has satisfied all the claims that are made of the concept of randomness. I, personally, doubt that any ever will.

Induction and detection

Up to this point I have argued that some of the intuitions that naive people have about randomness are not very different from the intuitions that have guided formal attempts by sophisticated people to characterize randomness. But it is not much use to show that naive people and sophisticated people agree about randomness unless what they agree about can also be shown to be useful in meeting the demands of ordinary living.

Toward this end, let me ask you to suppose that you own a company that manufactures random strings of 0's and 1's.[2] A worker reports that his random number machine is acting up, so you call in a random number expert to test the machine. The expert turns the crank on the machine and a 1 is produced. He observes, "Since in a random series 1 and 0 are equally likely, I cannot reject the hypothesis that this machine is functioning properly." The expert turns the crank again and a second 1 is produced. He observes, "Since in a random series 1 and 0 are equally likely following 1, I cannot reject the hypothesis that this machine is functioning properly." Again the expert turns the crank, and again a 1 appears. He observes, as you might have guessed by now, "Since in a random series 1 and 0 are equally likely following 11, I cannot reject the hypothesis that this machine is functioning properly." And so it goes – the series of 1's grows longer and longer, and still the expert maintains that he cannot reject the hypothesis that the machine is functioning properly.

There is clearly something strange about the random number expert – but the problem is not with his mathematics. Each of his statements is technically correct. What is incorrect is his framework. The expert is being asked to do induction – to distinguish between random and nonrandom events. But this is impossible in a framework that looks at the probabilities of the various *sequences*, for, as any beginning statistics student soon learns, all such sequences are equally likely.

Now some readers may be thinking that the scenario I have sketched is farfetched, to say the least. But it turns out that situations like this actually occur in real life. One particularly apt example was related by the renowned random number expert, Mark Kac of Rockefeller University, in a lecture titled "When is Random Random?" As he told it, shortly after the reinstatement of the draft lottery in December 1969, he received a telephone call from a graduate student asking him to testify in court that the sequence of birthdates chosen in the lottery was not random. The basis for the proposed court suit was given in a letter to the *New York Times* (December 11, 1969) in which F. T. Haddock of the University of Michigan pointed out that there were many more birthdates from the end of the year in early positions in the draft sequence than would be expected if the sequence were generated randomly. Kac declined the student's request in no uncertain terms, saying that he could not testify to the nonrandomness of the sequence since it is impossible to determine mathematically whether a given sequence has been generated by a random or a nonrandom process. However, as Dr. Kac wryly noted in his lecture, it turned out that the lottery had, indeed, been nonrandom; only

---

[2] I am using the term *random* to refer to a Bernoulli process with $p = .5$. This is in accord with common usage, particularly with respect to the generation of random numbers. However, von Mises's definition of randomness would admit Bernoulli processes with $0 < p < 1$.

the most cursory mixing of the capsules containing the birthdates had occurred, leaving the capsules that contained late birthdates in positions where they were likely to be drawn early in the lottery (Rosenbaum, 1970).

Choosing classes

In the preceding examples, induction fails because the events under consideration, that is, the various possible sequences, are all equally likely. This failure is not inherent in the situation but rather reflects an inappropriate choice in how the sequences are to be classified.

By its nature, all induction involves abstraction: Events occurring at different times and in different places, and perhaps having other distinguishing characteristics as well, must be grouped together into classes that can be treated as functionally equivalent. Consider a few of the ways that the five strings below might be classified:

```
1. 1  0  1  1  0  1  0  0
2. 1  1  1  1  0  0  0  0
3. 1  0  0  1  0  1  0  0
4. 0  1  1  1  1  1  1  1
5. 0  0  0  0  0  0  0  0
```

One way, obviously, would be to consider the strings each to belong to a separate group defined by the exact sequence of 1's and 0's. But other classifications are also possible. They might, for example, be classed according to the number of runs they contain. Thus, Strings 2 and 4 would be grouped together since they contain two runs, Strings 1 and 3 would be grouped together since they contain six, and String 5 would be in a separate group. Or they might be classed according to the proportion of 1's they contain, in which case only Strings 1 and 2 would be grouped together. Or they might be classed according to the length of their longest run, or according to their first symbol, or according to a great many other schemes.

The point to be made is that although there are many ways in which strings might be grouped into equivalence classes, these are not equally useful for doing induction. What is important for induction is that the possible distinct sequences be grouped into equivalence classes that are *not equally likely*. In fact, Carnap (1950) proved that for a person to assign equal prior probability to the possible distinct classes that might obtain in some universe of interest is "tantamount to the principle never to let our past experiences influence our expectations for the future" (p. 256).

Carnap's point can be illustrated nicely in the present context by modification of an example given by Kyburg (1970, p. 35). Consider our random number expert from the previous example having observed some number of 1's in a row, say seven. He is asked to calculate the probability that the next number generated will also be a 1. He proceeds by listing all the possible distinct 8–tuples of 1 and 0 that can occur.

S1	1	1	1	1	1	1	1	1
S2	1	1	1	1	1	1	1	0
S3	1	1	1	1	1	1	0	1

$$\cdots$$

| S256 | 0 | 0 | 0 | 0 | 0 | 0 | 0 | 0, |

and assigning to each the prior probability of 1/256. Then he applies Bayes' theorem to determine what his posterior probability should be. His calculations take the form below, with the various 8-tuples being designated by S1, S2, and so on, and the initial string of seven 1's, by S':

$$P(S1|S') = \frac{P(S'|S1) \cdot P(S1)}{\sum_{i=1}^{256} P(S'|S_i) \cdot P(S_i)}$$

$$= \frac{P(S'|S1) \cdot P(S1)}{\sum_{i=1}^{2} P(S'|S_i) \cdot P(S_i) + \sum_{i=3}^{256} P(S'|S_i) \cdot P(S_i)}$$

$$= \frac{(1)(1/256)}{\sum_{i=1}^{2} (1)(1/256) + \sum_{i=3}^{256}(0)(1/256)}$$

$$= 1/2.$$

Thus, the random number expert concludes that the probability of getting another 1 is 1/2. But this is exactly what he would have concluded without the evidence afforded by the seven previous 1's or, for that matter, by any other number of previous 1's, for no matter how many 1's the machine produces, the expert can never learn that the probability of the next number being a 1 is not equal to 1/2.

The reader may complain at this point, and fairly so, that our feckless random number expert has been "set up." We have repeatedly asked him to do induction, knowing full well that his habitual (and, admittedly, often useful) way of looking at the world will make this impossible. But the point cannot be made too strongly that the frameworks we adopt for analyzing and interpreting the events that occur around us have a major bearing on what we discover. And where induction is concerned, there is always something arbitrary in the choice of a framework.

Detecting nonrandomness

In my discussion so far, I have portrayed induction as a problem in detecting pattern (or nonrandomness) against a noisy (or random) background. In this section I argue that the theory of signal detection

(Green & Swets, 1966) provides a useful framework for thinking about some of the psychological factors that influence the ease or difficulty with which induction is done.

In the detection analysis, events can be either signal (i.e., generated by a nonrandom process) or noise (i.e., generated by a random process). When an event occurs, the observer classifies it as one or the other, depending on whether it exceeds some criterion value on a dimension that runs from subjective randomness or disorder to subjective nonrandomness or order. Events that seem more orderly than the criterion are classed as signal, and those that seem less orderly are classed as noise. If the criterion value is set low, then the proportion of hits (signal events classed as signals) will be high and the proportion of misses (signal events classed as noise) will be low, but this will be at the cost of a high proportion of false alarms (noise events classed as signal) and a low porportion of correct rejections (noise events classed as noise). If the criterion value is set high instead, the proportion of correct rejections will be high and the proportion of false alarms will be low, but at the cost of a low proportion of hits and a high proportion of misses.

One major advantage of the signal detection framework is that it changes the kinds of questions that are likely to be asked about human conceptions of randomness. What comes to matter is not whether particular beliefs are correct in a statistical sense. Rather, the important questions become, first, how do people's beliefs affect the decisions they must make, for example, in classifying events or in setting the criterion, and, second, how do these decisions, once made, affect the ease or difficulty people experience in detecting different types of nonrandomness?

Another advantage of the detection framework is that it invites needed consideration of the payoffs for induction. It is easy for psychologists working with artificial tasks in artificial settings to assume erroneously that rationality consists of being "right" as often as one can. A case in point is the bemoaning by some social psychologists (e.g., Mischel, 1968; Nisbett & Ross, 1980; Ross, 1977) of what has come to be called the *fundamental attribution error*, which (simply) is the predisposition of most of us to attribute the behavior of others to stable personality variables rather than to transient and often equivocal situational factors. But this may be no error at all. Both physical and social survival require that we learn as well as we can to predict and control the effects that other people have on us. Thus, if an effect is predictable, even weakly, by the presence of some individual, then it is important that we find this out. In terms of the detection analysis, misses are more consequential than false alarms. Accordingly, we set our criteria low and run the attendant risk of sometimes, or even often, being overconfident about our ability to predict what others will do.

The detection analysis can also lead to some surprises. I was intrigued early on by the question of just how poorly naive subjects would do in a "hostile" environment in which nonrandom events mimic the qualities associated with subjective randomness. I hypothesized, not surprisingly, that forms of nonrandomness involving biases toward alternation would play havoc with naive subjects' decision policies since, as was discussed earlier, naive subjects act as though they believe that random series alternate more often than they really do.

To test this hypothesis, I calculated theoretical probabilities for a detection-type task in which a naive observer judges "random" or "nonrandom" for a set of eight-character binary strings, half generated by a random (Bernoulli) process having $p = .5$ and half generated by a nonrandom process with a .8 probability of alternation.[3] In this task the observer is assumed to know that half of the strings will be generated by a random process and half by a nonrandom process, but no specific information is given about the particular characteristics of the nonrandom process.

The decision rule I used was based on the simplest sort of null hypothesis logic. The observer was assumed to call nonrandom any string with subjectively too few alternations (i.e., zero, one, or two) or subjectively too many alternations (i.e., six or seven). The remaining strings were assumed to be called random. Note that this rule captures the bias we expect of naive subjects: although strings with five alternations are just as unlikely to be generated by a random process as strings with two alternations ($p = .164$ for each), the former are judged to be random and the latter to be nonrandom.

The results of this exercise are in the first and second columns of Table 43.1. The first row gives the expected proportions of correct rejections (random strings called "random" by the subject) and false alarms (random strings called "nonrandom" by the subject). The second row gives the expected proportions of misses (nonrandom strings called "random" by the subject) and hits (nonrandom strings called "nonrandom" by the subject). The third row gives the overall values for percentage correct.

As anticipated, the biased observer has a sizable miss rate: Only 58% of the strings generated by the alternation biased process are recognized as nonrandom. But despite the bias, overall performance (64.6% correct) is relatively good, as can be seen by comparing the results for the biased observer with results from two nonbiased observers (shown in columns 3 and 4, and 5 and 6, respectively). These nonbiased observers differ from the biased observer in that they treat strings with five alternations in the

---

[3] The alternation biased process is, technically, a Markov process with a repetition probability of .2. Such processes are frequently called "random" in the psychological literature. But they are not random in von Mises's sense because the limiting frequency of 1, say, is not the same following 1 as it is following 0.

Table 43.1. *Theoretical detection probabilities for three different observers*

Generating process	Biased observer response		Nonbiased Observer 1 response		Nonbiased Observer 2 response	
	Random (3/4/5 alts)	Nonrandom (0/1/2/6/7 alts)	Random (3/4 alts)	Nonrandom (0/1/2/5/6/7 alts)	Random (2/3/4/5 alts)	Nonrandom (0/1/6/7 alts)
Random (Bernoulli, $p = .5$)	71.0 (CCR)	29.0 (FAR)	54.6 (CRR)	45.4 (FAR)	87.4 (CRR)	12.6 (FAR)
Nonrandom (p[alternation] $= .8$)	41.8 (MR)	58.2 (HR)	14.3 (MR)	85.7 (HR)	42.2 (MR)	57.8 (HR)
Overall % correct	64.6		70.2		72.6	

Note: The distribution of strings generated by the random process is symmetrical, so shifts in the criterion in either direction (relative to the biased observer) cause noticeable shifts in the correct rejection rate (CRR) and the false alarm rate (FAR). But the distribution of strings generated by the nonrandom process is negatively skewed so that despite the fact that Nonbiased Observer 2 has a stricter criterion for nonrandomness than the biased observer, the miss rates (MR) and the hit rates (HR) for the two are very similar. Nonbiased Observer 2 is using the rule that is optimal under the condition that nothing is known about the nonrandom process except that it generates 50% of the strings. Alts = alternations.

same way as they treat strings with two alternations. They differ from one another, however, in whether they call these strings "random" or "nonrandom."

As can be seen, the overall performances of the nonbiased observers (70.2% and 72.6% correct, respectively) are clearly better than that of the biased observer (64.6% correct). But the absolute difference is nowhere nearly so great as might have been expected from the fact that the present detection task was specially designed to handicap anyone with the naive bias. It is also worth remembering that the biased rule would actually do better than the unbiased rule in detecting forms of nonrandomness biased toward repetition. Thus, in order to evaluate fairly whether people's false expectations about alternation are helpful or harmful over a lifetime's opportunities for induction, one would have to know whether in the world nonrandom events are more often biased toward alternation or toward repetition – which raises tantalizing, but probably unanswerable, questions concerning the natural ecology of nonrandomness.

Sleight of mind

Before concluding this note, it is useful to digress briefly from the problem of evaluating human conceptions of randomness to consider an associated problem in visual perception. It is well known by psychologists – and certainly by stage magicians – that what we see is influenced by what we expect to see. "Given the slenderest of clues as to the nature of surrounding objects we identify them and act not so much according to what is directly sensed, *but to what is believed*" (Gregory, 1970, p. 11). "Magic is designed to fool the brains, not the eyes.... A bright and agile mind will furnish the details of a mystery which the magician has only suggested" (Mulholland, 1927, p. 79). The problem, of course, is how this fact about visual perception should be evaluated. One possibility would be for psychologists to stress the errors that can result and to emphasize the ways in which human perceptual processes are fallible and even irrational. But this has not happened. Psychologists have tended on the whole to be neutral in their evaluation of the "goodness" of perceptual processes.

That they have been so is undoubtedly to their credit since recent research in computer vision suggests that these potentially troublesome "expectancy errors" may play quite an important role in helping the perceiver cope with a complex and unavoidably "noisy" environment. In discussing the commonplace but remarkably complex perceptual process of adjusting visually to a room not previously seen, Winston (1975) commented, "One thing seems clear: the job must be done with sophisticated interlocking symbolic structures capable of holding onto information produced from visual analysis and capable of *supplying good guesses* about things either partly obscured or never looked at with the complete processing associated with full attention" (p. 15, emphasis added). In other words, in order to have a powerful visual system, bottom-up or sensory sources of information must be augmented by the very sorts of top-down or expectancy-driven information that occasionally cause humans to misperceive the visual scene. Thus, it may be an essential characteristic of intelligent visual systems that they be able to be fooled by a magician!

Psychologists must make a similar choice about how to evaluate the facts concerning people's beliefs about randomness. There is no doubt that psychological experiments like those reviewed at the beginning of this article can tell us much that is interesting and important about these beliefs, including, perhaps, the limitations of the beliefs relative to certain normative stnadards. But it must also be borne in mind, first, what these experiments *need* not tell us about human conceptions of randomness and, second, what they *cannot* tell us.

In the first place is the simple fact that people do not come equipped with knowledge of probability theory. Surely any of us who has ever taught an introductory course in statistics knows that. But a deeper point can be made concerning the slowness with which probability theory emerged as a branch of mathematics. Although people had been playing games of chance for thousands of years, it was not until the decade around 1660 that probability theory began to be developed (Hacking, 1975). And it should be noted as well, that the problems in the emerging theory that fascinated – and sometimes confounded – the great minds of the time were by today's standards extremely trivial. The probability that two tossed dice, for example, will fall to yield a particular sum is one we expect every statistics student to compute correctly. Yet there was once considerable scholarly correspondence concerning this problem, and no less a mathematical genius than Leibnitz once made the mistake of supposing that the set of equally probable alternatives in dice comprises the various combinations and not, what is actually correct, the various permutations (Hacking, 1975, p. 52). We should not, therefore, be particularly surprised that our mathematically unsophisticated subjects still stumble over such ideas.

In the second place is that psychological experiments, by their very nature, cannot tell us much about the functional role that people's beliefs about randomness play in helping them get along in the world. It is no doubt true that a great many people pass their lives without ever having to generate a random series or ever having to solve a problem in probability theory. So it should not surprise us that the conceptions they develop of randomness are inadequate for these tasks. But no one can avoid the necessity of doing induction. (Is your boss short-tempered on Mondays, or is this just a bad day? Is the battery in your car getting weak or not? Is your random number machine really producing too many 1's?) And for such purpose it is often sufficient to classify events rather crudely, into generic types that may correspond to mere notice that "there's something special here" or "there's nothing special here."

Consider the two experiments on use of the representativeness heuristic that were described earlier (Kahneman & Tversky, 1972). In the first, we saw subjects judging that one birth sequence (BGBBBB) is less likely than another (GBGBBG) when in fact both were equally likely, and in the second, we saw subjects judging that one distribution of marbles (A, B, and D get 4 each, C gets 5, and E gets 3) is more likely than another (all five get 4 each) when, in fact, just the opposite was true. In both these cases it is clear that the errors occurred because subjects based their judgments on generic information: relative proportion of boys in the first case and presence of variability in the second. And although it cannot be denied that the subjects in these experiments failed to correctly answer the questions they were asked, it seems equally undeniable that their view of the generic properties of the strings was dead accurate: Of families with six children there will be many more cases of three boys and three girls than of five boys and one girl, and of random distributions of 20 marbles to five children, there will be many more trials in which three children get 4 each, one gets 5, and one gets 3 than there will be trials in which each child gets 4. The examples that follow should suffice to suggest that both these generic properties have useful functions in induction.

When I was a child, I was greatly enamored of *Ripley's Believe It or Not!*. One of the strange facts I came across (and I do not swear that my numerical details are correct) concerned a sultan in some faraway place and time who, in quest of a son and heir, and with the aid of 100 or so wives, had fathered over 400 children, all girls. The sultan, of course, was greatly distressed, but was his case really unusual? I certainly would bet that if the sultan had the benefit of modern genetic counseling, the counselor would suspect that something was unusual about the case, perhaps a sex-linked lethal gene or something on that order. And surely I would be suspicious of any counselor who merely said, "Sorry, old man, you've had a run of bad luck, but you must grant that the sequence of births in your family is no less likely than any other." It simply goes without saying that unusual deviations from expected proportions in a process believed to be random can reasonably be taken as evidence that the process may be different than is supposed. They may also, importantly, be used as the basis for forming an alternative hypothesis against which further evidence can be evaluated.

My example of induction based on problems with variability is less dramatic, but it comes closer home for psychology. It is now widely believed among researchers in human intelligence that Cyril Burt supported his theories about the inheritance of intelligence with falsified data. Although Burt's views were always controversial, the most damning evidence against him came not from substantive problems, such as failures to replicate, but rather from the simple observation that his data were too consistent to be true. As Hearnshaw (1981) put it in his biography of Burt. "[Burt reported] remarkable, and indeed, wholly incredible, consistencies in correlation coefficients derived from changing sample sizes.... An occasional coincidence might have been acceptable, but not twenty such coincidences in a table of sixty correlations. There was obviously something wrong with Burt's work" (pp. 233–234). Burt's critics were clearly statistically more sophisticated than the average person; consequently, they were sensitive to problems in the data that were probably too subtle to be noticed by naive persons. But their intuition that reasonable amounts of random error are to be expected in all empirical work is no different in principle from the intuition of naive subjects that games of chance ought to show trial-to-trial variability in outcome.

There is probably no psychological process more fundamental to individual survival than the ability to do induction. And there is no part of the inductive process about which we know less than how it begins. What makes us notice some things and not others? And how are the things that we do notice linked to the hypotheses we generate about the world? The view expressed in this article is that the answers to these questions are intimately tied to people's beliefs about randomness. It is important, therefore, for psychologists to map out both the logical and the psychological consequences that these beliefs have on people's ability to distinguish between random and nonrandom events. In so doing, we may learn not only a lot about what people are like, but we may learn something, as well, about what it means to be rational.

Suggested readings

I. *Introduction*

Anderson, B. F., Deane, D. H., Hammond, K. R., McClelland, G. H., & Shanteau, J. C. (1981). *Concepts in judgment and decision research: Definition, sources, interrelations, comments.* New York: Praeger.

Einhorn, H. J., & Hogarth, R. M. (1981). Behavioral decision theory: Processes of judgment and choice. *Annual Review of Psychology, 32,* 53–88.

Hammond, K. R., McClelland, G. H., & Mumpower, J. (1980). *Human judgment and decision making: Theories, methods, and procedures.* New York: Praeger.

Hammond, K. R., & Wascoe, N. (Eds.). (1980). *New directions for methodology of social and behavioral science: No. 3. Realizations of Brunswik's representative design.* San Francisco: Jossey-Bass.

Janis, I. L., & Mann, L. (1977). *Decision making: A psychological analysis of conflict, choice, and commitment.* New York: Free Press.

Kahneman, D., Slovic, P., & Tversky, A. (Eds.). (1982). *Judgment under uncertainty: Heuristics and biases.* Cambridge: Cambridge University Press.

Pitz, G. F., & Sachs, N. J. (1984). Judgment and decision: Theory and application. *Annual Review of Psychology, 35,* 139–163.

Wright, G. (1984). *Behavioural decision theory: An introduction.* Beverly Hills, CA: Sage.

II. *Judgment and social policy*

Fischhoff, B. (1977). Cost benefit analysis and the art of motorcycle maintenance. *Policy Sciences, 8,* 177–202.

Kunreuther, H., Lathrop, J., & Linnerooth, J. (1982). A descriptive model of choice for siting facilities. *Behavioral Science, 27,* 281–297.

Stewart, T. R., Dennis, R. L., & Ely, D. W. (1984). Citizen participation and judgment in policy analysis: A case study of urban air quality policy. *Policy Sciences, 17,* 67–87.

III. Economics

Lopes, L. (1984). Risk and distributional inequality. *Journal of Experimental Psychology: Human Perception and Performance, 10,* 465–485.

Raiffa, H. (1968). *Decision analysis: Introductory lectures on choices under uncertainty.* Reading, MA: Addison-Wesley.

Slovic, P., & Lichtenstein, S. (1983). Preference reversals: A broader perspective. *American Economic Review, 73,* 596–605.

Thaler, R. (1980). Toward a positive theory of consumer choice. *Journal of Economic Behavior and Organization, 1,* 39–60.

IV. Law

Ebbesen, E. E., & Konečni, V. J. (1975). Decision making and information integration in the courts: The setting of bail. *Journal of Personality and Social Psychology, 32,* 805–821.

Saks, M., & Hastie, R. (1978). *Social psychology in court.* New York: Van Nostrand Reinhold.

Sigall, H., & Ostrove, N. (1975). Beautiful but dangerous: Effects of offender attractiveness and nature of the crime on juridic judgment. *Journal of Personality and Social Psychology, 31,* 410–414.

Stone, A. (1984). *Law, psychiatry, and morality.* Washington, DC: American Psychiatric Press.

V. Interpersonal conflict

Brehmer, B. (1976). Social judgment theory and the analysis of interpersonal conflict. *Psychological Bulletin, 83,* 985–1003.

Brehmer, B., & Garpebring, S. (1974). Social pressure and policy change in the "lens model" interpersonal conflict paradigm. *Scandinavian Journal of Psychology, 15,* 191–196.

Gillis, J., & Blevens, K. (1978). Sources of judgmental impairment in paranoid and nonparanoid schizophrenics. *Journal of Abnormal Psychology, 87,* 587–596.

Hammond, K. R., & Grassia, J. (1985). The cognitive side of conflict: From theory to resolution of policy disputes. In S. Oskamp (Ed.), *Applied social psychology annual: Vol. 6. International conflict and national public policy issues* (pp. 233–254). Beverly Hills, CA: Sage.

VI. Clinical judgment in medicine and psychology

Bunker, J., Barnes, B., & Mosteller, F. (1977). *Costs, risks, and benefits of surgery.* New York: Oxford University Press.

Hammond, K. R. (1955). Probabilistic functioning and the clinical method. *Psychological Review, 62,* 255–262.

Hoffman, P. J. (1960). The paramorphic representation of clinical judgment. *Psychological Bulletin, 57,* 116–131.

VII. *Social prediction and judgment*

Fischhoff, B. (1976). Hindsight foresight: The effect of outcome knowledge on judgment under uncertainty. *Journal of Experimental Psychology: Human Perception and Performance, 1,* 288–299.

Hamilton, D. L. (1981). Illusory correlation as a basis for stereotyping. In D. L. Hamilton (Ed.), *Cognitive processes in stereotyping and intergroup behavior* (pp. 115–144). Hillsdale, NJ: Erlbaum.

Ross, L., Lepper, M. R., Strack, F., & Steinmetz, J. L. (1977). Social explanation and social expectation: Effects of real and hypothetical explanations on subjective likelihood. *Journal of Personality and Social Psychology, 35,* 817–829.

VIII. *Experts*

Dawes, R. M., & Corrigan, B. (1974). Linear models in decision making. *Psychological Bulletin, 81,* 95–105.

Phelps, R. H., & Shanteau, J. (1978). Livestock judges: How much information can an expert use? *Organizational Behavior and Human Performance, 21,* 209–219.

IX. *Development and learning*

Einhorn, H. (1982). Learning from experience and suboptimal rules in decision making. In D. Kahneman, P. Slovic, & A. Tversky (Eds.), *Judgment under uncertainty: Heuristics and biases* (pp. 268–283). Cambridge: Cambridge University Press.

Leon, M. (1984). Rules mothers and sons use to integrate content and damage information in their moral judgments. *Child Development, 55,* 2106–2113.

Shavelson, R. J., & Stern, P. (1981). Research on teachers' pedagogical thoughts, judgments, decisions, and behavior. *Review of Educational Research, 51,* 455–498.

Surber, C. F. (1980). The development of reversible operations in judgments of ability, effort, and performance. *Child Development, 51,* 1018–1029.

X. *Research techniques*

Behn, R., & Vaupel, J. (1982). *Quick analysis for busy decision makers.* New York: Basic Books.

References

Abelson, R.P. (1976). Script processing in attitude formation and decision making. In J. S. Carroll & J. W. Payne (Eds.), *Cognition and social behavior* (pp. 33–45). Hillsdale, NJ: Erlbaum. (13)

Abraham, H. J. (1975). *The judicial process* (3rd ed.). New York: Oxford University Press. (14)

Ackoff, R. L. (1979). The future of operational research is past. *Journal of the Operational Research Society, 30*, 93–104. (41)

Aczel, J. (1966). *Lectures on functional equations and their applications.* New York: Academic Press. (4)

Adams, J. K. (1957). A confidence scale defined in terms of expected percentages. *American Journal of Psychology, 70*, 432–436. (40)

Adams, J. S. (1965). Inequity in social exchange. In L. Berkowitz (Ed.), *Advances in experimental social psychology* (Vol. 2). New York: Academic Press. (38)

Adelman, L., Stewart, T. R., & Hammond, K. R. (1975). A case history of the application of social judgment theory to policy formulation. *Policy Sciences, 6*, 137–159. (3, 15, 16)

Advisory Committee on Biological Effects of Ionizing Radiation. (1979). *BEIR III: The effects on populations of exposure to low levels of ionizing radiation.* Washington, DC: National Academy of Sciences. (28)

Ahlers, D. M. (1966). SEM: A security evaluation model. In K. J. Cohen & F. S. Hammer (Eds.), *Analytical methods in banking* (pp. 305–336). Homewood, IL: Irwin. (10)

Ainslie, G. (1975). Specious reward: A behavioral theory of impulsiveness and impulse control. *Psychological Bulletin, 82*, 463–496. (39)

Albert, D. A. (1978). Decision theory in medicine: A review and critique. *Milbank Memorial Fund Quarterly, 56*(3), 362–401. (22, 26)

Allais, M. (1953). Le comportement de l'homme rationnel devant le risque: Critique des postulate et axioms de l'école américaine. *Econometrica, 21*, 503–546. (10)

Allais, M., & Hagen, O. (Eds.). (1979). *Expected utility hypotheses and the Allais paradox.* Hingham, MA: Reidel. (11)

Allison, G. T. (1971). *Essence of decision: Explaining the Cuban missle crisis.* Boston: Little, Brown. (16)

Allport, G. W., Vernon, P. E., & Lindzey, G. (1951). *Study of values.* Boston: Houghton Mifflin. (38)

Alpert, M., & Raiffa, H. (1969). *A progress report on the training of probability assessors.* Unpublished manuscript, Harvard University, Graduate School of Business Administration, Cambridge. (2)

Alpert, M., & Raiffa, H. (1982). A progress report on the training of probability assessors. In D. Kahneman, P. Slovic, & A. Tversky (Eds.), *Judgment under uncertainty: Heuristics and biases* (pp. 294–305). Cambridge: Cambridge University Press. (40)

Amidon, A., & Carey, P. (1972). Why five-year-olds cannot understand before and after. *Journal of Verbal Learning and Verbal Behavior, 1,* 417–423. (31)

Anderson, B. F., Deane, D. H., Hammond, K. R., McClelland, G. H., & Shanteau, J. C. (1981). *Concepts in judgment and decision research: Definitions, sources, interrelations, comments.* New York: Praeger. (28)

Anderson, B. F., Hammond, K. R., Berg, J., Hamman, R., Johnson, C., Marine, W., & Sutherland, J. (1981). *Second report to the Rocky Flats Monitoring Committee* (Rep. No. 233) Boulder: University of Colorado, Joint report from the Center for Research on Judgment and Policy and the School of Medicine. (28)

Anderson, N. H. (1962). Application of an additive model to impression formation. *Science, 138,* 817–818. (4)

Anderson, N. H. (1971). Integration theory and attitude change. *Psychological Review, 78,* 171–206. (3, 37)

Anderson, N. H. (1974a). Algebraic models in perception. In E. C. Carterette & M. P. Friedman (Eds.), *Handbook of perception* (Vol. 2, pp. 215–298). New York: Academic Press. (4, 31)

Anderson, N. H. (1974b). Information integration theory: A brief survey. In D. H. Krantz, R. C. Atkinson, R. D. Luce, & P. Suppes (Eds.), *Contemporary developments in mathematical psychology* (Vol. 2). San Francisco: Freeman. (4, 14)

Anderson, N. H. (1976a). How functional measurement can yield validated interval scales of mental qualities. *Journal of Applied Psychology, 61,* 677–692. (38)

Anderson, N. H. (1976b). *Social perception and cognition* (Tech. Rep. No. 62). San Diego: University of California. (14)

Anderson, N. H. (1977). Note on functional measurement and data analysis. *Perception and Psychophysics, 21,* 201–215. (4)

Anderson, N. H. (1978a). Measurement of motivation and incentive. *Behavior Research Methods and Instrumentation, 10,* 360–375. (4)

Anderson, N. H. (1978b). Progress in cognitive algebra. In L. Berkowitz (Ed.), *Cognitive theories in social psychology* (pp. 103–126). New York: Academic Press. (4)

Anderson, N. H. (1979). *Introduction to cognitive algebra* (CHIP Tech. Rep. 85). San Diego: University of California, Center for Human Information Processing. (4)

Anderson, N. H. (1980). Information integration theory in developmental psychology. In F. Wilkening, J. Becker, & T. Trabasso (Eds.), *Information integration by children* (pp. 1–45). Hillsdale, NJ: Erlbaum. (4, 31)

Anderson, N. H. (1981). *Foundations of information integration theory.* New York: Academic Press. (31)

Anderson, N. H. (1982). *Methods of information integration theory.* New York:

Academic Press. (4)

Anderson, N. H., & Cuneo, D. O. (1978). The height + width rule in children's judgments of quantity. *Journal of Experimental Psychology: General, 107,* 335–378. (4, 31)

Archer, V. E., Gillam, J. D., Wagoner, J., & James, L. (1978). Factors in exposure–response relationships of radon daughter injury. In *Conference/workshop on lung cancer, epidemiology, and industrial applications of sputum cytology* (pp. 324–367). Golden: Colorado School of Mines Press. (28)

Areeda, P. (1974). *Antitrust analysis: Problems, text, cases* (2nd ed.). Boston: Little, Brown. (12)

Ares, C. E., Rankin, A., & Sturz, H. (1963). The Manhattan bail project: An interim report on the use of pre-trial parole. *New York University Law Review, 38,* 71–92. (14)

Arizona Daily Star. (1978, March 21). Editorial: Wrongful blame. Phoenix, AZ. (8)

Arizona Republic. (1978a, March 8). Flood losses blamed on state and SRP by Audubon chief. Phoenix, AZ. (8)

Arizona Republic. (1978b, March 21). Rhodes pushes for Orme Dam. Phoenix, AZ. (8)

Arizona Republic. (1978c, April 6). Arizona delegation presses panel to ressurrect Orme Dam. Phoenix, AZ. (8)

Arizona Republic. (1978d, April 6). Orme key to floods, Rudd told. Phoenix, AZ. (8)

Arizona Republic. (1978e, April 20). Editorial: Water or eagles. Phoenix, AZ. (8)

Arizona Republic. (1981a, March 21). Support grows for new Roosevelt dam, higher Orme structure. Phoenix, AZ. (8)

Arizona Republic. (1981b, October 22). Phoenix Council oks Orme alternative 6 at request of mayor. Phoenix, AZ. (8)

Arkes, H. R., & Harkness, A. R. (1980a). *Factors influencing estimates of contingency.* Manuscript submitted for publication. (36)

Arkes, H. R., & Harkness, A. R. (1980b). The effect of making a diagnosis on subsequent recognition of symptoms. *Journal of Experimental Psychology: Human Learning and Memory, 6,* 568–575. (36)

Arkes, H. R., Harkness, A. R., & Biber, D. (1980, May). *Salience and the judgment of contingency.* Paper presented at the meeting of the Midwestern Psychological Association, St. Louis, MO. (36)

Arkes, H. R., Wortmann, R. L., Saville, R. D., & Harkness, A. R. (1981). Hindsight bias among physicians weighing the likelihood of diagnoses. *Journal of Applied Psychology, 66,* 252–254. (36)

Armelius, K., & Armelius, B.-A. (1976). The effect of cue-criterion correlations, cue intercorrelations and the sign of the cue intercorrelation on performance in suppressor variable tasks. *Organizational Behavior and Human Performance, 17,* 241–250. (41)

Armstrong, J. S. (1978a). Forecasting with econometric methods: Folklore versus fact. *Journal of Business, 51,* 549–564. (41)

Armstrong, J. S. (1978b). *Long range forecasting: From crystal ball to computer.* New York: Wiley. (41)

Austin, W., Walster, E., & Utne, M. K. (1976). Liking and assigned punishment. In L. Berkowitz (Ed.), *Advances in experimental social psychology* (Vol. 9). New York: Academic Press. (38)

Axtell, L. M., Cutler, S. J., & Myers, M. H. (Eds.). (1972). *End results in cancer* (Rep. No. 4, DHEW Publication No. (NIH)73–272). Bethesda, MD: National Cancer Institute. (23)

Bailar, J. C., III, & Ederer, F. (1964). Significance factors for the ratio of a poisson variable to its expectation. *Biometrics, 20,* 639–643. (28)

Bakwin, H. (1945). Pseudodoxia pediatrica. *New England Journal of Medicine, 232,* 691–697. (10)

Baldus, D. C., & Cole, J. W. (1979). *Statistical proof of discrimination.* New York: McGraw–Hill. (12)

Balke, W. M., Hammond, K. R., & Meyer, G. D. (1973). An alternative approach to labor–management negotiations. *Administrative Science Quarterly, 18,* 311–327. (3, 15, 16)

Ball, J. A. (1980). Extraterrestrial intelligence: Where is everybody? *American Scientist, 68,* 656–663. (43)

Ball, O. J., & Khanna, O. K. (1977). The ISODATA method computation for the relative perception of similarities and differences in complex and real data. In K. Enstein, A. Ralston, & H. S. Wilf (Eds.), *Statistical methods for digital computers* (Vol. 3). New York: Wiley. (32)

Bandura, A. (1977). Self-efficacy: Toward a unifying theory of behavioral change. *Psychological Review, 84,* 191–215. (41)

Bar-Hillel, M. (1973). On the subjective probability of compound events. *Organizational Behavior and Human Performance, 9,* 396–406. (2, 12, 40, 41)

Bar-Hillel, M. (1979). The role of sample size in sample evaluation. *Organizational Behavior and Human Performance, 24,* 245–257. (41)

Bar-Hillel, M. (1980). The base rate fallacy in probability judgments. *Acta Psychologica, 44,* 211–233. (40)

Barker, C. J. (1981, October 21). *Historical comparison: Colorado Department of Health/ DOE Environmental Measurements Laboratory/Rocky Flats Plant: 1974–1978.* (Rocky Flats Plant Rep. No. ES–376–81–229). (28)

Barnoon, S., & Wolfe, H. (1972). *Measuring the effectiveness of medical decisions: An operations research approach.* Springfield, IL: Thomas. (20)

Barr, R. (1975). How children are taught to read: Grouping and pacing. *School Review, 83,* 479–498. (32)

Barry, W. (1970). Marriage research and conflict: An integrative review. *Psychological Bulletin, 73,* 41–54. (15)

Bartlett, F. C. (1932). *Remembering.* Cambridge: Cambridge University Press. (24)

Baucom, D. (1982, November). *The utility of cognitive restructuring as a supplement to behavioral marital therapy.* Paper presented at the meeting of the Association for the Advancement of Behavior Therapy, Los Angeles. (15)

Bauman, W. S. (1965). The less popular stocks versus the most popular stocks. *Financial Analysts Journal, 21,* 61–69. (10)

Bauman, W. S. (1967). Scientific investment analysis. *Financial Analysts Journal, 23,* 93–97. (10)

Bazelon, D. L. (1977). Coping with technology through the legal process. *Cornell Law Review, 62,* 817–832. (12)

Bazerman, M. H. (1982, August). *The framing of organizational behavior.* Paper presented at the meeting of the Academy of Management, New York. (17)

Bazerman, M. H., Beekun, R. K., & Schoorman, F. D. (1982). Peformance evaluation in a dynamic context: A laboratory study of the impact of a prior commitment to the ratee. *Journal of Applied Psychology, 67,* 873–876. (17)

Bazerman, M. H., & Neale, M. A. (1982). Improving negotiation effectiveness under final offer arbitration: The role of selection and training. *Journal of Applied Psychology, 67,* 543–548. (17)

Beach, L. R., & Mitchell, T. R. (1978). A contingency model for the selection of decision strategies. *Academy of Management Review, 3,* 439–449. (39)

Beach, L. R., Mitchell, T. R., Deaton, M. D., & Prothero, J. (1978). Information relevance, content, and source credibility in the revision of opinions. *Organizational Behavior and Human Performance, 21,* 1–16. (27)

Beach, L. R., & Scopp, T. S. (1968). Intuitive statistical inferences about variances. *Organizational Behavior and Human Peformance, 3,* 109–123. (10)

Beach, L. R., Wise, J. A., & Barclay, S. (1970). Sample proportion and subjective probability revisions. *Organizational Behavior and Human Performance, 5,* 183–190. (40)

Becker, G. M., & McClintock, C. G. (1967). Value: Behavioral decision theory. *Annual Review of Psychology, 18,* 239–286. (38)

Beer, S. (1966). *Decision and control.* New York: Wiley. (41)

Bendig, A. W. (1955). Rater experience and case history judgments of adjustment. *Journal of Clinical Psychology, 11,* 127–132. (35)

Berkeley, D., & Humphreys, P. (1982). Structuring decision problems and the 'bias heuristic.' *Acta Psychologica, 50,* 201–252. (39)

Berndt, T. J., & Wood, D. J. (1974). The development of time concepts through conflict based on a primitive duration capacity. *Child Development, 45,* 825–828. (31)

Bernhard, A. (1959). *The evaluation of common stocks.* New York: Simon & Schuster. (10)

Bernhard, A. (1967). Results of the second (1967) value line contest in stock market judgment. *Value Line Investment Survey, 23,* 236–242. (10)

Bernoulli, D. (1954). Exposition of a new theory on the measurement of risk. *Econometrica, 22,* 23–36. (Original work published 1738) (11)

Bernoulli, J. (1713). Ars conjectandi. Basel. (25)

Bernstein, W., & Davis, M. (1982). Perspective–taking, self-consciousness, and accuracy in person perception. *Basic and Applied Social Psychology, 3,* 1–19. (17)

Besner, D., & Coltheart, M. (1976). Mental size scaling examined. *Memory and Cognition, 4,* 525–531. (27)

Beuscher, J. H. (1941). The use of experts by the courts. *Harvard Law Review, 54,* 1105–1127. (12)

Beyth-Marom, R. (1981, October). *The subjective probability of conjunctions* (Rep. 81–12). Eugene, OR: Decision Research. (40)

Billings, A. (1979). Conflict resolution in distressed and nondistressed married couples. *Journal of Consulting and Clinical Psychology, 47,* 368–376. (15)

Birchler, G. R., Weiss, R. L., & Vincent, J. P. (1975). Multimethod analysis of social reinforcement exchange between maritally distressed and nondistressed spouse and stranger dyads. *Journal of Personality and Social Psychology, 31,* 349–360. (15)

Black, H. C. (1968). *Black's law dictionary* (4th ed.). St. Paul, MN: West Publishing. (37)

Bobrow, D. G., & Norman, D. A. (1975). Some principles of memory schemata. In D. G. Bobrow & A. Collins (Eds.), *Representation and understanding: Studies in cognitive science* (pp. 131–149). New York: Academic Press. (32)

Boffey, P. (1975). *The brain bank of America*. New York: McGraw-Hill. (7)

Bolton, N. (1972). *The psychology of thinking*. London: Methuen. (42)

Borke, H., & Fiske, D. W. (1957). Factors influencing the prediction of behavior from a diagnostic interview. *Journal of Consulting Psychology, 21*, 78–80. (19)

Borko, H., Cone, R., Russo, N. A., & Shavelson, R. J. (1979). Teachers' decision making. In P. L. Peterson & H. J. Walberg (Eds.), *Research on teaching: Concepts, findings, and implications* (pp. 136–160). Berkeley, CA: McCutchan. (32)

Boulding, K. E. (1975). Truth or power? *Science, 190*, 423. (7)

Bourne, L. E., Jr. (1966). *Human conceptual behavior*. Boston: Allyn & Bacon. (42)

Bourne, L. E., Jr., Dominowski, R. L., & Loftus, E. F. (1979). *Cognitive processes*. Englewood Cliffs, NJ: Prentice-Hall. (31)

Bowman, E. H. (1963). Consistency and optimality in managerial decision making. *Management Science, 9*, 310–321. (10, 12)

Brady, D., & Rappoport, L. (1973). Policy-capturing in the field: The nuclear safeguards problem. *Organizational Behavior and Human Performance, 9*, 253–266. (3, 15)

Braiker, H., & Kelley, H. H. (1979). Conflict in the development of close relationships. In R. L. Burgess & T. L. Huston (Eds.), *Social exchange in developing relationships*. (pp. 135–196). New York: Academic Press. (15)

Brainerd, C. (1978). The stage question in cognitive-developmental theory. *Behavioral and Brain Sciences, 2*, 173–182. (30)

Bray, J. (1975). Optimal control of a noisy economy with the UK as an example. *Journal of the Royal Statistical Society: Series A, 138*, 339–366. (41)

Bray, R. (1974). *Decision rules, attitude similarity, and jury decision making*. Unpublished doctoral dissertation, University of Illionis at Urbana. (37)

Brehmer, B. (1969a). *Sequence effects on conflict* (Umea Psychological Rep. No. 17). Umea, Sweden: University of Umea, Department of Psychology. (16)

Brehmer, B. (1969b). *The roles of policy differences and inconsistency in policy conflict* (Umea Psychological Rep. No. 18). Umea, Sweden: University of Umea, Department of Psychology. (3, 16)

Brehmer, B. (1971a). Effects of communication and feedback on cognitive conflict. *Scandinavian Journal of Psychology, 12*, 205–216. (3, 16)

Brehmer, B. (1971b). Subjects' ability to use functional rules. *Psychonomic Science, 24*, 259–260. (3)

Brehmer, B. (1972). Policy conflict as a function of policy differences and policy complexity. *Scandinavian Journal of Psychology, 13*, 208–221. (3, 16)

Brehmer, B. (1973a). Effects of cue validity on interpersonal learning of inference tasks with linear and nonlinear cues. *American Journal of Psychology, 86*, 29–48. (3)

Brehmer, B. (1973b). Effects of task predictability and cue validity on interpersonal learning of inference tasks including both linear and nonlinear cues. *Organizational Behavior and Human Performance, 10*, 24–46. (3)

Brehmer, B. (1973c). Policy conflict and policy change as a function of task characteristics: II. The effects of task predictability. *Scandinavian Journal of Psychology, 14*, 220–227. (3, 16)

Brehmer, B. (1974a). Effect of cue intercorrelations on interpersonal learning of probabilistic inference tasks. *Organizational Behavior and Human Performance, 12*, 397–412. (3)

Brehmer, B. (1974b). Effects of task predictability and cue validity on interpersonal learning of linear inference tasks. *Organizational Behavior and Human Performance, 12,* 17–29. (3)

Brehmer, B. (1974c). Hypotheses about relations between scaled variables in the learning of probabilistic inference tasks. *Organizational Behavior and Human Performance, 11,* 1–27. (42)

Brehmer, B. (1974d). A note on the cross-national differences in conflict found by Hammond et al. *International Journal of Psychology, 9,* 51–56. (16)

Brehmer, B. (1974e). Policy conflict and policy change as a function of task characteristics: III. The effect of the distribution of the validities of the cues in the conflict task. *Scandinavian Journal of Psychology, 15,* 135–138. (3, 16)

Brehmer, B. (1974f). Policy conflict, policy consistency, and interpersonal understanding. *Scandinavian Journal of Psychology, 15,* 273–276. (3, 16)

Brehmer, B. (1975). Policy conflict and policy change as a function of task characteristics: IV. The effect of cue intercorrelations. *Scandinavian Journal of Psychology, 16,* 85–96. (3, 16)

Brehmer, B. (1976a). Learning complex rules in probabilistic inference tasks. *Scandinavian Journal of Psychology, 17,* 309–312. (42)

Brehmer, B. (1976b). Note on clinical judgment and the formal characteristics of clinical tasks. *Psychological Bulletin, 83,* 778–782. (16, 42)

Brehmer, B. (1976c). Social judgment theory and the analysis of interpersonal conflict. *Psychological Bulletin, 83,* 985–1003. (16, 41)

Brehmer, B. (1978). Response consistency in probabilistic inference tasks. *Organizational Behavior and Human Performance, 22,* 103–115. (16, 41)

Brehmer, B. (1979). Preliminaries to a psychology of inference. *Scandinavian Journal of Psychology, 21,* 193–211. (16).

Brehmer, B. (1980a). Effect of cue validity on the learning of complex rules in probabilistic inference tasks. *Acta Psychologica, 44,* 201–210. (42)

Brehmer, B. (1980b). In a word: Not from experience. *Acta Psychologica, 45,* 223–241. (16)

Brehmer, B. (1980c). Probabilistic functionalism in the laboratory: Learning and interpersonal (cognitive) conflict. In K. R. Hammond & N. E. Wascoe (Eds.), *New directions for methodology of social and behavioral science: No. 3. Realizations of Brunswik's representative design* (pp. 13–24). San Francisco: Jossey-Bass. (32)

Brehmer, B., Azuma, H., Hammond, K. R., Kostron, L., & Varonos, D. D. (1970). A cross-national comparison of cognitive conflict. *Journal of Cross-Cultural Psychology, 1,* 5–20. (3, 16)

Brehmer, B., & Garpebring, S. (1974). Social pressure and policy change in the "lens model" interpersonal conflict paradigm. *Scandinavian Journal of Psychology, 15,* 191–196. (3)

Brehmer, B., Hagafors, R., & Johansson, R. (1980). Cognitive skills in judgment: Subjects' ability to use information about weights, function forms, and organizing principles. *Organizational Behavior and Human Performance, 26,* 373–385. (16)

Brehmer, B., & Hammond, K. R. (1973). Cognitive sources of interpersonal conflict: Analysis of interactions between linear and nonlinear cognitive systems. *Organizational Behavior and Human Performance, 10,* 290–313. (3, 16)

Brehmer, B., & Hammond, K. R. (1977). Cognitive factors in interpersonal conflict. In D. Druckman (Ed.), *Negotiations: Social-psychological perspectives* (pp.

79–103). Beverly Hills, CA: Sage. (16, 28)

Brehmer, B., & Kostron, L. (1973). Policy conflict and policy change as a function of task characteristics: I. The effects of cue validity and function form. *Scandinavian Journal of Psychology, 14,* 44–55. (3, 16)

Brehmer, B., & Kuylenstierna, J. (1978). Task information and performance in probabilistic inference tasks. *Organizational Behavior and Human Performance, 22,* 445–464. (16, 42)

Brehmer, B., & Kuylenstierna, J. (1979). Effect of the postfeedback interval on learning of complex rules in probabilistic inference tasks. *Scandinavian Journal of Psychology, 20,* 151–154. (42)

Brehmer, B., & Kuylenstierna, J. (1989). Content and consistency in probabilistic inference tasks. *Organizational Behavior and Human Performance, 26,* 54–64. (16, 42)

Brehmer, B., Kuylenstierna, J., & Liljergren, J. (1974). Effects of cue validity and function form of the subjects' hypotheses in probabilistic inference tasks. *Organizational Behavior and Human Performance, 11,* 338–354. (16, 36, 42)

Brehmer, B., & Qvarnström G. (1976). Information integration and subjective weights in multiple-cue judgments. *Organizational Behavior and Human Performance, 17,* 118–126. (16)

Brewer, J. K., & Owen, P. W. (1973). A note on the power of statistical tests in the "Journal of Educational Measurement." *Journal of Educational Measurement, 10,* 71–74. (12)

Brickman, P., & Campbell, D. T. (1971). Hedonic relativism and planning the good society. In M. H. Appley (Ed.), *Adaptation-level theory: A symposium* (pp. 287–302). New York: Academic Press. (11)

Brislin, R. W. (1970). Back-translation for cross-cultural research. *Journal of Cross-Cultural Psychology, 1,* 185–216. (25)

Brockner, J., Shaw, M. C., & Rubin, J. Z. (1979). Factors affecting withdrawal from an escalating conflict: Quitting before it's too late. *Journal of Experimental Social Psychology, 15,* 492–503. (17)

Brodie, C. M. (1964). Clinical prediction of personality traits displayed in specific situations. *Journal of Clinical Psychology, 20,* 459–461. (19)

Brooks, H. (1975). Expertise and politics: Problems and tensions. *American Philosophical Society Proceedings, 119,* 257–261. (28)

Brophy, J. E., & Good, T. L. (1970). Teachers' communication of differential expectations for children's classroom performance: Some behavioral data. *Journal of Educational Psychology, 61,* 365–374. (32)

Brophy, J. E., & Good, T. L. (1974). *Teacher–student relationships: Causes and consequences.* New York: Holt, Rinehart, & Winston. (32)

Broun, K. S., & Kelly, D. G. (1970). Playing the percentages and the law of evidence. *University of Illinois Law Forum, 1970,* 23–48. (12)

Brown, L., & Hammond, K. R. (1968). *A supra-linguistic method for reducing intragroup conflict* (Rep. No. 108). Boulder: University of Colorado, Center for Research on Judgment and Policy. (16)

Brown, R. V., Kahr, A. S., & Peterson, C. R. (1974a). *Decision analysis: An overview.* London: Holt-Blond. (25)

Brown, R. V., Kahr, A. S., & Peterson, C. R. (1974b). *Decision analysis for the manager.* New York: Holt, Rinehart, & Winston. (12)

Bruner, J. (1957). On perceptual readiness. *Psychological Review, 64,* 123–152. (15)

Bruner, J. S., Goodnow, J. J., & Austin, G. A. (1956). *A study of thinking.* New York: Wiley. (25, 42)

Bruner, J. S., & Tagiuri, R. (1954). The perception of people. In G. Lindzey (Ed.), *Handbook of social psychology* (Vol. 2). Reading, MA: Addison-Wesley. (12, 36)

Bruno, K. J., & Harris, R. J. (1980). The effect of repetition on the discrimination of asserted and implied claims in advertising. *Applied Psycholinguistics, 1,* 307–321. (27)

Brunswik, E. (1943). Organismic achievement and environmental probability. *Psychological Review, 50,* 255–272. (3, 41)

Brunswik, E. (1952). *The conceptual framework of psychology.* Chicago: University of Chicago Press. (3, 16, 34, 35, 41)

Brunswik, E. (1955). Representative design and probabilistic theory in a functional psychology. *Psychological Review, 62,* 193–217. (32, 34)

Brunswik, E. (1956). *Perception and the representative design of psychological experiments* (2nd ed.). Berkeley: University of California Press. (3, 34, 41)

Brunswik, E. (1957). Scope and aspects of the cognitive problem. In H. Gruber, R. Jessor, & K. Hammond (Eds.), *Cognition: The Colorado symposium* (pp. 5–31). Cambridge, MA: Harvard University Press. (3)

Bryan, J. H., Hunt, W. A., & Walker, R. E. (1966). Reliability of estimating intellectual ability from transcribed interviews. *Journal of Clinical Psychology, 22,* 360. (19)

Bryant, P. E., & Trabasso, T. (1971). Transitive inferences and memory in young children. *Nature, 232,* 456–458. (31)

Buchanan, J., & Tullock, G. (1962). *The calculus of consent.* Ann Arbor: University of Michigan Press. (9)

Buckhout, R. (1974). Eyewitness testimony. *Scientific American, 231,* 23–31. (12, 24)

Bundesen, C., & Larsen, A. (1975). Visual transformation of size. *Journal of Experimental Psychology: Human Perception and Performance, 1,* 214–220. (27)

Bureau of Reclamation. (1976). *Draft environmental statement, Orme dam and reservoir.* Lower Colorado Region, Boulder City, NV. (8)

Bureau of Reclamation. (1980). *CAWCS factbook: Public forums, November–December 1980.* Lower Colorado Region, Boulder City, NV. (8)

Bureau of Reclamation. (1981a). *CAWCS factbook.* Lower Colorado Region, Boulder City, NV. (8)

Bureau of Reclamation. (1981b). *CAWCS Appendix B, public values assessment.* Lower Colorado Region, Boulder City, NV. (8)

Bureau of Reclamation. (1982). *Summary and evaluation of CAWCS public involvement program, 1979–1981.* Lower Colorado Region, Boulder City, NV. (8)

Burgess, E., & Wallin, P. (1953). *Engagement and marriage.* Philadelphia: Lippincott. (15)

Buros, O. K. (1978). *Eighth mental measurements yearbook.* Highland Park, NJ: Gryphon Press. (34)

Bush, E. S., & Cohen, L. B. (1970). Effects of relevant and irrelevant labels on short-term memory in nursery-school children. *Psychonomic Science, 18,* 228–229. (27)

Butzin, C. A. (1978). *The effect of ulterior motive information on children's judgments.* Unpublished doctoral dissertation, University of California, San Diego. (4)

Campbell, D. T. (1959). Systematic error on the part of human links in communication systems. *Information and Control, 1,* 334–369. (41)

Campbell, D. T. (1960). Blind variation and selective retention in creative thought as in other knowledge processes. *Psychological Review, 67,* 380–400. (41)

Campbell, D. T. (1969). Reforms as experiments. *American Psychologist, 24,* 409–429. (41)

Campbell, D. T., & Fiske, D. W. (1959). Convergent and discriminant validation by the multitrait-multimethod matrix. *Psychological Bulletin, 56,* 81–105. (29)

Campbell, N. R. (1928). *An account of the principles of measurement and calculation.* London: Longmans, Green. (4)

Caplan, P. J. (1973). The role of classroom conduct in the promotion and retention of elementary school children. *Journal of Experimental Education, 41,* 8–10. (32)

Capon, N., & Kuhn, D. (1979). Logical reasoning in the supermarket: Adult female's use of a proportional reasoning strategy in an everyday context. *Developmental Psychology, 15,* 450–452. (30)

Caramazza, A., McCloskey, N., & Green, B. (1981). Naive beliefs in "sophisticated" subjects: Misconceptions about trajectories of objects. *Cognition, 9,* 117–123. (40)

Carment, D. W. (1974). Internal versus external control in India and Canada. *International Journal of Psychology, 9,* 45–50. (25)

Carnap, R. (1950). *Logical foundation of probability.* Chicago: University of Chicago Press. (43)

Carroll, J. S. (1978). Causal attributions in expert parole decisions. *Journal of Personality and Social Psychology, 36,* 1501–1511. (13)

Carroll, J. S. (1980). Judgments of recidivism risk: The use of base-rate information in parole decisions. In P. D. Lipsitt & B. D. Sales (Eds.), *New directions in psycholegal research* (pp. 68–86). New York: Van Nostrand Reinhold. (13)

Carroll, J. S., & Payne, J. W. (1976). The psychology of the parole decision process: A joint application of attribution theory and information-processing psychology. In J. S. Carroll & J. W. Payne (Eds.), *Cognition and social behavior* (pp. 13–32). Hillsdale, NJ: Erlbaum. (13)

Carroll, J. S., & Payne, J. W. (1977a). Judgments about crime and the criminal: A model and a method for investigating parole decisions. In B. D. Sales (Ed.), *Perspectives in law and psychology, Vol. 1: Criminal justice system.* New York: Plenum. (13)

Carroll, J. S., & Payne, J. W. (1977b). Crime seriousness, recidivism risk, and causal attribution in judgments of prison term by students and experts. *Journal of Applied Psychology, 62,* 595–602. (13)

Carroll, J. S., & Siegler, R. S. (1977). Strategies for the use of base rate information. *Organizational Behavior and Human Performance, 19,* 392–402. (40)

Carstairs, G. W. (1957). *The twice-born.* London: Hogarth Press. (25)

Carterette, E. C., & Anderson, N. H. (1979). Bisection of loudness. *Perception and Psychophysics, 26,* 265–280. (4)

Castellan, N. J., Jr. (1977). Decision making with multiple probabilistic cues. In N. J. Castellan, D. B. Pisoni, & G. R. Potts (Eds.), *Cognitive theory* (Vol. 2). Hillsdale, NJ: Erlbaum. (41)

Cattell, R. B. (1946). *Description and measurement of personality.* Yonkers, NY: World Book Company. (33)

Central Phoenix Sun. (1978, March 15). Editorial: We still say – Orme dam must be built. Phoenix, AZ. (8)

Chaitin, G. J. (1975). Randomness and mathematical proof. *Scientific American,*

232(5), 47–52. (43)

Chapman, L. J. (1967). Illusory correlation in observational report. *Journal of Verbal Learning and Verbal Behavior, 6,* 151–155. (19)

Chapman, L. J., & Chapman, J. P. (1967). Genesis of popular but erroneous psychodiagnostic observations. *Journal of Abnormal Psychology, 72,* 193–204. (2, 10, 12, 19, 36, 40)

Chapman, L. J., & Chapman, J. P. (1969). Illusory correlation as an obstacle to the use of valid psychodiagnostic signs. *Journal of Abnormal Psychology, 74,* 271–280. (2, 12, 29, 40)

Christensen, A. (1981). *Perceptual biases in couples' reports on their own interaction.* Paper presented at the meeting of the American Association for Advancement of Behavior Therapy, Toronto. (15)

Christensen-Szalanski, J. J. J. (1978). Problem-solving strategies: A selection mechanism, some implications, and some data. *Organizational Behavior and Human Performance, 22,* 307–323. (39)

Christensen–Szalanski, J. J. J. (1980). A further examination of the selection of problem-solving strategies: The effects of deadlines and analytic aptitudes. *Organizational Behavior and Human Performance, 25,* 107–122. (39)

Clark, E. V. (1971). On the acquisition of the meaning of before and after. *Journal of Verbal Learning and Verbal Behavior, 10,* 266–275. (31)

Clark, H. H., & Clark, E. V. (1977). *Psychology and language.* New York: Harcourt Brace Jovanovich. (11)

Clark, R. D., III. (1971). Group-induced shift toward risk: A critical appraisal. *Psychological Bulletin, 76,* 251–270. (10)

Clarke, G. R. (1936). *The study of soil in the field.* Oxford: Oxford University Press (Clarendon Press). (27)

Clarkson, G. P. E. (1962). *Portfolio selection: A simulation of trust investment.* Englewood Cliffs, NJ: Prentice-Hall. (10)

Clay, M. M. (1977). Reading acquisition: Do we get what we plan for? In *Proceedings of the third Australian reading conference: Literacy for life.* Melbourne: Australian Reading Association. (32)

Clay, M. M. (1979). *The early detection of reading difficulties: A diagnostic survey with recovery procedures.* Auckland, New Zealand: Heinemann Educational Books. (32)

Cobb, J. C., Eversole, B. C., Archer, P. G., Taggart. R., & Efurd, D. W. (1982, November). *Plutonium burdens in people living around the Rocky Flats Plant* (EPA-600/4–82–069). Washington, DC: U. S. Department of Commerce. (28).

Cochran, W. G., & Cox, G. M. (1957). *Experimental designs* (2nd ed.). New York: Wiley. (35)

Cohen, B., & Lee, I. (1979). A catalog of risks. *Health Physics, 36,* 707–722. (6)

Cohen, J. (1962). The statistical power of abnormal social psychological research. *Journal of Abnormal Social Psychology, 65,* 145–153. (12)

Cohen, J. (1972). *Psychological probability; or, The art of doubt.* London: Allen & Unwin. (41)

Cohen, J., & Chesnick, E. I. (1970). The doctrine of psychological chances. *British Journal of Psychology, 61,* 323–334. (10)

Cohen, J., Chesnick, E. I., & Haran, D. (1971). Evaluation of compound probabilities in sequential choice. *Nature, 232,* 414–416. (41)

Cohen, J., Chesnick, E. I., & Haran, D. (1972). A confirmation of the inertial-ψ effect in sequential choice and decision. *British Journal of Psychology, 63,* 41–46. (2, 41)

Cohen, J., & Hansel, C. E. M. (1957). The nature of decisions in gambling. *Acta Psychologica, 13,* 357–370. (40)

Cohen, J. J. (1972). A case for benefit–risk analysis. In H. J. Otway (Ed.), *Risk vs. benefit: Solution or dream?* (Rep. LA-4860-MS). Los Alamos: Los Alamos Scientific Laboratory. (40)

Cohen, K. J., Gilmore, T. C., & Singer, F. A. (1966). Bank procedures for analyzing business loan applications. In K. J. Cohen & F. S. Hammer (Eds.), *Analytical methods in banking* (pp. 218–251). Homewood, IL: Irwin. (10)

Cohen, L. J. (1977). *The probable and the provable.* Oxford: Oxford University Press (Clarendon Press). (12)

Cohen, L. J. (1979). On the psychology of prediction: Whose is the fallacy? *Cognition, 7,* 385–407. (12, 39)

Cohen, L. J. (1980). Whose is the fallacy? A rejoinder to Daniel Kahneman and Amos Tversky. *Cognition, 8,* 89–92. (12)

Cohen, M., Ronen, N., & Stepan, J. (1978). *Law and science: A selected bibliography.* Cambridge, MA: MIT Press. (12)

Collins, A. (1976). *Processes in acquiring knowledge* (Rep. No. 3231). Cambridge, MA: Bolt, Beranek, & Newman. (24)

Collins, A., Warnock, E. H., Aiello, N., & Miller, M. (1975). Reasoning from incomplete knowledge. In D. G. Bobrow & A. Collins (Eds.), *Representation and understanding: Studies in cognitive science* (pp. 383–415), New York: Academic Press. (24)

Colorado Department of Health. (1976). *A risk evaluation for the Colorado plutonium-in-soil standard.* Denver: Colorado Department of Health. (28)

Combs, B., & Slovic, P. (1979). Causes of death: Biased newspaper coverage and biased judgments. *Journalism Quarterly, 56,* 837–843. (6)

Committee on Public Engineering Policy, National Academy of Engineering. (1969). *A study of technology assessment.* Washington, DC: Government Printing Office. (7)

Congalton, A. A. (1969). *Status and prestige in Australia.* Melbourne: Cheshire Pty. (32)

Conlon, E. J., & Wolf, G. (1980). The moderating effects of strategy, visibility, and involvement on allocation behavior: An extension of Staw's escalation paradigm. *Organizational Behavior and Human Performance, 26,* 172–192. (17)

Connolly, T. (1980). Uncertainty, action, and competence: Some alternatives to omniscience in complex problem–solving. In S. Fiddle (Ed.), *Uncertainty: Behavioral and social dimensions* (pp. 69–91). New York: Praeger. (41)

Cooksey, R. W. (1982). *A modified version of the ISODATA program.* Armidale, NSW: University of New England, Centre for Behavioural Studies in Education. (32)

Cooksey, R. W., & Freebody, P. (1983). Judgments, policies, and decisions about the teaching of reading: New directions for research. *Reading Education, 8,* 42–50. (32)

Cooksey, R. W., & Freebody, P. (1984). *Social judgment theory and cognitive feedback: A general model for analyzing educational policies and decisions.* Manuscript submitted for publication. (32)

Cooksey, R. W., & Freebody, P. (1985). Generalized multivariate lens model analysis for complex human inference tasks. *Organizational Behavior and Human Decision Processes*, 35, 46–72. (32)

Coombs, C. H., & Pruitt, D. G. (1960). Components of risk in decision making: Probability and variance preferences. *Journal of Experimental Psychology*, 60, 265–277. (10)

Coppleson, L. W., Factor, R. M., Strum, S. B., Graff, P. W., & Rappaport, H. (1970). Observer disagreement in the classification and histology of Hodgkin's disease. *Journal of the National Cancer Institute*, 45, 731–740. (29)

Corbin, R. M. (1980). Decisions that might not get made. In T. S. Wallsten (Ed.), *Cognitive processes in choice and decision behavior* (pp. 47–67). Hillsdale, NJ: Erlbaum. (41)

Coser, L. (1956). *The function of social conflict*. Glencoe, IL: Free Press. (15)

Cowles, A. (1933). Can stock market forecasters forecast? *Econometrica*, 1, 309–324. (10, 41)

Cowles, A. (1944). Stock market forecasting. *Econometrica*, 12, 206–214. (10)

Coyle, R. G. (1977). *Management systems dynamics*. London: Wiley. (41)

Cragg, J. G., & Malkiel, B. G. (1968). The consensus and accuracy of some predictions of the growth of corporate earnings. *Journal of Finance*, 23, 67–84. (10)

Crépault, J. (1979). Organisation et genèse des relations temps, espace, et vitesse. In P. Fraisse (Ed.), *Du temps biologique au temps psychologique* (pp. 227–253). Paris: Presses Universitaires de France. (31)

Cronbach, L. J., & Meehl, P. E. (1955). Construct validity in psychological tests. *Psychological Bulletin*, 52, 281–302. (29)

Crow, W. J. (1957). The effect of training upon accuracy and variability in interpersonal perception. *Journal of Abnormal and Social Psychology*, 55, 355–359. (19)

Cullison, A. D. (1969). Probability analysis of judicial fact–finding: A preliminary outline of the subjective approach. *University of Toledo Law Review*, 1969(3), 538–598. (12)

Cuneo, D. O. (1978). *Children's judgments of numerical quantity: The role of length, density, and number cues*. Unpublished doctoral dissertation, University of California, San Diego. (4)

Cuneo, D. O. (1982). Children's judgments of numerical quantity: A new view of early quantification. *Cognitive Psychology*, 14, 13–44. (31)

Curlin, J. W. (1975). Mutatis mutandis: Congress, science, and law. *Science*, 190, 839. (7)

Cyert, R. M., & March, J. G. (1963). *A behavioral theory of the firm*. Englewood Cliffs, NJ: Prentice–Hall. (41)

Dailey, C. A. (1952). The effects of premature conclusions upon the acquisition of understanding of a person. *Journal of Psychology*, 33, 133–152. (36)

Darlington, R. B. (1968). Multiple regression in psychological research and practice. *Psychological Bulletin*, 69, 161–182.

Davis, J. H., Kerr, N. L., Atkin, R. S., Holt, R., & Meek, D. (1975). The decision processes of 6– and 12–person mock juries assigned unanimous and two–thirds majority rules. *Journal of Personality and Social Psychology*, 32, 1–14. (37)

Davis, K. B., Weisbrod, R. L., Freedy, A., & Weltman, G. (1975). *Adaptive computer aiding in dynamic decision processes: An experimental study of aiding effectiveness* (PTR–1016–75–5). Woodland Hills, CA: Perceptronics. (12)

Davis, M. (1981). A multidimensional approach to individual differences in empathy. *JSAS Catalogue of Selected Documents in Psychology, 10,* 85. (17)

Dawes, R. M. (1971). A case study of graduate admissions: Application of three principles of human decision making. *American Psychologist, 26,* 180–188. (10)

Dawes, R. M. (1972). *Fundamentals of attitude measurement.* New York: Wiley. (14)

Dawes, R. M. (1976). Shallow psychology. In J. S. Carroll & J. W. Payne (Eds.), *Cognition and social behavior* (pp. 3–11). Hillsdale, NJ: Erlbaum. (16)

Dawes, R. M. (1979). The robust beauty of improper linear models in decision making. *American Psychologist, 34,* 571–582. (12)

Dawes, R. M., & Corrigan, B. (1974). Linear models in decision making. *Psychological Bulletin, 81,* 95–106. (12, 29, 41, 42)

De Finetti, B. (1937). La prévision: Des logiques ses sources subjectives. *Annales de l'Institut Henri Poincaré, 7,* 1–68. English translation in M. E. Kyborg, Jr. & H. E. Smokler (Eds.), (1964), *Studies in subjective probability.* New York: Wiley. (25)

De Finetti, B. (1968). Probability: Interpretations. In D. E. Sills (Ed.), *International encyclopedia of the social sciences* (Vol. 12, pp. 496–504). New York: Macmillan. (2)

de Groot, A. D. (1965). *Thought and choice in chess.* The Hague: Mouton. (34)

de Groot, A. D. (1966). Perception and memory versus thought: Some old ideas and recent findings. In B. Kleinmuntz (Ed.), *Problem solving: Research, method and theory* (pp. 19–50). New York: Wiley. (34)

de Leeuw, J., Young, F. W., & Takane, Y. (1976). Additive structure in qualitative data: An alternating least squares method with optimal scaling features. *Psychometrika, 41,* 471–503. (4)

Dennis, R. L., Stewart, T. R., Middleton, P., Downton, M. W., Ely, D. W., & Keeling, M. C. (1983). Integration of technical and value issues in air quality policy formation: A case study. *Socio–Economic Planning Sciences, 17*(3), 95–108. (8)

Department of Interior. (1981, November 12). News release: Watt announces options for continuation of Central Arizona project. Washington, DC: Office of the Secretary. (8)

Dershowitz, A. (1968). Psychiatry in the legal process: A knife that cuts both ways. *Trial, 4*(2), 29–33. (12)

Dershowitz, A. (1971). Imprisonment by judicial hunch. *American Bar Association Journal, 57,* 560–564. (40)

DeSloovere, F. (1933). The functions of judge and jury in the interpretation of statutes. *Harvard Law Review, 46,* 1086–1110. (14)

deSmet, A. A., Fryback, D., & Thornbury, J. R. (1979). A second look at the utility of radiographic skull examination for trauma. *American Journal of Radiology, 132,* 75–99. (40)

Deutsch, M. (1969). Conflicts: Productive and destructive. *Journal of Social Issues, 25,* 7–41. (15)

Dhir, K. S. (1976). Design and implementation of a computer–oriented engineering design model for the cement industry. *Cement Technology, 7,* 52–58. (15)

DiVitto, B., & McArthur, L. (1978). Developmental differences in the use of distinctiveness, consensus, and consistency information for making causal attributions. *Developmental Psychology, 14,* 474–482. (30)

Doll, R., & Hill, A. B. (1964). Mortality in relation to smoking: Ten years observations of British doctors. *British Medical Journal, 1,* 1399–1410, 1460–1467. (28)

Doll, R., & Peto, R. (1978). Cigarette smoking and bronchial carcinoma: Dose and time relationships among regular smokers and lifelong non–smokers. *Journal of Epidemiological Community Health, 32,* 303–313. (28)

Donaldson, M., & Wales, R. J. (1970). On the acquisition of some relational terms. In J. R. Hayes (Ed.), *Cognition and the development of language* (pp. 235–268). New York: Wiley. (31)

Doob, A. N. (1976). Evidence, procedure, and psychological research. In G. Bermant, C. Nemeth, & N. Vidmar (Eds.), *Psychology and the law: Research frontiers* (pp. 135–168). Lexington, MA: Lexington. (37)

Doob, A. N., & Kirshenbaum, H. M. (1973). Bias in police lineups: Partial remembering. *Journal of Police Science and Administration, 1,* 287–293. (14)

Dörner, D. (1983). Heuristics and cognition in complex systems. In R. Groner, M. Groner, & W. F. Bischof (Eds.), *Methods of heuristics* (pp. 89–107). Hillsdale, NJ: Erlbaum. (39)

Dörner, D., Kreuzig, H. W., Reither, F., & Staudel, T. (Hrsg.). (1983). *Lohhausen.* Bern/Stuttgart/Wien: Hans Huber. (39)

Drew, G. A. (1941). *New methods for profit in the stock market.* Boston: Metcalf Press. (10)

Dudycha, A. L., & Naylor, J. C. (1966). The effect of variations in the cue R matrix upon the obtained policy equation of judges. *Educational and Psychological Measurement, 26,* 583–603. (34, 35)

Duncan, S., Jr., & Fiske, D. W. (1977). *Face–to–face interaction: Research, methods, and theory.* Hillsdale, NJ: Erlbaum. (41)

Dusek, J. B., & Joseph, G. (1983). The bases of teacher expectancies: A meta–analysis. *Journal of Educational Psychology, 75,* 327–346. (32)

Dyamour, J. (1959). Malay kinship and marriage in Singapore. *London School of Economics: Monographs on Social Anthropology, 21,* 35–55. (25)

Earle, T. C. (1973). Interpersonal learning. In L. Rappoport & D. A. Summers (Eds.), *Human judgment and social interaction* (pp. 240–266). New York: Holt, Rinehart, & Winston. (3)

Ebbesen, E. B., & Konečni, V. J. (1975). Decision–making and information integration in the courts: The setting of bail. *Journal of Personality and Social Psychology, 32,* 805–821. (14)

Ebbesen, E. B., & Konečni, V. J. (1976, September). *Fairness in sentencing: Severity of crime and judicial decision making.* Paper presented at the meeting of the American Psychological Association, Washington, DC. (14)

Ebbesen, E. B., & Konečni, V. J. (1980). On the external validity of decision–making research: What do we know about decisions in the real world? In T. Wallsten (Ed.), *Cognitive processes in choice and decision behavior* (pp. 21–45). Hillsdale, NJ: Erlbaum. (41)

Ebbesen, E. B., Parker, S., & Konečni, V. J. (1977). Laboratory and field analyses of decisions involving risk. *Journal of Experimental Psychology: Human Perception and Performance, 3,* 576–589. (31)

Eddy, D. M. (1982). Probabilistic reasoning in clinical medicine: Problems and opportunities. In D. Kahneman, P. Slovic, & A. Tversky (Eds.), *Judgment under uncertainty: Heuristics and biases* (pp. 249–267). Cambridge: Cambridge University Press. (40)

Edwards, W. (1954). The theory of decision making. *Psychological Bulletin, 51,* 380–417. (Gen. Int., 25)

Edwards, W. (1962). Dynamic decision theory and probabilistic information processing. *Human Factors, 4,* 59–73. (12, 40, 41)

Edwards, W. (1968). Conservatism in human information processing. In B. Kleinmuntz (Ed.), *Formal representation of human judgment* (pp. 17–52). New York: Wiley, (2, 3, 10, 34, 39, 40, 41)

Edwards, W. (1971). Bayesian and regression models of human information processing: A myopic perspective. *Organizational Behavior and Human Performance, 6,* 639–648. (34)

Edwards, W. (1980). Multiattribute utility for evaluation: Structures, uses, and problems. In M. W. Klein & K. S. Teilmann (Eds.), *Handbook of criminal justice evaluation.* (pp. 177–215). Beverly Hills, CA: Sage. (1)

Edwards, W. (1983). Human cognitive capabilities, representativeness, and ground rules for research. In P. C. Humphreys, O. Svenson, & A. Vari (Eds.), *Analysing and aiding decision processes* (pp. 507–513). Amsterdam: North Holland. (39, 40)

Edwards, W., Guttentag, K., & Snapper, K. (1975). A decision-theoretic approach to evaluation research. In E. L. Struening & M. Guttentag (Eds.), *Handbook of evaluation research* (Vol. 1, pp. 139–181). Beverly Hills, CA: Sage. (1, 7)

Edwards, W., Lindman, H., & Phillips, L. D. (1965). Emerging technologies for making decisions. In *New directions in psychology* 2 (pp. 261–325). New York: Holt, Rinehart, & Winston. (10)

Edwards, W., Lindman, H., & Savage, L. J. (1963). Bayesian statistical inference for psychological research. *Psychological Review, 70,* 193–242. (40)

Edwards, W., Phillips, L. D., Hays, W. L., & Goodman, B. C. (1968). Probabilistic information processing systems: Design and evaluation. *IEEE Transactions on Systems Science and Cybernetics, SSC-4,* 248–265. (10)

Eils, L., Seaver, D., & Edwards, W. (1977). *Developing the technology of probabilistic inference: Aggregating by averaging reduces conservatism* (Research Rep. 77–3). Los Angeles: University of Southern California, Social Science Research Institute. (40)

Eimas, P. D. (1966). Effects of overtraining on irrelevant stimuli and training task reversal on reversal discrimination learning in children. *Journal of Experimental Child Psychology, 3,* 315–323. (27)

Einhorn, H. J. (1972). Expert measurement and mechanical combination. *Organizational Behavior and Human Performance, 7,* 86–106. (10, 12, 29)

Einhorn, H. J. (1980a). Learning from experience and suboptimal rules in decision making. In T. Wallsten (Ed.), *Cognitive processes in choice and decision behavior* (pp. 1–20). Hillsdale, NJ: Erlbaum. (41, 42)

Einhorn, H. J. (1980b). Overconfidence in judgment. In R. A. Shweder & D. W. Fiske (Eds.), *New directions for methodology of social and behavioral science: No. 4. Fallible judgment in behavioral research* (pp. 1–16). San Francisco: Jossey-Bass. (17)

Einhorn, H. J., & Hogarth, R. M. (1975). Unit weighting schemes for decision making. *Organizational Behavior and Human Performance, 13,* 171–192. (41)

Einhorn, H. J., & Hogarth, R. M. (1978). Confidence in judgment: Persistence of the illusion of validity. *Psychological Review, 85,* 395–416. (17, 36, 41, 42)

Einhorn, H. J., & Hogarth, R. M. (1981). Behavioral decision theory: Processes of judgment and choice. *Annual Review of Psychology, 32,* 53–88. (27, 29, 41)

Einhorn, H. J., Hogarth, R. M., & Klempner, E. (1977). Quality of group judgment. *Psychological Bulletin, 84*, 158–172. (41)

Einhorn, H. J., Kleinmuntz, D. N., & Kleinmuntz, B. (1979). Linear regression *and* process-tracing models of judgment. *Psychological Review, 86*, 465–485. (16, 41)

Elashoff, J., & Snow, R. (1971). *Pygmalion reconsidered*. Worthington, OH: Charles A. Jones. (32)

Ellsberg, D. (1961). Risk, ambiguity, and the Savage axioms. *Quarterly Journal of Economics, 75*, 643–699. (9)

Elstein, A. S., Shulman, L. S., & Sprafka, S. A. (1978). *Medical problem solving: An analysis of clinical reasoning*. Cambridge, MA: Harvard University Press. (34, 36)

Elster, J. (1979). *Ulysses and the sirens*. Cambridge: Cambridge University Press; and Paris: Editions de la Maison des Sciences de l'Homme. (39)

Ennis, B. J., & Litwack, T. R. (1974). Psychiatry and the presumption of expertise: Flipping coins in the courtroom. *California Law Review, 62*, 693–752. (12)

Erakar, S. E., & Sox, H. C. (1981). Assessment of patients' preferences for therapeutic outcomes. *Medical Decision Making, 1*, 29–39. (11)

Erskine, H. (1974). The polls: Causes of crime. *Public Opinion Quarterly, 38*, 288–298. (13)

Estes, W. K. (1972). Research and theory in the learning of probabilities. *Journal of the American Statistical Association, 67*, 81–102. (41)

Evans, J. St. B. T. (1982). On statistical intuitions and inferential rules: A discussion of Kahneman and Tversky. *Cognition, 12*, 319–323. (39)

Evans, R. A., & Beedle, R. K. (1970). Discrimination learning in mentally-retarded children as a function of irrelevant dimension variability. *American Journal of Mental Deficiency, 74*, 568–573. (27)

Fairley, W. B., & Mosteller, F. (1974). A conversation about Collins. *University of Chicago Law Review, 41*, 242–253. (12)

Fama, E. F. (1965). The behavior of stock market prices. *Journal of Business, 38*, 34–105. (10)

Farber, H. S. (1981). An analysis of "splitting-the-difference" in interest arbitration. *Industrial and Labor Relations Review, 34*, 66–74. (17)

Farkas, A. J., & Anderson, N. H. (1979). Multidimensional input in equity theory. *Journal of Personality and Social Psychology, 37*, 879–896. (4)

Farrell, H., & Markman, H. J. (1986). Remarriage: A window in the role of communication in the etiology prevention of marital distress. In R. Gilmour & S. Duck (Eds.), *The emerging field of personal relationships*. Hillsdale, NJ: Erlbaum. (15)

Feather, N. T. (Ed.). (1982). *Expectations and actions*. Hillsdale, NJ: Erlbaum. (39)

Fechner, G. T. (1860). *Elemente der Psychophysik*. New York: Holt, Rinehart, & Winston (English edition, 1966). (4)

Feinberg, W. E. (1972). Teaching the Type I and Type II errors: The judicial process. *American Statistician, 26*, 21–23. (37)

Feinstein, A. R. (1970). What kind of basic science for clinical medicine? *New England Journal of Medicine, 283*, 847–852. (20)

Findler, N. V. (1977). Studies in machine cognition using the game of poker. *Communications of the ACM, 20*, 230–245. (41)

Finkelstein, M. O., & Fairley, W. B. (1970). A Bayesian approach to identification evidence. *Harvard Law Review, 83*, 489–517. (12)

Fisch, H.-U., Hammond, K. R., & Joyce, C. R. B. (1982). On evaluating the severity of depression: An experimental study of psychiatrists. *British Journal of Psychiatry, 140,* 378–383. (21)

Fisch, H.-U., Hammond, K. R., Joyce, C. R. B., & O'Reilly, M. (1981). An experimental study of the clinical judgment of general physicians in evaluating and prescribing for depression. *British Journal of Psychiatry, 138,* 100–109. (21)

Fischer, G. W. (1979). Utility models for multiple objective decisions: Do they accurately represent human preferences? *Decision Sciences, 10,* 451–479. (40)

Fischhoff, B. (1975). Hindsight ≠ foresight: The effect of outcome knowledge on judgment under uncertainty. *Journal of Experimental Psychology: Human Perception and Performance, 1,* 288–299. (12, 27, 36, 40, 41)

Fischhoff, B. (1976). Attribution theory and judgment under uncertainty. In N. H. Harvey, W. J. Ickes, & R. F. Kidd (Eds.), *New directions in attribution research* (pp. 421–452). Hillsdale, NJ: Erlbaum. (40, 41)

Fischhoff, B. (1977). Perceived informativeness of facts. *Journal of Experimental Psychology: Human Perception and Performance, 3,* 349–358. (36)

Fischhoff, B. (1980). For those condemned to study the past: Reflections on historical judgment. In R. A. Shweder & D. W. Fiske (Eds.), *New directions for methodology of social and behavioral science: No. 4. Fallible judgment in behavioral research* (pp. 79–93). San Francisco: Jossey-Bass. (40)

Fischhoff, B. (1982). Debiasing. In D. Kahneman, P. Slovic, & A. Tversky (Eds.), *Judgment under Uncertainty: Heuristics and biases* (pp. 422–444). Cambridge: Cambridge University Press. (17, 40)

Fischhoff, B. (1983a). Informed consent for transient nuclear workers. In R. Kasperson & M. Berberian (Eds.), *Equity issues in radioactive waste management* (pp. 301–328). Cambridge: Oelgeschlager, Gunn, & Hain. (6)

Fischhoff, B. (1983b). Predicting frames. *Journal of Experimental Psychology: Learning, Memory, and Cognition, 9,* 103–116. (11)

Fischhoff, B. (1983c). Reconstructive criticism. In P. C. Humphreys, O. Svenson, & A. Vari (Eds.), *Analysing and aiding decision processes* (pp. 515–523). Amsterdam: North Holland. (39)

Fischhoff, B., & Beyth, R. (1975). "I knew it would happen": Remembered probabilities of once-future things. *Organizational Behavior and Human Performance, 13,* 1–16. (12, 40)

Fischhoff, B., Goitein, B., & Shapira, Z. (1982). The experienced utility of expected utility approaches. In N. T. Feather (Ed.), *Expectations and actions* (pp. 315–339). Hillsdale, NJ: Erlbaum. (39)

Fischhoff, B., & Lichtenstein, S. (1977). *The effect of response mode and question format on calibration* (Rep. No. 77–1). Eugene. OR: Decision Research. (24)

Fischhoff, B., & Slovic, P. (1980). A little learning . . .: Confidence in multicue judgment tasks. In R. E. Nickerson (Ed.), *Attention and performance* (Vol. 8, pp. 779–800). Hillsdale, NJ: Erlbaum. (27, 41, 42)

Fischhoff, B., Slovic, P., & Lichtenstein, S. (1977). Knowing with certainty: The appropriateness of extreme confidence. *Journal of Experimental Psychology: Human Perception and Performance, 3,* 552–564. (27)

Fischhoff, B., Slovic, P., & Lichtenstein, S. (1978). Fault trees: Sensitivity of estimated failure probabilities to problem representation. *Journal of Experimental Psychology: Human Perception and Performance, 4,* 330–344. (6, 40)

Fischhoff, B., Slovic, P., & Lichtenstein, S. (1980). Knowing what you want: Measuring labile values. In T. Wallsten (Ed.), *Cognitive processes in choice and decision behavior* (pp. 117–141). Hillsdale, NJ: Erlbaum. (8, 11, 40, 41)

Fishburn, P. C., & Kochenberger, G. A. (1979). Two-piece von Neumann–Morgenstern utility functions. *Decision Sciences, 10,* 503–518. (11)

Fisher, I. (1906). *The nature of capital and income.* New York: Macmillan. (10)

Fisher, R. A., & Yates, F. (1938). *Statistical tables for biological, agricultural, and medical research.* London: Oliver & Boyd. (43)

Fiske, D. W. (1961). The inherent variability of behavior. In D. W. Fiske & S. R. Maddi (Eds.), *Functions of varied experience* (pp. 326–354). Homewood, IL: Dorsey Press. (41)

Flack, J. E., & Summers, D. A. (1971). Computer aided conflict resolution in water resource planning: An illustration. *Water Resources Research, 7,* 1410–1414. (3, 15)

Flavell, J. H. (1977). *Cognitive development.* Englewood Cliffs, NJ: Prentice-Hall. (40)

Floyd, F., & Markman, H. (1983). Observational biases in spouse observation: Toward a cognitive/behavioral model of marriage. *Journal of Consulting and Clinical Psychology, 51,* 450–457. (15)

Ford, J. M., Hink, R. F., Hopkins, W. F., Roth, W. T., Pfefferbaum, A., & Kopell, B. S. (1979). Age effects of event-related potentials in a selective attention task. *Journal of Gerontology, 34,* 388–395. (27)

Forston, R. F. (1970). Judges' instructions: A quantitative analysis of jurors' listening comprehension. *Today's Speech, 18,* 34–38. (14)

Frane, J. W. (1981). All possible subsets regression. In W. J. Dixon, M. B. Brown, L. Engleman, J. W. Frane, M. A. Hill, R. I. Jennrich, & J. D. Toporec (Eds.), *BMDP statistical software* (pp. 264–277). Berkeley: University of California Press. (21)

Frankena, W. K. (1963). *Ethics.* Englewood Cliffs, NJ: Prentice-Hall. (38)

Freebody, P., & Rust, P. (1985). Predicting reading achievement in the first year of schooling: A comparison of readiness tests and instructional programs. *Journal of School Psychology, 23,* 145–155. (32)

French, L. A., & Brown, A. L. (1977). Comprehension of before and after in logical and arbitrary sequences. *Journal of Child Language, 4,* 247–256. (31)

Fried, M., Kaplan, K. J., & Klein, K. W. (1975). Juror selection: An analysis of voir dire. In R. J. Simon (Ed.), *The jury system in America: A critical overview* (pp. 47–66). Beverly Hills, CA: Sage. (37)

Gaeth, G. J., & Shanteau, J. (1979). *Psychological analysis of the 1978 national soil judging contest* (Applied Psychology Rep. No. 79–10). Manhattan: Kansas State University, Department of Psychology. (27)

Gaeth, G. J., & Shanteau, J. (1980). *Hand method of soil texture assessment: A psychological analysis of accuracy.* Paper presented at the SCSS Conference, Fort Collins, CO. (27)

Gaeth, G. J., & Shanteau, J. (1981). *A bibliography of research on the effects of irrelevance in psychology* (Applied Psychology Rep. No. 81–13). Manhattan: Kansas State University, Department of Psychology. (27)

Gaeth, G. J., & Shanteau, J. (1982). Reducing the bias in hiring decisions by cognitive training [Abstract]. *Bulletin of the Psychonomic Society, 20,* 156. (27)

Galbraith, R. C., & Underwood, B. J. (1973). Perceived frequency of concrete and abstract words. *Memory and Cognition, 1,* 56–60. (2)

Galen, R. S., & Gambino, S. R. (1975). *Beyond normality: The predictive value and efficiency of medical diagnoses.* New York: Wiley. (36)

Galton, F. (1965). *Fingerprints*. New York: Da Capo Press. (12)

Gardiner, P. C., & Edwards, W. (1975). Public values: Multi-attribute utility measurement in social decisionmaking. In M. Kaplan & S. Schwartz (Eds.), *Human judgment and decision processes* (pp. 1–37). New York: Academic Press. (8)

Gardner, D. S. (1933). The perception and memory of witnesses. *Cornell Law Quarterly, 18*, 391–409. (12)

Gardner, M. (1976). On the fabric of inductive logic and some probability paradoxes. *Scientific American, 234*(3), 119–122. (43)

Gardner, M. (1979a). In some patterns of numbers or words there may be less than meets the eye. *Scientific American, 241*(3), 22–32. (43)

Gardner, M. (1979b). The random number omega bids fair to hold the mysteries of the universe. *Scientific American, 241*(5), 20–34. (43)

Garland, L. H. (1959). Studies of the accuracy of diagnostic procedures. *American Journal of Roentgenology, Radium Therapy, and Nuclear Medicine, 82*, 25–38. (19)

Garland, L. H. (1960). The problem of observer error. *Bulletin of the New York Academy of Medicine, 36*, 569–584. (10, 19)

Gasparski, W. (Ed.). (1980). *Decision making and action: Report*. Warsaw: Polish Academy of Sciences. (39)

Gaudet, F. J. (1938). Individual differences in the sentencing tendencies of judges. *Archives of Psychology, 32*(230). (14)

Gauron, E. G., & Dickinson, J. K. (1966). Diagnostic decision-making in psychiatry: 1. Information usage. *Archives of General Psychiatry, 14*, 225–232. (36)

Gelman, R. (1978). Cognitive development. *Annual Review of Psychology, 29*, 297–332. (31)

Gendlin, F. (1982, July/August). A talk with Mo Udall, Chair of the House Interior Committee. *Sierra*. (8)

Gettys, C. F., Kelly, C. W., III, & Peterson, C. R. (1973). The best guess hypothesis in multistage inference. *Organizational Behavior and Human Performance, 10*, 364–373. (24, 41)

Ghiselli, E. E. (1964). *Theory of psychological measurement*. New York: McGraw-Hill. (19)

Ghiselli, E. E., & Brown, C. W. (1955). *Personnel and industrial psychology*. New York: McGraw-Hill. (29)

Giedt, F. H. (1955). Comparison of visual, content, and auditory cues in interviewing. *Journal of Consulting Psychology, 19*, 407–416. (19)

Gilbert, J. P., McPeek, B., & Mosteller, F. (1977). Statistics and ethics in surgery and anesthesia. *Science, 198*, 684–689. (12)

Gillis, J. S. (1975). Effects of chlorpromazine and thiothixene on acute schizophrenic patients. In K. R. Hammond & C. R. B. Joyce (Eds.), *Psychoactive drugs and social judgment: Theory and research* (pp. 109–120, 147–155, 175–184). New York: Wiley. (3)

Gillis, J. S., Stewart, T. R., & Gritz, E. R. (1975). New procedures: Use of interactive computer graphics terminals with psychiatric patients. In K. R. Hammond & C. R. B. Joyce (Eds.), *Psychoactive drugs and social judgment: Theory and research* (pp. 217–237). New York: Wiley. (3)

Glackman, P. J. (1970). *A comparison of four subjective methods to classify data into conditionally independent complexes*. Unpublished master's thesis, University of Wisconsin. (26)

Goldberg, L. R. (1959). The effectiveness of clinicians' judgments: The diagnosis of organic brain damage from the Bender-Gestalt test. *Journal of Consulting Psychology*, *23*, 25–33. (19, 34, 35, 42)

Goldberg, L. R. (1965). Diagnosticians versus diagnostic signs: The diagnosis of psychosis versus neurosis from the MMPI. *Psychological Monographs*, *79*(9, Whole No. 602). (19, 35)

Goldberg, L. R. (1966). Reliability of Peace Corps selection boards: A study of interjudge agreement before and after board discussions. *Journal of Applied Psychology*, *50*, 400–408. (19, 35)

Goldberg, L. R. (1968). Simple models or simple processes? Some research on clinical judgments. *American Psychologist*, *23*, 483–496. (10, 16, 34, 42)

Goldberg, L. R. (1970). Man versus model of man: A rationale, plus some evidence, for a method of improving on clinical inferences. *Psychological Bulletin*, *73*, 422–432. (10, 12, 16, 41)

Goldberg, L. R., & Rorer, L. G. (1965, June). *Learning clinical inference: The results of intensive training on clinicians' ability to diagnose psychosis versus neurosis from the MMPI.* Paper presented at the meeting of the Western Psychological Association, Honolulu. (19)

Goldberg, L. R., & Werts, C. E. (1966). The reliability of clinicians' judgments: A multitrait-multimethod approach. *Journal of Consulting Psychology*, *30*, 199–206. (19, 36)

Golden M. (1964). Some effects of combining psychological tests on clinical inferences. *Journal of Consulting Psychology*, *28*, 440–446. (19)

Goldsmith, R. W. (1978). Assessing probabilities of compound events in a judicial context. *Scandinavian Journal of Psychology*, *19*, 103–110. (40)

Good, T. L., & Brophy, J. E. (1972). Behavioral expression of teacher attitudes. *Journal of Educational Psychology*, *63*, 617–624. (32)

Goodwin, W., & Sanders, J. (1969). *An exploratory study of the effect of selected variables upon teacher expectation of pupil success.* Paper presented at the meeting of the American Educational Research Association, Los Angeles. (32)

Gordon, I. E. (1970). Donders' c-reactions and irrelevant stimulus variety. *British Journal of Psychology*, *61*, 359–363. (27)

Gorry, G. A., Kassirer, J. P., Essig, A., & Schwartz, W. B. (1973). Decision analysis as the basis for computer-aided management of acute renal failure. *American Journal of Medicine*, *55*, 473–484. (20)

Gorsuch, R. L. (1983). *Factor analysis* (2nd ed.). Hillsdale, NJ: Erlbaum. (32)

Gottfredson, D. M. (1975). Some research needs. In D. M. Gottfredson (Ed.), *Decision-making in the criminal justice system: Reviews and essays* (pp. 124–132). Rockville, MD: National Institute of Mental Health. (13)

Gottman, J. (1979). *Empirical investigations of marriage.* New York: Academic Press. (15)

Gottman, J., Markman, H. J., & Notarius, C. (1977). The topography of marital conflict: A sequential analysis of verbal and nonverbal behavior. *Journal of Marriage and the Family*, *39*, 461–477. (15)

Gottman, J., Notarius, C. I., Gonso, J., & Markman, H. J. (1976). *A couple's guide to communication.* Champaign, IL: Research Press. (15)

Gottman, J., Notarius, C., Markman, H. J., Bank, D., Yoppi, B., & Rubin, M. (1976). Behavior exchange theory and marital decision-making. *Journal of Personality and Social Psychology*, *34*, 14–23. (15)

Gough, H. G. (1962). Clinical versus statistical prediction in psychology. In L.

Postman (Ed.), *Psychology in the making* (pp. 526–584). New york: Knopf. (19)

Graham, B., Dodd, D. L., Cottle, S., & Tatham, C. (1962). *Security analysis: Principles and technique.* New York: McGraw-Hill. (10)

Grant, M., Ives, V., & Ranzoni, J. (1952). Reliability and validity of judges' ratings of adjustment on the Rorschach. *Psychological Monographs, 66*(2, Whole No. 334). (19)

Gray, W. S. (1966). Measuring the analyst's performance. *Financial Analysts Journal, 22*, 56–60. (10)

Grebstein, L. C. (1963). Relative accuracy of actuarial prediction, experienced clinicians, and graduate students in a clinical judgment task. *Journal of Consulting Psychology, 27*, 127–132. (34, 35)

Green, A. E., & Bourne, A. J. (1972). *Reliability technology.* New York: Wiley-Interscience. (40)

Green, D. M., & Swets, J. A. (1966). *Signal detection theory and psychophysics.* New York: Wiley. (29, 43)

Greeno, J. G. (1980, July). *Development of processes for understanding problems.* Paper presented at the conference on The Development of Metacognition, the Formation of Attribution Style, and Learning, Heidelberg, Germany. (31)

Greeno, J. G., James, C. T., Da Polito, F., & Polson, P. G. (1978). *Associative learning: A cognitive analysis.* Englewood Cliffs, NJ: Prentice-Hall. (42)

Gregg, M. B., Bregman, D. J., O'Brien, R. J., & Millar, J. D. (1978). Influenza-related mortality. *Journal of the American Medical Association, 239*(2), 115–116 (22)

Gregory R. (1983). *Measures of consumer's surplus: Reasons for the disparity in observed values.* Keene, NH: Keene State College. (11)

Gregory, R. L. (1970). *The intelligent eye.* New York: McGraw-Hill. (43)

Greist, J. H., Gustafson, D. H., Strauss, F. F., Rowse, G. L., Laughren, T., & Chiles, J. A. (1973). A computer interview for suicide risk prediction. *American Journal of Psychiatry, 130*, 1327–1332. (26)

Grether, D. M., & Plott, C. R. (1979). Economic theory of choice and the preference reversal phenomenon. *American Economic Review, 69*, 623–638. (40, 41)

Griffitt, W., & Jackson, T. (1970). Influence of information about ability and nonability on personnel selection decisions. *Psychological Reports, 27*, 959–962. (27)

Grigg, A. E. (1958). Experience of clinicians, and speech characteristics and statements of clients as variables in clinical judgment. *Journal of Consulting Psychology, 22*, 315–319. (19)

Grinell, M., Keeley, S. M., & Doherty, M. E. (1971). Bayesian predictions of faculty judgments of graduate school success. *Organizational Behavior and Human Performance, 6*, 379–387. (26)

Griner, P. F., & Liptzin, B. (1971). Use of the laboratory in a teaching hospital: Implications for patient care, education, and hospital costs. *Annals of Internal Medicine, 75*, 157–163. (20)

Gritz, E. R. (1975). Effects of methylphenidate on mildly depressed hospitalized adults. In K. R. Hammond & C. R. B. Joyce (Eds.), *Psychoactive drugs and social judgment: Theory and research* (pp. 121–131, 157–163, 185–187). New York: Wiley. (3)

Grosz, H. J., & Grossman, K. G. (1964). The sources of observer variation and bias in clinical judgments: I. The item of psychiatric history. *Journal of Nervous and*

Mental Disease, 138, 105–113. (19)

Guilford, J. P. (1954). *Psychometric methods.* New York: McGraw-Hill. (29)

Gunderson, E. K. E. (1965a). Determinants of reliability in personality ratings. *Journal of Clinical Psychology, 21,* 164–169. (19)

Gunderson, E. K. E. (1965b). The reliability of personality ratings under varied assessment conditions. *Journal of Clinical Psychology, 21,* 161–164. (19)

Gustafson, D. H., Edwards, W., Phillips, L. D., & Slack, W. V. (1969). Subjective probabilities in medical diagnosis. *IEEE Transactions in Man–Machine Systems, 10,* 61–65. (26)

Gustafson, D. H., Greist, J. H., Strauss, F. F., Erdman, H., & Laughren, T. (1977). A probabilistic system for identifying suicide attemptors. *Computers and Biomedical Research, 10,* 83–89. (26)

Gustafson, D. H., Kestly, J. J., Greist, J. H., & Jensen, N. M. (1971). Initial evaluation of a subjective Bayesian diagnostic system. *Health Services Research, 86,* 204–213. (26)

Guttman, L. (1967). A basis for scaling qualitative data. In M. Fishbein (Ed.), *Readings in attitude theory and measurement* (pp. 96–107). New York: Wiley. (30)

Hacking, I. (1965). *Logic of statistical inference.* Cambridge: Cambridge University Press. (43)

Hacking, I. (1975). *The emergence of probability.* Cambridge: Cambridge University Press. (43)

Hagafors, R., & Brehmer, B. (1980a). Effects of information-presentation mode and task complexity on the learning of probabilistic inference tasks. *Scandinavian Journal of Psychology, 21,* 109–113. (16)

Hagafors, R., & Brehmer, B. (1980b). Effects of information-presentation mode and learning paradigm on the learning of probabilistic inference tasks under different levels of memory strain. *Scandinavian Journal of Psychology, 21,* 249–255. (16)

Hagan, J. (1974). Extra-legal attributes and criminal sentencing: An assessment of a sociological viewpoint. *Law and Society Review, 8,* 357–383. (14)

Hakeem, M. (1961). Prediction of parole outcomes from summaries of case histories. *Journal of Criminology, Criminal Law, and Police Science, 52,* 145–150. (13)

Hammack, J., & Brown, G. M., Jr. (1974). *Waterfowl and wetlands: Toward bioeconomic analysis.* Baltimore: Johns Hopkins University Press. (11)

Hammerton, M. (1973). A case of radical probability estimation. *Journal of Experimental Psychology, 101,* 252–254. (40)

Hammond, E. C. (1966). Smoking in relation to the death rates of one million men and women. *National Cancer Institute Monograph, 19,* 127–204. (28)

Hammond, K. R. (1955). Probabilistic functioning and the clinical method. *Psychological Review, 62*(4), 255–262. (Gen. Int., 3, 16, 29, 34, 35, 41)

Hammond, K. R. (1965). New directions in research on conflict resolution. *Journal of Social Issues, 21,* 44–66. (3, 15, 16, 41)

Hammond, K. R. (1966). Probabilistic functionalism: Egon Brunswik's integration of the history, theory, and method of psychology. In K. R. Hammond (Ed.), *The psychology of Egon Brunswik* (pp. 15–80). New York: Holt, Rinehart, & Winston. (3, 15, 34)

Hammond, K. R. (1971). Computer graphics as an aid to learning. *Science, 172,* 903–908. (3, 12, 15)

Hammond, K. R. (1972). Inductive knowing. In J. R. Royce & W. W. Rozeboom

(Eds.), *The psychology of knowing* (pp. 285–346). London: Gordon & Breach. (3, 41)

Hammond, K. R. (1974). *Human judgment and social policy* (Rep. No. 170). Boulder: University of Colorado, Center for Research on Judgment and Policy. (12, 16)

Hammond, K. R. (1978a). *Psychology's scientific revolution: Is it in danger?* (Rep. No. 211). Boulder: University of Colorado, Center for Research on Judgment and Policy. (41)

Hammond, K: R. (1978b). Toward increasing competence of thought in public policy formation. In K. R. Hammond (Ed.), *Judgment and decision in public policy formation, AAAS selected symposium* (pp. 11–32). Boulder, CO: Westview Press. (28)

Hammond, K. R., & Adelman, L. (1976). Science, values, and human judgment. *Science, 194*, 389–396. (8, 16, 28)

Hammond, K. R., Bonauito, G. B., Faucheux, C., Moscovici, S., Frohlich, W. D., Joyce, C. R. B., & DiMajo, G. (1968). A comparison of cognitive conflict between persons in Western Europe and the United States. *International Journal of Psychology, 3*, 1–12. (16)

Hammond, K. R., & Boyle, P. J. (1971). Quasi-rationality, quarrels, and new conceptions of feedback. *Bulletin of the British Psychological Society, 24*, 103–113. (15)

Hammond, K. R., & Brehmer, B. (1973). Quasi-rationality and distrust: Implications for international conflict. In L. Rappoport & D. A. Summers (Eds.), *Human judgment and social interaction* (pp. 338–391). New York: Holt, Rinehart, & Winston. (3, 15, 16, 28, 41)

Hammond, K. R., & Grassia, J. (1985). The cognitive side of conflict: From theory to resolution of policy disputes. In S. Oskamp (Ed.), *Applied social psychology annual: Vol 6. International conflict and national public policy issues* (pp. 233–254). Beverly Hills: Sage. (Pt. V Int.)

Hammond, K. R., Hamm, R. M., Grassia, J., & Pearson, T. (1984). *Direct comparison of intuitive, quasi-rational, and analytical cognition* (Rep. No. 248). Boulder: University of Colorado, Center for Research on Judgment and Policy. (40)

Hammond, K. R., Hursch, C. J., & Todd, F. J. (1964). Analyzing the components of clinical inference. *Psychological Review, 71*, 438–456. (19, 35)

Hammond, K. R., & Marvin, B. A. (1981). *Report to the Rocky Flats Monitoring Committee concerning scientists' judgments of cancer risk* (Rep. No. 232). Boulder: University of Colorado, Center for Research on Judgment and Policy. (16, 28).

Hammond, K. R., McClelland, G. H., & Mumpower, J. (1980). *Human judgment and decision making; Theories, methods, and procedures.* New York: Praeger. (Gen. Int., 41)

Hammond, K. R., Mumpower, J., Dennis, R. L., Fitch, J. S., & Crumpacker, D. W. (1983). Fundamental obstacles to the use of scientific information in public policy making. In F. Rossini, A. Porter, & C. Wolf (Eds.), *Integrated impact assessment* (pp. 168–183). Boulder, CO: Westview Press. (28)

Hammond, K. R., Rohrbaugh, J., Mumpower, J. L., & Adelman, L. (1977). Social judgment theory: Applications in policy formation. In M. F. Kaplan & S. Schwartz (Eds.), *Human judgment and decision processes in applied settings* (pp. 1–30). New York: Academic Press. (7, 16, 28, 32, 38)

Hammond, K. R., & Stewart, T. R. (1974). *The interaction between design and discovery in the study of human judgment* (Rep. No. 152). Boulder: University of Colorado, Center for Research on Judgment and Policy. (3, 41)

Hammond, K. R., Stewart, T. R., Adelman, L., & Wascoe, N. (1975). *Report to the Denver City Council and Mayor regarding the choice of handgun ammunition for the Denver police department* (Rep. No. 179). Boulder: University of Colorado, Center for Research on Judgment and Policy. (7)

Hammond, K. R., Stewart, T. R., Brehmer, B., & Steinmann, D. O. (1975). Social judgment theory. In M. F. Kaplan & S. Schwartz (Eds.), *Human judgment and decision processes* (pp. 271–312). New York: Academic Press. (7, 12, 15, 16, 21, 28, 32, 38, 41)

Hammond, K. R., & Summers, D. A. (1965). Cognitive dependence on linear and nonlinear cues. *Psychological Review, 72,* 215–224. (9, 35)

Hammond, K. R., & Summers, D. A. (1972). Cognitive control. *Psychological Review, 79,* 58–67. (3, 15)

Hammond, K. R., Summers, D. A., & Deane, D. H. (1973). Negative effects of outcome feedback in multiple-cue probability learning. *Organizational Behavior and Human Performance, 9,* 30–34. (3)

Hammond, K. R., & Wascoe, N. E. (Eds.). (1980). *New directions for methodology of social and behavioral science: No. 3. Realizations of Brunswik's respresentative design.* San Francisco: Jossey-Bass. (32)

Harré, R. (1970). *The principles of scientific thinking.* Chicago: University of Chicago Press. (43)

Harris, R. J. (1977). The comprehension of pragmatic implications in advertising. *Journal of Applied Psychology, 62,* 603–608. (27)

Harris, R. J., & Monaco, G. E. (1978). Psychology of pragmatic implication: Information processing between the lines. *Journal of Experimental Psychology: General, 107,* 1–22. (24)

Harsanyi, J. C. (1975). Nonlinear social welfare functions. *Theory and Decisions, 6,* 311–332. (38)

Harsanyi, J. C. (1976). *Essays on ethics, social behavior, and scientific explanation.* Boston: Reidel. (38)

Hattwick, M. A. W., O'Brien, R. J., Hoke, C. H., & Dowdle, W. R. (1976). *Pandemic influenza, the swine influenza virus, and the national influenza immunization program.* Washington, DC: DHEW, Center for Disease Control. (22)

Hausman, W. H. (1969). A note on "The value line contest: A test of the predictability of stockprice changes." *Journal of Business, 42,* 317–320. (10)

Hays, W. L. (1963). *Statistics for psychologists.* New York: Holt, Rinehart, & Winston. (19, 35)

Hearnshaw, L. S. (1981). *Cyril Burt, psychologist.* New York: Random House (Vintage Books). (43)

Heider, F. (1958). *The psychology of interpersonal relations.* New York: Wiley. (13, 30)

Helenius, M. (1973). Socially induced cognitive conflict: A study of disagreement over childrearing policies. In L. Rappoport & D. A. Summers (Eds.), *Human judgment and social interaction* (pp. 208–217). New York: Holt, Rinehart, & Winston. (3)

Hempel, C. G. (1949). The function of general laws in history. In H. Feigl & W. Sellars (Eds.), *Readings in philosophical analysis.* New York: Appleton-Century-Crofts. (33)

Hendrick, C., & Shaffer, D. (no date). *Murder: Effects of number of killers and victim mutilation on simulated jurors' judgments*. Unpublished manuscript, Kent State University. (37)

Henney, J. G. (1947). The jurors look at our judges. *Oklahoma Bar Association Journal, 18,* 1508–1513. (14)

Hersey, J. R. (1968). *Algiers motel incident*. New York: Knopf. (37)

Hershey, J. C., & Schoemaker, P. J. H. (1980). Risk taking and problem context in the domain of losses: An expected-utility analysis. *Journal of Risk and Insurance, 47,* 111–132. (11)

Hester, D. D. (1966). An empirical examination of a commercial bank loan offer function. In K. J. Cohen & F. S. Hammer (Eds.), *Analytical methods in banking* (pp. 178–217). Homewood, IL: Irwin. (10)

Hiler, E. W., & Nesvig, D. (1965). An evaluation of criteria used by clinicians to infer pathology from figure drawings. *Journal of Consulting Psychology, 29,* 520–529. (19)

Hilton, G. (1960). Present position relating to cancer of the lung: Results with radiotherapy alone. *Thorax, 15,* 17–18. (23)

Hochhaus, L. (1972). A table for the calculation of d' and B. *Psychological Bulletin, 77,* 375–376. (37)

Hoffman, P. B. (1973). *Paroling policy feedback* (Supp. Rep. 8). Davis, CA: National Council on Crime and Delinquency Research Center. (13)

Hoffman, P. J. (1960). The paramorphic representation of clinical judgment. *Psychological Bulletin, 57,* 116–131. (16, 19, 34, 35)

Hoffman, P. J. (1967, September). *Non-shrinkable, wrinkle-resistant configural prediction*. Paper presented at the meeting of the American Psychological Association, Washington, DC. (19)

Hoffman, P. J. (1968). Cue-consistency and configurality in human judgment. In B. Kleinmuntz (Ed.), *Formal representation of human judgment* (pp. 53–90). New York: Wiley. (19)

Hoffman, P. J., Earle, T. C., & Slovic, P. (1981). Multidimensional functional learning (MFL) and some new conceptions of feedback. *Organizational Behavior and Human Performance, 27,* 75–102. (41)

Hoffman, P. J., Slovic, P., & Rorer, L. G. (1968). An analysis-of-variance model for the assessment of configural cue utilization in clinical judgment. *Psychological Bulletin, 69,* 338–349. (10, 16, 19)

Hogarth, J. (1971). *Sentencing as a human process*. Toronto: University of Toronto Press. (13)

Hogarth, R. M. (1975a). Cognitive processes and the assessment of subjective probability distributions. *Journal of the American Statistical Association, 70,* 271–289. (41)

Hogarth, R. M. (1975b). Decision time as a function of task complexity. In D. Wendt & C. A. J. Vlek (Eds.), *Utility, probability, and human decision making* (pp. 321–338). Dordrecht: Reidel. (41)

Hogarth, R. M. (1980). *Judgment and choice: The psychology of decision*. Chichester: Wiley. (40, 41)

Hogarth, R. M. (1981). Beyond discrete biases: Functional and dysfunctional aspects of judgmental heuristics. *Psychological Bulletin, 90,* 197–217. (39)

Hogarth, R. M., & Makridakis, S. (1981). The value of decision making in a complex environment: An experimental approach. *Management Science, 27,* 92–107. (41)

Hogarth, R. M., Michaud, C., & Mery, J.-L. (1980). Decision behavior in urban development: A methodological approach and substantive considerations. *Acta Psychologica, 45*, 95–117. (41)

Hoiberg, B. C., & Stires, L. K. (1973). The effect of several types of pretrial publicity on the guilt attributions of simulated jurors. *Journal of Applied Social Psychology, 3*, 267–275. (37)

Holmes, O. W., Jr. (1881). *The common law*. Boston: Little, Brown. (13)

Holsopple, J. G., & Phelan, J. G. (1954). The skills of clinicians in analysis of projective tests. *Journal of Clinical Psychology, 10*, 307–320. (36)

Holt, C. C., Modigliani, F., Muth, J. R., & Simon, H. A. (1960). *Planning production, inventories, and work force*. Englewood Cliffs, NJ: Prentice-Hall. (5)

Holt, R. R. (1958). Clinical and statistical prediction: A reformulation and some new data. *Journal of Abnormal and Social Psychology, 56*, 1–12. (34)

Holt, R. R. (1978). *Methods in clinical psychology: Prediction and research* (Vol. 2). New York: Plenum. (34)

Holtzman, W. H., & Sells, S. B. (1954). Prediction of flying success by clinical analysis of test protocols. *Journal of Abnormal and Social Psychology, 49*, 485–490. (19, 35)

Homans, G. (1961). *Social behavior: Its elementary forms*. New York: Harcourt Brace & World. (38)

Housworth, J., & Langmuir, A. D. (1974). Excess mortality from epidemic influenza, 1957–1966. *American Journal of Epidemiology, 100*, 40–48. (22)

Housworth, J., & Spoon, M. M. (1971). The age distribution of excess mortality during A2 Hong Kong influenza epidemics compared with earlier A2 outbreaks. *American Journal of Epidemiology, 94*, 348–350. (22)

Howard, K. I. (1962). The convergent and discriminant validation of ipsative ratings from three projective instruments. *Journal of Clinical Psychology, 18*, 183–188. (19, 35)

Howard, K. I. (1963). Ratings of projective test protocols as a function of degree of inference. *Educational and Psychological Measurement, 23*, 267–275. (19)

Howard, R. A. (1966). Decision analysis: Applied decision theory. In D. B. Hertz & J. Melese (Eds.), *Proceedings of the Fourth International Conference on Operational Research* (pp. 55–71). New York: Wiley-Interscience. (7)

Howard, R. A., Matheson, J. E., & Miller, K. L. (1977). *Readings in decision analysis*. Menlo Park: Stanford Research Institute. (12)

Hoyer, W. J., Rebok, G. W., & Sved, S. M. (1979). Effects of varying irrelevant information on adult age differences in problem solving. *Journal of Gerontology, 34*, 553–560. (27)

Hume, D. (1977). *An enquiry concerning human understanding* (E. Steinberg, Ed.). Indianapolis, IN: Hackett. (Original work published 1748) (43)

Hunt, W. A., & Jones, N. F. (1958a). Clinical judgment of some aspects of schizophrenic thinking. *Journal of Clinical Psychology, 14*, 235–239. (19)

Hunt, W. A., & Jones, N. F. (1958b). The reliability of clinical judgments of asocial tendency. *Journal of Clinical Psychology, 14*, 233–235. (19)

Hunt, W. A., Jones, N. F., & Hunt, E. B. (1957). Reliability of clinical judgment as a function of clinical experience. *Journal of Clinical Psychology, 13*. 377–378. (19, 35)

Hunt, W. A., & Walker, R. E. (1966). Validity of diagnostic judgment as a function of amount of test information. *Journal of Clinical Psychology, 22*, 154–155. (19)

Hunt, W. A., Walker, R. E., & Jones, N. F. (1960). The validity of clinical ratings for estimating severity of schizophrenia. *Journal of Clinical Psychology, 16,* 391–393. (19)

Hunter, R. M. (1935). Law in the jury room. *Ohio State Law Journal, 2,* 1–19. (14)

Hursch, C. J., Hammond, K. R., & Hursch, J. L. (1964). Some methodological considerations in multiple-cue probability studies. *Psychological Review, 71,* 42–60. (16, 26, 34, 35)

Inhelder, B., & Piaget, J. (1958). *The growth of logical thinking from childhood to adolescence.* New York: Basic Books. (30, 40)

Jacobson, N. S. (1977). Problem-solving and contingency contracting in the treatment of marital discord. *Journal of Consulting and Clinical Psychology, 45,* 52–60. (15)

Jacobson, N. S., & Margolin, G. (1979). *Marital therapy: Strategies based on social learning and behavior exchange principles.* New York: Bruner/Mazel. (15)

Jacobson, N. S., McDonald, D., & Folletee, W. (1981, November). *Attributional differences between distressed and nondistressed married couples.* Paper presented at the meeting of the American Association of Advancement of Behavior Therapy, Toronto. (15)

Janis, I. L., & Mann, L. (1977). *Decision making: A psychological analysis of conflict, choice, and commitment.* New York: Free Press. (39)

Jenkins, H. M., & Ward, W. C. (1965). Judgment of contingency between responses and outcomes. *Psychological Monographs, 79* (1, Whole No. 594). (30, 42)

Jenkins, J. J. (1974). Remember that old theory of memory? Well, forget it! *American Psychologist, 29,* 785–795. (3)

Jennings, D. L., Amabile, T. M., & Ross, L. (1982). Informal covariation assessment: Data-based versus theory-based judgments. In D. Kahneman, P. Slovic, & A. Tversky (Eds.), *Judgment under uncertainty: Heuristics and biases* (pp. 211–230). Cambridge: Cambridge University Press. (40)

Jensen, M. C. (1968). The performance of mutual funds in the period 1945–1964. *Journal of Finance, 23,* 389–416. (10)

Johansson, R., & Brehmer, B. (1979). Inferences from incomplete information: A note. *Organizational Behavior and Human Performance, 24,* 141–145. (16, 42)

Johnson, C. J. (1981). Cancer incidence in areas contaminated with radionuclides near a nuclear installation. *Ambio, 10,* 176–182. (28)

Johnson, E. J. (1979, December). *Deciding how to decide: The effort of making a decision.* Unpublished manuscript, University of Chicago, Graduate School of Business. (39)

Johnson-Abercrombie, M. L. (1960). *The anatomy of judgment.* New York: Basic Books. (24)

Johnston, R., & McNeal, B. F. (1967). Statistical versus clinical prediction: Length of neuropsychiatric hospital stay. *Journal of Abnormal Psychology, 72,* 335–340. (19)

Jones, E., & Davis, K. (1965). From acts to dispositions. In L. Berkowitz (Ed.), *Advances in experimental social psychology* (Vol. 2). New York: Academic Press. (13)

Jones, N. F., Jr. (1959). The validity of clinical judgments of schizophrenic pathology based on verbal responses to intelligence test items. *Journal of Clinical Psychology, 15,* 396–400. (19)

Joyce, C. R. B., Berry, H., Chaput de Saintonge, D. M., Domenet, J., Fowler, P.,

& Mason, R. M. (1977). Judgment analysis of investigators' assessments: A way to reduce one important source of error in multi-centre trials. In K. Fehr, E. C. Huskisson, & E. Wilhelmi (Eds.), *International coordination of drug trials*. EULAR Bulletin Monograph, 1. (21)

Jungermann, H., von Ulardt, I., & Hausmann, L. (1983). The role of the goal for generating actions. In P. C. Humphreys, O. Svenson, & A. Vari (Eds.), *Analysing and aiding decision processes* (pp. 223–236). Amsterdam: North Holland. (39)

Kahneman, D., Slovic, P., & Tversky, A. (Eds.). (1982). *Judgment under uncertainty: Heuristics and biases*. Cambridge: Cambridge University Press. (9, 39, 40)

Kahneman, D., & Tversky A. (1972). Subjective probability: A judgment of representativeness. *Cognitive Psychology, 3*, 430–454. (2, 10, 12, 40, 41, 43)

Kahneman, D., & Tversky, A. (1973). On the psychology of prediction. *Psychological Review, 80*, 237–251. (2, 12, 34, 36, 40, 41, 42)

Kahneman, D., & Tversky, A. (1979a). Intuitive prediction: Biases and corrective procedures. *TIMS Studies in Management Sciences, 12*, 313–327. (40)

Kahneman, D., & Tversky, A. (1979b). Prospect theory: An analysis of decision under risk. *Econometrica, 47*, 263–291. (11, 12, 17, 23, 39, 41)

Kahneman, D., & Tversky, A. (1982a). On the study of statistical intuitions. *Cognition, 11*, 123–141. (39, 40)

Kahneman, D., & Tversky, A., (1982b). A reply to Evans. *Cognition, 12*, 325–326. (39)

Kahneman, D., & Tversky, A. (1982c). The simulation heuristic. In D. Kahneman, P. Slovic, & A. Tversky (Eds.), *Judgment under uncertainty: Heuristics and biases* (pp. 201–208). Cambridge: Cambridge University Press. (11)

Kahnemon, A. (1973). *Attention and effort*. Englewood Cliffs, NJ: Prentice-Hall. (27)

Kalven, H., Jr., & Zeisel, H. (1966). *The American jury*. Boston: Little, Brown. (14, 37)

Kalven, H., Jr., & Zeisel, H. (1967, May/June). The American jury: Notes for an English controversy. *Chicago Bar Record*, pp. 195–201. (14)

Kaplan, J. (1968). Decision theory and the factfinding process. *Stanford Law Review, 20*, 1065–1092. (12)

Kaplan, J. (1973). *Criminal justice: Introductory cases and materials*. Mineola, NY: Foundation Press. (14)

Kaplan, M., & Kemmerick, G. D. (1974). Juror judgment as information integration: Combining evidential and nonevidential information. *Journal of Personality and Social Psychology, 30*, 493–499. (37)

Kaplan, M. F., & Schwartz, S. (Eds.). (1975). *Human judgment and decision processes*. New York: Academic Press. (7)

Karplus, R., & Peterson, R. (1970). Intellectual development beyond elementary school: II. Ratio, a survey. *School Science and Mathematics, 70*, 813–820. (30)

Kauffman, K. G., & Shorett, A. (1977, September/October). A perspective on public involvement in water management decisionmaking. *Public Administration Review*, pp. 467–471. (8)

Kausler, D. H., & Kleim, D. M. (1978). Age differences in processing relevant versus irrelevant stimuli in multiple-item recognition learning. *Journal of Gerontology, 33*, 87–93. (27)

Keeney, R. L., & Kirkwood, C. W. (1975). Group decision making using cardinal social welfare functions. *Management Science, 22*, 430–437. (38)

Keeney, R. L., & Raiffa, H. (1976). *Decisions with multiple objectives: Preferences and value tradeoffs.* New York: Wiley. (23, 38)

Kelley, H. (1967). Attribution theory in social psychology. In D. Levine (Ed.), *Nebraska symposium on motivation* (pp. 192–241). Lincoln: University of Nebraska Press. (30)

Kelley, H. (1973). The processes of causal attribution. *American Psychologist, 28,* 107–128. (3, 13)

Kelley, H. (1979). *Personal relationships: Their structures and processes.* Hillsdale, NJ: Erlbaum. (15)

Kelley, H., & Thibaut, J. (1978). *Interpersonal relations: A theory of interdependence.* New York: Wiley. (15)

Kelly, E. L., & Fiske, D. W. (1951). *The prediction of performance in clinical psychology.* Ann Arbor: University of Michigan Press. (19)

Kelly, G. (1955). *The psychology of personal constructs* (2 vols.). New York: Norton. (15, 41)

Kendall, M. G., & Babington Smith, B. (1939). *Tables of random sampling numbers.* Cambridge: Cambridge University Press. (43)

Kerlinger, F. N., & Pedhazur, E. J. (1973). *Multiple regression in behavioral research.* New York: Holt, Rinehart, & Winston. (38)

Kerr, N. L., Atkin, R. S., Stasser, G., Meek, D., Holt, R. W., & Davis, J. H. (1976). Guilt beyond a reasonable doubt: Effects of concept definition and assigned decision rule on the judgments of mock jurors. *Journal of Personality and Social Psychology, 34,* 282–294. (37)

Kidd, J. B. (1970). The utilization of subjective probabilities in production planning. *Acta Psychologica, 34,* 338–347. (12)

Killeen, P. R. (1978). Superstition: A matter of bias, not detectability. *Science, 199,* 88–90. (41)

Kirwan, J. R., Chaput de Saintonge, D. M., Joyce, C. R. B., & Currey, H. L. F. (1983a). Clinical judgment in rheumatoid arthritis: I. Rheumatologists' opinions and the development of "paper patients." *Annals of the Rheumatic Diseases, 42,* 644–647. (21)

Kirwan, J. R., Chaput de Saintonge, D. M., Joyce, C. R. B., & Currey, H. L. F. (1983b). Clinical judgment analysis: Practical application in rheumatoid arthritis. *British Journal of Rheumatology, 22*(S), 18–23. (32)

Klein, M., & Teilmann, K. (Eds.). (1980). *Handbook of criminal justice evaluation.* Beverly Hills, CA: Sage. (1)

Kleinmuntz, B. (1963a). MMPI decision rules for the identification of college maladjustment: A digital computer approach. *Psychological Monographs, 77* (14, Whole No. 577). (19)

Kleinmuntz, B. (1963b). Personality test interpretation by digital computer. *Science, 139,* 416–418. (19, 34)

Kleinmuntz, B. (1963c). Profile analysis revisited: A heuristic approach. *Journal of Counseling Psychology, 10,* 315–324. (19)

Kleinmuntz, B. (1967). Sign and seer: Another example. *Journal of Abnormal Psychology, 72,* 163–165. (34)

Kleinmuntz, B. (1968). The processing of clinical information by man and machine. In B. Kleinmuntz (Ed.), *Formal representation of human judgment* (pp. 149–186). New York: Wiley. (29, 34)

Kleinmuntz, B. (1969). Personality test interpretation by computer and clinician.

In J. N. Butcher (Ed.), *MMPI: Research developments and clinical applications* (pp. 97–104). New York: McGraw-Hill. (34)

Kleinmuntz, B. (1970). Clinical information processing by computer. In K. H. Craik, B. Kleinmuntz, R. L. Rosnow, R. Rosenthal, J. A. Cheyne, & R. Walters (Eds.), *New directions in psychology 4* (pp. 123–210). New York: Holt, Rinehart, & Winston. (34)

Kleinmuntz, B. (1972). Medical information processing by computer. In J. A. Jacquez (Ed.), *Computer diagnosis and diagnostic methods* (pp. 45–72). Springfield, IL: Thomas. (34)

Kleinmuntz, B. (1975). The computer as clinician. *American Psychologist, 30,* 379–387. (34)

Kleinmuntz, B. (1984). Diagnostic problem solving by computer. *Computers in Biology and Medicine, 14,* 255–270. (34)

Kleinmuntz, D. N., & Kleinmuntz, B. (1981). Decision strategies in simulated environments. *Behavioral Science, 26,* 294–305. (41)

Kletz, T. A. (1981). Benefits and risks: Their assessment in relation to human needs. In R. F. Griffiths (Ed.), *Dealing with risk* (pp. 36–53). New York: Halsted Press/Wiley. (28)

Kluckhohn, F. R., & Strodtbeck, F. L. (1961). *Variations in value of orientation.* New York: Row, Peterson. (25)

Knetsch, J. L., & Sinden, J. A. (1984). Willingness to pay and compensation demanded: Experimental evidence of an unexpected disparity in measures of value. *Quarterly Journal of Economics, 99,* 507–521. (11)

Knuth, D. E. (1969). *The art of computer programming, Vol. II: Seminumerical algorithms.* Reading, MA: Addison-Wesley. (43)

Kochan, T. (1980). Collective bargaining and organizational behavior research. In B. Staw & L. Cummings (Eds.), *Research in organizational behavior* (Vol. 2). Greenwich, CT: JAI Press. (17)

Kochan, T., & Jick, T. (1978). The public sector mediation process: A theory and empirical examination. *Journal of Conflict Resolution, 22,* 209–240. (17)

Kogan, N., & Wallach, M. A. (1967). Risk taking as a function of the situation, the person, and the group. In *New directions in psychology 3* (pp. 111–278). New York: Holt, Rinehart, & Winston. (10)

Koopmans, T. C. (1964). On flexibility of future preferences. In M. W. Shelly & G. L. Bryan (Eds.), *Human judgments and optimality* (pp. 243–254). New York: Wiley. (41)

Koran, L. M. (1975). The reliability of clinical methods, data, and judgments. *New England Journal of Medicine, 293,* 642–646, 695–701. (34)

Koriat, A., Lichtenstein, S., & Fischhoff, B. (1980). Reasons for confidence. *Journal of Experimental Psychology: Human Learning and Memory, 6,* 107–118. (36, 40)

Kostlan, A. (1954). A method for the empirical study of psychodiagnosis. *Journal of Consulting Psychology, 18,* 83–88. (19)

Krechevsky, I. (1932). "Hypotheses" in rats. *Psychological Review, 39,* 516–532. (42)

Krieg, A. F., Gambino, R., & Galen, R. S. (1975). Why are clinical laboratory tests performed? When are they valid? *Journal of the American Medical Association, 233,* 76–78. (12, 20)

Kriger, S. F., & Kroes, W. H. (1972). Child rearing attitudes of Chinese, Jewish, and Protestant mothers. *Journal of Social Psychology, 86,* 205–210. (25)

Krupp, M. A., Sweet, N. J., Jawetz, E., Biglieri, E. G., Roe, R. L., & Camargo, C. A. (1979). *Physicians handbook*. Los Altos, CA: Lange Medical Publications. (12)

Kruskal, J. B. (1965). Analysis of factorial experiments by estimating monotone transformations of the data. *Journal of the Royal Statistical Society: Series B, 27*, 251–263. (4)

Kubovy, M., & Psotka, J. (1976). The predominance of seven and the apparent spontaneity of numerical choices. *Journal of Experimental Psychology: Human Perception and Performance, 2*, 291–294. (43)

Kunreuther, H. (1969). Extensions of Bowman's theory on managerial decision making. *Management Science, 15*, 415–439. (10)

Kurtz, P., & Karplus, R. (1979). Intellectual development beyond elementary school: VII. Teaching for proportional reasoning. *School Science and Mathematics, 79*, 387–398. (30)

Kurtz, R. M., & Garfield, S. L. (1978). Illusory correlation: A further exploration of Chapman's paradigm. *Journal of Consulting and Clinical Psychology, 46*, 1009–1015. (36)

Kuylenstierna, J., & Brehmer, B. (1981). Memory aids in the learning of probabilistic inference tasks. *Organizational Behavior and Human Performance, 28*, 415–424. (16)

Kyburg, H. E. (1970). *Probability and inductive logic*. London: Macmillan. (43)

Lakatos, I. (1970). Falsification and the methodology of scientific research programmes. In I. Lakatos & A. Musgrave (Eds.), *Criticism and the growth of knowledge* (pp. 91–195). Cambridge: Cambridge University Press. (43)

Landy, D., & Aronson, E. (1969). The influence of the character of the criminal and victim in the decisions of simulated jurors. *Journal of Experimental Social Psychology, 5*, 141–152. (37)

Langer, E. J. (1975). The illusion of control. *Journal of Personality and Social Psychology, 32*, 311–328. (41)

Langer, E. J. (1977). The psychology of chance. *Journal for the Theory of Social Behaviour, 7*, 185–207. (41)

Larntz, K. (1975). Reanalysis of Vidmar's data on the effects of decision alternatives on verdicts of simulated jurors. *Journal of Personality and Social Psychology, 31*, 123–125. (37)

Larsen, A., & Bundesen, C. (1978). Size scaling in visual pattern recognition. *Journal of Experimental Psychology: Human Perception and Performance, 4*, 1–20. (27)

Lathrop, R. G. (1967). Perceived variability. *Journal of Experimental Psychology, 73*, 498–502. (10)

Laughhunn, D. J., Payne, J. W., & Crum R. (1980). Managerial risk preferences for below-target returns. *Management Science, 26*, 1238–1249. (41)

Lazear, E. (1979). Why is there mandatory retirement? *Journal of Political Economy, 87*, 1261–1284. (9)

Ledley, R. S. (1972). Syntax-directed concept analysis in the reasoning foundations of medical diagnosis. In J. A. Jacquez (Ed.), *Computer diagnosis and diagnostic methods* (pp. 152–168). Springfield, IL: Thomas. (34)

Ledley, R. S., & Lusted, L. B. (1959a). Reasoning foundations of medical diagnosis. *Science, 130*, 9–22. (34)

Ledley, R. S., & Lusted, L. B. (1959b). The use of electronic computers to aid medical diagnosis. *Proceedings of the IRE, 47*, 1970–1977. (26)

774   REFERENCES

Lefevre, E. (1968). *Reminiscences of a stock operator.* New York: Pocket Books. (10)
Lempert, R. O. (1977). Modeling relevance. *Michigan Law Review, 75,* 1021–1057. (12)
Leon, M. (1980). Integration of intent and consequence information in children's moral judgments. In F. Wilkening, J. Becker, & T. Trabasso (Eds.), *Information integration by children* (pp. 71–98). Hillsdale, NJ: Erlbaum. (4)
Lepper, S. J. (1967). Effects of alternative tax structures on individuals' holdings of financial assets. In D. D. Hester & J. Tobin (Eds.), *Risk aversion and portfolio choice* (pp. 51–109). New York: Wiley. (10)
Leventhal, G. S. (1976). The distribution of rewards and resources in groups and organizations. In L. Berkowitz (Ed.), *Advances in experimental social psychology* (Vol. 9). New York: Academic Press. (38)
Leventhal, H. (1974). Environmental decisionmaking and the role of the courts. *University of Pennsylvania Law Review, 122,* 509–555. (12)
Levi, I. (1967). *Gambling with truth: An essay on induction and the aims of science.* Cambridge, MA: MIT Press. (43)
Levin, I. (1977). The development of time concepts in young children: Reasoning about duration. *Child Development, 48,* 435–444. (31)
Levin, I. (1979). Interference of time-related and unrelated cues with duration comparisons of young children: Analysis of Piaget's formulation of the relation of time and speed. *Child Development, 50,* 469–477. (31)
Levine, F. J., & Tapp, J. L. (1973). The psychology of criminal identification: The gap from Wade to Kirby. *University of Pennsylvania Law Review, 121,* 1079–1131. (12)
Levy, B. I., & Ulman, E. (1967). Judging psychopathology from painting. *Journal of Abnormal Psychology, 72,* 182–187. (19)
Lewontin, R. C. (1979). Sociobiology as an adaptationist program. *Behavioral Science, 24,* 5–14. (41)
Lichtenstein, S., & Fischhoff, B. (1977). Do those who know more also know more about how much they know? The calibration of probability judgments. *Organizational Behavior and Human Performance, 20,* 159–183. (24, 40)
Lichtenstein, S., & Fischhoff, B. (1980). Training for calibration. *Organizational Behavior and Human Performance, 26,* 149–171. (27, 40)
Lichtenstein, S., Fischhoff, B., & Phillips, L. D. (1977). Calibration of probabilities: The state of the art. In H. Jungermann & G. de Zeeuw (Eds.), *Decision making and change in human affairs* (pp. 275–324). Dordrecht: Reidel. (17, 24, 25, 40, 41)
Lichtenstein, S., Fischhoff, B., & Phillips, L. D. (1982). Calibration of probabilities: The state of the art to 1980. In D. Kahneman, P. Slovic, & A. Tversky (Eds.), *Judgment under uncertainty: Heuristics and biases* (pp. 306–334). Cambridge: Cambridge University Press. (40)
Lichtenstein, S., & Slovic, P. (1971). Reversals of preference between bids and choices in gambling decisions. *Journal of Experimental Psychology, 89,* 46–55. (10, 12, 40)
Lichtenstein, S., & Slovic, P. (1973). Response-induced reversals of preference in gambling: An extended replication in Las Vegas. *Journal of Experimental Psychology, 101,* 16–20. (6, 12, 40)
Lichtenstein, S., Slovic, P., Fischhoff, B., Combs, B., & Layman, M. (1976). *Perceived frequency of low probability, lethal events* (Rep. No. 76–2). Eugene, OR: Decision Research. (24)

Lichtenstein, S., Slovic, P., Fischhoff, B., Layman, M., & Combs, B. (1978). Judged frequency of lethal events. *Journal of Experimental Psychology: Human Learning and Memory, 4,* 551–578. (6)

Lindblom, C. E. (1959). The science of "muddling through." *Public Administration Review, 19,* 79–88. (41)

Lindell, M. K. (1974). *Differential effects of cognitive and outcome feedback in improving judgmental accuracy* (Rep. No. 178). Boulder: University of Colorado, Center for Research on Judgment and Policy. (3)

Lindley, D. V. (1971). *Making decisions.* New York: Wiley. (25)

Lindzey, G. (1965). Seer versus sign. *Journal of Experimental Research in Personality, 1,* 17–26. (34)

Little, K. B., & Schneidman, E. S. (1959). Congruencies among interpretations of psychological test and anamnestic data. *Psychological Monographs, 73*(6, Whole No. 476). (19, 36)

Livermore, J. M., Malmquist, C. P., & Meehl, P. E. (1968). On the justifications for civil commitment. *University of Pennsylvania Law Review, 117,* 75–96. (12)

Loeb, G. (1965). *The battle for investment survival.* New York: Simon & Schuster. (10)

Loftus, E. (1974). Reconstructing memory: The incredible eyewitness. *Psychology Today, 8*(7), 116–119. (24)

Loftus, E. F. (1980). Impact of expert psychological testimony on the unreliability of eyewitness identification. *Journal of Applied Psychology, 65,* 9–15. (12)

Loftus, G. R., & Loftus, E. F. (1976). *Human memory: The processing of information.* New York: Halsted Press. (12)

Long, B., & Henderson, E. (1972). *The effects of pupils' race, test scores, and classroom behavior on the academic expectancies of southern and non-southern white teachers.* Paper presented at the meeting of the American Educational Research Association, Chicago. (32)

Lopes, L. L. (1976). Model-based decision and inference in stud poker. *Journal of Experimental Psychology: General, 105,* 217–239. (4)

Lopes, L. L. (1980). *Doing the impossible: A note on induction and the experience of randomness.* Madison: University of Wisconsin, Department of Psychology. (41)

Lopes, L. L., & Ekberg, P.-H. S. (1980). Test of an ordering hypothesis in risky decision making. *Acta Psychologica, 45,* 161–167. (41)

Lord, C. G., Ross, L., & Lepper, M. R. (1979). Biased assimilation and attitude polarization: The effects of prior theories on subsequently considered evidence. *Journal of Personality and Social Psychology, 37,* 2098–2109. (36)

Lorie, J. H. (1966). Some comments on recent quantitative and formal research on the stock market. *Journal of Business, 39*(Part II), 107–110. (10)

Low, L. A., Coste, E., & Kirkup, C. (1980). Developmental differences in concept transfer as a function of variability of irrelevant features during acquisition. *Bulletin of the Psychonomic Society, 16,* 19–22. (27)

Lowrance, W. (1976). *Of acceptable risk: Science and the determination of safety.* Los Altos, CA: Kaufmann. (28)

Lowrance, W. (1981, July 6). Probing societal risk. *Chemical and Engineering News,* pp. 13–20. (28)

Lucas, R. E., Jr. (1976). Econometric policy evaluation: A critique. In K. Brunner & A. H. Meltzer (Eds.), *The Phillips curve and labor markets* (pp. 19–46). Amsterdam: North Holland. (41)

Luce, R. D., & Raiffa, H. (1957). *Games and decision: Introduction and critical survey.* New York: Wiley. (38)

Luce, R. D., & Tukey, J. W. (1964). Simultaneous conjoint measurement: A new type of fundamental measurement. *Journal of Mathematical Psychology, 1,* 1–27. (4)

Ludke, R. L., Stauss, F. Y., & Gustafson, D. H. (1977). Comparison of methods for estimating subjective probability distributions. *Organizational Behavior and Human Performance, 19,* 162–179. (40)

Lueger, R. J., & Petzel, T. P. (1979). Illusory correlation in clinical judgment: Effects of amount of information to be processed. *Journal of Consulting and Clinical Psychology, 47,* 1120–1121. (36)

Luft, J. (1950). Implicit hypotheses and clinical predictions. *Journal of Abnormal and Social Psychology, 45,* 756–760. (19)

Luft, J. (1951). Differences in prediction based on hearing versus reading verbatim clinical interviews. *Journal of Consulting Psychology, 15,* 115–119. (19)

Lunia, S., Parthasarathy, K. L., Bakshi, S., & Bender, M. A. (1975). An evaluation of ^{99m}Tc-sulfur colloid liver scintiscans and their usefulness in metastatic workup: A review of 1,424 studies. *Journal of Nuclear Medicine, 16,* 62–65. (20)

Lussier, R. J., Perlman, D., & Breen, L. J. (1977). Causal attributions, attitude similarity, and the punishment of drug offenders. *British Journal of Addiction, 72,* 357–364. (13)

Lusted, L. B. (1965). Computer techniques in medical diagnosis. In R. W. Stacy & B. D. Waxman (Eds.), *Computers in biomedical research* (Vol. 1, pp. 319–338). New York: Academic Press. (34)

Lusted, L. B. (1968). *Introduction to medical decision making.* Springfield, IL: Thomas. (36)

Lusted, L. B. (1975). In the process of solution. *New England Journal of Medicine, 293,* 255–256. (20)

Lusted, L. B., Roberts, H. V., Edwards, W., Wallace, P. L., Lahiff, M., Loop, J. W., Bell, R. S., Thornbury, J. R., Seale, D. L., Steele, J. P., & Fryback, D. G. (1980). *Efficacy of x-ray procedures.* American College of Radiology. (40)

Lykken, D. T. (1975). The right way to use a lie detector. *Psychology Today, 8*(10), 56–60. (40)

Lyon, D., & Slovic, P. (1976). Dominance of accuracy information and neglect of base rates in probability estimation. *Acta Psychologica, 40,* 287–298. (40, 41)

Mackinnon, A. J., & Wearing, A. J. (1980). Complexity and decision making. *Behavioral Science, 25,* 285–296. (41)

Magee, J. F. (1964). Decision trees for decision making. *Harvard Business Review, 42,* 126–138. (10)

Mahoney, M. J. (1977). Publication prejudices: An experimental study of confirmatory bias in the peer review system. *Cognitive Therapy and Research, 1,* 161–175. (36)

Makridakis, S. (1976). A survey of time series. *International Statistical Review, 44,* 29–70. (41)

Makridakis, S. (1978). Time-series analysis and forecasting: An update and evaluation. *International Statistical Review, 46,* 255–278. (41)

Makridakis, S., & Hibon, M. (1979). Accuracy of forecasting: An empirical investigation. *Journal of the Royal Statistical Society: Series A, 142,* 97–125. (41)

Mann, L., & Janis, I. L. (1982). Conflict theory of decision making and the expectancy-value approach. In N. T. Feather (Ed.), *Expectations and actions* (pp. 341–364). Hillsdale, NJ: Erlbaum. (39)

March, J. G. (1978). Bounded rationality, ambiguity, and the engineering of choice. *Bell Journal of Economics, 9,* 587–608. (11, 39, 41)

March, J., & Simon, H. (1958). *Organizations.* New York: Wiley. (17)

Markman, H. J. (1979). The application of a behavioral model of marriage in predicting relationship satisfaction for couples planning marriage. *Journal of Consulting and Clinical Psychology, 47,* 743–749. (15)

Markman, H. J. (1981). The prediction of marital distress: A five-year follow-up. *Journal of Consulting and Clinical Psychology, 49,* 760–762. (15)

Markman, H. J. (1984). The longitudinal study of couples' interactions: Implications for understanding and predicting the development of marital distress. In K. Hahlweg & N. S. Jacobson (Eds.), *Marital interaction: Analysis and modification* (pp. 253–281). New York: Guilford Press. (15)

Markman, H. J., Jamieson, K. J., & Floyd, F. J. (1983). The assessment of modification of premarital relationships: Preliminary findings on the etiology and prevention of marital and family distress. In J. Vincent (Ed.), *Advances in family intervention*, assessment and theory (Vol. 3). Greenwich, CT: JAI Press. (15)

Markman, H. J., Notarius, C. I., Stephen, T., & Smith, R. J. (1981). Behavioral observation systems for couples: The current status. In E. E. Filsinger & R. A. Lewis (Eds.), *Assessing marriage: New behavioral approaches* (pp. 234–262). Beverly Hills, CA: Sage. (15)

Markowitz, H. M. (1959). *Portfolio selection: Efficient diversification of investments.* New York: Wiley. (10)

Marks, D. F., & Clarkson, J. K. (1972). An explanation of conservatism in the bookbag-and-pokerchips situation. *Acta Psychologica, 36,* 145–160. (40)

Marks, P. A. (1961). An assessment of the diagnostic process in a child guidance setting. *Psychological Monographs, 75* (3, Whole No. 507). (19)

Marshall, J. (1968). *Intention in law and society.* New York: Funk & Wagnalls. (13)

Martin-Löf, P. (1966). The definition of random sequences. *Information and Control, 9,* 602–619. (43)

Martinson, R. (1974). What works? Questions and answers about prison reform. *Public Interest, 35,* 22–54. (13)

McAllister, D. W., Mitchell, T. R., & Beach, L. R. (1979). The contingency model for the selection of decision strategies: An empirical test of the effects of significance, accountability, and reversibility. *Organizational Behavior and Human Performance, 24,* 228–244. (39)

McArthur, C. (1954). Analyzing the clinical process. *Journal of Counseling Psychology, 1,* 203–208. (19)

McCall, R., & Appelbaum, M. (1973). Bias in the analysis of repeated-measures designs: Some alternative approaches. *Child Development, 44,* 401–415. (30)

McClelland, G. H., & Rohrbaugh, J. (1978). Who accepts the Pareto axiom? The role of utility and equity in arbitration decisions. *Behavioral Science, 23,* 446–456. (38)

McClintock, C. G. (1972). Social motivation: A set of propositions. *Behavioral Science, 17,* 438–454. (38)

McCloskey, M., Caramazza, A., & Green, B. (1980). Curvilinear motion in the absence of external forces: Naive beliefs about the motion of objects. *Science,*

210, 1139–1141. (40)

McDermott, R. P. (1976). Achieving school failure: An anthropological approach to illiteracy and social stratification. In H. Singer & R. B. Ruddell (Eds.), *Theoretical models and processes of reading* (2nd ed., pp. 389–428). Newark, DE: International Reading Association. (32)

McGargee, E. I. (1976). The prediction of dangerous behavior. *Criminal Justice and Behavior*, *3*, 3–22. (40)

McNeil, B. J., & Adelstein, S. J. (1975). Measures of clinical efficacy: The value of case finding in hypertensive renovascular disease. *New England Journal of Medicine*, *293*, 221–226. (20)

McNeil, B. J., Keeler, E., & Adelstein, S. J. (1976). Primer on certain elements of medical decision making. *New England Journal of Medicine*, *293*, 211–215. (20)

McNeil, B. J., Pauker, S., Sox, H., Jr., & Tversky, A. (1982). On the elicitation of preferences for alternative therapies. *New England Journal of Medicine*, *306*, 1259–1262. (11)

McNeil, B. J., Varady, P. D., Burrows, B. A., & Adelstein, S. J. (1975). Measures of clinical efficacy: Cost-effectiveness calculations in the diagnosis and treatment of hypertensive renovascular disease. *New England Journal of Medicine*, *293*, 216–221. (20)

McNeil, B. J., Weichselbaum, R., & Pauker, S. G. (1978). Fallacy of the five-year survival in lung cancer. *New England Journal of Medicine*, *299*, 1397–1401. (23)

Meehl, P. E. (1954). *Clinical versus statistical prediction: A theoretical analysis and a review of the evidence*. Minneapolis: University of Minnesota Press. (10, 12, 19, 34, 35, 36)

Meehl, P. E. (1956). Wanted: A good cookbook. *American Psychologist*, *11*, 263–272. (19)

Meehl, P. E. (1957). When shall we use our heads instead of the formula? *Journal of Counseling Psychology*, *4*, 268–273. (19)

Meehl, P. E. (1959). A comparison of clinicians with five statistical methods of identifying psychotic MMPI profiles. *Journal of Counseling Psychology*, *6*, 102–109. (19)

Meehl, P. E. (1960). The cognitive activity of the clinician. *American Psychologist*, *15*, 19–27. (19, 36)

Meehl, P. E. (1965). Seer over sign: The first good example. *Journal of Experimental Research in Personality*, *1*, 27–32. (34)

Meehl, P. E. (1973). *Psychodiagnosis: Selected papers*. Minneapolis: University of Minnesota Press. (34)

Meehl, P. E., & Rosen, A. (1955). Antecedent probability and the efficiency of psychometric signs, patterns, or cutting scores. *Psychological Bulletin*, *52*, 194–216. (36, 40)

Megargee, E. I. (1975). *Crime and delinquency*. Morristown, NJ: General Learning Press. (13)

Meyer, P. (1973). Evidence in the future. *Canadian Bar Review*, *51*, 107–118. (12)

Miller, D. W., & Starr, M. K. (1967). *The structure of human decisions*. Englewood Cliffs, NJ: Prentice-Hall. (39)

Miller, M. (1972). The indeterminate sentence paradigm: Resocialization or social control? *Issues in Criminology*, *7*, 101–121. (13)

Miller, M. J., Brehmer, B., & Hammond, K. R. (1970). Communication and conflict reduction: A cross-national study. *International Journal of Psychology*, 5, 44–56. (16)

Miller, W. (1973). Ideology and criminal justice policy: Some current issues. *Journal of Criminal Law and Criminology*, 64, 141–162. (13)

Minsky, M. (1975). A framework for representing knowledge. In P. H. Winston (Ed.), *The psychology of computer vision* (pp. 211–280). New York: McGraw-Hill. (32)

Mischel, W. (1968). *Personality and assessment*. New York: Wiley. (12, 14, 43)

Mischel, W. (1973). Toward a cognitive social learning reconceptualization of personality. *Psychological Review*, 80, 252–283. (41)

Mischel, W. (1979). On the interface of cognition and personality: Beyond the person–situation debate. *American Psychologist*, 34, 740–754. (41)

Mitchell, H. E., & Byrne, D. (1972, May). *Minimizing the influence of irrelevant factors in the courtroom: The defendant's character, judge's instructions, and authoritarianism.* Paper presented at the meeting of the Midwestern Psychological Association, Cleveland. (27)

Montague, W. E. (1965). Effect of irrelevant information on a complex auditory-discrimination task. *Journal of Experimental Psychology*, 69, 230–236. (27)

Montangero, J. (1977). *La notion de durée chez l'enfant de 5 à 9 ans.* Paris: Presses Universitaires de France. (31)

Montgomery, H., & Svenson, O. (1976). On decision rules and information processing strategies for choices among multiattribute alternatives. *Scandinavian Journal of Psychology*, 17, 283–291. (39)

Mori, I. (1976). A cross-cultural study on children's conception of speed and duration: A comparison between Japanese and Thai children. *Japanese Psychological Research*, 18, 105–112. (31)

Morrison, A., & McIntyre, D. (1969). *Teachers and teaching.* Baltimore, MD: Penguin Books. (32)

Morrison, D. (1976). *Multivariate statistical methods.* New York: McGraw-Hill. (30)

Mountain, C. F. (1976). The relationship of prognosis to morphology and the anatomic extent of disease: Studies of a new clinical staging system. In L. Israel & A. P. Chahinian (Eds.), *Lung cancer: Natural history, prognosis, and therapy* (pp. 107–140). New York: Academic Press. (23)

Mountain, C. F., Carr, D. T., & Anderson, W. A. D. (1974). A system for clinical staging of lung cancer. *American Journal of Roentgenology, Radium Therapy, and Nuclear Medicine*, 120, 130–138. (23)

Mowen, J. C., & Linder, D. E. (1976, April). *The theory of signal detection as an analogy to the jury decision making process.* Paper presented at the meeting of the Rocky Mountain Psychological Association, Phoenix, AZ. (37)

Mulholland, J. (1927). *Quicker than the eye.* Indianapolis, IN: Bobbs–Merrill. (43)

Mumpower, J. L., & Hammond, K. R. (1974). Entangled task-dimensions: An impediment to interpersonal learning. *Organizational Behavior and Human Performance*, 11, 377–389. (3)

Munsterberg, H. (1908). *On the witness stand.* New York: Doubleday, Page. (24)

Munsterberg, H. (1976). *On the witness stand: Essays on psychology and crime.* New York: AMS Press. (12)

Murphy, A. H., & Winkler, R. L. (1974). Probability forecasts: A survey of National Weather Service forecasters. *Bulletin of the American Meteorological Society*, 55, 1449–1453. (40)

Murphy, A. H., & Winkler, R. L. (1977a). Can weather forecasters formulate reliable forecasts of precipitation and temperature? *National Weather Digest*, 2, 2–9. (40)

Murphy, A. H., & Winkler, R. L. (1977b). The use of credible intervals in temperature forecasting: Some experimental results. In H. Jungermann & G. de Zeeuw (Eds.), *Decision making and change in human affairs* (pp. 45–56). Dordrecht: Reidel. (40)

Murphy, J. M. (1970). The value line contest: 1969. *Financial Analysts Journal, 26*, 94–100. (10)

Myers, D. K., & Newcomb, H. B. (1979). *Health effects of energy development*. Paper presented at the National Conference on Nuclear Issues in the Canadian Energy Context, Vancouver, B.C. (6)

Mynatt, C. R., Doherty, M. E., & Tweney, R. D. (1977). Confirmation bias in a simulated research environment: An experimental study of scientific inference. *Quarterly Journal of Experimental Psychology, 29*, 85–95. (42)

Nagel, E. (1952). Some issues in the logic of historical analysis. *Scientific Monthly, 74*, 162–169. (33)

Nagel, S. S. (1962). Judicial backgrounds and criminal cases. *Journal of Criminal Law, Criminology, and Police Science, 53*, 333–339. (14)

Nagy, C. (1981). *How are personnel selection decisions made? An analysis of decision strategies in a simulated personnel selection task*. Unpublished doctoral dissertation, Kansas State University. (27)

National Academy of Sciences. (1975a). *Decision making for regulating chemicals in the environment*. Washington, DC: National Academy of Sciences. (7)

National Academy of Sciences. (1975b). *Environmental impact of stratospheric flight*. Washington, DC: National Academy of Sciences. (7)

National Center for Health Statistics. (1976). *Vital statistics of the United States* (Vol. 11, Sec. 5). Rockville, MD: National Center for Health Statistics. (22)

Navon, D. (1978). The importance of being conservative: Some reflections on human Bayesian behavior. *British Journal of Mathematical and Statistical Psychology, 31*, 33–48. (40, 41)

Naylor, J. C., & Wherry, R. J., Sr. (1965). The use of simulated stimuli and the "JAN" technique to capture and cluster the policies of raters. *Educational and Psychological Measurement, 25*, 969–986. (29, 35)

Neale, M. A., & Bazerman, M. H. (1983a). The rule of perspective taking ability in negotiating under different forms of arbitration. *Industrial and Labor Relations Review, 36*, 378–388. (17)

Neale, M. A., & Bazerman, M. H. (1983b). *Systematic deviations from rationality in negotiator behavior: The framing of conflict and negotiator overconfidence* (working paper). Tucson: University of Arizona. (17)

Neisser, U. (1967). *Cognitive psychology*. New York: Appleton-Century-Crofts. (24)

Neisser, U. (1976). *Cognition and reality: Principles and implications of cognitive psychology*. San Francisco: Freeman. (41)

Neuhauser, D., & Lewicki, A. M. (1975). What do we gain from the sixth stool guaiac? *New England Journal of Medicine, 293*, 226–228. (20, 34)

New York Times. (1981, November 4). Cost and Indian opposition may halt Arizona dam plans. New York. (8)

Newcomb, T. M. (1929). *The consistency of certain extravert–introvert behavior patterns in 51 problem boys*. New York: Teachers College. (36)

Newell, A., Shaw, J. C., & Simon, H. A. (1958). The elements of a theory of human problem solving. *Psychological Review, 65*, 151–166. (34)

Newell, A., & Simon, H. A. (1961). Computer simulation of human thinking. *Science, 134*, 2011–2017. (34)

Newell, A., & Simon, H. A. (1972). *Human problem solving.* Englewood Cliffs, NJ: Prentice-Hall. (34)

Newman, D. J. (1956). Pleading guilty for consideration: A study of bargain justice. *Journal of Criminal Law, Criminology, and Police Science, 46*, 780–790. (14)

Newton, J. R. (1965). Judgment and feedback in a quasi-clinical situation. *Journal of Personality and Social Psychology, 1*, 336–342. (3)

Niemark, E. (1975). Longitudinal development of formal operations thought. *Genetic Psychology Monographs, 91*, 171–225. (30)

Nisbett, R. E., & Borgida, E. (1975). Attribution and the psychology of prediction. *Journal of Personality and Social Psychology, 32*, 932–943. (36, 40, 41)

Nisbett, R. E., Borgida, E., Crandall, R., & Reed, H. (1976). Popular induction: Information is not necessarily informative. In J. S. Carroll & J. W. Payne (Eds.), *Cognition and social behavior* (pp. 113–133). Hillsdale, NJ: Erlbaum. (40, 41)

Nisbett, R. E., Krantz, D. H., Jepson, C., & Kunda, Z. (1983). The use of statistical heuristics in everyday inductive reasoning. *Psychological Review, 90*, 339–363. (40)

Nisbett, R. E., & Ross, L. (1980). *Human inference: Strategies and shortcomings of social judgment.* Englewood Cliffs, NJ: Prentice-Hall. (17, 36, 39, 40, 41, 43)

Nisbett, R. E., & Temoshok, L. (1976). Is there an "external" cognitive style? *Journal of Personality and Social Psychology, 33*, 36–47. (12)

Nisbett, R. E., & Wilson, T. D. (1977). Telling more than we can know: Verbal reports on mental processes. *Psychological Review, 84*, 231–259. (16, 36)

Nishiyama, H., Lewis, J. T., Ashare, A. B., & Saenger, E. L. (1975). Interpretation of radionuclide liver images: Do training and experience make a difference? *Journal of Nuclear Medicine, 16*, 11–15. (20)

Niskanen, W. (1971). *Bureaucracy and representative government.* Chicago: Aldine-Atherton. (9)

Norman, D. A. (1981). Categorization of action slips. *Psychological Review, 88*, 1–15. (41)

Norris, H. (1965). *A casebook of complete criminal trials.* Detroit: Citation Press. (37)

O'Brien, J. W. (1970). How market theory can help investors set goals, select investment managers, and appraise investment performance. *Financial Analysts Journal, 26*(4), 91–103. (10)

Oden, G. C. (1977). Integration of fuzzy logical information. *Journal of Experimental Psychology: Human Perception and Performance, 3*, 565–575. (4)

Okrent, D. (1980). Comment of societal risk. *Science, 208*, 372–375. (28)

Olson, D. H., & Ryder, R. G. (1970). Inventory of marital conflicts (IMC): An experimental interaction procedure. *Journal of Marriage and the Family, 32*, 443–448. (15)

Ortolano, L. (1974). A process for federal water planning at the field level. *Water Resources Bulletin, 10*, 776–778. (8)

Orvis, B., Kelley, H., & Butler, D. (1976). Attributional conflict in young couples. In N. H. Harvey, W. J. Ickes, & R. F. Kidd (Eds.), *New directions in attribution research* (Vol. 1). Hillsdale, NJ: Erlbaum. (15)

Oskamp, S. (1962). The relationship of clinical experience and training methods to several criteria of clinical prediction. *Psychological Monographs, 76*(28, Whole No. 547). (19, 34)

Oskamp, S. (1965). Overconfidence in case-study judgments. *Journal of Consulting Psychology, 29,* 261–265. (10, 19, 36, 40, 41)

Oskamp, S. (1967). Clinical judgment from the MMPI: Simple or complex? *Journal of Clinical Psychology, 23,* 411–415. (19, 36)

Otten, A. L. (1975, April 3). Politics & people. *Wall Street Journal,* p. 12. (7)

Pankoff, L. D., & Roberts, H. V. (1968). Bayesian synthesis of clinical and statistical prediction. *Psychological Bulletin, 70,* 762–773. (10)

Parker, C. A. (1958). As a clinician thinks... *Journal of Counseling Psychology, 5,* 253–262. (19)

Parkinson, B. K. (1967). Non-economic factors in the economic retardation of the rural Malays. *Modern Asian Studies, 1,* 31–46. (25)

Parsons, O. A., & Schneider, J. M. (1974). Locus of control in university students from Eastern and Western societies. *Journal of Consulting and Clinical Psychology, 42,* 456–461. (25)

Partridge, A., & Eldridge, C. (1974). *The second circuit sentencing study: A report to the judges of the second circuit.* Washington, DC: Federal Judicial Center. (14)

Pauker, S. G., & Kassirer, J. P. (1975). Therapeutic decision making: A cost-benefit analysis. *New England Journal of Medicine, 293,* 229–234. (20)

Payne, J. W. (1976). Task complexity and contingent processing in decision making: An information search and protocol analysis. *Organizational Behavior and Human Performance, 16,* 366–387. (41)

Payne, J. W. (1982). Contingent decision behavior. *Psychological Bulletin, 92,* 382–402. (39)

Payne, J. W., Laughhunn, D. J., & Crum, R. (1980). Translation of gambles and aspiration level effects in risky choice behavior. *Management Science, 26,* 1039–1060. (11, 41)

Pearson, K. (1897). On the scientific measure of variability. *Natural Science, 11,* 115–118. (41)

Penny, D. M. (1967). Development opportunities in Indonesian agriculture. *Bulletin of Indonesian Economic Studies, 8,* 35–64. (25)

Pepitone, A. (1975). Social psychological perspectives on crime and punishment. *Journal of Social Issues, 31,* 197–216. (13)

Perlman, D. (1980). Attributions in the criminal justice process: Concepts and empirical illustrations. In P. D. Lipsitt & B. D. Sales (Eds.), *New directions in psycholegal research* (pp. 51–67). New York: Van Nostrand Reinhold. (13)

Peterson, C. R., & Beach, L. R. (1967). Man as an intuitive statistician. *Psychological Bulletin, 68,* 29–46. (39, 41)

Peterson, J. L., Fabricant, E. L., & Field, K. S. (1978). *Crime laboratory proficiency testing research program: Final report.* Washington, DC: U.S. Government Printing Office, U.S. Department of Justice. (12)

Phelan, J. G. (1964). Rationale employed by clinical psychologists in diagnostic judgment. *Journal of Clinical Psychology, 20,* 454–458. (19, 36)

Phelan, J. G. (1965). Use of matching method in measuring reliability of individual clinician's diagnostic judgment. *Psychological Reports, 16,* 491–497. (19)

Phelps, R. H. (1977). *Expert livestock judgment: A descriptive analysis of the development of expertise.* Unpublished doctoral dissertation, Kansas State University. (27)

Phillips, L. D. (1973). *Bayesian statistics for social scientists*. London: Nelson (New York: Crowell, 1974). (25)

Phillips, L. D. (1983). A theoretical perspective on heuristics and biases in probabilistic thinking. In P. C. Humphreys, O. Svenson, & A. Vari (Eds.), *Analysing and aiding decision processes* (pp. 525–543). Amsterdam: North Holland. (39)

Phillips, L. D., & Edwards, W. (1966). Conservatism in a simple probability inference task. *Journal of Experimental Psychology, 72*, 346–357. (40)

Phillips, L. D., Hays, W. L., & Edwards, W. (1966). Conservatism in complex probabilistic inference. *IEEE Transactions on Human Factors in Electronics, 7*, 7–18. (40)

Phillips, L. D., & Wright, G. N. (1976). *Group differences in probabilistic thinking* (Tech. Rep. 76–4). Uxbridge, Middlesex: Brunel University, Decision Analysis Unit, Brunel Institute of Organization and Social Studies. (25)

Phillips, L. D., & Wright, G. N. (1977). Cultural differences in viewing uncertainty and assessing probabilities. In H. Jungermann & G. de Zeeuw (Eds.), *Decision making and change in human affairs* (pp. 507–519). Dordrecht: Reidel. (25)

Phoenix Gazette. (1978, October 3). Governor's panel backs Waddell dam over Orme. Phoenix, AZ. (8)

Piaget, J. (1969). *The child's conception of time* (A. J. Pomerans, Trans.). London: Routledge & Kegan Paul. (Original work published 1946) (31)

Piaget, J. (1970). *The child's conception of movement and speed* (G. E. T. Holloway & M. J. Mackenzie, Trans.). New York: Basic Books. (Original work published 1946) (31)

Piaget, J. (1970). *Genetic epistemology* (E. Duckworth, Trans.). New York: Columbia University Press. (31, 41)

Piaget, J., & Inhelder, B. (1941). *Le développement des quantités chez l'enfant*. Neuchâtel: Delachaux et Niestle. (40)

Piaget, J., & Inhelder, B. (1975). *The origin of the idea of chance in children*. New York: Norton. (Original work published 1941) (40, 42)

Pitz, G. (1974). Subjective probability distributions for imperfectly known quantities. In L. W. Gregg (Ed.), *Knowledge and cognition* (pp. 29–41). New York: Wiley. (24, 40)

Pitz, G. (1977). Decision making and cognition. In H. Jungermann & G. de Zeeuw (Eds.), *Decision making and change in human affairs* (pp. 403–424). Dordrecht: Reidel. (39)

Pitz, G. F., Sachs, N. J., & Heerboth, J. (1980). Procedures for eliciting choices in the analysis of individual decisions. *Organizational Behavior and Human Performance, 26*, 396–408. (39)

Pliskin, J. S., & Beck, C. H. (1976). Decision analysis in individual clinical decision making: A real-world application in treatment of renal disease. *Methods of Information in Medicine, 15*, 43–46. (22)

Polsby, N. W. (1975). Questions of bias. *Science, 190*, 665–666. (7)

Pommerehne, W. W., Schneider, F., & Zweifel, P. (1982). Economic theory of choice and the preference reversal phenomenon: A reexamination. *American Economic Review, 72*, 569–574. (40)

Popper, K. R. (1959). *The logic of scientific discovery*. New York: Basic Books. (43)

Popper, K. R. (1963). *Conjectures and refutations: The growth of scientific knowledge*. London: Routledge & Kegan Paul. (42)

Postman, L., & Tolman, E. C. (1959). Brunswik's probabilistic functionalism. In S. Koch (Ed.), *Psychology: A study of a science* (Vol. 1). New York: McGraw-Hill. (41)

Poulton, E. C. (1974). *Tracking skill and manual control.* New York: Academic Press. (41)

Powers, W. T. (1973). Feedback: Beyond behaviorism. *Science, 179,* 351–356. (41)

Powers, W. T. (1978). Quantitative analysis of purposive systems: Some spadework at the foundations of scientific psychology. *Psychological Review, 85,* 417–435. (41)

Pratt, J. W., Wise, D., & Zeckhauser, R. (1979). Price differences in almost competitive markets. *Quarterly Journal of Economics, 93,* 189–211. (11)

President's Commission on Law Enforcement and Administration of Justice. (1967). *The challenge of crime and a free society.* Washington, DC: U.S. Government Printing Office. (14)

Prettyman, E. B. (1960). Jury instruction: First or last? *American Bar Association Journal, 46,* 1066. (14)

Pruitt, D. G. (1981). *Negotiation behavior.* New York: Academic Press. (17)

Public Broadcasting Service. (1975, February 16). *Black horizons.* (7)

Rabbitt, P. (1965). An age decrement in the ability to ignore irrelevant information. *Journal of Gerontology, 20,* 233–238. (27)

Raiffa, H. (1968). *Decision analysis: Introductory lectures on choices under uncertainty.* Reading, MA: Addison-Wesley. (7, 10, 12, 20, 22, 23, 25)

Rand Corporation. (1955). *One million random digits and 100,000 normal deviates.* New York: Free Press of Glencoe. (43)

Rapoport, A. (1975). Research paradigms for studying dynamic decision behavior. In D. Wendt & C. Vlek (Eds.), *Utility, probability, and human decision making.* Dordrecht: Reidel. (41)

Rappoport, L. (1969). Cognitive conflict as a function of socially-induced cognitive differences. *Journal of Conflict Resolution, 13,* 143–148. (3)

Rappoport, L., & Summers, D. A. (Eds.). (1973). *Human judgment and social interaction.* New York: Holt, Rinehart, & Winston. (3)

Raush, H. L., Barry, W. A., Hertel, R. K., & Swain, M. A. (1974). *Communication, conflict, and marriage.* San Francisco: Jossey-Bass. (15)

Rawls, J. (1958). Justice as fairness. *Philosophical Review, 67,* 164–194. (38)

Rawls, J. (1971). *A theory of justice.* Cambridge, MA: Harvard University Press. (7, 38)

Redding, S. G. (1978). Bridging the culture gap. *Asian Business and Investment, 4,* 45–52. (25)

Redding, S. G., & Martyn-Johns, T. A. (1978). *Paradigm differences and their relation to management functions, with reference to South-East Asia* (working paper). Hong Kong: University of Hong Kong, Centre of Asian Studies. (25)

Reichenbach, H. (1949). *The theory of probability* (E. Hutten & M. Reichenbach, Trans.). Berkeley: University of California. (Original work published 1934) (43)

Reilly, R. J. (1982). Preference reversal: Further evidence and some suggested modifications in experimental design. *American Economic Review, 72,* 576–584. (40)

Reissland, J., & Harries, V. (1979). A scale for measuring risks. *New Scientist, 83,* 809–811. (6)

Rethans, A. (1979). *An investigation of consumer perceptions of product hazards.* Unpublished doctoral dissertation, University of Oregon. (6)

Reynolds, D. E., & Sanders, M. S. (1973, May). *The effects of the defendant's attractiveness, age, and injury on severity of sentence given by simulated jurors.* Paper presented at the meeting of the Western Psychological Association, Anaheim, CA. (37)

Rice, M. F. (1975). Influence of irrelevant biographical information in teacher evaluation. *Journal of Educational Psychology, 67,* 658–662. (27)

Ridenour, L. N. (1952). Computers as information machines. *Scientific American, 187,* 116–118. (34)

Ringuette, E. L., & Kennedy, T. (1966). An experimental study of the double bind hypothesis. *Journal of Abnormal Psychology, 71,* 136–141. (19)

Rist, R. C. (1970). Student social class and teacher expectations: The self-fulfilling prophecy in ghetto education. *Harvard Educational Review, 40,* 411–451. (32)

Rohrbaugh, J., McClelland, G., & Quinn, R. (1980). Measuring the relative importance of utilitarian and egalitarian values: A study of individual differences about fair distribution. *Journal of Applied Psychology, 65,* 34–49. (38)

Rohrbaugh, J., & Wehr, P. (1978). Judgment analysis in policy formation: A new method for improving public participation. *Public Opinion Quarterly, 42,* 521–532. (8)

Rokeach, M. (1973). *The nature of human values.* New York: Free Press. (8, 38)

Ronen, J. (1973). Effects of some probability displays on choices. *Organizational Behavior and Human Performance, 9,* 1–15. (39, 41)

Rorer, L. G. (1967, September). *Conditions facilitating discovery of moderators.* Paper presented at the meeting of the American Psychological Association, Washington, DC. (19)

Rorer, L. G., Hoffman, P. J., Dickman, H. D., & Slovic, P. (1967). Configural judgments revealed. *Proceedings of the 75th Annual Convention of the American Psychological Association, 2,* 195–196. (19)

Rorer, L. G., & Slovic, P. (1966). The measurement of changes in judgmental strategy. *American Psychologist, 21,* 641–642. (19)

Rosen, B., & Jerdee, J. H. (1974). Factors influencing disciplinary judgments. *Journal of Applied Psychology, 59,* 327–331. (13)

Rosenbaum, D. E. (1970, December 11). Statisticians charge draft lottery was not random. *New York Times,* p. 66. (43)

Rosenberg, J. (1978). A question of ethics: The DNA controversy. *American Educator, 2,* 27–30. (6)

Rosenthal, R., & Jacobson, L. (1968). *Pygmalion in the classroom: Teacher expectation and pupils' intellectual development.* New York: Holt, Rinehart, & Winston. (32)

Rosett, A., & Cressey, D. R. (1976). *Justice by consent: Plea bargains in the American courthouse.* Philadelphia: Lippincott. (14)

Ross, L. (1977). The intuitive psychologist and his shortcomings: Distortions in the attribution process. In L. Berkowitz (Ed.), *Advances in experimental social psychology* (Vol. 10). New York: Academic Press. (41, 43)

Ross, L., Lepper, M. R., Strack, F., & Steinmetz, J. L. (1977). Social explanation and social expectation: Effects of real and hypothetical explanations on subjective likelihood. *Journal of Personality and Social Psychology, 35,* 817–829. (36)

Rothenberg, B. B. (1969). Preschool children's understanding of the coordinated concepts of distance, movement, number, and time. *Journal of Genetic Psychology, 115,* 263–276. (31)

Rotter, J. B. (1966). Generalized expectancies for internal versus external control of reinforcement. *Psychological Monographs, 80*(1, Whole No. 609). (13, 25, 41)

Royce, W., & Weiss, R. (1975). Behavioral cues in the judgment of marital satisfaction: A linear regression analysis. *Journal of Consulting and Clinical Psychology, 43,* 816–824. (15)

Rozelle, M. A. (1982). *The incorporation of public values into public policy.* Unpublished doctoral dissertation, Arizona State University. (8)

Rubin, J. (1980). Experimental research on third party intervention in conflict: Toward some generalizations. *Psychological Bulletin, 87,* 379–391. (17)

Rubin, J. Z., & Brown, B. R. (1975). *The social psychology of bargaining and negotiation.* New York: Academic Press. (17)

Rubovits, P., & Maehr, M. (1971). Pygmalion analyzed: Toward an explanation of the Rosenthal–Jacobson findings. *Journal of Personality and Social Psychology, 19,* 197–203. (32)

Ruffner, J. W., & Muchinsky, P. M. (1978). The influence of cue validity distributions and group discussion feedback on multiple cue probability learning. *Organizational Behavior and Human Performance, 21,* 189–208. (41)

Rumelhart, D. E., & Ortony, A. (1977). The representation of knowledge in memory. In R. C. Anderson, R. J. Spiro, & W. E. Montague (Eds.), *Schooling and the acquisition of knowledge* (pp. 99–135). Hillsdale, NJ: Erlbaum. (32)

Russo, J. E. (1978). Adaptation of cognitive processes to the eye movement system. In J. W. Senders, D. F. Fisher, & R. A. Monty (Eds.), *Eye movements and the higher psychological functions* (pp. 89–112). Hillsdale, NJ: Erlbaum. (41)

Ryback, D. (1967). Confidence and accuracy as a function of experience in judgment-making in the absence of systematic feedback. *Perceptual and Motor Skills, 24,* 331–334. (19)

Sabin, A. B. (1977). Mortality from pneumonia and risk conditions during influenza morbidity during nonepidemic years. *Journal of the American Medical Association, 237,* 2823–2828. (22)

Sager, C. (1976). *Marriage contracts and couples therapy.* New York: Brunner/Mazel. (15)

Saks, M. (1976). The limits of scientific jury selection: Ethical and empirical. *Jurimetrics Journal, 17,* 3–22. (12)

Saks, M. (1977). *Jury verdicts: The role of group size and social decision rule.* Lexington, MA: Heath. (12)

Sales, B. D., Elwork, A., & Alfini, J. J. (1977). Improving comprehension for jury instructions. In B. D. Sales (Ed.), *Perspectives in law and psychology: Vol. I. The criminal justice system* (pp. 23–90). New York: Plenum. (14)

Savage, L. J. (1954). *The foundations of statistics.* New York: Wiley. (2, 5, 11, 12, 25, 40, 41)

Savage, L. J. (1972). Diagnosis and the Bayesian viewpoint. In J. A. Jacquez (Ed.), *Computer diagnosis and diagnostic methods* (pp. 131–138). Springfield, IL: Thomas. (34)

Sawyer, J. (1966). Measurement *and* prediction, clinical *and* statistical. *Psychological Bulletin, 66,* 178–200. (10, 12, 19, 29, 35)

Scanzoni, J. (1979). A historical perspective on husband–wife bargaining power and marital dissolution. In G. Levinger & O. Moles (Eds.), *Divorce and separation: Context, causes, and consequences* (pp. 20–36). New York: Basic Books. (15)

Schaeffer, R. W. (1964). Clinical psychologists' ability to use the Draw-a-Person test as an indicator of personality adjustment. *Journal of Consulting Psychology, 28,* 383. (19)

Schafer, C. (1973). An exploratory study of teachers' descriptions of the "ideal" pupil. *Psychology in the Schools, 10,* 444–447. (32)

Schank, R., & Abelson, R. P. (1977). *Scripts, plans, goals, and understanding: An inquiry into human knowledge structures.* Hillsdale, NJ: Erlbaum. (32)

Schelling, T. C. (1978). Egonomics; or, The art of self-management. *American Economic Review, 68,* 290–294. (41)

Schierow, L., & Chesters, G. (1983). Enhancing the effectiveness of public participation in defining water resource policy. *Water Resources Bulletin, 19,* 107–114. (8)

Schlaifer, R. (1959). *Probability and statistics for business decisions.* New York: McGraw-Hill. (11)

Schlaifer, R. (1969). *Analysis of decisions under uncertainty.* New York: McGraw-Hill. (12)

Schmidt, R. A., Zelaznik, H., Hawkins, B., Frank, J. S., & Quinn, J. T., Jr. (1979). Motor-output variability: A theory for the accuracy of rapid motor acts. *Psychological Review, 86,* 415–451. (41)

Schneiderman, L. J., DeSalvo, L., Baylor, S., & Wolf, P. L. (1972). The "abnormal" screening laboratory results: Its effect on physician and patient. *Archives of Internal Medicine, 129,* 88–90. (20)

Schoemaker, P. J. H., & Kunreuther, H. C. (1979). An experimental study of insurance decisions. *Journal of Risk and Insurance, 46,* 603–618. (11)

Schoenbaum, S. C., McNeil, B. J., & Kavet, J. (1976). The swine-influenza decision. *New England Journal of Medicine, 295,* 759–765. (22)

Schrag, C. (1971). *Crime and justice: American style.* Rockville, MD: National Institute of Mental Health. (13)

Schreiber, S. (1967). *Product liability: Law, practice, science.* New York: Practicing Law Institute. (12)

Schum, D. A. (1979). A review of a case against Blaise Pascal and his heirs. *Michigan Law Review, 77,* 446–483. (12)

Schwartz, M. L. (1967). Validity and reliability in clinical judgments of C-V-S protocols as a function of amount of information and diagnostic category. *Psychological Reports, 20,* 767–774. (19)

Schwartz, W. B., Gorry, G. A., Kassirer, J. P., & Essig, A. (1973). Decision analysis and clinical judgment. *American Journal of Medicine, 55,* 459–472. (20, 36)

Scott, W. A. (1965). *Values and organizations.* Chicago: Rand McNally. (38)

Scottsdale Daily Progress. (1978, March 21). Editorial: Shootout over Orme. Scottsdale, AZ. (8)

Scottsdale Daily Progress. (1981, October 10). Leaders will support Waddell plan. Scottsdale, AZ. (8)

Seaver, D. A., von Winterfeldt, D., & Edwards, W. (1978). Eliciting subjective probability distributions on continuous variables. *Organizational Behavior and Human Performance, 21,* 379–391. (40)

Sechrest, L., Gallimore, R., & Hersch, P. D. (1967). Feedback and accuracy of clinical predictions. *Journal of Consulting Psychology, 31,* 1–11. (19)

Seggie, J., & Endersby, H. (1972). The empirical implications of Piaget's concept of correlation. *Australian Journal of Psychology, 24,* 3–8. (30)

Seligman, M. E. P. (1975). *Helplessness.* San Francisco: Freeman. (41)

Sellin, T. (1928). The Negro criminal: A statistical note. *Annals of the American Academy of Political and Social Science, 140,* 52–64. (14)

Sen, A. (1973). *On economic inequality.* New York: Norton. (38)

Shachtman, R. H., & Blau, R. A. (1974). *A syllabus for decision analysis.* Chapel Hill: University of North Carolina. (22)

Shaklee, H. (1979). Bounded rationality and cognitive development: Upper limits on growth? *Cognitive Psychology, 11,* 327–345. (30)

Shaklee, H. & Mims, M. (1980). *Sources of error in judging event covariations: Effects of memory demands.* Manuscript submitted for publication. (36)

Shaklee, H., & Tucker, D. (1980). A rule analysis of judgments of covariation between events. *Memory and Cognition, 8,* 459–467. (30)

Shanteau, J. (1974). Component processes in risky decision making. *Journal of Experimental Psychology, 103,* 680–691. (4)

Shanteau, J. (1977). Correlation as a deceiving measure of fit. *Bulletin of the Psychonomic Society, 10,* 134–136. (38)

Shanteau, J., & Phelps, R. H. (1977). Judgment and swine: Approaches and issues in applied judgment analysis. In M. F. Kaplan & S. Schwartz (Eds.), *Human judgment and decision processes in applied settings* (pp. 255–272). New York: Academic Press. (27)

Shantz, C. U. (1967). Effects of redundant and irrelevant information on children's seriation ability. *Journal of Experimental Child Psychology, 5,* 208–222. (27)

Shavelson, R. J., Caldwell, J., & Izu, T. (1977). Teachers' sensitivity to the reliability of information in making pedagogical decisions. *American Educational Research Journal, 14,* 83–97. (32)

Shavelson, R. J., & Stern, P. (1981). Research on teachers' pedagogical thoughts, judgments, decisions, and behavior. *Review of Educational Research, 51,* 455–498. (32)

Shaver, K. G., Gilbert, M. A., & Williams, M. C. (1975). Social psychology, criminal justice, and the principle of discretion: A selective review. *Personality and Social Psychological Bulletin, 1,* 471–484. (37)

Shaw, M. E., & Reitan, H. T. (1969). Attribution of responsibility as a basis for sanctioning behavior. *British Journal of Social and Clinical Psychology, 8,* 217–226. (13)

Shaw, M. E., & Sulzer, J. L. (1964). An empirical test of Heider's levels in attribution of responsibility. *Journal of Abnormal and Social Psychology, 69,* 39–46. (13)

Shepard, R. N. (1964). On subjectively optimum selections among multi-attribute alternatives. In M. W. Shelly & G. L. Bryan (Eds.), *Human judgments and optimality* (pp. 257–281). New York: Wiley. (41)

Shugan, S. M. (1980). The cost of thinking. *Journal of Consumer Research, 7,* 99–111. (39)

Shulman, L. S., & Elstein, A. S. (1975). Studies of problem solving, judgment, and decision making. In F. N. Kerlinger (Ed.), *Review of research in education* (Vol. 3). Itasca, IL: Peacock. (32)

Shultz, T., & Mendelson, R. (1975). Use of covariation as a principle of causal analysis. *Child Development, 46,* 394–399. (30)

Shweder, R. A. (1977). Likeness and likelihood in everyday thought: Magical thinking in judgments about personality. *Current Anthropology, 18,* 637–648. (36)

Sieber, J. E. (1974). Effects of decision importance on the ability to generate warranted subjective uncertainty. *Journal of Personality and Social Psychology, 30,* 688–694. (40)

Siegel, S. (1956). *Nonparametric statistics for the behavioral sciences*. New York: McGraw-Hill. (37)

Siegel, S., & Fouraker, L. E. (1960). *Bargaining and group decision making: Experiments in bilateral monopoly*. New York: McGraw-Hill. (17)

Siegler, R. S. (1975). Defining the locus of developmental differences in children's causal reasoning. *Journal of Experimental Child Psychology, 20*, 512–525. (30)

Siegler, R. S. (1976). Three aspects of cognitive development. *Cognitive Psychology, 8*, 481–520. (30, 31)

Siegler, R. S., & Richards, D. D. (1979). Development of time, speed, and distance concepts. *Developmental Psychology, 15*, 288–298. (31)

Siegler, R. S., & Vago, S. (1978). The development of a proportionality concept: Judging relative fullness. *Journal of Experimental Child Psychology, 25*, 371–395. (30)

Sigall, H., & Ostrove, N. (1975). Beautiful but dangerous: Effects of offender attractiveness and nature of the crime on juridic judgment. *Journal of Personality and Social Psychology, 31*, 410–414. (37)

Silberman, M. (1969). Behavioral expression of teachers' attitudes toward elementary school students. *Journal of Educational Psychology, 60*, 402–407. (32)

Silverman, L. H. (1959). A Q-sort study of the validity of evaluations made from projective techniques. *Psychological Monographs, 73*(7, Whole No. 477). (19)

Simon, H. A. (1953). *Models of man*. New York: Wiley. (16)

Simon, H. A. (1955). A behavioral model of rational choice. *Quarterly Journal of Economics, 69*, 99–118. (39, 41)

Simon, H. A. (1956). Rational choice and the structure of the environment. *Psychological Review, 63*, 129–138. (5)

Simon, H. A. (1959). Theories of decision making in economics and behavioral science. *American Economic Review, 49*, 253–280. (41)

Simon, H. A. (1972). On reasoning about actions. In H. A. Simon & L. Siklòssy (Eds.), *Representation and meaning: Experiments with information processing systems* (pp. 414–430). Englewood Cliffs, NJ: Prentice-Hall. (5)

Simon, H. A. (1977). *Models of discovery*. Dordrecht: Reidel. (5)

Simon, H. A. (1978). Rationality as process and as product of thought. *American Economic Review, 68*, 1–16. (39)

Simon, H. A. (1979a). Information processing models of cognition. *Annual Review of Psychology, 30*, 363–396. (34)

Simon, H. A. (1979b). *Models of thought*. New Haven, CT: Yale University Press. (5)

Simon, H. A. (1981). *The sciences of the artificial* (2nd ed.). Cambridge, MA: MIT Press. (5)

Simon, H. A., & Newell, A. (1964). Information processing in computer and man. *American Scientist, 53*, 281–300. (34)

Simon, H. A., & Newell, A. (1971). Human problem solving: The state of the theory in 1970. *American Psychologist, 26*, 145–159. (41)

Sines, L. K. (1959). The relative contribution of four kinds of data to accuracy in personality assessment. *Journal of Consulting Psychology, 23*, 483–492. (19)

Sjöberg, L. (1980). Volitional problems in carrying through a difficult decision. *Acta Psychologica, 45*, 123–132. (39)

Skinner, B. F. (1948). Superstition in the pigeon. *Journal of Experimental Psychology, 38*, 168–172. (10)

Skinner, B. F. (1966). The phylogeny and ontogeny of behavior. *Science, 153,* 1205–1213. (41)

Skinner, B. F. (1968). *The technology of teaching.* New York: Appleton-Century-Crofts. (19)

Skolnikoff, E. B., & Brooks, H. (1975). Science advice in the White House? Continuation of a debate. *Science, 187,* 35–41. (7)

Slovic, P. (1966a). Cue consistency and cue utilization in judgment. *American Journal of Psychology, 79,* 427–434. (19, 35)

Slovic, P. (1966b). Value as a determiner of subjective probability. *IEEE Transactions on Human Factors in Electronics, HFE-7,* 22–28. (10)

Slovic, P. (1967). The relative influence on probabilities and payoffs upon perceived risk of a gamble. *Psychonomic Science, 9,* 223–224. (10)

Slovic, P. (1968, March). *Analyzing the expert judge: A descriptive study of a stockbroker's decision processes.* Paper presented at the meeting of the Western Psychological Association, San Diego. (19)

Slovic, P. (1969a). Analyzing the expert judge: A descriptive study of a stockbroker's decision processes. *Journal of Applied Psychology, 53,* 255–263. (12, 16)

Slovic, P. (1969b). Manipulating the attractiveness of a gamble without changing its expected value. *Journal of Experimental Psychology, 79,* 139–145. (10)

Slovic, P. (1972a). From Shakespeare to Simon: Speculations—and some evidence —about man's ability to process information. *Oregon Research Institute Monograph, 12*(2). (39, 41)

Slovic, P. (1972b). Information processing, situation specificity, and the generality of risk-taking behavior. *Journal of Personality and Social Psychology, 22,* 128–134. (10)

Slovic, P., & Fischhoff, B. (1977). On the psychology of experimental surprises. *Journal of Experimental Psychology: Human Perception and Performance, 3,* 544–551. (27, 36)

Slovic, P., Fischhoff, B., & Lichtenstein, S. (1976a). Cognitive processes and societal risk taking. In J. S. Carroll & J. W. Payne (Eds.), *Cognition and social behavior* (pp. 165–184). Hillsdale, NJ: Erlbaum. (12)

Slovic, P., Fischhoff, B., & Lichtenstein, S. (1976b). *The certainty illusion* (Tech. Rep. DDI-2). Eugene, OR: Decision Research. (25)

Slovic, P., Fischhoff, B., & Lichtenstein, S. (1977). Behavioral decision theory. *Annual Review of Psychology, 28,* 1–39. (6, 7, 12, 27, 34, 40, 41)

Slovic, P., Fischhoff, B., & Lichtenstein, S. (1978). Accident probabilities and seat belt usage: A psychological perspective. *Accident Analysis and Prevention, 10,* 281–285. (6)

Slovic, P., Fischhoff, B., & Lichtenstein, S. (1980). Facts and fears: Understanding perceived risk. In R. Schwing & W. A. Albers, Jr. (Eds.), *Societal risk assessment: How safe is safe enough?* (pp. 181–216). New York: Plenum. (6)

Slovic, P., Fischhoff, B., & Lichtenstein, S. (1982). Response mode, framing, and information-processing effects in risk assessment. In R. Hogarth (Ed.), *New directions for methodology of social and behavioral science:* No. 11. *Question framing and response consistency* (pp. 21–36). San Francisco: Jossey-Bass. (11)

Slovic, P., Fleissner, D., & Bauman, W. S. (1972). Analyzing the use of information in investment decision making: A methodological proposal. *Journal of Business, 45,* 283–301. (10)

Slovic, P., Kunreuther, H., & White, G. F. (1974). Decision processes, rationality, and adjustment to natural hazards. In G. F. White (Ed.), *Natural hazards: Local, national, global* (pp. 187–205). New York: Oxford University Press. (6, 12, 43)

Slovic, P., & Lichtenstein, S. (1968). The importance of variance preferences in gambling decisions. *Journal of Experimental Psychology, 78,* 646–654. (10)

Slovic, P., & Lichtenstein, S. (1971). Comparison of Bayesian and regression approaches to the study of information processing in judgment. *Organizational Behavior and Human Performance, 6,* 649–744. (2, 10, 12, 14, 16, 26, 27, 29, 34, 38, 40, 41)

Slovic, P., & Lichtenstein, S. (1973). Comparison of Bayesian and regression approaches to the study of information processing in judgment. In L. Rappoport & D. A. Summers (Eds.), *Human judgment and social interaction* (pp. 16–108). New York: Holt, Rinehart, & Winston. (15)

Slovic, P., & Lichtenstein, S. (1983). Preference reversals: A broader perspective. *American Economic Review, 73,* 596–605. (40)

Slovic, P., & Tversky, A. (1974). Who accepts Savage's axiom? *Behavioral Science, 14,* 368–373. (41)

Smedslund, J. (1963). The concept of correlation in adults. *Scandinavian Journal of Psychology, 4,* 165–173. (10, 30, 36, 42)

Smith, A. (1968). *The money game.* New York: Random House. (10)

Smith, A. B., & Blumberg, A. S. (1967). The problem of objectivity in judicial decision-making. *Social Forces, 46,* 96–105. (14)

Smith, T. H. (1973). *A method for improving human judgment.* Unpublished doctoral dissertation, University of Colorado. (3, 15)

Snapper, K., & Seaver, D. (1978). *Application of decision analysis to program planning and evaluation* (Tech. Rep. 78–1). Reston, VA: Decision Science Consortium. (1)

Snedecor, G. W., & Cochran, W. G. (1967). *Statistical methods* (6th ed.). Ames: Iowa State University Press. (23)

Snow, R. E. (1968). Brunswikian approaches to research on teaching. *American Educational Research Journal, 5,* 475–489. (32)

Snyder, M. (1981). "Seek and ye shall find..." In E. T. Higgins, C. P. Herman, & M. P. Zanna (Eds.), *Social cognition: The Ontario symposium on personality and social psychology* (pp. 277–304). Hillsdale, NJ: Erlbaum. (36)

Snyder, M., & Swann, W. (1978). Hypothesis-testing processes in social interaction. *Journal of Personality and Social Psychology, 36,* 1202–1212. (30)

Snyder, M., Tanke, E. D., & Berscheid, E. (1977). Social perception and interpersonal behavior: On the self-fulfilling nature of social stereotypes. *Journal of Personality and Social Psychology, 35,* 656–666. (13)

Solomon, R. L. (1980). The opponent-process theory of acquired motivation: The costs of pleasure and the benefits of pain. *American Psychologist, 35,* 691–712. (41)

Sosis, R. (1974). Internal-external control and the perception of responsibility of another for an accident. *Journal of Personality and Social Psychology, 30,* 393–399. (13)

Soskin, W. F. (1954). Bias in postdiction from projective tests. *Journal of Abnormal and Social Psychology, 49,* 69–74. (19)

Soskin, W. F. (1959). Influence of four types of data on diagnostic conceptualization in psychological testing. *Journal of Abnormal and Social Psychology, 58,* 69–78. (19)

Sowby, F. D. (1965). Radiation and other risks. *Health Physics, 11,* 879–887. (6)

Spencer-Brown, G. (1957). *Probability and scientific inference.* London: Longmans, Green. (43)

Sprey, J. (1969). The family as a system in conflict. *Journal of Marriage and the Family, 31,* 699–706. (15)

Stanley, D. T. (1976). *Prisoners among us: The problem of parole.* Washington, DC: Brookings Institution. (13)

Stanley, J. C. (1961). Analysis of unreplicated three-way classifications with applications to rater bias and trait independence. *Psychometrika, 26,* 205–219. (29)

State Press–ASU. (1978, March 17). Orme controversy rekindles. Tempe, AZ. (8)

Staw, B. M. (1976). Knee-deep in the big muddy: A study of escalating commitment to a chosen course of action. *Organizational Behavior and Human Performance, 16,* 27–44. (17)

Staw, B. M. (1981). The escalation of commitment to a course of action. *Academy of Management Review, 6,* 577–587. (17)

Steadman, H. J., & Cocozza, J. J. (1974). *Careers of the criminally insane: Excessive social control of deviance.* Lexington, MA: Lexington Books. (12)

Steinmann, D. O. (1974). *The effects of cognitive feedback and task complexity in multiple-cue probability learning* (Rep. No. 175). Boulder: University of Colorado, Center for Research on Judgment and Policy. (3)

Steinmann, D. O., Smith, T. H., Jurdem, L., & Hammond, K. R. (1975). *Application and evaluation of social judgment theory in policy formulation: An example* (Rep. No. 174). Boulder: University of Colorado, Center for Research on Judgment and Policy. (3, 15)

Steinmann, D. O., & Stewart, T. R. (1973). *Measuring the relative importance of community goals* (Rep. No. 156). Boulder: University of Colorado, Center for Research on Judgment and Policy. (3, 15)

Stenson, H. H. (1974). The lens model with unknown cue structure. *Psychological Review, 81,* 257–264. (3)

Stephenson, W. (1953). *The study of behavior: Q technique and its methodology.* Chicago: University of Chicago Press. (34)

Stevens, S. S. (1974). Perceptual magnitude and its measurement. In E. C. Carterette & M. P. Friedman (Eds.), *Handbook of perception* (Vol. 2). New York: Academic Press. (4)

Stewart, R. B. (1975). The reformation of American administrative law. *Harvard Law Review, 88,* 1669–1813. (12)

Stewart, T. R., & Carter, J. (1973). *POLICY: An interactive computer program for externalizing, executing, and refining judgmental policy* (Rep. No. 159). Boulder: University of Colorado, Center for Research on Judgment and Policy. (3, 15, 16)

Stewart, T. R., Dennis, R. L., & Ely, D. W. (1984). Citizen participation and judgment in policy analysis: A case study of urban air quality policy. *Policy Sciences, 17,* 67–87. (8)

Stewart, T. R., & Gelberg, L. (1972). *Capturing judgment policy: A new approach for citizen participation in planning* (Rep. No. 151). Boulder: University of Colorado, Center for Research on Judgment and Policy. (3, 15)

Stewart, T. R., Joyce, C. R. B., & Lindell, M. K. (1975). New analyses: Application of judgment theory to physicians' judgments of drug effects. In K. R. Hammond & C. R. B. Joyce (Eds.), *Psychoactive drugs and social judgment: Theory and research* (pp. 249–262). New York: Wiley. (3, 15)

Stewart, T. R., West, R. E., Hammond, K. R., & Kreith, F. (1975). Improving human judgment in technology assessment. *Journal of the International Society for Technology Assessment, 1*(2), 37–43. (3, 15)

Stouffer, S. A. (1941). Notes on the case study and the unique case. *Sociometry, 4,* 349–357. (33)

Straus, M. A., & Tallman, I. (1971). SIMFAM: A technique for observational measurement and experimental study of families. In J. Aldous, T. Condon, R. Hill, M. Straus, & I. Tallman (Eds.), *Family problem solving: A symposium on theoretical, methodological, and substantive concerns* (pp. 381–438). Hinsdale, IL: Dryden. (15)

Stricker, G. (1967). Actuarial, naive clinical, and sophisticated clinical prediction of pathology from figure drawings. *Journal of Consulting Psychology, 31,* 492–494. (19)

Strodtbeck, F. (1951). Husband-wife interaction, over revealed differences. *American Sociological Review, 16,* 468–473. (15)

Stuart, R. B. (1969). Operant-interpersonal treatment for marital discord. *Journal of Consulting and Clinical Psychology, 33,* 675–682. (15)

Sue, S., Smith, R. E., & Caldwell, C. (1973). Effects of inadmissible evidence on the decisions of simulated jurors: A moral dilemma. *Journal of Applied Social Psychology, 3,* 345–353. (12, 14, 27)

Summers, D. A., Taliaferro, D. J., & Fletcher, D. J. (1970). Subjective vs. objective description of judgment policy. *Psychonomic Science, 18,* 249–250. (16, 32, 36)

Sutherland, J. V. (1983). Estimation of lung cancer risk from environmental exposure to airborne plutonium from the Rocky Flats Plant. In D. Fisher (Ed.), *Current concepts in lung dosimetry.* Washington, DC: U.S. Department of Energy, Technical Information Center, PNL-SA-11049. (28)

Svenson, O. (1970). A functional measurement approach to intuitive estimation as exemplified by estimated time savings. *Journal of Experimental Psychology, 86,* 204–210. (31)

Svenson, O. (1981). Are we all less risky and more skillful than our fellow drivers? *Acta Psychologica, 47,* 143–148. (6)

Swets, J. A. (1973). The relative operating characteristic in psychology. *Science, 182,* 990–1000. (37)

Swift, M. G. (1965). Malay peasant society in Jelebu. *London School of Economics Monographs on Social Anthropology, 29,* 31–61. (25)

Szucko, J. J., & Kleinmuntz, B. (1981). Statistical versus clinical lie detection. *American Psychologist, 36,* 488–496. (34)

Taylor, S., & Fiske, S. (1979). Salience, attention, and attribution: Top of the head phenomena. In L. Berkowitz (Ed.), *Advances in experimental social psychology.* New York: Academic Press. (13)

Teger, A. I. (1979). *Too much invested to quit: The psychology of the escalation of conflict.* Elmsford, NY: Pergamon Press. (17)

Thaler, R. (1980). Toward a positive theory of consumer choice. *Journal of Economic Behavior and Organization, 1,* 39–60. (9, 11, 17, 41)

Thaler, R. (1985). Mental accounting and consumer choice. *Marketing Science, 4*(3), 199–214. (11)

Thaler, R., & Shiffrin, H. M. (1981). An economic theory of self-control. *Journal of Political Economy, 89,* 392–406. (41)

The Times. (1981, August 27). Rhodes, Rudd visit reservation, still favor Orme. Fountain Hills, AZ. (8)

Thibaut, J., & Kelley, H. H. (1959). *The social psychology of groups.* New York: Wiley. (15)

Thibaut, J., & Walker, L. (1975). *Procedural justice: A psychological analysis.* Hillsdale, NJ: Erlbaum. (12, 14)

Thomas, E. A. C., & Hogue, A. (1976). Apparent weight of evidence, decision criteria, and confidence ratings in juror decision making. *Psychological Review, 83,* 442–465. (37)

Thorndike, E. L. (1918). Fundamental theorems in judging men. *Journal of Applied Psychology, 2,* 67–76. (Gen. Int.)

Thorndike, R. L. (1949). *Personnel selection.* New York: Wiley. (29)

Thorngate, W. (1980). Efficient decision heuristics. *Behavioral Science, 25,* 219–225. (41)

Thurstone, L. L. (1947). *Multiple factor analysis.* Chicago: University of Chicago Press. (33)

Timmers, H., & Wagenaar, W. A. (1977). Inverse statistics and misperception of exponential growth. *Perception and Psychophysics, 21,* 558–562. (41)

Toda, M. (1962). The design of a fungus eater: A model of human behavior in an unsophisticated environment. *Behavioral Science, 7,* 164–183. (41)

Toda, M. (1976). The decision process: A perspective. *International Journal of General Systems, 3,* 79–88. (41)

Toda, M. (1980). What happens at the moment of decision? Meta decisions, emotions, and volitions. In J. Sjöberg, T. Tyszka, & J. A. Wise (Eds.), *Human decision making* (Vol. 2). Bodafors, Sweden: Doxa. (41)

Todd, F. J., & Hammond, K. R. (1965). Differential feedback in multiple-cue probability learning tasks. *Behavioral Science, 10,* 429–435. (3, 19, 35)

Tolman, E. C. (1948). Cognitive maps in rats and men. *Psychological Review, 55,* 189–208. (3)

Tolman, E. C., & Brunswik, E. (1935). The organism and the causal texture of the environment. *Psychological Review, 42,* 43–77. (3)

Tompkins, C. B. (1956). Review of Rand Corporation's *One million random digits and 100,000 normal deviates. Mathematical Tables and Other Aids to Computation, 10,* 39–43. (43)

Torgenson, W. S. (1962). *Theory and methods of scaling.* New York: Wiley. (37)

Toronto, A. F., Veasey, L. G., & Warner, H. R. (1963). Evaluation of a computer program for diagnosis of congenital heart disease. *Progress in Cardiovascular Diseases, 5,* 362–377. (26)

Toulmin, S. E. (1972). The historical background to the anti-science movement. In G. E. W. Wolstenholme & M. O'Connor (Eds.), *Civilization and science: In conflict or collaboration?* Ciba Foundation Symposium 1. Amsterdam: Elsevier. (7)

Trabasso, T. (1977). The role of memory as a system in making transitive inferences. In R. V. Kail & J. W. Hagen (Eds.), *Perspectives on the development of memory and cognition* (pp. 333–366). Hillsdale, NJ: Erlbaum. (31)

Treynor, J. L., & Mazuy, K. K. (1966). Can mutual funds outguess the market? *Harvard Business Review, 44,* 131–136. (10)

Triandis, H. C. (1971). *Attitude and attitude change.* New York: Wiley. (41)

Tribe, L. (1971). Trial by mathematics: Precision and ritual in the legal process. *Harvard Law Review, 84,* 1329–1393. (12)

Tucker, L. R. (1964). A suggested alternative formulation in the developments by Hursch, Hammond, and Hursch, and by Hammond, Hursch, and Todd. *Psychological Review, 71,* 528–530. (16, 34, 35)

Tversky, A. (1974). Assessing uncertainty. *Journal of the Royal Statistical Society: Series B, 36,* 148–159. (12)

Tversky, A. (1977). On the elicitation of preferences: Descriptive and prescriptive considerations. In D. Bell, R. L. Keeney, & H. Raiffa (Eds.), *Conflicting objectives in decisions: International series on applied systems analysis* (pp. 209–222). New York: Wiley. (11)

Tversky, A., & Kahneman, D. (1971a). Belief in the law of small numbers. *Psychological Bulletin, 76,* 105–110. (2, 10, 12, 16, 40)

Tversky, A., & Kahneman, D. (1971b). The judgment of frequency and probability of availability of instances. *Oregon Research Institute Research Bulletin, 11*(6). (10)

Tversky, A., & Kahneman, D. (1973). Availability: A heuristic for judging frequency and probability. *Cognitive Psychology, 5,* 207–232. (2, 12, 24, 39, 40, 41)

Tversky, A., & Kahneman, D. (1974). Judgment under uncertainty: Heuristics and biases. *Science, 185,* 1124–1131. (3, 5, 6, 12, 16, 24, 39, 40, 41)

Tversky, A., & Kahneman, D. (1980). Causal schemas in judgments under uncertainty. In M. Fishbein (Ed.), *Progress in social psychology* (Vol. 1). Hillsdale, NJ: Erlbaum. (12, 40, 42)

Tversky, A., & Kahneman, D. (1981). The framing of decisions and the rationality of choice. *Science, 221,* 453–458. (6, 9, 11, 17, 23, 39, 40, 41)

Tversky, A., & Kahneman, D. (1983). Extensional versus intuitive reasoning: The conjunction fallacy in probability judgment. *Psychological Review, 90,* 293–315. (40)

Ulmer, S. S. (1971). *Courts as small and not so small groups.* Morristown, NJ: General Learning Press. (14)

United States Department of Energy. (1980). *Final environmental impact statement: Rocky Flats Plant site, Golden, Jefferson County, Colorado.* Washington, DC: U.S. Department of Energy. (28)

United States Nuclear Regulatory Commission. (1975). *Reactor safety study: An assessment of accident risks in U.S. commercial nuclear power plants* (NUREG-75/014). Washington, DC: Nuclear Regulatory Commission. (40)

United States Water Resources Council. (1973). Water and land resources: Establishment of principles and standards for planning. *Federal Register, 38*(174), 24779–24869. (8)

United States Water Resources Council. (1983). Economic and environmental principles and guidelines for water and related land resources implementation studies. *Federal Register, 48*(48), 10259. (8)

Valle, V. A., & Frieze, I. H. (1976). Stability of causal attributions as mediator in changing expectations for success. *Journal of Personality and Social Psychology, 33,* 579–587. (13)

Vandenberg, S. G., Rosenzweig, N., Moore, K. R., & Dukay, A. F. (1964). Diagnostic agreements among psychiatrists and "blind" Rorschach raters or the education of an interdisciplinary research team. *Psychological Reports, 15* 211–224. (19)

Vidmar, N. (1972). Effects of decision alternatives on the verdicts and social perceptions of simulated jurors. *Journal of Personality and Social Psychology, 22,* 211–218. (37)

Vlek, C., & Wagenaar, W. A. (1979). Judgment and decision under uncertainty. In J. A. Michon, E. G. Eijkman, & L. F. W. DeKlerk (Eds.), *Handbook of psychonomics II* (pp. 253–345). Amsterdam: North Holland. (40)

von Holstein, C. A. S. (1971). Two techniques for assessment of subjective probability distributions: An experimental study. *Acta Psychologica, 35,* 478–494. (2)

von Holstein, C. A. S. (1972). Probabilistic forecasting: An experiment related to the stock market. *Organizational Behavior and Human Performance, 8,* 139–158. (12)

von Mises, R. (1957). *Probability, statistics, and truth* (H. Geiringer, Ed. and Trans.). New York: Macmillan. (Original work published 1928) (43)

von Neumann, J., & Morgenstern, O. (1947). *Theory of games and economic behavior* (2nd ed.). Princeton: Princeton University Press. (11)

von Winterfeldt, D., & Edwards, W. (in press). *Decision analysis and behavioral research.* Cambridge: Cambridge University Press. (40)

Wagenaar, W. A. (1972). Generation of random sequences by human subjects: A critical survey of literature. *Psychological Bulletin, 77,* 65–72. (41, 43)

Wagenaar, W. A., & Sagaria, S. D. (1975). Misperception of exponential growth. *Perception and Psychophysics, 18,* 416–422. (40, 41)

Wagenaar, W. A., & Timmers, H. (1978a). Extrapolation of exponential time series is not enhanced by having more data points. *Perception and Psychophysics, 24,* 182–184. (41)

Wagenaar, W. A., & Timmers, H. (1978b). Intuitive prediction of growth. In D. F. Burkhardt & W. H. Ittelson (Eds.), *Environmental assessment of socioeconomic systems* (pp. 103–122). New York: Plenum Press. (40, 41)

Wagenaar, W. A., & Timmers, H. (1979). The pond-and-duckweed problem: Three experiments on the misperception of exponential growth. *Acta Psychologica, 43,* 239–251. (41)

Wagner, R., Tollison, R., Rabuska, A., & Noonan, J. T., Jr. (1982). *Balanced budgets, fiscal responsibility, and the Constitution.* Washington, DC: Cato Institute. (9)

Walker, L., Thibaut, J., & Andreoli, V. (1972). Order of presentation at trial. *Yale Law Journal, 82,* 216–226. (37)

Wallace, H. (1923). What is in the corn judge's mind? *Journal of the American Society of Agronomy, 15,* 300–304. (12)

Wallach, M. S., & Schooff, K. (1965). Reliability of degree of disturbance ratings. *Journal of Clinical Psychology, 21,* 273–275. (19, 36)

Walster, E., Berscheid, E., & Walster, G. W. (1973). New directions in equity research. *Journal of Personality and Social Psychology, 25,* 151–176. (38)

Walton, R. E., & McKersie, R. B. (1965). *A behavioral theory of labor negotiations: An analysis of a social interaction system.* New York: McGraw-Hill. (17)

Ward, W. C., & Jenkins, H. M. (1965). The display of information and the judgment of contingency. *Canadian Journal of Psychology, 19,* 231–241. (10, 36, 42)

Wason, P. C. (1960). On the failure to eliminate hypotheses in a conceptual task. *Quarterly Journal of Experimental Psychology, 12,* 129–140. (42)

Wason, P. C., & Johnson-Laird, P. N. (1972). *Psychology of reasoning: Structure and content.* Cambridge, MA: Harvard University Press. (24, 30, 42)

Watley, D. J. (1967). Counselor predictive skill and differential judgments of occupational suitability. *Journal of Counseling Psychology, 14,* 309–313. (19)

Watson, C. G. (1967). Relationship of distortion to DAP diagnostic accuracy among psychologists at three levels of sophistication. *Journal of Consulting Psychology, 31,* 142–146. (19)

Weichselbaum, H. F. (1975). New concepts: Effects of methadone maintenance on cognitive control. In K. R. Hammond & C. R. B. Joyce (Eds.), *Psychoactive drugs and social judgment: Theory and research* (pp. 239–248). New York: Wiley. (3)

Weick, K. E. (1977). Enactment processes in organizations. In B. M. Staw & G. R. Salancik (Eds.), *New directions in organizational behavior* (pp. 267–300). Chicago: St. Clair Press. (41)

Weinberg, A. (1976). The maturity and future of nuclear energy. *American Scientist, 64,* 16–21. (6)

Weinberg, A. (1979). *Energy policy and mathematics* (Rep. ORAU/IEA-79-5[0]). Oak Ridge, TN: Oak Ridge Associated Universities, Institute for Energy Analysis. (6)

Weiner, B. (1974). Achievement motivation as conceptualized by an attribution theorist. In B. Weiner (Ed.), *Achievement motivation and attribution theory.* Morristown, NJ: General Learning Press. (13)

Weiner, B., & Kukla, A. (1974). An attributional analysis of achievement motivation. *Journal of Personality and Social Psychology, 15,* 1–20. (13)

Weiner, B. Nierenberg, R., & Goldstein, M. (1976). Social learning (locus of control) versus attributional (causal stability) interpretations of expectancy of success. *Journal of Personality, 44,* 52–68. (13)

Weinreb, N., & Brainerd, C. J. (1975). A developmental study of Piaget's groupment model of the emergence of speed and time concepts. *Child Development, 46,* 176–185. (31)

Weinstein, N. D. (1979). Seeking reassuring or threatening information about environmental cancer. *Journal of Behavioral Medicine, 16,* 220–224. (6)

Weinstein, N. D. (1980). Unrealistic optimism about future life events. *Journal of Personality and Social Psychology, 39,* 806–820. (6)

Weiss, D. J. (1975). Quantifying private events: A functional measurement analysis of equisection. *Perception and Psychophysics, 17,* 351–357. (4)

Weiss, R. L. (1980). Strategic behavioral marital therapy: Toward a model for assessment and intervention. In J. Vincent (Ed.), *Advances in family intervention, assessment and theory* (Vol. 1, pp. 229–271). Greenwich, CT: JAI Press. (15)

Weitman, M. (1962). Some variables related to bias in clinical judgment. *Journal of Clinical Psychology, 18,* 504–506. (19)

Wendt, P. F. (1965). Current growth stock valuation methods. *Financial Analysts Journal, 21,* 91–103. (10)

Wharton School of Finance and Commerce. (1962). *A study of mutual funds: Report of the Committee on Interstate and Foreign Commerce, 87th Congress (House Report 2274).* Philadelphia: University of Pennsylvania. (10)

Wheeler, G. E., & Edwards, W. (1975). *Misaggregation explains conservative inference about normally distributed populations* (Research Rep. 75–11). Los Angeles: University of Southern California, Social Science Research Institute. (40)

Wickelgren, W. A. (1974). *How to solve problems: Elements of a theory of problems and problem solving.* San Francisco: Freeman. (17, 36)

Wiggins, J. (1981). Clinical and statistical prediction: Where are we and where do we go from here? *Clinical Psychology Review, 1,* 3–18. (34)

Wiggins, N., & Hoffman, P. J. (1968). Three models of clinical judgment. *Journal of Abnormal Psychology, 73,* 70–77. (16, 19, 35)

Wiggins, N., & Kolen, E. S. (1971). Man versus model of man revisited: The forecasting of graduate school success. *Journal of Personality and Social Psychology,* *19,* 100–106. (10, 12)

Wigmore, J. H. (1940). *Evidence in trials at common law.* Boston: Little, Brown. (12)

Wildavsky, A. (1979). *Speaking truth to power: The art and craft of policy analysis.* Boston: Little, Little. (8)

Wilford, J. N. (1976, February 19). Policy clashes stir interest in "court" for science. *New York Times,* p. 22. (7)

Wilkening, F. (1979). Combining of stimulus dimensions in children's and adults' judgments of area: An information integration analysis. *Developmental Psychology, 15,* 25–33. (31)

Wilkening, F. (1980). Development of dimensional integration in children's perceptual judgment: Experiments with area, volume, and velocity. In F. Wilkening, J. Becker, & T. Trabasso (Eds.), *Information integration by children* (pp. 47–69). Hillsdale, NJ: Erlbaum. (31)

Wilkening, F., & Anderson, N. H. (1980). *Comparison of two rule assessment methodologies for studying cognitive development* (Tech. Rep. CHIP94). La Jolla: University of California at San Diego, Center for Human Information Processing. (31)

Wilkins, L. T., Gottfredson, D. M., Robison, J. O., & Sadowsky, A. (1973). *Information selection and use in parole decision-making* (Supp. Rep. 5). Davis, CA: National Council on Crime and Delinquency Research Center. (13)

Williams, C. (1974). The effect of an irrelevant dimension on "same-different" judgments of multi-dimensional stimuli. *Quarterly Journal of Experimental Psychology, 26,* 26–31. (27)

Willis, S. L. (1972). *Formation of teacher expectations of students' academic performance.* Unpublished doctoral dissertation, University of Texas at Austin. (32)

Wilson, D. (1970). *Asia awakes.* London: Penguin Press. (25)

Wilson, R. (1979). Analyzing the daily risks of life. *Technology Review, 81,* 40–46. (6)

Winch, R. F., & More, D. M. (1956). Does TAT add information to interviews? Statistical analysis of the increment. *Journal of Clinical Psychology, 12,* 316–321. (19)

Winer, B. J. (1962). *Statistical principles in experimental design.* New York: McGraw-Hill. (29, 35)

Winkler, R. L. (1967). Assessment of prior distributions in Bayesian analysis. *Journal of the American Statistical Association, 62,* 776–800. (2)

Winkler, R. L., & Murphy, A. H. (1968). "Good" probability assessors. *Journal of Applied Meteorology, 1,* 751–758. (25)

Winkler, R. L., & Murphy, A. H. (1973). Experiments in the laboratory and the real world. *Organizational Behavior and Human Performance, 10,* 252–270. (40, 41)

Winslow, C. N., & Rapersand, I. (1964). Postdiction of the outcome of somatic therapy from the Rorschach records of schizophrenic patients. *Journal of Consulting Psychology, 28,* 243–247. (19)

Winston, P. H. (Ed.). (1975). *The psychology of computer vision.* New York: McGraw-Hill. (43)

Wishart, D. (1978). *CLUSTAN user manual* (3rd ed.). Edinburgh: Edinburgh University, Program Library Unit. (32)

Wolstenholme, G. E. W., & O'Connor, M. (Eds.). (1975). *The future as an academic discipline.* Ciba Foundation Symposium 36. Amsterdam: Elsevier. (7)

Wood, G. (1978). The knew-it-all-along effect. *Journal of Experimental Psychology: Human Perception and Performance, 4,* 345–353. (36)

Woodworth, R. S. (1899). The accuracy of voluntary movement. *Psychological Review Monograph, 3*(2, Whole No. 13). (41)

Wright, G. N., & Phillips, L. D. (1979). Personality and probabilistic thinking: An exploratory study. *British Journal of Psychology, 70,* 295–303. (25)

Wright, G. N., Phillips, L. D., Whalley, P. C., Choo, G. T., Ng, K. O., Tan, I., & Wisudha, A. (1978). Cultural differences in probabilistic thinking. *Journal of Cross-Cultural Psychology, 9,* 285–299. (25)

Wyer, R. S., Jr. (1970). Quantitative prediction of belief and opinion change: A further test of a subjective probability model. *Journal of Personality and Social Psychology, 16,* 559–570. (40)

Yamamoto, K. (1969). Images of the ideal pupil held by teachers in preparation. *Californian Journal of Educational Research, 20,* 221–232. (32)

Yankelovich, Skelly, & White, Inc. (1978). Highlights of a national survey of the general public, judges, lawyers, and community leaders. In T. J. Fetter (Ed.), *State courts: A blueprint for the future.* Williamsburg, VA: National Center for State Courts. (12)

Yntema, D. B., & Torgerson, W. S. (1961). Man-computer cooperation in decisions requiring common sense. *IRE Transactions of the Professional Group on Human Factors in Electronics, HFE-2*(1), 20–26. (19, 35)

Zachariadis, N., & Varonos, D. (1975). Effects of methylphenidate and barbiturate on normal subjects. In K. R. Hammond & C. R. B. Joyce (Eds.), *Psychoactive drugs and social judgment: Theory and research* (pp. 165–174, 189–194). New York: Wiley. (3)

Zadeh, L. A., Fu, K.-S., Tanaka, K., & Shimura, M. (1975). *Fuzzy sets and their applications to cognitive and decision processes.* New York: Academic Press. (4)

Zalkind, D. L., & Shachtman, R. H. (no date). *A non-economic personal value of life.* Unpublished manuscript, DHEW Office of Assistant Secretary for Planning and Evaluation, and University of North Carolina. (22)

Zalkind, D. L., & Shachtman, R. H. (1976a, November). *An introduction to decision analysis for health professionals.* Paper presented at the meeting of the American Public Health Association, Miami. (22)

Zalkind, D. L., & Shachtman, R. H. (1976b, November). *The swine flu vaccination decision for an individual.* Paper presented at the meeting of the American Public Health Association, Miami. (22)

Zeisel, H. (1971). . . . And then there were none: The diminution of the Federal Jury. *University of Chicago Law Review, 38,* 710–724. (12)

Ziskin, J. (1975). *Coping with psychiatric and psychological testimony.* Beverly Hills, CA: Law and Psychology Press. (12)

Zlotnick, J. (1968). A theorem for prediction. *Foreign Service Journal, 45,* 20. (40)

Name index

Abelson, R. P., 252, 531
Abraham, H. J., 257
Ackoff, R. L., 703
Aczel, J., 92
Adams, J. K., 654
Adams, J. S., 614
Adelman, L., 95, 127, 136, 151, 281, 307, 309, 466, 470, 532, 619
Adelstein, S. J., 355
Ahlers, D. M., 185
Aiello, N., 412
Ainslie, G., 630
Albert, D. A., 370, 433
Alfini, J. J., 270
Allais, M., 190, 197
Allison, G. T., 294
Allport, G. W., 613
Alpert, M., 52, 654
Amabile, T. M., 652
Amidon, A., 509
Anderson, B. F., 470, 472
Anderson, N. H., 11, 64, 77, 84–6, 91, 93–4, 261, 266, 509–10, 513, 519, 601, 619
Anderson, W. A. D., 387
Andreoli, V., 598
Applebaum, M., 501
Archer, V. E., 472–3, 478–9
Areeda, P., 232
Ares, C. E., 259
Arkes, H. R., 582–3, 587, 591
Armelius, B. A., 683
Armelius, K., 683
Armstrong, J. S., 696
Aronson, E., 597
Ashare, A. B., 359
Atkin, R. S., 594, 596
Austin, G., 417, 708–9
Austin, W., 614

Axtell, L. M., 387
Azuma, H., 70, 307

Babington Smith, B., 726
Bailer, J. C., 478
Bakshi, S., 358
Bakwin, H., 178
Baldus, D. C., 213, 232
Balke, W. M., 75, 281, 309–10
Ball, J. A., 721–2
Ball, O. J., 543
Bandura, A., 680
Bank, D., 278
Barclay, S., 647
Bar-Hillel, M., 50, 229, 648–651, 660, 667, 694, 700
Barker, C. J., 474, 476
Barnoon, S., 362
Barr, R., 525
Barry, W. A., 277
Bartlett, F. C., 413
Baucom, D., 278
Bauman, W. S., 175–6, 179, 182
Baylor, S., 358
Bazelon, D. L., 222
Bazerman, M., 313–4, 316–8
Beach, L. R., 187, 450, 629, 633–4, 647, 681
Beck, C. H., 370
Becker, G. M., 614
Beedle, R. K., 450
Beekun, R. K., 318
Beer, S., 683
Bender, M. A., 358
Bendig, A. W., 568
Bennett, J. V., 271
Berg, J., 472
Berkeley, D., 627, 632–3, 636, 640
Berndt, T. J., 507

800

Oden, G. C., 89–90
Okrent, D., 468
Olson, D. H., 278
O'Reilly, M., 367
Ortony, A., 531
Orvis, B., 278
Oskamp, S., 177, 336, 552, 585, 649, 680
Ostrove, N., 597
Otten, A. L., 128
Owen, P. W., 220

Pankoff, L. D., 179
Parker, C. A., 338
Parker, S., 518
Parkinson, B. K., 422
Parsons, O. A., 422
Parthasarathy, K. L., 358
Partridge, A., 272
Pauker, S., 203, 361, 387
Payne, J. W., 197, 245, 247–9, 252, 630, 633,
   641, 685, 691
Pearson, K., 703
Pearson, T., 670
Pedhazur, E. J., 619–20
Penny, D. M., 430
Pepitone, A., 251
Perlman, D., 251
Peterson, C. R., 220, 413, 417, 629, 681,
   694
Peterson, J. L., 240
Peterson, R., 506
Peto, R., 471–3, 478
Petzel, P. T., 592
Pfefferbaum, A., 450
Phelan, J. G., 338, 582, 585
Phelps, R., 450, 460
Phillips, L., 316, 397–8, 418–9, 421, 424,
   430, 433, 627, 633, 636–7, 646, 653–4,
   680
Piaget, J., 495–6, 498, 503–4, 507, 516, 661,
   664–5, 668, 682, 687, 690, 715
Pitz, G., 413, 631, 639, 654
Pliskin, J. S., 370
Plott, C. R., 664, 701
Polsby, N. W., 131
Polson, P. G., 706
Pommerehne, W. W., 664
Popper, K., 706–7, 721, 726–8
Postman, L., 683
Poulton, E. C., 697
Powers, W. T., 682, 685
Pratt, J. W., 206
Prettyman, E. B., 270
Prothero, J., 450
Pruitt, D. G., 190, 317, 321
Psotka, J., 723

Quinn, R., 620, 623
Qvarnstrom, G., 298

Rabbitt, P., 450
Rabuska, A., 171
Raiffa, H., 52, 183, 185, 216, 220, 359, 376,
   386, 417, 614, 622, 654
Rand Corporation, 720
Rankin, A., 259
Ranzoni, J., 336
Rapersand, I., 337
Rapoport, A., 681
Rappaport, H., 483
Rappoport, L., 68, 70, 75, 281
Rausch, H. L., 277–8, 292
Rawls, J., 142–3, 615–7, 620
Rebok, G. W., 450
Redding, S. G., 430
Reed, H., 650, 680
Reichenbach, H., 722
Reilly, R. J., 664
Reissland, J., 122
Reitan, H. T., 248
Reither, F., 632
Rethans, A., 117
Reynolds, D. E., 597
Rice, M. F., 450
Richards, D. D., 507–8, 516, 520
Ridenour, L. N., 565
Ringuette, E. L., 337
Rist, R. C., 524
Roberts, H. V., 179
Robison, J. O., 249
Roe, R. L., 217
Rohrbaugh, J., 151, 306, 470, 532, 615, 619–
   20, 623
Rokeach, M., 148, 613
Ronen, J., 634, 691
Ronen, N., 222
Rorer, L. G., 181, 299, 342, 345, 348–50
Rosen, A., 583, 648
Rosen, B., 251
Rosenbaum, D. E., 730
Rosenberg, J., 117
Rosenthal, R., 523
Rosenzweig, N., 338
Rosett, A., 268
Ross, L., 320, 582, 584–5, 588, 627, 629, 652,
   680, 732
Roth, W. T., 450
Rothenberg, B. B., 507
Rotter, J. B., 252, 418, 680
Rowse, G. L., 432
Royce, W., 279–80
Rozelle, M. A., 151
Rubin, J., 315, 317–8, 321
Rubin, M., 278
Rubovits, P., 524
Rumelhart, D. E., 531
Russo, J. E., 700
Russo, N. A., 524
Rust, P., 534–5

Subject index